PrincetonReview.com

COLLEGES THAT PAY YOU BACK

The 200 Schools That Give You the Best Bang for Your Tuition Buck

2017 Edition

By Robert Franek,
David Soto, Kristen O'Toole, and
the Staff of The Princeton Review

Penguin
Random
House

The Princeton Review
24 Prime Parkway, Suite 201
Natick, MA 01760
editorialsupport@review.com

ISBN: 978-0-451-48749-0
ISSN: 2376-1687

Production: Best Content Solutions, LLC
Production Editor: Melissa Duclos

Printed in the United States of America on partially recycled paper.

9 8 7 6 5 4 3 2 1

2017 Edition

Editorial
Robert Franek, Senior VP—Publisher
David Soto, Director of Content Development
Kristen O'Toole, Editorial Director
Steven Koch, Student Survey Manager
Pia Aliperti, Editor

Random House Publishing Team
Tom Russell, Publisher
Alison Stoltzfus, Publishing Director
Ellen L. Reed, Production Manager
Jake Eldred, Managing Editor
Suzanne Lee, Designer

CONTENTS

How Does College Pay You Back?

Introduction

The Princeton Review has long encouraged college applicants to seek out the schools that fit them best academically, culturally, and financially. As the cost of attending college continues to rise dramatically, applicants and their families are increasingly concerned about post-graduation job prospects. Tuition is an investment in the future, and like investors, students want to see a return on that investment. To continue our mission of helping students find the right college for them, we have combined alumni career outcome data with the institutional data and student surveys we collect to create a Return on Investment (ROI) rating for each of the 200 schools in this book. We know that students invest more than money in their educations, however—they invest their time, energy, and passion. The ROI on your education is much more than a high salary.

History

In 2008, we began publishing America's Best Value Colleges online (in partnership with USAToday), and in 2011, we turned that list into a book. The schools that we covered in *Best Value Colleges* were chosen based on more than thirty factors covering three areas: academics, cost of attendance, and financial aid, including student ratings of their financial aid packages. The aim of our Best Value Colleges franchise was to highlight schools that offer excellent academics as well as excellent need and non-need-based aid. We expanded our Best Value methodology to include information covering alumni careers in 2014, and renamed our book *Colleges That Pay You Back*.

Career Outcomes

Career outcomes have become as important to students and parents as academic quality and campus life when choosing a school. Increasingly, colleges and universities are moving their offices of career services closer to their admissions offices, providing visiting prospective students with a glimpse of what they can offer. Career services advisors are engaging with students earlier in their time on campus, often in the first few weeks of their first year. These trends in career services aren't a result of colleges pressuring students to plan out their futures before they are ready—rather, colleges and universities are beginning to help students identify their interests, strengths, and passions, and use those to build the foundation of an effective long-term career strategy.

In order to provide meaningful career metrics for each school profiled in this book, we partnered with PayScale.com, which surveys alumni about salary and career. On each of the 200 school profiles in *Colleges That Pay You Back*, you'll find PayScale.com's median starting salary and mid-career salary for graduates of that school. To cover professions that have high social value but may offer lower salary numbers, such as teaching or non-profit management, we have also included the percentage of alumni who feel that their job makes the world a better place. All of these statistics are printed on each school's profile, and were incorporated into the overall ROI rating for each school. When available, salary data is broken out for alumni who pursued further study, and the percentage of alumni with science/technology/engineering/math (STEM) majors appears in some school profiles.

The Real Cost of College

When we set out to develop our ROI rating and determine which schools to include in this book, we started with the same cost analysis we used to create our Best Value Colleges criteria: We calculate the the sticker price of each college (often referred to as "cost of attendance," that figure includes tuition, required fees and room and board), and subtract the average gift aid (scholarships and grants) awarded to students. We don't subtract work-study or student loans, since those are costs that students ultimately have to bear. Out of the 650 schools we considered for this project, the 200 we chose as our "Colleges That Pay You Back" offer great academics, combined with affordable cost, and stellar career outcomes.

Going Beyond Cold Hard Cash

Just as in our previous title *Best Value Colleges* we defined "value" as inclusive of excellent academics, facilities, and on-campus resources in addition to generous financial aid packages, we believe colleges pay you back in more than a high salary. The colleges and universities that appear in this book were chosen based on more than forty factors. These factors include PayScale.com's alumni career information, the cost of attendance, financial aid (based on both demonstrated need and merit), selectivity, academics, and student opinion surveys. This goes beyond the bottom line to provide a complete picture of a school's value, and as a result the 200 colleges that pay you back are diverse in academic programs, size, region, and type.

26 Tips for Getting Financial Aid, Scholarships, and Grants and for Paying Less for College

When it comes to actually paying for college, there is a lot of information out there. A great resource is our book *Paying for College Without Going Broke* by Kalman Chany. Here, we have some tips from Kal for applying for financial aid and trimming the costs of college.

Getting financial aid

1. Learn how financial aid works. The more and the sooner you know about how need-based aid eligibility is determined, the better you can take steps to maximize such eligibility.
2. Apply for financial aid no matter what your circumstances. Some merit-based aid can only be awarded if the applicant has submitted financial aid application forms.
3. Don't wait until you are accepted to apply for financial aid. Do it when applying for admission.
4. Complete all the required aid applications. All students seeking aid must submit the FAFSA (Free Application for Federal Student Aid); other forms may also be required. Check with each college to see what's required and when.
5. Get the best scores you can on the SAT or ACT. They are used not only in decisions for admission but they can also impact financial aid. If your scores and other stats exceed the school's admission criteria, you are likely to get a better aid package than a marginal applicant.
6. Apply strategically to colleges. Your chances of getting aid will be better at schools that have generous financial aid budgets. (Check the "Colleges That Pay You Back" list and Financial Aid Ratings for schools in this book and on princetonreview.com.)
7. Don't rule out any school as too expensive. A generous aid award from a pricey private school can make it less costly than a public school with a lower sticker price.
8. Take advantage of education tax benefits. A dollar saved on taxes is worth the same as a dollar in scholarship aid. Look into Coverdells, 529 Plans, education tax credits, and loan deductions.

Scholarships and grants

9. Get your best possible score on the PSAT: It is the National Merit Scholarship Qualifying Test and also used in the selection of students for other scholarships and recognition programs.
10. Check your eligibility for grants and scholarships from your state. Some (but not all) states will allow you to use such funds out of state.
11. Look for scholarships locally. Find out if your employer offers scholarships or tuition assistance plans for employees or family members. Also look into scholarships from your church, community groups, and high school.
12. Look for outside scholarships realistically: they account for less than five percent of aid awarded. Research them at princetonreview.com or other free sites. Steer clear of scholarship search firms that charge fees and "promise" scholarships.

Paying for college

13. It's never too late to start planning. If your parents started a fund for you, that's great, but even if they haven't, you can still start saving now. The more you save, the less you'll have to borrow.
14. Invest wisely. Considering a 529 plan? Compare your own state's plan which may have tax benefits with other states' programs. Get info at savingforcollege.com.
15. If you have to borrow, first pursue federal education loans (Stafford, PLUS). Avoid private loans at all costs.
16. Never put tuition on a credit card. The debt is more expensive than ever given recent changes to interest rates and other fees some card issuers are now charging.
17. Try not to take money from a retirement account or 401(k) to pay for college. In addition to likely early distribution penalties and additional income taxes, the higher income will reduce your aid eligibility.

Paying less for college

18. Attend a community college for two years and transfer to a pricier school to complete the degree. Plan ahead: Be sure the college you plan to transfer to will accept the community college credits.
19. Look into "cooperative education" programs. Over 900 colleges allow students to combine college education with a job. It can take longer to complete a degree this way, but graduates generally owe less in student loans and have a better chance of getting hired after graduation.
20. Take as many AP courses as possible and get high scores on AP exams. Many colleges award course credits for high AP scores. Some students have cut a year off their college tuition this way.
21. Earn college credit via "dual enrollment" programs available at some high schools. These allow students to take college level courses during their senior year.
22. Earn college credits by taking CLEP (College-Level Examination Program) exams. Depending on the college, a qualifying score on any of the thirty-three CLEP exams can earn students three to twelve college credits. (See Princeton Review's *Cracking the CLEP*, 5th Edition.)
23. Stick to your college and your major. Changing colleges can result in lost credits. Aid may be limited/not available for transfer students at some schools. Changing majors can mean paying for extra courses to meet requirements.
24. Finish college in three years if possible. Take the maximum number of credits every semester, attend summer sessions, and earn credits via online courses. Some colleges offer three-year programs for high-achieving students.
25. Let Uncle Sam pay for your degree. ROTC (Reserve Officer Training Corps) programs available from U.S. Armed Forces branches (except the Coast Guard) offer merit-based scholarships up to full tuition via participating colleges in exchange for military service after you graduate.
26. Better yet: Attend a tuition-free college. Check out the nine institutions in this book on the "Tuition-Free Schools" list on p. 41.

Note: As of this printing, the federal Perkins loan program has expired. It may be extended or replaced. Please visit PrincetonReview.com/college-advice online for the most up-to-date information on available financial aid programs.

Great Schools for the Highest Paying Majors

While choosing your major is not exactly choosing your fate, the major you choose can often impact your earning potential. There are certainly graduates who land in careers that are quite different from their college majors (we know a photojournalism major who became a statistical analyst, and a biology major who is now the chief technology officer at a start-up, just to name two examples). Your choice of major should not depend solely on your expected starting salary, but also on your academic interests, the subjects you are passionate about, and the type of career you're interested in. That said, in order to arm you with information you need to maximize the return on your education, below we have provided PayScale.com's Median starting and mid-career salary for forty-five of the highest paying majors, and lists of schools that report awarding the most degrees and having the most students currently enrolled in those majors. You can find median starting and mid-career salary information for many more majors on PayScale.com.

Biochemistry

Median starting salary: $44,700
Median mid-career salary: $83,000

Agnes Scott College
Arizona State University
   at the Tempe campus
Auburn University
Barnard College
Bates College
Beloit College
Boston College
Bowdoin College
Bradley University
Brandeis University
Brigham Young University (UT)
Brown University
Bucknell University
California State University—Long Beach
Carleton College
Case Western Reserve University
Claremont McKenna College
Clark University
Clemson University
Colgate University
The College of Wooster
Connecticut College
Cornell University
Dartmouth College
Denison University
DePauw University
Dickinson College
Drake University
Florida State University
Franklin and Marshall College
George Mason University
Georgetown University
Georgia Institute of Technology
Gettysburg College
Gonzaga University
Grinnell College

Grove City College
Gustavus Adolphus College
Hamilton College
Harvard College
Hobart and William Smith Colleges
Illinois Institute of Technology
Indiana University Bloomington
Iowa State University
Kenyon College
Knox College
Lafayette College
Lawrence University
Lehigh University
Lewis & Clark College
Loyola Marymount University
Miami University
Middlebury College
Mount Holyoke College
Muhlenberg College
New College of Florida
North Carolina State University
Northeastern University
Oberlin College
Occidental College
The Ohio State University—Columbus
Oklahoma State University
Penn State University Park
Pepperdine University
Pitzer College
Purdue University—West Lafayette
Reed College
Rensselaer Polytechnic Institute
Rice University
Rochester Institute of Technology
Rose-Hulman Institute of Technology
Rutgers, The State University
   of New Jersey—New Brunswick
Santa Clara University
Scripps College
Smith College

Southwestern University
St. Anselm College
St. Lawrence University
Saint Mary's College (CA)
State University of New York at
    Binghamton (Binghamton University)
State University of New York—College of
    Environmental Science and Forestry
State University of New York—
    Stony Brook University
State University of New York—
    University at Buffalo
Stevens Institute of Technology
Swarthmore College
Texas A&M University—College Station
Trinity College (CT)
Trinity University
Tufts University
Tulane University
Union College
University of Arizona
University of California, Los Angeles
University of California—Riverside
University of California—San Diego
University of Colorado Boulder
University of Dayton
University of Florida
University of Houston
University of Idaho
University of Illinois at Urbana-
    Champaign
University of Maryland, Baltimore County
University of Maryland, College Park
University of Michigan—Ann Arbor
University of Minnesota—
    Twin Cities Campus
University of Notre Dame
University of Oklahoma
University of Pennsylvania
University of Portland
University of Richmond
University of Rochester
University of Southern California
University of Tennessee—Knoxville
The University of Texas at Austin
The University of Texas at Dallas
The University of Tulsa
University of Wisconsin—Madison
Vassar College
Villanova University
Virginia Tech
Wabash College
Washington University in St. Louis
Wellesley College
Wesleyan University

William Jewell College
Worcester Polytechnic Institute
Yale University

Molecular Biology
Median starting salary: $45,500
Median mid-career salary: $90,100

Arizona State University
    at the Tempe campus
Auburn University
Beloit College
Boston University
Bradley University
Brigham Young University (UT)
Brown University
Bryn Mawr College
Bucknell University
California Institute of Technology
California State University—Long Beach
Centre College
Claremont McKenna College
Clark University
Colby College
Colgate University
Colorado College
The College of Wooster
Connecticut College
Gettysburg College
Harvard College
Harvey Mudd College
Illinois Institute of Technology
Iowa State University
Johns Hopkins University
Kenyon College
Lawrence University
Lehigh University
Michigan Technological University
Middlebury College
Princeton University
Purdue University—West Lafayette
Reed College
Rensselaer Polytechnic Institute
Rhodes College
Rutgers, The State University
    of New Jersey—New Brunswick
Scripps College
State University of New York at
    Binghamton (Binghamton University)
State University of New York—College of
    Environmental Science and Forestry
Texas A&M University—College Station
Trinity University
Tufts University
Tulane University
University of Arizona

University of California, Los Angeles
University of California—Berkeley
University of California-Irvine
University of California—San Diego
University of California—Santa Barbara
University of California—Santa Cruz
University of Colorado Boulder
University of Connecticut
University of Denver
University of Florida
University of Georgia
University of Idaho
University of Illinois
    at Urbana-Champaign
University of Maryland, Baltimore County
University of Massachusetts Amherst
University of Michigan—Ann Arbor
University of Pittsburgh—
    Pittsburgh Campus
University of Richmond
The University of Texas at Dallas
The University of Tulsa
University of Wisconsin—Madison
Vanderbilt University
Washington University in St. Louis
Wesleyan University
Whitman College
William Jewell College
Yale University

Biotechnology
Median starting salary: $47,500
Median mid-career salary: $84,000

Brigham Young University (UT)
Carnegie Mellon University
City University of New York—
    City College
Indiana University—Bloomington
James Madison University
Rochester Institute of Technology
Rutgers, The State University
    of New Jersey—New Brunswick
State University of New York—College of
    Environmental Science and Forestry
State University of New York—
    University at Buffalo
Tufts University
University of Arizona
University of California—Davis
University of Houston
University of Illinois
    at Urbana-Champaign
University of Maryland, Baltimore County
Worcester Polytechnic Institute

BUSINESS
Actuarial Science

Actuarial Mathematics
Median starting salary: $60,800
Median mid-career salary: $119,000

Bentley University
Bradley University
Brigham Young University (UT)
Carnegie Mellon University
City University of New York—
    Baruch College
Drake University
Florida State University
Michigan Technological University
The Ohio State University—Columbus
Purdue University—West Lafayette
State University of New York
    at Binghamton
University of Connecticut
University of Illinois
    at Urbana-Champaign
University of Minnesota—Twin Cities
University of Pennsylvania
The University of Texas at Dallas
University of Wisconsin—Madison
Worcester Polytechnic Institute

Construction Management
Median starting salary: $59,500
Median mid-career salary: $102,000

Arizona State University
Bradley University
Brigham Young University (UT)
Michigan Technological University
Purdue University—West Lafayette
State University of New York—College of
    Environmental Science and Forestry
University of Denver
University of Oklahoma
Virginia Polytechnic Institute
    and State University (Virginia Tech)

Finance
Median starting salary: $53,300
Median mid-career salary: $89,600

Auburn University
Bentley University
Boston College
City University of New York—
    Baruch College
Iowa State University
Lehigh University
Loyola Marymount University

The Ohio State University—Columbus
St. Anselm College
Saint Mary's College (CA)
University of Arkansas—Fayetteville
University of Connecticut
University of Delaware
University of Denver
University of Georgia
University of Notre Dame
University of Pennsylvania
University of Pittsburgh—
  Pittsburgh Campus
University of Portland
University of Utah
Villanova University
Wofford College

International Business
Median starting salary: $48,800
Median mid-career salary: $91,000

Auburn University
Bentley University
Bradley University
Bucknell University
California State University, Long Beach
Carnegie Mellon University
City University of New York—
  Baruch College
College of the Ozarks
Creighton University
Dickinson College
Drake University
Georgetown University
Gettysburg College
Gonzaga University
Grove City College
Illinois Wesleyan University
Iowa State University
James Madison University
Northeastern University
The Ohio State University—Columbus
Oklahoma State University
Pepperdine University
Rhodes College
Rochester Institute of Technology
St. Anselm College
Saint Mary's College (CA)
State University of New York
  at Binghamton
State University of New York—
  University at Buffalo
Trinity University
University of Arkansas—Fayetteville
University of Dayton
University of Delaware

University of Denver
University of Maryland, College Park
University of Minnesota—Twin Cities
University of Pennsylvania
The University of Texas at Dallas
The University of Tulsa
University of Wisconsin—Madison
Villanova University
Washington University in St. Louis
William Jewell College

Management Information Systems
Median starting salary: $58,100
Median mid-career salary: $97,400

Auburn University
Boston College
Bradley University
Brigham Young University (UT)
California State University, Long Beach
City University of New York—
  Baruch College
Clarkson University
Drake University
Florida State University
Furman University
Georgetown University
Gonzaga University
Iowa State University
Loyola Marymount University
Miami University
Michigan Technological University
Missouri University of Science and
  Technology
Northeastern University
The Ohio State University—Columbus
Purdue University—West Lafayette
Rochester Institute of Technology
Santa Clara University
State University of New York at
  Binghamton
Texas A&M University—College Station
University of Arizona
University of California—Irvine
University of Colorado—Boulder
University of Connecticut
University of Dayton
University of Delaware
University of Denver
University of Idaho
University of Illinois
  at Urbana-Champaign
University of Maryland, Baltimore County
University of Maryland, College Park
University of Minnesota—Twin Cities
University of Notre Dame

University of Oklahoma
University of Pennsylvania
The University of Texas at Dallas
The University of Tulsa
University of Utah
Villanova University
Worcester Polytechnic Institute

Marketing
Median starting salary: $45,400
Median mid-career salary: $94,800

Arizona State University
  at the Tempe campus
Auburn University
Bentley University
Boston College
Bucknell University
Drake University
Georgetown University
Gonzaga University
Lehigh University
Loyola Marymount University
Miami University
Northeastern University
Oklahoma State University
Pepperdine University
Santa Clara University
Trinity University
Tulane University
University of Arkansas—Fayetteville
University of Connecticut
University of Dayton
University of Denver
University of Georgia
University of Houston
University of Idaho
University of Notre Dame
University of Pennsylvania
The University of Texas at Dallas
The University of Tulsa
University of Utah

Supply Chain Management
Median starting salary: $52,600
Median mid-career salary: $92,200

Auburn University
Brigham Young University (UT)
Clarkson University
Iowa State University
Lehigh University
The Ohio State University—Columbus
State University of New York
  at Binghamton
Texas A&M University—College Station
University of Arkansas—Fayetteville

University of Houston
University of Illinois
  at Urbana-Champaign
University of Maryland, College Park
The University of Tennessee—Knoxville
The University of Texas at Dallas

COMPUTER AND INFORMATION SCIENCES

Computer Information Systems
Median starting salary: $54,300
Median mid-career salary: $89,500

Boston College
Boston University
Bradley University
Carnegie Mellon University
Clemson University
College of the Ozarks
Cornell University
Drake University
George Mason University
Georgetown University
Gettysburg College
Indiana University—Bloomington
Lawrence University
Michigan Technological University
Missouri University of Science
  and Technology
Montana Tech of the University
  of Montana
North Carolina State University
Northwestern University
Oberlin College
Oklahoma State University
Pennsylvania State University—
  University Park
Purdue University—West Lafayette
Rensselaer Polytechnic Institute
Rochester Institute of Technology
Rutgers, The State University
  of New Jersey—New Brunswick
Scripps College
State University of New York
  at Binghamton
State University of New York—College of
  Environmental Science and Forestry
State University of New York at Geneseo
Stevens Institute of Technology
Texas A&M University—College Station
Trinity University
Tulane University
University of Arizona
University of California—Berkeley

University of California—Davis
University of California—Santa Cruz
University of Dayton
University of Delaware
University of Florida
University of Georgia
University of Houston
University of Illinois
   at Urbana-Champaign
University of Maryland, College Park
University of Massachusetts Amherst
University of Minnesota—Twin Cities
University of Notre Dame
The University of Tennessee—Knoxville
University of Wisconsin—Madison
Virginia Polytechnic Institute
   and State University (Virginia Tech)
Washington University in St. Louis
Wellesley College
Worcester Polytechnic Institute

Computer Science
Median starting salary: $65,300
Median mid-career salary: $107,000

Arizona State University
Beloit College
Boston University
Bowdoin College
Bradley College
Brandeis University
Brigham Young University (UT)
Bryn Mawr College
Carnegie Mellon University
Case Western Reserve University
Centre College
City University of New York—
   Hunter College
Colby College
Colgate University
College of the Ozarks
Cornell University
Creighton University
Drake University
Emory University
George Mason University
Georgetown University
Gettysburg College
Gonzaga University
Grinnell College
Grove City College
Harvard College
Harvey Mudd College
Illinois Institute of Technology
Indiana University—Bloomington
Lake Forest College

Lawrence University
Lehigh University
Lewis & Clark College
Loyola University Maryland
Massachusetts Institute of Technology
Michigan Technological University
Middlebury College
Montana Tech of the University
   of Montana
Mount Holyoke College
North Carolina State University
Northwestern University
Pomona College
Purdue University—West Lafayette
Rhodes College
Rice University
Rochester Institute of Technology
Rose-Hulman Institute of Technology
Scripps College
St. Olaf College
Stanford University
State University of New York
   at Binghamton
State University of New York—
   Stony Brook University
State University of New York—
   University at Buffalo
Stevens Institute of Technology
Texas A&M University—College Station
Tufts University
University of Arizona
University of California—Davis
University of California—Irvine
University of California—Riverside
University of California—San Diego
University of California—Santa Barbara
University of California—Santa Cruz
The University of Chicago
University of Colorado—Boulder
University of Connecticut
University of Dayton
University of Delaware
University of Denver
University of Georgia
University of Idaho
University of Illinois
   at Urbana-Champaign
University of Maryland, Baltimore County
University of Massachusetts Amherst
University of Minnesota—Twin Cities
The University of North Carolina
   at Chapel Hill
University of Oklahoma
University of Pittsburgh—
   Pittsburgh Campus

University of Rochester
The University of Tennessee—Knoxville
The University of Tulsa
University of Washington
Vanderbilt University
Washington University in St. Louis
Wellesley College
Wofford College
Wheaton College (IL)
Willamette University
Worcester Polytechnic Institute
Yale University

Information Systems
Median starting salary: $56,300
Median mid-career salary: $92,200

Bradley University
City University of New York—
    Baruch College
City University of New York—
    Brooklyn College
George Mason University
James Madison University
Missouri University of Science and
    Technology
Northeastern University
Northwestern University
Pennsylvania State University—
    University Park
Purdue University—West Lafayette
Rutgers, The State University
    of New Jersey—New Brunswick
State University of New York—
    Stony Brook University
State University of New York—
    University at Buffalo
Stevens Institute of Technology
Tulane University
United States Military Academy
University of California—Santa Cruz
University of Houston
University of Maryland, Baltimore County
University of Maryland, College Park
The University of North Carolina
    at Chapel Hill
University of Oklahoma
University of Pittsburgh—Pittsburgh
    Campus
Washington University in St. Louis

Information Technology
Median starting salary: $53,000
Median mid-career salary: $84,300

Brigham Young University (UT)
Clarkson University

College of the Ozarks
Cornell University
Creighton University
Drake University
Florida State University
Furman University
George Mason University
Illinois Institute of Technology
Lehigh University
Missouri University of Science
    and Technology
Oklahoma State University
Purdue University—West Lafayette
Rensselaer Polytechnic Institute
Rochester Institute of Technology
United States Military Academy
United States Naval Academy
University of Arizona
University of Denver
University of Maryland, Baltimore County
The University of Tulsa

ENGINEERING

Aerospace Engineering
Median starting salary: $65,400
Median mid-career salary: $106,000

Arizona State University
Auburn University
Boston University
California Institute of Technology
California State University, Long Beach
Case Western Reserve University
Clarkson University
Georgia Institute of Technology
Illinois Institute of Technology
Iowa State University
Massachusetts Institute of Technology
Missouri University of Science
    and Technology
North Carolina State University
The Ohio State University—Columbus
Oklahoma State University
Pennsylvania State University—
    University Park
Purdue University—West Lafayette
Rensselaer Polytechnic Institute
Rochester Institute of Technology
Stanford University
State University of New York—
    University at Buffalo
Texas A&M University—College Station
United States Air Force Academy
United States Naval Academy

University of Arizona
University of California—Davis
University of California—Irvine
University of California—Los Angeles
University of California—San Diego
University of Colorado—Boulder
University of Florida
University of Houston
University of Illinois
   at Urbana-Champaign
University of Maryland, College Park
University of Michigan—Ann Arbor
University of Minnesota—Twin Cities
University of Notre Dame
University of Oklahoma
University of Southern California
The University of Tennessee—Knoxville
The University of Texas at Austin
University of Virginia
University of Washington
Virginia Polytechnic Institute
   and State University (Virginia Tech)
Worcester Polytechnic Institute

Architectural Engineering
Median starting salary: $61,700
Median mid-career salary: $89,800

Auburn University
George Mason University
Georgia Institute of Technology
Illinois Institute of Technology
Missouri University of Science
   and Technology
Oklahoma State University
Penn State University Park
Purdue University—West Lafayette
Tufts University
University of Colorado Boulder
University of Oklahoma
University of Pittsburgh—
   Pittsburgh Campus
The University of Texas at Austin
Washington University in St. Louis
Worcester Polytechnic Institute

Biomedical Engineering
Median starting salary: $62,700
Median mid-career salary: $104,000

Arizona State University
Brown University
Bucknell University
California State University, Long Beach
Case Western Reserve University
City University of New York—
   City College

Clemson University
The College of New Jersey
Duke University
George Mason University
Georgia Institute of Technology
Harvard College
Illinois Institute of Technology
Johns Hopkins University
Lehigh University
Massachusetts Institute of Technology
Miami University
Michigan Technological University
North Carolina State University
Northwestern University
The Ohio State University—Columbus
Pennsylvania State University—
   University Park
Rensselaer Polytechnic Institute
Rochester Institute of Technology
Rice University
Rose-Hulman Institute of Technology
Rutgers, The State University
   of New Jersey—New Brunswick
Santa Clara University
Stanford University
State University of New York
   at Binghamton
State University of New York—
   Stony Brook University
State University of New York—
   University at Buffalo
Stevens Institute of Technology
Texas A&M University—College Station
Tufts University
Tulane University
Union College (NY)
University of Arizona
University of Arkansas—Fayetteville
University of California—Berkeley
University of California—Davis
University of California—Irvine
University of California—Santa Cruz
University of Connecticut
University of Delaware
University of Florida
University of Houston
University of Illinois
   at Urbana-Champaign
University of Michigan—Ann Arbor
University of Pennsylvania
University of Pittsburgh—
   Pittsburgh Campus
University of Rochester
University of Southern California
The University of Tennessee—Knoxville

The University of Texas at Austin
The University of Texas at Dallas
University of Virginia
University of Washington
University of Wisconsin—Madison
Vanderbilt University
Washington University in St. Louis
Worcester Polytechnic Institute
Yale University

Chemical Engineering
Median starting salary: $69,800
Median mid-career salary: $119,000

Arizona State University
Auburn University
Brigham Young University (UT)
Bucknell University
California Institute of Technology
California State University, Long Beach
Carnegie Mellon University
Case Western Reserve University
City University of New York—
 City College
Clarkson University
Clemson University
The Cooper Union for the Advancement
 of Science and Art
Cornell University
Florida State University
Georgia Institute of Technology
Harvard College
Illinois Institute of Technology
Iowa State University
Johns Hopkins University
Lafayette College
Lehigh University
Massachusetts Institute of Technology
Michigan Technological University
Miami University
Missouri University of Science
 and Technology
North Carolina State University
Northeastern University
Northwestern University
The Ohio State University—Columbus
Oklahoma State University
Pennsylvania State University—
 University Park
Princeton University
Purdue University—West Lafayette
Rensselaer Polytechnic Institute
Rice University
Rochester Institute of Technology
Rose-Hulman Institute of Technology
Rutgers, The State University

of New Jersey—New Brunswick
Stanford University
State University of New York—College of
 Environmental Science and Forestry
State University of New York—
 Stony Brook University
State University of New York—
 University at Buffalo
Stevens Institute of Technology
Texas A&M University—College Station
Tufts University
Tulane University
United States Air Force Academy
United States Military Academy
University of Arizona
University of Arkansas—Fayetteville
University of California—Berkeley
University of California—Davis
University of California—Irvine
University of California—Los Angeles
University of California—Riverside
University of California—San Diego
University of California—Santa Barbara
University of Colorado—Boulder
University of Connecticut
University of Dayton
University of Delaware
University of Florida
University of Houston
University of Idaho
University of Illinois
 at Urbana-Champaign
University of Maryland, Baltimore County
University of Maryland, College Park
University of Massachusetts Amherst
University of Michigan—Ann Arbor
University of Minnesota—Twin Cities
University of Notre Dame
University of Oklahoma
University of Pennsylvania
University of Pittsburgh—
 Pittsburgh Campus
University of Rochester
University of Southern California
The University of Tennessee—Knoxville
The University of Texas at Austin
The University of Tulsa
University of Virginia
University of Washington
University of Wisconsin—Madison
Vanderbilt University
Villanova University
Virginia Polytechnic Institute
 and State University (Virginia Tech)
Washington University in St. Louis

Worcester Polytechnic Institute
Yale University

Civil Engineering
Median starting salary: $57,200
Median mid-career salary: $96,300

Arizona State University
Auburn University
Bradley University
Brigham Young University (UT)
Bucknell University
California State University, Long Beach
Carnegie Mellon University
Case Western Reserve University
City University of New York—
    City College
Clarkson University
Clemson University
The College of New Jersey
The Cooper Union for the Advancement
    of Science and Art
Cornell University
Duke University
Florida State University
George Mason University
Georgia Institute of Technology
Gonzaga University
Harvard College
Illinois Institute of Technology
Iowa State University
Johns Hopkins University
Lafayette College
Lehigh University
Loyola Marymount University
Massachusetts Institute of Technology
Michigan Technological University
Missouri University of Science
    and Technology
North Carolina State University
Northeastern University
Northwestern University
The Ohio State University—Columbus
Oklahoma State University
Pennsylvania State University—
    University Park
Princeton University
Purdue University—West Lafayette
Rensselaer Polytechnic Institute
Rice University
Rose-Hulman Institute of Technology
Rutgers, The State University
    of New Jersey—New Brunswick
Santa Clara University
Stanford University
State University of New York—College of
    Environmental Science and Forestry

State University of New York—
    Stony Brook University
State University of New York—
    University at Buffalo
Stevens Institute of Technology
Texas A&M University—College Station
Tufts University
United States Air Force Academy
United States Coast Guard Academy
United States Military Academy
University of Arizona
University of Arkansas—Fayetteville
University of California—Berkeley
University of California—Davis
University of California—Irvine
University of California—Los Angeles
University of California—San Diego
University of Colorado—Boulder
University of Connecticut
University of Dayton
University of Delaware
University of Florida
University of Georgia
University of Houston
University of Idaho
University of Illinois
    at Urbana-Champaign
University of Maryland, College Park
University of Massachusetts Amherst
University of Minnesota—Twin Cities
University of Oklahoma
University of Pennsylvania
University of Pittsburgh—
    Pittsburgh Campus
University of Southern California
The University of Tennessee—Knoxville
The University of Texas at Austin
University of Utah
University of Virginia
University of Washington
University of Wisconsin—Madison
Vanderbilt University
Villanova University
Virginia Polytechnic Institute
    and State University (Virginia Tech)
Worcester Polytechnic Institute

Computer Engineering
Median starting salary: $69,600
Median mid-career salary: $113,000

Arizona State University
Auburn University
Boston University
Bradley University
Brigham Young University (UT)
Bucknell University

California Institute of Technology
California State University, Long Beach
Carnegie Mellon University
Case Western Reserve University
Clarkson University
Clemson University
The College of New Jersey
Florida State University
George Mason University
Georgia Institute of Technology
Gonzaga University
Harvard College
Illinois Institute of Technology
Iowa State University
Johns Hopkins University
Lafayette College
Lehigh University
Miami University
Michigan Technological University
Missouri University of Science
and Technology
Montana Tech of the University
of Montana
North Carolina State University
Northeastern University
Northwestern University
Oklahoma State University
Pennsylvania State University—
University Park
Princeton University
Purdue University—West Lafayette
Rensselaer Polytechnic Institute
Rochester Institute of Technology
Rose-Hulman Institute of Technology
Santa Clara University
State University of New York
at Binghamton
State University of New York—
Stony Brook University
State University of New York—
University at Buffalo
Stevens Institute of Technology
Texas A&M University—College Station
Tufts University
Tulane University
United States Air Force Academy
United States Naval Academy
University of Arkansas—Fayetteville
University of California—Berkeley
University of California—Davis
University of California—Irvine
University of California—Los Angeles
University of California—Riverside
University of California—San Diego

University of California—Santa Barbara
University of California—Santa Cruz
University of Colorado—Boulder
University of Connecticut
University of Dayton
University of Delaware
University of Denver
University of Florida
University of Georgia
University of Houston
University of Idaho
University of Illinois
at Urbana-Champaign
University of Maryland, Baltimore County
University of Maryland, College Park
University of Massachusetts Amherst
University of Michigan—Ann Arbor
University of Minnesota—Twin Cities
University of Notre Dame
University of Oklahoma
University of Pennsylvania
University of Pittsburgh—
Pittsburgh Campus
University of Southern California
The University of Tennessee—Knoxville
The University of Texas at Dallas
University of Virginia
University of Washington
University of Wisconsin—Madison
Vanderbilt University
Villanova University
Virginia Polytechnic Institute
and State University (Virginia Tech)
Washington University in St. Louis
Worcester Polytechnic Institute

Electrical Engineering
Median starting salary: $67,000
Median mid-career salary: $110,000

Arizona State University
Auburn University
Bradley University
Boston University
Brigham Young University (UT)
Bucknell University
California Institute of Technology
California State University, Long Beach
Carnegie Mellon University
Case Western Reserve University
City University of New York—
City College
Clarkson University
Clemson University
The College of New Jersey

The Cooper Union for the Advancement
  of Science and Art
Cornell University
Duke University
Florida State University
Franklin W. Olin College of Engineering
George Mason University
Georgia Institute of Technology
Gonzaga University
Grove City College
Harvard College
Illinois Institute of Technology
Iowa State University
Johns Hopkins University
Lafayette College
Lehigh University
Loyola Marymount University
Massachusetts Institute of Technology
Miami University
Michigan Technological University
Missouri University of Science
  and Technology
Montana Tech of the University
  of Montana
North Carolina State University
Northeastern University
Northwestern University
The Ohio State University—Columbus
Oklahoma State University
Pennsylvania State University—University
  Park
Princeton University
Purdue University—West Lafayette
Rensselaer Polytechnic Institute
Rochester Institute of Technology
Rice University
Rose-Hulman Institute of Technology
Rutgers, The State University
  of New Jersey—New Brunswick
Santa Clara University
Stanford University
State University of New York
  at Binghamton
State University of New York—
  Maritime College
State University of New York—
  Stony Brook University
State University of New York—
  University at Buffalo
Stevens Institute of Technology
Texas A&M University—College Station
Tufts University
Union College (NY)
United States Air Force Academy
United States Coast Guard Academy

United States Military Academy
United States Naval Academy
University of Arkansas—Fayetteville
University of California—Berkeley
University of California—Davis
University of California—Irvine
University of California—Los Angeles
University of California—Riverside
University of California—San Diego
University of California—Santa Barbara
University of California—Santa Cruz
University of Colorado—Boulder
University of Connecticut
University of Dayton
University of Delaware
University of Denver
University of Florida
University of Georgia
University of Houston
University of Idaho
University of Illinois
  at Urbana-Champaign
University of Maryland, Baltimore County
University of Maryland, College Park
University of Massachusetts Amherst
University of Michigan—Ann Arbor
University of Minnesota—Twin Cities
University of Notre Dame
University of Oklahoma
University of Pennsylvania
University of Pittsburgh—Pittsburgh
  Campus
University of Rochester
University of Southern California
The University of Tennessee—Knoxville
The University of Texas at Austin
The University of Texas at Dallas
The University of Tulsa
University of Virginia
University of Washington
University of Wisconsin—Madison
Vanderbilt University
Villanova University
Virginia Polytechnic Institute
  and State University (Virginia Tech)
Washington University in St. Louis
Worcester Polytechnic Institute
Yale University

Industrial Engineering

Median starting salary: $63,800
Median mid-career salary: $104,000

Arizona State University
Auburn University
Bradley University

California State University, Long Beach
Clemson University
Florida State University
George Mason University
Georgia Institute of Technology
Gonzaga University
Iowa State University
Lehigh University
Missouri University of Science
   and Technology
North Carolina State University
Northeastern University
Northwestern University
The Ohio State University—Columbus
Oklahoma State University
Pennsylvania State University—
   University Park
Purdue University—West Lafayette
Rensselaer Polytechnic Institute
Rochester Institute of Technology
State University of New York
   at Binghamton
State University of New York—
   Maritime College
State University of New York—
   University at Buffalo
Texas A&M University—College Station
University of Arizona
University of Arkansas—Fayetteville
University of Connecticut
University of Florida
University of Houston
University of Idaho
University of Illinois
   at Urbana-Champaign
University of Massachusetts Amherst
University of Michigan—Ann Arbor
University of Minnesota—Twin Cities
University of Oklahoma
University of Pittsburgh—
   Pittsburgh Campus
University of Southern California
The University of Tennessee—Knoxville
University of Washington
University of Wisconsin—Madison
Virginia Polytechnic Institute
   and State University (Virginia Tech)
Worcester Polytechnic Institute

Materials Science and Engineering
Median starting salary: $65,800
Median mid-career salary: $108,000

Arizona State University
Bradley University
California Institute of Technology

California State University, Long Beach
Case Western Reserve University
Clarkson University
Clemson University
Cornell University
Georgia Institute of Technology
Harvard College
Illinois Institute of Technology
Iowa State University
Johns Hopkins University
Lehigh University
Massachusetts Institute of Technology
Michigan Institute of Technology
Missouri University of Science
   and Technology
North Carolina State University
Northwestern University
The Ohio State University—Columbus
Purdue University—West Lafayette
Rensselaer Polytechnic Institute
Rice University
Rochester Institute of Technology
Stanford University
University of California—Berkeley
University of California—Davis
University of California—Irvine
University of California—Los Angeles
University of California—Riverside
University of Florida
University of Houston
University of Idaho
University of Illinois
   at Urbana-Champaign
University of Maryland, College Park
University of Michigan—Ann Arbor
University of Minnesota—Twin Cities
University of Pennsylvania
University of Pittsburgh—
   Pittsburgh Campus
University of Rochester
The University of Tennessee—Knoxville
University of Virginia
University of Wisconsin—Madison
Virginia Polytechnic Institute and State
   University (Virginia Tech)

Mechanical Engineering
Median starting salary: $63,500
Median mid-career salary: $103,000

Auburn University
Bradley University
California Institute of Technology
Clarkson University
The Cooper Union for the Advancement
   of Science and Art

Cornell University
Franklin W. Olin College of Engineering
Georgia Institute of Technology
Grove City College
Illinois Institute of Technology
Iowa State University
Lafayette College
Lehigh University
Loyola Marymount University
Massachusetts Institute of Technology
Michigan Technological University
Missouri University of Science
  and Technology
North Carolina State University
Princeton University
Purdue University—West Lafayette
Rochester Institute of Technology
Rose-Hulman Institute of Technology
State University of New York—Maritime
  College
Stevens Institute of Technology
University of Arkansas—Fayetteville
University of Connecticut
University of Florida
University of Idaho
University of Maryland, Baltimore County
University of Portland
The University of Tulsa
University of Utah
Worcester Polytechnic Institute

Nuclear Engineering

Median starting salary: $68,500
Median mid-career salary: $116,000

Georgia Institute of Technology
Massachusetts Institute of Technology
Missouri University of Science
  and Technology
North Carolina State University
The Ohio State University—Columbus
Pennsylvania State University—
  University Park
Purdue University—West Lafayette
Rensselaer Polytechnic Institute
Texas A&M University—College Station
United States Military Academy
United States Naval Academy
University of California—Berkeley
University of Florida
University of Illinois
  at Urbana-Champaign
University of Michigan—Ann Arbor
The University of Tennessee—Knoxville
University of Wisconsin—Madison

Petroleum Engineering

Median starting salary: $96,700
Median mid-career salary: $172,000

Missouri University of Science
  and Technology
Montana Tech of the
  University of Montana
Pennsylvania State University—
  University Park
Texas A&M University—College Station
University of Houston
University of Oklahoma
University of Southern California
The University of Texas at Austin
The University of Tulsa
University of Utah

Software Engineering

Median starting salary: $64,700
Median mid-career salary: $98,100

Arizona State University
Auburn University
Carnegie Mellon University
Clarkson University
George Mason University
Harvard College
Iowa State University
Michigan Technological University
Montana Tech of the
  University of Montana
Purdue University—West Lafayette
Rochester Institute of Technology
Rose-Hulman Institute of Technology
University of California—Irvine
University of Illinois
  at Urbana-Champaign
University of Southern California
The University of Texas at Dallas

Systems Engineering

Median starting salary: $66,400
Median mid-career salary: $121,000

Case Western Reserve University
Cornell University
George Mason University
Harvard College
Purdue University—West Lafayette
Rochester Institute of Technology
Stevens Institute of Technology
United States Military Academy
United States Naval Academy
University of Arizona
University of California—Santa Cruz
University of Florida

University of Houston
University of Minnesota—Twin Cities
University of Pennsylvania
University of Virginia
Washington University in St. Louis

ENGINEERING TECHNOLOGIES

Electrical Engineering Technology
Median starting salary: $59,900
Median mid-career salary: $89,900

Arizona State University
George Mason University
Michigan Technological University
Oklahoma State University
Purdue University—West Lafayette
Rochester Institute of Technology
Texas A&M University—College Station
University of California—Irvine
University of Dayton
Environmental Engineering
Median starting salary: $53,900
Median mid-career salary: $92,800
California State University, Long Beach
North Carolina State University
Purdue University—West Lafayette
Rochester Institute of Technology
United States Military Academy

Industrial Technology
Median starting salary: $55,200
Median mid-career salary: $83,400

Arizona State University
Purdue University—West Lafayette
University of Dayton
University of Idaho
Mechanical Engineering Technology
Median starting salary: $57,600
Median mid-career salary: $87,400
Arizona State University
City University of New York—
   City College
City University of New York—
   Hunter College
Miami University
Michigan Technological University
Oklahoma State University
Purdue University—West Lafayette
Rochester Institute of Technology
United States Military Academy
University of Arizona
University of Dayton
University of Florida

University of Houston
University of Maryland, Baltimore County

Food Science
Median starting salary: $46,700
Median mid-career salary: $81,100

Amherst College
Auburn University
Brigham Young University (UT)
Case Western Reserve University
City University of New York—
   City College
City University of New York—
   Hunter College
Clemson University
Colby College
The College of Wooster
Colorado College
Cornell University
Dartmouth College
Emory University
George Mason University
Hamilton College
Indiana University—Bloomington
Lafayette College
Lawrence University
Miami University
Middlebury College
North Carolina State University
Oberlin College
Oklahoma State University
Pennsylvania State University—
   University Park
Pepperdine University
Purdue University—West Lafayette
Rhodes College
Scripps College
St. Olaf College
Texas A&M University—College Station
Trinity College (CT)
Tufts University
Tulane University
Union College (NY)
University of Arkansas—Fayetteville
University of California—Los Angeles
University of California—Riverside
University of California—San Diego
The University of Chicago
University of Colorado—Boulder
University of Dayton
University of Delaware
University of Florida
University of Georgia

University of Illinois at Urbana-
  Champaign
University of Maryland, College Park
University of Massachusetts Amherst
University of Michigan—Ann Arbor
University of Minnesota—Twin Cities
University of Richmond
University of Rochester
University of Southern California
The University of Tennessee—Knoxville
The University of Texas at Austin
The University of Tulsa
University of Wisconsin—Madison
Wellesley College
Yale University

Industrial and Product Design
Median starting salary: $48,600
Median mid-career salary: $82,100

Arizona State University
Auburn University
Brigham Young University (UT)
California State University, Long Beach
Carnegie Mellon University
City University of New York—
  Brooklyn College
Georgia Institute of Technology
North Carolina State University
The Ohio State University—Columbus
Purdue University—West Lafayette
Rochester Institute of Technology
Stanford University
University of Houston
University of Michigan—Ann Arbor
University of Washington
Virginia Polytechnic Institute
  and State University (Virginia Tech)

MATHEMATICS AND STATISTICS

Mathematics
Median starting salary: $53,700
Median mid-career salary: $95,300

Bowdoin College
Bryn Mawr College
California Institute of Technology
Carleton College
Harvey Mudd College

Applied Mathematics
Median starting salary: $56,100
Median mid-career salary: $110,000

Arizona State University
Auburn University

Barnard College
Bradley University
Berea College
Boston College
Brown University
California Institute of Technology
California State University, Long Beach
Carnegie Mellon University
Case Western Reserve University
City University of New York—
  Baruch College
City University of New York—
  Brooklyn College
Clark University
Clarkson University
Colgate University
Creighton University
Emory University
Georgia Institute of Technology
Gettysburg College
Harvard College
Illinois Institute of Technology
Iowa State University
Loyola University Maryland
Missouri University of Science
  and Technology
New College of Florida
North Carolina State University
Northwestern University
Purdue University—West Lafayette
Rensselaer Polytechnic Institute
Rice University
Southwestern University
Stanford University
State University of New York—
  Stony Brook University
State University of New York—
  University at Buffalo
Stevens Institute of Technology
Texas A&M University—College Station
Tufts University
Tulane University
University of Arizona
University of California—Berkeley
University of California—Davis
University of California—Los Angeles
University of California—San Diego
University of California—Santa Barbara
University of California—Santa Cruz
University of Colorado—Boulder
University of Connecticut
University of Houston
University of Idaho
University of Illinois
  at Urbana-Champaign

University of Maryland, Baltimore County
University of Minnesota—Twin Cities
University of Rochester
University of Southern California
The University of Texas at Dallas
The University of Tulsa
University of Wisconsin—Madison
Vanderbilt University
Washington University in St. Louis
Whitman College
Willamette University
Worcester Polytechnic Institute
Yale University

Statistics
Median starting salary: $57,400
Median mid-career salary: $97,500

Arizona State University
Auburn University
Barnard College
Bradley University
Brigham Young University (UT)
California State University, Long Beach
Carnegie Mellon University
Case Western Reserve University
City University of New York—
    Baruch College
Colby College
Cornell University
Florida State University
George Mason University
Hampden-Sydney College
Harvard College
Indiana University—Bloomington
Iowa State University
Lehigh University
Loyola University Maryland
Miami University
Michigan Technological University
Missouri University of Science
    and Technology
Montana Tech of the
    University of Montana
Mount Holyoke College
North Carolina State University
Northwestern University
Oklahoma State University
Purdue University—West Lafayette
Rice University
Rochester Institute of Technology
Rutgers, The State University
    of New Jersey—New Brunswick
Stanford University
Stevens Institute of Technology
United States Military Academy

University of Arizona
University of California—Berkeley
University of California—Davis
University of California—Los Angeles
University of California—Riverside
University of California—San Diego
University of California—Santa Barbara
The University of Chicago
University of Connecticut
University of Delaware
University of Denver
University of Florida
University of Illinois
    at Urbana-Champaign
University of Maryland, Baltimore County
University of Michigan—Ann Arbor
University of Minnesota—Twin Cities
University of Pennsylvania
University of Rochester
The University of Tennessee—Knoxville
University of Virginia
University of Washington
University of Wisconsin—Madison
Virginia Polytechnic Institute
    and State University (Virginia Tech)
Wake Forest University
Washington University in St. Louis
Williams College

HEALTH PROFESSIONS

Environmental Health and Safety
Median starting salary: $51,200
Median mid-career salary: $89,800

Purdue University—West Lafayette
State University of New York—College of
    Environmental Science and Forestry
Tulane University
University of Arizona
University of Georgia
University of Minnesota—Twin Cities
University of North Carolina
    at Chapel Hill
University of Washington
Willamette University

Nursing
Median starting salary: $57,500
Median mid-career salary: $74,100

Arizona State University
Auburn University
Boston College
Bradley University
Case Western Reserve University
College of the Ozarks

Creighton University
Emory University
Florida State University
George Mason University
Gonzaga University
Indiana University—Bloomington
Northeastern University
St. Anselm College
St. Olaf College
State University of New York at
    Binghamton
State University of New York—
    Stony Brook University
State University of New York—
    University at Buffalo
Truman State University
University of Arizona
University of Arkansas—Fayetteville
University of California—Irvine
University of California—Los Angeles
University of Connecticut
University of Delaware
University of Massachusetts Amherst
University of Michigan—Ann Arbor
University of Pennsylvania
University of Pittsburgh—
    Pittsburgh Campus
University of Portland
The University of Tennessee—Knoxville
The University of Tulsa
University of Utah
University of Wisconsin—Madison
Villanova University
William Jewell College

Physical Therapy
Median starting salary: $60,300
Median mid-career salary: $86,600

Clarkson University
Northeastern University
Purdue University—West Lafayette
University of Florida
University of Minnesota—Twin Cities
University of Utah

Physician Assistant Studies
Median starting salary: $85,200
Median mid-career salary: $103,000

Purdue University—West Lafayette
Rochester Institute of Technology
University of Florida
University of Washington
Wake Forest University

PHYSICAL SCIENCES
Geology
Median starting salary: $44,800
Median mid-career salary: $79,800

Amherst College
Arizona State University
    at the Tempe campus
Bates College
Boston College
Boston University
Bowdoin College
Brigham Young University (UT)
Brooklyn College,
    City University of New York
Brown University
Bryn Mawr College
Bucknell University
California Institute of Technology
California State University—Long Beach
Carleton College
Case Western Reserve University
Clemson University
Colby College
Colgate University
The College of William and Mary
The College of Wooster
Colorado College
Cornell University
Dartmouth College
Denison University
DePauw University
Dickinson College
Duke University
Florida State University
Furman University
George Mason University
Gustavus Adolphus College
Hamilton College
Haverford College
Indiana University Bloomington
Iowa State University
James Madison University
Johns Hopkins University
Lawrence University
Macalester College
Massachusetts Institute of Technology
Miami University
Michigan Technological University
Middlebury College
Missouri University of Science
    and Technology
Mount Holyoke College
North Carolina State University
Northeastern University

Northwestern University
Oberlin College
Occidental College
Oklahoma State University
Pennsylvania State University—
  University Park
Purdue University—West Lafayette
The Ohio State University—Columbus
Rensselaer Polytechnic Institute
Rice University
Rutgers, The State University
  of New Jersey—New Brunswick
Scripps College
Skidmore College
Smith College
St. Lawrence University
Stanford University
State University of New York at
  Binghamton (Binghamton University)
State University of New York—
  Stony Brook University
State University of New York—
  University at Buffalo
Texas A&M University—College Station
Trinity University
Tufts University
Tulane University
Union College
University of Arizona
University of California, Davis
University of California, Los Angeles
University of California-Irvine
University of California—Riverside
University of California—San Diego
University of California—Santa Barbara
University of California—Santa Cruz
University of Colorado Boulder
University of Dayton
University of Delaware
University of Florida
University of Georgia
University of Houston
University of Idaho
University of Illinois
  at Urbana-Champaign
University of Maryland, College Park
University of Massachusetts Amherst
University of Michigan—Ann Arbor
University of Minnesota—
  Twin Cities Campus
The University of North Carolina
  at Chapel Hill
University of Oklahoma
University of Pennsylvania

University of Pittsburgh—
  Pittsburgh Campus
University of Rochester
University of Southern California
The University of Tennessee—Knoxville
The University of Texas at Austin
The University of Texas at Dallas
The University of Tulsa
University of Washington
University of Wisconsin—Madison
Vanderbilt University
Vassar College
Virginia Tech
Washington University in St. Louis
Wellesley College
Wesleyan University
Wheaton College (IL)
Whitman College
Yale University

Meteorology
Median starting salary: $43,600
Median mid-career salary: $82,700

Cornell University
Creighton University
Florida State University
George Mason University
Iowa State University
North Carolina State University
Penn State University Park
Purdue University—West Lafayette
Rutgers, The State University
  of New Jersey—New Brunswick
State University of New York—College of
  Environmental Science and Forestry
State University of New York—
  Maritime College
State University of New York—
  Stony Brook University
Texas A&M University—College Station
United States Air Force Academy
University of Arizona
University of California, Davis
University of Houston
University of Illinois
  at Urbana-Champaign
University of Maryland, College Park
University of Michigan—Ann Arbor
University of Oklahoma
University of Washington
University of Wisconsin—Madison
Virginia Tech

Physics
Median starting salary: $55,100
Median mid-career salary: $108,000

Bryn Mawr College
California Institute of Technology
Carleton College
The College of Wooster
Colorado College
Furman University
Gustavus Adolphus College
Harvey Mudd College
Haverford College
Kalamazoo College
Massachusetts Institute of Technology
Pitzer College
Princeton University
Rhodes College
St. Olaf College
United States Coast Guard Academy
United States Naval Academy
The University of Chicago
Wabash College
Whitman College
Willamette University
Williams College

SOCIAL SCIENCES

Economics
Median starting salary: $53,900
Median mid-career salary: $100,000

Amherst College
Boston College
Bowdoin College
Brandeis University
Brown University
Bucknell University
Centre College
Claremont McKenna College
Colby College
Colgate University
College of the Holy Cross
Colorado College
Connecticut College
Cornell University
Dartmouth College
Denison University
DePauw University
Duke University
Emory University
Grinnell College
Hamilton College
Hampden-Sydney College
Harvard College

Hobart and William Smith Colleges
Kalamazoo College
Kenyon College
Knox College
Lafayette College
Macalester College
Middlebury College
Mount Holyoke College
Northwestern University
Occidental College
Pitzer College
Princeton University
Rice University
Smith College
St. Lawrence University
St. Olaf College
Swarthmore College
Trinity College (CT)
Tufts University
Union College (NY)
United States Military Academy
United States Naval Academy
University of California—Davis
University of California—San Diego
University of California—Santa Barbara
The University of Chicago
University of Maryland, College Park
University of Michigan—Ann Arbor
The University of North Carolina
   at Chapel Hill
University of Pennsylvania
University of Rochester
University of Wisconsin—Madison
Vassar College
Wellesley College
Wesleyan University
Willamette University
Williams College
Yale University

International Relations
Median starting salary: $46,500
Median mid-career salary: $86,400

Boston University
Brigham Young University (UT)
Brown University
Bucknell University
Carleton College
Carnegie Mellon University
Case Western Reserve University
City University of New York—
   City College
Claremont McKenna College
Colgate University
The College of New Jersey

The College of William & Mary
The College of Wooster
Connecticut College
Creighton University
Denison University
Dickinson College
Drake University
Florida State University
George Mason University
Georgetown University
Georgia Institute of Technology
Gettysburg College
Gonzaga University
Hamilton College
Hampden-Sydney College
Harvard College
Hobart and William Smith Colleges
Indiana University—Bloomington
James Madison University
Johns Hopkins University
Lafayette College
Lake Forest College
Lehigh University
Lewis & Clark College
Miami University
Middlebury College
Mount Holyoke College
Muhlenberg College
Northeastern University
Northwestern University
Occidental College
The Ohio State University—Columbus
Reed College
Rhodes College
Skidmore College
Southwestern University
Stanford University
State University of New York
   at Binghamton
State University of New York at Geneseo
Trinity University
Tufts University
United States Military Academy
University of Arizona
University of California—Davis
The University of Chicago
University of Delaware
University of Denver
University of Florida
University of Minnesota—Twin Cities
University of Pennsylvania
University of Southern California
The University of Tulsa
University of Virginia

Vassar College
Virginia Polytechnic Institute
   and State University (Virginia Tech)
Washington University in St. Louis
Wellesley College
Wheaton College (IL)
William Jewell College
Yale University

POLITICAL SCIENCE AND GOVERNMENT

Political Science
Median starting salary: $44,300
Median mid-career salary: $79,900

Agnes Scott College
Amherst College
Arizona State University
Auburn University
Barnard College
Bates College
Beloit College
Berea College
Boston College
Boston University
Bowdoin College
Bradley University
Brigham Young University (UT)
Brown University
Bryn Mawr College
Bucknell University
California Institute of Technology
California State University—Long Beach
Carleton College
Case Western Reserve University
Centre College
City University of New York—
   Baruch College
City University of New York—
   Brooklyn College
City University of New York—
   City College
City University of New York—
   Hunter College
Claremont McKenna College
Clarkson University
Clark University
Clemson University
Colby College
Colgate University
College of the Holy Cross
The College of New Jersey
College of William and Mary
College of Wooster

Colorado College
Columbia University
Connecticut College
Cornell University
Creighton University
Dartmouth College
Davidson College
Denison University
DePauw University
Dickinson College
Drake University
Duke University
Emory University
Florida State University
Franklin & Marshall College
Furman University
Georgetown University
Gettysburg College
Gonzaga University
Grinnell College
Grove City College
Gustavus Adolphus College
Hamilton College
Hampden-Sydney College
Harvard College
Haverford College
Illinois Institute of Technology
Illinois Wesleyan University
Indiana University—Bloomington
Iowa State University
James Madison University
Johns Hopkins University
Kalamazoo College
Kenyon College
Knox College
Lafayette College
Lake Forest College
Lehigh University
Lewis & Clark College
Loyola Marymount University
Macalester College
Massachusetts Institute of Technology
Miami University
Middlebury College
Mount Holyoke College
Muhlenberg College
New College of Florida
Northeastern University
North Carolina State University
Northwestern University
Oberlin College
Occidental College
Ohio State University—Columbus
Pennsylvania State University—
   University Park
Pepperdine University

Pitzer College
Princeton University
Purdue University—West Lafayette
Reed College
Rhodes College
Rice University
Rutgers, The State University
   of New Jersey—New Brunswick
Saint Mary's College (CA)
Santa Clara University
Scripps College
Skidmore College
Smith College
Southwestern University
Stanford University
St. Anselm College
State University of New York
   at Binghamton
State University of New York at Geneseo
State University of New York—
   Stony Brook University
State University of New York—
   University at Buffalo
St. Lawrence University
St. Olaf College
Swarthmore College
Texas A&M University—College Station
Trinity College (CT)
Trinity University
Truman State University
Tulane University
Union College (NY)
United States Coast Guard Academy
United States Military Academy
United States Naval Academy
University of Arizona
University of Arkansas—Fayetteville
University of California—Berkeley
University of California—Davis
University of California-Irvine
University of California—Los Angeles
University of California—Riverside
University of California—San Diego
University of California—Santa Cruz
University of Chicago
University of Colorado—Boulder
University of Connecticut
University of Dayton
University of Delaware
University of Denver
University of Florida
University of Georgia
University of Houston
University of Idaho
University of Maryland, Baltimore County
University of Maryland, College Park

University of Massachusetts-Amherst
University of Michigan—Ann Arbor
University of Minnesota—Twin Cities
University of North Carolina
 at Chapel Hill
University of Notre Dame
University of Oklahoma
University of Pennsylvania
University of Pittsburgh—
 Pittsburgh Campus
University of Portland
University of Richmond
University of Rochester
University of Southern California
University of Tennessee- Knoxville
University of Texas at Austin
The University of Texas at Dallas
University of Tulsa
University of Utah
University of Virginia
University of Washington
University of Wisconsin-Madison
Vanderbilt University
Vassar College
Villanova University
Virginia Tech
Wabash College
Wake Forest University
Washington University in St. Louis
Wellesley College
Wesleyan University
Wheaton College (IL)
Willamette University
William Jewell College
Williams College
Wofford College
Yale University

Government
Median starting salary: $49,600
Median mid-career salary: $105,000

Amherst College
Barnard College
Bates College
Bowdoin College
Claremont McKenna College
Clark University
College of the Holy Cross
Columbia University
Connecticut College
Dartmouth College
Davidson College
Dickinson College
Franklin & Marshall College

Furman University
Georgetown University
Gettysburg College
Grinnell College
Hamilton College
Hampden-Sydney College
Harvard College
Hobart and William Smith Colleges
Lafayette College
Middlebury College
New College of Florida
Pepperdine University
Princeton University
Scripps College
Smith College
St. Lawrence University
Swarthmore College
Trinity College (CT)
United States Coast Guard Academy
United States Naval Academy
University of Arizona
University of California—Berkeley
The University of Chicago
University of Illinois
 at Urbana-Champaign
University of Notre Dame
University of Wisconsin—Madison
Vassar College
Wake Forest University
Wellesley College
Yale University

About Our Student Survey

Surveying tens of thousands of students on hundreds of campuses is a mammoth undertaking. In 1992, our survey was a paper survey. We worked with school administrators to set up tables in centrally-trafficked locations on their campuses at which students filled out the surveys. To reach a range of students, freshmen to seniors, this process sometimes took place over several days and at various on-campus locations. That process yielded about 125 surveys per college.

However, the launch of our online survey several years ago made our survey process more efficient, secure, and representative. Our student survey is also now a continuous process. Students submit surveys online from all schools in the book and they can submit their surveys at any time at http://survey.review.com. (However, our site will accept only one survey from a student per academic year per school (it's not possible to "stuff" the ballot box, as it were).) In addition to those surveys we receive from students on an ongoing basis, we also conduct "formal" surveys of students at each school in the book at least once every three years. (We conduct these more often once every three years if the colleges request that we do so (and we can accommodate that request) or we deem it necessary.)

How do we do conduct those "formal" surveys? First, we notify our administrative contacts at the schools we plan to survey. We depend upon these contacts for assistance in informing the student body of our survey (although we also get the word out to students about our survey via other channels independent of the schools). An increasing number of schools have chosen to send an e-mail to the entire student body about the availability of our online survey; in such cases this has yielded robust response rates. Our average number of student surveys (per college) is now 375 students per campus (and at some schools we hear from more than 3,000 students).

And of course, surveys we receive from students outside of their schools' normal survey cycles are always factored into the subsequent year's ranking calculations, so our pool of student survey data is continuously refreshed.

The survey has more than eighty questions divided into four sections: "About Yourself," "Your School's Academics/Administration," "Students," and "Life at Your School." We ask about all sorts of things, from "How many out-of-class hours do you spend studying each day?" to "How do you rate your campus food?" Most questions offer students a five-point grid on which to indicate their answer choices (headers may range from "Excellent" to "Awful"). Eight questions offer students the opportunity to expand on their answers with narrative comment. These essay-type responses are the sources of the student quotations that appear in the school profiles. Once the surveys have been completed and responses stored in our database, every college is given a score (similar to a grade point average) for its students' answers to each question. This score enables us to compare students' responses to a particular question from one college to the next. We use these scores as an underlying data point in our calculation of the ratings in the profile sidebars and the ranking lists in the section of the book titled "School Rankings and Lists."

Once we have the student survey information in hand, we write the college profiles. Student quotations in each profile are chosen because they represent the sentiments expressed by the majority of survey respondents from the college; or, they illustrate one side or another of a mixed bag of student opinion, in which case there will also appear a counterpoint within the text. In order to guard against producing a write-up that's off the mark for any particular college, we send our administrative contact at each school a copy of the profile we intend to publish prior to its publication date, with ample opportunity to respond with corrections, comments, and/or outright objections. In every case in which we receive requests for changes, we take careful measures to review the school's suggestions against the student survey data we collected and make appropriate changes when warranted.

How To Use This Book

It's pretty self-explanatory. We have done our best to include lots of helpful information about choosing colleges and gaining admission. The profiles we have written contain the same basic information for each school and follow the same basic format. The Princeton Review collects all of the data you see in the sidebars of each school. As is customary with college guides, our numbers usually reflect the figures for the academic year prior to publication. Since college offerings and demographics significantly vary from one institution to another and some colleges report data more thoroughly than others, some entries will not include all of the individual data described. Please know that we take our data-collection process seriously. We reach out to schools numerous times through the process to ensure we can present you with the most accurate and up-to-date facts, figures, and deadlines. Even so, a book is dated from the moment it hits the printing press. Be sure to double-check with any schools to which you plan to apply to make sure you are able to get them everything they need in order to meet their deadlines.

How This Book Is Organized

Each of the colleges and universities in this book has its own two-page profile. To make it easier to find and compare information about the schools, we've used the same profile format for every school. First, at the very top of the profile you will see the school's address, telephone, and fax numbers for the admissions office, the telephone number for the financial aid office, and the school's website and/or e-mail address. Second, there are two sidebars (the narrow columns on the outside of each page, which consist mainly of statistics) divided into the categories of Campus Life, Academics, Selectivity, and Financial Facts. Third, at the bottom of the page you will find a PayScale.com Career Information box with the each school's ROI rating and salary figures. Finally, there are seven headings in the narrative text: About the School, Bang for Your Buck, Student Life, Career, General Info, Financial Aid, and The Bottom Line.

Sidebars

The sidebars contain various statistics culled from our surveys of students attending the school and from questionnaires that school administrators complete at our request in the fall of each year. Keep in mind that not every category will appear for every school—in some cases the information is not reported or not applicable. We compile the eight ratings— Quality of Life, Fire Safety, Green Rating, Academic, Profs Interesting, Profs Accessible, Admissions Selectivity, and Financial Aid—listed in the sidebars based on the results from our student surveys and/or institutional data we collect from school administrators.

These ratings are on a scale of 60–99. If a 60* (60 with an asterisk) appears as any rating for any school, it means that the school reported so few of the rating's underlying data points by our deadline that we were unable to calculate an accurate rating for it. (These measures are outlined in the ratings explanation below.) Be advised that, because the Admissions Selectivity Rating is a factor in the computation that produces the Academic Rating, a school that has 60* (60 with an asterisk) as its Admissions Selectivity Rating will have an Academic Rating that is lower than it should be. Also bear in mind that each rating places each college on a continuum for purposes of comparing colleges within this edition only. Since our ratings computations may change from year to year, it is invalid to compare the ratings in this edition to those that appear in any prior or future edition.

PayScale.com Career Information Box

This box includes up to seven data points: our unique ROI rating; median starting salary reported by alumni and median mid-career salary reported by alumni, both those holding a bachelor's degree and those with at least a bachelor's degree which includes students who have gone on to a higher degree; the percentage of alumni that report having high job meaning (i.e., feeling that their job makes the world a better place); and the percentage of degrees the school awarded in STEM (science, engineering, technology, and math). Alumni survey information comes from PayScale.com's 2015–2016 College Salary Report. Some school profiles do not include all of these data points, as PayScale.com only reports survey results based on a statistically significant sample of responses. The data used for PayScale.com's annual College Salary Report is collected through their ongoing, online compensation survey. You can read more about their survey and methodology online at www.PayScale.com/college-salary-report/ methodology.

Our ROI rating is based on data we collected from fall 2015 through fall 2016 via our institutional and student surveys. It is calculated using more than forty data points covering academics, costs, financial aid, career outcomes, and student and alumni survey data.

We asked students to rate their schools career services office, the opportunities for internships and experiential learning, and the strength of their alumni network on campus. Starting and mid-career salary data was taken from PayScale.com's 2015–16 College Salary Report. In addition to salary data, PayScale.com provided data on alumni who reported high job meaning.

Also considered are the percentage of graduating seniors who borrowed from any loan program and the average debt those students had at graduation. The percentage of students graduating within four and six years was also taken into account.

Additional criteria included the following breakdown of Princeton Review's ratings:

Academic Rating

To tally this rating, we analyze a large amount of data the schools report to us about their academic selectivity and admissions, plus opinion data we collect from students reporting on the education they are receiving at their schools. The admissions statistics shed light on how difficult it is to gain acceptance: they include average SAT/ACT scores and high school GPA of enrolled freshmen as well as other data factors. The student data reveals how students at the school rate their professors' teaching ability as well as how accessible the professors are outside of class.

Financial Aid Rating

This rating measures how much financial aid a school awards and how satisfied students are with that aid. This rating is based on school-reported data on the percentage of students who were determined to have need and received aid, the percentage of need met for those students, and the percentage of students whose need was fully met. Student survey data that measures students' satisfaction with the financial aid they receive is also considered.

Nota Bene: *The following ratings appear in each school profile, but were not included in the ROI methodology.*

Quality of Life Rating:

On a scale of 60–99, this rating is a measure of how happy students are with their campus experiences outside the classroom. To compile this rating, we weighed several factors, all based on students' answers to questions on our survey. They included the students' assessments of: their overall happiness; the beauty, safety, and location of the campus; comfort of dorms; quality of food; ease of getting around campus and dealing with administrators; friendliness of fellow students; and the interaction of different student types on campus and within the greater community.

Fire Safety Rating:

On a scale of 60–99, this rating measures how well prepared a school is to prevent or respond to campus fires, specifically in residence halls. We asked schools several questions about their efforts to ensure fire safety for campus residents. We developed the questions in consultation with the Center for Campus Fire Safety (www.campusfiresafety. org). Each school's responses to seven questions were considered when calculating its Fire Safety Rating. They cover:

1. The percentage of student housing sleeping rooms protected by an automatic fire sprinkler system with a fire sprinkler head located in the individual sleeping rooms.

2. The percentage of student housing sleeping rooms equipped with a smoke detector connected to a supervised fire alarm system.

3. The number of malicious fire alarms that occur in student housing per year.

4. The number of unwanted fire alarms that occur in student housing per year.

5. The banning of certain hazardous items and activities in residence halls, like candles, smoking, halogen lamps, etc.

6. The percentage of student housing fire alarm systems that, if activated, result in a signal being transmitted to a monitored location, where security investigates before notifying the fire department.

7. The percentage of student housing fire alarm systems that, if activated, result in a signal being transmitted immediately to a continuously monitored location.

Schools that did not report answers to a sufficient number of questions receive a Fire Safety Rating of 60* (60 with an asterisk). You can also find Fire Safety Ratings for our *Colleges That Pay You Back* (and several additional schools) in *The Complete Book of Colleges*, 2017 Edition and in *Best 381 Colleges* book.

Green Rating:

We asked all the schools we collect data from annually to answer a number of questions that evaluate the comprehensive measure of their performance as an environmentally aware and responsible institution. The questions were first developed in consultation with ecoAmerica (www.ecoAmerica.org), a research and partnership-based environmental nonprofit that convened an expert committee to design this comprehensive rating system, and cover: 1) whether students have a campus quality of life that is both healthy and sustainable; 2) how well a school is preparing students not only for employment in the clean energy economy of the twenty-first century, but also for citizenship in a world now defined by environmental challenges; and 3) how environmentally responsible a school's policies are.

Additionally, The Princeton Review, the Association for the Advancement of Sustainability in Higher Education (AASHE) and Sierra magazine have now collaborated on an effort to streamline the reporting process for institutions that choose to participate in various higher education sustainability assessments. The intent of this initiative is to reduce and streamline the amount of time campus staff spend tracking sustainability data and completing related surveys.

To address this issue these four groups have worked to establish the Campus Sustainability Data Collector (CSDC). The CSDC is based off of the STARS Reporting Tool and is available for all schools (free of charge) that would like to submit data to these groups in one single survey.

Please find more information here:

http://www.princetonreview.com/green-data-partnership

Each school's responses to ten questions were considered when calculating The Princeton Review's Green Rating.

They include:

1. The percentage of food expenditures that go toward local, organic, or otherwise environmentally preferable food.

2. Whether the school offers programs including mass transit programs, bike sharing, facilities for bicyclists, bicycle and pedestrian plan, car sharing, carpool discount, carpool/vanpool matching, cash-out of parking, prohibiting idling, local housing, telecommuting, and condensed work week.

3. Whether the school has a formal committee that is devoted to advancing sustainability on campus.

4. Whether school buildings that were constructed or underwent major renovations in the past three years are LEED certified.

5. The schools overall waste-diversion rate.

6. Whether the school offers at least one sustainability-focused undergraduate major, degree program, or equivalent.

7. Whether the school's students graduate from programs that include sustainability as a required learning outcome or include multiple sustainability learning outcomes.

8. Whether the school has a formal plan to mitigate its greenhouse gas emissions.

9. What percentage of the school's energy consumption is derived from renewable resources.

10. Whether the school employs a dedicated full-time (or full-time equivalent) sustainability officer.

Colleges that did not supply answers to a sufficient number of the green campus questions for us to fairly compare them to other colleges receive a Green Rating of 60*.

Check out our free downloadable resource, The Princeton Review's *Guide to 361 Green Colleges* at www.princetonreview.com/green-guide.

In addition to these ratings, we have compiled the following information about each school. Keep in mind that not all schools responded to our requests for information, so not all of this information will appear in every profile.

Type of school: Whether the school is public or private.

Affiliation: Any religious order with which the school is affiliated.

Environment: Whether the campus is located in an urban, suburban, or rural setting.

Total undergrad enrollment: The total number of degree-seeking undergraduates who attend the school. The total number of undergraduates who attend the school.

"% male/female" through "# countries represented": Demographic information about the full-time undergraduate student body, including male to female ratio, ethnicity, and the number of countries represented by the student body. Also included are the percentages of the student body who are from out of state, attended a public high school, freshmen living on campus, and belong to Greek organizations.

Academic Rating: On a scale of 60–99, this rating is a measure of how hard students work at the school and how much they get back for their efforts. The rating is based on results from our surveys of students and data we collect from administrators. Factors weighed included how many hours students reported that they study each day outside of class, students' assessments of their professors' teaching abilities and of their accessibility outside the classroom and the quality of students the school attracts as measured by admissions statistics.

4-year graduation rate: The percentage of degree-seeking undergraduate students graduating in four years or less.

6-year graduation rate: The percentage of degree-seeking undergraduate students graduating within six years.

Calendar: The school's schedule of academic terms. A "semester" schedule has two long terms, usually starting in September and January. A "trimester" schedule has three terms, one usually beginning before Christmas and two after. A "quarterly" schedule has four terms, which go by very quickly: the entire term, including exams, usually lasts only nine or ten weeks. A "4-1-4" schedule is like a semester schedule, but with a month-long term in between the fall and spring semesters. (Similarly, a "4-4-1" has a short term following two longer semesters.) It is always best to call the admissions office for details.

Student/faculty ratio: The ratio of full-time undergraduate instructional faculty members to all undergraduates.

Profs interesting rating: On a scale of 60–99, this rating is based on levels of surveyed students' agreement or disagreement with the statement: "Your instructors are good teachers."

Profs accessible rating: On a scale of 60–99, this rating is based on levels of surveyed students' agreement or disagreement with the statement: "Your instructors are accessible outside the classroom."

Most common regular class size; Most common lab size: The most commonly occurring class size for regular courses and for labs/discussion sections.

Most popular majors: The majors with the highest enrollments at the school.

Admissions Selectivity Rating: On a scale of 60–99, this rating is a measure of how competitive admission is at the school. This rating is determined by several factors, including the class rank of entering freshmen, test scores, and percentage of applicants accepted.

% of applicants accepted: The percentage of applicants to whom the school offered admission.

% of acceptees attending: The percentage of accepted students who eventually enrolled at the school.

 # accepting a place on wait list: The number of students who decided to take a place on the wait list when offered this option.

% admitted from wait list: The percentage of applicants who opted to take a place on the wait list and were subsequently offered admission. These figures will vary tremendously from college to college, and should be a consideration when deciding whether to accept a place on a college's wait list.

# of early decision applicants: The number of students who applied under the college's early decision or early action plan.

% accepted early decision: The percentage of early decision or early action applicants who were admitted under this plan. By the nature of these plans, the vast majority who are admitted ultimately enroll.

Range SAT Critical Reading, Range SAT Math, Range SAT Writing, Range ACT Composite. The average and the middle fifty percent range of test scores for entering freshmen.

Nota Bene: The score ranges published in this edition are from the old SAT, administered prior to March 2016. For the most up-to-date information on SAT score concordance, college and university admission policies and the new SAT, please visit PrincetonReview.com.

Don't be discouraged from applying to the school of your choice even if your combined SAT scores are 80 or even 120 points below the average, because you may still have a chance of getting in. Remember that many schools value other aspects of your application (e.g., your grades, how good a match you make with the school) more heavily than test scores.

Minimum TOEFL: The minimum test score necessary for entering freshmen who are required to take the TOEFL (Test of English as a Foreign Language). Most schools will require all international students or non-native English speakers to take the TOEFL in order to be considered for admission.

Average HS GPA: The average grade point average of entering freshman. We report this on a scale of 1.0–4.0 (occasionally colleges report averages on a 100 scale, in which case we report those figures). This is one of the key factors in college admissions.

% graduated top 10%, top 25%, top 50% of class: Of those students for whom class rank was reported, the percentage of entering freshmen who ranked in the top tenth, quarter, and half of their high school classes.

Early decision/action deadlines: The deadline for submission of application materials under the early decision or early action plan.

Early decision, early action, priority, and regular admission deadlines: The dates by which all materials must be postmarked (we suggest "received in the office") in order to be considered for admission under each particular admissions option/cycle for matriculation in the fall term.

Early decision, early action, priority, and regular admission notification: The dates by which you can expect a decision on your application under each admissions option/cycle.

Nonfall registration: Some schools will allow incoming students to register and begin attending classes at times other than the fall term, which is the traditional beginning of the academic calendar year. Other schools will allow you to register for classes only if you can begin in the fall term. A simple "yes" or "no" in this category indicates the school's policy on nonfall registration.

Financial Aid Rating: On a scale of 60–99, this rating is a measure of the financial aid the school awards and how satisfied students are with the aid they receive. It is based on school-reported data on financial aid and students' responses to the survey question, "If you receive financial aid, how satisfied are you with your financial aid package?"

Annual in-state tuition: The tuition at the school, or for public colleges, the cost of tuition for a resident of the school's state. Usually much lower than out-of-state tuition for state-supported public schools.

Annual out-of-state tuition: For public colleges, the tuition for a non-resident of the school's state. This entry appears only for public colleges, since tuition at private colleges is generally the same regardless of state of residence.

Room and board: Estimated annual room and board costs.

Required fees: Any additional costs students must pay beyond tuition in order to attend the school. These often include fitness center fees and the like. A few state schools may not officially charge in-state students tuition, but those students are still responsible for hefty fees.

Tuition and fees: In cases when schools do not report separate figures for tuition and required fees, we offer this total of the two.

Comprehensive fee: A few schools report one overall fee that reflects the total cost of tuition, room and board, and required fees. If you'd like to see how this figure breaks down, we recommend contacting the school.

Books and supplies: Estimated annual cost of necessary textbooks and/or supplies.

Average need-based scholarship: The average need-based scholarship and grant aid awarded to students with need.

% needy frosh receiving need-based scholarship or grant aid: The percentage of all degree-seeking freshmen who were determined to have need and received any need-based scholarship or grant.

% needy UG receiving need-based scholarship or grant aid: The percentage of all degree-seeking undergraduates who were determined to have need and received any need-based scholarship or grant.

% needy frosh receiving non-need-based scholarship or grant aid: The percentage of all degree-seeking freshmen, determined to have need, receiving any non-need based scholarship or grant aid.

% needy UG receiving non-need-based scholarship or grant aid: The percentage of all degree-seeking undergraduates, determined to have need, receiving any non-need based scholarship or grant aid.

% needy frosh receiving need-based self-help aid: The percentage of all degree-seeking freshmen, determined to have need, who received any need-based self-help aid.

% needy UG receiving need-based self-help aid: The percentage of all degree-seeking undergraduates, determined to have need, who received any need-based self-help aid.

% frosh receiving any financial aid: The percentage of all degree-seeking freshmen receiving any financial aid (need-based, merit-based, gift aid).

% UG receiving any financial aid: The percentage of all degree-seeking undergraduates receiving any financial aid (need-based, merit-based, gift aid).

% UG borrow to pay for school: The percentage who borrowed at any time through any loan programs (institutional, state, Federal Stafford Subsidized and Unsubsidized, private loans that were certified by your institution, etc., exclude parent loans). Includes both Federal Direct Student Loans and Federal Family Education Loans (prior to the FFEL program ending in June 2010).

Average Indebtedness: The average per-borrower cumulative undergraduate indebtedness of those who borrowed at any time through any loan programs (institutional, state, Federal Stafford Subsidized and Unsubsidized, private loans that were certified by your institution, etc.; excluding parent loans).

% frosh and ugrad need fully met: The percentage of needy degree-seeking students whose needs were fully met (excludes PLUS loans, unsubsidized loans and private alternative loans).

Average % of frosh and ugrad need met: On average, the percentage of need that was met of students who were awarded any need-based aid. Excludes any aid that was awarded in excess of need as well as any resources that were awarded to replace EFC (PLUS loans, unsubsidized loans and private alternative loans).

Nota Bene: *The statistical data reported in this book, unless otherwise noted, was collected from the profiled colleges from fall 2015 through the fall of 2016. In some cases, we were unable to publish the most recent data because schools did not report the necessary statistics to us in time, despite our repeated outreach efforts. Because the enrollment and financial statistics, as well as application and financial aid deadlines, fluctuate from one year to another, we recommend that you check with the schools to make sure you have the most current information before applying.*

The Narrative

These sections share the straight-from-the-campus feedback we get from the school's most important customers: The students attending them. They summarize the opinions of freshmen through seniors we've surveyed and they include direct quotes from scores of them. When appropriate, they also incorporate statistics provided by the schools. The sections based on student survey responses are divided into four subsections:

About the School

This section provides a general overview of the school including student descriptions of the school environment and often tells you which programs or academic departments students rated most favorably and how professors interact with students. Student opinion regarding administrative departments also works its way into this section.

Bang For Your Buck

Here you will find information about scholarship and fellowship programs, the school's commitment to meeting demonstrated need, and student opinion regarding financial aid. Details on particular offerings related to funding are also included.

Student Life

The student life section describes life outside the classroom and addresses questions ranging from "How comfortable are the dorms?" to "How popular are fraternities and sororities?" In this section, students describe what they do for entertainment both on-campus and off, providing a clear picture of the social environment at their particular school. This section will also give you the lowdown on the types of students the school attracts and how the students view the level of interaction among various groups, including those of different ethnic, socioeconomic, and religious backgrounds.

Career

In this section, you will find information about the career resources at each school including career services departments, job fairs, and internship programs. We spotlight specific experiential learning opportunities that could have real-world advantages in terms of your career and include student opinions about the career services offered to them.

The other three sections included in the profile are:

General Info
This section lists student activities, organizations, athletics, and other campus highlights that each school's admissions office would you to know about their institution.

Financial Aid
Here you'll find out what you need to know about the financial aid process at the school, namely what forms you need and what types of merit-based aid and loans are available. Information about need-based aid is contained in the financial aid sidebar. This section includes specific deadline dates for submission of materials as reported by the colleges. We strongly encourage students seeking financial aid to file all forms— federal, state, and institutional—carefully, fully, and on time.

The Bottom Line
Here we breakdown the cost of attendance for each school by tuition, fees, and housing, and give you the final totals for in-state and out-of-state students.

Ranking Lists

Colleges That Pay You Back contains seven ranking lists, all of which focus on different aspects of financial aid and career preparation. For lists that cover sixty-two topics on academics, facilities, and campus culture, check out our book *Best 381 Colleges*, or visit PrincetonReview.com.

Top 50 Colleges That Pay You Back

The fifty schools that received the highest ROI rating (described on page 29), ranked in order. Each of these school's profiles also includes a banner with its rank.

1. Princeton University
2. Stanford University
3. Massachusetts Institute of Technology
4. Harvey Mudd College
5. California Institute of Technology
6. Harvard College
7. Yale University
8. The Cooper Union for the Advancement of Science and Art
9. University of California—Berkeley
10. Amherst College
11. Duke University
12. University of Virginia
13. Rice University
14. Brown University
15. Dartmouth College
16. Vanderbilt University
17. Colgate University
18. Brigham Young University (UT)
19. Cornell University
20. The University of Chicago
21. Hamilton College
22. University of California—Los Angeles
23. University of Michigan—Ann Arbor
24. Columbia University
25. Williams College
26. Haverford College
27. Washington University in St. Louis
28. Carleton College
29. Rose-Hulman Institute of Technology
30. University of Pennsylvania
31. Tufts University
32. Claremont McKenna College
33. Bowdoin College
34. Swarthmore College
35. Carnegie Mellon University
36. Worcester Polytechnic Institute
37. Pomona College
38. Wabash College
39. Johns Hopkins University
40. Grinnell College
41. Reed College
42. Emory University
43. Lafayette College
44. Case Western Reserve University
45. University of California—Santa Barbara
46. Babson College
47. University of California—San Diego
48. University of Richmond
49. New College of Florida
50. Union College (NY)

Top 25 Colleges That Pay You Back for Students With No Demonstrated Need

To create this list, we used the same methodology for our ROI rating, but removed need-based aid information. If you don't qualify for financial aid, these are your twenty-five best value schools.

1. California Institute of Technology
2. Harvey Mudd College
3. Massachusetts Institute of Technology
4. Brigham Young University (UT)
5. Princeton University
6. University of California—Berkeley
7. Stanford University
8. University of Virginia
9. University of Michigan—Ann Arbor
10. Duke University
11. Rice University
12. University of California—Los Angeles
13. State University of New York—Maritime College
14. Yale University
15. New College of Florida
16. Harvard College
17. University of California—Santa Barbara
18. College of William and Mary
19. University of California—San Diego
20. Carnegie Mellon University
21. The Cooper Union for the Advancement of Science and Art
22. Dartmouth College
23. University of Texas at Austin
24. Vanderbilt University
25. Rose-Hulman Institute of Technology

Best Alumni Network

These twenty-five schools have the strongest and most active alumni networks, based on current students' ratings of alumni activity and visibility on campus.

1. Wabash College
2. Dartmouth College
3. Pennsylvania State University—University Park
4. Texas A&M University—College Station
5. Claremont McKenna College
6. Clemson University
7. St. Lawrence University
8. Wellesley College
9. Hampden-Sydney College
10. University of Virginia
11. Virginia Tech
12. College of the Holy Cross
13. Bucknell University
14. Ohio State University—Columbus
15. Gettysburg College
16. University of Florida
17. Union College (NY)
18. DePauw University
19. Florida State University
20. University of Georgia
21. Cornell University
22. New College of Florida
23. Agnes Scott College
24. Colgate University
25. Stanford University

Best Schools for Internships

This top twenty-five list is based on students' ratings of accessibility of internships at their school.

1. Bentley University
2. Claremont McKenna College
3. Wabash College
4. Connecticut College
5. Rose-Hulman Institute of Technology
6. Wake Forest University
7. Pennsylvania State University—University Park
8. Northeastern University
9. Barnard College
10. Clemson University
11. Franklin W. Olin College of Engineering
12. Smith College
13. Dartmouth College
14. University of Dayton
15. Missouri University of Science and Technology
16. Rhodes College
17. University of Notre Dame
18. University of Richmond
19. Stevens Institute of Technology
20. Amherst College
21. Scripps College
22. University of Pennsylvania
23. Massachusetts Institute of Technology
24. Virginia Tech
25. Worcester Polytechnic Institute

Best Career Placement

This top twenty-five list is based on students' ratings of career services at their school, and on PayScale.com's median starting and mid-career salary information.

1. Massachusetts Institute of Technology
2. Harvey Mudd College
3. State University of New York—Maritime College
4. California Institute of Technology
5. Stanford University
6. Princeton University
7. Carnegie Mellon University
8. Rose-Hulman Institute of Technology
9. Babson College
10. University of Pennsylvania
11. Stevens Institute of Technology
12. Harvard College
13. Rensselaer Polytechnic Institute
14. Dartmouth College
15. Worcester Polytechnic Institute
16. Georgia Institute of Technology
17. Duke University
18. Cornell University
19. Rice University
20. University of California—Berkeley
21. Yale University
22. Clarkson University
23. Santa Clara University
24. The Cooper Union for the Advancement of Science and Art
25. Colgate University

Best Financial Aid

The twenty-five schools in this book that receive the highest financial aid rating (described on page 29).

1. Pomona College
2. Vassar College
3. Princeton University
4. Colgate University
5. Haverford College
6. Middlebury College
7. Reed College
8. Bowdoin College
9. Vanderbilt University
10. Macalester College
11. St. Olaf College
12. Stanford University
13. The Cooper Union for the Advancement of Science and Art
14. Trinity College (CT)
15. Wellesley College
16. Yale University
17. Bates College
18. Columbia University
19. Pitzer College
20. Amherst College
21. Claremont McKenna College
22. Rice University
23. Cornell University
24. Franklin W. Olin College of Engineering
25. Grinnell College

Best Schools for Making an Impact

These twenty-five schools were selected based on student ratings and responses to our survey questions covering community service opportunities at their school, student government, sustainability efforts, and on-campus student engagement. We also took into account PayScale.com's percentage of alumni from each school that reported that they had high job meaning.

1. Wesleyan University
2. Middlebury College
3. University of California—Santa Cruz
4. Oberlin College
5. University of Portland
6. Yale University
7. Bates College
8. Brandeis University
9. Lawrence University
10. Smith College
11. Southwestern University
12. Washington University in St. Louis
13. Macalester College
14. Tufts University
15. Kalamazoo College
16. Clark University
17. Stanford University
18. Whitman College
19. St. Olaf College
20. Colorado College
21. Union College (NY)
22. Willamette University
23. Brown University
24. Furman University
25. St. Lawrence University

Tuition-Free Schools

Berea College
College of the Ozarks
Deep Springs College
United States Air Force Academy
United States Coast Guard Academy
United States Merchant Marine Academy
United States Military Academy (West Point)
United States Naval Academy
Webb Institute

Nota Bene: *For tuition-free schools, we have included neither Financial Aid or ROI ratings. Because our ratings are calculated on a continuum for each edition, giving tuition-free schools ratings of 99 would drastically skew the ratings for the other 200 schools in this book. Rest assured, each of these nine schools will provide an excellent return on each student's education.*

Berea College

CPO 2220, BEREA, KY 40404 • ADMISSIONS: 859-985-3500 • FAX: 859-985-3512

CAMPUS LIFE

Quality of Life Rating	**84**
Fire Safety Rating	**95**
Green Rating	**89**
Type of school	Private
Affiliation	No Affiliation
Environment	Village

STUDENTS

Total undergrad enrollment	1,643
% male/female	43/57
% from out of state	53
% frosh live on campus	97
% ugrads live on campus	85
% African American	16
% Asian	2
% Caucasian	60
% Hispanic	8
% Native American	<1
% Pacific Islander	<1
% Two or more races	5
% Race and/or ethnicity unknown	1
% international	8
# of countries represented	70

ACADEMICS

Academic Rating	**85**
% students returning for sophomore year	86
% students graduating within 4 years	45
% students graduating within 6 years	63
Calendar	Semester
Student/faculty ratio	10:1
Profs interesting rating	79
Profs accessible rating	79
Most classes have 10–19 students.	

MOST POPULAR MAJORS
Business/Commerce; Family and Consumer Sciences/Human Sciences; Biology

ABOUT THE SCHOOL

Perhaps best known for its tuition-free, four-year education, Berea has a whole lot more goin' on. At this predominantly Appalachian school in Kentucky, students can select from a curriculum that includes undergraduate research, service learning, and numerous study abroad opportunities, and expect to receive the full support of the school along the way. Since Berea's objective is to provide an education to students of limited economic resources, the school makes it clear that there is no slacking off; your spot here is an opportunity that could have gone to someone else. Academics are rigorous, classroom attendance is mandatory, and students are happy to be given an opportunity.

With such a distinct and regional mission, students here are not just faces in the crowd. All classes are taught by full professors, and everyone has access to the learning center, math and language labs, and tutors for assistance with papers, presentations, and homework. Service is also a way of life here, and Berea is one of the top schools in the nation for service learning. When students do need a rest from their studies, do-gooding, and work, there are more than 50 clubs and organizations available, as well as performing arts programs, theaters, and plenty of nature nearby.

Berea College is "about bringing underprivileged high school graduates from the Appalachian region and beyond together for a chance at a higher education, a career, and a better life." Thanks to a labor program that requires all students to work ten to fifteen hours each week (not to mention a ton of donated cash), tuition is entirely covered for each student, with a laptop thrown in for the duration of the school year to boot. In addition to a decent range of liberal arts and sciences majors, there are several career-oriented programs, all of which combines to make "a comfortable place for students to learn and grow."

BANG FOR YOUR BUCK

The school doesn't think your income should dictate your outcome, which is why it only admits students who have financial need. The school's endowment is what allows it to be so generous in awarding full scholarships to deserving students, and these scholarships work in conjunction with any other grants or scholarships students receive to completely cover the cost of tuition (as well as that laptop). In many cases, the school can even offer additional financial aid to assist with room, board, and other fees—not loans—according to each student's need. Simply put, students at Berea College pay what they can afford.

STUDENT LIFE

The student body at Berea is "so genuinely diverse" (though most are from Appalachia) that the only unifying ribbon is "the desire to learn and a craving for knowledge, and . . . a certain drive for self-improvement." That being said, "We also have an unusually high number of what you might call 'hipsters'," says a student. Though town life is admittedly slow, there is a regular shuttle to Richmond, and the campus is almost never quiet. Student organizations "are constantly holding events to keep Berea students occupied and having fun." "We still find ways to keep ourselves entertained," says one. For example, every semester a game called humans versus zombies is held, where people chase each other all over campus with Nerf guns and "sometimes even the professors join in." For those into hiking and being outdoors, "the Pinnacles (a popular hiking spot) are beautiful."

Berea College

FINANCIAL AID: 859-985-3310 • E-MAIL: ADMISSIONS@BEREA.EDU • WEBSITE: WWW.BEREA.EDU

CAREER

The job program at Berea inherently infuses students with a "rigorous, real world experience" that they might not receive elsewhere, and students are afforded "so much opportunity," such as internships, study/travel abroad, and the ability to attend conferences and workshops off-campus. The Center for Transformative Learning centralizes all of the school's career development resources in one place, and offers peer consultations, workshops, alumni networking, and job search tools. The volunteer program at the Center for Excellence and Learning Through Service (CELTS) also offers students the chance to develop leadership and social justice backgrounds through academic service learning and student-led community service.

GENERAL INFO

Activities: Choral groups, dance, drama/theater, jazz band, literary magazine, music ensembles, pep band, student government, student newspaper, yearbook, campus ministries, international student organization. **Organizations:** 75 registered organizations, 14 honor societies, 5 religious organizations. **Athletics (Intercollegiate):** *Men:* Baseball, basketball, cross-country, golf, soccer, swimming, tennis, track/field (outdoor). *Women:* Basketball, cross-country, soccer, softball, swimming, tennis, track/field (outdoor), volleyball. **On-Campus Highlights:** Carillon (in Draper building tower), EcoVillage (married and single parent housing), Alumni Building (cafeteria, lounge, gameroom), Woods-Penn Complex (post office, cafe, etc.), Seabury Center (gym). **Environmental Initiatives:** 1. Sustainability and Environmental Studies academic program; 2. Ecological Renovations (including 1st LEED-certified building in Kentucky and the Ecovillage residential complex for student families); 3. Local Food Initiative.

FINANCIAL AID

Students should submit: FAFSA. Regular filing deadline is 5/1. The Princeton Review suggests that all financial aid forms be submitted as soon as possible after October 1. *Need-based scholarships/grants offered:* Federal Pell, FSEOG, State scholarships/grants, Private scholarships, College/university scholarship or grant aid from institutional funds. *Loan aid offered:* Direct Subsidized Stafford Loans, Direct Unsubsidized Stafford Loans, Direct PLUS loans, College/university loans from institutional funds. Applicants will be notified of awards on a rolling basis beginning 11/1. Federal Work-Study Program available. Institutional employment available.

BOTTOM LINE

Tuition costs are quite simple: every admitted student is provided with a four-year tuition scholarship, knocking tuition down to zero. No tuition does not mean a full ride, however, and extra costs such as technology fees, insurance, food plans, etc., add up quickly (room, board, and fees run around $7,100 a year). However, about two-thirds of the students receive additional financial aid to help offset these costs. Each student is required to take an on-campus job for a certain number of hours per week as part of the school's work program, giving them valuable experience that translates into real-world skills, as well as a salary (about $1,200 in the first year) to assist with living expenses.

SELECTIVITY

Admissions Rating	**94**
# of applicants	1,637
% of applicants accepted	36
% of acceptees attending	72

FRESHMAN PROFILE

Range SAT Critical Reading	550–635
Range SAT Math	515–620
Range SAT Writing	500–605
Range ACT Composite	22–26
Minimum paper TOEFL	520
Minimum internet-based TOEFL	68
Average HS GPA	3.4
% graduated top 10% of class	24
% graduated top 25% of class	67
% graduated top 50% of class	96

DEADLINES

Regular	
Deadline	4/30
Nonfall registration?	No

FINANCIAL FACTS

Financial Aid Rating	**60***
Annual tuition	$0
Room and board	$6,472
Required fees	$570
Average need-based scholarship	$27,810
% needy frosh rec. need-based scholarship or grant aid	100
% needy UG rec. need-based scholarship or grant aid	100
% needy frosh rec. non-need-based scholarship or grant aid	0
% needy UG rec. non-need-based scholarship or grant aid	0
% needy frosh rec. need-based self-help aid	100
% needy UG rec. need-based self-help aid	100
% frosh rec. any financial aid	100
% UG rec. any financial aid	100
% UG borrow to pay for school	68
Average cumulative indebtedness	$7,928
% frosh need fully met	0
% ugrads need fully met	0
Average % of frosh need met	96
Average % of ugrad need met	93

CAREER INFORMATION FROM PAYSCALE.COM

ROI rating	**N/A**
Bachelor's and No Higher	
Median starting salary	$32,600
Median mid-career salary	$58,200
At Least Bachelor's	
Median starting salary	$32,600
Median mid-career salary	$58,200

College of the Ozarks

OFFICE OF ADMISSIONS, P.O. BOX 17, POINT LOOKOUT, MO 65726 • ADMISSIONS: 417-690-2636 • FAX: 417-335-2618

CAMPUS LIFE

Quality of Life Rating	92
Fire Safety Rating	89
Green Rating	70
Type of school	Private
Affiliation	Interdenominational
Environment	Rural

STUDENTS

Total undergrad enrollment	1,452
% male/female	47/53
% from out of state	19
% frosh from public high school	74
% frosh live on campus	92
% ugrads live on campus	82
% African American	1
% Asian	1
% Caucasian	93
% Hispanic	2
% Native American	<1
% Pacific Islander	<1
% Two or more races	2
% Race and/or ethnicity unknown	0
% international	2
# of countries represented	16

ACADEMICS

Academic Rating	80
% students returning for sophomore year	73
% students graduating within 4 years	63
% students graduating within 6 years	73
Calendar	Semester
Student/faculty ratio	14:1
Profs interesting rating	84
Profs accessible rating	81

Most classes have 10–19 students.
Most lab/discussion sessions have
10–19 students.

MOST POPULAR MAJORS

Elementary Education and Teaching;
Business Administration and Management;
Agricultural Business and Management

ABOUT THE SCHOOL

Welcome to Hard Work U., where students work for an education, graduate without debt, develop character, value God and country, and don't pay tuition. Debt is openly discouraged, and instead of paying tuition, all full-time students work campus jobs to defray the cost of education. Opportunities for gaining life and career skills abound through this program, ranging from landscaping to operating a four-star restaurant, and students learn to show up on time, finish the job right, and be a team player—skills that translate well into any profession. Students are graded by their work supervisors each semester, and their work grades become a part of their permanent transcript, so good students have a great track record to provide to prospective employers.

The school is one of the most difficult private schools to gain acceptance to in the Midwest, and not just because it's free. While there are almost too many singular aspects of this small Christian college to name, one popular program in particular stands out: the Patriotic Education Travel Program, which offers students the opportunity to accompany WWII Veterans to Pacific and European battle sites. It's this type of unique educational experience that makes College of the Ozarks unique and an outstanding value in higher education.

Christian values and character, hard work, and financial responsibility comprise the fundamental building blocks of the "Hard Work U." experience. C of O is committed to its founding mission of providing a quality, Christian education to those who are found worthy, but who are without sufficient means to obtain such training. "My family didn't have enough money to send me to any other college, and I'm not afraid of a little hard work!" says a student.

BANG FOR YOUR BUCK

Generous donors who believe in what College of the Ozarks represents enable the college to provide tuition scholarships in exchange for work on campus (if you paid cash for instructional expenses at C of O, it would cost you $18,500 per year!). The Christian atmosphere keeps students away from the more party-heavy aspects of college life, so students stay focused on school and work. Whereas a lot of students approach prospective employers without much in the way of demonstrated work ethic, this is obviously not the case for College of the Ozarks alumni. Even during the economic downturn, 82 percent of graduates found employment upon graduation, and 13 percent pursued graduate school.

STUDENT LIFE

College of the Ozarks is a school with a strong religious foundation and "a huge sports and agriculture backing." There are a fair number of "aggies" (agricultural studies students), homeschooled students, and the typical student "is what would have been the 'the good one' in every clique in high school." Work stations and academics dominate most everyone's free time and "a lot of students work off campus as well as the required fifteen hours per week during the semester," but when students do emerge from their dorm rooms for a night on the town there's tons to do. "Whether you hang out with your friends, go to shows in Branson, go to campus-sponsored events, or just go play ping-pong," there are "plenty of things to keep a student occupied." Various organizations hold events for the whole campus like Senate Movie Night, and there are "plenty of interesting speakers for convocations."

College of the Ozarks

FINANCIAL AID: 417-690-3292 • E-MAIL: E-MAIL: ADMISS4@COFO.EDU • WEBSITE: WWW.COFO.EDU

CAREER

The College of the Ozarks automatically provides students with the opportunity to gain hands on experience in their desired field through the required work study at any one of ninety job stations across campus. Between the work stations and the prevalence of off-campus jobs, "good job references after graduation" are pretty much a lock. "Employers see the College of the Ozarks name [and] they know they are getting a very good worker," says a student. "We have credibility in the workforce, so it is easy for students to pursue their careers, or even just get a part-time job." The school does "an excellent job" at letting everyone know when there are internships and other opportunities to pursue and students are often able to customize their work study to areas that pertain to their intended careers. The Career Center provides guidance throughout, and offers a course in Career Planning, Career Placement, and two Career Days each year.

GENERAL INFO

Activities: Choral groups, concert band, drama/theater, jazz band, literary magazine, music ensembles, musical theater, pep band, radio station, student government, student newspaper, yearbook, campus ministries. **Organizations:** 45 registered organizations, 6 honor societies, 10 religious organizations. **Athletics (Intercollegiate):** *Men:* Baseball, basketball, cheerleading, cross country, golf, track. *Women:* Basketball, cheerleading, cross country, track, volleyball. **On-Campus Highlights:** Howell W. Keeter Athletic Complex, Ralph Foster Museum, Williams Memorial Chapel, The Keeter Center, Agriculture, Edwards Mill, Fruitcake and Jelly Kitchen. **Environmental Initiatives:** The College ensures proper management of hazardous, special and universal waste. There is campus-wide recycling: plastic bottles, corrugated cardboard, aluminum cans, tin cans, batteries, tires, light bulbs and electronic products. Light bulb reclamation (recycle of bulbs) and energy efficient lights. Agricultural Livestock Waste Containment program (protects area lakes). Lake water cools many buildings.

FINANCIAL AID

Students should submit: FAFSA. Priority filing deadline is 2/15. The Princeton Review suggests that all financial aid forms be submitted as soon as possible after October 1. *Need-based scholarships/grants offered:* Federal Pell, FSEOG, State scholarships/grants, Private scholarships, College/university scholarship or grant aid from institutional funds. Federal Work Program available. Institutional employment available.

BOTTOM LINE

College of the Ozarks students do not pay a penny of tuition. Each student participates in the on-campus Work Education Program fifteen hours each week and two forty-hour work weeks. Upon full completion of the Work Education Program, the college guarantees to meet the remaining balance through a combination of private scholarships and grants. Room and board still runs $6,800 a year, as well as $430 in additional fees, but there are additional scholarships available for students unable to pay these costs.

CAREER INFORMATION FROM PAYSCALE.COM

ROI rating	N/A
Bachelor's and No Higher	
Median starting salary	$35,200
Median mid-career salary	$71,800
At Least Bachelor's	
Median starting salary	$36,300
Median mid-career salary	$78,100
% STEM	6%

SELECTIVITY

Admissions Rating	96
# of applicants	3,122
% of applicants accepted	12
% of acceptees attending	89
# offered a place on the wait list	865
% accepting a place on wait list	99
% admitted from wait list	0

FRESHMAN PROFILE

Range SAT Critical Reading	455–498
Range SAT Math	495–561
Range SAT Writing	485–534
Range ACT Composite	21–25
Minimum paper TOEFL	550
Minimum internet-based TOEFL	79
Average HS GPA	3.6
% graduated top 10% of class	23
% graduated top 25% of class	61
% graduated top 50% of class	91

DEADLINES

Regular	
Priority	2/15
Nonfall registration?	No

FINANCIAL FACTS

Financial Aid Rating	90
Annual tuition	$0
Room and board	$6,800
Required fees	$430
Average need-based scholarship	$14,917
% needy frosh rec. need-based scholarship or grant aid	100
% needy UG rec. need-based scholarship or grant aid	100
% needy frosh rec. non-need-based scholarship or grant aid	7
% needy UG rec. non-need-based scholarship or grant aid	12
% needy frosh rec. need-based self-help aid	93
% needy UG rec. need-based self-help aid	87
% frosh rec. any financial aid	100
% UG rec. any financial aid	100
% UG borrow to pay for school	7
Average cumulative indebtedness	$5,339
% frosh need fully met	22
% ugrads need fully met	36
Average % of frosh need met	86
Average % of ugrad need met	89

Deep Springs College

Applications Committee, HC 72 Box 45001, Dyer, NV 89010 • Admissions: 760-872-2000 • Fax: 760-872-4466

CAMPUS LIFE

Quality of Life Rating	**96**
Fire Safety Rating	**88**
Green Rating	**60***
Type of school	Private
Affiliation	No Affiliation
Environment	Rural

STUDENTS

Total undergrad enrollment	28
% male/female	100/0
% from out of state	82
% frosh from public high school	64
% frosh live on campus	100
% ugrads live on campus	100
% African American	0
% Asian	14
% Caucasian	64
% Hispanic	4
% Native American	0
% Pacific Islander	0
% Two or more races	4
% Race and/or ethnicity unknown	0
% international	14
# of countries represented	3

ACADEMICS

Academic Rating	**99**
% students returning for sophomore year	92
% students graduating within 4 years	0
Calendar	Semester
Student/faculty ratio	4:1
Profs interesting rating	99
Profs accessible rating	99
Most classes have fewer than 10 students.	

MOST POPULAR MAJORS
Liberal Arts and Sciences

ABOUT THE SCHOOL

You know the feeling you get when you look back at your second-grade class picture and you can remember every single person's name, no matter how long ago that was? That is the level of camaraderie that is achieved at Deep Springs College, a teeny-tiny, uber-selective, all-male school in the middle of the California desert. The school operates on the belief that manual labor and political deliberation are integral parts of a comprehensive liberal arts education, and every student must also work on the school's ranch and farm, which helps drive home the school's unique mission of service. After two years at Deep Springs (with full scholarship), the school's twenty-six students go on to complete a four-year degree at the world's most prestigious universities.

Whereas at some colleges, professors' doors are always open, at Deep Springs, professors' porch lights are always on. Classes are intense and bleed into activities around the clock, and they're sometimes also held in unconventional locations, like professors' homes or the irrigation ditch. Some students must wake up early to feed the cattle; some must stay up late to mend fences on the alfalfa farm. At every hour of the day, there are at least a few people awake and discussing Heidegger, playing chess, or strumming guitars. There is no other school like it, and students receive an education that transcends simply learning from books, as well as an unprecedented education in citizenship.

Deep Springs is an all-male liberal arts college located on a cattle ranch and alfalfa farm in California's High Desert. Founded in 1917, the curriculum is based on the three pillars of academics, labor, and self-governance, offering "a unique liberal arts education that gives you very much freedom and requires a lot of responsibility for your classmates and environment." To say that the school's twenty-eight students (along with its staff and faculty) form a close community would be an understatement. Everyone is on a first-name basis and knows each other like the back of their own hand.

BANG FOR YOUR BUCK

Deep Springs is one of the best educations a student can receive after high school, and though you may not have heard of the school before, the nation's top universities certainly have. Although percentages are somewhat moot for a school that has only twenty-five students over two class years, in the past five years, nearly 45 percent of students have gone on to Harvard, Yale, Brown, and the University of Chicago, as well as winning numerous prestigious scholarships and fellowships.

Deep Springs College

E-MAIL: APCOM@DEEPSPRINGS.EDU • WEBSITE: WWW.DEEPSPRINGS.EDU

STUDENT LIFE

With only twenty-six people, one student's life is every student's life here. Students play a significant part in running the college, which means that from day one, every student is involved in some meaningful and essential way in the everyday workings of the college. "When you are helping hire faculty, review applications, milk cows, cook meals for the community, and working in the organic garden, it's hard not to fit in or find a place where you belong," says a student. The typical student here is "driven and deeply committed to the 'common project'." He is also "permanently exhausted." Most people here "think about thinking, though of course there are students who exist more in feeling, but they aren't the majority." Hikes and horseback riding tend are popular ways to get away, physically and mentally.

CAREER

The academic rigor and work ethic required to get into Deep Springs is well-known, and mandatory public speaking and composition studies only further set the intellectual foundation. As men learning to be citizens of the world, many eventually go on to "a life of service" following the completion of a degree. Since Deep Springs is a two-year school, most everyone transfers to a more typical four-year institution, and Deep Springers are generally successful in their transfers. Of forty-seven students transferring from the entering years 2007–2011, over half transferred to either Yale, Brown, or the University of Chicago.

GENERAL INFO

Activities: Student government. **Organizations:** 1 registered organization. **On-Campus Highlights:** Boarding House, Dairy Barn, Horse Stables, The Upper Reservoir, The Druid.

FINANCIAL AID

Students should submit: The Princeton Review suggests that all financial aid forms be submitted as soon as possible after October 1.

BOTTOM LINE

Every single student accepted at Deep Springs receives a comprehensive scholarship that covers tuition and room and board in full, an estimated value of over $50,000. Students are only expected to pay for books, incidentals, and travel, which the school estimates run less than $2,800 per year.

CAREER INFORMATION FROM PAYSCALE.COM
ROI rating	N/A

SELECTIVITY

Admissions Rating	99
# of applicants	200
% of applicants accepted	10
% of acceptees attending	84
# offered a place on the wait list	5
% accepting a place on wait list	100
% admitted from wait list	100

FRESHMAN PROFILE

Range SAT Critical Reading	740–800
Range SAT Math	670–740
% graduated top 10% of class	100
% graduated top 25% of class	100
% graduated top 50% of class	100

DEADLINES

Regular	
Deadline	11/7
Notification	4/15
Nonfall registration?	No

FINANCIAL FACTS

Financial Aid Rating	60*
Annual tuition	$0
Books and supplies	$1,200
Average frosh need-based scholarship	$0
% frosh rec. any financial aid	100
% UG rec. any financial aid	100

United States Air Force Academy

HQ USAFA/RRS, 2304 Cadet Drive, Suite 2400, USAF Academy, CO 80840-5025 • Admissions: 719-333-2520

CAMPUS LIFE

Quality of Life Rating	83
Fire Safety Rating	91
Green Rating	71
Type of school	Public
Affiliation	No Affiliation
Environment	Metropolis

STUDENTS

Total undergrad enrollment	4,111
% male/female	0/0
% from out of state	88
% frosh live on campus	100
% ugrads live on campus	100
% African American	6
% Asian	5
% Caucasian	63
% Hispanic	10
% Native American	<1
% Pacific Islander	1
% Two or more races	7
% Race and/or ethnicity unknown	7
% international	1
# of countries represented	25

ACADEMICS

Academic Rating	93
% students returning for sophomore year	93
% students graduating within 4 years	79
% students graduating within 6 years	81
Calendar	Semester
Student/faculty ratio	8:1
Profs interesting rating	81
Profs accessible rating	94

Most classes have 10–19 students.

Most lab/discussion sessions have 10–19 students.

MOST POPULAR MAJORS

Business/Commerce; Social Sciences; Aerospace, Aeronautical and Astronautical/Space Engineering

ABOUT THE SCHOOL

As you might expect, most of those who attend this prestigious military academy have designs on becoming officers in the Air Force and/or becoming pilots one day and are willing to devote years and years of their life to receive top training. Not only are graduates guaranteed employment when they leave (each cadet will owe at least five years of service as an active-duty officer upon graduation), they leave with what amounts to a really cool skill set, between military free-fall parachute training, combat survival, internships at national labs, and, of course, the best flying programs in the solar system. USAFA is on the cutting edge of cyber training as well as aerospace technology with students having the opportunity to launch and control satellites. The academy has one of the greatest locations of all of the U.S. service academies, and it offers extensive recreational facilities and a wide range of seasonal programs to help make Colorado and its seasons enjoyable for not just the cadets, but the entire base community.

The unyielding dedication to student success and character development is felt in every class, activity, and tradition. Constant professionalism is the minimum standard, and nothing is easy, but cadets are happy to rise to the challenge and bring their brothers and sisters in planes along. Everyone is a leader, and all are working towards a common cause and belief regardless of ranking or position. If you can get in to the USAFA, the tools are there to help you stay.

BANG FOR YOUR BUCK

The Air Force puts a high premium on leaders with vision, dedication, and ability, and the pay and allowances of a new officer compare favorably with starting salaries in business, industry and the professions. All career officers are eligible to apply for further education through AFIT at civilian colleges and universities, and selected officers attend on a full-time basis, receive pay and allowances, have their tuition and fixed fees paid, and receive some reimbursement for books and thesis expenses, among other benefits. A certain percentage of students can become eligible for medical, law, or dental school upon graduation, and a few graduates will receive scholarships to attend civilian graduate schools immediately after graduation. Graduates in the top 15 percent of their class on overall performance average will normally be considered future graduate education for a master's degree if they meet two important criteria: they must perform well as officers, and the Air Force must need people from the degree program they wish to pursue.

STUDENT LIFE

Life at the Academy is undoubtedly busy, so in the little free time they have ("free time and fun doesn't mean the same thing here as at a civilian college"), and most days follow a pattern of "wake up, march, eat, classes, march, eat, classes, study/homework, sleep, repeat." For fun, students "watch movies, hang out, and workout." "Work work work, then on the weekends you go out and have fun in the [Springs] or in Denver or even go to the mountains to snowboard," says a cadet. The area surrounding USAFA is "an outdoor paradise with something to do in every season" such as snowboarding, skiing, hiking, camping, fishing, rock climbing, mountain biking, white water rafting, canoeing, and snowshoeing, though freshmen and sophomores aren't allowed to leave campus on weekdays or own cars. Most students do try to get away for the weekend, usually to nearby Denver or Colorado Springs. The school itself offers great athletic facilities with a wide range of activities, and "a quarter to half of the campus body ends up at the gym at some point toward the end of the day."

United States Air Force Academy

Fax: 719-333-3012 • E-mail: rr_webmail@usafa.edu • Website: www.academyadmissions.com

CAREER

Understandably, there's a pretty well-beaten path from the Academy into the Air Force, and it is all about the education and development of officers. Graduates receive a Bachelor of Science and are commissioned as second lieutenants in the U.S. Air Force, and must serve out a several-year military commitment. The Academy offers a number of Airmanship programs that ready students for flying and non-flying careers, and depending on ability and desire, students can receive more specialized training or certifications. Of the Academy graduates who visited PayScale.com, the starting salary averaged $66,700 and 62 percent reported feeling that their jobs had a meaningful impact on the world.

GENERAL INFO

Activities: Choral groups, dance, drama/theater, marching band, musical theater, pep band, radio station, yearbook, campus ministries. **Organizations:** 93 registered organizations, 12 honor societies, 14 religious organizations. **Athletics (Intercollegiate):** *Men:* Baseball, basketball, boxing, cheerleading, cross-country, diving, fencing, football, golf, gymnastics, ice hockey, lacrosse, riflery, soccer, swimming, tennis, track/field (outdoor), track/field (indoor), water polo, wrestling. *Women:* Basketball, cheer- leading, cross-country, diving, fencing, gymnastics, riflery, soccer, swimming, tennis, track/ field (outdoor), track/field (indoor), volleyball. **On-Campus Highlights:** USAF Academy Chapel, Thunderbird Lookout and Air Field, Falcon Stadium, Cadet Sports Complex, Visitor Center. **Environmental Initiatives:** Solar Hydro Geo Thermal.

FINANCIAL AID

Students should submit: The Princeton Review suggests that all financial aid forms be submitted as soon as possible after October 1. *Loan aid offered:* Federal Work-Study Program available. Institutional employment available.

BOTTOM LINE

Aside from the free tuition, students receive a nominal monthly stipend. Each cadet will owe at least five years of service as an active-duty officer upon graduation, though additional programs (such as attending higher education, or becoming a pilot) can add to the commitment. The current law enables an officer to retire after completing twenty years of active service. Cadets enjoy other benefits like military commissaries and exchanges, and space available seats on military aircraft around the world.

CAREER INFORMATION FROM PAYSCALE.COM	
ROI rating	N/A
Bachelor's and No Higher	
Median starting salary	$71,900
Median mid-career salary	$116,000
At Least Bachelor's	
Median starting salary	$72,600
Median mid-career salary	$115,000
% alumni with high job meaning	51%
% STEM	48%

SELECTIVITY

Admissions Rating	**98**
# of applicants	9,122
% of applicants accepted	17
% of acceptees attending	80

FRESHMAN PROFILE

Range SAT Critical Reading	600–690
Range SAT Math	630–710
Range ACT Composite	29–32
Average HS GPA	3.8
% graduated top 10% of class	52
% graduated top 25% of class	81
% graduated top 50% of class	97

DEADLINES

Early action	
Deadline	11/1
Notification	1/15
Regular	
Deadline	12/31
Nonfall registration?	No

FINANCIAL FACTS

Financial Aid Rating	**60***
Annual in-state tuition	$0
Annual out-of-state tuition	$0
Average frosh need-based scholarship	$0
% needy frosh rec. need-based scholarship or grant aid	0
% needy UG rec. need-based scholarship or grant aid	0
% needy frosh rec. non-need-based scholarship or grant aid	0
% needy UG rec. non-need-based scholarship or grant aid	0
% needy frosh rec. need-based self-help aid	0
% needy UG rec. need-based self-help aid	0
Average % of frosh need met	0
Average % of ugrad need met	0

United States Coast Guard Academy

31 Mohegan Avenue, New London, CT 06320-8103 • Admissions: 860-444-8503 • Fax: 860-701-6700

CAMPUS LIFE

Quality of Life Rating	85
Fire Safety Rating	91
Green Rating	63
Type of school	Public
Affiliation	No Affiliation
Environment	City

STUDENTS

Total undergrad enrollment	898
% male/female	65/35
% from out of state	95
% frosh from public high school	76
% frosh live on campus	100
% ugrads live on campus	100
% African American	4
% Asian	7
% Caucasian	67
% Hispanic	10
% Native American	<1
% Pacific Islander	<1
% Two or more races	8
% Race and/or ethnicity unknown	2
% international	2
# of countries represented	12

ACADEMICS

Academic Rating	89
% students returning for sophomore year	90
% students graduating within 4 years	84
Calendar	Semester
Student/faculty ratio	8:1
Profs interesting rating	78
Profs accessible rating	99

Most classes have 10–19 students.
Most lab/discussion sessions have 10–19 students.

MOST POPULAR MAJORS

Oceanography; Political Science and Government; Business Administration and Management

ABOUT THE SCHOOL

There is a special sense of pride at the Coast Guard Academy—pride in America, service, each class, each company, and in one's accomplishments. With a student body of less than 1,000, it's easy to see why graduates of the Coast Guard Academy form such a lifelong dedication to the school and each other. The USCGA graduates young men and women with "sound bodies, stout hearts, and alert minds, [and] with a liking for the sea and its lore," not to mention a four-year Bachelor of Science degree. The curriculum is heavily oriented toward math, science, and engineering, with a nationally recognized engineering program, as well as other programs in government, management, marine and environmental sciences, and more.

Given the intensity of academy life, most cadets are eager for the opportunity to participate in extracurricular activities, and social events and organized activities are an integral part of the cadet experience. There are a number of long-standing traditions that cement the Coast Guard bond, from organized dress-white formals to playful hazing between classes. While the opportunities afforded by a degree from this highly selective institution are impressive enough, top performers spend their senior summer traveling on exciting internships around the nation and overseas, and graduates have unmatched opportunities to attend flight school and graduate school.

BANG FOR YOUR BUCK

All graduates go on to become commissioned officers in the U.S. Coast Guard, and every junior officer in the Coast Guard can apply for the opportunity to obtain advanced education at Coast Guard expense (and additional service obligation). While in school, officers continue to receive full pay and benefits—their only job is to study and earn a degree. While acceptance into these programs is based on job performance and academic potential, there is such a broad range of opportunities offered that any academy graduate has a good chance of being selected for one of the programs. In the last ten years, every academy engineering graduate who has applied for an engineering postgraduate program has been accepted and has gone on to complete a master's degree. Also of interest: up to 10 percent (approximately twenty cadets) of the graduating class may attend flight training immediately upon completion of the four-year academy program.

STUDENT LIFE

Most of the people that choose to come here are of the same mindset: "determined to become good officers." It's a military academy, so "life is orderly and predictable from day to day, but very busy." Students have time in the afternoons for sports and other activities, and after 10:30 P.M. the halls are quiet and empty (sleeping hours are regulated: students can't sleep between 6:20 A.M. and 4 P.M. without special permission). The dorms reflect this, and "cleanliness is great, and things get fixed (if anything breaks) rather quickly." "Getting off campus is a top priority to have fun," since the rules to be followed are very stringent. Every weekend, cadets leave campus whenever they can: the mall is a huge hot spot for freshman/sophomores, and the surrounding area up to Boston and down to New York is popular for juniors/seniors. When not in class or at military trainings, "students are either working on academic work or watching movies, playing video games, or working out to de-stress from cadet life."

United States Coast Guard Academy

CAREER

The Academy opens doors and equips cadets with the skills and resume they need to get upper echelon jobs. All students go on to become officers in the U.S. Coast Guard once they graduate and report for duty aboard cutters and at sector offices in ports around the country, and serve out a five year commitment to the military. "I will have a guaranteed job once I graduate. And I am now a part of the military family that takes care of its own," says a student. Students are eager to begin their "very noble career" and many go on past their five years to become lifetime military.

GENERAL INFO

Activities: Choral groups, concert band, dance, drama/theater, jazz band, marching band, pep band, yearbook, campus ministries. **Organizations:** 2 honor societies, 7 religious organizations. **Athletics (In-tercollegiate):** *Men:* Baseball, basketball, crew/rowing, cross-country, diving, football, pistol, riflery, sailing, soccer, swimming, tennis, track/field (outdoor), track/field (indoor), wrestling. *Women:* Basketball, cheerleading, crew/rowing, cross-country, diving, pistol, riflery, sailing, soccer, softball, swimming, track/ field (outdoor), track/field (indoor), volleyball. **On-Campus Highlights:** Coast Guard Barque EAGLE, Coast Guard Museum, Sailing Center and Waterfront, Souvenier Shop (Military Exchange), Coast Guard Academy Chapel and Crown Park. **Environmental Initiatives:** Federal Electronic Recycling Challenge Participant. RecycleMania.

FINANCIAL AID

Students should submit: The Princeton Review suggests that all financial aid forms be submitted as soon as possible after October 1.

BOTTOM LINE

Cadets don't pay a penny for tuition, room, or board at the Coast Guard Academy. All candidates who accept an appointment must submit $3,000 to purchase uniforms, a laptop computer, school supplies, and other necessary items. Other than this initial deposit, there are no additional fees, and all cadets receive pay totaling $11,530 per year. Students have a five-year service commitment after graduation, but that can be lengthened by the many available postgraduate degrees and training made available to USCGA alum. Approximately 80 percent of academy graduates go to sea after graduation, and the other 20 percent of academy graduates go to marine-safety offices, ashore operations, or flight training.

CAREER INFORMATION FROM PAYSCALE.COM

ROI rating	N/A
Bachelor's and No Higher	
Median starting salary	$67,400
Median mid-career salary	$95,800
At Least Bachelor's	
Median starting salary	$67,400
Median mid-career salary	$95,800

SELECTIVITY

Admissions Rating	97
# of applicants	2,214
% of applicants accepted	18
% of acceptees attending	75
# offered a place on the wait list	148
% accepting a place on wait list	100
% admitted from wait list	24
# of early decision applicants	648
% accepted early decision	24

FRESHMAN PROFILE

Range SAT Critical Reading	570–660
Range SAT Math	610–690
Range SAT Writing	560–650
Range ACT Composite	26–31
Minimum paper TOEFL	560
Minimum internet-based TOEFL	90
Average HS GPA	3.8
% graduated top 10% of class	45
% graduated top 25% of class	79
% graduated top 50% of class	96

DEADLINES

Early action	
Deadline	11/15
Notification	2/1
Regular	
Priority	11/15
Deadline	2/1
Notification	4/15
Nonfall registration?	No

FINANCIAL FACTS

Financial Aid Rating	60*
Annual in-state tuition	$0
Annual out-of-state tuition	$0
Required fees	$978
Books and supplies	$2,199
% needy frosh rec. need-based scholarship or grant aid	0
% needy UG rec. need-based scholarship or grant aid	0
% needy frosh rec. non-need-based scholarship or grant aid	0
% needy UG rec. non-need-based scholarship or grant aid	0
% needy frosh rec. need-based self-help aid	0
% needy UG rec. need-based self-help aid	0
% frosh rec. any financial aid	0
% UG rec. any financial aid	0

United States Merchant Marine Academy

Office of Admissions, Kings Point, NY 11024-1699 • Admissions: 516-773-5391 • Fax: 516-773-5390

CAMPUS LIFE

Quality of Life Rating	68
Fire Safety Rating	98
Green Rating	64
Type of school	Public
Affiliation	No Affiliation
Environment	Village

STUDENTS

Total undergrad enrollment	904
% male/female	83/17
% from out of state	90
% frosh from public high school	75
% frosh live on campus	100
% ugrads live on campus	100
% African American	3
% Asian	7
% Caucasian	74
% Hispanic	10
% Native American	2
% Pacific Islander	0
% Two or more races	0
% Race and/or ethnicity unknown	4
% international	1
# of countries represented	4

ACADEMICS

Academic Rating	67
% students returning for sophomore year	94
% students graduating within 4 years	74
% students graduating within 6 years	83
Calendar	Trimester
Student/faculty ratio	13:1
Profs interesting rating	65
Profs accessible rating	64
Most classes have 10–19 students.	

MOST POPULAR MAJORS

Logistics; Engineering; Systems;
Transportation and Management

ABOUT THE SCHOOL

Known for having the hardest academics out of all the military academies, the United States Merchant Marine Academy offers students free tuition, rigorous academics, and the widest range of career options available to graduates of U.S. service academies following graduation (including officers in any branch of the armed forces, or a number of civilian occupations). Professors are undoubtedly more than qualified in their fields of study, ranging from former NASA scientists to highly decorated and accomplished officers in the military.

The notorious freshman year is spent inducting students into a completely new way of life, in which they learn new terms, the quality of endurance, how to perform under pressure, and the definition of a wakeup call at "0-dark-thirty." The "sea year" spent studying on merchant vessels gives students a hands-on perspective that not many other engineering schools offer, and students typically visit ten to fifteen countries in the course of the school year. When liberty time is allowed, students have access to New York City, as well as a multimillion-dollar waterfront packed with powerboats (not to mention the know-how to use them). At the end of it all, students graduate with a Bachelor of Science degree, as well as the specialized training for licensing as a merchant marine officer, the military knowledge for commissioning in a reserve component of the armed forces, and a strong network of alumni that know how capable a USMMA graduate really is.

The United States is a maritime nation, and every hour of every day, ships of all types ply the waters in and around it. It's a dangerous and lucrative business, and that's why the country relies on graduates of the United States Merchant Marine Academy in Kings Point, New York, to serve the economic and defense interests of the United States through the maritime industry and armed forces. This "prestigious academy, paid for by the federal government" offers "opportunities upon graduation [that] are endless."

BANG FOR YOUR BUCK

After graduation, students are automatically qualified to enter any branch of the armed forces as an officer, including Army, Navy, Air Force, Marines, Coast Guard, or NOAA. Virtually 100 percent of graduates obtain well-paying employment within six months of commencement, with the majority at work within three months, and most with offers of employment before graduation day. Most students that attend the USMMA have their sights set on a solid job that only requires them to work six months out of the year. The Academy's four-year program centers on a regimental system that turns its students—called midshipmen (a term used for both men and women)—into "top notch officers who are not only capable at sea, but have the ability to work under stress in any situation."

STUDENT LIFE

The ratio of men to women is around 10:1, and can be classified into two groups: those who want to serve in the military and serve their country, and those who want to sail commercially for a living after graduation. The first year is designed to build unity in each graduating class, so camaraderie is apparent from the start. "Because of the regimental/military experience here everyone is smashed together and forced to work together to some extent so for the most part everyone gets along and or works together," says a student. The typical student "has tons on his plate," whether it be regimental duties or academic ones, and "people strongly focus on graduating and doing whatever it takes to reach that big goal." Students are restricted to the campus grounds during the week until senior year, so "most time is spent either in class, studying or working out."

United States Merchant Marine Academy

FINANCIAL AID: 516-773-5295 • E-MAIL: ADMISSIONS@USMMA.EDU • WEBSITE: WWW.USMMA.EDU

CAREER

Depending on whether one's focus was on transportation or engineering, a graduate can sit for different licenses and certifications that determine their career. Unlike the other military academies, USMMA graduates are required to fulfill their service obligation on their own in a wide variety of occupations, and must just provide proof of employment. Acceptable options include employment on any U.S. flagged merchant vessels, as civilians in the maritime industry, or as active duty officers in any branch of the U.S. armed forces. All graduates must maintain their merchant marine officer's license for six years.

GENERAL INFO

Activities: Choral groups, concert band, drama/theater, marching band, student government, student newspaper, yearbook, campus ministries. **Organizations:** 3 religious organizations. **Athletics (Intercollegiate):** *Men:* Baseball, basketball, crew/rowing, cross-country, diving, football, golf, lacrosse, riflery, sailing, soccer, swimming, tennis, track/field (outdoor), volleyball, water polo, wrestling. *Women:* Basketball, crew/rowing, cross-country, diving, golf, riflery, sailing, softball, swimming, tennis, track/field (outdoor), volleyball.

FINANCIAL AID

Students should submit: FAFSA. The Princeton Review suggests that all financial aid forms be submitted as soon as possible after October 1. *Need-based scholarships/grants offered:* Federal Pell, State scholarships/grants, Private Scholarships. *Loan aid offered:* Direct Subsidized Stafford Loans, Direct Unsubsidized Stafford Loans, Direct PLUS Loans. Applicants will be notified of awards on a rolling basis beginning 5/1.

BOTTOM LINE

The federal government pays for all of a student's education, room and board, uniforms, and books; however, midshipmen are responsible for the payment of fees for mandatory educational supplies not provided by the government, such as the prescribed personal computer, activity fees (athletic, cultural events, health services, student newspaper, yearbook, etc.), and personal fees. These fees along with books and supplies come to approximately $4,000, though totals may vary depending on class year (loans are available). The service commitment for each student is determined by their choice of career following graduation.

CAREER INFORMATION FROM PAYSCALE.COM

ROI rating	**N/A**
Bachelor's and No Higher	
Median starting salary	$75,300
Median mid-career salary	$121,000
At Least Bachelor's	
Median starting salary	$77,900
Median mid-career salary	$128,000
% alumni with high job meaning	71%
% STEM	47%

SELECTIVITY

Admissions Rating	**97**
# of applicants	1,662
% of applicants accepted	22
% of acceptees attending	71
# offered a place on the wait list	197
% accepting a place on wait list	100

FRESHMAN PROFILE

Range SAT Critical Reading	570–660
Range SAT Math	620–690
Range ACT Composite	26–30
Minimum paper TOEFL	540
Minimum internet-based TOEFL	83
Average HS GPA	3.6
% graduated top 10% of class	33
% graduated top 25% of class	57
% graduated top 50% of class	92

DEADLINES

Regular	
Deadline	3/1
Nonfall registration?	No

FINANCIAL FACTS

Financial Aid Rating	**60***
Annual in-state tuition	$0
Annual out-of-state tuition	$0
Required fees	$1,167
Books and supplies	$2,887
Average frosh need-based scholarship	$0
% needy frosh rec. need-based scholarship or grant aid	100
% needy UG rec. need-based scholarship or grant aid	100
% needy frosh rec. non-need-based scholarship or grant aid	100
% needy UG rec. non-need-based scholarship or grant aid	100
% needy frosh rec. need-based self-help aid	100
% needy UG rec. need-based self-help aid	100
% frosh rec. any financial aid	33
% UG rec. any financial aid	30
% UG borrow to pay for school	34
Average cumulative indebtedness	$7,500
% frosh need fully met	100
% ugrads need fully met	100
Average % of frosh need met	100
Average % of ugrad need met	100

United States Military Academy—West Point

646 Swift Road, West Point, NY 10996-1905 • Admissions: 845-938-4041 • Fax: 845-938-3021

CAMPUS LIFE

Quality of Life Rating	86
Fire Safety Rating	91
Green Rating	60*
Type of school	Public
Affiliation	No Affiliation
Environment	Village

STUDENTS

Total undergrad enrollment	4,348
% male/female	0/0
% from out of state	93
% frosh from public high school	79
% frosh live on campus	100
% ugrads live on campus	100
% African American	10
% Asian	6
% Caucasian	65
% Hispanic	12
% Native American	1
% Pacific Islander	1
% Two or more races	3
% Race and/or ethnicity unknown	1
% international	1
# of countries represented	33

ACADEMICS

Academic Rating	99
% students returning for sophomore year	93
% students graduating within 4 years	80
% students graduating within 6 years	83
Calendar	Semester
Student/faculty ratio	7:1
Profs interesting rating	97
Profs accessible rating	99

Most classes have 10–19 students.
Most lab/discussion sessions have
10–19 students.

MOST POPULAR MAJORS

Economics; Business Administration and
Management; Engineering/Industrial
Management

ABOUT THE SCHOOL

There's just a little history behind this one, you see. Founded in 1802, the United States Military Academy—West Point is integral to the military and political history of the United States of America, having produced Generals Grant, Lee, Pershing, MacArthur, Eisenhower, Patton, Schwarzkopf, and Petraeus. The school is all about transforming regular citizens into intellectual soldiers with unparalleled skills of leadership who will be fit to lead America into battle. If it sounds like a tall order, that's because it is, and one that West Point has fulfilled time and time again over three centuries.

USMA is all about the leadership, and the school is very open about the grueling process involved in producing West Point-grade leaders that can make it to the front lines and back. The large core curriculum ensures that cadets are at the very least jacks of all trades, and mandatory sports events keep cadets in peak performance shape. Ethical, social, and spiritual development are also on the docket, and the school's staff and faculty role models and a vigorous guest-speaker program help to provide living proof of the values the school wishes to impart. These jam-packed schedules produce well-rounded students who are able to apply a wide range of analytical skills to life as a military officer, as well as a decision maker in all contexts.

Renowned as one of the world's preeminent leader-development institutions, West Point's mission is to educate, train, and inspire the student body (called the Corps of Cadets) through a "strenuous schedule that requires hard work and sacrifice." Luckily, there "are absolutely excellent" instructors who "put an incredible amount of effort and work into making sure the students succeed." All cadets receive a Bachelor of Science degree, and each year, approximately 1,000 cadets who make it through all four years "join the Long Gray Line" as they graduate and are commissioned as second lieutenants in the U.S. Army.

BANG FOR YOUR BUCK

The doors West Point opens are innumerable, and those doors don't just lead to military careers. Joining "the Long Gray Line" of West Point graduates is a mark of distinction, and one that can carry over into civilian life. Training for a future career outside of the military can begin during the service obligation, as during senior year, cadets find out which specialized field, or "branch," they will enter (options include combat branches, support branches and intelligence, and even the Medical Service Corps). Both the needs of the Army and cadet preferences will be considered.

STUDENT LIFE

The Corps is divided into companies of about 160 students of all classes that function as ad hoc families, and the general mindset is focused solely towards personal development and the development of younger students. Cadets "average five hours of sleep through all four years of their undergraduate degree" and march to every meal, adhering to "a rigid system in which they carry out their day to day activities." For fun, "most people run or workout during the week" and on weekends many students travel to New York City by train. "As a plebe I watch movies and just hang out with my classmates on the weekends," says one student. Playing sports is also a big release for most cadets, and there are two bars on campus for juniors and seniors to use once they are of age.

United States Military Academy—West Point

E-MAIL: ADMISSIONS@USMA.EDU • WEBSITE: WWW.WESTPOINT.EDU

CAREER

Upon graduation, all cadets receive a Bachelor of Science degree and most are commissioned as second lieutenants in the Army (foreign cadets are commissioned into the armies of their home countries), though a small number apply for a cross-commission, in which they request another branch of the armed services. "It's a free education, opportunities to study abroad (FOR FREE) among other amazing opportunities, and a job guaranteed to us at the end of the line," says a cadet. The precise courses and wide range of majors are "good preparation for a both a military and civilian career in the future." Of the West Point graduates who visited PayScale.com, sixty-six percent reported feeling their job had a meaningful impact on the world. The median starting salary was $75,100.

GENERAL INFO

Activities: Choral groups, drama/theater, jazz band, music ensembles, pep band, radio station, student government, student newspaper, television station, yearbook, campus ministries, international student organization. **Organizations:** 105 registered organizations, 7 honor societies, 13 religious organizations. **Athletics (Intercollegiate):** *Men:* Baseball, basketball, cross-country, football, golf, gymnastics, ice hockey, lacrosse, riflery, soccer, swimming, tennis, track/field (outdoor), track/field (indoor), wrestling. *Women:* Basketball, cross-country, riflery, soccer, softball, swimming, tennis, track/field (outdoor), track/field (indoor), volleyball. **On-Campus Highlights:** Cadet Chapel, West Point Museum, Eisenhower Hall, Michie Stadium, Trophy Point, Fort Putnam, West Point Cemetery.

FINANCIAL AID

Students should submit: The Princeton Review suggests that all financial aid forms be submitted as soon as possible after October 1.

BOTTOM LINE

Tuition is free, and all cadets receive a monthly stipend of approximately $10,000 a year. All graduates must serve at least five years of active duty (beginning as a second lieutenant in the Army) and three years in a Reserve Component, a total of eight years, after graduation. Cadets are expected to pay a fee upon admission to the academy. This $2,000 is not only a commitment to attend, but will be used to defray the costs of uniforms, books, and a computer—essential items for every cadet. The active-duty obligation is the nation's return on a West Point graduate's fully funded, four-year college education that is valued in excess of $225,000.

CAREER INFORMATION FROM PAYSCALE.COM	
ROI rating	N/A
Bachelor's and No Higher	
Median starting salary	$78,500
Median mid-career salary	$120,000
At Least Bachelor's	
Median starting salary	$82,800
Median mid-career salary	$127,000
% alumni with high job meaning	61%
% STEM	39%

SELECTIVITY

Admissions Rating	98
# of applicants	14,635
% of applicants accepted	10
% of acceptees attending	83

FRESHMAN PROFILE

Range SAT Critical Reading	580–680
Range SAT Math	610–710
Range SAT Writing	560–670
Range ACT Composite	26–31
Minimum paper TOEFL	500
Minimum internet-based TOEFL	75
% graduated top 10% of class	52
% graduated top 25% of class	76
% graduated top 50% of class	94

DEADLINES

Regular	
Deadline	2/28
Nonfall registration?	No

FINANCIAL FACTS

Financial Aid Rating	60*
Annual in-state tuition	$0
Annual out-of-state tuition	$0
Average frosh need-based scholarship	$0
% needy frosh rec. need-based scholarship or grant aid	0
% needy UG rec. need-based scholarship or grant aid	0
% needy frosh rec. non-need-based scholarship or grant aid	0
% needy UG rec. non-need-based scholarship or grant aid	0
% needy frosh rec. need-based self-help aid	0
% needy UG rec. need-based self-help aid	0
% frosh rec. any financial aid	0
% UG rec. any financial aid	0
Average % of frosh need met	0
Average % of ugrad need met	0

United States Naval Academy

117 Decatur Road, Annapolis, MD 21402 • Admissions: 410-293-1914 • Fax: 410-293-4348

CAMPUS LIFE

Quality of Life Rating	90
Fire Safety Rating	77
Green Rating	60*
Type of school	Public
Affiliation	No Affiliation
Environment	Town

STUDENTS

Total undergrad enrollment	4,525
% male/female	75/25
% from out of state	93
% frosh from public high school	60
% frosh live on campus	100
% ugrads live on campus	100
% African American	7
% Asian	7
% Caucasian	64
% Hispanic	11
% Native American	<1
% Pacific Islander	1
% Two or more races	8
% Race and/or ethnicity unknown	1
% international	1
# of countries represented	28

ACADEMICS

Academic Rating	91
% students returning for sophomore year	98
% students graduating within 4 years	86
% students graduating within 6 years	86
Calendar	Semester
Student/faculty ratio	8:1
Profs interesting rating	76
Profs accessible rating	97
Most classes have 10–19 students.	

MOST POPULAR MAJORS

Economics; Political Science and Government; Systems Engineering

ABOUT THE SCHOOL

The deeply historic United States Naval Academy is one of the few colleges in the world that prepares students morally, mentally, and physically. There's an intense focus not only on regimentation, but also on the shaping of students' moral character, and students here thrive on the academic and militaristic discipline required to make it as a midshipman. Those that decide to apply here—and receive the necessary congressional recommendation to do so—are looking for more than a college degree, and so this self-selecting pool of the best and the brightest young men and women are ready to become the next military leaders of the world from the second they set foot in the Yard.

Through the school's well-worn system, students learn to take orders from practically everyone (Plebe Summer Training certainly provides an introduction to this) but before long acquire the responsibility for making decisions that can affect hundreds of other midshipmen. Small class sizes, protected study time, academic advising, and a sponsor program for newly arrived midshipmen all help ensure that students are given the tools to succeed at this tough school. After four years at the Naval Academy, the life and customs of the naval service become second nature, and most midshipmen go on to careers as officers in the Navy or Marines.

The scenic Naval Academy campus, known as the Yard, is located in historic Annapolis, Maryland, and has been the home to some of the country's foremost leaders, astronauts, scholars, and military heroes. With its combination of early-twentieth-century and modern buildings ("the facilities are unmatched"), the USNA is a blend of tradition and state-of-the-art technology, and the school's history is felt even in the most high tech of classrooms.

BANG FOR YOUR BUCK

All graduates go on to become an ensign in the Navy or a second lieutenant in the Marine Corps and serve five years as an officer, followed by reserve commissions. Many also go on for additional training, including nuclear power, aviation, submarine warfare, and special operations. Especially capable and highly motivated students are able to enroll in the school's challenging honors programs, which provide opportunities to start work on postgraduate degrees while still at the academy. Graduates of USNA tend to spread themselves beyond the military, and the school has produced one president and numerous astronauts, and more than 990 noted scholars in a variety of academic fields are academy graduates, including forty-six Rhodes Scholars and twenty-four Marshall Scholars.

STUDENT LIFE

Monday to Friday midshipmen "put every hour of their lives into their development" and weekdays are scheduled tightly with a "six-period class schedule, lunch together, sports period from 3:45 to 6:00, dinner together, then study period from 8:00 to 10:00." World conflicts are always being discussed "because in a few short years that is where we are possibly going to be." Fun activities involve Army Week, Halloween trick-or-treating, walking around downtown Annapolis ("a beautiful, quaint little town"), or going to the mall. While free time is extremely scarce, most students spend the afternoon working out or participating on varsity or intramural teams and head into DC or Baltimore on the weekends during one of their allotted weekends away. "Eating out and going to the movies" are also always popular activities on the weekends. Friendships are forged by fire during freshman year: "When you get the same haircut and wear the same outfit, 'fitting in' never seems to be a problem."

United States Naval Academy

FINANCIAL AID: 909-621-8205 • E-MAIL: STROOP@USNA.EDU • WEBSITE: WWW.USNA.EDU

CAREER

Midshipmen life is very difficult, but "the rewards are so great in four short years." "It [is] a fantastic opportunity to serve my country and to secure a fantastic education and job immediately after I finish my undergraduate degree," says one midshipman. Those who make it through all four years receive a Bachelor of Science degree and then are commissioned as Ensigns in the Navy or Second Lieutenants in the Marine Corps, and must fulfill a minimum military commitment of five years. Graduates of the academy who visited PayScale.com had an median starting salary of $80,700, and sixty-nine percent reported feeling that their job had a meaningful impact on the world.

GENERAL INFO

Activities: Choral groups, concert band, drama/theater, jazz band, literary magazine, marching band, musical theater, pep band, radio station, student government, yearbook, campus ministries, international student organization. **Organizations:** 70 registered organizations, 10 honor societies, 8 religious organizations. **Athletics (Intercollegiate):** *Men:* Baseball, basketball, crew/rowing, cross-country, diving, football, golf, gymnastics, lacrosse, light weight football, riflery, sailing, soccer, squash, swimming, tennis, track/field (outdoor), track/field (indoor), water polo, wrestling. *Women:* Basketball, crew/ rowing, cross-country, diving, lacrosse, riflery, sailing, soccer, swimming, tennis, track/field (outdoor), track/field (indoor), volleyball. **On-Campus Highlights:** Bancroft Hall, U.S. Naval Academy Museum, Armel-Leftwich Visitor Center, U.S. Naval Academy Chapel, Lejeune Hall.

FINANCIAL AID

Students should submit: The Princeton Review suggests that all financial aid forms be submitted as soon as possible after October 1.

BOTTOM LINE

The Navy pays for the tuition, room and board, and medical and dental care of Naval Academy midshipmen. Midshipmen also enjoy regular active-duty benefits, including access to military commissaries and exchanges, commercial transportation and lodging discounts, and the ability to fly space-available in military aircraft around the world. Midshipmen are also given a monthly salary of $864, from which laundry, barber, cobbler, activities fees, yearbook, and other service charges are deducted. Actual cash pay is less than $100 per month your first year, increasing each year to $400 per month in your fourth year.

CAREER INFORMATION FROM PAYSCALE.COM	
ROI rating	N/A
Bachelor's and No Higher	
Median starting salary	$78,200
Median mid-career salary	$126,000
At Least Bachelor's	
Median starting salary	$81,700
Median mid-career salary	$134,000
% alumni with high job meaning	59%
% STEM	54%

SELECTIVITY

Admissions Rating	98
# of applicants	16,101
% of applicants accepted	9
% of acceptees attending	87
# offered a place on the wait list	187
% accepting a place on wait list	76
% admitted from wait list	3

FRESHMAN PROFILE

Range SAT Critical Reading	570–680
Range SAT Math	610–700
% graduated top 10% of class	58
% graduated top 25% of class	81
% graduated top 50% of class	94

DEADLINES

Regular	
Deadline	1/31
Notification	4/15
Nonfall registration?	No

FINANCIAL FACTS

Financial Aid Rating	60*
Annual in-state tuition	$0
Annual out-of-state tuition	$0
Average frosh need-based scholarship	$0
% needy frosh rec. need-based scholarship or grant aid	0
% needy UG rec. need-based scholarship or grant aid	0
% needy frosh rec. non-need-based scholarship or grant aid	0
% needy UG rec. non-need-based scholarship or grant aid	0
% needy frosh rec. need-based self-help aid	0
% needy UG rec. need-based self-help aid	0
% frosh rec. any financial aid	0
% UG rec. any financial aid	0
Average % of frosh need met	0
Average % of ugrad need met	0

Webb Institute

298 Crescent Beach Road, Glen Cove, NY 11542 • Admissions: 516-671-8355 • Fax: 516-674-9838

CAMPUS LIFE

Quality of Life Rating	95
Fire Safety Rating	98
Green Rating	66
Type of school	Private
Affiliation	No Affiliation
Environment	Village

STUDENTS

Total undergrad enrollment	91
% male/female	81/19
% from out of state	80
% frosh from public high school	81
% frosh live on campus	100
% ugrads live on campus	100
% African American	0
% Asian	11
% Caucasian	77
% Hispanic	0
% Native American	0
% Pacific Islander	0
% Two or more races	8
% Race and/or ethnicity unknown	3
% international	1
# of countries represented	4

ACADEMICS

Academic Rating	98
% students returning for sophomore year	83
% students graduating within 4 years	63
% students graduating within 6 years	74
Calendar	Semester
Student/faculty ratio	8:1
Profs interesting rating	93
Profs accessible rating	99
Most classes have 20–29 students.	

ABOUT THE SCHOOL

Ever wondered what goes into designing an America's Cup yacht, U.S. Navy destroyer, or a cruise liner? That's the exact sort of curiosity that brings students to Webb Institute, an engineering college that has produced the nation's leading ship designers for more than a century. Imagine a tiny student body living, eating, sleeping, and learning ship design in a mansion in a residential area overlooking the beautiful Long Island Sound. Then imagine that when that tiny student body leaves their manse, they find a 100 percent placement rate in careers and graduate schools. That's Webb Institute.

As the only school of its kind in the country, Webb enjoys an unrivaled reputation within the marine industry, which is also where students (happily) complete their mandatory two-month internships each January and February. Life—and that includes study, work, and play—on a twenty-six-acre beachfront estate with just 100 students and eleven full-time professors is a rare combination of challenge, focus, and adventure, so in a sense, every day at Webb is a beach day.

Webb Institute is a four-year, fully accredited engineering college that has specialized in naval architecture and marine engineering for the last 123 years. Founded in 1889 by prominent New York shipbuilder William H. Webb, the school's rigorous curriculum couples seamlessly with a total immersion in real-world experience. The school's curriculum goes beyond mechanical, electrical, and civil engineering, taking a systems-engineering approach to problem-solving, meaning Webb graduates are capable of working across engineering disciplines. "If you're passionate about architecture and engineering, you cannot hope for a better learning environment." Everyone majors in naval architecture and marine engineering, although nonengineering electives are available to juniors and seniors, and Webbies are exposed to a smattering of the liberal arts and a ton of advanced math and physics.

BANG FOR YOUR BUCK

Webb's full-tuition scholarship creates the lowest average student loan indebtedness of any four-year college in the nation besides the military academies. Job prospects are phenomenal; every Webb student goes to work in the marine industry for two months every year, creating a professional network and résumé content of eight months or more industry experience. In part due to this experience, as well as the school's specialized nature and excellent reputation, every graduate has a job at graduation or within two months after.

STUDENT LIFE

Classes are so small that "you learn to like everyone to an extent" (everyone being "obsessed about boats" also helps), and from the start "every student fits right into the freshman class through a week of dedicated trips and activities." "When you're going to spend four years with the same people in a room that's not very big, you learn to appreciate all types of people," says a student. This "very hardworking" group "knows how to have a good time when we put our minds to it," and students will often go sailing, fishing, or kayaking on the Long Island Sound with the school-funded boats. Webb students are given a lot of freedom outside of their classes (which "must be attended"), and "[New York City] is never too far away and offers anything you could want." Sports are also a great way to relax, and "anyone can join."

Webb Institute

FINANCIAL AID: 516-671-2213 • E-MAIL: ADMISSIONS@WEBB-INSTITUTE.EDU • WEBSITE: WWW.WEBB-INSTITUTE.EDU

CAREER

With only one academic major and a mandatory internship program, Webb has a pretty established reputation for the students it sends out into the world, and a one hundred percent job placement rate reflects this. "Webb Institute is THE college for Naval Architecture, and a job offer is basically guaranteed after graduating." The focus is on preparing the students for a marine engineering or naval architecture job by teaching them everything they might need to know, and students can expect one-on-one attention when lining up a post-graduation job. "Webb students are very prepared for a future career," says one.

GENERAL INFO

Activities: Choral groups, drama/theater, music ensembles, student government, yearbook. **Organizations:** 2 registered organizations. **Athletics (Intercollegiate):** *Men:* Basketball, cross-country, sailing, soccer, tennis, volleyball. *Women:* Basketball, cross-country, sailing, soccer, tennis, volleyball. **On-Campus Highlights:** Stevenson Taylor Hall, Brockett Pub, Waterfront Facility.

FINANCIAL AID

Students should submit: FAFSA, Institution's own financial aid form, Business/Farm Supplement. Regular filing deadline is 7/1. The Princeton Review suggests that all financial aid forms be submitted as soon as possible after October 1. *Need-based scholarships/grants offered:* Federal Pell, State scholarships/grants, Private scholarships, College/university scholarship or grant aid from institutional funds. *Loan aid offered:* Direct Subsidized Stafford Loans, Direct Unsubsidized Stafford Loans, Direct PLUS Loans. Applicants will be notified of awards on or about 8/1.

BOTTOM LINE

Every Webb student receives a full-tuition scholarship founded by Mr. Webb, and continued by the generous contributions of alumni/ae, friends of Webb, parents, corporations, and the U.S. government. All admitted students also get paid for two months of internships every year. The only costs are room, board, books, and supplies, which come to $15,500 each year. You can also expect to pay another $4,850 in personal expenses (including transportation and a laptop). There are some additional scholarships available to deserving students to help defray these costs, and if a student needs additional financial assistance, the school recommends pursuing federal grants and loans (and they'll help you do so).

CAREER INFORMATION FROM PAYSCALE.COM	
ROI rating	N/A
Bachelor's and No Higher	
Median starting salary	$65,400
Median mid-career salary	$105,000
At Least Bachelor's	
Median starting salary	$65,400
Median mid-career salary	$105,000

SELECTIVITY

Admissions Rating	97
# of applicants	105
% of applicants accepted	36
% of acceptees attending	68
# of early decision applicants	27
% accepted early decision	30

FRESHMAN PROFILE

Range SAT Critical Reading	670–730
Range SAT Math	750–770
Range SAT Writing	680–730
Range ACT Composite	30–33
Average HS GPA	4.2
% graduated top 10% of class	71
% graduated top 25% of class	21
% graduated top 50% of class	8

DEADLINES

Early decision	
Deadline	10/15
Notification	12/15
Regular	
Priority	10/15
Deadline	2/15
Nonfall registration?	No

FINANCIAL FACTS

Financial Aid Rating	60*
Annual tuition	$47,000
Room and board	$14,400
Required fees	$400
Average need-based scholarship	$2,000
% needy frosh rec. need-based scholarship or grant aid	100
% needy UG rec. need-based scholarship or grant aid	100
% needy frosh rec. non-need-based scholarship or grant aid	33
% needy UG rec. non-need-based scholarship or grant aid	53
% needy frosh rec. need-based self-help aid	100
% needy UG rec. need-based self-help aid	100
% frosh rec. any financial aid	23
% UG rec. any financial aid	18
% frosh need fully met	0
% ugrads need fully met	0
Average % of frosh need met	80
Average % of ugrad need met	79

School Profiles

Agnes Scott College

141 East College Avenue, Decatur, GA 30030-3770 • Admissions: 404-471-6285 • Fax: 404-471-6414

CAMPUS LIFE

Quality of Life Rating	**94**
Fire Safety Rating	**96**
Green Rating	**91**
Type of school	Private
Affiliation	Presbyterian
Environment	Metropolis

STUDENTS

Total undergrad enrollment	902
% male/female	1/99
% from out of state	45
% frosh from public high school	76
% frosh live on campus	93
% ugrads live on campus	87
% African American	34
% Asian	6
% Caucasian	33
% Hispanic	10
% Native American	<1
% Pacific Islander	0
% Two or more races	8
% Race and/or ethnicity unknown	2
% international	8
# of countries represented	32

ACADEMICS

Academic Rating	**90**
% students returning for sophomore year	87
% students graduating within 4 years	61
% students graduating within 6 years	68
Calendar	Semester
Student/faculty ratio	10:1
Profs interesting rating	91
Profs accessible rating	87
Most classes have 10–19 students.	
Most lab/discussion sessions have 10–19 students.	

MOST POPULAR MAJORS
Psychology; Public Health; Business Management

ABOUT THE SCHOOL

At Agnes Scott College, a women's liberal arts college in Decatur, Georgia, students find a "warm student body, beautiful campus, great location" and a "small close knit community that is always there for [you]." This "fun, quirky little college" focuses on "educating women in a caring and intellectual atmosphere." Students benefit from individual attention and don't "feel like a number or just another face in the crowd." Instead, Agnes Scott faculty "actually take the time to get to know you" and "are very accommodating of differences in learning style." Students say that this level of support "has contributed to [their] academic success." The college offers thirty-four degrees and maintains affiliations with nearby universities, including Emory University and Georgia Tech, that allow students to earn dual degrees in fields such as computer science, engineering, and nursing. In the end, Scotties enjoy being "part of a community of ferocious women leaders who will, single-handedly, not just address but resolve the 'intellectual and social challenges of our time.'"

BANG FOR YOUR BUCK

Agnes Scott offers a number of merit-based scholarships to incoming first-years that are renewable throughout the student's four years of college. Two scholarships are reserved for students with demonstrated financial need: the Goizueta Foundation scholarships and the Nannette Hopkins Music Scholarships. Additionally, the school provides need-based aid in the form of grants. One senior majoring in psychology and education said "the scholarships and grants that were offered" made it possible for her to attend. "When searching for schools," she explained, "Agnes Scott was one of my top choices but was quickly brushed aside when I saw how much it cost to attend." Luckily, a counselor convinced her to apply, and "needless to say I ended up choosing Agnes Scott. My out of pocket cost will be less than $2,000 for a full year."

STUDENT LIFE

These "feisty intellectuals ready to make their mark on society" describe themselves as "academically driven" and "ambitious women who think critically about difficult issues." While "academics are a little demanding," this "close-knit community" enjoys blowing off some steam together. Sometimes "President Kiss (pronounced 'quiche') will take a group of us to Stone Mountain to hike up the side of it," one student explained. For cash strapped students, entertainment on campus is easy: "Most everything at Agnes is free for the students," including a Wednesday craft night and free movie screenings with the film club. Students take their clubs seriously, leveraging their experiences to network and build their résumés. One student explained that, through her involvement with Agnes's modern dance club, Studio Dance Theatre, she has met "professional lighting designers and electricians in Atlanta" who have helped her get some "very nice jobs in town."

CAREER

The Office of Internship and Career Development maintains an online database, HireAScottie, that connects students and alumnae with internship and employment opportunities. This office also hosts a speaker series that covers topics like career management, networking, and interviewing. Students also find career help from among their peers and their professors. It helps being around a bunch of driven Scotties who say, "I think about my future on a daily basis" because Agnes students can count on each other to "support one another's career plans." And small class sizes mean that Agnes students develop close relationships with their professors who, as one student sums up, "have helped me reach out to the community for experience and connections that have helped me start my career while in school." Agnes Scott grads who visited PayScale.com reported a median starting salary of $38,800.

Agnes Scott College

FINANCIAL AID: 404-471-6395 • E-MAIL: ADMISSION@AGNESSCOTT.EDU • WEBSITE: WWW.AGNESSCOTT.EDU

GENERAL INFO

Activities: Choral groups, dance, drama/theater, literary magazine, marching band, music ensembles, musical theater, pep band, student government, student newspaper, symphony orchestra, television station, yearbook, Campus Ministries, International Student Organization, Model UN. **Organizations:** 80 registered organizations, 12 honor societies, 12 religious organizations. **Athletics (Intercollegiate):** *Women:* basketball, cross-country, soccer, softball, tennis, volleyball. **On-Campus Highlights:** Recent Campbell Hall Living and Learning community renovation anticipating LEED Gold Certification, Alston Campus Center, Bradley Observatory and Planetarium, five solar arrays, McCain Library.

FINANCIAL AID

Students should submit: FAFSA. Regular filing deadline is 5/1. The Princeton Review suggests that all financial aid forms be submitted as soon as possible after October 1. *Need-based scholarships/grants offered:* Federal Pell, FSEOG, State scholarships/grants, Private scholarships, College/university scholarship or grant aid from institutional funds. *Loan aid offered:* Direct Subsidized Stafford Loans, Direct Unsubsidized Stafford Loans, Direct PLUS Loans. Applicants will be notified of awards on a rolling basis beginning 3/1. Federal Work-Study Program available. Institutional employment available.

BOTTOM LINE

An education at this small women's college will cost $38,232 in tuition per year. With $240 in fees and $1,000 to cover the average cost of books and supplies, the total cost should come to $39,472. Don't forget to factor in the cost of room and board, which adds another $11,520.

CAREER INFORMATION FROM PAYSCALE.COM

ROI rating	87
Bachelor's and No Higher	
Median starting salary	$38,800
Median mid-career salary	$91,900
At Least Bachelor's	
Median starting salary	$38,800
Median mid-career salary	$91,900

SELECTIVITY

Admissions Rating	87
# of applicants	1,461
% of applicants accepted	62
% of acceptees attending	30
# of early decision applicants	29
% accepted early decision	100

FRESHMAN PROFILE

Range SAT Critical Reading	550–690
Range SAT Math	510–640
Range SAT Writing	550–670
Range ACT Composite	24–29
Minimum internet-based TOEFL	80
Average HS GPA	3.7
% graduated top 10% of class	29
% graduated top 25% of class	62
% graduated top 50% of class	93

DEADLINES

Early decision	
Deadline	11/1
Notification	12/1
Early action	
Deadline	11/15
Notification	12/15
Regular	
Priority	1/15
Deadline	3/15
Notification	4/15
Nonfall registration?	No

FINANCIAL FACTS

Financial Aid Rating	85
Annual tuition	$38,232
Room and board	$11,520
Required fees	$240
Average need-based scholarship	$27,336
% needy frosh rec. need-based scholarship or grant aid	100
% needy UG rec. need-based scholarship or grant aid	100
% needy frosh rec. non-need-based scholarship or grant aid	26
% needy UG rec. non-need-based scholarship or grant aid	25
% needy frosh rec. need-based self-help aid	80
% needy UG rec. need-based self-help aid	83
% frosh rec. any financial aid	100
% UG rec. any financial aid	99
% UG borrow to pay for school	76
Average cumulative indebtedness	$33,050
% frosh need fully met	27
% ugrads need fully met	25
Average % of frosh need met	84

Amherst College

CAMPUS BOX 2231, AMHERST, MA 01002 • ADMISSIONS: 413-542-2328 • FAX: 413-542-2040

CAMPUS LIFE
Quality of Life Rating	90
Fire Safety Rating	84
Green Rating	76
Type of school	Private
Affiliation	No Affiliation
Environment	Town

STUDENTS
Total undergrad enrollment	1,795
% male/female	50/50
% from out of state	86
% frosh from public high school	62
% frosh live on campus	100
% ugrads live on campus	98
% African American	12
% Asian	14
% Caucasian	42
% Hispanic	13
% Native American	<1
% Pacific Islander	<1
% Two or more races	5
% Race and/or ethnicity unknown	4
% international	10
# of countries represented	54

ACADEMICS
Academic Rating	98
% students returning for sophomore year	98
% students graduating within 4 years	88
% students graduating within 6 years	95
Calendar	Semester
Student/faculty ratio	8:1
Profs interesting rating	94
Profs accessible rating	93

Most classes have 10–19 students.
Most lab/discussion sessions have
10–19 students.

MOST POPULAR MAJORS
Economics; Biology; History

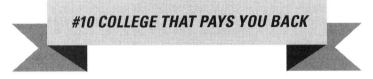

#10 COLLEGE THAT PAYS YOU BACK

ABOUT THE SCHOOL
Situated on a lush 1,015-acre campus in Amherst, Massachusetts, Amherst College offers students an intellectual atmosphere fostered by friendly and supportive faculty members. Amherst College has an exploratory vibe with a virtually requirement-free curriculum that gives students unprecedented academic freedom. There are no core or general requirements. Beyond the first-year seminar and major coursework, students can choose what they want to study. One student told us, "I love the open curriculum and that you can do whatever you want here." That doesn't mean you can slack off, though: students say you must be "willing to read a text forward and backward and firmly grasp it" and "skimming will do you no good." The most popular majors are economics, political science, and English, and alumni have a solid track record in gaining admission to postgraduate programs. In fact, some students view Amherst as "prep school for grad school." Students can also receive credit for courses at neighboring colleges Smith, Mount Holyoke, Hampshire, and the University of Massachusetts Amherst for a total selection of more than 6,000 courses. Students say that they love the "abundant academic and social opportunities" provided by the consortium. Almost half of Amherst students also pack their bags during junior year to study abroad. Students say that professors "are always available, and they want to spend time with us outside of the classroom."

BANG FOR YOUR BUCK
Amherst College is a no-loan institution, which means the college does not include loans in its financial aid packages but focuses on providing grant and scholarship aid instead. It is possible to graduate from Amherst with no debt. In addition to a need-blind admissions policy, Amherst meets 100 percent of students' demonstrated need, be they international or domestic. Every year, Amherst awards grants and scholarships to more than half the student body. All students who apply for financial aid are automatically considered for grant and scholarship funds. In 2014-15, the school provided just over $52 million in scholarship and grant aid to students, and the average award was just over $47,000.

STUDENT LIFE
While students at Amherst are "focused first and foremost on academics, nearly every student is active and enjoys life outside of the library." In their spare time, "students love to get involved in extracurriculars. It seems like everyone plays a sport, is a member of an a cappella group, and has joined an affinity group." "There's a club or organization for every interest" here, and students assure us that if there isn't one that you're interested in, "the school will find the money for it." Amherst's small size "means that no group is isolated, and everyone interacts and more or less gets along." And truly, "diversity—racial, ethnic, geographic, socioeconomic—is more than a buzzword here." The campus is also "a politically and environmentally conscious" place, and the town of Amherst and the surrounding areas are "incredibly intellectual." Still, the "awesome" dorms tend to serve as the school's social hubs, as Amherst did away with its Greek system in 1984.

Amherst College

FINANCIAL AID: 413-542-2296 • E-MAIL: ADMISSION@AMHERST.EDU • WEBSITE: WWW.AMHERST.EDU

CAREER

The Career Center at Amherst is focused on empowering students to think about their futures reflectively and strategically. The Amherst Select Internship Program allows students to get a taste of different fields over the summer and truly test out their options. Other resources like Quest, Career Beam, and the Liberal Arts Career Network list job and internship opportunities for gaining professional experience. Students can easily connect with alumni through Pathways, the alumni-student mentoring program that helps undergrads set goals and make informed career decisions. Those grads who visited PayScale.com report starting salaries of about $53,000, and 30 percent believe their work makes the world a better place.

GENERAL INFO

Activities: Choral groups, concert band, dance, drama/theater, jazz band, literary magazine, music ensembles, musical theater, opera, radio station, student government, student newspaper, student-run film society, symphony orchestra, yearbook, international student organization. **Organizations:** 100-plus registered organizations, 2 honor societies, 7 religious organizations. **Athletics (Intercollegiate):** *Men:* Baseball, basketball, cross-country, football, golf, ice hockey, lacrosse, soccer, squash, swimming and diving, tennis, track/field (outdoor), track/field (indoor). *Women:* Basketball, cross-country, field hockey, golf, ice hockey, lacrosse, soccer, softball, squash, swimming and diving, tennis, track/field (outdoor), track/field (indoor), volleyball. **On-Campus Highlights:** Mead Art Museum, Beneski Museum of Natural History, Center for Russian Culture, Japanese Yushien Garden, Wilder Observatory.

FINANCIAL AID

Students should submit: FAFSA, CSS/Financial Aid PROFILE, Noncustodial PROFILE, Business/Farm Supplement. Priority filing deadline is 2/15. The Princeton Review suggests that all financial aid forms be submitted as soon as possible after October 1. *Need-based scholarships/grants offered:* Federal Pell, FSEOG, State scholarships/grants, Private scholarships, College/university scholarship or grant aid from institutional funds. *Loan aid offered:* Direct Subsidized Stafford Loans, Direct Unsubsidized Stafford Loans, Direct PLUS loans, Federal Perkins Loans, College/university loans from institutional funds. Applicants will be notified of awards on or about 4/1. Federal Work-Study Program available. Institutional employment available.

BOTTOM LINE

Annual tuition, fees, and room and board cost roughly $63,000 at Amherst. Once you consider books, supplies, personal expenses, and transportation, you can expect to spend anywhere from $66,000 to $70,000 per year. In the end, you'll get much more than what you pay for. The school meets 100 percent of its student body's demonstrated need without loans, and those who choose to take them out graduate with little debt (relative to the indebtedness of graduates of many similar schools). Students feel it is "hard to find somewhere better" and believe Amherst is "the best of the small, elite New England colleges."

CAREER INFORMATION FROM PAYSCALE.COM

ROI rating	94
Bachelor's and No Higher	
Median starting salary	$53,000
Median mid-career salary	$104,000
At Least Bachelor's	
Median starting salary	$59,800
Median mid-career salary	$98,600
% alumni with high job meaning	54%
% STEM	15%

SELECTIVITY

Admissions Rating	98
# of applicants	8,568
% of applicants accepted	14
% of acceptees attending	39
# offered a place on the wait list	1,398
% accepting a place on wait list	46
% admitted from wait list	5
# of early decision applicants	483
% accepted early decision	36

FRESHMAN PROFILE

Range SAT Critical Reading	680–780
Range SAT Math	680–780
Range SAT Writing	680–770
Range ACT Composite	31–34
Minimum internet-based TOEFL	100
% graduated top 10% of class	86
% graduated top 25% of class	96
% graduated top 50% of class	100

DEADLINES

Early decision	
Deadline	11/15
Notification	12/15
Regular	
Deadline	1/1
Notification	4/1
Nonfall registration?	No

FINANCIAL FACTS

Financial Aid Rating	96
Annual tuition	$51,620
Room and board	$13,710
Required fees	$856
Average need-based scholarship	$49,134
% needy frosh rec. need-based scholarship or grant aid	100
% needy UG rec. need-based scholarship or grant aid	99
% needy UG rec. non-need-based scholarship or grant aid	0
% needy frosh rec. need-based self-help aid	80
% needy UG rec. need-based self-help aid	88
% frosh rec. any financial aid	54
% UG rec. any financial aid	58
% UG borrow to pay for school	25
Average cumulative indebtedness	$15,756
% frosh need fully met	100
% ugrads need fully met	100
Average % of frosh need met	100
Average % of ugrad need met	100

Arizona State University

PO Box 870112, Tempe, AZ 85287-0112 • Admissions: 480-965-7788 • Fax: 480-965-3610

CAMPUS LIFE

Quality of Life Rating	**85**
Fire Safety Rating	**92**
Green Rating	**96**
Type of school	Public
Affiliation	No Affiliation
Environment	Metropolis

STUDENTS

Total undergrad enrollment	57,272
% male/female	53/47
% frosh live on campus	72
% ugrads live on campus	21
# of fraternities (% ugrad men join)	37 (5)
# of sororities (% ugrad women join)	28 (8)
% African American	4
% Asian	6
% Caucasian	52
% Hispanic	21
% Native American	1
% Pacific Islander	<1
% Two or more races	4
% Race and/or ethnicity unknown	1
% international	9
# of countries represented	112

ACADEMICS

Academic Rating	**71**
% students returning for sophomore year	86
% students graduating within 4 years	45
% students graduating within 6 years	65
Calendar	Semester
Student/faculty ratio	21:1
Profs interesting rating	71
Profs accessible rating	70
Most classes have 10–19 students.	
Most lab/discussion sessions have 20–29 students.	

MOST POPULAR MAJORS

Business, Management, Marketing; Biology/
Biological Sciences; Psychology

ABOUT THE SCHOOL

Arizona State University is a top-ranked research university in the greater Phoenix metropolitan area. With over 70,000 students—making it the largest public university in the United States by enrollment—ASU offers a wide range of majors and takes advantage of its urban setting. Within the university, Barrett, the Honors College, and the Walter Cronkite School of Journalism and Mass Communication are popular, and provide the more academically inclined with targeted education, with students taking advantage of ASU's position as a noted research university. Students agree that while ASU is "a large university," it "offers small seminar classes through the Honors College," giving students the intimate feeling of a smaller university within a larger collegiate environment. The professors are "very diverse" and within discussion sections students note that "there are people from many various backgrounds that offer many new and interesting insights." With class sizes averaging ten to nineteen students—slightly more for labs and subsections—ASU's top majors include business, management, marketing, biology/biological sciences, and psychology.

BANG FOR YOUR BUCK

Financial aid plays an important role in students' decisions to attend ASU, with one noting that the school "provided enough financial aid for me to graduate without debt," while another said ASU "offered me the most financial aid out of the universities I applied to." While ASU offers a number of scholarship opportunities, many come from the New American University Scholarship Program, which the school's website emphasizes as targeted at students who are "highly accomplished, match the university's quest for excellence and who would be ideal students to join ASU in meeting challenges that make a difference in the world." ASU also offers the Barack Obama Scholars Program, which, according to the school's website, "promote[s] equal access to education for all Arizonans." For incoming freshmen looking to get an idea of available aid, the ASU website provides the Freshman Merit Scholarship Estimator, which takes into account factors like GPA, class rank, and SAT/ACT scores.

STUDENT LIFE

Students praise the recently added "mass-transit system that runs through campus and connects it to downtown Phoenix" and call it "crucial and definitely useful." There's much to do off-campus, with "cultural events around ASU and in the surrounding community [making] student life even richer." On campus, "there is always something to do, someone to hang out with or places to be [and there] is always someplace that is open with students there around the clock." For those in Barrett, The Honors College, there's the added benefit of "extracurricular activities only for honors students." Those who prefer athletic activities will find that many ASU students enjoy "outdoor activities, [like] hiking, skydiving, running, [and] mountain climbing." A benefit of ASU's size is that "there are activities for just about anyone; [it's] almost guaranteed that no matter how obscure your hobby is that there is probably a club devoted to it." There are more than 1,000 registered student organizations, thirty honor societies, twenty-eight social sororities, and thirty-seven social fraternities (approximately 6 percent of students join a fraternity, with 10 percent joining a sorority).

Arizona State University

FINANCIAL AID: 855-278-5080 • E-MAIL: ADMISSIONS@ASU.EDU • WEBSITE: WWW.ASU.EDU

CAREER

ASU provides live online career advisement, and the school puts on events such as the Fall Career and Internship Fair. Students praise "companies offering internship opportunities" and note that they are "encouraged to get internships and are trained/treated as professionals in school to ensure they have the experience necessary to obtain top jobs and thrive in the work environment." According to PayScale.com, the average post-graduation salary is $47,700; the most popular and most profitable careers include software engineer, mechanical engineer, marketing manager, and software developer. Fifty-four percent of ASU graduates report on PayScale.com that their work and careers "make the world a better place."

GENERAL INFO

Activities: Choral groups, concert band, dance, drama/theater, jazz band, marching band, music ensembles, musical theater, pep band, radio station, student government, student newspaper, student-run film society, symphony orchestra, television station, Campus Ministries, International Student Organization, Model UN. **Organizations:** 1,069 registered organizations, 30 honor societies, 66 religious organizations, 37 fraternities, 28 sororities. **Athletics (Intercollegiate):** *Men:* baseball, basketball, cross-country, diving, football, golf, ice hockey, swimming, track/field (outdoor), wrestling. *Women:* basketball, cross-country, diving, golf, gymnastics, lacrosse, soccer, softball, swimming, tennis, track/field (outdoor), volleyball, water polo.

FINANCIAL AID

Students should submit: FAFSA. Priority filing deadline is 1/1. The Princeton Review suggests that all financial aid forms be submitted as soon as possible after October 1. *Need-based scholarships/grants offered:* Federal Pell, FSEOG, State scholarships/grants, private scholarships, college/university scholarship or grant aid from institutional funds, United Negro College Fund. *Loan aid offered:* Direct Subsidized Stafford Loans, Direct Unsubsidized Stafford Loans, Direct PLUS Loans, Federal Perkins Loans, State Loans. Applicants will be notified of awards on a rolling basis beginning 3/1. Federal Work-Study Program available. Institutional employment available.

BOTTOM LINE

In-state tuition for Arizona residents is roughly $9,684 annually, with out-of-state students paying approximately $25,784 per year. Seventy-four percent of first-year students live on campus, with that percentage dropping to 22 for all undergraduates. On-campus room and board fees average $11,386, with books, supplies, and fees adding an additional $1,789. Overall, an average in-state student pays roughly $23,115 per year versus $39,215 annually for out-of-state students. To help offset the fees, ASU provides general financial aid to 85 percent of undergraduates, with need-based scholarships averaging $12,181 for first years and $9,596 for all undergraduates. A number of students stress that ASU "provided enough financial aid for me to graduate without debt" and "offered me the most financial aid out of the universities I applied to."

CAREER INFORMATION FROM PAYSCALE.COM

ROI rating	85
Bachelor's and No Higher	
Median starting salary	$48,400
Median mid-career salary	$83,600
At Least Bachelor's	
Median starting salary	$49,300
Median mid-career salary	$85,800
% alumni with high job meaning	53%
% STEM	12%

SELECTIVITY

Admissions Rating	80
# of applicants	33,575
% of applicants accepted	82
% of acceptees attending	38

FRESHMAN PROFILE

Range SAT Critical Reading	500–620
Range SAT Math	510–630
Range ACT Composite	22–28
Minimum paper TOEFL	500
Minimum internet-based TOEFL	61
Average HS GPA	3.5
% graduated top 25% of class	61
% graduated top 50% of class	90

DEADLINES

Regular	
Priority	2/1
Nonfall registration?	Yes

FINANCIAL FACTS

Financial Aid Rating	82
Annual in-state tuition	$9,684
Annual out-of-state tuition	$25,784
Room and board	$11,642
Required fees	$686
Average need-based scholarship	$9,349
% needy frosh rec. need-based scholarship or grant aid	98
% needy UG rec. need-based scholarship or grant aid	92
% needy frosh rec. non-need-based scholarship or grant aid	14
% needy UG rec. non-need-based scholarship or grant aid	8
% needy frosh rec. need-based self-help aid	57
% needy UG rec. need-based self-help aid	71
% frosh rec. any financial aid	91
% UG rec. any financial aid	85
% UG borrow to pay for school	57
Average cumulative indebtedness	$23,210
% frosh need fully met	23
% ugrads need fully met	19
Average % of frosh need met	70
Average % of ugrad need met	60

Auburn University

108 Mary Martin Hall, Auburn, AL 36849-5149 • Admissions: 334-844-4080 • Fax: 334-844-6436

ABOUT THE SCHOOL

This Alabama research university is more than just a football stalwart; Auburn University offers more than 140 academic majors spread across thirteen colleges and schools, including pharmacy and nursing schools, as well as an accelerated bachelor's/master's program for outstanding students. As the heart of "one of the friendliest towns in the county," Auburn provides the best of both worlds: "a large school in terms of opportunities and recognition, and . . . a small school in terms of class size and campus feel." The "very hands-on professors" and administration have "genuine concern for the well-being of students, and it is apparent." The administration places equal emphasis on the university's undergraduate, graduate, and professional schools, and it stresses a shared academic experience through its undergraduate Core Curriculum and initiatives such as the Common Book program, which asks first-year students to read the same book prior to matriculation and incorporates themes and author talks into September programming.

BANG FOR YOUR BUCK

Though out-of-state is three times the in-state rate, there are plenty of scholarships and grants available for all types of students including both need-based and merit-based aid. The Auburn University Scholarship Manager (AUSOM) helps students keep track of scholarships they are eligible for using a general match system, including the Academic Charter ($6,000 a year), Heritage ($12,000 a year), and Presidential Scholarships ($16,000 a year) for incoming non-resident freshmen with high GPAs and standardized test scores; the McWane Foundation Annual Scholarship ($10,000 per year) for a student with a minimum 34 ACT or comparable SAT score and a 3.5 high school GPA; and the All Auburn Scholarship ($2,000 per year) for academic excellence.

STUDENT LIFE

Located in namesake Auburn, a "small town with a big heart and a pretty darn good football team," this university of 27,000 is a Deep South bastion of traditions, including the Tree Roll, Hey Day, War Eagle, and of course, Greek life. The over 300 student organizations are "well-organized and allowed to regulate themselves," and the student body "thrives on campus involvement and community service." "The opportunities that every individual at Auburn is given is fantastic. There are so many avenues to get involved in that it makes it hard to choose," says one student. One popular option is study abroad, taken by more than 800 students each year. The most popular weekend activities are "of course, football games."

CAREER

Students agree that Auburn "produces credible degrees and excels in most fields," including excellent leadership development programs. The Auburn University Career Center provides a centralized place for students considering all post-graduate paths through its Handshake job database, and offers services ranging from broad and specialized career fairs (such as Aviation Management) to Grad School Info Day. The center offers electronic resume review, career assessments, and an online interview practice program that allows students to record mock interviews for feedback from career counselors or employers. "Auburn gives you to tools that will help you succeed," says a student. "Overall, I know that I am well-prepared for both graduate school and work from my Auburn education." For those Auburn University

Auburn University

FINANCIAL AID: 334-844-4634 • E-MAIL: ADMISSIONS@AUBURN.EDU • WEBSITE: WWW.AUBURN.EDU

graduates who visited PayScale.com, the average early career salary was $48,700, with 54 percent of alumni feeling that their job makes the world a better place.

GENERAL INFO

Activities: Choral groups, concert band, dance, drama/theater, jazz band, literary magazine, marching band, music ensembles, musical theater, opera, pep band, radio station, student government, student newspaper, student-run film society, symphony orchestra, television station, yearbook, International Student Organization 300 registered organizations, 50 honor societies, 15 religious organizations. 30 fraternities, 19 sororities. **Athletics (Intercollegiate):** *Men:* baseball, basketball, cheerleading, cross-country, diving, football, golf, swimming, tennis, track/field (outdoor), track/field (indoor). *Women:* basketball, cheerleading, cross-country, diving, equestrian sports, golf, gymnastics, soccer, softball, swimming, tennis, track/field (outdoor), track/field (indoor), volleyball. **On-Campus Highlights:** Telfair B. Peet Theatre, Student Activity Center, Haley Center Concourse, Library Coffee Shop, War Eagle Dining, Student Center; Arboretum; Agricultural Heritage Park; Forest Ecology Preserve.

FINANCIAL AID

Students should submit: FAFSA. Priority filing deadline is 3/1. The Princeton Review suggests that all financial aid forms be submitted as soon as possible after October 1. *Need-based scholarships/grants offered:* Federal Pell, FSEOG, State scholarships/grants, Private scholarships, College/university scholarship or grant aid from institutional funds. *Loan aid offered:* Direct Subsidized Stafford Loans, Direct Unsubsidized Stafford Loans, Direct PLUS loans, Federal Perkins Loans, Federal Nursing Loans, College/university loans from institutional funds. Applicants will be notified of awards on a rolling basis beginning 10/2. Federal Work-Study Program available. Institutional employment available.

BOTTOM LINE

Alabama residents can expect to pay a steal of $5,348 a year in tuition and fees; non-residents have a heftier price tag of $14,420. Students residing on campus can expect to pay anywhere from $3,895 to $6,595 a semester in room and board. Fortunately, approximately 60 percent of first years are awarded some form of financial assistance.

CAREER INFORMATION FROM PAYSCALE.COM

ROI rating	86
Bachelor's and No Higher	
Median starting salary	$48,300
Median mid-career salary	$89,800
At Least Bachelor's	
Median starting salary	$49,200
Median mid-career salary	$90,700
% alumni with high job meaning	52%
% STEM	20%

SELECTIVITY

Admissions Rating	85
# of applicants	19,414
% of applicants accepted	78
% of acceptees attending	33

FRESHMAN PROFILE

Range SAT Critical Reading	530–630
Range SAT Math	540–650
Range SAT Writing	520–620
Range ACT Composite	24–30
Minimum paper TOEFL	550
Minimum internet-based TOEFL	79
Average HS GPA	3.8
% graduated top 10% of class	31
% graduated top 25% of class	62
% graduated top 50% of class	89

DEADLINES

Early action	
Deadline	10/1
Notification	10/15
Regular	
Priority	2/1
Deadline	6/1
Notification	2/15
Nonfall registration?	Yes

FINANCIAL FACTS

Financial Aid Rating	81
Annual in-state tuition	$9,072
Annual out-of-state tuition	$27,216
Room and board	$12,898
Required fees	$1,624
Average need-based scholarship	$7,440
% needy frosh rec. need-based scholarship or grant aid	81
% needy UG rec. need-based scholarship or grant aid	72
% needy frosh rec. non-need-based scholarship or grant aid	15
% needy UG rec. non-need-based scholarship or grant aid	9
% needy frosh rec. need-based self-help aid	66
% needy UG rec. need-based self-help aid	77
% frosh rec. any financial aid	50
% UG rec. any financial aid	44
% UG borrow to pay for school	41
Average cumulative indebtedness	$27,782
% frosh need fully met	19
% ugrads need fully met	13
Average % of frosh need met	50
Average % of ugrad need met	44

Babson College

231 FOREST STREET, BABSON PARK, MA 02457 • ADMISSION: 781-239-5522 • FAX: 781-239-4006

CAMPUS LIFE

Quality of Life Rating	93
Fire Safety Rating	95
Green Rating	93
Type of school	Private
Affiliation	No Affiliation
Environment	Village

STUDENTS

Total undergrad enrollment	2,141
% male/female	52/48
% from out of state	73
% frosh live on campus	100
% ugrads live on campus	78
# of fraternities (% ugrad men join)	3 (14)
# of sororities (% ugrad women join)	3 (27)
% African American	5
% Asian	12
% Caucasian	38
% Hispanic	10
% Native American	<1
% Pacific Islander	<1
% Two or more races	2
% Race and/or ethnicity unknown	6
% international	26
# of countries represented	77

ACADEMICS

Academic Rating	88
% students returning for sophomore year	96
% students graduating within 4 years	85
% students graduating within 6 years	89
Calendar	Semester
Student/faculty ratio	14:1
Profs interesting rating	92
Profs accessible rating	89
Most classes have 30-39 students.	

MOST POPULAR MAJORS

Business Administration and Management

#46 COLLEGE THAT PAYS YOU BACK

ABOUT THE SCHOOL

If you're set on becoming the next Michael Bloomberg or Warren Buffet, Babson College just might be the school for you! Babson deftly balances a liberal arts curriculum with a "world-class business education." Many students truly value how the college pushes both "entrepreneurship and creative thinking" and encourages applying these to "all aspects of life." Perhaps even more importantly, "every student graduating from Babson has taken part in running a business, [attaining] a background in all aspects of business (law, accounting, marketing, finance, organizational behavior, etc.), and [gaining] exposure to an international community." Students also appreciate that instructors "devote majority of their classes to discussion." In turn, this "makes the academic experience that much better because you are learning with the professor instead of just listening to them talk for two hours." They also continually "demonstrate a real interest" in their students. An astonished senior shares, "Professors that I had freshman year still know me by name and ask how I'm doing."

BANG FOR YOUR BUCK

Though on paper the cost might seem high, Babson is known for offering "excellent financial aid." A grateful senior notes, "[For] an independent paying my own tuition, the financial aid office has made Babson College affordable." More specifically, the average financial aid package awarded is approximately $37,060. Impressively, Babson doles out $39 million in undergraduate aid, with $32 million coming directly from scholarships and grants. Roughly 34 percent of the student population receives some sort of aid. And, most importantly, Babson is able to meet nearly 98 percent of incoming students' demonstrated need.

STUDENT LIFE

Students at Babson happily report that life on this bustling campus is fairly "fast paced." Undergrads here typically "get involved with the campus in as many ways as possible...athletics, special interest groups, community service organizations, etc." To kick back, many of these students love to attend "school wide parties as well as different social events hosted by Greek life." Indeed, we're told that fraternities and sororities "are very prevalent on campus." Additionally, the "Thursday Night Series" provides fun alternatives to drinking. The events can involve "anything from salsa dancing or karaoke to making cards for prisoners in Africa." Of course, close proximity to Boston virtually guarantees "a good number of people will head into the city on weekends."

CAREER

There's no question that a degree from Babson helps lead to professional success. As one highly content junior explains, "Because of the professors' connections as well as school reputation in the business world, job and internship opportunities are abundant." In fact, "99 percent of Babson students either have a job or are pursuing higher education six months after graduation...in this economy/job market that's fantastic!" Certainly, the Career Development Office helps to fuel this success. The office hosts many industry

Babson College

FINANCIAL AID: 781-239-4015 • E-MAIL: UGRADADMISSION@BABSON.EDU • WEBSITE: WWW.BABSON.EDU

spotlights (for accounting, finance, etc.) and even has employers-in-residence! Students can hobnob with representatives from Ernst & Young and Fidelity Investments (just to name a few). Finally, given all the business acumen acquired at this school, it's no surprise that the average starting salary of recent grads is $59,700 (according to PayScale.com).

GENERAL INFO

Activities: Dance, drama/theater, jazz band, literary magazine, musical theater, radio station, student government, student newspaper, television station. **Organizations.** 115 registered organizations, 3 religious organizations. 3 fraternities, 3 sororities. **Athletics (Intercollegiate):** *Men:* baseball, basketball, cross-country, diving, golf, ice hockey, lacrosse, skiing (downhill/alpine), soccer, swimming, tennis, track/field (outdoor), track/field (indoor). *Women:* basketball, cross-country, diving, field hockey, lacrosse, skiing (downhill/alpine), soccer, softball, swimming, tennis, track/field (outdoor), track/field (indoor), volleyball. **On-Campus Highlights:** Sorenson Arts Center, Blank Center for Entrepeneurship, Glavin Family Chapel, Reynolds Student Center, Webster Athletic Center, Cutler Center for Investments and Finance, Center for Women's Entrepreneurial Leadership.

FINANCIAL AID

Students should submit: FAFSA, CSS/Financial Aid PROFILE, Noncustodial PROFILE. Regular filing deadline is 2/15. The Princeton Review suggests that all financial aid forms be submitted as soon as possible after October 1. *Need-based scholarships/grants offered:* Federal Pell, FSEOG, State scholarships/grants, Private scholarships, College/university scholarship or grant aid from institutional funds. *Loan aid offered:* Direct Subsidized Stafford Loans, Direct Unsubsidized Stafford Loans, Direct PLUS loans, State Loans. Applicants will be notified of awards on or about 4/1. Federal Work-Study Program available. Institutional employment available.

BOTTOM LINE

Tuition at Babson is $45,120. On-campus housing (note: the average room is a double) will cost roughly $9,354. The meal plan will run students an additional $5,140. Books and supplies are anticipated to cost $1,020. Lastly, it's recommended that undergrads set aside another $1,750 to cover personal expenses that are bound to pop up throughout the year.

CAREER INFORMATION FROM PAYSCALE.COM

ROI rating	90
Bachelor's and No Higher	
Median starting salary	$60,700
Median mid-career salary	$121,000
At Least Bachelor's	
Median starting salary	$60,800
Median mid-career salary	$128,000
% alumni with high job meaning	30%
% STEM	0%

SELECTIVITY

Admissions Rating	94
# of applicants	7,516
% of applicants accepted	26
% of acceptees attending	27
# offered a place on the wait list	1,384
% accepting a place on wait list	43
% admitted from wait list	0
# of early decision applicants	354
% accepted early decision	43

FRESHMAN PROFILE

Range SAT Critical Reading	580–720
Range SAT Math	620–720
Range SAT Writing	590–660
Range ACT Composite	27–30
Minimum paper TOEFL	600
Minimum internet-based TOEFL	100

DEADLINES

Early decision	
Deadline	11/1
Notification	12/15
Early action	
Deadline	11/1
Notification	1/1
Regular	
Priority	11/1
Deadline	1/1
Notification	4/1
Nonfall registration?	Yes

FINANCIAL FACTS

Financial Aid Rating	90
Annual tuition	$48,288
Room and board	$15,376
Average need-based scholarship	$36,320
% needy frosh rec. need-based scholarship or grant aid	89
% needy UG rec. need-based scholarship or grant aid	96
% needy frosh rec. non-need-based scholarship or grant aid	11
% needy UG rec. non-need-based scholarship or grant aid	15
% needy frosh rec. need-based self-help aid	84
% needy UG rec. need-based self-help aid	82
% frosh rec. any financial aid	53
% UG rec. any financial aid	50
% UG borrow to pay for school	42
Average cumulative indebtedness	$32,982
% frosh need fully met	60
% ugrads need fully met	55
Average % of frosh need met	98
Average % of ugrad need met	97

B rnard Coll ge

3009 BROADWAY, NEW YORK, NY 10027 • ADMISSIONS: 212-854-2014 • FINANCIAL AID: 212-854-2154

CAMPUS LIFE

Quality of Life Rating	**92**
Fire Safety Rating	**79**
Green Rating	**71**
Type of school	Private
Affiliation	No Affiliation
Environment	Metropolis

STUDENTS

Total undergrad enrollment	2,556
% male/female	0/100
% from out of state	74
% frosh from public high school	55
% frosh live on campus	99
% ugrads live on campus	91
# of sororities	10
% African American	7
% Asian	14
% Caucasian	53
% Hispanic	12
% Native American	<1
% Pacific Islander	<1
% Two or more races	6
% Race and/or ethnicity unknown	1
% international	8
# of countries represented	51

ACADEMICS

Academic Rating	**91**
% students returning for sophomore year	95
% students graduating within 4 years	85
% students graduating within 6 years	91
Calendar	Semester
Student/faculty ratio	10:1
Profs interesting rating	87
Profs accessible rating	83

Most classes have 10–19 students.
Most lab/discussion sessions have
  10–19 students.

MOST POPULAR MAJORS
Psychology; English; Economics

ABOUT THE SCHOOL

Students of Barnard College say wonderful things about the school, such as "I loved the idea of a small liberal arts college in New York City." "Barnard is a school where students are challenged and given countless opportunities but are given support and guidance from professors, advisors, administrators, and other students to achieve their goals." When asked about her choice, another student tells us, "I wanted to attend a school that had very small classes (two-thirds have nineteen or fewer students), a community, and was still in the heart of New York City, specifically Manhattan, a wonderful island of activity." The academic environment is one where all students are able to find something of value. A sophomore mentions, "Barnard is all about educating young women in the most effective ways to help create the future leaders of the world." A student in her senior year adds, "At Barnard, you are not a face in the crowd. Professors want to get to know their students, even if the class is a larger lecture. The professors are extremely passionate about their specialties and go out of their way to make sure students benefit from their classes. Another added benefit is having access to all of Columbia University's classes."

BANG FOR YOUR BUCK

The value of the school is in the people, the location, and the satisfaction found throughout the years by successful Barnard graduates. One recent graduate tells us, "The school has a strong faculty, outstanding students, fabulous career-development services, a great alumnae network, and an important mission." Barnard College practices need-blind admissions for U.S. citizens and permanent residents, which means that admissions officers are unaware of a student's financial circumstances when evaluating an application or debating an application in committee. Financial need is not considered when considering the qualifications of potential Barnard students. Once accepted, undergraduates have access to many financial-assistance options; also included are study-abroad opportunities for qualified students.

STUDENT LIFE

"Barnard has so many resources for the students to live healthy, academically and socially strong lives," and students praise its "vibrant culture" and long-standing traditions, like Midnight Breakfast "a breakfast buffet served by administrators on the night before finals each semester" and Spirit Day, "a full day of programming each Spring which celebrates everything Barnard." Students also take advantage of Barnard's proximity to Columbia University and its shared resources: "I loved the way Barnard empowers women . . . and how it's a small school while still having the resources and accessibility of a big university across the street." The school's Manhattan location is also a big draw, with students noting that "in New York City the opportunities are really endless." An added perk is that as a "Barnard or Columbia student you get into almost all of the museums in New York City for free."

CAREER

Barnard's Career Development department strives to "support women in cultivating a career of their own invention that connects a liberal arts education, leadership and work-life planning," according to the school's website. In addition to career fairs held every semester, Barnard also offers the Senior Initiative Program, which the school says "provides graduating seniors with the tools to navigate today's job market in order to prepare for life post-Barnard." Likewise, free Leadership Lab workshops, put on by the Athena Center for

Barnard College

E-MAIL: ADMISSIONS@BARNARD.EDU 2038 • FAX: 212-854-6220 • WEBSITE: WWW.BARNARD.EDU

Leadership Studies, and the three-year Athena Scholars Program engage students to develop their leadership potential. Students note that "internships in finance and publishing are popular" and praise the "strong alumnae network." According to PayScale.com, 58 percent of Barnard graduates report that their jobs are of high social value. The average starting salary for a Barnard graduate is $46,000, with popular jobs including director of a non-profit, research analyst, and marketing director. PayScale.com reports that the most popular majors at Barnard include Economics, Psychology, English, and Art History.

GENERAL INFO

Activities: Choral groups, concert band, dance, drama/theater, jazz band, literary magazine, marching band, music ensembles, musical theater, opera, pep band, radio station, student government, student newspaper, student-run film society, symphony orchestra, television station, yearbook, campus ministries. **Organizations:** 100 registered organizations, 1 honor society. **Athletics (Intercollegiate):** Archery, basketball, crew/rowing, cross-country, diving, fencing, field hockey, golf, lacrosse, soccer, softball, swimming, tennis, track/field (outdoor), volleyball. **On-Campus Highlights:** Diana Center Art Gallery, Arthur Ross Greenhouse, Held Auditorium, Smart Media Classrooms, Liz's Place Cafe.

FINANCIAL AID

Students should submit: FAFSA, CSS/Financial Aid PROFILE, State aid form, Noncustodial PROFILE. Regular filing deadline is 2/15. The Princeton Review suggests that all financial aid forms be submitted as soon as possible after October 1. *Need-based scholarships/grants offered:* Federal Pell, FSEOG, State scholarships/grants, Private scholarships, College/university scholarship or grant aid from institutional funds. *Loan aid offered:* Direct Subsidized Stafford Loans, Direct Unsubsidized Stafford Loans, Direct PLUS loans, Federal Perkins Loans. Applicants will be notified of awards on or about 3/31. Federal Work-Study Program available. Institutional employment available.

BOTTOM LINE

An education as valuable as one from Barnard College does not come without its costs; yearly tuition is $48,614. With fees and room and board totaling $17,378 (not to mention books, supplies, and other personal expenses), students are making a substantial investment. Forty-eight percent of all students benefit from some form of financial aid. Over forty percent of recent graduates needed to pay for school, and they can expect an average indebtedness upon graduating from Barnard of about $20,000—extremely reasonable given the cost of attending the college.

CAREER INFORMATION FROM PAYSCALE.COM

ROI rating	**88**
Bachelor's and No Higher	
Median starting salary	$48,300
Median mid-career salary	$81,400
At Least Bachelor's	
Median starting salary	$49,300
Median mid-career salary	$81,100
% alumni with high job meaning	58%
% STEM	10%

SELECTIVITY

Admissions Rating	98
# of applicants	6,655
% of applicants accepted	20
% of acceptees attending	49
# offered a place on the wait list	1,195
% accepting a place on wait list	11
% admitted from wait list	5
# of early decision applicants	748
% accepted early decision	43

FRESHMAN PROFILE

Range SAT Critical Reading	640–730
Range SAT Math	620–720
Range SAT Writing	650–740
Range ACT Composite	29–32
Minimum paper TOEFL	600
Minimum internet-based TOEFL	100
Average HS GPA	3.9
% graduated top 10% of class	81
% graduated top 25% of class	94
% graduated top 50% of class	99

DEADLINES

Early decision	
Deadline	11/1
Notification	12/15
Regular	
Deadline	1/1
Notification	4/1
Nonfall registration?	No

FINANCIAL FACTS

Financial Aid Rating	94
Annual tuition	$48,614
Room and board	$15,598
Required fees	$1,780
Average need-based scholarship	$40,661
% needy frosh rec. need-based scholarship or grant aid	98
% needy UG rec. need-based scholarship or grant aid	98
% needy frosh rec. non-need-based scholarship or grant aid	0
% needy UG rec. non-need-based scholarship or grant aid	0
% needy frosh rec. need-based self-help aid	100
% needy UG rec. need-based self-help aid	100
% frosh rec. any financial aid	53
% UG rec. any financial aid	48
% UG borrow to pay for school	44
Average cumulative indebtedness	$20,008
% frosh need fully met	98
% ugrads need fully met	98
Average % of frosh need met	100
Average % of ugrad need met	100

B tes College

23 Campus Avenue, Lindholm House, Lewiston, ME 04240 • Admissions: 207-786-6000 • Fax: 207-786-6025

CAMPUS LIFE

Quality of Life Rating	91
Fire Safety Rating	98
Green Rating	60*
Type of school	Private
Affiliation	No Affiliation
Environment	Town

STUDENTS

Total undergrad enrollment	1,773
% male/female	0/0
% from out of state	89
% frosh from public high school	53
% frosh live on campus	100
% ugrads live on campus	91
% African American	5
% Asian	5
% Caucasian	72
% Hispanic	7
% Native American	<1
% Pacific Islander	0
% Two or more races	4
% Race and/or ethnicity unknown	1
% international	7
# of countries represented	71

ACADEMICS

Academic Rating	92
% students returning for sophomore year	95
% students graduating within 4 years	89
% students graduating within 6 years	88
Calendar	Semester
Student/faculty ratio	10:1
Profs interesting rating	93
Profs accessible rating	92

Most classes have 10–19 students.

Most lab/discussion sessions have 10–19 students.

MOST POPULAR MAJORS
Political Science and Government; Psychology; History

ABOUT THE SCHOOL

Bates was founded in 1855, more than 150 years ago, by people who believed strongly in freedom, civil rights, and the importance of a higher education for all who could benefit from it. Bates is devoted to undergraduates in the arts and science, and commitment to teaching excellence is central to the college's mission. The college is recognized for its inclusive social character; there are no fraternities or sororities, and student organizations are open to all. Bates College has stood firmly for the ideals of academic rigor, intellectual curiosity, egalitarianism, social justice, and freedom since its founding just before the Civil War. "The willingness of everyone to hear differing viewpoints and opinions even if they disagree" is very attractive to one student. Another is impressed that "Bates is an institution that challenges me to critically think in a way I never have before."

Students who can demonstrate the intellectual soundness and potential value of an initiative—whether it's for a senior thesis project, a performance, or an independent study—will receive every possible backing from the college. And one enrollee is very pleased to find that "you will not find it hard to gain access to resources." Bates has long understood that the privilege of education carries with it responsibility to others. Commitment to social action and the environment is something students here take seriously. Learning at Bates is connected to action and to others beyond the self. Bates faculty routinely incorporate service-learning into their courses, and about half of students take part in community-based projects in the Lewiston-Auburn region.

BANG FOR YOUR BUCK

With 200 instructors at the school, those students fortunate enough to actually enroll can expect to find an outstanding student-to-faculty ratio of 10:1. More than 90 percent of freshmen return as sophomores and just a few percent less graduate within four years. Diversity is paramount at Bates; 89 percent of students are from out-of-state, and fifty-five different countries are represented on campus—extremely impressive for such a small institution. Internships and experiential learning opportunities are heavily encouraged; through the Purposeful Work Internship program, for example, students explore the world of work throughout their four years. Ninety-eight percent of students complete a senior thesis and the other 2 percent complete a capstone project. More than two-thirds of alumni enroll in graduate study within ten years. Bates highly values its study-abroad programs, unique calendar (4-4-1), and the many opportunities available for one-on-one collaboration with faculty. "The size of the student body allows for a relationship beyond that of typical professor-student and creates a sense of academic equality that produces incredible levels of scholarship at the undergraduate level."

STUDENT LIFE

Bates undergrads promise you'll never have a dull moment on this campus. A lot of the fun can be attributed to the industrious "Student Activities Office, [which] puts on a tremendous [number] of exciting events/shows/trips for students to participate in." For example, they sponsored "the Snoop Dog concert last year, D.E.A.P. ('drop everything and play') concert in May, [the] weekly 'Village Club Series' concerts where up-and-coming artists perform café-style shows [and] the annual Winter Carnival in January." There are also nearly 100 student-run clubs to join, ranging "from Chess Club to Environmental Club to the DJ Society and, of course, the champion debating society." Additionally, you'll find "wild dances with all different themes, as well as crazy traditions like the puddle jump." And, of course, the minute that first snow fall hits, plenty of Batesies will head to the slopes to ski and/or snowboard.

Bates College

FINANCIAL AID: 207-786-6096 • WEBSITE: WWW.BATES.EDU

CAREER

Bates' tremendous Career Development Center really helps undergrads plot their post-collegiate life. To begin with, the office provides the standard workshops in resume building, cover letter writing and interviewing techniques. Students can also participate in a new, short-term job shadowing program that offers both career insight and networking opportunities. Additionally, undergrads have access to JobCat, an exclusive Bates-only site that gives them the opportunity to browse a number of job postings/openings. Batesies looking to continue their education can attend the office's annual graduate and professional school fair. This event usually brings around 100 admissions representatives to campus. And, of course, the Career Development Center invites numerous employers (from various industries) to campus each year to conduct interviews and information sessions. Finally, recent graduates have managed to nab jobs with companies such as Sony Music Entertainment, Boston Consulting Group, GoldmanSachs, The Metropolitan Museum of Art, High Mountain Institute, and Trapeze School New York.

GENERAL INFO

Activities: Choral groups, dance, drama/theater, jazz band, literary magazine, music ensembles, pep band, radio station, student government, student newspaper, student-run film society, symphony orchestra, yearbook, campus ministries, international student organization. **Organizations:** 99 registered organizations, 3 honor societies, 9 religious organizations.

FINANCIAL AID

Students should submit: FAFSA, CSS/Financial Aid PROFILE, Noncustodial PROFILE. Regular filing deadline is 2/15. The Princeton Review suggests that all financial aid forms be submitted as soon as possible after October 1. *Need-based scholarships/grants offered:* Federal Pell, FSEOG, State scholarships/grants, Private scholarships, College/university scholarship or grant aid from institutional funds. *Loan aid offered:* Direct Subsidized Stafford Loans, Direct Unsubsidized Stafford Loans, Direct PLUS loans, Federal Perkins Loans. Applicants will be notified of awards on or about 4/1. Federal Work-Study Program available. Institutional employment available.

BOTTOM LINE

The education that one receives at an institution like Bates College does not come without a price. The total cost of tuition, room, board, and fees comes to $62,540. But, have no fear, students and parents: on average Bates College also meets 100 percent of need. The average total need-based grant package is a whopping $38,921. Forty-six percent of all undergrads receive financial aid. The average graduate can expect to leave school with about $19,917 of loan debt. Additionally, scholarships and grants are plentiful, for international as well as domestic students. One student was excited that Bates "provided me the greatest amount of financial aid. It was very generous."

CAREER INFORMATION FROM PAYSCALE.COM

ROI rating	88
Bachelor's and No Higher	
Median starting salary	$44,700
Median mid-career salary	$91,500
At Least Bachelor's	
Median starting salary	$44,700
Median mid-career salary	$91,500
% alumni with high job meaning	53%
% STEM	13%

SELECTIVITY

Admissions Rating	96
# of applicants	5,044
% of applicants accepted	25
% of acceptees attending	38
# offered a place on the wait list	1,595
% accepting a place on wait list	44
% admitted from wait list	4
# of early decision applicants	589
% accepted early decision	42

FRESHMAN PROFILE

Range SAT Critical Reading	640–720
Range SAT Math	640–710
Range SAT Writing	640–710
Range ACT Composite	29–32
% graduated top 10% of class	69
% graduated top 25% of class	95
% graduated top 50% of class	100

DEADLINES

Early decision	
Deadline	11/15
Notification	12/20
Other ED	
Deadline	11/15
Other ED	
Notification	12/20
Regular	
Deadline	1/1
Notification	4/1
Nonfall registration?	Yes

FINANCIAL FACTS

Financial Aid Rating	97
Annual comprehensive fee	$62,540
Average need-based scholarship	$38,921
% needy frosh rec. need-based scholarship or grant aid	100
% needy UG rec. need-based scholarship or grant aid	100
% needy frosh rec. non-need-based scholarship or grant aid	0
% needy UG rec. non-need-based scholarship or grant aid	0
% needy frosh rec. need-based self-help aid	99
% needy UG rec. need-based self-help aid	98
% frosh rec. any financial aid	42
% UG rec. any financial aid	42
% frosh need fully met	100
% ugrads need fully met	100
Average % of frosh need met	100
Average % of ugrad need met	100

Beloit College

700 College Street, Beloit, WI 53511 • Admissions: 608-363-2500 • Fax: 608-363-2075

CAMPUS LIFE
Quality of Life Rating	84
Fire Safety Rating	84
Green Rating	71
Type of school	Private
Affiliation	No Affiliation
Environment	Town

STUDENTS
Total undergrad enrollment	1,358
% male/female	45/55
% from out of state	83
% frosh from public high school	75
% frosh live on campus	98
% ugrads live on campus	87
# of fraternities (% ugrad men join)	3 (19)
# of sororities (% ugrad women join)	3 (20)
% African American	5
% Asian	3
% Caucasian	66
% Hispanic	9
% Native American	<1
% Pacific Islander	<1
% Two or more races	3
% Race and/or ethnicity unknown	4
% international	9
# of countries represented	28

ACADEMICS
Academic Rating	89
% students returning for sophomore year	85
% students graduating within 4 years	69
% students graduating within 6 years	81
Calendar	Semester
Student/faculty ratio	11:1
Profs interesting rating	95
Profs accessible rating	95
Most classes have 10–19 students.	

MOST POPULAR MAJORS
Psychology; Science, Technology and Society; Anthropology

ABOUT THE SCHOOL

A "prestigious liberal arts college" with "Midwestern flair," Beloit College in southern Wisconsin is all about "cultivating critical thinkers" and truly preparing students "for success in the world." Undergrads here appreciate that the college pushes them "to think outside the box, work closely with others, and pursue the academic interests they are most passionate about." Students certainly benefit from "small class sizes" and "individualized attention" as well. Perhaps that's one reason why Beloit students are quick to declare their "academic experience [is] phenomenal." Of course, credit also goes to "wonderful" professors who "work hard to put together classes that are meaningful and interesting." Just as important, these instructors are also "very personable and always make an extra effort to help you with whatever you need, whether it's for internships or special needs particular to their class." Overall, as one thrilled philosophy major concludes, "Beloit has allowed me to care about school and my education in a way that I have never felt before."

BANG FOR YOUR BUCK

Beloit undergrads happily report that financial aid is one of the college's "great strength[s]." And we can understand why. After all, over 95 percent of students here receive some type of assistance. Undergrads are especially grateful that the institution sponsors a handful of generous merit-based scholarships. For example, the Wisconsin Distinguished Scholars Award provides a whopping $100,000 (to be distributed over the course of four years). The award is given to Wisconsin residents who have earned a GPA of 3.5 or higher. Additionally, the Eaton Scholarship is another generous award. It offers students anywhere from $40,000 to $72,000 (across four years). Recipients are selected based upon both outstanding academic achievement and proven leadership ability. Finally, it's important to mention that Beloit is a partner in the Yellow Ribbon GI Education Enhancement Program. Eligible veterans (or their dependents) can have nearly all tuition expenses covered through this program.

STUDENT LIFE

There's rarely a dull moment at Beloit. That's because extracurricular activities and opportunities abound. For starters, we're told that the college is "an aggressively creative place" with a "top-notch" theater program and "insane" music scene. As an excited math major adds, "C-Haus, our music venue, gets incredible acts to swing by school, while we have an impressive array of on campus artists as well." And if the arts aren't your thing, fear not. The "sports center is great for intramurals, basic weight room activities, and swimming." Of course, once the weekend rolls around you'll find "both large official parties and small get-togethers with a few friends." Though that's probably to be expected given that roughly "one-third of Beloit is in a Greek organization." Finally, if you're looking to escape campus life for a bit, both "Madison and Chicago are less than an hour drive away."

CAREER

Beloit grads are certainly able to capitalize on their degree. After all, according to PayScale.com, the average starting salary for alums is $38,400 and the average mid-career salary is $79,500. Of course, some of this success can be attributed to a "good . . . career center." Indeed, the staff in the Liberal Arts in Practice Center work closely with undergrads to help them develop a career trajectory. For example, Beloit students are privy to individual career counseling. They can

Beloit College

FINANCIAL AID: 608-363-2663 • E-MAIL: ADMISS@BELOIT.EDU • WEBSITE: WWW.BELOIT.EDU

also tap into the Beloit Career Network (BCN), which allows them to connect with alumni for job opportunities, mentorships, etc. Students can also use the career center to find internships, opportunities for job shadowing or simply receive help writing a cover letter. Whatever you need, the Liberal Arts in Practice Center will have your back.

GENERAL INFO

Activities: Choral groups, dance, drama/theater, jazz band, literary magazine, music ensembles, musical theater, radio station, student government, student newspaper, student-run film society, symphony orchestra, television station, yearbook, International Student Organization 95 registered organizations, 6 honor societies, 3 religious organizations. 3 fraternities, 3 sororities. **Athletics (Intercollegiate):** *Men:* baseball, basketball, cross-country, football, golf, soccer, swimming, tennis, track/field (outdoor), track/field (indoor). *Women:* basketball, cross-country, soccer, softball, swimming, tennis, track/field (outdoor), track/field (indoor), volleyball. **On-Campus Highlights:** Logan Museum of Anthropology, Wright Museum of Art, Center for the Sciences, Alfred S. Thompson Observatory, Laura H. Idrich Neese Theatre Complex, Other popular spaces include the Poetry Garden, the Java Joint, Morse Library, Sports Center, and Pearsons Hall.

FINANCIAL AID

Students should submit: FAFSA. Regular filing deadline is 3/1. The Princeton Review suggests that all financial aid forms be submitted as soon as possible after October 1. *Need-based scholarships/grants offered:* Federal Pell, FSEOG, State scholarships/grants, Private scholarships, College/university scholarship or grant aid from institutional funds. *Loan aid offered:* Direct Subsidized Stafford Loans, Direct Unsubsidized Stafford Loans, Direct PLUS loans, Federal Perkins Loans, College/university loans from institutional funds. Applicants will be notified of awards on a rolling basis beginning 3/1. Federal Work-Study Program available. Institutional employment available.

BOTTOM LINE

Full tuition at Beloit will cost undergrads (and their families) $46,596 for the academic year. Housing costs an additional $4,626 and a full meal plan runs $3,520 (this plan is required for all first year students). Further, there's a $280 student activity fee and a $184 health and wellness charge. Families can expect to pay another $1,502 in estimated health insurance costs. Books and supplies often run around $1,000. Finally, it is recommended students set aside another $1,300 for personal expenses.

CAREER INFORMATION FROM PAYSCALE.COM

ROI rating	86
Bachelor's and No Higher	
Median starting salary	$38,400
Median mid-career salary	$79,500
At Least Bachelor's	
Median starting salary	$40,000
Median mid-career salary	$80,700
% alumni with high job meaning	69%
% STEM	16%

SELECTIVITY

SELECTIVITY

Admissions Rating	86
# of applicants	3,552
% of applicants accepted	69
% of acceptees attending	16
# offered a place on the wait list	81
% accepting a place on wait list	40
% admitted from wait list	9

FRESHMAN PROFILE

Range SAT Critical Reading	540–695
Range SAT Math	540–645
Range ACT Composite	24–30
Minimum paper TOEFL	550
Minimum internet-based TOEFL	80
Average HS GPA	3.4
% graduated top 10% of class	29
% graduated top 25% of class	64
% graduated top 50% of class	91

DEADLINES

Early decision	
Deadline	11/1
Notification	11/30
Other ED	
Deadline	11/1
Other ED	
Notification	11/30
Early action	
Deadline	11/1
Notification	12/15
Regular	
Priority	1/15
Nonfall registration?	Yes

FINANCIAL FACTS

Financial Aid Rating	89
Annual tuition	$46,596
Room and board	$8,146
Required fees	$464
Average need-based scholarship	$28,199
% needy frosh rec. need-based scholarship or grant aid	99
% needy UG rec. need-based scholarship or grant aid	98
% needy frosh rec. non-need-based scholarship or grant aid	52
% needy UG rec. non-need-based scholarship or grant aid	51
% needy frosh rec. need-based self-help aid	81
% needy UG rec. need-based self-help aid	79
% frosh rec. any financial aid	99
% UG rec. any financial aid	99
% UG borrow to pay for school	70
Average cumulative indebtedness	$31,308
% frosh need fully met	31
% ugrads need fully met	32

Bentley University

175 Forest Street, Waltham, MA 02452 • Admissions: 781-891-2244 • Fax: 781-891-3414

CAMPUS LIFE

Quality of Life Rating	**91**
Fire Safety Rating	**99**
Green Rating	**97**
Type of school	Private
Affiliation	No Affiliation
Environment	Town

STUDENTS

Total undergrad enrollment	4,203
% male/female	59/41
% from out of state	55
% frosh from public high school	66
% frosh live on campus	98
% ugrads live on campus	79
# of fraternities (% ugrad men join)	8 (11)
# of sororities (% ugrad women join)	3 (11)
% African American	3
% Asian	8
% Caucasian	61
% Hispanic	7
% Native American	0
% Pacific Islander	<1
% Two or more races	2
% Race and/or ethnicity unknown	3
% international	16
# of countries represented	101

ACADEMICS

Academic Rating	**85**
% students returning for sophomore year	95
% students graduating within 4 years	83
% students graduating within 6 years	89
Calendar	Semester
Student/faculty ratio	12:1
Profs interesting rating	85
Profs accessible rating	83
Most classes have 20–29 students.	

MOST POPULAR MAJORS

Marketing/Marketing Management; Finance; Business, Management, Marketing

ABOUT THE SCHOOL

The Bentley curriculum is an integration of business and the liberal arts, offering twenty-four majors, the most popular of which being accounting, finance, and marketing. The school boasts a student to faculty ratio of twelve to one, and "the average class size is capped at thirty-five" reports a student, while another notes that "[there are] larger classes than that (forty-two to forty-four) for General Business classes." Students feel that "the administration at Bentley is ok; however, the professors are phenomenal. They are great role models and have had a lot of experience in the business world. Office hours are always available. My academic experience has been great." One student sums up the widely held sentiment: "I love the Bentley curriculum. Everything is business focused which is exactly what I came here for." Another reports, "Bentley has phenomenal facilities: a brilliant library, wired classrooms with the latest in learning technology, and access to the most awesome software and academic resources."

BANG FOR YOUR BUCK

Most students feel that Bentley gives "great financial aid." "Although it is very true that most students are either rich and foreign, rich and smart, or smart and foreign, in recent years there has been an uprising in the 'smart and poor' category." "Someone once told me, 'If you want to be rich, then Bentley is the place for you.' Thus I am here. Also, I got a full scholarship." Many students report receiving a partial, if not full, scholarship. With tuition at about $40,990, and the average aid package working out to $32,722, this is backed up by the numbers.

STUDENT LIFE

"Bentley University is a very expensive, diverse business school, where people love to party but take their academics seriously as well." "As for students cracking down on weekdays to get their work done, yes the library is definitely much busier during the week, however that does not prevent students from going out on a given weeknight. As for the city, my friends and I will venture in there every once in a while, but I wouldn't call it Bentley's main attraction. In addition to registered parties, there's also an abundance of unregistered ones that usually don't get broken up until the start of quiet hours."

Bentley University

FINANCIAL AID: 781-891-3441 • E-MAIL: UGADMISSION@BENTLEY.EDU • WEBSITE: WWW.BENTLEY.EDU

CAREER

The typical Bentley University graduate has a starting salary of around $58,000, and 38 percent report that their job has a great deal of meaning. Students report that "Bentley also has a wonderful career services department that seems to take networking pretty seriously, and I owe it a lot of credit for helping me find a very attractive internship my Sophomore year with a large CPA firm." "The Career Services Office provides unique, one-on-one aid to students in finding fantastic internships and jobs after graduation," and "offers many internships to get a foot in the door with top corporations." Overall, the school is "very business oriented and they have great career placement. As long as you did pretty well in school, you will get a job by the time you graduate."

GENERAL INFO

Activities: Academic Groups, debating club, international student groups, literary magazine, music ensembles, radio station, student government, student film society, student newspaper, television station, campus ministries, Model UN. **Organizations:** 104 registered organizations, 4 honor societies, 4 religious organizations. 8 fraternities, 3 sororities. **Athletics (Intercollegiate):** *Men:* baseball, basketball, cross-country, diving, football, golf, ice hockey, lacrosse, soccer, swimming, tennis, track/field (outdoor), track/field (indoor). *Women:* basketball, cross-country, diving, field hockey, lacrosse, soccer, softball, swimming, tennis, track/field (outdoor), track/field (indoor), volleyball. **On-Campus Highlights:** Student Center, Dana Athletic Center, Currito Burrito, Einstein's Coffee Shop, Library.

FINANCIAL AID

Students should submit: FAFSA, CSS/Financial Aid PROFILE, Noncustodial PROFILE, Business/Farm Supplement. Regular filing deadline is 2/1. The Princeton Review suggests that all financial aid forms be submitted as soon as possible after October 1. *Need-based scholarships/grants offered:* Federal Pell, FSEOG, State scholarships/grants, Private scholarships, College/university scholarship or grant aid from institutional funds. *Loan aid offered:* Direct Subsidized Stafford Loans, Direct Unsubsidized Stafford Loans, Direct PLUS loans, Federal Perkins Loans, State Loans. Applicants will be notified of awards on or about 3/31. Federal Work-Study Program available. Institutional employment available.

BOTTOM LINE

The sticker price for tuition, fees, and room and board at Bentley University comes to about $60,890 per year. But you don't have to be an historical Bentleyian to be able to afford to go here. The average need-based financial aid package is $32,722, with 73 percent of undergraduates receiving at least some form of financial aid, and an average of 94 percent of demonstrated need met.

CAREER INFORMATION FROM PAYSCALE.COM

ROI rating	89
Bachelor's and No Higher	
Median starting salary	$58,600
Median mid-career salary	$97,200
At Least Bachelor's	
Median starting salary	$59,300
Median mid-career salary	$100,000
% alumni with high job meaning	35%
% STEM	4%

SELECTIVITY

Admissions Rating	91
# of applicants	8,346
% of applicants accepted	42
% of acceptees attending	26
# offered a place on the wait list	1,898
% accepting a place on wait list	30
% admitted from wait list	16
# of early decision applicants	158
% accepted early decision	00

FRESHMAN PROFILE

Range SAT Critical Reading	540–640
Range SAT Math	600–690
Range SAT Writing	550–650
Range ACT Composite	26–30
Minimum paper TOEFL	577
Minimum internet-based TOEFL	90
% graduated top 10% of class	38
% graduated top 25% of class	72
% graduated top 50% of class	93

DEADLINES

Early decision	
Deadline	11/15
Regular	
Deadline	1/7
Nonfall registration?	Yes

FINANCIAL FACTS

Financial Aid Rating	87
Annual tuition	$44,210
Room and board	$15,130
Required fees	$1,550
Average need-based scholarship	$29,755
% needy frosh rec. need-based scholarship or grant aid	98
% needy UG rec. need-based scholarship or grant aid	98
% needy frosh rec. non-need-based scholarship or grant aid	25
% needy UG rec. non-need-based scholarship or grant aid	15
% needy frosh rec. need-based self-help aid	94
% needy UG rec. need-based self-help aid	96
% frosh rec. any financial aid	73
% UG rec. any financial aid	66
% UG borrow to pay for school	54
Average cumulative indebtedness	$29,547
% frosh need fully met	43
% ugrads need fully met	39
Average % of frosh need met	94
Average % of ugrad need met	93

Boston Colleg

140 Commonwealth Avenue, Devlin Hall 208, Chestnut Hill, MA 02467-3809 • Admissions: 617-552-3100

CAMPUS LIFE

Quality of Life Rating	**91**
Fire Safety Rating	**98**
Green Rating	**82**
Type of school	Private
Affiliation	Roman Catholic
Environment	City

STUDENTS

Total undergrad enrollment	9,192
% male/female	47/53
% from out of state	75
% frosh from public high school	45
% frosh live on campus	100
% ugrads live on campus	84
% African American	4
% Asian	10
% Caucasian	63
% Hispanic	10
% Native American	<1
% Pacific Islander	<1
% Two or more races	3
% Race and/or ethnicity unknown	4
% international	6
# of countries represented	68

ACADEMICS

Academic Rating	**88**
% students returning for sophomore year	95
% students graduating within 4 years	89
% students graduating within 6 years	92
Calendar	Semester
Student/faculty ratio	12:1
Profs interesting rating	84
Profs accessible rating	84
Most classes have 10–19 students.	

MOST POPULAR MAJORS

Communication and Media Studies; Finance; Economics

ABOUT THE SCHOOL

Boston, one of the finest college towns in the United States, is home to some of the most prestigious institutions of higher learning around. Boston College shoulders this pedigree effortlessly. Within a rich and challenging environment, while promoting "Jesuit ideals in the modern age," the school offers a rigorous and enlightening education. A student says, "Upon my first visit I knew this was the place for me." Students benefit greatly from Boston College's location just outside of downtown Boston, which affords them internship, service-learning, and career opportunities that give them world-class, real-world experiences before they graduate. In addition, Boston College has an excellent career-services office that works in concert with BC's renowned network of more than 150,000 alumni to assist students in career placement. Unique Jesuit-inspired service and academic reflection in core courses develop teamwork and analytical-thinking skills. Many students are amazed at their own development: "I have never been so challenged and motivated to learn in my life." "I leave virtually every class with useful knowledge and new opinions."

BANG FOR YOUR BUCK

Boston College is one of a very few elite private universities that is strongly committed to admitting students without regard to their family's finances and that also guarantees to meet a student's full demonstrated financial need through to graduation. (That means your aid won't dry up after the heady generosity of freshman year.) For the 2011–2012 school year, Boston College awarded $129.6 million in student financial aid, including $87 million in need-based undergraduate financial aid. In addition, BC offers a highly selective program of merit-based aid that supports selected students from among the top 1 or 2 percent of high school achievers in the country. While Boston College is committed to helping superior students attend with need-based financial aid, it is also highly selective. The college's Presidential Scholars Program, in existence since 1995, selects candidates who are academically exceptional and who exhibit through personal interviews the leadership potential for high achievement at a Jesuit university. In addition to offering four-year, full-tuition scholarships to students, the program offers built-in supports for a wide range of cocurricular opportunities, including summer placements for advanced internships and independent study. The Office of International Programs is extremely helpful in getting students interested in and ready for studying abroad and "encourages a 'citizen of the world' mindset."

STUDENT LIFE

Of Boston College, one student says "being just outside of Boston is a huge draw for BC students. As a student, I often go into the city to hang out, run errands, go to a sporting event, eat, or shop." As for staying on campus, "BC has an awesome sports program that semi-dominates the social scene in the Fall and Winter (football, hockey and basketball seasons) and the school also hosts a variety of weekend events like concerts, student dances and dance/theater shows that many people attend," while another adds, of the school's mission of "men and women for others," "BC doesn't force Catholicism on anyone. Rather, BC simply presents this simple mission of helping one another," and still another says, "Once you've settled in, you'll find that it's not at all difficult to find a group of friends" no matter who you are. Students feel that "Boston College seeks to educate the whole person with an emphasis on giving back to those who are unable to receive such a privileged education." In addition, Boston College's Division I ranking means there are plenty of athletes and sports fans.

Boston College

FAX: 617-552-0798 • FINANCIAL AID: 617-552-3300 • WEBSITE: WWW.BC.EDU

CAREER

The typical Boston College graduate has a starting salary of around $51,900, and 44 percent of graduates feel their jobs have a lot of meaning in their lives. Students feel that Boston College has "an excellent career center," both for current students and alumni, and a "great alumni network." In particular, the alumni network is "very supportive and strong ... They really try to help students find internships and jobs." Some students feel that the career center is "really good for students in the business school, but it could be better in helping students in the humanities find internships."

GENERAL INFO

Activities: Choral groups, concert band, dance, drama/theater, jazz band, literary magazine, marching band, music ensembles, musical theater, pep band, radio station, student government, student newspaper, student-run film society, symphony orchestra, television station, yearbook, campus ministries, international student organization. **Organizations:** 225 registered organizations, 12 honor societies, 14 religious organizations. **Athletics (Intercollegiate):** *Men:* Baseball, basketball, cross-country, diving, fencing, football, golf, ice hockey, lacrosse, sailing, skiing (downhill/alpine), soccer, swimming, tennis, track/field (outdoor), track/field (indoor). *Women:* Basketball, crew/rowing, cross-country, diving, fencing, field hockey, golf, ice hockey, lacrosse, sailing, skiing (downhill/alpine), soccer, softball, swimming, tennis, track/field (outdoor), track/field (indoor), volleyball.

FINANCIAL AID

Students should submit: FAFSA, CSS/Financial Aid PROFILE, Noncustodial PROFILE, Business/Farm Supplement. Priority filing deadline is 2/1. The Princeton Review suggests that all financial aid forms be submitted as soon as possible after October 1. *Need-based scholarships/grants offered:* Federal Pell, FSEOG, State scholarships/grants, Private scholarships, College/university scholarship or grant aid from institutional funds. *Loan aid offered:* Direct Subsidized Stafford Loans, Direct Unsubsidized Stafford Loans, Direct PLUS loans, Federal Perkins Loans, Federal Nursing Loans, State Loans. Applicants will be notified of awards on or about 4/1. Federal Work-Study Program available. Institutional employment available.

BOTTOM LINE

The sticker price for tuition, fees, room and board, and everything else at Boston College comes to about $65,100 per year. But you don't have to be an old-guard Bostonian to be able to afford to go here. The average need-based financial aid package is $36,929. "Their stellar academics and their generous financial aid were a combination that I couldn't find anywhere else," one grateful student exclaims.

CAREER INFORMATION FROM PAYSCALE.COM

ROI rating	90
Bachelor's and No Higher	
Median starting salary	$53,100
Median mid-career salary	$104,000
At Least Bachelor's	
Median starting salary	$55,500
Median mid-career salary	$109,000
% alumni with high job meaning	45%
% STEM	10%

SELECTIVITY

Admissions Rating	96
# of applicants	29,486
% of applicants accepted	29
% of acceptees attending	26
# offered a place on the wait list	7,072
% accepting a place on wait list	56
% admitted from wait list	9

FRESHMAN PROFILE

Range SAT Critical Reading	620–720
Range SAT Math	640–750
Range SAT Writing	640–730
Range ACT Composite	30–33
Minimum paper TOEFL	600
Minimum internet-based TOEFL	100
% graduated top 10% of class	79
% graduated top 25% of class	95
% graduated top 50% of class	99

DEADLINES

Early action	
Deadline	11/1
Notification	12/25
Regular	
Deadline	1/1
Notification	4/15
Nonfall registration?	Yes

FINANCIAL FACTS

Financial Aid Rating	94
Annual tuition	$50,480
Room and board	$13,818
Required fees	$816
Average need-based scholarship	$36,929
% needy frosh rec. need-based scholarship or grant aid	88
% needy UG rec. need-based scholarship or grant aid	87
% needy frosh rec. non-need-based scholarship or grant aid	3
% needy UG rec. non-need-based scholarship or grant aid	2
% needy frosh rec. need-based self-help aid	94
% needy UG rec. need-based self-help aid	93
% frosh rec. any financial aid	63
% UG rec. any financial aid	66
% frosh need fully met	100
% ugrads need fully met	100
Average % of frosh need met	100
Average % of ugrad need met	100

Boston University

233 Bay State Road, Boston, MA 02215 • Admissions: 617-353-2300 • Fax: 617-353-9695

CAMPUS LIFE

Quality of Life Rating	**92**
Fire Safety Rating	**64**
Green Rating	**93**
Type of school	Private
Affiliation	No Affiliation
Environment	Metropolis

STUDENTS

Total undergrad enrollment	17,932
% male/female	40/60
% from out of state	80
% frosh from public high school	65
% frosh live on campus	99
% ugrads live on campus	75
# of fraternities (% ugrad men join)	9 (5)
# of sororities (% ugrad women join)	12 (15)
% African American	4
% Asian	13
% Caucasian	42
% Hispanic	10
% Native American	<1
% Pacific Islander	<1
% Two or more races	3
% Race and/or ethnicity unknown	7
% international	20
# of countries represented	106

ACADEMICS

Academic Rating	**86**
% students returning for sophomore year	93
% students graduating within 4 years	80
% students graduating within 6 years	85
Calendar	Semester
Student/faculty ratio	12:1
Profs interesting rating	80
Profs accessible rating	83

Most classes have 10–19 students.
Most lab/discussion sessions have
20–29 students.

MOST POPULAR MAJORS

Communication; Engineering; Business
Administration and Management

ABOUT THE SCHOOL

Boston University provides "a high-quality education in an atmosphere that promotes creativity and diversity," "plus it's in BOSTON!" BU's location in one of America's greatest college cities is certainly an attraction for students who crave big city energy. "BU has so many choices when it comes to majors and classes that I find myself struggling to pick just four classes a semester," one student proclaims. The "very passionate" and "dedicated" professors "make special efforts to challenge you, because our programs are so competitive." BU's faculty includes multiple Pulitzer Prize winners, Nobel Prize laureates, and a MacArthur Fellow. The school's alumni also include multiple Nobel laureates—such as Martin Luther King, Jr.—and thirty-five Pulitzer Prize winners. The student population is around 30,000 and split evenly between graduates and undergraduates. The average class size is twenty-seven. A political science major says, "Boston University has the perfect balance of everything I expected from college—school spirit, academic opportunity, and a diverse student population."

BANG FOR YOUR BUCK

Although the price of a BU education is not cheap, the school doles out more than $209 million in need-based aid for undergrads. The school also has numerous merit scholarships, including Presidential Scholarships and National Merit Scholarships. Most merit scholarships are handed out based on admissions applications being submitted by December 1, and do not require any special application. There are several specialized scholarships as well, such as the Boston Community Service Award Scholarship. If you are applying to BU, make sure to check the full list of scholarships to see if you are eligible.

STUDENT LIFE

While "school is definitely a priority at BU," students here know how to have fun too. "The campus is safe and there is a ton to do both on and off campus." Students love hanging out around Boston, which is "a great city with tons of stuff to do every weekend," or seeing friends at other nearby colleges. On campus, "there are an amazing [number] of clubs" such as "astronomy, camping, [and] religious/ethnic clubs." The average student can be described as "intuitive, intelligent, and has his/her own niche at college." BU is so large and diverse that there really is "no 'typical' BU student." "I think my favorite part about being in Boston is that there is ALWAYS something to do," one happy student says.

CAREER

BU's location in Boston provides numerous "job and internship opportunities" for students. "The fact that BU doesn't have a 'traditional' college campus… is one of the best parts" of attending BU if you are attracted to the energy and opportunities of a large city. Students say that most undergrads get "involved with research/on-campus jobs" or intern in the city. The BU CareerLink website posts opportunities daily and employers frequently come to campus to recruit students. PayScale.com reports an average starting salary of $50,600 for BU graduates. Most of the graduates find work in Boston with New York City being the second most common career destination.

Boston University

FINANCIAL AID: 617-353-4176 • E-MAIL: ADMISSIONS@BU.EDU • WEBSITE: WWW.BU.EDU

GENERAL INFO

Activities: Choral groups, concert band, dance, drama/theater, jazz band, literary magazine, marching band, music ensembles, musical theater, opera, radio station, pep band, student government, student newspaper, student-run film society, symphony orchestra, television station, yearbook, international student organization. **Organizations:** 450+ registered organizations, 11 honor societies, 21 religious organizations. 11 fraternities, 10 sororities. **Athletics (Intercollegiate):** *Men:* basketball, crew/rowing, cross-country, diving, golf, ice hockey, lacrosse, soccer, swimming, tennis, track/field (outdoor), track/field (indoor). *Women:* basketball, crew/rowing, cross-country, diving, field hockey, golf, ice hockey, lacrosse, soccer, softball, swimming, tennis, track/field (outdoor), track/field (indoor). **On-Campus Highlights:** Marsh Chapel Plaza, Mugar Memorial Library special collections, DeWolfe Boathouse, George Sherman Student Union, The Photonics Center, New Balance Athletics Field, Engineering Product Innovation Center, Yawkey Center for Student Services.

FINANCIAL AID

Students should submit: FAFSA, CSS/Financial Aid PROFILE, Noncustodial PROFILE. Regular decision filing deadline is 2/1. The Princeton Review suggests that all financial aid forms be submitted as soon as possible after October 1. *Need-based scholarships/grants offered:* Federal Pell, FSEOG, State scholarships/grants, Private scholarships, College/university scholarship or grant aid from institutional funds. *Loan aid offered:* Direct Subsidized Stafford Loans, Direct Unsubsidized Stafford Loans, Direct PLUS loans, Federal Perkins Loans, State Loans. Applicants will be notified of awards on a rolling basis beginning 4/1. Federal Work-Study Program available. Institutional employment available.

BOTTOM LINE

A BU education can cost a pretty penny without aid. Currently, tuition is $49,176 dollars for the 2016–2017 academic year. That total comes up to $65,110 with estimated fees, books, and room and board—and with rents on the rise in Boston, living off-campus likely won't produce any savings. That said, BU's many financial aid and merit scholarships can reduce this significantly. The total average award package for freshmen with need is $40,005. Students should make sure to fully research their aid options and follow the application deadlines.

CAREER INFORMATION FROM PAYSCALE.COM

ROI rating	86
Bachelor's and No Higher	
Median starting salary	$50,600
Median mid-career salary	$91,000
At Least Bachelor's	
Median starting salary	$51,400
Median mid-career salary	$93,900
% alumni with high job meaning	49%
% STEM	16%

SELECTIVITY

Admissions Rating	94
# of applicants	57,441
% of applicants accepted	33
% of acceptees attending	20
# offered a place on the wait list	4,381
% accepting a place on wait list	51
% admitted from wait list	<1
# of early decision applicants	1,643
% accepted early decision	43

FRESHMAN PROFILE

Range SAT Critical Reading	580–680
Range SAT Math	620–730
Range SAT Writing	600–690
Range ACT Composite	27–31
Average HS GPA	3.6
% graduated top 10% of class	58
% graduated top 25% of class	89
% graduated top 50% of class	99

DEADLINES

Early Decisio ; Early Decision 2	
Deadline	11/1; 1/3
Notification	12/15; 2/15
Regular	
Priority	11/1
Deadline	1/3
Notification	4/1
Nonfall registration?	Yes

FINANCIAL FACTS

Financial Aid Rating	86
Annual tuition	$49,176
Room and board	$14,870
Required fees	$1,064
Average need-based scholarship	$32,397
% needy frosh rec. need-based scholarship or grant aid	100
% needy UG rec. need-based scholarship or grant aid	100
% needy frosh rec. non-need-based scholarship or grant aid	8
% needy UG rec. non-need-based scholarship or grant aid	5
% needy frosh rec. need-based self-help aid	88
% needy UG rec. need-based self-help aid	89
% frosh rec. any financial aid	54
% UG rec. any financial aid	54
% UG borrow to pay for school	53
Average cumulative indebtedness	$40,365
% frosh need fully met	40
% ugrads need fully met	30
Average % of frosh need met	93
Average % of ugrad need met	88

Bowdoin College

5000 COLLEGE STATION, BOWDOIN COLLEGE, BRUNSWICK, ME 04011-8441 • ADMISSIONS: 207-725-3100

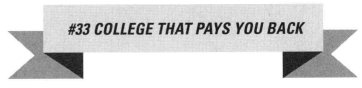

#33 COLLEGE THAT PAYS YOU BACK

ABOUT THE SCHOOL

Bowdoin College has a lot to offer its happy students, including rigorous and varied academic offerings, a picturesque setting, and a vibrant community of faculty and fellow students. It even has great food; Bowdoin is particularly well-known for its dining services. The college has two major dining halls, and every academic year Bowdoin welcomes students back to campus with a lobster bake, "a venerable Bowdoin institution in and of itself." Small, discussion-oriented classes are the norm; professors are accessible and genuinely invested in student's success, often making time to meet with students one-on-one. Students say that "between the professors, students, deans, and other faculty, we have a really great support system."

Campus life is pretty cushy at Bowdoin. Dorms are beautiful. Dining services are top-notch. Hometown Brunswick is lovely, and students say they "love how Bowdoin is integrated in the community." Many of the students here hail from the Northeast. Initially, they might come across as a little preppy, but dig a little deeper and you'll see the diversity lying just beneath the surface. Here, you'll find your jocks and frat boys, but you'll also find skaters, rockers, artsy types, and everything else in between. Students here are very athletic, and 50 percent are involved in some kind of sport. One student athlete says that the relationship between academics and athletics is ideal because students are "able to get a phenomenal education while having an amazing athletic experience, neither at the expense of the other." Bowdoin's outdoorsy student body loves to get outside and explore its surrounding environs through the popular Outing Club, which "goes out on numerous trips every week" to explore the countryside.

BANG FOR YOUR BUCK

Bowdoin meets students' demonstrated need with grant money from federal, state, and institutional sources. All admitted students who qualify for need-based financial aid receive grants that meet 100 percent of their need, and 45 percent of enrolled students receive some amount of grant assistance to help pay for college costs. Several students have said that the school gave them "more financial aid than I even thought I'd qualify for," and others say that Bowdoin gave them as much as "$10,000 a year more than any other school" they applied to. Eligibility for Bowdoin grant assistance is "need-based." If necessary, first-year students may elect to borrow up to $5,500 in low-interest, federal Stafford loan money. On average, students who choose to borrow graduate with approximately $20,000 in debt.

STUDENT LIFE

"There's a little bit of an idealist philosopher in almost every Bowdoin student," and it's not hard for them to find an outlet for their musings in one of the plethora of clubs and organizations at Bowdoin. There's "an eclectic mix from the Republican club to the Film Society and its debauchery." In other words, "it's easy to find your niche." Also, student athletes are common, from varsity and intramural teams to the Outing Club. For those seeking indoor alternatives, there are "film screenings and art shows every weekend" as well as "DJ's, casino nights and roller blading around the Union building." Overall, at Bowdoin students work hard, but on campus "life is certainly filled with fun."

Bowdoin College

Fax: 207-725-3101 • Financial Aid: 207-725-3273 • E-mail: ADMISSIONS@BOWDOIN.EDU • Website: WWW.BOWDOIN.EDU

CAREER

"The Career Planning Center and the Head of Student Activities are by far the greatest assets of Bowdoin." "If you are motivated, Bowdoin will provide you with wonderful opportunities." The resources, which include a fellowship office, career planning, grants and great professors, are all quite accessible due to the college's small size. There is also an "extensive alumni network," plenty of study abroad options, and opportunities for special internships funded by donors. Students have the chance to attend conferences and assist in research off campus. Half of the alumni who visited the website PayScale.com listed their careers as meaningful. On the same site, the average starting salary for Bowdoin graduates was reported at $48,500.

GENERAL INFO

Activities: Choral groups, concert band, dance, drama/theater, jazz band, literary magazine, music ensembles, musical theater, radio station, student government, student newspaper, student-run film society, symphony orchestra, television station, yearbook, international student organization. **Organizations:** 109 registered organizations, 1 honor society, 4 religious organizations. **Athletics (Intercollegiate):** *Men:* Baseball, basketball, cross-country, diving, football, golf, ice hockey, lacrosse, sailing, skiing (nordic/cross-country), soccer, squash, swimming, tennis, track/field (outdoor), track/field (indoor). *Women:* Basketball, cross-country, diving, field hockey, golf, ice hockey, lacrosse, rugby, sailing, skiing (nordic/cross-country), soccer, softball, squash, swimming, tennis, track/field (outdoor), track/field (indoor), volleyball.

FINANCIAL AID

Students should submit: FAFSA, CSS/Financial Aid PROFILE, Noncustodial PROFILE, Business/Farm Supplement. Regular filing deadline is 2/15. The Princeton Review suggests that all financial aid forms be submitted as soon as possible after October 1. *Need-based scholarships/grants offered:* Federal Pell, FSEOG, State scholarships/grants, Private scholarships, College/university scholarship or grant aid from institutional funds. *Loan aid offered:* Direct Subsidized Stafford Loans, Direct Unsubsidized Stafford Loans, Federal Perkins Loans, State Loans. Applicants will be notified of awards on or about 3/20. Federal Work-Study Program available. Institutional employment available.

BOTTOM LINE

Incoming freshmen at Bowdoin can expect to pay about $47,744 in tuition and another $468 in required fees. On-campus room and board totals more than $13,140. When you factor in other costs like, books, personal expenses, and travel, that brings the total sticker price to more than $61,350.

CAREER INFORMATION FROM PAYSCALE.COM

ROI rating	92
Bachelor's and No Higher	
Median starting salary	$48,500
Median mid-career salary	$103,000
At Least Bachelor's	
Median starting salary	$48,500
Median mid-career salary	$103,000

SELECTIVITY

Admissions Rating	98
# of applicants	6,790
% of applicants accepted	15
% of acceptees attending	50
# of early decision applicants	950
% accepted early decision	26

FRESHMAN PROFILE

Range SAT Critical Reading	690–765
Range SAT Math	685–770
Range SAT Writing	690–770
Range ACT Composite	31–34
Minimum paper TOEFL	600
Minimum internet-based TOEFL	100
% graduated top 10% of class	84
% graduated top 25% of class	98
% graduated top 50% of class	100

DEADLINES

Early decision	
Deadline	11/15
Notification	12/15
Regular	
Deadline	1/1
Notification	3/20
Nonfall registration?	No

FINANCIAL FACTS

Financial Aid Rating	99
Annual tuition	$49,416
Room and board	$13,600
Required fees	$484
Average need-based scholarship	$41,582
% needy frosh rec. need-based scholarship or grant aid	100
% needy UG rec. need-based scholarship or grant aid	100
% needy frosh rec. non-need-based scholarship or grant aid	0
% needy UG rec. non-need-based scholarship or grant aid	0
% needy frosh rec. need-based self-help aid	95
% needy UG rec. need-based self-help aid	96
% frosh rec. any financial aid	49
% UG rec. any financial aid	48
% UG borrow to pay for school	34
Average cumulative indebtedness	$20,883
% frosh need fully met	100
% ugrads need fully met	100
Average % of frosh need met	100
Average % of ugrad need met	100

Bradley University

1501 WEST BRADLEY AVENUE, PEORIA, IL 61625 • ADMISSIONS: 309-677-1000 • FAX: 309-677-2797

CAMPUS LIFE

Quality of Life Rating	91
Fire Safety Rating	91
Green Rating	62
Type of school	Private
Affiliation	No Affiliation
Environment	City

STUDENTS

Total undergrad enrollment	4,439
% male/female	49/51
% from out of state	16
% frosh from public high school	83
% frosh live on campus	92
% ugrads live on campus	51
# of fraternities (% ugrad men join)	17 (34)
# of sororities (% ugrad women join)	11 (36)
% African American	5
% Asian	3
% Caucasian	64
% Hispanic	6
% Native American	<1
% Pacific Islander	<1
% Two or more races	1
% Race and/or ethnicity unknown	19
% international	1
# of countries represented	33

ACADEMICS

Academic Rating	78
% students returning for sophomore year	86
% students graduating within 4 years	53
% students graduating within 6 years	74
Calendar	Semester
Student/faculty ratio	12:1
Profs interesting rating	85
Profs accessible rating	89
Most classes have 10–19 students.	

MOST POPULAR MAJORS
Business, Management, Marketing;
Engineering; Health Professions

ABOUT THE SCHOOL

Bradley University, in Peoria, Illinois, provides "a phenomenal education" with opportunities to gain "real-world experiences in your career field." It is "easier to be social" at this mid-sized school of 4,439 undergraduates where the "family-like atmosphere" encourages students to "grow personal and professional relationships with the faculty and staff" and "meet friendly, influential people." Bradley's "strong focus on individual students" includes the "research opportunities" that students are "offered as a freshman" and the Academic Exploration Program that one student says "allowed me to remain undecided while guiding me in what career fit best for my personality and interests." With over 185 majors and areas of study, including a "prestigious engineering program," students have plenty of options. Students praise the Bradley faculty, who go "above and beyond," including coming "in on the weekend just to help us all study." Students say Bradley professors grant them the "ability to explore what [they] would enjoy doing as a lifelong career" and provide them with opportunities that lead to careers.

BANG FOR YOUR BUCK

Bradley offers a number of academic scholarships that range from $28,000 to $48,000, distributed over four years. Bradley also offers several scholarships based on family background, talent and interest, including scholarships for dependent children of Caterpillar Inc. employees, scholarships for the children or siblings of Bradley alums, and scholarships for students in the performing arts. The celebrated engineering department at Bradley offers a number of departmental scholarships, including ones for women pursuing degrees in engineering. Bradley also offers need-based grants, because, according to the Statement of Ethical Principles that guides their financial aid distribution, the school is "committed to removing financial barriers" and to "make every effort to assist students with financial need." Students say that Bradley scholarships allow them "to get a great education for a reasonable price."

STUDENT LIFE

Students at Bradley are "passionate about their grades" but maintain "a healthy balance between their academic and social lives." With more than "240 different organizations on campus," students can "[enjoy] a vivacious social life" and find "a lot of volunteering opportunities." Greek life is popular on campus, and "everyone is involved in at least one" club. On Friday night, students flock to "free movies in the basement of the student center" or to Late Night BU, "an event hosted once a month where a ton of free activities are provided to Bradley students." The school's "rec center is very popular and state-of-the-art," and "the library is busy all day." Students also like to "hike through the abundant nature preserves and parks, spend time in the quads on campus," and participate in monthly "campus-wide service projects."

CAREER

Bradley's Smith Career Center hosts a job and internship fair that attracts over 190 organizations and employers from a range of industries. The SCC also hosts events for students interested in graduate and professional school, as well as a career fair for students entering the nursing and physical therapy fields. The Springer Center also helps students get career related work experience through internships and cooperative education programs, and the Bradley Internship Fund helps defray the cost of unpaid summer internships with a stipend. Students say that providing "assistance in obtaining a career and internships" is one of the school's greatest strengths and that, in addition to the SCC, their Bradley "professors have been excellent resources during [their] college career[s] and have helped land internships." Bradley grads who visited PayScale.com reported an average starting salary of $49,900 and 49 percent described their job as being meaningful.

Bradley University

Financial Aid: 309-677-3089 • E-mail: admissions@bradley.edu • Website: www.bradley.edu

GENERAL INFO

Activities: Choral groups, concert band, dance, drama/theater, jazz band, literary magazine, music ensembles, musical theater, pep band, radio station, student government, student newspaper, student-run film society, symphony orchestra, television station, Campus Ministries, International Student Organization. **Organizations:** 220 registered organizations, 31 honor societies, 17 religious organizations. 16 fraternities, 11 sororities. **Athletics (Intercollegiate):** *Men:* baseball, basketball, cross-country, golf, soccer, track/field. *Women:* basketball, cross-country, golf, softball, tennis, track/field (outdoor), track/field (indoor), volleyball. **On-Campus Highlights:** Markin Family Student Recreation Center, Caterpillar Global Communications Center, Olin Hall of Science, Michel Student Center, Cullom-Davis Library. Bradley's eighty-five-acre campus is in the heart of a residential neighborhood just one mile from downtown. Peoria is the largest metropolitan area in Illinois south of Chicago.

FINANCIAL AID

Students should submit: FAFSA. Priority filing deadline is 3/1. The Princeton Review suggests that all financial aid forms be submitted as soon as possible after October 1. *Need-based scholarships/grants offered:* Federal Pell, FSEOG, State scholarships/grants, Private scholarships, College/university scholarship or grant aid from institutional funds. *Loan aid offered:* Direct Subsidized Stafford Loans, Direct Unsubsidized Stafford Loans, Direct PLUS loans, Federal Perkins Loans, Federal Nursing Loans. Applicants will be notified of awards on a rolling basis beginning 3/1. Federal Work-Study Program available. Institutional employment available.

BOTTOM LINE

Getting an education at Bradley University will cost $31,740 in tuition per year. Add to that $380 in required fees and an average of $1,200 for books and supplies and the yearly cost comes to $32,680. Don't forget to factor in the cost of room and board, an additional $10,010.

CAREER INFORMATION FROM PAYSCALE.COM

ROI rating	85
Bachelor's and No Higher	
Median starting salary	$50,100
Median mid-career salary	$88,100
At Least Bachelor's	
Median starting salary	$50,400
Median mid-career salary	$90,100
% alumni with high job meaning	49%
% STEM	21%

SELECTIVITY

Admissions Rating	83
# of applicants	9,186
% of applicants accepted	66
% of acceptees attending	15
# offered a place on the wait list	0

FRESHMAN PROFILE

Range SAT Critical Reading	500–620
Range SAT Math	520–650
Range SAT Writing	470–610
Range ACT Composite	23–28
Minimum paper TOEFL	550
Minimum internet-based TOEFL	79
Average HS GPA	3.7
% graduated top 10% of class	22
% graduated top 25% of class	58
% graduated top 50% of class	89

DEADLINES

Regular	
Priority	2/1
Nonfall registration?	Yes

FINANCIAL FACTS

Financial Aid Rating	83
Annual tuition	$31,740
Room and board	$10,010
Required fees	$380
Average need-based scholarship	$15,801
% needy frosh rec. need-based scholarship or grant aid	99
% needy UG rec. need-based scholarship or grant aid	96
% needy frosh rec. non-need-based scholarship or grant aid	14
% needy UG rec. non-need-based scholarship or grant aid	11
% needy frosh rec. need-based self-help aid	77
% needy UG rec. need-based self-help aid	80
% frosh rec. any financial aid	95
% UG rec. any financial aid	88
% UG borrow to pay for school	80
Average cumulative indebtedness	$28,093
% frosh need fully met	18
% ugrads need fully met	17
Average % of frosh need met	70
Average % of ugrad need met	67

Brandeis University

415 SOUTH ST, MS003, WALTHAM, MA 02454-9110 • ADMISSIONS: 781-736-3500 • FINANCIAL AID: 781-736-3700

CAMPUS LIFE

Quality of Life Rating	91
Fire Safety Rating	97
Green Rating	87
Type of school	Private
Affiliation	No Affiliation
Environment	City

STUDENTS

Total undergrad enrollment	3,621
% male/female	43/57
% from out of state	74
% frosh from public high school	57
% frosh live on campus	99
% ugrads live on campus	79
% African American	5
% Asian	13
% Caucasian	47
% Hispanic	7
% Native American	<1
% Pacific Islander	<1
% Two or more races	3
% Race and/or ethnicity unknown	5
% international	20
# of countries represented	54

ACADEMICS

Academic Rating	89
% students returning for sophomore year	92
% students graduating within 4 years	80
% students graduating within 6 years	87
Calendar	Semester
Student/faculty ratio	10:1
Profs interesting rating	90
Profs accessible rating	86
Most classes have 10–19 students.	

MOST POPULAR MAJORS
Biology; Economics; Psychology

ABOUT THE SCHOOL

The distinctive elements of a Brandeis University education are the intense intellectual engagement students share with faculty who are at the cutting-edge of their disciplines, in addition to the interdisciplinary connections and perspectives that unite teachers and students in such majors as international and global studies, health and science, society and policy, film, television, and interactive media. "Attending classes at Brandeis is only part of my education," shares one sophomore, "because the students and faculty are interested and involved in social issues and we relate our education to the world around us. The focus is on producing globally and socially aware members of society." Another undergraduate tells us that "Brandeis cares—about learning both inside and outside the classroom, about other people, and about the world around us." A new student adds, "I was impressed by . . . the many opportunities for experiential learning. There is more to my education than sitting in a classroom, and Brandeis opens many doors for hands-on learning."

BANG FOR YOUR BUCK

When considering costs, Brandeis has many benefits. This New England campus has financial aid awards that meet the full demonstrated need for nearly all admitted undergraduate students. Additionally, Brandeis has a policy for the treatment of outside scholarships that allows recipients to replace loans and work first, before any adjustment is made to Brandeis need-based scholarship. Most Brandeis students participate in internships connected with their liberal arts interests, either for credit or not. By graduation, students have participated, on average, in three internships and have had the experiences sought by top graduate schools and employers. A recent graduate explains, "My résumé was well-rounded and I had a lot to offer employers." Students have had a placement rate of approximately 97 percent within six months of graduation, and with free alumni career services for life, students are more than prepared for life in the workforce. "I really feel prepared and excited to graduate," a senior tells us.

STUDENT LIFE

"There is definitely a strong campus life" at Brandeis, says a student. "There is always something going on." Others echo that sentiment, saying that, "the truth is Brandeis is a place where just about anyone can find someone like them." "There is definitely a party life if that's what you're looking for, though I wouldn't call Brandeis a 'party school,' but if you're not interested it's easy to not partake and find other things to do." As for those other things, "many students spend their time outside of class [participating] in clubs and other activities such as intramural sports or hobbies. Many students ice skate, dance, sing in an a cappella group, perform in a play, play a club or intramural sport, work on campus, [or] have an internship off campus." The school also sponsors major concerts and seasonal festivals, and students looking to get away can "use the Brandeis Shuttle to go into Boston on the weekends [. . .] I would say that the average students makes it into Boston once or twice a month."

CAREER

The Hiatt Career Center at Brandeis University offers many resources for students planning for life beyond college. The school holds a large number of career fairs, recruiting events, and other networking opportunities on campus (similar off-campus events for students and alumni are sponsored in major cities across the country), and the Center provides a great deal of advice for students on how build and manage professional relationships. Brandeis is also generous with funding for internship experiences. For example, The World of Work fellowship program awards approximately forty stipends annually to undergraduates who pursue summer internships

Brandeis University

E-MAIL: ADMISSIONS@BRANDEIS.EDU • FAX: 781-736-3536 • WEBSITE: WWW.BRANDEIS.EDU

with organizations that are not be able to provide a salary. Likewise, the Eli J. Segal Citizen Leadership Program provides financial support to students assigned to government and non-profit agencies in Washington D.C., Boston, and New York City. Out of Brandeis alumni visiting PayScale.com, 53 percent report that they derive a high level of meaning from their jobs.

GENERAL INFO

Activities: Choral groups, concert band, dance, drama/theater, jazz band, literary magazine, music ensembles, musical theater, radio station, student government, student newspaper, student-run film society, symphony orchestra, television station, yearbook, campus ministries, international student organization. **Organizations:** 253 registered organizations, 4 honor societies, 19 religious organizations. **Athletics (Intercollegiate):** *Men:* Baseball, basketball, cross-country, diving, fencing, soccer, tennis, track/field (outdoor), track/field (indoor). *Women:* Basketball, cheerleading, cross-country, diving, fencing, soccer, softball, tennis, track/field (outdoor), track/field (indoor), volleyball. **On-Campus Highlights:** Shapiro Science Center, Spingold Theater, Shapiro Campus Center, Rapaporte Treasure Hall. **Environmental Initiatives:** The Brandeis University Climate Action Plan has aggressive goals for future energy and climate impact reductions. Brandeis has invested significantly in energy reduction efforts.

FINANCIAL AID

Students should submit: FAFSA, CSS/Financial Aid PROFILE, Noncustodial PROFILE. Regular filing deadline is 1/1. The Princeton Review suggests that all financial aid forms be submitted as soon as possible after October 1. *Need-based scholarships/grants offered:* Federal Pell, FSEOG, State scholarships/grants, Private scholarships, College/university scholarship or grant aid from institutional funds. *Loan aid offered:* Direct Subsidized Stafford Loans, Direct Unsubsidized Stafford Loans, Direct PLUS loans, Federal Perkins Loans, State Loans, College/university loans from institutional funds. Applicants will be notified of awards on or about 4/1. Federal Work-Study Program available. Institutional employment available.

BOTTOM LINE

Brandeis University, while providing a diverse curriculum and fantastic educational experience, has a yearly tuition of about $45,600. After including another $15,700 for room, board, books, and fees, one becomes quickly aware that financial support is essential for many students. Fortunately, need-based scholarships and grants are provided to nearly 97 percent of needy freshman, 65 percent of the student body being recipients of financial aid. Approximately three-fifths of undergrads will borrow to pay for school; their average total debt will be more than $28,600 upon leaving Brandeis.

CAREER INFORMATION FROM PAYSCALE.COM

ROI rating	87
Bachelor's and No Higher	
Median starting salary	$45,300
Median mid-career salary	$96,200
At Least Bachelor's	
Median starting salary	$48,400
Median mid-career salary	$98,800
% alumni with high job meaning	45%
% STEM	16%

SELECTIVITY

Admissions Rating	96
# of applicants	10,528
% of applicants accepted	34
% of acceptees attending	22
# offered a place on the wait list	1,553
% accepting a place on wait list	38
% admitted from wait list	4
# of early decision applicants	698
% accepted early decision	35

FRESHMAN PROFILE

Range SAT Critical Reading	600–700
Range SAT Math	650–770
Range SAT Writing	640–710
Range ACT Composite	29–32
Minimum paper TOEFL	600
Minimum internet-based TOEFL	100
Average HS GPA	4.0
% graduated top 10% of class	71
% graduated top 25% of class	91
% graduated top 50% of class	98

DEADLINES

Early decision	
Deadline	11/1
Notification	12/15
Regular	
Deadline	1/1
Notification	4/1
Nonfall registration?	Yes

FINANCIAL FACTS

Financial Aid Rating	90
Annual tuition	$49,586
Room and board	$14,380
Required fees	$1,659
Average need-based scholarship	$35,798
% needy frosh rec. need-based scholarship or grant aid	97
% needy UG rec. need-based scholarship or grant aid	94
% needy frosh rec. non-need-based scholarship or grant aid	8
% needy UG rec. non-need-based scholarship or grant aid	4
% needy frosh rec. need-based self-help aid	89
% needy UG rec. need-based self-help aid	94
% frosh rec. any financial aid	63
% UG rec. any financial aid	65
% UG borrow to pay for school	58
Average cumulative indebtedness	$30,850
% frosh need fully met	84
% ugrads need fully met	75
Average % of frosh need met	97

Brigham Young University

A-153 ASB, Provo, UT 84602-1110 • Admissions: 801-422-2507 • Fax: 801-422-0005

CAMPUS LIFE

Quality of Life Rating	92
Fire Safety Rating	76
Green Rating	60*
Type of school	Private
Affiliation	Church of Jesus Christ of Latter-day Saints
Environment	City

STUDENTS

Total undergrad enrollment	30,221
% male/female	52/48
% from out of state	66
% frosh live on campus	79
% ugrads live on campus	19
% African American	<1
% Asian	2
% Caucasian	83
% Hispanic	6
% Native American	<1
% Pacific Islander	1
% Two or more races	4
% Race and/or ethnicity unknown	1
% international	3
# of countries represented	105

ACADEMICS

Academic Rating	83
% students returning for sophomore year	86
% students graduating within 4 years	31
% students graduating within 6 years	80
Calendar	Semester
Student/faculty ratio	20:1
Profs interesting rating	82
Profs accessible rating	80
Most classes have 10–19 students.	

MOST POPULAR MAJORS

Business/Commerce; Exercise Physiology; Elementary Education and Teaching

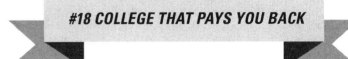

#18 COLLEGE THAT PAYS YOU BACK

ABOUT THE SCHOOL

Owned by the Church of Jesus Christ of Latter-Day Saints, BYU is all about "high moral standards" and "educating the best LDS students efficiently." Students love the "religious atmosphere" that helps in "isolating its students from what they believe will wrongly influence their choices." Also, "the tuition cost is relatedly cheap." The "academically accomplished" professors are "smart and interesting people" and "very well trained in their field." The school offers a "large variety of majors" with almost 200 in total. Popular majors include exercise science, elementary education, psychology, management, and English. The roughly 30,000 students on campus—about 28,000 of which are undergraduates—make it the largest religious university in the United States. "It offers everything I wanted," one student says, "good education, my major, people who would support me in my beliefs and morals, large campus, and it was all at a great price!"

BANG FOR YOUR BUCK

Tuition is affordable, especially if you are an LDS member. BYU cuts tuition in half for LDS members, claiming it is the equivalent of in-state tuition for state universities. In addition, BYU offers about one quarter of their incoming freshmen academic scholarships of varying amounts. These scholarships are mostly paid for by tithes on LDS church members. The scholarships do not renew, but instead are awarded on a yearly basis. Students must apply every year, which also means that you may receive a scholarship in later years even if you do not get one initially. Students may also apply for federal grants and loans.

STUDENT LIFE

BYU's student population "is pretty homogeneous due to the fact that 98 percent of us are LDS." "The average student is kind, conservative, dedicated to school, and very religious," one student explains. "Everyone pretty much fits in," "as long as a person doesn't wear clothes or have a hairstyle that stands out obnoxiously." Student life is shaped in large part by the school's religious rules, which enforce standards of appearance and ban alcohol, drugs, and premarital sex. Consequentially, many "people think about getting married...[and] for fun, people go on dates." "Good clean fun" is the rule, and students enjoy outdoor activities "like skiing, mountain biking, hiking, climbing, etc." "There are many social activities either through the church you attend or through the school" and students "like to watch movies, dance, cook, play games, sing, or make up their own ways to have fun."

Brigham Young University

FINANCIAL AID: 801-422-4104 • E-MAIL: ADMISSIONS@BYU.EDU • WEBSITE: WWW.BYU.EDU

CAREER

"Professors are very attuned to career opportunities" at BYU and help students get connected with jobs. "The alumni network is amazing" although "there needs to be more help for incoming freshman to figure out what they want to do." PayScale.com reports an average starting salary of $51,800 for BYU graduates. "BYU does emphasize book smarts but that is not the main emphasis," one student explains. "Hands-on experience, internships, and study abroad are highly encouraged," which helps students get a jump start on their post-college career.

GENERAL INFO

Activities: Choral groups, concert band, dance, drama/theater, jazz band, literary magazine, marching band, music ensembles, musical theater, opera, pep band, radio station, student government, student newspaper, student-run film society, symphony orchestra, television station. **Organizations:** 390 registered organizations, 22 honor societies, 25 religious organizations. **Athletics (Intercollegiate):** *Men:* baseball, basketball, cheerleading, cross-country, diving, football, golf, swimming, tennis, track/field (outdoor), track/field (indoor), volleyball. *Women:* basketball, cheerleading, cross-country, diving, golf, gymnastics, soccer, softball, swimming, tennis, track/field (outdoor), track/field (indoor), volleyball. **On-Campus Highlights:** Monte L. Bean Life Science Museum, The Museum of Art, Gordon B. Hinckley Alumni & Visitors Cen, Harold B. Lee Library, Wilkinson Student Center, Creamery on 9th, the Marriott Center.

FINANCIAL AID

Students should submit: FAFSA. Priority filing deadline is 4/15. The Princeton Review suggests that all financial aid forms be submitted as soon as possible after October 1. *Need-based scholarships/grants offered:* Federal Pell, Private scholarships, College/university scholarship or grant aid from institutional funds. *Loan aid offered:* Direct Subsidized Stafford Loans, Direct Unsubsidized Stafford Loans, Direct PLUS loans. Federal Work-Study Program available. Institutional employment available.

BOTTOM LINE

The cost of BYU depends on your religious affiliation. LDS members pay $5,000 a year while members of any other church pay roughly double that amount. Room, board, books, and supplies will bring those totals to just over $13,300 for LDS members and about $18,300 for non-LDS students.

CAREER INFORMATION FROM PAYSCALE.COM

ROI rating	93
Bachelor's and No Higher	
Median starting salary	$51,700
Median mid-career salary	$93,000
At Least Bachelor's	
Median starting salary	$53,900
Median mid-career salary	$97,900
% alumni with high job meaning	60%
% STEM	20%

SELECTIVITY

Admissions Rating	94
# of applicants	13,376
% of applicants accepted	48
% of acceptees attending	80

FRESHMAN PROFILE

Range SAT Critical Reading	570–680
Range SAT Math	68–680
Range SAT Writing	550–660
Range ACT Composite	27–31
Minimum paper TOEFL	500
Average HS GPA	3.8
% graduated top 10% of class	54
% graduated top 25% of class	85
% graduated top 50% of class	98

DEADLINES

Regular	
Priority	12/1
Deadline	2/1
Notification	2/28
Nonfall registration?	Yes

FINANCIAL FACTS

Financial Aid Rating	78
Annual tuition	$5,300
Room and board	$7,448
Average need-based scholarship	$5,068
% needy frosh rec. need-based scholarship or grant aid	57
% needy UG rec. need-based scholarship or grant aid	80
% needy frosh rec. non-need-based scholarship or grant aid	69
% needy UG rec. non-need-based scholarship or grant aid	45
% needy frosh rec. need-based self-help aid	27
% needy UG rec. need-based self-help aid	30
% frosh rec. any financial aid	53
% UG rec. any financial aid	64
% UG borrow to pay for school	27
Average cumulative indebtedness	$15,720
% frosh need fully met	1
% ugrads need fully met	2
Average % of frosh need met	30
Average % of ugrad need met	34

Brown University

Box 1876, 45 Prospect St, Providence, RI 02912 • Admissions: 401-863-2378 • Fax: 401-863-9300

CAMPUS LIFE

Quality of Life Rating	**95**
Fire Safety Rating	**92**
Green Rating	**91**
Type of school	Private
Affiliation	No Affiliation
Environment	City

STUDENTS

Total undergrad enrollment	6,652
% male/female	47/53
% from out of state	94
% frosh from public high school	57
% frosh live on campus	100
% ugrads live on campus	76
# of fraternities (% ugrad men join)	10 (12)
# of sororities (% ugrad women join)	4 (9)
% African American	7
% Asian	13
% Caucasian	43
% Hispanic	11
% Native American	<1
% Pacific Islander	<1
% Two or more races	6
% Race and/or ethnicity unknown	7
% international	12
# of countries represented	111

ACADEMICS

Academic Rating	**94**
% students returning for sophomore year	98
% students graduating within 4 years	83
% students graduating within 6 years	96
Calendar	Semester
Student/faculty ratio	9:1
Profs interesting rating	93
Profs accessible rating	88
Most classes have 19–29 students.	

MOST POPULAR MAJORS

Economics; Biology; Computer and Information Sciences

#14 COLLEGE THAT PAYS YOU BACK

ABOUT THE SCHOOL

Located in historic Providence, Rhode Island, and founded in 1764, Brown University is the seventh-oldest college in the United States. Brown is an independent, coeducational Ivy League institution. With its talented and motivated student body and accomplished faculty, Brown is a leading research university that maintains a particular commitment to exceptional undergraduate instruction. Known for its somewhat unconventional (but still highly regarded) approaches to life and learning, Brown University remains the slightly odd man out of the Ivy League, and the school wouldn't have it any other way. The school's willingness to employ and support different methods—such as the shopping period, the first two weeks of the semester where anyone can drop into any class to "find out if it's something they're interested in enrolling in," or the *Critical Review*, a student publication that produces reviews of courses based on evaluations from students who have completed the course—is designed to treat students "like adult[s]" through "freedom and choice." This open-minded environment allows them "to practice passion without shame or fear of judgment," the hallmark of a Brown education. Even if students do find themselves exploring the wrong off-the-beaten path, "there are multitudes of built-in support measures to help you succeed despite any odds." Other students tell us, "I have always considered the goal of college to teach students how to think, and Brown does exactly that"; "Brown, among all else, values knowledge and the independent pursuit of it."

BANG FOR YOUR BUCK

The Brown community forges an original relationship with the world and makes a distinctive contribution to global research, service, and education. Brown's global reach extends beyond the gates of campus to establish the university's place as a positive force in a complex and interconnected world. Brown students, staff, and faculty are engaged in local schools, hospitals, religious groups, charities, and social-justice organizations. Students are encouraged to get involved in the diverse and dynamic communities beyond the campus gates. The independent nature of the school in general "is one of the things that makes it such a strong institution," according to a student here. Because of the open curriculum, "we have the freedom to study what we want to study, unhindered by a core curriculum, with the connections and resources that an Ivy provides." Another undergrad is pleased that "it allows me to truly figure out what I would love to study and pursue." "It may seem intimidating because there is not much of a guide as to what a student should take, but it depends on the student to pave his or her own way."

STUDENT LIFE

Students are diligent in their academic pursuits and feel assured they're "getting a wonderful education with the professors"; most agree that their education is "really more about the unique student body and learning through active participation in other activities." It's a pretty unique crowd here, where "athletes, preps, nerds, and everyone in between come together" because they "love learning for the sake of learning, and [they] love Brown equally as much." "The 'mainstream' is full of people who are atypical in sense of fashion, taste in music, and academic interests," says a junior. Unsurprisingly, everyone here's "very smart," as well as "very quirky and often funny," and "a great [number] are brilliant and passionate about their interests"; "most

Brown University

FINANCIAL AID: 401-863-2721 • E-MAIL: ADMISSION_UNDERGRADUATE@BROWN.EDU • WEBSITE: WWW.BROWN.EDU

have interesting stories to tell." People here are "curious and open about many things," which is perhaps why diversity is a "strong theme" among Brown interactions and events. The overall culture "is pretty laid-back and casual," and "most of the students are friendly and mesh well with everyone."

CAREER

CareerLAB is the colloquial name for the Center for Careers and Life after Brown, where students can meet with advisors, polish their cover letters and LinkedIn profiles, explore career fields, or get information about Brown's on-campus recruiting process. Any student organization or athletic team can request a specialized CareerLAB-staffed program just for their group on topics like "How to Network" or "How to Find An Internship." Students use the online resource BrownConnect to network with alumni and to find internships, research opportunities, mentorship, and career advice. For those interested in graduate school, pre-professional advising is offered in areas like Health, Law, and Business. According to PayScale.com, the median starting salary for Brown graduates is $57,100, and 54 percent of alumni derive a high level of meaning from their work.

GENERAL INFO

Activities: Choral groups, concert band, dance, drama/theater, jazz band, literary magazine, marching band, music ensembles, musical theater, opera, pep band, radio station, student government, student newspaper, student-run film society, symphony orchestra, television station, yearbook, campus ministries, international student organization.

FINANCIAL AID

Students should submit: FAFSA, CSS/Financial Aid PROFILE, Noncustodial PROFILE. Regular filing deadline is 2/1. The Princeton Review suggests that all financial aid forms be submitted as soon as possible after October 1. *Need-based scholarships/grants offered:* Federal Pell, FSEOG, State scholarships/grants, Private scholarships, College/university scholarship or grant aid from institutional funds. *Loan aid offered:* Direct Subsidized Stafford Loans, Direct Unsubsidized Stafford Loans, Direct PLUS loans, Federal Perkins Loans, College/university loans from institutional funds. Applicants will be notified of awards on or about 4/1. Federal Work-Study Program available. Institutional employment available.

BOTTOM LINE

Obviously, the stellar education and overall academic experience a student receives from such an impressive institution as Brown University does not come without a cost. Tuition is over $50,200 per year, with room and board adding another $13,200. With over $1,000 for required fees, total costs are approximately $66,500. However, Brown University generously meets 100 percent of the demonstrated need of all undergraduates; 57 percent of undergrads receive financial aid, and the average need-based gift aid is more than $40,000.

CAREER INFORMATION FROM PAYSCALE.COM

ROI rating	93
Bachelor's and No Higher	
Median starting salary	$57,100
Median mid-career salary	$108,000
At Least Bachelor's	
Median starting salary	$60,800
Median mid-career salary	$113,000
% alumni with high job meaning	54%
% STEM	22%

SELECTIVITY

Admissions Rating	99
# of applicants	30,396
% of applicants accepted	9
% of acceptees attending	56
# of early decision applicants	3,043
% accepted early decision	21

FRESHMAN PROFILE

Range SAT Critical Reading	680–780
Range SAT Math	690–780
Range SAT Writing	690–780
Range ACT Composite	31–34
Minimum paper TOEFL	600
Minimum internet-based TOEFL	100
% graduated top 10% of class	91
% graduated top 25% of class	100
% graduated top 50% of class	100

DEADLINES

Early decision	
Deadline	11/1
Notification	12/15
Regular	
Deadline	1/1
Nonfall registration?	No

FINANCIAL FACTS

Financial Aid Rating	95
Annual tuition	$50,224
Room and board	$13,200
Required fees	$1,142
Average need-based scholarship	$43,045
% needy frosh rec. need-based scholarship or grant aid	96
% needy UG rec. need-based scholarship or grant aid	96
% needy frosh rec. non-need-based scholarship or grant aid	0
% needy UG rec. non-need-based scholarship or grant aid	0
% needy frosh rec. need-based self-help aid	84
% needy UG rec. need-based self-help aid	89
% frosh rec. any financial aid	55
% UG rec. any financial aid	57
% UG borrow to pay for school	34
Average cumulative indebtedness	$22,197
% frosh need fully met	100
% ugrads need fully met	100
Average % of frosh need met	100
Average % of ugrad need met	100

Bryn Mawr College

101 North Merion Avenue, Bryn Mawr, PA 19010-2859 • Admissions: 610-526-5152 • Fax: 610-526-7471

CAMPUS LIFE

Quality of Life Rating	**92**
Fire Safety Rating	**86**
Green Rating	**76**
Type of school	Private
Affiliation	No Affiliation
Environment	Suburban

STUDENTS

Total undergrad enrollment	1,346
% male/female	0/100
% from out of state	83
% frosh from public high school	64
% frosh live on campus	100
% ugrads live on campus	93
% African American	6
% Asian	12
% Caucasian	36
% Hispanic	9
% Native American	<1
% Pacific Islander	<1
% Two or more races	5
% Race and/or ethnicity unknown	8
% international	24
# of countries represented	60

ACADEMICS

Academic Rating	**93**
% students returning for sophomore year	94
% students graduating within 4 years	78
% students graduating within 6 years	85
Calendar	Semester
Student/faculty ratio	8:1
Profs interesting rating	87
Profs accessible rating	90
Most classes have 10–19 students.	

MOST POPULAR MAJORS
Biology; Mathematics; Psychology

ABOUT THE SCHOOL

An intellectually engaging college like Bryn Mawr delivers an invaluable experience. This all-women's college delivers professors that "are not only passionate about their respective fields but are also incredibly accessible," and many are on a first-name basis with the students. Labs and facilities are state-of-the-art. Classes here are intense and small, and students emphasize that "the social science and hard science departments are very strong." Stress is a way of life, especially when midterms and finals roll around, but the "passionate" women here say they "manage to find time to form a tight community, despite mounds of schoolwork." The administration is well liked, not least because it gives students all manner of support in their academic endeavors. Bryn Mawr has a bi-college relationship with Haverford College, meaning that students from either school can live, study, and even major at both schools. Bryn Mawr and Haverford are also part of the Tri-College Consortium with Swarthmore College, which allows students from all three schools to use libraries and attend social functions, performances, and lectures on any campus. Cross-registration with Haverford, Swarthmore, and the University of Pennsylvania gives students access to more than 5,000 courses. Students praise the "vast resources offered through the Tri-Co," as well as the opportunities this system provides to "to grow culturally, academically, socially, and politically." Upon graduation, Mawrters can take advantage of a loyal network of successful alumnae who maintain a strong connection to the school.

BANG FOR YOUR BUCK

Bryn Mawr College is deeply committed to enrolling outstanding scholars. To eliminate financial barriers to attendance, the college meets 100 percent of the demonstrated financial need of enrolling students. In 2016–2016 alone, the college awarded $28.6 million dollars in grant assistance to 71 percent of undergraduate students. The average grant is approximately $30,000. If you are a veteran— or will soon be one—Bryn Mawr offers very generous benefits. In addition, graduates of Bryn Mawr are very competitive when the time comes to find a job.

STUDENT LIFE

Life at Bryn Mawr has somehow achieved the perfect balance of being both "relaxed" yet "busy." Certainly, these undergrads are quite focused on their studies. Yet they also manage to carve out time to kick back. And, fortunately, there are plenty of "musical, poetic and comedy events" as well as a movie series for those who "prefer a low-key night." Indeed, prospective students looking for a raucous scene be warned; "there are only a few big parties a year at Bryn Mawr, so if you want a party scene you have to go to one of the other schools in the area." However, a political science major counters that "you can find groups of people drinking with friends on any night of the week, and campus-wide parties for birthdays etc. are relatively common." Finally, since the college is in close proximity to Philadelphia, students love to "take advantage of everything going on in the city from concerts to restaurants."

Bryn Mawr College

FINANCIAL AID: 610-526-5245 • E-MAIL: ADMISSIONS@BRYNMAWR.EDU • WEBSITE: WWW.BRYNMAWR.EDU

CAREER

Bryn Mawr's Leadership Innovation and Liberal Arts Center integrates the Office of Civic Engagement and Career and Professional Development to prepare liberal arts and sciences students to become effective, self-aware leaders in their chosen life pursuits through experiential education. Undergrads here can schedule one-on-one appointments at any time and receive assistance in crafting their personal job strategy. Of course, they can get help both crafting and tweaking their résumés and cover letters. And they can learn the secrets to successful networking. Importantly, they may also participate in the college's recruiting program. Here, undergrads can meet with prospective employers interested in hiring Bryn Mawr students for internships, entry-level positions and gap-year fellowships. According to PayScale.com, the typical starting salary for alumnae after graduation is $44,600. Companies that have recently recruited undergrads include J.P. Morgan and Cornerstone Research.

GENERAL INFO

Environment: Metropolis. **Activities:** Choral groups, dance, drama/theater, jazz band, literary magazine, music ensembles, musical theater, radio station, student government, student newspaper, student-run film society, yearbook. **Organizations:** 158 registered organizations, 13 religious organizations. **Athletics (Intercollegiate):** Badminton, basketball, crew/rowing, cross-country, field hockey, lacrosse, soccer, swimming, tennis, track/field (outdoor), track/field (indoor), volleyball. **On-Campus Highlights:** Thomas Great Hall (National Historic Landmark), Erdman Hall (designed by famed architect, Louis Kahn), The Cloisters, Taft Garden, Rhys Carpenter Library, Goodhart Theater.

FINANCIAL AID

Students should submit: FAFSA, CSS/Financial Aid PROFILE. Regular filing deadline is 1/15. The Princeton Review suggests that all financial aid forms be submitted as soon as possible after October 1. *Need-based scholarships/grants offered:* Federal Pell, FSEOG, State scholarships/grants, College/university scholarship or grant aid from institutional funds. *Loan aid offered:* Direct Subsidized Stafford Loans, Direct Unsubsidized Stafford Loans, Direct PLUS loans, Federal Perkins Loans. Federal Work-Study Program available. Institutional employment available.

BOTTOM LINE

Tuition, fees, room and board costs approximately $64,000 each year. While that may seem like a lot, the college's need-based financial aid programs are among the most generous in the country.

CAREER INFORMATION FROM PAYSCALE.COM

ROI rating	**86**
Bachelor's and No Higher	
Median starting salary	$44,600
Median mid-career salary	$69,800
At Least Bachelor's	
Median starting salary	$44,600
Median mid-career salary	$69,800
% alumni with high job meaning	
% STEM	21%

SELECTIVITY

Admissions Rating	**94**
# of applicants	2,890
% of applicants accepted	39
% of acceptees attending	35
# offered a place on the wait list	872
% accepting a place on wait list	49
% admitted from wait list	0
# of early decision applicants	279
% accepted early decision	50

FRESHMAN PROFILE

Range SAT Critical Reading	620–730
Range SAT Math	620–730
Range SAT Writing	630–730
Range ACT Composite	28–32
Minimum paper TOEFL	600
Minimum internet-based TOEFL	100
% graduated top 10% of class	63
% graduated top 25% of class	88
% graduated top 50% of class	98

DEADLINES

Early decision	
Deadline	11/15
Notification	12/15
Regular	
Deadline	1/15
Notification	4/1
Nonfall registration?	No

FINANCIAL FACTS

Financial Aid Rating	**96**
Annual tuition	$47,640
Room and board	$15,370
Required fees	$1,150
Average need-based scholarship	$38,637
% needy frosh rec. need-based scholarship or grant aid	100
% needy UG rec. need-based scholarship or grant aid	100
% needy frosh rec. non-need-based scholarship or grant aid	5
% needy UG rec. non-need-based scholarship or grant aid	4
% needy frosh rec. need-based self-help aid	94
% needy UG rec. need-based self-help aid	91
% frosh rec. any financial aid	74
% UG rec. any financial aid	74
% UG borrow to pay for school	60
Average cumulative indebtedness	$22,914
% frosh need fully met	100
% ugrads need fully met	100
Average % of frosh need met	100
Average % of ugrad need met	100

Bucknell University

FREAS HALL, BUCKNELL UNIVERSITY, LEWISBURG, PA 17837 • ADMISSIONS: 570-577-1101 • FINANCIAL AID: 570-577-1331

CAMPUS LIFE

Quality of Life Rating	89
Fire Safety Rating	94
Green Rating	94
Type of school	Private
Affiliation	No Affiliation
Environment	Village

STUDENTS

Total undergrad enrollment	3,569
% male/female	48/52
% from out of state	77
% frosh from public high school	64
% frosh live on campus	100
% ugrads live on campus	91
# of fraternities (% ugrad men join)	8 (42)
# of sororities (% ugrad women join)	8 (49)
% African American	3
% Asian	4
% Caucasian	77
% Hispanic	6
% Native American	<1
% Pacific Islander	0
% Two or more races	4
% Race and/or ethnicity unknown	<1
% international	5
# of countries represented	51

ACADEMICS

Academic Rating	93
% students returning for sophomore year	93
% students graduating within 4 years	85
% students graduating within 6 years	90
Calendar	Semester
Student/faculty ratio	9:1
Profs interesting rating	92
Profs accessible rating	90

Most classes have 10–19 students.
Most lab/discussion sessions have
10–19 students.

MOST POPULAR MAJORS

Economics; Biology; Political Science and
Government

ABOUT THE SCHOOL

Bucknell University delivers the quintessential East Coast college experience, and one student says it offers a balanced combination of "great academics, a liberal arts education, sterling reputation, and a great social scene." Lewisburg is located in central Pennsylvania, and the campus is described as both beautiful and safe. Another student shares his experience, saying, "Bucknell was the perfect next step from my high school; it is small enough that your teachers know your name but big enough that you don't know every person on campus. I felt the most comfortable at Bucknell, and I felt that the school actually cared about me as a person, compared to some of the larger state schools to which I applied." Overall, Bucknell balances reputation with accessibility in a neat package. "It's extremely prestigious, beautiful, and the perfect size," shares one junior. A recent graduate sums up by saying, "Bucknell University is small enough to affect change, but big enough to attract national attention. It is a school where academics are amazing, school spirit is everywhere, and the people genuinely care." Another new student is excited that "campus pride is obvious, and as a large liberal arts college there are a myriad of opportunities, but I don't have to compete with a ton of people to take advantage of them."

BANG FOR YOUR BUCK

Bucknell pride extends into the community, and students become involved socially in many area projects and activities. One student relates, "Bucknell just felt like home. It is big enough where alumni and community connections are a huge benefit, but the campus is small enough that I'm not just a number. Professors take time to know me, and being included in class discussions is not a challenge." Another resident "wanted a small school where I could form close relationships with faculty and have the opportunity to do undergraduate research. So far it has exceeded my expectations, and the faculty and administration have made sure opportunities are within my reach." As another student notes appreciatively, "I also received a scholarship that allowed me to have an internship on campus, giving me work experience on top of my education."

STUDENT LIFE

At Bucknell "more than half of eligible students are members of a Greek Organization." "The typical student at Bucknell is upper/middle class, friendly, driven, well educated and preppy." Still, "people tend to be very accepting of alternate cultures and lifestyles." "Generally, academics are the number one priority" and "Bucknellians work extremely hard all week." In addition to Greek life, Bucknell hosts "engaging guest speakers" and concerts at the Weis Performance Center. "Lewisburg, a quaint town, feels like a true metropolis" with "an adorable old fashioned movie theater" and late night carnivals. In general, student sentiment echoes that at Bucknell, "there is a place for everyone." "Most people find one, two, or 100 extracurricular activities to join."

CAREER

"Bucknell University allows students, no matter what their academic or social preferences are, to find opportunities to really explore their interests. Students are encouraged to develop projects or clubs to enhance the campus community." Most are "impressed" with the career services and "networking opportunities" available, especially the alumni "dedication." Alumni are "valuable" assets to future Bucknellians and

Bucknell University

E-MAIL: ADMISSIONS@BUCKNELL.EDU • FAX: 570-577-3538 • WEBSITE: WWW.BUCKNELL.EDU

remain involved with the school and students long after graduation. Also, the career development center is "amazing" as are the study abroad programs, internships, and undergrad research opportunities. Bucknell "has a huge focus on service learning and community service which is phenomenal." Students receive guidance and opportunities through their professors and pre-professional advisors. According to the website PayScale.com, the average starting salary for graduates is $56,800 with a mid-career average at $101,000.

GENERAL INFO

Activities: Choral groups, concert band, dance, drama/theater, jazz band, literary magazine, music ensembles, musical theater, opera, pep band, radio station, student government, student newspaper, student-run film society, symphony orchestra, yearbook, campus ministries, international student organization. **Organizations:** 150 registered organizations, 23 honor societies, 11 religious organizations. 8 fraternities, 8 sororities. **Athletics (Intercollegiate):** *Men:* Baseball, basketball, cross-country, diving, football, golf, lacrosse, soccer, swimming, tennis, track/field, water polo, wrestling. *Women:* Basketball, crew/rowing, cross-country, diving, field hockey, golf, lacrosse, soccer, softball, swimming, tennis, track/field, volleyball, water polo.

FINANCIAL AID

Students should submit: FAFSA, CSS/Financial Aid PROFILE. Regular filing deadline is 1/15. The Princeton Review suggests that all financial aid forms be submitted as soon as possible after October 1. *Need-based scholarships/grants offered:* Federal Pell, FSEOG, State scholarships/grants, Private scholarships, College/university scholarship or grant aid from institutional funds. *Loan aid offered:* Direct Subsidized Stafford Loans, Direct Unsubsidized Stafford Loans, Direct PLUS loans, Federal Perkins Loans. Applicants will be notified of awards on or about 4/1. Federal Work-Study Program available. Institutional employment available.

BOTTOM LINE

Bucknell University provides students with a fine educational experience. The yearly tuition does reflect that monetarily, at $51,676 a year. With room, board, and books adding another $12,656, students are making a large but wise investment in their future. The school does provide a variety of options to offset the cost of attending here, with 89 percent of needy freshmen receiving need-based scholarships or grants. Fifty-five percent of students borrow to pay for school, and around 52 percent of students receive some form of financial aid. Upon graduating, for those who take out loans, the average total loan debt is $22,500. "The school has been generous and fair in financial assistance, and easy to work with," relates a satisfied undergraduate.

CAREER INFORMATION FROM PAYSCALE.COM

ROI rating	89
Bachelor's and No Higher	
Median starting salary	$57,100
Median mid-career salary	$99,600
At Least Bachelor's	
Median starting salary	$58,600
Median mid-career salary	$107,000
% alumni with high job meaning	46%
% STEM	30%

SELECTIVITY

Admissions Rating	96
# of applicants	10,967
% of applicants accepted	25
% of acceptees attending	35
# offered a place on the wait list	2,427
% accepting a place on wait list	38
% admitted from wait list	6
# of early decision applicants	830
% accepted early decision	53

FRESHMAN PROFILE

Range SAT Critical Reading	590–680
Range SAT Math	620–710
Range SAT Writing	590–690
Range ACT Composite	28–32
Minimum paper TOEFL	600
Minimum internet-based TOEFL	100
Average HS GPA	3.5
% graduated top 10% of class	65
% graduated top 25% of class	91
% graduated top 50% of class	99

DEADLINES

Early decision	
Deadline	11/15
Notification	12/15
Regular	
Deadline	1/15
Notification	4/1
Nonfall registration?	No

FINANCIAL FACTS

Financial Aid Rating	93
Annual tuition	$51,676
Room and board	$12,656
Required fees	$284
Average need-based scholarship	$25,000
% needy frosh rec. need-based scholarship or grant aid	89
% needy UG rec. need-based scholarship or grant aid	95
% needy frosh rec. non-need-based scholarship or grant aid	24
% needy UG rec. non-need-based scholarship or grant aid	22
% needy frosh rec. need-based self-help aid	100
% needy UG rec. need-based self-help aid	100
% frosh rec. any financial aid	62
% UG rec. any financial aid	62
% UG borrow to pay for school	52
Average cumulative indebtedness	$22,500
% frosh need fully met	91
% ugrads need fully met	91
Average % of frosh need met	91
Average % of ugrad need met	91

California Institute of Technology

1200 EAST CALIFORNIA BOULEVARD, PASADENA, CA 91125 • ADMISSIONS: 626-395-6341

#5 COLLEGE THAT PAYS YOU BACK

ABOUT THE SCHOOL

Caltech's swagger is completely out of proportion with its small size of about 1,000 students. Thirty-four Caltech alumni and faculty have won the Nobel Prize; fifty-eight have won the National Medal of Science; thirteen have won the National Medal of Technology and Innovation; and 125 have been elected to the National Academies combined. To say that this science and engineering powerhouse is world-class is an understatement. Located in the suburbs of Los Angeles ("Where else do you have beaches, mountains, and desert all within a two-hour drive?"), Caltech boasts a long history of excellence, with a list of major research achievements that reads like a textbook in the history of science. It goes without saying that academics are highly rigorous and competitive; if you are used to getting straight As, Caltech may be a shock to the system. "If you were the top student all your life, prepare to experience a big dose of humility, because you'll have to work hard just to stay in the middle of the pack," says a student. Techers say the learning experience here is "like trying to drink from a firehose," which is "as accurate a statement as can be made, given the breadth, intensity, and amount of coursework required."

BANG FOR YOUR BUCK

Caltech is extremely affordable, while the school's immense reputation and plethora of opportunities ensure a bright future in research or academia for Caltech graduates. Caltech operates need-blind admissions for all U.S. citizens and permanent residents. Every year, financial aid awards meet 100 percent of demonstrated student need. Of particular note, the school makes every effort to limit a student's debt, awarding aid packages with little work-study or loans. Across the board, the maximum loan expectation for Caltech students is just around $5,500 annually, and the average loan debt for Caltech students is just over $20,677 for all four years. The school also offers substantial need-based packages for international students, a rarity among private institutions. Caltech scholarships are awarded based on demonstrated financial need.

STUDENT LIFE

We're told that at Caltech, most "of the social interaction is centered around the eight student houses, which are somewhere between dorms and frats/sororities, but closest to the houses in Harry Potter." Indeed, undergrads here can participate in a myriad of activities through their respective houses. Events might include "scavenger hunts, inter-house dodgeball [and] frisbee, paint balling…pumpkin carving competition, Project Euler new problem solving session and New Yorker caption contest." Outside of the houses, "there are many music and theatre groups on campus, and countless clubs" in which students can participate. It's common for "most people [to be] involved with at least one non-academic thing." And while there is a small party scene, it's "much less traditional…than at other schools." A senior clarifies, "We're more likely to throw themed parties, with things to do other than dance, because we're kind of awkward."

California Institute of Technology

FINANCIAL AID: 626-395-6280 • E-MAIL: UGADMISSIONS@CALTECH.EDU • WEBSITE: ADMISSIONS.CALTECH.EDU

CAREER

We'll get right to the point—Caltech students do very well for themselves. In fact, according to PayScale.com, the average starting salary for recent graduates is $74,800. Certainly, the school's Career Development Center should take some of the credit for this success. After all, the office provides some stellar career counseling. It also hosts a number of workshops covering an array of topics such as connecting with recruiters, projecting confidence in interviews and social media networking. Undergrads also have access to the TecherLink which connects them with job, internship and work study opportunities as well as the career center's activities. Perhaps most importantly, the office hosts two big career fairs each year (one in the fall, one in the winter). Finally, companies that frequently hire Caltech grads include Google, Inc., National Institutes of Health (NIH) and Oracle Corp.

GENERAL INFO

Activities: Choral groups, concert band, dance, drama/theater, jazz band, literary magazine, music ensembles, musical theater, opera, pep band, student government, student newspaper, student-run film society, symphony orchestra, yearbook. **Organizations:** 113 registered organizations, 2 honor societies, 7 religious organizations. **Athletics (Intercollegiate):** *Men:* Baseball, basketball, cross-country, diving, fencing, soccer, swimming, tennis, track/field (outdoor), water polo. *Women:* Basketball, cross-country, diving, fencing, swimming, tennis, track/field (outdoor), volleyball, water polo.

FINANCIAL AID

Students should submit: FAFSA, Institution's own financial aid form, CSS/Financial Aid PROFILE, State aid form, Noncustodial PROFILE, Business/Farm Supplement. Priority filing deadline is 3/2. The Princeton Review suggests that all financial aid forms be submitted as soon as possible after October 1. *Need-based scholarships/grants offered:* Federal Pell, FSEOG, State scholarships/grants, Private scholarships, College/university scholarship or grant aid from institutional funds. *Loan aid offered:* Direct Subsidized Stafford Loans, Direct Unsubsidized Stafford Loans, Direct PLUS loans, College/university loans from institutional funds. Applicants will be notified of awards on a rolling basis beginning 4/15. Federal Work-Study Program available. Institutional employment available.

THE BOTTOM LINE

In 2015 Caltech's endowment was just under $2.1 billion. It's no wonder generous financial aid and scholarship packages are commonplace here. Tuition at Caltech is $45,846 annually, plus another $1,700-plus in student fees. Once you factor in $14,100 for room and board and $1,300 more for books and supplies, the estimated annual cost is $62,977 per year. Few students pay the full cost, while everyone benefits from the world-class education, making this school a best buy. Financial aid packages for freshman include a $38,983 need-based grant on average.

CAREER INFORMATION FROM PAYSCALE.COM

ROI rating	97
Bachelor's and No Higher	
Median starting salary	$72,600
Median mid-career salary	$125,000
At Least Bachelor's	
Median starting salary	$77,000
Median mid-career salary	$126,000
% alumni with high job meaning	66%
% STEM	93%

SELECTIVITY

Admissions Rating	99
# of applicants	6,506
% of applicants accepted	9
% of acceptees attending	42
# offered a place on the wait list	615
% accepting a place on wait list	70
% admitted from wait list	0

FRESHMAN PROFILE

Range SAT Critical Reading	730–800
Range SAT Math	770–800
Range SAT Writing	730–790
Range ACT Composite	34–35
Minimum internet-based TOEFL	110
% graduated top 10% of class	99
% graduated top 25% of class	100
% graduated top 50% of class	100

DEADLINES

Early action	
Deadline	11/1
Notification	12/15
Regular	
Deadline	1/3
Notification	Mid March
Nonfall registration?	No

FINANCIAL FACTS

Financial Aid Rating	96
Annual tuition	$45,846
Room and board	$14,100
Required fees	$1,731
Average need-based scholarship	$38,983
% needy frosh rec. need-based scholarship or grant aid	100
% needy UG rec. need-based scholarship or grant aid	100
% needy frosh rec. non-need-based scholarship or grant aid	1
% needy UG rec. non-need-based scholarship or grant aid	2
% needy frosh rec. need-based self-help aid	60
% needy UG rec. need-based self-help aid	67
% frosh rec. any financial aid	75
% UG rec. any financial aid	60
% UG borrow to pay for school	39
Average cumulative indebtedness	$20,677
% frosh need fully met	100
% ugrads need fully met	100
Average % of frosh need met	100
Average % of ugrad need met	100

California State University—Long Beach

1250 Bellflower Boulevard, Long Beach, CA 90840 • Admissions: 562-985-5471 • Fax: 562-985-4973

CAMPUS LIFE

Quality of Life Rating	89
Fire Safety Rating	67
Green Rating	60*
Type of school	public
Affiliation	No affiliation

STUDENTS

Total undergrad enrollment	31,523
% male/female	44/56
% from out of state	1
% frosh from public high school	82
% frosh live on campus	38
% ugrads live on campus	9
# of fraternities (% ugrad men join)	16 (2)
# of sororities (% ugrad women join)	15 (2)
% African American	4
% Asian	23
% Caucasian	20
% Hispanic	38
% Native American	0
% Pacific Islander	0
% Two or more races	5
% Race and/or ethnicity unknown	4
% international	6

ACADEMICS

Academic Rating	73
% students returning for sophomore year	90
% students graduating within 4 years	14
% students graduating within 6 years	65
Student/faculty ratio	24:1
Profs interesting rating	71
Profs accessible rating	72

Most classes have 20–29 students.
Most lab/discussion sessions have
 20–29 students.

MOST POPULAR MAJORS
Psychology; Corrections and Criminal
Justice; Management Information Systems

ABOUT THE SCHOOL

As "one of the top CSU schools," California State University Long Beach boasts eight undergraduate colleges, including "one of the top film schools in Southern California," "one of CSU's top business programs," and a College of the Arts that is "renowned across the globe and much cheaper than exclusive art schools." With more than 30,000 students, CSULB offers plenty of choices when it comes to courses like majors in creative writing or fashion, and "the best outdoor recreation classes of any school I know," including classes in "kayaking, surfing, rock climbing, desert expedition, [and] ultimate Frisbee." Despite its size, students cultivate close and productive relationships with faculty, which one senior described as "great in shaping the career path I decided to take." Students describe their professors as "a very close-knit group that really present their students with the opportunity to flourish" by "[offering] many opportunities for internships and projects outside of class." One student explained, "I have had the chance to network with countless speakers and explore career options just by showing up to class." Many of the students are commuters, but nevertheless students feel CSULB is "one of the only schools where the students [are] actively involved in just about everything: sports, government, clubs, and their education."

BANG FOR YOUR BUCK

Students name "financial aid and scholarship awareness" among the university's greatest strengths. For top performing California residents, the President's Scholars Program at CSULB offers tons of financial support, including a full-ride scholarship, yearly book allowance, paid housing, and such perks as priority registration and parking privileges. Once you're in the door, there are scholarships at the university, college, and department levels as well as scholarships sponsored by the California State University system. For example, the CSU Future Scholars program awards $1,000 to first-years and transfer students from disadvantaged backgrounds. Many of the university's scholarships show a commitment to need-based financial aid like their Study Abroad Scholarships that are made available to students who receive Pell Grants. Additionally, the Educational Opportunity Program offers a range of services, like help applying for financial aid and career guidance to low-income and first generation college students.

STUDENT LIFE

One nickname for CSULB is "The Beach," which aptly describes the university's easygoing style. Living close to the ocean, many students "get around with long boards and bikes" and enjoy "the beautiful Japanese garden . . . a great place to relax and study, if you have a few hours between classes." Students are "very welcoming" and, "as a commuter school, most people try joining clubs and organizations to make connections." Twice a week students are treated to a free movie night, and "escort and shuttle services" are available to help students get home safely. Students also benefit from free access to the Long Beach city transit, which has a route right through campus. Daycare is available "for single parent[s] who [are] also student[s]," and the "library is open until midnight" to help accommodate work schedules.

California State University—Long Beach

E-MAIL: ESLB@CSULB.EDU • WEBSITE: WWW.CSULB.EDU

CAREER

The Career Development Center helps students throughout the college to career process. From picking a major to locating internships to considering grad school, CDC offers workshops, one-on-one counseling sessions and special events. Internship Week is an extended event on campus with info sessions, panel discussions, and presentations from employers looking for interns. Past events have brought in employers from many different career fields, ranging from NASA to BET Networks. Students describe the school as generally "very career-oriented," living up to its motto, "Graduation begins today," by encouraging students to "think about their careers" from the beginning of their college experience and by teaching "transitional skills that can be used right away in life and work." Among CSULB grads who visited PayScale.com, the median starting salary is $43,600, and 52 percent rate their job as being meaningful.

GENERAL INFO

Activities: Choral groups, concert band, dance, drama/theater, jazz band, literary magazine, music ensembles, musical theater, opera, radio station, student government, student newspaper, student-run film society, symphony orchestra, television station, yearbook. **Organizations:** 300 registered organizations, 25 honor societies, 20 religious organizations. 16 fraternities, 15 sororities. **Athletics (Intercollegiate):** *Men:* baseball, basketball, cross-country, golf, track/field (outdoor), volleyball, water polo. *Women:* basketball, cross-country, golf, soccer, softball, tennis, track/field (outdoor), volleyball, water polo.

FINANCIAL AID

Students should submit: FAFSA. Applicants will be notified of awards on a rolling basis beginning 4/1. The Princeton Review suggests that all financial aid forms be submitted as soon as possible after October 1. *Need-based scholarships/grants offered:* Federal Pell, SEOG, State scholarships/grants, Private scholarships, College/university scholarship or grant aid from institutional funds. *Loan aid offered:* Direct Subsidized Stafford Loans, Direct Unsubsidized Stafford Loans, Direct PLUS loans, Federal Perkins Loans Applicants will be notified of awards on a rolling basis beginning 4/1. Federal Work-Study Program available. Institutional employment available.

BOTTOM LINE

Full-time students who are California residents will pay $5,472 per year in tuition, and out-of-state students pay $11,160. With an additional $980 in fees, $1,828 for books and supplies, $11,880 for room and board, the total yearly cost comes to $20,160 for in-state tuition and $25,848 for out-of-state students (less for commuters). The average loan debt is $16,579 per graduate.

SELECTIVITY

Admissions Rating	89
# of applicants	56,357
% of applicants accepted	36
% of acceptees attending	21

FRESHMAN PROFILE

SAT Critical Reading	460–570
Range SAT Math	480–600
Range ACT Composite	20–25
Minimum paper TOEFL	525
Average HS GPA	3.52

DEADLINES

Deadline	11/30
Notification	12/1
Nonfall registration?	No

FINANCIAL FACTS

Financial Aid Rating	82
Annual in-state tuition	$5,472
Annual out-of-state tuition	$11,160
Room and board	$11,880
Required fees	$980
Average need-based scholarship	$6,538
% needy frosh rec. need-based scholarship or grant aid	80
% needy UG rec. need-based scholarship or grant aid	80
% needy frosh rec. non-need-based scholarship or grant aid	25
% needy UG rec. non-need-based scholarship or grant aid	26
% needy frosh rec. need-based self-help aid	71
% needy UG rec. need-based self-help aid	79
% frosh need fully met	73
% ugrads need fully met	45
Average % of frosh need met	80
Average % of ugrad need met	83

CAREER INFORMATION FROM PAYSCALE.COM

ROI rating	86
Bachelor's and No Higher	
Median starting salary	$43,800
Median mid-career salary	$88,000
At Least Bachelor's	
Median starting salary	$44,200
Median mid-career salary	$88,200
% alumni with high job meaning	48%
% STEM	11%

Carleton College

100 SOUTH COLLEGE STREET, NORTHFIELD, MN 55057 • ADMISSIONS: 507-222-4190 • FAX: 507-222-4526

CAMPUS LIFE

Quality of Life Rating	96
Fire Safety Rating	79
Green Rating	93
Type of school	Private
Affiliation	No Affiliation
Environment	Village

STUDENTS

Total undergrad enrollment	1,995
% male/female	49/51
% from out of state	82
% frosh from public high school	60
% frosh live on campus	100
% ugrads live on campus	96
% African American	4
% Asian	8
% Caucasian	63
% Hispanic	7
% Native American	<1
% Pacific Islander	<1
% Two or more races	5
% Race and/or ethnicity unknown	2
% international	10
# of countries represented	38

ACADEMICS

Academic Rating	98
% students returning for sophomore year	96
% students graduating within 4 years	91
% students graduating within 6 years	95
Calendar	Trimester
Student/faculty ratio	9:1
Profs interesting rating	98
Profs accessible rating	97

Most classes have 10–19 students.
Most lab/discussion sessions have
10–19 students.

MOST POPULAR MAJORS
Biology; Economics; Computer and
Information Sciences

#28 COLLEGE THAT PAYS YOU BACK

ABOUT THE SCHOOL

Carleton College emphasizes rigor and intellectual growth without competition or hubris. Students attracted to Carleton's campus seek meaningful collaboration without the distraction of divisive academic one-upping. The opportunities to work with bright and engaged students and professors are plentiful. One student explains that "Carleton is not a research college, so while professors do some research, they are much more focused on students." Carleton operates on a trimester calendar, which many students enjoy, saying that "it's nice to be only taking three classes, though more intensely, rather than spreading yourself over four or five." An endless array of social and cocurricular activities is on offer at Carleton, as well as numerous programs for off-campus studies. These opportunities combine rural and urban experiences in a friendly Midwestern environment; students can master Chinese, Japanese, Arabic, and modern Hebrew; they can study in the shadow of a wind turbine generating electricity for the campus; they can choose to live in an environmentally conscious way from their dorm arrangements to the food they eat. Students love the "great study abroad office," which provides students here with "opportunities to travel to China, Thailand, Spain, and Africa." Experiential learning opportunities are immense here. Carleton Scholars is Carleton's highest-visibility experiential learning program and consists of taste-of-industry tours that introduce a variety of organizations in a particular field of interest, through site visits, panel discussions, receptions, and social activities. The 30 Minutes initiative provides students with access to one-on-one time, group discussion, and candid interviews with Carleton alumni luminaries in many fields. Carleton's Mentor Externships program connects students with alumni for one- to four-week short internships, most with a focus project, and generally including home-stays with their alumni hosts.

BANG FOR YOUR BUCK

Carleton's financial aid program is primarily need-based, and the college commits to meeting the need of admitted students fully. This means that a student's aid award will include grants and scholarships from Carleton, applicable government grants, on-campus work, and a reasonable amount of loan. Students graduate with about $20,000 in loan debt on average. Carleton's financial aid program helps support the unique culture and character of this college through its goal of enrolling diverse students regardless of their ability to pay for college. With nearly three-fifths of the student body receiving need-based grant aid, there is a broad socioeconomic representation across the student body, and students laud Carleton for its "generous financial aid."

STUDENT LIFE

The "creative, warm, compassionate, and helpful" undergrads of Carleton are "quirky," but "everyone is accepting of these little eccentricities." One Physics major praises the inclusive nature of the school, noting that "the moment that I first stepped foot on campus I felt as if I belong here." The "average Carl is . . . very physically active and loves to spend time outdoors." Even the cold Minnesota weather can be a good thing: "Minnesota winters teach you how to appreciate sunny, forty degree Spring days!" Carleton is "everything I wanted in a school: small, Midwest, great campus community, professors who really care," notes an English major. Despite the academically rigorous atmosphere, on the weekends there are "movie screenings, plays, dance performances, lectures, [and] musicians [on] campus." "Carleton boasts a tight-knit community, strong

Carleton College

FINANCIAL AID: 507-222-4138 • E-MAIL: ADMISSIONS@CARLETON.EDU • WEBSITE: WWW.CARLETON.EDU

academics and fun campus life." One undergrad details weekend plans—"on Fridays I go to the Sci-Fi interest house . . . then go to an improv/sketch comedy group"—and highlights the general camaraderie of the school: "Conversations are often simultaneously totally goofy and deeply intellectual. I just love it here, and I'm convinced there's no better place for me."

CAREER

PayScale.com reports that 43 percent of Carleton graduates feel their careers help make the world a better place. The average starting salary for a Carleton grad is $11,700, with popular jobs including executive director, research analyst, and art director. Economics, Political Science, and Computer Sciences are three of the most popular majors at the school. A Biology major notes that "there are great resources for academic and career help, and all kinds of interests are encouraged." Carleton's Career Center offers assistance to students at all levels of the job (and internship) hunting process. According to the school's website, two online resources, The Tunnel and Going Global, give students the opportunity to search for internships, participate in on-campus recruiting, and learn about international job and internship opportunities, respectively. Students note that Carleton professors "are very helpful in finding students summer . . . job opportunities."

GENERAL INFO

Activities: Choral groups, concert band, dance, drama/theater, jazz band, literary magazine, music ensembles, musical theater, radio station, student government, student newspaper, student-run film society, symphony orchestra, yearbook, campus ministries, international student organization.

FINANCIAL AID

Students should submit: FAFSA, CSS/Financial Aid PROFILE, Noncustodial PROFILE. Regular filing deadline is 2/15. The Princeton Review suggests that all financial aid forms be submitted as soon as possible after October 1. *Need-based scholarships/grants offered:* Federal Pell, FSEOG, State scholarships/grants, Private scholarships, College/university scholarship or grant aid from institutional funds. *Loan aid offered:* Direct Subsidized Stafford Loans, Direct Unsubsidized Stafford Loans, Direct PLUS loans, Federal Perkins Loans, State Loans, College/university loans from institutional funds. Applicants will be notified of awards on or about 3/31. Federal Work-Study Program available. Institutional employment available.

BOTTOM LINE

At Carleton College, the total cost for tuition and fees and room and board comes to just over $64,000 annually. Fortunately, the folks writing the checks at Carleton believe that cost should not be an obstacle to achieving a Carleton education. The average financial aid package for freshman includes scholarships and grants totaling $39,854—that gets you halfway there. When you factor in Carleton's other financial aid offerings in the form of work-study and loans, the dollar amount will seem much more manageable.

CAREER INFORMATION FROM PAYSCALE.COM

ROI rating	92
Bachelor's and No Higher	
Median starting salary	$44,000
Median mid-career salary	$107,000
At Least Bachelor's	
Median starting salary	$45,500
Median mid-career salary	$106,000
% alumni with high job meaning	52%
% STEM	34%

SELECTIVITY

Admissions Rating	97
# of applicants	6,722
% of applicants accepted	21
% of acceptees attending	35
# offered a place on the wait list	1,350
% accepting a place on wait list	33
% admitted from wait list	4
# of early decision applicants	689
% accepted early decision	31

FRESHMAN PROFILE

Range SAT Critical Reading	660–750
Range SAT Math	660–770
Range SAT Writing	660–750
Range ACT Composite	29–33
Minimum paper TOEFL	600
% graduated top 10% of class	71
% graduated top 25% of class	96
% graduated top 50% of class	100

DEADLINES

Early decision	
Deadline	11/15
Notification	12/15
Regular	
Deadline	1/15
Notification	3/31
Nonfall registration?	No

FINANCIAL FACTS

Financial Aid Rating	96
Annual tuition	$50,580
Room and board	$13,197
Required fees	$294
Average need-based scholarship	$36,482
% needy frosh rec. need-based scholarship or grant aid	100
% needy UG rec. need-based scholarship or grant aid	100
% needy frosh rec. non-need-based scholarship or grant aid	10
% needy UG rec. non-need-based scholarship or grant aid	14
% needy frosh rec. need-based self-help aid	97
% needy UG rec. need-based self-help aid	97
% frosh rec. any financial aid	54
% UG rec. any financial aid	56
% UG borrow to pay for school	41
Average cumulative indebtedness	$20,063
% frosh need fully met	100
% ugrads need fully met	100
Average % of frosh need met	100
Average % of ugrad need met	100

Carnegie Mellon University

5000 FORBES AVENUE, PITTSBURGH, PA 15213 • ADMISSIONS: 412-268-2082 • FAX: 412-268-7838

CAMPUS LIFE

Quality of Life Rating	88
Fire Safety Rating	96
Green Rating	99
Type of school	Private
Affiliation	No Affiliation
Environment	Metropolis

STUDENTS

Total undergrad enrollment	6,454
% male/female	54/46
% from out of state	84
% frosh live on campus	99
% ugrads live on campus	61
# of fraternities (% ugrad men join)	15 (17)
# of sororities (% ugrad women join)	10 (14)
% African American	4
% Asian	26
% Caucasian	30
% Hispanic	8
% Native American	<1
% Pacific Islander	<1
% Two or more races	4
% Race and/or ethnicity unknown	5
% international	22
# of countries represented	60

ACADEMICS

Academic Rating	89
% students returning for sophomore year	98
% students graduating within 4 years	72
% students graduating within 6 years	88
Calendar	Semester
Profs interesting rating	78
Profs accessible rating	89

Most classes have 10–19 students.
Most lab/discussion sessions have 20–29 students.

MOST POPULAR MAJORS

Computer Science; Electrical and Electronics Engineering; Mechanical Engineering

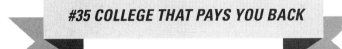

#35 COLLEGE THAT PAYS YOU BACK

ABOUT THE SCHOOL

Primarily known for its incredibly strong STEM and drama programs, Carnegie Mellon University enjoys a worldwide reputation as a research university. Professors are experts in their respective fields, and the difficulty of the classes and high expectations from faculty push students to do their best work. In return, they are given "a lot of trust from the administration" in regards to self-governance and their courses of study. "I am not limited to take classes in any one particular college," says a student. "It is nice to know I will get a good degree, but that it is also unique to me." The school offers "more opportunities to excel than you could possibly use in one four-year period" and most here treat the university as an intellectual and creative playground. "Carnegie Mellon is the only place where you will see engineers working while an art installation goes in above their heads," says a student.

BANG FOR YOUR BUCK

Students who fill out and submit the requisite forms and materials for federal and state grants and the CSS financial aid profile will be considered for a Carnegie Mellon Undergraduate Grant. Incoming freshman also have the opportunity to receive a Carnegie Scholarship, which goes to academically and artistically talented middle income students who qualify for little to no need-based financial aid. Forty-two percent of students receive some form of need-based financial aid, and 82 percent of all such need is met. Additionally, there are many student employment opportunities on campus, both need-based and non-need based.

STUDENT LIFE

Students report that "there are a million ways to find your niche on campus" beginning with orientation, and "eventually the labels 'artist' or 'scientist' fade and you become friends with people from all over campus." The challenging academics put everyone in the same time constrained boat, and so "the work-heavy culture becomes a social thing." The student body "isn't so small that you'll know everyone… [but] it's not so big that you'll disappear either." Everyone here fits in somewhere, and even people who were outcasts in high school "easily find large groups of people just like them on campus." Students at CMU are very dedicated to a variety of clubs and interests, and adhere to the logic "study or be trampled, but make sure you still have some fun."

CAREER

At CMU, the interdisciplinary approach to education means that students are taught to be versatile problem solvers with a key sense of community. The school is "great for engineering, math, science, or physics students (or drama or design)," who find that the world "practically throws opportunities (internships, guidance) at these majors." You would be hard-pressed to find a junior or senior who did not have an internship in the summer; "it almost seems expected of you because of the caliber of student you are." CMU's academic diversity and rigor "put its students in an excellent position to start their careers." "People will hire you because they know you can work since you have been doing nothing but working the past four years of your life," says a student. For those students who visited PayScale. com, forty-nine percent reported feeling that their job was making a meaningful impact on the world.

Carnegie Mellon University

FINANCIAL AID: 412-268-8186 • E-MAIL: UNDERGRADUATE-ADMISSIONS@ANDREW.CMU.EDU • WEBSITE: WWW.CMU.EDU

GENERAL INFO

Activities: Choral groups, concert band, dance, drama/theater, literary magazine, marching band, music ensembles, musical theater, pep band, radio station, student government, student newspaper, student-run film society, symphony orchestra, television station, yearbook, Campus Ministries, International Student Organization. **Organizations:** 303 registered organizations, 29 religious organizations. 13 fraternities, 10 sororities. **Athletics (Intercollegiate):** *Men:* basketball, cheerleading, cross-country, diving, football, golf, soccer, swimming, tennis, track/field (outdoor). *Women:* basketball, cheerleading, cross country, diving, golf, soccer, swimming, tennis, track/field (outdoor), volleyball. **On-Campus Highlights:** Cohon Center, Hunt Library, The Cut, The Fence, The Underground, Pausch Bridge, Gates Café, Skibo Café, Bagpiping.

FINANCIAL AID

Students should submit: FAFSA, CSS/Financial Aid PROFILE, Noncustodial PROFILE. Priority filing deadline is 2/15. The Princeton Review suggests that all financial aid forms be submitted as soon as possible after October 1. *Need-based scholarships/grants offered:* Federal Pell, FSEOG, State scholarships/grants, Private scholarships, College/university scholarship or grant aid from institutional funds. *Loan aid offered:* Direct Subsidized Stafford Loans, Direct Unsubsidized Stafford Loans, Direct PLUS loans. Applicants will be notified of awards on or about 4/15. Federal Work-Study Program available. Institutional employment available.

BOTTOM LINE

As a private institution, the cost of tuition is set at $51,196 for all students regardless of state residence; add on another $12,960 for room and board (all incoming freshmen are required to live on campus). Once all fees and additional expenses (such as books and supplies) are factored in, incoming freshmen can expect to pay about $67,980. International students are not eligible to receive financial aid.

CAREER INFORMATION FROM PAYSCALE.COM

ROI rating	91
Bachelor's and No Higher	
Median starting salary	$64,700
Median mid-career salary	$118,000
At Least Bachelor's	
Median starting salary	$68,200
Median mid-career salary	$125,000
% alumni with high job meaning	46%
% STEM	51%

SELECTIVITY

Admissions Rating	98
# of applicants	20,547
% of applicants accepted	24
% of acceptees attending	32
# offered a place on the wait list	5,526
% accepting a place on wait list	51
% admitted from wait list	0
# of early decision applicants	1,143
% accepted early decision	29

FRESHMAN PROFILE

Range SAT Critical Reading	650–740
Range SAT Math	710–800
Range SAT Writing	670–760
Range ACT Composite	31–34
Minimum internet-based TOEFL	102
Average HS GPA	3.8
% graduated top 10% of class	78
% graduated top 25% of class	95
% graduated top 50% of class	99

DEADLINES

Early decision	
Deadline	11/1
Notification	12/15
Regular	
Deadline	1/1
Notification	4/15
Nonfall registration?	No

FINANCIAL FACTS

Financial Aid Rating	83
Annual tuition	$51,196
Room and board	$12,960
Required fees	$844
Average need-based scholarship	$31,417
% needy frosh rec. need-based scholarship or grant aid	96
% needy UG rec. need-based scholarship or grant aid	96
% needy frosh rec. non-need-based scholarship or grant aid	19
% needy UG rec. non-need-based scholarship or grant aid	11
% needy frosh rec. need-based self-help aid	79
% needy UG rec. need-based self-help aid	87
% frosh need fully met	29
% ugrads need fully met	24
Average % of frosh need met	84
Average % of ugrad need met	82

Case Western Reserve University

WOLSTEIN HALL, CLEVELAND, OH 44106-7055 • ADMISSIONS: 216-368-4450 • FAX: 216-368-5111

CAMPUS LIFE

Quality of Life Rating	89
Fire Safety Rating	87
Green Rating	94
Type of school	Private
Affiliation	No Affiliation
Environment	Metropolis

STUDENTS

Total undergrad enrollment	5,121
% male/female	55/45
% from out of state	60
% frosh from public high school	70
% frosh live on campus	99
% ugrads live on campus	80
# of fraternities (% ugrad men join)	18 (34)
# of sororities (% ugrad women join)	9 (39)
% African American	5
% Asian	20
% Caucasian	52
% Hispanic	6
% Native American	<1
% Pacific Islander	<1
% Two or more races	4
% Race and/or ethnicity unknown	2
% international	11
# of countries represented	35

ACADEMICS

Academic Rating	87
% students returning for sophomore year	94
% students graduating within 4 years	63
% students graduating within 6 years	81
Calendar	Semester
Student/faculty ratio	11:1
Profs interesting rating	75
Profs accessible rating	81

Most classes have 10–19 students.
Most lab/discussion sessions have
fewer than 10 students.

MOST POPULAR MAJORS
Mechanical Engineering; Biology;
Psychology

#44 COLLEGE THAT PAYS YOU BACK

ABOUT THE SCHOOL
More than seventy-five majors, small class sizes, and a 11:1 student-to-faculty ratio guarantee that students at Case Western Reserve University have access to a unique combination of all the opportunities of a big school with all of the individual attention of a small school. The research behemoth stresses a lot of interdisciplinary learning from a research, clinical, experiential, classroom, and social perspective, and the strong SAGES program (Seminar Approach to General Education and Scholarship) offers undergrads a series of small, interdisciplinary seminars throughout the entirety of their time at CWRU. Professors are "sociable and eminently approachable" and "truly believe that their job is to educate students, be it in the laboratory or in the classroom." CWRU relies heavily on student initiative, creating "a close knit community centered around the cultivation of the intellect."

BANG FOR YOUR BUCK
CWRU doesn't want sticker prices to deter any student from receiving an education, and is "very generous with aid, whether it is financial or merit-based," working with each student to develop a tailored assistance package. Eighty-seven percent of students receive financial aid of some form, with the average freshman scholarship/grant package coming in at $29,932. In addition to need-based scholarships, students may receive general academic scholarships, including a variety of awards based on specific academic interests, such as the Bolton Scholarship, Michelson-Morley STEM Scholarship, and University Scholarship. Students are automatically considered for most available scholarships when they apply to CWRU.

STUDENT LIFE
Case Western Reserve's location in Cleveland offers a campus that still feels "collegiate" with the cultural benefits of a city; the school has a free access program to most museums, and the programming board "does a great job of planning events to restaurants, events, and concerts." In the summer, the beach is nearby, and skiing and snowboarding are equally a cinch in the winter. Students tend to be "Renaissance men and women," "jack[s]-of-all-trades" who get along "because there is something we end up working on together at some point." Most balance a full schedule, multiple campus organizations, and "still find time to go out and have fun on weekends." Leaders on campus often talk about how CWRU is "over-programmed"; there are "so many active organizations putting together events all the time that it's impossible to go to everything."

CAREER
The academic atmosphere at CWRU is "competitive and full of opportunities for research or internship experience." Opportunities for co-ops, lab experience, shadowing, and volunteering with some of the world's top organizations help to overlay classroom theory with hands-on applications, and Case Western Reserve's science and tech programs act as a natural feeder to the booming healthcare and biotechnology industries in Cleveland. "A student need only simply look, or ask career services," says one. In addition to being academics, professors include "professionals in the work force who bring those experiences to the classroom for a much more enhanced education," and can become the foundation of a contact network for jobs after graduation. Many engineering students at Case Western Reserve also take part in a co-op, which is a full-time, two-semester-long,

Case Western Reserve University

FINANCIAL AID: 216-368-4530 • E-MAIL: ADMISSION@CASE.EDU • WEBSITE: WWW.CASE.EDU

paid work experience that gives students a head start with potential employers. Students in the College of Arts & Sciences can take part in a similar (but shorter) experience called a practicum. The average starting salary for graduates who visited PayScale.com was $58,000, and 52 percent of these same graduates reported feeling that their job had a meaningful impact on the world.

GENERAL INFO

Activities: Choral groups, concert band, dance, drama/theater, jazz band, literary magazine, marching band, music ensembles, musical theater, pep band, radio station, student government, student newspaper, student-run film society, symphony orchestra, yearbook, Campus Ministries, International Student Organization, Model UN. **Organizations:** 150 registered organizations, 8 honor societies, 4 religious organizations. 18 fraternities, 9 sororities. **Athletics (Intercollegiate):** *Men:* baseball, basketball, cross-country, football, soccer, swimming, tennis, track/field (outdoor), track/field (indoor), wrestling. *Women:* basketball, cross-country, soccer, softball, swimming, tennis, track/field (outdoor), track/field (indoor), volleyball. **On-Campus Highlights:** North Residential Village, Peter B. Lewis Building, Kelvin Smith Library, Veale Convocation and Athletic Center, Tinkham Veale University Center.

FINANCIAL AID

Students should submit: FAFSA, CSS/Financial Aid PROFILE, Noncustodial PROFILE. Priority filing deadline is 11/15. The Princeton Review suggests that all financial aid forms be submitted as soon as possible after October 1. *Need-based scholarships/grants offered:* Federal Pell, FSEOG, State scholarships/grants, Private scholarships, College/university scholarship or grant aid from institutional funds. *Loan aid offered:* Direct Subsidized Stafford Loans, Direct Unsubsidized Stafford Loans, Direct PLUS loans, Federal Perkins Loans, College/university loans from institutional funds. Applicants will be notified of awards on a rolling basis beginning 12/15. Federal Work-Study Program available. Institutional employment available.

BOTTOM LINE

Tuition runs at $45,592, with $14,298 being added on for room and board. With all fees incorporated, the total cost for freshman year is $63,929. CWRU suggests that students all live on campus, but those returning students who choose to commute typically receive less need-based grant assistance (around $12,300 less) than those who live on campus. Sixty percent of students also choose to borrow through a loan program to cover costs, graduating with an average loan debt of $30,561.

CAREER INFORMATION FROM PAYSCALE.COM

ROI rating	**90**
Bachelor's and No Higher	
Median starting salary	$58,400
Median mid-career salary	$103,000
At Least Bachelor's	
Median starting salary	$58,600
Median mid-career salary	$108,000
% alumni with high job meaning	47%
% STEM	52%

SELECTIVITY

Admissions Rating	94
# of applicants	22,807
% of applicants accepted	36
% of acceptees attending	15
# offered a place on the wait list	9,446
% accepting a place on wait list	54
% admitted from wait list	10
# of early decision applicants	341
% accepted early decision	32

FRESHMAN PROFILE

Range SAT Critical Reading	620–720
Range SAT Math	680–770
Range SAT Writing	620–720
Range ACT Composite	30–33
Minimum paper TOEFL	577
Minimum internet-based TOEFL	90
% graduated top 10% of class	71
% graduated top 25% of class	91
% graduated top 50% of class	99

DEADLINES

Early decision	
Deadline	11/1
Notification	12/15
Early action	
Deadline	11/1
Notification	12/15
Regular	
Deadline	1/15
Notification	3/20
Nonfall registration?	Yes

FINANCIAL FACTS

Financial Aid Rating	91
Annual tuition	$45,592
Room and board	$14,298
Required fees	$414
Average need-based scholarship	$28,347
% needy frosh rec. need-based scholarship or grant aid	97
% needy UG rec. need-based scholarship or grant aid	97
% needy frosh rec. non-need-based scholarship or grant aid	25
% needy UG rec. non-need-based scholarship or grant aid	13
% needy frosh rec. need-based self-help aid	80
% needy UG rec. need-based self-help aid	85
% frosh rec. any financial aid	83
% UG rec. any financial aid	87
% UG borrow to pay for school	57
Average cumulative indebtedness	$28,562

Centre College

600 West Walnut Street, Danville, KY 40422 • Admissions: 800-423-6236 • Fax: 859-238-5373

CAMPUS LIFE

Quality of Life Rating	91
Fire Safety Rating	76
Green Rating	60*
Type of school	Private
Affiliation	Presbyterian
Environment	Village

STUDENTS

Total undergrad enrollment	1,367
% male/female	50/50
% from out of state	47
% frosh from public high school	66
% frosh live on campus	99
% ugrads live on campus	98
# of fraternities (% ugrad men join)	6 (40)
# of sororities (% ugrad women join)	4 (41)
% African American	5
% Asian	4
% Caucasian	77
% Hispanic	3
% Native American	<1
% Pacific Islander	<1
% Two or more races	3
% Race and/or ethnicity unknown	1
% international	7
# of countries represented	13

ACADEMICS

Academic Rating	91
% students returning for sophomore year	89
% students graduating within 4 years	83
% students graduating within 6 years	86
Calendar	4/1/4
Student/faculty ratio	10:1
Profs interesting rating	97
Profs accessible rating	98

Most classes have 10–19 students.
Most lab/discussion sessions have 10–19 students.

MOST POPULAR MAJORS
Economics & Finance; Psychology; Biology

ABOUT THE SCHOOL

Centre College provides its students with a personal education that enables them to achieve extraordinary success in advanced study and their careers, "bringing a worldwide cultural intellect and perspective to a small town in Kentucky," according to a grateful undergraduate. Professors challenge their students and give them the individual attention and support they need. Courses are "pertinent to modern issues and thought," says a student. This results in graduates with a can-do attitude and the ability to accomplish their goals. "Preparing students to be actively engaged global citizens" is important here, one student tells us. Academics are of course paramount, but Centre also puts emphasis on community involvement and the social development of its students; there is "a big movement on getting out of the classroom with the community-based learning." "If a professor doesn't require that kind of learning," a student explains, "then they almost always will still make connections outside the classroom whether to real life or to other classes." While Centre is in a small town in rural Kentucky, "there is never a dull moment." Centre College has an active campus life. Fraternities and sororities have a big presence, but one student says, "There are a lot of students who are involved in Greek life, but there are a fair amount who are not involved in any way."

BANG FOR YOUR BUCK

Centre offers a multitude of advantages, such as a recognized academic reputation, a plethora of majors to choose from, and exposure to internationally known artists and scholars; benefits like these produce extraordinary success. For example, entrance to top graduate and professional schools; the most prestigious postgraduate scholarships (Rhodes, Fulbright, Goldwater); interesting, rewarding jobs (97 percent of graduates are either employed or engaged in advance study within ten months of graduation). Centre has an impressively strong study abroad program, and about eighty-five percent of their students take advantage; it "allows every student the chance to study abroad, regardless of major or financial situation," reports one student. Another undergrad states proudly that Centre "looks toward the future...of our world and the need for students to be prepared for it." Just about everyone gets a job or accepted into some sort of graduate school after graduation. "They took a chance by letting me attend. I had a below average ACT score than the college accepted. They offered me a great scholarship that allowed attending their school financially feasible. I honor their decision by doing my best, which has led me not only to good grades but also a life changing experience."

STUDENT LIFE

"When you go to Centre," says one behavioral neuroscience major, "you know that there is always someone to keep you accountable, to listen to you, and to help you when you need it." With eighty-one student organizations to choose from and 98 percent of students living on campus, this small Kentucky school—enrollment is roughly 1,400—provides many options for its students. Greek life plays a large role on campus, with four sororities and six fraternities available to pledge; nearly half the students (40 percent of women and 42 percent of men) join a sorority or fraternity. While weekends are often dominated by frat parties, "during the week, there are sporting events and tailgates sponsored by the Student Activities Council, religious group meetings, Midnight Movie events, convocations, and concerts at the Norton Center for the Arts." One English and Religion major noted that "we have this phrase at Centre called 'The Centre Bubble'—we get...wrapped up in life at Centre." While students agree that there aren't many social opportunities in the town of Danville, the "Student Activities Council always has something up [its sleeve] that is fun."

Centre College

FINANCIAL AID: 859-238-5365 • E-MAIL: ADMISSION@CENTRE.EDU • WEBSITE: WWW.CENTRE.EDU

CAREER

The Center for Career & Professional Development at Centre promises students that its staff "are here to help you apply for internships, jobs and graduate school, as well as explore your career options and interests." From the career center's website, students can watch tutorial videos from CareerSpots.com, which provides "a series of short videos on career related topics such as networking, interviewing, job fairs, etiquette, and more." One Computer Science major raved that Centre "guarantees an internship" or research experience, and other students praise the professors' helpfulness in tracking down and applying for internships. After graduating, a Biology major noted that the "alumni network is HUGE, and really helpful once you leave Centre." Popular majors for Centre students include economics and finance, philosophy, and history with popular post-Centre fields like financial services, education, and health/medicine.

GENERAL INFO

Activities: Choral groups, dance, drama/theater, jazz band, literary magazine, music ensembles, musical theater, opera, pep band, student government, student newspaper, symphony orchestra, television station, Campus Ministries, International Student Organization, 70 registered organizations, 12 honor societies, 6 religious organizations. 6 fraternities, 4 sororities. **Athletics (Intercollegiate):** *Men:* baseball, basketball, cross-country, diving, football, golf, lacrosse, soccer, swimming, tennis, track/field (outdoor). *Women:* basketball, cross-country, diving, field hockey, golf, lacrosse, soccer, softball, swimming, tennis, track/field (outdoor), volleyball.

FINANCIAL AID

Students should submit: FAFSA, Institution's own financial aid form. Regular filing deadline is 1/31. The Princeton Review suggests that all financial aid forms be submitted as soon as possible after October 1. *Need-based scholarships/grants offered:* Federal Pell, FSEOG, State scholarships/grants, Private scholarships, College/university scholarship or grant aid from institutional funds. *Loan aid offered:* Direct Subsidized Stafford Loans, Direct Unsubsidized Stafford Loans, Direct PLUS loans, Federal Perkins Loans, College/university loans from institutional funds. Applicants will be notified of awards on a rolling basis beginning 3/19. Federal Work-Study Program available. Institutional employment available.

BOTTOM LINE

Centre's small but capable student body reflects solid academic preparation from high school. If you're ranked in the top quarter of your graduating class and have taken challenging courses throughout high school, you should have no difficulties with the admissions process. Tuition, room, board, books, and supplies will come to $47,800 at Centre College. However, since Centre meets on average 83 percent of student need, an education of the caliber provided by the school is still within reach for most applicants. The average need-based financial aid package is substantial, at around $26,886. Centre College provided one undergraduate with a "good financial aid package and made it possible for a student with little financial means to study abroad." Upon graduation, student loan debt is a very reasonable $25,269.

CAREER INFORMATION FROM PAYSCALE.COM

ROI rating	88
Bachelor's and No Higher	
Median starting salary	$39,700
Median mid-career salary	$86,700
At Least Bachelor's	
Median starting salary	$40,900
Median mid-career salary	$87,900
% STEM	17%

SELECTIVITY

Admissions Rating	**89**
# of applicants	2,716
% of applicants accepted	71
% of acceptees attending	19
# offered a place on the wait list	183
% accepting a place on wait list	23
% admitted from wait list	45
# of early decision applicants	100
% accepted early decision	68

FRESHMAN PROFILE

Range SAT Critical Reading	540–660
Range SAT Math	570–740
Range ACT Composite	26–31
Minimum paper TOEFL	580
Minimum internet-based TOEFL	90
Average HS GPA	3.6
% graduated top 10% of class	54
% graduated top 25% of class	84
% graduated top 50% of class	97

DEADLINES

Early decision	
Deadline	11/15
Notification	12/15
Early action	
Deadline	12/1
Notification	1/15
Regular	
Deadline	1/15
Notification	3/15
Nonfall registration?	No

FINANCIAL FACTS

Financial Aid Rating	**86**
Annual tuition	$39,300
Room and board	$9,950
Average need-based scholarship	$26,886
% needy frosh rec. need-based scholarship or grant aid	100
% needy UG rec. need-based scholarship or grant aid	100
% needy frosh rec. non-need-based scholarship or grant aid	0
% needy UG rec. non-need-based scholarship or grant aid	0
% needy frosh rec. need-based self-help aid	62
% needy UG rec. need-based self-help aid	65
% frosh rec. any financial aid	97
% UG rec. any financial aid	96
% UG borrow to pay for school	55
Average cumulative indebtedness	$28,515
% frosh need fully met	37
% ugrads need fully met	31

City University of New York—Baruch College

UNDERGRADUATE ADMISSIONS, 151 EAST 25TH STREET, NEW YORK, NY 10010 • ADMISSIONS: 646-312-1400 • FAX: 646-312-1363

CAMPUS LIFE

Quality of Life Rating	**82**
Fire Safety Rating	**60***
Green Rating	**62**
Type of school	Public
Affiliation	No Affiliation
Environment	Metropolis

STUDENTS

Total undergrad enrollment	15,254
% male/female	51/49
% from out of state	3
% frosh from public high school	89
% ugrads live on campus	2
% African American	9
% Asian	32
% Caucasian	23
% Hispanic	23
% Native American	<1
% Pacific Islander	<1
% Two or more races	2
% Race and/or ethnicity unknown	0
% international	11
# of countries represented	174

ACADEMICS

Academic Rating	**80**
% students returning for sophomore year	91
% students graduating within 4 years	42
% students graduating within 6 years	70
Calendar	Semester
Student/faculty ratio	17:1
Profs interesting rating	80
Profs accessible rating	71

Most classes have 20–29 students.

Most lab/discussion sessions have 20–29 students.

MOST POPULAR MAJORS
Accounting; Finance

ABOUT THE SCHOOL

Baruch College consists of three schools, and while its Wiessman School of Arts and Sciences and Austin W. Marxe School of Public and International Affairs both have strong reputations, it's the Zicklin School of Business that garners nearly all the attention here (as well over three-quarters of the student body). Zicklin offers a "very demanding business-oriented program that provides a great education" and "professionalism and real life experiences prior to graduation, especially being in the middle of the financial center of the world." Baruch has no campus, just a collection of six buildings scattered over four city blocks. Most of the action centers around the "beautiful" seventeen-story Newman Vertical Campus facility. It may not offer the traditional on-campus experience, but it does have a faculty filled with professors at the cutting edge of their fields, a simulated trading floor for future brokers, a three-floor athletic and recreation complex, and the myriad opportunities for entertainment, cultural enrichment, volunteering, networking, and just plain fun that fill New York City.

BANG FOR YOUR BUCK

Baruch's location and connections provide "a gateway to the world of finance," and with many students citing its low cost relative to other schools in the area and a "large [number] of students [with] full scholarships or heavy financial aid," Baruch is widely considered "the best college value in New York City." The career office "works tirelessly to prepare its students for the working world. Not only do they offer workshops on how to make yourself an attractive candidate, they also offer counseling and even résumé reviews to make sure your résumé is perfect, as well as mock interviews that help you analyze your strengths and weaknesses as an interviewer."

STUDENT LIFE

Baruch is really a "commuter" school, so there might not be quite as much campus unity as you'd find at a residential college. However, that doesn't mean that the school shuts down as soon as classes are over. Indeed, we're told that there are "an abundance of clubs" in which many students participate. And undoubtedly, in between classes, numerous undergrads can be found lounging around the "game room [playing] . . . ping pong, pool and foosball." Many students also rave about Baruch's gym, which is replete with "swimming pool, tennis court and handball court." And they can always catch one of the many shows "playing at the beautiful Performing Arts Center." Of course, these students don't necessarily need to rely on their school for fun. Being located in New York City means endless possibilities "from museum visits, to the best restaurants and bars, parks, the best shopping, concerts [all] . . . just a ten minute train ride away!"

City University of New York—Baruch College

FINANCIAL AID: 646-312-1360 • E-MAIL: ADMISSIONS@BARUCH.CUNY.EDU • WEBSITE: WWW.BARUCH.CUNY.EDU

CAREER

Baruch does a fantastic job of "preparing students for very successful careers." Certainly, some of this stems from the fact that the college really "enforce[s] networking as an important [search] tool." Beyond the usual networking and resume tutorials, the Starr Career Development Center runs a number of programs to help undergrads jumpstart their professional lives. For example, Executives On Campus pairs students with mentors who can advise them on interviewing, managing career trajectories and other soft skills. This helps to ensure that Baruch undergrads enter competitive job markets fully prepared. Additionally, programs like the Max Berger Pre-Law Program provide students with pre-law advising, workshops and practical information regarding legal careers. And, fortunately, Baruch's robust On Campus Recruiting (OCR) program helps undergrads find and secure internships and entry-level jobs.

GENERAL INFO

Activities: Choral groups, dance, drama/theater, literary magazine, musical theater, radio station, student government, student newspaper, yearbook, Campus Ministries, Model UN 172 registered organizations, 9 honor societies, 7 religious organizations. 9 fraternities, 7 sororities. **Athletics (Intercollegiate):** *Men:* baseball, basketball, cross-country, soccer, swimming, tennis, volleyball. *Women:* basketball, cheerleading, cross-country, softball, swimming, tennis, volleyball. **On-Campus Highlights:** Student Club Area—Vertical Campus Build, NewMan Library, Lobby—23 St. Building, Food Court—Vertical Campus Building, College Fitness Center—Vertical Campus.

FINANCIAL AID

Students should submit: FAFSA, State aid form. Priority filing deadline is 4/15. The Princeton Review suggests that all financial aid forms be submitted as soon as possible after October 1. *Need-based scholarships/ grants offered:* Federal Pell, FSEOG, State scholarships/grants, Private scholarships, College/university scholarship or grant aid from institutional funds. *Loan aid offered:* Direct Subsidized Stafford Loans, Direct Unsubsidized Stafford Loans, Direct PLUS loans, Federal Perkins Loans. Applicants will be notified of awards on a rolling basis beginning 4/15. Federal Work-Study Program available. Institutional employment available.

THE BOTTOM LINE

Many, many students cite Baruch's generous financial aid packages as their reason for choosing to attend. Even if you're paying out of pocket, tuition here is low—and factoring in the school's strong reputation and awesome location, it's a truly amazing deal. If you're a New York state resident, annual tuition for a full-time undergrad is about $6,330, or for part-timers, $275 per credit. Full-time out-of-staters will pay $16,800 annually, which is significantly lower than many northeast colleges, both public and private.

CAREER INFORMATION FROM PAYSCALE.COM

ROI rating	89
Bachelor's and No Higher	
Median starting salary	$50,700
Median mid-career salary	$86,200
At Least Bachelor's	
Median starting salary	$51,200
Median mid-career salary	$87,000
% alumni with high job meaning	32%
% STEM	4%

SELECTIVITY

Admissions Rating	91
# of applicants	19,864
% of applicants accepted	32
% of acceptees attending	23

FRESHMAN PROFILE

Range SAT Critical Reading	520–630
Range SAT Math	580–690
Minimum paper TOEFL	550
Minimum internet-based TOEFL	80
Average HS GPA	3.3
% graduated top 10% of class	48
% graduated top 25% of class	78
% graduated top 50% of class	93

DEADLINES

Early decision	
Deadline	12/13
Notification	1/7
Other ED	
Deadline	12/13
Other ED	
Notification	1/7
Regular	
Priority	12/1
Deadline	2/1
Notification	5/1
Nonfall registration?	Yes

FINANCIAL FACTS

Financial Aid Rating	80
Annual in-state tuition	$6,330
Annual out-of-state tuition	$16,800
Room and board	$13,768
Required fees	$531
Average need-based scholarship	$7,269
% needy frosh rec. need-based scholarship or grant aid	100
% needy UG rec. need-based scholarship or grant aid	100
% needy frosh rec. non-need-based scholarship or grant aid	6
% needy UG rec. non-need-based scholarship or grant aid	2
% needy frosh rec. need-based self-help aid	15
% needy UG rec. need-based self-help aid	27
% frosh rec. any financial aid	59
% UG rec. any financial aid	61
% frosh need fully met	11
% ugrads need fully met	10
Average % of frosh need met	65
Average % of ugrad need met	56

City University of New York—Brooklyn College

2900 BEDFORD AVENUE, BROOKLYN, NY 11210 • ADMISSIONS: 718-951-5001 • FAX: 718-951-4506

CAMPUS LIFE

Quality of Life Rating	**83**
Fire Safety Rating	**60***
Green Rating	**60***
Type of school	Public
Affiliation	No Affiliation
Environment	Metropolis

STUDENTS

Total undergrad enrollment	14,207
% male/female	41/59
% from out of state	2
% frosh from public high school	83
% frosh live on campus	0
% ugrads live on campus	0
# of fraternities (% ugrad men join)	7 (3)
# of sororities (% ugrad women join)	9 (3)
% African American	22
% Asian	18
% Caucasian	33
% Hispanic	22
% Native American	<1
% Pacific Islander	<1
% Two or more races	2
% Race and/or ethnicity unknown	0
% international	4
# of countries represented	150

ACADEMICS

Academic Rating	**73**
% students returning for sophomore year	82
% students graduating within 4 years	24
% students graduating within 6 years	54
Calendar	Semester
Student/faculty ratio	16:1
Profs interesting rating	70
Profs accessible rating	68
Most classes have 20–29 students.	

MOST POPULAR MAJORS

Psychology; Accounting; Business Administration and Management

ABOUT THE SCHOOL

Respected nationally for its rigorous academic standards, the college takes pride in such innovative programs as its award-winning Freshman Year College; the Honors Academy, which houses six programs for high achievers; and its nationally recognized core curriculum. Its School of Education is ranked among the top twenty in the country, for graduates who go on to be considered among the best teachers in New York City. Brooklyn College's strong academic reputation has attracted an outstanding faculty of nationally renowned teachers and scholars. Among the awards they have won are Pulitzers, Guggenheims, Fulbrights, and many National Institutes of Health grants. The Brooklyn College campus, considered to be among the most beautiful in the nation, is in the midst of an ambitious program of expansion and renewal.

Education at the college is taken seriously, and the curriculum is challenging. Students mention that "the material is engaging and interesting while the professors are first-rate"; "I find myself learning beyond the course description." There is respect for the opinions of their students, and "each professor allows students to have free reign of their thoughts and ideas," one student says admiringly. Another satisfied undergrad tells us that "it is hard to estimate my academic gains, but they have been substantial." Additionally, each student is assigned a peer mentor and a counseling class that "helps us adapt to college life. I think that it helped me to be a more active student."

STUDENT LIFE

"The typical student at Brooklyn College is hardworking, from the New York metro area, and a commuter." Many "hold part-time jobs and pay at least part of their own tuition, so they are usually in a rush because they have a lot more responsibility on their shoulders than the average college student." Like Brooklyn itself, "the student body is very diversified," with everyone from "an aspiring opera singer to quirky film majors to single mothers looking for a better life for their children," and so "no student can be described as being typical. Everyone blends in as normal, and little segregation is noticed (if it exists)." Students here represent more than 100 nations and speak nearly as many languages. There are even students "that come from Long Island to North Carolina, from Connecticut to even Hong Kong." The college's accessibility by subway or bus allows students to further enrich their educational experience through New York City's many cultural events and institutions. It should be noted that there are now new dorms for students, and that this is very exciting.

CAREER

The typical Brooklyn College graduate has a starting salary of around $43,400, and 43 percent of graduates feel their jobs have a lot of meaning in their lives. Students feel that Brooklyn College "is an outstanding school with a very good reputation of successful alumni," and that "there are a lot of volunteering programs and internships available." Students feel that "Brooklyn College is a school that attempts to provide an effective education for people in need of career advancement." The Magner Career Center partners with employers, faculty and staff, alumni and students to provide career programs, services and resources.

City University of New York—Brooklyn College

FINANCIAL AID: 718-951-5045 • WEBSITE: WWW.BROOKLYN.CUNY.EDU

GENERAL INFO

Activities: dance, drama/theater, literary magazine, music ensembles, musical theater, radio station, student government, student newspaper, television station, yearbook, international student organization. **Organizations:** 171 registered organizations, 7 honor societies, 8 fraternities, 9 sororities. **Athletics (Intercollegiate):** *Men:* Basketball, cross-country, soccer, tennis, track/field (outdoor), track/field (indoor), volleyball. *Women:* Basketball, cross-country, softball, tennis, track/field (outdoor), track/field (indoor), volleyball. **On-Campus Highlights:** Library, Student Center, Lily Pond, Library Cafe, Cafeteria, Dining Hall, Magner Center, James Hall. **Environmental Initiatives:** Reduce consumption; awareness.

FINANCIAL AID

Students should submit: FAFSA. Priority filing deadline is 4/1. The Princeton Review suggests that all financial aid forms be submitted as soon as possible after October 1. *Need-based scholarships/grants offered:* Federal Pell, FSEOG, State scholarships/grants, Private scholarships, College/university scholarship or grant aid from institutional funds. *Loan aid offered:* Direct Subsidized Stafford Loans, Direct Unsubsidized Stafford Loans, Direct PLUS loans, Federal Perkins Loans. Applicants will be notified of awards on a rolling basis beginning 5/1. Federal Work-Study Program available. Institutional employment available.

BOTTOM LINE

Brooklyn College provides students with an excellent education for a cost that will not break any banks—piggy or otherwise. Fortunately, in-state tuition runs only $6,330 or so; out-of-state tuition comes to $16,800. Perhaps most importantly, the institution is able to meet 92 percent of all need. Undergraduates average $3,400 in need-based gift aid; financial aid packages generally come to about $7,500.

CAREER INFORMATION FROM PAYSCALE.COM

ROI rating	84
Bachelor's and No Higher	
Median starting salary	$42,000
Median mid-career salary	$77,800
At Least Bachelor's	
Median starting salary	$42,400
Median mid-career salary	$80,700
% alumni with high job meaning	47%
% STEM	10%

SELECTIVITY

Admissions Rating	88
# of applicants	20,324
% of applicants accepted	37
% of acceptees attending	18

FRESHMAN PROFILE

Range SAT Critical Reading	470–570
Range SAT Math	500–610
Minimum paper TOEFL	500
Average HS GPA	3.3
% graduated top 10% of class	18
% graduated top 25% of class	50
% graduated top 50% of class	78

DEADLINES

Regular	
Priority	2/1
Nonfall registration?	Yes

FINANCIAL FACTS

Financial Aid Rating	89
Annual in-state tuition	$6,330
Annual out-of-state tuition	$16,800
Required fees	$508
Average need-based scholarship	$3,400
% needy frosh rec. non-need-based scholarship or grant aid	23
% needy UG rec. non-need-based scholarship or grant aid	24
% needy frosh rec. need-based self-help aid	68
% needy UG rec. need-based self-help aid	77
% frosh rec. any financial aid	80
% UG rec. any financial aid	79
% UG borrow to pay for school	18
Average cumulative indebtedness	$14,313
% frosh need fully met	65
% ugrads need fully met	71
Average % of frosh need met	88
Average % of ugrad need met	89

City University of New York—City College

160 Convent Avenue, Wille Administration Building, New York, NY 10031 • Admissions: 212-650-6977 • Fax: 212-650-6417

CAMPUS LIFE

Quality of Life Rating	86
Fire Safety Rating	97
Green Rating	92
Type of school	Public
Environment	Metropolis

STUDENTS

Total undergrad enrollment	13,436
% male/female	49/51
% from out of state	1
% frosh from public high school	85
% ugrads live on campus	4
# of fraternities	2
# of sororities	1
% African American	16
% Asian	25
% Caucasian	15
% Hispanic	35
% Native American	<1
% Pacific Islander	<1
% Two or more races	2
% Race and/or ethnicity unknown	0
% international	6
# of countries represented	100

ACADEMICS

Academic Rating	75
% students returning for sophomore year	86
% students graduating within 4 years	11
% students graduating within 6 years	44
Calendar	Quarter
Student/faculty ratio	12:1
Profs interesting rating	71
Profs accessible rating	68

Most classes have 20–29 students.
Most lab/discussion sessions have
20–29 students.

MOST POPULAR MAJORS
Communication and Media Studies;
Mechanical Engineering; Psychology

ABOUT THE SCHOOL

Founded in 1847, City College offers a prestigious education to a diverse student body. With its "astonishingly low cost," "great engineering program," "strong ties to research collaborators and institutions," and an art program that's "also one of the best" in the metro area, indeed, City College earns its claim of being one of "America's finest democratic achievements." When it comes to the school's main draws, students cite the three C's: "convenience, cost, and concentration." The school "is known for its rigorous academic programs," which "rival that of the nation's premier universities." Additionally, "it is affordable," which students are quick to note "is an important factor in these tough economic times." With total undergraduate enrollment at just under 13,000, City College is all about embracing diversity and harnessing personal dedication. Professors are "attentive" and classes are "challenging." Professors "exhibit great love for the materials they teach and generally go above and beyond to ensure that students are able to grasp and apply the material." What's better? All this learning takes place in New York City, with its wealth of professional opportunities.

BANG FOR YOUR BUCK

More than 80 percent of the entering class at City College receives some type of financial aid. In addition, in the last three years, City has increased the dollar amount going to student scholarships by 35 percent. It pays to be an exceptional student when your application comes through the admissions office, as many of the students receiving merit-based awards are members of the City College Honors program. In addition, the Macaulay Honors College at City College offers students a free laptop computer, a cultural passport to New York City, and a $7,500 educational expense account. Many scholarships are awarded on the basis of the major or entrance to a specific school of the college.

STUDENT LIFE

As one student proudly contends, "We (the student body in the aggregate) speak over 100 languages and come from places most people have never heard of." The diversity at CCNY is not just limited to ethnicity—it also spans political leanings, economic background, academic interest, age, and professional experience, and—regardless of their origins—most CCNY students "identify first and foremost as New Yorkers." One student says, "CCNY is definitely a diamond in the rough. It should be considered by any student who wants to experience New York City college life at an affordable rate without sacrificing education quality," but warns that one should "expect to hunt for an apartment or a roommate on your own IN ADDITION TO, and not instead of, opting for on-campus housing." Most CCNY students are not looking for the "typical college experience," but rather are interested "in the intellectual and emotional growth that comes with higher education."

CAREER

The typical City College graduate has a starting salary of around $52,500, and 60 percent of graduates feel their jobs have a lot of meaning in their lives. Students feel that City College "thoroughly prepares its students for their future careers, with emphasis placed on the effects of the current economic climate," and that there are veritable "tons of internship/research opportunities," which students receive frequent e-mail updates about. City College's Career and Professional Development Institute offers a number of services to students and alumni including individual career counseling, internship and job opportunities, resume writing, career fairs, and workshops aimed at developing the professional identity of students and alumni.

City University of New York—City College

FINANCIAL AID: 212-650-5819 • E-MAIL: ADMISSIONS@CCNY.CUNY.EDU • WEBSITE: WWW.CCNY.CUNY.EDU

GENERAL INFO

Activities: Choral groups, concert band, dance, drama/theater, jazz band, literary magazine, radio station, student government, student newspaper, student-run film society, yearbook. **Organizations:** International Student Organization, Model UN. 145 registered organizations, 8 religious organizations. 2 fraternities, 1 sorority. **Athletics (Intercollegiate):** *Men:* baseball, basketball, cross-country, soccer, tennis, track/field (outdoor), track/field (indoor), volleyball. *Women:* basketball, fencing, soccer, tennis, track/field (outdoor), track/field (indoor), volleyball. **On-Campus Highlights:** NAC Rotunda and Plaza, Spitzer School of Architecture, Wingate Hall Athletic Center, North Campus Quad in warm weather, The Towers—Residence Hall. **Environmental Initiatives:** Signed on to ACUPCC and NYC Mayor's Campus 30in10 Challenge to reduce GHG emissions; task force to place sustainability at forefront in all operations, outreach and educational mission; undergraduate and graduate programs in sustainability, interdisciplinary with science, engineering, architecture, and economics.

FINANCIAL AID

Students should submit: FAFSA, State aid form. Priority filing deadline is 3/15. The Princeton Review suggests that all financial aid forms be submitted as soon as possible after October 1. *Need-based scholarships/grants offered:* Federal Pell, FSEOG, State scholarships/grants, College/university scholarship or grant aid from institutional funds. *Loan aid offered:* Direct Subsidized Stafford Loans, Direct Unsubsidized Stafford Loans, Direct PLUS Loans. Applicants will be notified of awards on a rolling basis beginning 4/1. Federal Work-Study Program available. Institutional employment available.

BOTTOM LINE

With in-state tuition holding steady at $6,330 and out-of-state tuition at $16,800 (15 credits per semester), for many, CCNY offers a real opportunity to realize their future at a remarkably affordable cost. Due to its "close ties to the business community of New York City," CCNY "provides an extensive array of contacts and networking opportunities leading to internships and real-life work experiences." Located in historic West Harlem, "students are minutes away from leading organizations in the fields of business, theatre, music, art, law, education, finance, retail, engineering, architecture, science, and medicine." For those career-minded individuals looking to get a jumpstart in the workforce, CCNY provides "true work experience in day-to-day settings."

CAREER INFORMATION FROM PAYSCALE.COM

ROI rating	**87**
Bachelor's and No Higher	
Median starting salary	$51,400
Median mid-career salary	$86,600
At Least Bachelor's	
Median starting salary	$51,800
Median mid-career salary	$87,700
% alumni with high job meaning	49%
% STEM	30%

SELECTIVITY

Admissions Rating	**82**
# of applicants	24,735
% of applicants accepted	40
% of acceptees attending	17

FRESHMAN PROFILE

Range SAT Critical Reading	460–590
Range SAT Math	510–640
Range SAT Writing	450–580
Minimum paper TOEFL	500
Minimum internet-based TOEFL	61

DEADLINES

Regular	
Priority	2/1
Nonfall registration?	Yes

FINANCIAL FACTS

Financial Aid Rating	**91**
Annual in-state tuition	$6,330
Annual out-of-state tuition	$16,800
Room and board	$11,516
Required fees	$410
Average need-based scholarship	$8,145
% needy frosh rec. need-based scholarship or grant aid	91
% needy UG rec. need-based scholarship or grant aid	96
% needy frosh rec. non-need-based scholarship or grant aid	54
% needy UG rec. non-need-based scholarship or grant aid	61
% needy frosh rec. need-based self-help aid	44
% needy UG rec. need-based self-help aid	61
% frosh rec. any financial aid	80
% UG rec. any financial aid	79
% frosh need fully met	74
% ugrads need fully met	82
Average % of frosh need met	84
Average % of ugrad need met	83

City University of New York—Hunter College

695 Park Ave, Room N203, New York, NY 10065 • Admissions: 212-772-4490 • Fax: 212-650-3472

CAMPUS LIFE

Quality of Life Rating	**84**
Fire Safety Rating	**97**
Green Rating	**93**
Type of school	Public
Environment	Metropolis

STUDENTS

Total undergrad enrollment	16,550
% male/female	36/64
% from out of state	3
% frosh from public high school	70
# of fraternities	2
# of sororities	2
% African American	11
% Asian	28
% Caucasian	33
% Hispanic	21
% Native American	<1
% Pacific Islander	0
% Two or more races	0
% Race and/or ethnicity unknown	0
% international	6
# of countries represented	151

ACADEMICS

Academic Rating	**72**
% students returning for sophomore year	82
% students graduating within 4 years	25
% students graduating within 6 years	54
Calendar	Semester
Student/faculty ratio	13:1
Profs interesting rating	69
Profs accessible rating	70
Most classes have 20–29 students.	

MOST POPULAR MAJORS
Psychology; English; Chemistry

ABOUT THE SCHOOL

The City University of New York—Hunter College has a lot to offer beyond its miniscule tuition. For many New Yorkers seeking a top-notch college degree, Hunter offers the best, most affordable option available. Hunter's 15,000-plus students choose from more than seventy undergraduate programs. Regardless of their area of concentration, all Hunter students are encouraged to have broad exposure to the liberal arts: "Hunter is all about bringing people from all different parts of the world together in one place to learn from one another and to be exposed to almost every subject imaginable to help one find their true calling in life," says one sophomore. Though a Hunter College education doesn't come with a lot of frills, the school's faculty is a huge asset. Professors are very often experts in their fields, and they work hard to accommodate undergraduates. One student says, "Many of the professors teach at other, more expensive universities. Throughout my Hunter career, I have had professors who also teach at NYU, Hofstra, Cooper Union, and Yale! So it really is quite the bargain . . . I am not missing out on a challenging, intellectual educational process by attending a public school."

BANG FOR YOUR BUCK

Extraordinarily low tuition makes Hunter affordable, and more than 1,000 scholarships, awards, and special program opportunities offered throughout the CUNY campuses complement that affordability. The usual combination of work-study jobs, need-based grants, scholarships, and credit-bearing internships helps students fund their educations. Need-based grants from the state of New York are available. Hunter offers a variety of scholarship programs for entering freshman who have maintained a high level of academic achievement while in high school and who demonstrate potential for superior scholarship at the college level. Institutional scholarships [at Hunter College] are offered to more than 50 percent of the aid-eligible population. The Macaulay Honors College is definitely one of the highlights. Accepted students receive a full-ride scholarship (except for fees), a laptop computer, and additional funds to pursue research, internships, or service activities. One student boasts: "The Macaulay Honors College allows me access to the best Hunter and CUNY has to offer, and to the wide resources of New York City itself, while paying no tuition." Also, financial sessions are offered at Hunter to incoming students and cover topics such as loans, credit cards, and budgeting. All new students are considered for Hunter College sponsored scholarships automatically—no separate application is required.

STUDENT LIFE

Like many of the CUNY institutions, Hunter College is primarily a commuter school. Fortunately, there's still plenty of camaraderie among these undergrads. Indeed, "Hunter encourages student interaction through Student Government run parties and other student-run activities." And many undergrads are quick to take advantage of the numerous "great events, visiting authors and scientists, guest lectures" happening around campus. Of course, being located in the heart of New York City is also a boon for these students. As one political science major boasts, "It's nearly impossible not to find stuff to do, no matter what your tastes are. The city is our campus, and it's up to you to use it to the fullest."

City University of New York—Hunter College

FINANCIAL AID: 212-772-4820 • E-MAIL: ADMISSIONS@HUNTER.CUNY.EDU • WEBSITE: WWW.HUNTER.CUNY.EDU

CAREER

Hunter's Career Development Services truly does a tremendous job for its students. Undergrads have the opportunity to attend a variety of career panels throughout the year, featuring guest speakers and assorted alumni from a number of industries. Hunter also presents students with many chances to attend different career expos. There, undergrads are able to network, learn about specific corporations and career fields and discover potential job openings. Naturally, the college also works hard to capitalize on its New York City location. Each semester, Hunter invites companies to campus to meet with students regarding internships, part-time jobs and entry-level positions. Undergrads can attend recruiting events in a number of areas: social services, public affairs, film and media, financial services, scientific research, etc. All students, no matter their interests, are bound to find an opening that piques their curiosity.

GENERAL INFO

Activities: Choral groups, concert band, dance, drama/theater, jazz band, literary magazine, music ensembles, musical theater, radio station, student government, student newspaper, student-run film society, symphony orchestra, television station, yearbook. **Organizations:** 150 registered organizations, 20 honor societies, 2 fraternities, 2 sororities. **Athletics (Intercollegiate):** *Men:* Basketball, cross-country, fencing, soccer, tennis, track/field (outdoor), track/field (indoor), volleyball, wrestling. *Women:* Basketball, cross-country, diving, fencing, softball, swimming, tennis, track/field (outdoor), track/field (indoor), volleyball. **On-Campus Highlights:** More than 100 campus clubs, CARSI Geography Lab, Television Studio, Learning Center and Computer Lab, Sports Complex.

FINANCIAL AID

Students should submit: FAFSA, State aid form. Priority filing deadline is 5/1. The Princeton Review suggests that all financial aid forms be submitted as soon as possible after October 1. *Need-based scholarships/ grants offered:* Federal Pell, State scholarships/grants, College/ university scholarship or grant aid from institutional funds. *Loan aid offered:* Direct Subsidized Stafford Loans, Direct Unsubsidized Stafford Loans, Direct PLUS loans, Federal Perkins Loans, State Loans, College/university loans from institutional funds. Applicants will be notified of awards on a rolling basis beginning 5/15. Federal Work-Study Program available. Institutional employment available.

BOTTOM LINE

Full-time tuition for New York residents comes to approximately $6,330. That's ridiculously cheap. If you can't claim state residency, you'll pay about three times that amount. Also, as you know if you are a New Yorker and probably have heard if you aren't, New York City can be a painfully expensive place to live. But that shouldn't dissuade prospective students, since about 94 percent of students receive aid.

SELECTIVITY

Admissions Rating	**84**
# of applicants	28,041
% of applicants accepted	39
% of acceptees attending	20

FRESHMAN PROFILE

Range SAT Critical Reading	520–620
Range SAT Math	510–610
Minimum paper TOEFL	500

DEADLINES

Regular	
Deadline	3/15
Nonfall registration?	Yes

FINANCIAL FACTS

Financial Aid Rating	**84**
Annual in-state tuition	$6,330
Annual out-of-state tuition	$16,800
Room and board	$8,655
Required fees	$450
Average need-based scholarship	$7,202
% needy frosh rec. need-based scholarship or grant aid	89
% needy UG rec. need-based scholarship or grant aid	82
% needy frosh rec. non-need-based scholarship or grant aid	89
% needy UG rec. non-need-based scholarship or grant aid	14
% needy frosh rec. need-based self-help aid	21
% needy UG rec. need-based self-help aid	22
% frosh rec. any financial aid	91
% UG rec. any financial aid	94
% frosh need fully met	20
% ugrads need fully met	13
Average % of frosh need met	73
Average % of ugrad need met	72

CAREER INFORMATION FROM PAYSCALE.COM

ROI rating	**85**
Bachelor's and No Higher	
Median starting salary	$45,800
Median mid-career salary	$78,200
At Least Bachelor's	
Median starting salary	$46,000
Median mid-career salary	$79,500
% alumni with high job meaning	58%
% STEM	6%

Claremont McKenna College

888 COLUMBIA AVENUE, CLAREMONT, CA 91711 • ADMISSIONS: 909-621-8088 • FAX: 909-621-8516

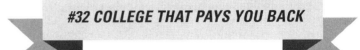

#32 COLLEGE THAT PAYS YOU BACK

ABOUT THE SCHOOL

Part of a new generation of liberal arts colleges, Claremont McKenna was founded in 1946—more than a century later than many of its East Coast counterparts—but it has steadily built a reputation as one of the nation's best small schools. With a total enrollment of just 1,200 students, the average class size is under twenty, making it easy for students to work directly with the school's talented faculty. One literature and government major gushes that her "academic experience has been so rich—full of dinners with professors outside of class and conversations that make me a better scholar and person. I have been doing research on Robert Frost's letters that would usually be reserved for graduate students." Despite the comfortable environment, academics are surprisingly rigorous and varied. Offering a pragmatic approach to the liberal arts, the college is divided into twelve academic departments offering major programs in fields like biochemistry and history, as well as minor programs or "sequences" in unusual areas such as Asian-American studies and leadership. The most popular majors are economics, accounting, finance, government, and international relations. A psychology major relates that "the campus environment is extremely friendly, open, and career-focused. Students at CMC are motivated to make something of themselves in the world." As a part of the five Claremont colleges, Claremont McKenna offers students the intimacy of a small college with the variety of a larger system. Jointly, the colleges offer more than 2,500 courses, and cross-registration is encouraged (as is eating in neighboring colleges' dining halls.)

BANG FOR YOUR BUCK

Not only is CMC need-blind in its admission policies, but the college is committed to meeting every student's financial need through a combination of merit-based scholarships and need-based awards. There is a no-packaged-loan policy. In addition to state and federal grants, the school offers a number of merit-based scholarship awards derived from gifts and endowments given to the college. Army ROTC Scholarships are also available. The school's website offers detailed information about the amount of aid granted to incoming students in recent years based on their family's income level. Furthermore, for students interested in an unpaid internship with a public or nonprofit organization, the Sponsored Internship Program will provide funding for students to pursue internships anywhere in the world.

STUDENT LIFE

The incredibly content undergrads here happily declare that "life at CMC is unbeatable." For starters, students love to take advantage of the beautiful SoCal weather. And many an individual "can often be found throwing around a Frisbee, playing bocce ball, or setting up a slip-n-slide." Of course, these smart students also enjoy intellectual pursuits. Indeed, "there are numerous 'academic' things that people do for fun, such as Mock Trial or attending lectures." Students also rave about the welcoming and fun party scene. Unlike a lot of other schools, the "student government sends out emails weekly informing the students of the parties taking place that weekend." This helps to "unify the whole school and creates a really fun community." Lastly,

Claremont McKenna College

FINANCIAL AID: 909-621-8356 • E-MAIL: ADMISSION@CMC.EDU • WEBSITE: WWW.CMC.EDU

when undergrads are itching to get away, they can head to "amazing places...such as Los Angeles, the beaches, the San Gabriel Mountains, and even as far as Las Vegas and Lake Tahoe."

CAREER

Undergrads at Claremont McKenna love to shower the "AMAZING career services center" with praise. And it's no secret why! The office is with students every step of the way, from initial career exploration to landing that first job offer. Through their alumni career contacts database, the office makes it fairly simple for current students to connect with alums working in industries of interest. Even better, Mentor Connect allows students to find an accomplished alumn and enlist him/her as a mentor. The mentor can provide insight into his/her working world, offer professional (and educational) guidance and networking opportunities. Beyond alumni, CMC's extensive internship database allows undergrads to search through a myriad of interesting opportunities. With all of these outlets, it's no wonder CMC grads are so successful.

FINANCIAL AID

Students should submit: FAFSA, CSS/Financial Aid PROFILE, State aid form, Noncustodial PROFILE, Business/Farm Supplement. Regular filing deadline is 2/1. The Princeton Review suggests that all financial aid forms be submitted as soon as possible after October 1. *Need-based scholarships/grants offered:* Federal Pell, FSEOG, State scholarships/grants, Private scholarships, College/university scholarship or grant aid from institutional funds. *Loan aid offered:* Direct Subsidized Stafford Loans, Direct Unsubsidized Stafford Loans, Direct PLUS loans, Federal Perkins Loans, College/university loans from institutional funds. Applicants will be notified of awards on or about 4/1. Federal Work-Study Program available. Institutional employment available.

BOTTOM LINE

Full-time tuition at Claremont McKenna College is $50,700 annually. Meal plans and housing range in price, but together room and board generally run about $15,740 per semester. As at any private school, the annual cost to attend CMC can be a bit pricey; however, the school offers aid to students in a wide range of financial situations.

CAREER INFORMATION FROM PAYSCALE.COM

ROI rating	92
Bachelor's and No Higher	
Median starting salary	$54,400
Median mid-career salary	$105,000
At Least Bachelor's	
Median starting salary	$50,100
Median mid-career salary	$96,000
% alumni with high job meaning	47%
% STEM	12%

SELECTIVITY

Admissions Rating	98
# of applicants	6,043
% of applicants accepted	11
% of acceptees attending	50
# offered a place on the wait list	614
% accepting a place on wait list	57
% admitted from wait list	11
# of early decision applicants	675
% accepted early decision	26

FRESHMAN PROFILE

Range SAT Critical Reading	660–750
Range SAT Math	690–770
Range SAT Writing	680–760
Range ACT Composite	30–33
Minimum paper TOEFL	600
Minimum internet-based TOEFL	100
% graduated top 10% of class	78
% graduated top 25% of class	97
% graduated top 50% of class	100

DEADLINES

Early decision	
Deadline	11/1
Notification	12/15
Regular	
Deadline	1/1
Notification	4/1
Nonfall registration?	No

FINANCIAL FACTS

Financial Aid Rating	96
Annual tuition	$50,700
Room and board	$15,740
Required fees	$245
Average need-based scholarship	$40,781
% needy frosh rec. need-based scholarship or grant aid	97
% needy UG rec. need-based scholarship or grant aid	98
% needy frosh rec. non-need-based scholarship or grant aid	58
% needy UG rec. non-need-based scholarship or grant aid	45
% needy frosh rec. need-based self-help aid	88
% needy UG rec. need-based self-help aid	91
% frosh rec. any financial aid	43
% UG rec. any financial aid	45
% frosh need fully met	100
% ugrads need fully met	91
Average % of frosh need met	100
Average % of ugrad need met	100

Clark University

950 Main Street, Worcester, MA 01610-1477 • Admissions: 508-793-7431 • Fax: 508-793-8821

CAMPUS LIFE

Quality of Life Rating	90
Fire Safety Rating	98
Green Rating	90
Type of school	Private
Affiliation	No Affiliation
Environment	City

STUDENTS

Total undergrad enrollment	2,397
% male/female	40/60
% from out of state	63
% frosh from public high school	75
% frosh live on campus	97
% ugrads live on campus	70
% African American	4
% Asian	7
% Caucasian	57
% Hispanic	7
% Native American	<1
% Pacific Islander	<1
% Two or more races	2
% Race and/or ethnicity unknown	8
% international	15
# of countries represented	64

ACADEMICS

Academic Rating	90
% students returning for sophomore year	87
% students graduating within 4 years	77
% students graduating within 6 years	83
Calendar	Semester
Student/faculty ratio	10:1
Profs interesting rating	91
Profs accessible rating	88

Most classes have 10–19 students.
Most lab/discussion sessions have
10–19 students.

MOST POPULAR MAJORS
Biology; Political Science and Government;
Psychology

ABOUT THE SCHOOL
Students come to Clark University in Worcester, Massachusetts, "for an intimate and comfortable classroom environment" and a "diverse atmosphere" that nurtures a "dynamic community of socially conscious students." Throughout each of its thirty-two majors, four undergraduate professional programs, and fourteen accelerated BA/Master's degree programs (which students refer to as "5th year" programs), Clark focuses on getting its 2,300 students hands-on training with a career focus. Clarkies rave about the school's Liberal Education & Effective Practice program, which "gives us immense opportunities to explore careers in different fields" through projects that pair curriculum and independent study with internships or volunteer work with outside organizations. Through LEEP, Clark students find that they are "graduating as a much more rounded and employable student." Students universally praise the faculty as "really good, caring professors, who are legitimately interested in their students' academic progress," but who also care about their "overall achievement and well-being." One junior in psychology even "spent Thanksgiving this year at a professor's home."

BANG FOR YOUR BUCK
First-year applicants can apply for a four-year Presidential LEEP Scholarship, one of the school's most prominent awards, which comes with a full-ride scholarship and paid room and board. In addition to other merit scholarships, the school offers a number of need-based grants. The school's "5th year" accelerated Master's program is also available, tuition-free, to any student who meets the academic requirements. One junior explains that "the fifth year [masters in teaching] program at Clark is fantastic to prepare for a job as an educator."

STUDENT LIFE
Clarkies are both laid back and rigorous; one student sums it up: "We take our academics seriously, but we don't take ourselves too seriously." These liberally minded students are generally concerned with the environment, and "the average Clarkie cares deeply about social justice issues." The school offers students plenty of ways to get around for free: "There are buses that go to nearby malls for free every week, and a bus that goes to Boston every two weeks, [and] also the Clark Student Safety Escort service can take you to nearby restaurants." On campus there are tons of clubs, and student organizations that host well-attended "events every week including things like CUFS movie screenings, Big Prize Bingo, and outing club trips." Students say they "don't know anyone who doesn't go to at least three to four club events a month."

CAREER
The LEEP Center organizes a number of career and résumé building opportunities, including mentorship, job shadowing, internships, and community-based work study, among others. The school also awards academic credit for internships and offers a limited number of $2,500 stipends for students who want to take an unpaid summer internship. Students appreciate that "Clark offers the research and internship opportunities of a large research institution with the personal instruction and help of a small liberal arts school." As a result Clark students "tend to think about what they want to do in the future and how they can incorporate what they learned in class in real life." One student elaborates, "I know a few students who also work on their own personal projects such as the development of a mobile app, a nonprofit organization, or even a short film to enhance their education and career." The average starting salary of Clark grads is $40,700, and 54 percent say they have high job meaning.

Clark University

FINANCIAL AID: 508-793 7478 • E-MAIL: ADMISSIONS@CLARKU.EDU • WEBSITE: WWW.CLARKU.EDU

GENERAL INFO

Activities: Choral groups, concert band, dance, drama/theater, jazz band, literary magazine, marching band, music ensembles, musical theater, pep band, radio station, student government, student newspaper, student-run film society, symphony orchestra, television station, yearbook, Campus Ministries, International Student Organization, Model UN. **Organizations:** 110 registered organizations, 10 honor societies, 7 religious organizations. **Athletics (Intercollegiate):** *Men:* baseball, basketball, crew/rowing, cross-country, diving, lacrosse, soccer, swimming, tennis. *Women:* basketball, crew/rowing, cross-country, diving, field hockey, soccer, softball, swimming, tennis, volleyball. **On-Campus Highlights:** Larger than life statue of Freud, rare book room, Goddard Library, Traina Center for the Arts, Dolan Field House and updated fields, The Green on a warm spring day.

FINANCIAL AID

Students should submit: FAFSA, CSS/Financial Aid PROFILE, Noncustodial PROFILE. Regular filing deadline is 1/15. The Princeton Review suggests that all financial aid forms be submitted as soon as possible after October 1. *Need-based scholarships/grants offered:* Federal Pell, FSEOG, State scholarships/grants, College/university scholarship or grant aid from institutional funds. *Loan aid offered:* Direct Subsidized Stafford Loans, Direct Unsubsidized Stafford Loans, Direct PLUS loans, Federal Perkins Loans, State Loans. Applicants will be notified of awards about the same time as admissions decisions. Federal Work-Study Program available. Institutional employment available.

BOTTOM LINE

The annual tuition for a liberal arts education at Clark University is $41,590. Depending on the options you choose, food and housing on campus will cost between $7,300 and $10,600. Adding $350 for fees and $800 for books and supplies, the total comes to between $50,040 and $53,340.

CAREER INFORMATION FROM PAYSCALE.COM

ROI rating	88
Bachelor's and No Higher	
Median starting salary	$40,700
Median mid-career salary	$86,100
At Least Bachelor's	
Median starting salary	$44,300
Median mid-career salary	$92,800
% alumni with high job meaning	54%
% STEM	13%

SELECTIVITY

Admissions Rating	90
# of applicants	8,045
% of applicants accepted	55
% of acceptees attending	15
# offered a place on the wait list	670
% accepting a place on wait list	47
% admitted from wait list	4
# of early decision applicants	48
% accepted early decision	73

FRESHMAN PROFILE

Range SAT Critical Reading	560–670
Range SAT Math	560–670
Range SAT Writing	560–670
Range ACT Composite	26–30
Minimum paper TOEFL	550
Average HS GPA	3.7
% graduated top 10% of class	44
% graduated top 25% of class	77
% graduated top 50% of class	99

DEADLINES

Early decision	
Deadline	11/1
Notification	12/15
Early action	
Deadline	11/1
Notification	12/15
Regular	
Deadline	1/15
Notification	4/1
Nonfall registration?	Yes

FINANCIAL FACTS

Financial Aid Rating	92
Annual tuition	$42,800
Room and board	$8,450
Required fees	$350
Average need-based scholarship	$26,628
% needy frosh rec. need-based scholarship or grant aid	98
% needy UG rec. need-based scholarship or grant aid	98
% needy frosh rec. non-need-based scholarship or grant aid	39
% needy UG rec. non-need-based scholarship or grant aid	40
% needy frosh rec. need-based self-help aid	78
% needy UG rec. need-based self-help aid	82
% frosh rec. any financial aid	91
% UG rec. any financial aid	89
% frosh need fully met	59
% ugrads need fully met	65

Clarkson University

HOLCROFT HOUSE, POTSDAM, NY 13699 • ADMISSIONS: 315-268-6480 • FAX: 315-268-7647

CAMPUS LIFE

Quality of Life Rating	**81**
Fire Safety Rating	**96**
Green Rating	**88**
Type of school	Private
Affiliation	No Affiliation
Environment	Village

STUDENTS

Total undergrad enrollment	3,257
% male/female	70/30
% from out of state	26
% frosh from public high school	86
% frosh live on campus	97
% ugrads live on campus	84
# of fraternities (% ugrad men join)	9 (10)
# of sororities (% ugrad women join)	4 (12)
% African American	2
% Asian	3
% Caucasian	84
% Hispanic	4
% Native American	<1
% Pacific Islander	<1
% Two or more races	2
% Race and/or ethnicity unknown	2
% international	3
# of countries represented	22

ACADEMICS

Academic Rating	**73**
% students returning for sophomore year	90
% students graduating within 4 years	53
% students graduating within 6 years	73
Calendar	Semester
Student/faculty ratio	15:1
Profs interesting rating	70
Profs accessible rating	75
Most classes have 10–19 students.	
Most lab/discussion sessions have 20–29 students.	

MOST POPULAR MAJORS

Business Administration and Management; Mechanical Engineering; Engineering/Industrial Management

ABOUT THE SCHOOL

Students at Clarkson love the environment of a small campus in the Adirondacks, but some warn that they were not fully prepared for the winters. In terms of academics, there are thirty-nine majors offered, and the school boasts a 14.5:1 student to faculty ratio. Students feel that "the majority of the professors at Clarkson work extremely well with the students to ensure that everyone fully understands the material, while maintaining a relaxed presence among the students," with one student noting that their professors have gone so far as to "actually answer questions in lecture." Students feel that "academically, Clarkson is very difficult, but you get a lot out of it." The top majors are business administration and management, civil engineering, and mechanical engineering, and the student body is predominantly white (82 percent) and male (72 percent).

BANG FOR YOUR BUCK

At Clarkson, 98 percent of students received some form of financial aid, and the average aid package comes to about $29,683. It is a private institution, and tuition runs $45,132, and the school makes an effort to make sure that up to 90 percent of financial aid need is met, demonstrating a commitment to meeting demonstrated need. Students feel that "they have a high tuition, but attract kids here by giving them high scholarships." Clarkson "has a great reputation as an engineering school in the corporate world which reflects its high job placement percentage for students after they graduate." Most students report receiving scholarships that they rate from "great" to "excellent." With their high rate of financial aid and reportedly excellent job placement, one could say that Clarkson offers an excellent bang for ones buck.

STUDENT LIFE

Students at Clarkson feel that they "defy convention" and do so "daily." More than a few students are "outdoorsy," and many would identify as "gamers," if not outright "nerds." In fact some students responding to our survey said they'd like to see more quiet study spaces on campus. As Clarkson is in the Adirondacks, "a lot of people participate in winter sports like skiing and snowboarding on the weekends. Also, intramural sports are very common. During the week, however, most people can be found either studying, or working on different assignments for clubs and organizations." Clarkson provides "some activities for students on the weekend, but there are quite a few parties nonetheless" although "none of the parties seem too out of control."

Clarkson University

FINANCIAL AID: 315-268-6480 • E-MAIL: ADMISSION@CLARKSON.EDU • WEBSITE: WWW.CLARKSON.EDU

CAREER

The typical Clarkson University graduate has a starting salary of around $59,936, and 58 percent report that their job has a great deal of meaning. Students feel that Clarkson has "an amazing placement rate" but that it could do a better job with "non-engineering majors." Some students report that Clarkson has "a huge alumni network which helps the current students find internships and research opportunities." Really? you ask. "Really," they say, "You have to try to not get one."

GENERAL INFO

Activities: Choral groups, drama/theater, jazz band, musical theater, pep band, radio station, student government, student newspaper, symphony orchestra, television station, yearbook, International Student Organization. **Organizations:** 219 registered organizations, 21 honor societies, 4 religious organizations. 9 fraternities, 4 sororities. **Athletics (Intercollegiate):** *Men:* baseball, basketball, cross-country, diving, golf, ice hockey, lacrosse, skiing (downhill/alpine), skiingnordiccross-country, soccer, swimming. *Women:* basketball, cross-country, diving, ice hockey, lacrosse, skiing (downhill/alpine), skiingnordiccross-country, soccer, softball, swimming, volleyball. **On-Campus Highlights:** Snell Hall Shipley Center for Innovation, Adirondack Lodge, Cheel Campus Center Club 99, CAMP Building SPEED Labs, Java City/Library, Fitness Center, Student Center, Educational Resource Center, Residence Hall Rooms, Cheel Campus Center and Arena.

FINANCIAL AID

Students should submit: FAFSA, State aid form. Regular filing deadline is 3/1. The Princeton Review suggests that all financial aid forms be submitted as soon as possible after October 1. *Need-based scholarships/grants offered:* Federal Pell, FSEOG, State scholarships/grants, Private scholarships, College/university scholarship or grant aid from institutional funds. *Loan aid offered:* Direct Subsidized Stafford Loans, Direct Unsubsidized Stafford Loans, Direct PLUS loans, Federal Perkins Loans, College/university loans from institutional funds. Applicants will be notified of awards on a rolling basis beginning 3/14. Federal Work-Study Program available. Institutional employment available.

BOTTOM LINE

The tuition at Clarkson University comes to $45,132 per year, without fees and room and board. But Clarkson does its best to meet its students' needs, with an average need-based financial aid package of $29,663. Ninety-eight percent of students receive some form of aid, and on average 90 percent of students' financial aid needs are met. The school offers a lot of aid, and has a respected job placement rate.

CAREER INFORMATION FROM PAYSCALE.COM

ROI rating	**88**
Bachelor's and No Higher	
Median starting salary	$61,900
Median mid-career salary	$111,000
At Least Bachelor's	
Median starting salary	$63,400
Median mid-career salary	$117,000
% alumni with high job meaning	62%
% STEM	72%

SELECTIVITY

Admissions Rating	**87**
# of applicants	6,906
% of applicants accepted	68
% of acceptees attending	17
# offered a place on the wait list	56
% accepting a place on wait list	18
% admitted from wait list	60
# of early decision applicants	180
% accepted early decision	81

FRESHMAN PROFILE

Range SAT Critical Reading	520–630
Range SAT Math	560–660
Range SAT Writing	490–600
Range ACT Composite	24–30
Minimum paper TOEFL	550
Minimum internet-based TOEFL	80
Average HS GPA	3.7
% graduated top 10% of class	36
% graduated top 25% of class	72
% graduated top 50% of class	95

DEADLINES

Early decision	
Deadline	12/1
Notification	1/1
Regular	
Deadline	1/15
Nonfall registration?	Yes

FINANCIAL FACTS

Financial Aid Rating	**86**
Annual tuition	$45,132
Room and board	$14,558
Required fees	$1,000
Average need-based scholarship	$29,663
% needy frosh rec. need-based scholarship or grant aid	99
% needy UG rec. need-based scholarship or grant aid	99
% needy frosh rec. non-need-based scholarship or grant aid	14
% needy UG rec. non-need-based scholarship or grant aid	14
% needy frosh rec. need-based self-help aid	82
% needy UG rec. need-based self-help aid	82
% frosh rec. any financial aid	97
% UG rec. any financial aid	97
% UG borrow to pay for school	84
Average cumulative indebtedness	$29,000
% frosh need fully met	20
% ugrads need fully met	21
Average % of frosh need met	89
Average % of ugrad need met	90

Clemson University

105 Sikes Hall, Box 345124, Clemson, SC 29634-5124 • Admissions: 864-656-2287 • Financial Aid: 864-656-2280

CAMPUS LIFE

Quality of Life Rating	95
Fire Safety Rating	96
Green Rating	60*
Type of school	Public
Affiliation	No Affiliation
Environment	Village

STUDENTS

Total undergrad enrollment	18,016
% male/female	53/47
% from out of state	35
% frosh from public high school	89
% frosh live on campus	98
% ugrads live on campus	41
# of fraternities (% ugrad men join)	26 (10)
# of sororities (% ugrad women join)	17 (15)
% African American	7
% Asian	2
% Caucasian	83
% Hispanic	3
% Native American	<1
% Pacific Islander	<1
% Two or more races	3
% Race and/or ethnicity unknown	1
% international	1
# of countries represented	84

ACADEMICS

Academic Rating	78
% students returning for sophomore year	93
% students graduating within 4 years	61
% students graduating within 6 years	82
Calendar	Semester
Student/faculty ratio	18:1
Profs interesting rating	81
Profs accessible rating	90

Most classes have 10–19 students.
Most lab/discussion sessions have
  20–29 students.

MOST POPULAR MAJORS
Engineering; Business/Commerce; Biology

ABOUT THE SCHOOL

Located in sunny South Carolina, Clemson University is "the total package: challenging academics, beautiful campus, sports, a thriving Greek life, Southern edge, and that extra something that just makes me excited to be here every morning when I wake up," according to one happy undergrad. The atmosphere is laid-back yet competitive; learning is fostered often for its own sake, and financial aid, alumni connections, and relationships within the community help put the learning within reach for all. Clemson is also very flexible in allowing its motivated students to achieve dual degrees, double majors, and five-year master's degree options.

Professors at Clemson strike an amazing balance between their lives as researchers and teachers. They manage to make themselves fully accessible to students while still engaging in valuable research, which provides great opportunities for undergraduates. One student tells us, "Overall, my professors at Clemson have been engaging, encouraging students to not only learn the information being presented, but also to apply it. Many of my courses have been solely discussion-based, and those with predominately lectures encourage class participation. I truly enjoy attending class at Clemson because the professors make the topics interesting." Overall, students feel that the value is unbeatable. "The scholarship money was great, the location picture-perfect, the atmosphere friendly, and the quality of education among the best in the nation," according to a current freshman. "I have been challenged throughout my college career," another student informs us.

BANG FOR YOUR BUCK

Clemson University works to engage students and provide them with advantages in the workforce that begin with their undergraduate experience. Students have worked at more than 375 companies through cooperative education, providing them with the ability to apply what is learned in class to real-life situations, while making invaluable contacts in the field they have chosen to pursue. This makes them strong contenders in today's job market. As one student relates, "Being able to research as an undergraduate has been exceedingly helpful in obtaining a job after graduation." One junior reports, "At Clemson, I'm earning a respected degree working alongside the leading researcher in my field, gaining valuable leadership experience while serving the community, and having the time of my life with my best friends. What's not to love?" Yet another student adds, "Clemson has put a large emphasis on recruiting the best faculty over the past ten years, and it shows."

STUDENT LIFE

"My life at school is great because my classes are interesting and my professors are friendly," says one student. But for those looking beyond academics, there is a balance: "During finals week, or the week before spring/fall break, it's all about the library. Other than that, Clemson students know how to have fun. Football, basketball and baseball games are big. Intramural sports are pretty popular as well. Campus ministries are prominent." The campus, on the whole, is "really into sports" and some complain that "too much of campus life revolves around the Greeks." However, students also report participating in movie nights and "many concerts, classical and modern." Additionally Clemson "is located on the lake, not far from the mountains and some excellent camping spots," so "many students also take advantage of our geographic location." "Students vacation [in the mountains] for the weekend to go hiking. Some students also go to the lake or beach (which isn't too far) when the weather is warm. Sports and outdoor activities are extremely popular for leisure activities, and they are constantly taking place on campus."

Clemson University

E-MAIL: CUADMISSIONS@CLEMSON.EDU • FAX: 864-656-2464 • WEBSITE: WWW.CLEMSON.EDU

CAREER

Clemson's Center for Career and Professional Development is generally well regarded and offers many programs, from the standard job fairs and career counseling to more unique events, such as a "Diversity Networking Night." The career center also runs the school's Cooperative Education Program, which allows students to alternate semesters of traditional academic work with "paid, career-related, engaged-learning experience," according to its website. Most students think highly of the center as "providing unmatched career services and opportunities." Out of Clemson alumni visiting PayScale.com, 52 percent report that they derive meaning from their jobs.

GENERAL INFO

Activities: Choral groups, concert band, dance, drama/theater, jazz band, literary magazine, marching band, music ensembles, pep band, radio station, student government, student newspaper, television station, yearbook. **Organizations:** 292 registered organizations, 23 honor societies, 24 religious organizations. 26 fraternities, 17 sororities. **Athletics (Intercollegiate):** *Men:* Baseball, basketball, cheerleading, cross-country, diving, football, golf, soccer, swimming, tennis, track/field (outdoor), track/field (indoor). *Women:* Basketball, cheerleading, crew/rowing, cross-country, diving, soccer, swimming, tennis, track/field (outdoor), track/field (indoor), volleyball. **On-Campus Highlights:** SC Botanical Garden/Discovery Center/Geology Muse, Hendrix Student Center–Clemson Ice Cream, Conference Center and Inn at Clemson/Walker Golf Course, Fort Hill–John C. Calhoun House, Lee Art Gallery.

FINANCIAL AID

Students should submit: FAFSA. Priority filing deadline is 4/1. The Princeton Review suggests that all financial aid forms be submitted as soon as possible after October 1. *Need-based scholarships/grants offered:* Federal Pell, FSEOG, State scholarships/grants, Private scholarships, College/university scholarship or grant aid from institutional funds, Federal Nursing Scholarships. *Loan aid offered:* Direct Subsidized Stafford Loans, Direct Unsubsidized Stafford Loans, Direct PLUS loans, Federal Perkins Loans, State Loans, College/university loans from institutional funds. Applicants will be notified of awards on a rolling basis beginning 4/1. Federal Work-Study Program available. Institutional employment available.

BOTTOM LINE

Clemson University provides a diverse yet comprehensive educational experience at an affordable cost. One satisfied student shares, "I wanted to be a part of the Clemson family, and the price was right. I received full scholarship and stipend, and thus Clemson became the best value for an education." Yearly tuition is about $13,186 for students from in-state. Undergraduates from elsewhere will be looking at an increase to more than $32,700; nonetheless, 35 percent of students do come from out-of-state. Another $9,100 or so will cover room and board, as well as books and supplies for all students.

CAREER INFORMATION FROM PAYSCALE.COM

ROI rating	**89**
Bachelor's and No Higher	
Median starting salary	$51,900
Median mid-career salary	$90,800
At Least Bachelor's	
Median starting salary	$53,000
Median mid-career salary	$90,900
% alumni with high job meaning	59%
% STEM	23%

SELECTIVITY

Admissions Rating	92
# of applicants	22,396
% of applicants accepted	51
% of acceptees attending	30
# offered a place on the wait list	2,249
% accepting a place on wait list	35
% admitted from wait list	99

FRESHMAN PROFILE

Range SAT Critical Reading	560–660
Range SAT Math	590–690
Range ACT Composite	27–31
Minimum paper TOEFL	550
Average HS GPA	4.0
% graduated top 10% of class	56
% graduated top 25% of class	86
% graduated top 50% of class	98

DEADLINES

Regular	
Priority	12/1
Deadline	5/1
Nonfall registration?	Yes

FINANCIAL FACTS

Financial Aid Rating	82
Annual in-state tuition	$13,186
Annual out-of-state tuition	$32,738
Room and board	$9,144
Required fees	$1,132
Average need-based scholarship	$8,946
% needy frosh rec. need-based scholarship or grant aid	92
% needy UG rec. need-based scholarship or grant aid	81
% needy frosh rec. non-need-based scholarship or grant aid	71
% needy UG rec. non-need-based scholarship or grant aid	52
% needy frosh rec. need-based self-help aid	67
% needy UG rec. need-based self-help aid	75
% frosh rec. any financial aid	87
% UG rec. any financial aid	71
% UG borrow to pay for school	49
Average cumulative indebtedness	$30,270
% frosh need fully met	21
% ugrads need fully met	17
Average % of frosh need met	61
Average % of ugrad need met	55

Colby College

4000 Mayflower Hill, Waterville, ME 04901-8848 • Admissions: 207-859-4800 • Fax: 207-859-4828

CAMPUS LIFE

Quality of Life Rating	**90**
Fire Safety Rating	**98**
Green Rating	**99**
Type of school	Private
Affiliation	No Affiliation
Environment	Village

STUDENTS

Total undergrad enrollment	1,857
% male/female	48/52
% from out of state	88
% frosh from public high school	49
% frosh live on campus	100
% ugrads live on campus	95
% African American	3
% Asian	6
% Caucasian	62
% Hispanic	6
% Native American	<1
% Pacific Islander	<1
% Two or more races	5
% Race and/or ethnicity unknown	9
% international	11
# of countries represented	74

ACADEMICS

Academic Rating	**92**
% students returning for sophomore year	93
% students graduating within 4 years	88
Calendar	4/1/4
Student/faculty ratio	9:1
Profs interesting rating	95
Profs accessible rating	99

Most classes have 10–19 students.
Most lab/discussion sessions have
  10–19 students.

MOST POPULAR MAJORS
Biology; Economics; English

ABOUT THE SCHOOL

Challenging academics and professors who work closely with students are the backbone of Colby College's reputation as a small and desirable liberal arts college. The school's location in Waterville, Maine, may have some applicants asking, "Where?" But what that means is that students and professors who go to Colby do so because they want to be there. Academics are the focus here, so the work is challenging. Incoming students should be prepared to deal with a hefty workload, but those who are aiming high will find that Colby is "heaven for students who excel at everything." Studying abroad is also a major part of most Colby programs, and some two-thirds of students here spend time abroad. "Colby's greatest strengths lie in its people," one student notes. "From the administrators to the faculty, staff, students, and alumni, Colby's community is one that is genuinely caring, genuinely smart, and genuinely engaging." The dorms are mixed-class, and most activities at Colby center around the self-contained campus, so that sense of community is essential for student contentment. Nightlife here isn't necessarily thriving or hectic, with outdoor activities such as skiing and hiking the focus of much off-campus entertainment. Students who don't enjoy the outdoors or extra study time—a major pastime among Colby students—may find the campus "suffocating." Colby does not sponsor Greek life, so partying tends to be limited to small dorm parties or drinking at local pubs. Colby does offer a wide array of school-sponsored events, though, a natural extension of the community feeling fostered here. Most students find the intimacy of the campus to be a positive, not a negative.

BANG FOR YOUR BUCK

Colby College has a highly selective admissions process that sees fewer than a third of applicants accepted. However, Colby will meet the financial needs of students they accept, and it does so via grants rather than loans so as to alleviate the burden of loan debt. The school also sponsors National Merit Scholarships. Loan aid is available in the form of Direct Subsidized Stafford, Direct Unsubsidized Stafford, Direct PLUS, state loans, university loans from institutional funds. An array of campus jobs are available for those interested in student employment.

STUDENT LIFE

Due to its challenging academics and driven student body, "during the week, people think about finishing their homework, meeting deadlines, and attending lectures." Due to its small-town setting, "our campus has a great sense of community because most students spend all their time on campus." Colby provides no shortage of things for students to do, with "activities going on every day of the week such as lectures, dances, theatre productions, musical productions, and guest performers." Once the week is over, students cite Colby as having a "work hard, play hard" mentality and "have a blast on weekends." "There is a huge party culture," says a student "but also supportive friend groups and activities sponsored on the weekends for students to participate in." And though social life is largely centered on campus, "plenty of people take advantage of being in Maine. Without too much effort, you can spend a day on the coast or in the mountains regardless of the season." "Skiing is the big thing to do" and many students cite nearby Sugarloaf Mountain as an extremely enjoyable weekend excursion. No matter what their hobbies or how intense the workload, students agree that "life at Colby is a whole lot of fun!"

CAREER

The Colby Career Center offers a variety of services to prepare students for success, including Colby Connect, a four-year, career development program that features workshops, career counseling, job shadowing,

Colby College

FINANCIAL AID: 207-859-4832 • E-MAIL: ADMISSIONS@COLBY.EDU • WEBSITE: WWW.COLBY.EDU

and internships; the Entrepreneurial Alliance, a program that provides practical support for student entrepreneurs and prepares students to compete for $15,000 in an annual business competition; and career immersion programs that provide opportunities to explore career fields through site visits, career panels, mock interviews, and networking receptions with alumni. Reactions to Career Center offerings are mixed, but the sentiment of some is that it's "substantial" and "excellent" and that "it guides us, through different workshops, in the right direction to be a successful person and fill in our doubts about our career paths." Out of Colby alumni visiting PayScale.com, 47 percent report that they derive meaning from their careers.

GENERAL INFO
Activities: Choral groups, concert band, dance, drama/theater, jazz band, literary magazine, music ensembles, musical theater, radio station, student government, student newspaper, student-run film society, symphony orchestra, yearbook, international student organization. **Organizations:** 106 registered organizations, 4 honor societies, 5 religious organizations. **Athletics (Intercollegiate):** *Men:* Baseball, basketball, crew/rowing, cross-country, diving, football, golf, ice hockey, lacrosse, skiing (downhill/alpine), skiing (nordic/cross-country), soccer, squash, swimming, tennis, track/field (outdoor), track/field (indoor). *Women:* Basketball, crew/rowing, cross-country, diving, field hockey, golf, ice hockey, lacrosse, skiing (downhill/alpine), skiing (nordic/cross-country), soccer, softball, squash, swimming, tennis, track/field (outdoor), track/field (indoor), volleyball.

FINANCIAL AID
Students should submit: FAFSA, CSS/Financial Aid PROFILE, Business/Farm Supplement. Regular filing deadline is 2/1. The Princeton Review suggests that all financial aid forms be submitted as soon as possible after October 1. *Need-based scholarships/grants offered:* Federal Pell, FSEOG, State scholarships/grants, Private scholarships, College/university scholarship or grant aid from institutional funds. *Loan aid offered:* Direct Subsidized Stafford Loans, Direct Unsubsidized Stafford Loans, Direct PLUS loans, Federal Perkins Loans, State Loans. Applicants will be notified of awards on or about 4/1. Federal Work-Study Program available. Institutional employment available.

BOTTOM LINE
Yearly comprehensive fees at Colby College are $61,730, plus another $700 for books, though officials there say, "We don't want any student not to come to Colby because of concerns about paying off student loans." The college meets all calculated need with grants and scholarships. Limited off-campus job opportunities mean many students will look toward aid and on-campus jobs. Students graduate with an average debt of $23,343.

CAREER INFORMATION FROM PAYSCALE.COM

ROI rating	88
Bachelor's and No Higher	
Median starting salary	$48,700
Median mid-career salary	$95,100
At Least Bachelor's	
Median starting salary	$52,100
Median mid-career salary	$96,000
% alumni with high job meaning	34%
% STEM	26%

SELECTIVITY
Admissions Rating	95
# of applicants	7,593
% of applicants accepted	23
% of acceptees attending	30
# offered a place on the wait list	1,497
# of early decision applicants	576
% accepted early decision	50

FRESHMAN PROFILE
Range SAT Critical Reading	630–720
Range SAT Math	640–740
Range SAT Writing	630–730
Range ACT Composite	29–32
Minimum internet-based TOEFL	100
% graduated top 10% of class	63
% graduated top 25% of class	93
% graduated top 50% of class	97

DEADLINES
Early decision	
Deadline	11/15
Notification	12/15
Regular	
Deadline	1/1
Notification	4/1
Nonfall registration?	Yes

FINANCIAL FACTS
Financial Aid Rating	96
Annual tuition	$48,820
Room and board	$13,100
Required fees	$2,140
Average need-based scholarship	$42,468
% needy frosh rec. need-based scholarship or grant aid	100
% needy UG rec. need-based scholarship or grant aid	100
% needy frosh rec. non-need-based scholarship or grant aid	2
% needy UG rec. non-need-based scholarship or grant aid	2
% needy frosh rec. need-based self-help aid	65
% needy UG rec. need-based self-help aid	72
% frosh rec. any financial aid	45
% UG rec. any financial aid	40
Average cumulative indebtedness	$23,343
% frosh need fully met	100
% ugrads need fully met	100
Average % of frosh need met	100
Average % of ugrad need met	100

Colgate University

13 Oak Drive, Hamilton, NY 13346 • Admissions: 315-228-7401 • Fax: 315-228-7544

CAMPUS LIFE

Quality of Life Rating	86
Fire Safety Rating	95
Green Rating	96
Type of school	Private
Affiliation	No Affiliation
Environment	Rural

STUDENTS

Total undergrad enrollment	2,853
% male/female	45/55
% from out of state	73
% frosh from public high school	54
% frosh live on campus	100
% ugrads live on campus	92
# of fraternities	5
# of sororities	3
% African American	4
% Asian	4
% Caucasian	67
% Hispanic	9
% Native American	<1
% Pacific Islander	<1
% Two or more races	3
% Race and/or ethnicity unknown	4
% international	9
# of countries represented	48

ACADEMICS

Academic Rating	94
% students returning for sophomore year	95
% students graduating within 4 years	86
% students graduating within 6 years	90
Calendar	Semester
Student/faculty ratio	9:1
Profs interesting rating	89
Profs accessible rating	94

Most classes have 10–19 students.
Most lab/discussion sessions have
    10–19 students.

MOST POPULAR MAJORS
Economics; Political Science; History

#17 COLLEGE THAT PAYS YOU BACK

ABOUT COLGATE UNIVERSITY

Since 1819, Hamilton, New York, has hosted Colgate University, a small liberal arts college that has a "very rigorous academic curriculum" and that will prove challenging to students—gratifyingly so, since those who choose Colgate tend to be looking for a focus on "high-intensity" academics. The science, medicine and health, music, and other programs at this "prestigious institution" win praise from those who attend. Students will be taught by professors who "love being at Colgate as much as the students do." Incoming students should expect small classrooms and hands-on teaching by professors, with class sizes that "allow for personal attention and a higher level of learning." Yet it's not all academics at Colgate. Those attending will also enjoy "strong Division I athletics, a wide variety of extracurricular activities, and a very special community." Football, softball, tennis, and other sports give students challenges to overcome outside the classroom. Students say Colgate offers "the perfect balance between academics and extracurricular activities." A strong sense of community helps. Success both in school and beyond is attributed to the "Colgate connection," a bond among the school's 2,900 students that lasts beyond their years here. The school's philosophical core, and by extension its student body, is career-minded. This is reflected in an extensive set of career-development programs and services. Among others, these include shadowing programs, internship recruiting and off-campus recruiting, and the innovative Colgate on the Cuyahoga program, which gives those accepted an unprecedented opportunity to network with executives, politicians, and business owners. According to the school administration, "These programs offer many dynamic opportunities for students to connect with alumni, staff, faculty, and others to learn about and discuss interests and goals."

BANG FOR YOUR BUCK

Financial aid packages can be sizable at Colgate, averaging just more than $49,442 for the class of 2020. The list of available grants and scholarships is extensive; graduating students call it "strong" and "generous." Over the next several years, school administration aims to lower the average debt for exiting students—and even that may be washed away easily for many students. One year after graduation, 80.5 percent of the class of 2015 is employed. early 15 percent are attending graduate school.

STUDENT LIFE

Colgate boasts a "happy and enthusiastic student body" that "follows the motto 'work hard, play hard.'" A sophomore says, "Imagine J. Crew models. Now give them brains, and that is who is walking around Colgate's campus." Fraternities and sororities are popular: "Greek life does have a huge presence in the social life at Colgate," but "it is not exclusive to just those who are members," a sentiment backed up by an art history major who states that "many students do not take part in the preppy, Greek, party-every-night lifestyle that dominates Colgate's reputation," and that "there IS diversity at Colgate, but you have to work quite hard to find it. It is nice to know that it DOES exist if you want to seek it out," while an English major adds that "with the addition of the new Ho Science Building, the science department is getting more popular, but be warned because the chemistry major is one of the toughest in the country. No one tells

Colgate University

FINANCIAL AID: : 315-228-7431 • E-MAIL: ADMISSION@COLGATE.EDU • WEBSITE: WWW.COLGATE.EDU

you this before you apply but it falls just behind MIT and CalTech in difficulty."

CAREER

The typical Colgate University graduate has a starting salary of around $54,000, and 42 percent of graduates feel their jobs have a lot of meaning in their lives. Students feel that Colgate University has "good financial aid and good career prep." One student feels that "the alumni system is amazing," and that said alumni would "jump over any hurdle for you." Students feel that "the Career Services is phenomenal," due to offering "an incredible selection of opportunities for students to prepare for life after graduation, starting with a major event for sophomores called Sophomore Connections which gives students an opportunity to connect with the alumni network and learn more about career paths, job opportunities, and networking in general." Colgate also offers many grants to support summer career exploration, internships, and research.

GENERAL INFO

Activities: Choral groups, concert band, dance, drama/theater, jazz band, literary magazine, music ensembles, musical theater, pep band, radio station, student government, student newspaper, student-run film society, symphony orchestra, television station, yearbook, campus ministries, international student organization. **Organizations:** 280 registered organizations, 3 honor societies, 10 religious organizations. 5 fraternities, 3 sororities. **Athletics (Intercollegiate):** *Men:* Baseball, basketball, cross-country, diving, football, golf, soccer, swimming, tennis, track/field (outdoor), water polo. *Women:* Basketball, cross-country, diving, golf, lacrosse, soccer, softball, swimming, tennis, track/field (outdoor), volleyball, water polo.

FINANCIAL AID

Students should submit: FAFSA, CSS/Financial Aid PROFILE, Noncustodial PROFILE. Regular filing deadline is 1/15. The Princeton Review suggests that all financial aid forms be submitted as soon as possible after October 1. *Need-based scholarships/grants offered:* Federal Pell, FSEOG. *Loan aid offered:* Direct Subsidized Stafford Loans, Direct Unsubsidized Stafford Loans, Direct PLUS loans, Federal Perkins Loans. Applicants will be notified of awards on or about 4/1. Federal Work-Study Program available. Institutional employment available.

BOTTOM LINE

If the $51,635 in annual tuition seems daunting, your fears should be offset by the fact that the school's generous need-based financial aid programs help carry a large share of that burden. Colgate meets 100 percent of student need through need-based scholarships, grants, and self-help aid.

CAREER INFORMATION FROM PAYSCALE.COM

ROI rating	93
Bachelor's and No Higher	
Median starting salary	$53,700
Median mid-career salary	$115,000
At Least Bachelor's	
Median starting salary	$54,000
Median mid-career salary	$116,000
% alumni with high job meaning	47%
% STEM	16%

SELECTIVITY

Admissions Rating	97
# of applicants	8,724
% of applicants accepted	27
% of acceptees attending	32
# offered a place on the wait list	1,896
% accepting a place on wait list	48
% admitted from wait list	5
# of early decision applicants	879
% accepted early decision	47

FRESHMAN PROFILE

Range SAT Critical Reading	620–720
Range SAT Math	630–730
Range ACT Composite	30–33
Average HS GPA	3.7
% graduated top 10% of class	75
% graduated top 25% of class	94
% graduated top 50% of class	99

DEADLINES

Early decision	
Deadline	11/15
Notification	12/15
Regular	
Deadline	1/15
Notification	4/1
Nonfall registration?	No

FINANCIAL FACTS

Financial Aid Rating	99
Annual tuition	$51,635
Room and board	$13,075
Required fees	$320
Average need-based scholarship	$49,442
% needy frosh rec. need-based scholarship or grant aid	100
% needy UG rec. need-based scholarship or grant aid	99
% needy frosh rec. non-need-based scholarship or grant aid	0
% needy UG rec. non-need-based scholarship or grant aid	0
% needy frosh rec. need-based self-help aid	66
% needy UG rec. need-based self-help aid	74
% frosh rec. any financial aid	38
% UG rec. any financial aid	38
% frosh need fully met	100
% ugrads need fully met	100
Average % of frosh need met	100
Average % of ugrad need met	100

College of the Holy Cross

ADMISSIONS OFFICE, 1 COLLEGE STREET, WORCESTER, MA 01610-2395 • ADMISSIONS: 508-793-2443 • FAX: 508-793-3888

CAMPUS LIFE

Quality of Life Rating	84
Fire Safety Rating	97
Green Rating	86
Type of school	Private
Affiliation	Roman Catholic
Environment	City

STUDENTS

Total undergrad enrollment	2,916
% male/female	50/50
% from out of state	62
% frosh from public high school	51
% frosh live on campus	99
% ugrads live on campus	91
# of fraternities (% ugrad men join)	(0)
# of sororities (% ugrad women join)	(0)
% African American	3
% Asian	5
% Caucasian	70
% Hispanic	10
% Native American	<1
% Pacific Islander	<1
% Two or more races	3
% Race and/or ethnicity unknown	5
% international	2
# of countries represented	15

ACADEMICS

Academic Rating	91
% students returning for sophomore year	96
% students graduating within 4 years	89
% students graduating within 6 years	92
Calendar	Semester
Student/faculty ratio	9:1
Profs interesting rating	93
Profs accessible rating	96
Most classes have 10–19 students.	
Most lab/discussion sessions have fewer than 10 students.	

MOST POPULAR MAJORS
Economics; Political Science; Psychology

ABOUT THE SCHOOL

The College of the Holy Cross is a small liberal arts college of fewer than 3,000 students offering rigorous academic preparation in more than thirty degree programs. Students are thrilled to discover the value of a Holy Cross education. "I realized with a degree from here, I can get a job almost anywhere," and the "large and strong" alumni network provides further professional connections. Students say that College of the Holy Cross "does an incredible job of giving its students a very broad education [and] preparing them with the tools for the real world."

But it's the professors that make students' four years at Holy Cross an extraordinary value. "The emphasis here is on teaching and learning, not research," enthused a freshman. All first-year students take part in full-year seminars that are heavy on intellectual development, and the college values effective communication skills. Faculty is accessible in and out of the classrooms. "At Holy Cross, the professors will keep you busy throughout the week." "Classes are hard," warns a biology major. Good grades are hard to come by. "You have to work your tail off to just get an A–." At the same time, students love their "caring" and "amazing" professors.

Holy Cross has a top-notch Career Planning Center and Summer Internship Program that connect students with alumni working in business, government, media, medicine, law, public policy, research, and many other fields. In fact, the alumni network at Holy Cross is legendary for its willingness to mentor and assist students and graduates throughout their careers. Opportunities such as academic internships, community-based learning courses, a prestigious Washington semester, and experiences through study abroad and immersion trips also provide students with invaluable "real-world" experience. Holy Cross has extensive summer internship and study abroad opportunities.

BANG FOR YOUR BUCK

No student or family should be dissuaded from applying to Holy Cross because of the price tag. Holy Cross is need-blind in its admissions policy, which means the decision to admit students to this highly selective liberal arts college is made without regard to a student's ability to pay. Additionally, Holy Cross meets 100 percent of a student's demonstrated financial need with a combination of scholarship grants, loans, and work-study.

STUDENT LIFE

The campus is exceptionally beautiful, and the sense of community within the first-year dorms is "outstanding." Students love going to sporting events (especially football and basketball), and Boston is a shuttle ride away. Though academics and extracurriculars dominate weekdays, "the weekends are the time to relax from the hectic pace of the week." "The library is full all week, but that nerdy chem major you see working hard all week can turn into the girl riding the mechanical bull at a local bar." For those who don't want to partake in the going out scene, SGA-sponsored events such as trivia nights, karaoke and dances are "a blast," and there are "plenty of comedians and musical performers to satisfy us on Friday nights." It is not unusual to find a group of friends hanging out watching movies and ordering in food on a lazy weekend night.

College of the Holy Cross

FINANCIAL AID: 508-793-2265 • E-MAIL: ADMISSIONS@HOLYCROSS.EDU • WEBSITE: WWW.HOLYCROSS.EDU

CAREER

"Holy Cross equips their students with an intangible set of skills that not only prepares them for a job, but for life," says a student. There are a ton of good connections to jobs after college, and students "have a lot of good programs to prepare us for those opportunities." Alumni networking, research and internship opportunities and career planning services all make going to Holy Cross "a fulfilling and active experience." The Career Planning Office's annual fall career fair and the "Crusader Connections" portal help students link up with employers, and the Career Advisor Network helps them to network with alumni. Of those Holy Cross graduates who visited PayScale.com, 48 percent said they felt their job had a meaningful impact on the world. The average starting salary for these same graduates is $50,700.

GENERAL INFO

Activities: Choral groups, concert band, dance, drama/theater, jazz band, literary magazine, marching band, music ensembles, musical theater, pep band, radio station, student government, student newspaper, yearbook, campus ministries, international student organization. **Organizations:** 105 registered organizations, 20 honor societies, 4 religious organizations. **Athletics (Intercollegiate):** *Men:* Baseball, basketball, crew/rowing, cross-country, diving, football, golf, ice hockey, lacrosse, soccer, swimming, tennis, track/field (outdoor), track/field (indoor). *Women:* Basketball, crew/rowing, cross-country, diving, field hockey, golf, ice hockey, lacrosse, soccer, softball, swimming, tennis, track/field (outdoor), track/field (indoor), volleyball. **On-Campus Highlights:** Library, Smith Hall, St. Joseph Chapel, Hart Recreation Center, Hogan Campus Center.

FINANCIAL AID

Students should submit: FAFSA, CSS/Financial Aid PROFILE, Noncustodial PROFILE, Business/Farm Supplement. Regular filing deadline is 2/1. The Princeton Review suggests that all financial aid forms be submitted as soon as possible after October 1. *Need-based scholarships/grants offered:* Federal Pell, FSEOG, State scholarships/grants, Private scholarships, College/university scholarship or grant aid from institutional funds. *Loan aid offered:* Direct Subsidized Stafford Loans, Direct Unsubsidized Stafford Loans, Direct PLUS loans, Federal Perkins Loans. Applicants will be notified of awards on or about 4/1. Federal Work-Study Program available. Institutional employment available.

BOTTOM LINE

At Holy Cross, the total cost for tuition and fees and room and board comes to about $62,200 annually. Don't fret; financial aid is generous here. The average need-based financial aid package for freshman includes gift aid totaling approximately $34,000. Additional aid is available in the form of work-study and loans.

CAREER INFORMATION FROM PAYSCALE.COM

ROI rating	**89**
Bachelor's and No Higher	
Median starting salary	$50,700
Median mid-career salary	$92,000
At Least Bachelor's	
Median starting salary	$52,400
Median mid-career salary	$97,500
% alumni with high job meaning	61%
% STEM	16%

SELECTIVITY

Admissions Rating	92
# of applicants	6,595
% of applicants accepted	37
% of acceptees attending	30
# offered a place on the wait list	1,307
% accepting a place on wait list	38
% admitted from wait list	2
# of early decision applicants	442
% accepted early decision	75

FRESHMAN PROFILE

Range SAT Critical Reading	600–690
Range SAT Math	620–690
Range SAT Writing	610–700
Range ACT Composite	28–31
Minimum paper TOEFL	600
Minimum internet-based TOEFL	100
% graduated top 10% of class	61
% graduated top 25% of class	89
% graduated top 50% of class	100

DEADLINES

Early decision	
Deadline	12/15
Other ED Deadline	12/15
Regular	
Deadline	1/15
Nonfall registration?	No

FINANCIAL FACTS

Financial Aid Rating	94
Annual tuition	$48,295
Room and board	$13,225
Required fees	$645
Average need-based scholarship	$33,714
% needy frosh rec. need-based scholarship or grant aid	85
% needy UG rec. need-based scholarship or grant aid	84
% needy frosh rec. non-need-based scholarship or grant aid	3
% needy UG rec. non-need-based scholarship or grant aid	3
% needy frosh rec. need-based self-help aid	90
% needy UG rec. need-based self-help aid	93
% frosh rec. any financial aid	61
% UG rec. any financial aid	56
% UG borrow to pay for school	59
Average cumulative indebtedness	$25,613
% frosh need fully met	100
% ugrads need fully met	100
Average % of frosh need met	100
Average % of ugrad need met	100

The College of New Jersey

PO Box 7718, Ewing, NJ 08628-0718 Admissions: 609-771-2131 • Financial Aid: 609-771-2211

CAMPUS LIFE

Quality of Life Rating	87
Fire Safety Rating	98
Green Rating	90
Type of school	Public
Affiliation	No Affiliation
Environment	Village

STUDENTS

Total undergrad enrollment	6,758
% male/female	41/59
% from out of state	6
% frosh from public high school	70
% frosh live on campus	95
% ugrads live on campus	60
# of fraternities (% ugrad men join)	11 (14)
# of sororities (% ugrad women join)	13 (11)
% African American	6
% Asian	10
% Caucasian	66
% Hispanic	12
% Native American	<1
% Pacific Islander	<1
% Two or more races	<1
% Race and/or ethnicity unknown	5
% international	<1
# of countries represented	32

ACADEMICS

Academic Rating	83
% students returning for sophomore year	95
% students graduating within 4 years	72
% students graduating within 6 years	85
Calendar	Semester
Student/faculty ratio	13:1
Profs interesting rating	81
Profs accessible rating	84

Most classes have 20–29 students.
Most lab/discussion sessions have
10–19 students.

MOST POPULAR MAJORS

Biology; Psychology; Business
Administration and Management

ABOUT THE SCHOOL

The College of New Jersey is situated on 289 acres in Ewing. The small, state-run public school starts incoming freshmen off on the right foot with a strong foundation of core requirements, which eventually leads to a final capstone course their senior year. Students who sign up for the First Year Experience will participate in the program for the duration of the year and receive support related to their transition from high school to college. The group is required to sign up for a First Seminar course, where they will discuss issues that may arise while adjusting and be housed on the same floor in their dorm.

No courses are complete without outstanding professors, and students at TCNJ say theirs are the best. "I think the personal attention is the greatest strength," a student shares. "I loved that all of my professors knew my name. The classes are small and you really get to know both your professor and the other students in the class." The faculty goes above and beyond, even inviting their students in on the hiring process. "Whenever a position opens up in a department, the students are encouraged to attend lectures by prospective candidates and offer their input," one student writes. They also "find no cake-walk when it comes to classes."

BANG FOR YOUR BUCK

Over 60 percent of full-time undergraduates benefit from financial aid, which can come in the form of merit-based scholarships, work-study programs, loans, or government or institutional grants. Title IV students may compete for the college's merit scholarships, which are funded by the state government as well as private donors. These awards are offered to those applicants with top SAT scores and class rankings. Over the last six years, TCNJ has given scholarships totaling more than $12 million. Almost three-quarters of students graduate within four years, and more than a third pursue graduate studies. In addition to "top-notch faculty and the newest technology," students have the opportunity to develop their own special-interest learning communities on campus. Also, commitment to sustainability has been incorporated into the curriculum at TCNJ. The college's Municipal Land Use Center is authoring the state's sustainability and climate neutrality plans, and the school has committed to offsetting greenhouse gas produced by faculty and staff travel on an annual basis through the purchase of carbon offsets

STUDENT LIFE

At the College of New Jersey, it's "not uncommon [for] someone who you don't know [to] say hello and ask [how] day is going—that's pretty much [the] norm around campus." With approximately 6,600 students—the majority of them New Jersey residents—there are roughly 223 registered student organizations on campus. A little more than half the students live on campus and the school does assist in finding off-campus housing for those who don't want to live in dorms. Greek life is a presence at the school, particularly sororities: there are thirteen sororities and eleven fraternities at the College of New Jersey, with 11 percent of women joining a sorority and 14 percent of men joining a fraternity. Despite these numbers, students note that while the Greek system is "definitely a presence on campus," they "don't feel obliged to join in order to have a social life" and the "College Union Board offers plenty of weekend entertainment for people who do not want to go out to parties." According to one Marketing major, "There is no way to define the typical student at TCNJ. With [so many] clubs and activities, there is something for everyone."

CAREER

According to PayScale.com, 44 percent of College of New Jersey graduates would describe their careers as helping to improve the

The College of New Jersey

E MAIL: TCNJINFO@TCNJ.EDU • FAX: 609-637-5174 • WEBSITE: WWW.TCNJ.EDU

world. With an average starting salary of $50,300, the most popular post-TCNJ jobs include software engineer, project engineer, and marketing coordinator. The most popular majors are Computer Science, Finance, and Psychology. Professors "often email students with internship...opportunities" and students praise the plethora of internships available and the study abroad options, which help connect them to the global job market. With its strong "academic focus," The College of New Jersey produces "successful and prepared graduates." The school's Career Center puts on events such as the Fall Engineering and Computer Science Networking event, the Fall Opportunities Fair, and Student Career Forums. According to one Political Science major, students "think about their futures here at TCNJ, and they're always wondering what the next step will be" when it comes to jobs or graduate school.

GENERAL INFO

Environment: Village. **Activities:** Choral groups, concert band, dance, drama/theater, jazz band, literary magazine, music ensembles, musical theater, opera, pep band, radio station, student government, student newspaper, symphony orchestra, television station, yearbook, campus ministries, international student organization, Model UN. **Organizations:** 205 registered organizations, 16 honor societies, 11 religious organizations. 11 fraternities, 13 sororities.

FINANCIAL AID

Students should submit: FAFSA, CSS/Financial Aid PROFILE. Regular filing deadline is 10/1. The Princeton Review suggests that all financial aid forms be submitted as soon as possible after October 1. *Need-based scholarships/grants offered:* Federal Pell, FSEOG, State scholarships/grants, Private scholarships, College/university scholarship or grant aid from institutional funds, Federal Nursing Scholarships. *Loan aid offered:* Direct Subsidized Stafford Loans, Direct Unsubsidized Stafford Loans, Direct PLUS loans, Federal Perkins Loans, Federal Nursing Loans. Applicants will be notified of awards on a rolling basis beginning 6/1. Federal Work-Study Program available. Institutional employment available.

BOTTOM LINE

"A smaller school that is a bargain for its quality of education," the College of New Jersey lives up to these words, according to one happy undergrad. With in-state tuition and fees amounting to just more than $15,000, and plenty of aid available, the school makes college a possibility for most every budget. Seventy percent of freshmen receive financial aid, with the average total need-based package being close to $14,000. Out-of-state students are looking at a bit more than $22,300 per year; room and board for all students is just over $12,880. The college meets on average 46 percent of all need, and the average need-based gift aid is more than $12,000. "Many of my friends... got into very prestigious schools...but chose TCNJ because of its unbeatable cost," reports one undergrad. There is also a respectable 13:1 student-to-faculty ratio, within such a large campus; there are 6,500 students in all.

CAREER INFORMATION FROM PAYSCALE.COM

ROI rating	86
Bachelor's and No Higher	
Median starting salary	$51,000
Median mid-career salary	$79,800
At Least Bachelor's	
Median starting salary	$51,700
Median mid-career salary	$85,200
% alumni with high job meaning	42%
% STEM	18%

SELECTIVITY

Admissions Rating	89
# of applicants	11,290
% of applicants accepted	49
% of acceptees attending	26
# offered a place on the wait list	1,837
% accepting a place on wait list	29
% admitted from wait list	18
# of early decision applicants	600
% accepted early decision	69

FRESHMAN PROFILE

Range SAT Critical Reading	550–640
Range SAT Math	570–670
Range SAT Writing	550–650
Range ACT Composite	26–30
Minimum paper TOEFL	550
Minimum internet-based TOEFL	90
% graduated top 10% of class	39
% graduated top 25% of class	79
% graduated top 50% of class	97

DEADLINES

Early decision	
Deadline	11/1
Notification	12/1
Regular	
Priority	11/1
Deadline	2/1
Nonfall registration?	Yes

FINANCIAL FACTS

Financial Aid Rating	78
Annual in-state tuition	$11,124
Annual out-of-state tuition	$22,301
Room and board	$12,881
Required fees	$4,670
Average need-based scholarship	$12,074
% needy frosh rec. need-based scholarship or grant aid	37
% needy UG rec. need-based scholarship or grant aid	39
% needy frosh rec. non-need-based scholarship or grant aid	31
% needy UG rec. non-need-based scholarship or grant aid	27
% needy frosh rec. need-based self-help aid	66
% needy UG rec. need-based self-help aid	75
% frosh rec. any financial aid	70
% UG rec. any financial aid	62
% frosh need fully met	8
% ugrads need fully met	11
Average % of frosh need met	42
Average % of ugrad need met	46

College of William & Mary

ADMISSIONS, PO Box 8795, WILLIAMSBURG, VA 23187-8795 • ADMISSIONS: 757-221-4223 • FAX: 757-221-1242

CAMPUS LIFE

Quality of Life Rating	94
Fire Safety Rating	91
Green Rating	76
Type of school	Public
Affiliation	No Affiliation
Environment	Village

STUDENTS

Total undergrad enrollment	6,301
% male/female	44/56
% from out of state	30
% frosh from public high school	77
% frosh live on campus	100
% ugrads live on campus	74
# of fraternities (% ugrad men join)	17 (26)
# of sororities (% ugrad women join)	13 (34)
% African American	7
% Asian	8
% Caucasian	59
% Hispanic	9
% Native American	<1
% Pacific Islander	0
% Two or more races	4
% Race and/or ethnicity unknown	6
% international	6
# of countries represented	46

ACADEMICS

Academic Rating	89
% students returning for sophomore year	96
% students graduating within 4 years	82
% students graduating within 6 years	90
Calendar	Semester
Student/faculty ratio	12:1
Profs interesting rating	89
Profs accessible rating	93

MOST POPULAR MAJORS
Business, English, Psychology

ABOUT THE SCHOOL

The College of William & Mary was founded in 1693 by a couple of English monarchs, King William III and Queen Mary II (hence the name). It's the second-oldest college in the United States. "I absolutely loved the feeling of community on campus," one student says. Another contends that "the traditions at William & Mary really ground students in campus life." The long list of prominent alumni who have graced the hallowed halls of this stately southern campus runs the gamut from Thomas Jefferson to Jon Stewart. The academic atmosphere here is intense and occasionally daunting. However, one student argues, "everyone at William & Mary cares about each other. People are competitive, but by no means cutthroat." At the same time, the faculty is tremendous pretty much across the board, and professors are widely available outside of class, "as they generally care about the students," says one sophomore. "From e-mailing to texting students with concerns, the professors at William & Mary are invested in the success of their students." One student says, "Even in my lecture class of over 200, the professor knows me by name. I think that speaks volumes about the atmosphere and expectations of William & Mary." A student describes her experience: "Professors actively involve undergraduates in their research—I even got to cowrite and present a paper at an academic conference last year!" Social life is strong. One senior explains, "I was excited about the prospect of entering an atmosphere where intellectualism and levity are considered compatible. While [William & Mary] students are intelligent hard-workers, they aren't obnoxious or über-competitive (grades are rarely discussed), and even if their brows are often furrowed, their lips are often smiling." "There's a certain intensity here: people are world-aware, involved, hard-working, motivated, and genuinely caring."

BANG FOR YOUR BUCK

William & Mary does a stellar job of meeting the financial need of its students: 100 percent of demonstrated financial need is met for Virginian residents, and approximately 64 percent of demonstrated need is met for nonresidents. In addition, the William & Mary Promise guarantees in-state tuition will remain the same for all four years for each incoming class. In addition to need-based aid, William & Mary offers merit-based scholarships. The 1693 Scholarship provides the equivalent of in-state tuition and general fees, room and board, and a $5,000 stipend for research. In addition, the William & Mary Scholar Award is presented each year to a select group of students who have overcome unusual adversity and/or would add to the diversity of the campus community. This award provides the equivalent of in-state tuition and general fees. Both the 1693 Scholars Award and the William & Mary Scholars Award are awarded through the admission process. The Howard Hughes Medical Institute offers support through "Mentored Research Experiences" where students receive real-world experience. First-years may apply for Howard Hughes Medical Institute award once enrolled.

STUDENT LIFE

Students tell us that the real "T.W.A.M.P., or Typical William & Mary Person" is "open-minded, outgoing, charismatic, driven, dedicated, caring, and unique." The school is full of "well-rounded people who are in touch with their inner nerd," and undergrads are quick to note that "intellectual people who care about the world find the zaniest ways to have fun." On campus, Alma Mater Productions, the college programming board, "sponsors a lot of different events that are well-attended, including [...] comedians, music artists, movies, etc." Student organizations are also very strong, from intramural sports, some form of which "almost everyone plays," to arts organizations such as "the William & Mary Symphony Orchestra, three university

The College of William & Mary

FINANCIAL AID: 757-221-2420 • E-MAIL: ADMISSION@WM.EDU • WEBSITE: WWW.WM.EDU

choirs, the Middle Eastern Music Ensemble, an Early Music Ensemble, an Appalachian string band, a small chamber orchestra, eleven a cappella groups and [...] two all-student theater companies." Campus is buzzing, and students agree: "There's a certain intensity here: people are world-aware, involved, hard-working, motivated, and genuinely caring."

CAREER

The Cohen Career Center begins educating students about their opportunities in the early days of freshman and sophomore year with Compass, a "menu" of events for underclassmen, like Majors, Milk and Cookies that demystifies the major selection process. The Center hosts a fair number of recruiting events on campus including the Fall Recruiting consortium which gives students the chance to apply for an interview with various companies all in one location. Tribe pride is fierce at William & Mary, and students are encouraged to speed network or seek one-on-one mentorship through the Tribe Partners Program, made up of alumni, parents, and friends of the college. Grads who visited PayScale.com report an average starting salary of $44,500, and 47 percent believe their work holds a high level of meaning.

GENERAL INFO

Activities: Choral groups, concert band, dance, drama/theater, jazz band, literary magazine, music ensembles, musical theater, opera, pep band, radio station, student government, student newspaper, student-run film society, symphony orchestra, television station, yearbook, campus ministries, international student organization. **Organizations:** 375 registered organizations, 32 honor societies, 32 religious organizations. 17 fraternities, 13 sororities.

FINANCIAL AID

Students should submit: FAFSA, CSS/Financial Aid PROFILE. The Princeton Review suggests that all financial aid forms be submitted as soon as possible after October 1. *Need-based scholarships/grants offered:* Federal Pell, FSEOG, State scholarships/grants, Private scholarships, College/university scholarship or grant aid from institutional funds. *Loan aid offered:* Direct Subsidized Stafford Loans, Direct Unsubsidized Stafford Loans, Direct PLUS loans, Federal Perkins Loans. Federal Work-Study Program available. Institutional employment available.

BOTTOM LINE

William & Mary is truly a steal for Virginia residents. The cost of in-state tuition, room and board, and fees is about $30,350 per year. Students from outside Virginia pay about 40 percent more than that amount. Financial aid is ample with 75 percent of student need met on average.

CAREER INFORMATION FROM PAYSCALE.COM

ROI rating	90
Bachelor's and No Higher	
Median starting salary	$45,900
Median mid-career salary	$92,500
At Least Bachelor's	
Median starting salary	$48,000
Median mid-career salary	$99,300
% alumni with high job meaning	53%
% STEM	15%

SELECTIVITY

Admissions Rating	96
# of applicants	14,952
% of applicants accepted	34
% of acceptees attending	29
# offered a place on the wait list	3,552
% accepting a place on wait list	47
% admitted from wait list	11
# of early decision applicants	1,070
% accepted early decision	50

FRESHMAN PROFILE

Range SAT Critical Reading	630–730
Range SAT Math	630–730
Range SAT Writing	620–720
Range ACT Composite	28–32
Minimum paper TOEFL	600
Minimum internet-based TOEFL	100
Average HS GPA	4.2
% graduated top 10% of class	81
% graduated top 25% of class	96
% graduated top 50% of class	100

DEADLINES

Early decision	
Deadline	11/1
Notification	12/1
Regular	
Deadline	1/1
Notification	4/1
Nonfall registration?	No

FINANCIAL FACTS

Financial Aid Rating	82
Annual in-state tuition	$15,674
Annual out-of-state tuition	$36,158
Room and board	$11,382
Required fees	$5,560
Average need-based scholarship	$15,073
% needy frosh rec. need-based scholarship or grant aid	0
% needy UG rec. need-based scholarship or grant aid	0
% needy frosh rec. non-need-based scholarship or grant aid	0
% needy UG rec. non-need-based scholarship or grant aid	0
% needy frosh rec. need-based self-help aid	0
% needy UG rec. need-based self-help aid	0
% frosh rec. any financial aid	54
% UG rec. any financial aid	53

The College of Wooster

847 COLLEGE AVENUE, WOOSTER, OH 44691 • ADMISSIONS: 330-263-2322 • FAX: 330-263-2621

CAMPUS LIFE

Quality of Life Rating	92
Fire Safety Rating	86
Green Rating	85
Type of school	Private
Affiliation	Historically Presbyterian
Environment	Town

STUDENTS

Total undergrad enrollment	2,058
% male/female	45/55
% from out of state	61
% frosh from public high school	69
% frosh live on campus	100
% ugrads live on campus	99
# of fraternities (% ugrad men join)	4 (15)
# of sororities (% ugrad women join)	6 (20)
% African American	8
% Asian	5
% Caucasian	69
% Hispanic	5
% Native American	1
% Pacific Islander	<1
% Two or more races	0
% Race and/or ethnicity unknown	3
% international	9
# of countries represented	35

ACADEMICS

Academic Rating	94
% students returning for sophomore year	88
% students graduating within 4 years	78
% students graduating within 6 years	82
Calendar	Semester
Student/faculty ratio	12:1
Profs interesting rating	93
Profs accessible rating	97

Most classes have fewer than 10 students.
Most lab/discussion sessions have 10–19 students.

MOST POPULAR MAJORS

History; Psychology; English

ABOUT THE SCHOOL

The College of Wooster provides "a small, liberal-arts education" with "a great balance between good academics, athletics and other student activities." The 240-acre suburban campus has "gorgeous" large trees and "buildings...straight out of a fairy tale book." The school is famous for its mentored research program for undergrads. The "well-known independent study (capstone) project," or I.S., has seniors work on a project with a faulty advisor on a one-on-one basis. The small school has about 2,000 undergraduates and a "home-like atmosphere" with "friendly students" and "approachable faculty." "The administration is open to student input" and the "professors at the College of Wooster clearly care deeply that their students." "During my first semester two of my Professors invited me to their house for dinner," one student says. Another sums up the Wooster experience: "My school provides students with rigorous academics and prepares us for life after college, all while encouraging a bit of weirdness—Wooster is quirky, in a good way."

BANG FOR YOUR BUCK

Students admire Wooster's "commitment to making scholarships available," and the school says that over 75 percent of Wooster students receive financial assistance. There are $1 million in on-campus employment opportunities for students each year. The overall aid from need-based and merit totals about $46 million. In addition to Dean's scholarships, the school has three "competition-based scholarships." These are the Clarence Beecher Allen Scholarship for African-American students, the Covenant Scholarship for members of the Presbyterian Church, and a College Scholar Award that is open to all high-achieving students. In addition, the school offers Performing Arts Scholarships in Dance, Music, Theater, and Scottish Arts.

STUDENT LIFE

"The typical College of Wooster student is in one word NORMAL yet unique" and "everyone fits in here." "The student body is definitely more liberal overall, with a pretty relaxed feel," a History major says. Although small, the student body is still divided into "a lot of little social groups" that do not necessarily interact. Students aim for "a healthy balance of work and play." "There are often day trips to neighboring regions that have fun things to do like skiing or amusement parks," one student says. "For fun we go to sporting events, we golf on our campus course, and on the weekends we go to the campus pub," an Archeology major explains. Students do say that "the town is kind of small, so without a car there isn't much to do." On campus, "the school also does a great job of providing student activities" such as "concerts, comedians, and crafts."

The College of Wooster

FINANCIAL AID: 800-877-3688 • E-MAIL: ADMISSIONS@WOOSTER.EDU • WEBSITE: WWW.WOOSTER.EDU

CAREER

Students rave about the aforementioned Independent Study program. "The fact that I would be doing graduate level research on a subject that I wanted to learn about which would potentially help me land my dream job" was a major selling point to one Sociology student. Because of I.S., every senior graduates with an impressive research project already completed. The school has created a web-based tool called WooLink to help students land internships and jobs. Students do wish that there were more "experiential learning opportunities and emphasis on internships." The website PayScale.com reports a typical starting salary of $41,800 for Wooster alums.

GENERAL INFO

Activities: Choral groups, concert band, dance, drama/theater, jazz band, literary magazine, marching band, music ensembles, musical theater, pep band, radio station, student government, student newspaper, student-run film society, symphony orchestra, yearbook, Campus Ministries, International Student Organization, Model UN. **Organizations:** 100 registered organizations, 6 honor societies, 9 religious organizations. 4 fraternities, 6 sororities. **Athletics (Intercollegiate):** *Men:* baseball, basketball, cross-country, diving, football, golf, lacrosse, soccer, swimming, tennis, track/field (outdoor), track/field (indoor). *Women:* basketball, cross-country, diving, field hockey, lacrosse, soccer, softball, swimming, tennis, track/field (outdoor), track/field (indoor), volleyball. **On-Campus Highlights:** Kauke Hall, Severance Hall Chemistry Bldg., Timken Science Library, Ebert Art Center, Burton D. Morgan Hall, Gault Manor (residence hall).

FINANCIAL AID

Students should submit: FAFSA, Institution's own financial aid form, CSS/Financial Aid PROFILE. Priority filing deadline is 2/15. The Princeton Review suggests that all financial aid forms be submitted as soon as possible after October 1. *Need-based scholarships/grants offered:* Federal Pell, FSEOG, State scholarships/grants, Private scholarships, College/university scholarship or grant aid from institutional funds, United Negro College Fund. *Loan aid offered:* Direct Subsidized Stafford Loans, Direct Unsubsidized Stafford Loans, Direct PLUS loans, Federal Perkins Loans. Applicants will be notified of awards on a rolling basis beginning 3/15. Federal Work-Study Program available. Institutional employment available.

BOTTOM LINE

Tuition for Wooster currently stands at about $44,520 per year. Room and board brings that to $55,170 a year, plus fees and books. While that figure is not exactly pocket change, financial aid offerings are extremely strong here, and the average need-based package is $37,614—which knocks that annual price tag down to less than $20,000!

CAREER INFORMATION FROM PAYSCALE.COM

ROI rating	87
Bachelor's and No Higher	
Median starting salary	$38,000
Median mid-career salary	$74,800
At Least Bachelor's	
Median starting salary	$39,600
Median mid-career salary	$74,000
% alumni with high job meaning	66%
% STEM	18%

SELECTIVITY

Admissions Rating	88
# of applicants	5,748
% of applicants accepted	55
% of acceptees attending	18
# offered a place on the wait list	726
% accepting a place on wait list	9
% admitted from wait list	15
# of early decision applicants	130
% accepted early decision	65

FRESHMAN PROFILE

Range SAT Critical Reading	540–670
Range SAT Math	560–680
Range SAT Writing	540–650
Range ACT Composite	25–30
Minimum internet-based TOEFL	81
Average HS GPA	3.7
% graduated top 10% of class	46
% graduated top 25% of class	70

DEADLINES

Early decision	
Deadline	11/1
Notification	11/15
Other ED	
Deadline	1/15
Notification	2/1
Early action	
Deadline	11/15
Notification	12/31
Regular	
Deadline	2/15
Notification	4/1
Nonfall registration?	Yes

FINANCIAL FACTS

Financial Aid Rating	90
Annual tuition	$46,430
Room and board	$11,040
Required fees	$430
Average need-based scholarship	$29,842
% needy frosh rec. need-based scholarship or grant aid	97
% needy UG rec. need-based scholarship or grant aid	98
% needy frosh rec. non-need-based scholarship or grant aid	23
% needy UG rec. non-need-based scholarship or grant aid	14
% needy frosh rec. need-based self-help aid	73
% needy UG rec. need-based self-help aid	81
% frosh rec. any financial aid	99
% UG rec. any financial aid	99
% UG borrow to pay for school	62

Colorado College

14 East Cache la Poudre Street, Colorado Springs, CO 80903 • Phone: 719-389-6344 • Financial Aid Phone: 719-389-6651

CAMPUS LIFE

Quality of Life Rating	**90**
Fire Safety Rating	**95**
Green Rating	**92**
Type of school	Private
Affiliation	No Affiliation
Environment	Metropolis

STUDENTS

Total undergrad enrollment	2,118
% male/female	46/54
% from out of state	82
% frosh live on campus	100
% ugrads live on campus	75
# of fraternities (% ugrad men join)	3 (9)
# of sororities (% ugrad women join)	3 (11)
% African American	3
% Asian	5
% Caucasian	64
% Hispanic	9
% Native American	<1
% Pacific Islander	0
% Two or more races	9
% Race and/or ethnicity unknown	3
% international	7
# of countries represented	69

ACADEMICS

Academic Rating	**94**
% students returning for sophomore year	96
% students graduating within 4 years	82
% students graduating within 6 years	87
Calendar	Semester
Student/faculty ratio	10:1
Profs interesting rating	94
Profs accessible rating	90
Most classes have 10–19 students.	

MOST POPULAR MAJORS

Economics; Ecology and Evolutionary Biology; Political Science and Government

ABOUT THE SCHOOL

Colorado College provides an education without boundaries. With an average class size of sixteen students and a 10:1 student/faculty ratio, students have access to an intimate learning experience where the focus is on immersion and independence. Pair a liberal arts education with the college's signature feature, the "Block Plan" (students take, and professors teach, one course at a time in intensive three-and-a-half week segments), locate the school in Colorado Springs, and you create unparalleled opportunities for field studies and experiential learning, as well as total subject immersion. "Taking one class at a time allows you to devote all of your time to it. It is definitely nice when you are in a class that you love, because you don't have to sacrifice any time for another class that you may like less, or that you have a harder time with."

On average, there are 750 independent study blocks completed by students each year. Colorado College also offers $100,000 annually in Venture Grants, enabling students to pursue original research or an academic project of their choosing. "CC students care about the world. They are idealists and dreamers [who] want to change the world for the better. CC fosters an arena where dreams can grow and students can learn how to go about pursuing them." A Public Interest Fellowship Program awards students paid summer and year-long postgraduate fellowships annually, a number of which have evolved into permanent positions.

BANG FOR YOUR BUCK

Overall, Colorado College provides a nontraditional learning opportunity where young adults can develop their passions in a beautiful and supportive environment. Not only is the educational opportunity perfect for individual learners, it is attainable. Great financial aid is a major selling point. The school is committed to the philosophy that cost should not deter a student from considering Colorado College. "The staff is very nice. If you go into to any office to ask anything they are very helpful. Financial Aid has been exceptionally helpful." Once Colorado College determines a student's eligibility for CC grant and scholarship funds, the school will make a four-year commitment to the family (except in limited circumstances) and renew the CC funds automatically each year at the same level. Funds have been specially designated to assist families who have been adversely impacted by the downturn in the economy.

STUDENT LIFE

Due to the unusual "Block Plan" academic structure, "life at CC is filled with class from 9–12, then the rest of the day is open for activities or resting or doing homework." Beyond studying, campus life involves "a ridiculously large array of different student groups, and there's a lot of good programming put on by them (concerts, speeches, performers, etc.). Also, the Student Activities office on campus also does a lot of its own events and they're always pretty good." Off campus events are popular too: "Due to the glorious set up of the block plan, we get five day adventures every three and a half weeks. These include rafting trips in Utah, backpacking trips throughout Colorado, skiing in the mountains or doing just about anything you'd like to do for five days." Partying plays a role in on and off campus fun as well. "Drinking is a big part of the culture here. That being said people are really good about looking out for each other, and I feel really safe." But while there is definitely an active party scene "it's not overwhelming and a large portion of the student body doesn't participate." The bottom line is that students are involved and friendly: "Most people are extremely outgoing, social, and because it is such a small school there are few faces that aren't familiar."

Colorado College

E-MAIL: ADMISSION@COLORADOCOLLEGE.EDU • FAX: 719-389-6816 • WEBSITE: WWW.COLORADOCOLLEGE.EDU

CAREER

The Colorado College Career Center offers many services: advising and counseling to help students explore their interests; professional services such as resume, cover letter, and interview coaching; opportunities for networking; and internship and job search resources. Colorado College also offers funding for student internships both through the Career Center and through certain academic departments. Most students agree that Colorado College gives students "a unique academic experience that provides you with the tools and foundation for your future career." Out of CC alumni visiting PayScale.com, 53 percent report that they derive a high level of meaning from their jobs.

GENERAL INFO

Activities: Choral groups, concert band, dance, drama/theater, jazz band, literary magazine, music ensembles, musical theater, radio station, student government, student newspaper, student-run film society, yearbook, campus ministries, international student organization. **Organizations:** 147 registered organizations, 13 honor societies, 20 religious organizations. 3 fraternities, 3 sororities. **Athletics (Intercollegiate):** *Men:* Basketball, cross-country, ice hockey, lacrosse, soccer, swimming, tennis, track/field (outdoor). *Women:* Basketball, cross-country, lacrosse, soccer, swimming, tennis, track/field (outdoor), track/field (indoor), volleyball. **On-Campus Highlights:** Worner Student Center, Palmer Hall, Shove Chapel, Cutler Hall–Admission, View of Pikes Peak. **Environmental Initiatives:** Campus-wide, semester-long resource conservation and waste reduction campaign, "aCClimate14," which challenges campus community to adapt to shifting environmental and economic conditions.

FINANCIAL AID

Students should submit: FAFSA, CSS/Financial Aid PROFILE, Noncustodial PROFILE. Regular filing deadline is 2/15. The Princeton Review suggests that all financial aid forms be submitted as soon as possible after October 1. *Need-based scholarships/grants offered:* Federal Pell, FSEOG, State scholarships/grants, Private scholarships, College/university scholarship or grant aid from institutional funds. *Loan aid offered:* Direct Subsidized Stafford Loans, Direct Unsubsidized Stafford Loans, Direct PLUS loans, Federal Perkins Loans. Applicants will be notified of awards on or about 3/15. Federal Work-Study Program available. Institutional employment available.

BOTTOM LINE

Students are attracted to Colorado College for more than its stunning landscape. "Life at Colorado College is intense—everything from class to social life to long-weekend vacations— have yet to meet someone who doesn't meet every opportunity with enthusiastic energy." Tuition and fees at Colorado College may total close to $50,000, but on average the school meets 100 percent of student need through financial aid.

CAREER INFORMATION FROM PAYSCALE.COM

ROI rating	88
Bachelor's and No Higher	
Median starting salary	$44,100
Median mid-career salary	$85,100
At Least Bachelor's	
Median starting salary	$43,600
Median mid-career salary	$85,700
% alumni with high job meaning	65%
% STEM	20%

SELECTIVITY

Admissions Rating	**97**
# of applicants	8,062
% of applicants accepted	17
% of acceptees attending	42
# offered a place on the wait list	1,119
% accepting a place on wait list	21
% admitted from wait list	10
# of early decision applicants	875
% accepted early decision	30

FRESHMAN PROFILE

Range SAT Critical Reading	630–710
Range SAT Math	620–710
Range SAT Writing	620–700
Range ACT Composite	28–32
% graduated top 10% of class	68
% graduated top 25% of class	91
% graduated top 50% of class	100

DEADLINES

Early decision	
Deadline	11/15
Notification	12/15
Early action	
Deadline	11/15
Notification	12/18
Regular	
Priority	1/15
Deadline	1/15
Notification	4/1
Nonfall registration?	Yes

FINANCIAL FACTS

Financial Aid Rating	**96**
Annual tuition	$50,472
Room and board	$11,668
Required fees	$420
Average need-based scholarship	$40,539
% needy frosh rec. need-based scholarship or grant aid	97
% needy UG rec. need-based scholarship or grant aid	96
% needy frosh rec. non-need-based scholarship or grant aid	31
% needy UG rec. non-need-based scholarship or grant aid	19
% needy frosh rec. need-based self-help aid	71
% needy UG rec. need-based self-help aid	76
% frosh rec. any financial aid	57
% UG rec. any financial aid	54
% UG borrow to pay for school	37
Average cumulative indebtedness	$22,068
% frosh need fully met	100
% ugrads need fully met	99
Average % of frosh need met	100
Average % of ugrad need met	100

Columbia University

212 Hamilton Hall MC 2807, 1130 Amsterdam Ave., New York, NY 10027 • Phone: 212-854-2522

CAMPUS LIFE
Quality of Life Rating	**95**
Fire Safety Rating	**85**
Green Rating	**96**
Type of school	Private
Affiliation	No Affiliation
Environment	Metropolis

STUDENTS
Total undergrad enrollment	6,102
% male/female	52/48
% from out of state	77
% frosh from public high school	56
% frosh live on campus	100
% ugrads live on campus	94
# of fraternities (% ugrad men join)	17 (8)
# of sororities (% ugrad women join)	11 (10)
% African American	12
% Asian	22
% Caucasian	34
% Hispanic	12
% Native American	2
% Race and/or ethnicity unknown	4
% international	14
# of countries represented	99

ACADEMICS
Academic Rating	**94**
% students returning for sophomore year	99
% students graduating within 4 years	89
% students graduating within 6 years	96
Calendar	Semester
Student/faculty ratio	6:1
Profs interesting rating	79
Profs accessible rating	79
Most classes have 10–19 students.	

MOST POPULAR MAJORS
Political Science and Economics; English; Engineering

#24 COLLEGE THAT PAYS YOU BACK

ABOUT THE SCHOOL
Columbia University provides prestigious academics and top-of-the-line resources for an Ivy League education with a liberal arts college feel in the heart of one of the greatest cities in the world. Nestled on the Upper West Side of New York City, one student tells us that the campus itself is "an inspiration and a motivation to push and excel academically." The core curriculum is a large draw, providing students with a solid liberal arts education on which to base their future studies. Pair this with a location that provides unparalleled access to internships, community service, and research opportunities and you have a recipe for a melting pot of possibility.

Columbia undergraduates represent every socioeconomic, racial, and ethnic background and hail from all fifty states and all over the world. Students' distinct interests and talents are reflected by their diverse academic pursuits: undergraduates study in more than ninety different academic fields. Engagement within the global community is central to the Columbia experience, and being in the heart of the city is like holding a passport to opportunity with a side of arts, culture, and entertainment.

BANG FOR YOUR BUCK
With nearly all undergraduate students living on campus, students are active participants in campus life through participation in hundreds of student clubs, community-service organizations, and athletic teams. One student tells us, "The opportunities Columbia has to offer, not only on campus but also throughout New York City, attracted me to its gates. The dichotomy of a self-contained campus in the largest city in the U.S. is truly unique and cannot be surpassed by any other American university." Another student adds, "I am big on the sciences, and I knew that if I did not attend a school that had a core curriculum (required set of classes that surveys the humanities and the sciences), all I would take are science classes. With Columbia's core, I am able to have a more holistic education. Also, the location of Columbia is perfect—the university still has a campus feel even though it is in the middle of New York City!"

STUDENT LIFE
Despite its location in one of the most iconic cities in the world, "life at Columbia is surprisingly similar to the typical college experience." While students love to take advantage of the activities in the city, they are also very passionate about events on-campus. "From concerts to opera, finding restaurants in the local area to watching sports games, people can find ways to relax both on campus and in the city at large," says one. The school's various arts programs also provide the chance to get discounted tickets to Broadway shows and concerts. People here are "fairly ambitious (though not cutthroat) high achievers" and the general air of the university is very conducive to working hard and doing well.

CAREER
The Columbia University brand goes far in this country, even though many students only need it to work downtown. Students are thankful for the wealth of resources (referring primarily to internships) available to a student at Columbia University, as well as the professors that are

Columbia University

FAX: 212-894-1209 • WEBSITE: UNDERGRAD.ADMISSIONS.COLUMBIA.EDU

"keen to let you work with them through research." Internships in New York are an excellent entry point for students trying to make themselves known to employers, and it doesn't hurt that the city is rife with Columbia alumni. The Center for Career Education offers a boatload of resources to get students on their way, including counseling sessions, practice interviews, dossier assessments, and old reliable career fairs. Graduates who visited PayScale.com reported an average starting salary of $59,200; 57 percent of these students said they felt their job had a meaningful impact on the world.

GENERAL INFO

Activities: Choral groups, concert band, dance, drama/theater, jazz band, literary magazine, marching band, music ensembles, musical theater, opera, pep band, radio station, student government, student newspaper, student-run film society, symphony orchestra, television station, yearbook, campus ministries, international student organization. **Athletics (Intercollegiate):** *Men:* Baseball, basketball, crew/rowing, cross-country, diving, fencing, football, golf, soccer, squash, swimming, tennis, track/field (outdoor), track/field (indoor), wrestling. *Women:* Archery, basketball, crew/rowing, cross-country, diving, fencing, field hockey, golf, lacrosse, soccer, softball, squash, swimming, tennis, track/field (outdoor), track/field (indoor), volleyball.

FINANCIAL AID

Students should submit: FAFSA, CSS/Financial Aid PROFILE, Noncustodial PROFILE. Regular filing deadline is 2/15. The Princeton Review suggests that all financial aid forms be submitted as soon as possible after October 1. *Need-based scholarships/grants offered:* Federal Pell, FSEOG, State scholarships/grants, Private scholarships, College/university scholarship or grant aid from institutional funds. *Loan aid offered:* Direct Subsidized Stafford Loans, Direct Unsubsidized Stafford Loans, Direct PLUS loans, Federal Perkins Loans, College/university loans from institutional funds. Applicants will be notified of awards on or about 4/1. Federal Work-Study Program available. Institutional employment available.

BOTTOM LINE

Earning an acceptance letter from Columbia is no easy feat. Admissions officers are looking to build a diverse class that will greatly contribute to the university. It's the Ivy League, folks, and it's New York City, and there is a price tag that goes with both. A year's tuition is $52,478. Additionally, count on $13,244 in room and board (such a deal for NYC!). Columbia's New York City campus means that every manner of distraction is literally at your fingertips, so you'll want to factor in another nice chunk of change for things like transportation, personal expenses, outings, etc. These figures are nothing to sneeze at. Take heart: If you get over the first hurdle and manage to gain admittance to this prestigious university, you can be confident that the university will help you pay for it.

CAREER INFORMATION FROM PAYSCALE.COM

ROI rating	92
Bachelor's and No Higher	
Median starting salary	$60,200
Median mid-career salary	$104,000
At Least Bachelor's	
Median starting salary	$62,000
Median mid-career salary	$109,000
% alumni with high job meaning	56%
% STEM	29%

SELECTIVITY

Admissions Rating	99
# of applicants	36,250
% of applicants accepted	6
% of acceptees attending	63
# of early decision applicants	3,337
% accepted early decision	19

FRESHMAN PROFILE

Range SAT Critical Reading	700–790
Range SAT Math	700–800
Range SAT Writing	700–790
Range ACT Composite	32–35
Minimum paper TOEFL	600

DEADLINES

Early decision	
Deadline	11/1
Notification	12/15
Regular	
Deadline	1/1
Notification	4/1
Nonfall registration?	No

FINANCIAL FACTS

Financial Aid Rating	97
Annual tuition	$52,478
Room and board	$13,244
Required fees	$2,578
Average need-based scholarship	$47,490
% needy frosh rec. need-based scholarship or grant aid	97
% needy UG rec. need-based scholarship or grant aid	97
% needy frosh rec. non-need-based scholarship or grant aid	1
% needy UG rec. non-need-based scholarship or grant aid	1
% needy frosh rec. need-based self-help aid	78
% needy UG rec. need-based self-help aid	86
% frosh rec. any financial aid	55
% UG rec. any financial aid	60
% UG borrow to pay for school	27
Average cumulative indebtedness	$25,167
% frosh need fully met	100
% ugrads need fully met	100
Average % of frosh need met	100
Average % of ugrad need met	100

Connecticut College

270 MOHEGAN AVENUE, NEW LONDON, CT 06320 • ADMISSIONS: 860-439-2200 • FAX: 860-439-4301

CAMPUS LIFE
Quality of Life Rating	**86**
Fire Safety Rating	**60***
Green Rating	**80**
Type of school	Private
Affiliation	No Affiliation
Environment	Town

STUDENTS
Total undergrad enrollment	1,918
% male/female	38/62
% from out of state	82
% frosh from public high school	50
% frosh live on campus	100
% ugrads live on campus	99
% African American	4
% Asian	4
% Caucasian	71
% Hispanic	9
% Native American	<1
% Pacific Islander	<1
% Two or more races	3
% Race and/or ethnicity unknown	3
% international	6
# of countries represented	43

ACADEMICS
Academic Rating	**92**
% students returning for sophomore year	90
% students graduating within 4 years	79
% students graduating within 6 years	83
Calendar	Semester
Student/faculty ratio	9:1
Profs interesting rating	85
Profs accessible rating	82

Most classes have 10–19 students.
Most lab/discussion sessions have
10–19 students.

MOST POPULAR MAJORS
Economics; Psychology; Biology

ABOUT THE SCHOOL

Founded in 1911 as a liberal arts college for women, Connecticut College has been coed since 1969. Conn has been particularly aggressive in recent years in fundraising and expanding. The college's mission statement lays forth its goal to educate "students to put the liberal arts into action as citizens in a global society." The global focus is embraced by the students, over half of whom study abroad around the globe. Even on campus, the global focus is clear. As the administration puts it: "Virtually every academic discipline has an international dimension, including environmental studies, literature, religion, economics, and the arts." Academics at Conn are very strong, as evidenced by the fact that Conn students received more Fulbright Scholarships in 2012 than any other liberal arts college. The school is also very committed to interdisciplinary education. Everyone who comes to Conn receives "a completely unique and entirely interdisciplinary experience here," one student explains. For example, a new Connections curriculum encourages students to explore linkages between academic courswework and work in the world, among others. Classes at Conn often revolve around discussion, allowing "students to express their own opinions while hearing from their fellow students and professors." "Professors are very dedicated to their students" at Conn and "often very innovative with class materials." The faculty "teach and encourage intellectual and meaningful class discussions." The honor code at Conn is taken very seriously, and is "beloved" by students. In general, Conn offers "a close-knit, supportive community" where "everyone knows one another—between offices, custodial staff, campus safety, and students." Community is important at Conn. Socially, students "attend each others' events, attend social functions in the student center, grab some coffee at one of our coffee shops, and generally hang out with each other." Conn views the "education of the entire person" as a major goal and has a "great commitment to being sustainable, to promoting community service, and to learning."

BANG FOR YOUR BUCK

Connecticut College is proud to boast about its status as one of the top producers of Peace Corps members, Fulbright Scholars, and Teach for America educators in the country. It provides students with excellent career services and study abroad options. Four certificate-granting centers provide students with opportunities for interdisciplinary study and supplement students' degrees with certificates in arts and technology, environmental studies, community action and public policy, or international studies. While Conn features a 9:1 student/faculty ratio and the small class sizes in line with a traditional liberal arts education, interested students can also collaborate with faculty on research and are often cited as co-authors in publications. Located in New London, Connecticut, this suburban campus is situated between Boston and New York City, and day trips let students experience all they have to offer.

STUDENT LIFE

Many students at Conn are generally "smart, probably upper-class, well-dressed, and white," though the school "embraces diversity." The common theme among all Conn students is "their active involvement both on campus and off and their desire to be challenged in all aspects of their educations." "At a community-service level, students are regularly interacting with the people who live in" New

Connecticut College

FINANCIAL AID: 860-439-2058 • E-MAIL: ADMISSION@CONNCOLL.EDU • WEBSITE: WWW.CONNCOLL.EDU

London. Students fit in by "showing an interest in their studies but also carrying on an active social life." It is fairly easy to find one's niche within the community, and "while it might take a semester to become adjusted, there are many groups, teams, and other resources . . . that help freshmen find a place here."

CAREER

Conn College has a unique career services program that combines one-on-one counseling, workshops, and career advising, and guarantees a stipend of $3,000 to fund a summer internship to all students who participate in the four-year career and professional development program. For seniors, the new "Now Hiring!" program offers intensive training, mock interviews, and practice sessions covering technology, communications, and finances. Outside the career services office, aspiring i-bankers can participate in the Peggotty Investment Club, which provides real-world experience by allowing students to manage a portion of the college endowment. All of these programs drive serious results: According to the school, 96 percent of one-year out grads report being employed or enrolled in graduate school.

FINANCIAL AID

Students should submit: FAFSA, CSS/Financial Aid PROFILE, Noncustodial PROFILE. Priority filing deadline is 2/15. The Princeton Review suggests that all financial aid forms be submitted as soon as possible after October 1. *Need-based scholarships/grants offered:* Federal Pell, FSEOG, State scholarships/grants *Loan aid offered:* Direct Subsidized Stafford Loans, Direct Unsubsidized Stafford Loans, Direct PLUS loans, Federal Perkins Loans. Applicants will be notified of awards on or about 4/1. Federal Work-Study Program available. Institutional employment available.

BOTTOM LINE

The price tag for the great education that Conn offers is not cheap. In fact, it is one of the most expensive schools in the country with an annual tuition of $50,620. Students can expect to spend about $14,060 on room and board as well. That said, Conn is very committed to helping students pay for school. Over half of the freshmen class receives financial aid, and in the most recent school year, Conn awarded over $39 million in need-based aid. The average need-based aid package was $38,709, and has been increasing annually in recent years. The vast majority of students also participate in funded internships at some point in their Conn career.

CAREER INFORMATION FROM PAYSCALE.COM

ROI rating	86
Bachelor's and No Higher	
Median starting salary	$47,000
Median mid-career salary	$69,000
At Least Bachelor's	
Median starting salary	$46,500
Median mid-career salary	$88,700
% alumni with high job meaning	33%
% STEM	17%

SELECTIVITY

Admissions Rating	90
# of applicants	5,182
% of applicants accepted	40
% of acceptees attending	23
# offered a place on the wait list	1,306
% accepting a place on wait list	49
% admitted from wait list	10
# of early decision applicants	347
% accepted early decision	70

FRESHMAN PROFILE

Range SAT Critical Reading	610–700
Range SAT Math	610–700
Range SAT Writing	610–698
Range ACT Composite	28–31
% graduated top 10% of class	49
% graduated top 25% of class	79
% graduated top 50% of class	99

DEADLINES

Early decision	
Deadline	11/15
Notification	12/15
Regular	
Deadline	1/1
Notification	3/31
Nonfall registration?	Yes

FINANCIAL FACTS

Financial Aid Rating	94
Annual tuition	$50,620
Room and board	$14,060
Required fees	$320
Average need-based scholarship	$35,847
% needy frosh rec. need-based scholarship or grant aid	96
% needy UG rec. need-based scholarship or grant aid	95
% needy frosh rec. non-need-based scholarship or grant aid	0
% needy UG rec. non-need-based scholarship or grant aid	0
% needy frosh rec. need-based self-help aid	91
% needy UG rec. need-based self-help aid	89
% frosh rec. any financial aid	59
% UG rec. any financial aid	54
% UG borrow to pay for school	47
Average cumulative indebtedness	$34,098
% frosh need fully met	100
% ugrads need fully met	100
Average % of frosh need met	100
Average % of ugrad need met	100

The Cooper Union for the Advancement of Science and Art

30 Cooper Square, New York, NY 10003 • Admissions: 212-353-4120 • Fax: 212-353-4342

CAMPUS LIFE	
Quality of Life Rating	**84**
Fire Safety Rating	**97**
Green Rating	**60***
Type of school	Private
Affiliation	No Affiliation
Environment	Metropolis

STUDENTS	
Total undergrad enrollment	899
% male/female	67/33
% from out of state	47
% frosh from public high school	65
% frosh live on campus	90
% ugrads live on campus	30
# of fraternities (% ugrad men join)	2 (5)
% African American	3
% Asian	18
% Caucasian	32
% Hispanic	9
% Native American	0
% Pacific Islander	0
% Two or more races	9
% Race and/or ethnicity unknown	12
% international	16

ACADEMICS	
Academic Rating	**92**
% students returning for sophomore year	96
% students graduating within 4 years	70
% students graduating within 6 years	81
Calendar	Semester
Student/faculty ratio	9:1
Profs interesting rating	74
Profs accessible rating	76
Most classes have 10–19 students.	

MOST POPULAR MAJORS
Electrical and Electronics Engineering;
Mechanical Engineering; Art/Art Studies

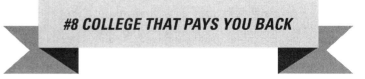

#8 COLLEGE THAT PAYS YOU BACK

ABOUT THE SCHOOL
Believe it or not, the generous scholarship policy isn't the only reason gifted students clamor for a spot at The Cooper Union for the Advancement of Science and Art. The school's reputable, rigorous academics and location in the heart of New York's East Village are equally big draws. Classes are small (total enrollment is fewer than 900), and students must handle a highly demanding workload. The size of the school allows for very close relationships between the professors and the students, and the faculty is the intellectual pulse of the institution. Most come to The Cooper Union while continuing their own personal research and work at various points in their academic careers, giving students frontline access to real-world experience and insight from professors who want to teach. Group projects are a major part of the curriculum, regardless of academic discipline, furthering the school's problem-solving philosophy of education. A degree from The Cooper Union is enormously valuable in the job market, and many graduates become world-class leaders in the disciplines of architecture, fine arts, design, and engineering. As an all-honors private college, The Cooper Union offers talented students rigorous, humanistic learning enhanced by the process of design and augmented by the urban setting. In addition to outstanding academic programs in architecture, art, and engineering, it offers a Faculty of Humanities and Social Sciences. "An institution of the highest caliber," the school has a narrow academic focus, conferring degrees only in fine arts, architecture, and engineering, with "plenty of opportunities for independent study in your field." All students take a core curriculum of required courses in the humanities and social sciences in their first two years, and those that go on to the School of Art have easy "access to established and interesting artists."

BANG FOR YOUR BUCK
The school's founder, Peter Cooper, believed that an "education of the first rank" should be "as free as air and water," and while the current economic climate has recently changed the school's scholarship practices, The Cooper Union remains committed to providing financial support to its accomplished, ambitious student body. An example of this is every enrolled student receives a minimum half-tuition scholarship. The engineering program is considered one of the best in the nation, and a degree from The Cooper Union is a ticket into an excellent professional career. Forty percent of graduates go on to top-tier graduate programs, and the small school has produced thirty-four Fulbright scholars since 2001. The Cooper Union's location in the East Village adds value to students' experience as well. In the limited time they spend outside of the lab or the studio, students here have access to the nearly infinite range of cultural events, restaurants, museums, and other adventures available in New York City.

STUDENT LIFE
Artists, engineers, and architects abound on this East Village campus filled with "very unique, interesting people" eager to learn and cross-pollinate between departments. This goal is supported by the architecture of The Cooper Union's distinctive academic building which was designed by Thom Mayne to enhance interaction between enrollees of all three schools. Across the board, students in every major are serious about their studies, and most of The Cooper Union's selective admits are "super intelligent, super creative, and/or just super hardworking." Still, The Cooper Union's prime location allows the City That Never Sleeps to act as The Cooper Union's extended campus with plenty of "comedy

The Cooper Union for the Advancement of Science and Art

FINANCIAL AID: 212-353-4130 • E-MAIL: ADMISSIONS@COOPER.EDU • WEBSITE: WWW.COOPER.EDU

clubs, movies, bowling, lounges, and bars" to entice students to take a break from their studies. Students say their school will "push you to your limits, push you to succeed, and this common goal unites all the students as well," which makes for a "close-knit community," not to mention an exciting, motivating experience.

CAREER

The Center for Career Development encourages "self-accountability," "initiative," and "autonomy" in all Cooper students as they transition to a professional practice. With that in mind, the Center offers ample resources to help students find their way, like online timelines and career counseling tailored to each school as well as the Cooper Career Connection that informs students about all career-related events, programs, and forums. The Career Resource Library is another excellent way to keep abreast of trends and ideas in your relevant field. Alumni lead by example, and the CU @ Lunch program allows recent grads to "speak about the vital issues they face following graduation." Those graduates who visited PayScale.com report an average starting salary of $61,400, and 50 percent believe their work makes the world a better place.

GENERAL INFO

Activities: Choral groups, concert band, dance, drama/theater, jazz band, literary magazine, music ensembles, student government, student newspaper, student-run film society, symphony orchestra, yearbook. **Organizations:** 90 registered organizations, 18 honor societies, 8 religious organizations. 2 fraternities. **Athletics (Intercollegiate):** *Men:* Baseball, basketball, cross-country, soccer, tennis, volleyball. *Women:* Basketball, cross-country, soccer, tennis, volleyball.

FINANCIAL AID

Students should submit: FAFSA. Recommended filing deadline for early decision applicants is 12/1 and 3/1 for regular decision applicants. The Princeton Review suggests that all financial aid forms be submitted as soon as possible after October 1. *Need-based scholarships/grants offered:* Federal Pell, FSEOG, State scholarships/grants, Private scholarships, College/university scholarship or grant aid from institutional funds. *Loan aid offered:* Direct Subsidized Stafford Loans, Direct Unsubsidized Stafford Loans, Direct PLUS loans, Federal Perkins Loans, College/university loans from institutional funds. Applicants will be notified of awards with admissions packets. Federal Work-Study Program available. Institutional employment available.

BOTTOM LINE

Students are accepted on the basis of merit alone, and as of Fall 2015 every admitted student receives a half-tuition scholarship valued at $21,000 annually. For remaining expenses, including room and board, The Cooper Union provides additional aid based upon financial need. Health insurance adds an additional $1,200 for those that require it. Financial aid is available to assist with payment of all fees.

CAREER INFORMATION FROM PAYSCALE.COM

ROI rating	95
Bachelor's and No Higher	
Median starting salary	$62,700
Median mid-career salary	$114,000
At Least Bachelor's	
Median starting salary	$63,500
Median mid-career salary	$120,000
% alumni with high job meaning	39%
% STEM	59%

SELECTIVITY

Admissions Rating	98
# of applicants	3,258
% of applicants accepted	13
% of acceptees attending	55
# offered a place on the wait list	315
% accepting a place on wait list	97
% admitted from wait list	4
# of early decision applicants	228
% accepted early decision	30

FRESHMAN PROFILE

Range SAT Critical Reading	610–720
Range SAT Math	630–790
Range SAT Writing	600–720
Range ACT Composite	31–34
Minimum paper TOEFL	600
Minimum internet-based TOEFL	100
Average HS GPA	3.5
% graduated top 10% of class	85
% graduated top 25% of class	90
% graduated top 50% of class	95

DEADLINES

Early decision	
Deadline	12/1
Notification	12/23
Other ED	
Deadline	12/1
Other ED	
Notification	12/23
Regular	
Priority	12/1
Deadline	1/9
Notification	4/1
Nonfall registration?	No

FINANCIAL FACTS

Financial Aid Rating	97
Annual tuition	$42,000
Room and board	$15,910
Required fees	$1,850
Average need-based scholarship	$12,603
% needy frosh rec. need-based scholarship or grant aid	84
% needy UG rec. need-based scholarship or grant aid	81
% needy frosh rec. non-need-based scholarship or grant aid	100
% needy UG rec. non-need-based scholarship or grant aid	100
% needy frosh rec. need-based self-help aid	54
% needy UG rec. need-based self-help aid	60
% frosh rec. any financial aid	100
% UG rec. any financial aid	100

Cornell University

UNDERGRADUATE ADMISSIONS, 410 THURSTON AVE, ITHACA, NY 14850 • ADMISSIONS: 607-255-5241 • FAX: 607-255-0659

CAMPUS LIFE

Quality of Life Rating	92
Fire Safety Rating	89
Green Rating	99
Type of school	Private
Affiliation	No Affiliation
Environment	Town

STUDENTS

Total undergrad enrollment	14,315
% male/female	48/52
% from out of state	65
% frosh live on campus	100
% ugrads live on campus	55
# of fraternities (% ugrad men join)	47 (33)
# of sororities (% ugrad women join)	18 (34)
% African American	6
% Asian	18
% Caucasian	41
% Hispanic	12
% Native American	<1
% Pacific Islander	<1
% Two or more races	4
% Race and/or ethnicity unknown	8
% international	10
# of countries represented	82

ACADEMICS

Academic Rating	91
% students returning for sophomore year	97
% students graduating within 4 years	86
% students graduating within 6 years	93
Calendar	Semester
Student/faculty ratio	9:1
Profs interesting rating	81
Profs accessible rating	79

Most classes have 10–19 students.
Most lab/discussion sessions have 10–19 students.

MOST POPULAR MAJORS

Biology; Hotel Administration/Management; Industrial and Labor Relations

#19 COLLEGE THAT PAYS YOU BACK

ABOUT THE SCHOOL

"Any person, any study." Perhaps no motto does a better job of summing up the spirit of a school than Ithaca, New York's Cornell University, an Ivy League school in upstate New York consisting of seven undergraduate colleges and schools. Cornell University is not just Ivy League, it's the largest of the Ivy League schools—and it has a curriculum to match. The "unbelievably broad curriculum" at Cornell offers a "large variety of academic programs" and "a plethora of classes to chose from," giving credence to the school's famous motto. There are more than forty different majors at the College of Arts and Sciences alone. Factor in six other colleges and schools, and it's clear that students have a wealth of options before them. Specializations in science, agriculture, and environmental studies are especially popular here, though engineering, premed, and other studies receive just as much attention by attendees. "The research opportunities have been incredible," one student says. Another notes that, thanks to the hard work it demands of students and the school's great reputation, Cornell is a "difficult school with great job placement after." With all the educational opportunities Cornell has to offer, it should come as no surprise that the campus features an "intellectually mature student body" who are intent on focusing on the school's "rigorous" academics. "The intellectual caliber of the student body here is really unmatched." When study time ends, students exploring the "bustling student life" will see that "diversity here is definitely apparent . . . I love the fact that you can be surrounded by dairy farmers and Wall Street wannabes all in the same quad." About the only thing tying Cornell's student population together is the fact that everyone is "very focused on performing well in the classroom." Outside the classroom, recreation is just as diverse as the classes. Being in Ithaca, New York, opportunities for outdoor adventure abound, and Greek life thrives. Sports are as popular here as partying—wrestling, track, and hockey are the school's top sports—and students note that "if I want to go study in a library at 3 A.M. on Saturday night, I will find a busy library full of other eager students, but if I want to go to a hockey game on a Saturday afternoon, I will find just as many screaming fans to share the fun."

BANG FOR YOUR BUCK

Need-based Federal Pell, SEOG, state scholarships/grants, private scholarships, school scholarship, or grant aid from institutional funds are all available to prospective students. Loan aid is also available in the form of Direct Subsidized Stafford loans, Direct Unsubsidized Stafford, Direct PLUS, and university loans from institutional funds.

STUDENT LIFE

Since Cornell is such a rigorous school, it's not surprising that "most of the time people are thinking about studying and getting their work done." "People are always thinking about the next prelim or paper they have to suffer through, but it's not always immediately at the forefront of their mind," says a student, so "people work hard here, and people certainly know how to play hard as well. "People here do anything and everything they can for fun: sports, parties, hanging out with friends or even getting involved with the clubs here on campus." With 30 to 40 percent of kids participating, "Greek life is big here. Not overwhelming, but definitely big." "Frat parties are really popular freshman and sophomore years, but then the crowd tends to migrate to the bars in Collegetown during junior and senior years." But while "it is not hard to find alcohol on campus,

Cornell University

FINANCIAL AID: 607-255-5147 • E-MAIL: ADMISSIONS@CORNELL.EDU • WEBSITE: WWW.CORNELL.EDU

there really is no pressure to drink, [and] there are also a lot of campus run events on the weekends and also throughout the week to encourage students to do other things." "The campus is so diverse and the range of activities is endless. You will find a club or organization here that interests you, and there's always the possibility of establishing something new if that's what you're interested in here." So even if "the size of the student body may be overwhelming at first," students will find that "it's easy to find a close group of people."

CAREER

Cornell students are definitely a career-focused bunch: "People are kind of paranoid of failure," says a student. "They go crazy looking for internships and career opportunities as early as second semester freshman year." Fortunately for those students, consensus seems to be that "Cornell offers great career assistance to help students write resumes, cover letters, and find jobs/internships." The center offers counseling for students looking to explore their interests and determine a career path, resources for finding jobs and internships, career fairs and on campus recruiting, and even resources for those seeking international work experience. In addition to a central office in Barnes Hall that serves all students, each of Cornell's seven undergraduate colleges has its own office with resources tailored to the students in that college.

GENERAL INFO

Environment: Town. **Activities:** Choral groups, concert band, dance, drama/theater, jazz band, literary magazine, marching band, music ensembles, musical theater, pep band, radio station, student government, student newspaper, student-run film society, symphony orchestra, television station, yearbook, campus ministries, international student organization.

FINANCIAL AID

Students should submit: FAFSA, CSS/Financial Aid PROFILE, Noncustodial PROFILE. Regular filing deadline is 2/15. The Princeton Review suggests that all financial aid forms be submitted as soon as possible after October 1. *Need-based scholarships/grants offered:* Federal Pell, FSEOG, State scholarships/grants, Private scholarships, College/university scholarship or grant aid from institutional funds. *Loan aid offered:* Direct Subsidized Stafford Loans, Direct Unsubsidized Stafford Loans, Direct PLUS loans, Federal Perkins Loans, College/university loans from institutional funds. Applicants will be notified of awards on or about 4/1. Federal Work-Study Program available. Institutional employment available.

BOTTOM LINE

An Ivy League education at Cornell University will cost attendees just more than $47,000 per year in tuition. Add to that $13,680 for room and board, and another $1,086 for books, fees, and supplies, and costs come to about $61,800 annually. Students are graduating from Cornell with an average accumulated debt of $20,557.

CAREER INFORMATION FROM PAYSCALE.COM

ROI rating	92
Bachelor's and No Higher	
Median starting salary	$59,700
Median mid-career salary	$109,000
At Least Bachelor's	
Median starting salary	$61,900
Median mid-career salary	$114,000
% alumni with high job meaning	54%
% STEM	33%

SELECTIVITY

Admissions Rating	97
# of applicants	41,900
% of applicants accepted	15
% of acceptees attending	50
# offered a place on the wait list	3,583
% accepting a place on wait list	62
% admitted from wait list	4
# of early decision applicants	4,560
% accepted early decision	26

FRESHMAN PROFILE

Range SAT Critical Reading	650–750
Range SAT Math	680–780
Range ACT Composite	30–34
Minimum paper TOEFL	600
Minimum internet-based TOEFL	100
% graduated top 10% of class	89
% graduated top 25% of class	97
% graduated top 50% of class	100

DEADLINES

Early decision	
Deadline	11/1
Regular	
Deadline	1/2
Nonfall registration?	No

FINANCIAL FACTS

Financial Aid Rating	96
Annual tuition	$50,712
Room and board	$13,950
Required fees	$241
Average need-based scholarship	$38,377
% needy frosh rec. need-based scholarship or grant aid	98
% needy UG rec. need-based scholarship or grant aid	98
% needy frosh rec. non-need-based scholarship or grant aid	0
% needy UG rec. non-need-based scholarship or grant aid	0
% needy frosh rec. need-based self-help aid	88
% needy UG rec. need-based self-help aid	92
% frosh rec. any financial aid	60
% UG rec. any financial aid	57
% UG borrow to pay for school	43
Average cumulative indebtedness	$24,394
% frosh need fully met	100
% ugrads need fully met	100
Average % of frosh need met	100
Average % of ugrad need met	100

Creighton University

2500 CALIFORNIA PLAZA, OMAHA, NE 68178 • ADMISSIONS: 402-280-2703 • FAX: 402-280-2685

CAMPUS LIFE
Quality of Life Rating	**90**
Fire Safety Rating	**96**
Green Rating	**86**
Type of school	Private
Affiliation	Roman Catholic Jesuit
Environment	Metropolis

STUDENTS
Total undergrad enrollment	4,163
% male/female	43/57
% from out of state	75
% frosh from public high school	51
% frosh live on campus	95
% ugrads live on campus	60
# of fraternities (% ugrad men join)	5 (30)
# of sororities (% ugrad women join)	7 (46)
% African American	2
% Asian	10
% Caucasian	71
% Hispanic	8
% Native American	<1
% Pacific Islander	<1
% Two or more races	4
% Race and/or ethnicity unknown	1
% international	3
# of countries represented	33

ACADEMICS
Academic Rating	**84**
% students returning for sophomore year	90
% students graduating within 4 years	72
% students graduating within 6 years	79
Calendar	Semester
Student/faculty ratio	11:1
Profs interesting rating	83
Profs accessible rating	86

Most classes have 10–19 students.
Most lab/discussion sessions have 10–19 students.

MOST POPULAR MAJORS
Nursing; Biology; Psychology

ABOUT THE SCHOOL
A Catholic school that thoroughly embraces its Jesuit values, it's no surprise that Creighton provides undergraduates with a "welcoming community that focuses on giving each student a quality education." Indeed, "Creighton cares about the whole person, pushing you to do your best and learn things you never expected to." Undergrads benefit from a "small student-[to-professor] ratio" which helps to ensure personalized attention. They also rave about "the highly ranked" physical therapy and nursing departments as well as the "excellent and unique pre-pharmacy/pharmacy program." No matter the course of study, Creighton undergrads are full of praise for their professors. An English major gushes, "They're always willing to talk outside of class and offer suggestions about subjects of study that might make what is learned in the classroom more interesting and applicable to the individual." It's clearly evident that they "are passionate about their subjects and genuinely care about the success of their students."

BANG FOR YOUR BUCK
While some families might initially balk at the price tag ascribed to Creighton, rest assured that the university does all that it can in helping to ease the financial burden. Indeed, many students receive "generous financial aid package[s]." A freshman wholeheartedly agrees sharing, "[Creighton] love[s] to give everyone a chance with their scholarships and financial aid." After all, an astounding 96 percent of the undergraduate population receives some form of need-based aid, with the average package around $27,934. While some of that definitely derives from loans, plenty of scholarship and grant money gets distributed. For example, students at the top of the applicant pool are considered for the Presidential Scholarship, which provides a renewable $25,000 award. And Diversity Scholarships offer a staggering $30,000 in renewable tuition scholarships to students who demonstrate a continuous commitment to diversity.

STUDENT LIFE
There are plenty of distractions to be found when Creighton undergrads are looking to take a study break. As an eager sophomore shares, "There are tons of activities all the time, [both] campus-wide, and dorm specific. There is [always something] to do." More specifically, basketball is "huge" at Creighton and most students can be found attending games. Lots of undergrads are "involved in Greek life here and participate in community service [as well]." Students also report that "Omaha is a great city to live in." There "always seems to be cultural festivals going on [and] the food scene is really fun too because there are so many different restaurants."

Creighton University

FINANCIAL AID: 402-280-2731 • E-MAIL: ADMISSIONS@CREIGHTON.EDU • WEBSITE: WWW.CREIGHTON.EDU

CAREER

Armed with a great reputation in Omaha and beyond, Creighton undergrads quickly assert that their alma mater "has a great return on investment." And given that the average starting salary for recent grads is $46,100, we'd say that statement is wholly accurate. Creighton's Career Center works tirelessly to help create professional opportunities. In fact, more than 774 interviews take place in the office each year. And students interact with nearly 400 employers at campus networking events. Events like these have led to Creighton undergrads working at companies such as Berkshire Hathaway, Yahoo!, Ameritrade, Mutual of Omaha, First National Bank, Under Armour and Macy's.

GENERAL INFO

Activities: Campus ministries, choral groups, dance, drama/theatre, international student organization,model UN, music ensembles, musical theatre, pep band, radio station, student government, student newspaper, symphony orchestra. **Organizations:** 222 registered organizations, 15 honor societies, 18 religious organizations. 5 fraternities, 7 sororities. **Athletics (Intercollegiate):** *Men:* baseball, basketball, cross-country, golf, soccer, tennis. *Women:* basketball, crew/rowing, cross-country, golf, soccer, softball, tennis, volleyball. **On-Campus Highlights:** Harper Center, Championship Center, Hixson-Lied Science Building, Morrison Soccer Stadium, Jesuit Gardens, Ryan Athletics Center and D.J.Sokol Arena.

FINANCIAL AID

Students should submit: FAFSA, Institution's own financial aid form. Priority filing deadline is 3/1. The Princeton Review suggests that all financial aid forms be submitted as soon as possible after October 1. *Need-based scholarships/grants offered:* Federal Pell, FSEOG, State scholarships/grants, Private scholarships, College/university scholarship or grant aid from institutional funds. *Loan aid offered:* Direct Subsidized Stafford Loans, Direct Unsubsidized Stafford Loans, Direct PLUS loans, Federal Perkins Loans, Federal Nursing Loans. Applicants will be notified of awards on a rolling basis beginning 3/15. Federal Work-Study Program available. Institutional employment available.

BOTTOM LINE

Students interested in enrolling at Creighton will face a tuition bill of $35,942. Additionally, on-campus room and board should run students around $10,600. Finally, students will also have to pay another $1,664 in required fees.

CAREER INFORMATION FROM PAYSCALE.COM

ROI rating	**86**
Bachelor's and No Higher	
Median starting salary	$45,200
Median mid-career salary	$84,700
At Least Bachelor's	
Median starting salary	$46,100
Median mid-career salary	$87,500
% alumni with high job meaning	67%
% STEM	17%

SELECTIVITY

Admissions Rating	87
# of applicants	9,747
% of applicants accepted	70
% of acceptees attending	16
# offered a place on the wait list	0

FRESHMAN PROFILE

Range SAT Critical Reading	510–630
Range SAT Math	540–650
Range SAT Writing	510–620
Range ACT Composite	24–29
Minimum paper TOEFL	550
Minimum internet-based TOEFL	80
Average HS GPA	3.8
% graduated top 10% of class	37
% graduated top 25% of class	68
% graduated top 50% of class	92

DEADLINES

Regular	
Priority	12/1
Deadline	2/15
Nonfall registration?	Yes

FINANCIAL FACTS

Financial Aid Rating	85
Annual tuition	$35,942
Room and board	$10,600
Required fees	$1,664
Average need-based scholarship	$21,283
% needy frosh rec. need-based scholarship or grant aid	100
% needy UG rec. need-based scholarship or grant aid	96
% needy frosh rec. non-need-based scholarship or grant aid	22
% needy UG rec. non-need-based scholarship or grant aid	18
% needy frosh rec. need-based self-help aid	81
% needy UG rec. need-based self-help aid	82
% frosh rec. any financial aid	99
% UG rec. any financial aid	96
% UG borrow to pay for school	57
Avg indebtedness	$33,792
% frosh need fully met	28
% UG need full met	27
Avg % frosh need met	85
Avg % UG need met	81

Dartmouth College

6016 McNutt Hall, Hanover, NH 03755 • Admissions: 603-646-2875 • Fax: 603-646-1216

#15 COLLEGE THAT PAYS YOU BACK

ABOUT THE SCHOOL

A member of the Ivy League, Dartmouth is a small, student-centered undergraduate and graduate college, with three leading professional schools—Geisel School of Medicine, Thayer School of Engineering, and the Tuck School of Business. It is known for its commitment to excellence in undergraduate education and has a reputation as a place where intellectual rigor and creativity collide. This comes from a flexible academic curriculum that emphasizes an interdisciplinary approach. The campus community is generally relaxed, accepting, a bit outdoorsy, and usually bundled up under eight layers of clothing to get through the New Hampshire winters. What students learn outside the classroom is often as meaningful as what they learn inside. All incoming freshmen live in residential housing clusters located throughout the campus, and more than 80 percent of upperclassmen choose to do so as well. Almost all of the student body comes from outside the college's New Hampshire base. Greek groups add to the social mix because everyone is welcome to attend fraternity and sorority parties and events. Intramural athletics are insanely popular on campus as well.

BANG FOR YOUR BUCK

Dartmouth's approximately 4,300 undergraduate students enjoy the college's strong reputation as a member of the Ivy League, as well as its high-quality academics through twenty-nine departments and ten multidisciplinary programs. Academics at New Hampshire's preeminent college, comparable with other Ivy League schools, are demanding, but Dartmouth students feel they are up to the challenge. Unlike many of the other Ivies, though, the student-faculty ratio of 8:1 favors the undergrads, who find graduate assistants in their classes to have the same open willingness to help them learn as the regular professors do.

STUDENT LIFE

Dartmouth students are continually on the go and they "wouldn't have it any other way." As one senior shares, "After attending classes in the morning, we run from meetings to debates to the library and finally to Frat Row. It is a relentless, fast-paced cycle, but it is so unbelievably fun and rewarding." More specifically, undergrads can enjoy "movies playing at our arts center . . . activities night (games, movies, etc. . . .), performance groups (dance troupes, a cappella groups, plays), outdoor activities (skiing, camping, hiking, sailing, etc.), and much more." We're told that "a very large percentage" of the student body chooses to go Greek. Fortunately, it's a "unique and VERY welcoming [scene] and much more low key than at other schools." And, of course, these undergrads love participating in Dartmouth traditions like "running around a giant three-story bonfire hundreds of times or streaking the green or singing karaoke with a milkshake close by."

CAREER

A Dartmouth degree and professional success typically go hand-in-hand. After all, according to PayScale.com, the average starting salary for Dartmouth grads is an impressive $55,000. Some of this success can indeed be attributed to the college's extensive alumni network. As one grateful psych major shares, "Alumni are . . . a HUGE resource; they love to stay involved with the college and are often willing to talk to current students about careers (and many have been known to give

Dartmouth College

FINANCIAL AID: 603-646-2451 • WEBSITE: WWW.DARTMOUTH.EDU

internships and jobs to Dartmouth students).” Certainly, students can also turn to the fantastic Center for Professional Development as well. Undergrads may use the office to find funding for unpaid internships, receive graduate and professional school advising and even get help finding housing for when they head out into the world. And, perhaps most important, the center hosts numerous recruiting sessions throughout the year.

GENERAL INFO

Activities: Choral groups, concert band, dance, drama/theater, jazz band, literary magazine, marching band, music ensembles, musical theater, opera, pep band, radio station, student government, student newspaper, student-run film society, symphony orchestra, television station, yearbook, campus ministries, international student organization. **Organizations:** 330 registered organizations, 26 religious organizations. 17 fraternities, 11 sororities. **Athletics (Intercollegiate):** *Men:* Baseball, basketball, crew/rowing, cross-country, diving, equestrian sports, fencing, football, golf, ice hockey, lacrosse, sailing, skiing (downhill/alpine), skiing (nordic/cross-country), soccer, squash, swimming, tennis, track/field (outdoor), track/field. *Women:* Basketball, crew/rowing, cross-country, diving, equestrian sports, fencing, field hockey, golf, ice hockey, lacrosse, sailing, skiing (downhill/alpine), skiing (nordic/cross-country), soccer, softball, squash, swimming, tennis, track/field (outdoor), track/ field, volleyball.

FINANCIAL AID

Students should submit: FAFSA, CSS/Financial Aid PROFILE, Noncustodial PROFILE, Business/Farm Supplement. Regular filing deadline is 2/1. The Princeton Review suggests that all financial aid forms be submitted as soon as possible after October 1. *Need-based scholarships/grants offered:* Federal Pell, FSEOG, State scholarships/ grants, Private scholarships, College/university scholarship or grant aid from institutional funds. *Loan aid offered:* Direct Subsidized Stafford Loans, Direct Unsubsidized Stafford Loans, Direct PLUS loans, Federal Perkins Loans, State Loans, College/university loans from institutional funds. Applicants will be notified of awards on or about 4/2. Federal Work-Study Program available. Institutional employment available.

BOTTOM LINE

To enjoy an Ivy League education with a nod to the New England collegiate experience, incoming freshmen at Dartmouth can expect to pay about $49,998 in tuition and roughly another $1,440 in required fees. On-campus room and board totals more than $14,736. Over half of Dartmouth students receive financial aid to help defray these costs, as the school maintains the philosophy that no one should hesitate to apply for fear they won’t be able to afford it. A recent graduate shares her experience: “The administration is great to work with. Opportunities for funding to travel and do research, internships, volunteer, etc. are AMAZING.”

CAREER INFORMATION FROM PAYSCALE.COM

ROI rating	93
Bachelor's and No Higher	
Median starting salary	$56,300
Median mid-career salary	$111,000
At Least Bachelor's	
Median starting salary	$58,800
Median mid-career salary	$113,000
% alumni with high job meaning	45%
% STEM	20%

SELECTIVITY

Admissions Rating	98
# of applicants	20,675
% of applicants accepted	11
% of acceptees attending	52
# offered a place on the wait list	2,064
% accepting a place on wait list	67
% admitted from wait list	1
# of early decision applicants	1,928
% accepted early decision	26

FRESHMAN PROFILE

Range SAT Critical Reading	670–780
Range SAT Math	680–780
Range SAT Writing	670–790
Range ACT Composite	30–34
Minimum paper TOEFL	600
Minimum internet-based TOEFL	100
% graduated top 10% of class	93
% graduated top 25% of class	98
% graduated top 50% of class	100

DEADLINES

Early decision	
Deadline	11/1
Notification	12/15
Regular	
Deadline	1/1
Notification	4/10
Nonfall registration?	No

FINANCIAL FACTS

Financial Aid Rating	96
Annual tuition	$49,998
Room and board	$14,736
Required fees	$1,440
Average need-based scholarship	$46,917
% needy frosh rec. need-based scholarship or grant aid	98
% needy UG rec. need-based scholarship or grant aid	96
% needy frosh rec. non-need-based scholarship or grant aid	0
% needy UG rec. non-need-based scholarship or grant aid	0
% needy frosh rec. need-based self-help aid	86
% needy UG rec. need-based self-help aid	91
% frosh rec. any financial aid	58
% UG rec. any financial aid	54
% frosh need fully met	100
% ugrads need fully met	100
Average % of frosh need met	100
Average % of ugrad need met	100

Davidson College

PO Box 7156, Davidson, NC 28035-7156 • Admissions: 704-894-2230 • Fax: 704-894-2016

CAMPUS LIFE

Quality of Life Rating	88
Fire Safety Rating	60*
Green Rating	60*
Type of school	Private
Affiliation	Presbyterian
Environment	Village

STUDENTS

Total undergrad enrollment	1,784
% male/female	50/50
% from out of state	75
% frosh from public high school	47
% frosh live on campus	100
% ugrads live on campus	94
# of fraternities (% ugrad men join)	8 (39)
# of sororities (% ugrad women join)	6 (70)
% African American	7
% Asian	5
% Caucasian	68
% Hispanic	8
% Native American	1
% Pacific Islander	0
% Two or more races	4
% Race and/or ethnicity unknown	1
% international	6
# of countries represented	42

ACADEMICS

Academic Rating	90
% students returning for sophomore year	96
% students graduating within 4 years	90
% students graduating within 6 years	93
Calendar	Semester
Student/faculty ratio	10:1
Profs interesting rating	84
Profs accessible rating	86

Most classes have 10–19 students.
Most lab/discussion sessions have
  10–19 students.

MOST POPULAR MAJORS
Biology; Political Science and Government;
Psychology

ABOUT THE SCHOOL

Davidson is a place where serious students can thrive and really throw themselves into the world of academia, all while surrounded by similarly energetic, curious, and quirky students. At this small, "really beautiful" school north of Charlotte, North Carolina, students come from nearly every state in the union and from dozens of foreign countries to immerse themselves in the "intellectually challenging, academically rigorous" cocoon that Davidson provides. The school offers a classic liberal arts education, encouraging students to take classes in all areas, and "all of these people come out smarter than they came in." Classes are small and intensive, with significant contact between students and faculty both in and out of the classroom, and faculty, while emphasizing teaching, involve students in significant research projects. There is a lot of work, but it "is accompanied by even more resources with which it can be successfully managed." "I have never witnessed people so eager to come do their job every day. [Professors] are almost too willing to help," says a student. The honor code also helps contribute "to having a safe and reliable environment."

BANG FOR YOUR BUCK

Davidson is consistently regarded as one of the top liberal arts colleges in the country, and its small size (and twenty-person class limits) give students access to a level of academic guidance and greatness that most college students can only dream of, at a price that students can afford. The school has just 1,700 undergraduates but offers $17 million a year in financial aid. On top of the holy triumvirate of financial aid, Davidson offers merit scholarships ranging from $1,000 to the full cost of education. The school is also need-blind to life experience: Need and merit aid can go with students on approved study-abroad programs, thereby eliminating a potential barrier to having an international experience.

STUDENT LIFE

Davidson is "an amalgamation of all types of people, religiously, ethnically, politically, economically, etc.," all "united under the umbrella of intellectual curiosity" and their devotion to the school as a community. The typical Davidson student is "probably white," but in the past few years, admissions has been making progress in racially diversifying the campus, which students agree is necessary. Though there are plenty of Southern, preppy, athletic types to fit the brochure examples, there are many niches for every type of "atypical" student. "There are enough people that one can find a similar group to connect with, and there are few enough people that one ends up connecting with dissimilar [people] anyway," says a student. Everyone here is smart and well-rounded; admissions "does a good job . . . so if you're in, you'll probably make the cut all the way through the four years." Most students have several extracurriculars to round out their free time, and they have a healthy desire to enjoy themselves when the books shut. "During the week we work hard. On the weekends we play hard. We don't do anything halfway," says a senior. Though the majority of students lean to the left, there's a strong conservative contingent, and there are no real problems between the two.

CAREER

Davidson's Center for Career Development keeps its student body on track with thorough career planning checklists for each class year (Step One: Sign up for career services announcements!). Students can drop-in to get advice on topics like career exploration and major selection or they can take part in a Job Shadowing Program over winter break when they will spend time with alumni at work. WildcatLink is the online gateway to Davidson-specific opportunities like fellowships,

Davidson College

E-MAIL: ADMISSION@DAVIDSON.EDU • WEBSITE: WWW.DAVIDSON.EDU

jobs, and internships. Recent graduates have also participated in the Davidson Impact Fellows program, working for a year with organizations focused on the environment, social entrepreneurship, and other issues. Alumni visiting PayScale.com reported a median starting salary of $47,200.

GENERAL INFO

Activities: Choral groups, concert band, dance, drama/theater, jazz band, literary magazine, music ensembles, musical theater, pep band, radio station, student government, student newspaper, symphony orchestra, yearbook, campus ministries, international student organization. **Organizations:** 151 registered organizations, 15 honor societies, 16 religious organizations. 8 fraternities, 6 sororities. **Athletics (Intercollegiate):** *Men:* Baseball, basketball, cross-country, diving, football, golf, soccer, swimming, tennis, track/field (outdoor), wrestling. *Women:* Basketball, cross-country, diving, field hockey, lacrosse, soccer, swimming, tennis, track/field (outdoor), volleyball. **On-Campus Highlights:** Belk Visual Arts Center, Baker-Watt Science Complex, Baker Sports Complex, Campus Center, Lake Campus.

FINANCIAL AID

Students should submit: FAFSA, CSS/Financial Aid PROFILE, Noncustodial PROFILE, Business/Farm Supplement. Regular filing deadline is 2/15. The Princeton Review suggests that all financial aid forms be submitted as soon as possible after October 1. *Need-based scholarships/grants offered:* Federal Pell, FSEOG, State scholarships/grants, Private scholarships, College/university scholarship or grant aid from institutional funds. *Loan aid offered:* Direct Subsidized Stafford Loans, Direct Unsubsidized Stafford Loans, Direct PLUS Loans. Applicants will be notified of awards on or about 4/1. Federal Work-Study Program available. Institutional employment available.

BOTTOM LINE

Tuition runs about $47,897, with an additional $13,547 or so needed for room and board. However, the school hits the three major financial aid points: it admits domestic students on a need-blind basis, meets 100 percent of all students' calculated need, and does so with grant and work funds only, not requiring students to utilize loans to have their need met. Aid is also guaranteed throughout the four years if a family's financial circumstances stay the same.

CAREER INFORMATION FROM PAYSCALE.COM

ROI rating	90
Bachelor's and No Higher	
Median starting salary	$48,800
Median mid-career salary	$88,100
At Least Bachelor's	
Median starting salary	$49,300
Median mid-career salary	$90,600
% alumni with high job meaning	59%
% STEM	15%

SELECTIVITY

Admissions Rating	96
# of applicants	5,382
% of applicants accepted	22
% of acceptees attending	43
# of early decision applicants	638
% accepted early decision	48

FRESHMAN PROFILE

Range SAT Critical Reading	630–720
Range SAT Math	630–720
Range SAT Writing	610–720
Range ACT Composite	29–32
Minimum paper TOEFL	600
Minimum internet-based TOEFL	100
Average HS GPA	4.0
% graduated top 10% of class	55
% graduated top 25% of class	91
% graduated top 50% of class	91

DEADLINES

Early decision	
Deadline	11/15
Notification	12/15
Regular	
Deadline	1/2
Notification	4/1
Nonfall registration?	No

FINANCIAL FACTS

Financial Aid Rating	96
Annual tuition	$47,897
Room and board	$13,547
Required fees	$479
Average need-based scholarship	$40,140
% needy frosh rec. need-based scholarship or grant aid	99
% needy UG rec. need-based scholarship or grant aid	99
% needy frosh rec. non-need-based scholarship or grant aid	34
% needy UG rec. non-need-based scholarship or grant aid	32
% needy frosh rec. need-based self-help aid	62
% needy UG rec. need-based self-help aid	70
% frosh rec. any financial aid	52
% UG rec. any financial aid	52
% UG borrow to pay for school	27
Average cumulative indebtedness	$19,929
% frosh need fully met	100
% ugrads need fully met	100
Average % of frosh need met	100
Average % of ugrad need met	100

Denison University

Box H, Granville, OH 43023 • Admissions: 740-587-6276 • Fax: 740-587-6306

CAMPUS LIFE

Quality of Life Rating	**89**
Fire Safety Rating	**96**
Green Rating	**91**
Type of school	Private
Affiliation	No Affiliation
Environment	Suburban

STUDENTS

Total undergrad enrollment	2,282
% male/female	43/57
% from out of state	72
% frosh from public high school	66
% frosh live on campus	99
% ugrads live on campus	99
# of fraternities (% ugrad men join)	9 (21)
# of sororities (% ugrad women join)	9 (34)
% African American	7
% Asian	4
% Caucasian	66
% Hispanic	10
% Native American	<1
% Pacific Islander	<1
% Two or more races	4
% Race and/or ethnicity unknown	2
% international	8
# of countries represented	34

ACADEMICS

Academic Rating	**91**
% students returning for sophomore year	89
% students graduating within 4 years	78
% students graduating within 6 years	80
Calendar	Semester
Student/faculty ratio	10:1
Profs interesting rating	89
Profs accessible rating	92
Most classes have 10–19 students.	

MOST POPULAR MAJORS
Economics; Psychology; Biology

ABOUT THE SCHOOL

For those seeking out "a small, liberal arts school with quality academics as well as a penchant for producing students who are well-rounded citizens," Denison University deserves a closer look. The school is "set in a beautiful and very safe town" in Ohio, just outside the state capital of Columbus, and offers "an intelligent and welcoming community ready and willing to help others" as well as "a great support system." Denison offers a campus filled with "continuous construction of new facilities" where "students have diverse opportunities to explore their talents and improve their skills through campus jobs, clubs, internships, and the election of double majors and minors that don't necessarily fit together." One student raves, "At Denison, we have professors that can make a poem out of a picture and a mountain out of a math problem. We are so privileged to be surrounded by scholars who are passionate about teaching and learning what they love." Students get a chance to form close bonds with their professors thanks to the "small student-to-faculty ratio" as well as the high accessibility of the professors outside of the classroom. According to one student, "As far as professor availability goes, I see my professors on campus so often that I'm starting to suspect they sleep in their offices..." Students keep it all in perspective and recognize that "although academics are certainly important here, Denison teaches you how to shape what you know so that you become a more curious, passionate, and interesting individual."

Outside the classroom, Denison offers a large Greek scene as well as "more and more non-Greek [social] options." "There are plenty of people who prefer to chill with friends in the dorm rooms and just watch movies." Off campus, "Granville is small but cute, [and] there's plenty to eat at a good price," and for those seeking a larger city, Columbus is close by.

BANG FOR YOUR BUCK

Among the reasons students cite for choosing Denison, the beauty of the campus, the rigor of academics, and the broad range of academic opportunities provided by a liberal arts education are first on everyone's lips. Classes are small, evidencing "a commitment to close professor-student relationships" and tight-knit community. Students are also thrilled with their generous financial aid packages, and access to resources and opportunities. Many note that their offers were simply too good to refuse, and that their aid makes Denison even more affordable than many state schools.

STUDENT LIFE

During the week, people "are mostly good students and take academics seriously." As soon as classes end on Fridays, "people tend to let loose." The size of the school and its nearly entirely residential student body makes for a friendly foxhole, as "you are living with your friends, either in the same dorm room or they are at most a ten minute walk away." "From Greek life to school sponsored events, I never want to leave campus in fear of missing a beat," says a student. While most people have their core group of close friends, there are "many opportunities to branch out beyond that group either through class, leadership retreats or campus organizations." Granville itself feels like "a quaint New England town" with "good, local food," and Columbus is only around thirty minutes by car for those who want a touch of the big city now and then.

Denison University

FINANCIAL AID: 800-336-4766 • E-MAIL: ADMISSIONS@DENISON.EDU • WEBSITE: WWW.DENISON.EDU

CAREER

Students at Denison have "diverse opportunities to explore their talents and improve their skills through campus jobs, clubs, internships, and the election of double majors and minors that don't necessarily fit together." The various summer research programs pay for dozens of students from all academic areas to stay on campus and conduct research; the service-learning organization has a fleet of cars used to provide transportation for local service; and the school provides a good number of internship stipends that are connected to the student, not a specific internship. The Knowlton Office of Career Exploration puts together on-campus recruitment events, career fairs, mock interviews, and cover letter/resume critiques for students, supporting them on their career path. Of the Denison graduates who visited PayScale.com, 44 percent said they felt their job was meaningful to the world; the average starting salary was $47,500.

FINANCIAL AID

Students should submit: FAFSA. Priority filing deadline is 3/15. The Princeton Review suggests that all financial aid forms be submitted as soon as possible after October 1. *Need-based scholarships/grants offered:* Federal Pell, FSEOG, State scholarships/grants, Private scholarships, College/university scholarship or grant aid from institutional funds. *Loan aid offered:* Direct Subsidized Stafford Loans, Direct Unsubsidized Stafford Loans, Direct PLUS loans, Federal Perkins Loans, College/university loans from institutional funds. Applicants will be notified of awards on a rolling basis beginning 3/28. Federal Work-Study Program available. Institutional employment available.

BOTTOM LINE

Denison's price tag is $56,850 once you factor in housing, board, and fees. It's not cheap, but it is in line with many small private liberal arts colleges around the country. What sets Denison apart is the high percentage of the student body that finds its financial need met. In addition to completing the all-important FAFSA, students interested in attending Denison should aim high academically—the school offers more than 1,000 merit-based scholarships for first year students.

CAREER INFORMATION FROM PAYSCALE.COM

ROI rating	88
Bachelor's and No Higher	
Median starting salary	$45,900
Median mid-career salary	$84,800
At Least Bachelor's	
Median starting salary	$47,000
Median mid-career salary	$88,500
% alumni with high job meaning	34%
% STEM	17%

SELECTIVITY

Admissions Rating	90
# of applicants	6,110
% of applicants accepted	48
% of acceptees attending	22
# offered a place on the wait list	515
% accepting a place on wait list	85
% admitted from wait list	5
# of early decision applicants	246
% accepted early decision	88

FRESHMAN PROFILE

Range SAT Critical Reading	580–680
Range SAT Math	580–680
Range ACT Composite	26–31
Minimum paper TOEFL	599
Average HS GPA	3.6
% graduated top 10% of class	55
% graduated top 25% of class	23
% graduated top 50% of class	96

DEADLINES

Early decision	
Deadline	11/15
Regular	
Priority	11/15
Deadline	1/15
Notification	3/15
Nonfall registration?	Yes

FINANCIAL FACTS

Financial Aid Rating	88
Annual tuition	$46,250
Room and board	$11,570
Required fees	$1,040
Average need-based scholarship	$34,812
% needy frosh rec. need-based scholarship or grant aid	100
% needy UG rec. need-based scholarship or grant aid	100
% needy frosh rec. non-need-based scholarship or grant aid	93
% needy UG rec. non-need-based scholarship or grant aid	93
% needy frosh rec. need-based self-help aid	78
% needy UG rec. need-based self-help aid	77
% frosh rec. any financial aid	99
% UG rec. any financial aid	98
% UG borrow to pay for school	50
Average cumulative indebtedness	$28,146
% frosh need fully met	21
% ugrads need fully met	22
Average % of frosh need met	90
Average % of ugrad need met	92

DePauw University

204 E. SEMINARY, GREENCASTLE, IN 46135 • ADMISSIONS: 765-658-4006 • FAX: 765-658-4067

CAMPUS LIFE

Quality of Life Rating	87
Fire Safety Rating	73
Green Rating	91
Type of school	Private
Affiliation	Methodist
Environment	Village

STUDENTS

Total undergrad enrollment	2,264
% male/female	46/54
% from out of state	63
% frosh from public high school	83
% frosh live on campus	100
% ugrads live on campus	100
# of fraternities (% ugrad men join)	13 (77)
# of sororities (% ugrad women join)	11 (63)
% African American	6
% Asian	5
% Caucasian	69
% Hispanic	3
% Native American	<1
% Pacific Islander	0
% Two or more races	6
% Race and/or ethnicity unknown	2
% international	9
# of countries represented	34

ACADEMICS

Academic Rating	93
% students returning for sophomore year	93
% students graduating within 4 years	81
Calendar	Semester
Student/faculty ratio	10:1
Profs interesting rating	90
Profs accessible rating	97

Most classes have 10–19 students.
Most lab/discussion sessions have
10–19 students.

MOST POPULAR MAJORS
Economics and Management,
Communication and Theatre, Biology,
Psychology

ABOUT THE SCHOOL

Serious-minded students are drawn to DePauw University for its "small classes," "encouraging" professors, and the "individual academic attention" they can expect to receive. Academically, DePauw is "demanding but rewarding" and "requires a lot of outside studying and discipline" in order to keep up. Professors lead small, discussion-based classes and hold their students firmly to high academic standards. Professors' "expectations are very high," which means "you can't slack off and get good grades." Be prepared to pull your "fair share of all-nighters."

Beyond stellar professors, DePauw's other academic draws include "extraordinary" study-abroad opportunities and a "wonderful" alumni network great for "connections and networking opportunities." Alums also "keep our endowment pretty high, making it easy for the school to give out merit scholarships," which undergraduates appreciate. DePauw emphasizes life outside the classroom, too. The school operates several fellowships to support independent projects by high-achieving students, and four out of five DePauw students will complete a professional internship during college. The DePauw curriculum includes an Extended Studies requirement. These can be completed during a Winter Term or May Term course, approved externship, travel experience or service learning program, semester-long off-campus study opportunity or internship, and/or independent study, research project or creative project. Arts and culture are at the forefront of campus life, and the school's annual ArtsFest allows students and invited artists to exhibit or perform for the campus and community.

BANG FOR YOUR BUCK

Small class sizes, close community, athletic opportunities, alumni network, great scholarships, and campus involvement make DePauw a good value. Need-based aid is available, and DePauw is also strong in the area of merit-based awards. All first-year applicants are automatically considered for scholarships, and awards are determined based on a student's GPA, course load, class rank, and standardized test scores. Almost 80 percent of the school's scholarship assistance comes from institutional funds rather than state or federal sources. Once a student is enrolled at DePauw, the only scholarships available come through individual academic departments. In addition to these general scholarships, the school operates several scholarship programs for students that meet specific criteria. To apply for need-based aid, students must submit the FAFSA as well as the DePauw application for financial aid. More than half of DePauw's student body receives some form of need-based financial aid through grants, loans, and work-study. The average financial aid package totals $28,000. Students who aren't eligible for work-study may still apply for campus jobs through the financial aid office.

STUDENT LIFE

Students at DePauw are a hardworking lot and many say that there's "a heavy emphasis on studying" around here. Of course, even intellectual types need to relax every once in awhile and there's certainly plenty of fun to be had on campus. Undergrads here report that the "majority of social life is centered around fraternity parties." However, they immediately explain that it's "mostly because fraternities provide a large gathering space for people." And they insist that Greek life "is a very open and non-exclusive environment." Aside from fraternities and sororities, lots of students can be found "work[ing] out . . . running outside or play[ing] football and frisbee in the park." And "every weekend there is some philanthropy event, music school concert, or speaker brought in by the school."

DePauw University

FINANCIAL AID: 765-658-4030 • E-MAIL: ADMISSION@DEPAUW.EDU • WEBSITE: WWW.DEPAUW.EDU

CAREER

DePauw students "are very focused on getting their degrees and [landing] really good jobs." Considering that the average starting salary of recent grads is $46,200 (source: PayScale.com), we'd say they're achieving their goals. This is no doubt due to DePauw's "amazing" resources to help students find internships, jobs, etc. To begin with, undergrads love to highlight the "alumni database [which is teeming with] successful people." Additionally, students can scour TigerTracks, an internal site that allows undergrads to search for jobs and internships listed specifically for DePauw students. The Hubbard Center for Student Engagement also offers some really unique programs beyond the traditional resume workshops and mock interviews. For example, collaborating with Indiana University's Kelly School of Business, DePauw offers the Liberal Arts Management Program, which teaches how businesses are created and how they function. The insight gleaned from programs like this is enormous.

GENERAL INFO

Activities: Choral groups, concert band, dance, drama/theater, jazz band, literary magazine, music ensembles, musical theater, opera, pep band, radio station, student government, student newspaper, student-run film society, symphony orchestra, television station, campus ministries, international student organization. **Organizations:** 119 registered organizations, 13 honor societies, 10 religious organizations. 13 fraternities, 11 sororities. **Athletics (Intercollegiate):** *Men:* Baseball, basketball, cross-country, diving, football, golf, lacrosse, soccer, swimming, tennis, track/field (outdoor), track/field (indoor). *Women:* Basketball, cross-country, diving, field hockey, golf, lacrosse, soccer, softball, swimming, tennis, track/field (outdoor), track/field (indoor), volleyball.

FINANCIAL AID

Students should submit: FAFSA, CSS/Financial Aid PROFILE. Regular filing deadline is 2/1. The Princeton Review suggests that all financial aid forms be submitted as soon as possible after October 1. *Need-based scholarships/grants offered:* Federal Pell, FSEOG, State scholarships/grants, Private scholarships, College/university scholarship or grant aid from institutional funds. *Loan aid offered:* Direct Subsidized Stafford Loans, Direct Unsubsidized Stafford Loans, Direct PLUS loans, Federal Perkins Loans, College/university loans from institutional funds. Applicants will be notified of awards on a rolling basis beginning 3/10. Federal Work-Study Program available. Institutional employment available.

BOTTOM LINE

DePauw tuition and fees are about $45,600 with an additional $12,240 for room and board. Incoming students are also required to purchase a laptop. Families have the option of paying their college costs monthly (with no deferred payment charge) or each semester. Although DePauw does not guarantee meeting full demonstrated need for each student, the school's track record is good, with many students receiving all the funding they need.

CAREER INFORMATION FROM PAYSCALE.COM

ROI rating	88
Bachelor's and No Higher	
Median starting salary	$46,200
Median mid-career salary	$88,500
At Least Bachelor's	
Median starting salary	$46,900
Median mid-career salary	$90,300
% alumni with high job meaning	29%
% STEM	17%

SELECTIVITY

Admissions Rating	90
# of applicants	4,831
% of applicants accepted	65
% of acceptees attending	18
# of early decision applicants	52
% accepted early decision	88

FRESHMAN PROFILE

Range SAT Critical Reading	530–640
Range SAT Math	560–660
Range SAT Writing	520–630
Range ACT Composite	25–29
Minimum paper TOEFL	560
Average HS GPA	3.8
% graduated top 10% of class	48
% graduated top 25% of class	83
% graduated top 50% of class	97

DEADLINES

Early decision	
Deadline	11/1
Notification	1/1
Early action	
Deadline	12/1
Notification	1/31
Regular	
Deadline	2/1
Nonfall registration?	Yes

FINANCIAL FACTS

Financial Aid Rating	87
Annual tuition	$45,660
Room and board	$12,240
Required fees	$788
Average need-based scholarship	$28,320
% needy frosh rec. need-based scholarship or grant aid	100
% needy UG rec. need-based scholarship or grant aid	100
% needy frosh rec. non-need-based scholarship or grant aid	24
% needy UG rec. non-need-based scholarship or grant aid	19
% needy frosh rec. need-based self-help aid	75
% needy UG rec. need-based self-help aid	80
% frosh need fully met	33
% ugrads need fully met	27
Average % of frosh need met	89
Average % of ugrad need met	89

SCHOOL PROFILES ■ 157

Dickinson College

PO Box 1773, Carlisle, PA 17013-2896 • Admissions: 717-245-1231 • Fax: 717-245-1442

CAMPUS LIFE

Quality of Life Rating	**87**
Fire Safety Rating	**92**
Green Rating	**99**
Type of school	Private
Affiliation	No Affiliation
Environment	Town

STUDENTS

Total undergrad enrollment	2,420
% male/female	42/58
% from out of state	78
% frosh from public high school	56
% frosh live on campus	100
% ugrads live on campus	94
# of fraternities (% ugrad men join)	5 (14)
# of sororities (% ugrad women join)	5 (26)
% African American	4
% Asian	3
% Caucasian	72
% Hispanic	6
% Native American	<1
% Pacific Islander	<1
% Two or more races	4
% Race and/or ethnicity unknown	2
% international	10
# of countries represented	46

ACADEMICS

Academic Rating	**89**
% students returning for sophomore year	92
% students graduating within 4 years	81
% students graduating within 6 years	85
Calendar	Semester
Student/faculty ratio	9:1
Profs interesting rating	91
Profs accessible rating	89
Most classes have 10–19 students.	

MOST POPULAR MAJORS
International Business/Trade/Commerce;
Political Science and Government;
Economics

ABOUT THE SCHOOL

It's a good endorsement for any school if a prospective student says "upon visiting campus, I got the best gut feeling about the students, the professors, and the environment." Located in the Cumberland Valley region of south-central Pennsylvania, Dickinson is ideal for students who want "a small school where it [is] possible to get involved with different aspects of the [college] experience" and who desire "a traditional campus and great professors." According to the school's website, "Dickinsonians are guided by a core set of tenets—to be decisive, useful, curious and unafraid to take risks." Dickinson also holds the distinction of being the first college chartered in the United States, in 1783. Though some students note the lack of diversity on campus, others highlight the school as a place that "promotes and actively [pursues] the mission of bettering the world by graduating world class, globally engaged citizens who want to help sustain all facets of society." In general, "Dickinson students work hard, have fun hard, and are a close-knit community."

BANG FOR YOUR BUCK

While 76 percent of Dickinson undergraduates receive some sort of financial aid, some students note that the "academic scholarships start out as a great deal, but are not adjusted for Dickinson's . . . tuition increases, meaning they become less and less impressive." But the offer of a merit- or need-based scholarship is a key reason many students choose to attend the college: "I knew that Dickinson was the place I wanted to be [and what] was truly amazing . . . was the generosity of the Financial Aid office, [which] granted me a scholarship that made it possible for me to attend [the school]." According to the school's website, Dickinson awards more than $45 million annually in scholarships and financial aid. The cornerstone of Dickinson's Financial Aid and scholarship office is the "[commitment] to the principle that if a student possesses the academic ability and maturity to succeed, is excited about learning, passionate about engagement and includes us in his or her considered set of colleges, we'll do whatever we can to see that he or she is able to attend the school," according to the college's website.

STUDENT LIFE

Even if, as one student describes the Dickinson community, "almost all of us are a little [weird]," the majority of students "are all passionate [and] it's generally pretty easy to get along." Greek life does play a role on campus, where there are five sororities and four fraternities; 14 percent of students join a fraternity while 26 percent join a sorority. While opinions are mixed on the appeal of the town of Carlisle, many students note that it's nice to have access to close-by restaurants and describe the small town as "quaint with . . . two theaters . . . bars, and shops, museums and historical sites." It's easy to make like-minded friends, as one English major reports: "For a small school, Dickinson offers so many clubs and activities that it is not hard to find people with similar interests and passions."

CAREER

Dickinson's Career Center offers general assistance and help with the nuts and bolts of crafting the perfect resume and cover letter. Along with nearby Franklin & Marshall College and Gettysburg College, Dickinson hosts Graduate and Professional School Fairs that give students the opportunity to meet face-to-face with prospective employers and learn more about internship opportunities. Students participate in community activities such as "a non-profit organization in Carlisle called Project SHARE" and even go on service trips to places like New Orleans "with Serve the World to help rebuild houses

Dickinson College

FINANCIAL AID: 717-245-1308 • E-MAIL: ADMISSIONS@DICKINSON.EDU • WEBSITE: WWW.DICKINSON.EDU

affected by Hurricane Katrina." The average starting salary for a Dickinson graduate is $44,400, according to PayScale.com, and 46 percent of graduates report that their careers help make the world a better place. Popular careers for Dickinson graduates include social media marketing manager and program coordinator for a non-profit, and popular majors include political science, international business and management, and economics.

GENERAL INFO

Activities: Choral groups, concert band, dance, drama/theater, jazz band, literary magazine, music ensembles, musical theater, radio station, student government, student newspaper, student-run film society, symphony orchestra, yearbook, International Student Organization, Model UN. **Organizations:** 100+ registered organizations, 16 honor societies, 8 religious organizations. 5 fraternities, 5 sororities. **Athletics (Intercollegiate):** *Men:* baseball, basketball, cross-country, football, golf, lacrosse, soccer, squash, swimming, tennis, track/field (outdoor), track/field (indoor). *Women:* basketball, cross-country, field hockey, golf, lacrosse, soccer, softball, squash, swimming, tennis, track/field (outdoor), track/field (indoor), volleyball. **On-Campus Highlights:** Old West (designed by Benjamin Latrobe), Holland Union Building, Waidner Spahr Library/Biblio Cafe, newly expanded Kline Athletic Center, Rector Science Complex, The Quarry (coffee shop; Mermaid Society Trellis and late night party/gathering space), Weiss Center for the Arts, Trout Gallery.

FINANCIAL AID

Students should submit: FAFSA, CSS/Financial Aid PROFILE, State aid form, Noncustodial PROFILE. Regular filing deadline is 2/1. The Princeton Review suggests that all financial aid forms be submitted as soon as possible after October 1. *Need-based scholarships/ grants offered:* Federal Pell, FSEOG, State scholarships/grants, Private scholarships, College/university scholarship or grant aid from institutional funds. *Loan aid offered:* Direct Subsidized Stafford Loans, Direct Unsubsidized Stafford Loans, Direct PLUS loans, Federal Perkins Loans, College/university loans from institutional funds. Applicants will be notified of awards on or about 3/20. Federal Work-Study Program available. Institutional employment available.

BOTTOM LINE

A Dickinson education costs roughly $50,730 annually for tuition, plus an additional $1,580 for books, supplies, and fees. Eighty-one percent of freshmen receive some sort of financial assistance, while 76 percent of other undergraduates receive financial aid. The school reports that it meets 97 percent of student financial need. Tuition costs can be offset by an average freshman need-based gift aid of $36,639. On average, a Dickinson graduate leaves the school with a debt of approximately $28,108. One Dickinson student summed up the school as "a small-sized liberal arts college" that "offered [me] the greatest scholarship."

CAREER INFORMATION FROM PAYSCALE.COM

ROI rating	87
Bachelor's and No Higher	
Median starting salary	$44,500
Median mid-career salary	$89,200
At Least Bachelor's	
Median starting salary	$49,000
Median mid-career salary	$94,900
% alumni with high job meaning	41%
% STEM	12%

SELECTIVITY

Admissions Rating	91
# of applicants	6,031
% of applicants accepted	47
% of acceptees attending	26
# offered a place on the wait list	848
% accepting a place on wait list	31
% admitted from wait list	0
# of early decision applicants	406
% accepted early decision	77

FRESHMAN PROFILE

Range SAT Critical Reading	590–680
Range SAT Math	600–700
Range SAT Writing	590–690
Range ACT Composite	27–30
Minimum internet-based TOEFL	90

DEADLINES

Early decision	
Deadline	11/15
Notification	12/15
Early action	
Deadline	12/1
Notification	2/15
Regular	
Deadline	2/1
Notification	3/20
Nonfall registration?	No

FINANCIAL FACTS

Financial Aid Rating	94
Annual tuition	$50,730
Room and board	$12,794
Required fees	$450
Average need-based scholarship	$35,343
% needy frosh rec. need-based scholarship or grant aid	98
% needy UG rec. need-based scholarship or grant aid	97
% needy frosh rec. non-need-based scholarship or grant aid	7
% needy UG rec. non-need-based scholarship or grant aid	7
% needy frosh rec. need-based self-help aid	91
% needy UG rec. need-based self-help aid	90
% frosh rec. any financial aid	81
% UG rec. any financial aid	76
% UG borrow to pay for school	55
Average cumulative indebtedness	$28,108
% frosh need fully met	88
% ugrads need fully met	84
Average % of frosh need met	99
Average % of ugrad need met	99

Drake University

2507 UNIVERSITY AVENUE, IA 50311-4505 • ADMISSIONS: 515-271-3181 • FAX: 515-271-2831

CAMPUS LIFE

Quality of Life Rating	**78**
Fire Safety Rating	**98**
Green Rating	**60***
Type of school	Private
Affiliation	No affiliation
Environment	Metropolis

STUDENTS

Total undergrad enrollment	3,338
% male/female	44/56
% from out of state	69
% frosh live on campus	97
% ugrads live on campus	70
# of fraternities (% ugrad men join)	9 (36)
# of sororities (% ugrad women join)	5 (29)
% African American	4
% Asian	3
% Caucasian	79
% Hispanic	4
% Native American	0
% Pacific Islander	0
% Two or more races	2
% Race and/or ethnicity unknown	0
% international	7
# of countries represented	43

ACADEMICS

Academic Rating	**85**
% students graduating within 4 years	68
% students graduating within 6 years	75
Student/faculty ratio	13:1
Profs interesting rating	82
Profs accessible rating	84
Most classes have 10–19 students.	•
Most lab/discussion sessions have 10–19 students.	

MOST POPULAR MAJORS
Marketing/Marketing Management;
Actuarial Science; Psychology

ABOUT THE SCHOOL

Located in Iowa, Drake University adheres to the Drake Curriculum, which is designed to send students into the world with the critical thinking abilities needed to succeed in a professional capacity. Or, as a student puts it: "Prepares [its] students to not be just another member of society, but an effective member of society." All students take part in a small, discussion-based First Year Seminar; take courses in the ten basic core Areas of Inquiry (such as The Engaged Citizen and Scientific Literacy); and complete a Senior Capstone project. "Classes can be tough but professors give ample resources to do well," and the school procures influential speakers and a "wide variety of leadership development opportunities" to help shape students' skill sets. "Each classroom experience is unique which keeps the classes and material interesting," says a student.

BANG FOR YOUR BUCK

Ninety-eight percent of Drake students receive scholarships and financial aid, with an average financial aid package running $20,605. The school offers generous merit-based scholarships: academic scholarships abound, including the Presidential Scholarships (ranging from $8,500 to $14,000 per year), National Alumni Scholarships (versions of which cover everything from tuition to fees and board), and Trustee Scholarships of $1,000, which are awarded to all eligible students who complete the National Alumni Scholarship application process and participate in a Scholarship Day. Scholarships are also available for specific areas of study, athletic teams, and state origins, and $1,000 Legacy Awards are available for descendants of alumni.

STUDENT LIFE

This "close-knit community full of familiar faces" is composed mostly of small town Midwesterners who are "generally friendly, kind and helpful to other students and staff." There is "plenty to do in Des Moines" including a "great nightlife scene," and bus transportation is free for Drake students. Intramural sports and student government groups are common extracurriculars on-campus, concerts are held frequently, and the Student Activities board "is always hosting fun events that are free to students." "A strong Greek presence" rounds out the social and philanthropic needs of students. Since it's a relatively small school, "every student can easily get involved in something and fit in somewhere."

Drake University

FINANCIAL AID: 515-271-2905 • E-MAIL: ADMISSION@DRAKE.EDU • WEBSITE: WWW.DRAKE.EDU

CAREER

"Great opportunities are available for internships and intellectual growth outside the classroom" and the school ensures that the student has a chance to partake in real-world experiences and that "anything learned in the classroom is applicable to the world outside of the college atmosphere." "You have all the resources to get exactly what you want out of your education," says a student. Forty-eight percent of Drake graduates who visited PayScale.com reported feeling that their jobs had a meaningful impact on the world, and "the percentage of Drake graduates getting jobs in their fields after school is very high." The Professional & Career Development Services Office hosts an All-University Career Fair each spring.

GENERAL INFO

Activities: Choral groups, concert band, drama/theater, jazz band, literary magazine, marching band, music ensembles, musical theater, pep band, radio station, student government, student newspaper, symphony orchestra, Campus Ministries, International Student Organization, Model UN. **Organizations:** 160 registered organizations, 24 honor societies, 10 religious organizations. 9 fraternities, 6 sororities. **Athletics (Intercollegiate):** *Men:* basketball, cheerleading, cross-country, football, golf, soccer, tennis, track/field (outdoor), track/field (indoor). *Women:* basketball, cheerleading, crew/rowing, cross-country, golf, soccer, softball, tennis, track/field (outdoor), track/field (indoor), volleyball. **On-Campus Highlights:** Athletic Facilities, Olmsted Center, Anderson Gallery, Helmick Commons, Residence Halls / Residence Life.

FINANCIAL AID

Students should submit: FAFSA. Applicants will be notified of awards on a rolling basis beginning 3/1. The Princeton Review suggests that all financial aid forms be submitted as soon as possible after October 1. *Need-based scholarships/grants offered:* Federal Pell, SEOG, State scholarships/grants, Private scholarships, College/university scholarship or grant aid from institutional funds. *Loan aid offered:* Direct Subsidized Stafford Loans, Direct Unsubsidized Stafford Loans, Direct PLUS loans, Federal Perkins Loans, College/university loans from institutional funds. Applicants will be notified of awards on a rolling basis beginning 3/1. Federal Work-Study Program available. Institutional employment available.

BOTTOM LINE

Tuition for all students at Drake is just over $35,000 a year, with room and board running another $9,850, and additional fees are slight. Very few students see this full sticker price at the bottom of their bill, thanks to financial aid and a plethora of scholarships. Des Moines is also an excellent town for college grads, meaning that additional costs of living can be minimized.

CAREER INFORMATION FROM PAYSCALE.COM

ROI rating	87
Bachelor's and No Higher	
Median starting salary	$44,300
Median mid-career salary	$92,300
At Least Bachelor's	
Median starting salary	$45,100
Median mid-career salary	$92,700
% alumni with high job meaning	55%
% STEM	10%

SELECTIVITY

Admissions Rating	88
# of applicants	6,514
% of applicants accepted	67
% of acceptees attending	18

FRESHMAN PROFILE

Range SAT Critical Reading	520–670
Range SAT Math	550–690
Range ACT Composite	24–30
Minimum paper TOEFL	530
Minimum internet-based TOEFL	71
Average HS GPA	3.71
% graduated top 10% of class	37
% graduated top 25% of class	69
% graduated top 50% of class	93

DEADLINES

Notification	10/15
Nonfall registration?	Yes

FINANCIAL FACTS

Financial Aid Rating	84
Annual tuition	$35,060
Room and board	$9,850
Required fees	$146
Average need-based scholarship	$17,770
% needy frosh rec. need-based scholarship or grant aid	99
% needy UG rec. need-based scholarship or grant aid	98
% needy frosh rec. non-need-based scholarship or grant aid	22
% needy UG rec. non-need-based scholarship or grant aid	18
% needy frosh rec. need-based self-help aid	80
% needy UG rec. need-based self-help aid	84
% frosh rec. any financial aid	99
% UG rec. any financial aid	97
% UG borrow to pay for school	65
Average cumulative indebtedness	$30,742
% frosh need fully met	28
% ugrads need fully met	27
Average % of frosh need met	76
Average % of ugrad need met	80

Duke University

2138 CAMPUS DRIVE, BOX 90586, DURHAM, NC 27708-0586 • ADMISSIONS: 919-684-3214

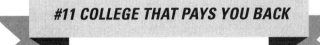

#11 COLLEGE THAT PAYS YOU BACK

CAMPUS LIFE

Quality of Life Rating	77
Fire Safety Rating	60*
Green Rating	96
Type of school	Private
Affiliation	Methodist
Environment	City

STUDENTS

Total undergrad enrollment	6,646
% male/female	50/50
% from out of state	88
% frosh from public high school	65
% frosh live on campus	100
% ugrads live on campus	82
# of fraternities (% ugrad men join)	21 (29)
# of sororities (% ugrad women join)	14 (42)
% African American	10
% Asian	21
% Caucasian	49
% Hispanic	6
% Native American	1
% Pacific Islander	<1
% Two or more races	2
% Race and/or ethnicity unknown	3
% international	9
# of countries represented	89

ACADEMICS

Academic Rating	95
% students returning for sophomore year	97
% students graduating within 4 years	87
% students graduating within 6 years	94
Calendar	Semester
Student/faculty ratio	7:1
Profs interesting rating	81
Profs accessible rating	81
Most classes have 10–19 students.	
Most lab/discussion sessions have 10–19 students.	

MOST POPULAR MAJORS
Psychology; Public Policy Analysis; Economics

ABOUT THE SCHOOL

Duke University offers students a word-class education and freedom in choosing the academic path that best meets their needs. The school's research expenditures rank in the top ten nationally, the library system is extensive, and the school's Division I sports teams are legendary. Still, the undergraduate experience is the heart and soul of the school. Students are required to live on campus for three years. First-year students live together on East Campus, where about a quarter of them participate in FOCUS, a living/learning program organized around academic themes, which gives them access to faculty mentoring and a smaller community of students they get to know well. Maybe it's the mild North Carolina climate, but the students say their campus is way more laid-back than what you'd find at any of the Ivy League schools. It's also breathtakingly beautiful, featuring soaring Gothic buildings, modern teaching and research facilities, accessible athletic fields and recreational spaces, and a lush botanical garden. It's true that Duke students are focused on academics, but they are just as enthusiastic about attending campus events, participating in Greek functions, or cheering on the teams at Duke sporting events, especially when it's the school's top-ranked basketball team that's playing.

BANG FOR YOUR BUCK

Duke is dedicated to making its outstanding education affordable. More than half of undergraduates receive some sort of financial assistance, including need-based aid, and merit or athletic scholarships. Students are evaluated for admission without regard to their ability to pay. If admitted, Duke pledges to meet 100 percent of need. There are no loans or parental contributions required for families with incomes under $40,000. Families with incomes under $60,000 are not required to make a parental contribution, and the school offers capped loans for eligible families with incomes of more than $100,000. The biggest value is the academic experience. One student explains, "Every single one of my professors actually knows me very well. They know where I'm from; they know what I actually find funny in class; they know when I'm sick and are incredibly parental in making sure that I get all of my work done and stay healthy; they know ME. How many other students can say that in any university?" Another student adds, "I wanted a medium college that was not too large but had research opportunities. I liked the culture at Duke and the choice was easy because they also gave me the best financial package."

STUDENT LIFE

Life involves "getting a ton of work done first and then finding time to play and have fun," and the typical student here wears five or more hats: "He/she is studious but social, athletic but can never be seen in the gym, job hunting but not worrying, and so on and so forth." Of course, "Duke basketball games are a must" and sorority/fraternity life is popular but not necessary. The school has an on-campus movie theater and events happening all the time, and students also can just do their own thing, such as "exploring, going skiing or to the beach for a weekend, [or] making a bonfire in the forest." No matter what your weekend plan is, "people will be hitting the books on Sundays (all-nighters are common) in order to maintain their grades."

Duke University

FINANCIAL AID: 919 684 6225 • E MAIL: UNDERGRAD-ADMISSIONS@DUKE.EDU • WEBSITE: WWW.DUKE.EDUWWW.DUKE.EDU

CAREER

Duke students "are focused on graduating and obtaining a lucrative and prosperous career." The "engaged Career Center" provides a range of services (such as seminars, workshops, and online databases) that help students fine-tune their skills. Career fairs are held throughout the year (including the "Just-in-Time" Career Fair in the spring, for employers who have immediate openings for graduating students. Drop-in advising is always available. Fifty-three percent of Duke graduates who visited PayScale.com reported feeling their jobs had a meaningful impact on the world, and averaged a starting salary of $59,500.

GENERAL INFO

Activities: Choral groups, concert band, dance, drama/theater, jazz band, literary magazine, marching band, music ensembles, musical theater, opera, pep band, radio station, student government, student newspaper, student-run film society, symphony orchestra, television station, yearbook. **Organizations:** 200 registered organizations, 10 honor societies, 25 religious organizations. 21 fraternities, 14 sororities. **Athletics (Intercollegiate):** *Men:* Baseball, basketball, cross-country, diving, fencing, football, golf, lacrosse, soccer, swimming, tennis, track/field (outdoor), track/field (indoor), volleyball, wrestling. *Women:* Basketball, crew/rowing, cross-country, diving, fencing, field hockey, golf, lacrosse, soccer, swimming, tennis, track/field (outdoor), track/field (indoor), volleyball. **On-Campus Highlights:** Primate Center, Sarah P. Duke Gardens, Duke Forest, Levine Science Research Center.

FINANCIAL AID

Students should submit: FAFSA, CSS/Financial Aid PROFILE, Noncustodial PROFILE, Business/Farm Supplement. Regular filing deadline is 3/1. The Princeton Review suggests that all financial aid forms be submitted as soon as possible after October 1. *Need-based scholarships/grants offered:* Federal Pell, FSEOG, State scholarships/grants, Private scholarships, College/university scholarship or grant aid from institutional funds. *Loan aid offered:* Direct Subsidized Stafford Loans, Direct Unsubsidized Stafford Loans, Direct PLUS loans, Federal Perkins Loans, College/university loans from institutional funds. Applicants will be notified of awards on or about 4/1. Federal Work-Study Program available. Institutional employment available.

BOTTOM LINE

With a moderately sized campus of almost 7,000 undergraduates, students have the opportunity to work closely with the school's accomplished faculty. Academics are challenging, especially in the quantitative majors like science and mathematics. However, there are plentiful student resources, including a writing center and a peer-tutoring program, not to mention the constant support from the school's teaching staff. Innovation and independence are encouraged; the school offers grants for undergraduate research projects, as well as travel grants and awards for artistic endeavors.

CAREER INFORMATION FROM PAYSCALE.COM

ROI rating	94
Bachelor's and No Higher	
Median starting salary	$60,600
Median mid-career salary	$111,000
At Least Bachelor's	
Median starting salary	$62,000
Median mid-career salary	$122,000
% alumni with high job meaning	59%
% STEM	35%

SELECTIVITY

Admissions Rating	98
# of applicants	30,546
% of applicants accepted	12
% of acceptees attending	45
# of early decision applicants	2,439
% accepted early decision	31

FRESHMAN PROFILE

Range SAT Critical Reading	670–760
Range SAT Math	690–790
Range SAT Writing	680–780
Range ACT Composite	31–34
% graduated top 10% of class	90
% graduated top 25% of class	8
% graduated top 50% of class	2

DEADLINES

Early decision	
Deadline	11/1
Notification	12/15
Regular	
Priority	12/20
Deadline	1/2
Notification	4/1
Nonfall registration?	No

FINANCIAL FACTS

Financial Aid Rating	95
Annual tuition	$45,800
Room and board	$13,290
Required fees	$1,443
Average need-based scholarship	$39,275
% needy frosh rec. need-based scholarship or grant aid	85
% needy UG rec. need-based scholarship or grant aid	87
% needy frosh rec. non-need-based scholarship or grant aid	11
% needy UG rec. non-need-based scholarship or grant aid	8
% needy frosh rec. need-based self-help aid	84
% needy UG rec. need-based self-help aid	89
% frosh need fully met	100
% ugrads need fully met	100
Average % of frosh need met	100
Average % of ugrad need met	100

Emory University

1390 Oxford Road NE, Atlanta, GA 30322 • Admissions: 404-727-6036 • Fax: 404-727-6039

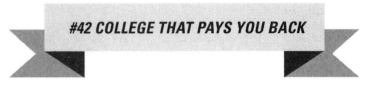

#42 COLLEGE THAT PAYS YOU BACK

ABOUT THE SCHOOL

Emory University is known for demanding academics, highly ranked professional schools, and state-of-the-art research facilities. One student insightfully defines Emory as a place that "seeks to bring together intelligent, well-rounded students and prepare them to positively impact the world around them." Students are taught by Emory's distinguished faculty, which includes President Jimmy Carter, Salman Rushdie, and the Dalai Lama. "The professors are very accessible and open to students, and the classes are small enough that I cannot really go unnoticed" writes one sophomore. At Emory, students take learning seriously but also have the time for extracurricular pursuits as athletes, leaders of clubs and organizations, and community-service participants. Campus traditions help create a close-knit community through all years; Dooley, "the spirit of Emory" and unofficial mascot can often be seen releasing students from classes. As one student puts it: "Everywhere I go, I see people I know, but I am constantly meeting new people as well." Students who receive on-campus housing have access to "several academic advisors" throughout the school year, and that kind of attention will definitely appeal to undecided academics. Downtown Atlanta is just a few miles from campus, and students head there to catch a concert at Philips Arena or toss a frisbee in Centennial Olympic Park. Research opportunities are available to undergraduates in all fields.

BANG FOR YOUR BUCK

Need-blind admission is a cornerstone of Emory's financial aid philosophy. A family's ability to pay is not considered in the admission process. Emory further enhances access and affordability with special financial aid initiatives such as Emory Advantage. Emory Advantage provides additional need-based grant assistance to eligible families with total annual incomes of $100,000 or less. Emory Advantage funding is designed to reduce a student's dependence on educational borrowing normally required to attain an undergraduate degree. Competitive merit-based scholarships are also offered to incoming first-year students. Through the Emory University Scholars Programs, which can cover up to the full cost of tuition and fees, students receive enriched intellectual, cultural, and social programs throughout their college years. Recipients of these competitive awards represent an impressive range of academic, cultural, and extracurricular interests and achievements themselves. Most of the students have been National Merit finalists or semifinalists, and almost all have won distinction beyond the classroom. In addition, some merit scholarships are available to continuing Emory students on a competitive basis after their first or second year of study at Emory.

STUDENT LIFE

Extracurricular options abound at Emory! Truly, on "any given night you can go see a friend in a show [...] go to a soccer game, a frat party, a club, a movie set up on the field by college council, etc." An amazed neuroscience major further explains, "There's always a bunch of stuff [to participate in] whether it's free tango lessons from Tangueros Emory or a free Indian food at Hindu Students Association's Diwali celebration." Additionally, the university frequently hosts "programs... with [fabulous] guest speakers." And "on-campus concerts by a cappella groups and other musical ensembles are [also quite] popular."

Emory University

FINANCIAL AID: 404-727-6039 • E-MAIL: ADMISSION@EMORY.EDU • WEBSITE: WWW.EMORY.EDU

Finally, undergrads love to capitalize on their urban location. As a content music major shares, "There's a lot to do in Atlanta at night and places like Piedmont Park...make for a great escapes on the weekend."

CAREER

A degree from Emory University is definitely a boon to any job search. Looking for evidence to support that claim? Well, according to PayScale.com, the average starting salary for recent grads is $51,100. Of course, with all the resources Emory makes available, this success is no surprise. To begin with, students may access Eagle Ops, Emory's online career management system which helps undergrads connect with hiring organizations. The Career Center also hosts information sessions with a variety of companies throughout the academic year. These events continually provide great networking opportunities for students. And, naturally, undergrads are quick to take advantage of the handful of career fairs held on campus. Students are able to meet with representatives from companies such as Teach for America, SunTrust Bank, L'Oreal USA, Deloitte, Bank of America, Porsche Cars North America, and Turner Broadcasting.

GENERAL INFO

Activities: Choral groups, concert band, dance, drama/theater, jazz band, literary magazine, marching band, music ensembles, musical theater, opera, pep band, radio station, student government, student newspaper, student-run film society, symphony orchestra, television station, campus ministries, international student organization. **Organizations:** 400+ registered organizations. 17 fraternities, 12 sororities. **Athletics (Intercollegiate):** *Men:* Baseball, basketball, cross-country, diving, golf, soccer, swimming, tennis, track/field (outdoor). *Women:* Basketball, cross-country, diving, soccer, softball, swimming, tennis, track/field (outdoor), volleyball.

FINANCIAL AID

Students should submit: FAFSA, CSS/Financial Aid PROFILE, Noncustodial PROFILE. Regular filing deadline is 3/1. The Princeton Review suggests that all financial aid forms be submitted as soon as possible after October 1. *Need-based scholarships/grants offered:* Federal Pell, FSEOG, Private scholarships, College/university scholarship or grant aid from institutional funds. *Loan aid offered:* Direct Subsidized Stafford Loans, Direct Unsubsidized Stafford Loans, Direct PLUS loans, Federal Perkins Loans, Federal Nursing Loans, State Loans, College/university loans from institutional funds. Applicants will be notified of awards on or about 4/1. Federal Work-Study Program available. Institutional employment available.

BOTTOM LINE

The sticker price for tuition, room and board, and fees at Emory is more than $61,400 a year. Financial aid is generous, though, so don't let the numbers scare you away from applying.

CAREER INFORMATION FROM PAYSCALE.COM

ROI rating	91
Bachelor's and No Higher	
Median starting salary	$51,300
Median mid-career salary	$89,800
At Least Bachelor's	
Median starting salary	$53,400
Median mid-career salary	$95,100
% alumni with high job meaning	58%
% STEM	14%

SELECTIVITY

Admissions Rating	97
# of applicants	20,492
% of applicants accepted	24
% of acceptees attending	28
# offered a place on the wait list	3,809
% accepting a place on wait list	50
% admitted from wait list	2
# of early decision applicants	2,437
% accepted early decision	30

FRESHMAN PROFILE

Range SAT Critical Reading	620–720
Range SAT Math	650–770
Range SAT Writing	640–730
Range ACT Composite	29–33
Minimum paper TOEFL	600
Average HS GPA	3.7
% graduated top 10% of class	83
% graduated top 25% of class	96
% graduated top 50% of class	99

DEADLINES

Early decision	
Deadline	11/1
Notification	12/15
Regular	
Deadline	1/1
Notification	4/1
Nonfall registration?	No

FINANCIAL FACTS

Financial Aid Rating	94
Annual tuition	$47,300
Room and board	$13,486
Required fees	$654
Average need-based scholarship	$39,440
% needy frosh rec. need-based scholarship or grant aid	90
% needy UG rec. need-based scholarship or grant aid	91
% needy frosh rec. non-need-based scholarship or grant aid	32
% needy UG rec. non-need-based scholarship or grant aid	29
% needy frosh rec. need-based self-help aid	95
% needy UG rec. need-based self-help aid	95
% frosh rec. any financial aid	55
% UG rec. any financial aid	54
% frosh need fully met	100
% ugrads need fully met	93
Average % of frosh need met	100
Average % of ugrad need met	97

Florida State University

PO Box 3062400, Tallahassee, FL 32306-2400 • Admissions: 850-644-6200 • Fax: 850-644-0197

CAMPUS LIFE

Quality of Life Rating	91
Fire Safety Rating	86
Green Rating	60*
Type of school	Public
Affiliation	No Affiliation
Environment	City

STUDENTS

Total undergrad enrollment	32,706
% male/female	45/55
% from out of state	10
% frosh from public high school	84
% frosh live on campus	63
% ugrads live on campus	19
# of fraternities (% ugrad men join)	31 (19)
# of sororities (% ugrad women join)	26 (25)
% African American	8
% Asian	2
% Caucasian	64
% Hispanic	19
% Native American	<1
% Pacific Islander	<1
% Two or more races	3
% Race and/or ethnicity unknown	1
% international	2
# of countries represented	106

ACADEMICS

Academic Rating	71
% students returning for sophomore year	93
% students graduating within 4 years	62
% students graduating within 6 years	79
Calendar	Semester
Student/faculty ratio	25:1
Profs interesting rating	76
Profs accessible rating	80

Most classes have 20–29 students.
Most lab/discussion sessions have
20–29 students.

MOST POPULAR MAJORS
Psychology; Criminal Justice/Safety Studies;
English

ABOUT THE SCHOOL

Opportunity, diversity, and choice: these terms define the undergraduate experience at Florida State University. One student says, "I chose FSU because it is affordable, the campus is beautiful, I received excellent scholarships, and it's in a perfect location for gaining internship experience." In addition to intense academic competition at FSU, "the professors at Florida State are very interested in the success of their students and are available for office hours and outside help for a wide spectrum of times convenient for you." FSU also awards research fellowships to promising undergraduates, with numerous grants available to help offset the costs of studying overseas. "The Student Government Association is very active on campus. There are great student organizations to get involved in." When they aren't studying, many FSU undergrads will tell you that lots of students equals lots of fun. Football games and Greek parties are all a big part of life at FSU. "The Greek life here at FSU has a strong influence that challenges students to better their campus and college experience." "Aside from having a great football team and incredible academics, FSU also has a top-notch international program." One junior says that "a lot of people don't know about FSU's great international programs. I spent a semester abroad at FSU's campus in central London, which is one of the best decisions I've made in college." A research giant, the school's faculty includes Nobel laureates, members of the National Academy of Sciences, Guggenheim Fellows, and Pulitzer Prize winners. "All of my professors continuously push our mental abilities to ensure that students are thinking outside of the box and improving our problem-solving capabilities." Opportunities abound. "The professors are very learned individuals that support the growth of their students in and out of the classroom. Overall, the academic experience is a challenging course through a wide array of studies."

BANG FOR YOUR BUCK

For a low in-state tuition, FSU offers unmatched resources, diverse academic opportunities, access to major research facilities, and a bustling campus environment. All things considered, this school is a steal for Florida residents. In addition to the low price tag, students may submit the FAFSA to apply for need-based loans, grants, and work-study. Students with AP, IB, or dual enrollment course credit can receive an FSU degree within just three years of study, thereby saving a year's tuition and expenses. The school awards numerous scholarships for academic merit, as well as for athletics and the arts. The top admitted students may apply for the Presidential Scholarship Program, which includes $19,200 in scholarship funding distributed over four years as well as $12,000 for educational enrichment opportunities. All applicants to Florida State University are automatically considered for merit scholarships.

Florida State University

FINANCIAL AID: 850-644-0539 • E-MAIL: ADMISSIONS@ADMISSIONS@FSU.EDU • WEBSITE: WWW.FSU.EDU

STUDENT LIFE

Your average FSU student is a "football fan, partier, into academics and community service, [and] passionate." Students tend to be "extremely involved," whether it's in athletics, "Greek life or community service, or one of the other hundreds of groups and clubs here at FSU." "Greek is a huge part of campus, but you are fine if you are not in one." Although "the majority of students are Caucasians," "students of all races and religions work together here to make FSU an enjoyable environment," and "the school continues to become more diverse each year." No matter what their background, every FSU student has "a colossal amount of school spirit and loves to go out and support the team."

GENERAL INFO

Activities: Choral groups, concert band, dance, drama/theater, jazz band, literary magazine, marching band, music ensembles, musical theater, opera, pep band, radio station, student government, student newspaper, student-run film society, symphony orchestra, television station, yearbook, campus ministries, international student organization. **Organizations:** 520 registered organizations, 23 honor societies, 30 religious organizations. 30 fraternities, 27 sororities. **Athletics (Intercollegiate):** *Men:* Baseball, basketball, cross country, football, golf, swimming & diving, tennis, track & field. *Women:* Basketball, cross country, golf, soccer, softball, swimming & diving, tennis, track & field, volleyball, beach volleyball.

FINANCIAL AID

Students should submit: FAFSA, State aid form. The Princeton Review suggests that all financial aid forms be submitted as soon as possible after October 1. *Need-based scholarships/grants offered:* Federal Pell, FSEOG, State scholarships/grants, Private scholarships, College/university scholarship or grant aid from institutional funds. *Loan aid offered:* Direct Subsidized Stafford Loans, Direct Unsubsidized Stafford Loans, Direct PLUS loans, Federal Perkins Loans. Applicants will be notified of awards on a rolling basis beginning 4/5. Federal Work-Study Program available. Institutional employment available.

BOTTOM LINE

FSU is affordable. For state residents, annual tuition and fees run a little more than $6,500. The school estimates that students will spend another $10,000 or so on room and board. Nonresidents pay $21,600 in tuition and fees, a significant increase from the in-state rate, yet still cheaper than many private institutions. One student remarks on "how inexpensive FSU is. FSU offered me a scholarship on top of my Bright Futures and Florida Prepaid. I actually have enough money left over each semester to pay for my sorority." To secure the best aid package and scholarships, the school recommends that prospective students apply as early as possible.

CAREER INFORMATION FROM PAYSCALE.COM

ROI rating	86
Bachelor's and No Higher	
Median starting salary	$42,400
Median mid-career salary	$77,600
At Least Bachelor's	
Median starting salary	$43,700
Median mid-career salary	$78,900
% alumni with high job meaning	48%
% STEM	11%

SELECTIVITY

Admissions Rating	89
# of applicants	29,828
% of applicants accepted	56
% of acceptees attending	37

FRESHMAN PROFILE

Range SAT Critical Reading	560–640
Range SAT Math	560–640
Range SAT Writing	560–640
Range ACT Composite	25–29
Minimum paper TOEFL	550
Minimum internet-based TOEFL	80
Average HS GPA	3.9
% graduated top 10% of class	38
% graduated top 25% of class	75
% graduated top 50% of class	97

DEADLINES

Regular	
Deadline	1/15
Nonfall registration?	Yes

FINANCIAL FACTS

Financial Aid Rating	80
Annual in-state tuition	$4,640
Annual out-of-state tuition	$19,806
Room and board	$10,304
Required fees	$1,867
Average need-based scholarship	$7,917
% needy frosh rec. need-based scholarship or grant aid	94
% needy UG rec. need-based scholarship or grant aid	90
% needy frosh rec. non-need-based scholarship or grant aid	76
% needy UG rec. non-need-based scholarship or grant aid	66
% needy frosh rec. need-based self-help aid	61
% needy UG rec. need-based self-help aid	65
% frosh rec. any financial aid	96
% UG rec. any financial aid	87
% UG borrow to pay for school	52
Average cumulative indebtedness	$22,912
% frosh need fully met	14
% ugrads need fully met	9
Average % of frosh need met	62
Average % of ugrad need met	61

Franklin & Marshall College

PO Box 3003, Lancaster, PA 17604-3003 • Admissions: 717-358-3953 • Fax: 717-358-4389

CAMPUS LIFE

Quality of Life Rating	**88**
Fire Safety Rating	**97**
Green Rating	**90**
Type of school	Private
Affiliation	No Affiliation
Environment	Town

STUDENTS

Total undergrad enrollment	2,249
% male/female	48/52
% from out of state	73
% frosh from public high school	62
% frosh live on campus	100
% ugrads live on campus	99
# of fraternities (% ugrad men join)	7 (20)
# of sororities (% ugrad women join)	4 (30)
% African American	6
% Asian	5
% Caucasian	59
% Hispanic	8
% Native American	<1
% Pacific Islander	<1
% Two or more races	2
% Race and/or ethnicity unknown	6
% international	14
# of countries represented	49

ACADEMICS

Academic Rating	**94**
% students returning for sophomore year	92
% students graduating within 4 years	81
% students graduating within 6 years	87
Calendar	Semester
Student/faculty ratio	9:1
Profs interesting rating	90
Profs accessible rating	93

Most classes have 10–19 students.
Most lab/discussion sessions have
  10–19 students.

MOST POPULAR MAJORS
Political Science and Government;
Psychology; Business Administration and
Management

ABOUT THE SCHOOL

Located in Lancaster, Pennsylvania, Franklin & Marshall College is "a small, liberal arts school" that "offers a great education and a leg up in today's competitive job marketplace." The school's small class sizes and 9:1 student to faculty ratio means "professor accessibility." "I've been able to meet personally with all of my professors outside of class multiple times," an astronomy major attests. The school has about 2,300 undergraduates and a faculty of 250. Students like the "general atmosphere of academic excellence" and say professors "challenge students in order to provide the best future opportunities." "The professors at F&M are the best at what they do" and each one "brings his or her own spin to a class." "F&M is such a happy school," one student explains. "I immediately felt welcomed on campus because it has such a warm, friendly, and happy vibe."

BANG FOR YOUR BUCK

"We all know that we're paying $52,000 a year to be here, it's no secret," one student says. However, roughly half of the student body receives needs-based financial aid. F&M is committed to meeting 100 percent of student's financial needs. The school determines those needs "based on an institutional methodology that analyzes family income, assets, and other circumstances." The school eliminated merit-based scholarships—which one student calls "a huge mistake"—in order to commit to enrolling "highly qualified students who could not otherwise afford a Franklin & Marshall College education." The school does provide students with resources to find merit-based scholarships awarded by outside institutions.

STUDENT LIFE

At F&M, "the typical student is clean-cut, perhaps a little preppy, [and] dedicated to academics," while the student body as a whole is increasingly diverse. School is a priority, but when the weekend roles around students let loose. The social life of the school is heavily dominated by Greek life and "everyone goes to the frats every weekend." However, "it's not a huge deal if you decide not to be a part of it." Students say that downtown Lancaster offers a lot of things, "but students rarely take advantage of them." There's plenty to do on campus though, such as "orchestra concerts," "regular documentary screenings," and "guest lecturers." Students are very involved in campus life at F&M. Most undergrads are "either in a fraternity/sorority, sports team, the house system or a theme house, or a time-consuming club" such as "debate, ultimate Frisbee, and French Club."

CAREER

"F&M is all about good undergrad programs and tight-knit networking," one student says. Students praise the alumni network that helps F&M get a leg-up in their post-college careers. One says, "there are interesting opportunities for volunteer activities and internships everywhere I look." PayScale.com reports an average starting salary of $46,300 and a mid-career average of $98,200 for F&M graduates. Lancaster is the third most common post-college employment location after New York and Philadelphia. Popular companies for F&M grads include Morgan Stanley, Citi, Deloitte, and Merrill Lynch.

Franklin & Marshall College

FINANCIAL AID: 717-291-3991 • E-MAIL: ADMISSION@FANDM.EDU • WEBSITE: WWW.FANDM.EDU

GENERAL INFO

Activities: Choral groups, concert band, dance, drama/theater, jazz band, literary magazine, music ensembles, musical theater, radio station, student government, student newspaper, symphony orchestra, yearbook, Campus Ministries, International Student Organization, Model UN. **Organizations:** 90 registered organizations, 13 honor societies, 8 religious organizations. 8 fraternities, 4 sororities. **Athletics (Intercollegiate):** *Men:* baseball, basketball, crew/rowing, cross-country, football, golf, lacrosse, soccer, squash, swimming, tennis, track/field (outdoor), track/field (indoor), wrestling. *Women:* basketball, crew/rowing, cross country, field hockey, golf, lacrosse, soccer, softball, squash, swimming, tennis, track/field (outdoor), track/field (indoor), volleyball. **On-Campus Highlights:** Alumni Sports and Fitness Center, Barshinger Center in Hensel Hall, Barnes and Noble Bookstore and Zime Cafe, Roschel Performing Arts Center, Writers House, International Center, Center for Jewish Life.

FINANCIAL AID

Students should submit: FAFSA, CSS/Financial Aid PROFILE, Noncustodial PROFILE. Regular filing deadline is 2/15. The Princeton Review suggests that all financial aid forms be submitted as soon as possible after October 1. *Need-based scholarships/grants offered:* Federal Pell, FSEOG, State scholarships/grants, Private scholarships, College/university scholarship or grant aid from institutional funds. *Loan aid offered:* Direct Subsidized Stafford Loans, Direct Unsubsidized Stafford Loans, Direct PLUS loans, Federal Perkins Loans, College/university loans from institutional funds. Applicants will be notified of awards on or about 4/1. Federal Work-Study Program available.

BOTTOM LINE

The basic tuition at F&M currently stands at $50,300. Student housing costs range from $7,550 to $8,850 depending on the rooming situation. Meal plans and other fees bring up the room and board total to an average of $12,770. While F&M meets 100 percent of students' financial needs, they do not offer merit-based scholarships.

CAREER INFORMATION FROM PAYSCALE.COM

ROI rating	**90**
Bachelor's and No Higher	
Median starting salary	$46,500
Median mid-career salary	$106,000
At Least Bachelor's	
Median starting salary	$47,300
Median mid-career salary	$109,000
% alumni with high job meaning	32%
% STEM	16%

SELECTIVITY

Admissions Rating	**93**
# of applicants	7,146
% of applicants accepted	32
% of acceptees attending	26
# offered a place on the wait list	1,944
# of early decision applicants	555
% accepted early decision	61

FRESHMAN PROFILE

Range SAT Critical Reading	580–670
Range SAT Math	630–730
Range ACT Composite	28–31
Minimum paper TOEFL	600
% graduated top 10% of class	48
% graduated top 25% of class	80
% graduated top 50% of class	97

DEADLINES

Early decision	
Deadline	11/15
Notification	12/15
Regular	
Deadline	1/15
Notification	4/1
Nonfall registration?	Yes

FINANCIAL FACTS

Financial Aid Rating	**96**
Annual tuition	$52,190
Room and board	$13,120
Required fees	$100
Average need-based scholarship	$41,659
% needy frosh rec. need-based scholarship or grant aid	100
% needy UG rec. need-based scholarship or grant aid	99
% needy frosh rec. non-need-based scholarship or grant aid	20
% needy UG rec. non-need-based scholarship or grant aid	22
% needy frosh rec. need-based self-help aid	93
% needy UG rec. need-based self-help aid	95
% frosh rec. any financial aid	51
% UG rec. any financial aid	53
% UG borrow to pay for school	51
Average cumulative indebtedness	$26,162
% frosh need fully met	100
% ugrads need fully met	100
Average % of frosh need met	100
Average % of ugrad need met	100

Franklin W. Olin College of Engineering

OLIN WAY, NEEDHAM, MA 02492-1245 • ADMISSIONS: 781-292-2222 • FAX: 781-292-2210

CAMPUS LIFE

Quality of Life Rating	**95**
Fire Safety Rating	**91**
Green Rating	**68**
Type of school	Private
Affiliation	No Affiliation
Environment	Town

STUDENTS

Total undergrad enrollment	370
% male/female	50/50
% from out of state	86
% frosh live on campus	100
% ugrads live on campus	100
% African American	<1
% Asian	16
% Caucasian	53
% Hispanic	5
% Native American	<1
% Pacific Islander	0
% Two or more races	7
% Race and/or ethnicity unknown	11
% international	8
# of countries represented	13

ACADEMICS

Academic Rating	**98**
% students returning for sophomore year	91
% students graduating within 4 years	76
% students graduating within 6 years	93
Calendar	Semester
Student/faculty ratio	8:1
Profs interesting rating	99
Profs accessible rating	92
Most classes have 20–29 students.	

MOST POPULAR MAJORS

Engineering; Electrical and Electronics Engineering; Mechanical Engineering

ABOUT THE SCHOOL

Olin College offers a rigorous engineering curriculum that prepares students to be "twenty-first century engineers." At Olin, which only opened in 2002, the spirit of hands-on collaboration transcends the classroom. Though the school's history is short, the vision has long been evolving, and this "tight-knit community of eager learners and tinkerers" thrives on a sense of "innovation and initiative." Located fourteen miles outside of Boston, the school is "small, quirky, and somewhat in a bubble," but "full of amazing adventures and opportunities." A typical day includes everything from "watching a movie" to a "midnight bike expedition," not to mention "experimental baking, pickup soccer, zombie video games, auditorium movie screenings, [and] midnight dump raids."

Professors are "one of the best—if not the best—part of Olin" and are frequently described as "always available, always knowledgeable, [and] always approachable." The school's curriculum is designed to create "engineers who understand the entire development process with a deep understanding of engineering's business impact." Programs emphasize inquiry-based learning and team-based projects in a community of self-directed learners, and the focus on "experiential education" and "entrepreneurial implementation" provides students with "the ability to help design the curriculum and the school culture." All Olin students receive real-world experience through the senior-year capstone experience, when they complete a project for a company or organization. In addition, the Office of Post Graduate Planning is very active in helping students find internships. Combined with an extraordinary level of financial aid for all students, Olin provides an unusual opportunity for talented engineering students.

BANG FOR YOUR BUCK

All enrolled students receive a 50 percent scholarship, and Olin works to meet 100 percent of demonstrated need beyond that. This makes the school quite the bargain, especially considering its reputation among employers. The senior-year capstone project is quite a foot in the door for young engineers entering the workforce, and many students convert their experience into a job. In addition to institutional grants, National Merit Finalists who win a scholarship or corporate sponsorship can use their scholarship at Olin; finalists who designate Olin College as their first choice college but do not receive a NMSC or corporate-sponsored scholarship will be designated as Olin National Merit Scholars and will be awarded a $1,000 scholarship, renewable for three years, funded by Olin College.

STUDENT LIFE

"Take the nation's top engineering students, mix with awesome personalities, add a dash of amazing resources, and shake vigorously." When it comes to describing the typical student, there is no status quo. "There are all sorts of people at Olin. Some of us avoid homework by discussing metaphysics and ethics. Others watch old episodes of Firefly . . . some people read books in their spare time," however "the 'run-of-the-mill' activities aren't just DDR and videogames . . . Olin students love to go outside and play sports too!" The commonality? "Students care about their educations," and "everyone takes their own paths." Students feel that "what distinguishes Olin is its openness to innovation and tight-knit community."

Franklin W. Olin College of Engineering

FINANCIAL AID: 781-292-2343 • E-MAIL: INFO@OLIN.EDU • WEBSITE: WWW.OLIN.EDU

CAREER

The typical Franklin W. Olin College of Engineering graduate has a starting salary of around $68,200. Students feel that Olin does a great job at "providing students with opportunities such as jobs, internships, and research." One student says, "I got a paid internship after my first year here. How many undergraduates can say they made $20/hr right after freshman year?" Nearly all students agree that Olin's project-based learning model is fantastic for "preparing students for jobs in the real world." The Office of Post-Graduate Planning does its part to help students plan for the future by hosting job and internship fairs, career exploration workshops as well as offering a database of job and internship leads.

GENERAL INFO

Activities: Choral groups, dance, drama/theater, jazz band, music ensembles, musical theater, student government, student-run film society, symphony orchestra, yearbook. **Organizations:** 55 registered organizations. Large Project Building provides workspace for large-scale, hands-on student projects.

FINANCIAL AID

Students should submit: FAFSA. Regular filing deadline is 2/15. The Princeton Review suggests that all financial aid forms be submitted as soon as possible after October 1. *Need-based scholarships/grants offered:* Federal Pell, FSEOG, College/university scholarship or grant aid from institutional funds. *Loan aid offered:* Direct Subsidized Stafford Loans, Direct Unsubsidized Stafford Loans, Direct PLUS Loans. Applicants will be notified of awards on or about 3/21. Institutional employment available.

BOTTOM LINE

Olin was founded on the premise that financial considerations should not stand in the way of an excellent engineering education, and hence all enrolled students receive a 50 percent tuition scholarship, making tuition $22,500 a year, with an additional estimated $15,600 in additional expenses and fees. In addition to the tuition scholarship, need-based aid is available for those who qualify. Olin meets, on average, 99 percent of demonstrated need.

CAREER INFORMATION FROM PAYSCALE.COM

ROI rating	88
Bachelor's and No Higher	
Median starting salary	$68,200
At Least Bachelor's	
Median starting salary	$68,200

SELECTIVITY

Admissions Rating	98
# of applicants	1,075
% of applicants accepted	11
% of acceptees attending	64
# offered a place on the wait list	57
% accepting a place on wait list	82
% admitted from wait list	28

FRESHMAN PROFILE

Range SAT Critical Reading	710–800
Range SAT Math	730–800
Range SAT Writing	680–770
Range ACT Composite	32–35
Average HS GPA	3.9

DEADLINES

Regular	
Deadline	1/1
Notification	3/21
Nonfall registration?	No

FINANCIAL FACTS

Financial Aid Rating	96
Annual tuition	$46,800
Room and board	$15,800
Required fees	$530
Average need-based scholarship	$40,374
% needy frosh rec. need-based scholarship or grant aid	100
% needy UG rec. need-based scholarship or grant aid	100
% needy frosh rec. non-need-based scholarship or grant aid	100
% needy UG rec. non-need-based scholarship or grant aid	100
% needy frosh rec. need-based self-help aid	81
% needy UG rec. need-based self-help aid	88
% frosh rec. any financial aid	100
% UG rec. any financial aid	100
% UG borrow to pay for school	43
Average cumulative indebtedness	$19,196
% frosh need fully met	97
% ugrads need fully met	97
Average % of frosh need met	100
Average % of ugrad need met	99

Furman University

3300 POINSETT HIGHWAY, GREENVILLE, SC 29613 • ADMISSIONS: 864-294-2034 • FAX: 864-294-2018

CAMPUS LIFE

Quality of Life Rating	**93**
Fire Safety Rating	**90**
Green Rating	**97**
Type of school	Private
Affiliation	No Affiliation
Environment	City

STUDENTS

Total undergrad enrollment	2,731
% male/female	43/57
% from out of state	72
% frosh from public high school	59
% frosh live on campus	98
% ugrads live on campus	96
# of fraternities (% ugrad men join)	7 (33)
# of sororities (% ugrad women join)	7 (58)
% African American	5
% Asian	2
% Caucasian	78
% Hispanic	4
% Native American	<1
% Pacific Islander	0
% Two or more races	2
% Race and/or ethnicity unknown	2
% international	6
# of countries represented	54

ACADEMICS

Academic Rating	**86**
% students returning for sophomore year	89
% students graduating within 4 years	79
% students graduating within 6 years	83
Calendar	Semester
Student/faculty ratio	11:1
Profs interesting rating	88
Profs accessible rating	96
Most classes have 20–29 students.	

MOST POPULAR MAJORS

Political Science and Government; Business/Commerce; Health Professions

ABOUT THE SCHOOL

This small, highly-acclaimed liberal arts university offers its 2,600 students "an intense undergraduate experience" both in and out of the classroom and boasts a "great capacity for supporting students." Students are "constantly challenged to do better, learn more subjects, and get more involved in the community," and professors "encourage self-teaching" and are willing to meet with students and work around their schedules. "I've been to dinner with my professors before and they are always willing to help you in your journey," says one. The administration "knows what its doing and is neither overbearing nor a non-existent presence." Not for the academically faint-of-heart, students work hard in the hopes of being rewarded with a well-reputed undergraduate education. "I wake up every day thrilled to be a part of this community," says a happy student.

BANG FOR YOUR BUCK

The school also offers more than 100 renewable merit-based scholarships such as the four Herman W. Lay Scholarships for full tuition and partial other costs; ten James B. Duke Scholarships for full tuition; up to twenty John D. Hollingsworth Scholarships for incoming students from South Carolina; and ten Charles H. Townes Scholarships for students coming from outside South Carolina. Additionally, Furman offers scholarships for students pursuing specific courses of study such as engineering, chemistry, and teaching.

STUDENT LIFE

The typical Furman student in this "close-knit, southern community" is "very studious but still very active in social life." "Pulling all-nighters is not uncommon but neither is staying out late." The school "has a lot of interesting things to do on campus, from music concerts to improv shows to sports games"; people visit "fun and safe" downtown Greenville on the weekends to shop or go to dinner. Football games are well-attended and most everyone is "overinvolved in many clubs." "Studying is a necessity," and students say Furman has done a good job at making studying convenient with "two coffee shops, four parlors, and fifteen–twenty study rooms in the library."

Furman University

FINANCIAL AID: 864-294-2204 • E-MAIL: ADMISSIONS@FURMAN.EDU • WEBSITE: WWW.FURMAN.EDU

CAREER

This "bubble community" allows for "strong research/internships if you want them"; "graduate schools like the Furman name," and the professors associated with the school serve as great references and connections to a broader future. "Furman has given me a great opportunity to learn, challenge myself, and find incredible internships," says one student. The Malone Career Center organizes job fairs and campus recruiting to help aid students in their search. For those Furman graduates who visited PayScale.com, 52 percent reported feeling that their career had a high social value. Ninety-seven percent of graduates gain admission to graduate school or find a job within six months of graduation.

GENERAL INFO

Activities: Choral groups, concert band, dance, drama/theater, jazz band, literary magazine, marching band, music ensembles, musical theater, opera, pep band, radio station, student government, student newspaper, student-run film society, symphony orchestra, television station, yearbook, Campus Ministries, International Student Organization. **Organizations:** 143 registered organizations, 29 honor societies, 17 religious organizations. 7 fraternities, 7 sororities. **Athletics (Intercollegiate):** *Men:* baseball, basketball, cheerleading, cross-country, football, golf, soccer, tennis, track/field (outdoor), track/field (indoor). *Women:* basketball, cheerleading, cross-country, golf, soccer, softball, tennis, track/field (outdoor), track/field (indoor), volleyball. **On-Campus Highlights:** Charles Townes Science Center, Timmons Arena, Library, 18-hole Golf Course, Physical Activities Center, Place of Peace, David Shi Center for Sustainability.

FINANCIAL AID

Students should submit: FAFSA, Institution's own financial aid form, CSS/Financial Aid PROFILE, State aid form. Regular filing deadline is 1/15. The Princeton Review suggests that all financial aid forms be submitted as soon as possible after October 1. *Need-based scholarships/grants offered:* Federal Pell, FSEOG, State scholarships/grants, Private scholarships, College/university scholarship or grant aid from institutional funds. *Loan aid offered:* Direct Subsidized Stafford Loans, Direct Unsubsidized Stafford Loans, Direct PLUS loans, Federal Perkins Loans, State Loans. Applicants will be notified of awards on or about 4/1. Federal Work-Study Program available. Institutional employment available.

BOTTOM LINE

Tuition costs $45,632 with $11,522 being added on for room and board. The vast majority of students receive need-based financial aid, with packages averaging $31,665, and merit-based scholarships are in no short supply for the eligible. Thirty-seven percent of students will graduate with loans, with the average debt coming in at $32,594.

CAREER INFORMATION FROM PAYSCALE.COM

ROI rating	87
Bachelor's and No Higher	
Median starting salary	$42,800
Median mid-career salary	$87,400
At Least Bachelor's	
Median starting salary	$44,400
Median mid-career salary	$88,200
% alumni with high job meaning	57%
% STEM	16%

SELECTIVITY

Admissions Rating	87
# of applicants	5,043
% of applicants accepted	65
% of acceptees attending	21
# offered a place on the wait list	208
% accepting a place on wait list	51
% admitted from wait list	14
# of early decision applicants	126
% accepted early decision	94

FRESHMAN PROFILE

Range SAT Critical Reading	550–660
Range SAT Math	550–660
Range SAT Writing	550–660
Range ACT Composite	25–30
% graduated top 10% of class	39
% graduated top 25% of class	71
% graduated top 50% of class	92

DEADLINES

Early decision	
Deadline	11/1
Notification	11/15
Other ED	
Deadline	11/1
Other ED	
Notification	11/15
Early action	
Deadline	11/15
Notification	12/20
Regular	
Deadline	1/15
Notification	3/1
Nonfall registration?	No

FINANCIAL FACTS

Financial Aid Rating	86
Annual tuition	$45,632
Room and board	$11,522
Required fees	$380
Average need-based scholarship	$33,774
% needy frosh rec. need-based scholarship or grant aid	100
% needy UG rec. need-based scholarship or grant aid	100
% needy frosh rec. non-need-based scholarship or grant aid	100
% needy UG rec. non-need-based scholarship or grant aid	100
% needy frosh rec. need-based self-help aid	71
% needy UG rec. need-based self-help aid	71
% frosh rec. any financial aid	98
% UG rec. any financial aid	94
% UG borrow to pay for school	37

George Mason University

4400 University Drive, Fairfax, VA 22030-4444 • Admissions: 703-993-2400 • Fax: 703-993-4622

CAMPUS LIFE

Quality of Life Rating	95
Fire Safety Rating	94
Green Rating	90
Type of school	Public
Affiliation	No Affiliation
Environment	City

STUDENTS

Total undergrad enrollment	23,062
% male/female	49/51
% from out of state	10
% frosh from public high school	89
% frosh live on campus	69
% ugrads live on campus	26
# of fraternities (% ugrad men join)	19 (1)
# of sororities (% ugrad women join)	16 (3)
% African American	11
% Asian	19
% Caucasian	43
% Hispanic	13
% Native American	<1
% Pacific Islander	<1
% Two or more races	5
% Race and/or ethnicity unknown	5
% international	5
# of countries represented	97

ACADEMICS

Academic Rating	78
% students returning for sophomore year	87
% students graduating within 4 years	46
% students graduating within 6 years	69
Calendar	Semester
Student/faculty ratio	16:1
Profs interesting rating	88
Profs accessible rating	85
Most classes have 20–29 students.	
Most lab/discussion sessions have 20–29 students.	

MOST POPULAR MAJORS

Biology; Psychology; Information Technology

ABOUT THE SCHOOL

Located in Virginia, right on the doorstep of D.C., the relatively new George Mason University boasts a strong sense of community. Professors not only have huge insight on the material of the courses they teach, but they bring it to life, encouraging the discussion of opinions. "All the classes I have taken so far have grabbed my full attention and [have] challenged me to think about topics I never thought to be interested in," says one student. A student at Mason has every opportunity imaginable to learn in different atmospheres, from both academics and professionals, via methods that offer "eye-opening perspectives." Proactivity is a noticeable strength of the school: "From smaller problems, to significantly larger ones, the school will take action immediately to fix any problems that arise."

BANG FOR YOUR BUCK

The majority of students at Mason are in-state residents, and so pay a sharply discounted tuition rate, and the school also gives out millions of dollars in need-and merit-based scholarships. All those who apply for admission by the first of November are automatically considered for merit-based scholarships. In addition, Mason offers internal, athletic, and department-based scholarships. On average, 59 percent of financial need is met.

STUDENT LIFE

Life at GMU is "exciting and engaging." There are "always different student organizations putting events together," and if there is nothing interesting happening on campus, "Washington D.C. is a metro stop away!" Indeed, D.C. is utilized to its fullest, with "shuttles provided by Mason, the Mason to metro, and the Fairfax Cue buses, one can always make their way out to DC." Students spend a lot of free time volunteering and becoming involved in on-and off-campus student activities; Greek life and men's basketball games are extremely popular. Regardless of race, ethnicity, country of origin, religion, or language, there are hundreds of student orgs that embrace the highly diverse student body's interests and views. "Two exciting things I've seen at Mason were an underwater hockey game as well as Quidditch games being played on the lawn," says a student.

CAREER

Mason is a career-preparatory school (with a top-notch Career Services Office to boot), where a student graduates with "an exemplary education, a phenomenal resume and worthwhile life experiences." "Mason is about teaching its students the fundamentals to life, while offering opportunities to work in their field and be prepared for the world ahead," says a student. The school has many specific and unique programs that are constructed in an innovative fashion, and don't necessarily follow traditional methods. The proximity to the nation's capital is certainly a boon, and "helps immensely with internships." "I intern on Capitol Hill, something you can't do in other regions of the country," says a student. Fifty-three percent of GMU graduates who visited PayScale.com report feeling that their jobs had a high level of meaningful impact on the world, and averaged $49,800 as a starting salary.

George Mason University

FINANCIAL AID: 703-993-2353 • E-MAIL: ADMISSIONS@GMU.EDU • WEBSITE: WWW.GMU.EDU

GENERAL INFO

Activities: Choral groups, concert band, dance, drama/theater, jazz band, literary magazine, music ensembles, musical theater, opera, pep band, radio station, student government, student newspaper, student-run film society, symphony orchestra, television station, yearbook, Campus Ministries, International Student Organization. **Organizations:** 487 registered organizations, 32 honor societies, 29 religious organizations. 19 fraternities, 16 sororities. **Athletics (Intercollegiate):** *Men:* baseball, basketball, cross-country, diving, golf, soccer, swimming, tennis, track/field (outdoor), track/field (indoor), volleyball, wrestling. *Women:* basketball, crew/rowing, cross-country, diving, lacrosse, soccer, softball, swimming, tennis, track/field (outdoor), track/field (indoor), volleyball. **On-Campus Highlights:** Johnson Center, Aquatic and Fitness Center, Center for the Arts, Patriot Center, Freedom Aquatic Center at Prince William, Hylton Performing Arts Center.

FINANCIAL AID

Students should submit: FAFSA. Priority filing deadline is 3/1. The Princeton Review suggests that all financial aid forms be submitted as soon as possible after October 1. *Need-based scholarships/grants offered:* Federal Pell, FSEOG, State scholarships/grants, Private scholarships, College/university scholarship or grant aid from institutional funds. *Loan aid offered:* Direct Subsidized Stafford Loans, Direct Unsubsidized Stafford Loans, Direct PLUS loans, Federal Perkins Loans, Federal Nursing Loans. Applicants will be notified of awards on a rolling basis beginning 4/1. Federal Work-Study Program available. Institutional employment available.

BOTTOM LINE

GMU is a public university, so in-state tuition runs $7,976 per year while out-of-state is $28,622 per year. Expect room and board to run about $10,510, though many students choose to live at home and commute. Fifty-nine percent of undergraduates receive some form of financial aid, with the average freshman need-based gift running $5,889.

CAREER INFORMATION FROM PAYSCALE.COM

ROI rating	86
Bachelor's and No Higher	
Median starting salary	$51,400
Median mid-career salary	$89,700
At Least Bachelor's	
Median starting salary	$51,700
Median mid-career salary	$91,300
% alumni with high job meaning	44%
% STEM	10%

SELECTIVITY

Admissions Rating	82
# of applicants	21,981
% of applicants accepted	69
% of acceptees attending	21
# offered a place on the wait list	1,884
% accepting a place on wait list	50
% admitted from wait list	37

FRESHMAN PROFILE

Range SAT Critical Reading	520–620
Range SAT Math	520–630
Range ACT Composite	23–29
Minimum paper TOEFL	570
Minimum internet-based TOEFL	80
Average HS GPA	3.7
% graduated top 10% of class	21
% graduated top 25% of class	56
% graduated top 50% of class	92

DEADLINES

Early action	
Deadline	11/1
Notification	12/15
Regular	
Priority	11/1
Deadline	1/15
Nonfall registration?	Yes

FINANCIAL FACTS

Financial Aid Rating	79
Annual in-state tuition	$8,204
Annual out-of-state tuition	$29,486
Room and board	$10,730
Required fees	$3,096
Average need-based scholarship	$6,092
% needy frosh rec. need-based scholarship or grant aid	77
% needy UG rec. need-based scholarship or grant aid	76
% needy frosh rec. non-need-based scholarship or grant aid	35
% needy UG rec. non-need-based scholarship or grant aid	17
% needy frosh rec. need-based self-help aid	76
% needy UG rec. need-based self-help aid	77
% frosh rec. any financial aid	70
% UG rec. any financial aid	59
% UG borrow to pay for school	58
Average cumulative indebtedness	$27,373
% frosh need fully met	5
% ugrads need fully met	5
Average % of frosh need met	64
Average % of ugrad need met	57

Georgetown University

37TH AND O STREETS, NW, 103 WHITE-GRAVEN, WASHINGTON, D.C. 20057 • ADMISSIONS: 202-687-3600

CAMPUS LIFE

Quality of Life Rating	**68**
Fire Safety Rating	**88**
Green Rating	**60***
Type of school	Private
Affiliation	Roman Catholic
Environment	Metropolis

STUDENTS

Total undergrad enrollment	7,562
% male/female	45/55
% from out of state	98
% frosh from public high school	49
% frosh live on campus	100
% ugrads live on campus	65
% African American	6
% Asian	10
% Caucasian	56
% Hispanic	8
% Native American	<1
% Pacific Islander	<1
% Two or more races	5
% Race and/or ethnicity unknown	2
% international	12
# of countries represented	138

ACADEMICS

Academic Rating	**86**
% students returning for sophomore year	96
% students graduating within 4 years	90
% students graduating within 6 years	94
Calendar	Semester
Student/faculty ratio	11:1
Profs interesting rating	70
Profs accessible rating	64

Most classes have 10–19 students.
Most lab/discussion sessions have 10–19 students.

MOST POPULAR MAJORS
Political Science and Government;
International Relations and Affairs; English

ABOUT THE SCHOOL

Georgetown was founded in 1789 by John Carroll, who concurred with his contemporaries Benjamin Franklin and Thomas Jefferson in believing that the success of the young democracy depended upon an educated and virtuous citizenry. Carroll founded the school with the dynamic Jesuit tradition of education, characterized by humanism and committed to the assumption of responsibility and action. Georgetown is a national and international university, enrolling students from all fifty states and more than 100 foreign countries. Undergraduate students are enrolled in one of four undergraduate schools: the College of Arts and Sciences, School of Foreign Service, Georgetown School of Business, and Georgetown School of Nursing and Health Studies. All students share a common liberal arts core and have access to the entire university curriculum.

This moderately sized elite academic establishment stays true to its Jesuit foundations by educating its students with the idea of "cura personalis," or "care for the whole person." The "well-informed" student body perpetuates upon itself, creating an atmosphere full of vibrant intellectual life that is "also balanced with extracurricular learning and development." "Georgetown is . . . a place where people work very, very hard without feeling like they are in direct competition," says an international politics major.

BANG FOR YOUR BUCK

Professors tend to be "fantastic scholars and teachers" and are "generally available to students," as well as often being "interested in getting to know you as a person (if you put forth the effort to talk to them and go to office hours)." Though Georgetown has a policy of grade deflation, meaning "As are hard to come by," there are "a ton of interesting courses available," and TAs are used only for optional discussion sessions and help with grading. The academics "can be challenging, or they can be not so much (not that they are ever really easy, just easier);" it all depends on the courses you choose and how much you actually do the work. Internship opportunities in the DC area are valuable and often take place "in the heart of the nation's capital." People know the importance of connections and spend time making sure they get to know the people here. One student is very enthusiastic about these opportunities. "The location in DC and the pragmatism of people who come here make for people that are fun to be around but are serious about their ambitions. There's a reason that Georgetown tends to draw political junkies. It's because there's no better place in the United States to get involved with politics on a national level."

STUDENT LIFE

There are "a lot of wealthy students on campus," and preppy-casual is the fashion de rigueur; this is "definitely not a 'granola' school," but students from diverse backgrounds are typically welcomed by people wanting to learn about different experiences. Indeed, everyone here is well-traveled and well-educated, and there are "a ton of international students." "You better have at least some interest in politics, or you will feel out-of-place," says a student. The school can also be "a bit cliquish, with athletes at the top," but there are "plenty of groups for everybody to fit into and find their niche," and "there is much crossover between groups."

CAREER

The Cawley Career Education Center can help students answer that perennial question: "What can I do with my major?" The Career Exploration resource on its website allows students to learn about the

Georgetown University

FINANCIAL AID: 202-687-4547 • FAX: 202-687-5084 • E-MAIL: GUADMISS@GEORGETOWN.EDU • WEBSITE: WWW.GEORGETOWN.EDU

transferable skills that different majors at Georgetown will help them develop and see jobs and internships that alumni from those programs have held. The Hoya Career Connection and the iNet Internship network are the Career Education Center's online management systems that allow students to search and apply for jobs, internships, fellowships and volunteer gigs. Finally, the Center brings a number of potential employers to campus through the Career Fair, Government & Nonprofit Expo, and various Industry Weeks. Graduates who visited PayScale.com report a median starting salary of $53,000.

GENERAL INFO

Activities: Choral groups, concert band, dance, drama/theater, jazz band, literary magazine, music ensembles, musical theater, pep band, radio station, student government, student newspaper, student-run film society, symphony orchestra, television station, yearbook. **Organizations:** 139 registered organizations, 14 honor societies, 20 religious organizations. **Athletics (Intercollegiate):** *Men:* Baseball, basketball, crew/rowing, cross-country, diving, football, golf, lacrosse, sailing, soccer, swimming, tennis, track/field (outdoor), track/field (indoor). *Women:* Basketball, crew/rowing, cross-country, diving, field hockey, golf, lacrosse, sailing, soccer, softball, swimming, tennis, track/field (outdoor), track/field (indoor), volleyball. **On-Campus Highlights:** Yates Field House, Uncommon Grounds, The Observatory, The Quadrangle, Healy Hall.

FINANCIAL AID

Students should submit: FAFSA, CSS/Financial Aid PROFILE, Business/Farm Supplement. Priority filing deadline is 2/1. The Princeton Review suggests that all financial aid forms be submitted as soon as possible after October 1. *Need-based scholarships/grants offered:* Federal Pell, FSEOG, State scholarships/grants, Private scholarships, College/university scholarship or grant aid from institutional funds. *Loan aid offered:* Direct Subsidized Stafford Loans, Direct Unsubsidized Stafford Loans, Direct PLUS loans, Federal Perkins Loans, Federal Nursing Loans. Applicants will be notified of awards on or about 4/1. Federal Work-Study Program available. Institutional employment available.

BOTTOM LINE

Georgetown University has a well-deserved reputation for the outstanding quality of its curriculum and the fantastic overall educational experience it provides. Of course, the cost of tuition reflects that to a great extent, amounting to nearly $50,547 with fees. Room and board tacks on another $14,962. At the same time, Georgetown meets 100 percent of student need; with an average need-based scholarship of $40,104, it is easy to see that a Georgetown education is still accessible to a large segment of potential students. Students can envision a loan debt of about $23,067 once they graduate from the university.

CAREER INFORMATION FROM PAYSCALE.COM

ROI rating	89
Bachelor's and No Higher	
Median starting salary	$51,800
Median mid-career salary	$110,000
At Least Bachelor's	
Median starting salary	$54,400
Median mid-career salary	$116,000
% alumni with high job meaning	48%
% STEM	7%

SELECTIVITY

Admissions Rating	98
# of applicants	19,478
% of applicants accepted	17
% of acceptees attending	47
# offered a place on the wait list	2,184
% accepting a place on wait list	57
% admitted from wait list	12

FRESHMAN PROFILE

Range SAT Critical Reading	660–750
Range SAT Math	660–750
Range ACT Composite	30–34
% graduated top 10% of class	89
% graduated top 25% of class	98
% graduated top 50% of class	100

DEADLINES

Early action	
Deadline	11/1
Notification	12/15
Regular	
Deadline	1/10
Notification	4/1
Nonfall registration?	No

FINANCIAL FACTS

Financial Aid Rating	93
Annual tuition	$49,968
Room and board	$14,962
Required fees	$579
Average need-based scholarship	$40,104
% needy frosh rec. need-based scholarship or grant aid	89
% needy UG rec. need-based scholarship or grant aid	90
% needy frosh rec. non-need-based scholarship or grant aid	40
% needy UG rec. non-need-based scholarship or grant aid	30
% needy frosh rec. need-based self-help aid	84
% needy UG rec. need-based self-help aid	9
% UG borrow to pay for school	38
Average cumulative indebtedness	$23,067
% frosh need fully met	100
Average % of frosh need met	100
Average % of ugrad need met	100

SCHOOL PROFILES ■ 177

Georgia Institute of Technology

GEORGIA INSTITUTE OF TECHNOLOGY, ATLANTA, GA 30332-0320 • ADMISSIONS: 404-894-4154 • FAX: 404-894-9511

CAMPUS LIFE

Quality of Life Rating	**72**
Fire Safety Rating	**96**
Green Rating	**98**
Type of school	Public
Affiliation	No Affiliation
Environment	Metropolis

STUDENTS

Total undergrad enrollment	15,142
% male/female	66/34
% from out of state	34
% frosh live on campus	98
% ugrads live on campus	53
# of fraternities (% ugrad men join)	40 (25)
# of sororities (% ugrad women join)	16 (30)
% African American	7
% Asian	19
% Caucasian	51
% Hispanic	7
% Native American	<1
% Pacific Islander	<1
% Two or more races	4
% Race and/or ethnicity unknown	2
% international	11
# of countries represented	95

ACADEMICS

Academic Rating	**67**
% students returning for sophomore year	97
% students graduating within 4 years	40
% students graduating within 6 years	85
Calendar	Semester
Student/faculty ratio	19:1
Profs interesting rating	67
Profs accessible rating	66

Most classes have 20–29 students.
Most lab/discussion sessions have 20–29 students.

MOST POPULAR MAJORS

Mechanical Engineering; Industrial Engineering; Computer and Information Sciences

ABOUT THE SCHOOL

Firmly rooted in research, Georgia Tech teaches its students to be independent learners who are able to recognize when it's time to ask for help. "If you're organized and get help when you need it, you'll be okay, because we have tons of free tutoring on campus… If you need help with anything, there are countless different places that offer tutoring." The best resource is usually fellow students. The school "is extremely challenging, academically," a student tells us. "Because everyone knows how tough of a school it is, there is a spirit of camaraderie here that you don't find anywhere else," one student says.

BANG FOR YOUR BUCK

Almost 97 percent of freshman students return for their sophomore year—always an encouraging sign. Programs on the Atlanta campus include design, business, computing, engineering, liberal arts, and the sciences. Graduates of Georgia Tech often find themselves well prepared once they enter the workforce. Undergraduates are offered countless opportunities to earn valuable work experience through the institution's co-op and internship programs. For those with international interests, immersions are available through study abroad, work abroad, or the international plan. Forty-five percent of Georgia Tech students participate in a study abroad experience. The Career Services department is said by students to be "outstanding," and Georgia Tech is "one of the only schools in the country that offers the BS distinction for liberal arts majors because we [get] such a rigorous grounding in math and science." There are also more than twenty different honor societies.

STUDENT LIFE

"The greatest strength of Georgia Tech is its diversity," undergrads report. "Students, activities, opportunities, teachers—all are diverse." One observes that the school offers "a great sense of school spirit and a great feeling of cohesion with the student body." Another student explains, "Unlike at high school, no one looks down upon you if you know the entire periodic table, if you can do differential equations, or you can speak three languages; rather, you are respected." At Georgia Tech there is "a little something for everyone. Salsa club on weekends, musical groups, intramural sports—even a skydiving club!" Other options include "a 'good enough' NCAA Division I sports program, a good social scene," a welcoming Greek community, "and for everyone else, there's the city of Atlanta right at your doorstep." One sore spot: Men outnumber women here by greater than a two-to-one ratio. The situation is most pronounced in engineering (three-to-one) and computing (more than four-to-one) disciplines. Women actually outnumber men in the liberal arts and science colleges.

CAREER

The school's prime location in midtown Atlanta is a boon to Georgia Tech students, who have great access to paid co-op and internship opportunities right in the city. Finding opportunities couldn't be simpler with CareerBuzz, a one-stop online database for all full-time, part-time, seasonal, cooperative education, internship, and undergraduate research positions. Additionally, a co-op and internship fair attracts approximately 100 or more employers to campus. For students wanting to work abroad, the Office of International Education facilitates paid work opportunities in multiple countries. Finally, a packed calendar of workshops put on by the Center for Career Discovery and Development ("Resume Blitz," "Evaluating Job Offers," and "Success on the Job" are a few offerings) gives students insight into the job hunt from every angle. Alumni who visited PayScale.com reported a median starting salary of $62,500.

Georgia Institute of Technology

FINANCIAL AID: 404 894-4160 • E-MAIL: ADMISSION@GATECH.EDU • WEBSITE: WWW.GATECH.EDU

GENERAL INFO

Activities: Choral groups, concert band, dance, drama/theater, jazz band, literary magazine, marching band, music ensembles, musical theater, pep band, radio station, student government, student newspaper, student-run film society, symphony orchestra, television station, yearbook, campus ministries, international student organization. **Organizations:** 548 registered organizations, 22 honor societies, 41 religious organizations. 40 fraternities, 16 sororities. **Athletics (Intercollegiate):** *Men:* Baseball, basketball, cheerleading, cross-country, diving, football, golf, swimming, tennis, track/field (outdoor), track/field (indoor). *Women:* Basketball, cheerleading, cross-country, diving, softball, swimming, tennis, track/field (outdoor), track/ field (indoor), volleyball.

FINANCIAL AID

Students should submit: FAFSA, CSS/Financial Aid PROFILE and Institute's Application for Scholarships & Financial Aid. Regular filing deadline is 1/31. The Princeton Review suggests that all financial aid forms be submitted as soon as possible after October 1. *Need-based scholarships/grants offered:* Federal FSEOG, State scholarship/grants, and Scholarship and grants from institutional and foundation support. *Loan aid offered:* Federal Direct Subsidized and Unsubsidized Loans. Direct PLUS; and Institute loans from institutional funds. Applicants will be notified of awards in early April. Both Federal Work-Study Program and Institutional employment available.

BOTTOM LINE

In-state tuition is extremely affordable, at approximately $9,812 per year. While out-of-state tuition is substantially higher at more than $30,004 each year, there are a variety of ways to reduce that total through various financial aid and scholarship opportunities. Nearly 74 percent of all undergraduates receive some form of financial aid, and the average need-based package for students is $10,108. On-campus room and board is $13,640, with required fees, books, and supplies running in the neighborhood of $4,000.

CAREER INFORMATION FROM PAYSCALE.COM

ROI rating	89
Bachelor's and No Higher	
Median starting salary	$62,500
Median mid-career salary	$112,000
At Least Bachelor's	
Median starting salary	$63,400
Median mid-career salary	$114,000
% alumni with high job meaning	44%
% STEM	71%

SELECTIVITY

Admissions Rating	97
# of applicants	27,277
% of applicants accepted	32
% of acceptees attending	35
# offered a place on the wait list	3,397
% accepting a place on wait list	60
% admitted from wait list	2

FRESHMAN PROFILE

Range SAT Critical Reading	630–730
Range SAT Math	680–770
Range SAT Writing	640–730
Range ACT Composite	30–33
Average HS GPA	4.0
% graduated top 10% of class	81
% graduated top 25% of class	96
% graduated top 50% of class	99

DEADLINES

Early action	
Deadline	10/15
Notification	1/10
Regular	
Priority	10/15
Deadline	1/10
Notification	3/14
Nonfall registration?	Yes

FINANCIAL FACTS

Financial Aid Rating	81
Annual in-state tuition	$9,812
Annual out-of-state tuition	$30,004
Room and board	$13,640
Required fees	$2,400
Average need-based scholarship	$10,108
% needy frosh rec. need-based scholarship or grant aid	86
% needy UG rec. need-based scholarship or grant aid	86
% needy frosh rec. non-need-based scholarship or grant aid	53
% needy UG rec. non-need-based scholarship or grant aid	61
% needy frosh rec. need-based self-help aid	66
% needy UG rec. need-based self-help aid	65
% frosh rec. any financial aid	63
% UG rec. any financial aid	72
% UG borrow to pay for school	40
Average cumulative indebtedness	$25,182
% frosh need fully met	35
% ugrads need fully met	24
Average % of frosh need met	84
Average % of ugrad need met	74

Gettysburg College

ADMISSIONS OFFICE, EISENHOWER HOUSE, GETTYSBURG, PA 17325-1484 • ADMISSIONS: 717-337-6100 • FAX: 717-337-6145

CAMPUS LIFE

Quality of Life Rating	**94**
Fire Safety Rating	**91**
Green Rating	**80**
Type of school	Private
Affiliation	Lutheran
Environment	Village

STUDENTS

Total undergrad enrollment	2,454
% male/female	47/53
% from out of state	74
% frosh from public high school	70
% frosh live on campus	100
% ugrads live on campus	94
# of fraternities (% ugrad men join)	9 (31)
# of sororities (% ugrad women join)	6 (33)
% African American	3
% Asian	2
% Caucasian	79
% Hispanic	5
% Native American	<1
% Pacific Islander	0
% Two or more races	2
% Race and/or ethnicity unknown	3
% international	5
# of countries represented	36

ACADEMICS

Academic Rating	**94**
% students returning for sophomore year	91
% students graduating within 4 years	80
Calendar	Semester
Student/faculty ratio	10:1
Profs interesting rating	86
Profs accessible rating	93
Most classes have 10–19 students.	

MOST POPULAR MAJORS
Psychology; Political Science and Government; Business/Commerce

ABOUT THE SCHOOL

Gettysburg is a national college of liberal arts and sciences located in Gettysburg, Pennsylvania. Gettysburg's 2,500 students are actively involved in an academically rigorous and personally challenging educational experience offered through a wonderful "combination of small student-body and world-class faculty and administrative" members. "The small class sizes are a huge benefit for students, as they get individual attention, [something] so hard to find at most other institutions." With an average class size of eighteen and a student-to-faculty ratio of 10:1, there are no passive learners here—personal interactions and supports are part of the educational process. Don't be surprised if professors here know you by first name. One visiting, prospective undergraduate explains: "I met a biology professor in the college parking lot [who] took two hours out of his day to show us around the Science Center, the labs, and classrooms and even introduce me to the chair of the biology department." At Gettysburg, all first-years participate in the First-Year Seminar, in which students analyze, investigate, research, discuss, and debate a diverse range of topics and themes. "The small environment provides the best conditions for participating in class, getting to know professors on a personal basis, and having a voice on campus," all while brazenly engaging whatever academic pursuits the student desires. "There is something for everyone," a sophomore expresses, "from trumpet performance to Latin studies to globalization to health sciences." Gettysburg's world-famous Sunderman Conservatory of Music attracts many artists to its campus and enables students to "seriously study music while allowing [them] to explore other areas of study as well." Research opportunities are copious, and students graduate from Gettysburg with hands-on learning experiences attractive to employers and graduate schools alike. "The Center for Career Development does a great job of helping students of all class years find internships, externships, and job-shadowing opportunities."

BANG FOR YOUR BUCK

Gettysburg College awards about $47 million in scholarships and grants each year. Both need-based and merit-based awards are available. Merit-based scholarships range from $7,000 to $25,000 per year. A separate application is not required; decisions on merit scholarship recipients are made as part of the admissions process. Talent scholarships are also available. Gettysburg College grants vary from $500 to $38,690, based on financial need. The average freshman grant is $28,000.

STUDENT LIFE

Students at Gettysburg love the place get involved in order to continue to improve it, so a lot of these students "spend a significant amount of time volunteering and are involved in on-campus groups during the week." There's always something going on at Gettysburg, meaning "it is never 'what is there to do tonight?' but instead 'what am I going to choose to do?'" The Campus Activities Board usually has something going on, whether they are hosting a concert, showing a movie, or having a dance in the Attic (an on-campus hangout spot), and the diverse Greek-oriented social life makes "a place for everyone regardless of who you are." Studying abroad is hugely popular, and

Gettysburg College

FINANCIAL AID: 717-337-6611 • E mail: ADMISS@GETTYSBURG.EDU • WEBSITE: WWW.GETTYSBURG.EDU

most students "participate in sports on some level or take advantage of our amazing fitness facility."

CAREER

There is excellent financial support for students who "want to do really cool things with their education" such as study abroad, unpaid internships, or academic conferences. The study abroad program is "impressively large," and the opportunities for gaining work experience both in the United States and abroad are "endless." The Center for Career Development "does a great job of helping students find internships, externships and job shadowing opportunities" and "the support from the alumni helps with having lots of options for internships and jobs," says a student. Aside from job fairs, resume reviews, and online resources, the center's Career Immersion Trips are three-day intensive career programs that offer students a chance to get firsthand insight into their possible career up close and in person. Of the Gettysburg graduates who visited PayScale.com 41 percent reported a feeling that their job had a meaningful impact on the world, and an average starting salary of $47,600.

GENERAL INFO

Athletics (Intercollegiate): *Men:* Baseball, basketball, cheerleading, cross-country, football, golf, lacrosse, soccer, swimming, tennis, track/field (outdoor), track/field (indoor), wrestling. *Women:* Basketball, cheerleading, cross-country, field hockey, golf, lacrosse, soccer, softball, swimming, tennis, track/field (outdoor), track/field (indoor), volleyball.

FINANCIAL AID

Students should submit: FAFSA, CSS/Financial Aid PROFILE. Regular filing deadline is 1/15. The Princeton Review suggests that all financial aid forms be submitted as soon as possible after October 1. *Need-based scholarships/grants offered:* Federal Pell, FSEOG, State scholarships/grants, Private scholarships, College/university scholarship or grant aid from institutional funds. *Loan aid offered:* Direct Subsidized Stafford Loans, Direct Unsubsidized Stafford Loans, Direct PLUS loans, Federal Perkins Loans, College/university loans from institutional funds. Applicants will be notified of awards on or about 4/1. Federal Work-Study Program available. Institutional employment available.

BOTTOM LINE

At Gettysburg College, tuition and fees cost about $50,860 per year. Room and board on campus costs about $12,140. Prospective students should also factor in the annual cost of books, supplies, transportation, and personal expenses. Overall, about 60 percent of Gettysburg students receive some sort of funding from their "irresistible . . . and generous financial aid program."

CAREER INFORMATION FROM PAYSCALE.COM

ROI rating	**90**
Bachelor's and No Higher	
Median starting salary	$48,900
Median mid-career salary	$100,000
At Least Bachelor's	
Median starting salary	$50,500
Median mid-career salary	$102,000
% alumni with high job meaning	50%
% STEM	19%

SELECTIVITY

Admissions Rating	**92**
# of applicants	6,386
% of applicants accepted	40
% of acceptees attending	28
# of early decision applicants	444
% accepted early decision	68

FRESHMAN PROFILE

Range SAT Critical Reading	600–670
Range SAT Math	610–680
% graduated top 10% of class	56
% graduated top 25% of class	71
% graduated top 50% of class	98

DEADLINES

Early decision	
Deadline	11/15
Notification	12/15
Regular	
Priority	1/15
Deadline	1/15
Notification	4/1
Nonfall registration?	Yes

FINANCIAL FACTS

Financial Aid Rating	**94**
Annual tuition	$50,860
Room and board	$12,140
Average need-based scholarship	$33,139
% needy frosh rec. need-based scholarship or grant aid	96
% needy UG rec. need-based scholarship or grant aid	95
% needy frosh rec. non-need-based scholarship or grant aid	55
% needy UG rec. non-need-based scholarship or grant aid	50
% needy frosh rec. need-based self-help aid	87
% needy UG rec. need-based self-help aid	86
% frosh rec. any financial aid	60
% UG rec. any financial aid	60
% UG borrow to pay for school	61
Average cumulative indebtedness	$30,544
% frosh need fully met	88
% ugrads need fully met	87
Average % of frosh need met	90
Average % of ugrad need met	90

Gonzaga University

502 East Boone Avenue, Spokane, WA 99258 • Admissions: 509-313-6572 • Fax: 509-313-5780

CAMPUS LIFE

Quality of Life Rating	**88**
Fire Safety Rating	**89**
Green Rating	**94**
Type of school	Private
Affiliation	Roman Catholic
Environment	City

STUDENTS

Total undergrad enrollment	5,041
% male/female	46/54
% from out of state	50
% frosh from public high school	63
% frosh live on campus	98
% ugrads live on campus	60
% African American	1
% Asian	5
% Caucasian	72
% Hispanic	10
% Native American	1
% Pacific Islander	<1
% Two or more races	6
% Race and/or ethnicity unknown	3
% international	2
# of countries represented	34

ACADEMICS

Academic Rating	**82**
% students returning for sophomore year	95
% students graduating within 4 years	73
% students graduating within 6 years	83
Calendar	Semester
Student/faculty ratio	12:1
Profs interesting rating	81
Profs accessible rating	86

Most classes have 20–29 students.
Most lab/discussion sessions have
10–19 students.

MOST POPULAR MAJORS
Business, Social Science, Engineering

ABOUT THE SCHOOL

Students uniformly stress the strong sense of community at Gonzaga, a Jesuit university boasting a reported 12:1 student to faculty ratio. Of its seventy-three offered majors, the most popular are Business, Social Science, and Engineering. Gonzaga is a Division I athletic program and the home of the Bulldogs. The makeup is 54 percent female, 46 percent male, and 72 percent white. Students feel that each professor has at least "some background in research and is able to provide their personal experience in the classroom." Students note that Gonzaga "requires a broad mix of classes for any major," and that being there is about "developing as a whole person." Many students stress Gonzaga's commitment to social justice. Students feel that the professors are primarily "awesome," "very personable," and "helpful and accessible outside of the classroom," although some stress that not all students "approve of the religious lean most of the professors take." One student notes of Gonzaga that "sometimes it's so liberal it bothers people, sometimes it's so conservative it bothers people."

BANG FOR YOUR BUCK

Tuition at Gonzaga runs about $38,980, and the average aid package is about $25,839. Gonzaga reportedly meets 81 percent of freshman financial need; however, 99 percent of freshman receive at least some form of aid. Students rate the scholarships received from "good" to "great" to "very generous." One student feels that "the number of students who survive because of financial aid or merit based scholarships is bigger than most people think." A few students report that Gonzaga "generally matches 100 percent of your [financial] need."

STUDENT LIFE

Ninety percent of the campus is accessible to physically disabled students and 100 percent of classrooms are wireless. In addition to being huge fans of the men's basketball team ("go Bulldogs!"), students at Gonzaga really like participating in intramural sports. Students warn that registration can be "a bit of a nightmare." Students at Gonzaga "like to do volunteer work and are pretty friendly. They also like to party as soon as Thursday comes around," but be wary, partiers, for a student notes that that the administration goes "pretty hard with writing kids up on the weekends and getting caught with weed is very bad news." A current student wants you all to know about "the new dorms, new science building and new business building. Even though Gonzaga isn't a major research or state university, the science department is really strong, with lots of great opportunities to get involved as undergrads."

Gonzaga University

FINANCIAL AID: 509-313-6582 • E-MAIL: ADMISSIONS@GONZAGA.EDU • WEBSITE: WWW.GONZAGA.EDU

CAREER

The typical Gonzaga University graduate has a starting salary of around $47,600, and 53 percent report that their job has a great deal of meaning. Students feel that Gonzaga "does a great job looking up internships and job openings for you as well," especially in the Biology department. "A lot of students enter Teach for America, JVC, or the Peace Corps post graduation." One Business major notes, "The business school has great opportunities for their students; Everything from internships with Boeing to incredible alumni relations to jobs in the big four accounting firms," and many students feel that "the Career Center and GAMP (Gonzaga Alumni Mentorship Program) are two the greatest things GU has to offer students (especially seniors)."

GENERAL INFO

Activities: Choral groups, concert band, dance, drama/theater, jazz band, literary magazine, music ensembles, pep band, radio station, student government, student newspaper, symphony orchestra, television station, yearbook, Campus Ministries. **Organizations:** 86 registered organizations, 10 honor societies, 4 religious organizations. **Athletics (Intercollegiate):** *Men:* baseball, basketball, crew/rowing, cross-country, golf, soccer, tennis, track/field (outdoor). *Women:* basketball, crew/rowing, cross-country, golf, soccer, tennis, track/field (outdoor), volleyball. **On-Campus Highlights:** John J. Hemmingson Center, St Aloysius Cathedral, McCarthy Athletic Center, Jundt Art Museum, Bing Crosby Museum in the Crosby Student Center, The Gonzaga University Bookstore.

FINANCIAL AID

Students should submit: FAFSA. Priority filing deadline is 2/1. The Princeton Review suggests that all financial aid forms be submitted as soon as possible after October 1. *Need-based scholarships/grants offered:* Federal Pell, FSEOG, State scholarships/grants, Private scholarships, College/university scholarship or grant aid from institutional funds. *Loan aid offered:* Direct Subsidized Stafford Loans, Direct Unsubsidized Stafford Loans, Direct PLUS loans, Federal Perkins Loans, Federal Nursing Loans, College/university loans from institutional funds. Applicants will be notified of awards on a rolling basis beginning 3/1. Federal Work-Study Program available. Institutional employment available.

BOTTOM LINE

The tuition at Gonzaga University comes to $38,980, excluding fees and room and board. The average need-based aid scholarship offered to undergraduates at Gonzaga comes to about $20,609 with 80 percent of undergraduate financial aid need reported as being met. In addition, 99 percent of freshmen and 98 percent of undergrads receive some form of financial aid.

CAREER INFORMATION FROM PAYSCALE.COM

ROI rating	86
Bachelor's and No Higher	
Median starting salary	$50,300
Median mid-career salary	$89,000
At Least Bachelor's	
Median starting salary	$51,700
Median mid-career salary	$89,400
% alumni with high job meaning	53%
% STEM	16%

SELECTIVITY

Admissions Rating	87
# of applicants	6,729
% of applicants accepted	73
% of acceptees attending	27
# offered a place on the wait list	332
% accepting a place on wait list	39
% admitted from wait list	0

FRESHMAN PROFILE

Range SAT Critical Reading	540–640
Range SAT Math	550–650
Range ACT Composite	25–29
Minimum paper TOEFL	550
Average HS GPA	3.7
% graduated top 10% of class	39
% graduated top 25% of class	71
% graduated top 50% of class	95

DEADLINES

Early action	
Deadline	11/15
Notification	1/15
Regular	
Priority	11/15
Deadline	2/1
Notification	3/15
Nonfall registration?	Yes

FINANCIAL FACTS

Financial Aid Rating	85
Annual tuition	$38,980
Room and board	$11,158
Required fees	$750
Average need-based scholarship	$20,609
% needy frosh rec. need-based scholarship or grant aid	100
% needy UG rec. need-based scholarship or grant aid	100
% needy frosh rec. non-need-based scholarship or grant aid	22
% needy UG rec. non-need-based scholarship or grant aid	19
% needy frosh rec. need-based self-help aid	67
% needy UG rec. need-based self-help aid	70
% frosh rec. any financial aid	99
% UG rec. any financial aid	98
% UG borrow to pay for school	65
Average cumulative indebtedness	$29,459
% frosh need fully met	26
% ugrads need fully met	23
Average % of frosh need met	79
Average % of ugrad need met	78

Grinnell College

1103 PARK STREET, GRINNELL, IA 50112 • ADMISSIONS: 641-269-3600 • FAX: 641-269-4800

CAMPUS LIFE

Quality of Life Rating	90
Fire Safety Rating	92
Green Rating	79
Type of school	Private
Affiliation	No Affiliation
Environment	Village

STUDENTS

Total undergrad enrollment	1,705
% male/female	45/55
% from out of state	88
% frosh from public high school	67
% frosh live on campus	100
% ugrads live on campus	88
% African American	6
% Asian	7
% Caucasian	56
% Hispanic	7
% Native American	<1
% Pacific Islander	0
% Two or more races	5
% Race and/or ethnicity unknown	3
% international	16
# of countries represented	47

ACADEMICS

Academic Rating	97
% students returning for sophomore year	94
% students graduating within 4 years	79
% students graduating within 6 years	86
Calendar	Semester
Student/faculty ratio	9:1
Profs interesting rating	95
Profs accessible rating	97

Most classes have 10–19 students.
Most lab/discussion sessions have
10–19 students.

MOST POPULAR MAJORS
Political Science and Government;
Economics; Biology

#40 COLLEGE THAT PAYS YOU BACK

ABOUT THE SCHOOL

Grinnell College is a smorgasbord of intellectual delights in a tiny, quintessential Iowa town that is surrounded by cornfields. The arts and sciences facilities here are world-class. The academic atmosphere is extremely challenging and stressful. Classes are hard and demanding. The ability to handle a lot of reading and writing is vital. Even though Grinnell boasts of an "open curriculum [and] low faculty-to-student ratio," the setting demands that students "work hard [and] play hard." Undergrads here often complete work that would be considered graduate-level at other institutions. At the same time, there isn't much in the way of competition; students bring the pressure on themselves. Classes are small and intimate. Professors are crazy accessible. The curriculum is completely open except for a freshman tutorial—a writing-intensive course that introduces academic thinking and research. Beyond that, there are no subject- matter requirements for obtaining a degree from Grinnell, as the school "encourages liberal arts academic exploration." Students are free to design their own paths to graduation. Mentored advanced projects provide a chance to work closely with a faculty member on scholarly research or the creation of a work of art. Fifty to 60 percent of every graduating class is accepted onto a wide range of off-campus study programs both domestic and abroad. On campus, Scholars' Convocation enriches the college's academic community by bringing notable speakers to campus.

BANG FOR YOUR BUCK

Grinnell was founded by a group of Iowa pioneers in 1843, and that pioneering spirit still informs the college's approach to education. Grinnell's endowment these days is in the range of a billion dollars. That's billion, with a B, so admission here is in no way contingent on your economic situation. If you can get admitted here (no small feat), Grinnell will meet 100 percent of your financial need. The college is even moving to meet the full demonstrated institutional need of select international students. In a typical year, Grinnell awards over ten times more in grants than in loans. As part of the culture of alumni support, the college also raises specific funds from alumni to reduce, at the time of graduation, the indebtedness of seniors who have demonstrated a solid work ethic both academically and cocurricularly. Eligible students may designate one summer devoted to either an approved Grinnell-sponsored internship or summer research at Grinnell. In return, the expected summer earnings contribution of $2,500 will be eliminated for that one summer only. One student notes that "on-campus employment is virtually guaranteed."

STUDENT LIFE

Undergrads here seem to live at fairly frenzied clip. Indeed, "Grinnellians pride themselves on working hard, but also playing hard." And, thankfully, there's plenty of fun to be had. To begin with, "every weekend there are movies, concerts, and parties planned and run by students all going on in addition to other events planned by the college." Additionally, "a lot of students volunteer for fun at the animal shelter or our Liberal Arts in Prison program, or they join an organization to learn something new or change the world." Moreover, Grinnell definitely has a party scene, one that is viewed as "thriving, quirky, welcoming, and casual." And "even [when it does get] raucous . . . you will [still] find people discussing 17th century literature or debating hot political

Grinnell College

FINANCIAL AID: 641-269-3250 • E-MAIL: ASKGRIN@GRINNELL.EDU • WEBSITE: WWW.GRINNELL.EDU

topics." Overall, Grinnell provides "an amazing mix of silly times and very smart people."

CAREER

Grinnell undergrads do pretty well for themselves. Indeed, according to PayScale.com, the average starting salary for these students is $43,100. Students are thankful that the "Grinnell College alumni . . . are very proactive in providing students with assistance in the form of . . . employment, or mentorship." And, even if undergrads are unable to hook up with an alum, they can always turn to the Center for Careers, Life and Service (CLS). Besides interview prep, job shadowing programs, and on-campus recruiting, the center also houses the Service Learning and Civic Engagement Program, which helps students find co-curricular service learning opportunities. Grinnellink internships are specific (and paid!) opportunities with college alumni and friends and are open exclusively to Grinnell students. Off-campus study experiences, whether abroad like Grinnell-in-London, or at a U.S. location like Grinnell-in Washington, offer more ways for experiential learning to complement coursework.

GENERAL INFO

Activities: Choral groups, concert band, dance, drama/theater, jazz band, literary magazine, music ensembles, musical theater, pep band, radio station, student government, student newspaper, student-run film society, symphony orchestra, yearbook, campus ministries, international student organization. **Organizations:** 240 registered organizations, 2 honor societies, 12 religious organizations. **Athletics (Intercollegiate):** *Men:* Baseball, basketball, cross-country, diving, football, golf, soccer, swimming, tennis, track/field (outdoor), track/field (indoor). *Women:* Basketball, cross-country, diving, golf, soccer, softball, swimming, tennis, track/field (outdoor), track/field (indoor), volleyball.

FINANCIAL AID

Students should submit: FAFSA, CSS/Financial Aid PROFILE, Noncustodial PROFILE. Regular filing deadline is 2/1. The Princeton Review suggests that all financial aid forms be submitted as soon as possible after October 1. *Need-based scholarships/grants offered:* Federal Pell, FSEOG, State scholarships/grants, Private scholarships, College/ university scholarship or grant aid from institutional funds. *Loan aid offered:* Direct Subsidized Stafford Loans, Direct Unsubsidized Stafford Loans, Direct PLUS loans, Federal Perkins Loans, College/university loans from institutional funds. Applicants will be notified of awards on or about 4/1. Federal Work-Study Program available. Institutional employment available.

BOTTOM LINE

The tab for tuition, fees, room and board, and everything else at Grinnell comes to about $59,298 per year. About 86 percent of Grinnell's students receive some form of financial aid, though. Need-based financial aid packages for freshman includes $37,153 in gift aid on average.

CAREER INFORMATION FROM PAYSCALE.COM

ROI rating	91
Bachelor's and No Higher	
Median starting salary	$42,500
Median mid-career salary	$84,200
At Least Bachelor's	
Median starting salary	$44,400
Median mid-career salary	$92,100
% alumni with high job meaning	38%
% STEM	28%

SELECTIVITY

Admissions Rating	97
# of applicants	6,414
% of applicants accepted	25
% of acceptees attending	28
# offered a place on the wait list	1,224
% accepting a place on wait list	39
% admitted from wait list	4
# of early decision applicants	316
% accepted early decision	53

FRESHMAN PROFILE

Range SAT Critical Reading	640–740
Range SAT Math	660–770
Range ACT Composite	30–33
% graduated top 10% of class	81
% graduated top 25% of class	96
% graduated top 50% of class	100

DEADLINES

Early decision	
Deadline	11/15
Regular	
Deadline	1/15
Nonfall registration?	No

FINANCIAL FACTS

Financial Aid Rating	96
Annual tuition	$48,322
Room and board	$11,980
Required fees	$436
Average need-based scholarship	$38,612
% needy frosh rec. need-based scholarship or grant aid	99
% needy UG rec. need-based scholarship or grant aid	99
% needy frosh rec. non-need-based scholarship or grant aid	16
% needy UG rec. non-need-based scholarship or grant aid	10
% needy frosh rec. need-based self-help aid	83
% needy UG rec. need-based self-help aid	87
% frosh rec. any financial aid	88
% UG rec. any financial aid	87
% UG borrow to pay for school	59
Average cumulative indebtedness	$15,982
% frosh need fully met	100
% ugrads need fully met	100
Average % of frosh need met	100
Average % of ugrad need met	100

Grove City College

100 Campus Drive, Grove City, PA 16127-2104 • Admissions: 724-458-2100 • Fax: 724-458-3395

CAMPUS LIFE

Quality of Life Rating	**87**
Fire Safety Rating	**93**
Green Rating	**69**
Type of school	Private
Affiliation	Christian (Nondenominational)
Environment	Rural

STUDENTS

Total undergrad enrollment	2,444
% male/female	50/50
% from out of state	46
% frosh from public high school	62
% frosh live on campus	98
% ugrads live on campus	96
# of fraternities (% ugrad men join)	10 (18)
# of sororities (% ugrad women join)	8 (19)
% African American	1
% Asian	2
% Caucasian	92
% Hispanic	1
% Native American	<1
% Pacific Islander	0
% Two or more races	3
% Race and/or ethnicity unknown	0
% international	1
# of countries represented	14

ACADEMICS

Academic Rating	**81**
% students returning for sophomore year	89
% students graduating within 4 years	80
% students graduating within 6 years	85
Calendar	Semester
Student/faculty ratio	13:1
Profs interesting rating	80
Profs accessible rating	90

Most classes have 10–19 students.
Most lab/discussion sessions have 20–29 students.

MOST POPULAR MAJORS

Mechanical Engineering; Biology;
Communication Studies; Accounting;
Electrical Engineering

ABOUT THE SCHOOL

Grove City College, located an hour north of Pittsburgh, is reputed by students to be an "excellent liberal arts program, maintaining an authentically Christian atmosphere while being intellectually challenging." Students praise both the biology program and the "strong Christian values." It boasts a 13:1 student to faculty ratio. Students feel that "a Small Christian School With a Marching Band," like Grove City, "is hard to find," and they are not wrong. "The typical Grover is extremely hard working in his or her classes, but still maintains time to spend with God. Every student here can relate." The student body is evenly split between genders, and it is predominantly white at 92 percent of students.

BANG FOR YOUR BUCK

Tuition at Grove City College is currently $16,630, and the average aid package is about $7,103. Grove City reportedly meets 51 percent of financial need, and although their scholarships are not enormous, their tuition is low enough that most students are not uncomfortable, with one student testifying that they "chose Grove City College because their campus was enchanting, their reputation as a top-notch Christian school really appealed to my beliefs in moral development through my years in college, and their tuition was low enough that I wasn't vying for every drop of scholarship money in order to attend."

STUDENT LIFE

One hundred percent of the campus is wireless, and 94 percent of undergrads live on campus where they participate in "a large [number]" of intramural sports (ping pong, volleyball, soccer, Frisbee, etc.), and where "academic-based clubs are available (mock trial, debate, Student Government, Law Society, etc.) along with artistic programs such as theater, Ballroom Club, and Swing Club." As for why such a high rate of students live on-campus, one student notes that "you CAN live off-campus but ONLY if you are a) living with a direct relative b) married or c) only a part-time student." Students feel that "because of the high level of academic commitment, many students spend the majority of their time studying." Therefore, leisure time is limited. Drinking on-campus is not permitted, so "parties are typically low-key." One student notes that "Grove City has created a student body that is easily stereotyped and lacks diversity. While a strength in the sense that it creates a strong community, it is also a weakness in that there is very little to challenge that stereotype." Overall students identify as Christian and as politically conservative.

Grove City College

Financial Aid: 724-458-3300 • E-mail: admissions@gcc.edu • Website: www.gcc.edu

CAREER

The typical Grove City College graduate has a starting salary of around $47,200, and 54 percent report that their job has a great deal of meaning. Many students feel that there are "lots of influential alumni that are still connected the school and are available," and that there is an "excellent" and "accessible alumni network." Career services is "great" for "engineering," "business, marketing, and communications" majors. A student notes "the number of internship opportunities, and the connections professors have with employers, especially in the Political Science department." Grove has a comprehensive alumni directory to aid students in networking and career placements.

GENERAL INFO

Activities: Choral groups, concert band, dance, drama/theater, jazz band, literary magazine, marching band, music ensembles, musical theater, opera, pep band, radio station, student government, student newspaper, symphony orchestra, television station, yearbook, Campus Ministries, International Student Organization. **Organizations:** More than 130 registered organizations, 26 honor societies, 19 religious organizations. 10 fraternities, 8 sororities. **Athletics (Intercollegiate):** *Men:* baseball, basketball, cross-country, diving, football, golf, soccer, swimming, tennis, track/field (indoor and outdoor). *Women:* basketball, cross-country, diving, golf, soccer, softball, swimming, tennis, track/field (indoor and outdoor), volleyball, water polo. **On-Campus Highlights:** Student Union, Chapel, Hall of Arts and Letters, Fitness Center, Ketler Recreation Room.

FINANCIAL AID

Students should submit: Institution's own financial aid form. Regular filing deadline is 4/15. The Princeton Review suggests that all financial aid forms be submitted as soon as possible after October 1. *Need-based scholarships/grants offered:* State scholarships/grants, Private scholarships, College/university scholarship or grant aid from institutional funds. *Loan aid offered:* State and private loans. First-time freshman applicants will be notified of rewards on a rolling basis beginning 3/15. Institutional employment available.

BOTTOM LINE

The tuition at Grove City College comes to $16,630, excluding room, board, and books, which come to an additional $10,062. The average need-based financial aid package offered to undergraduates at Grove City comes to about $7,103. In addition, 77 percent of freshman and 79 percent of undergrads receive some form of financial aid.

CAREER INFORMATION FROM PAYSCALE.COM

ROI rating	87
Bachelor's and No Higher	
Median starting salary	$48,100
Median mid-career salary	$84,700
At Least Bachelor's	
Median starting salary	$48,900
Median mid-career salary	$86,800
% alumni with high job meaning	45%
% STEM	31%

SELECTIVITY

Admissions Rating	87
# of applicants	1,541
% of applicants accepted	81
% of acceptees attending	44
# offered a place on the wait list	160
% accepting a place on wait list	93
% admitted from wait list	37
# of early decision applicants	282
% accepted early decision	84

FRESHMAN PROFILE

Range SAT Critical Reading	536–655
Range SAT Math	650–654
Range ACT Composite	24–29
Minimum paper TOEFL	550
Minimum internet-based TOEFL	79
Average HS GPA	3.7
% graduated top 10% of class	40
% graduated top 25% of class	68
% graduated top 50% of class	91

DEADLINES

Early decision	
Deadline	11/15
Notification	12/15
Regular	
Deadline	2/1
Notification	3/1
Nonfall registration?	Yes

FINANCIAL FACTS

Financial Aid Rating	78
Annual tuition	$16,630
Room and board	$9,062
Required fees	
Average need-based scholarship	$7,103
% needy frosh rec. need-based scholarship or grant aid	100
% needy UG rec. need-based scholarship or grant aid	98
% needy frosh rec. non-need-based scholarship or grant aid	14
% needy UG rec. non-need-based scholarship or grant aid	9
% needy frosh rec. need-based self-help aid	52
% needy UG rec. need-based self-help aid	66
% frosh rec. any financial aid	77
% UG rec. any financial aid	79
% UG borrow to pay for school	57
Average cumulative indebtedness	$36,997
% frosh need fully met	14
% ugrads need fully met	9
Average % of frosh need met	56
Average % of ugrad need met	52

Gustavus Adolphus College

800 College Avenue, Saint Peter, MN 56082 • Admissions: 507-933-7676 • Fax: 507-933-7474

CAMPUS LIFE

Quality of Life Rating	94
Fire Safety Rating	96
Green Rating	60*
Type of school	Private
Affiliation	Lutheran
Environment	Village

STUDENTS

Total undergrad enrollment	2,386
% male/female	47/53
% from out of state	18
% frosh from public high school	94
% frosh live on campus	100
% ugrads live on campus	88
# of fraternities (% ugrad men join)	5 (16)
# of sororities (% ugrad women join)	6 (18)
% African American	2
% Asian	4
% Caucasian	82
% Hispanic	4
% Native American	0
% Pacific Islander	0
% Two or more races	3
% Race and/or ethnicity unknown	0
% international	4
# of countries represented	22

ACADEMICS

Academic Rating	97
% students returning for sophomore year	89
% students graduating within 4 years	82
% students graduating within 6 years	83
Student/faculty ratio	11:1
Profs interesting rating	96
Profs accessible rating	94

Most classes have 10–19 students.
Most lab/discussion sessions have
10–19 students.

MOST POPULAR MAJORS
Psychology; Business/Commerce; Biology/
Biological Sciences

ABOUT THE SCHOOL

With its "gorgeous campus" and great "sense of community," Gustavus Adolphus College in Minnesota manages to be "just as fun as it [is] academically challenging." Moreover, as a liberal arts college, Gustavus Adolphus is an institution that truly allows students to "explore their interests." And while there are a number of great departments, Gustavus undergrads are especially quick to highlight the "amazing" and "welcoming" music program. Fortunately, regardless of what they study, undergrads profit from "small, discussion based" classes. They also benefit from "extremely passionate" professors who "all really seem to enjoy the subjects they teach." Additionally, it's quite evident that they "want you . . . to succeed." As an astounded physics major shares, "I have a professor who will call you if you are not in class." A biology major agrees, "There are so many professors that live for this job. They are not here for the pay check . . . they are here because they love students and their areas of expertise."

BANG FOR YOUR BUCK

Students at Gustavus Adolphus happily report that financial aid is "excellent" here. As one grateful communications major shares, "You can get all the help that you need simply by asking because [the administration] genuinely want you to stay." This sentiment is supported by the fact that over 90 percent of the students receive some type of aid. And, impressively, the college doles out over $14 million in scholarships and grants to incoming students. Even better, when applying for admission, candidates are automatically considered for scholarships. These include the Dean's Scholarship, which can range from $13,000 to $23,000 annually; the President's Scholarship, which awards up to $26,000 annually; and the Diversity Scholarship, which provides between $1,000 and $5,000 annually.

STUDENT LIFE

If you attend Gustavus Adolphus, you'll quickly discover that your peers are "VERY involved." After all, according to a nursing major, "Most students are a part of at least one or two student organizations." And with "more than 120 special interest groups, [. . .] including a sauna club, intramural sports, choirs, an improv comedy troupe, Greek life, religious organizations, [etc.]" it's easy to understand why. Many of these clubs also receive funding to host various events on Saturday nights. Dubbed "SNL," these could involve everything from "free Chipotle" to "giant inflatable obstacle courses." In addition, "the Campus Activities Board regularly brings comedians, famous musicians, and big speakers to Gustavus." And they even sponsor "free movies." As if that wasn't enough, the college periodically busses "students to and from the Twin cities [Minneapolis and St. Paul] to see professional theater performances at the Orpheum and Ordway theaters." All in all, you'd have to work very diligently to be bored here.

CAREER

Undergrads at Gustavus Adolphus are privy to a "wonderful" Office of Career Development. Indeed, thanks to Career Development's hard and work and dedication, by the time graduation rolls around, "over 90 percent [of students have] participat[ed] in some type of experiential education [be it an] internship, career exploration, clinical, student-teaching…service-learning, etc." These opportunities certainly help ensure that Gustavus students are ready for the working world. Of course, Career Development's numerous interview and

Gustavus Adolphus College

FINANCIAL AID: 507-933-7527 • E-MAIL: ADMISSION@GUSTAVUS.EDU • WEBSITE: WWW.GUSTAVUS.EDU

resume writing workshops are also integral to student success. If you need any more proof, just consider the fact that the average starting salary for Gustavus grads is $41,100 and the average mid-career salary is $84,100, according to PayScale.com.

GENERAL INFO

Activities: Choral groups, concert band, dance, drama/theater, jazz band, literary magazine, music ensembles, musical theater, pep band, radio station, student government, student newspaper, symphony orchestra, television station, yearbook 120 registered organizations, 11 honor societies, 0 religious organizations. 5 fraternities, 5 sororities. **Athletics (Intercollegiate):** *Men:* baseball, basketball, cross-country, diving, football, golf, ice hockey, skiingnordiccross-country, soccer, swimming, tennis, track/field (outdoor), track/field (indoor). *Women:* basketball, cross-country, diving, golf, gymnastics, ice hockey, skiingnordiccross-country, soccer, softball, swimming, tennis, track/field (outdoor), track/field (indoor), volleyball. **On-Campus Highlights:** Campus Center, Courtyard Cafe, Lund Athletic Center, Christ Chapel, Linnaeus Arboretum, With over 75% of students remaining on campus during a typical weekend (according to our Dining Service), our students actively use the entire campus. As there are no city streets intersecting our campus, Gusties enjoy their home on the hill.

FINANCIAL AID

Students should submit: FAFSA. Applicants will be notified of awards on a rolling basis beginning 3/15. The Princeton Review suggests that all financial aid forms be submitted as soon as possible after October 1. *Need-based scholarships/grants offered:* Federal Pell, SEOG, State scholarships/grants, Private scholarships, College/university scholarship or grant aid from institutional funds. *Loan aid offered:* Direct Subsidized Stafford Loans, Direct Unsubsidized Stafford Loans, Direct PLUS loans, State Loans. Applicants will be notified of awards on a rolling basis beginning 3/15. Federal Work-Study Program available. Institutional employment available.

THE BOTTOM LINE

If you decide to attend Gustavus Adolphus, you'll receive a tuition bill for $42,360. In addition, you (and your family) can expect to pay $5,990 for housing and another $3,410 for a meal plan. The college also charges $673 in fees. And, finally, you should set aside $1,850 for miscellaneous expenses.

SELECTIVITY

Admissions Rating	85
# of applicants	4,657
% of applicants accepted	67
% of acceptees attending	20

FRESHMAN PROFILE

Range SAT Critical Reading	550–620
Range SAT Math	530–675
Range ACT Composite	24–30
Minimum paper TOEFL	550
Minimum internet-based TOEFL	80
Average HS GPA	3.60
% graduated top 10% of class	30
% graduated top 25% of class	65
% graduated top 50% of class	94

DEADLINES

Notification	11/15
Priority Deadline	4/1
Nonfall registration?	Yes

FINANCIAL FACTS

Financial Aid Rating	86
Annual tuition	$42,360
Room and board	$9,400
Required fees	$673
Average need-based scholarship	$27,435
% needy frosh rec. need-based scholarship or grant aid	100
% needy UG rec. need-based scholarship or grant aid	100
% needy frosh rec. non-need-based scholarship or grant aid	14
% needy UG rec. non-need-based scholarship or grant aid	9
% needy frosh rec. need-based self-help aid	100
% needy UG rec. need-based self-help aid	100
% frosh rec. any financial aid	96
% UG rec. any financial aid	95
% UG borrow to pay for school	81
Average cumulative indebtedness	$35,247
% frosh need fully met	40
% ugrads need fully met	33
Average % of frosh need met	93
Average % of ugrad need met	90

CAREER INFORMATION FROM PAYSCALE.COM

ROI rating	87
Bachelor's and No Higher	
Median starting salary	$41,100
Median mid-career salary	$84,100
At Least Bachelor's	
Median starting salary	$42,100
Median mid-career salary	$83,900
% alumni with high job meaning	48%
% STEM	21%

Hamilton College

OFFICE OF ADMISSION, CLINTON, NY 13323 • ADMISSIONS: 315-859-4421 • FAX: 315-859-4457

CAMPUS LIFE

Quality of Life Rating	**91**
Fire Safety Rating	**92**
Green Rating	**60***
Type of school	Private
Affiliation	No Affiliation
Environment	Rural

STUDENTS

Total undergrad enrollment	1,872
% male/female	49/51
% from out of state	70
% frosh from public high school	61
% frosh live on campus	100
% ugrads live on campus	100
# of fraternities (% ugrad men join)	10 (28)
# of sororities (% ugrad women join)	7 (21)
% African American	5
% Asian	7
% Caucasian	63
% Hispanic	7
% Native American	<1
% Pacific Islander	0
% Two or more races	3
% Race and/or ethnicity unknown	8
% international	6
# of countries represented	45

ACADEMICS

Academic Rating	**98**
% students returning for sophomore year	93
% students graduating within 4 years	87
% students graduating within 6 years	92
Calendar	Semester
Student/faculty ratio	9:1
Profs interesting rating	98
Profs accessible rating	96
Most classes have 10–19 students.	
Most lab/discussion sessions have 10–19 students.	

MOST POPULAR MAJORS
Economics; Biology; International Relations and Affairs

#21 COLLEGE THAT PAYS YOU BACK

ABOUT THE SCHOOL
Hamilton provides about 155 research opportunities for students to work closely with science and nonscience faculty mentors each summer. Many students' choice of college depends on the strength of the school's academic department most relevant to their major: "I am amazed by the incredible resources—especially for the sciences—and couldn't believe all of the opportunities and grants they offer to students who are passionate about pursuing their studies outside of the classroom," says one sophomore. Oftentimes, the work leads to a paper published in a professional journal and gives the student a leg-up when competing for national postgraduate fellowships and grants. The college also provides about sixty to seventy stipends each summer so students can get career-related experience pursuing internships that are otherwise unpaid. A student contends that "the school has a lot of active alumni, so the networking opportunities are great. Many students find internships or jobs just through the alumni connections."

BANG FOR YOUR BUCK
Once you are accepted, the financial aid office will make your Hamilton education affordable through a comprehensive program of scholarships, loans, and campus jobs. The financial aid budget is approximately $36 million annually, enabling the school to make good on its commitment to meet 100 percent of students' demonstrated need. One student says, "The school offered me a generous amount of financial aid." The average financial aid package for students is $45,553. The average Hamilton College grant is $41,170 and does not have to be repaid.

STUDENT LIFE
There are two types of students at Hamilton: "Light-siders" are more preppy, and "dark-siders" are typically more artistic or hipster. No matter which group they fall into, students "are incredibly devoted to their school work, but they are also devoted to having a good time." People attend athletic events, student improv comedy shows, poetry readings, community service events, plays and concerts, and "very successfully compensate for our isolated location with themed parties, clubs, and other eclectic activities." In addition to all-campus parties, Hamilton has "Late Nights" every weekend, which are alcohol-free events "like a Glowstick party or a MarioKart Tournament where students can enjoy great local Indian takeout and a fun night." Hamilton has "a very intellectually stimulating academic environment," and it is not at all uncommon to find a whole dorm room debating about an economic theory. People who have cars can also go downtown or into New Hartford in their free time, but most students choose to spend their time on campus.

CAREER
At Hamilton, there is "a real investment in ensuring that every student is successful and happy both here and after graduation." The Career Center suggests that every student have two career-related experiences before they graduate, and the HamNet system helps to link students up with internships or jobs that come via Hamilton

Hamilton College

FINANCIAL AID: 800-859-4413 • E-MAIL: ADMISSION@HAMILTON.EDU • WEBSITE: WWW.HAMILTON.EDU

alumni or alumni recommendations. There are many workshops, fairs, and employer visits held throughout the year, including the half-day Sophomore Jumpstart! for second-year students beginning their career or internship search. Peer Advisors are students who are available to critique cover letters and resumes, and offer advice on all aspects of finding jobs through events such as the popular How I Got My Internship lunch series. Beginning with the Class of 2020, all incoming students are assigned a dedicated career advisor to work with during their four years at Hamilton. Of the Hamilton graduates who visited PayScale.com, the average starting salary was $57,600.

GENERAL INFO

Activities: Choral groups, dance, drama/theater, jazz band, literary magazine, music ensembles, musical theater, radio station, student government, student newspaper, student-run film society, symphony orchestra, television station, yearbook, Campus Ministries, International Student Organization. **Organizations:** 189 registered organizations, 8 honor societies, 6 religious organizations. 10 fraternities, 7 sororities. **Athletics (Intercollegiate):** *Men:* baseball, basketball, crew/rowing, cross-country, diving, football, golf, ice hockey, lacrosse, soccer, squash, swimming, tennis, track/field (outdoor), track/field (indoor). *Women:* basketball, crew/rowing, cross-country, diving, field hockey, golf, ice hockey, lacrosse, soccer, softball, squash, swimming, tennis, track/field (outdoor), track/field (indoor), volleyball. **On-Campus Highlights:** Wellin Museum of Art, Root Glen/Outdoor Leadership Center, Café Opus and Café Opus 2, Arthur Levitt Public Affairs Center.

FINANCIAL AID

Students should submit: FAFSA, Institution's own financial aid form, CSS/Financial Aid PROFILE, State aid form, Noncustodial PROFILE, Business/Farm Supplement. Regular filing deadline is 2/15. The Princeton Review suggests that all financial aid forms be submitted as soon as possible after October 1. *Need-based scholarships/ grants offered:* Federal Pell, FSEOG, State scholarships/grants, Private scholarships, College/university scholarship or grant aid from institutional funds. *Loan aid offered:* Direct Subsidized Stafford Loans, Direct Unsubsidized Stafford Loans, Direct PLUS loans, Federal Perkins Loans, College/university loans from institutional funds. Applicants will be notified of awards on or about 4/1. Federal Work-Study Program available. Institutional employment available.

THE BOTTOM LINE

Hamilton College is one of the nation's top liberal arts colleges, and you certainly get what you pay for here. The total cost of tuition, room and board, and everything else adds up to about $64,250 per year. Hamilton is need-blind and pledges to meet 100 percent of students' demonstrated need.

CAREER INFORMATION FROM PAYSCALE.COM

ROI rating	92
Bachelor's and No Higher	
Median starting salary	$54,700
Median mid-career salary	$94,600
At Least Bachelor's	
Median starting salary	$55,300
Median mid-career salary	$97,200
% alumni with high job meaning	47%
% STEM	14%

SELECTIVITY

Admissions Rating	96
# of applicants	5,434
% of applicants accepted	25
% of acceptees attending	35
# offered a place on the wait list	958
% accepting a place on wait list	38
% admitted from wait list	13
# of early decision applicants	616
% accepted early decision	38

FRESHMAN PROFILE

Range SAT Critical Reading	650–740
Range SAT Math	650–730
Range SAT Writing	650–750
Range ACT Composite	31–33
% graduated top 10% of class	77
% graduated top 25% of class	96
% graduated top 50% of class	100

DEADLINES

Early decision	
Deadline	11/15
Notification	12/15
Regular	
Deadline	1/1
Notification	4/1
Nonfall registration?	Yes

FINANCIAL FACTS

Financial Aid Rating	96
Annual tuition	$50,730
Room and board	$13,010
Required fees	$510
Average need-based scholarship	$41,170
% needy frosh rec. need-based scholarship or grant aid	100
% needy UG rec. need-based scholarship or grant aid	100
% needy frosh rec. non-need-based scholarship or grant aid	0
% needy UG rec. non-need-based scholarship or grant aid	0
% needy frosh rec. need-based self-help aid	85
% needy UG rec. need-based self-help aid	82
% frosh rec. any financial aid	53
% UG rec. any financial aid	48
% UG borrow to pay for school	39
Average cumulative indebtedness	$17,654
% frosh need fully met	100
% ugrads need fully met	100
Average % of frosh need met	100
Average % of ugrad need met	100

Hampden-Sydney College

PO Box 667, Hampden-Sydney, VA 23943-0667 • Admissions: 434-223-6120 • Fax: 434-223-6346

CAMPUS LIFE

Quality of Life Rating	**84**
Fire Safety Rating	**88**
Green Rating	**71**
Type of school	Private
Affiliation	Presbyterian
Environment	Rural

STUDENTS

Total undergrad enrollment	1,087
% male/female	100/0
% from out of state	29
% frosh from public high school	73
% frosh live on campus	100
% ugrads live on campus	95
# of fraternities (% ugrad men join)	11 (34)
# of sororities (% ugrad women join)	(0)
% African American	6
% Asian	1
% Caucasian	81
% Hispanic	2
% Native American	<1
% Pacific Islander	0
% Two or more races	6
% Race and/or ethnicity unknown	3
% international	0
# of countries represented	11

ACADEMICS

Academic Rating	**83**
% students returning for sophomore year	83
% students graduating within 4 years	57
% students graduating within 6 years	63
Calendar	Semester
Student/faculty ratio	10:1
Profs interesting rating	90
Profs accessible rating	97
Most classes have 10–19 students.	

MOST POPULAR MAJORS
Economics; History; Business/Managerial Economics

ABOUT THE SCHOOL

Established in 1775, Hampden-Sydney was the last college founded before the American Revolution took place. The faculty and students are understandably proud of their school's traditions and history. Hampden-Sydney is also notable as one of the only all-male liberal arts schools in America. The school provides "a small, intimate setting that fosters individualized learning." Students like "the rural setting," "beautiful campus," and "the instant brotherhood" that an all-male education provides. "My school is a strong, intellectual community that seeks to transform boys into good men and good citizens," a Mathematics major says. The "great professors" are "incredible helpful" and always accessible even outside of class. "Many even invite their students to have dinner at their homes," another student confirms. The school is also known for its strict "student-run honor code." "You will not get an education like this anywhere else," attests one Biology major.

BANG FOR YOUR BUCK

Although tuition alone is just over $38,000, Hampden-Sydney offers plenty of opportunities for scholarships and aid. The school offered over $31 million in financial assistance to the roughly 1,100 undergraduates last year. The school has several academic and "Citizen-Leader Scholarships." The academic scholarships are awarded based on GPA and SAT or ACT scores. The Citizen-Leadership Scholarships are the Eagle Scout Scholarship, the Boys State Participant Scholarship, and the Student Government President Scholarship. Hampden-Sydney has federal, state, and institutional work-study programs available. Virginia residents can also apply for the Virginia Tuition Assistance Grant.

STUDENT LIFE

The average Hampden-Sydney student is "smart, white, preppy, [and] male." "The style of HSC is very southern prep," one student explains, adding that "the vast majority have Republican views and like to hunt, fish, and generally spend time outdoors." "Topsiders, Khakis and Button Down Oxfords" are the required look. "Students here are very friendly because we like to promote an environment of gentlemanliness," and "brotherhood" rules the day here. "Farmville is a small town that is really about an hour away from anything that could be considered a major city," one student says. This means that students have to make their own fun. Luckily, the school provides a "plethora of extracurricular activities" and students enjoy going "to concerts that our activities committee provides" or "hang[ing] out with friends in their dorms" and, of course, "Greek life." "The Tiger Inn is a great hang-out place with couches, TVs, ping-pong tables, pool, arcade games, and computers."

Hampden-Sydney College

FINANCIAL AID: 434-223-6119 • E-MAIL: HSAPP@HSC.EDU • WEBSITE: WWW.HSC.EDU

CAREER

Hampden-Sydney's motto is "you can do anything with a degree from Hampden-Sydney College." The school works hard to help students get a leg up in an ever-competitive job market and the "reputation [of the] alumni network" at Hampden-Sydney is a major draw for applicants. One way that the school uses its impressive alumni network is TigerConnections. This online job board allows alumni to post job openings for other Hampden-Sydney alums to see. The Internship Scholarship Program provides thousands of dollars to students who may not be able to afford an unpaid internship. PayScale.com reports an average starting salary of $49,800 for Hampden-Sydney grads.

GENERAL INFO

Activities: Choral groups, drama/theater, literary magazine, music ensembles, pep band, radio station, student government, student newspaper, yearbook, Campus Ministries, International Student Organization. **Organizations:** 45 registered organizations, 14 honor societies, 6 religious organizations. 11 fraternities. **Athletics (Intercollegiate):** *Men:* baseball, basketball, cross-country, football, golf, lacrosse, soccer, swimming, tennis, wrestling. **On-Campus Highlights:** Bortz Library.

FINANCIAL AID

Students should submit: FAFSA, State aid form. Priority filing deadline is 3/1. The Princeton Review suggests that all financial aid forms be submitted as soon as possible after October 1. *Need-based scholarships/ grants offered:* Federal Pell, FSEOG, State scholarships/grants, Private scholarships, College/university scholarship or grant aid from institutional funds. *Loan aid offered:* Direct Subsidized Stafford Loans, Direct Unsubsidized Stafford Loans, Direct PLUS loans, Federal Perkins Loans, College/university loans from institutional funds. New student applicants will be notified of awards beginning in mid-December. Applicants will be notified of awards on or about 3/15. Federal Work-Study Program available. Institutional employment available.

BOTTOM LINE

Tuition for the 2015 academic term is $39,920. On-campus room and board averages about $13,060. Combined with other fees, students can expect a total of over $56,000 before any aid. The school's TigerWeb system lets students pay bills easily online.

CAREER INFORMATION FROM PAYSCALE.COM

ROI rating	87
Bachelor's and No Higher	
Median starting salary	$49,800
Median mid-career salary	$89,400
At Least Bachelor's	
Median starting salary	$49,800
Median mid-career salary	$89,400
% alumni with high job meaning	64%

SELECTIVITY

Admissions Rating	86
# of applicants	3,683
% of applicants accepted	55
% of acceptees attending	15
# of early decision applicants	108
% accepted early decision	35

FRESHMAN PROFILE

Range SAT Critical Reading	500–620
Range SAT Math	500–610
Range SAT Writing	460–580
Range ACT Composite	21–27
Minimum paper TOEFL	600
Minimum internet-based TOEFL	100
Average HS GPA	3.4
% graduated top 10% of class	12
% graduated top 25% of class	37
% graduated top 50% of class	77

DEADLINES

Early decision	
Deadline	11/15
Notification	12/15
Early action	
Deadline	1/15
Notification	2/15
Regular	
Deadline	3/1
Notification	4/15
Nonfall registration?	Yes

FINANCIAL FACTS

Financial Aid Rating	84
Annual tuition	$41,516
Room and board	$13,286
Required fees	$1,446
Average need-based scholarship	$28,086
% needy frosh rec. need-based scholarship or grant aid	100
% needy UG rec. need-based scholarship or grant aid	100
% needy frosh rec. non-need-based scholarship or grant aid	16
% needy UG rec. non-need-based scholarship or grant aid	14
% needy frosh rec. need-based self-help aid	83
% needy UG rec. need-based self-help aid	80
% frosh rec. any financial aid	100
% UG rec. any financial aid	99
% UG borrow to pay for school	65
Average cumulative indebtedness	$33,153
% frosh need fully met	20
% ugrads need fully met	18
Average % of frosh need met	77

Harvard College

86 BRATTLE STREET, CAMBRIDGE, MA 02138 • ADMISSIONS: 617-495-1551 • FAX: 617-495-8821

#6 COLLEGE THAT PAYS YOU BACK

ABOUT THE SCHOOL

Here you will find a faculty of academic rock stars, intimate classes, a cosmically vast curriculum, world-class facilities (including what is arguably the best college library in the United States), a diverse student body from across the country and around the world ("The level of achievement is unbelievable"), and a large endowment that allows the college to support undergraduate and faculty research projects. When you graduate, you'll have unlimited bragging rights and the full force and prestige of the Harvard brand working for you for the rest of your life. All first-year students live on campus, and Harvard guarantees housing to its students for all four years. All freshmen also eat in the same place, Annenberg Hall, and there are adult residential advisers living in the halls to help students learn their way around the vast resources of this "beautiful, fun, historic, and academically alive place." Social and extracurricular activities at Harvard are pretty much unlimited: "Basically, if you want to do it, Harvard either has it or has the money to give to you so you can start it." With more than 400 student organizations on campus, whatever you are looking for, you can find it here. The off-campus scene is hopping, too. Believe it or not, Harvard kids do party, and "there is a vibrant social atmosphere on campus and between students and the local community," with Cambridge offering art and music, not to mention more than a couple of great bars. Downtown Boston and all of its attractions is just a short ride across the Charles River on the "T" (subway).

BANG FOR YOUR BUCK

Harvard is swimming in cash, and financial need simply isn't a barrier to admission. In fact, the admissions staff here often looks especially favorably upon applicants who have stellar academic and extracurricular records despite having to overcome considerable financial obstacles. About 90 percent of the students who request financial aid qualify for it. If you qualify, 100 percent of your financial need will be met. Just so we're clear: by aid, we mean free money—not loans. Harvard doesn't do loans. Instead, Harvard asks families that qualify for financial aid to contribute somewhere between zero and 10 percent of their annual income each year. If your family income is less than $65,000, the odds are very good that you and your family won't pay a dime for you to attend. It's also worth noting that Harvard extends its commitment to full financial aid for all four undergraduate years. Families with higher incomes facing unusual financial challenges may also qualify for need–based scholarship assistance. Home equity is no longer considered in Harvard's assessment of the expected parent contribution.

STUDENT LIFE

As you might expect, ambition and achievement are the ties that bind at Harvard. Most every student can be summed up in three bullet points: "Works really hard. Doesn't sleep. Involved in a million extracurriculars." Diversity is found in all aspects of life, from ethnicities to religion to ideology, and "there is a lot of tolerance and acceptance at Harvard for individuals of all races, religions, socioeconomic backgrounds, life styles, etc." Campus on the Charles River is a "beautiful, fun, historic, and academically alive place," with close to 400 student organizations to stoke your interests. "Arts First Week" annually showcases the talents of the arts and culture groups, and students gather each June (in Connecticut) for the Harvard-

Harvard College

FINANCIAL AID: 617 495 1581 • E-MAIL: COLLEGE@FAS.HARVARD.EDU • WEBSITE: WWW.COLLEGE.HARVARD.EDU

Yale Regatta. Nearby Cambridge and Boston are quintessential college towns, so students never lack for options. As one satisfied undergrad puts it, "Boredom does not exist here. There are endless opportunities and endless passionate people to do them with."

CAREER

As befits a school known for graduating presidents, CEOs, and literary legends, Harvard's Office of Career Service is tireless in working to educate, connect, and advise students about their options and opportunities. At its three locations, OCS offers specialized resources for finding internships, jobs, global opportunities, research and funding opportunities, or just getting your foot in the door of the field of your choice. Crimson Careers lists jobs and internships tailored for Harvard students only, including listings posted by alumni, and an impressive career fair and expo lineup ensures students always have access to hiring companies. Alumni who visited PayScale.com report an average starting salary of $57,700 and 65 percent believe their work makes the world a better place.

GENERAL INFO

Activities: Choral groups, concert band, dance, drama/theater, jazz band, literary magazine, marching band, music ensembles, musical theater, opera, pep band, radio station, student government, student newspaper, student-run film society, symphony orchestra, television station, yearbook, campus ministries, international student organization. **Organizations:** 393 registered organizations, 1 honor societies, 28 religious organizations.

FINANCIAL AID

Students should submit: FAFSA, CSS/Financial Aid PROFILE, Noncustodial PROFILE, Business/Farm Supplement. Regular filing deadline is 3/1. The Princeton Review suggests that all financial aid forms be submitted as soon as possible after October 1. *Need-based scholarships/ grants offered:* Federal Pell, FSEOG, State scholarships/grants, Private scholarships, College/university scholarship or grant aid from institutional funds. *Loan aid offered:* Direct Subsidized Stafford Loans, Direct Unsubsidized Stafford Loans, Direct PLUS loans, Federal Perkins Loans, State Loans, College/university loans from institutional funds. Applicants will be notified of awards on or about 4/1. Federal Work-Study Program available. Institutional employment available.

THE BOTTOM LINE

The sticker price to attend Harvard is as exorbitant as its opportunities. Tuition, fees, room and board, and expenses cost about $63,025 a year. However, financial aid here is so unbelievably ample and generous that you just shouldn't worry about that. The hard part about going to Harvard is getting in. If you can accomplish that, Harvard will help you find a way to finance your education. Period.

CAREER INFORMATION FROM PAYSCALE.COM

ROI rating	96
Bachelor's and No Higher	
Median starting salary	$61,400
Median mid-career salary	$126,000
At Least Bachelor's	
Median starting salary	$62,600
Median mid-career salary	$131,000
% alumni with high job meaning	65%
% STEM	28%

SELECTIVITY

Admissions Rating	99
# of applicants	37,307
% of applicants accepted	6
% of acceptees attending	80
# offered a place on the wait list	0

FRESHMAN PROFILE

Range SAT Critical Reading	700–800
Range SAT Math	700–800
Range SAT Writing	710–790
Range ACT Composite	32–35
Average HS GPA	4.1
% graduated top 10% of class	95
% graduated top 25% of class	99
% graduated top 50% of class	100

DEADLINES

Early action	
Deadline	11/1
Notification	12/16
Regular	
Deadline	1/1
Notification	4/1
Nonfall registration?	No

FINANCIAL FACTS

Financial Aid Rating	96
Annual tuition	$43,280
Room and board	$15,951
Required fees	$3,794
Average need-based scholarship	$46,409
% needy frosh rec. need-based scholarship or grant aid	100
% needy UG rec. need-based scholarship or grant aid	99
% needy frosh rec. non-need-based scholarship or grant aid	0
% needy UG rec. non-need-based scholarship or grant aid	0
% needy frosh rec. need-based self-help aid	71
% needy UG rec. need-based self-help aid	85
% frosh rec. any financial aid	54
% UG rec. any financial aid	56
% UG borrow to pay for school	24
Average cumulative indebtedness	$16,723
% frosh need fully met	100
% ugrads need fully met	100
Average % of frosh need met	100
Average % of ugrad need met	100

arvey Mudd College

301 Platt Boulevard, 301 Platt Blvd, Claremont, CA 91711-5990 • Admissions: 909-621-8011 • Fax: 909-621-8360

#4 COLLEGE THAT PAYS YOU BACK

CAMPUS LIFE

Quality of Life Rating	91
Fire Safety Rating	84
Green Rating	60*
Type of school	Private
Affiliation	No Affiliation
Environment	Town

STUDENTS

Total undergrad enrollment	804
% male/female	54/46
% from out of state	58
% frosh from public high school	59
% frosh live on campus	100
% ugrads live on campus	99
% African American	2
% Asian	21
% Caucasian	44
% Hispanic	10
% Native American	<1
% Pacific Islander	0
% Two or more races	6
% Race and/or ethnicity unknown	4
% international	12

ACADEMICS

Academic Rating	97
% students graduating within 4 years	90
% students graduating within 6 years	94
Calendar	Semester
Student/faculty ratio	8:1
Profs interesting rating	98
Profs accessible rating	97

Most classes have 10–19 students.
Most lab/discussion sessions have
10–19 students.

MOST POPULAR MAJORS
Engineering; Computer and Information
Sciences; Mathematics

ABOUT THE SCHOOL

A member of the Claremont Consortium, Harvey Mudd shares resources with Pitzer, Scripps, Claremont McKenna, and Pomona Colleges. It is the "techie" school of the bunch and focuses on educating future scientists, engineers, and mathematicians. "Mudd is a place where everyone is literate in every branch of science." The college offers four-year degrees in chemistry, mathematics, physics, computer science, biology, and engineering, as well as interdisciplinary degrees in mathematical and computational biology, and a few joint majors for students seeking extra challenges. Harvey Mudd is "small, friendly, and tough. Professors and other students are very accessible. The honor code is an integral part of the college." The honor code is so entrenched in campus culture that the college entrusts the students to twenty-four-hour-per-day access to many buildings, including some labs, and permits take-home exams, specified either as open-book or closed-book, timed or untimed. "Our honor code really means something," insists one student. "It isn't just a stray sentence or two that got put into the student handbook; it's something that the students are really passionate about." Academics at Harvey Mudd may seem "excessive [and] soul-crushing," but there are "great people and community," nonetheless. In order to ensure that all students receive a well-rounded education, students enrolled at Harvey Mudd are required to take a core component of humanities courses. Research opportunities are literally limitless. The Clinic program is open to students of all majors, who collaborate to satisfy the requests of an actual company. Best of all, these opportunities are available without the cutthroat competition of other similar schools.

BANG FOR YOUR BUCK

Harvey Mudd believes that college choice is more about fit than finances. That's why the college offers a robust program of need-based and merit-based awards to help insure that a Harvey Mudd education is accessible to all who qualify. Eighty-two percent of students receive financial aid, and 40 percent qualify for merit-based awards. In determining who will receive merit-based awards, the Office of Admission looks primarily at academic achievement—financial need is not considered. While these awards are granted independent of financial need, students who receive a merit-based award and are also eligible for need-based aid. Standout programs include the Harvey S. Mudd Merit Award, in which students receive a $40,000 scholarship distributed annually in the amount of $10,000 per year. The President's Scholars Program is a renewable, four-year, full-tuition scholarship that promotes excellence and diversity at Harvey Mudd by recognizing outstanding young men and women from populations that are traditionally underrepresented at HMC.

STUDENT LIFE

Mudders say they are united by "a brimming passion for science and a love of knowledge for its own sake." "All students are exceptionally intelligent and are able to perform their work in a professional manner." Beyond that, there's "a really diverse group of personalities" at Mudd, who are "not afraid to show their true colors" and who all have "a unique sense of humor." Students say they "are all friendly, smart, and talented, which brings us together. Upperclassmen look out for underclassmen, and students tend to bond together easily over difficult homework." In such a welcoming community, "students primarily fit

Harvey Mudd College

FINANCIAL AID: 909 621-8055 • E-MAIL: ADMISSION@HMC.EDU • WEBSITE: WWW.HMC.EDU

in by not fitting in—wearing pink pirate hats, or skateboarding while playing harmonica, or practicing unicycle jousting are all good ways to fit in perfectly," though it should be noted that several student have "never seen a dorm swordfight." The speed of the Wi-Fi network on campus has been deemed "great."

CAREER

The typical Harvey Mudd College graduate has a starting salary of around $75,600, and 55 percent of graduates feel their jobs have a lot of meaning in their lives. Students feel that at Mudd, "the Office of Career Services finds more than enough summer internships," and one student in particular notes that one dedicated adviser "worked very hard to help me find a summer internship, calling many of his friends and passing around my resume." Students especially feel that their professors have been very helpful about finding them jobs and internships, and that Mudd provides "first-rate preparation for graduate study or (especially for the engineering major) success in the job market."

GENERAL INFO

Activities: Choral groups, concert band, dance, drama/theater, jazz band, literary magazine, music ensembles, musical theater, pep band, radio station, student government, student newspaper, student-run film society, symphony orchestra, yearbook, campus ministries, international student organization. **Organizations:** 109 registered organizations, 4 honor societies, 6 religious organizations. **Athletics (Intercollegiate):** *Men:* Baseball, basketball, cross-country, diving, football, golf, soccer, swimming, tennis, track/ field (outdoor), water polo. *Women:* Basketball, cross-country, diving, golf, lacrosse, soccer, softball, swimming, tennis, track/field (outdoor), volleyball, water polo.

FINANCIAL AID

Students should submit: FAFSA, CSS/Financial Aid PROFILE, State aid form, Noncustodial PROFILE, Business/Farm Supplement. Regular filing deadline is 2/1. The Princeton Review suggests that all financial aid forms be submitted as soon as possible after October 1. *Need-based scholarships/grants offered:* Federal Pell, FSEOG, State scholarships/ grants, Private scholarships, College/university scholarship or grant aid from institutional funds. *Loan aid offered:* Direct Subsidized Stafford Loans, Direct Unsubsidized Stafford Loans, Direct PLUS loans, Federal Perkins Loans, College/university loans from institutional funds. Applicants will be notified of awards on or about 4/1. Federal Work-Study Program available. Institutional employment available.

BOTTOM LINE

The retail price for tuition, room and board, and fees at Harvey Mudd ends up being a little more than $69,717 a year. Financial aid is plentiful here, though, so please don't let cost scare you away from applying. The average need-based scholarship is $37,874, and some students report receiving "excellent financial aid packages," including a "full-tuition scholarship."

CAREER INFORMATION FROM PAYSCALE.COM

ROI rating	97
Bachelor's and No Higher	
Median starting salary	$78,200
Median mid-career salary	$133,000
At Least Bachelor's	
Median starting salary	$78,800
Median mid-career salary	$134,000
% alumni with high job meaning	63%
% STEM	86%

SELECTIVITY

Admissions Rating	98
# of applicants	3,678
% of applicants accepted	14
% of acceptees attending	37
# offered a place on the wait list	596
% accepting a place on wait list	67
% admitted from wait list	4
# of early decision applicants	377
% accepted early decision	17

FRESHMAN PROFILE

Range SAT Critical Reading	678–770
Range SAT Math	740–800
Range SAT Writing	680–760
Range ACT Composite	33–35
Minimum paper TOEFL	600
Minimum internet-based TOEFL	100
% graduated top 10% of class	88
% graduated top 25% of class	99
% graduated top 50% of class	100

DEADLINES

Early decision	
Deadline	11/15
Notification	12/15
Regular	
Deadline	1/1
Notification	4/1
Nonfall registration?	No

FINANCIAL FACTS

Financial Aid Rating	96
Annual tuition	$52,383
Room and board	$17,051
Required fees	$283
Average need-based scholarship	$37,874
% needy frosh rec. need-based scholarship or grant aid	98
% needy UG rec. need-based scholarship or grant aid	97
% needy frosh rec. non-need-based scholarship or grant aid	21
% needy UG rec. non-need-based scholarship or grant aid	12
% needy frosh rec. need-based self-help aid	55
% needy UG rec. need-based self-help aid	72
% frosh rec. any financial aid	84
% UG rec. any financial aid	76
% frosh need fully met	100
% ugrads need fully met	100
Average % of frosh need met	100
Average % of ugrad need met	100

averford ▪ ollege

370 LANCASTER AVENUE, HAVERFORD, PA 19041 • ADMISSIONS: 610-896-1350 • FINANCIAL AID: 610-896-1350

CAMPUS LIFE

Quality of Life Rating	93
Fire Safety Rating	88
Green Rating	86
Type of school	Private
Affiliation	No Affiliation
Environment	Town

STUDENTS

Total undergrad enrollment	1,233
% male/female	49/51
% from out of state	87
% frosh from public high school	54
% frosh live on campus	100
% ugrads live on campus	99
% African American	7
% Asian	10
% Caucasian	61
% Hispanic	10
% Native American	<1
% Pacific Islander	0
% Two or more races	4
% Race and/or ethnicity unknown	1
% international	7
# of countries represented	36

ACADEMICS

Academic Rating	96
% students returning for sophomore year	97
% students graduating within 4 years	85
% students graduating within 6 years	90
Calendar	Semester
Student/faculty ratio	9:1
Profs interesting rating	92
Profs accessible rating	97

Most classes have 10–19 students.
Most lab/discussion sessions have
fewer than 10 students.

MOST POPULAR MAJORS
Biology; English; Psychology

#26 COLLEGE THAT PAYS YOU BACK

ABOUT THE SCHOOL

Haverford College prides itself on the type of student that it draws. Academically minded and socially conscious are two words that often describe the typical Haverford student. Many are drawn to the college due to the accessibility of the professors and attention each student receives in the classroom. They don't have to fight for attention in a large lecture hall, since the most common class size is around fourteen students, and most professors live on or around campus and regularly invite students over for a lively talk over dinner or tea. There is also a larger sense of community on campus that is proliferated by the much-lauded honor code, which, according to one surprised student, "really works, and we actually do have things like closed-book, timed, take-home tests." Many find that the honor code (which includes proctorless exams) brings a certain type of student looking for a mature academic experience that helps prepare students by treating them as intellectual equals. In fact, even comparing grades with other students is discouraged, which tends to limit competitiveness and creates a greater sense of community. This sense of togetherness is prevalent throughout campus. Students are actively involved in student government since they have Plenary twice a year, where at least two-thirds of students must be present to make any changes to documents such as the student constitution and the honor code.

BANG FOR YOUR BUCK

Students with family income below $60,000/year will not have loans included in their financial aid package; loan levels for incomes above this line range from $1,500–$3,000 each year. Though they don't offer any merit-based aid, the school does meet the demonstrated need of all students who were deemed eligible according to the college. Many students are able to find on-campus jobs to help support themselves. Haverford also encourages students to take internships through one of its three Academic Centers, which connect students with opportunities for paid research or internship experiences. The Center for Peace and Global Citizenship, for example, helps Haverfordians find fields that are simpatico with the college's ideals of trust and creating civically minded adults. The Center for Career and Professional Advising also has numerous programs that coordinate with alumni and help students expand their networking abilities and create job opportunities for when they graduate.

STUDENT LIFE

Many students describe themselves as a little "nerdy" or "quirky," but in the best possible way. "For the most part, Haverfordians are socially awkward, open to new friends, and looking for moral, political, [or] scholarly debate." As for the honor code in place at Haverford—"students who are not fully committed to abiding by Haverford's academic and social honor code will feel out of place. Students here are really in love with the atmosphere the honor code creates and feel uncomfortable with those who feel differently." Most are "liberal-minded" and "intellectual" and "want to save the world after they graduate." Some students found that "a lot of people were actually way more mainstream than I expected—not everyone is an awkward nerd with no social skills!" and in addition, "the party scene is open to everyone, and generally consists of music provided by student DJs, some dancing, the options to drink hard alcohol or beer (or soft drinks) and a generally fun environment."

Haverford College

E-MAIL: ADMISSIONS@HAVERFORD.EDU • FAX: 610-896-1338 • WEBSITE: WWW.HAVERFORD.EDU

CAREER

The typical Haverford College graduate has a starting salary of around $38,600. Students feel that Haverford offers a great deal of internship opportunities, especially ones with financial support. Koshland Integrated Natural Sciences Center and the Hurford Center for Arts and Humanities act as grant-making organizations to fund internships and research experiences on-campus, locally in the city of Philadelphia, across the U.S. and abroad. The Integrated Natural Science Center offers "plenty of internship opportunities." The Center for Career and Professional Advising, with a mission to "empower" past and enrolled students to "translate their Haverford liberal arts education into a rewarding life," offers several job boards like CareerConnect as well as other helpful resources.

GENERAL INFO

Activities: Choral groups, dance, drama/theater, literary magazine, music ensembles, musical theater, student government, student newspaper, yearbook, campus ministries, international student organization. **Organizations:** 144 registered organizations, 1 honor societies, 6 religious organizations. **Athletics (Intercollegiate):** *Co-ed:* Cricket. *Men:* Baseball, basketball, cross-country, fencing, lacrosse, soccer, squash, tennis, track/field (outdoor), track/field (indoor). *Women:* Basketball, cross-country, fencing, field hockey, lacrosse, soccer, softball, squash, tennis, track/field (outdoor), track/field (indoor), volleyball. **On-Campus Highlights:** Integrated Natural Sciences Center, John Whitehead Campus Center, Cantor Fitzgerald Gallery, Arboreteum. **Environmental Initiatives:** Our athletic center is the first gold LEED-certified recreation center in the United States (opened in 2005). We have reached 75 to 85 percent for grounds recycling. We have completed a master plan to identify utility and powerhouse improvements, and will commence work on these improvements immediately.

FINANCIAL AID

Students should submit: FAFSA, CSS/Financial Aid PROFILE, Noncustodial PROFILE, Business/Farm Supplement. Regular filing deadline is 2/1. The Princeton Review suggests that all financial aid forms be submitted as soon as possible after October 1. *Need-based scholarships/grants offered:* Federal Pell, FSEOG, State scholarships/grants, College/university scholarship or grant aid from institutional funds. *Loan aid offered:* Direct Subsidized Stafford Loans, Direct Unsubsidized Stafford Loans, Direct PLUS Loans. Applicants will be notified of awards on or about 4/1. Federal Work-Study Program available. Institutional employment available.

BOTTOM LINE

Though the annual tuition is $50,564 per year, Haverford offers more than half of its students financial aid. The average cumulative indebtedness is around $15,000. The price may seem high on paper, but Haverford helps its students afford the education.

CAREER INFORMATION FROM PAYSCALE.COM

ROI rating	92
Bachelor's and No Higher	
Median starting salary	$38,600
Median mid-career salary	$115,000
At Least Bachelor's	
Median starting salary	$38,600
Median mid-career salary	$115,000
% STEM	27%

SELECTIVITY

Admissions Rating	98
# of applicants	3,467
% of applicants accepted	25
% of acceptees attending	41
# offered a place on the wait list	883
% accepting a place on wait list	40
% admitted from wait list	3
# of early decision applicants	323
% accepted early decision	46

FRESHMAN PROFILE

Range SAT Critical Reading	660–760
Range SAT Math	660–770
Range SAT Writing	670–770
Range ACT Composite	31–34
Minimum internet-based TOEFL	100
% graduated top 10% of class	96
% graduated top 25% of class	100
% graduated top 50% of class	100

DEADLINES

Early decision	
Deadline	11/15
Notification	12/15
Deadline	1/1
Notification	2/15
Regular	
Deadline	1/15
Notification	4/1
Nonfall registration?	No

FINANCIAL FACTS

Financial Aid Rating	99
Annual tuition	$50,564
Room and board	$15,466
Required fees	$460
Average need-based scholarship	$45,390
% needy frosh rec. need-based scholarship or grant aid	98
% needy UG rec. need-based scholarship or grant aid	97
% needy frosh rec. non-need-based scholarship or grant aid	0
% needy UG rec. non-need-based scholarship or grant aid	0
% needy frosh rec. need-based self-help aid	91
% needy UG rec. need-based self-help aid	91
% frosh rec. any financial aid	51
% UG rec. any financial aid	51
% UG borrow to pay for school	28
Average cumulative indebtedness	$14,750
% frosh need fully met	100
% ugrads need fully met	100
Average % of frosh need met	100
Average % of ugrad need met	100

Hobart and William Smith Colleges

629 SOUTH MAIN STREET, GENEVA, NY 14456 • ADMISSIONS: 315-781-3622 • FAX: 315-781-3914

CAMPUS LIFE

Quality of Life Rating	85
Fire Safety Rating	94
Green Rating	91
Type of school	Private
Affiliation	No Affiliation
Environment	Village

STUDENTS

Total undergrad enrollment	2,344
% male/female	51/49
% from out of state	58
% frosh from public high school	60
% frosh live on campus	100
% ugrads live on campus	90
# of fraternities (% ugrad men join)	7 (18)
# of sororities (% ugrad women join)	0 (0)
% African American	5
% Asian	3
% Caucasian	72
% Hispanic	6
% Native American	<1
% Pacific Islander	<1
% Two or more races	0
% Race and/or ethnicity unknown	7
% international	6
# of countries represented	30

ACADEMICS

Academic Rating	89
% students returning for sophomore year	86
% students graduating within 4 years	76
% students graduating within 6 years	81
Calendar	Semester
Student/faculty ratio	10:1
Profs interesting rating	89
Profs accessible rating	90

Most classes have 10–19 students.
Most lab/discussion sessions have
  10–19 students.

MOST POPULAR MAJORS
Biology, Environmental Studies; Economics;
Media and Society

ABOUT THE SCHOOL
Hobart and William Smith Colleges were founded separately in 1822 and 1908 respectively, but now operate together as a coordinate system. Men graduate from Hobart and women graduate from William Smith. The Colleges share the same campus and teachers, but have separate traditions and athletic departments. Students love their "beautiful campus"—located on about 320 acres in Geneva, New York—and "the GORGEOUS LAKE outside my window!" The Colleges have about 2,300 students between them, which means "the atmosphere is beyond friendly" within this "close-knit community." Students also recommend the "fantastic study abroad opportunities" and "personal relationships between the faculty and students." "Professors are always accessible, and a good number of them reach out to their students as opposed to simply expecting students to take initiative for help. They easily become friends with students and keep in touch with and mentor them after graduation." These professors show themselves to be "very respectful while simultaneously maintaining high standards of work," and one student comments, "I've never had a professor that did not inspire me while here."

BANG FOR YOUR BUCK
HWS's website states that they view financial aid as "a partnership": staff work "one-on-one with each accepted student and his or her family to create a total financial aid package that makes sense." In addition to federal and state need-based awards, there are numerous merit and scholarships available. Examples include the Elizabeth Blackwell Scholarships for students doing advanced science coursework and the Environmental Sustainability Trustee Scholarship for students dedicated to environmental leadership. On average, 79 percent of undergraduate financial need is fully met.

STUDENT LIFE
Students love the sense of inclusiveness at HWS. As one geoscience major explains about her decision to attend: "I did not want to be a number in a classroom; I wanted to be a person." "As soon as I got on campus it felt like 'my people' were here," a sociology major added. Students who are attracted to HWS include those who are interested in developing their own approach to their education, as the school's popular interdisciplinary curriculum allows (they are a high-achieving bunch for sure: A top Fulbright producer, HWS boasts fourteen Fulbright U.S. Student Award recipients in 2015 and 2016). Plenty of students engage with the Colleges' offerings in "athletics, leadership and entrepreneurship, study abroad opportunities, alum network and connections," but they also enjoy weekend excursions off-campus. "Many people are involved in outing club trips" or drive to spots where they can "go hiking, kayaking, ice climbing," or just "go shopping at the Outlets fifteen minutes away."

Hobart and William Smith Colleges

FINANCIAL AID: 315-781 3315 • E-MAIL: ADMISSIONS@HWS.EDU • WEBSITE: WWW.HWS.EDU

CAREER

Students say HWS has "an extensive alumni network" that helps students find work after college. They also report excellent "access to great internships." In fact, in 2014 HWS started a "guaranteed internship program" where every student of "good academic and social standing" who completes their Pathways Program is assured an internship or research experience. HWS provides a stipend if the internship is unpaid. Students also say Career Services is very good at "helping students access . . . jobs during and after graduation." PayScale.com reports an average starting salary of $49,000 for HWS graduates and a mid career average of $94,600.

GENERAL INFO

Activities: Choral groups, dance, drama/theater, jazz band, literary magazine, music ensembles, radio station, student government, student newspaper, student-run film society, symphony orchestra, yearbook. **Organizations:** 98 registered organizations, 12 honor societies, 7 religious organizations. 7 fraternities. **Athletics (Intercollegiate):** *Men:* basketball, crew/rowing, cross-country, football, golf, ice hockey, lacrosse, sailing, soccer, squash, tennis. *Women:* basketball, crew/rowing, cross-country, field hockey, golf, ice hockey, lacrosse, sailing, soccer, squash, swimming and diving, tennis. **On-Campus Highlights:** Scandling Campus Center, de Cordova Hall, Stern Hall, Caird Hall, Bristol Field House, Trinity Hall, the Gearan Center for the Performing Arts, Perkin Observatory, Elliott Studio Arts Building and HWS Fribolin Farm.

FINANCIAL AID

Students should submit: FAFSA, CSS/Financial Aid PROFILE, State aid form, Noncustodial PROFILE. Regular filing deadline is 2/1. The Princeton Review suggests that all financial aid forms be submitted as soon as possible after October 1. *Need-based scholarships/ grants offered:* Federal Pell, FSEOG, State scholarships/grants, Private scholarships, College/university scholarship or grant aid from institutional funds. *Loan aid offered:* Direct Subsidized Stafford Loans, Direct Unsubsidized Stafford Loans, Direct PLUS loans, Federal Perkins Loans. Federal Work-Study Program available. Institutional employment available.

BOTTOM LINE

Tuition at HWS is $50,432. Room, board, and fees bring that total to $64,609. The school estimates an additional $1,300 for books and other supplies. Don't let that price tag detour you though, at HWS 89 percent of students receive some form of financial assistance.

CAREER INFORMATION FROM PAYSCALE.COM

ROI rating	87
Bachelor's and No Higher	
Median starting salary	$49,000
Median mid-career salary	$94,600
At Least Bachelor's	
Median starting salary	$48,900
Median mid-career salary	$98,100
% alumni with high job meaning	43%
% STEM	15%

SELECTIVITY

Admissions Rating	88
# of applicants	4,488
% of applicants accepted	57
% of acceptees attending	25
# offered a place on the wait list	622
% accepting a place on wait list	29
% admitted from wait list	12
# of early decision applicants	389
% accepted early decision	82

FRESHMAN PROFILE

Range SAT Critical Reading	570–670
Range SAT Math	600–670
Range ACT Composite	26–30
Minimum paper TOEFL	550
Minimum internet-based TOEFL	80
Average HS GPA	3.4
% graduated top 10% of class	30
% graduated top 25% of class	65
% graduated top 50% of class	92

DEADLINES

Early decision	
Deadline	11/15
Notification	12/15
Regular	
Deadline	2/1
Notification	4/1
Nonfall registration?	Yes

FINANCIAL FACTS

Financial Aid Rating	89
Annual tuition	$50,432
Room and board	$13,050
Required fees	$1,127
Average need-based scholarship	$28,981
% needy frosh rec. need-based scholarship or grant aid	99
% needy UG rec. need-based scholarship or grant aid	99
% needy frosh rec. non-need-based scholarship or grant aid	25
% needy UG rec. non-need-based scholarship or grant aid	18
% needy frosh rec. need-based self-help aid	73
% needy UG rec. need-based self-help aid	80
% frosh rec. any financial aid	90
% UG rec. any financial aid	88
% UG borrow to pay for school	61
Average cumulative indebtedness	$34,504
% frosh need fully met	82
% ugrads need fully met	79
Average % of frosh need met	80
Average % of ugrad need met	78

Illinois Institute of Technology

10 West Thirty-third Street, Chicago, IL 60616 • Admissions: 312-567-3025 • Fax: 312-567-6939

CAMPUS LIFE

Quality of Life Rating	**80**
Fire Safety Rating	**83**
Green Rating	**62**
Type of school	Private
Affiliation	No Affiliation
Environment	Metropolis

STUDENTS

Total undergrad enrollment	2,991
% male/female	70/30
% from out of state	21
% frosh from public high school	90
% frosh live on campus	71
% ugrads live on campus	64
# of fraternities (% ugrad men join)	7 (11)
# of sororities (% ugrad women join)	3 (15)
% African American	6
% Asian	13
% Caucasian	33
% Hispanic	16
% Native American	<1
% Pacific Islander	<1
% Two or more races	2
% Race and/or ethnicity unknown	4
% international	26
# of countries represented	74

ACADEMICS

Academic Rating	**77**
% students returning for sophomore year	92
% students graduating within 4 years	39
% students graduating within 6 years	73
Calendar	Semester
Student/faculty ratio	13:1
Profs interesting rating	69
Profs accessible rating	67

Most classes have 10–19 students.
Most lab/discussion sessions have 20–29 students.

MOST POPULAR MAJORS

Architecture; Mechanical Engineering; Computer and Information Sciences

ABOUT THE SCHOOL

The Illinois Institute of Technology is "an amazing place for people passionate about technology," and "with the great city of Chicago as its backdrop, [it's] a close-knit community dedicated to academic excellence, sustainability, and hands-on experience." Those looking to cruise through college should look elsewhere, with its rigorous coursework, this "academically demanding technical school" is nonetheless "a small, intimate campus that allows for a large number of opportunities for gaining experience academically, professionally and culturally." While it's impossible for every professor to earn the highest marks, one psychology major raves, "The professors at IIT have been no less than amazing both in and out of the classroom. They take the necessary time to cover complex topics but do not water the material down or go at too slow of a pace. Everyone has helped me tremendously, and I owe my success to them." Students do stress that "teaching styles vary a lot but all courses are very demanding in terms of homework."

BANG FOR YOUR BUCK

Students highlight "substantial financial aid" as a key reason for choosing the Illinois Institute of Technology. "The financial aid here is great," says one electrical and computer engineering major, and 56 percent of IIT students have borrowed through some sort of loan program. For Chicago-area graduating high school seniors, IIT offers the Collens Scholarship, which provides full tuition, books, and fees to an academically qualified and dedicated student. Incoming first-years may apply for the Duchossois Leadership Scholarship, which seeks extraordinary young people who will work across disciplines at IIT to further leadership goals. These scholarship recipients are awarded full tuition, a room and board allowance, and a summer educational experience. Other students praise the school's generous Presidential Scholarship.

STUDENT LIFE

Students say that life at IIT is "almost entirely what you make of it. On the surface lies an awkward engineering school on the south side of Chicago but the 'college experience' is not hard to come by." Greek life plays a key role in social life on campus. As one architecture major puts it, "Life at IIT only exists as a member of a fraternity"—but students stress that, "Mostly, students here are those who are concerned with their grades and graduate school outlook." With Chicago as a backdrop, "there are lots of things to do [and] students are given a U-Pass once they enroll so they can get around using the CTA. With so many student [organizations], there is always something to do." Other students say that with the school's rigorous course load, "We mainly just talk about school, it is very challenging and there isn't much time for anything else." In terms of registered student organizations, there are 100 on campus, along with four honor societies. For the athletically minded, IIT and its Scarlet Hawks are Division III.

CAREER

While still attending IIT, students praise the "many internship opportunities as well as opportunities for networking within [their] community." The school encourages students to meet with a Career Development Coach sooner rather than later and provides an online job and résumé posting database—Jobs4Hawks—that can be accessed through its extensive Career Services website. Internships and Co-Ops (Cooperative Education, which are multi-semester programs that are work-integrated) are offered to students who meet the general GPA requirements; students are encouraged to attend career fairs to connect with potential internship contacts, which could lead to future employers. Students also cite the school's "high job placement after graduation." As

Illinois Institute of Technology

FINANCIAL AID: 312-567-7219 • E-MAIL: ADMISSION@IIT.EDU • WEBSITE: WWW.IIT.EDU

one mechanical engineering major puts it, "If you want internships, its almost impossible not to find one. The support for students to get a leg up in the working world after college is one of this school's strengths, if the student chooses to take advantage of it." IIT grads who visited PayScale.com reported a median starting salary of $58,300.

GENERAL INFO

Activities: Choral groups, concert band, dance, drama/theater, literary magazine, music ensembles, musical theater, radio station, student government, student newspaper, student-run film society, television station, yearbook, Campus Ministries, International Student Organization. **Organizations:** 100 registered organizations, 4 honor societies, 10 religious organizations. 7 fraternities, 3 sororities. **Athletics (Intercollegiate):** *Men:* baseball, cross-country, diving, soccer, swimming. *Women:* cross-country, diving, soccer, swimming, volleyball. **On-Campus Highlights:** S.R. Crown Hall (Architecture Building), McCormick Tribune Center, Keating Athletic Center, Hermann Hall, State Street Village.

FINANCIAL AID

Students should submit: FAFSA. Priority filing deadline is 2/1. The Princeton Review suggests that all financial aid forms be submitted as soon as possible after October 1. *Need-based scholarships/grants offered:* Federal Pell, FSEOG, State scholarships/grants, Private scholarships, College/university scholarship or grant aid from institutional funds. *Loan aid offered:* Direct Subsidized Stafford Loans, Direct Unsubsidized Stafford Loans, Direct PLUS loans, Federal Perkins Loans. Applicants will be notified of awards on a rolling basis beginning 3/15. Federal Work-Study Program available. Institutional employment available.

BOTTOM LINE

Tuition at IIT is $43,500, with an additional $1,714 in fees and an average of $1,250 in books and supplies. Don't forget to factor in room and board, an additional $11,898. The average freshman total need-based gift aid is $32,136 while the undergraduate total is $29,733.

CAREER INFORMATION FROM PAYSCALE.COM

ROI rating	87
Bachelor's and No Higher	
Median starting salary	$59,400
Median mid-career salary	$98,300
At Least Bachelor's	
Median starting salary	$60,300
Median mid-career salary	$102,000
% alumni with high job meaning	52%
% STEM	69%

SELECTIVITY

Admissions Rating	89
# of applicants	4,403
% of applicants accepted	53
% of acceptees attending	21

FRESHMAN PROFILE

Range SAT Critical Reading	520–650
Range SAT Math	630–730
Range SAT Writing	520–640
Range ACT Composite	25–30
Minimum paper TOEFL	550
Minimum internet-based TOEFL	80
Average HS GPA	4.0
% graduated top 10% of class	56
% graduated top 25% of class	70
% graduated top 50% of class	98

DEADLINES

Regular	
Priority	12/1
Deadline	8/1
Nonfall registration?	Yes

FINANCIAL FACTS

Financial Aid Rating	82
Annual tuition	$43,500
Room and board	$11,898
Required fees	$1,714
Average need-based scholarship	$29,733
% needy frosh rec. need-based scholarship or grant aid	100
% needy UG rec. need-based scholarship or grant aid	99
% needy frosh rec. non-need-based scholarship or grant aid	19
% needy UG rec. non-need-based scholarship or grant aid	10
% needy frosh rec. need-based self-help aid	63
% needy UG rec. need-based self-help aid	76
% frosh rec. any financial aid	100
% UG rec. any financial aid	99
% UG borrow to pay for school	59
Average cumulative indebtedness	$30,569
% frosh need fully met	22
% ugrads need fully met	13
Average % of frosh need met	83
Average % of ugrad need met	75

Illinois Wesleyan University

PO Box 2900, Bloomington, IL 61702-2900 • Admissions: 309-556-3031 • Fax: 309-556-3820

CAMPUS LIFE

Quality of Life Rating	**92**
Fire Safety Rating	**94**
Green Rating	**66**
Type of school	Private
Affiliation	No Affiliation
Environment	City

STUDENTS

Total undergrad enrollment	1,842
% male/female	44/56
% from out of state	13
% frosh from public high school	73
% frosh live on campus	100
% ugrads live on campus	70
# of fraternities (% ugrad men join)	5 (28)
# of sororities (% ugrad women join)	4 (32)
% African American	4
% Asian	4
% Caucasian	71
% Hispanic	7
% Native American	<1
% Pacific Islander	<1
% Two or more races	3
% Race and/or ethnicity unknown	2
% international	9
# of countries represented	24

ACADEMICS

Academic Rating	**85**
% students returning for sophomore year	93
% students graduating within 4 years	78
% students graduating within 6 years	83
Calendar	Semester
Student/faculty ratio	11:1
Profs interesting rating	89
Profs accessible rating	96
Most classes have 10–19 students.	
Most lab/discussion sessions have fewer than 10 students.	

MOST POPULAR MAJORS

Business/Commerce; Psychology; Biology

ABOUT THE SCHOOL

"The population of IWU may be tiny, but the passions, interests and talents of its students are anything but." This small—roughly 1,900 students—liberal arts school in Bloomington, Illinois, "is a friendly community where your professors become mentors, your classmates become lifelong friends, and you graduate prepared to make a real difference in the world." Students say IWU is "a small school that oozes big opportunities." The "small class size really allows [students] to get personal attention from [the] professors" and students say that "the professors at Illinois Wesleyan University are not only insightful individuals who are the best in their field, but the exuberance they have for their subject area and their students is very evident." Says one history major, "I know I am ready for the rigors of law school because my [p]rofessors pushed me to develop strong writing and analytical skills."

BANG FOR YOUR BUCK

Students note the school's "generous financial aid" as a reason for choosing the school, with one psychology major noting that the IWU "admissions staff...worked well to accommodate my financial needs." Sixty-eight percent of students at IWU have borrowed through some sort of loan program. Scholarships include merit-based Alumni scholarships in amounts ranging from $2,500 to $20,000 and based on an entering student's high school performance, as well as need-based Alumni Grants, awarded in various amounts. IWU also offers Pre-Theology grants to Methodist pre-ministerial students and Ministerial Grants to dependent sons and daughters of active United Methodist ministers. Merit-based scholarships are also offered to international and fine arts students at IWU.

STUDENT LIFE

"For a small school, there are usually a lot of events going on at school on the weekends for students to have fun." Students say that there's the usual college divide between work and play at IWU, and that Greek life "...is a fun and easy way to become more involved both on campus and in the community as well." Off campus, "the community of Bloomington-Normal also has shopping and movie theaters, so there are lots of opportunities for fun." Students praise the school's efforts to provide a wide variety of activities, underscoring that "because of the small school environment, the Office of Student Activities does a great job having entertainment available for students."

CAREER

When it comes to planning for a career after college, IWU students note that their "career center staff are also constantly working to reach out and provide internship and post-graduation employment opportunities for students." The school's Hart Career Center is focused on "career guidance, internship facilitation, graduate school advising, and job search assistance." Students feel confident about getting job straight out of college and note that career fairs are often co-sponsored with nearby Illinois State University, which offers students even more opportunities to meet potential employers: "Some career fairs are sponsored by both schools, but held at ISU since they have bigger buildings than we do." Using Titan CareerLink from the Career Center's website, IWU students can search for internships and employment opportunities related to their major; the website also offers information about upcoming career fairs and resources for preparing for interviews and graduate school.

Illinois Wesleyan University

FINANCIAL AID: 309-556-3096 • E-MAIL: IWUADMIT@IWU.EDU • WEBSITE: WWW.IWU.EDU

GENERAL INFO

Activities: Choral groups, concert band, dance, drama/theater, jazz band, literary magazine, music ensembles, musical theater, opera, pep band, radio station, student government, student newspaper, student-run film society, symphony orchestra, television station, yearbook, Campus Ministries, International Student Organization, Model UN. **Organizations:** 165 registered organizations, 29 honor societies, 15 religious organizations. 5 fraternities, 4 sororities. **Athletics (Intercollegiate):** *Men:* baseball, basketball, cross-country, diving, football, golf, soccer, swimming, tennis, track/field (outdoor), track/field (indoor). *Women:* basketball, cross-country, diving, golf, soccer, softball, swimming, tennis, track/field (outdoor), track/field (indoor), volleyball. **On-Campus Highlights:** Ames Library, Hansen Student Center, Shirk Center for Athletics and Wellness, Center for Natural Science, The Dugout (snack bar and coffee shop).

FINANCIAL AID

Students should submit: FAFSA, Institution's own financial aid form. Priority filing deadline is 3/1. The Princeton Review suggests that all financial aid forms be submitted as soon as possible after October 1. *Need-based scholarships/grants offered:* Federal Pell, FSEOG, State scholarships/grants, Private scholarships, College/university scholarship or grant aid from institutional funds. *Loan aid offered:* Direct Subsidized Stafford Loans, Direct Unsubsidized Stafford Loans, Direct PLUS loans, Federal Perkins Loans, Federal Nursing Loans, College/university loans from institutional funds. Applicants will be notified of awards on a rolling basis beginning 3/1. Federal Work-Study Program available. Institutional employment available.

BOTTOM LINE

Tuition is roughly $43,940, with an additional $202 in fees and approximately $800 in books and supplies. The average amount a freshman with demonstrated need receives in gift aid is $26,251, with the undergraduate amount dropping to $24,220. Financial aid is available to international students.

CAREER INFORMATION FROM PAYSCALE.COM

ROI rating	**86**
Bachelor's and No Higher	
Median starting salary	$45,900
Median mid-career salary	$81,000
At Least Bachelor's	
Median starting salary	$45,500
Median mid-career salary	$89,200
% alumni with high job meaning	44%
% STEM	12%

SELECTIVITY

Admissions Rating	**87**
# of applicants	3,744
% of applicants accepted	62
% of acceptees attending	39
# offered a place on the wait list	193
% accepting a place on wait list	21
% admitted from wait list	53

FRESHMAN PROFILE

Range ACT Composite	25–30
Minimum paper TOEFL	550
Minimum internet-based TOEFL	80
Average HS GPA	3.7
% graduated top 10% of class	34
% graduated top 25% of class	69
% graduated top 50% of class	97

DEADLINES

Early action	
Deadline	11/15
Notification	1/15
Regular	
Nonfall registration?	Yes

FINANCIAL FACTS

Financial Aid Rating	**87**
Annual tuition	$43,940
Room and board	$10,178
Required fees	$202
Average need-based scholarship	$24,220
% needy frosh rec. need-based scholarship or grant aid	100
% needy UG rec. need-based scholarship or grant aid	100
% needy frosh rec. non-need-based scholarship or grant aid	15
% needy UG rec. non-need-based scholarship or grant aid	11
% needy frosh rec. need-based self-help aid	76
% needy UG rec. need-based self-help aid	83
% frosh rec. any financial aid	100
% UG rec. any financial aid	100
% UG borrow to pay for school	69
Average cumulative indebtedness	$35,219
% frosh need fully met	45
% ugrads need fully met	41
Average % of frosh need met	87
Average % of ugrad need met	85

Indiana University—Bloomington

300 North Jordan Avenue, Bloomington, IN 47405-1106 • Admissions: 812-855-0661 • Fax: 812-855-5102

CAMPUS LIFE

Quality of Life Rating	**86**
Fire Safety Rating	**88**
Green Rating	**97**
Type of school	Public
Affiliation	No Affiliation
Environment	City

STUDENTS

Total undergrad enrollment	38,364
% male/female	49/51
% from out of state	33
% frosh live on campus	95
% ugrads live on campus	35
# of fraternities (% ugrad men join)	40 (21)
# of sororities (% ugrad women join)	31 (19)
% African American	4
% Asian	4
% Caucasian	71
% Hispanic	5
% Native American	<1
% Pacific Islander	<1
% Two or more races	4
% Race and/or ethnicity unknown	<1
% international	11
# of countries represented	133

ACADEMICS

Academic Rating	**79**
% students returning for sophomore year	89
% students graduating within 4 years	60
% students graduating within 6 years	77
Calendar	Semester
Student/faculty ratio	17:1
Profs interesting rating	79
Profs accessible rating	83
Most classes have 20–29 students.	
Most lab/discussion sessions have 20–29 students.	

MOST POPULAR MAJORS
Business/Commerce; Kinesiology and Exercise Science; Public Administration

ABOUT THE SCHOOL

Indiana University—Bloomington offers a quintessential college town, campus, and overall academic experience. Students enjoy all of the advantages, opportunities, and resources that a larger school can offer, while still receiving personal attention and support. Indiana is a "Big Ten research university that offers a huge variety of classes and majors . . . within a surprisingly diverse student body," says one student. Quite accurate, and exemplified by undergrads from 133 different countries being represented throughout the campus. Indiana offers more than 4,000 courses and more than 200 undergraduate majors, of which many are known nationally and internationally. Students can tailor academic programs to meet their needs, and enjoy research opportunities and state-of-the-art technology throughout all university departments. Students love the curriculum at IU. "The best combination of academics and extracurriculars one could ask for in a school." Many majors require students to hold an internship before graduating, so "you really have to be self-motivated."

BANG FOR YOUR BUCK

Above-average high school performers traditionally meet little resistance from the IU admissions office. Providing tradition and complete academic excellence in one package, one undergraduate is pleased that "the best part is that IU prepares you for a well-rounded go at life but focuses on giving you a solid academic foundation." Also, IU's music program is highly competitive; a successful audition is imperative. Representatives from businesses, government agencies, and not-for-profit organizations come to campus frequently to recruit IU students.

STUDENT LIFE

It's a large school with a little something for everyone, so the most common characteristics of students here are as basic as "everyone enjoying an IU basketball game, not wanting to walk through the snow to classes on occasion, and loving Bloomington." During the week, the campus is very active, with a good number of students working out or running, and on the weekends the "very fun social scene" kicks into high gear. The restaurants off-campus are "amazing," and the local bowling alleys and movie theater are popular haunts. The Greek system, although it only encompasses roughly 20 percent of the student body, provides a strong social scene. "Most students here are very respectful of one another and ready to help out a fellow Hoosier," says one.

CAREER

The school "wants to see [students] succeed and land jobs" and to that end, "there are so many resources for internships." "With such highly praised professors, a student will be sure to have an 'in' when the time is needed," says one. Students can make the most out of their time here at IU with drop-in advising and hands-on experience, from civil rights immersion trips to volunteer opportunities in other countries. More than 1,500 hiring organizations recruit students from IU, and there are thirteen separate specialized career centers that help build industry-specific employer relationships. Of the Indiana University—Bloomington alums who visited PayScale.com, the average starting salary was $45,100 and 51 percent reported feeling their job had a meaningful impact on the world.

Indiana University—Bloomington

FINANCIAL AID: 812-855-0321 • E-MAIL: IUADMIT@INDIANA.EDU • WEBSITE: WWW.INDIANA.EDU

GENERAL INFO

Activities: Choral groups, concert band, dance, drama/theater, jazz band, literary magazine, marching band, music ensembles, musical theater, opera, radio station, student government, student newspaper, symphony orchestra, television station, yearbook, campus ministries, international student organization. **Organizations:** 750-plus registered organizations, 10 honor societies, 48 religious organizations. 40 fraternities, 31 sororities. **Athletics (Intercollegiate):** *Men:* Baseball, basketball, cheerleading, cross-country, diving, football, golf, soccer, swimming, tennis, track/field (outdoor), wrestling. *Women:* Basketball, cheerleading, cross country, diving, field hockey, golf, rowing, soccer, softball, swimming, tennis, track/field (outdoor), volleyball, water polo.

FINANCIAL AID

Students should submit: FAFSA. Priority filing deadline is 3/10. The Princeton Review suggests that all financial aid forms be submitted as soon as possible after October 1. *Need-based scholarships/grants offered:* Federal Pell, FSEOG, State scholarships/grants, Private scholarships, College/university scholarship or grant aid from institutional funds. *Loan aid offered:* Direct Subsidized Stafford Loans, Direct Unsubsidized Stafford Loans, Direct PLUS loans, Federal Perkins Loans, Federal Nursing Loans, College/university loans from institutional funds. Applicants will be notified of awards on a rolling basis beginning in March. Federal Work-Study Program available. Institutional employment available.

BOTTOM LINE

A very large institution, Indiana University has a total undergraduate enrollment of more than 38,000 students; almost one-third of students are originally from another part of the country. In-state tuition is $9,087; for out-of-state students tuition runs $32,945. Room, board, fees, and supplies will add an extra $14,420. One student was excited that although "my financial resources were limited, I was in-state . . . IU was a great deal." There is also plenty of financial assistance available; 77 percent of needy freshmen receive some form of need-based scholarship or grant aid. Upon graduation, enrollees can expect to have in the area of $27,681 in cumulative indebtedness.

CAREER INFORMATION FROM PAYSCALE.COM

ROI rating	**86**
Bachelor's and No Higher	
Median starting salary	$45,400
Median mid-career salary	$80,600
At Least Bachelor's	
Median starting salary	$46,600
Median mid-career salary	$83,100
% alumni with high job meaning	47%
% STEM	9%

SELECTIVITY

Admissions Rating	85
# of applicants	34,483
% of applicants accepted	78
% of acceptees attending	29
# offered a place on the wait list	1,843
% accepting a place on wait list	21
% admitted from wait list	7

FRESHMAN PROFILE

Range SAT Critical Reading	520–630
Range SAT Math	540–660
Range SAT Writing	510–620
Range ACT Composite	24–30
Minimum paper TOEFL	550
Minimum internet-based TOEFL	79
Average HS GPA	3.6
% graduated top 10% of class	34
% graduated top 25% of class	68
% graduated top 50% of class	95

DEADLINES

Early action	
Deadline	11/1
Regular	
Priority	2/1
Nonfall registration?	Yes

FINANCIAL FACTS

Financial Aid Rating	82
Annual in-state tuition	$9,087
Annual out-of-state tuition	$32,945
Room and board	$10,041
Required fees	$1,301
Average need-based scholarship	$10,575
% needy frosh rec. need-based scholarship or grant aid	77
% needy UG rec. need-based scholarship or grant aid	80
% needy frosh rec. non-need-based scholarship or grant aid	16
% needy UG rec. non-need-based scholarship or grant aid	15
% needy frosh rec. need-based self-help aid	62
% needy UG rec. need-based self-help aid	63
% frosh rec. any financial aid	72
% UG rec. any financial aid	75
% UG borrow to pay for school	48
Average cumulative indebtedness	$27,681
% frosh need fully met	26
% ugrads need fully met	24
Average % of frosh need met	66
Average % of ugrad need met	66

Iowa State University

100 ENROLLMENT SERVICES CENTER, AMES, IA 50011-2011 • ADMISSIONS: 515-294-5836 • FAX: 515-294-2592

CAMPUS LIFE

Quality of Life Rating	93
Fire Safety Rating	92
Green Rating	98
Type of school	Public
Affiliation	No Affiliation
Environment	Town

STUDENTS

Total undergrad enrollment	30,034
% male/female	57/43
% from out of state	31
% frosh from public high school	93
% frosh live on campus	94
% ugrads live on campus	41
# of fraternities (% ugrad men join)	36 (12)
# of sororities (% ugrad women join)	25 (20)
% African American	3
% Asian	3
% Caucasian	76
% Hispanic	5
% Native American	<1
% Pacific Islander	<1
% Two or more races	2
% Race and/or ethnicity unknown	5
% international	7
# of countries represented	116

ACADEMICS

Academic Rating	74
% students returning for sophomore year	87
% students graduating within 4 years	41
% students graduating within 6 years	71
Calendar	Semester
Student/faculty ratio	19:1
Profs interesting rating	70
Profs accessible rating	71

Most classes have 20–29 students.
Most lab/discussion sessions have
  20–29 students.

MOST POPULAR MAJORS

Mechanical Engineering; Kinesiology and
Exercise Science; Finance

ABOUT THE SCHOOL

Iowa State University has the reputation of being a "large university with a small-town feel." With more than 100 undergraduate programs to choose from, many students are drawn to the ISU campus due to interests in agriculture, food science, preveterinary studies, or architecture. Not to be overlooked is the university's engineering program, which students boast is exceptionally supportive of its female engineering students. Undergraduates at Iowa State, known as Cyclones, say they always feel like they have full support of faculty and professors. Though accomplished, including Rhodes Scholars, Fulbright Scholars, and National Academy of Sciences and National Academy of Engineering members, the majority of Iowa State's 1,700 faculty members are easily accessible.

"There are so many services on campus to help students, it is almost unreal. From tutoring to study sessions and counseling to mock interviews and résumé building, ISU offers a wide variety of services to students." This superior support is not limited to the classroom, though, "there are a lot of opportunities for student research and hands-on learning"; some students insist that ISU is "the best 'outside of class' university in the nation." ISU offers a Freshman Honors Program, which promotes an enhanced academic environment for students of high ability. Benefits include unique courses, small class sizes, research opportunities and funding, access to graduate-level courses, and priority registration. The University is heavily focused on the environment, too. The Commitment to Sustainable Operations, highlighted by a joint contract with the City of Ames, and Campus Green Teams, dedicated to increasing sustainability efforts, are two of the most noteworthy initiatives.

BANG FOR YOUR BUCK

With an enrollment of more than 23,000 students, 4,500 of those being freshmen, Iowa State University "holds true to its initial mission of providing affordable, practical education with a special focus on agriculture." As would befit an agricultural school, the campus encompasses 1,800 acres. Nearly 60 percent of students are male; full-time students account for 95 percent of the enrollees at the university, although distance education undergraduate degree programs are also offered. Iowa State employs 1,600 full-time faculty members, and there is a comfortable seventeen to one student-to-faculty ratio–excellent for such a large school. Additionally, nearly a quarter of all students continue on to pursue graduate school studies.

STUDENT LIFE

Most of the students here come from the Midwest (most popularly Iowa), so nice is the default setting. "If someone gets off of the campus and city bus system without thanking the bus driver, it's practically a sin," says a student. Ames is a relatively small community by itself, but with the college it grows to about 60,000 people. Downtown is "full of fast food and chain restaurants, bars, movie theaters, a mall, as well as locally owned businesses, restaurants, and novelty shops." Most students live on campus the first couple years, and the school hosts quite a few bands and late night activities such as Bingo, hypnotists, speakers, and free food, and "just about everyone is involved in at least one intramural sport." The "awesome bus system" CyRide takes you "within two blocks of everything," and so a lot of students go out in town on the weekends.

Iowa State University

FINANCIAL AID: 515-294-2223 • E-MAIL: ADMISSIONS@IASTATE.EDU • WEBSITE: WWW.IASTATE.EDU

CAREER

Students say one of the school's greatest strengths is getting students involved in internships, which makes it "extremely easy to find a job." Each of the university's colleges maintains its own Career Service Office, and the centralized Career Exploration Services helps those students who don't know what they want to do with their lives look at different majors and occupations, and offers career coaching and counseling. Career fairs are offered year-round, and the "very large engineering, agriculture and business/LAS career fairs allow students to find internships and full time jobs easily." Of the Iowa State University alumni who visited PayScale.com, an average starting salary rang in at $49,300 and 51 percent said they felt their job had a meaningful impact on society.

GENERAL INFO

Activities: Choral groups, concert band, dance, drama/theater, jazz band, literary magazine, marching band, music ensembles, musical theater, opera, pep band, radio station, student government, student newspaper, student-run film society, symphony orchestra, television station **Organizations:** 799 registered organizations, 43 honor societies, 34 religious organizations. 32 fraternities, 20 sororities. **Athletics (Intercollegiate):** *Men:* Basketball, cross-country, football, golf, track/field (outdoor), track/field (indoor), wrestling. *Women:* Basketball, cross-country, diving, golf, gymnastics, soccer, softball, swimming, tennis, track/field (outdoor), track/field (indoor), volleyball.

FINANCIAL AID

Students should submit: FAFSA. Priority filing deadline is 3/1. The Princeton Review suggests that all financial aid forms be submitted as soon as possible after October 1. *Need-based scholarships/grants offered:* Federal Pell, FSEOG, State scholarships/grants, College/university scholarship or grant aid from institutional funds. *Loan aid offered:* Direct Subsidized Stafford Loans, Direct Unsubsidized Stafford Loans, Direct PLUS loans, Federal Perkins Loans, College/university loans from institutional funds. Applicants will be notified of awards on a rolling basis beginning 4/1. Federal Work-Study Program available. Institutional employment available.

BOTTOM LINE

Tuition at Iowa State University is an excellent value for in-state students, with tuition being just $6,648. Room and board will come to about $7,721; books, supplies, and required fees will add another $2,100. Students from out-of-state can expect an overall tuition of $19,768—still a very affordable total for a school providing such a wealth of educational opportunities. Plus, 87 percent of freshmen receive some manner of financial support, with 98 percent of needy freshman receiving some form of need-based aid. Average financial aid packages average $11,800; for most freshman, the total need-based gift aid approaches $7,700, with the average amount of loan debt per graduate at about $28,880.

CAREER INFORMATION FROM PAYSCALE.COM

ROI rating	86
Bachelor's and No Higher	
Median starting salary	$49,500
Median mid-career salary	$84,300
At Least Bachelor's	
Median starting salary	$50,000
Median mid-career salary	$86,500
% alumni with high job meaning	51%
% STEM	26%

SELECTIVITY

Admissions Rating	79
# of applicants	19,164
% of applicants accepted	87
% of acceptees attending	37

FRESHMAN PROFILE

Range SAT Critical Reading	460–620
Range SAT Math	500–640
Range ACT Composite	22–28
Minimum paper TOEFL	530
Minimum internet-based TOEFL	71
Average HS GPA	3.5
% graduated top 10% of class	22
% graduated top 25% of class	54
% graduated top 50% of class	91

DEADLINES

Nonfall registration?	Yes

FINANCIAL FACTS

Financial Aid Rating	83
Annual in-state tuition	$6,648
Annual out-of-state tuition	$19,768
Room and board	$8,070
Required fees	$1,088
Average need-based scholarship	$7,059
% needy frosh rec. need-based scholarship or grant aid	98
% needy UG rec. need-based scholarship or grant aid	98
% needy frosh rec. non-need-based scholarship or grant aid	46
% needy UG rec. non-need-based scholarship or grant aid	45
% needy frosh rec. need-based self-help aid	66
% needy UG rec. need-based self-help aid	75
% frosh rec. any financial aid	88
% UG rec. any financial aid	79
% UG borrow to pay for school	64
Average cumulative indebtedness	$27,571
% frosh need fully met	35
% ugrads need fully met	33
Average % of frosh need met	82
Average % of ugrad need met	80

James Madison University

SONNER HALL, MSC 0101, HARRISONBURG, VA 22807 • ADMISSIONS: 540-568-5681 • FAX: 540-568-3332

CAMPUS LIFE

Quality of Life Rating	92
Fire Safety Rating	85
Green Rating	93
Type of school	Public
Affiliation	No Affiliation
Environment	Town

STUDENTS

Total undergrad enrollment	19,396
% male/female	41/59
% from out of state	24
% frosh from public high school	60
% frosh live on campus	91
% ugrads live on campus	13
# of fraternities (% ugrad men join)	15 (1)
# of sororities (% ugrad women join)	13 (5)
% African American	4
% Asian	4
% Caucasian	76
% Hispanic	6
% Native American	<1
% Pacific Islander	<1
% Two or more races	4
% Race and/or ethnicity unknown	3
% international	2
# of countries represented	68

ACADEMICS

Academic Rating	75
% students returning for sophomore year	91
% students graduating within 4 years	66
% students graduating within 6 years	83
Calendar	Semester
Student/faculty ratio	16:1
Profs interesting rating	82
Profs accessible rating	82

Most classes have 20–29 students.
Most lab/discussion sessions have
20–29 students.

MOST POPULAR MAJORS
Community Health Services/Liaison/
Counseling; Speech Communication and
Rhetoric; Psychology

ABOUT THE SCHOOL

James Madison University is located on 785 acres in Virginia's breathtaking Shenandoah Valley. "The moment I walked on campus I was captured by the student spirit and how beautiful it is," one student says. The university itself, however, offers its students much more than the "benefits of walking in the mountains." There is an impressive balance of educational, social, and extracurricular activities to enrich students' experiences, including more than 100 majors to choose from spanning everything from musical theater, to business, to an innovative information security program. Both students and professors alike contribute to the feeling of community on campus. Students love the "positive, enriching, and supportive learning environment." Most who take classes here can agree that the faculty is always "available to help" and constantly proving they're "interested in student achievement." While most of the programs offered at JMU are rigorous, teachers "are very down-to-earth, approachable, and huge supporters of discussion-based classes." In fact, most go the extra mile and are "willing to facilitate your education in any way possible"; one student believes that "the greatest strength of the school is the ability to get any sort of assistance when needed." JMU offers extensive academic and cocurricular experiences that allow students hands-on exploration of sustainability. JMU's president formed a Commission on Environmental Stewardship and Sustainability to coordinate campus environmental stewardship efforts.

BANG FOR YOUR BUCK

Having an enrollment of 4,000 freshmen, and more than 19,000 undergraduate students overall, James Madison University includes representation from more than eighty countries. Ninety-five percent of students are full-time, with 60 percent being female and almost 30 percent from out-of-state. With almost 1,400 faculty on campus, students are pleased to find two-thirds have PhDs. Impressively, nine out of every ten students return to the university for sophomore year.

STUDENT LIFE

Students at JMU seem committed to enjoying themselves outside their studies, and the school offers many opportunities. "Many students on a nice day will lay out on the quad, throw Frisbee, go swimming at Blue Hole, study on the quad, go downtown, hike in the Shenandoah Valley. People for fun hangout with their friends in extracurricular groups, but a large majority of students go out to parties since JMU has an 'open door policy.'" While many report that JMU has a "party atmosphere" on weekends, others don't feel that way: "Although many people believe that the students at JMU thrive on the party scene I would strongly disagree!! The students here are all very intelligent, passionate, friendly people who truly want to succeed in life!" Sports and intramurals are very popular due to the school's "outdoorsy" vibe, and many cultural events are offered: "On Friday nights the University sponsors comedians and other performers and once a month on Thursdays the University Program Board sponsors a movie or game night." So whatever you're into, you'll find something to do at JMU.

James Madison University

FINANCIAL AID: 540-568-7820 • E-MAIL: ADMISSIONS@JMU.EDU • WEBSITE: WWW.JMU.EDU

CAREER

JMU's office of Career and Academic Planning offers a variety of resources for students exploring their post-graduation options. Academic and career advising is available for students looking to explore their interests; career fairs and recruiting events are held on campus; job and internship opportunities are listed online through Recruit-A-Duke; and resources are available for help with résumés, cover letters, and interviews. Beyond the Career and Academic Planning office, students cite their professors as a source of guidance: "They are a great resource for preparing for graduate school, and always do their best to make sure you are on track for your career." Of JMU alumni visiting PayScale.com, 44 percent feel as though they derive a high level of meaning from their jobs.

GENERAL INFO

Activities: Choral groups, concert band, dance, drama/theater, jazz band, literary magazine, marching band, music ensembles, musical theater, opera, pep band, radio station, student government, student newspaper, student-run film society, symphony orchestra, yearbook, campus ministries, international student organization. **Organizations:** 330 registered organizations, 21 honor societies, 28 religious organizations. 15 fraternities, 9 sororities. **Athletics (Intercollegiate):** *Men:* Baseball, basketball, cheerleading, football, golf, soccer, tennis. *Women:* Basketball, cheerleading, cross-country, diving, field hockey, golf, lacrosse, soccer, softball, swimming, tennis, track/field (outdoor), volleyball.

FINANCIAL AID

Students should submit: FAFSA. Priority filing deadline is 3/1. The Princeton Review suggests that all financial aid forms be submitted as soon as possible after October 1. *Need-based scholarships/grants offered:* Federal Pell, FSEOG, State scholarships/grants, Private scholarships, College/university scholarship or grant aid from institutional funds. *Loan aid offered:* Direct Subsidized Stafford Loans, Direct Unsubsidized Stafford Loans, Direct PLUS loans, Federal Perkins Loans. Applicants will be notified of awards on a rolling basis beginning 4/1. Federal Work-Study Program available. Institutional employment available.

BOTTOM LINE

With in-state tuition being just over $9,600 per year, James Madison University is an exceptionally affordable school. Another $9,396 will provide students with full room and board; books and educational supplies will increase this figure by almost $900, and required school fees are $4,294. Out-of-state tuition is just more than $24,500. About half of undergrads receive need-based financial aid, with the average need-based gift aid being in the neighborhood of $7,500. Need-based financial aid packages will generally provide freshman with over $8,000 in support.

CAREER INFORMATION FROM PAYSCALE.COM

ROI rating	**86**
Bachelor's and No Higher	
Median starting salary	$49,100
Median mid-career salary	$85,300
At Least Bachelor's	
Median starting salary	$49,900
Median mid-career salary	$86,100
% alumni with high job meaning	43%
% STEM	9%

SELECTIVITY

Admissions Rating	82
# of applicants	21,439
% of applicants accepted	73
% of acceptees attending	28
# offered a place on the wait list	2,500
% accepting a place on wait list	48
% admitted from wait list	42

FRESHMAN PROFILE

Range SAT Critical Reading	520–610
Range SAT Math	520–610
Range ACT Composite	23–27
Minimum paper TOEFL	550
% graduated top 10% of class	23
% graduated top 25% of class	41
% graduated top 50% of class	97

DEADLINES

Early action	
Deadline	11/1
Notification	1/15
Regular	
Deadline	1/15
Notification	4/1
Nonfall registration?	No

FINANCIAL FACTS

Financial Aid Rating	83
Annual in-state tuition	$5,896
Annual out-of-state tuition	$21,670
Room and board	$9,334
Required fees	$4,446
Average need-based scholarship	$7,080
% needy frosh rec. need-based scholarship or grant aid	53
% needy UG rec. need-based scholarship or grant aid	51
% needy frosh rec. non-need-based scholarship or grant aid	9
% needy UG rec. non-need-based scholarship or grant aid	10
% needy frosh rec. need-based self-help aid	76
% needy UG rec. need-based self-help aid	70
% frosh rec. any financial aid	59
% UG rec. any financial aid	56
% UG borrow to pay for school	100
Average cumulative indebtedness	$25,677
% frosh need fully met	78
% ugrads need fully met	68
Average % of frosh need met	40
Average % of ugrad need met	43

Johns Hopkins University

OFFICE OF UNDERGRADUATE ADMISSIONS, MASON HALL, 3400 N. CHARLES STREET, BALTIMORE, MD 21218 • ADMISSIONS: 410-516-8171

CAMPUS LIFE

Quality of Life Rating	91
Fire Safety Rating	98
Green Rating	92
Type of school	Private
Affiliation	No Affiliation
Environment	Metropolis

STUDENTS

Total undergrad enrollment	5,386
% male/female	51/49
% from out of state	88
% frosh from public high school	57
% frosh live on campus	99
% ugrads live on campus	52
# of fraternities (% ugrad men join)	11 (17)
# of sororities (% ugrad women join)	11 (26)
% African American	6
% Asian	23
% Caucasian	40
% Hispanic	13
% Native American	<1
% Pacific Islander	<1
% Two or more races	5
% Race and/or ethnicity unknown	3
% international	10
# of countries represented	65

ACADEMICS

Academic Rating	91
% students returning for sophomore year	97
% students graduating within 4 years	88
% students graduating within 6 years	94
Calendar	4/1/4
Profs interesting rating	78
Profs accessible rating	76
Most classes have 10–19 students.	

MOST POPULAR MAJORS

Bioengineering and Biomedical Engineering; Neuroscience; Public Health

#39 COLLEGE THAT PAYS YOU BACK

ABOUT THE SCHOOL

Without a doubt, Johns Hopkins University's reputation for academic rigor and its wide array of programs in the sciences and humanities make it a magnet for its top-notch students. In addition to its lauded biochemical engineering and international studies programs, this research university also offers opportunities for its students to study at its other divisions, including the Peabody Conservatory, the Nitze School of Advanced International Studies, the Carey Business School, and the Bloomberg School of Public Health. Students appreciate the school's lack of a core curriculum, small class size, and emphasis on academic exploration and hands-on learning. Around two-thirds of the students are involved in some kind of research opportunity, and an equal amount of students end up with internships. Many of the distinguished professors at Johns Hopkins often serve as mentors and collaborators on these research projects. According to one student, "Johns Hopkins puts you shoulder-to-shoulder with some of the greatest minds in the world while promoting a work ethic that forces you to push yourself to your intellectual limits."

BANG FOR YOUR BUCK

To apply for financial aid, students must submit the FAFSA. Johns Hopkins distributes more than 90 percent of its financial aid awards on the basis of need and also provides need- and merit-based scholarships, including the Hodson Trust Scholarships as well as Bloomberg Scholarships. Along with financial aid, students receive a lot of support from the school's Career Center and Office of Pre-Professional Programs and Advising, as well as the extensive and loyal alumni network, to help them tackle their career-development and postgraduation goals.

STUDENT LIFE

For some reason, Hopkins developed a reputation as a school where "fun comes to die." However, many undergrads here balk at that notion and insist that it couldn't be further from the truth. Indeed, while the academics are certainly rigorous there's also plenty of fun to be had. As one international studies major asserts, "There's never a dull moment at Johns Hopkins: you just have to step outside your room and look for five seconds." For starters, there are plenty of "free on-campus movies, plays, dance and a cappella performances" to catch. Additionally, the MSE symposium "always has interesting speakers (like Will Ferrell)." Moreover, about "one fourth of the school population is involved in Greek life." Of course, should students (temporarily) grow weary of campus life, they have the option of exploring Baltimore. And, as an added bonus, D.C. and Philadelphia are both roughly an hour away.

CAREER

If you asked Hopkins undergrads to summarize their career services office in one word, it would likely be "awesome." And that's no surprise. After all, when the average starting salary for graduates is $58,700 (source: PayScale.com), you know the school is doing something right. The Career Center truly bends over backwards to help students prepare for the job market. Impressively, undergrads can request customized workshops on any career-related topic they

Johns Hopkins University

FAX: 410-516-6025 • FINANCIAL AID: 410-516-8028 • E-MAIL: GOTOJHU@JHU.EDU • WEBSITE: WWW.JHU.EDU

deem important. They can also participate in unique programs during the university's intersession. For example, there's "Financial Literacy" which combines classroom lectures regarding specific areas of finance (venture capital, IPOs, etc.) with a visit to NYC and meetings at firms such as Goldman Sachs, Morgan Stanley, etc. The office hosts similar for programs for students interested in PR/media, globalization and public health. And, of course, undergrads can receive more traditional assistance such as resume critiques and mock interviews.

GENERAL INFO

Activities: Choral groups, concert band, dance, drama/theater, jazz band, literary magazine, music ensembles, musical theater, pep band, radio station, student government, student newspaper, student-run film society, symphony orchestra, yearbook, campus ministries. **Organizations:** 250 registered organizations, 17 honor societies, 20 religious organizations. 12 fraternities, 11 sororities. **Athletics (Intercollegiate):** *Men:* Baseball, basketball, cross-country, fencing, football, lacrosse, soccer, swimming, tennis, track/field (outdoor), track/field (indoor), water polo, wrestling. *Women:* Basketball, cross-country, fencing, field hockey, lacrosse, soccer, swimming, tennis, track/field (outdoor), track/field (indoor), volleyball. **On-Campus Highlights:** Mattin Student Arts Center, Homewood House Museum, Undergraduate Teaching Labs, Ralph S. O'Connor Recreation Center, Charles Commons, Brody Learning Commons, a state-of-the-art collaborative learning space. **Environmental Initiatives:** Commitment to reduce greenhouse gas emissions by 51 percent by 2025.

FINANCIAL AID

Students should submit: FAFSA, CSS/Financial Aid PROFILE, Noncustodial PROFILE. The Princeton Review suggests that all financial aid forms be submitted as soon as possible after October 1. *Need-based scholarships/grants offered:* Federal Pell, FSEOG, State scholarships/grants, Private scholarships, College/university scholarship or grant aid from institutional funds. *Loan aid offered:* Direct Subsidized Stafford Loans, Direct Unsubsidized Stafford Loans, Direct PLUS loans, Federal Perkins Loans, College/university loans from institutional funds. Applicants will be notified of awards on or about 4/1. Federal Work-Study Program available. Institutional employment available.

BOTTOM LINE

Johns Hopkins tuition fees hover at the $50,410 mark, with an additional $14,976 for room and board. This does not include books, supplies, personal expenses, or transportation. Nearly 60 percent of first years receive some form of financial aid.

CAREER INFORMATION FROM PAYSCALE.COM

ROI rating	91
Bachelor's and No Higher	
Median starting salary	$57,500
Median mid-career salary	$97,500
At Least Bachelor's	
Median starting salary	$61,200
Median mid-career salary	$107,000
% alumni with high job meaning	63%
% STEM	26%

SELECTIVITY

Admissions Rating	99
# of applicants	24,716
% of applicants accepted	13
% of acceptees attending	40
# offered a place on the wait list	2,752
% accepting a place on wait list	63
% admitted from wait list	11
# of early decision applicants	1,000
% accepted early decision	29

FRESHMAN PROFILE

Range SAT Critical Reading	690–760
Range SAT Math	710–790
Range SAT Writing	690–770
Range ACT Composite	32–34
Minimum paper TOEFL	600
Average HS GPA	3.9
% graduated top 10% of class	92
% graduated top 25% of class	99
% graduated top 50% of class	100

DEADLINES

Early decision	
Deadline	11/1
Notification	12/15
Regular	
Deadline	1/1
Notification	4/1
Nonfall registration?	No

FINANCIAL FACTS

Financial Aid Rating	93
Annual tuition	$50,410
Room and board	$14,976
Required fees	$500
Average need-based scholarship	$36,687
% needy frosh rec. non-need-based scholarship or grant aid	33
% needy UG rec. non-need-based scholarship or grant aid	20
% needy frosh rec. need-based self-help aid	80
% needy UG rec. need-based self-help aid	84
% frosh rec. any financial aid	63
% UG rec. any financial aid	57
% UG borrow to pay for school	42
Average cumulative indebtedness	$24,702
% frosh need fully met	100
% ugrads need fully met	100
Average % of frosh need met	100
Average % of ugrad need met	100

Kalamazoo College

1200 ACADEMY STREET, KALAMAZOO, MI 49006 • ADMISSIONS: 269-337-7166 • FAX: 269-337-7390

CAMPUS LIFE

Quality of Life Rating	**89**
Fire Safety Rating	**79**
Green Rating	**60***
Type of school	Private
Affiliation	No Affiliation
Environment	City

STUDENTS

Total undergrad enrollment	1,443
% male/female	44/56
% from out of state	34
% frosh from public high school	82
% frosh live on campus	100
% ugrads live on campus	66
% African American	6
% Asian	7
% Caucasian	59
% Hispanic	9
% Native American	<1
% Pacific Islander	<1
% Two or more races	5
% Race and/or ethnicity unknown	6
% international	9
# of countries represented	32

ACADEMICS

Academic Rating	**89**
% students returning for sophomore year	92
% students graduating within 4 years	77
Calendar	Quarter
Student/faculty ratio	13:1
Profs interesting rating	95
Profs accessible rating	95
Most classes have 10–19 students.	
Most lab/discussion sessions have 10–19 students.	

MOST POPULAR MAJORS
English; Psychology; Economics

ABOUT THE SCHOOL

"Kalamazoo College," says a Chemistry major, "is all about diversity and creating an accepting environment for its students." Located in the mid-size Michigan city of the same name, Kalamazoo College's mission is "to prepare graduates to better understand, live successfully within, and provide enlightened leadership to a richly diverse and increasingly complex world," according to its website. The school is nationally known for its *K-Plan*, which integrates "depth and breadth in the liberal arts and sciences, learning through experience, international engagement, and [a] senior individualized project." It's this drive that causes students to admire a college that "challenges its student[s] in more than academics, it pushes you to rethink what you've already learned in all areas of life, then encourages you [to] apply that thinking to make a difference." The small school—enrollment is approximately 1,450—boasts a diverse mix, with students from thirty-three countries and forty-three states.

BANG FOR YOUR BUCK

According to the school's website, nearly 80 percent of Kalamazoo students complete an internship or an externship. "Through internships, externships, study abroad and the Senior Individualized Project," says a student, "all [Kalamazoo] students graduate completely ready to pursue a career in what they are passionate about or to continue their education on the next level." One student praised the Financial Aid office, saying the "department is wonderful [and does] a great job helping students find the aid they need." Kalamazoo College reports that it meets an average of 91 percent of student financial need.

STUDENT LIFE

"K students are highly motivated, but it's not just about academics," says one Spanish major. "People participate [in a wide variety of extracurricular activities] and are encouraged to do so by the school." These include "activities that either compliment [one's] academic study or contribute to a [well-rounded] life." With no Greek life presence and modest offerings in downtown Kalamazoo, the campus becomes the nexus of social life. According to one Classical Studies major, "we cook, we do art, [and] we certainly make our own fun." Life on campus is perfection for many students: "Whether one is sprawled out studying on the gorgeous Quad or curled up with a book by one of the many fireplaces, one is never far from thoughtful friends, scenic escapes, or exciting activities." Summing up Kalamazoo College's "work hard, play hard" motto, "[students are] crazy studying during the week and mad-hopping with all sorts of activities the rest of the time."

CAREER

PayScale.com reports that 52 percent of Kalamazoo College graduates consider their careers to be bettering the world in some way. The school's Center for Career and Professional Development offers resources like the Recruiting Expo, a café-style gathering where students can interact with potential employers or internship supervisors. Regardless of what job you choose, "Kalamazoo College not only educates you to be successful in a career, but in all aspects of life." According to Payscale, one of the most popular jobs for Kalamazoo graduates is district sales manager, with an average starting salary for graduates of $36,300. Economics, Business Economics, Computer Science, and Psychology are among the school's most popular majors. Students praise the *K-Plan*, noting that it's "practical for both career and grad-school preparation. Most of all, [Kalamazoo

Kalamazoo College

FINANCIAL AID: 269-337-7192 • E-MAIL: ADMISSION@KZOO.EDU • WEBSITE: WWW.KZOO.EDU

College] has one of the strongest study abroad programs in the country," helping connect students with future job opportunities abroad. More than 80 percent of K students study abroad for three, six, or nine months.

GENERAL INFO

Activities: Choral groups, concert band, dance, drama/theater, jazz band, literary magazine, music ensembles, musical theater, pep band, radio station, student government, student newspaper, symphony orchestra, yearbook, Campus Ministries, International Student Organization, Model UN. **Organizations:** 60 registered organizations, 3 honor societies, 5 religious organizations. **Athletics (Intercollegiate):** *Men:* baseball, basketball, cross-country, diving, football, golf, lacrosse, soccer, swimming, tennis. *Women:* basketball, cross-country, diving, golf, lacrosse, soccer, softball, swimming, tennis, volleyball. **On-Campus Highlights:** Upjohn Library Commons, The Quad, Water Street Coffee Joint, Hicks Student Center, Anderson Athletic Center, Arcus Center for Social Justice Leadership.

FINANCIAL AID

Students should submit: FAFSA. Priority filing deadline is 2/15. The Princeton Review suggests that all financial aid forms be submitted as soon as possible after October 1. *Need-based scholarships/grants offered:* Federal Pell, FSEOG, State scholarships/grants, Private scholarships, College/university scholarship or grant aid from institutional funds. *Loan aid offered:* Direct Subsidized Stafford Loans, Direct Unsubsidized Stafford Loans, Direct PLUS loans, Federal Perkins Loans. Applicants will be notified of awards on a rolling basis beginning 1/15. Federal Work-Study Program available. Institutional employment available.

BOTTOM LINE

Annual tuition is $44,418, with 97 percent of undergrads receiving some form of financial aid. Add to the tuition another $9,714 for room and board, books, and fees and a year at Kalamazoo College is over $53,931. The average need-based scholarship is approximately $28,294. The average senior graduates from Kalamazoo College with around $28,764 in debt. One student singles out the financial aid offered—"[Kalamazoo College] gave me the best financial aid package"—as a key reason for attending the school.

CAREER INFORMATION FROM PAYSCALE.COM

ROI rating	**87**
Bachelor's and No Higher	
Median starting salary	$36,300
Median mid-career salary	$75,000
At Least Bachelor's	
Median starting salary	$36,300
Median mid-career salary	$75,000
% alumni with high job meaning	52%

SELECTIVITY

Admissions Rating	**88**
# of applicants	2,455
% of applicants accepted	72
% of acceptees attending	21
# offered a place on the wait list	228
% accepting a place on wait list	28
# of early decision applicants	37
% accepted early decision	84

FRESHMAN PROFILE

Range SAT Critical Reading	530–660
Range SAT Math	540–690
Range SAT Writing	510–650
Range ACT Composite	26–30
Minimum paper TOEFL	550
Minimum internet-based TOEFL	84
Average HS GPA	3.8
% graduated top 10% of class	40
% graduated top 25% of class	79
% graduated top 50% of class	97

DEADLINES

Early decision	
Deadline	11/1
Notification	12/1
Early action	
Deadline	11/1
Notification	12/20
Regular	
Deadline	1/15
Notification	4/1

FINANCIAL FACTS

Financial Aid Rating	**89**
Annual tuition	$44,418
Room and board	$9,714
Required fees	$339
Average need-based scholarship	$28,294
% needy frosh rec. need-based scholarship or grant aid	97
% needy UG rec. need-based scholarship or grant aid	98
% needy frosh rec. non-need-based scholarship or grant aid	28
% needy UG rec. non-need-based scholarship or grant aid	20
% needy frosh rec. need-based self-help aid	75
% needy UG rec. need-based self-help aid	81
% frosh rec. any financial aid	98
% UG rec. any financial aid	97
% UG borrow to pay for school	61
Average cumulative indebtedness	$28,764
% frosh need fully met	58
% ugrads need fully met	47
Average % of frosh need met	94
Average % of ugrad need met	92

Kenyon College

KENYON COLLEGE, ADMISSION OFFICE, GAMBIER, OH 43022-9623 • ADMISSIONS: 740-427-5776 • FAX: 740-427-5770

CAMPUS LIFE

Quality of Life Rating	90
Fire Safety Rating	89
Green Rating	80
Type of school	Private
Affiliation	Episcopal,
but non-denominational in practice	
Environment	Rural

STUDENTS

Total undergrad enrollment	1,698
% male/female	45/55
% from out of state	83
% frosh from public high school	51
% frosh live on campus	100
% ugrads live on campus	100
# of fraternities (% ugrad men join)	7 (18)
# of sororities (% ugrad women join)	4 (20)
% African American	4
% Asian	4
% Caucasian	73
% Hispanic	7
% Native American	<1
% Pacific Islander	0
% Two or more races	4
% Race and/or ethnicity unknown	3
% international	5
# of countries represented	41

ACADEMICS

Academic Rating	96
% students returning for sophomore year	93
% students graduating within 4 years	84
% students graduating within 6 years	88
Calendar	Semester
Student/faculty ratio	10:1
Profs interesting rating	97
Profs accessible rating	97
Most classes have 10–19 students.	

MOST POPULAR MAJORS
Economics; Psychology; English

ABOUT KENYON COLLEGE

Kenyon College, the oldest private college in Ohio, was founded in 1824 by Episcopalian Bishop Philander Chase. This small liberal arts college—about 1,600 students attend—sports an idyllic hilltop campus that is considered one of the most beautiful in the United States. The school's collegiate Gothic architecture is especially renowned. Kenyon College's strong academic reputation in the liberal arts and sciences rests on the back of its faculty. "The professors are what make Kenyon so great," as one student says. In addition to being "intelligent and stimulating," they "encourage discussion and constantly [ask] provoking questions." These are professors who "legitimately care about students." It is not uncommon for Kenyon professors to "invite [students] over for dinner, bring snacks to class, plan extracurricular departmental events, and . . . always [be] willing to help with schoolwork." Professors and students get to know each other here instead of being mere faces in giant, crowded lecture halls. In 2006, the college opened the Kenyon Athletic Center, a 263,000-square-foot building that is home to school athletics and a popular hangout spot for students. One of Kenyon College's strengths is its long and proud literary tradition, which includes the celebrated and still active *The Kenyon Review* magazine. Founded in 1937 by the poet John Crowe Ransom, *The Kenyon Review* has published such leading literary figures as Robert Lowell (also a Kenyon alum), Robert Penn Warren, Flannery O'Connor, and Dylan Thomas. The college believes its "small classes, dedicated teachers, and friendly give-and-take set the tone" of college life. Kenyon is a school that fosters a sense of community in which cooperation and shared intellectual growth is valued over competition. As one student sums up a common sentiment: "It just feels like a tight-knit, loving family, and it has made me feel at home here."

BANG FOR YOUR BUCK

The small classroom sizes and talented and personable faculty are real draws for Kenyon's students. With about 200 faculty members and only 1,600 students, the faculty-to-student ratio is simply outstanding. A full 94 percent of freshmen return for sophomore year, and 83 percent graduate within four years. The college boasts a diverse student body, "ethnically but also in terms of types of people and personality," that makes for a stimulating atmosphere. As the administration explains, "Life in this small college community is fueled by the talents and enthusiasm of our students, so the admission staff seeks students who have a range of talents and interests." Kenyon also has a commitment to student success beyond college. All seniors work with the career-development office to help plan their postcollege life and career, whatever path the student chooses to take.

STUDENT LIFE

At this rural Ohio liberal arts school, students "don't have much around [them] besides corn fields, so student life revolves around student groups, large [all-campus] parties, and lectures and performances." The parties are "welcoming and there is practically no exclusion in social life." With roughly, 1,700 students, Kenyon is an insular community and there are approximately 128 registered student organizations. Greek life plays a presence on campus—which has four sororities and nine fraternities—and roughly 10 percent of men and women pledge. Ninety-nine percent of the undergraduates live on campus, adding to the close-knit feeling. One International Studies major notes that students "mostly stay on campus, so [it's] a very social place. This gives most people a chance to get involved in

Kenyon College

FINANCIAL AID: 740-427-5240 • E-MAIL: ADMISSIONS@KENYON.EDU • WEBSITE: WWW.KENYON.EDU

some way," such as in "clubs [and] [intramural] sports." Aside from clubs to join and sports to play, "almost every week there is a cool concert . . . or a movie screening" on campus.

CAREER

Forty-three percent of Kenyon graduates would classify their careers as jobs that help make the world a better place, according to PayScale. com. The most popular career choices for Kenyon graduates are high school teacher, digital marketing manager, and attorney. Popular degrees include Economics, Political Science, and English. One Kenyon Biochemistry major praises the school's professors, who provide "amazing resources both inside and outside the classroom" and "can provide insight not only [about] classroom topics, but on life and careers as well." Kenyon's Career Development office—whose mission is to "facilitate [students'] career success"—regularly brings in alumni for career-oriented presentations, such as the Kenyon Finance Panel led by Kenyon alumni working in the finance industry. According to the school's website, Kenyon offers lifetime services for alumni, which include networking opportunities and the ability to search, as an employer, for a Kenyon graduate to fill a position.

FINANCIAL AID

Students should submit: FAFSA, CSS/Financial Aid PROFILE, Noncustodial PROFILE. Regular filing deadline is 2/15. The Princeton Review suggests that all financial aid forms be submitted as soon as possible after October 1. *Need-based scholarships/grants offered:* Federal Pell, FSEOG, State scholarships/grants, Private scholarships, College/university scholarship or grant aid from institutional funds. *Loan aid offered:* Direct Subsidized Stafford Loans, Direct Unsubsidized Stafford Loans, Direct PLUS loans, Federal Perkins Loans, College/university loans from institutional funds. Federal Work-Study Program available. Institutional employment available.

BOTTOM LINE

Kenyon College has an annual tuition of $49,220, and students can expect to spend an additional $12,130 on room and board. However, Kenyon has a strong commitment to bringing in talented students regardless of their financial situation. All students with financial aid needs can expect to find help at Kenyon. The school makes sure they meet students' financial needs for all their years attending the school, even if those needs change over the course of the student's college career. About half of students will take out loans to attend Kenyon. All told, the average Kenyon student can expect to accrue $27,000 of debt over the course of their college career.

CAREER INFORMATION FROM PAYSCALE.COM

ROI rating	90
Bachelor's and No Higher	
Median starting salary	$45,800
Median mid-career salary	$97,600
At Least Bachelor's	
Median starting salary	$46,300
Median mid-career salary	$101,000
% alumni with high job meaning	44%
% STEM	15%

SELECTIVITY

Admissions Rating	95
# of applicants	7,076
% of applicants accepted	24
% of acceptees attending	29
# offered a place on the wait list	2,876
% accepting a place on wait list	35
% admitted from wait list	2
# of early decision applicants	428
% accepted early decision	58

FRESHMAN PROFILE

Range SAT Critical Reading	630–730
Range SAT Math	610–690
Range SAT Writing	620–720
Range ACT Composite	28–32
Minimum internet-based TOEFL	100
Average HS GPA	4.0
% graduated top 10% of class	61
% graduated top 25% of class	54
% graduated top 50% of class	97

DEADLINES

Early decision	
Deadline	11/15
Notification	12/15
Regular	
Priority	1/15
Deadline	1/15
Notification	4/1
Nonfall registration?	No

FINANCIAL FACTS

Financial Aid Rating	92
Annual tuition	$49,220
Room and board	$12,130
Required fees	$1,980
Average need-based scholarship	$39,628
% needy frosh rec. need-based scholarship or grant aid	97
% needy UG rec. need-based scholarship or grant aid	96
% needy frosh rec. non-need-based scholarship or grant aid	26
% needy UG rec. non-need-based scholarship or grant aid	17
% needy frosh rec. need-based self-help aid	83
% needy UG rec. need-based self-help aid	80
% frosh rec. any financial aid	53
% UG rec. any financial aid	42
% UG borrow to pay for school	36
Average cumulative indebtedness	$27,000
% frosh need fully met	64
% ugrads need fully met	63
Average % of frosh need met	100
Average % of ugrad need met	100

Knox College

2 East South Street, Campus Box 148, Galesburg, IL 61401 • Admissions: 309-341-7100 • Fax: 309-341-7070

CAMPUS LIFE

Quality of Life Rating	88
Fire Safety Rating	96
Green Rating	86
Type of school	Private
Affiliation	No Affiliation
Environment	Town

STUDENTS

Total undergrad enrollment	1,397
% male/female	41/59
% from out of state	45
% frosh from public high school	70
% frosh live on campus	98
% ugrads live on campus	87
# of fraternities (% ugrad men join)	6 (32)
# of sororities (% ugrad women join)	4 (18)
% African American	8
% Asian	6
% Caucasian	52
% Hispanic	14
% Native American	<1
% Pacific Islander	0
% Two or more races	3
% Race and/or ethnicity unknown	5
% international	12
# of countries represented	44

ACADEMICS

Academic Rating	88
% students returning for sophomore year	83
% students graduating within 4 years	71
% students graduating within 6 years	77
Calendar	Trimester
Student/faculty ratio	11:1
Profs interesting rating	95
Profs accessible rating	92

Most classes have 10–19 students.
Most lab/discussion sessions have
  10–19 students.

MOST POPULAR MAJORS
Creative Writing; Economics; Education

ABOUT THE SCHOOL

This small, liberal arts college in Galesburg, Illinois grants students "ownership" of their educations by giving them "the freedom and resources to make something truly great out of your college experience." Knox "encourages its students to formulate their own educational goals" with over sixty different majors and minors, including student designed majors and minors. In addition, the school offers pre-professional programs for fields ranging from forestry, optometry, and law, as well as more specialized programs, like their Peace Corps preparatory program. Students appreciate that Knox only serves undergraduate students: "I also really liked the fact that only undergrads go to Knox because I felt like I would get more attention and opportunities to work on internships and research than I would at a larger school where I would have to compete for attention not only against other undergrads but against the graduate students as well." Students enjoy a relaxed and intimate relationship with professors who are "dedicated" and "incredibly informed." "Half of the time you don't even need to make an appointment," one student describes. "You can just walk into their office and strike up a conversation!"

BANG FOR YOUR BUCK

While the college has in recent years moved away from meeting 100 percent of demonstrated financial need, Knox still offer need-blind admittance and have moved toward making a Knox education as affordable as possible. Eighty-three percent of first-year students qualified for need-based financial aid in 2015, and Knox offers a generous array of scholarships that range from a few thousand dollars to full tuition. Scholarship categories include academic scholarships; writing, visual and performing arts awards; leadership scholarships; regional scholarships; and scholarships for transfer students. Students find the aid packages compelling: "Knox gave me a really good financial aid and scholarship package and money talks."

STUDENT LIFE

"Knox College students like to describe themselves as 'Knox Awkward,'" a term of endearment that acknowledges and embraces the quirky, "nerdiness" of the student body. "It is easy to make friends at Knox, because nobody is pretentious . . . We do our homework, do community service, and find awesome things to do in our spare time. One weekend I helped build a cottage-sized structure out of boxes outside of a dorm." Students like to keep busy with their studies and extracurriculars during the week, but "the weekend is most often when many of the on-campus activities take place." Events include "theater productions," "concerts," charity events and outdoor activities. Flunk Day, the much-anticipated annual festival (for which the date is kept secret) is, according to students, "the best day of the year."

CAREER

The Bastian Family Career Center offers students a gateway to internships, career fairs, and experiential learning opportunities. The school lists nearly 200 different organizations that offered internships to Knox students during the 2015-16 academic year. Knox also offers financial assistance to a limited number of students pursuing internships with nonprofits and environmental organizations. In addition to on-campus recruiting, Knox students are connected to exclusive job opportunities via the Illinois Small College Placement Association, through which students and alumni can post their

Knox College

FINANCIAL AID: 309-341-7149 • E-MAIL: ADMISSION@KNOX.EDU • WEBSITE: WWW.KNOX.EDU

resumes, browse jobs and internships, and get exclusive access to job fairs and interviews. A strong alumni and parent network helps to connect students with job opportunities, and student point to "alumni loyalty and willingness to help current students with internships" among the school's greatest strengths. Faculty help students plan for the future as well: "They are also incredible about doing everything in their power to help the students realize their academic and professional goals." Graduates have an average early career salary of $43,000 and a mid-career salary of $75,500. According to PayScale.com, 44 percent of alumni say their job makes the world a better place.

GENERAL INFO

Activities: Choral groups, dance, drama/theater, jazz band, literary magazine, music ensembles, radio station, student government, student newspaper, symphony orchestra, Campus Ministries, International Student Organization, Model UN 102 registered organizations, 8 honor societies, 6 religious organizations. 5 fraternities, 3 sororities. **Athletics (Intercollegiate):** *Men:* baseball, basketball, cross-country, football, golf, soccer, swimming, tennis, track/field (outdoor), track/field (indoor), wrestling. *Women:* basketball, cross-country, golf, soccer, softball, swimming, tennis, track/field (outdoor), track/field (indoor), volleyball. **On-Campus Highlights:** Gizmo Snack Bar, Andrew Fitness Center, Hard Knox Cafe, Gizmo Patio, Seymour Library.

FINANCIAL AID

Students should submit: FAFSA, Institution's own financial aid form. Priority filing deadline is 2/1. The Princeton Review suggests that all financial aid forms be submitted as soon as possible after October 1. *Need-based scholarships/grants offered:* Federal Pell, FSEOG, State scholarships/grants, Private scholarships, College/university scholarship or grant aid from institutional funds. *Loan aid offered:* Direct Subsidized Stafford Loans, Direct Unsubsidized Stafford Loans, Direct PLUS loans, Federal Perkins Loans, College/university loans from institutional funds. Applicants will be notified of awards on a rolling basis beginning 2/15. Federal Work-Study Program available. Institutional employment available.

BOTTOM LINE

Tuition at Knox runs $42,532, add to that $9,330 for room and board and $753 and it is clear that most students will need some assistance. The average first year student's need-based gift aid package is $32,565, while the average first year student's need-based student loan is $5,322, and 60 percent of all undergraduates borrow from some kind of loan program. On average, graduates leave Knox with student loan debt of $32,644.

CAREER INFORMATION FROM PAYSCALE.COM

ROI rating	**86**
Bachelor's and No Higher	
Median starting salary	$38,900
Median mid-career salary	$81,800
At Least Bachelor's	
Median starting salary	$40,900
Median mid-career salary	$81,500
% alumni with high job meaning	38%
% STEM	19%

SELECTIVITY

Admissions Rating	**85**
# of applicants	3,445
% of applicants accepted	64
% of acceptees attending	18
# offered a place on the wait list	123
% accepting a place on wait list	19
% admitted from wait list	13

FRESHMAN PROFILE

Range SAT Critical Reading	580–630
Range SAT Math	590–660
Range SAT Writing	580–630
Range ACT Composite	23–29
Minimum paper TOEFL	550
Minimum internet-based TOEFL	80
% graduated top 10% of class	34
% graduated top 25% of class	67
% graduated top 50% of class	97

DEADLINES

Early action	
Deadline	11/1
Notification	11/30
Regular	
Deadline	1/15
Notification	3/30
Nonfall registration?	No

FINANCIAL FACTS

Financial Aid Rating	**87**
Annual tuition	$42,532
Room and board	$9,330
Required fees	$753
Average need-based scholarship	$29,393
% needy frosh rec. need-based scholarship or grant aid	99
% needy UG rec. need-based scholarship or grant aid	98
% needy frosh rec. non-need-based scholarship or grant aid	10
% needy UG rec. non-need-based scholarship or grant aid	11
% needy frosh rec. need-based self-help aid	88
% needy UG rec. need-based self-help aid	86
% frosh rec. any financial aid	99
% UG rec. any financial aid	98
% UG borrow to pay for school	60
Average cumulative indebtedness	$32,644
% frosh need fully met	23
% ugrads need fully met	26
Average % of frosh need met	91
Average % of ugrad need met	88

L f yette College

118 Markle Hall, Easton, PA 18042 • Admissions: 610-330-5100 • Fax: 610-330-5355

CAMPUS LIFE

Quality of Life Rating	89
Fire Safety Rating	97
Green Rating	91
Type of school	Private
Affiliation	No Affiliation
Environment	Village

STUDENTS

Total undergrad enrollment	2,533
% male/female	51/49
% from out of state	81
% frosh from public high school	61
% frosh live on campus	100
% ugrads live on campus	94
# of fraternities (% ugrad men join)	4 (17)
# of sororities (% ugrad women join)	6 (34)
% African American	5
% Asian	4
% Caucasian	67
% Hispanic	6
% Native American	<1
% Pacific Islander	<1
% Two or more races	2
% Race and/or ethnicity unknown	7
% international	9
# of countries represented	46

ACADEMICS

Academic Rating	91
% students returning for sophomore year	95
% students graduating within 4 years	87
Calendar	Semester
Student/faculty ratio	10:1
Profs interesting rating	88
Profs accessible rating	93

Most classes have 10–19 students.
Most lab/discussion sessions have 10–19 students.

MOST POPULAR MAJORS

Economics; Mechanical Engineering; Biology

#43 COLLEGE THAT PAYS YOU BACK

ABOUT LAFAYETTE COLLEGE

Thinking across disciplines has defined the Lafayette College experience since its founding in 1826. With a total student body of just under 2,500, the focus is exclusively on undergraduates at this top liberal arts college. Lafayette graduates are well-trained in cross-disciplinary thinking and practical application. Here's what that looks like in real terms: computer science, art, biology, and neuroscience students might work together on brain research. A team of engineering, economics, psychology, and English students might take on a consulting project to redesign a new arts and cultural center in New Orleans. Lafayette sees the world through this interdisciplinary lens, and an ability to pursue those intersections in a practical way is a big reason Lafayette students land top research, academic, and employment opportunities. Students love that "even though the school is a small liberal arts college, its strengths in math, science, and engineering give it a very practical feel," and students also "think our greatest strength is our academic diversity." Undergrads are quite pleased to discover that "classes are mostly small and even our lecture classes don't get bigger than roughly seventy-five students." The small student-to-teacher ratio allows students to build a relationship with their professors and, according to a contented undergrad, "creates a spectacular class dynamic and sense of trust."

BANG FOR YOUR BUCK

Lafayette College is part of a very small group of colleges and universities throughout the United States, that provide reduced-loan or no-loan financial aid awards to lower- and middle-income students who gain admission and seek financial assistance. Scholarships are also offered to top applicants (no additional application needed). There are two major merit-based programs: The Marquis Fellowship, worth $40,000 per year and the Marquis Scholarship, worth $24,000 per year. The majority of Marquis winners are selected solely on the merits presented in their application. Both awards come with special mentoring activities with faculty and other campus scholars, and an additional $4,000 scholarship for an off-campus course during the interim period (in winter or summer). These awards are based on superior academic performance and evidence of leadership and major contribution to school or community activities. Said one thankful student, "I was lucky enough to be chosen as a Marquis Scholar, giving me ample opportunity to study abroad."

STUDENT LIFE

Life at Lafayette "is everything you make it. There are as many or as few social opportunities as any one person can handle." With 250 registered student organizations—at a school with only roughly 2,500 students—there really is something for everyone. Greek life plays a role in the social scene, with six sororities and four fraternities on campus. Roughly 38 percent of women join a sorority and 17 percent of men join a fraternity. According to one Mathematics major, "Greek life and [Division I] sports teams dominate the social scene after freshmen year." Lafayette students "work hard . . . but also know how to have a good time" and "tend to go to a lot of events on campus[,] whether it be musicians or comedians." There is "very little to do in Easton itself," so most students stick to campus activities sponsored by the school, various sports teams, or one of the Greek houses.

Lafayette College

FINANCIAL AID: 610-330-5055 • E-MAIL: ADMISSIONS@LAFAYETTE.EDU • WEBSITE: WWW.LAFAYETTE.EDU

CAREER

The average starting salary for a Lafayette graduate is roughly $57,000, according to PayScale.com, which also reports that 47 percent of Lafayette graduates consider their careers to be in keeping with making the world a better place. Popular jobs after graduation include project engineer, civil engineer, and marketing coordinator, with the most popular majors being Mechanical Engineering, Economics, and Civil Engineering. "Career counseling services start freshman year and are readily available to any student who wants to utilize them," says one Government/Law and Spanish double major. The Office of Career Services is "proud to be a national leader in career development," according to the school's website, and is ranked as one of the top twenty higher education career services offices. Students are encouraged to join Gateway, the school's four-year individualized career exploration program, and Lafayette's website reports that 85 percent of each undergraduate class signs up. A Psychology and Government double major praises the school's "strong career services program that provides excellent opportunities and . . . works closely with alumni to provide career exposure opportunities even to first year students."

GENERAL INFO

Activities: Choral groups, concert band, dance, drama/theater, jazz band, literary magazine, music ensembles, musical theater, pep band, radio station, student government, student newspaper, student-run film society, symphony orchestra, yearbook, campus ministries, international student organization.

FINANCIAL AID

Students should submit: FAFSA, CSS/Financial Aid PROFILE, Noncustodial PROFILE. Regular filing deadline is 3/1. The Princeton Review suggests that all financial aid forms be submitted as soon as possible after October 1. *Need-based scholarships/grants offered:* Federal Pell, FSEOG, State scholarships/grants, Private scholarships, College/university scholarship or grant aid from institutional funds. *Loan aid offered:* Direct Subsidized Stafford Loans, Direct Unsubsidized Stafford Loans, Direct PLUS loans, Federal Perkins Loans, College/university loans from institutional funds. Applicants will be notified of awards on or about 4/1. Federal Work-Study Program available. Institutional employment available.

BOTTOM LINE

The tab for tuition, fees, and room and board at Lafayette College comes to about $63,355 per year. Fortunately, Lafayette's strong endowment enables the college to aggressively offset costs for students. Financial aid packages are generous and the average need-based gift package for freshmen is $33,311. Students thoroughly understand and appreciate the value of a Lafayette College education. "It's no secret that the education is expensive, but I feel like I'm really getting my money's worth from Lafayette."

CAREER INFORMATION FROM PAYSCALE.COM

ROI rating	91
Bachelor's and No Higher	
Median starting salary	$58,900
Median mid-career salary	$102,000
At Least Bachelor's	
Median starting salary	$60,800
Median mid-career salary	$103,000
% alumni with high job meaning	46%
% STEM	33%

SELECTIVITY

Admissions Rating	95
# of applicants	7,465
% of applicants accepted	30
% of acceptees attending	30
# offered a place on the wait list	1,532
% accepting a place on wait list	28
% admitted from wait list	1
# of early decision applicants	704
% accepted early decision	49

FRESHMAN PROFILE

Range SAT Critical Reading	580–670
Range SAT Math	620–710
Range SAT Writing	590–690
Range ACT Composite	27–31
Minimum paper TOEFL	550
Minimum internet-based TOEFL	80
Average HS GPA	3.5
% graduated top 10% of class	70
% graduated top 25% of class	93
% graduated top 50% of class	98

DEADLINES

Early decision	
Deadline	11/15
Notification	12/15
Regular	
Deadline	1/15
Notification	4/1
Nonfall registration?	Yes

FINANCIAL FACTS

Financial Aid Rating	95
Annual tuition	$48,450
Room and board	$14,470
Required fees	$435
Average need-based scholarship	$37,495
% needy frosh rec. need-based scholarship or grant aid	95
% needy UG rec. need-based scholarship or grant aid	93
% needy frosh rec. non-need-based scholarship or grant aid	33
% needy UG rec. non-need-based scholarship or grant aid	23
% needy frosh rec. need-based self-help aid	88
% needy UG rec. need-based self-help aid	93
% frosh rec. any financial aid	61
% UG rec. any financial aid	58
% UG borrow to pay for school	55
Average cumulative indebtedness	$31,154
% frosh need fully met	100
% ugrads need fully met	100
Average % of frosh need met	100

Lake Forest College

555 NORTH SHERIDAN ROAD, LAKE FOREST, IL 60045 • ADMISSIONS: 847-735-5000 • FAX: 847-735-6291

CAMPUS LIFE

Quality of Life Rating	90
Fire Safety Rating	82
Green Rating	60*
Type of school	Private
Affiliation	No Affiliation
Environment	Village

STUDENTS

Total undergrad enrollment	1,572
% male/female	44/56
% from out of state	36
% frosh from public high school	70
% frosh live on campus	89
% ugrads live on campus	74
# of fraternities (% ugrad men join)	3 (19)
# of sororities (% ugrad women join)	4 (21)
% African American	7
% Asian	5
% Caucasian	58
% Hispanic	17
% Native American	<1
% Pacific Islander	0
% Two or more races	3
% Race and/or ethnicity unknown	3
% international	8
# of countries represented	76

ACADEMICS

Academic Rating	89
% students returning for sophomore year	85
% students graduating within 4 years	66
% students graduating within 6 years	72
Calendar	Semester
Student/faculty ratio	12:1
Profs interesting rating	90
Profs accessible rating	93

Most classes have 10–19 students.
Most lab/discussion sessions have
  10–19 students.

MOST POPULAR MAJORS
Business/Commerce; Speech
Communication and Rhetoric; Biology

ABOUT THE SCHOOL

When students enroll in Lake Forest College, they join a "close-knit [community] of intellectuals" who are truly passionate about their school. And it's easy to understand why. Indeed, undergrads quickly point out that they benefit from a "liberal arts education that is centered around student and professor relationships." This can partially be ascribed to "small class sizes" which virtually guarantee "individualized attention." Undergrads also highly value "the great opportunities available to [both] . . . study abroad and obtain hands on experience." And they rave about their professors who are "very passionate about what they are teaching" and "have very high expectations for student performance." Perhaps most importantly, professors here are "great at facilitating discussion and making students think deeply about issues." All in all, as one ecstatic senior concludes, "Lake Forest College is about expanding your horizons, your intellectual abilities, and opening your eyes to the world wider than imaginable."

BANG FOR YOUR BUCK

At first glance, Lake Forest might seem a tad pricey on paper. Thankfully, an active and caring financial aid office strives to help families mitigate costs. These efforts don't go unnoticed. After all, a handful of students report that their "financial aid [package] was a big factor" in deciding to attend Lake Forest. As a sociology major explains, "the financial aid office bends over backwards to help students and offers many grants. It was cheaper to attend LFC than the other private schools I was accepted to." In fact, 95 percent of undergraduates receive some form of need-based aid. Some of this money comes from the Lake Forest College Grant which awards gifts ranging from $5,000 to $30,000 each year. The Illinois Monetary Award Program also helps students meet their need with grants up to $4,720. Of course, we'd be remiss if we didn't also point out that the average need-based loan is $5,000.

STUDENT LIFE

Academics usually take priority at Lake Forest. Therefore, it's not surprising that "during the week life revolves around studying and classes." But don't let these workhorses fool you! They find plenty of ways to kick back as well. On the weekends, students head to the Mohr Student Center for "Mohr at Midnight" events, such as Casino Night and Silent Dance Party as well as student-sponsored All Campus Parties (ACPs). School sponsored events such as "'Global Fest' [and] 'Casino Night' are also well attended. And undergrads love to take advantage of the fact that Lake Michigan, and a beautiful beach, are only half a mile from campus." Lastly, "Chicago is [merely] a train ride away so many weekends are spent exploring the city."

Lake Forest College

FINANCIAL AID: 847-735-5103 • E-MAIL: ADMISSIONS@LAKEFOREST.EDU • WEBSITE: WWW.LAKEFOREST.EDU

CAREER

Rest assured that when it comes time to cross the dais on graduation day, Lake Forest students are prepared to meet the future head on! In fact, more than 90 percent of these newly minted alums landed jobs or secured admission to grad school. More specifically, over 90 percent of Lake Forest students who applied to medical school were accepted. And 95 percent of education majors immediately found school gigs. This success is certainly made possible through the guiding hand of a fantastic career services office. For example, undergrads here can participate in the Forester Career Plan, which helps students develop and implement career strategies throughout each academic year. This action plan really helps undergrads to focus their goals and professional aspirations. And, of course, the office hosts plenty of fun (and effective!) events from major and career exploration workshops, industry-focused events, to Speed Networking.

GENERAL INFO

Activities: Choral groups, concert band, dance, drama/theater, jazz band, literary magazine, music ensembles, musical theater, radio station, student government, student newspaper, symphony orchestra, Campus Ministries, International Student Organization, Model UN. **Organizations:** 80 registered organizations, 12 honor societies, 6 religious organizations. 3 fraternities, 4 sororities. **Athletics (Intercollegiate):** *Men:* basketball, cross-country, diving, football, handball, ice hockey, soccer, swimming, tennis. *Women:* basketball, cross-country, diving, handball, ice hockey, soccer, softball, swimming, tennis, volleyball. **On-Campus Highlights:** Donnelley and Lee Library, Mohr Student Center, Sports Center, Center for Chicago Programs, Career Advancement Center.

FINANCIAL AID

Students should submit: FAFSA. Regular filing deadline is 5/1. The Princeton Review suggests that all financial aid forms be submitted as soon as possible after October 1. *Need-based scholarships/grants offered:* Federal Pell, FSEOG, State scholarships/grants, Private scholarships, College/university scholarship or grant aid from institutional funds. *Loan aid offered:* Direct Subsidized Stafford Loans, Direct Unsubsidized Stafford Loans, Direct PLUS loans, Federal Perkins Loans, College/university loans from institutional funds. Applicants will be notified of awards on a rolling basis beginning 3/1. Federal Work-Study Program available. Institutional employment available.

BOTTOM LINE

Students choosing to enroll in Lake Forest College will receive a tuition bill of $41,920. Undergrads face an additional $724 in required fees. They can also expect to spend roughly $1,000 for books and various academic supplies. And, of course, room and board is estimated to cost $9,570. Fortunately, these figures become a little more palatable after learning that the average financial aid package is $35,800.

CAREER INFORMATION FROM PAYSCALE.COM

ROI rating	87
Bachelor's and No Higher	
Median starting salary	$43,100
Median mid-career salary	$85,400
At Least Bachelor's	
Median starting salary	$43,100
Median mid-career salary	$85,400
% alumni with high job meaning	47%
% STEM	15%

SELECTIVITY

Admissions Rating	87
# of applicants	3,373
% of applicants accepted	55
% of acceptees attending	19
# of early decision applicants	58
% accepted early decision	67

FRESHMAN PROFILE

Range SAT Critical Reading	480–610
Range SAT Math	500–600
Range SAT Writing	460–580
Range ACT Composite	22–28
Minimum paper TOEFL	550
Minimum internet-based TOEFL	83
Average HS GPA	3.7
% graduated top 10% of class	39
% graduated top 25% of class	64
% graduated top 50% of class	91

DEADLINES

Early decision	
Deadline	11/15
Early action	
Deadline	11/15
Regular	
Priority	2/15
Nonfall registration?	Yes

FINANCIAL FACTS

Financial Aid Rating	87
Annual tuition	$43,392
Room and board	$9,810
Required fees	$724
Average need-based scholarship	$30,270
% needy frosh rec. need-based scholarship or grant aid	100
% needy UG rec. need-based scholarship or grant aid	100
% needy frosh rec. need-based self-help aid	90
% needy UG rec. need-based self-help aid	88
% frosh rec. any financial aid	94
% UG rec. any financial aid	95
% frosh need fully met	21
% ugrads need fully met	26
Average % of frosh need met	85
Average % of ugrad need met	83

Lawrence University

711 EAST BOLDT WAY, APPLETON, WI 54911-5699 • ADMISSIONS: 920-832-6500 • FAX: 920-832-6782

CAMPUS LIFE

Quality of Life Rating	**92**
Fire Safety Rating	**83**
Green Rating	**70**
Type of school	Private
Affiliation	No Affiliation
Environment	City

STUDENTS

Total undergrad enrollment	1,561
% male/female	45/55
% from out of state	71
% frosh live on campus	99
% ugrads live on campus	96
# of fraternities (% ugrad men join)	4 (20)
# of sororities (% ugrad women join)	4 (14)
% African American	3
% Asian	5
% Caucasian	70
% Hispanic	7
% Native American	<1
% Pacific Islander	<1
% Two or more races	4
% Race and/or ethnicity unknown	1
% international	11
# of countries represented	42

ACADEMICS

Academic Rating	**92**
% students returning for sophomore year	89
% students graduating within 4 years	63
% students graduating within 6 years	76
Calendar	Trimester
Student/faculty ratio	9:1
Profs interesting rating	94
Profs accessible rating	94
Most classes have fewer than 10 students.	

MOST POPULAR MAJORS
Music Performance; Biology; Psychology

ABOUT THE SCHOOL

Lawrence University extolls the values of a liberal education as a means by which to build character, think critically, and create opportunities for choice. It has recently been cited as one of the most rigorous U.S. colleges, the top college in Wisconsin, and a top liberal arts college in the country. In addition to offering a Bachelor of Music degree through the Lawrence Conservatory of Music (known colloquially as "the Con"), Lawrence offers programs in approximately forty fields of study, as well as opportunities for students to build their own majors and participate in interdisciplinary programs. Conservatory students have the option to pursue a five-year double degree that combines a B.Mus with a BA in another field. Additionally, 90 percent of students take part in an independent study program that allows them to build their own courses. Boasting an extremely low student-to-teacher ratio, Lawrence students feel that they are receiving "an amazing education here, and a lot of that is due to the one on one interaction we can get with our professors." In addition to their accessibility, students find professors to be "passionate," "interesting," "willing to take the time to make sense of even the most difficult questions," and occasionally even "hilarious." Between faculty involvement and customizable academic programs, Lawrence provides an "overall academic experience [that] has been extremely enriching, interactive, and flexible."

BANG FOR YOUR BUCK

Lawrence offers gift aid such as merit scholarships and need-based grants offered based on the FAFSA, in addition to "self-help" aid derived from federal loans and student employment. It offers several Academic and Music scholarships of up to $23,000 per year. Recognizing that prospective students come from many different academic environments, the school emphasizes that it takes a "holistic approach" to evaluating students for scholarships, rather than applying a standardized formula to evaluating candidates. Lawrence also offers smaller scholarships via diverse programs such as National Merit and the National Hispanic Recognition Program. Prospective students are also eligible for a More Light! Scholarship program that rewards applicants for excellence in areas such as Community Engagement or Environmental Leadership. Many students report receiving "generous" and "significant" financial aid packages, and others note that "almost everyone here has some financial aid from the school." That casual observation is supported by fact—97 percent of undergraduates at Lawrence are receiving some form of financial aid.

STUDENT LIFE

Lawrence offers a rigorous academic experience, but students note that "people here are just as serious at having a good time as they are at their academic endeavors" and that "life at Lawrence is generally happy, if busy with work." "As a small college, we're a very close-knit community," notes one student, but another reassures that while "the number of students is small but you still get to meet new people all the time." Students report that most of their peers "are involved in some sort of activity, whether it is a sport, a musical group (orchestra, band, choir, etc.), or clubs of some sort." Concerts are a popular way for students to have fun, because in addition to student performances Lawrence "[brings] great performing artists to the conservatory." A free cinema on campus offers themed movie nights, and a wide number of campus groups, teams, and clubs throw parties and other recreational events on the weekends. Though some students report that "social life revolves around campus; there's very little to do off-campus," others are adamant that "Appleton is a great little town with a lot of good restaurants, bars and cafes," as well as "the performing arts center, an art gallery, and at least three cafes with live music."

Lawrence University

FINANCIAL AID: 920-832-6583 • E-MAIL: ADMISSIONS@LAWRENCE.EDU • WEBSITE: WWW.LAWRENCE.EDU

CAREER

Of Lawrence University Alumni visiting PayScale.com, an extremely solid 65 percent report deriving a high level of meaning from their careers. For current students, Lawrence offers a career services department to help students navigate internship programs, graduate education, and employment opportunities. In spite of this, several students listed the career center as being "hard to navigate" or as generally needing improvement, while others praise the department as being "very helpful" and fostering strong alumni relationships. There is far less disagreement on the value of a Lawrence education, however, which is praised for "[preparing] students for any career path through the power of individualized learning" and "preparing students for the future by broadening the way we think."

GENERAL INFO

Activities: Choral groups, concert band, dance, drama/theater, jazz band, literary magazine, music ensembles, musical theater, opera, pep band, radio station, student government, student newspaper, student-run film society, symphony orchestra, International Student Organization, Model UN. **Organizations:** 105 registered organizations, 4 honor societies, 3 religious organizations. 4 fraternities, 4 sororities. **Athletics (Intercollegiate):** *Men:* baseball, basketball, cross-country, diving, fencing, football, ice hockey, soccer, swimming, tennis, track/field (outdoor), track/field (indoor). *Women:* basketball, cross-country, diving, fencing, soccer, softball, swimming, tennis, track/field (outdoor), track/field (indoor), volleyball. **On-Campus Highlights:** Wriston Art Gallery, Music Conservatory, Warch Campus Center, Bjorklunden(451-acre campus in Door County, WI), newly renovated Banta Bowl (football and soccer stadium).

FINANCIAL AID

Students should submit: FAFSA, CSS/Financial Aid PROFILE, Noncustodial PROFILE. Priority filing deadline is 2/1. The Princeton Review suggests that all financial aid forms be submitted as soon as possible after October 1. *Need-based scholarships/grants offered:* Federal Pell, FSEOG, State scholarships/grants, Private scholarships, College/university scholarship or grant aid from institutional funds. *Loan aid offered:* Direct Subsidized Loans, Direct Unsubsidized Loans, Direct PLUS loans, Federal Perkins Loans. Applicants will be notified of awards on a rolling basis beginning 2/1. Federal Work-Study Program available. Institutional employment available.

BOTTOM LINE

Tuition at Lawrence currently runs just over $44,500 with room and board adding close to $9,600. Required fees come to $300, putting the total cost of a year at Lawrence University at somewhere around $54,400. However, the school's many scholarships and financial aid programs, which grant an average of more than $29,000 in need-based scholarship aid to freshmen and $5,400 in loans, can significantly offset these costs.

CAREER INFORMATION FROM PAYSCALE.COM

ROI rating	88
Bachelor's and No Higher	
Median starting salary	$36,400
Median mid-career salary	$89,500
At Least Bachelor's	
Median starting salary	$36,400
Median mid-career salary	$89,500
% alumni with high job meaning	64%

SELECTIVITY

Admissions Rating	89
# of applicants	3,014
% of applicants accepted	68
% of acceptees attending	19
# offered a place on the wait list	249
% accepting a place on wait list	28
% admitted from wait list	10
# of early decision applicants	12
% accepted early decision	92

FRESHMAN PROFILE

Range SAT Critical Reading	560–690
Range SAT Math	610–730
Range SAT Writing	580–690
Range ACT Composite	26–32
Minimum paper TOEFL	577
Minimum internet-based TOEFL	90
Average HS GPA	3.6
% graduated top 10% of class	42
% graduated top 25% of class	77
% graduated top 50% of class	97

DEADLINES

Early action I	
Deadline	11/1
Notification	12/15
Early action II	
Deadline	12/1
Notification	1/25
Regular	
Deadline	1/15
Notification	4/1
Nonfall registration?	Yes

FINANCIAL FACTS

Financial Aid Rating	89
Annual tuition	$44,544
Room and board	$9,654
Required fees	$300
Average need-based scholarship	$29,622
% needy UG rec. non-need-based scholarship or grant aid	0
% needy frosh rec. need-based self-help aid	80
% needy UG rec. need-based self-help aid	80
% frosh rec. any financial aid	97
% UG rec. any financial aid	97
% UG borrow to pay for school	62
Average cumulative indebtedness	$33,343
% frosh need fully met	46
% ugrads need fully met	45
Average % of frosh need met	97

Lehigh University

27 MEMORIAL DRIVE WEST, BETHLEHEM, PA 18015 • ADMISSIONS: 610-758-3100 • FAX: 610-758-4361

CAMPUS LIFE

Quality of Life Rating	83
Fire Safety Rating	90
Green Rating	89
Type of school	Private
Affiliation	No Affiliation
Environment	City

STUDENTS

Total undergrad enrollment	5,075
% male/female	56/44
% from out of state	73
% frosh live on campus	99
% ugrads live on campus	67
# of fraternities (% ugrad men join)	20 (40)
# of sororities (% ugrad women join)	11 (45)
% African American	4
% Asian	9
% Caucasian	66
% Hispanic	9
% Native American	<1
% Pacific Islander	<1
% Two or more races	3
% Race and/or ethnicity unknown	3
% international	8
# of countries represented	60

ACADEMICS

Academic Rating	86
% students returning for sophomore year	95
% students graduating within 4 years	74
% students graduating within 6 years	88
Calendar	Semester
Student/faculty ratio	10:1
Profs interesting rating	75
Profs accessible rating	79

Most classes have 10–19 students.
Most lab/discussion sessions have 10–19 students.

MOST POPULAR MAJORS

Mechanical Engineering; Finance; Chemical Engineering

ABOUT THE SCHOOL

Located in Bethlehem, Pennsylvania, Lehigh University is "a magical place, not unlike Hogwarts." Students say the "extremely beautiful" campus is "the perfect size" with "a friendly, community oriented atmosphere." The "very helpful" professors "have been well-travelled in their given field" and are "good at engaging students even when it's a 200 student lecture." "They try to apply real life scenarios to allow further understanding of the material," one student says. "Lehigh has a rich history of tradition and passionate, engaging students," says another. "A nice research institute/university that lives up to its academic reputation" and strong liberal arts offerings, Lehigh is especially notable for its "one-of-a-kind engineering" program. Many notable engineers have graduated from Lehigh including Jesse Wilford Reno, who invented the first working escalator, and James Packard of Packard automobiles. In addition to the P.C. Rossin College of Engineering and Applied Science, Lehigh undergrads can enroll in the College of Arts and Sciences or the College of Business and Economics.

BANG FOR YOUR BUCK

Lehigh is fully committed to offering need-based financial aid to accepted applicants. In addition to federal Pell grants and Pennsylvania state grants, Lehigh offers endowed and sponsored grants to students who could not otherwise afford to attend. The latter can be swapped out with a scholarship. The school has many merit awards and scholarships. Examples of academic merit awards are the Academic Merit Awards that cover half of tuition and the Alice P. Gast STEM Scholarships for women pursuing STEM careers. Lehigh also offers arts merit scholarships for students in Choral Arts, Marching Band, Instrumental Music, and Theatre.

STUDENT LIFE

Lehigh students are "very well-rounded, highly intelligent, and motivated people" who know how to "work hard, and play hard." Many students are "preppy and upper class" and "a big part of our campus is Greek life." Students report a "gap between Greeks and non-Greeks" that divides the student body. Students who eschew Greek life often join one of "the multitude[s] of student clubs and orgs." "There is a club for everyone" and students "have a ton of school spirit and value athletics greatly." There are about 4,900 undergraduates between the three colleges. "We're all smart enough to get in here, but we know school isn't the only thing in the world," a Mechanical Engineering major says.

CAREER

Some of the biggest reasons students apply to Lehigh are "the opportunities for advanced learning such as research on campus as well as externship, internship, and co-op programs." Lehigh has many programs that help students get real-world experience before graduation. "There are students who get internships at the UN" and "extensive international programs and opportunities." One student tells us that Career Services helps some majors more than others and needs to offer "more opportunities for social sciences." The university reports that 95 percent of undergraduates get at least one career-

Lehigh University

FINANCIAL AID: 610-758-3181 • E-MAIL: ADMISSIONS@LEHIGH.EDU • WEBSITE: WWW.LEHIGH.EDU

related experience, such as an internship, before graduation. They also report that a full 97 percent of students from the class of 2013 are employed or in graduate school. PayScale.com reports an impressive average starting salary of $60,400 for Lehigh graduates.

GENERAL INFO

Activities: Choral groups, concert band, dance, drama/theater, jazz band, literary magazine, marching band, music ensembles, musical theater, pep band, radio station, student government, student newspaper, student-run film society, symphony orchestra, yearbook, Campus Ministries, International Student Organization, Model UN. **Organizations:** 18 honor societies, 12 religious organizations. 20 fraternities, 11 sororities. **Athletics (Intercollegiate, Division I):** *Men:* baseball, basketball, cross-country, diving, football, golf, lacrosse, soccer, swimming, tennis, track/field (outdoor), track/field (indoor), wrestling. *Women:* basketball, crew/rowing, cross-country, diving, field hockey, golf, lacrosse, soccer, softball, swimming, tennis, track/field (outdoor), track/field (indoor), volleyball. **On-Campus Highlights:** Zoellner Arts Center LU Art Galleries, Campus Square, Taylor Gymnasium, Ulrich Student Center, Goodman Campus.

FINANCIAL AID

Students should submit: FAFSA, CSS/Financial Aid PROFILE, Noncustodial PROFILE. Deadlines vary with admission options. The Princeton Review suggests that all financial aid forms be submitted as soon as possible after October 1. *Need-based scholarships/grants offered:* Federal Pell, FSEOG, State scholarships/grants, College/university scholarship or grant aid from institutional funds. *Loan aid offered:* Direct Subsidized Stafford Loans, Direct Unsubsidized Stafford Loans, Direct PLUS loans, College/university loans from institutional funds. Applicants will be notified of awards at time of admission. Federal Work-Study Program available. Institutional employment available.

BOTTOM LINE

For the 2015–16 academic year, Lehigh tuition stands at $45,860. Room and board comes to $12,280. Adding those up with fees, books, and supplies gives a grand total of $59,510. Students accepted to the P.C. Rossin College of Engineering and Applied Science must pay an additional $480 fee. Lehigh offers a payment plan that allows students to pay their bill in four monthly installments.

CAREER INFORMATION FROM PAYSCALE.COM

ROI rating	**90**
Bachelor's and No Higher	
Median starting salary	$60,400
Median mid-career salary	$108,000
At Least Bachelor's	
Median starting salary	$61,400
Median mid-career salary	$111,000
% alumni with high job meaning	43%
% STEM	37%

SELECTIVITY

Admissions Rating	**94**
# of applicants	12,843
% of applicants accepted	30
% of acceptees attending	32
# offered a place on the wait list	4,232
% accepting a place on wait list	44
% admitted from wait list	0
# of early decision applicants	999
% accepted early decision	58

FRESHMAN PROFILE

Range SAT Critical Reading	590–680
Range SAT Math	640–740
Range ACT Composite	29–32
Minimum paper TOEFL	570
Minimum internet-based TOEFL	90
% graduated top 10% of class	60
% graduated top 25% of class	89
% graduated top 50% of class	98

DEADLINES

Early decision	
Deadline	11/15
Notification	12/15
Regular	
Deadline	1/1
Notification	4/1
Nonfall registration?	Yes

FINANCIAL FACTS

Financial Aid Rating	**91**
Annual tuition	$47,920
Room and board	$12,690
Required fees	$400
Average need-based scholarship	$34,878
% needy frosh rec. need-based scholarship or grant aid	96
% needy UG rec. need-based scholarship or grant aid	98
% needy frosh rec. non-need-based scholarship or grant aid	16
% needy UG rec. non-need-based scholarship or grant aid	15
% needy frosh rec. need-based self-help aid	94
% needy UG rec. need-based self-help aid	95
% frosh rec. any financial aid	57
% UG rec. any financial aid	62
% UG borrow to pay for school	54
Average cumulative indebtedness	$34,940
% frosh need fully met	51
% ugrads need fully met	63
Average % of frosh need met	95
Average % of ugrad need met	97

Lewis & Clark College

0615 SOUTHWEST PALATINE HILL ROAD, PORTLAND, OR 97219-7899 • ADMISSIONS: 503-768-7040 • FAX: 503-768-7055

CAMPUS LIFE

Quality of Life Rating	**92**
Fire Safety Rating	**87**
Green Rating	**99**
Type of school	Private
Affiliation	No Affiliation
Environment	City

STUDENTS

Total undergrad enrollment	2,209
% male/female	39/61
% from out of state	89
% frosh from public high school	75
% frosh live on campus	98
% ugrads live on campus	70
% African American	2
% Asian	6
% Caucasian	66
% Hispanic	10
% Native American	1
% Pacific Islander	<1
% Two or more races	4
% Race and/or ethnicity unknown	6
% international	5
# of countries represented	80

ACADEMICS

Academic Rating	**91**
% students returning for sophomore year	83
% students graduating within 4 years	66
% students graduating within 6 years	72
Calendar	Semester
Student/faculty ratio	12:1
Profs interesting rating	92
Profs accessible rating	92
Most classes have 10–19 students.	
Most lab/discussion sessions have 20–29 students.	

MOST POPULAR MAJORS
Psychology; Biology; International Relations and Affairs

ABOUT THE SCHOOL

Portland, Oregon's, Lewis & Clark is a "Northwest paradise filled with flannel, beards, hipsters, and hippies, all "liberally" sprinkled with granola." As one Biochemistry major puts it, "If you want it, [Lewis & Clark] has it: academic rigor, good athletics, study abroad opportunities, individual attention from your professors, research opportunities, and so on." Students stress the school's "global and environmental awareness," as well as taking advantage of "all that Portland has to offer." Says one French Studies major, "Lewis & Clark College is a school completely dedicated to the liberal arts education, and through offering a wide range of classes and [subjects] from which to choose, it encourages discovery, both personally and academically." The professors "care about the performance of their students and encourage students to come and meet with them regularly to talk about class work but also about outside interests, research opportunities and so on." Students underscore that Lewis & Clark "has a rigorous academic program. People here care about school." The school's small size—there are roughly 2,200 students—leads to a 12:1 student to faculty ratio and "Small class sizes allow one-on-one contact with the professors, which, in turn, allows students to ask questions, attend office hours, and succeed in class."

BANG FOR YOUR BUCK

While most students praise the "good" financial aid and cite the "excellent financial aid offers" as reasons for choosing Lewis & Clark, some say the Financial Aid office is "terrible." Many students note they were offered merit scholarships, which influenced their decisions to attend. Fifty-five percent of undergraduates have borrowed from some sort of loan program. The average freshman receives $28,655 in need-based gift aid (the average undergraduate receives $29,334) and the average amount a Lewis & Clark student receives in need-based loan is $5,047. Lewis & Clark's highest merit-based award is the Barbara Hirschi Neely Scholarship, which is awarded to first-year students of "exceptional academic achievement and distinctive personal accomplishment." The Herbert Templeton National Merit Scholarship is a "merit-based scholarship...awarded to entering first-year students who have been selected as National Merit Scholars and who have designated Lewis & Clark as their first choice college." Oregon Opportunity Grants are available to qualified Oregon residents and the Helen Sanders Scholarship is awarded to Native American students or those who demonstrate an interest in Native American issues.

STUDENT LIFE

Students "tend to be artsy, free spirits who are globally minded" however "don't mistake their funky hair and clothes for not being serious and competitive about academics." As one Sociology major puts it, "At [Lewis & Clark,] students are not afraid to show their multiple interests and be accepted for who they are, in their various ways. Everyone is unique and quirky." Students seem to agree that it's hard to pin down the "typical" Lewis & Clark student; as one Biology major puts it, "The only thing that I can say that transcends through all students is the commitment that we all have to figuring out who we are, what gets us excited, and what we want to do with our lives." There are always things happening on the campus "that looks like a park" and students take advantage of the "outdoor activities in the area around the college," as well as Portland itself. According to one International Affairs major, "People generally at this stage are thinking about the weekend and thesis in equal measure."

CAREER

"Many students have internships with companies or non-profits in Portland" and there are "lots of opportunities for research and internships" at Lewis & Clark. "The resources available for career and community engagement are great," says one Sociology major and "Students are able to develop very personal relationships with professors, which can be key in pursuing careers following school," adds a Psychology major. At the

Lewis & Clark College

FINANCIAL AID: 503-768-7090 • E-MAIL: ADMISSIONS@LCLARK.EDU • WEBSITE: WWW.LCLARK.EDU

school's Career Development Center, students are encouraged to consult a handout (also available online) known as the Road Map, which helps them plan out their college and post-college careers. Lewis & Clark encourages students to engage with the surrounding Portland community and students can drop by the Office of Student and Leadership Service to learn more. The school's Alumni Career Corps helps put current Lewis & Clark students in touch with past graduates who could be potential employers or internship leaders. The Career Development Center also helps students with questions related to graduate school applications— Lewis & Clark itself boasts a well-known law school.

GENERAL INFO

Activities: Choral groups, concert band, dance, drama/theater, jazz band, literary magazine, music ensembles, musical theater, radio station, student government, student newspaper, symphony orchestra, television station, yearbook, Campus Ministries, International Student Organization, Model UN. **Organizations:** 70 registered organizations, 5 honor societies, 9 religious organizations. **Athletics (Intercollegiate):** *Men:* baseball, basketball, crew/rowing, cross-country, football, golf, swimming, tennis, track/field (outdoor). *Women:* basketball, crew/rowing, cross-country, golf, soccer, softball, swimming, tennis, track/field (outdoor), volleyball. **On-Campus Highlights:** Gallery of Contemporary Art, New residence halls/Maggie's Cafe, Library, Templeton Student Center, Pamplin Sports Center, Howard Hall, newest academic building.

FINANCIAL AID

Students should submit: FAFSA, CSS/Financial Aid PROFILE. Priority filing deadline is 2/15. The Princeton Review suggests that all financial aid forms be submitted as soon as possible after October 1. *Need-based scholarships/grants offered:* Federal Pell, FSEOG, State scholarships/grants, Private scholarships, College/university scholarship or grant aid from institutional funds. *Loan aid offered:* Direct Subsidized Stafford Loans, Direct Unsubsidized Stafford Loans, Direct PLUS loans, Federal Perkins Loans. Applicants will be notified of awards on a rolling basis beginning 3/15. Federal Work-Study Program available. Institutional employment available.

BOTTOM LINE

Tuition is roughly $46,534, with an additional $360 in fees and approximately $1,050 in books and supplies. Room and board is roughly $11,540 and approximately 70 percent of Lewis & Clark undergraduates live on campus. Tuition and fees do not vary by year. The average Lewis & Clark undergraduate graduates with $29,836 in loan debt. Financial aid is available to international students.

CAREER INFORMATION FROM PAYSCALE.COM

ROI rating	86
Bachelor's and No Higher	
Median starting salary	$41,200
Median mid-career salary	$79,000
At Least Bachelor's	
Median starting salary	$44,300
Median mid-career salary	$79,900
% alumni with high job meaning	74%
% STEM	16%

SELECTIVITY

Admissions Rating	90
# of applicants	7,368
% of applicants accepted	63
% of acceptees attending	14
# offered a place on the wait list	775
% accepting a place on wait list	29
% admitted from wait list	0
# of early decision applicants	65
% accepted early decision	86

FRESHMAN PROFILE

Range SAT Critical Reading	600–720
Range SAT Math	590–670
Range SAT Writing	580–630
Range ACT Composite	27–31
Minimum paper TOEFL	575
Minimum internet-based TOEFL	91
Average HS GPA	3.9
% graduated top 10% of class	48
% graduated top 25% of class	82
% graduated top 50% of class	97

DEADLINES

Early decision	
Deadline	11/1
Notification	12/15
Early action	
Deadline	11/1
Notification	12/31
Regular	
Priority	1/15
Deadline	3/1
Notification	4/1
Nonfall registration?	Yes

FINANCIAL FACTS

Financial Aid Rating	85
Annual tuition	$46,534
Room and board	$11,540
Required fees	$360
Average need-based scholarship	$29,836
% needy frosh rec. need-based scholarship or grant aid	98
% needy UG rec. need-based scholarship or grant aid	99
% needy frosh rec. non-need-based scholarship or grant aid	10
% needy UG rec. non-need-based scholarship or grant aid	6
% needy frosh rec. need-based self-help aid	89
% needy UG rec. need-based self-help aid	93
% frosh rec. any financial aid	94
% UG rec. any financial aid	91
% UG borrow to pay for school	57

Loyola Marymount University

ONE LMU DRIVE, SUITE 100, LOS ANGELES, CA 90045-8350 • ADMISSIONS: 310-338-2750 • FAX: 310-338-2797

CAMPUS LIFE

Quality of Life Rating	**95**
Fire Safety Rating	**89**
Green Rating	**93**
Type of school	Private
Affiliation	Roman Catholic
Environment	Metropolis

STUDENTS

Total undergrad enrollment	6,259
% male/female	44/56
% from out of state	24
% frosh from public high school	48
% frosh live on campus	94
% ugrads live on campus	51
# of fraternities (% ugrad men join)	9 (22)
# of sororities (% ugrad women join)	12 (37)
% African American	6
% Asian	11
% Caucasian	45
% Hispanic	21
% Native American	<1
% Pacific Islander	<1
% Two or more races	8
% Race and/or ethnicity unknown	<1
% international	9
# of countries represented	74

ACADEMICS

Academic Rating	**83**
% students returning for sophomore year	91
% students graduating within 4 years	70
% students graduating within 6 years	79
Calendar	Semester
Student/faculty ratio	11:1
Profs interesting rating	82
Profs accessible rating	93
Most classes have 10–19 students.	
Most lab/discussion sessions have 10–19 students.	

MOST POPULAR MAJORS

Speech Communication and Rhetoric;
Psychology; English

ABOUT THE SCHOOL

Undergrads at Loyola Marymount in Los Angeles, California proudly report that their university is "the embodiment of its mission statement: the encouragement of learning, the education of the whole person, and the service of faith and the promotion of justice." This private Catholic university in the Jesuit and Marymount traditions also places a "big importance on philanthropy and interdisciplinary work." And while the academics are "rigorous," students benefit from "small class sizes" which allow them to truly "get to know their professors." An engineering undergrad adds, "Professors know your name and remember who you are. They also take a step further and talk with other professors . . . to make sure you are doing well academically." Instructors at LMU also tend to be "passionate." In turn, that "makes it much more interesting to learn from them." And, perhaps most importantly, professors "actually care that a student is prepared for . . . post-grad life. They focus on your goals and needs and . . . they work toward your strengths."

BANG FOR YOUR BUCK

Loyola Marymount strives to ensure that the education it offers is affordable. To that end, 86 percent of all undergrads receive some type of financial assistance. For example, Loyola Marymount provides LMU Grants to eligible individuals who demonstrate both academic achievement and financial need. Looking beyond grants, students may also qualify for a number of scholarships. One of the most prestigious is the Trustee Scholarship, which covers full tuition, room and board. Additionally, top applicants may be named Presidential Scholars and receive $25,000 per year for four years. There's also the Jesuit Community Scholarships, which provides $10,000 annually. This scholarship is given to graduates of Catholic secondary schools who have made significant contributions to their community through service.

STUDENT LIFE

There's no denying it— life at Loyola Marymount can be busy. And these students wouldn't have it any other way. As a finance major reveals, "The motto of LMU students is if you're not doing too much, you're not doing enough." Fortunately, there's plenty of which to take advantage. Aside from hitting the books, "there are many service organizations to join." Additionally, "Greek life is very popular at LMU, so there are always Greek events happening on campus." Of course, the "on-campus programming is spectacular," as well. As a psych major explains, "There are several opportunities for fun events on campus such as carnivals, craft nights, karaoke, etc." Undergrads also love to explore the surrounding area. An electrical engineering student concludes, "People tend to go to Santa Monica, Venice Beach, or Manhattan Beach to spend time in places that are very unique to Los Angeles."

Loyola Marymount University

FINANCIAL AID: 310-338-2753 • E-MAIL: ADMISSIONS@LMU.EDU • WEBSITE: WWW.LMU.EDU

CAREER

Loyola Marymount graduates do quite well for themselves. The average starting salary for recent alums is $50,700. Even better, the median mid-career salary is $96,000 (both statistics according to PayScale.com). LMU's Career and Professional Development office does a stellar job of attracting big name companies for on-campus recruiting and career events, such as Amazon, Deloitte, Honda, NBCUniversal, and Yelp. Known as the "University of Silicon Beach," LMU is in close proximity to Playa Vista, home to over 500 technology start-up companies, including global giants Belkin, Facebook, Google, Snapchat, and YouTube.

GENERAL INFO

Activities: Choral groups, dance, drama/theater, literary magazine, music ensembles, musical theater, pep band, radio station, student government, student newspaper, student-run film society, television station, yearbook. **Organizations:** 173 registered organizations, 22 honor societies, 10 religious organizations. 9 fraternities, 12 sororities. **Athletics (Intercollegiate):** *Men:* baseball, basketball, cheerleading, crew/rowing, cross-country, golf, soccer, tennis, track, water polo. *Women:* basketball, cheerleading, crew/rowing, cross-country, soccer, softball, swimming, tennis, track, volleyball, water polo. **On-Campus Highlights:** William H. Hannon Library, Malone Student Center, Burns Recreation Center, Lion's Den and Living Room, Life Sciences Building.

FINANCIAL AID

Students should submit: FAFSA. Priority filing deadline is 2/1. The Princeton Review suggests that all financial aid forms be submitted as soon as possible after October 1. *Need-based scholarships/grants offered:* Federal Pell, FSEOG, State scholarships/grants, Private scholarships, College/university scholarship or grant aid from institutional funds. *Loan aid offered:* Direct Subsidized Stafford Loans, Direct Unsubsidized Stafford Loans, Direct PLUS loans, Federal Perkins Loans, College/university loans from institutional funds. Applicants will be notified of awards in mid-December, late January, and late-March beginning 12/20. Federal Work-Study Program available. Institutional employment available.

THE BOTTOM LINE

LMU students and their families will face a hefty tuition bill of $43,526 plus $704 in required fees. Moreover, students choosing to live on-campus can look forward to paying $14,485 for room and board. Individuals opting to live off-campus can likely expect to pay an additional $1,107 for parking and transportation. Finally, all undergrads will need to set aside an additional $1,791 for books and supplies.

CAREER INFORMATION FROM PAYSCALE.COM

ROI rating	86
Bachelor's and No Higher	
Median starting salary	$50,700
Median mid-career salary	$96,000
At Least Bachelor's	
Median starting salary	$51,300
Median mid-career salary	$99,600
% alumni with high job meaning	44%
% STEM	10%

SELECTIVITY

Admissions Rating	89
# of applicants	13,288
% of applicants accepted	51
% of acceptees attending	20
# offered a place on the wait list	2,037
% accepting a place on wait list	25
% admitted from wait list	35

FRESHMAN PROFILE

Range SAT Critical Reading	550–640
Range SAT Math	560–660
Range SAT Writing	550–650
Range ACT Composite	25–30
Minimum paper TOEFL	550
Minimum internet-based TOEFL	80
Average HS GPA	3.8
% graduated top 10% of class	44
% graduated top 25% of class	76
% graduated top 50% of class	93

DEADLINES

Early decision	
Deadline	11/1
Notification	12/1
Early action	
Deadline	11/1
Notification	12/20
Regular	
Deadline	1/15
Nonfall registration?	Yes

FINANCIAL FACTS

Financial Aid Rating	83
Annual tuition	$43,526
Room and board	$14,485
Required fees	$704
Average need-based scholarship	$19,970
% needy frosh rec. need-based scholarship or grant aid	97
% needy UG rec. need-based scholarship or grant aid	95
% needy frosh rec. non-need-based scholarship or grant aid	16
% needy UG rec. non-need-based scholarship or grant aid	12
% needy frosh rec. need-based self-help aid	76
% needy UG rec. need-based self-help aid	80
% frosh rec. any financial aid	92
% UG rec. any financial aid	87
% UG borrow to pay for school	56
Average cumulative indebtedness	$30,487
% frosh need fully met	23
% ugrads need fully met	19
Average % of frosh need met	68
Average % of ugrad need met	66

Loyola University Maryland

4501 North Charles Street, Baltimore, MD 21210 • Admissions: 410-617-5012 • Fax: 410-617-2176

CAMPUS LIFE

Quality of Life Rating	92
Fire Safety Rating	94
Green Rating	76
Type of school	Private
Affiliation	Roman Catholic
Environment	Village

STUDENTS

Total undergrad enrollment	4,068
% male/female	42/58
% from out of state	82
% frosh from public high school	51
% frosh live on campus	98
% ugrads live on campus	81
% African American	6
% Asian	4
% Caucasian	78
% Hispanic	9
% Native American	<1
% Pacific Islander	<1
% Two or more races	2
% Race and/or ethnicity unknown	<1
% international	<1
# of countries represented	37

ACADEMICS

Academic Rating	86
% students returning for sophomore year	87
% students graduating within 4 years	76
% students graduating within 6 years	81
Calendar	Semester
Student/faculty ratio	11:1
Profs interesting rating	91
Profs accessible rating	90

Most classes have 20–29 students.
Most lab/discussion sessions have
10–19 students.

MOST POPULAR MAJORS
Business Administration and Management;
Psychology; Communication

ABOUT THE SCHOOL

A Jesuit institution that emphasizes "service and social justice," Loyola University immediately conjures a "supportive" atmosphere. Indeed, a "sense of community" permeates the campus and students happily report studying within a "nurturing" environment. Undergrads here truly feel that Loyola "cares deeply about each individual student's success." They also appreciate that the university really "makes an effort to use [the city of] Baltimore as an extension of the classroom." And they value the "Core curriculum, which requires that [students] explore a variety of disciplines in the humanities." Certainly, a lot of their academic happiness derives from "fantastic" professors. For the most part, instructors are "very enthusiastic and passionate about what they teach." Perhaps even more important, "They are very accessible and use a lot of different learning techniques to cater to everyone's different learning styles." Overall, "Loyola is an excellent institution [that] strongly encourages academic growth inside and outside the classroom."

BANG FOR YOUR BUCK

Loyola University truly believes that a high quality education should be available to anyone, no matter their financial circumstances. And the financial aid office works tirelessly to help students in whatever manner they can. To that end, the university offers undergrads a variety of scholarships and grants. For example, the Presidential Scholarship, which is awarded on the basis of academic merit, provides students with between $16,000 and $26,000 in funds. This scholarship is good for four years, provided the recipient maintains a certain GPA. Additionally, the Marion Burk Knott Scholarship, also awarded on the basis of academic merit, covers all four years of tuition for Catholic students residing in the Archdiocese of Baltimore. And, fortunately, students with exceptional financial need typically qualify for Loyola Grants. These grants can range anywhere from $200 to $38,350, depending on need and availability of funds.

SCHOOL LIFE

Life at Loyola moves at a fairly hectic pace. Indeed, there are always events to attend, "rang[ing] from educational and thought-provoking to fun and exciting." Not surprisingly, community service is rather popular here. Athletic contests are also well attended. As one psychology major shares, "Students have excellent school spirit and we're always in green cheering on the Greyhounds, either in lacrosse, basketball, swimming or soccer." We're also told that "there is not a party scene on campus because of the strict rules regarding alcohol, which many students uphold." However, a handful of undergrads counter that plenty of students "go to bars on the weekend." Lastly, students also love to take advantage of Baltimore, especially the inner harbor which is "close by and great for weekend dinners or shopping."

CAREER

Loyola grads tend to do pretty well for themselves. According to PayScale.com, the average starting salary for these alums is $52,000. Not too shabby right? Of course, this success likely wouldn't be achieved without some assistance from the fabulous Career Center. For starters, the career office manages HireLOYOLA, an online portal that helps students coordinate job postings, on-campus interviews and resume development. Further, through the Alumni Career Network (ACN), current students can connect with alumni to network and receive professional guidance. The Career Center also runs a fantastic "Interviewing for Success" workshop. Undergrads must attend this three-part series before they sit for actual on-campus interviews. And,

Loyola University Maryland

FINANCIAL AID: 410-617-2576 • WEBSITE: WWW.LOYOLA.EDU

as if all that weren't enough, Loyola also hosts numerous career fairs such as the Maryland Career Consortium. With all this guidance, Loyola students can certainly face the job market with confidence!

GENERAL INFO

Activities: Choral groups, dance, drama/theater, literary magazine, music ensembles, musical theater, radio station, student government, student newspaper, television station, yearbook, Campus Ministries, International Student Organization. **Organizations:** 185 registered organizations, 25 honor societies, 4 religious organizations. **Athletics (Intercollegiate).** *Men:* basketball, crew/rowing, cross-country, diving, golf, lacrosse, soccer, swimming, tennis. *Women:* basketball, crew/rowing, cross-country, diving, lacrosse, soccer, swimming, tennis, track/field (outdoor), track/field (indoor), volleyball. **On-Campus Highlights:** Loyola/Notre Dame Library, The Loyola University Art Gallery, Fitness and Aquatic Center, Boulder Garden Cafe, Primo's: The New Marketplace.

FINANCIAL AID

Students should submit: FAFSA, CSS/Financial Aid PROFILE, Noncustodial PROFILE. Regular filing deadline is 2/15. The Princeton Review suggests that all financial aid forms be submitted as soon as possible after October 1. *Need-based scholarships/grants offered:* Federal Pell, FSEOG, State scholarships/grants, Private scholarships, College/university scholarship or grant aid from institutional funds. *Loan aid offered:* Direct Subsidized Stafford Loans, Direct Unsubsidized Stafford Loans, Direct PLUS loans, Federal Perkins Loans, College/university loans from institutional funds. Applicants will be notified of awards on or about 3/15. Federal Work-Study Program available. Institutional employment available.

BOTTOM LINE

Loyola University charges undergraduates $43,800 for tuition. Beyond that bill, students can expect an additional $1,400 in fees. Undergrads choosing to live on-campus will have to pay $13,310 for room and board. Off-campus living expenses are often cheaper; students can anticipate spending roughly $7,300. Finally, those students residing on-campus will likely need another $1,200 to cover transportation and personal expenses. Those living off-campus will require an additional $1,430.

CAREER INFORMATION FROM PAYSCALE.COM

ROI rating	**87**
Bachelor's and No Higher	
Median starting salary	$51,100
Median mid-career salary	$102,000
At Least Bachelor's	
Median starting salary	$51,100
Median mid-career salary	$104,000
% alumni with high job meaning	48%
% STEM	12%

SELECTIVITY

Admissions Rating	**87**
# of applicants	13,867
% of applicants accepted	61
% of acceptees attending	12
# offered a place on the wait list	2,347
% accepting a place on wait list	18
% admitted from wait list	35

FRESHMAN PROFILE

Range SAT Critical Reading	550–650
Range SAT Math	560–640
Range ACT Composite	25–29
Minimum paper TOEFL	550
Minimum internet-based TOEFL	79
Average HS GPA	3.4
% graduated top 10% of class	26
% graduated top 25% of class	62
% graduated top 50% of class	91

DEADLINES

Early action	
Deadline	11/1
Notification	1/15
Regular	
Priority	11/1
Deadline	1/15
Notification	3/15
Nonfall registration?	Yes

FINANCIAL FACTS

Financial Aid Rating	**94**
Annual tuition	$43,800
Room and board	$14,200
Required fees	$1,400
Average need-based scholarship	$22,245
% needy frosh rec. need-based scholarship or grant aid	89
% needy UG rec. need-based scholarship or grant aid	89
% needy frosh rec. non-need-based scholarship or grant aid	33
% needy UG rec. non-need-based scholarship or grant aid	29
% needy frosh rec. need-based self-help aid	96
% needy UG rec. need-based self-help aid	95
% frosh rec. any financial aid	75
% UG rec. any financial aid	70
% UG borrow to pay for school	61
Average cumulative indebtedness	$34,375
% frosh need fully met	92
% ugrads need fully met	90
Average % of frosh need met	93
Average % of ugrad need met	92

Macalester College

1600 Grand Avenue, St. Paul, MN 55105 • Admissions: 651-696-6357 • Fax: 651-696-6724

CAMPUS LIFE

Quality of Life Rating	94
Fire Safety Rating	98
Green Rating	94
Type of school	Private
Affiliation	No Affiliation
Environment	Metropolis

STUDENTS

Total undergrad enrollment	2,172
% male/female	40/60
% from out of state	82
% frosh from public high school	63
% frosh live on campus	100
% ugrads live on campus	61
% African American	2
% Asian	7
% Caucasian	65
% Hispanic	6
% Native American	<1
% Pacific Islander	<1
% Two or more races	5
% Race and/or ethnicity unknown	<1
% international	15
# of countries represented	91

ACADEMICS

Academic Rating	94
% students returning for sophomore year	95
% students graduating within 4 years	86
% students graduating within 6 years	90
Calendar	Semester
Student/faculty ratio	10:1
Profs interesting rating	96
Profs accessible rating	96
Most classes have 10–19 students.	
Most lab/discussion sessions have 10–19 students.	

MOST POPULAR MAJORS

Biology; Economics; Political Science and Government

ABOUT THE SCHOOL

Macalester College has been preparing its students for world citizenship and providing a rigorous, integrated international education for over six decades. (Kofi Annan is an alumnus.) With a total campus size of just over 2,000 undergraduates, students benefit from a curriculum designed to include international perspectives, a multitude of semester-long study abroad programs, faculty with worldwide experience, and a community engaged in issues that matter. With more than 90 countries represented on campus, Macalester has one of the highest percentages of international-student enrollment of any U.S. college. Students affirm that the school's "commitment to internationalism is unmatched by any other institution." As a result, Macalester immerses students in a microcosm of the global world from the day each moves into a dorm room, walks into the first classroom, and begins to make friends over global cuisine in Café Mac. One student notes that the student body is "diverse and interesting; some of my best friends are from countries I had hardly heard of before I got here." A fifth of students on campus are people of color, further contributing to diverse perspectives in the classroom.

Macalester's location in a major metropolitan city offers students a wealth of research and internship opportunities in business, finance, medicine, science, government, law, the arts, and more. The internship program and career-development center help students gain experience and connections that frequently lead to employment opportunities in the United States and around the world. Students say that "one of Macalester's greatest strengths is its commitment to providing students with opportunities to apply their learning in real settings. Most students do an internship and/or participate in some kind of civic engagement during their time here, and the school is great about supporting that." In addition to teaching, Macalester's science and math faculty are very active in research. The college ranks number one among U.S. liberal arts colleges for active National Science Foundation (NSF) grants relative to faculty size. This results in incredible opportunities for students to work with their professors on cutting-edge, real-world research projects.

BANG FOR YOUR BUCK

Macalester meets the full demonstrated financial need of every admitted student in order to ensure that classes are filled with talented, high-achieving students from a broad variety of backgrounds. Support is provided by the college's endowment and gifts to the college, which remains fiscally strong. Every student benefits both academically and financially from this support.

STUDENT LIFE

Life at Macalester "is ruled by randomness," and these undergrads wouldn't have it any other way. As one delighted political science major shares, "Studying in the Campus Center can be broken up by an impromptu performance by one of our a cappella groups, or the water polo team running through to raise awareness about a match." The fun and whimsy doesn't end there. As another contented undergrad tells us, "I've gone sledding in full-body trash bag 'sleds', held election night viewing parties in the dorm lounges, and sat around talking until 3:30 in the morning about different religions with people who each brought a different experience to the table." Naturally, there are

Macalester College

FINANCIAL AID: 651-696-6214 • E-MAIL: ADMISSIONS@MACALESTER.EDU • WEBSITE: WWW.MACALESTER.EDU

plenty of more structured and school-sponsored activities. Indeed, "there's usually at least one dance a week as well as a healthy variety of other performances, sporting events, or discussions." Lastly, the surrounding Twin Cities offer plenty of entertainment should students decide to venture off-campus.

CAREER

Macalester provides its undergrads with "many opportunities and [lots of] encouragement [in finding] internships, research [opportunities], careers [paths], etc." And a lot of that is supplied by the awesome Career Development Center. To begin with, students unsure of what they might want to pursue can reap the benefits of career counseling. They can meet with counselors to discuss their passions and take career assessment tests. The office also helps undergrads to connect with alumni for both mentoring and networking purposes. Through the Macalester Career Connection, students can search through numerous job postings. And for those undergrads confident they want to attend grad school—fear not! The Career Development Center offers plenty of guidance in that department as well.

GENERAL INFO

Athletics (Intercollegiate): *Men:* Baseball, basketball, cross-country, diving, football, golf, soccer, swimming, tennis, track/field (outdoor), track/field (indoor). *Women:* Basketball, cross-country, diving, golf, soccer, softball, swimming, tennis, track/field (outdoor), track/field (indoor), volleyball, water polo.

FINANCIAL AID

Students should submit: FAFSA, CSS/Financial Aid PROFILE, Noncustodial PROFILE. Regular filing deadline is 2/1. The Princeton Review suggests that all financial aid forms be submitted as soon as possible after October 1. *Need-based scholarships/grants offered:* Federal Pell, FSEOG, State scholarships/grants, Private scholarships, College/university scholarship or grant aid from institutional funds. *Loan aid offered:* Direct Subsidized Stafford Loans, Direct Unsubsidized Stafford Loans, Direct PLUS loans, State Loans, College/university loans from institutional funds. Applicants will be notified of awards on or about 4/1. Federal Work-Study Program available. Institutional employment available.

BOTTOM LINE

The cost of tuition for a year at Macalester is about $50,418. Room and board is approximately $11,266. Daunting though that may seem, the college is committed to helping. The average need-based financial aid package is $44,085. Not to mention additional aid offered through scholarships and loans.

CAREER INFORMATION FROM PAYSCALE.COM

ROI rating	89
Bachelor's and No Higher	
Median starting salary	$40,300
Median mid-career salary	$89,300
At Least Bachelor's	
Median starting salary	$41,200
Median mid-career salary	$89,400
% alumni with high job meaning	54%
% STEM	18%

SELECTIVITY

Admissions Rating	94
# of applicants	6,030
% of applicants accepted	39
% of acceptees attending	25
# offered a place on the wait list	350
% accepting a place on wait list	51
% admitted from wait list	0
# of early decision applicants	227
% accepted early decision	53

FRESHMAN PROFILE

Range SAT Critical Reading	620–730
Range SAT Math	620–740
Range SAT Writing	630–720
Range ACT Composite	29–32
Minimum paper TOEFL	600
Minimum internet-based TOEFL	100
% graduated top 10% of class	65
% graduated top 25% of class	95
% graduated top 50% of class	100

DEADLINES

Early decision	
Deadline	11/15
Notification	12/15
Regular	
Deadline	1/15
Notification	3/30
Nonfall registration?	No

FINANCIAL FACTS

Financial Aid Rating	97
Annual tuition	$50,418
Room and board	$11,266
Required fees	$221
Average need-based scholarship	$35,887
% needy frosh rec. need-based scholarship or grant aid	99
% needy UG rec. need-based scholarship or grant aid	99
% needy frosh rec. non-need-based scholarship or grant aid	6
% needy UG rec. non-need-based scholarship or grant aid	5
% needy frosh rec. need-based self-help aid	89
% needy UG rec. need-based self-help aid	93
% frosh rec. any financial aid	79
% UG rec. any financial aid	79
% UG borrow to pay for school	69
Average cumulative indebtedness	$21,544
% frosh need fully met	100
% ugrads need fully met	100
Average % of frosh need met	100
Average % of ugrad need met	100

Massachusetts Institute of Technology

77 MASSACHUSETTS AVENUE, CAMBRIDGE, MA 02139 • ADMISSIONS: 617-253-3400 • FAX: 617-258-8304

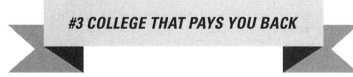

#3 COLLEGE THAT PAYS YOU BACK

ABOUT THE SCHOOL

The essence of Massachusetts Institute of Technology is its appetite for problems. Students here tend to be game-changers, capable of finding creative solutions to the world's big, intractable, complicated problems. A chemical engineering major says that "MIT is different from many schools in that its goal is not to teach you specific facts in each subject. MIT teaches you how to think, not about opinions but about problem-solving. Facts and memorization are useless unless you know how to approach a tough problem." While MIT is a research university committed to world-class inquiry in math, science, and engineering, MIT has equally distinguished programs in architecture, the humanities, management, and the social sciences. No matter what their field, almost all MIT students get involved in research during their undergraduate career, making contributions in fields as diverse as biochemistry, artificial intelligence, and urban planning. "Research opportunities for undergrads with some of the nation's leading professors" is a real highlight for students here. The school also operates an annual Independent Activities Period during the month of January, during which MIT faculty offer hundreds of noncredit activities and short for-credit classes, from lecture and film series to courses like Ballroom Dance or Introduction to Weather Forecasting (students may also use this period to work on research or independent projects). Students are frequently encouraged to unite MIT's science and engineering excellence with public service. Recent years have focused on projects using alternative forms of energy, and machines that could be used for sustainable agriculture. MIT's D-Lab, Poverty Action Lab, and Public Service Center all support students and professors in the research and implementation of culturally sensitive and environmentally responsible technologies and programs that alleviate poverty.

BANG FOR YOUR BUCK

Aid from all sources totals more than $115.6 million, and 72 percent of that total is provided by MIT Scholarships. Sixty-two percent of undergraduates qualify for need-based MIT Scholarships, and the average scholarship award exceeds $32,000. MIT is one of only a few number of institutions that have remained wholly committed to need-blind admissions and need-based aid. (There are no purely merit-based scholarships.) What truly sets MIT apart, however, is the percentage of students from lower-income households. Twenty-eight percent of MIT undergraduates are from families earning less than $75,000 a year, and 19 percent qualify for a federal Pell Grant. MIT also educates a high proportion of first-generation college students, including 16 percent of the current freshman class.

STUDENT LIFE

"As soon as you arrive on campus," students say, "you are bombarded with choices." Extracurricular options range from "building rides" (recent projects have included a motorized couch and a human-sized hamster wheel) "to partying at fraternities to enjoying the largest collection of science fiction novels in the United States at the MIT Science Fiction Library." Students occasionally find time to "pull a hack," which is an ethical prank, like changing digital construction signs on Mass Ave to read "Welcome to Bat Country," or building a "life-size Wright brothers' plane that appeared on top of the Great Dome for the 100th anniversary of flight." Luckily, "there actually isn't one typical student at MIT,"

Massachusetts Institute of Technology

FINANCIAL AID: 617-258-4917 • E-MAIL: ADMISSIONS@MIT.EDU • WEBSITE: WEB.MIT.EDU

students here assure us. "The one thing students all have in common is that they are insanely smart and love to learn. Pretty much anyone can find the perfect group of friends to hang out with at MIT."

CAREER

MIT's Global Education & Career Development "seeks to empower" students and alumni by taking a holistic approach to career services. A few offerings (among many) include career counseling and mock interviews, study abroad informational sessions, and graduate school advising. Frequent career fairs connect undergrads with potential employers (and the Career Fair Online Workshop will help you make the most of your time with them) or you can also peruse job and internship listings on CareerBridge. Students definitely get a hand-up from the rock-solid alumni network, and the surrounding areas of Cambridge and Boston abound with tech and research companies, offering students abundant opportunities for networking and internships. Alumni who visited PayScale.com reported starting salaries at about $70,300 and 58 percent felt that they do meaningful work.

GENERAL INFO

Activities: Choral groups, concert band, dance, drama/theater, jazz band, literary magazine, marching band, music ensembles, musical theater, radio station, student government, student newspaper.

FINANCIAL AID

Students should submit: FAFSA, CSS/Financial Aid PROFILE, Noncustodial PROFILE, Business/Farm Supplement. Regular filing deadline is 2/15. The Princeton Review suggests that all financial aid forms be submitted as soon as possible after October 1. *Need-based scholarships/grants offered:* Federal Pell, FSEOG, State scholarships/grants, Private scholarships, College/university scholarship or grant aid from institutional funds. *Loan aid offered:* Direct Subsidized Stafford Loans, Direct Unsubsidized Stafford Loans, Direct PLUS loans, Federal Perkins Loans, College/university loans from institutional funds. Applicants will be notified of awards on or about 3/15. Federal Work-Study Program available. Institutional employment available.

BOTTOM LINE

For the fall and spring terms, MIT tuition is about $46,400. Room and board averages about $13,730 per academic year, though those costs vary depending on a student's living situation. Books run about $1,000. MIT admits students without regard to their familys' circumstances and awards financial aid to students solely on the basis of need. The school is very clear that its sticker price not scare away applicants; approximately 75 percent of undergrads receive some form of aid. They also try to limit the amount of aid provided in loan form, aiming to meet the first $6,000 of need with loans or on-campus work, and covering the remainder of a student's demonstrated need with a scholarship.

CAREER INFORMATION FROM PAYSCALE.COM

ROI rating	99
Bachelor's and No Higher	
Median starting salary	$74,900
Median mid-career salary	$124,000
At Least Bachelor's	
Median starting salary	$78,000
Median mid-career salary	$137,000
% alumni with high job meaning	55%
% STEM	79%

SELECTIVITY

Admissions Rating	99
# of applicants	18,306
% of applicants accepted	8
% of acceptees attending	73
# offered a place on the wait list	652
% accepting a place on wait list	88
% admitted from wait list	9

FRESHMAN PROFILE

Range SAT Critical Reading	680–780
Range SAT Math	750–800
Range SAT Writing	690–780
Range ACT Composite	33–35
Minimum internet-based TOEFL	90
% graduated top 10% of class	98
% graduated top 25% of class	100
% graduated top 50% of class	100

DEADLINES

Early action	
Deadline	11/1
Notification	12/20
Regular	
Deadline	1/1
Notification	3/20
Nonfall registration?	No

FINANCIAL FACTS

Financial Aid Rating	95
Annual tuition	$46,400
Room and board	$13,730
Required fees	$304
Average need-based scholarship	$39,775
% needy frosh rec. need-based scholarship or grant aid	96
% needy UG rec. need-based scholarship or grant aid	96
% needy frosh rec. non-need-based scholarship or grant aid	2
% needy UG rec. non-need-based scholarship or grant aid	1
% needy frosh rec. need-based self-help aid	82
% needy UG rec. need-based self-help aid	87
% frosh rec. any financial aid	86
% UG rec. any financial aid	76
% UG borrow to pay for school	32
Average cumulative indebtedness	$23,485
% frosh need fully met	100
% ugrads need fully met	100
Average % of frosh need met	100
Average % of ugrad need met	100

Miami University (OH)

301 South Campus Avenue, Oxford, OH 45056 • Admissions: 513-529-2531 • Fax: 513-529-1550

CAMPUS LIFE

Quality of Life Rating	93
Fire Safety Rating	91
Green Rating	85
Type of school	Public
Affiliation	No Affiliation
Environment	Village

STUDENTS

Total undergrad enrollment	16,387
% male/female	49/51
% from out of state	35
% frosh from public high school	69
% frosh live on campus	98
% ugrads live on campus	46
# of fraternities (% ugrad men join)	29 (23)
# of sororities (% ugrad women join)	20 (31)
% African American	3
% Asian	2
% Caucasian	77
% Hispanic	4
% Native American	<1
% Pacific Islander	<1
% Two or more races	3
% Race and/or ethnicity unknown	<1
% international	10
# of countries represented	84

ACADEMICS

Academic Rating	81
% students returning for sophomore year	90
% students graduating within 4 years	65
% students graduating within 6 years	80
Calendar	Semester
Student/faculty ratio	17:1
Profs interesting rating	89
Profs accessible rating	90

Most classes have 20–29 students.
Most lab/discussion sessions have 10–19 students.

MOST POPULAR MAJORS

Accounting; Marketing/Marketing Management; Finance

ABOUT THE SCHOOL

Oxford, Ohio's Miami University offers students a number of opportunities to gain practical, hands-on experience through "education, student activities, networking, and preparation for the future." The school maintains a strong core academic curriculum (called the Global Miami Plan for Liberal Education) and keeps the standards expected of students consistent. This education "insists students take classes to make them a well-rounded individual rather than focus only on their major," which pushes students to interact and learn in areas they wouldn't normally encounter outside of the major they select from more than the one hundred on offer. The "very accessible and teaching-focused" professors make learning meaningful and provide "many resources to help us to achieve our goals in their class as well as outside of their class." "Miami does a good job of providing a small college feel all the while encompassing over 15,000 students," says a student.

BANG FOR YOUR BUCK

Each year Miami gives out millions of dollars of scholarships based on academics, special achievements, and financial need; the application for admissions to Miami University doubles as an application for academic scholarships. Numerous scholarships, including up to full tuition, are available to high-achieving Ohio and non-resident students who have demonstrated academic merit. Miami's University Academic Scholars Program offers additional scholarship opportunities to exceptional students pursuing academic and professional interests in specific areas like Sustainability or the Humanities or Mathematic, and Statistics. Need-based grants and scholarships include full tuition for first-time, academically competitive freshmen from Ohio who have been admitted to the Oxford campus and who have a total family income of less than $35,000 (courtesy of the Miami Access Initiative). Several academic departments and athletic teams also offer financial awards.

STUDENT LIFE

Everyone is required to live on-campus for the first two years, and "the residence halls put a lot of effort into providing different activities for their students." Late night programming is also offered through Miami, as well as athletic events and other cultural events; people are often studying or "just hanging out on Miami's beautiful campus." On weekends, many choose to go uptown or take part in Greek life (more than 30 percent are involved); Oxford "may be a small town but it is the perfect college town to be in." Students can also travel to nearby Hueston Woods to engage in outdoor activities such as, hiking, boating, swimming, camping, and horseback riding.

CAREER

Miami University has a strong focus on preparing students for the workplace after graduation, "many of the students treat their education like a job—dress code and all." They applaud the commitment of the school in providing tools to help them to find jobs after college, including "career fairs, relationships with recruiters, supporting alumni, mock interview/resume workshops/career services, and teaching material that is applicable to future endeavors," as well as the Miami CAREERlink database. "Career Services will help anyone find an internship or job," says a student. Forty-seven percent of Miami graduates who visited PayScale.com reported feeling their jobs highly impacted the world.

Miami University (OH)

FINANCIAL AID: 513-529-8734 • E-MAIL: ADMISSION@MIAMIOH.EDU • WEBSITE: WWW.MIAMIOH.EDU

GENERAL INFO

Activities: Choral groups, concert band, dance, drama/theater, Engineers Without Borders, Genetics Club, Greenhawks Media (sustainability publication), literary magazine, marching band, MU Dropouts Skydiving Club, music ensembles, radio station, student government, Quidditch, student newspaper, student-run film society, symphony orchestra, television station, varsity eSports, yearbook, campus ministries, international student organization, Model UN. **Organizations:** 400 registered organizations, 20 honor societies, 26 religious organizations. 29 fraternities, 21 sororities. **Athletics (Intercollegiate):** *Men:* baseball, basketball, cross-country, diving, football, golf, ice hockey, swimming, track/field (outdoor). *Women:* basketball, cross-country, diving, field hockey, soccer, softball, swimming, tennis, track/field (outdoor), volleyball. **On-Campus Highlights:** Armstrong Student Center, Institute for Entrepreneurship, Center for Student Engagement and Leadership, Howe Writing Center, Office of Research for Undergraduates, Human Immersive Virtual Environment, Center for the Performing Arts, Recreational Sports Center, Outdoor Pursuit Center.

FINANCIAL AID

Students should submit: FAFSA. The Princeton Review suggests that all financial aid forms be submitted as soon as possible after October 1. *Need-based scholarships/grants offered:* Federal Pell, FSEOG, State scholarships/grants, Private scholarships, College/university scholarship or grant aid from institutional funds. *Loan aid offered:* Direct Subsidized Stafford Loans, Direct Unsubsidized Stafford Loans, Direct PLUS loans, Federal Perkins Loans, College/university loans from institutional funds. Applicants will be notified of awards on a rolling basis. Federal Work-Study Program available. Institutional employment available.

BOTTOM LINE

In-state students pay $14,233 for base tuition, while out-of-state students pay $31,538; room and board is an additional $12,014. With all associated fees and living costs added in, the total annual cost for in-state Ohio residents is $27,011, and out-of-state residents is $44,306. Around 62 percent of students borrow money to pay for school.

CAREER INFORMATION FROM PAYSCALE.COM

ROI rating	87
Bachelor's and No Higher	
Median starting salary	$49,700
Median mid-career salary	$90,200
At Least Bachelor's	
Median starting salary	$50,200
Median mid-career salary	$91,500
% alumni with high job meaning	48%
% STEM	14%

SELECTIVITY

Admissions Rating	88
# of applicants	27,454
% of applicants accepted	65
% of acceptees attending	21
# offered a place on the wait list	3,269
% accepting a place on wait list	28
% admitted from wait list	0
# of early decision applicants	1,030
% accepted early decision	71

FRESHMAN PROFILE

Range SAT Critical Reading	550–650
Range SAT Math	590–690
Range SAT Writing	540–650
Range ACT Composite	26–30
Minimum paper TOEFL	550
Minimum internet-based TOEFL	80
Average HS GPA	3.8
% graduated top 10% of class	36
% graduated top 25% of class	68
% graduated top 50% of class	94

DEADLINES

Early decision	
Deadline	11/15
Notification	12/15
Early action	
Deadline	12/1
Notification	2/1
Regular	
Deadline	2/1
Notification	3/15
Nonfall registration?	Yes

FINANCIAL FACTS

Financial Aid Rating	81
Annual in-state tuition	$14,233
Annual out-of-state tuition	$31,538
Room and board	$12,014
Required fees	$754
Average need-based scholarship	$8,754
% needy frosh rec. need-based scholarship or grant aid	88
% needy UG rec. need-based scholarship or grant aid	87
% needy frosh rec. non-need-based scholarship or grant aid	18
% needy UG rec. non-need-based scholarship or grant aid	12
% needy frosh rec. need-based self-help aid	72
% needy UG rec. need-based self-help aid	78
% frosh need fully met	22
% ugrads need fully met	17
Average % of frosh need met	60
Average % of ugrad need met	58

Michigan Technological University

1400 Townsend Drive, Houghton, MI 49931 • Admissions: 906-487-2335 • Fax: 906-487-2125

CAMPUS LIFE

Quality of Life Rating	89
Fire Safety Rating	92
Green Rating	77
Type of school	Public
Affiliation	No Affiliation
Environment	Village

STUDENTS

Total undergrad enrollment	5,721
% male/female	73/27
% from out of state	23
% frosh live on campus	92
% ugrads live on campus	47
# of fraternities (% ugrad men join)	12 (8)
# of sororities (% ugrad women join)	8 (14)
% African American	1
% Asian	1
% Caucasian	86
% Hispanic	2
% Native American	<1
% Pacific Islander	<1
% Two or more races	3
% Race and/or ethnicity unknown	3
% international	4
# of countries represented	38

ACADEMICS

Academic Rating	74
% students returning for sophomore year	87
% students graduating within 4 years	23
% students graduating within 6 years	65
Calendar	Semester
Student/faculty ratio	12:1
Profs interesting rating	69
Profs accessible rating	73

Most classes have fewer than 10 students.
Most lab/discussion sessions have
  10–19 students.

MOST POPULAR MAJORS
Mechanical Engineering; Electrical and
Electronics Engineering; Civil Engineering

ABOUT THE SCHOOL

Michigan Technological University gives students a "big city education in a small town setting." Some students say this public research university in Michigan's "often snowy" Upper Peninsula boils down to "Engineering, Nerds, and the Great Outdoors" while others stress that "Michigan Tech was a school created for engineering but [its] other departments are just as strong and the education you receive is great." For students looking to pursue an engineering focus, though, Michigan Tech excels at "preparing [tomorrow's] engineers to create the future today." With its small, rural campus, "Michigan Tech is the type of school where you're not just a student, you're a family." According to one Civil Engineering major, "The experience gets better with more time you put into your program, the professors become more interactive and the experience becomes more meaningful." Students say the professors are mostly "helpful and accommodating" while "a few have been dull, but those are the minority;" the fact that the majority "have high expectations…helps in learning." Small class sizes (usually between two and nine students) for non-general education classes and a 12:1 student-to-faculty ratio "allows for a great professor-student relationships."

BANG FOR YOUR BUCK

Though some students say that "Financial Aid usually does a good job at keeping us covered," other students wish that Michigan Tech would "allocate financial resources more effectively" and "consider [its] students more when making financial decisions." Seventy-three percent of Michigan Tech undergraduates have borrowed through some sort of loan program. The average Michigan Tech freshman receives a total of $9,417 in need-based gift aid (the average for a Michigan Tech undergrad is $7,728) and the average amount received in need-based loans is $3,218. Scholarships are available to qualifying Michigan residents, including the Presidential Scholars program, the Wade McCree scholarship, and the School of Business Impact Scholarship. Since Michigan Tech is located so close to Canada, there are special scholarship opportunities, such as through the McAllister Foundation, available to qualified incoming Canadian students.

STUDENT LIFE

"They are smart, studious, but know how to have fun," Michigan Tech students say of their classmates. They are "great at balancing school and hanging out." Some say it's hard to define the "typical" student and that "it all depends on the department. There is a great deal of diversity apart from the large white male majority." According to one Biology major, "There's little diversity ethnically, but everyone feels welcome. There's many more men than women, so girls get doors opened for them across campus. If you have any problems, anyone will help you. It's easy to fit in." Around campus, "students play a lot of intramural sports and are in a lot of student organizations." There are a total of 225 registered student organizations on campus. Some students say "embrace the Greek system" because "it is a big thing here"—8 percent of men at Michigan Tech join a fraternity, while 14 percent of women join a sorority. Winter sports are especially popular, "[skiing], snowboarding, snowshoeing, ice fishing and [snowmobiling] are all very popular" during Michigan's long, snowy winter months.

CAREER

"Career services are unbelievable here. If you work for your degree and earn it, participate in co-ops or internships (and the opportunities to do so are ample), you are almost guaranteed a job out of college." Not all students have quite such high praise, saying that they wished there were "more internships etc. for majors that are not engineering."

Michigan Technological University

Financial Aid: 906-487-2622 • E-mail: mtu4u@mtu.edu • Website: www.mtu.edu

But overall, Michigan Tech gets high marks, with students saying "the [school's] biggest strength is the Career Services...There is a fall and spring career fair so getting internships and co-ops is slightly better than other universities." The Career Services department is "really helpful in working with you to find a job/internship/co-op." During the month of the career fair, Michigan Tech also offers lots of informal events that make up CareerFEST, which helps prepare students for interviews, résumé-writing, and more. From the school's website, students can access the online HuskyJobs system that helps connect students and potential employers and internship leaders.

GENERAL INFO

Activities: Choral groups, concert band, dance, drama/theater, jazz band, literary magazine, music ensembles, musical theater, pep band, radio station, student government, student newspaper, student-run film society, symphony orchestra, Campus Ministries, International Student Organization. **Organizations:** 225 registered organizations, 12 honor societies, 9 religious organizations. 12 fraternities, 8 sororities. **Athletics (Intercollegiate):** *Men:* basketball, cross-country, football, ice hockey, skiing (nordic/cross-country), tennis, track/field (outdoor). *Women:* basketball, cross-country, skiing (nordic/cross-country), soccer, tennis, track/field (outdoor), volleyball. **On-Campus Highlights:** Student Development Complex, Rozsa Center for the Performing Arts, Mont Ripley Ski Hill, Portage Lake Golf Course, Memorial Union Building.

FINANCIAL AID

Students should submit: FAFSA. Priority filing deadline is 3/1. The Princeton Review suggests that all financial aid forms be submitted as soon as possible after October 1. *Need-based scholarships/grants offered:* Federal Pell, FSEOG, State scholarships/grants, Private scholarships, College/university scholarship or grant aid from institutional funds. *Loan aid offered:* Direct Subsidized Stafford Loans, Direct Unsubsidized Stafford Loans, Direct PLUS loans, Federal Perkins Loans, College/university loans from institutional funds. Applicants will be notified of awards on a rolling basis beginning 3/15. Federal Work-Study Program available. Institutional employment available.

BOTTOM LINE

Tuition for in-state students is roughly $14,334, with an additional $300 in fees and approximately $1,200 in books and supplies. Tuition for out-of-state students is roughly $30,668. In terms of scholarships and grants, the average freshman receives roughly $10,566 and the average loan debt per Michigan Tech graduate is $35,741. Financial aid is available to international students.

CAREER INFORMATION FROM PAYSCALE.COM

ROI rating	87
Bachelor's and No Higher	
Median starting salary	$62,800
Median mid-career salary	$99,900
At Least Bachelor's	
Median starting salary	$63,400
Median mid-career salary	$101,000
% alumni with high job meaning	48%
% STEM	76%

SELECTIVITY

Admissions Rating	84
# of applicants	5,386
% of applicants accepted	75
% of acceptees attending	31

FRESHMAN PROFILE

Range SAT Critical Reading	545–665
Range SAT Math	565–690
Range SAT Writing	505–625
Range ACT Composite	24–29
Minimum paper TOEFL	550
Minimum internet-based TOEFL	79
Average HS GPA	3.7
% graduated top 10% of class	28
% graduated top 25% of class	62
% graduated top 50% of class	92

DEADLINES

Regular	
Priority	1/15
Nonfall registration?	Yes

FINANCIAL FACTS

Financial Aid Rating	81
Annual in-state tuition	$14,334
Annual out-of-state tuition	$30,668
Room and board	$10,105
Required fees	$300
Average need-based scholarship	$7,728
% needy frosh rec. need-based scholarship or grant aid	85
% needy UG rec. need-based scholarship or grant aid	79
% needy frosh rec. non-need-based scholarship or grant aid	84
% needy UG rec. non-need-based scholarship or grant aid	74
% needy frosh rec. need-based self-help aid	78
% needy UG rec. need-based self-help aid	84
% frosh rec. any financial aid	97
% UG rec. any financial aid	91
% UG borrow to pay for school	73
Average cumulative indebtedness	$35,741
% frosh need fully met	22
% ugrads need fully met	19
Average % of frosh need met	81
Average % of ugrad need met	73

ıddlebury College

EMMA WILLARD HOUSE, MIDDLEBURY, VT 05753-6002 • ADMISSIONS: 802-443-3000 • FAX: 802-443-2056

CAMPUS LIFE

Quality of Life Rating	**96**
Fire Safety Rating	**96**
Green Rating	**98**
Type of school	Private
Affiliation	No Affiliation
Environment	Village

STUDENTS

Total undergrad enrollment	2,542
% male/female	47/53
% from out of state	93
% frosh from public high school	52
% frosh live on campus	100
% ugrads live on campus	95
% African American	3
% Asian	6
% Caucasian	65
% Hispanic	9
% Native American	<1
% Pacific Islander	0
% Two or more races	5
% Race and/or ethnicity unknown	1
% international	11
# of countries represented	74

ACADEMICS

Academic Rating	**99**
% students returning for sophomore year	97
% students graduating within 4 years	92
% students graduating within 6 years	94
Calendar	4/1/4
Student/faculty ratio	8:1
Profs interesting rating	98
Profs accessible rating	96

Most classes have 10–19 students.

MOST POPULAR MAJORS
Economics; Environmental Studies; Political Science

ABOUT THE SCHOOL

Home to "smart people who enjoy Aristotelian ethics and quantum physics, but aren't too stuck up to go sledding in front of Mead Chapel at midnight," Middlebury College is a small, exclusive liberal arts school with "excellent foreign language programs" as well as standout offerings in environmental studies, the sciences, theatre, and writing. The successful Middlebury candidate excels in a variety of areas, including academics, athletics, the arts, leadership, and service to others. These strengths and interests permit students to grow beyond their traditional comfort zones and conventional limits. The classrooms are as varied as the Green Mountains, the Metropolitan Museum of Art, or the great cities of Russia and Japan. Outside the classroom, students informally interact with professors in activities such as intramural basketball games and community service. At Middlebury, students develop critical-thinking skills, enduring bonds of friendship, and the ability to challenge themselves. Middlebury offers majors and programs in forty-five different fields, with particular strengths in languages, international studies, environmental studies, literature and creative writing, and the sciences. Opportunities for engaging in individual research with faculty abound at Middlebury.

BANG FOR YOUR BUCK

Distribution requirements and other general requirements ensure that a Middlebury education "is all about providing students with a complete college experience, including excellent teaching, exposure to many other cultures, endless opportunities for growth and success, and a challenging (yet relaxed) environment." Its "small class size and friendly yet competitive atmosphere make for the perfect college experience," as do "the best facilities of a small liberal arts college in the country." A new squash center and new field house recently opened. Students are grateful for the stellar advantages the school is able to provide them with. "I think that even if I didn't have classes or homework, I wouldn't be able to take advantage of all of the opportunities available on campus on a day-to-day basis." "The academics here are unbeatable. I'd come here over an Ivy League school any day."

STUDENT LIFE

Middlebury students are, in three words: "Busy, friendly, and busy." Everyone "will talk about how stressed they are, but it's not just from preparing for a Chinese exam while also trying to finish up a lab report for biology; it's doing both of those while also playing a club or a varsity sport and finding time to enjoy long meals in the cafeteria with friends." Weekends are for much-deserved relaxation: hiking or skiing (the school has its own ski mountain, the Snow Bowl, and cross-country ski area, Rikert Nordic Center), attending shows and concerts, film screenings, dance parties, and parties are put on by sports teams and other clubs on campus. The student activity board "does a pretty good job, but if you don't like it, you are always welcome to apply to be on the board." Many here are politically active in some way, and "the environment is big for most."

Middlebury College

E-MAIL: ADMISSIONS@MIDDLEBURY.EDU • WEBSITE: WWW.MIDDLEBURY.EDU

CAREER

Middlebury students "know how to take advantage of resources that aid their success." The Center for Careers & Internships helps students to find internships or even develop their own, and the online resources include a comprehensive series of Five-Minute Workshops. Funding is even available for unpaid internships, conferences, service projects, international volunteer programs, and local public service projects. Experiential learning is a heavy focus of the college, and there are numerous centers for students to enhance academic work, or explore possible career paths. Middlebury College graduates who visited PayScale.com had an average starting salary of $51,900; 56 percent said they felt their job had a meaningful impact on the world.

GENERAL INFO

Activities: Choral groups, dance, drama/theater, jazz band, literary magazine, music ensembles, musical theater, radio station, student government, student newspaper, student-run film society, symphony orchestra, yearbook. **Organizations:** 185 registered organizations. **Athletics (Intercollegiate):** *Men:* Baseball, basketball, cross-country, diving/swimming, football, golf, ice hockey, lacrosse, skiing (downhill/alpine), skiing (nordic/cross-country), soccer, squash. tennis, track/field (outdoor), track/field (indoor). *Women:* Basketball, cross-country, diving/swimming, field hockey, golf, ice hockey, lacrosse, skiing (downhill/alpine), skiing (nordic/cross-country), soccer, softball, squash, tennis, track/field (outdoor), track/field (indoor), volleyball.

FINANCIAL AID

Students should submit: FAFSA, Institution's own financial aid form, CSS/Financial Aid PROFILE, Noncustodial PROFILE. Regular filing deadline is 2/1. The Princeton Review suggests that all financial aid forms be submitted as soon as possible after October 1. *Need-based scholarships/grants offered:* Federal Pell, FSEOG, State scholarships/grants, Private scholarships, College/university scholarship or grant aid from institutional funds. *Loan aid offered:* Direct Subsidized Stafford Loans, Direct Unsubsidized Stafford Loans, Direct PLUS loans, College/university loans from institutional funds. Applicants will be notified of awards on or about 4/1. Federal Work-Study Program available. Institutional employment available.

BOTTOM LINE

Middlebury College is not the most expensive institution in the country, but it is a substantial investment. Fortunately, the opportunity for financial aid and other support is provided for needy students. Tuition is $47,418 per year, and Middlebury meets full demonstrated need for all admitted students. About 42 percent of enrollees receive some form of financial aid. Forty-four percent of students borrow to help offset the cost of their education and, upon graduating, are looking at a total loan debt of under $17,975; extremely reasonable for an education of the caliber provided by Middlebury.

CAREER INFORMATION FROM PAYSCALE.COM

ROI rating	90
Bachelor's and No Higher	
Median starting salary	$50,100
Median mid-career salary	$93,900
At Least Bachelor's	
Median starting salary	$51,900
Median mid-career salary	$96,300
% alumni with high job meaning	55%
% STEM	12%

SELECTIVITY

Admissions Rating	97
# of applicants	8,891
% of applicants accepted	17
% of acceptees attending	38
# offered a place on the wait list	1,304
% accepting a place on wait list	41
% admitted from wait list	6
# of early decision applicants	961
% accepted early decision	33

FRESHMAN PROFILE

Range SAT Critical Reading	630–750
Range SAT Math	640–750
Range SAT Writing	650–760
Range ACT Composite	29–33

DEADLINES

Early decision	
Deadline	11/1
Regular	
Deadline	1/1
Nonfall registration?	Yes

FINANCIAL FACTS

Financial Aid Rating	99
Annual tuition	$49,648
Room and board	$14,269
Required fees	$415
Average need-based scholarship	$41,778
% needy frosh rec. need-based scholarship or grant aid	100
% needy UG rec. need-based scholarship or grant aid	98
% needy frosh rec. non-need-based scholarship or grant aid	0
% needy UG rec. non-need-based scholarship or grant aid	0
% needy frosh rec. need-based self-help aid	94
% needy UG rec. need-based self-help aid	92
% frosh rec. any financial aid	48
% UG rec. any financial aid	42
% UG borrow to pay for school	41
Average cumulative indebtedness	$17,797
% frosh need fully met	100
% ugrads need fully met	100
Average % of frosh need met	100
Average % of ugrad need met	100

Missouri University of Science and Technology

300 West 13th Street; 106 Parker Hall, Rolla, MO 65409-1060 • Admissions: 573-341-4165 • Fax: 573-341-4082

CAMPUS LIFE

Quality of Life Rating	**87**
Fire Safety Rating	**88**
Green Rating	**83**
Type of school	Public
Affiliation	No Affiliation
Environment	Village

STUDENTS

Total undergrad enrollment	6,841
% male/female	77/23
% from out of state	19
% frosh from public high school	85
% ugrads live on campus	40
# of fraternities (% ugrad men join)	23 (21)
# of sororities (% ugrad women join)	5 (19)
% African American	3
% Asian	3
% Caucasian	77
% Hispanic	3
% Native American	<1
% Pacific Islander	<1
% Two or more races	0
% Race and/or ethnicity unknown	3
% international	4
# of countries represented	38

ACADEMICS

Academic Rating	**74**
% students graduating within 4 years	23
% students graduating within 6 years	63
Calendar	Semester
Student/faculty ratio	18:1
Profs interesting rating	77
Profs accessible rating	77

Most classes have 20–29 students.
Most lab/discussion sessions have 10–19 students.

MOST POPULAR MAJORS
Civil Engineering; Electrical and Electronics Engineering; Mechanical Engineering

ABOUT THE SCHOOL

Missouri University of Science and Technology is one of the premier engineering and science-centered institutions in the Midwest. Though a "small school compared to other public universities," we've been assured that "the quality of education and availability of resources here is second to none." Of course, given the engineering focus, prospective students should anticipate a rigorous curriculum. Fortunately, students truly seem to value that their "classes really push you to learn and master the content." Undergrads also appreciate that they have the ability to participate in "lots of undergraduate research." Yes, these Miners love their time in the classroom. That's due in large part to some "incredibly capable and accessible" professors who really "want [to see] you succeed." Perhaps most impressively "they are always willing to spend time with you to understand the material [and they don't] hesitate to get to know you outside of the classroom at social events and such."

BANG FOR YOUR BUCK

If you're looking for a school that won't break the proverbial bank, Missouri S&T just might be the university for you. As one thrilled sophomore explains, "Missouri S&T offers a quality degree at a low price." And it's not just a bargain for Missouri residents. A relieved senior shares, "[Missouri S&T is even] affordable for an out-of-state student like myself; [it was actually cheaper] than some [of my] in-state institutions." Beyond just a state school price tag, undergrads often benefit from generous financial aid packages. A lot of that generosity can be attributed to the numerous merit scholarships available. For example, S&T offers the Excellence Scholarship, which provides a minimum of $5,500 for in-state students and $11,000 for out-of-state students. The Trustees Scholarship offers a minimum of $4,000 and $10,000 respectively. There are also many departmental awards to be had. Upon receiving an acceptance letter, students are encouraged to inquire with their intended degree program.

SCHOOL LIFE

Undergrads here don't mince words; "academics are everyone's top priority." As one knowledgeable senior admits, "People are usually very weighed down by classes." However, even the most diligent students need to take the occasional break. And when these undergrads do, there's plenty of fun to be had. Indeed, "for a school as small as S&T, our range of student organizations is mind-boggling. Who knew a small school in the middle of Missouri would have a thriving salsa club?" Students can also participate in activities such as "scavenger hunts, video game nights, cooking classes, viewing parties, dance lessons, and much more." Additionally, we're told that "Greek life is pretty big here [...] it feels like everyone is Greek." Thankfully, undergrads assure us that there's a friendly vibe and everyone is welcome at parties no matter their affiliation.

Missouri University of Science and Technology

FINANCIAL AID: 573-341-4282 • E-MAIL: ADMISSIONS@MST.EDU • WEBSITE: WWW.MST.EDU

CAREER

Success is often synonymous with Missouri S&T graduates. And this does not go unnoticed by current students. As one senior boasts, "Many employers place Missouri S&T candidates at the top of their list." A fellow senior concurs adding, "Missouri S&T provides a first class education and employers know the quality of student that graduates from this institution so finding a job is no problem at all!" Certainly, some of this professional achievement can be chalked up to a "fantastic" career services office. After all, the industrious individuals who work here put up some remarkable statistics. For starters, the office facilitates roughly 4,700 on-campus interviews a year. It also arranges approximately 3,330 job postings for Missouri S&T students and provides access to an additional 16 million job postings worldwide. And, as if that all weren't enough, according to PayScale. com, the median starting salary of S&T graduates is $62,400.

GENERAL INFO

Activities: Choral groups, concert band, dance, drama/theater, jazz band, literary magazine, marching band, music ensembles, musical theater, pep band, radio station, student government, student newspaper, symphony orchestra, yearbook, Campus Ministries, International Student Organization. **Organizations:** 202 registered organizations, 29 honor societies, 13 religious organizations. 23 fraternities, 5 sororities. **Athletics (Intercollegiate):** *Men:* baseball, basketball, cross-country, football, soccer, swimming, track/field (outdoor), track/field (indoor). *Women:* basketball, cross-country, soccer, softball, track/field (outdoor), track/field (indoor), volleyball. **On-Campus Highlights:** Havener Student Center, Residential College, Student Design Team Center, Castleman Performing Arts Center, Student Recreation Center.

FINANCIAL AID

Students should submit: FAFSA. Priority filing deadline is 2/1. The Princeton Review suggests that all financial aid forms be submitted as soon as possible after October 1. *Need-based scholarships/grants offered:* Federal Pell, FSEOG, State scholarships/grants, Private scholarships, College/university scholarship or grant aid from institutional funds. *Loan aid offered:* Federal Loans, State Loans, College/university loans from institutional funds. Federal Work-Study Program available. Institutional employment available.

BOTTOM LINE

Missouri residents attending Missouri S&T will receive a tuition bill of $7,734. Undergrads hailing from out-of-state face a higher bill, one priced at $23,850. Additionally, all students must pay another $1,520 in required fees. And undergrads should anticipate spending around $836 for books and supplies. Finally, students can expect to pay $9,780 for on-campus room and board.

CAREER INFORMATION FROM PAYSCALE.COM

ROI rating	**89**
Bachelor's and No Higher	
Median starting salary	$62,700
Median mid-career salary	$102,000
At Least Bachelor's	
Median starting salary	$63,200
Median mid-career salary	$104,000
% alumni with high job meaning	58%
% STEM	89%

SELECTIVITY

Admissions Rating	85
# of applicants	3,592
% of applicants accepted	88
% of acceptees attending	47
# offered a place on the wait list	0

FRESHMAN PROFILE

Range SAT Critical Reading	520–660
Range SAT Math	560–640
Range ACT Composite	25–31
Minimum internet-based TOEFL	79
Average HS GPA	3.71
% graduated top 10% of class	44
% graduated top 25% of class	74
% graduated top 50% of class	94

DEADLINES

Regular	
Deadline	Rolling
Notification	Rolling
Nonfall registration?	Yes

FINANCIAL FACTS

Financial Aid Rating	87
Annual in-state tuition	$7,734
Annual out-of-state tuition	$23,850
Room and board	$9,780
Required fees	$1,520
Average need-based scholarship	$7,724
% needy frosh rec. need-based scholarship or grant aid	95
% needy UG rec. need-based scholarship or grant aid	91
% needy frosh rec. non-need-based scholarship or grant aid	28
% needy UG rec. non-need-based scholarship or grant aid	33
% needy frosh rec. need-based self-help aid	17
% needy UG rec. need-based self-help aid	29
% frosh rec. any financial aid	91
% UG rec. any financial aid	85
% frosh need fully met	96
% ugrads need fully met	94
Average % of frosh need met	28
Average % of ugrad need met	36

Montana Tech of the University of Montana

1300 WEST PARK STREET, BUTTE, MT 59701 • ADMISSIONS: 406-496-4256 • FAX: 406-496-4710

CAMPUS LIFE

Quality of Life Rating	**81**
Fire Safety Rating	**98**
Green Rating	**60***
Type of school	Public
Affiliation	No Affiliation
Environment	Town

STUDENTS

Total undergrad enrollment	2,751
% male/female	60/40
% from out of state	15
% frosh live on campus	46
% ugrads live on campus	12
% African American	1
% Asian	1
% Caucasian	81
% Hispanic	2
% Native American	2
% Pacific Islander	0
% Two or more races	<1
% Race and/or ethnicity unknown	5
% international	9
# of countries represented	14

ACADEMICS

Academic Rating	**72**
% students returning for sophomore year	71
% students graduating within 4 years	17
% students graduating within 6 years	43
Calendar	Semester
Student/faculty ratio	15:1
Profs interesting rating	72
Profs accessible rating	78

Most classes have 10–19 students.
Most lab/discussion sessions have fewer than 10 students.

MOST POPULAR MAJORS
Petroleum Engineering; Engineering; Management Information Systems and Services

ABOUT THE SCHOOL

Originally founded as Montana State School of Mines, Montana Tech of the University of Montana now houses four schools and colleges and offers more than sixty undergraduate degrees (as well as a variety of minor and certificates programs). It stands as one of only two U.S. schools that offer a Bachelor of Science degree in geophysical engineering. This "very personal university" stresses the importance of knowing current technologies and obtaining summer internships, and its approach strongly benefits those "who know what they want to major in, and strongly desire work after graduation." Though Montana Tech is primarily known for its engineering programs and STEM disciplines, professors "teach at a high level" in all programs, and students who are willing to put in the effort find that the school is "more than happy to help [students] find internships, school jobs, and research opportunities."

BANG FOR YOUR BUCK

Montana Tech offers "a high education at [a] lower cost school model," providing over $1.4 million in scholarships to each new incoming class via a simple application process. The average freshman grant/scholarship package totals $6,068. Western University Exchange (WUE) awards are offered to students who achieve high academic excellence and provide up to 150 percent of in-state tuition for up to 4.5 years. The Advantage Scholarship offers 150 percent of in-state tuition for the student's entire undergraduate term at Montana Tech and is available to all out-of-state students (equating to over $8,800 per year). For first-years with academic and extracurricular achievements, the Marie Moebus Presidential Scholarship is the school's highest honor and is a combination of a fee waiver, a WUE or Advantage Scholarship, and a cash supplement of up to $3,000 per year.

STUDENT LIFE

The historic town of Butte is full of rich history and access to the great outdoors. On weekends students can "hunt, fish, snowboard, ski, ice fish, mountain bike, camp, rock climb" and "basically just enjoy Montana's beauty." The town itself "isn't big, but bowling alleys and nice restaurants with bars make for [a] pleasant evening with friends." Students tend to form cliques based on their major, but community can always be found at the Mill Building, which has "pool tables, ping pong tables, shuffleboard, a seventy-inch TV, and a place to get coffee." Course work is incredibly challenging "but not life-consuming," and "despite the bitterly cold weather, people are warm and friendly" and are active in extracurriculars and clubs.

Montana Tech of the University of Montana

FINANCIAL AID: 406-496-4213 • E-MAIL: ENROLLMENT@MTECH.EDU • WEBSITE: WWW.MTECH.EDU

CAREER

Most students attend Montana Tech with aspirations of a decent paying job upon graduation, and "students work hard to try and obtain this goal." The school "takes pride in the overall job placement of the students after graduation" and boasts a ten-year average placement rate of 93 percent. The university maintains strong connections with a host of companies that "create great internship and job opportunities" as well as "high wages immediately after graduation." As a small school, most career help occurs on a personal level between faculty, staff, and students, such as the coordination of on-campus and off-campus interviewing opportunities, job search strategies, and internships. The school's online career management system DIGGERecruiting also provides a centralized location for all job-seeking resources and listings and connects students and alumni with employers and internships. For those Montana Tech graduates who visited PayScale.com, 65 percent reported feeling that their career had a high social value.

GENERAL INFO

Activities: concert band, pep band, radio station, student government, student newspaper, yearbook, Campus Ministries. **Organizations:** 58 registered organizations, 2 honor societies, 3 religious organizations. **Athletics (Intercollegiate):** *Men:* basketball, football, golf. *Women:* basketball, golf, volleyball. **On-Campus Highlights:** Mineral Museum, Mil Building (which houses Starbucks and, HPER (athletic facility), Student Union, Mall area.

FINANCIAL AID

Students should submit: FAFSA. Priority filing deadline is 3/1. The Princeton Review suggests that all financial aid forms be submitted as soon as possible after October 1. *Need-based scholarships/grants offered:* Federal Pell, FSEOG, State scholarships/grants, Private scholarships, College/university scholarship or grant aid from institutional funds. *Loan aid offered:* Direct Subsidized Stafford Loans, Direct Unsubsidized Stafford Loans, Direct PLUS loans, Federal Perkins Loans, College/university loans from institutional funds. Applicants will be notified of awards on a rolling basis beginning 3/15. Fed

BOTTOM LINE

Though the $6,881 annual tuition for in-state residents is a downright steal, out-of-staters are still getting a bargain at $21,008. Room and board will run an additional $8,932, with an additional $1,050 in books and supplies. As a bonus, all students applying to Montana Tech can avail themselves of the Student Assistance Foundation, which is a Montana-based non-profit that helps students find scholarships and budget for their college careers within the state.

CAREER INFORMATION FROM PAYSCALE.COM

ROI rating	**86**
Bachelor's and No Higher	
Median starting salary	$62,100
Median mid-career salary	$86,700
At Least Bachelor's	
Median starting salary	$65,500
Median mid-career salary	$88,100
% alumni with high job meaning	68%
% STEM	72%

SELECTIVITY

Admissions Rating	77
# of applicants	952
% of applicants accepted	90
% of acceptees attending	52

FRESHMAN PROFILE

Range SAT Critical Reading	490–590
Range SAT Math	540–630
Range SAT Writing	450–560
Range ACT Composite	22–27
Minimum paper TOEFL	525
Minimum internet-based TOEFL	71
Average HS GPA	3.5
% graduated top 10% of class	24
% graduated top 25% of class	57
% graduated top 50% of class	85

DEADLINES

Nonfall registration?	Yes

FINANCIAL FACTS

Financial Aid Rating	81
Annual in-state tuition	$6,881
Annual out-of-state tuition	$21,008
Room and board	$8,932
Required fees	
Average need-based scholarship	$5,485
% needy frosh rec. need-based scholarship or grant aid	90
% needy UG rec. need-based scholarship or grant aid	89
% needy frosh rec. non-need-based scholarship or grant aid	10
% needy UG rec. non-need-based scholarship or grant aid	5
% needy frosh rec. need-based self-help aid	73
% needy UG rec. need-based self-help aid	80
% frosh rec. any financial aid	72
% UG rec. any financial aid	67
% frosh need fully met	21
% ugrads need fully met	12
Average % of frosh need met	68
Average % of ugrad need met	63

Mount Holyoke College

NEWHALL CENTER, SOUTH HADLEY, MA 01075 • ADMISSIONS: 413-538-2023 • FAX: 413-538-2409

CAMPUS LIFE

Quality of Life Rating	93
Fire Safety Rating	88
Green Rating	92
Type of school	Private
Affiliation	No Affiliation
Environment	Town

STUDENTS

Total undergrad enrollment	2,099
% male/female	0/100
% from out of state	75
% frosh from public high school	65
% frosh live on campus	100
% ugrads live on campus	95
% African American	6
% Asian	10
% Caucasian	45
% Hispanic	8
% Native American	<1
% Pacific Islander	<1
% Two or more races	4
% Race and/or ethnicity unknown	1
% international	26
# of countries represented	69

ACADEMICS

Academic Rating	96
% students returning for sophomore year	90
% students graduating within 4 years	78
% students graduating within 6 years	85
Calendar	Semester
Student/faculty ratio	10:1
Profs interesting rating	98
Profs accessible rating	95

Most classes have 10–19 students.
Most lab/discussion sessions have 10–19 students.

MOST POPULAR MAJORS
English; Economics; Psychology

ABOUT THE SCHOOL

At this original member of the Seven Sisters schools, founded in 1837, young women find "an ideal environment for curious and engaged students of different backgrounds." Mount Holyoke College reinforces the idea of a global, twenty-first century education for its students, giving them the broad education of a true liberal arts curriculum while providing the practical tools needed to adapt to different career paths and jobs. More than 200 faculty members guide over 2,100 students (about 25 percent of whom are international citizens) through the halls of academia, providing "a vastly engaging classroom experience" that "excels in empowering students to lead on-campus organizations and programs." There are fifty majors to choose from (as well as an option to design your own), and professors "not only help you with your homework, but often give you words of wisdom about life in general."

BANG FOR YOUR BUCK

Despite the high sticker price, Mount Holyoke does everything in its power to make sure that "significant financial aid" is given to students who require it. The school is highly focused on the employability of its students down the road, so the return on whatever level of investment students do end up making is solid. Numerous merit-based scholarships are available on top of grants. The Trustee Scholarship offers full tuition to a select group of high-achieving first-year students; around twenty-five freshman Twenty-First Century Scholars also receive $25,000 annually based upon scholarship, extracurricular achievement, and leadership potential. Scholarships ranging from $10,000 to $20,000 are also available via the Mount Holyoke Leadership Awards.

STUDENT LIFE

From the bond of sisterhood to the numerous college traditions, this "truly unique" campus community is very close knit. The "racially and ethnically diverse, internationally representative" student body is also "inclusive of many sexual orientations and gender identities," embraces variety in terms of student organizations and social life, and is "pretty active socially on campus." "If you want to be considered a MoHo, you have to be intelligent and love to raise dialogue." There is "always plenty going on here" and at the other colleges in the Five College Consortium, from lectures to theatre to concerts to exhibits to parties. Students can "take a walk around the lake, see an a cappella performance, go to a celebration of the scientific measurement . . . or a lecture on ancient manuscripts," or attend one of the "big five-college parties in Chapin Auditorium."

CAREER

Many who attend Mount Holyoke choose to go on to a secondary degree (nearly 80 percent enroll in grad school within ten years of graduation), and 84 percent of the class of 2014 reported being employed or in school six months after graduation. The college has adapted to the needs of students facing a volatile job market with curriculum-to-career classes and other job training endeavors (The Lynk), and students are able to call on an alumnae network of more than 35,000 to supplement the already "excellent internship and career resources" provided. The active Career Development Center helps connect students with internships, advisers, preparatory workshops, and funding for unpaid internships and research opportunities, and an employer partnership with Smith and Amherst Colleges helps bolster job opportunities. For those Mount Holyoke graduates who visited PayScale.com, 58 percent reported that they had a career with high job meaning.

Mount Holyoke College

FINANCIAL AID: 413-538-2291 • E-MAIL: ADMISSION@MTHOLYOKE.EDU • WEBSITE: WWW.MTHOLYOKE.EDU

GENERAL INFO

Activities: Choral groups, dance, drama/theater, jazz band, literary magazine, music ensembles, musical theater, radio station, student government, student newspaper, student-run film society, symphony orchestra, yearbook, Campus Ministries, International Student Organization, Model UN. **Organizations:** 130 registered organizations, 5 honor societies, 9 religious organizations. **Athletics (Intercollegiate):** *Women:* basketball, crew/rowing, cross-country, diving, equestrian sports, field hockey, golf, horseback riding, lacrosse, soccer, squash, swimming, tennis, track/field (outdoor), track/field (indoor), volleyball. **On-Campus Highlights:** Unified Science Center, Kendall Sports and Dance Complex, The Equestrian Center, Blanchard Campus Center, Williston Memorial Library. The entire campus is an exquisitely maintained botanic garden which includes an arboretum, numerous gardens, and the Talcott Greenhouse.

FINANCIAL AID

Students should submit: FAFSA, CSS/Financial Aid PROFILE, Noncustodial PROFILE. Regular filing deadline is 3/1. The Princeton Review suggests that all financial aid forms be submitted as soon as possible after October 1. *Need-based scholarships/grants offered:* Federal Pell, FSEOG, State scholarships/grants, Private scholarships, College/university scholarship or grant aid from institutional funds. *Loan aid offered:* Direct Subsidized Stafford Loans, Direct Unsubsidized Stafford Loans, Direct PLUS loans, Federal Perkins Loans, State Loans, College/university loans from institutional funds. Applicants will be notified of awards on or about 4/1. Federal Work-Study Program available. Institutional employment available.

BOTTOM LINE

Tuition at this private school runs $45,680 across the board, with room and board adding an additional $13,440 to the bill; however, financial aid, scholarships (both need- and merit-based), and financing opportunities are plentiful. Most students receive some sort of financial assistance, with the average undergraduate total need-based gift running $31,101.

CAREER INFORMATION FROM PAYSCALE.COM

ROI rating	89
Bachelor's and No Higher	
Median starting salary	$44,400
Median mid-career salary	$65,000
At Least Bachelor's	
Median starting salary	$45,600
Median mid-career salary	$79,400
% alumni with high job meaning	71%
% STEM	20%

SELECTIVITY

Admissions Rating	93
# of applicants	3,858
% of applicants accepted	50
% of acceptees attending	27
# offered a place on the wait list	785
% accepting a place on wait list	58
% admitted from wait list	2
# of early decision applicants	321
% accepted early decision	50

FRESHMAN PROFILE

Range SAT Critical Reading	620–730
Range SAT Math	610–735
Range SAT Writing	630–720
Range ACT Composite	29–32
Minimum internet-based TOEFL	100
Average HS GPA	3.8
% graduated top 10% of class	58
% graduated top 25% of class	90
% graduated top 50% of class	97

DEADLINES

Early decision	
Deadline	11/15
Notification	1/1
Other ED	
Deadline	1/1
Notification	2/1
Regular	
Deadline	1/15
Notification	4/1
Nonfall registration?	Yes

FINANCIAL FACTS

Financial Aid Rating	96
Annual tuition	$45,680
Room and board	$13,440
Required fees	$186
Average need-based scholarship	$31,101
% needy frosh rec. need-based scholarship or grant aid	100
% needy UG rec. need-based scholarship or grant aid	99
% needy frosh rec. non-need-based scholarship or grant aid	28
% needy UG rec. non-need-based scholarship or grant aid	20
% needy frosh rec. need-based self-help aid	85
% needy UG rec. need-based self-help aid	88
% frosh rec. any financial aid	81
% UG rec. any financial aid	80
% UG borrow to pay for school	69
Average cumulative indebtedness	$25,339
% frosh need fully met	100

Muhlenberg College

2400 WEST CHEW STREET, ALLENTOWN, PA 18104-5596 • ADMISSIONS: 484-664-3200 • FAX: 484-664-3032

CAMPUS LIFE

Quality of Life Rating	91
Fire Safety Rating	96
Green Rating	79
Type of school	Private
Affiliation	Lutheran
Environment	City

STUDENTS

Total undergrad enrollment	2,397
% male/female	40/60
% from out of state	73
% frosh from public high school	74
% frosh live on campus	98
% ugrads live on campus	91
# of fraternities (% ugrad men join)	4 (19)
# of sororities (% ugrad women join)	4 (27)
% African American	3
% Asian	3
% Caucasian	75
% Hispanic	7
% Native American	<1
% Pacific Islander	<1
% Two or more races	2
% Race and/or ethnicity unknown	8
% international	3
# of countries represented	18

ACADEMICS

Academic Rating	87
% students returning for sophomore year	93
% students graduating within 4 years	82
% students graduating within 6 years	85
Calendar	Semester
Student/faculty ratio	11:1
Profs interesting rating	88
Profs accessible rating	88

Most classes have 10–19 students.
Most lab/discussion sessions have
   fewer than 10 students.

MOST POPULAR MAJORS

Business/Commerce; Psychology; Drama
and Dramatics/Theatre Arts

ABOUT THE SCHOOL

At this private Lutheran college in Allentown, Pennsylvania, "the education is wonderful, and there isn't a day that goes by without learning something." This small school—enrollment is roughly 2,400—is "an excellent place to go if you're serious about academics, and you want to try a lot of different things throughout your undergraduate career. There are tons of options for extra-curriculars, and there are many majors and minors to explore." The liberal arts mentality appeals to students who praise "strong academics" and the ability to sample lots of different classes by professors who "are willing to help and listen, which significantly [increases] the learning experience." The "highly accepting and friendly" environment and the ease of access to professors "is extremely encouraging" and students find that "[they] work harder" because of it.

BANG FOR YOUR BUCK

In addition to offering an online catalogue of current internship opportunities, the school's website also provides students with the Muhlenberg College Internship Manual, which includes "tips on how to make the most of your internship, various guidelines, as well as important forms." One Environmental Science and Sociology major praised the "strong science program and honors program," where students "could conduct research and take part in an internship" instead of having to sacrifice internship opportunities for academic ones. Muhlenberg meets roughly 91 percent of students' need for aid, with students praising "generous" and "incredible" financial aid packages. Muhlenberg students are also encouraged to participate in the Student Research and Scholarship program, where they take part in "a variety of extracurricular experiences in which students conduct an independent scholarly investigation of a field under the guidance of a faculty member," according to the school's website.

STUDENT LIFE

Students describe Muhlenberg campus life as "a bubble" with little venturing out to downtown Allentown. Even for a small school, "there is such a wide variety of talented students here at Muhlenberg." Greek life does play a role on campus, where there are five sororities and four fraternities; approximately 24 percent of women join a sorority, while roughly 18 percent of men join a fraternity. "When the weather is nice," says one Neuroscience and Spanish major, "everyone is outside, whether playing pickup Frisbee, lacrosse, football or just relaxing on a blanket in the sun." Most students don't have classes on Friday, so the weekend begins on Thursday evening. One Political Science major described the school as "very accepting and open" and if "students want to try something new (clubs, etc.), they're welcome to. At Muhlenberg, the sky is the limit." There are roughly 100 registered student organizations and around 92 percent of all undergraduates living on campus, making for a college that "works hard to make sure that there are always fun events going on."

CAREER

PayScale.com reports that 42 percent of Muhlenberg graduates would describe their careers as helping to improve society. With an average starting salary of around $44,800, popular careers for graduates include web project manager, high school teacher, and software developer. The most popular majors reflect the school's dual strengths in the humanities and the sciences, with three common majors being business administration, communication, and biology. The Muhlenberg website offers two helpful services to students looking to gain traction in the work world: Collegefeed.com, where

Muhlenberg College

FINANCIAL AID: 484-664-3175 • E-MAIL: ADMISSION@MUHLENBERG.EDU • WEBSITE: WWW.MUHLENBERG.EDU

students upload a profile and the site "connect[s] [students] directly to hiring managers and founders at 500+ great companies;" and Interviewstream.com, a "virtual interviewing system" where students can "record an unlimited amount of practice interviews before seeking employment" and view "video clips on interviewing with tips from experts." A French and Business double major says that "Muhlenberg is very strong in academics and I feel that I will be well prepared for whatever career I [choose]."

GENERAL INFO

Activities: concert band, dance, drama/theater, jazz band, literary magazine, music ensembles, musical theater, pep band, radio station, student government, student newspaper, student-run film society, symphony orchestra, yearbook. **Organizations:** 100 registered organizations, 12 honor societies, 7 religious organizations. 4 fraternities, 5 sororities. **Athletics (Intercollegiate):** *Men:* baseball, basketball, cheerleading, cross-country, football, golf, lacrosse, soccer, tennis, track/field (outdoor), track/field (indoor), wrestling. *Women:* basketball, cheerleading, cross-country, field hockey, golf, lacrosse, soccer, softball, tennis, track/field (outdoor), track/field (indoor), volleyball. **On-Campus Highlights:** Seegers Union by fireplace & Java Joe's, The Life Sports Center-Athletic Facility, Parents Plaza-Outdoor Courtyard, GQ, Seegers Union, Trexler Pavilion for Threatre & Dance.

FINANCIAL AID

Students should submit: FAFSA, Institution's own financial aid form, CSS/Financial Aid PROFILE, State aid form, Noncustodial PROFILE, Business/Farm Supplement. Regular filing deadline is 2/15. The Princeton Review suggests that all financial aid forms be submitted as soon as possible after October 1. *Need-based scholarships/grants offered:* Federal Pell, FSEOG, State scholarships/grants, Private scholarships, College/university scholarship or grant aid from institutional funds. *Loan aid offered:* Direct Subsidized Stafford Loans, Direct Unsubsidized Stafford Loans, Direct PLUS loans, Federal Perkins Loans. Applicants will be notified of awards on or about 4/1. Federal Work-Study Program available. Institutional employment available.

BOTTOM LINE

Tuition is roughly $45,875 annually, with an additional $10,770 for room and board, and around $1,550 for books and fees, making a year at Muhlenberg cost $58,195. Eighty-nine percent of freshmen receive some sort of financial aid, with 86 percent of other undergraduates receiving aid. The average need-based gift aid awarded is $26,007. The typical Muhlenberg student graduates with approximately $29,761 in debt.

CAREER INFORMATION FROM PAYSCALE.COM

ROI rating	86
Bachelor's and No Higher	
Median starting salary	$49,100
Median mid-career salary	$81,500
At Least Bachelor's	
Median starting salary	$50,500
Median mid-career salary	$83,300
% alumni with high job meaning	47%
% STEM	13%

SELECTIVITY

Admissions Rating	90
# of applicants	5,015
% of applicants accepted	48
% of acceptees attending	24
# offered a place on the wait list	1,690
% accepting a place on wait list	19
% admitted from wait list	13
# of early decision applicants	354
% accepted early decision	81

FRESHMAN PROFILE

Range SAT Critical Reading	560–660
Range SAT Math	560–660
Range SAT Writing	560–660
Range ACT Composite	25–31
Minimum paper TOEFL	550
Minimum internet-based TOEFL	80
Average HS GPA	3.3
% graduated top 10% of class	41
% graduated top 25% of class	71
% graduated top 50% of class	94

DEADLINES

Early decision	
Deadline	2/15
Other ED	
Deadline	2/15
Regular	
Priority	2/15
Deadline	2/15
Notification	3/15
Nonfall registration?	Yes

FINANCIAL FACTS

Financial Aid Rating	89
Annual tuition	$47,825
Room and board	$11,090
Required fees	$485
Average need-based scholarship	$26,007
% needy frosh rec. need-based scholarship or grant aid	90
% needy UG rec. need-based scholarship or grant aid	91
% needy frosh rec. non-need-based scholarship or grant aid	75
% needy UG rec. non-need-based scholarship or grant aid	68
% needy frosh rec. need-based self-help aid	71
% needy UG rec. need-based self-help aid	73
% frosh rec. any financial aid	89
% UG rec. any financial aid	88
% UG borrow to pay for school	57
Average cumulative indebtedness	$30,527
% frosh need fully met	31

New College of Florida

5800 Bay Shore Road, Sarasota, FL 34243-2109 • Admissions: 941-487-5000 • Fax: 941-487-5001

CAMPUS LIFE

Quality of Life Rating	91
Fire Safety Rating	91
Green Rating	74
Type of school	Public
Affiliation	No Affiliation
Environment	Town

STUDENTS

Total undergrad enrollment	861
% male/female	39/61
% from out of state	13
% frosh from public high school	82
% frosh live on campus	98
% ugrads live on campus	76
% African American	3
% Asian	3
% Caucasian	69
% Hispanic	16
% Native American	0
% Pacific Islander	0
% Two or more races	4
% Race and/or ethnicity unknown	3
% international	2
# of countries represented	23

ACADEMICS

Academic Rating	96
% students returning for sophomore year	81
% students graduating within 4 years	63
% students graduating within 6 years	71
Calendar	4/1/4
Student/faculty ratio	10:1
Profs interesting rating	98
Profs accessible rating	90
Most classes have 10–19 students.	

MOST POPULAR MAJORS
Psychology; Anthropology; Economics

#49 COLLEGE THAT PAYS YOU BACK

ABOUT THE SCHOOL
New College of Florida distinguishes itself from other elite colleges and universities through its unique collaborative curriculum, emphasis on independent learning, and "deep and stimulating academics." With a total enrollment of fewer than 1,000 students, New College offers a "small, intimate atmosphere" in which faculty and students engage collaboratively in in-depth exploration of ideas and subject matter, all at a public college price. "It [feels] like a family," says a student. With no graduate students on campus, undergraduates receive the full attention of their professors and work one-on-one with them to map their own intellectual journey, which culminates in a senior thesis. There is no rigid core curriculum required of all students ("Our school has been tailored to us"). The cornerstone of the New College experience is that, in addition to traditional course offerings, the student has the ability to work with "dedicated and wise professors" to design their own independent study and research projects during the month of January, which is set aside for independent projects. Course work at NCF is intense and can be stressful. However, with fewer than 1,000 students on campus, all students are guaranteed to receive plenty of personal attention from passionate and accessible professors. The student body takes "active participation in the running of the school," and The Center for Engagement and Opportunity helps students coordinate internships, make career decisions, conduct job searches, apply to graduate and professional schools, and network with New College alumni. This leads to impressive outcomes, as evidenced by the seventy Fulbright Scholarships that have been awarded to NCF students since 2001 (there were eight in 2011 alone).

BANG FOR YOUR BUCK
The combination of NCF's incredibly low tuition and rigorous, individualized academic program make it a tremendous value for both in-state and out-of-state students. Students and their families can take advantage of many funding opportunities, including grants, loans, book advances, and work-study. Scholarships are guaranteed to all admitted applicants meeting the February 15 application deadline. Additional scholarship opportunities may be available to students based upon their specialized high school curriculum. In addition to an academic scholarship, gift assistance is available for qualifying students who submit the FAFSA by the February 15 priority deadline.

STUDENT LIFE
New College students share "a few things in common: Most […] are friendly, passionate about the things they believe in, very hard workers, liberal, and most of all, try to be open to new experiences." Put another way: "New College is a bunch of incredibly intelligent hippies exploring every facet of existence." On campus, students enjoy everything "from club meetings to public speakers to 'hip' bands playing shows. There's usually something to do and usually free food to be found!" Weekends usually mean going to see "the Wall," which are the "school-wide parties every Friday and Saturday night in a courtyard outside of the dorms" or a visit to nearby Lido and Siesta Beaches, "where [students] enjoy unlimited swimming, sunning and Frisbee playing." Undergrads praise the overall emphasis on "freedom, intelligence, creativity, and challenging yourself" that permeates student culture in class and out.

New College of Florida

FINANCIAL AID: 941-487-5000 • E-MAIL: ADMISSIONS@NCF.EDU • WEBSITE: WWW.NCF.EDU

CAREER

The Center for Engagement and Opportunity (CEO), a new office in 2014–2015, houses everything related to career services, internships, and fellowships for students thinking strategically about their future. Beyond CEO, faculty advisors also act as career mentors and help their students locate experiential learning opportunities like study abroad or off-campus research—students have recently interned at the Jane Goodall Institute in Washington, D.C., and the Early Intervention Program in Massachusetts. The Alumnae/i Association boasts professional connections at University of Florida, University of South Florida, UC Berkeley, and Apple and serves as another resource for students seeking opportunities or advice about life after graduation.

GENERAL INFO

Activities: Choral groups, dance, drama/theater, literary magazine, music ensembles, musical theater, radio station, student government, student newspaper, student-run film society, campus ministries. **Organizations:** 90 registered organizations, 5 religious organizations. **Athletics (Intercollegiate):** *Men:* Sailing. *Women:* Sailing. **On-Campus Highlights:** The R.V. Heiser Natural Sciences Complex, Pritzker Marine Biology Research Center, The Caples Fine Arts Complex, Four Winds Cafe (Student owned and operated), Jane Bancroft Cook Library, Historic bay-front mansions. **Environmental Initiatives:** Waste management efforts—recycling of all paper, newsprint, cardboard, phone books, magazines, junk mail, soft-cover books, cotton goods, cans (all types), glass and plastic, jars and bottles, auto batteries, used oil and filters, used antifreeze, toner cartridges, chemicals and solvents, white goods, scrap metal, precious metals, wastewater solids, used pallets, yard debris, masonry and concrete, fluorescent tubes, used lumber, etc. Purchasing efforts—all new appliances are EnergyStar.

FINANCIAL AID

Students should submit: FAFSA. Priority filing deadline is 2/15. The Princeton Review suggests that all financial aid forms be submitted as soon as possible after October 1. *Need-based scholarships/grants offered:* Federal Pell, FSEOG, State scholarships/grants, Private scholarships, College/university scholarship or grant aid from institutional funds. *Loan aid offered:* Direct Subsidized Stafford Loans, Direct Unsubsidized Stafford Loans, Direct PLUS Loans. Applicants will be notified of awards on a rolling basis beginning 3/15. Federal Work-Study Program available. Institutional employment available.

THE BOTTOM LINE

Even in the era of rising higher education costs, tuition at New College of Florida is still incredibly low, as evidenced by the comparatively low average debt for graduating students: just under $15,000. The sticker price is further offset by loans, grants, and scholarships. The average scholarship and grant package for students with demonstrated need is $8,752, and the average need-based loan is $3,591. The school estimates that books and supplies may run another $1,200 per year. Independent study projects and senior theses may involve additional costs for travel, research expenses, and equipment.

CAREER INFORMATION FROM PAYSCALE.COM

ROI rating	**90**
Bachelor's and No Higher	
Median starting salary	$39,800
Median mid-career salary	$85,000
At Least Bachelor's	
Median starting salary	$39,800
Median mid-career salary	$85,000

SELECTIVITY

Admissions Rating	**89**
# of applicants	1,655
% of applicants accepted	61
% of acceptees attending	26
# offered a place on the wait list	178
% accepting a place on wait list	29
% admitted from wait list	59

FRESHMAN PROFILE

Range SAT Critical Reading	610–720
Range SAT Math	560–660
Range SAT Writing	570–670
Range ACT Composite	27–31
Minimum paper TOEFL	560
Minimum internet-based TOEFL	83
Average HS GPA	4.0
% graduated top 10% of class	43
% graduated top 25% of class	79
% graduated top 50% of class	97

DEADLINES

Regular	
Priority	11/1
Deadline	4/15
Nonfall registration?	No

FINANCIAL FACTS

Financial Aid Rating	**87**
Annual in-state tuition	$6,916
Annual out-of-state tuition	$29,944
Room and board	$9,060
Average need-based scholarship	$8,752
% needy frosh rec. need-based scholarship or grant aid	91
% needy UG rec. need-based scholarship or grant aid	92
% needy frosh rec. non-need-based scholarship or grant aid	16
% needy UG rec. non-need-based scholarship or grant aid	12
% needy frosh rec. need-based self-help aid	79
% needy UG rec. need-based self-help aid	82
% frosh rec. any financial aid	100
% UG rec. any financial aid	98
% UG borrow to pay for school	48
Average cumulative indebtedness	$14,929
% frosh need fully met	48
% ugrads need fully met	37
Average % of frosh need met	89
Average % of ugrad need met	83

rth Carolina State University

Raleigh, NC 27695 • Admissions: 919-515-2434 • Fax: 919-515-5039

PUS LIFE

lity of Life Rating	**91**
Fire Safety Rating	**98**
Green Rating	**96**
Type of school	Public
Affiliation	No Affiliation
Environment	Metropolis

STUDENTS

Total undergrad enrollment	24,111
% male/female	55/45
% from out of state	10
% frosh from public high school	84
% frosh live on campus	79
% ugrads live on campus	32
# of fraternities (% ugrad men join)	29 (11)
# of sororities (% ugrad women join)	21 (17)
% African American	6
% Asian	5
% Caucasian	73
% Hispanic	5
% Native American	<1
% Pacific Islander	<1
% Two or more races	4
% Race and/or ethnicity unknown	2
% international	4
# of countries represented	107

ACADEMICS

Academic Rating	**76**
% students returning for sophomore year	94
% students graduating within 4 years	44
% students graduating within 6 years	76
Calendar	Semester
Student/faculty ratio	14:1
Profs interesting rating	73
Profs accessible rating	78

Most classes have 10–19 students.
Most lab/discussion sessions have 20–29 students.

MOST POPULAR MAJORS
Biology; Business Administration and Management; Engineering

ABOUT THE SCHOOL

Science and technology are big at North Carolina State University, a major research university and the largest four-year institution in its state. While the College of Engineering and the College of Sciences form the backbone of the academic program, the school also boasts nationally reputable majors in architecture, design, textiles, management, agriculture, humanities and social sciences, education, physical and mathematical sciences, natural resources, and veterinary medicine, providing "big-school opportunity with a small-school feel." The "vicinity to top-of-the-line research" is palpable, as more than 70 percent of NC State's faculty is involved in sponsored research, and the school is "an incubator for outstanding engineering and scientific research." For undergraduates, many of whom grew up wanting to attend the school, this opportunity to participate in important research is a major advantage. It makes sense, given that NC State "is all about developing skills in school that will help you throughout your professional career." In addition, an education at NC State includes many opportunities for students to get a head start on a real-world job, and the school also has "a great [Exploratory Studies] for students . . . who aren't sure what major they want to go into." The university's co-op program is one of the largest in the nation, with more than 1,000 work rotations a year, all due to the school's excellent reputation. "I want my degree to pack a punch when people see it, without having to be ridiculously rich or a prodigy of some sort," says a student of his decision to go to NC State.

BANG FOR YOUR BUCK

NC State continues to be a bargain for North Carolina residents. Offering financial assistance to qualified students is an integral part of NC State's history. In fact, this school was one of the first universities in the nation to create a scholarship program for students with the greatest financial need. The school's program, Pack Promise, guarantees that North Carolina's most disadvantaged students will receive 100 percent of their financial aid needs met through scholarships, grants, federal work-study employment, and need-based loans.

STUDENT LIFE

North Carolina State offers a lot for students to do both on and off campus. Though students report that they spend a great deal of time studying, social life is very big as well: "Although sleep deprivation seems to be very popular, everyone manages to have some fun doing what they want to do while maintaining their GPA. And there is something for everyone here at State." "The school offers various activities throughout each semester that are usually lots of fun, and the best part is they're free," says a student. "There are also a lot of club events. Outdoor Adventures usually does something about every weekend, involving a trip to the mountains or something. There's always a lot of support for the sports teams and tons of school spirit." In addition to attending sporting events, "it's easy to get out and play yourself" through a variety of intramural teams and clubs. For those looking to venture out at night, "students love to go to downtown Raleigh to have fun in clubs or wander Hillsborough Street. There is opportunity to do just about anything in the area."

CAREER

Students at NC State work hard and are concerned about their future careers, and most feel that the school prepares them very well for life after college. The Career Development Center offers one-on-one academic advising and career planning; job and internship search resources; career fairs and on-campus recruiting in many different

North Carolina State University

FINANCIAL AID: 919-515-2421 • E-MAIL: UNDERGRAD_ADMISSIONS@NCSU.EDU • WEBSITE: WWW.NCSU.EDU

fields; and help with resume building, job interviews, and other professional skills. The school also offers a Cooperative Education program that allows students to pursue paid work in their field while studying for their degree. "I have had several good academic advisors that have helped me decide what courses I should take based on the different career paths I have been considering," says a student. "Also, all of my professors always wish to do whatever they can in order to help out the students." Out of NC State alumni visiting PayScale. com, 55 percent report that they derive a high level of meaning from their jobs.

GENERAL INFO

Activities: Choral groups, concert band, dance, drama/theater, jazz band, literary magazine, marching band, music ensembles, musical theater, pep band, radio station, student government, student newspaper, symphony orchestra, yearbook, campus ministries, international student organization. **Organizations:** 637 registered organizations, 26 honor societies, 50 religious organizations. 30 fraternities, 20 sororities. **Athletics (Intercollegiate):** *Men:* Baseball, basketball, cheerleading, cross-country, diving, football, golf, riflery, soccer, swimming, tennis, track/field (outdoor), track/field (indoor), wrestling. *Women:* Basketball, cheerleading, cross-country, diving, golf, gymnastics, riflery, soccer, softball, swimming, tennis, track/ field (outdoor), track/field (indoor), volleyball.

FINANCIAL AID

Students should submit: FAFSA. Priority filing deadline is 3/1. The Princeton Review suggests that all financial aid forms be submitted as soon as possible after October 1. *Need-based scholarships/grants offered:* Federal Pell, FSEOG, State scholarships/grants, Private scholarships, College/university scholarship or grant aid from institutional funds, United Negro College Fund. *Loan aid offered:* Direct Subsidized Stafford Loans, Direct Unsubsidized Stafford Loans, Direct PLUS loans, Federal Perkins Loans, State Loans, College/university loans from institutional funds. Applicants will be notified of awards on a rolling basis beginning 3/1. Federal Work-Study Program available. Institutional employment available.

BOTTOM LINE

Annual tuition and fees for North Carolina residents are $8,880. For nonresidents, tuition and fees reach $26,399. For both residents and nonresidents, room and board runs about $10,635 per year, while books and supplies average just over $1,000 annually. Around 55 percent of all NC State students take out loans—students who borrow money graduate with an average loan debt of roughly $17,461.

CAREER INFORMATION FROM PAYSCALE.COM

ROI rating	**90**
Bachelor's and No Higher	
Median starting salary	$50,600
Median mid-career salary	$87,800
At Least Bachelor's	
Median starting salary	$51,400
Median mid-career salary	$90,000
% alumni with high job meaning	51%
% STEM	41%

SELECTIVITY

Admissions Rating	91
# of applicants	21,099
% of applicants accepted	50
% of acceptees attending	40
# offered a place on the wait list	2,433
% accepting a place on wait list	42
% admitted from wait list	2

FRESHMAN PROFILE

Range SAT Critical Reading	570–650
Range SAT Math	590–680
Range SAT Writing	540–630
Range ACT Composite	27–31
Minimum paper TOEFL	563
Minimum internet-based TOEFL	85
Average HS GPA	3.7
% graduated top 10% of class	51
% graduated top 25% of class	87
% graduated top 50% of class	99

DEADLINES

Early action	
Deadline	10/15
Notification	1/30
Regular	
Priority	10/15
Deadline	1/15
Nonfall registration?	Yes

FINANCIAL FACTS

Financial Aid Rating	85
Annual in-state tuition	$6,407
Annual out-of-state tuition	$23,926
Room and board	$10,635
Required fees	$2,473
Average need-based scholarship	$9,913
% needy frosh rec. need-based scholarship or grant aid	93
% needy UG rec. need-based scholarship or grant aid	90
% needy frosh rec. non-need-based scholarship or grant aid	21
% needy UG rec. non-need-based scholarship or grant aid	13
% needy frosh rec. need-based self-help aid	70
% needy UG rec. need-based self-help aid	72
% frosh rec. any financial aid	75
% UG rec. any financial aid	68
% UG borrow to pay for school	55
Average cumulative indebtedness	$17,461
% frosh need fully met	24
% ugrads need fully met	24
Average % of frosh need met	80
Average % of ugrad need met	78

Northeastern University

360 Huntington Avenue, Boston, MA 02115 • Admissions: 617-373-2200 • Fax: 617-373-8780

CAMPUS LIFE

Quality of Life Rating	**94**
Fire Safety Rating	**94**
Green Rating	**95**
Type of school	Private
Affiliation	No Affiliation
Environment	Metropolis

STUDENTS

Total undergrad enrollment	17,990
% male/female	50/50
% from out of state	70
% frosh live on campus	99
% ugrads live on campus	48
# of fraternities (% ugrad men join)	18 (8)
# of sororities (% ugrad women join)	14 (12)
% African American	4
% Asian	12
% Caucasian	49
% Hispanic	7
% Native American	<1
% Pacific Islander	<1
% Two or more races	4
% Race and/or ethnicity unknown	6
% international	19
# of countries represented	121

ACADEMICS

Academic Rating	**83**
% students returning for sophomore year	97
% students graduating within 6 years	84
Calendar	Semester
Student/faculty ratio	14:1
Profs interesting rating	76
Profs accessible rating	75

Most classes have 10–19 students.
Most lab/discussion sessions have 10–19 students.

MOST POPULAR MAJORS

Engineering; Health Services; Business/Commerce

ABOUT THE SCHOOL

Northeastern University is a school full of big ideas and big opportunity. The school's incredibly unique and dynamic co-op program allows students to gain "real-world experiences coupled with classroom guidance." As one thankful marketing major explains, "[It's] an amazing opportunity to apply what you learn in the class room to a real, full-time job for six months." She continues, "It's incredibly refreshing to take off school for six months and learn in a completely different environment. It's also quite fulfilling to take what you've learned in work and bring it back with you into the classroom." What's more, Northeastern has a wide array of fantastic programs. Indeed, students excitedly highlight the "amazing" political science, criminal justice, engineering, and physical therapy programs. By and large undergrads speak glowingly of their "knowledgeable" professors who "are eager to engage students in their courses." And, importantly, they "all either have practiced or currently practice what they teach, which makes their lectures that much more interesting and valuable."

BANG FOR YOUR BUCK

Overall, students at Northeastern give the financial aid office a thumbs up. Undergrads report receiving "solid financial aid packages" which definitely help families alleviate what otherwise might feel like a big burden. Clearly, the university's efforts pay off, as 100% of first year students' demonstrated need is met, and the school says it is committed to meeting full demonstrated need for all incoming students. Moreover, the average package awarded is approximately $25,281. Also available are federal or state grants; federal work-study; loans for particular academic programs; low-interest, need-based federal loans; and university scholarships. These include the Global Scholars Award, the Dean's Scholarship, and other merit-based scholarships. Finalists in the national Merit Scholarship Program or scholars in the National Hispanic Scholarship program are eligible for merit scholarships.

SCHOOL LIFE

Students at Northeastern are constantly on the go. And considering there's so much to take advantage of it's easy to understand why! After all, undergrads assert that "there are performances, movies, club meetings, and programs every night of the week," not to mention more than 380+ campus organizations to keep them busy. Students can frequently see "comedians like Andy Samberg" or attend "large scale concerts [featuring artists such as] Drake." Additionally, undergrads here are generally a health conscious group. One senior confirms this stating, "The fitness centers are always full and have plenty of people working out all the time." Changing the subject, a fellow senior quickly interjects, "There is always a party (or ten) off campus and never far, but it is easy to avoid them if you choose." And, certainly, "Boston is at our disposal and many students choose to take advantage of our fantastic city."

CAREER

There's no question that Northeastern's "world class co-op program," which includes 3,000 employers worldwide, "really gives students a leg up in finding a career." In fact, according to the school, 50 percent of 2015 graduates received a job offer from a previous co-op employer. It also helps that the university's Career Development Office is top notch! Indeed, the office is continually hosting events such as "LinkedIn 1: Build Your Profile" and "Interviewing 101." On-Campus Recruiting also does a phenomenal job, bringing

Northeastern University

FINANCIAL AID: 617-373-3190 • E-MAIL: ADMISSIONS@NEU.EDU • WEBSITE: WWW.NORTHEASTERN.EDU

numerous companies to Northeastern every year. As if that wasn't enough, the school also hosts several big career fairs. Students have the opportunity to meet with companies like Amazon, Dana-Farber Cancer Institute, Bose Corporation & Johnson and Johnson. Another unique aspect of this career office—it helps prepare students in the art of salary negotiation. And that very well might be why the average starting salary for recent grads is an impressive $54,100 (according to PayScale.com).

GENERAL INFO

Activities: Choral groups, dance, drama/theater, jazz band, literary magazine, music ensembles, musical theater, radio station, student government, student newspaper, symphony orchestra, television station, yearbook, International Student Organization, Model UN. **Organizations:** 380+ registered organizations, 14 honor societies, 20 religious organizations. 12 fraternities, 11 sororities. **Athletics (Intercollegiate):** *Men:* baseball, basketball, crew/rowing, cross-country, ice hockey, soccer, track/field (outdoor), track/field (indoor). *Women:* basketball, crew/rowing, cross-country, diving, field hockey, ice hockey, soccer, swimming, track/field (outdoor), track/field (indoor), volleyball. **On-Campus Highlights:** International Village, Curry Student Center, Marino Health and Fitness Center, Levine Marketplace & Stetson West Dining, Cyber Cafe.

FINANCIAL AID

Students should submit: FAFSA, CSS/Financial Aid PROFILE, Noncustodial PROFILE. Priority filing deadline is 2/15. The Princeton Review suggests that all financial aid forms be submitted as soon as possible after October 1. *Need-based scholarships/grants offered:* Federal Pell, FSEOG, State scholarships/grants, Private scholarships, College/university scholarship or grant aid from institutional funds. *Loan aid offered:* Direct Subsidized Stafford Loans, Direct Unsubsidized Stafford Loans, Direct PLUS loans, Federal Perkins Loans, Federal Nursing Loans, State Loans. Applicants will be notified of awards on or about 4/1. Federal Work-Study Program available. Institutional employment available.

BOTTOM LINE

Northeastern undergraduates and their families can expect a tuition bill of $46,720. Students choosing to reside on-campus will pay $15,600 for room and board. An additional $1,000 will be needed for books and other academic supplies. Further, students face another $933 in required fees.

CAREER INFORMATION FROM PAYSCALE.COM

ROI rating	84
Bachelor's and No Higher	
Median starting salary	$55,000
Median mid-career salary	$89,600
At Least Bachelor's	
Median starting salary	$56,000
Median mid-career salary	$91,900
% alumni with high job meaning	53%
% STEM	23%

SELECTIVITY

Admissions Rating	95
# of applicants	50,523
% of applicants accepted	28
% of acceptees attending	19
# of early decision applicants	773
% accepted early decision	31

FRESHMAN PROFILE

Range SAT Critical Reading	660–740
Range SAT Math	680–770
Range SAT Writing	640–730
Range ACT Composite	31–34
Minimum internet-based TOEFL	92
% graduated top 10% of class	70
% graduated top 25% of class	94
% graduated top 50% of class	99

DEADLINES

Early decision	
Deadline	11/1
Notification	12/15
Early action	
Deadline	11/1
Notification	12/31
Regular	
Deadline	1/1
Notification	4/1
Nonfall registration?	Yes

FINANCIAL FACTS

Financial Aid Rating	85
Annual tuition	$46,720
Room and board	$15,600
Required fees	$933
Average need-based scholarship	$25,281
% needy frosh rec. need-based scholarship or grant aid	98
% needy UG rec. need-based scholarship or grant aid	94
% needy frosh rec. non-need-based scholarship or grant aid	47
% needy UG rec. non-need-based scholarship or grant aid	34
% needy frosh rec. need-based self-help aid	89
% needy UG rec. need-based self-help aid	87
% frosh need fully met	100
% ugrads need fully met	37
Average % of frosh need met	100
Average % of ugrad need met	85

Northwestern University

PO Box 3060, 1801 Hinman Avenue, Evanston, IL 60204-3060 • Admissions: 847-491-7271

CAMPUS LIFE

Quality of Life Rating	73
Fire Safety Rating	83
Green Rating	60*
Type of school	Private
Affiliation	No Affiliation
Environment	Town

STUDENTS

Total undergrad enrollment	8,315
% male/female	50/50
% from out of state	67
% frosh from public high school	65
% frosh live on campus	99
% ugrads live on campus	50
# of fraternities (% ugrad men join)	17 (29)
# of sororities (% ugrad women join)	12 (32)
% African American	6
% Asian	17
% Caucasian	53
% Hispanic	11
% Native American	<1
% Pacific Islander	<1
% Two or more races	5
% Race and/or ethnicity unknown	2
% international	9
# of countries represented	80

ACADEMICS

Academic Rating	92
% students returning for sophomore year	97
% students graduating within 4 years	0
Calendar	Semester
Student/faculty ratio	7:1
Profs interesting rating	77
Profs accessible rating	77

Most classes have fewer than 10 students.
Most lab/discussion sessions have
   10–19 students.

MOST POPULAR MAJORS
Economics; Engineering; Journalism

ABOUT THE SCHOOL

One student relates that Northwestern University "is all about balance—academically it excels across the academic spectrum, its location is just the right balance between urban and suburban, and its student body, while not incredibly ethnically diverse, still has a range of people." The total undergraduate enrollment is more than 8,000 students; adding to the school's diversity, nearly three-quarters of kids come from out-of-state. Northwestern University is a school built on communities, be they social, political, or academic. It's a rigorous, "very challenging" multidisciplinary school that is preprofessional and stimulating, and students are pleased by the fact that "Northwestern is not an easy school. It takes hard work to be average here." Northwestern not only has a varied curriculum, but "everything is given fairly equal weight." Northwestern students and faculty "do not show a considerable bias" toward specific fields. Excellence in competencies that transcend any particular field of study is highly valued.

BANG FOR YOUR BUCK

Northwestern University works hard to empower students to become leaders in their professions and communities. People are goal-oriented and care about their academic success, and they're pleased that Northwestern helps provide "so many connections and opportunities during and after graduation." Numerous resources established by administrators and professors, including tutoring programs such as Northwestern's Gateway Science Workshop, provide needy students with all of the support they desire.

STUDENT LIFE

The typical Northwestern student "was high school class president with a 4.0, swim team captain, and on the chess team." So it makes sense everyone here "is an excellent student who works hard" and "has a leadership position in at least two clubs, plus an on-campus job." Students also tell us "there's [a] great separation between North Campus (think: fraternities, engineering, state-school mentality) and South Campus (think: closer to Chicago and its culture, arts and letters, liberal arts school mentality). Students segregate themselves depending on background and interests, and it's rare for these two groups to interact beyond a superficial level." The student body here includes sizeable Jewish, Indian, and East-Asian populations.

CAREER

The University Career Services at Northwestern aims to empower students to "assess, explore, decide and act" on their future professional goals, according to its website. The office offers resources on finding a major, an internship, or a job, applying to graduate school, and on honing employment skills like writing resumes and cover letters or being a fantastic interviewee. CareerCat is the online internship and job database through which students and alumni also get updates on programming, special events, and other services. If students are unsure about which career path is for them, they can participate in a Career Trek to cities like New York City or Washington D.C. where they meet with professionals and are given some perspective on industries like Finance, Media & Marketing or Law, Government & Policy. Northwestern graduates who visited PayScale.com report a median starting salary of $54,200.

Northwestern University

FINANCIAL AID: 847-491-7400 • E-MAIL: UG-ADMISSION@NORTHWESTERN.EDU • WEBSITE: WWW.NORTHWESTERN.EDU

GENERAL INFO

Activities: Choral groups, concert band, dance, drama/theater, jazz band, literary magazine, marching band, music ensembles, musical theater, opera, pep band, radio station, student government, student newspaper, student-run film society, symphony orchestra, television station, yearbook, campus ministries, international student organization. **Organizations:** 415 registered organizations, 23 honor societies, 29 religious organizations. 17 fraternities, 12 sororities. **Athletics (Intercollegiate):** *Men:* Baseball, basketball, cheerleading, diving, football, golf, soccer, swimming, tennis, wrestling. *Women:* Basketball, cheerleading, cross-country, diving, fencing, field hockey, golf, lacrosse, soccer, softball, swimming, tennis, volleyball. **On-Campus Highlights:** Shakespeare Garden, Dearborn Observatory, Norris Student Center, Henry Crown Sports Pavilion and Aquatic Center, the lakefill on Lake Michigan. **Environmental Initiatives:** Commitment to purchase of renewable energy credits for 20 percent of the University's usage. Commitment to LEED certifications awarded (LEED NC Silver and LEED CI Gold).

FINANCIAL AID

Students should submit: FAFSA, CSS/Financial Aid PROFILE, Noncustodial PROFILE. Regular filing deadline is 3/5. The Princeton Review suggests that all financial aid forms be submitted as soon as possible after October 1. *Need-based scholarships/grants offered:* Federal Pell, FSEOG, State scholarships/grants, College/university scholarship or grant aid from institutional funds. *Loan aid offered:* Direct Subsidized Stafford Loans, Direct Unsubsidized Stafford Loans, Direct PLUS loans, Federal Perkins Loans, College/university loans from institutional funds. Applicants will be notified of awards on or about 4/15. Federal Work-Study Program available. Institutional employment available.

BOTTOM LINE

Northwestern is among the nation's most expensive undergraduate institutions, a fact that sometimes discourages some qualified students from applying. The school is increasing its efforts to attract more low-income applicants by increasing the number of full scholarships available for students whose family income is less than $45,000. Low-income students who score well on the ACT may receive a letter from the school encouraging them to apply. With tuition more than $50,000 a year, any and all support is greatly appreciated by undergrads and their parents.

CAREER INFORMATION FROM PAYSCALE.COM

ROI rating	89
Bachelor's and No Higher	
Median starting salary	$56,300
Median mid-career salary	$102,000
At Least Bachelor's	
Median starting salary	$58,400
Median mid-career salary	$105,000
% alumni with high job meaning	54%
% STEM	23%

SELECTIVITY

Admissions Rating	98
# of applicants	32,122
% of applicants accepted	13
% of acceptees attending	48
# offered a place on the wait list	2,614
% accepting a place on wait list	55
% admitted from wait list	2
# of early decision applicants	3,102
% accepted early decision	35

FRESHMAN PROFILE

Range SAT Critical Reading	690–760
Range SAT Math	710–800
Range ACT Composite	31–34
% graduated top 10% of class	91
% graduated top 25% of class	100
% graduated top 50% of class	100

DEADLINES

Early decision	
Deadline	11/1
Notification	12/15
Regular	
Deadline	1/1
Notification	4/1
Nonfall registration?	Yes

FINANCIAL FACTS

Financial Aid Rating	93
Annual tuition	$50,424
Room and board	$15,489
Required fees	$431
Average need-based scholarship	$40,208
% needy frosh rec. need-based scholarship or grant aid	98
% needy UG rec. need-based scholarship or grant aid	97
% needy frosh rec. non-need-based scholarship or grant aid	0
% needy UG rec. non-need-based scholarship or grant aid	0
% needy frosh rec. need-based self-help aid	75
% needy UG rec. need-based self-help aid	78
% frosh need fully met	100
% ugrads need fully met	100
Average % of frosh need met	100
Average % of ugrad need met	100

Oberlin College

101 North Professor Street, Oberlin, OH 44074 • Admissions: 440-775-8411 • Fax: 440-775-6905

ABOUT THE SCHOOL

Oberlin is known as a school that emphasizes the "liberal" in liberal arts. Oberlin's forward thinking and progressive values can be seen in its history. It was the first school to institute a policy of admitting students without regard to race and was the first coeducational school to grant bachelor's degrees to women. Academics are excellent here. An Oberlin education "focus[es] on learning for learning's sake rather than making money in a career." Oberlin can boast having more graduates earn PhDs than any other liberal arts college. Oberlin's academics are strong all around, but "the sciences, English, politics, religion, music, environmental studies, and East Asian studies are particularly noteworthy." The campus is also home to the Oberlin Conservatory of Music, which is the oldest continually active conservatory in America. Consequentially, music is a huge part of campus, and there are "400-plus musical performances every year, due to the conservatory." "I am lucky to be involved in the music scene at Oberlin," one student says, "so most of my social life revolves around the numerous house parties that host live bands." Oberlin alumni have gone on to perform in such bands as Deerhoof, Tortoise, Liz Phair, and Yeah Yeah Yeahs. The professors are the "heart and soul of the school" and "an absolute dream." The dedicated faculty "treat you more like collaborators." "Academically, my classes are stimulating and my professors are engaging," one student says.

BANG FOR YOUR BUCK

With an undergrad population of about 2,800 students, Oberlin is a small and selective school. The "excellent instructors" are easily accessible to students, as Oberlin boasts an impressive nine to one student-to-faculty-ratio. "Because of the small-town atmosphere, you can get to know professors quite personally," one student explains. Oberlin students tend to love their experience: a full 94 percent of freshmen return for sophomore year. Sixty-nine percent of students graduate in four years. "The beautiful campus" has, in addition to the worldclass music conservatory, a great art museum with a peculiar art rental program. For a mere five dollars, students are able to rent out original works of art by such renowned artists as Pablo Picasso, Salvador Dali, and Andy Warhol to hang in their dorm rooms. This is just one example of the kind of unique and forward-thinking ideas that you will find while receiving Oberlin's one-of-a-kind education.

STUDENT LIFE

"If you're a liberal, artsy, indie loner," then Oberlin might be the place for you. "We're all different and unusual, which creates a common bond between students." "Musicians, jocks, science geeks, creative writing majors, straight, bi, questioning, queer, and trans [students]," all have their place here, alongside "straight-edge, international, local, and joker students." Oberlin has a reputation for a left-leaning and active student body. One undergrad observes, "They are less active politically than they would like to think, but still more active than most people elsewhere." Another adds, "Most students are very liberal, but the moderates and (few) Republicans have a fine time of it. Every student has different interests and isn't afraid to talk about them."

CAREER

Oberlin offers abundant opportunities for students to gain experience that may be valuable to future employers. The Career Center, for example, coordinates Winter Term internships in various fields (past sites have included the Smithsonian Institution, Global Green, and Discovery Communications), usually sponsored by Oberlin alumni. Oberlin's recruiting database, ObieOpps, makes the sometimes daunting search for internships and jobs a simple process. The Office of Undergraduate Research provides support for students interested in faculty-mentored research, and OSU has special scholars programs

Oberlin College

FINANCIAL AID: 440-775-8142 • E-MAIL: COLLEGE.ADMISSIONS@OBERLIN.EDU • WEBSITE: WWW.OBERLIN.EDU

in areas like law, business, and entrepreneurship for undergraduates who wish to hone their skills. To draw upon the experience of Oberlin graduates, students can visit TAPPAN, an online directory with thousands of alumni career profiles. Finally, there are frequent information sessions about anything you might be interested in pursuing after graduation from Google to grad school. Oberlin graduates who visited PayScale.com reported an average starting salary of about $40,200.

GENERAL INFO
Activities: Choral groups, concert band, dance, drama/theater, jazz band, literary magazine, marching band, music ensembles, musical theater, opera, radio station, student government, student newspaper, student-run film society, symphony orchestra, yearbook, Campus Ministries, International Student Organization. **Organizations:** 125 registered organizations, 3 honor societies, 10 religious organizations. **Athletics (Intercollegiate):** *Men:* baseball, basketball, cross-country, diving, football, golf, lacrosse, soccer, swimming, tennis, track/field (outdoor), track/field (indoor). *Women:* basketball, cross-country, diving, field hockey, golf, lacrosse, soccer, softball, swimming, tennis, track/field (outdoor), track/field (indoor), volleyball. **On-Campus Highlights:** Allen Art Museum, Oberlin College Science Center, Adam Joseph Lewis Center for Environmental Studies, Mudd Library, Jesse Philips Recreational Center.

FINANCIAL AID
Students should submit: FAFSA, Institution's own financial aid form, CSS/Financial Aid PROFILE, Noncustodial PROFILE. Regular filing deadline is 2/15. The Princeton Review suggests that all financial aid forms be submitted as soon as possible after October 1. *Need-based scholarships/grants offered:* Federal Pell, FSEOG, State scholarships/grants, Private scholarships, College/university scholarship or grant aid from institutional funds, United Negro College Fund. *Loan aid offered:* Direct Subsidized Stafford Loans, Direct Unsubsidized Stafford Loans, Federal Perkins Loans, College/university loans from institutional funds. Applicants will be notified of awards on or about 4/1. Federal Work-Study Program available. Institutional employment available.

BOTTOM LINE
Oberlin's top-notch education does not come free. The annual tuition is $49,928 and students will spend another $15,400 a year on housing, books, and required fees. That said, Oberlin is very committed to helping students financially. Ninety-six percent of needy freshmen receive need-based financial aid here, and 60 percent of the undergraduate population as a whole receive some form of financial aid. The average grant was $34,557 to students who needed aid last year. Oberlin is also one of the few American universities that offer a substantial amount of aid to international students. Those who get into Oberlin will get a truly unique education. As one student exclaims, "Oberlin has let me expand my horizons in ways I never would have imagined before I got to college!"

CAREER INFORMATION FROM PAYSCALE.COM

ROI rating	88
Bachelor's and No Higher	
Median starting salary	$41,700
Median mid-career salary	$100,000
At Least Bachelor's	
Median starting salary	$43,400
Median mid-career salary	$98,900
% alumni with high job meaning	45%
% STEM	14%

SELECTIVITY

Admissions Rating	95
# of applicants	7,227
% of applicants accepted	33
% of acceptees attending	34
# of early decision applicants	431
% accepted early decision	62

FRESHMAN PROFILE

Range SAT Critical Reading	640–730
Range SAT Math	620–720
Range SAT Writing	640–730
Range ACT Composite	28–32
Minimum paper TOEFL	600
Average HS GPA	3.6
% graduated top 10% of class	61
% graduated top 25% of class	91
% graduated top 50% of class	100

DEADLINES

Early decision	
Deadline	11/15
Notification	12/15
Regular	
Deadline	1/15
Notification	4/1
Nonfall registration?	No

FINANCIAL FACTS

Financial Aid Rating	95
Annual tuition	$49,928
Room and board	$13,630
Required fees	$428
Average need-based scholarship	$34,557
% needy frosh rec. need-based scholarship or grant aid	96
% needy UG rec. need-based scholarship or grant aid	99
% needy frosh rec. non-need-based scholarship or grant aid	81
% needy UG rec. non-need-based scholarship or grant aid	73
% needy frosh rec. need-based self-help aid	79
% needy UG rec. need-based self-help aid	89
% frosh rec. any financial aid	61
% UG rec. any financial aid	60
% frosh need fully met	100
% ugrads need fully met	100
Average % of frosh need met	100
Average % of ugrad need met	100

Occidental College

1600 CAMPUS ROAD, OFFICE OF ADMISSION, LOS ANGELES, CA 90041-3314 • ADMISSIONS: 323-259-2700 • FAX: 323-341-4875

CAMPUS LIFE

Quality of Life Rating	91
Fire Safety Rating	81
Green Rating	90
Type of school	Private
Affiliation	No Affiliation
Environment	Metropolis

STUDENTS

Total undergrad enrollment	2,112
% male/female	43/57
% from out of state	52
% frosh from public high school	60
% frosh live on campus	100
% ugrads live on campus	82
# of fraternities (% ugrad men join)	4 (12)
# of sororities (% ugrad women join)	4 (21)
% African American	5
% Asian	13
% Caucasian	49
% Hispanic	15
% Native American	<1
% Pacific Islander	<1
% Two or more races	9
% Race and/or ethnicity unknown	2
% international	5
# of countries represented	28

ACADEMICS

Academic Rating	91
% students returning for sophomore year	93
% students graduating within 4 years	82
Calendar	Semester
Student/faculty ratio	10:1
Profs interesting rating	90
Profs accessible rating	89

Most classes have 10–19 students.
Most lab/discussion sessions have
  10–19 students.

MOST POPULAR MAJORS
Economics; International Relations and
Affairs; Biology

ABOUT THE SCHOOL

Although the curriculum is reportedly difficult, students actually appreciate it. It's a "very prestigious school," and "tough academically," but "the benefits of getting an education here are worth all the work." Professors really care about their students and desperately want them to be successful. Undergrads are pleased that profs here don't exist to "publish or perish"; "they actually are at Oxy to teach—and not to teach so they can research." Students say it is "really easy" to get "independent study, internships, and grants" that would "not be offered anywhere else to undergraduates." "I've been working with postdoctoral researchers as an undergraduate. It's very rewarding." There is also the highly respected Center for Academic Excellence, which provides free tutoring. With a total student body of only 2,100 or so students—women being more highly represented—individual attention is a wonderful advantage for all undergrads.

Occidental offers a semester-long, residential United Nations program, one of the few programs of its kind; the country's only Campaign Semester program, which every two years offers students the opportunity to earn academic credit while working on House, Senate, and presidential campaigns; one of the few opportunities to pursue fully funded undergraduate research overseas (almost 50 percent of Occidental students study overseas); and one of the country's best undergraduate research programs, which has sent more than 170 students to the National Conference on Undergraduate Research over the past six years.

BANG FOR YOUR BUCK

Occidental emphasizes experiential learning. Internships for academic credit are available for sophomores, juniors, and seniors through the Hameetman Career Center; the Center also offers a limited number of paid summer internships through its Intern LA and Intern PDX programs. The Center also offers a career-shadowing program with alumni professionals (the Walk in My Shoes program). "I've gotten a broader sense of self and have been able to fulfill my learning goals," said one student appreciatively. The admission team at Occidental is adamant about not adhering to formulas. They rely heavily on essays and recommendations in their mission to create a talented and diverse incoming class. The college attracts some excellent students, so a demanding course load in high school is essential for the most competitive candidates. Successful applicants tend to be creative and academically motivated. A stellar total of 80 percent of students graduate within four years.

STUDENT LIFE

There's no doubt that Occidental students lead full and fulfilling lives. After all, there's so much of which to take advantage. For starters, "the school brings amazing speakers and musicians to campus...and every weekend [features] a movie screening." There are also "regular campus-wide dances...that everyone attends." Even better, the "Office of Student Life...[frequently] organizes outdoor pool parties, theme parties like Toga...[and events such as] Septemberween." For those undergrads wishing to remain substance free, the residence "halls usually provide alternative event/activities for people who do not partake in drinking/partying." And, naturally, students "love to [simply] explore Los Angeles [whether it involves] going to the beach, farmers market, museums, or hiking." Oxy undergrads truly have it all!

Occidental College

FINANCIAL AID: 323-259-2548 • E-MAIL: ADMISSION@OXY.EDU • WEBSITE: WWW.OXY.EDU

CAREER

Overall, "Occidental does a great job of providing its students with excellent resources and opportunities." And this certainly extends to career services. Indeed, as one happy junior succinctly states, the "career development support is fantastic." Undergrads really appreciate the fact that Oxy runs a robust internship program, one in which they can earn course credit. Students also have the unique opportunity to participate in job shadowing. More specifically, the "Walk in My Shoes (WIMS)" program matches undergrads with alumni and professionals from the surrounding area. They can experience a day-in-the-life of all types of jobs—from marine biology and green business to jobs within the fine arts. Ultimately, WIMS provides students with invaluable insight into potential career tracks. Lastly, according to PayScale.com, the median starting salary for recent Oxy graduates is $45,600.

GENERAL INFO

Activities: Choral groups, concert band, dance, drama/theater, jazz band, literary magazine, music ensembles, musical theater, radio station, student government, student newspaper, student-run film society, symphony orchestra, yearbook, international student organization. **Organizations:** 8 honor societies, 5 religious organizations. 4 fraternities, 4 sororities. **Athletics (Intercollegiate):** *Men:* Baseball, basketball, cross-country, diving, football, golf, soccer, swimming, tennis, track/field (outdoor), water polo. *Women:* Basketball, cross-country, diving, golf, lacrosse, soccer, softball, swimming, tennis, track/field (outdoor), volleyball, water polo.

FINANCIAL AID

Students should submit: FAFSA, CSS/Financial Aid PROFILE, State aid form, Noncustodial PROFILE. Regular filing deadline is 2/1. The Princeton Review suggests that all financial aid forms be submitted as soon as possible after October 1. *Need-based scholarships/grants offered:* Federal Pell, FSEOG, State scholarships/grants, Private scholarships, College/university scholarship or grant aid from institutional funds. *Loan aid offered:* Direct Subsidized Stafford Loans, Direct Unsubsidized Stafford Loans, Direct PLUS loans, Federal Perkins Loans, College/university loans from institutional funds. Applicants will be notified of awards on or about 4/1. Federal Work-Study Program available. Institutional employment available.

BOTTOM LINE

About three out of four Occidental students receive some form of financial aid, including need-based aid and merit scholarships. The average need-based financial aid package is $44,918. Oxy actively seeks out talented students from all backgrounds. There are more than 300 student scholarships available. "They gave me gave me extraordinary financial aid," says one undergrad.

CAREER INFORMATION FROM PAYSCALE.COM

ROI rating	88
Bachelor's and No Higher	
Median starting salary	$46,200
Median mid-career salary	$112,000
At Least Bachelor's	
Median starting salary	$46,500
Median mid-career salary	$111,000
% alumni with high job meaning	49%
% STEM	18%

SELECTIVITY

Admissions Rating	92
# of applicants	5,911
% of applicants accepted	45
% of acceptees attending	20
# offered a place on the wait list	705
% accepting a place on wait list	51
% admitted from wait list	7
# of early decision applicants	255
% accepted early decision	41

FRESHMAN PROFILE

Range SAT Critical Reading	600–690
Range SAT Math	600–690
Range SAT Writing	605–690
Range ACT Composite	28–31
Minimum paper TOEFL	600
Average HS GPA	3.6
% graduated top 10% of class	55
% graduated top 25% of class	90
% graduated top 50% of class	99

DEADLINES

Early decision	
Deadline	11/15
Notification	12/15
Regular	
Deadline	1/15
Notification	3/25
Nonfall registration?	No

FINANCIAL FACTS

Financial Aid Rating	95
Annual tuition	$48,690
Room and board	$13,946
Required fees	$558
Average need-based scholarship	$35,814
% needy frosh rec. need-based scholarship or grant aid	90
% needy UG rec. need-based scholarship or grant aid	91
% needy frosh rec. non-need-based scholarship or grant aid	32
% needy UG rec. non-need-based scholarship or grant aid	35
% needy frosh rec. need-based self-help aid	86
% needy UG rec. need-based self-help aid	85
% frosh rec. any financial aid	72
% UG rec. any financial aid	74
% UG borrow to pay for school	55
Average cumulative indebtedness	$29,947
% frosh need fully met	100
% ugrads need fully met	99
Average % of frosh need met	100
Average % of ugrad need met	100

The Ohio State University—Columbus

Student Academic Svcs. Bldg. 281 West Lane Ave., Columbus, OH 43210 • Admissions: 614-292-3980 • Fax: 614-292-4818

CAMPUS LIFE

Quality of Life Rating	89
Fire Safety Rating	60*
Green Rating	96
Type of school	Public
Affiliation	No Affiliation
Environment	Metropolis

STUDENTS

Total undergrad enrollment	45,289
% male/female	52/48
% from out of state	17
% frosh from public high school	85
% frosh live on campus	94
% ugrads live on campus	26
# of fraternities	42
# of sororities	25
% African American	6
% Asian	6
% Caucasian	71
% Hispanic	4
% Native American	<1
% Pacific Islander	<1
% Two or more races	3
% Race and/or ethnicity unknown	3
% international	7
# of countries represented	112

ACADEMICS

Academic Rating	75
% students returning for sophomore year	94
% students graduating within 4 years	59
% students graduating within 6 years	83
Calendar	Semester
Student/faculty ratio	19:1
Profs interesting rating	74
Profs accessible rating	77

Most classes have 20–29 students.
Most lab/discussion sessions have 20–29 students.

MOST POPULAR MAJORS
Psychology; Finance; Communication

ABOUT THE SCHOOL

Twelve thousand courses, more than 200 majors and a student-to-faculty ratio of 19:1 help convey just how solid an institution The Ohio State University—Columbus is. This first tier research university "hires the best and the brightest" faculty from around the world, and provides its student with many opportunities to become involved. The facilities are "state of the art," the administration is "extremely approachable," and "Ohio State is always trying to stay ahead of the game." "Ohio State combines the love of tradition with the excellence of modern facilities and technology," says an undergrad. Students praise the work ethic instilled in them by a blue-chip education, and "the spirit instilled by citizenship in the living experience that is Buckeye Nation." "No two students leave Ohio State with the same experience, proving you are not just a number," says a student.

BANG FOR YOUR BUCK

Seventy-nine percent of undergraduate students receive some form of financial aid, with the average freshman need-based award being $10,107. There are numerous merit-based scholarships available to qualified students, including those associated with the Eminence Fellows Scholarship, the Morrill Scholarship Program, and the Maximus, Provost, and Trustees scholarships, which consider those students who graduate high school within various rankings of their class. Non-Ohio residents attending the Columbus campus may be eligible for the National Buckeye Scholarship, worth $12,500 per year. At least one student from each of Ohio's eighty-eight counties receives the equivalent of in-state tuition thanks to the Land Grant Opportunity Scholarship. Departmental scholarships are also available.

STUDENT LIFE

People here like to have a good time. In the fall "campus is in a frenzy for Buckeye Football," and in the spring "the Oval turns into a beach." Columbus is a major metro area, so "there is never a shortage of stuff to do." Athletics play a big role here, and this is "a sport fan's paradise. Campus is bursting with Buckeye spirit and it's infectious." Not only do students love attending games, but "we also have so many intramural sports that students get involved in for fun." Though the size of OSU can be daunting, students say not to worry, as there are more than 1,000 student organizations, which really facilitate students in finding people with similar interests. Students have free transportation provided to downtown Columbus, and the Ohio Union Activities Board also does a great job of bringing in speakers and comedians, and hosting free movie events on campus. "OSU has a great way of breaking down the large school into much smaller communities," says a student.

CAREER

The sheer size of the school results in an overflow of resources and opportunities, and "the alumni base is outstanding." The university is committed to helping students advance themselves academically and personally through club/organization involvement and career/internship services, and maintains the Buckeye Careers Network online database for helping to foster such connections. There are also plenty of "top-notch research opportunities for undergraduates in every academic area on campus." The "international recognition" automatically attracts employers, and there are plenty of Career Days throughout the year for this to happen. Of those graduates who visited PayScale.com, 52 percent reported feeling that their job had a high level of meaning in the world, and averaged a starting salary of $48,000.

The Ohio State University—Columbus

FINANCIAL AID: 614-292-0300 • E-MAIL: ASKABUCKEYE@OSU.EDU • WEBSITE: WWW.OSU.EDU

GENERAL INFO

Activities: Choral groups, dance, drama/theater, jazz band, literary magazine, marching band, music ensembles, musical theater, opera, pep band, student government, student newspaper, student-run film society, symphony orchestra, television station, yearbook, international student organizations. **Organizations:** 1,000+ registered organizations, 39 honor societies, 93 religious organizations. 42 fraternities, 25 sororities. **Athletics (Intercollegiate):** *Men:* baseball, basketball, cheerleading, cross-country, diving, fencing, football, golf, gymnastics, ice hockey, lacrosse, pistol, riflery, soccer, swimming, tennis, track/field (outdoor), track/field (indoor), volleyball, wrestling. *Women:* baseball, basketball, cheerleading, crew/rowing, cross-country, diving, fencing, field hockey, golf, gymnastics, ice hockey, lacrosse, pistol, riflery, soccer, softball, swimming, synchronized swimming, tennis, track/field (outdoor), track/field (indoor), volleyball. **On-Campus Highlights:** Hale Cultural Center, Chadwick Arboretum, Jack Nicklaus Golf Museum, Schottenstein Center and Value City Arena, Wexner Center for the Arts.

FINANCIAL AID

Students should submit: FAFSA. Priority filing deadline is 2/1. The Princeton Review suggests that all financial aid forms be submitted as soon as possible after October 1. *Need-based scholarships/grants offered:* Federal Pell, FSEOG, State scholarships/grants, Private scholarships, College/university scholarship or grant aid from institutional funds. *Loan aid offered:* Direct Subsidized Stafford Loans, Direct Unsubsidized Stafford Loans, Direct PLUS loans, Federal Perkins Loans, Federal Nursing Loans, State Loans, College/university loans from institutional funds. Applicants will be notified of awards by late Feb. Federal Work-Study Program available. Institutional employment available.

BOTTOM LINE

Ohio residents pay $10,036 in tuition each year; non-Ohio residents pay $28,229, including an out-of-state surcharge. The most popular room and board plan runs $11,666, though cheaper options are available. Over 80 percent of OSU students are Ohio residents, and 55 percent graduate with some form of loan debt.

CAREER INFORMATION FROM PAYSCALE.COM

ROI rating	88
Bachelor's and No Higher	
Median starting salary	$49,300
Median mid-career salary	$81,200
At Least Bachelor's	
Median starting salary	$49,800
Median mid-career salary	$83,600
% alumni with high job meaning	49%
% STEM	17%

SELECTIVITY

Admissions Rating	91
# of applicants	40,240
% of applicants accepted	49
% of acceptees attending	30
# offered a place on the wait list	1,556
% accepting a place on wait list	20
% admitted from wait list	100

FRESHMAN PROFILE

Range SAT Critical Reading	560–670
Range SAT Math	610–720
Range SAT Writing	560–660
Range ACT Composite	27–31
Minimum paper TOEFL	550
Minimum internet-based TOEFL	79
% graduated top 10% of class	62
% graduated top 25% of class	95
% graduated top 50% of class	99

DEADLINES

Early action	
Deadline	11/1
Regular	
Deadline	2/1
Notification	2/28
Nonfall registration?	Yes

FINANCIAL FACTS

Financial Aid Rating	82
Annual in-state tuition	$10,036
Annual out-of-state tuition	$28,229
Room and board	$11,666
Required fees	
Average need-based scholarship	$9,633
% needy frosh rec. need-based scholarship or grant aid	90
% needy UG rec. need-based scholarship or grant aid	83
% needy frosh rec. non-need-based scholarship or grant aid	9
% needy UG rec. non-need-based scholarship or grant aid	5
% needy frosh rec. need-based self-help aid	77
% needy UG rec. need-based self-help aid	87
% frosh rec. any financial aid	90
% UG rec. any financial aid	79
% UG borrow to pay for school	55
Average cumulative indebtedness	$27,400
% frosh need fully met	29
% ugrads need fully met	19
Average % of frosh need met	74
Average % of ugrad need met	68

Pennsylvania State University

201 Shields Building, Box 3000, University Park, PA 16802-3000 • Admissions: 814-865-5471 • Fax: 814-863-7590

CAMPUS LIFE	
Quality of Life Rating	94
Fire Safety Rating	98
Green Rating	95
Type of school	Public
Affiliation	No Affiliation
Environment	Town

STUDENTS	
Total undergrad enrollment	40,742
% male/female	54/46
% from out of state	31
% ugrads live on campus	34
# of fraternities (% ugrad men join)	56 (18)
# of sororities (% ugrad women join)	27 (19)
% African American	4
% Asian	6
% Caucasian	69
% Hispanic	6
% Native American	<1
% Pacific Islander	<1
% Two or more races	3
% Race and/or ethnicity unknown	2
% international	11
# of countries represented	110

ACADEMICS	
Academic Rating	77
% students returning for sophomore year	93
% students graduating within 4 years	64
% students graduating within 6 years	86
Calendar	Semester
Student/faculty ratio	16:1
Profs interesting rating	77
Profs accessible rating	79

Most classes have 20–29 students.
Most lab/discussion sessions have 20–29 students.

MOST POPULAR MAJORS
Business, Management, Marketing; Engineering; Communication

ABOUT THE SCHOOL

At 8,556 acres, the campus at Pennsylvania State University is enormous. 54 percent of the students are male, 46 percent are female, 69 percent are white, and 69 percent hail from the great keystone state. Penn State offers a whopping 160 majors, with students having special commendations for the well-regarded Smeal College of Business and the Schreyer Honors College. What is big on Penn State besides the campus itself? Football. Football and School Spirit. Cries of "We! Are! Penn State!" echo across the campus, and the nation itself. Students note that the initial core classes "had such a huge amount of students in the classes that it was hard to get much professor interaction," but that as you progress through the school classes get "down to about fifteen to forty people and there are a lot more discussions." Students find the faculty and administration to be available, but advise that, given the size of the school, students should take the initiative to reach out.

BANG FOR YOUR BUCK

Tuition at the Penn State comes to $16,952 for in-state students and $31,434 for out-of-state students, with the average aid package coming to around $11,175. Students note that 60 percent of their financial needs are met, and of these students whose needs are met, 68 percent are freshman. Students feel that the "fantastic alumni association" provides them with "financial funds for scholarships and programs," though some note that due to the enormous size of the campus, "scholarships, grants, and student recognition is extremely competitive," adding "don't expect much in terms of financial aid." The school offers solid value for in-state students.

STUDENT LIFE

Students at Penn State attend many football games, and after football season comes THON, the "forty-six-hour dance marathon for children with pediatric cancer" at Hershey's Children's Hospital, one of the largest student run philanthropies in the country with "almost 15,000 students involved each year." State College contains multitudes "of restaurants and stores," and malls and movie theaters that can all be reached on the CATA bus. The CATA bus-system is "high tech" with an iPhone/Android application that "shows real time tracking of every bus on every loop, which is very convenient." As for social life, students feel that "Greek Life dominates the social scene. There are fifty plus fraternities and twenty plus sororities on and off campus." And again, for students not that wild about the large size of the school, "you really do need to get involved to meet people and really find your place at PSU. Coming from smaller high schools it can be a little overwhelming and hard to transition at first, but once you find your niche it makes all the difference."

CAREER

The typical Penn State graduate has a starting salary of around $51,500, and 49 percent report that their job has a great deal of meaning. Past that, students choose Penn State for its vast alumni network. How vast, you ask? Students boast of "access to an alumni network of over half a million, and . . . of its job recruiting power out of major metropolitan areas such as Philadelphia, New York, Pittsburgh, Baltimore, Washington D.C., and across the country." A student notes that the "giant alumni and brand name make getting internships so much easier. I loved our career fair when just about every company was here. I was offered four summer internships . . . as a freshman!" and this theme is reiterated by a member of the Smeal College of Business, who notes, "One of the best things about Penn State overall is the

Pennsylvania State University

FINANCIAL AID: 814-865-6301 • E-MAIL: ADMISSIONS@PSU.EDU • WEBSITE: WWW.PSU.EDU

fact that the alumni network is one of the largest in the United States. Because of this, PSU alums seek out Penn State grads for jobs at their companies."

GENERAL INFO

Activities: Choral groups, concert band, dance, drama/theater, jazz band, literary magazine, marching band, music ensembles, musical theater, opera, pep band, radio station, student government, student newspaper, student-run film society, symphony orchestra, television station, yearbook, Campus Ministries, International Student Organization, Model UN. **Organizations:** 1,062 registered organizations, 40 honor societies, 58 religious organizations. 56 fraternities, 27 sororities. **Athletics (Intercollegiate):** *Men:* baseball, basketball, cheerleading, cross-country, diving, fencing, football, golf, gymnastics, lacrosse, soccer, swimming, tennis, track/field (outdoor), track/field (indoor), volleyball, wrestling. *Women:* basketball, cheerleading, cross-country, diving, fencing, field hockey, golf, gymnastics, lacrosse, soccer, softball, swimming, tennis, track/field (outdoor), track/field (indoor), volleyball. **On-Campus Highlights:** HUB-Robeson Union Building, Pattee Paterno Library, The Creamery, Old Main, The Lion Shrine.

FINANCIAL AID

Students should submit: FAFSA. Priority filing deadline is 2/15. The Princeton Review suggests that all financial aid forms be submitted as soon as possible after October 1. *Need-based scholarships/grants offered:* Federal Pell, FSEOG, State scholarships/grants, Private scholarships, College/university scholarship or grant aid from institutional funds. *Loan aid offered:* Direct Subsidized Stafford Loans, Direct Unsubsidized Stafford Loans, Direct PLUS loans, Federal Perkins Loans, College/university loans from institutional funds. Federal Work-Study Program available. Institutional employment available.

BOTTOM LINE

The tuition at Pennsylvania State University comes to about $16,952 for in-state students and $31,434 for out-of-state students. The average aid package comes to $11,175, with 60 percent of students reporting their demonstrated financial need was met. And with its intense, dedicated, and enormous alumni network at your back, a Penn State grad will have a good shot out there in the employment market.

CAREER INFORMATION FROM PAYSCALE.COM

ROI rating	87
Bachelor's and No Higher	
Median starting salary	$52,500
Median mid-career salary	$88,000
At Least Bachelor's	
Median starting salary	$53,300
Median mid-career salary	$91,300
% alumni with high job meaning	49%
% STEM	26%

SELECTIVITY

Admissions Rating	89
# of applicants	53,472
% of applicants accepted	51
% of acceptees attending	28
# offered a place on the wait list	1,473
% accepting a place on wait list	100
% admitted from wait list	98

FRESHMAN PROFILE

Range SAT Critical Reading	530–630
Range SAT Math	560–670
Range SAT Writing	540–640
Range ACT Composite	25–29
Minimum paper TOEFL	550
Minimum internet-based TOEFL	80
Average HS GPA	3.6
% graduated top 10% of class	41
% graduated top 25% of class	82
% graduated top 50% of class	98

DEADLINES

Regular	
Priority	11/30
Nonfall registration?	Yes

FINANCIAL FACTS

Financial Aid Rating	77
Annual in-state tuition	$16,952
Annual out-of-state tuition	$31,434
Room and board	$11,860
Required fees	$948
Average need-based scholarship	$7,144
% needy frosh rec. need-based scholarship or grant aid	43
% needy UG rec. need-based scholarship or grant aid	51
% needy frosh rec. non-need-based scholarship or grant aid	47
% needy UG rec. non-need-based scholarship or grant aid	36
% needy frosh rec. need-based self-help aid	72
% needy UG rec. need-based self-help aid	81
% frosh rec. any financial aid	66
% UG rec. any financial aid	67
% UG borrow to pay for school	56
Average cumulative indebtedness	$35,972
% frosh need fully met	8
% ugrads need fully met	8
Average % of frosh need met	58
Average % of ugrad need met	59

Pepperdine University

24255 PACIFIC COAST HIGHWAY, MALIBU, CA 90263 • ADMISSIONS: 310-456-4392 • FAX: 310-506-4861

CAMPUS LIFE

Quality of Life Rating	**92**
Fire Safety Rating	**85**
Green Rating	**75**
Type of school	Private
Affiliation	Church of Christ
Environment	Suburban

STUDENTS

Total undergrad enrollment	3,533
% male/female	41/59
% from out of state	42
% frosh live on campus	98
% ugrads live on campus	57
# of fraternities (% ugrad men join)	5 (6)
# of sororities (% ugrad women join)	8 (9)
% African American	6
% Asian	12
% Caucasian	47
% Hispanic	16
% Native American	<1
% Pacific Islander	<1
% Two or more races	5
% Race and/or ethnicity unknown	4
% international	10
# of countries represented	76

ACADEMICS

Academic Rating	**84**
% students returning for sophomore year	94
% students graduating within 4 years	76
% students graduating within 6 years	84
Calendar	Semester
Student/faculty ratio	13:1
Profs interesting rating	85
Profs accessible rating	89
Most classes have 10–19 students.	
Most lab/discussion sessions have 10–19 students.	

MOST POPULAR MAJORS
Business Administration and Management;
Psychology; Economics

ABOUT THE SCHOOL

Located in beautiful sunny Malibu, California, Pepperdine, a private Christian university, is a place to have "a good time" and where "everyone can find a place where he or she fits in." With roughly 3,500 students, the school is small enough to be intimate and large enough to offer a wide array of academic and social options. One Integrated Marketing and Communication major summed it up: "Pepperdine is all about service and giving back to the community while creating [well-rounded] people through education." The school's religious affiliation is a draw for some students—"I wanted an exceptional education with small classes and Christian values"—while others see the school simply as somewhere to receive "a quality education [in] a friendly atmosphere. [It's an all-around] wonderful experience." The small class sizes—the average student to professor ratio is thirteen to one—help "each student develop into a unique individual [with] lots of [one-on-one] connections with faculty." The professors themselves also get high marks: they "go out of their way to get to know you . . . they seriously care." The university is divided into two undergraduate programs: Seaver College of Arts, Letters and Science and the Graziadio School of Business and Management.

BANG FOR YOUR BUCK

While the school has a reputation for attracting only wealthy students, scholarship opportunities are plentiful and the aid offered is often what seals a prospective student's decision to attend Pepperdine. On average, the school meets 84 percent of students' demonstrated financial need. One English major notes that "financial aid awards are generous, as are scholarships for students with [exceptional] high school [GPAs], test scores, and [a demonstrated history of] service work." Sixty-three percent of undergraduates have borrowed through various loan programs, and the average need-based gift aid for freshman is $33,140 (and roughly $37,300 for other undergraduates). For students in Seaver College, Pepperdine contributed approximately $54 million in university-funded grants and scholarships for undergraduate students during the 2012-2013 academic year, according to the school's website. Within the business school, several scholarship opportunities exist, from merit-based awards to Bridge Scholarships, which help fill in the monetary gap between the cost of tuition and the family's contribution.

STUDENT LIFE

Despite its glamorous name, students note that the city of Malibu "shuts down early" and one's social life will be much improved by having a car in order to drive to nearby Los Angeles or Santa Monica. Fifty-eight percent of undergraduates live on campus and the school does offer assistance for students wishing to live outside the dorm system. Students love the view, with one Nutrition major underscoring that "the campus is on Malibu Beach on a hill overlooking the beach. You cannot ask for a more picturesque setting." The school organizes trips to local amusement parks and opportunities for surfing are literally across the street. On campus, there are 121 registered student organizations and a Psychology major notes that "there are so many clubs and organizations or [you can] even start your own so it [isn't] hard to find your niche." Greek life does play a role at Pepperdine, which has eight sororities and five fraternities, with 31 percent of women joining a sorority and 18 percent of men joining a fraternity. In general, students "fit in by getting involved with [Greek] life, social action groups and musical groups on campus."

Pepperdine University

FINANCIAL AID: 310-506-4301 • E-MAIL: ADMISSION-SEAVER@PEPPERDINE.EDU • WEBSITE: WWW.PEPPERDINE.EDU

CAREER

According to PayScale.com, 46 percent of Pepperdine graduates consider their careers vital to making the world a better place. The average starting salary for a Pepperdine graduate is $48,300 and popular jobs include human resources director, communications manager, and financial analyst. In terms of majors, the most popular include business administration, psychology, and economics. Pepperdine "is focused on helping you discover a career that you will love not only love but be able to become successful in," according to one Public Relations major. While the school helps "developing students to do well in their careers," it also emphasizes "serving the community." With offerings like Career Fair—in both the spring and fall semesters—the Career Center offers students, alumni, and prospective employers search for and post job and internship opportunities. Students can also meet with a career counselor to help tune-up resumes, and register for career and internship events online. Students praise Pepperdine's "unique opportunities" such as "internships and study abroad" programs all over the world.

GENERAL INFO

Activities: Choral groups, concert band, dance, drama/theater, jazz band, literary magazine, music ensembles, musical theater, opera, pep band, radio station, student government, student newspaper, student-run film society, symphony orchestra, television station, yearbook, Campus Ministries, International Student Organization, Model UN. **Organizations:** 102 registered organizations, 3 honor societies, 14 religious organizations. 5 fraternities, 8 sororities. **Athletics (Intercollegiate):** *Men:* baseball, basketball, cross-country, golf, tennis, volleyball, water polo. *Women:* basketball, cross-country, golf, soccer, swimming, tennis, track/field (outdoor), volleyball. **On-Campus Highlights:** Theme Tower, Smother'sTheatre, The Sandbar, Payson Library, Alumni Park.

FINANCIAL AID

Students should submit: FAFSA. Priority filing deadline is 2/15. The Princeton Review suggests that all financial aid forms be submitted as soon as possible after October 1. *Need-based scholarships/grants offered:* Federal Pell, FSEOG, State scholarships/grants, Private scholarships, College/university scholarship or grant aid from institutional funds, United Negro College Fund. *Loan aid offered:* Direct Subsidized Stafford Loans, Direct Unsubsidized Stafford Loans, Direct PLUS loans, Federal Perkins Loans, College/university loans from institutional funds. Applicants will be notified of awards on or about 4/15. Federal Work-Study Program available. Institutional employment available.

BOTTOM LINE

An average year at Pepperdine's Seaver College costs $64,352, this includes room, board, and required fees. The average need-based scholarship is $37,026. Financial assistance is not available for international students. Pepperdine students will graduate with an average of $34,820 in debt.

SELECTIVITY	
Admissions Rating	**91**
# of applicants	9,923
% of applicants accepted	38
% of acceptees attending	20

FRESHMAN PROFILE	
Range SAT Critical Reading	550–650
Range SAT Math	550–670
Range SAT Writing	550–650
Range ACT Composite	25–30
Minimum paper TOEFL	550
Minimum internet-based TOEFL	80
Average HS GPA	3.6
% graduated top 10% of class	48
% graduated top 25% of class	80
% graduated top 50% of class	97

DEADLINES	
Regular	
Deadline	1/5
Notification	4/1
Nonfall registration?	Yes

FINANCIAL FACTS	
Financial Aid Rating	**85**
Annual tuition	$49,770
Room and board	$14,330
Required fees	$252
Average need-based scholarship	$37,026
% needy frosh rec. need-based scholarship or grant aid	99
% needy UG rec. need-based scholarship or grant aid	97
% needy frosh rec. need-based self-help aid	99
% needy UG rec. need-based self-help aid	71
% frosh rec. any financial aid	94
% UG rec. any financial aid	81
% UG borrow to pay for school	57
Average cumulative indebtedness	$34,820
% frosh need fully met	16
% ugrads need fully met	21
Average % of frosh need met	73
Average % of ugrad need met	77

CAREER INFORMATION FROM PAYSCALE.COM

ROI rating	**86**
Bachelor's and No Higher	
Median starting salary	$48,300
Median mid-career salary	$87,500
At Least Bachelor's	
Median starting salary	$50,100
Median mid-career salary	$88,700
% alumni with high job meaning	51%
% STEM	4%

Pitzer College

1050 NORTH MILLS AVENUE, CLAREMONT, CA 91711-6101 • ADMISSIONS: 909-621-8129 • FAX: 909-621-8770

CAMPUS LIFE

Quality of Life Rating	93
Fire Safety Rating	88
Green Rating	96
Type of school	Private
Affiliation	No Affiliation
Environment	Town

STUDENTS

Total undergrad enrollment	1,067
% male/female	43/57
% from out of state	51
% frosh live on campus	100
% ugrads live on campus	76
% African American	5
% Asian	9
% Caucasian	48
% Hispanic	15
% Native American	<1
% Pacific Islander	<1
% Two or more races	9
% Race and/or ethnicity unknown	6
% international	7
# of countries represented	33

ACADEMICS

Academic Rating	93
% students returning for sophomore year	93
% students graduating within 4 years	80
% students graduating within 6 years	89
Calendar	Semester
Student/faculty ratio	10:1
Profs interesting rating	92
Profs accessible rating	94

Most classes have 10–19 students.

MOST POPULAR MAJORS
Psychology; Environmental Analysis;
Political Studies

ABOUT THE SCHOOL

As one of the five undergraduate institutions comprising The Claremont Colleges in California, Pitzer College gives its more than 1,000 students access to all of the major university resources (such as 2,500 classes across the consortium) while still offering an "intimate" liberal arts experience—not to mention a ten to one student-to-faculty ratio. Professors "will answer any and every question you have" in Pitzer's challenging classes, most of which are writing-based, and "professors and deans milling about the dining hall is not an uncommon sight." The school's required First-Year Seminars for all incoming students are a set of writing-intensive courses that teach students about the writing process, including drafting, peer review, and revision. Students say Pitzer's cohesive set of guiding educational objectives combines "the right mix of motivated students, dynamic faculty, and a progressive administration."

BANG FOR YOUR BUCK

Pitzer, as part of The Claremont Colleges, has excellent resources and explains to students how to make the most of them: Events are well publicized and well attended. Students are encouraged to participate in one of forty-eight international study abroad exchanges, which cost the same as a semester at Pitzer. Approximately 37 percent of the student body receives some form of financial assistance, and aid comes from federal, state, and institutional grants. Numerous Pitzer Scholarships are based on financial need and various other factors (such as intended major), and the school also awards two merit scholarships to first-year students based on academic performance: the Trustee Community Scholarship and the Academic Achievement Scholarship.

STUDENT LIFE

Pitzer and the other Claremont Colleges strongly encourage campus life, and school-sponsored events, both educational and recreational, take place on the campuses. Another good thing about Pitzer's membership in the consortium is that students "can experience a lot of diversity of thought" between institutions (Pitzer tends to be liberal). The eco-friendly campus lifestyle is very much representative of southern California: "The sun is always out and people are always on the mounds, at the Grove House, or on a hiking trip." There are over 200 student organizations and "any club that you want to start is an option," plus plenty of campus-sponsored trips to LA or outdoor destinations are available. Even though there is "a lot of work to do," life "is not very stressful . . . because the atmosphere is so laid back and everyone is supportive."

CAREER

A Pitzer education emphasizes internships, hands-on learning, and community outreach (community service is actually required for graduation); to that end, the Career Services Office hosts numerous career fairs, and the Pitzer Internship Fund provides money to students taking otherwise unfunded internships. (The internship does not need to be in place in order to apply.) The school uses the online job database Handshake to let students search for employment and internships, and there is also the Pitzer Professional Directory, an online, searchable database of Pitzer alumni and current parents, useful for career planning purposes. Career counseling sessions, assessments, and workshops are also available. Field learning is also encouraged; on Fridays throughout the academic year, the office

Pitzer College

FINANCIAL AID: 909-621-8208 • E-MAIL: ADMISSION@PITZER.EDU • WEBSITE: WWW.PITZER.EDU

arranges field trips for small groups to visit employers throughout southern California, and the Pitzer Shadowing Program lets students spend one to five days with alumni or parents at their place of work.

GENERAL INFO

Activities: Choral groups, dance, drama/theater, literary magazine, music ensembles, radio station, student government, student newspaper, symphony orchestra, Campus Ministries, International Student Organization, Model UN 120 registered organizations, 1 honor societies.
Athletics (Intercollegiate): *Men:* baseball, basketball, cross-country, diving, football, golf, soccer, swimming, tennis, track/field (outdoor), water polo. *Women:* basketball, cross-country, diving, soccer, softball, swimming, tennis, track/field (outdoor), volleyball, water polo. **On-Campus Highlights:** Grove House, McConnell Center, Gloria and Peter Gold Student Center, Marquis Library, The Mounds, The Claremont Colleges Consortium. Pitzer students may cross-register at any of The Claremont Colleges, and may utilize all Claremont facilities, including Honnold Library, the third-largest academic library in the state, with more than 2 million volumes; Huntley Bookstore; Baxter Medical Center; McAlister Center for Religious Activities and Monsour Counseling Center. Pitzer sponsors the Joint Science Program with Claremont McKenna and Scripps colleges, and the five undergraduate colleges offer a wide range of recreational facilities, student gathering places and dining areas. Pitzer combines with Pomona College for NCAA Division III sports.

FINANCIAL AID

Students should submit: FAFSA, CSS/Financial Aid PROFILE, State aid form, Noncustodial PROFILE. Regular filing deadline is 1/1. The Princeton Review suggests that all financial aid forms be submitted as soon as possible after October 1. *Need-based scholarships/grants offered:* Federal Pell, FSEOG, State scholarships/grants, Private scholarships, College/university scholarship or grant aid from institutional funds. *Loan aid offered:* Direct Subsidized Stafford Loans, Direct Unsubsidized Stafford Loans, Direct PLUS loans, Federal Perkins Loans, College/university loans from institutional funds. Applicants will be notified of awards on or about 4/1. Federal Work-Study Program available. Institutional employment available.

BOTTOM LINE

Tuition at Pitzer College runs $50,160 a year, and about 76 percent of students live on campus, which will run an additional $15,762 a year in room and board. Additionally, each student is expected to budget about $2,000 for books and personal expenses. Fortunately, plenty of aid is available to those in need (as well as federal work study opportunities), and California state residents can also apply for need-based Cal Grants, which can cover up to $10,740 a year.

CAREER INFORMATION FROM PAYSCALE.COM

ROI rating	86
Bachelor's and No Higher	
Median starting salary	$45,000
Median mid-career salary	$71,200
At Least Bachelor's	
Median starting salary	$48,400
Median mid-career salary	$71,100
% STEM	2%

SELECTIVITY

Admissions Rating	97
# of applicants	4,149
% of applicants accepted	13
% of acceptees attending	47
# offered a place on the wait list	1,022
% accepting a place on wait list	90
% admitted from wait list	2
# of early decision applicants	405
% accepted early decision	29

FRESHMAN PROFILE

Range SAT Critical Reading	620–720
Range SAT Math	630–720
Range ACT Composite	29–32
Minimum paper TOEFL	190
Minimum internet-based TOEFL	70
Average HS GPA	3.9

DEADLINES

Early decision	
Deadline	11/15
Notification	12/18
Regular	
Deadline	1/1
Notification	4/1
Nonfall registration?	No

FINANCIAL FACTS

Financial Aid Rating	97
Annual tuition	$50,160
Room and board	$15,762
Required fees	$270
Average need-based scholarship	$40,220
% needy frosh rec. need-based scholarship or grant aid	100
% needy UG rec. need-based scholarship or grant aid	100
% needy frosh rec. non-need-based scholarship or grant aid	7
% needy UG rec. non-need-based scholarship or grant aid	7
% needy frosh rec. need-based self-help aid	90
% needy UG rec. need-based self-help aid	88
% frosh rec. any financial aid	34
% UG rec. any financial aid	41
% UG borrow to pay for school	37
Average cumulative indebtedness	$21,951
% frosh need fully met	100
% ugrads need fully met	100
Average % of frosh need met	100
Average % of ugrad need met	100

Pomona College

333 North College Way, Claremont, CA 91711-6312 • Admissions: 909-621-8134 • Fax: 909-621-8952

#37 COLLEGE THAT PAYS YOU BACK

ABOUT THE SCHOOL

Students here are among the most happy and comfortable in the nation. To help ease the transition to college life, first-year students are assigned to sponsor groups of ten to twenty fellow first-years who live in adjacent rooms, with two sophomore sponsors who help them learn the ropes of college life. Students rave that the sponsor program is "the single best living situation for freshmen." It "makes you feel welcome the second you step on campus as a new student" and is "amazing at integrating the freshmen into the community smoothly." Greek life is almost nonexistent, but you'll never hear a complaint about a lack of (usually free and awesome) things to do. There's virtually always an event or a party happening either on campus or just a short walk away on one of the other Claremont campuses (Scripps, Pitzer, Claremont McKenna, and Harvey Mudd). Students say that the Claremont Consortium offers "an abundance of nightlife that you wouldn't expect at a small elite liberal arts school." There are also quite a few quirky traditions here throughout the academic year. If you find yourself craving some big-city life, Los Angeles is just a short train ride away.

BANG FOR YOUR BUCK

The financial aid program here is exceedingly generous and goes beyond just covering tuition, room and board, and fees, for which Pomona can and does meet 100 percent of students' demonstrated financial need. The financial aid packages consist wholly of grants and scholarships, probably along with a campus job that you work maybe ten hours a week. For students on financial aid who wish to participate in study abroad, Pomona ensures that cost is not a barrier. All programs carry academic credit and no extra cost for tuition or room and board. To ensure that all Pomona students are able to participate in the college's internship program, funding is provided in the form of an hourly wage for semester-long internships, making it possible for students to take unpaid positions. The Career Development Office (CDO) also subsidizes transportation to and from internships. In addition, the college offers funding, based on need, to students with job interviews on the East Coast during the Winter Break Recruiting Days program.

STUDENT LIFE

Due to its location in Southern California, "life [at Pomona] consists of a lot of school work but always done out in the beautiful sun. I think most people love it here." "People usually are athletic or at least interested in outdoor activities like hiking, camping, and rock climbing." For those with access to cars "the beach, the mountains, and Joshua Tree National Park are other popular locations for a day or weekend," and many students will venture into nearby Los Angeles for fun. However it's not necessary to get away to have a good time, as "at Pomona, there's usually so much happening on campus that you don't need to venture out." "While partying is a big deal—as it is at almost any college—it certainly isn't the only deal. There are movie nights all over campus, music festivals, plays, impromptu games of Frisbee going on at all times of the year." Many students also say that talking the night away with their friends is one of the things they love about Pomona. "Deep conversations" are a frequent occurrence and "people engage in AMAZING conversations

Pomona College

FINANCIAL AID: 909-621-8205 • E-MAIL: ADMISSIONS@POMONA.EDU • WEBSITE: WWW.POMONA.EDU

about EVERYTHING." "Whatever you like to do for fun," students say, "there's a good chance that you'll find others who like to do the same."

CAREER

Pomona's Career Development Office offers advising and counseling to help students explore their interests and discover careers to which they might be suited; hosts career fairs and recruiting events; and provides resources for networking job searches. It also hosts a Prestigious Scholarships and Fellowships Expo that brings representatives from foundations and universities to discuss post-graduate opportunities. However despite the number of offerings, many students list the Career Office as an area that "could definitely be better" and say that the school needs "more resources for internships and career development." On the other hand, several students cite their professors as a helpful resource to "get the internships and jobs that we want or need for our desired careers," and more than 200 students conduct mentored research, with a stipend, each summer. Overall, students say that Pomona provides "a diverse education that will prepare students for whatever they choose to do afterward" and out of alumni visiting PayScale.com, 43 percent report that they derive meaning from their career.

GENERAL INFO

Activities: Choral groups, concert band, dance, drama/theater, jazz band, literary magazine, music ensembles, musical theater, pep band, radio station, student government, student newspaper, student-run film society, symphony orchestra, television station, yearbook, campus ministries, international student organization.

FINANCIAL AID

Students should submit: FAFSA, CSS/Financial Aid PROFILE, Noncustodial PROFILE, Business/Farm Supplement. Regular filing deadline is 3/1. The Princeton Review suggests that all financial aid forms be submitted as soon as possible after October 1. *Need-based scholarships/grants offered:* Federal Pell, FSEOG, State scholarships/grants, Private scholarships, College/university scholarship or grant aid from institutional funds. *Loan aid offered:* Direct Subsidized Stafford Loans, Direct Unsubsidized Stafford Loans, Direct PLUS loans, College/university loans from institutional funds. Applicants will be notified of awards on or about 4/1. Federal Work-Study Program available. Institutional employment available.

THE BOTTOM LINE

Tuition, fees, and room and board at Pomona run about $60,500 for a year. At the same time, the mantra here is that no one should hesitate to apply because of the cost. Pomona College has need-blind admissions and meets the full, demonstrated financial aid need of every accepted student with scholarships and work-study. Students say that Pomona "has a reputation of providing great financial aid packages."

CAREER INFORMATION FROM PAYSCALE.COM

ROI rating	91
Bachelor's and No Higher	
Median starting salary	$46,700
Median mid-career salary	$92,000
At Least Bachelor's	
Median starting salary	$49,700
Median mid-career salary	$105,000
% alumni with high job meaning	75%
% STEM	21%

SELECTIVITY

Admissions Rating	98
# of applicants	8,099
% of applicants accepted	10
% of acceptees attending	48
# offered a place on the wait list	842
% accepting a place on wait list	58
% admitted from wait list	5
# of early decision applicants	1,187
% accepted early decision	15

FRESHMAN PROFILE

Range SAT Critical Reading	670–760
Range SAT Math	690–770
Range SAT Writing	680–770
Range ACT Composite	30–34
Minimum paper TOEFL	600
Minimum internet-based TOEFL	100
% graduated top 10% of class	92
% graduated top 25% of class	100
% graduated top 50% of class	100

DEADLINES

Early decision	
Deadline	11/1
Notification	12/15
Regular	
Deadline	1/1
Notification	4/1
Nonfall registration?	No

FINANCIAL FACTS

Financial Aid Rating	99
Annual tuition	$47,280
Room and board	$15,150
Required fees	$340
Average need-based scholarship	$41,443
% needy frosh rec. need-based scholarship or grant aid	100
% needy UG rec. need-based scholarship or grant aid	100
% needy frosh rec. non-need-based scholarship or grant aid	0
% needy UG rec. non-need-based scholarship or grant aid	0
% needy frosh rec. need-based self-help aid	100
% needy UG rec. need-based self-help aid	100
% frosh rec. any financial aid	57
% UG rec. any financial aid	56
% UG borrow to pay for school	39
Average cumulative indebtedness	$13,381
% frosh need fully met	100
% ugrads need fully met	100
Average % of frosh need met	100
Average % of ugrad need met	100

Princeton University

PO Box 430, Admission Office, Princeton, NJ 08542-0430 • Admissions: 609-258-3060 • Fax: 609-258-6743

#1 COLLEGE THAT PAYS YOU BACK

ABOUT THE SCHOOL
Princeton offers its 5,000 undergraduate students a top-notch liberal arts education, taught by some of the best minds in the world. The university is committed to undergraduate teaching, and all faculty, including the president, teach undergraduates. "You get the attention you deserve—if you seek it," says a student. Supporting these efforts are exceptional academic and research resources, including the world-class Firestone Library, the new Frick Chemistry Laboratory that emphasizes hands-on learning in teaching labs, a genomics institute, the Woodrow Wilson School of Public and International Affairs that trains leaders in public service, and an engineering school that enrolls more than 900 undergraduates. Freshman seminars take students into a variety of settings, such as to theaters on Broadway, geological sites in the West, art museums, and more. Princeton students can choose between more than seventy-five fields of concentration (majors) and interdisciplinary certificate programs, of which history, political science, economics, and international affairs are among the most popular. The school's excellent faculty-student ratio of five to one means that many classes are discussion-based, giving students a direct line to their brilliant professors, and "once you take upper-level courses, you'll have a lot of chances to work closely with professors and study what you are most interested in." All "unfailingly brilliant, open, and inspirational" faculty members also work closely with undergraduates in the supervision of junior-year independent work and senior theses. "Professors love teaching, and there are many fantastic lecturers," giving students a chance "to meet and take classes from some of the most brilliant academic minds in the world." Even before they start taking Princeton classes, select students each year are chosen for the Bridge Year Program, which provides funding for students to engage in public-service opportunities in one of four countries: India, Peru, Ghana, or Serbia. There are "pools of resources available for students for all sorts of nonacademic or extracurricular pursuits."

BANG FOR YOUR BUCK
Princeton operates need-blind admissions, as well as one of the strongest need-based financial aid programs in the country. Once a student is admitted, Princeton meets 100 percent of each student's demonstrated financial need. One of the first schools in the country to do so, Princeton has eliminated all loans for students who qualify for aid—it is possible to graduate from this Ivy League school without debt. Financial awards come in the form of grants, which do not need to be repaid. About 60 percent of Princeton students receive financial aid, with an average grant of about $44,890. No need to pinch yourself, you're not dreaming. In recent years, the amount of grant aid available at Princeton has outpaced the annual increase in school fees. Good news for international students: Financial aid packages extend to international admits as well.

STUDENT LIFE
"Academics come first" at this hallowed Ivy, but an "infinite number of clubs" on campus means that "almost everyone at Princeton is involved with something other than school about which they are extremely passionate." Students "tend to participate in a lot of different activities from varsity sports (recruits), intramural sports (high school athletes) . . . [to] Engineers Without Borders, and the

Princeton University

FINANCIAL AID: 609-258-3330 • E-MAIL: UAOFFICE@PRINCETON.EDU • WEBSITE: WWW.PRINCETON.EDU

literary magazine." If you need to relax, "sporting events, concerts, recreational facilities," "a movie theater that frequently screens current films for free," and "arts and crafts at the student center" will help you de-stress. Others enjoy Princeton's eating clubs—private houses that service as social clubs and cafeterias for upperclassmen. Campus is located in a quaint little bubble of a New Jersey town and is full of traditions (some dating back hundreds of years), but if you crave some city-life "there's NJ transit if you want to go to New York, Philly, or even just the local mall."

CAREER

As one student tells us, "Princeton is a place that prepares you for anything and everything, providing you with a strong network every step of the way." Career Services lends a hand the moment students arrive on campus by guiding undergrads through self-assessments, educating about majors and careers, updating HireTigers—which holds hundreds of listings for jobs, fellowships, and internships—and, of course, strategize regarding resumes, cover letters, and online profiles. "Princeternships" allow students to experience " a day in the life" by shadowing an alumnus at their workplace for a few days. According to PayScale.com, the average starting salary for recent grads is $60,000.

GENERAL INFO

Activities: Choral groups, concert band, dance, drama/theater, jazz band, literary magazine, marching band, music ensembles, musical theater, opera, pep band, radio station, student government, student newspaper, student-run film society, symphony orchestra, yearbook, campus ministries, international student organization. **Organizations:** 250 registered organizations, 30 honor societies, 28 religious organizations.

FINANCIAL AID

Students should submit: FAFSA, Institution's own financial aid form. Priority filing deadline is 11/1. The Princeton Review suggests that all financial aid forms be submitted as soon as possible after October 1. *Need-based scholarships/grants offered:* Federal Pell, FSEOG, State scholarships/grants, Private scholarships, College/university scholarship or grant aid from institutional funds. *Loan aid offered:* Direct Subsidized Stafford Loans, Direct Unsubsidized Stafford Loans, Direct PLUS loans, College/university loans from institutional funds. Applicants will be notified of awards on or about 4/1. Federal Work-Study Program available. Institutional employment available.

THE BOTTOM LINE

If you can afford it, Princeton is far from cheap. A year's tuition is $45,320, plus about $14,160 in room and board. These figures are nothing to scoff at. However, if you qualify for aid, you'll be granted the amount you need, without loans.

CAREER INFORMATION FROM PAYSCALE.COM

ROI rating	99
Bachelor's and No Higher	
Median starting salary	$61,300
Median mid-career salary	$122,000
At Least Bachelor's	
Median starting salary	$64,000
Median mid-career salary	$128,000
% alumni with high job meaning	58%
% STEM	32%

SELECTIVITY

Admissions Rating	99
# of applicants	27,290
% of applicants accepted	7
% of acceptees attending	68
# offered a place on the wait list	1,206
% accepting a place on wait list	71
% admitted from wait list	5

FRESHMAN PROFILE

Range SAT Critical Reading	690–790
Range SAT Math	700–800
Range SAT Writing	710–790
Range ACT Composite	32–35
Minimum paper TOEFL	600
Average HS GPA	3.9
% graduated top 10% of class	94
% graduated top 25% of class	98
% graduated top 50% of class	100

DEADLINES

Early action	
Deadline	11/1
Notification	12/15
Regular	
Deadline	1/1
Notification	4/1
Nonfall registration?	No

FINANCIAL FACTS

Financial Aid Rating	99
Annual tuition	$45,320
Room and board	$14,160
Average need-based scholarship	$44,890
% needy frosh rec. need-based scholarship or grant aid	100
% needy UG rec. need-based scholarship or grant aid	100
% needy frosh rec. non-need-based scholarship or grant aid	0
% needy UG rec. non-need-based scholarship or grant aid	0
% needy frosh rec. need-based self-help aid	100
% needy UG rec. need-based self-help aid	100
% frosh rec. any financial aid	59
% UG rec. any financial aid	60
% UG borrow to pay for school	16
Average cumulative indebtedness	$8,577
% frosh need fully met	100
% ugrads need fully met	100
Average % of frosh need met	100
Average % of ugrad need met	100

Purdue University—West Lafayette

1080 Schleman Hall, West Lafayette, IN 47907-2050 • Admissions: 765-494-1776 • Fax: 765-494-0544

CAMPUS LIFE

Quality of Life Rating	**92**
Fire Safety Rating	**95**
Green Rating	**94**
Type of school	Public
Affiliation	No Affiliation
Environment	Town

STUDENTS

Total undergrad enrollment	29,497
% male/female	57/43
% from out of state	34
% frosh live on campus	94
% ugrads live on campus	38
# of fraternities (% ugrad men join)	50 (19)
# of sororities (% ugrad women join)	31 (21)
% African American	3
% Asian	6
% Caucasian	64
% Hispanic	4
% Native American	<1
% Pacific Islander	<1
% Two or more races	2
% Race and/or ethnicity unknown	2
% international	18
# of countries represented	123

ACADEMICS

Academic Rating	**79**
% students graduating within 4 years	52
% students graduating within 6 years	75
Calendar	Semester
Student/faculty ratio	12:1
Profs interesting rating	70
Profs accessible rating	83
Most classes have 10–19 students.	
Most lab/discussion sessions have 20–29 students.	

MOST POPULAR MAJORS

Mechanical Engineering; Biology; Business Administration and Management

ABOUT THE SCHOOL

Though it is wedged between the cornfields of rural Indiana, Purdue, having over 30,000 students, is one of the most educationally and ethnically diverse universities in the United States. Purdue has rich tradition and has one of the oldest colleges of agriculture in the nation. "An institution filled with brain power and immense achievement, yet at the same time exceedingly humble and saturated with the warm-hearted hospitality of the Midwest," a contented undergrad tells us. Academics are taken seriously here. Purdue is research-intensive but retains great faculty-student interaction inside and outside of the classroom. "It allows undergraduates to enter laboratory research very early in their college career," says one student excitedly. Purdue has excellent research opportunities that are open to almost anyone who shows interest and dedication, and prides itself on being strong in STEM (science, technology, engineering, and math) education, with heavy emphasis on real-world practical research and knowledge. When combined with an emphasis on innovation and creative thinking, Purdue becomes a great choice for anyone looking to have a successful future. A well-networked university, that is incorporated into the surrounding town through collaborative learning, field experiences, and service opportunities, allows students to learn in and out of the classroom.

BANG FOR YOUR BUCK

One student describes the value of a Purdue education by saying, "I considered the problem mathematically. Math + science + social skills = engineering. Engineering + Midwest = Purdue." Others add, "I knew that I would be receiving an excellent education and that I would be prepared for my chosen career field," and explain that Purdue offers "a great education that will prepare you for a career, and it won't break the bank," and "tries its hardest to ensure everyone comes out of college with a job lined up." Purdue also draws a lot of employers for internships and full-time positions at many of their career fairs; the school produces marketable graduates who are in high demand by a number of top employers. Students are not hesitant with their praise. "I love Purdue and all of the doors it has opened for me in terms of engineering jobs and opportunities." The school's "emphasis on real-world practical research and knowledge, combined with an emphasis on innovation and creative thinking, make Purdue a great choice for anyone looking to have a successful future." High expectations ensure that the students at Purdue are well prepared for the future. "Nurturing a strong work ethic and high moral accountability" is important at Purdue, one student tells us. "It's been extremely tough, and a lot of work, but I feel like a much better engineer than I would have been had I gone anywhere else," says another appreciative enrollee.

STUDENT LIFE

"Students do work hard in the classroom throughout the week because we know that we are getting an outstanding education here. Come weekend time though, we definitely like to cut loose." Football and basketball games are major draws at the school, and "a lot of people on our campus think about when the next sporting event is. Big Ten Sports are huge here on campus. But not so huge that those who are uninterested in sports feel left out." When students are looking for ways to unwind that don't involve either sporting events or parties, they can choose from "so many different organizations" that are designed to "meet whatever your interests are whether it be sports, music, art, or may be even medieval jousting." A student raves that "Lafayette has plenty of restaurants, movie theatres, bowling, shopping, etc. . . . Chicago and Indianapolis are also near enough for day trips! I am so busy on campus because there are so many great organizations to join! I could be busy every night, if I wanted!" General consensus about life at Purdue seems to be that "there's always something going on on-campus, no one can TRULY say they have NOTHING to do."

Purdue University—West Lafayette

FINANCIAL AID: 765-494-0998 • E-MAIL: ADMISSIONS@PURDUE.EDU • WEBSITE: WWW.PURDUE.EDU

CAREER

"The programs to help people out with career development are countless. That's definitely a strength at Purdue," raves one student, and students definitely seem to feel that the school leaves them well prepared to navigate life after graduation. The Center for Career Opportunities offers counseling on academic majors and career paths, networking and recruiting opportunities, resources for job and internship searches, and coaching on résumés, cover letters, and interviews. Overall, "Purdue has an outstanding reputation for developing difference makers, role models, and individuals who can think outside the box." Out of Purdue alumni visiting PayScale.com, 50 percent report feeling as though they derive a high level of meaning from their careers.

GENERAL INFO

Activities: Choral groups, concert band, dance, drama/theater, jazz band, literary magazine, marching band, music ensembles, musical theater, opera, pep band, radio station, student government, student newspaper, student-run film society, symphony orchestra, television station, yearbook, campus ministries, international student organization. **Organizations:** 970 registered organizations, 51 honor societies, 58 religious organizations. 50 fraternities, 31 sororities. **Athletics (Intercollegiate):** *Men:* Baseball, basketball, cross-country, diving, football, golf, swimming, tennis, track/field (outdoor), track/field (indoor), wrestling. *Women:* Basketball, cross-country, diving, golf, soccer, softball, swimming, tennis, track/field (outdoor), track/field (indoor), volleyball.

FINANCIAL AID

Students should submit: FAFSA. Priority filing deadline is 3/1. The Princeton Review suggests that all financial aid forms be submitted as soon as possible after October 1. *Need-based scholarships/grants offered:* Federal Pell, FSEOG, State scholarships/grants, Private scholarships, College/university scholarship or grant aid from institutional funds. *Loan aid offered:* Direct Subsidized Stafford Loans, Direct Unsubsidized Stafford Loans, Direct PLUS loans, Federal Perkins Loans, College/university loans from institutional funds. Applicants will be notified of awards on or about 3/15. Federal Work-Study Program available. Institutional employment available.

BOTTOM LINE

Tuition is about $9,200 for in-state students, with those from other states looking at a substantial increase to over $28,000. Room, board, books, and fees will increase this amount by another $12,000. "The financial aid package was the best offered to me, along with a very good scholarship." Purdue is "cheaper than a private school but it is a world-renowned engineering school at the same time." One student reports, "[Purdue] gave me a very generous scholarship package."

CAREER INFORMATION FROM PAYSCALE.COM

ROI rating	90
Bachelor's and No Higher	
Median starting salary	$55,500
Median mid-career salary	$92,900
At Least Bachelor's	
Median starting salary	$56,400
Median mid-career salary	$95,200
% alumni with high job meaning	51%
% STEM	31%

SELECTIVITY

Admissions Rating	89
# of applicants	45,023
% of applicants accepted	59
% of acceptees attending	26

FRESHMAN PROFILE

Range SAT Critical Reading	520–630
Range SAT Math	560–700
Range SAT Writing	520–640
Range ACT Composite	25–31
Minimum paper TOEFL	550
Minimum internet-based TOEFL	79
Average HS GPA	3.7
% graduated top 10% of class	43
% graduated top 25% of class	79
% graduated top 50% of class	97

DEADLINES

Early action	
Deadline	11/1
Notification	Rolling
Regular	
Priority	1/1
Notification	Rolling
Nonfall registration?	Yes

FINANCIAL FACTS

Financial Aid Rating	88
Annual in-state tuition	$9,208
Annual out-of-state tuition	$28,010
Room and board	$10,030
Required fees	$794
Average need-based scholarship	$12,834
% needy frosh rec. need-based scholarship or grant aid	62
% needy UG rec. need-based scholarship or grant aid	66
% needy frosh rec. non-need-based scholarship or grant aid	45
% needy UG rec. non-need-based scholarship or grant aid	39
% needy frosh rec. need-based self-help aid	76
% needy UG rec. need-based self-help aid	83
% frosh rec. any financial aid	74
% UG rec. any financial aid	77
% UG borrow to pay for school	48
Average cumulative indebtedness	$27,711
% frosh need fully met	48
% ugrads need fully met	42
Average % of frosh need met	83
Average % of ugrad need met	86

Reed College

3203 SE Woodstock Boulevard, Portland, OR 97202-8199 • Admissions: 503-777-7511 • Fax: 503-777-7553

CAMPUS LIFE

Quality of Life Rating	92
Fire Safety Rating	96
Green Rating	60*
Type of school	Private
Affiliation	No Affiliation
Environment	Metropolis

STUDENTS

Total undergrad enrollment	1,430
% male/female	46/54
% from out of state	92
% frosh from public high school	59
% frosh live on campus	99
% ugrads live on campus	67
% African American	2
% Asian	6
% Caucasian	60
% Hispanic	11
% Native American	<1
% Pacific Islander	<1
% Two or more races	8
% Race and/or ethnicity unknown	5
% international	7
# of countries represented	46

ACADEMICS

Academic Rating	99
% students returning for sophomore year	88
% students graduating within 4 years	69
% students graduating within 6 years	82
Calendar	Semester
Student/faculty ratio	9:1
Profs interesting rating	99
Profs accessible rating	97

Most classes have 10–19 students.
Most lab/discussion sessions have
10–19 students.

MOST POPULAR MAJORS
English; Anthropology; Psychology

#41 COLLEGE THAT PAYS YOU BACK

ABOUT THE SCHOOL

Students greatly enjoy the nontraditional aspects of a Reed educational experience. The "unique and quirky atmosphere," in a "beautiful" part of the country with a "gorgeous" campus, provides students with a "traditional, classical, highly structured curriculum–yet, at the same time, a progressive, free-thinking, decidedly unstructured community culture." Reed students tend to be "smart, intellectually curious, and a little quirky." Politics tilt strongly to the left. Though the academics are incredibly intense, students are still playful and funky. Members of the student body here tell us that "Reed met my every desire with characteristic zeal; I received the financial aid I needed, I was able to sign up for challenging classes, and the living situation is ideal." Also, Reed doesn't "pad your ego." "Getting an A is a hard-fought battle here, but it means more because of it." Reed exalts the individual and the independent thinker. Even if a student doesn't start off with these qualities, they will likely develop them. Although the workload is intense, Reed enrollees are fiercely intellectual and more concerned with academic pursuits for their own sake than for any financial rewards their educations will produce. "I wanted to challenge myself and what I believed. I didn't want that passive undergraduate experience I see so much in other college students." "I was intrigued by the idea of an environment where people study because they care and participate in class because they feel that education is a worthwhile endeavor." It's a place where one comes to learn for the sake of learning, not to earn good grades, in a supportive environment. It is a place that is genuinely dedicated to the life of the mind and teaches the student to approach all aspects of life with a scholarly attitude.

BANG FOR YOUR BUCK

Of fundamental importance at Reed is how you contribute to the intellectual life of the college. "I am challenged to work hard and I strive to meet the very high expectations for Reed students." Students seek out an "academic rigor that definitely prepares us for graduate school and scholarly work." High-level research and scholarship at the cutting edge of each academic discipline are important to the school. With outstanding professors, and a healthy social environment, "for students who are interested both in exploring great ideas and in developing personal autonomy, it makes very good sense." Aptly put by another undergrad, "I wanted a challenge—if college isn't hard, you're doing something wrong."

STUDENT LIFE

"Intellectual discussion and debates are more definitely woven into the fabric of life here." With no Greek system or varsity sports, and student groups that change year to year based on students' interest, freedom and flexibility abound on campus. Students note there is "a growing population of minority students (minority in various senses), and they are making efforts constantly to establish themselves as a social presence on campus. Student groups like the Latino, Asian, and Black and African Student Unions and places like the Multicultural Resource Center offer places for support."

Reed College

FINANCIAL AID: 503-777-7223 • E-MAIL: ADMISSION@REED.EDU • WEBSITE: WWW.REED.EDU

CAREER

The aptly named Center for Life After Reed is dedicated to connecting students with experiential learning experiences during their time in college and with professional contacts for their future careers. Paid summer internships abound through the Internship Advantage Initiative, and winter Externships let Reedies learn even more about interesting career paths. SEEDS links students to service learning gigs throughout the year, and the weekly e-mail digest Beyond Campus Opportunities reminds them about upcoming fellowship deadlines, interesting employment opportunities, and more. Graduates report average starting salaries of $47,500, and 56 percent derive a high level of meaning from their work.

GENERAL INFO

Activities: A capella groups, theatre productions, literary magazine, radio station, foreign language clubs, student government, student newspaper, symphony orchestra, feminist student union, social activist groups, international student organization. **Organizations:** 105 registered organizations, 1 honor society, 5 religious organizations. **On-Campus Highlights:** Thesis Tower, Nuclear Research Reactor, Crystal Springs Canyon, Cerf Amphitheatre, Paradox and Paradox Lost Cafes. **Environmental Initiatives:** LEED construction, recycling, installation for energy efficiency across campus (i.e., lighting, windows, heating).

FINANCIAL AID

Students should submit: FAFSA, CSS/Financial Aid PROFILE, Noncustodial PROFILE, Business/Farm Supplement. Regular filing deadline is 2/1. The Princeton Review suggests that all financial aid forms be submitted as soon as possible after October 1. *Need-based scholarships/grants offered:* Federal Pell, FSEOG, State scholarships/grants, Private scholarships, College/university scholarship or grant aid from institutional funds. *Loan aid offered:* Direct Subsidized Stafford Loans, Direct Unsubsidized Stafford Loans, Direct PLUS loans, Federal Perkins Loans, College/university loans from institutional funds. Federal Work-Study Program available. Institutional employment available.

BOTTOM LINE

Annual tuition is $49,640; with books, room, board, and fees, you can tack another $13,940 onto that total. However, about 99 percent of needy Reed students are recipients of need-based scholarships or grant assistance; it is commonly heard from students, "I received generous financial aid." And not only in-state students benefit from these advantages. "Reed was really generous with my financial aid package and made it possible for me to go out of state to college."

CAREER INFORMATION FROM PAYSCALE.COM

ROI rating	91
Bachelor's and No Higher	
Median starting salary	$47,600
Median mid-career salary	$103,000
At Least Bachelor's	
Median starting salary	$49,200
Median mid-career salary	$103,000
% alumni with high job meaning	55%
% STEM	25%

SELECTIVITY

Admissions Rating	94
# of applicants	5,396
% of applicants accepted	35
% of acceptees attending	22
# offered a place on the wait list	1,468
% accepting a place on wait list	30
% admitted from wait list	1

FRESHMAN PROFILE

Range SAT Critical Reading	670–760
Range SAT Math	620–720
Range SAT Writing	640–730
Range ACT Composite	29–33
Minimum paper TOEFL	600
Minimum internet-based TOEFL	100
Average HS GPA	3.9
% graduated top 10% of class	53
% graduated top 25% of class	87
% graduated top 50% of class	98

DEADLINES

Early decision	
Deadline	11/15
Notification	12/15
Regular	
Deadline	1/1
Notification	2/1
Nonfall registration?	No

FINANCIAL FACTS

Financial Aid Rating	99
Annual tuition	$49,640
Room and board	$12,590
Required fees	$300
Average need-based scholarship	$39,304
% needy frosh rec. need-based scholarship or grant aid	98
% needy UG rec. need-based scholarship or grant aid	99
% needy frosh rec. non-need-based scholarship or grant aid	0
% needy UG rec. non-need-based scholarship or grant aid	0
% needy frosh rec. need-based self-help aid	94
% needy UG rec. need-based self-help aid	93
% frosh rec. any financial aid	53
% UG rec. any financial aid	54
% frosh need fully met	99
% ugrads need fully met	100
Average % of frosh need met	100
Average % of ugrad need met	100

Rensselaer Polytechnic Institute

110 EIGHTH STREET, TROY, NY 12180-3590 • ADMISSIONS: 518-276-6216 • FAX: 518-276-4072

CAMPUS LIFE

Quality of Life Rating	84
Fire Safety Rating	93
Green Rating	60*
Type of school	Private
Affiliation	No Affiliation
Environment	City

STUDENTS

Total undergrad enrollment	5,864
% male/female	69/31
% from out of state	67
% frosh from public high school	70
% frosh live on campus	100
% ugrads live on campus	57
# of fraternities (% ugrad men join)	29 (30)
# of sororities (% ugrad women join)	5 (16)
% African American	3
% Asian	10
% Caucasian	59
% Hispanic	8
% Native American	<1
% Pacific Islander	<1
% Two or more races	7
% Race and/or ethnicity unknown	2
% international	11
# of countries represented	44

ACADEMICS

Academic Rating	85
% students returning for sophomore year	94
% students graduating within 4 years	63
% students graduating within 6 years	81
Calendar	Semester
Student/faculty ratio	16:1
Profs interesting rating	70
Profs accessible rating	84
Most classes have 10–19 students.	

MOST POPULAR MAJORS
Computer Engineering; Electrical and Electronics Engineering; Business/Commerce

ABOUT THE SCHOOL

As the oldest technological research university in the country, Rensselaer Polytechnic Institute has some legs to stand on in the higher education world. Though primarily an engineering institution, RPI offers degrees through five schools and encourages its students to take part in interdisciplinary programs that combine work from different areas of study. A focus on bringing the skills and technology from the lab to the real world has kept the school current and provided many a career showpiece for students. For instance, according to the school, in the last thirty years RPI has helped launch almost 300 start-up companies, many of which grew out of class projects. Classes are sized so that students can get to know their professors, who "make it a point to be accessible to students, either personally or through other venues like phone or email."

BANG FOR YOUR BUCK

Ninety-three percent of Rensselaer students receive need-based financial aid, and the school meets an average of 77 percent of need. The school offers numerous merit-based scholarships and grants, most prominently the Rensselaer Leadership Award for academic and personal achievements, and the Rensselaer Medal, which offers a minimum of $15,000 per year to students who have distinguished themselves in mathematics and science. A relatively large number of RPI students receive the Rensselaer Medal (13 percent of the most recently admitted class). International students are eligible to receive financial aid.

STUDENT LIFE

RPI draws a significant portion (nearly one-third) of its "very diverse" students from outside of the northeast. The typical student "may be considered 'nerdy' by the liberal arts world, but being a nerd is totally cool here," says a student. "Everyone has quirks that are appreciated here, and people with similar quirks tend to flock together." There "is always something going on, especially with all the student clubs,"of which there are over 180, and the intramural sports (hockey is especially big at Rensselaer), and most people stay on campus over the weekends (even those who are local) since it is "packed full of concerts, sporting events, plays, and club events." Students often split up the weekend with some homework and pick and choose which events to attend; they "are really focused and goal-oriented, but know when and how to have a good time."

CAREER

RPI is all about ensuring every student gets legitimate experience in his or her field of study as soon as possible, and looks to "equip each student with the skills needed to be a valuable member of any research team or company." The focus on problem-solving and "opportunities to be involved in hands-on research" are just two of the ways the school accomplishes this, and "the research buildings are amazing." The RPI name has a great reputation with science and tech employers, and many take part in co-ops throughout the academic year. The Center for Career & Professional Development maintains JobLink, an online job recruiting and posting system, offers career programming tailored to your class year, and hosts a Spring Career Fair. Fifty percent of the RPI graduates who visited PayScale.com reported feeling that their jobs had a high level of meaningful impact on the world, and brought in an average starting salary of $62,300.

Rensselaer Polytechnic Institute

FINANCIAL AID: 518-276-6813 • E-MAIL: ADMISSIONS@RPI.EDU • WEBSITE: WWW.RPI.EDU

GENERAL INFO

Activities: Choral groups, concert band, dance, drama/theater, jazz band, literary magazine, music ensembles, musical theater, pep band, radio station, student government, student newspaper, student-run film society, symphony orchestra, television station, yearbook, Campus Ministries, International Student Organization. **Organizations:** 177 registered organizations, 40 honor societies, 11 religious organizations. 29 fraternities, 5 sororities. **Athletics (Intercollegiate):** *Men:* baseball, basketball, cross-country, diving, football, golf, ice hockey, lacrosse, soccer, swimming, tennis, track/field (outdoor), track/field (indoor). *Women:* basketball, cross country, diving, field hockey, ice hockey, lacrosse, soccer, softball, swimming, tennis, track/field (outdoor), track/field (indoor). **On-Campus Highlights:** Rensselaer Union, Mueller Fitness Center, Experimental Media & Performing Arts Ctr, Houston Field House (hockey arena), ECAV.

FINANCIAL AID

Students should submit: FAFSA, CSS/Financial Aid PROFILE. Priority filing deadline is 2/1. The Princeton Review suggests that all financial aid forms be submitted as soon as possible after October 1. *Need-based scholarships/grants offered:* Federal Pell, FSEOG, State scholarships/grants, Private scholarships, College/university scholarship or grant aid from institutional funds. *Loan aid offered:* Direct Subsidized Stafford Loans, Direct Unsubsidized Stafford Loans, Direct PLUS loans, Federal Perkins Loans, State Loans. Applicants will be notified of awards on or about 3/15. Federal Work-Study Program available. Institutional employment available.

BOTTOM LINE

Tuition runs a hefty $49,520, with an additional $14,630 needed for room and board. With fees and supplies added in the estimated cost of attendance is $68,244, but the vast majority of students receive aid so as not to pay the sticker price. The average need-based scholarship award is $30,943.

CAREER INFORMATION FROM PAYSCALE.COM

ROI rating	90
Bachelor's and No Higher	
Median starting salary	$63,300
Median mid-career salary	$110,000
At Least Bachelor's	
Median starting salary	$64,300
Median mid-career salary	$115,000
% alumni with high job meaning	48%
% STEM	74%

SELECTIVITY

Admissions Rating	95
# of applicants	17,752
% of applicants accepted	42
% of acceptees attending	19
# offered a place on the wait list	4,087
% accepting a place on wait list	54
% admitted from wait list	3
# of early decision applicants	554
% accepted early decision	65

FRESHMAN PROFILE

Range SAT Critical Reading	610–720
Range SAT Math	670–770
Range ACT Composite	28–32
Minimum paper TOEFL	570
Minimum internet-based TOEFL	88
Average HS GPA	3.9
% graduated top 10% of class	72
% graduated top 25% of class	94
% graduated top 50% of class	99

DEADLINES

Early decision	
Deadline	11/1
Notification	12/12
Regular	
Deadline	1/15
Notification	3/14
Nonfall registration?	Yes

FINANCIAL FACTS

Financial Aid Rating	83
Annual tuition	$49,520
Room and board	$14,630
Required fees	$1,277
Average need-based scholarship	$30,943
% needy frosh rec. need-based scholarship or grant aid	100
% needy UG rec. need-based scholarship or grant aid	100
% needy frosh rec. non-need-based scholarship or grant aid	21
% needy UG rec. non-need-based scholarship or grant aid	14
% needy frosh rec. need-based self-help aid	99
% needy UG rec. need-based self-help aid	97
% frosh rec. any financial aid	89
% UG rec. any financial aid	89
% frosh need fully met	27
% ugrads need fully met	21
Average % of frosh need met	87
Average % of ugrad need met	79

Rhodes College

2000 North Parkway, Memphis, TN 38112 • Admissions: 901-843-3700 • Fax: 901-843-3631

CAMPUS LIFE

Quality of Life Rating	97
Fire Safety Rating	87
Green Rating	72
Type of school	Private
Affiliation	Presbyterian
Environment	Metropolis

STUDENTS

Total undergrad enrollment	2,046
% male/female	43/57
% from out of state	74
% frosh from public high school	46
% frosh live on campus	97
% ugrads live on campus	71
# of fraternities (% ugrad men join)	8 (40)
# of sororities (% ugrad women join)	7 (62)
% African American	6
% Asian	6
% Caucasian	74
% Hispanic	5
% Native American	<1
% Pacific Islander	<1
% Two or more races	4
% Race and/or ethnicity unknown	2
% international	3
# of countries represented	18

ACADEMICS

Academic Rating	97
% students returning for sophomore year	91
% students graduating within 4 years	76
% students graduating within 6 years	83
Calendar	Semester
Student/faculty ratio	10:1
Profs interesting rating	97
Profs accessible rating	98

Most classes have 10–19 students.
Most lab/discussion sessions have
20–29 students.

MOST POPULAR MAJORS

Biology; Business Administration and
Management; Psychology

ABOUT THE SCHOOL

Located in the heart of Memphis, Tennessee, Rhodes College was founded in 1848 by Freemasons, but came to be affiliated with the Presbyterian Church. This private liberal arts college encourages students to study "as many different disciplines as possible in order to gain a broader understanding of the world." Rhodes students can expect small classes—averaging ten to nineteen students—and "rigorous" academics. Students who put in the work can expect to succeed: "Most people here work hard and see it academically pay off." The school's "very dedicated professors" "really care about their students and make an effort to get to know us and help us succeed." One student proudly explains that "Rhodes offers a close, personalized environment where teachers and faculty are not just willing, but enthusiastic to help you find your unique path to achievement." The school's 110-acre campus, situated right in the middle of historic Memphis, is known for its "beautiful" grounds and architecture. Over a dozen of Rhodes's buildings are listed in the National Register of Historic Places. The campus is located near Overton Park and the Memphis Zoo, and a short walk to many entertainment, internship, and research opportunities, including institutions such as St. Jude Children's Research Hospital and the National Civil Rights Museum.

BANG FOR YOUR BUCK

"Memphis is a city with character, and Rhodes is an institution [that] helps foster it," one student explains. The city of Memphis offers it all to students, from internships to "great restaurants" and weekend activities. Despite being located in a city, the college provides a secluded college atmosphere for those who want it. The professors are "great and helpful," and with a faculty-to-student ratio of 10:1, they are easily accessible. The student body is "actually really diverse and tends to have some great opportunities for students to learn about other cultures and countries."

STUDENT LIFE

"Stereotypically, Rhodes is a white, private college full of men in sweater-vests and women in pearls. But, there is an incredible diversity at Rhodes between upper socioeconomic backgrounds to lower socioeconomic backgrounds, between different races, between different ethnic backgrounds, between political backgrounds, and between genders. There are 'preppy' students, 'hippies,' 'punks,' and 'nerds.' The one thing that unites us all is that, on the inside, we're all just a bunch of geeks who love to learn and want to broaden our horizons." The school is full of hard workers ("academic but not full of nerds") and its honor code is taken very seriously. One thing is for certain—students here are "busy" in all areas of their life: studying, taking advantage of the "countless service opportunities," arts, athletics, and Greek life. At Rhodes, "there is an emphasis on academics, a friendly atmosphere, and plenty of extra-curriculars to get involved in."

CAREER

The typical Rhodes College graduate has a starting salary of around $40,600, and 60 percent report that their job has a great deal of meaning. Students feel that Rhodes "is the epitome of opportunity: from service to sports to academics to internships and jobs to career services and professors. Rhodes has it all." A Biochemistry major notes that "I get to do cutting edge biomedical Cancer research at St. Jude Children's Research hospital. This is an invaluable internship I got through Rhodes." Many students feel that the internship opportunities at Rhodes are not only "invaluable," but the sort of things that "helped pull us here."

Rhodes College

FINANCIAL AID: 901-843-3810 • E-MAIL: ADMINFO@RHODES.EDU • WEBSITE: WWW.RHODES.EDU

GENERAL INFO

Activities: Choral groups, dance, drama/theater, jazz band, literary magazine, music ensembles, musical theater, pep band, radio station, student government, student newspaper, student-run film society, symphony orchestra, television station, yearbook. **Organizations:** Campus Ministries, International Student Organization, Model UN, 115 registered organizations, 14 honor societies, 8 religious organizations. 8 fraternities, 7 sororities. **Athletics (Intercollegiate):** *Men:* baseball, basketball, cross-country, football, golf, lacrosse, soccer, swimming, tennis, track/field (outdoor). *Women:* basketball, cross-country, field hockey, golf, lacrosse, soccer, softball, swimming, tennis, track/field (outdoor), volleyball. **On-Campus Highlights:** Barret Library (includes a Starbucks coffee shop), Burrow Center for Student Opportunity, Bryan Campus Life Center (home to the Lynx Lair pub, East Village (apartment-style dorms), McCoy Theater, The Burrow Center for Student Opportunity opened in Spring, 2008. It consolidates most student services under one roof, including a one-stop transaction center, enrolling and financing, student development and academic support, and out of class experiences. It also includes space for student organizations and is open to students 24x7. **Environmental Initiatives:** $500,000 Andrew W. Mellon Foundation grant to expand environmental studies initiatives through community partnerships; comprehensive campuswide recycling program; centralized energy management system; Green Power Switch.

FINANCIAL AID

Students should submit: FAFSA, CSS/Financial Aid PROFILE, Noncustodial PROFILE. Regular filing deadline is 3/1. The Princeton Review suggests that all financial aid forms be submitted as soon as possible after October 1. *Need-based scholarships/grants offered:* Federal Pell, FSEOG, State scholarships/grants, Private scholarships, College/university scholarship or grant aid from institutional funds. *Loan aid offered:* Direct Subsidized Stafford Loans, Direct Unsubsidized Stafford Loans, Direct PLUS loans, Federal Perkins Loans. Federal Work-Study Program available. Institutional employment available.

BOTTOM LINE

Annual tuition at Rhodes is $44,632 to which a student should expect to add another $11,068 for living and other school expenses. However, in addition to working hard to meet students with financial needs—a full 94 percent of undergraduates receive aid—the school offers many merit-based scholarships. Fifty-one percent of students will take out loans, and the average cumulative student debt is $28,008. The Rhodes Student Associate Program is a unique work program that matches students with "meaningful employment that requires advanced skills and dedication." The program currently offers more than 100 positions in a variety of both academic and administrative departments. Rhodes also facilitates many off-campus student employment opportunities with local non-profits.

CAREER INFORMATION FROM PAYSCALE.COM

ROI rating	**89**
Bachelor's and No Higher	
Median starting salary	$43,200
Median mid-career salary	$90,700
At Least Bachelor's	
Median starting salary	$44,900
Median mid-career salary	$90,700
% alumni with high job meaning	49%
% STEM	21%

SELECTIVITY

Admissions Rating	**93**
# of applicants	4,666
% of applicants accepted	47
% of acceptees attending	26
# offered a place on the wait list	1,290
% accepting a place on wait list	21
% admitted from wait list	16
# of early decision applicants	188
% accepted early decision	76

FRESHMAN PROFILE

Range SAT Critical Reading	600–700
Range SAT Math	580–680
Range ACT Composite	27–32
Minimum paper TOEFL	550
Average HS GPA	3.9
% graduated top 10% of class	54
% graduated top 25% of class	83
% graduated top 50% of class	98

DEADLINES

Early decision	
Deadline	11/1
Notification	12/1
Early action	
Deadline	11/15
Notification	1/15
Regular	
Priority	1/15
Notification	4/1
Nonfall registration?	Yes

FINANCIAL FACTS

Financial Aid Rating	**88**
Annual tuition	$44,632
Room and board	$11,068
Required fees	$310
Average need-based scholarship	$27,938
% needy frosh rec. need-based scholarship or grant aid	99
% needy UG rec. need-based scholarship or grant aid	99
% needy frosh rec. non-need-based scholarship or grant aid	52
% needy UG rec. non-need-based scholarship or grant aid	34
% needy frosh rec. need-based self-help aid	42
% needy UG rec. need-based self-help aid	60
% frosh rec. any financial aid	95
% UG rec. any financial aid	94
% UG borrow to pay for school	51
Average cumulative indebtedness	$28,008
% frosh need fully met	56
% ugrads need fully met	40

Rice University

MS 17, PO Box 1892, Houston, TX 77251-1892 • Admissions: 713-348-7423 • Fax: 713-348-5952

CAMPUS LIFE

Quality of Life Rating	**97**
Fire Safety Rating	**95**
Green Rating	**90**
Type of school	Private
Affiliation	No Affiliation
Environment	Metropolis

STUDENTS

Total undergrad enrollment	3,910
% male/female	53/47
% from out of state	50
% frosh live on campus	99
% ugrads live on campus	72
% African American	7
% Asian	24
% Caucasian	37
% Hispanic	14
% Native American	<1
% Pacific Islander	<1
% Two or more races	4
% Race and/or ethnicity unknown	1
% international	12
# of countries represented	46

ACADEMICS

Academic Rating	**93**
% students returning for sophomore year	97
% students graduating within 4 years	80
% students graduating within 6 years	91
Calendar	Semester
Student/faculty ratio	6:1
Profs interesting rating	84
Profs accessible rating	86
Most classes have 10–19 students.	

MOST POPULAR MAJORS
Biology; Psychology; Economics

#13 COLLEGE THAT PAYS YOU BACK

ABOUT THE SCHOOL

The culture at Rice is uniquely student-focused. The eleven colleges in the school's residential college system—"the greatest thing ever"—each have their own history and traditions and their own system of self (student) governance, and the "super-strong sense of community" created by the system affords students a greater than usual amount of influence regarding University policies and academic offerings. With students taking such a unique hand in shaping their experience ("the amount of trust and responsibilities put in the hands of students is unparalleled"), you can imagine that the level of school pride positively soars here: "Rice is a place where everyone is smart, the professors are accessible, the community is strong, and you'll always feel like you belong somewhere and that people care about you."

Academics are well-integrated into student culture, making the environment feel "open and welcome socially, and not cutthroat." "We all help each other out academically, and as a result we all become great friends," says a student. The premed program, located next to the largest medical center in the world, is one of the country's finest, and the engineering program is beyond excellent (to single out a couple of strengths among many). With so many research opportunities (including mentored lab work, independent projects, and social-science internships), students often develop a strong rapport with their instructors. One details, "Most Rice professors love what they're doing, and you can tell that they are truly passionate about the material." They may show this "by literally dancing around in the front of the classroom or by simply being available at any time to help students."

BANG FOR YOUR BUCK

In addition to their terrific financial aid policy, Rice offers a number of merit scholarships to incoming students. No additional application is required, and students are selected for merit scholarships based on their admission applications, meaning that when the big envelope comes, it can sometimes offer double the fun. In addition to the monetary value, some scholarships include the opportunity to do individual research under the direction of a faculty member, adding even greater value to the Rice experience. Even for students who receive no financial assistance, Rice remains one of the best values in higher education. With tuition set at thousands of dollars lower than Ivy League and other peer institutions, Rice walks the walk of keeping the highest caliber of education affordable for all.

STUDENT LIFE

Students at Rice "are generally very driven to either make a ton of money or change the world." A current undergraduate details, "Rice genuinely has a diverse community that accepts people of all backgrounds," and is "a school that is not only diverse in interest, religious background and political stance, but that . . . also [has] a very diverse socioeconomic community." Nonetheless, Rice students do share some common traits, generally described as "liberal (for Texas)," low-key, and "good-natured." It should be noted that "students at Rice work hard and accomplish great things in academics

Rice University

FINANCIAL AID: 713-348-4958 • E-MAIL: ADMI@RICE.EDU • WEBSITE: WWW.RICE.EDU

and extracurriculars. But this is complemented and supported by a thriving social life. From Thursday pub nights to Friday and Saturday night parties, including large public parties thrown by residential colleges." That said, "Rice's alcohol policy fosters a culture of care in which students look out for each other and generally help each other stay safe and make good decisions."

CAREER

The typical Rice University graduate has a starting salary of around $60,000, and 53 percent report that their job has a great deal of meaning. Students feel that the career services at Rice "are incredibly geared toward oil and gas, consulting, and computer science," and note that "the Sport Management department is very good with connections and internships in the Houston sport industry." Some add that "the Gateway Program provides phenomenal resources to students who want to study abroad or do internships in the social sciences," and "the Baker Institute brings in a wide range of speakers and often gives students the opportunity to meet these world leaders and scholars in small groups of fifteen to twenty prior to larger events. The Baker Institute also has several research internships for social sciences majors."

FINANCIAL AID

Students should submit: FAFSA, CSS/Financial Aid PROFILE, Noncustodial PROFILE, Business/Farm Supplement. Priority filing deadline is 2/15. The Princeton Review suggests that all financial aid forms be submitted as soon as possible after October 1. *Need-based scholarships/grants offered:* Federal Pell, FSEOG, State scholarships/grants, Private scholarships, College/university scholarship or grant aid from institutional funds. *Loan aid offered:* Direct Subsidized Stafford Loans, Direct Unsubsidized Stafford Loans, Direct PLUS loans, Federal Perkins Loans, State Loans. Applicants will be notified of awards on or about 4/1. Federal Work-Study Program available. Institutional employment available.

THE BOTTOM LINE

Tuition runs $43,220 a year, with an additional $15,278 or so in fees, room and board, and expenses. But, Rice meets 100 percent of demonstrated need for all admitted students. As of 2009, Rice eliminated loans to students whose family income is below $80,000, instead meeting their need through a combination of grants, work-study, merit aid (if qualified), and institutional funds. For students with need eligibility whose family income is above $80,000, Rice will award a small subsidized loan in combination with grants, work- study, merit aid (if qualified), and institutional funds to cover 100 percent of the student's unmet need. The subsidized loan cap for students who show need is $2,500 each year, significantly limiting the debt at graduation for the small number of students in this category.

CAREER INFORMATION FROM PAYSCALE.COM

ROI rating	93
Bachelor's and No Higher	
Median starting salary	$63,900
Median mid-career salary	$114,000
At Least Bachelor's	
Median starting salary	$65,500
Median mid-career salary	$112,000
% alumni with high job meaning	60%
% STEM	43%

SELECTIVITY

Admissions Rating	97
# of applicants	17,951
% of applicants accepted	16
% of acceptees attending	34
# offered a place on the wait list	2,237
% accepting a place on wait list	74
% admitted from wait list	8
# of early decision applicants	1,389
% accepted early decision	20

FRESHMAN PROFILE

Range SAT Critical Reading	680–760
Range SAT Math	710–800
Range SAT Writing	680–770
Range ACT Composite	32–35
Minimum paper TOEFL	600
Minimum internet-based TOEFL	100
% graduated top 10% of class	89
% graduated top 25% of class	96
% graduated top 50% of class	100

DEADLINES

Early decision	
Deadline	11/1
Notification	12/15
Regular	
Deadline	1/1
Notification	4/1
Nonfall registration?	No

FINANCIAL FACTS

Financial Aid Rating	96
Annual tuition	$43,220
Room and board	$13,750
Required fees	$683
Average need-based scholarship	$36,025
% needy frosh rec. need-based scholarship or grant aid	97
% needy UG rec. need-based scholarship or grant aid	97
% needy frosh rec. non-need-based scholarship or grant aid	5
% needy UG rec. non-need-based scholarship or grant aid	3
% needy frosh rec. need-based self-help aid	65
% needy UG rec. need-based self-help aid	75
% frosh rec. any financial aid	41
% UG rec. any financial aid	39
% frosh need fully met	99
% ugrads need fully met	99
Average % of frosh need met	100
Average % of ugrad need met	100

Rochester Institute of Technology

60 LOMB MEMORIAL DRIVE, ROCHESTER, NY 14623-5604 • ADMISSIONS: 585-475-5502 • FAX: 585-475-7424

CAMPUS LIFE

Quality of Life Rating	**89**
Fire Safety Rating	**89**
Green Rating	**96**
Type of school	Private
Affiliation	No Affiliation
Environment	City

STUDENTS

Total undergrad enrollment	13,543
% male/female	68/32
% from out of state	46
% frosh from public high school	85
% frosh live on campus	96
% ugrads live on campus	55
# of fraternities (% ugrad men join)	19 (5)
# of sororities (% ugrad women join)	10 (6)
% African American	5
% Asian	8
% Caucasian	66
% Hispanic	7
% Native American	<1
% Pacific Islander	<1
% Two or more races	3
% Race and/or ethnicity unknown	5
% international	6
# of countries represented	68

ACADEMICS

Academic Rating	**80**
% students returning for sophomore year	89
% students graduating within 4 years	34
% students graduating within 6 years	70
Calendar	Semester
Student/faculty ratio	13:1
Profs interesting rating	76
Profs accessible rating	74
Most classes have 10–19 students.	
Most lab/discussion sessions have 10–19 students.	

MOST POPULAR MAJORS
Mechanical Engineering; Mechanical Engineering Technology; Game Design and Development

ABOUT THE SCHOOL

Though it has certainly made a name for itself with its STEM programs, Rochester Institute of Technology rounds itself out as an interdisciplinary institution where "a unique blend of amazing design students, computing technology, and business students" come together to find innovation with an entrepreneurial focus. The "rich RIT culture" offers students a versatile curriculum where professors "are engaging and really stimulate [your] creativity and mind," buoyed by a 12:1 student to faculty ratio. Employers trust the RIT brand implicitly, and the school stresses experiential learning and creativity as a part of every curriculum. Although RIT is a larger private school with 11,691 undergraduates, "it feels much smaller than it is because of its tight-knit community," and students are afforded "many opportunities to branch out, work with other majors, and pursue non-technical interests."

BANG FOR YOUR BUCK

The school has one of the largest co-op programs in the world (drawing from more than 2,100 employers "at the types of places you grow up dreaming of working for"), and most of the school's majors offer these paid career-related work experiences that prepare students "to be a key asset at any job." Additionally, there are numerous merit-based scholarships up for grabs, including the RIT Presidential Scholarship, which awards first-years above a certain SAT score and academic rank up anywhere from $10,000 to $16,000 per year; Achievement Scholarships for various programs of study that award $7,000 to $10,000 per year to students of distinguished academic marks and involvement; as well as other $7,000 annual awards for specific study interests such as robotics and computing.

STUDENT LIFE

RIT has "an amazing number of clubs, groups, events and opportunities" that bring together all of the people "who love to innovate using technology and intellect." Everyone has a niche here; "nerdy and plays video games" is a common but proud badge worn by some, but "everybody fits in and has friends because there is such a large student body and no one is afraid to be themselves." The pool of students is big enough to find any interests, "from a powerlifting team and on-campus rock climbing club to various intramural sports," and on the weekends many head to downtown Rochester via the bus RIT provides. Hockey is a popular pastime, and people like to go to the gym and rent equipment or "meet at one of the more than twelve places on campus to share a meal."

CAREER

RIT has "a great focus on what students will do once they leave the classroom," and all professors have experience in the real world and "use that experience and those connections to help us anyway they can." The attention paid to making sure students get more than just a formal education helps students to graduate with real-world connections and skills that employers recognize and desire. The Office of Career Services and Cooperative Education helps arrange for counseling, mentors, job prep, portfolio reviews, and career fairs, keeping the hire rate straight out of college well above 90 percent. The average starting salary for those graduates who visited PayScale.com was $55,900 with 45 percent of these graduates reporting they felt their jobs had high social meaning.

Rochester Institute of Technology

FINANCIAL AID: 585-475-5502 • E-MAIL: ADMISSIONS@RIT.EDU • WEBSITE: WWW.RIT.EDU

GENERAL INFO

Activities: Choral groups, concert band, dance, drama/theater, jazz band, literary magazine, music ensembles, musical theater, pep band, radio station, student government, student newspaper, student-run film society, symphony orchestra, yearbook, Campus Ministries, International Student Organization. **Organizations:** 175 registered organizations, 9 honor societies, 5 religious organizations. 19 fraternities, 10 sororities. **Athletics (Intercollegiate):** *Men:* baseball, basketball, crew/rowing, cross-country, diving, ice hockey, lacrosse, soccer, swimming, tennis, track/field (outdoor), track/field (indoor), wrestling. *Women:* basketball, cheerleading, crew/rowing, cross-country, diving, ice hockey, lacrosse, soccer, softball, swimming, tennis, track/field (outdoor), track/field (indoor), volleyball. **On-Campus Highlights:** Java Wally's (Wallace Library coffee shop, Student Life Center/Field House/Ice Arena, ESPN Zone @ RIT Student Alumni Union, Ben and Jerry's (RIT Student Alumni Union, The Cafe and Market at Crossroads.

FINANCIAL AID

Students should submit: FAFSA, Institution's own financial aid form, State aid form. Priority filing deadline is **2/15.** The Princeton Review suggests that all financial aid forms be submitted as soon as possible after October 1. *Need-based scholarships/grants offered:* Federal Pell, FSEOG, State scholarships/grants, Private scholarships, College/university scholarship or grant aid from institutional funds. *Loan aid offered:* Direct Subsidized Stafford Loans, Direct Unsubsidized Stafford Loans, Direct PLUS loans, Federal Perkins Loans. Applicants will be notified of awards on a rolling basis beginning 3/1. Federal Work-Study Program available. Institutional employment available.

BOTTOM LINE

Tuition is set at $38,024 for all students, with an additional room and board cost of $12,274. Fortunately, around 77 percent of undergraduates receive merit- or need-based financial aid, with first-years receiving an average gift-based award of $18,500. As many undergrads earn money for their cooperative rotations, tuition costs are often offset by earnings while matriculated.

CAREER INFORMATION FROM PAYSCALE.COM

ROI rating	**86**
Bachelor's and No Higher	
Median starting salary	$56,900
Median mid-career salary	$85,400
At Least Bachelor's	
Median starting salary	$58,000
Median mid-career salary	$88,200
% alumni with high job meaning	44%
% STEM	52%

SELECTIVITY

Admissions Rating	88
# of applicants	18,598
% of applicants accepted	57
% of acceptees attending	27
# offered a place on the wait list	376
% accepting a place on wait list	98
% admitted from wait list	22
# of early decision applicants	1,329
% accepted early decision	64

FRESHMAN PROFILE

Range SAT Critical Reading	550–660
Range SAT Math	580–690
Range SAT Writing	520–630
Range ACT Composite	26–31
Minimum paper TOEFL	550
Minimum internet-based TOEFL	79
Average HS GPA	3.6
% graduated top 10% of class	36
% graduated top 25% of class	69
% graduated top 50% of class	96

DEADLINES

Early decision	
Deadline	11/15
Notification	1/15
Regular	
Priority	1/15
Deadline	2/1
Nonfall registration?	Yes

FINANCIAL FACTS

Financial Aid Rating	92
Annual tuition	$38,024
Room and board	$12,274
Required fees	$544
Average need-based scholarship	$20,000
% needy UG rec. need-based scholarship or grant aid	90
% needy frosh rec. non-need-based scholarship or grant aid	29
% needy UG rec. non-need-based scholarship or grant aid	29
% needy frosh rec. need-based self-help aid	88
% needy UG rec. need-based self-help aid	82
% frosh rec. any financial aid	87
% UG rec. any financial aid	77
% frosh need fully met	81
% ugrads need fully met	82
Average % of frosh need met	87
Average % of ugrad need met	87

Rose-Hulman Institute of Technology

5500 Wabash Ave., IN 47803 • Admissions: 812-877-8213 • Fax: 812-877-8941

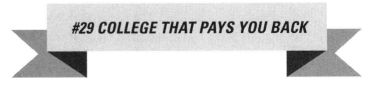

#29 COLLEGE THAT PAYS YOU BACK

ABOUT THE SCHOOL

Though ostensibly dedicated to the study of engineering, science and mathematics, the Rose-Hulman Institute of Technology seeks to create a "collaborative rather than competitive" environment that sends its graduates into the real world with the tools needed to secure employment. "Everyone from the housekeepers and residence life to professors and staff truly wants you to succeed, academically and at life in general," says a student. The professors in the small classes "genuinely care about your learning and advancing you in your career path," the "accommodating" administration creates an "intimate family atmosphere," and there is an open door policy that extends "from your fellow students all the way up to the president." Additionally, there are many resources for students who are struggling, and the school makes it a point to encourage students to take advantage of the artwork and cultural opportunities available at the school (including the Rose-Hulman art collection and the Performing Arts Series).

BANG FOR YOUR BUCK

Almost every single student attending Rose-Hulman receives aid of some sort, and the college makes the application process as ingrained with the admissions process as possible. In addition to federal grants and scholarships, there are several institutional scholarships available. Rose-Hulman Merit Scholarships are based on both academic and non-academic measures (such as extracurricular activities, leadership and community service), and all admitted students are automatically considered. Rose-Hulman Named Scholarships are more limited in number and have specific restrictions placed on them by the donor; all students are also considered upon admission.

STUDENT LIFE

Students at this 2,100 strong school "are time- and efficiency-oriented" and while they may put a lot of hours into school, they all "choose a few extracurriculars with which to get very involved." Rose-Hulman "is a sort of social oasis for the kids that knew everything in high school" and "we are all proud to be nerds together," beams a student. "Students are pretty goofy and creative" so "random games like 'owling' and fruit golf pop up," says one. The excellent residential life program means that "floor residents become extremely close and participate in many events together" and people call it the "Rose bubble" because "life on campus is amazing (although unrealistic to the outside world because of how nice everyone is)." Indeed, there's so much to do on campus that people leave very rarely: "If we aren't busy studying or getting homework done, we are out participating in intramurals, varsity athletics, community service, religious groups, gaming groups, campus jobs, greek life...the list goes on and on," says a student.

Rose-Hulman Institute of Technology

FINANCIAL AID: 812-877-8259 • E-MAIL: ADMISSIONS@ROSE-HULMAN.EDU • WEBSITE: WWW.ROSE-HULMAN.EDU

CAREER

This is one of the top undergraduate engineering schools in the country, and "the job placement rate and average starting salary are amazing." The importance is set strictly on academics and employers recognize that, and "the opportunities for gaining experience in your field of study are endless." Career Services brings in numerous companies to help provide jobs, co-ops, and internships to students, and sets up mock interviews, résumé reviews, and numerous career and graduate school fairs to help the job hunt process run smoothly. Fifty-six percent of Rose-Hulman graduates who visited PayScale.com felt their job had a meaningful impact on the world; an average starting salary of $66,600 was reported.

GENERAL INFO

Activities: Choral groups, concert band, dance, drama/theater, jazz band, literary magazine, music ensembles, musical theater, pep band, radio station, student government, student newspaper, International Student Organization. **Organizations:** 105 registered organizations, 7 honor societies, 2 religious organizations. 8 fraternities, 3 sororities. **Athletics (Intercollegiate):** *Men:* baseball, basketball, cross-country, diving, football, golf, riflery, soccer, swimming, tennis, track/field (outdoor), track/field (indoor). *Women:* basketball, cross-country, diving, golf, riflery, soccer, softball, swimming, tennis, track/field (outdoor), track/field (indoor), volleyball. **On-Campus Highlights:** Sports and Recreation Center, Hatfield Hall, White Chapel, Moench Hall, Chauncey's Place.

FINANCIAL AID

Students should submit: FAFSA. Priority filing deadline is 3/1. The Princeton Review suggests that all financial aid forms be submitted as soon as possible after October 1. *Need-based scholarships/grants offered:* Federal Pell, FSEOG, State scholarships/grants, College/university scholarship or grant aid from institutional funds. *Loan aid offered:* Direct Subsidized Stafford Loans, Direct Unsubsidized Stafford Loans, Direct PLUS loans, Federal Perkins Loans. Applicants will be notified of awards on or about 3/10. Federal Work-Study Program available. Institutional employment available.

BOTTOM LINE

Tuition rings in at $41,865, with another $12,660 going towards room and board. Fortunately, 96 percent of students receive financial aid. Of the 64 percent of students who borrow through a loan program, the average debt upon graduation is $35,420. About 60 percent of Rose-Hulman students also participate in Federal Work-Study or Work Opportunity to help offset costs while they are at school.

CAREER INFORMATION FROM PAYSCALE.COM

ROI rating	92
Bachelor's and No Higher	
Median starting salary	$67,200
Median mid-career salary	$107,000
At Least Bachelor's	
Median starting salary	$68,600
Median mid-career salary	$117,000
% alumni with high job meaning	51%
% STEM	97%

SELECTIVITY

Admissions Rating	93
# of applicants	4,331
% of applicants accepted	58
% of acceptees attending	22
# offered a place on the wait list	326
% accepting a place on wait list	46
% admitted from wait list	25

FRESHMAN PROFILE

Range SAT Critical Reading	550–670
Range SAT Math	630–750
Range SAT Writing	550–660
Range ACT Composite	28–32
Minimum paper TOEFL	550
Minimum internet-based TOEFL	80
Average HS GPA	4.0
% graduated top 10% of class	69
% graduated top 25% of class	90
% graduated top 50% of class	99

DEADLINES

Early action	
Deadline	11/1
Notification	12/15
Regular	
Priority	2/1
Deadline	2/1
Notification	3/15
Nonfall registration?	No

FINANCIAL FACTS

Financial Aid Rating	83
Annual tuition	$43,122
Room and board	$13,293
Required fees	$888
Average need-based scholarship	$24,373
% needy frosh rec. need-based scholarship or grant aid	83
% needy UG rec. need-based scholarship or grant aid	84
% needy frosh rec. non-need-based scholarship or grant aid	100
% needy UG rec. non-need-based scholarship or grant aid	99
% needy frosh rec. need-based self-help aid	88
% needy UG rec. need-based self-help aid	87
% frosh rec. any financial aid	99
% UG rec. any financial aid	97
% UG borrow to pay for school	64
Average cumulative indebtedness	$41,804
% frosh need fully met	25
% ugrads need fully met	20
Average % of frosh need met	77
Average % of ugrad need met	73

Rutgers University—New Brunswick

100 Sutphen Road, Piscataway, NJ 08854-8097 • Admissions: 732-445-4636 • Fax: 732-445-0237

CAMPUS LIFE

Quality of Life Rating	83
Fire Safety Rating	88
Green Rating	60*
Type of school	Public
Affiliation	No Affiliation
Environment	Town

STUDENTS

Total undergrad enrollment	35,484
% male/female	50/50
% from out of state	6
% frosh live on campus	87
% ugrads live on campus	48
# of fraternities	29
# of sororities	15
% African American	7
% Asian	26
% Caucasian	42
% Hispanic	13
% Native American	<1
% Pacific Islander	<1
% Two or more races	3
% Race and/or ethnicity unknown	2
% international	7
# of countries represented	117

ACADEMICS

Academic Rating	75
% students returning for sophomore year	93
% students graduating within 4 years	58
% students graduating within 6 years	80
Calendar	Semester
Student/faculty ratio	12:1
Profs interesting rating	67
Profs accessible rating	71

Most classes have 10–19 students.
Most lab/discussion sessions have 20–29 students.

MOST POPULAR MAJORS
Business; Engineering

ABOUT THE SCHOOL

As New Jersey's premiere state institution, Rutgers attracts "friendly and intelligent students" bursting with "school pride [and] spirit." And it's no surprise why. After all, undergrads here immediately tout Rutgers as "a diverse university in all aspects of the word—academically, culturally, politically, ethnically, linguistically, and socially." And they find that this "enriches" their collegiate experience tenfold. Aside from diversity, students happily report that opportunities abound for "undergraduates to conduct research and work with professors in any number of fields." However, they do caution that since the university "is so big, you have to learn to make your own way . . . no one is going to hold your hand for you." Despite the need for assertiveness, students do enjoy their academic experience. Many find their professors "engaging" and state that they know how to make "course material interesting." And, thankfully, they "are very accessible outside of classes in their office hours and by email."

BANG FOR YOUR BUCK

If forced to summarize Rutgers in one word, many undergraduates would likely say "affordable." Indeed, students here wholeheartedly agree that "the price is right" at their alma mater. In fact one very contented senior even brags, "I am getting an Ivy League education at an in-state tuition price!" Certainly, it's not just state school prices that leave these students grateful. The financial aid office also works hard to make higher education affordable for all undergraduates. In fact, 72 percent of Rutgers undergraduates receive some form of need-based aid. Even more impressive, the average freshman need-based gift aid is a whopping $10,698. Not too shabby, eh?

STUDENT LIFE

Undergrads at Rutgers have to work extremely hard if they want to find themselves bored. That's because there's "ALWAYS something going on, whether it's a football game . . . arcade games at the RutgersZone, performing arts [shows] . . . [a] university-sponsored concert, free food events, community service days, Greek life . . . EVERYTHING!" An ecstatic math major rushes to add, "RUPA, our programming association, plans many different events . . . anything from movie nights to Rock, Paper, Scissor tournaments." Undergrads can also enjoy "free ice cream on Thursdays, free seminars . . . and the attractions of downtown New Brunswick." In addition, students readily admit that "Rutgers has a great party scene. Every night is an adventure in one of the many fraternities or house parties going on." Fortunately, there's a place for drinkers and non-drinkers alike. Lastly, students love that Rutgers is close to the Jersey Shore and "half-way between NYC and Philly, so getting away for the weekend is easy."

CAREER

Employment opportunities are plentiful for both Rutgers students and alums. Of course, this should probably be expected. After all, a Middle Eastern studies major emphatically tells us that, "Career Services is awesome." And many undergrads are able to land "amazing internships." One thrilled journalism major confirms this stating, "I work at NBC in 30 Rockefeller Plaza, and will continue my internship for my last semester." Numerous students attribute this success to Career Service's robust internship and co-op program. Beyond internships, the office also hosts a massive fall career fair featuring over 250 companies from a variety of industries as well as government and nonprofit organizations. And undergrads are also privy to a bevy

Rutgers University—New Brunswick

FINANCIAL AID: 848-932-7305 • E-MAIL: ADMISSIONS@UGADM.RUTGERS.EDU • WEBSITE: WWW.RUTGERS.EDU

of career events—including everything from drop-in resume clinics to sixty-minute job search boot camps. Finally, prospective (and current!) students should be pleased to discover that, according to PayScale.com, the average starting salary for a Rutgers alum is $51,000.

GENERAL INFO

Activities: Choral groups, concert band, dance, drama/theater, jazz band, literary magazine, marching band, music ensembles, musical theater, opera, pep band, radio station, student government, student newspaper, student-run film society, symphony orchestra, television station, yearbook, Campus Ministries, International Student Organization. **Organizations:** 400 registered organizations, 24 honor societies. 29 fraternities and 18 sororities. **Athletics (Intercollegiate):** *Men:* baseball, basketball, cheerleading, cross-country, football, golf, lacrosse, soccer, track/field (outdoor), track/field (indoor), wrestling. *Women:* basketball, cheerleading, crew/rowing, cross-country, diving, field hockey, golf, gymnastics, lacrosse, soccer, softball, swimming, tennis, track/field (outdoor), track/field (indoor), volleyball. **On-Campus Highlights:** Geology Museum, Jane Voorhees Zimmereli Art Museum, Rutgers Display Gardens and Heylar Woods, Hutcheson Memorial Forest.

FINANCIAL AID

Students should submit: FAFSA. Priority filing deadline for freshman is 12/1. The Princeton Review suggests that all financial aid forms be submitted as soon as possible after October 1. *Need-based scholarships/grants offered:* Federal Pell, FSEOG, State scholarships/grants, College/university scholarship or grant aid from institutional funds, Federal Nursing Scholarships. *Loan aid offered:* Direct Subsidized Stafford Loans, Direct Unsubsidized Stafford Loans, Direct PLUS loans, Federal Perkins Loans, Federal Nursing Loans, State Loans, College/university loans from institutional funds. Freshman applicants will be notified of awards on a rolling basis beginning 1/15. Federal Work-Study Program available. Institutional employment available.

THE BOTTOM LINE

New Jersey residents joining Rutgers ranks will face a tuition bill of $11,408. Students hailing from out-of-state have a tuition bill that comes in at $27,059. Further, undergraduates who decide to live on-campus will have to pay another $12,260 in room and board. Students (and their families) must also pay $2,964 in required fees. And they'll need an additional $1,350 for books and supplies. Finally, those undergraduates commuting from off-campus should expect roughly $1,872 in transportation fees.

CAREER INFORMATION FROM PAYSCALE.COM

ROI rating	87
Bachelor's and No Higher	
Median starting salary	$50,800
Median mid-career salary	$94,800
At Least Bachelor's	
Median starting salary	$51,400
Median mid-career salary	$98,200
% alumni with high job meaning	43%
% STEM	23%

SELECTIVITY

Admissions Rating	87
# of applicants	35,340
% of applicants accepted	58
% of acceptees attending	32
# offered a place on the wait list	0

FRESHMAN PROFILE

Range SAT Critical Reading	530–640
Range SAT Math	580–700
Range SAT Writing	540–660
Minimum paper TOEFL	550
% graduated top 10% of class	38
% graduated top 25% of class	76
% graduated top 50% of class	97

DEADLINES

Early Action	
Deadline	11/1
Notification	1/31
Regular	
Deadline	12/1
Notification	2/28
Nonfall registration?	Yes

FINANCIAL FACTS

Financial Aid Rating	79
Annual in-state tuition	$11,408
Annual out-of-state tuition	$27,059
Room and board	$12,260
Required fees	$2,964
Average need-based scholarship	$10,698
% needy frosh rec. need-based scholarship or grant aid	69
% needy UG rec. need-based scholarship or grant aid	72
% needy frosh rec. non-need-based scholarship or grant aid	28
% needy UG rec. non-need-based scholarship or grant aid	17
% needy frosh rec. need-based self-help aid	84
% needy UG rec. need-based self-help aid	83
% frosh rec. any financial aid	79
% UG rec. any financial aid	85
Average cumulative indebtedness	$25,334
% frosh need fully met	5
% ugrads need fully met	4
Average % of frosh need met	56
Average % of ugrad need met	51

Saint Mary's College (CA)

PO Box 4800, Moraga, CA 94575-4800 • Admissions: 925-631-4224 • Fax: 925-376-7193

CAMPUS LIFE

Quality of Life Rating	88
Fire Safety Rating	92
Green Rating	60*
Type of school	Private
Affiliation	Roman Catholic
Environment	Village

STUDENTS

Total undergrad enrollment	2,958
% male/female	41/59
% from out of state	11
% frosh from public high school	61
% frosh live on campus	99
% ugrads live on campus	56
% African American	4
% Asian	10
% Caucasian	46
% Hispanic	25
% Native American	<1
% Pacific Islander	1
% Two or more races	7
% Race and/or ethnicity unknown	5
% international	2
# of countries represented	20

ACADEMICS

Academic Rating	83
% students returning for sophomore year	89
% students graduating within 4 years	54
% students graduating within 6 years	65
Calendar	4/1/4
Student/faculty ratio	12:1
Profs interesting rating	84
Profs accessible rating	86
Most classes have 20–29 students.	

MOST POPULAR MAJORS

Business Administration and Management; Psychology; Communication and Media Studies

ABOUT THE SCHOOL

This small Lasallian liberal arts school boasts small class sizes, a 4-1-4 semester system, and forty majors across four schools. At the heart of the Saint Mary's curriculum is the required Collegiate Seminar series, in which students examine the Great Books of Western civilization in a small, discussion-based setting (almost all classes are seminar-style). The intimacy among students and faculty is a motivating force: "Professors help students learn by engaging one another in meaningful dialogue and debate," and "class is very discussion-based, so you learn how to talk more in public settings and it gives you life skills that you can rely on." These soft skills and the close on-campus network come in handy as students apply for scholarships, internships, and grad schools. Students enjoy classes that encourage them to form opinions, make arguments and listen. "We are not only getting an education, we [are] learning how to think, a philosophy that will go with you wherever you end up in life," says a student.

BANG FOR YOUR BUCK

A large amount of need-based aid is available for those who demonstrate need on the FAFSA, and there are many merit-based scholarships also up for grabs, including departmental scholarships; the Presidential Scholarship ($24,000 annually), the Honors at Entrance Scholarship ($18,000 annually), and the Gael Scholar's Award ($14,000 annually). Merit awards are not typically separate applications, but are included with the initial financial aid letter. Saint Mary's January Term lets students explore one topic in depth through hands-on learning (such as "The Science of Cooking"), community service, and even travel courses that take small groups across the country (during which students can still access the school's "amazing online research database"); scholarship assistance is available for students who would otherwise be unable to afford a travel course. Around 55 percent of undergraduates participate in the study abroad program, for which scholarships are also available.

STUDENT LIFE

It's "a small university but contains everything a person needs to keep themselves occupied," ranging from numerous student clubs to a "very competitive" athletics program. Students can often be found attending basketball or rugby games, interesting discussions on campus, or events held by the campus activities board and the school (such as movie and documentary showings, BBQs, carnivals, and free field trips around the Bay Area).The beautiful setting is right at the foot of the mountains, lending itself to "great hiking, biking, and running trails," and Oakland and Berkeley are just twenty minutes away by car. The common thread between classroom life and social life is talk; "We all work very hard so when there is downtime we tend to be discussing anything and everything," says a student.

CAREER

These "deep thinkers" are being given "a strong education and foundation for their future," and "life on campus is centered on helping us build a career." The small size means "you can network easily and quickly" in order to get one of the "tons of internships" available, and

Saint Mary's College (CA)

FINANCIAL AID: 925-631-4522 • E-MAIL: SMCADMIT@STMARYS-CA.EDU • WEBSITE: WWW.STMARYS-CA.EDU

"a really good career center" helps prepare students for the real world." This Career and Professional Development Services office offers an online database of jobs and internships, as well as career fairs and workshops, and takes the "storytelling approach" to job placement: how students can tell their story through resumes, internships, elevator pitches, and volunteer work. For those graduates who visited Payscale.com, the average starting salary was $50,000, with 51 percent reporting that their job had a high level of meaning to the world.

GENERAL INFO
Activities: Choral groups, dance, drama/theater, jazz band, music ensembles, musical theater, pep band, radio station, student government, student newspaper, Campus Ministries, International Student Organization 56 registered organizations, 3 religious organizations. **Athletics (Intercollegiate):** *Men:* baseball, basketball, cheerleading, cross-country, golf, soccer, tennis. *Women:* basketball, cheerleading, crew/rowing, cross-country, lacrosse, soccer, softball, tennis, volleyball. **On-Campus Highlights:** Br. Alfred Brousseau Hall, Cassin Student Union and LeFevre Quad, College Chapel, Hearst Art Gallery, Oliver Dining Hall, Power Plant (exercise facility) McKeon Pavilion, "St. Patty's Cathedral".

FINANCIAL AID
Students should submit: FAFSA. Priority filing deadline is 2/15. The Princeton Review suggests that all financial aid forms be submitted as soon as possible after October 1. Need-based scholarships/grants offered: Federal Pell, FSEOG, State scholarships/grants, Private scholarships, College/university scholarship or grant aid from institutional funds. Loan aid offered: Direct Subsidized Stafford Loans, Direct Unsubsidized Stafford Loans, Direct PLUS loans, Federal Perkins Loans. Applicants will be notified of awards on a rolling basis beginning 2/1. Federal Work-Study Program available. Institutional employment available.

BOTTOM LINE
A full year's tuition (including the January term) runs $44,210, with room and board running an additional $14,880. California residents (who make up 89 percent of the student body) can apply for Cal Grants to offset these costs. Seventy-four percent of Saint Mary's students do receive some form of financial aid, and the average undergraduate need-based package rings in at $27,902.

SELECTIVITY
Admissions Rating	81
# of applicants	4,864
% of applicants accepted	69
% of acceptees attending	18
# offered a place on the wait list	680
% accepting a place on wait list	33
% admitted from wait list	19

FRESHMAN PROFILE
Range SAT Critical Reading	490–600
Range SAT Math	490–600
Range ACT Composite	22–27
Minimum paper TOEFL	550
Minimum internet-based TOEFL	79
Average HS GPA	3.6

DEADLINES
Early action	
Deadline	11/15
Notification	1/15
Regular	
Priority	11/15
Deadline	2/1
Notification	3/15
Nonfall registration?	Yes

FINANCIAL FACTS
Financial Aid Rating	72
Annual tuition	$44,210
Room and board	$14,880
Required fees	$150
Average need-based scholarship	$23,443
% needy frosh rec. need-based scholarship or grant aid	100
% needy UG rec. need-based scholarship or grant aid	96
% needy frosh rec. non-need-based scholarship or grant aid	59
% needy UG rec. non-need-based scholarship or grant aid	0
% needy frosh rec. need-based self-help aid	99
% needy UG rec. need-based self-help aid	97
% frosh rec. any financial aid	77
% UG rec. any financial aid	74
% frosh need fully met	8
% ugrads need fully met	8
Average % of frosh need met	85
Average % of ugrad need met	78

CAREER INFORMATION FROM PAYSCALE.COM
ROI rating	**86**
Bachelor's and No Higher	
Median starting salary	$51,400
Median mid-career salary	$101,000
At Least Bachelor's	
Median starting salary	$51,300
Median mid-career salary	$101,000
% alumni with high job meaning	42%
% STEM	5%

Santa Clara University

500 EL CAMINO REAL, SANTA CLARA, CA 95053 • ADMISSIONS: 408-554-4700 • FAX: 408-554-5255

CAMPUS LIFE

Quality of Life Rating	**92**
Fire Safety Rating	**91**
Green Rating	**99**
Type of school	Private
Affiliation	Roman Catholic
Environment	City

STUDENTS

Total undergrad enrollment	5,385
% male/female	51/49
% from out of state	27
% frosh from public high school	46
% frosh live on campus	94
% ugrads live on campus	52
% African American	3
% Asian	16
% Caucasian	49
% Hispanic	17
% Native American	<1
% Pacific Islander	<1
% Two or more races	7
% Race and/or ethnicity unknown	4
% international	3
# of countries represented	44

ACADEMICS

Academic Rating	**86**
% students returning for sophomore year	95
% students graduating within 4 years	77
% students graduating within 6 years	84
Calendar	Quarter
Student/faculty ratio	12:1
Profs interesting rating	84
Profs accessible rating	89
Most classes have 10–19 students.	
Most lab/discussion sessions have 10–19 students.	

MOST POPULAR MAJORS
Finance; Marketing/Marketing Management; Psychology

ABOUT THE SCHOOL

Santa Clara University is a mid-sized Jesuit University that offers undergraduate and graduate degrees through six different colleges on a beautiful campus in Silicon Valley. Though Jesuit philosophy and spirituality are central to the school's identity, students hail from many different backgrounds and "other than occasionally seeing a Jesuit walking around campus, you can make it four years without any contact with religion" if that is your preference. Rather, the emphasis is firmly on academic excellence, and Santa Clara has received many accolades in undergraduate education. Fifty-two undergraduate majors are offered through the schools of Arts and Sciences, Engineering, and Business. The University offers abundant opportunities for undergraduate research, and a third of students take advantage of study abroad programs in more than fifty countries. While large lectures are fairly common, 72 percent of classes contain under thirty students, and though some professors "don't connect to students" the majority "invest their out of class time to help students achieve their academic and personal development goals." "I have been able to form personal relationships with all of my professors if I make the effort," so if "you are willing to put in work, your professor is likely to be willing to work as hard as you towards your success."

BANG FOR YOUR BUCK

Santa Clara offers many opportunities for Federal or State aid via well-known programs like the Pell Grant, and boasts that nearly two-thirds of undergraduates receive scholarships directly from the University. Its prestigious Johnson Scholars Program offers full tuition, room, and board, along with a number of specialized academic opportunities, to a small selection of top-tier applicants for four years. The University's other top award is the Presidential at Entry Scholarship, which also offers full tuition to outstanding applicants and is likewise renewable for four years. Several smaller awards, both need and merit based, are offered through the University or through specific departments such as Music, Theater and Dance, or Military Science. In addition to scholarships students can qualify for loans and Federal Work Study, and opportunities for student employment are available through the Career Center. Eighty-nine percent of students at Santa Clara receive some manner of financial aid.

STUDENT LIFE

Due to its location in sunny California and an appealing outdoor campus, "the social scene really takes life when the weather is nice." "It's not uncommon to see kids sitting outside the cafeteria or the library doing homework on any given day," and during less studious moments "going to school in California means lots of day-parties, lots of time spent tanning on the lawn." Santa Clara has a fairly robust party scene on and off campus, "but no more or less than I think you'd find at a school of comparable size." The school has a top-tier athletic program and many activities are available through the University: "the typical student is very active on campus in all sorts of clubs and groups, and usually works out at least once a week." A special feature of life at the school is the beautiful regional geography, and students with access to a car can enjoy "so many incredible things, just distant from school: hiking in the Santa Cruz mountains, the Santa Cruz beach, travelling to Lick Observatory, exploring Marin County, and of course, skiing at Tahoe!" Trips to nearby San Francisco on the weekends are also common. So while Santa Clara offers a great deal on campus, one of the best features of student life may be the fun of getting away.

Santa Clara University

FINANCIAL AID: 408-554-4505 • E-MAIL: ADMISSION@SCU.EDU • WEBSITE: WWW.SCU.EDU

CAREER

Santa Clara University has an "exceptionally helpful" Career Center which offers counseling, networking opportunities, and professional development services from traditional resume building to how to craft a great LinkedIn profile. Praise for career services is widespread, with many students citing it as one of the school's strengths. "The University has a phenomenal career center that was able to find me a top notch internship" and "they have so many connections [that] there is no reason why anyone should not have a job or internship because of all the resources they provide." Outside of the Career Center, students praise an environment where "my professors all have access to the type of resources that will help us further our careers" and the Business and Engineering schools are particularly known for "placing graduates at top firms throughout the valley."

GENERAL INFO

Activities: Choral groups, dance, drama/theater, jazz band, literary magazine, music ensembles, musical theater, opera, pep band, radio station, student government, student newspaper, symphony orchestra, yearbook, Campus Ministries, International Student Organization, Model UN. **Organizations:** 84 registered organizations, 24 honor societies, 10 religious organizations. **Athletics (Intercollegiate):** *Men:* baseball, basketball, crew/rowing, cross-country, golf, soccer, tennis, track/field (outdoor), water polo. *Women:* basketball, crew/rowing, cross-country, golf, soccer, softball, tennis, track/field (outdoor), volleyball, water polo.

FINANCIAL AID

Students should submit: FAFSA, CSS/Financial Aid PROFILE. Priority filing deadline is 2/1. The Princeton Review suggests that all financial aid forms be submitted as soon as possible after October 1. *Need-based scholarships/grants offered:* Federal Pell, FSEOG, State scholarships/grants, Private scholarships, College/university scholarship or grant aid from institutional funds. *Loan aid offered:* Direct Subsidized Stafford Loans, Direct Unsubsidized Stafford Loans, Direct PLUS loans, Federal Perkins Loans. Applicants will be notified of awards on or about 4/1. Federal Work-Study Program available. Institutional employment available.

BOTTOM LINE

Tuition and fees for a year at Santa Clara University are listed at $47,112, with room and board totaling $13,965. Combined with books, supplies, and expenses, students can expect to spend approximately $61,000 per year to attend Santa Clara. That's not cheap, and while some students describe their peers as largely "upper middle class," others refer to students "who are on almost complete full scholarship and financial aid." Sixty-three percent of students receive need-based financial aid. The average need-based award package for all undergraduates is around $24,937 in scholarships or grants and $5,003 in loans, and for students who land one of the school's substantial merit scholarships the deal is even sweeter.

CAREER INFORMATION FROM PAYSCALE.COM

ROI rating	89
Bachelor's and No Higher	
Median starting salary	$58,900
Median mid-career salary	$113,000
At Least Bachelor's	
Median starting salary	$59,800
Median mid-career salary	$117,000
% alumni with high job meaning	49%
% STEM	15%

SELECTIVITY

Admissions Rating	91
# of applicants	14,899
% of applicants accepted	49
% of acceptees attending	17
# offered a place on the wait list	2,203
% accepting a place on wait list	50
% admitted from wait list	25
# of early decision applicants	215
% accepted early decision	63

FRESHMAN PROFILE

Range SAT Critical Reading	590–690
Range SAT Math	620–710
Range ACT Composite	27–32
Minimum paper TOEFL	575
Minimum internet-based TOEFL	90
Average HS GPA	3.7
% graduated top 10% of class	50
% graduated top 25% of class	83
% graduated top 50% of class	98

DEADLINES

Early decision	
Deadline	11/1
Early action	
Deadline	11/1
Regular	
Deadline	1/7
Nonfall registration?	No

FINANCIAL FACTS

Financial Aid Rating	82
Annual tuition	$47,112
Room and board	$13,965
Required fees	
Average need-based scholarship	$24,937
% needy frosh rec. need-based scholarship or grant aid	80
% needy UG rec. need-based scholarship or grant aid	70
% needy frosh rec. non-need-based scholarship or grant aid	43
% needy UG rec. non-need-based scholarship or grant aid	32
% needy frosh rec. need-based self-help aid	47
% needy UG rec. need-based self-help aid	45
% frosh rec. any financial aid	70
% UG rec. any financial aid	77
% UG borrow to pay for school	47
Average cumulative indebtedness	$27,407
% frosh need fully met	42
% ugrads need fully met	32
Average % of frosh need met	81
Average % of ugrad need met	75

Scripps College

1030 COLUMBIA AVENUE, CLAREMONT, CA 91711 • ADMISSIONS: 909-621-8149 • FAX: 909-607-7508

ABOUT THE SCHOOL

As the women's college within a consortium that also includes four schools within walking distance of one another, Scripps offers the intimacy and intense focus of a small college campus with the academic and co-curricular offerings of a larger university. You can use all the facilities at the other four schools in the Claremont Colleges and cross-register for all manner of courses. Students find this system "very beneficial because it offers opportunities and resources that a small school would not otherwise have access to, and makes for interesting class discussions with people from very diverse academic backgrounds." Scripps' innovative Money Wise Women program includes a financial literacy course that covers everything from buying a first home to signing a prenuptial agreement. Professors at Scripps are always accessible and consistently excellent. There's a demanding, three-semester, interdisciplinary Core Curriculum that sets the academic tone when you arrive. Students say they appreciate how the core program "strengthens your understanding of Western thought in ways you'd never imagined." Every student also completes a thesis or senior project prior to graduation. Eighty-two percent of students hold at least one internship during their undergraduate years.

BANG FOR YOUR BUCK

Scripps College meets 100 percent of an eligible student's demonstrated financial need for all four years with the combination of grants, scholarships, part-time employment, and loans. Additionally, all applicants are considered for merit funds ranging from $10,000 a year to $20,000 a year. No separate application is required in order to be considered for these merit awards. The pick of the litter is the New Generation Award. It's renewable, and it's a full ride in the truest sense. In addition to tuition, fees, and room and board, you get three round-trip airfares home annually and a $3,000 one-time summer research stipend. The James E. Scripps Award is a $20,000 annual, renewable award. There are 75–100 of them offered each year. New Trustee, Founder's, and Presidential Scholarships offer students whose "strong academic performance and school or community involvement indicate that they will add vitality and intellectual value to the campus" and a four-year renewable award worth between $10,000 and $17,500. A biology major says that she chose Scripps College "because of the fantastic merit scholarships. Not only did they defray the expense of attending a private college, but they convinced me I could be a big fish in a small pond here."

STUDENT LIFE

Prospective students interested in Scripps will be delighted to discover that there's rarely a dull moment on this campus. As one knowing senior shares, "There are so many activities to become involved in. Whether you're interested in feminist issues, journalism, baking, sports or music, Scripps has a place for you to belong." When it comes to simply kicking back, "Scripps women love sunning on the lawn or at the pool...[and] they also love grabbing a cup of coffee at our amazing student run and eco-friendly coffee shop, the Motley!" While the college itself doesn't have a big party scene, the "surrounding schools in the consortiums throw great parties every weekend...[including] 'art after hours' and 'Thursday Night Club' on Thursdays." And, as another senior boasts, "there are many off campus activities like trips to LA, rock climbing, and skiing [...] You can be on the slopes and at the beach on the same day! How do you beat that?"

Scripts College

FINANCIAL AID: : 909-621-8275 • E-MAIL: ADMISSION@SCRIPPSCOLLEGE.EDU • WEBSITE: WWW.SCRIPPSCOLLEGE.EDU

CAREER

Scripps alums are a successful lot and can be found working across a variety of industries. In fact, over 50 percent of students begin full-time work within three months after graduation. Recent graduates have landed plum with gigs with companies such as 21st Century Fox, Facebook, Ernst & Young, Los Angeles County Museum of Art, Johnson & Johnson, National Institute of Health and Morgan Stanley. Moreover, within the first year of graduation, roughly 20 percent of students pursue graduate and/or professional degrees. Scripps alums have enrolled in institutions such as Cornell University, Duke University, Boston College, UCLA, Georgetown University and Rice University. Other resources unique to Scripps include a personalized freshman orientation to the Career Planning & Resources office and an online Resume Book for seniors embarking on their job hunts. Approximately 8 percent of graduating seniors receive prestigious fellowships and grants like the Fulbright and Watson Fellowship to continue their studies/research.

GENERAL INFO

Activities: Choral groups, dance, drama/theater, literary magazine, music ensembles, radio station, student government, student newspaper, symphony orchestra, yearbook, campus ministries, international student organization. **Organizations:** 200 registered organizations, 5 honor societies, 7 religious organizations. **Athletics (Intercollegiate):** *Women:* Basketball, cross-country, diving, golf, lacrosse, soccer, softball, swimming, tennis, track/field (outdoor), volleyball, water polo. **On-Campus Highlights:** Williamson Gallery, Motley Coffee House, Denison Library, Margaret Fowler Garden, Malott Commons, Graffiti Wall, Sallie Tiernan Field House.

FINANCIAL AID

Students should submit: FAFSA, CSS/Financial Aid PROFILE, State aid form, Noncustodial PROFILE, Business/Farm Supplement. Regular filing deadline is 2/1. The Princeton Review suggests that all financial aid forms be submitted as soon as possible after October 1. *Need-based scholarships/grants offered:* Federal Pell, FSEOG, State scholarships/grants, Private scholarships, College/university scholarship or grant aid from institutional funds. *Loan aid offered:* Direct Subsidized Stafford Loans, Direct Unsubsidized Stafford Loans, Direct PLUS loans, Federal Perkins Loans, College/university loans from institutional funds. Applicants will be notified of awards on or about 4/1. Federal Work-Study Program available. Institutional employment available.

BOTTOM LINE

The retail price for tuition, room and board, and fees at Scripps is around $66,664 a year. Financial aid is superabundant here, though, so please don't let cost keep you from applying. Also worth noting: the average total need-based indebtedness for Scripps graduates is $18,692—well below the national average at private colleges and universities.

CAREER INFORMATION FROM PAYSCALE.COM

ROI rating	89
Bachelor's and No Higher	
Median starting salary	$43,000
Median mid-career salary	$101,000
At Least Bachelor's	
Median starting salary	$43,000
Median mid-career salary	$101,000

SELECTIVITY

Admissions Rating	97
# of applicants	2,613
% of applicants accepted	28
% of acceptees attending	38
# offered a place on the wait list	641
% accepting a place on wait list	44
% admitted from wait list	0
# of early decision applicants	219
% accepted early decision	47

FRESHMAN PROFILE

Range SAT Critical Reading	650–730
Range SAT Math	630–718
Range SAT Writing	653–730
Range ACT Composite	29–32
Minimum paper TOEFL	600
Minimum internet-based TOEFL	100
Average HS GPA	4.1
% graduated top 10% of class	72
% graduated top 25% of class	95
% graduated top 50% of class	98

DEADLINES

Early decision	
Deadline	11/15
Regular	
Deadline	1/1
Notification	4/1
Nonfall registration?	Yes

FINANCIAL FACTS

Financial Aid Rating	94
Annual tuition	$50,766
Room and board	$15,682
Required fees	$216
Average need-based scholarship	$36,444
% needy frosh rec. need-based scholarship or grant aid	100
% needy UG rec. need-based scholarship or grant aid	98
% needy frosh rec. non-need-based scholarship or grant aid	3
% needy UG rec. non-need-based scholarship or grant aid	3
% needy frosh rec. need-based self-help aid	86
% needy UG rec. need-based self-help aid	91
% UG borrow to pay for school	44
Average cumulative indebtedness	$18,692
% frosh need fully met	100
% ugrads need fully met	91
Average % of frosh need met	100
Average % of ugrad need met	100

,kidmore College

315 North Broadway, Saratoga Springs, NY 12866-1632 • Admissions: 518-580-5570 • Fax: 518-580-5584

ABOUT THE SCHOOL

Set on a pristine 890-acre campus in Saratoga Springs, New York, this prestigious liberal arts hamlet is celebrated for its creative arts, student-centered learning, low student/faculty ratio, and multidisciplinary academic approach. Skidmore's strong majors in the liberal arts and sciences are complemented by an "excellent and intimate" theater program, as well as strong programs in art, music, and dance. Faculty here are "accessible, interested and most importantly—student-centered." Students at Skidmore are well aware that they are attending a "first-rate academic institution," and tell us that the learning atmosphere on campus fosters a "relaxed intensity." The library "is packed on weeknights" and "many people would be surprised to find how often a Skidmore student is cramming his or her weekend with serious studying." The low student-to-teacher ratio offers "smaller class sizes for more personalized and individual attention." Beyond the caliber of its academics, Skidmore is "the perfect size in the perfect town." The surrounding city of Saratoga Springs is "beautiful and vibrant."

BANG FOR YOUR BUCK

From the moment students step onto campus freshman year, they are embraced by the school's commitment to student-centered learning and community involvement. The journey begins with Skidmore's First-Year Experience, which places students from each seminar in close proximity to one another in the residence halls, where they can cohabitate intellectually and creatively with their peers while establishing lasting relationships with close faculty mentors. Skidmore is one of few liberal arts colleges to offer majors in preprofessional disciplines, including business, education, exercise science, and social work. In fact, business consistently ranks as a popular major alongside English and psychology. Always ready to extend learning beyond the classroom, more than 60 percent of students study abroad at some point. Many Skidmore students complete a culminating project in their major—70 percent complete senior capstones, 62 percent complete independent studies, and 32 percent complete theses or advanced research projects. In addition, the Career Development Center provides one-on-one career counseling for life, including pre-health, pre-law, and graduate school preparation advising. More than 60 percent of students do an internship—often for academic credit—and the school's network boasts approximately 80 funded internships and more than 2,200 alumni mentors, which extends Skidmore's community well beyond graduation.

STUDENT LIFE

"I love life at Skidmore," says one sociology major. "There is no excuse to be bored because something is [always] going on. If you're not into the [party] scene, student clubs always have events going on during the weekend." The fairly small student body—roughly 2,400 students—makes for a close community feeling, particularly with 89 percent of undergraduates living on campus. There are 110 registered student organizations on campus and no Greek life presence at the school. Performances, particularly by visiting musicians and DJs, are a "big thing" at Skidmore, especially near the "end of the semester [when] a typical weekend night would be a performance and then the after party." One History and Theater major notes that "Skidmore students are very involved in the Saratoga community through everything from sustainability efforts to mentoring local children." The town of Saratoga Springs can be "a great town" with "amazing food options."

CAREER

According to PayScale.com, the average starting salary for a Skidmore graduate is roughly $43,200. Popular jobs and majors include research associate, financial analyst, graphic designer, software engineer, and marketing manager, and business, English and psychology, respectively.

Skidmore College

FINANCIAL AID: 518-580-5750 • E-MAIL: ADMISSIONS@SKIDMORE.EDU • WEBSITE: WWW.SKIDMORE.EDU

Thirty-five percent of Skidmore graduates consider their careers to be instrumental in helping improve the world. According to the school's website, Skidmore's "Career Development Center helps students develop a holistic view of their career development plan, offering programs and services for students in each year to foster enhanced self-awareness, exposure to a variety of career fields, participation in off-campus experiential activities, [and] effective career decision-making." A Summer Funded Internship program provides grants to students interning locally, nationally, or abroad. Another unique feature on the school's website is the "What Can I Do With This Major?" section, where students can "learn about the typical career areas and the types of employers that hire people with each major, as well as strategies to make [them] more marketable candidate[s]."

GENERAL INFO

Activities: Admissions ambassador, campus committees, chorus, collaborative faculty-student research, community garden, community service, dance, drama/theater, student-run EMS program, jazz ensemble, literary and art magazines, music ensembles (guitar, vocal, concert band, small jazz, chamber), peer mentor, peer tutor, radio station, residential life, student government, student newspaper, orchestra, television station, yoga. **Athletics (Intercollegiate):** *Men:* baseball, basketball, rowing, golf, ice hockey, lacrosse, soccer, swimming and diving, tennis. *Women:* basketball, rowing, riding, field hockey, lacrosse, soccer, softball, swimming and diving, tennis, volleyball.

FINANCIAL AID

Students should submit: CSS/Financial Aid PROFILE, Noncustodial PROFILE. Regular filing deadline is 2/1. The Princeton Review suggests that all financial aid forms be submitted as soon as possible after October 1. *Need-based scholarships/grants offered:* Federal Pell, FSEOG, State scholarships/grants, Private scholarships, College/university scholarship or grant aid from institutional funds. *Loan aid offered:* Direct Subsidized Stafford Loans, Direct Unsubsidized Stafford Loans, Direct PLUS loans, Federal Perkins Loans, State Loans. Applicants will be notified of awards on or about 4/1. Federal Work-Study Program available. Institutional employment available.

BOTTOM LINE

With a price tag in line with other prestigious liberal arts colleges, Skidmore culls an annual tuition of $49,716, and students can expect to spend an additional $13,530 on room and board. However, with 100 percent of needy incoming freshmen receiving either need-based scholarship or grant aid, the school recognizes the significance of a hefty academic price tag for many and works hard to make sure all eligible students find their needs met. Forty-six percent of undergraduates borrow to finance their education. Upon graduation, the average Skidmore student can expect to shoulder about $22,557 of debt.

CAREER INFORMATION FROM PAYSCALE.COM

ROI rating	88
Bachelor's and No Higher	
Median starting salary	$43,200
Median mid-career salary	$97,600
At Least Bachelor's	
Median starting salary	$46,300
Median mid-career salary	$98,000
% alumni with high job meaning	60%
% STEM	8%

SELECTIVITY

Admissions Rating	**92**
# of applicants	8,508
% of applicants accepted	36
% of acceptees attending	22
# offered a place on the wait list	1,742
% accepting a place on wait list	22
% admitted from wait list	3
# of early decision applicants	415
% accepted early decision	67

FRESHMAN PROFILE

Range SAT Critical Reading	550–670
Range SAT Math	560–673
Range SAT Writing	560–670
Range ACT Composite	26–30
Minimum paper TOEFL	590
% graduated top 10% of class	41
% graduated top 25% of class	72
% graduated top 50% of class	96

DEADLINES

Early decision	
Deadline	11/15
Notification	12/15
Regular	
Deadline	1/15
Notification	4/1
Nonfall registration?	No

FINANCIAL FACTS

Financial Aid Rating	**95**
Annual tuition	$49,716
Room and board	$13,530
Required fees	$968
Average need-based scholarship	$39,300
% needy frosh rec. need-based scholarship or grant aid	100
% needy UG rec. need-based scholarship or grant aid	100
% needy frosh rec. non-need-based scholarship or grant aid	7
% needy UG rec. non-need-based scholarship or grant aid	8
% needy frosh rec. need-based self-help aid	77
% needy UG rec. need-based self-help aid	72
% frosh rec. any financial aid	49
% UG rec. any financial aid	51
% UG borrow to pay for school	42
Average cumulative indebtedness	$22,557
% frosh need fully met	100
% ugrads need fully met	93
Average % of frosh need met	100
Average % of ugrad need met	95

SCHOOL PROFILES ■ 299

,mith College

VEN COLLEGE LANE, NORTHAMPTON, MA 01063 • ADMISSIONS: 413-585-2500 • FAX: 413-585-2527

CAMPUS LIFE

Quality of Life Rating	95
Fire Safety Rating	84
Green Rating	99
Type of school	Private
Affiliation	No Affiliation
Environment	Town

STUDENTS

Total undergrad enrollment	2,478
% male/female	0/100
% from out of state	82
% frosh from public high school	63
% frosh live on campus	100
% ugrads live on campus	95
% African American	5
% Asian	12
% Caucasian	45
% Hispanic	10
% Native American	<1
% Pacific Islander	<1
% Two or more races	5
% Race and/or ethnicity unknown	9
% international	14
# of countries represented	68

ACADEMICS

Academic Rating	94
% students returning for sophomore year	90
% students graduating within 4 years	82
% students graduating within 6 years	87
Calendar	Semester
Student/faculty ratio	9:1
Profs interesting rating	91
Profs accessible rating	90

MOST POPULAR MAJORS
Psychology; Political Science and Government; Economics

ABOUT THE SCHOOL

Located in western Massachusetts in the idyllic college town of Northampton, Smith College boasts "extremely challenging academics" in a setting where "women come first." Along with the school's "global and interdisciplinary focus," women at Smith enjoy an "excellent academic atmosphere, close-knit community, small class size, top-notch professors, [and] fantastic resources" in a "beautiful New England" setting. Smith's "open curriculum" "doesn't have course requirements," and the school boasts "lots of unique traditions that make it enjoyable." Smith professors are "strikingly committed to their students." Students routinely attend "class dinners with professors," where mentors "volunteer to read drafts, and help with research." As one student attests, "not only that, but [professors] always get excited when you visit office hours—the one-on-one is not only available here, but encouraged." Another incoming freshman recalls, "Walking onto Smith College campus was like a breath of fresh air. The old brick buildings (mixed in with the newer ones), the gorgeous campus (designed by Fredrick Law Olmsted), and atmosphere pulled me in. The academics were superb and the people welcoming." In a nutshell, this highly prestigious women's college is "all about being socially aware and making a positive impact in the environment, economy, politics, and everyday life."

BANG FOR YOUR BUCK

One of the cornerstones of a Smith education is the ability to design your own academic experience within a plethora of curricular opportunities. Students here are routinely engaged in one-on-one research as undergraduates, with professors in the arts, humanities, sciences, and social sciences. There are no required courses outside of the freshman year writing-intensive seminar. In addition, students have the added benefit of the larger academic community of the Five Colleges Consortium, which includes Amherst, Hampshire, Mount Holyoke, and the University of Massachusetts Amherst. Smith is the only women's college in the country with an accredited degree in engineering, and more than 30 percent of Smithies major in the hardcore sciences. Praxis, Smith's unique internship program, guarantees all students access to at least one college-funded internship during their four years at the college.

STUDENT LIFE

Undergrads at Smith certainly cultivate full and varied lives. Of course, it helps that "a range of social activities" abound. The student government continually sponsors a number of events "like movie showings, outdoor activities [and] bowling nights." As you might expect, these ladies are also incredibly politically savvy. Hence, there's also "a lot of involvement in community service and activism for global issues, women's rights, LGBTQ rights, the environment, and pretty much anything that fights oppression." Further, during the weekend "there are always house parties on campus and students can go to other college parties at surrounding campuses." Additionally, "downtown Northampton [is] always bustling with events. Indeed, "there are . . . concerts, restaurants, and cute shops . . . to provide us with distractions."

CAREER

Hands down, "Smith provides so many opportunities for [undergrads]!" Indeed, from "on-campus resources to internship and job opportunities—Smith gives students the means to thrive in the world." To begin with, it's definitely not uncommon for professors to "[go] out of their way to help [students] find contacts and resources for jobs." What's more, according to a grateful American

Smith College

FINANCIAL AID: 413-585-2530 • E-MAIL: ADMISSION@SMITH.EDU • WEBSITE: WWW.SMITH.EDU

studies major, "The Career Development Office will do everything in its power to help you get a job/internship." With its myriad of workshops, Preparing for Finance Interviews or Marketing Your Study Abroad Experience for example, Smith students can confidently enter the job market. They can visit the office to get assistance in tweaking their resumes and cover letters or to gain insight in the grad school admissions process. And they may definitely take advantage of the career fairs the college hosts. Organizations in attendance have included the Peace Corps, Bloomingdale's, Verizon Wireless and Teach for America.

GENERAL INFO

Activities: Choral groups, concert band, dance, drama/theater, jazz band, literary magazine, music ensembles, musical theater, radio station, student government, student newspaper, television station, yearbook, International Student Organization, Model UN. **Organizations:** 120 registered organizations, 3 honor societies, 13 religious organizations. **Athletics (Intercollegiate):** *Women:* basketball, crew/rowing, cross-country, diving, equestrian sports, field hockey, lacrosse, soccer, softball, swimming, tennis, track/field (outdoor), track/field (indoor), volleyball. **On-Campus Highlights:** Smith Art Museum, The Botanical Gardens, Campus Center, Mendenhall Center for Performing Arts, Lyman Plant House.

FINANCIAL AID

Students should submit: FAFSA, Institution's own financial aid form, CSS/Financial Aid PROFILE, Noncustodial PROFILE. Regular filing deadline is 2/15. The Princeton Review suggests that all financial aid forms be submitted as soon as possible after October 1. *Need-based scholarships/grants offered:* Federal Pell, FSEOG, State scholarships/grants, Private scholarships, College/university scholarship or grant aid from institutional funds. *Loan aid offered:* Direct Subsidized Stafford Loans, Direct Unsubsidized Stafford Loans, Direct PLUS loans, Federal Perkins Loans, College/university loans from institutional funds. Applicants will be notified of awards on or about 4/1. Federal Work-Study Program available. Institutional employment available.

BOTTOM LINE

Smith makes no bones about its commitment to finding inroads to making a serious private education available to women of all stripes, no matter their financial background. Though the cost of education here doesn't come at a discount—annual tuition is currently $47,620, with room and board tallying an additional $16,010—according to our recent statistics, over the past several years Smith has boasted a 100 percent success rate when it comes to meeting not just freshman financial need but financial need across all four years. The average student indebtedness after four years totals $20,154, with 68 percent of undergraduates receiving some form of need-based financial aid.

CAREER INFORMATION FROM PAYSCALE.COM

ROI rating	89
Bachelor's and No Higher	
Median starting salary	$42,400
Median mid-career salary	$78,000
At Least Bachelor's	
Median starting salary	$43,600
Median mid-career salary	$78,000
% alumni with high job meaning	44%
% STEM	15%

SELECTIVITY

Admissions Rating	**95**
# of applicants	5,006
% of applicants accepted	38
% of acceptees attending	32
# offered a place on the wait list	773
% accepting a place on wait list	51
% admitted from wait list	33
# of early decision applicants	409
% accepted early decision	57

FRESHMAN PROFILE

Range SAT Critical Reading	620–740
Range SAT Math	620–720
Range SAT Writing	630–720
Range ACT Composite	28–32
Minimum paper TOEFL	600
Minimum internet-based TOEFL	90
Average HS GPA	3.9
% graduated top 10% of class	64
% graduated top 25% of class	90
% graduated top 50% of class	100

DEADLINES

Early decision	
Deadline	11/15
Notification	12/15
Regular	
Deadline	1/15

FINANCIAL FACTS

Financial Aid Rating	**96**
Annual tuition	$47,620
Room and board	$16,010
Required fees	$284
Average need-based scholarship	$38,040
% needy frosh rec. need-based scholarship or grant aid	97
% needy UG rec. need-based scholarship or grant aid	97
% needy frosh rec. non-need-based scholarship or grant aid	2
% needy UG rec. non-need-based scholarship or grant aid	1
% needy frosh rec. need-based self-help aid	92
% needy UG rec. need-based self-help aid	93
% frosh rec. any financial aid	68
% UG rec. any financial aid	68
% UG borrow to pay for school	63
Average cumulative indebtedness	$20,514
% frosh need fully met	100
% ugrads need fully met	100
Average % of frosh need met	100
Average % of ugrad need met	100

Southwestern University

OFFICE OF ADMISSION, GEORGETOWN, TX 78627-0770 • OFFICE OF ADMISSION: 512-863-1200 • FAX: 512-863-9601

CAMPUS LIFE

Quality of Life Rating	**91**
Fire Safety Rating	**91**
Green Rating	**91**
Type of school	Private
Affiliation	Methodist
Environment	Town

STUDENTS

Total undergrad enrollment	1,538
% male/female	42/58
% from out of state	12
% frosh from public high school	75
% frosh live on campus	100
% ugrads live on campus	77
# of fraternities (% ugrad men join)	4 (22)
# of sororities (% ugrad women join)	4 (21)
% African American	5
% Asian	5
% Caucasian	64
% Hispanic	19
% Native American	<1
% Pacific Islander	<1
% Two or more races	3
% Race and/or ethnicity unknown	1
% international	3
# of countries represented	6

ACADEMICS

Academic Rating	**85**
% students graduating within 4 years	65
Calendar	Semester
Student/faculty ratio	12:1
Profs interesting rating	94
Profs accessible rating	91
Most classes have 10–19 students.	
Most lab/discussion sessions have 10–19 students.	

MOST POPULAR MAJORS
Business/Commerce; Biology; Psychology

ABOUT THE SCHOOL

A "top ranked" Texas university, Southwestern provides undergraduates with a "welcoming environment" and a "beautiful" campus. The university's "small" size allows students to feel as though they are truly receiving a "personalized" education. In addition, the liberal arts curriculum fosters a "holistic" and "well rounded" experience. While there are a number of disciplines to pursue, students speak glowingly of the "stunning" psychology department, "incredible" music department and a fantastic pre-med program. Though undergrads find their classes "challenging," most also relish the fact that they "have learned a great deal." This joy of learning can, at least partially, be attributed to "wonderful" professors who clearly "love what they teach." They also "encourage discussion and participation, whether it is a class discussion or in the middle of a lecture, which allows you to get a feel for the real core of whatever topic you're studying." Overall, as one senior concludes, "My academic experience is amazing, and I could not have chosen a better school."

BANG FOR YOUR BUCK

Southwestern acknowledges that the price of a college education can be rather exorbitant. In an effort to counter these high costs, the university has created some "generous" policies. Indeed, Southwestern offers "a great deal of . . . both merit and need-based [financial aid]." And "many students" benefit from some type of assistance. The college's scholarship program includes the Brown Scholarship, which starts at $30,000 per year, the Cody Scholarship, which starts at $25,000 per year; the Mood Scholarship, which provides $20,000 per year; the Ruter Scholarship, which starts at $16,000 per year; and the Southwestern Award, which grants up to $15,000 each year. Of course, we should also highlight the fact that there are many smaller scholarships to be had such as the Fine Arts Scholarships, which begin at $2,000 a year.

SCHOOL LIFE

Students here excitedly proclaim that "life at Southwestern is awesome!" And how could it not be? For starters, there are "plenty of opportunities to see shows put on by the theatre department, concerts of all types, or recitals." Additionally, "the school also brings in music groups like Cake or Spoon or comedians like Eric O'Shea for Friday Night Live every week." Undergrads also report that events such as movie screenings and casino nights are typically well attended. Moreover, Greek life is fairly big here, and we're told that "frats are really popular on the weekends because there's not much entertainment very late in town." Finally, when looking for a change of scenery, many students decamp for Austin, "which is only twenty minutes away."

Southwestern University

FINANCIAL AID: 512-863-1259 • E-MAIL: ADMISSION@SOUTHWESTERN.EDU • WEBSITE: WWW.SOUTHWESTERN.EDU

CAREER

Students at Southwestern proudly report that the "Career Services office puts an extraordinary amount of effort into helping students find good jobs." A grateful senior further explains that "the vast amount of resources available through counseling and career services [means that] job placement right out of school is nearly guaranteed." More specifically, the office hosts numerous panels about getting into grad school, interview preparation and internship advising. Undergraduates can also meet one-on-one with career advisors to explore potential fields and industries that might complement both their major and their passions. And they can definitely receive assistance crafting a strong resume. Lastly, all of this helps to explain why, according to PayScale.com, the average starting salary for a Southwestern graduate is a solid $42,400.

GENERAL INFO

Activities: Choral groups, concert band, dance, drama/theatre, jazz band, literary magazine, music ensembles, musical theater, student government, student newspaper, student-run film society. **Organizations:** 99 registered organizations, 17 honor societies, 9 religious organizations. 4 fraternities, 4 sororities. **Athletics (Intercollegiate):** *Men:* baseball, basketball, cross-country, diving, football, golf, lacrosse, soccer, swimming, tennis, track/field (outdoor). *Women:* basketball, cross-country, diving, golf, lacrosse, soccer, softball, swimming, tennis, track/field (outdoor), volleyball. **On-Campus Highlights:** Robertson Center—indoor Olympic size pool, McCombs Center—Student Center, Fountainwood Observatory, Korouva Milkbar—student run coffee house, Academic Mall.

FINANCIAL AID

Students should submit: FAFSA. Regular filing deadline is 3/1. The Princeton Review suggests that all financial aid forms be submitted as soon as possible after October 1. *Need-based scholarships/grants offered:* Federal Pell, FSEOG, State scholarships/grants, Private scholarships, College/university scholarship or grant aid from institutional funds. *Loan aid offered:* Direct Subsidized Stafford Loans, Direct Unsubsidized Stafford Loans, Direct PLUS loans, Federal Perkins Loans, State Loans, College/university loans from institutional funds. Applicants will be notified of awards on a rolling basis beginning 3/1. Federal Work-Study Program available. Institutional employment available.

THE BOTTOM LINE

Tuition at Southwestern University will cost undergraduates $37,560. Beyond tuition, students can anticipate spending $12,108 for room and board. Undergrads should also set aside roughly $1,200 for books and academic supplies. Additionally, those students who will be commuting can expect to spend around $450 for transportation. Fortunately, the average financial aid package is usually $26,126.

CAREER INFORMATION FROM PAYSCALE.COM

ROI rating	87
Bachelor's and No Higher	
Median starting salary	$44,800
Median mid-career salary	$83,900
At Least Bachelor's	
Median starting salary	$44,700
Median mid-career salary	$85,300
% alumni with high job meaning	58%
% STEM	16%

SELECTIVITY

Admissions Rating	88
# of applicants	3,487
% of applicants accepted	49
% of acceptees attending	23
# offered a place on the wait list	92
% accepting a place on wait list	11
% admitted from wait list	50

FRESHMAN PROFILE

Range SAT Critical Reading	520–630
Range SAT Math	530–630
Range ACT Composite	23–28
Minimum paper TOEFL	570
Minimum internet-based TOEFL	88
% graduated top 10% of class	36
% graduated top 25% of class	66
% graduated top 50% of class	95

DEADLINES

Early action	
Deadline	11/14
Notification	2/15
Regular	
Priority	2/1
Notification	4/1
Nonfall registration?	No

FINANCIAL FACTS

Financial Aid Rating	87
Annual tuition	$39,060
Room and board	$12,288
Required fees	
Average need-based scholarship	$27,580
% needy frosh rec. need-based scholarship or grant aid	100
% needy UG rec. need-based scholarship or grant aid	99
% needy frosh rec. non-need-based scholarship or grant aid	99
% needy UG rec. non-need-based scholarship or grant aid	96
% needy frosh rec. need-based self-help aid	83
% needy UG rec. need-based self-help aid	85
% frosh rec. any financial aid	99
% UG rec. any financial aid	97
% frosh need fully met	26
% ugrads need fully met	27
Average % of frosh need met	90
Average % of ugrad need met	88

St. Anselm College

100 Saint Anselm Drive, Manchester, NH 03102-1310 • Admissions: 603-641-7500 • Fax: 603-641-7550

CAMPUS LIFE

Quality of Life Rating	92
Fire Safety Rating	85
Green Rating	60*
Type of school	Private
Affiliation	Roman Catholic
Environment	City

STUDENTS

Total undergrad enrollment	1,927
% male/female	40/60
% from out of state	77
% frosh from public high school	65
% frosh live on campus	93
% ugrads live on campus	92
% African American	2
% Asian	1
% Caucasian	83
% Hispanic	3
% Native American	<1
% Pacific Islander	0
% Two or more races	2
% Race and/or ethnicity unknown	9
% international	1
# of countries represented	7

ACADEMICS

Academic Rating	82
% students returning for sophomore year	90
% students graduating within 4 years	70
% students graduating within 6 years	73
Calendar	Semester
Student/faculty ratio	11:1
Profs interesting rating	82
Profs accessible rating	86

Most classes have 10–19 students.
Most lab/discussion sessions have
  fewer than 10 students.

MOST POPULAR MAJORS
Registered Nursing/Registered Nurse;
Biology; Psychology

ABOUT THE SCHOOL

This picturesque, quaint, Catholic college is located on a New Hampshire hilltop, offering its almost 2,000 students a traditional liberal arts education while emphasizing preparation for real-world careers. The school has forty-five majors and forty-three minors, as well as several pre-professional programs for advanced studies. All freshmen begin in the humanities program (Conversatio) and follow a core curriculum throughout their four years (including required philosophy and theology courses), with average class sizes of eighteen students and a focus on "improving the academic skills of the student to the maximum." Students get out what they put in, but "there is a strong sense of encouragement to do well," and students agree that one of the best parts about the college is the personal interaction between students and both administrators and faculty members. "They are ready and willing to meet with you at a time convenient for you."

BANG FOR YOUR BUCK

Plenty of need- and merit-based scholarships are available to students to offset the cost of the private school: Chancellor Honors Scholarships provide academically strong students with Honors Program admission and up to $20,000 annually; the Presidential Scholarship offers up to $17,000 a year; and the Dean's Scholarship is up to $10,000 a year. Furthermore, the school has multiple scholarships set aside for talent-based achievements, and for families who have two or more children attending the college.

STUDENT LIFE

The campus is separate from the city of Manchester so students tend to stay local for their fun, and most are "very involved in activities here, especially sports (a lot of people do intramurals) and service activities" (indeed, "volunteering is HUGE here at Saint Anselm College"). During the week, there are usually club-run events students can go to, as well as "a lot of speakers and political candidates who come to the New Hampshire Institute of Politics." Students are typically from a religious private high school, and the environment at the college is "very intellectual," with "debates and discussions on politics, philosophy and society in general [being] typical."

CAREER

The college is heavily vested in its students' future careers, and employment readiness is incorporated into the curriculum from day one. Credit-bearing internships, study abroad, and faculty-student research opportunities abound, and the Career Development Center also offers personal guidance, professional development workshops, and HawkCareers, a Saint-Anselm specific job and internship database. Additionally, the Meelia Center for Community Engagement helps connect students with agencies throughout the Greater Manchester area, in order to gain service experience. For the Class of 2014, 97 percent were employed, in graduate school, or engaged in service within six months of graduation. Saint Anselm graduates who visited Payscale.com reported an early career salary of $49,000 annually.

St. Anselm College

FINANCIAL AID: 603-641-7110 • E-MAIL: ADMISSION@ANSELM.EDU • WEBSITE: WWW.ANSELM.EDU

GENERAL INFO

Activities: Choral groups, dance, drama/theater, jazz band, literary magazine, musical theater, radio station, student government, student newspaper, television station, yearbook, Campus Ministries, International Student Organization, Model UN 120 registered organizations, 11 honor societies, 7 religious organizations. **Athletics (Intercollegiate):** *Men:* baseball, basketball, cross-country, football, golf, ice hockey, lacrosse, skiing (downhill/alpine), soccer, tennis. *Women:* basketball, cross-country, field hockey, golf, ice hockey, lacrosse, skiing (downhill/alpine), soccer, softball, tennis, volleyball. **On-Campus Highlights:** Joseph Hall Academic Building, Chapel Arts Center, Davidson Hall Dining Hall, Sullivan Ice Arena & Fitness Center, Abbey Church, Coffee Shop and Pub Cushing Student Center.

FINANCIAL AID

Students should submit: FAFSA, CSS/Financial Aid PROFILE, Noncustodial PROFILE. Regular filing deadline is 3/15. The Princeton Review suggests that all financial aid forms be submitted as soon as possible after October 1. *Need-based scholarships/grants offered:* Federal Pell, FSEOG, State scholarships/grants, Private scholarships, College/university scholarship or grant aid from institutional funds. *Loan aid offered:* Direct Subsidized Stafford Loans, Direct Unsubsidized Stafford Loans, Direct PLUS loans, Federal Perkins Loans. Applicants will be notified of awards on a rolling basis beginning 3/1. Federal Work-Study Program available. Institutional employment available.

BOTTOM LINE

It costs $37,826 in tuition and $13,734 in room and board (as well as an additional $1,560 in fees) to attend Saint Anselm, but a whopping 98% of first-year students are awarded some form of financial aid, with the average need-based grant/scholarship coming in at $20,800. All averages considered, a first-year student receiving need-based aid can expect a total price of around $25,575.

CAREER INFORMATION FROM PAYSCALE.COM

ROI rating	86
Bachelor's and No Higher	
Median starting salary	$49,600
Median mid-career salary	$89,800
At Least Bachelor's	
Median starting salary	$49,600
Median mid-career salary	$89,900
% alumni with high job meaning	52%
% STEM	10%

SELECTIVITY

Admissions Rating	84
# of applicants	3,955
% of applicants accepted	73
% of acceptees attending	18
# offered a place on the wait list	472
% accepting a place on wait list	37
% admitted from wait list	16

FRESHMAN PROFILE

Range SAT Critical Reading	530–620
Range SAT Math	540–630
Range SAT Writing	530–640
Range ACT Composite	24–28
Minimum paper TOEFL	550
Minimum internet-based TOEFL	80
Average HS GPA	3.3
% graduated top 10% of class	31
% graduated top 25% of class	62
% graduated top 50% of class	89

DEADLINES

Early decision	
Deadline	12/1
Notification	1/1
Early action	
Deadline	11/15
Notification	1/15
Regular	
Deadline	2/1
Notification	3/15
Nonfall registration?	Yes

FINANCIAL FACTS

Financial Aid Rating	85
Annual tuition	$37,826
Room and board	$13,734
Required fees	$1,000
Average need-based scholarship	$21,681
scholarship or grant aid	99
% needy UG rec. need-based	
scholarship or grant aid	99
% needy frosh rec. non-need-based	
scholarship or grant aid	24
% needy UG rec. non-need-based	
scholarship or grant aid	19
% needy frosh rec. need-based	
self-help aid	81
% needy UG rec. need-based	
self-help aid	84
% frosh rec. any financial aid	98
% UG rec. any financial aid	98
% UG borrow to pay for school	83
Average cumulative indebtedness	$38,583
% frosh need fully met	30
% ugrads need fully met	28
Average % of frosh need met	81
Average % of ugrad need met	80

St. Lawrence University

PAYSON HALL, CANTON, NY 13617 • ADMISSIONS: 315-229-5261 • FAX: 315-229-5818

CAMPUS LIFE

Quality of Life Rating	**91**
Fire Safety Rating	**81**
Green Rating	**91**
Type of school	Private
Affiliation	No Affiliation
Environment	Village

STUDENTS

Total undergrad enrollment	2,435
% male/female	45/55
% from out of state	54
% frosh from public high school	69
% frosh live on campus	100
% ugrads live on campus	99
# of fraternities (% ugrad men join)	2 (10)
# of sororities (% ugrad women join)	4 (15)
% African American	3
% Asian	2
% Caucasian	79
% Hispanic	5
% Native American	<1
% Pacific Islander	<1
% Two or more races	2
% Race and/or ethnicity unknown	<1
% international	9
# of countries represented	51

ACADEMICS

Academic Rating	**92**
% students returning for sophomore year	89
% students graduating within 4 years	82
% students graduating within 6 years	87
Calendar	Semester
Student/faculty ratio	11:1
Profs interesting rating	93
Profs accessible rating	90
Most classes have 10–19 students.	
Most lab/discussion sessions have 10–19 students.	

MOST POPULAR MAJORS

Economics; Psychology; Biology; Government; English

ABOUT THE SCHOOL

Located on the St. Lawrence River in the far reaches of Northern NY, St. Lawrence University is a small, private university with a 11:1 student-to-faculty ratio and professors who "genuinely care about the success of all of their students and put forth an effort to produce those results." The school is "guided by tradition" and inspires students to make a sustainable and meaningful impact in communities, and the "rigorous curriculum accompanied by unceasing co-curricular amenities" and "well-developed study abroad programs" help to spread this idea. Classroom participation is highly encouraged and easy to do in "a comfortable and engaging classroom environment." "Very rarely will a professor lecture for the full amount of class time," says a student. Many students here are "environmentally minded with a tendency toward political activism and community involvement."

BANG FOR YOUR BUCK

The "very generous" university states that it will do everything possible to help students plan their SLU education in an affordable way, and to that end, gives out more than $43 million in financial aid each year. Many, many merit-based scholarships are available also, including the full tuition offered through the Trustee Scholarship for the top male and female in each first-year class; the $32,000 per year Momentum Scholarships, which reward academic and co-curricular achievements; and the Sesquicentennial and University Scholarships. Leaderships Scholarships and Community Service Scholarship recipients get $10,000 per year. For those who need assistance while working, the various Internship Fellowship Awards help offset living and travel costs incurred during a student's internship (specific awards are given for certain fields or regions).

STUDENT LIFE

"Welcome to the North Country, bring mittens!" warns a student. Whether the "tundra" weather in the winter plays a factor or not, people always stay on campus on weekends, "creating a vibrant social life and involvement." The First-Year program is designed for students to have a smooth transition academically and socially into college and allows students "the opportunity to fit it with a group of students right away." There are plenty of events on campus and in the community, and people take advantage of the area to hike in the Adirondacks, float down the river, go apple picking, and generally "take advantage of what the North Country has to offer." Not only are students outdoorsy, but "a lot of us are involved in sports whether at the varsity, club, or intramural level." Fairly often students will also go to Ottawa or Montreal and Burlington for concerts.

CAREER

The "absolutely excellent" Career Services Office offers a host of resources for students looking for jobs, internships, or research opportunities, including online tools, career fairs, and a new Business Case Study Course. The school's Shadow A Saint program allows current undergraduates to spend work time during the summer with an alumni in their area of career interest, and the Laurentians in Residence program brings alumni and parent leaders to the school throughout the year for panels, networking, and mentoring. "Networking and alumni contact is HUGE! Alumni are very helpful and are proud to lend a hand," says a student. Ninety-five percent of the most recent graduating class had a job or was enrolled in graduate school within a year after commencement. Forty-one percent of SLU graduates who visited PayScale.com felt their job was meaningful to the world, and visitors reported an average starting salary of $42,600.

St. Lawrence University

FINANCIAL AID: 315-229-5265 • E-MAIL: ADMISSIONS@STLAWU.EDU • WEBSITE: WWW.STLAWU.EDU

GENERAL INFO

Activities: Choral groups, concert band, dance, drama/theater, jazz band, literary magazine, music ensembles, radio station, student government, student newspaper, student-run film society, yearbook, Campus Ministries, International Student Organization, Model UN, Outdoor Club. **Organizations:** 117 registered organizations, 22 honor societies, 4 religious organizations. 2 fraternities, 4 sororities. **Athletics (Intercollegiate):** *Men:* baseball, basketball, crew/rowing, cross-country, equestrian sports, football, golf, ice hockey, lacrosse, skiing (downhill/alpine), skiing (nordic/cross-country), soccer, squash, swimming, tennis, track/field (outdoor), track/field (indoor). *Women:* basketball, crew/rowing, cross-country, equestrian sports, field hockey, golf, ice hockey, lacrosse, skiing (downhill/alpine), skiing nordic cross-country, soccer, softball, squash, swimming, tennis, track/field (outdoor), track/field (indoor), volleyball. **On-Campus Highlights:** Newell Field House, Brewer Bookstore, Johnson Hall of Science, Owen D. Young Library, Student Center, Newell Center for Arts Technology.

FINANCIAL AID

Students should submit: FAFSA, Noncustodial PROFILE. Regular filing deadline is 2/1. The Princeton Review suggests that all financial aid forms be submitted as soon as possible after October 1. *Need-based scholarships/grants offered:* Federal Pell, FSEOG, State scholarships/grants, Private scholarships, College/university scholarship or grant aid from institutional funds. *Loan aid offered:* Direct Subsidized Stafford Loans, Direct Unsubsidized Stafford Loans, Direct PLUS loans, Federal Perkins Loans, College/university loans from institutional funds. Applicants will be notified of awards on or about 3/30. Federal Work-Study Program available. Institutional employment available.

BOTTOM LINE

Tuition for all students runs $50,830 and room and board is another $13,190. Ninety-three percent of all SLU undergrads receive financial aid, with the average need-based package running $33,515. Sixty-seven percent of students take out some form of loan, graduating with an average of $26,792 in loan debt.

CAREER INFORMATION FROM PAYSCALE.COM

ROI rating	**88**
Bachelor's and No Higher	
Median starting salary	$49,100
Median mid-career salary	$69,300
At Least Bachelor's	
Median starting salary	$50,100
Median mid-career salary	$81,800
% alumni with high job meaning	55%
% STEM	19%

SELECTIVITY

Admissions Rating	**92**
# of applicants	5,876
% of applicants accepted	46
% of acceptees attending	25
# offered a place on the wait list	73
% accepting a place on wait list	18
% admitted from wait list	0
# of early decision applicants	351
% accepted early decision	90

FRESHMAN PROFILE

Range SAT Critical Reading	550–650
Range SAT Math	550–660
Range SAT Writing	540–640
Range ACT Composite	26–30
Minimum paper TOEFL	600
Minimum internet-based TOEFL	82
Average HS GPA	3.6
% graduated top 10% of class	45
% graduated top 25% of class	77
% graduated top 50% of class	95

DEADLINES

Early decision	
Deadline	11/1
Regular	
Deadline	2/1
Nonfall registration?	Yes

FINANCIAL FACTS

Financial Aid Rating	**87**
Annual tuition	$50,830
Room and board	$13,190
Required fees	$370
Average need-based scholarship	$37,312
% needy frosh rec. need-based scholarship or grant aid	100
% needy UG rec. need-based scholarship or grant aid	100
% needy frosh rec. non-need-based scholarship or grant aid	76
% needy UG rec. non-need-based scholarship or grant aid	72
% needy frosh rec. need-based self-help aid	75
% needy UG rec. need-based self-help aid	79
% frosh rec. any financial aid	100
% UG rec. any financial aid	96
% UG borrow to pay for school	60
Average cumulative indebtedness	$26,792
% frosh need fully met	28
% ugrads need fully met	26
Average % of frosh need met	87
Average % of ugrad need met	85

St. Olaf College

1520 St. Olaf Avenue, Northfield, MN 55057 • Admissions: 507-786-3025 • Fax: 507-786-3832

CAMPUS LIFE

Quality of Life Rating	94
Fire Safety Rating	80
Green Rating	60*
Type of school	Private
Affiliation	Lutheran
Environment	Village

STUDENTS

Total undergrad enrollment	3,046
% male/female	43/57
% from out of state	58
% frosh from public high school	73
# of fraternities (% ugrad men join)	0
# of sororities (% ugrad women join)	0
% African American	2
% Asian	6
% Caucasian	75
% Hispanic	5
% Native American	<1
% Pacific Islander	<1
% Two or more races	4
% Race and/or ethnicity unknown	1
% international	7
# of countries represented	80

ACADEMICS

Academic Rating	93
% students returning for sophomore year	93
% students graduating within 4 years	84
% students graduating within 6 years	87
Calendar	4/1/4
Student/faculty ratio	12:1
Profs interesting rating	91
Profs accessible rating	90

Most classes have 10–19 students.
Most lab/discussion sessions have 10–19 students.

MOST POPULAR MAJORS
Biology; Economics; Psychology

ABOUT THE SCHOOL

Located in Northfield, Minnesota, a historic river town conveniently situated near the Twin Cities of Minneapolis and St. Paul, St. Olaf offers exceptional students with a civic mindset a rigorous college experience in a positive "community atmosphere." With a reputation for "strong academics" and a "beautiful campus," the school's aim of "fostering the development of mind, body, and spirit" stems from its tradition as a college of the Evangelical Lutheran Church in America. Lauded for its commitment to "interdisciplinary study" and "global education," St. Olaf offers particularly strong programs in science, math, and music. With a small but dedicated community of around 3,000 students and 340 faculty members, the opportunity to develop close mentor relationships with professors in nearly any department is a standing invitation from the moment students step on campus. In addition, a "great reputation for study abroad" is a hallmark of this "utopian community." As one student attests, "Through providing fresh food and fun athletic opportunities, challenging academic stimulation, and a healthy religious and spiritual conversation, St. Olaf demonstrates that it is a learning institution truly driven by educating the whole person."

BANG FOR YOUR BUCK

At St. Olaf, opportunity begins with community. The celebrated Piper Center offers a staggering number of vocational services to students across their four years, providing "a resource center for students . . . to help determine vocational goals and devise well-informed postgraduation [goals]." Collaboration between the Piper Center, faculty members, and community partners "enhances learning and encourages students to develop the skills, knowledge, and experience necessary to become engaged citizens." In addition, the Innovation Scholars program is "dedicated to education, research, and service within the liberal arts" and "supports student creativity through innovation grants, courses, internships, business-plan development, startup support, and networking events."

STUDENT LIFE

"Because Northfield is a small town and there is not easy transit to the cities," St. Olaf is a school where "social life happens on campus, at events or at houses and dorms." However, that doesn't seem to be a problem for most students. "The student government association is great at providing entertainment on the weekends," an opinion shared by many. "We have a lot of dances in our club, school events all the time like live bands, magicians, comedians, etc., and movies that are not out on DVD play in the theater every weekend." Though St. Olaf has a dry campus policy that many of the students abide by, "a lot of students still use alcohol on a regular basis, so it's not hard to find a party" should you be so inclined. Students also speak fondly about a communal atmosphere that makes it easy to unwind and have fun with their peers. "Everyone's door is always open, so I spend a lot of nights just hanging in friends rooms, watching TV, or playing video games." So while the school provides its students with many things to do, most agree that "the fun at St. Olaf comes not from doing specific things, but rather simply hanging out with the amazing people here."

CAREER

The Piper Center for Vocation and Career at St. Olaf provides students with a number of resources to help them plan for life after graduation. Academic advising, career counseling, on-campus recruiting, extensive alumni networking opportunities, and job and internship search resources are just a sampling of the Center's many offerings. Other noteworthy programs include funding for students taking unpaid or underpaid internships, and several special internship

St. Olaf College

FINANCIAL AID: 507-786-3019 • E-MAIL: ADMISSIONS@STOLAF.EDU • WEBSITE: WWW.STOLAF.EDU

programs that engage with nearby businesses and institutions, such as the Mayo Clinic. While a few students cite the Piper Center as an area that could do with some improvement, the majority opinion seems to be that it offers "awesome resources for career planning and networking." A few students say that their professors "are also helpful as career and internship counselors and references." Of St. Olaf alumni visiting PayScale.com, 50 percent report that they derive a high level of meaning from their careers.

GENERAL INFO

Activities: Choral groups, concert band, dance, drama/theater, jazz band, literary magazine, music ensembles, musical theater, opera, pep band, radio station, student government, student newspaper, student-run film society, symphony orchestra. **Organizations:** Campus Ministries, International Student Organization, Model UN, 257 registered organizations, 20 honor societies, 19 religious organizations. **Athletics (Intercollegiate):** *Men:* baseball, basketball, cross-country, diving, football, golf, ice hockey, skiing (downhill/alpine), skiing (nordic/cross-country), soccer, swimming, tennis, track/field (outdoor), track/field (indoor), wrestling. *Women:* basketball, cross-country, diving, golf, ice hockey, skiing (downhill/alpine), skiing (nordic/cross-country), soccer, softball, swimming, tennis, track/field (outdoor), track/field (indoor), volleyball.

FINANCIAL AID

Students should submit: FAFSA, CSS/Financial Aid PROFILE, Noncustodial PROFILE. Regular filing deadline is 3/1. The Princeton Review suggests that all financial aid forms be submitted as soon as possible after October 1. *Need-based scholarships/grants offered:* Federal Pell, FSEOG, State scholarships/grants, Private scholarships, College/university scholarship or grant aid from institutional funds. *Loan aid offered:* Direct Subsidized Stafford Loans, Direct Unsubsidized Stafford Loans, Direct PLUS loans, Federal Nursing Loans, State Loans, College/university loans from institutional funds. Applicants will be notified of awards on or about 4/1. Federal Work-Study Program available. Institutional employment available.

BOTTOM LINE

If you're a spiritually minded, environmentally conscious individual who excels at academics and enjoys studying in a small, fastidious community, this liberal arts bastion will provide a challenging but idyllic backdrop. The school is serious about its commitment to study abroad and postgraduate education and its graduates often enjoy much success in their pursuit of competitive postgraduate fellowships. St. Olaf is committed to creating and supporting stewards of the global world through its comprehensive financial aid packages, which meet 97 percent of undergraduate need across all four years. The $42,940 tuition and $9,790 room and board costs reflect the caliber of the institution, with the average cumulative undergraduate indebtedness tallying up to $28,396.

CAREER INFORMATION FROM PAYSCALE.COM

ROI rating	90
Bachelor's and No Higher	
Median starting salary	$45,300
Median mid-career salary	$89,400
At Least Bachelor's	
Median starting salary	$46,700
Median mid-career salary	$87,900
% alumni with high job meaning	50%
% STEM	26%

SELECTIVITY

Admissions Rating	92
# of applicants	7,571
% of applicants accepted	36
% of acceptees attending	28
# offered a place on the wait list	729
% accepting a place on wait list	21
% admitted from wait list	75
# of early decision applicants	245
% accepted early decision	73

FRESHMAN PROFILE

Range SAT Critical Reading	560–710
Range SAT Math	580–700
Range ACT Composite	26–31
Minimum internet-based TOEFL	90
Average HS GPA	3.6
% graduated top 10% of class	43
% graduated top 25% of class	77
% graduated top 50% of class	96

DEADLINES

Early decision	
Deadline	11/15
Notification	12/15
Regular	
Deadline	1/15
Notification	3/20
Nonfall registration?	Yes

FINANCIAL FACTS

Financial Aid Rating	97
Annual tuition	$44,180
Room and board	$10,080
Required fees	
Average need-based scholarship	$30,182
% needy frosh rec. need-based scholarship or grant aid	100
% needy UG rec. need-based scholarship or grant aid	99
% needy frosh rec. non-need-based scholarship or grant aid	24
% needy UG rec. non-need-based scholarship or grant aid	23
% needy frosh rec. need-based self-help aid	100
% needy UG rec. need-based self-help aid	100
% frosh rec. any financial aid	92
% UG rec. any financial aid	93
% UG borrow to pay for school	57
Average cumulative indebtedness	$29,617
% frosh need fully met	91
% ugrads need fully met	90
Average % of frosh need met	99
Average % of ugrad need met	98

Stanford University

UNDERGRADUATE ADMISSION, MONTAG HALL, 355 GALVEZ STREET, STANFORD, CA 94305-6106 • ADMISSION: 650-723-2091

CAMPUS LIFE

Quality of Life Rating	95
Fire Safety Rating	89
Green Rating	99
Type of school	Private
Affiliation	No Affiliation
Environment	City

STUDENTS

Total undergrad enrollment	6,999
% male/female	52/48
% from out of state	61
% frosh from public high school	57
% frosh live on campus	100
% ugrads live on campus	93
# of fraternities (% ugrad men join)	16 (20)
# of sororities (% ugrad women join)	14 (20)
% African American	6
% Asian	20
% Caucasian	37
% Hispanic	15
% Native American	1
% Pacific Islander	<1
% Two or more races	10
% Race and/or ethnicity unknown	<1
% international	9
# of countries represented	90

ACADEMICS

Academic Rating	95
% students returning for sophomore year	98
% students graduating within 4 years	75
% students graduating within 6 years	93
Calendar	Quarter
Student/faculty ratio	4:1
Profs interesting rating	85
Profs accessible rating	84

Most classes have 10–19 students.
Most lab/discussion sessions have
fewer than 10 students.

MOST POPULAR MAJORS
Computer Science; Human Biology;
Engineering

#2 COLLEGE THAT PAYS YOU BACK

ABOUT THE SCHOOL
Stanford University is widely recognized as one of the nation's most outstanding universities, considered by many to be the West Coast's answer to the Ivy League. Stanford alumni, who can be found in 143 countries, eighteen territories, and all fifty states, have distinguished themselves in many fields, from government service to innovation to business to arts and entertainment. Academics are simply top-notch, and despite the fact that this is a research-driven university, professors are seriously interested in getting to know their undergrads. Students say that teachers at Stanford are "wonderful resources for guidance and tutoring," and there is "an opportunity to engage with them on a regular basis." The classroom experience is discussion-oriented and otherwise awesome. There are tons of majors, and, if you don't like any of the ones on offer, it's a breeze to design your own. The dorms are like palaces. The administration runs the school like a finely tuned machine. There's very little not to like about this place. "The classes, campus, and faculty are amazing," reports one contented undergrad; another is happy to find that Stanford "has incredible resources, incredible people . . . and an unrivaled atmosphere of openness and collaboration."

BANG FOR YOUR BUCK
Like a handful of other spectacularly wealthy schools in the United States, Stanford maintains a wholly need-blind admission policy, and it demonstrates a serious commitment to making its world-class education available to talented and well-prepared students regardless of economic circumstances. All of Stanford's scholarship funds are need-based. For parents with total annual income and typical assets below $65,000, Stanford will not expect a parent contribution toward educational costs. For parents with total annual income and typical assets below $125,000, the expected parent contribution will be low enough to ensure that all tuition charges are covered with need-based scholarship, federal and state grants, and/or outside scholarship funds. Families with incomes at higher levels (typically up to $200,000) may also qualify for assistance, especially if more than one family member is enrolled in college. The hard part is getting admitted. If you can do that, the school will make sure you have a way to pay. The vast majority of successful applicants will be among the strongest students (academically) in their secondary schools.

STUDENT LIFE
"People often use the duck metaphor to describe Stanford," says a student, "on the surface they are calm and serene, under the surface they are paddling really hard." But it's not all hard work and studying for the student body, as "life at Stanford has the potential to be both extremely stressful (due to the strenuous academics) and very carefree (due to the wide variety of 'releases' available to students)." "We aren't a typical party school, but about a third of the student body tries to party enough for everyone else." For the other two-thirds, "there are tons of ways to be involved" and "clubs for every type of person." "Some dance, some sing, some play instruments, some plan events" and "students constantly 'roll out' to whatever performance, sports event, or talk they can in order to support their fellow classmates and the hard work that is put in to it." And of course, students can turn to the beautiful natural surroundings when in need of a little relaxation. "Life at Stanford is like a vacation. The campus with its palm trees and

Stanford University

Financial Aid: 650-723-3058 • E-mail: admission@stanford.edu • Fax: 650-725-2846 • Website: www.stanford.edu

surrounding foothills is the most beautiful in the world." But while "anything you could possibly need is pretty much on campus" getting away can be great too: "Only at Stanford can you go from snowy mountains, to sunny beaches, to bustling city life [in San Francisco] all in one day."

CAREER

As a top-notch school, Stanford can lead to "great job opportunities" for motivated students looking to enter a wide variety of careers. Stanford students tend to be very focused on the future, with "about a 50/50 divide of people who are planning for careers to make money and people who are planning for careers to 'make a difference.'" Stanford's Career Development Center provides standard services such as job fairs and recruiting events, resume critique, and one-on-one counseling. The Center also offers "career communities" in specific fields, and a special community devoted solely to the needs of underclassmen still a few years from their job search. Most agree that Stanford "provides a great opportunity to pursue greater careers with a wide array of resources and support." Out of Stanford alumni visiting PayScale.com, 57 percent report that they derive meaning from their jobs.

GENERAL INFO

Activities: Choral groups, concert band, dance, drama/theater, jazz band, literary magazine, marching band, music ensembles, musical theater, opera, pep band, radio station, student government, student newspaper, student-run film society, symphony orchestra, television station, yearbook, campus ministries, international student organization. **Organizations:** 625 registered organizations, 40 religious organizations. 16 fraternities, 14 sororities.

FINANCIAL AID

Students should submit: FAFSA, CSS/Financial Aid PROFILE, Noncustodial PROFILE. Priority filing deadline is 2/15. The Princeton Review suggests that all financial aid forms be submitted as soon as possible after October 1. *Need-based scholarships/grants offered:* Federal Pell, FSEOG, State scholarships/grants, Private scholarships, College/university scholarship or grant aid from institutional funds. *Loan aid offered:* Direct Subsidized Stafford Loans, Direct Unsubsidized Stafford Loans, Direct PLUS loans, Federal Perkins Loans. Applicants will be notified of awards on a rolling basis beginning 4/1. Federal Work-Study Program available. Institutional employment available.

BOTTOM LINE

A year of tuition, fees, room and board, and basic expenses at Stanford costs about $62,541. While that figure is staggering, you have to keep in mind that few students pay anywhere near that amount. Financial packages here are very generous. Most aid comes with no strings attached. Only 22 percent of undergrads borrow to pay for school, and those who do walk away with an average of $21,238 in loan debt.

CAREER INFORMATION FROM PAYSCALE.COM

ROI rating	99
Bachelor's and No Higher	
Median starting salary	$65,900
Median mid-career salary	$123,000
At Least Bachelor's	
Median starting salary	$70,100
Median mid-career salary	$130,000
% alumni with high job meaning	62%
% STEM	29%

SELECTIVITY

Admissions Rating	99
# of applicants	42,167
% of applicants accepted	5
% of acceptees attending	78
# offered a place on the wait list	1,256
% accepting a place on wait list	74
% admitted from wait list	0

FRESHMAN PROFILE

Range SAT Critical Reading	690–780
Range SAT Math	700–800
Range SAT Writing	690–780
Range ACT Composite	31–35
Average HS GPA	4.0
% graduated top 10% of class	96
% graduated top 25% of class	99
% graduated top 50% of class	100

DEADLINES

Early action	
Deadline	11/1
Notification	12/15
Regular	
Deadline	1/3
Notification	4/1
Nonfall registration?	No

FINANCIAL FACTS

Financial Aid Rating	97
Annual tuition	$47,331
Room and board	$14,601
Required fees	$609
Average need-based scholarship	$43,167
% needy frosh rec. need-based scholarship or grant aid	95
% needy UG rec. need-based scholarship or grant aid	100
% needy frosh rec. non-need-based scholarship or grant aid	0
% needy UG rec. non-need-based scholarship or grant aid	1
% needy frosh rec. need-based self-help aid	58
% needy UG rec. need-based self-help aid	75
% frosh rec. any financial aid	86
% UG rec. any financial aid	85
% UG borrow to pay for school	22
Average cumulative indebtedness	$21,238
% frosh need fully met	91
% ugrads need fully met	91
Average % of frosh need met	100
Average % of ugrad need met	100

ate University of New York at Binghamton

PO Box 6001, BINGHAMTON, NY 13902-6001 • ADMISSIONS: 607-777-2171 • FAX: 607-777-4445

CAMPUS LIFE

Quality of Life Rating	82
Fire Safety Rating	92
Green Rating	97
Type of school	Public
Affiliation	No Affiliation
Environment	City

STUDENTS

Total undergrad enrollment	13,491
% male/female	52/48
% from out of state	8
% frosh from public high school	88
% frosh live on campus	98
% ugrads live on campus	51
# of fraternities (% ugrad men join)	34 (14)
# of sororities (% ugrad women join)	17 (10)
% African American	5
% Asian	14
% Caucasian	56
% Hispanic	10
% Native American	<1
% Pacific Islander	<1
% Two or more races	2
% Race and/or ethnicity unknown	2
% international	10
# of countries represented	115

ACADEMICS

Academic Rating	73
% students returning for sophomore year	91
% students graduating within 4 years	69
% students graduating within 6 years	81
Calendar	Semester
Student/faculty ratio	20:1
Profs interesting rating	67
Profs accessible rating	69
Most classes have 10–19 students.	
Most lab/discussion sessions have 20–29 students.	

MOST POPULAR MAJORS

Business Administration and Management;
Engineering; Psychology

ABOUT THE SCHOOL

Binghamton University (a State University of New York institution) offers its students a true value: this medium-sized university is more competitive than many of the Northeast's private schools, yet its top-notch education is available for a low state-school price. Undergraduate students choose Binghamton because of its value, but also because every semester they experience a great return on their investment. Binghamton students aspire to more than bachelor's degrees, often earning dual degrees or double majors and minors from the "great range of course offerings." Binghamton's Fleishman Center for Career and Professional Development (CCPD) reaches out to students, parents, alumni, faculty and campus administrators to provide information and advice about the realities of the job market as well as strategies for becoming competitive candidates for employment or graduate school. "I feel like I am learning things that I will be using in further education as well as in a future career," says a student. Although the quality of a Binghamton education depends upon which school within the university you attend, top-notch departments include a good management program, a strong science departments (especially in biology, premed, and psychology), stellar political science and philosophy programs, and a pre-law program that yields high law school acceptance rates. Engineering and nursing programs provide good real-world prep. Professors run the gamut from research-minded to student-focused and are "very accommodating and [try] to make their classes as engaging as possible." "I feel like my teachers genuinely care about me and my future," says a student.

BANG FOR YOUR BUCK

When all is said and done, a Binghamton degree will cost a student literally one-third of what they can expect to pay at other comparable schools. The school also offers a plethora of student opportunities for experiential education through research, study abroad, and internships, along with the third highest four-year graduation rate in the nation among peer public institutions. In addition to the low price, the school further assists students through need-based financial aid and grant/scholarship packages. Binghamton targets the vast majority of its institutional, alumni, and donor-funded scholarships primarily toward those students who would not be able to attend college without financial assistance. In most cases, new and current undergraduate students are required to complete only the Free Application for Financial Student Aid (FAFSA) to assist in determining financial need and scholarship eligibility. If you receive an award, the school makes every effort to offer you a similar financial aid package in subsequent years as long as your ability to pay remains unchanged. Binghamton students find numerous opportunities for on- and off-campus employment as well.

STUDENT LIFE

Nearly everyone at Binghamton "takes their classes very seriously, which provides an intellectually stimulating environment," but because "everyone works so hard during the week, people basically go crazy once Thursday and Friday hit." But if partying hard isn't what you're in the mood for, "there are many people who choose to stay in on weekends, get work done, or only go out once." "There are concerts, sports games, and Late Nite Bing, which is for the people that don't like to go out, or don't drink." With the abundance of things going on, students are "always on the move. If not in class or studying, they will be off to some sort of club or team meeting, volunteer project, athletic training, or even heading out to a party, whether it is a small dorm party or a bar bash." And while some may be inclined to find the University's large size intimidating, the variety also means that "nearly everyone can find their own niche."

State University of New York at Binghamton

FINANCIAL AID: 607-777-2428 • E-MAIL: ADMIT@BINGHAMTON.EDU • WEBSITE: WWW.BINGHAMTON.EDU

CAREER

At Binghamton, students are heavily invested in career opportunities to get "ahead of the game." The Fleishman Center for Career and Professional Development offers a wide variety of services that cover counseling, resume and cover letter preparation, career fairs and job search resources, and advice on personal branding and networking though social media. It also offers resources specifically for those looking to pursue work overseas. Many students point to "awesome" career services as Binghamton's greatest strength, while others don't seem entirely satisfied, despite the considerable offerings. "The alumni connection is very good but not excellent," says one, and another elaborates that the Career and Professional Development Center "is not significantly helpful, especially for the professional schools." Still, the typical starting salary for an alum is about $47,200. Out of Binghamton alumni visiting PayScale.com, 48 percent report feeling as though they derive meaning from their jobs.

GENERAL INFO

Activities: Choral groups, concert band, dance, drama/theater, jazz band, literary magazine, music ensembles, musical theater, opera, pep band, radio station, student government, student newspaper, student-run film society, symphony orchestra, television station, yearbook, campus ministries, international student organization.

FINANCIAL AID

Students should submit: FAFSA, State aid form. Priority filing deadline is 2/1. The Princeton Review suggests that all financial aid forms be submitted as soon as possible after October 1. *Need-based scholarships/ grants offered:* Federal Pell, FSEOG, State scholarships/grants, Private scholarships, College/university scholarship or grant aid from institutional funds. *Loan aid offered:* Direct Subsidized Stafford Loans, Direct Unsubsidized Stafford Loans, Direct PLUS loans, Federal Perkins Loans, Federal Nursing Loans, College/university loans from institutional funds. Applicants will be notified of awards on a rolling basis beginning 3/4. Federal Work-Study Program available. Institutional employment available.

THE BOTTOM LINE

At this reasonably priced public school, in-state tuition is just over $6,470, while out-of-state and international students pay roughly $21,550. Tuition aside, students are required to pay an additional $2,801 in mandatory fees and about $1,000 for books. For students who live on campus, the school charges approximately $13,590 for room and board, though these expenses can be reduced if the student chooses to live at home. It is important to note that, unlike undergraduates at many state schools, the vast majority of Binghamton students graduate in four years; therefore, they are not saddled with an additional year of tuition and fees.

CAREER INFORMATION FROM PAYSCALE.COM

ROI rating	87
Bachelor's and No Higher	
Median starting salary	$49,100
Median mid-career salary	$86,500
At Least Bachelor's	
Median starting salary	$49,900
Median mid-career salary	$91,400
% alumni with high job meaning	48%
% STEM	22%

SELECTIVITY

Admissions Rating	**90**
# of applicants	30,616
% of applicants accepted	42
% of acceptees attending	20
# offered a place on the wait list	3,961

FRESHMAN PROFILE

Range SAT Critical Reading	600–690
Range SAT Math	630–703
Range SAT Writing	580–670
Range ACT Composite	27–31
Minimum paper TOEFL	560
Minimum internet-based TOEFL	83
Average HS GPA	3.7

DEADLINES

Early action	
Deadline	11/1
Notification	1/15
Regular	
Priority	1/15
Nonfall registration?	Yes

FINANCIAL FACTS

Financial Aid Rating	**80**
Annual in-state tuition	$6,470
Annual out-of-state tuition	$21,550
Room and board	$13,590
Required fees	$2,801
Average need-based scholarship	$8,551
% needy frosh rec. need-based scholarship or grant aid	80
% needy UG rec. need-based scholarship or grant aid	84
% needy frosh rec. non-need-based scholarship or grant aid	13
% needy UG rec. non-need-based scholarship or grant aid	6
% needy frosh rec. need-based self-help aid	97
% needy UG rec. need-based self-help aid	97
% frosh rec. any financial aid	81
% UG rec. any financial aid	70
% UG borrow to pay for school	53
Average cumulative indebtedness	$25,844
% frosh need fully met	16
% ugrads need fully met	16
Average % of frosh need met	66
Average % of ugrad need met	73

ते University of New York
t Geneseo

LLEGE CIRCLE, GENESEO, NY 14454-1401 • ADMISSIONS: 585-245-5571 • FINANCIAL AID: 585-245-5731

CAMPUS LIFE

Quality of Life Rating	89
Fire Safety Rating	98
Green Rating	71
Type of school	Public
Affiliation	No Affiliation
Environment	Village

STUDENTS

Total undergrad enrollment	5,583
% male/female	40/60
% from out of state	2
% frosh live on campus	98
% ugrads live on campus	56
# of fraternities (% ugrad men join)	12 (22)
# of sororities (% ugrad women join)	15 (26)
% African American	3
% Asian	6
% Caucasian	74
% Hispanic	7
% Native American	<1
% Pacific Islander	<1
% Two or more races	3
% Race and/or ethnicity unknown	4
% international	2
# of countries represented	26

ACADEMICS

Academic Rating	75
% students returning for sophomore year	89
% students graduating within 4 years	69
% students graduating within 6 years	82
Calendar	Semester
Student/faculty ratio	20:1
Profs interesting rating	75
Profs accessible rating	80

Most classes have 20–29 students.
Most lab/discussion sessions have 10–19 students.

MOST POPULAR MAJORS

Business Administration and Management; Biology; Psychology

ABOUT THE SCHOOL

The State University of New York at Geneseo sits in a small town in the Finger Lakes region of upstate New York. Proudly sporting the title of the "Ivy of the SUNYs," this university is the place for students looking for all the prestige of a posh private school on a public-school budget. Small classes and enthusiastic professors make it easy to excel at SUNY Geneseo. "I truly feel that Geneseo's greatest strength is its sense of community. This is true when it comes to professor-student interactions, student-student interactions and all others. Everyone is very receptive to new ideas and to learning from each other," one student shares. Professors "seek to challenge" their students, and the "course load is tough," according to members of the student body. Beyond campus, students have the option to study abroad (nearly 44 percent take part) at one of Geneseo's partner universities or through another SUNY sponsored program, totaling 500 opportunities across seven continents.

BANG FOR YOUR BUCK

Students are thrilled that SUNY Geneseo provides them with "an outstanding education [at] an affordable price;" also, over two-thirds of faculty at the school have PhDs. An intimate environment, which promotes close student-teacher interaction, provides students with the chance to explore the varied curriculum in an in-depth and comprehensive manner. With over1,300 freshman enrolling last year, virtually everyone is a full-time student and lives on campus; there are only 5,583 students in all. There are a number of scholarships targeted at freshman, and awards range from $1,000 to some that cover full tuition. "Geneseo has a great atmosphere, challenging classes, a wonderful student population, and the best price!"

STUDENT LIFE

Geneseo students are "every[thing] from carefree-casual to business suit and tie." "It's really a good mix that supports all aspects of your own personality and doesn't pressure you to be any one particular way." Monday through Thursday comprise "straight academics for most people," though there's "always something to do at Geneseo on any night of the week." Ice Hockey games are usually a hit, "there are active clubs everywhere," a huge portion of the student body is involved in intramural, sports, and the school organizes "plenty of the Late Knight activities" to keep students busy on Friday and Saturday. Off-campus, Geneseo has a bowling alley, movie theater, and about half a dozen bars (for those over twenty-one), and Rochester and Buffalo are within reach (the county provides bus service to the former). There are also trips throughout the year to mountains for skiing, Syracuse basketball games, musicals, white water rafting and "many other things." Still, "most students stay on in Geneseo for the weekends because there is so much to do."

CAREER

The Department of Career Development offers the full gamut of career assessment and fulfillment resources; the office's extensive library of career-related materials is just the tip of the job hunt preparation iceberg. Services that students and alumni can utilize include drop-in hours, online internship/job databases, on-campus recruiting, mock interviews, and alumni mentoring. Career Partners, the Winter Shadow Program, and other externships also connect students with alumni, and numerous large career fairs are held throughout the year to facilitate employer and student interaction. Service learning opportunities are also available in Geneseo's partner communities and NGOs. Fifty-three percent of Geneseo graduates who visited PayScale.com reported feeling a high level of impact on the world.

State University of New York at Geneseo

E-mail: ADMISSIONS@GENESEO.EDU • Fax: 585-245-5550 • Website: WWW.GENESEO.EDU

GENERAL INFO

Environment: Village. **Activities:** Choral groups, dance, drama/theater, jazz band, literary magazine, music ensembles, musical theater, pep band, radio station, student government, student newspaper, symphony orchestra, television station, campus ministries, international student organization. **Organizations:** 197 registered organizations, 9 honor societies, 7 religious organizations. 12 fraternities, 15 sororities. **Athletics (Intercollegiate):** *Men:* Basketball, cross-country, diving, ice hockey, lacrosse, soccer, swimming, track/field (outdoor), track/field (indoor). *Women:* Basketball, cross-country, diving, equestrian sports, field hockey, lacrosse, soccer, softball, swimming, tennis, track/field (outdoor), track/field (indoor), volleyball. **On-Campus Highlights:** MacVittie College Union, The Gazebo, Milne Library, Alumni Fieldhouse (Workout Center), College Green. **Environmental Initiatives:** Signing of the Presidents Climate Commitment. Currently developing our Climate Action Plan. Establishment of Geneseo's Environmental Impact and Sustainability Task Force. Gold Lecture Series–Live Green Task Force Work/Initiatives.

FINANCIAL AID

Students should submit: FAFSA, State aid form. Regular filing deadline is 2/15. The Princeton Review suggests that all financial aid forms be submitted as soon as possible after October 1. *Need-based scholarships/grants offered:* Federal Pell, FSEOG, State scholarships/grants *Loan aid offered:* Direct Subsidized Stafford Loans, Direct Unsubsidized Stafford Loans, Direct PLUS loans, Federal Perkins Loans. Applicants will be notified of awards on a rolling basis beginning 3/15. Federal Work-Study Program available. Institutional employment available.

BOTTOM LINE

SUNY Geneseo provides a comprehensive education while not digging deeply into students' pockets. In-state tuition comes to $6,470, while out-of-state students can expect to pay closer to $16,320 annually. There are plenty of ways to lower costs at the school, however. Half of all freshmen receive financial assistance, and the average need-based aid package is $6,116. Undergrads here can expect to graduate with approximately $22,300 in loan debt.

CAREER INFORMATION FROM PAYSCALE.COM

ROI rating	87
Bachelor's and No Higher	
Median starting salary	$41,000
Median mid-career salary	$80,700
At Least Bachelor's	
Median starting salary	$44,900
Median mid-career salary	$81,600
% alumni with high job meaning	49%
% STEM	16%

SELECTIVITY

Admissions Rating	86
# of applicants	9,118
% of applicants accepted	73
% of acceptees attending	20
# offered a place on the wait list	542
% accepting a place on wait list	33
% admitted from wait list	27
# of early decision applicants	238
% accepted early decision	90

FRESHMAN PROFILE

Range SAT Critical Reading	550–640
Range SAT Math	550–650
Range ACT Composite	25–29
Minimum paper TOEFL	525
Minimum internet-based TOEFL	71
Average HS GPA	3.7
% graduated top 10% of class	36
% graduated top 25% of class	74
% graduated top 50% of class	95

DEADLINES

Early decision	
Deadline	11/15
Notification	12/15
Regular	
Deadline	1/1
Notification	3/1
Nonfall registration?	Yes

FINANCIAL FACTS

Financial Aid Rating	88
Annual in-state tuition	$6,470
Annual out-of-state tuition	$16,320
Room and board	$12,264
Required fees	$1,706
Average need-based scholarship	$6,116
% needy frosh rec. need-based scholarship or grant aid	51
% needy UG rec. need-based scholarship or grant aid	78
% needy frosh rec. non-need-based scholarship or grant aid	18
% needy UG rec. non-need-based scholarship or grant aid	26
% needy frosh rec. need-based self-help aid	48
% needy UG rec. need-based self-help aid	78
% UG borrow to pay for school	49
Average cumulative indebtedness	$22,300
% frosh need fully met	60
% ugrads need fully met	60
Average % of frosh need met	60
Average % of ugrad need met	60

State University of New York—College of Environmental Science and Forestry

Office of Undergraduate Admissions, SUNY-ESF, Syracuse, NY 13210 • Admissions: 315-470-6600

CAMPUS LIFE

Quality of Life Rating	90
Fire Safety Rating	98
Green Rating	99
Type of school	Public
Affiliation	No Affiliation
Environment	City

STUDENTS

Total undergrad enrollment	1,727
% male/female	55/45
% from out of state	18
% frosh from public high school	90
% frosh live on campus	95
% ugrads live on campus	30
# of fraternities (% ugrad men join)	26 (5)
# of sororities (% ugrad women join)	21 (5)
% African American	1
% Asian	3
% Caucasian	84
% Hispanic	4
% Native American	<1
% Pacific Islander	0
% Two or more races	3
% Race and/or ethnicity unknown	3
% international	2
# of countries represented	11

ACADEMICS

Academic Rating	79
% students returning for sophomore year	85
% students graduating within 4 years	47
% students graduating within 6 years	68
Calendar	Semester
Student/faculty ratio	13:1
Profs interesting rating	87
Profs accessible rating	78

Most classes have 10–19 students.

Most lab/discussion sessions have 10–19 students.

MOST POPULAR MAJORS

Environmental Science; Environmental Biology; Landscape Architecture

ABOUT THE SCHOOL

Located in Syracuse, SUNY's nationally renowned College of Environmental Science and Forestry offers twenty-four unique undergraduate programs, including a variety of specialties in addition to the obvious two within its name; fisheries science, landscape architecture, construction management, paper engineering, and wildlife sciences are just a few of them. Master's and PhD programs are also offered in these subjects. Students are often involved in research projects, and field trips are prominent in most classes. Undergraduates tell us ESF is "a small, personal school" with "tough" coursework. "Challenging but also very interesting and real." "They connect real-life problems to all the coursework." Professors are "fantastic" and "brilliant in their fields," as well as "supportive and easy to find and speak to." Students are impressed by faculty members who "can back up their teaching with real experiences." Discipline is a prized trait at ESF, as students find that "class schedules are very rigid," and that the "academic program is very specialized, so there is not a lot of flexibility with general studies and choosing minors." Students who put in a concerted effort regarding their studies and involvement in class will find ESF to be a fine match for them.

BANG FOR YOUR BUCK

ESF awards approximately half of its total institutional scholarships based on academic merit, with the other half based on financial need. There are many special scholarships available for students who live outside New York State to help them cover tuition costs. All students in the bioprocess engineering program, and the paper science and engineering programs, are required to complete a summer internship in a related industry, and they are encouraged to complete a semester-long paid internship. More than 95 percent of students in these programs are placed in a related job or graduate study within nine months of graduation. As a member of Raise, ESF offers "micro-scholarships" for students who pursue specific activities (like Eagle Scouts) and courses in high school. A long-standing partnership with Syracuse University just across the street means students can take classes there at no additional cost.

STUDENT LIFE

People at ESF universally "love the outdoors." To grossly generalize, "there are two loose groups at ESF." The "more populous" group is the "vegan, save-the-world" "tree huggers." Not surprisingly, these students "lean more toward the left." The other, smaller group is comprised of "fairly conservative" "hunters," who have "a management view of the environment." They "often major in forestry resources management, construction management, paper science engineering, or some such thing." "Somehow," members of both groups manage to get along pretty well. A student sums up campus life this way: "People think about saving the environment here. We are the people who genuinely care about where we live. The community here is great. There are clubs and organizations for everyone. There is a real sense of community within and outside of the school. Mostly, people enjoy the outdoors (no matter the weather) and enjoy healthful meals together. The music life is superb here." In general, most students are white and from the state of New York. The typical student "is conservationally minded, friendly and not afraid to show and be who they are at heart."

CAREER

Most students feel that ESF, and especially the faculty there, are "very helpful when it comes to finding jobs and internships." For example, ESF's partnership with the NY Department of Environmental Conservation produces fifty paid summer internships each year. The Career Services Office puts on an Environmental Career Fair for students "to gather employer and graduate school information, develop

State University of New York—College of Environmental Science and Forestry

FINANCIAL AID: 315-470-6706 • E-MAIL: ESFINFO@ESF.EDU • FAX: 315-470-6933 • WEBSITE: WWW.ESF.EDU

networks and meet organizations from a variety of sectors, including corporate, environmental, and not-for-profit." Students feel that their awareness of the environment and tough classes are what "will get SUNY-ESF students top notch jobs and lives after college."

GENERAL INFO

Activities: Choral groups, concert band, dance, drama/theater, jazz band, literary magazine, marching band, music ensembles, musical theater, pep band, radio station, student government, student newspaper, student-run film society, symphony orchestra, television station, yearbook, Campus Ministries, International Student Organization, 300 registered organizations. **Athletics (Intercollegiate):** *Men:* basketball, cross-country, golf, soccer, track. *Women:* cross-country, golf, soccer, track. **On-Campus Highlights:** Library, Green houses, Wildlife collection, Laboratories & Studios, Gateway Center, snack bar, student store. SUNY-ESF is on the campus of Syracuse University. Popular sites include: Carrier Dome, Crouse College (a historic building), Schine Student Center, Hendricks Chapel. **Environmental Initiatives:** (1) ESF's new student center is a LEED platinum rated building with a wood pellet fueled heating system. (2) Photovoltaic arrays/green roof. (3) College owns and manages 25,000 acres of forest (providing carbon offsets). Faculty are conducting government supported research in the development of ethanol and other renewable products from wood biomass. ESF has partnered with the NY State government and private industry to develop the state's first "biorefinery" aimed at producing ethanol and other chemical products from wood sugars. ESF has also developed a genetically engineered species of fast growth willow that is being grown as an alternative to corn use in ethanol production. Forty percent of all College vehicles (cars, maintenance vehicles, buses, GEM, etc.) are powered with renewable fuels, electric or hybrid technologies.

FINANCIAL AID

Students should submit: FAFSA, State aid form. Priority filing deadline is 3/1. The Princeton Review suggests that all financial aid forms be submitted as soon as possible after October 1. *Need-based scholarships/ grants offered:* Federal Pell, FSEOG, State scholarships/grants, Private scholarships, College/university scholarship or grant aid from institutional funds. *Loan aid offered:* Direct Subsidized Stafford Loans, Direct Unsubsidized Stafford Loans, Direct PLUS loans, Federal Perkins Loans. Applicants will be notified of awards on a rolling basis beginning 3/15. Federal Work-Study Program available. Institutional employment available.

BOTTOM LINE

ESF is highly specialized and selective; it is the oldest and largest environmental college in the country. The school enjoys a unique partnership with Syracuse University that gives ESF students special access to Syracuse classes, academic facilities, student clubs and organizations and other services while paying low state-supported tuition. SUNY's in-state and out-of-state tuition rates are among the lowest in the Northeast for public colleges.

CAREER INFORMATION FROM PAYSCALE.COM

ROI rating	86
Bachelor's and No Higher	
Median starting salary	$45,800
Median mid-career salary	$84,100
At Least Bachelor's	
Median starting salary	$44,800
Median mid-career salary	$79,300

SELECTIVITY

Admissions Rating	89
# of applicants	1,538
% of applicants accepted	51
% of acceptees attending	37
# offered a place on the wait list	151
% accepting a place on wait list	28
% admitted from wait list	40
# of early decision applicants	128
% accepted early decision	66

FRESHMAN PROFILE

Range SAT Critical Reading	530–630
Range SAT Math	550–630
Range ACT Composite	22–26
Minimum paper TOEFL	550
Minimum internet-based TOEFL	79
Average HS GPA	3.7
% graduated top 10% of class	30
% graduated top 25% of class	66
% graduated top 50% of class	95

DEADLINES

Early decision	
Deadline	12/1
Notification	1/15
Regular	
Priority	2/1
Nonfall registration?	Yes

FINANCIAL FACTS

Financial Aid Rating	90
Annual in-state tuition	$6,470
Annual out-of-state tuition	$16,320
Room and board	$15,040
Required fees	$1,633
Average need-based scholarship	$4,700
% needy frosh rec. need-based scholarship or grant aid	89
% needy UG rec. need-based scholarship or grant aid	93
% needy frosh rec. non-need-based scholarship or grant aid	53
% needy UG rec. non-need-based scholarship or grant aid	46
% needy frosh rec. need-based self-help aid	88
% needy UG rec. need-based self-help aid	87
% frosh rec. any financial aid	91
% UG rec. any financial aid	93
% frosh need fully met	45
% ugrads need fully met	69
Average % of frosh need met	83
Average % of ugrad need met	86

State University of New York—Maritime College

6 Pennyfield Ave, Throggs Neck, NY 10465 • Admissions: 718-409-7200 • Fax: 718-409-7465

CAMPUS LIFE

Quality of Life Rating	69
Fire Safety Rating	89
Green Rating	65
Type of school	Public
Affiliation	No affiliation
Environment	Metropolis

STUDENTS

Total undergrad enrollment	1,676
% male/female	90/10
% from out of state	24
% frosh live on campus	96
% ugrads live on campus	85
% African American	4
% Asian	5
% Caucasian	71
% Hispanic	11
% Native American	0
% Pacific Islander	0
% Two or more races	2
% Race and/or ethnicity unknown	5
% international	3
# of countries represented	14

ACADEMICS

Academic Rating	68
% students returning for sophomore year	87
% students graduating within 4 years	32
% students graduating within 6 years	56
Student/faculty ratio	17:1
Profs interesting rating	71
Profs accessible rating	75

Most classes have 20–29 students.
Most lab/discussion sessions have
20–29 students.

MOST POPULAR MAJORS

Transportation/Mobility Management; Naval
Architecture and Marine Engineering;
Mechanical Engineering

ABOUT THE SCHOOL

Located on the waterfront just north of New York City, SUNY Maritime College is the oldest and largest maritime school in the country, offering five engineering degrees, four Bachelor of Science degrees, and an Associate degree that can be completed in combination with preparation for a professional license as a United States Merchant Marine Officer. Every summer, cadets complete a Summer Sea Term, traveling the world on a 565-foot training ship in order to learn about the maritime industry and ship operations; cadets will visit at least twelve countries over the course of their studies at Maritime. "If you wish to work on ships or love the sea, this is the place for you." Students choose between the Civilian Program or the Regiment Program, with the Civilian program offering a more traditional college experience, as compared to the "very structured environment" of the Regiment, which does requires students to wear a uniform and live on campus.

BANG FOR YOUR BUCK

The historically high employment placement rate of 90% within three months of graduation is a heavy hitter in the value equation, and "Maritime College is a great school to go to if you want to be prepared for your real job upon graduation." The Coast Guard license and highly desired skills "gives the ticket for a student to pick where he or she wants to live after graduation" (and get paid handsomely). All incoming first-years and transfer students are automatically considered for the merit-based New Student Scholarships, which range from $2,500 to $7,500 per year, and the Cadet Appointment Program (CAP) allows elected officials to nominate a select few New York State residents to receive a four-year, full tuition scholarship.

STUDENT LIFE

"Life at Maritime is for sure different than life at any other college," to say the least. From a social perspective, "the uniform acts as an equalizer and people from various backgrounds and social strata tend to form friendships that might otherwise not have occurred." Students universally agree that the greatest part about going to Maritime is the Summer Sea Term. "Going to different countries abroad and learning seamanship skills are the best," says a student. Keeping up with the school work is essential and "takes up a lot of free time," but "sports help escape that" and this physically fit NCAA Division III school has fifteen varsity athletic teams, three club sport teams, a robust intramural program, a newly renovated gym and baseball court, and a military obstacle course. There are over one hundred clubs and sport options in total, and New York City is a bus or train ride away.

CAREER

Let's not bury the lede: Maritime College boasts a 90 percent job placement rate for its graduates, assisted by the fact that around 50 percent go on to utilize their license as a merchant marine (others go on to government, military, and private industry positions). The "very specific academic and practical learning" makes graduates highly employable (in both regiment and civilian programs), and employers recognize that Maritime graduates come equipped with life skills "like discipline and chain of command" that can be applied to the real world. Maritime graduates who visited PayScale.com reported an average starting salary of $62,100.

State University of New York— Maritime College

FINANCIAL AID: 718-409-7268 • E-MAIL: ADMISSIONS@SUNYMARITIME.EDU • WEBSITE: WWW.SUNYMARITIME.EDU

GENERAL INFO

Activities: Choral groups, jazz band, marching band, music ensembles, pep band, student government, yearbook, Campus Ministries, International Student Organization. **Organizations:** 30 registered organizations, 4 religious organizations. **Athletics (Intercollegiate):** *Men:* baseball, basketball, cross-country, football, ice hockey, lacrosse, riflery, soccer, swimming. *Women:* basketball, crew/rowing, cross-country, lacrosse, riflery, soccer, softball, swimming, volleyball. **On-Campus Highlights:** Fort Schuyler.

FINANCIAL AID

Students should submit: FAFSA. Applicants will be notified of awards on a rolling basis beginning in February. The Princeton Review suggests that all financial aid forms be submitted as soon as possible after October 1. *Need-based scholarships/grants offered:* Federal Pell, SEOG, State scholarships/grants, Private scholarships, College/ university scholarship or grant aid from institutional funds. *Loan aid offered:* Federal Perkins Loans, State Loans. Applicants will be notified of awards on a rolling basis beginning in February. Federal Work-Study Program available. Institutional employment available.

BOTTOM LINE

As with all of the SUNY schools, in-state residents get a big price cut on tuition, which runs $6,470, as compared to the $16,320 that out-of-staters will pay. For new students that are "in region" (see the school's website for eligible states), the cost is $9,710. Those in the Regiment of Cadets are required to live on campus all four years, with room and board (in a double) running an additional $11,516. On top of merit-based awards, financial aid is available; more than 75 percent of students receive some aid, with the average freshman scholarship/ grant coming to $4,263.

CAREER INFORMATION FROM PAYSCALE.COM

ROI rating	89
Bachelor's and No Higher	
Median starting salary	$65,200
Median mid-career salary	$134,000
At Least Bachelor's	
Median starting salary	$65,400
Median mid-career salary	$139,000
% alumni with high job meaning	65%
% STEM	46%

SELECTIVITY

Admissions Rating	84
# of applicants	1,342
% of applicants accepted	68
% of acceptees attending	36
# offered a place on the wait list	89
% accepting a place on wait list	98
% admitted from wait list	0
# of early decision applicants	134
% accepted early decision	51

FRESHMAN PROFILE

Range SAT Critical Reading	500–590
Range SAT Math	530–610
Range SAT Writing	470–550
Range ACT Composite	22–26
Minimum paper TOEFL	550
Minimum internet-based TOEFL	79
Average HS GPA	85.00
% graduated top 10% of class	13
% graduated top 25% of class	34
% graduated top 50% of class	79

DEADLINES

Notification	12/15
Other ED Deadline	11/1
Other ED Notification	12/15
Priority Deadline	1/31
Nonfall registration?	Yes

FINANCIAL FACTS

Financial Aid Rating	70
Annual in-state tuition	$6,470
Annual out-of-state tuition	$16,320
Room and board	$11,516
Required fees	$1,339
Average need-based scholarship	$5,521
% needy frosh rec. need-based scholarship or grant aid	54
% needy UG rec. need-based scholarship or grant aid	65
% needy frosh rec. non-need-based scholarship or grant aid	42
% needy UG rec. non-need-based scholarship or grant aid	33
% needy frosh rec. need-based self-help aid	68
% needy UG rec. need-based self-help aid	75
% frosh rec. any financial aid	83
% UG rec. any financial aid	78
% frosh need fully met	9
% ugrads need fully met	6
Average % of frosh need met	43
Average % of ugrad need met	44

ate University of New York—
Stony Brook University

Office of Admissions, Stony Brook, NY 11794-1901 • Admissions: 631-632-6868 • Financial Aid: 631-632-6840

CAMPUS LIFE

Quality of Life Rating	84
Fire Safety Rating	81
Green Rating	97
Type of school	Public
Affiliation	No Affiliation
Environment	Town

STUDENTS

Total undergrad enrollment	16,831
% male/female	54/46
% from out of state	8
% frosh from public high school	90
% frosh live on campus	85
% ugrads live on campus	51
# of fraternities (% ugrad men join)	18 (3)
# of sororities (% ugrad women join)	14 (3)
% African American	7
% Asian	24
% Caucasian	36
% Hispanic	11
% Native American	<1
% Pacific Islander	<1
% Two or more races	2
% Race and/or ethnicity unknown	7
% international	13
# of countries represented	90

ACADEMICS

Academic Rating	73
% students returning for sophomore year	90
% students graduating within 4 years	47
% students graduating within 6 years	68
Calendar	Semester
Student/faculty ratio	17:1
Profs interesting rating	68
Profs accessible rating	66

Most classes have 10–19 students.
Most lab/discussion sessions have 20–29 students.

MOST POPULAR MAJORS
Biology; Business Management; Health Science; Psychology

ABOUT THE SCHOOL

Stony Brook University with a total student population of about 25,000, sits on 1,040 acres of woodlands on the north shore of Long Island. The Research and Development Campus encompasses 246 acres adjacent to the main campus; there is also Southampton location. The university boasts more than 200 undergraduate majors, minors, and joint-degree programs, including rich research opportunities and a Fast Track MBA program. This creates an unparalleled first-year experience program for incoming freshmen. "The breadth of the school's curriculum is impressive," says one contented undergrad.

BANG FOR YOUR BUCK

Stony Brook "combines affordability and excellence with academic prestige," where students can learn from "world-renowned professors for a great price." The school offers many merit-based scholarships including those to valedictorians, salutatorians, and Intel Science Talent Search winners. There is a highly respected honors college, study-abroad opportunities in more than 30 countries and undergrads may pursue their master's through combined-degree programs. Students can also work with faculty on interesting projects; "it is relatively easy to find internships and research opportunities" as an undergraduate, especially with over 2,500 faculty members and centers like the Brookhaven National Laboratory nearby. First-year resident members of each college are housed together in the same residential quad, and there are also new undergraduate apartments. "I feel that the balance between independence and assistance has prepared me well," one student relates.

STUDENT LIFE

Most students agree that while there are definitely ways to have fun at Stony Brook University, you have to be proactive about finding them. "You can have fun, but it's not going to come to you," says a student. "You have to find the people that interest you, you have to go to the office and ask what's available." Part of the issue is that many students grew up near the campus, so they often head home for the weekends, leaving those who stay behind wondering how to entertain themselves. "I think that you have to be adventurous and go out and explore," says a student. "Some students are suckered into just staying in their dorms, but if they joined a club they would become incredibly happy." For those who seek them out, "there are programs every day, social events, and of course on and off-campus parties." There are also "AMAZING shows at our campus theater." There are also plenty of ways that small groups of friends can entertain themselves: "Most people either go to the mall, go to the restaurant located on campus, head over to the University Cafe or watch movies in their rooms." So while student activities might not be as plentiful as they would be at a more campus-oriented school, "if you are willing to seek out activities and events, you will never be bored."

CAREER

Students at Stony Brook are, for the most part "very serious about achieving whatever goal they have set for post graduation" and find the Career Center to be "really useful and the people extremely helpful." The Center provides career services to help students choose an area of academic interest and explore related fields; hosts industry-specific job fairs; connects students with alumni mentors; and provides online resources for job and internship services and networking. It also runs an Internship Contest that provides monetary awards and special recognition to students who "provide outstanding evidence of

State University of New York—Stony Brook University

E-MAIL: ENROLL@STONYBROOK.EDU • FAX: 631-632-9898 • WEBSITE: WWW.STONYBROOK.EDU

professionalism and the intrinsic value of career-related experience" during an off-campus internship. All in all, Stony Brook "provides a lot of opportunities for students who wish to get that extra something upon entering the working world." Of alumni who visit PayScale.com, 48 percent report feeling that they derive a high level of meaning from their jobs.

GENERAL INFO

Activities: Choral groups, concert band, dance, drama/theater, jazz band, literary magazine, marching band, music ensembles, musical theater, pep band, radio station, student government, student newspaper, student-run film society, yearbook, campus ministries. **Organizations:** 401 registered organizations, 21 honor societies, 24 religious organizations. 18 fraternities, 14 sororities. **Athletics (Intercollegiate):** *Men:* Baseball, basketball, cross-country, diving, football, lacrosse, soccer, swimming, tennis, track/field (outdoor), track/field (indoor). *Women:* Basketball, cross-country, diving, lacrosse, soccer, softball, swimming, tennis, track/field (outdoor), track/field (indoor), volleyball. **On-Campus Highlights:** Staller Center for the Arts, Sports Complex (including a new 4,000-seat arena) and Stadium, Student Activities Center, University Hospital, The Charles B. Wang Center.

FINANCIAL AID

Students should submit: FAFSA, State aid form. Priority filing deadline is 3/1. The Princeton Review suggests that all financial aid forms be submitted as soon as possible after October 1. *Need-based scholarships/grants offered:* Federal Pell, FSEOG, State scholarships/grants, Private scholarships, College/university scholarship or grant aid from institutional funds. *Loan aid offered:* Direct Subsidized Stafford Loans, Direct Unsubsidized Stafford Loans, Direct PLUS loans, Federal Perkins Loans. Applicants will be notified of awards on a rolling basis beginning 4/1. Federal Work-Study Program available. Institutional employment available.

BOTTOM LINE

There are more than 16,800 undergraduates at the school, with about 2,900 freshmen enrolling each year. In-state tuition is very reasonable, at just over $6,400; out-of-state students can expect that figure to rise to nearly $24,000. On-campus room and board is approximately $13,000. Books, supplies, and required fees will add another $3,400. However, options for aid are prevalent. About 69 percent of undergrads receive some manner of financial support, with 70 percent of average need being met. In general, aid packages tend to be about $12,100 per student; need-based gift aid averages $7,800. Students can expect to graduate with about $24,000 in loan debt.

CAREER INFORMATION FROM PAYSCALE.COM

ROI rating	88
Bachelor's and No Higher	
Median starting salary	$49,700
Median mid-career salary	$94,700
At Least Bachelor's	
Median starting salary	$49,900
Median mid-career salary	$98,100
% alumni with high job meaning	54%
% STEM	26%

SELECTIVITY

Admissions Rating	90
# of applicants	34,146
% of applicants accepted	41
% of acceptees attending	20
# offered a place on the wait list	3,512
% accepting a place on wait list	41
% admitted from wait list	22

FRESHMAN PROFILE

Range SAT Critical Reading	550–660
Range SAT Math	600–720
Range SAT Writing	540–660
Range ACT Composite	26–31
Minimum paper TOEFL	550
Minimum internet-based TOEFL	80
Average HS GPA	3.8
% graduated top 10% of class	46
% graduated top 25% of class	79
% graduated top 50% of class	96

DEADLINES

Regular	
Priority	1/15
Notification	4/1
Nonfall registration?	Yes

FINANCIAL FACTS

Financial Aid Rating	81
Annual in-state tuition	$6,470
Annual out-of-state tuition	$23,710
Room and board	$12,882
Required fees	$2,529
Average need-based scholarship	$7,765
% needy frosh rec. need-based scholarship or grant aid	89
% needy UG rec. need-based scholarship or grant aid	83
% needy frosh rec. non-need-based scholarship or grant aid	12
% needy UG rec. non-need-based scholarship or grant aid	6
% needy frosh rec. need-based self-help aid	89
% needy UG rec. need-based self-help aid	90
% frosh rec. any financial aid	76
% UG rec. any financial aid	69
% UG borrow to pay for school	58
Average cumulative indebtedness	$23,592
% frosh need fully met	19
% ugrads need fully met	17
Average % of frosh need met	71
Average % of ugrad need met	66

State University of New York— University at Buffalo

12 Capen Hall, Buffalo, NY 14260-1660 • Admissions: 716-645-6900 • Financial Aid: 716-645-2450

CAMPUS LIFE

Quality of Life Rating	**70**
Fire Safety Rating	**62**
Green Rating	**98**
Type of school	Public
Affiliation	No affiliation
Environment	City

STUDENTS

Total undergrad enrollment	19,951
% male/female	56/44
% from out of state	3
% frosh live on campus	75
% ugrads live on campus	35
# of fraternities (% ugrad men join)	19 (1)
# of sororities (% ugrad women join)	13 (2)
% African American	7
% Asian	14
% Caucasian	48
% Hispanic	6
% Native American	0
% Pacific Islander	0
% Two or more races	2
% Race and/or ethnicity unknown	5
% international	16
# of countries represented	87

ACADEMICS

Academic Rating	**79**
% students returning for sophomore year	88
% students graduating within 4 years	55
% students graduating within 6 years	74
Student/faculty ratio	13:1
Profs interesting rating	69
Profs accessible rating	66

Most classes have 20–29 students.
Most lab/discussion sessions have 20–29 students.

MOST POPULAR MAJORS

Social Sciences; Business Administration and Management; Engineering

ABOUT THE SCHOOL

Offering more than 400 undergraduate, graduate and professional degree programs, SUNY—Buffalo (UB for short) is one of the nation's premier public research universities. UB is divided into three campuses: South Campus in Northeast Buffalo, North Campus in the suburban enclave of Amherst, and the downtown campus. A school with this much to offer is bound to be large, making it "easy not to attend class and fall through the cracks, so one must be self-motivated to do well." "If you're not serious about what you're doing, you will get left behind." The school puts a lot of emphasis on research, and there are labs that are open twenty-four hours a day. "There really isn't an extreme concerning politics, but it mostly seems to be a pretty moderate campus. You have your liberal groups and your right-wingers, but no one is really outspoken." We're also informed that the school has grown in their environmental awareness and are clearly trying to become more environmentally sound.

BANG FOR YOUR BUCK

The talented freshmen of UB are considered for merit-based scholarships, which range from $2,500 to the total cost of attendance depending on academic performance. The university awards about $12.6 million in merit-based scholarships to their incoming class. Scholarship receipiants may also be invited to participate in scholarly communities. These programs offer expanded educational opportunities both in and out of the classroom. The University at Buffalo has a variety of internship and experiential-education programs, which allow students to gain an advantage in the marketplace upon graduation. One student relates that "programs are all of the highest quality, translating [into] a best-value education for students."

STUDENT LIFE

School life at UB is "blissful, mainly due to the level of freedom" that students are given. The sheer size of the school gives students a natural need for autonomy, and the daily routine beyond classes is what you make of it. As a Division I school, sporting events are always a popular point of relaxation, and students have more than 300 clubs and organizations to choose from. Whatever your passion or passing interest, "everyone has a place in this large and diverse student population"; most students do hail from New York State, but there is a sizable international population. Students "often congregate to chat or watch movies when there is nothing to do," and the university's location in western New York provides easy access to Niagara Falls, Canada (the "skiing is excellent" for those who take advantage during the long winters).

State University of New York—University at Buffalo

E-MAIL: UB-ADMISSIONS@BUFFALO.EDU • FAX: 716-645-6411 • WEBSITE: WWW.BUFFALO.EDU

CAREER

The university "is known for its research" and carries quite the cachet with science, engineering, and tech employers. The Career Services department maintains a comprehensive list of jobs and internships, and provides services such as advising, an online résumé/job bank, and interview/résumé planning, and job fairs throughout the year. UB has an extensive Mentor Network for students to utilize, and alumni can even take advantage of Career Services' resources. Of the graduates who visited PayScale.com, 47 percent reported feeling that their job had a meaningful impact on the world, and the starting salary came in at $47,800.

GENERAL INFO

Activities: Choral groups, concert band, dance, drama/theater, jazz band, literary magazine, marching band, music ensembles, musical theater, pep band, radio station, student government, student newspaper, student-run film society, symphony orchestra, television station, campus ministries, international student organization. **Organizations:** 215 registered organizations, 29 honor societies, 35 religious organizations. 24 fraternities, 16 sororities. **Athletics (Intercollegiate):** *Men:* Baseball, basketball, cross-country, football, soccer, swimming, tennis, track/field (outdoor), wrestling. *Women:* Basketball, crew/rowing, cross-country, soccer, softball, swimming, tennis, track/field (outdoor), volleyball. **On-Campus Highlights:** Center for the Arts, Alumni Arena and Athletic Stadium, Center for Computational Research, apartment-style student housing, The Commons (on-campus shopping).

FINANCIAL AID

Students should submit: FAFSA. Applicants will be notified of awards on a rolling basis beginning 2/1. The Princeton Review suggests that all financial aid forms be submitted as soon as possible after October 1. *Need-based scholarships/grants offered:* Federal Pell, SEOG, State scholarships/grants, Private scholarships, College/university scholarship or grant aid from institutional funds, Federal Nursing Scholarships. *Loan aid offered:* Direct Subsidized Stafford Loans, Direct Unsubsidized Stafford Loans, Direct PLUS loans, Federal Perkins Loans, Federal Nursing Loans. Applicants will be notified of awards on a rolling basis beginning 2/1. Federal Work-Study Program available. Institutional employment available.

BOTTOM LINE

SUNY–Buffalo is able to provide great education at a low price. And at a fraction of the cost of comparable private colleges and universities, a UB education is also an exceptional value. Tuition for in-state students is $6,470; those from out-of-state can expect to pay $23,710 per year. Room and board will add another $13,548 or so. Eighty-five percent of needy freshmen receive need-based scholarship or grant aid, with the average gift aid package being close to $5,500; the school is also able to meet 63 percent of demonstrated student need.

CAREER INFORMATION FROM PAYSCALE.COM

ROI rating	**86**
Bachelor's and No Higher	
Median starting salary	$47,500
Median mid-career salary	$82,100
At Least Bachelor's	
Median starting salary	$48,800
Median mid-career salary	$85,200
% alumni with high job meaning	52%
% STEM	24%

SELECTIVITY

Admissions Rating	**85**
# of applicants	23,629
% of applicants accepted	60
% of acceptees attending	26
# offered a place on the wait list	1,657
% accepting a place on wait list	34
% admitted from wait list	32
# of early decision applicants	384
% accepted early decision	92

FRESHMAN PROFILE

Range SAT Critical Reading	510–610
Range SAT Math	550–660
Range ACT Composite	24–29
Minimum paper TOEFL	550
Minimum internet-based TOEFL	79
Average HS GPA	3.60
% graduated top 10% of class	27
% graduated top 25% of class	61
% graduated top 50% of class	91

DEADLINES

Deadline	11/15
Priority	11/15
Notification	2/1
Nonfall registration?	yes

FINANCIAL FACTS

Financial Aid Rating	**91**
Annual in-state tuition	$6,470
Annual out-of-state tuition	$23,710
Room and board	$13,548
Required fees	$3,104
Average need-based scholarship	$5,435
% needy frosh rec. need-based scholarship or grant aid	85
% needy UG rec. need-based scholarship or grant aid	57
% needy frosh rec. non-need-based scholarship or grant aid	22
% needy UG rec. non-need-based scholarship or grant aid	28
% needy frosh rec. need-based self-help aid	80
% needy UG rec. need-based self-help aid	60
% frosh rec. any financial aid	65
% UG rec. any financial aid	64
% ugrads need fully met	26
Average % of frosh need met	64
Average % of ugrad need met	63

Stevens Institute of Technology

CASTLE POINT ON HUDSON, HOBOKEN, NJ 07030 • ADMISSIONS: 201-216-5194 • FAX: 201-216-8348

CAMPUS LIFE

Quality of Life Rating	89
Fire Safety Rating	98
Green Rating	78
Type of school	Private
Affiliation	No Affiliation
Environment	Town

STUDENTS

Total undergrad enrollment	2,976
% male/female	71/29
% from out of state	37
% frosh from public high school	72
% frosh live on campus	91
% ugrads live on campus	71
# of fraternities (% ugrad men join)	12 (25)
# of sororities (% ugrad women join)	6 (25)
% African American	2
% Asian	10
% Caucasian	66
% Hispanic	9
% Native American	<1
% Pacific Islander	0
% Two or more races	0
% Race and/or ethnicity unknown	8
% international	4
# of countries represented	30

ACADEMICS

Academic Rating	78
% students returning for sophomore year	94
% students graduating within 4 years	38
% students graduating within 6 years	82
Calendar	Semester
Student/faculty ratio	10:1
Profs interesting rating	66
Profs accessible rating	67

Most classes have 20–29 students.
Most lab/discussion sessions have
20–29 students.

MOST POPULAR MAJORS

Mechanical Engineering; Bioengineering
and Biomedical Engineering; Computer
Science

ABOUT THE SCHOOL

Stevens Institute of Technology is a private institution in Hoboken, New Jersey. It boasts a student to faculty ratio of ten to one, and it offers thirty-five different majors, the most popular of which are Biomedical Engineering, Computer Science, and Mechanical Engineering. The student body is 71 percent male and 66 percent white, and a vast majority of students are full-time. At fifty-five acres, it is a relatively small campus. Students feel that the professors are extremely knowledgeable and have "relevant, often recent real world experience," noting that they are also "accessible and generally helpful." However, some students say that "the administration seems more interested in bringing in professors who are good at research." Stevens, students note, "is all about technology and getting every student the exact job they want or getting every student into the graduate program they want." Overall, "Stevens gets students ready for professional careers and is a good starting place for smart and self-motivated people."

BANG FOR YOUR BUCK

Tuition at Stevens Institute of Technology comes to $49,016, with the average aid package coming to around $29,139. Students note that 67 percent of their needs are met, and of these students whose needs are met, 74 percent are freshman. Past that, students choose Stevens "because of its interdisciplinary engineering curriculum," and "sizable alumni scholarship offers." Many students remark upon the "good" to "great" scholarships they received from Stevens. A business student remarks, "The connections that I have been able to establish outside the classroom are truly invaluable. Stevens Professors and Administrators provide an excellent support network." An example of such is "the support network for fellowships and scholarship like the Rhodes and Marshall Scholarships."

STUDENT LIFE

Students at Stevens Institute feel that the average students is someone who "plays video games and hangs out with friends in between classes," and "probably plays on a club sports team." At Stevens, "engineering dominates the school, and the course load is demanding in its math, physics and engineering classes." Students feel that there are "a great deal of athletes," and that "there is a place for everyone here but it is not your average clique oriented school, there isn't really the 'popular kid' and the 'nerds.' Everyone here is a little nerdy and it bodes for a strong community on campus."

CAREER

The average starting salary of a Stevens Institute of Technology graduate is $66,800, and 48 percent report that their job has a great deal of meaning. Students feel that Stevens, given its location in Hoboken supplies students with "more opportunities for internships and jobs due to having the better of both worlds with New York City and New Jersey that can offer so much." A Civil Engineering major notes that "the job placement percentage is also very high, and is one of the school's biggest appeals." In addition, the cooperative education and internship programs allow students to work with professionals in corporate and laboratory settings, with employers such as Colgate, Exxon Mobil, L'Oreal, Goldman Sachs, Citigroup, MICRO, Palmolive, and Panasonic.

Stevens Institute of Technology

FINANCIAL AID: 201-216-5555 • E-MAIL: ADMISSIONS@STEVENS.EDU • WEBSITE: WWW.STEVENS.EDU

GENERAL INFO

Activities: Choral groups, concert band, dance, drama/theater, jazz band, literary magazine, music ensembles, musical theater, pep band, radio station, student government, student newspaper, student-run film society, symphony orchestra, television station, yearbook, Campus Ministries, International Student Organization. **Organizations:** 120 registered organizations, 10 honor societies, 5 religious organizations. 12 fraternities, 6 sororities. **Athletics (Intercollegiate):** *Men:* baseball, basketball, cross-country, fencing, golf, lacrosse, soccer, swimming, tennis, track/field (outdoor), track/field (indoor), volleyball, wrestling. *Women:* basketball, cross-country, equestrian sports, fencing, field hockey, lacrosse, soccer, softball, swimming, tennis, track/field (outdoor), track/field (indoor), volleyball. **On-Campus Highlights:** Schaefer Athletic Center, DeBaun Auditorium, Castle Point Lookout, NYC skyline views, Babbio Center, Wesley J. Howe Center.

FINANCIAL AID

Students should submit: FAFSA, CSS/Financial Aid PROFILE. Priority filing deadline is 2/15. The Princeton Review suggests that all financial aid forms be submitted as soon as possible after October 1. *Need-based scholarships/grants offered:* Federal Pell, FSEOG, State scholarships/grants, Private scholarships, College/university scholarship or grant aid from institutional funds, United Negro College Fund. *Loan aid offered:* Direct Subsidized Stafford Loans, Direct Unsubsidized Stafford Loans, Direct PLUS loans, Federal Perkins Loans, State Loans. Federal Work-Study Program available. Institutional employment available.

BOTTOM LINE

The tuition at the Stevens Institute of Technology comes to about $49,016, and is up to $65,070 with fees, room and board, and everything else. Stevens meets an average of 67 percent of student need. The average need-based scholarship comes to $13,299; 99 percent of freshmen and 91 percent of all undergraduates receive some form of financial aid.

CAREER INFORMATION FROM PAYSCALE.COM

ROI rating	87
Bachelor's and No Higher	
Median starting salary	$66,800
Median mid-career salary	$120,000
At Least Bachelor's	
Median starting salary	$67,200
Median mid-career salary	$120,000
% alumni with high job meaning	47%
% STEM	84%

SELECTIVITY

Admissions Rating	94
# of applicants	6,540
% of applicants accepted	44
% of acceptees attending	24
# offered a place on the wait list	1,047
% accepting a place on wait list	34
% admitted from wait list	52
# of early decision applicants	798
% accepted early decision	56

FRESHMAN PROFILE

Range SAT Critical Reading	590–680
Range SAT Math	650–745
Range ACT Composite	29–32
Minimum paper TOEFL	550
Minimum internet-based TOEFL	80
Average HS GPA	3.9
% graduated top 10% of class	62
% graduated top 25% of class	92
% graduated top 50% of class	99

DEADLINES

Early decision	
Deadline	11/15
Notification	12/15
Regular	
Deadline	2/1
Notification	4/1
Nonfall registration?	No

FINANCIAL FACTS

Financial Aid Rating	82
Annual tuition	$49,016
Room and board	$14,350
Required fees	$1,704
Average need-based scholarship	$13,299
% needy frosh rec. need-based scholarship or grant aid	43
% needy UG rec. need-based scholarship or grant aid	61
% needy frosh rec. non-need-based scholarship or grant aid	97
% needy UG rec. non-need-based scholarship or grant aid	94
% needy frosh rec. need-based self-help aid	62
% needy UG rec. need-based self-help aid	72
% frosh rec. any financial aid	99
% UG rec. any financial aid	91
% UG borrow to pay for school	75
Average cumulative indebtedness	$48,244
% frosh need fully met	28
% ugrads need fully met	20
Average % of frosh need met	74
Average % of ugrad need met	67

Swarthmore College

500 College Avenue, Swarthmore, PA 19081 • Admissions: 610-328-8300 • Fax: 610-328-8580

#34 COLLEGE THAT PAYS YOU BACK

ABOUT THE SCHOOL
Swarthmore College is among the most renowned liberal arts schools in the country. The locus of Swarthmore's greatness lies in the quality and passion of its faculty ("Some of my professors have knocked me to the floor with their brilliance"). A student/faculty ratio of eight to one ensures that students have close, meaningful engagement with their professors. "It's where to go for a real education—for learning for the sake of truly learning, rather than just for grades," says a student. The college's Honors Program features small groups of dedicated and accomplished students working closely with faculty, with an emphasis on independent learning, and helps further the school's reputation as "a community where everyone pushes each other toward success." External examiners who are experts in their fields, such as theater professionals from the Tisch School at NYU and Google software engineers, evaluate seniors in the Honors Program through written and oral examinations. Swatties are a bright and creative lot "who don't get enough sleep because they're too busy doing all they want to do in their time here." Professors and administrators are extremely supportive and "view the students as responsible adults, and thus leave them to their own devices when they are out of class." Students also enjoy an expansive curriculum—about 600 course offerings each year. Swarthmore is part of the Tri-College Consortium (along with Bryn Mawr and Haverford), which means that students can take courses at those schools and use their facilities.

BANG FOR YOUR BUCK
Swarthmore College maintains a need-blind admission policy. Admission here is not contingent on your economic situation, and financial aid awards meet 100 percent of admitted students' demonstrated need. Financial aid is also available for some international students. Best of all, all Swarthmore financial aid awards are loan-free (though some students choose to borrow to cover their portion). In most cases, Swarthmore students may apply their financial aid toward the cost of participation in a study abroad program. Finally, the annual activity fee covers everything from digital printing to sports matches, campus movie screenings to lectures and dance performances, making for a cash-free campus.

STUDENT LIFE
Students are "not sure if there is a typical Swattie," but suspect that "the defining feature among us is that each person is brilliant at something: maybe dance, maybe quantum physics, maybe philosophy." One undergrad sums up, "While it is tough to generalize … one word definitely applies to us all: busy." Swarthmore's small size combined with its vast number of clubs and organizations provide opportunities to participate in pretty much whatever you want, and if not "you can start your own club." "There are student musical performances, drama performances, movies, speakers, and comedy shows," along with all kinds of school-sponsored events, so "there is almost always something to do on the weekend." When they can spare a couple of hours, many Swatties like to blow off steam in nearby Philadelphia, which is easily accessible by public transportation, including the train station located right on campus.

Swarthmore College

FINANCIAL AID: 610-328-8358 • E-MAIL: ADMISSIONS@SWARTHMORE.EDU • WEBSITE: WWW.SWARTHMORE.EDU

CAREER

Swarthmore's Career Services does its part to help students reach their fullest potential by offering a variety of useful resources. Personalized career counseling advises undergrads on their options for major selection, internships, externships, and graduate school applications. The Career Cafés engage the community on broad topics, like women in leadership or sustainable farming, that may have career implications. And, of course, a packed events calendar lets students network with alumni, attend panel discussions, and impress potential employers at recruiting consortiums. Take note of Swarthmore's extensive externship program. It matches students with alumni volunteers for week-long job-shadowing experiences in laboratories, museums, publishing companies, labor unions, leading think-tanks, and other places where you might like to work someday. Alumni who visited PayScale.com reported an average starting salary of $51,000, and 49 percent think their work makes the world a better place.

GENERAL INFO

Activities: Choral groups, dance, drama/theater, jazz band, literary magazine, music ensembles, opera, student government, student newspaper, student-run film society, symphony orchestra, yearbook, campus ministries, international student organization. **Organizations:** 150 registered organizations, 3 honor societies, 12 religious organizations. 2 fraternities, 1 sorority. **Athletics (Intercollegiate):** *Men:* Baseball, basketball, cross-country, golf, lacrosse, soccer, swimming, tennis, track/field (outdoor), track/field (indoor). *Women:* Badminton, basketball, cross-country, field hockey, lacrosse, soccer, softball, swimming, tennis, track/field (outdoor), track/field (indoor), volleyball.

FINANCIAL AID

Students should submit: FAFSA, CSS/Financial Aid PROFILE, State aid form, Noncustodial PROFILE, Business/Farm Supplement. Priority filing deadline is 2/18. The Princeton Review suggests that all financial aid forms be submitted as soon as possible after October 1. *Need-based scholarships/grants offered:* Federal Pell, FSEOG, State scholarships/grants, Private scholarships, College/university scholarship or grant aid from institutional funds. *Loan aid offered:* Direct Subsidized Stafford Loans, Direct Unsubsidized Stafford Loans, Direct PLUS loans, Federal Perkins Loans, State Loans, College/university loans from institutional funds. Applicants will be notified of awards on or about 4/1. Federal Work-Study Program available. Institutional employment available.

THE BOTTOM LINE

Swarthmore has staggeringly generous financial aid resources, and it will meet 100 percent of your demonstrated need without loans. The average need-based financial aid award here is more than $45,000. Don't assume you won't receive aid because your family is too wealthy and definitely—please!—don't assume you can't afford Swarthmore because your family isn't wealthy enough.

CAREER INFORMATION FROM PAYSCALE.COM

ROI rating	**91**
Bachelor's and No Higher	
Median starting salary	$48,000
Median mid-career salary	$109,000
At Least Bachelor's	
Median starting salary	$50,400
Median mid-career salary	$115,000
% alumni with high job meaning	51%
% STEM	25%

SELECTIVITY

Admissions Rating	**98**
# of applicants	7,818
% of applicants accepted	12
% of acceptees attending	42
# of early decision applicants	567
% accepted early decision	36

FRESHMAN PROFILE

Range SAT Critical Reading	670–760
Range SAT Math	670–770
Range SAT Writing	680–760
Range ACT Composite	30–34
% graduated top 10% of class	88
% graduated top 25% of class	99
% graduated top 50% of class	100

DEADLINES

Early decision	
Deadline	11/15
Notification	12/15
Regular	
Deadline	1/1
Notification	4/1
Nonfall registration?	No

FINANCIAL FACTS

Financial Aid Rating	**95**
Annual tuition	$48,720
Room and board	$14,446
Required fees	$384
Average need-based scholarship	$45,907
% needy frosh rec. need-based scholarship or grant aid	100
% needy UG rec. need-based scholarship or grant aid	100
% needy frosh rec. non-need-based scholarship or grant aid	0
% needy UG rec. non-need-based scholarship or grant aid	0
% needy frosh rec. need-based self-help aid	97
% needy UG rec. need-based self-help aid	98
% frosh rec. any financial aid	58
% UG rec. any financial aid	52
% frosh need fully met	100
% ugrads need fully met	100
Average % of frosh need met	100
Average % of ugrad need met	100

Texas A&M University—College Station

PO Box 30014, College Station, TX 77842-3014 • Admissions: 979-845-3741 • Fax: 979-847-8737

CAMPUS LIFE

Quality of Life Rating	**91**
Fire Safety Rating	**95**
Green Rating	**92**
Type of school	Public
Affiliation	No Affiliation
Environment	City

STUDENTS

Total undergrad enrollment	48,960
% male/female	51/49
% from out of state	4
% frosh live on campus	70
% ugrads live on campus	23
# of fraternities (% ugrad men join)	36 (3)
# of sororities (% ugrad women join)	26 (6)
% African American	3
% Asian	6
% Caucasian	65
% Hispanic	22
% Native American	<1
% Pacific Islander	<1
% Two or more races	3
% Race and/or ethnicity unknown	<1
% international	1
# of countries represented	81

ACADEMICS

Academic Rating	**72**
% students returning for sophomore year	90
% students graduating within 4 years	51
% students graduating within 6 years	79
Calendar	Semester
Student/faculty ratio	20:1
Profs interesting rating	74
Profs accessible rating	74

Most classes have 20–29 students.
Most lab/discussion sessions have 20–29 students.

MOST POPULAR MAJORS
Engineering; Biomedical Sciences; Business Administration and Management

ABOUT THE SCHOOL

As one of the ten largest universities in the country—the school is home to over 50,000 students, about 40,000 of whom are undergraduates—Texas A&M may embody the idea that everything is bigger in Texas. However, that doesn't mean that students don't feel at home here. The community of Texas A&M bonds over its traditions and pervasive school spirit. Students at Texas A&M have a great "sense of pride that . . . motivates them to do well because they're part of something bigger than themselves." Students tend to feel that they are "part of a huge family" at Texas A&M. As one student says, "From the outside looking in, you can't understand it. From the inside looking out, you can't explain it." Perhaps part of that mysterious spirit lies in the school's devotion to their "Aggies" athletic teams. From women's volleyball to baseball, Texas A&M fields top-quality athletic teams, and of course, "Saturdays in the fall are owned by football." Founded back in the 1890s, the Aggies Football team has appeared in thirty bowls, winning thirteen of them as well as three national championships. The professors "all have life experiences working with the topics that they teach, making them the perfect resource for information," one student says. Another sums up the Texas A&M experience thusly: "Texas A&M University is not only one of the best universities in terms of higher education. At Texas A&M you learn to be a well-rounded, moral, and ethical person."

BANG FOR YOUR BUCK

If you love college sports, and especially football, it is hard to do better than Texas A&M. About 650 student athletes compete in twenty varsity sports. In 2012, Texas A&M officially joined the storied Southeastern Conference (SEC). Kyle Field is always "packed for home games." This is all part of the Aggie school spirit which extends to the vast Aggie alumni network. "Aggie alumni are loyal to their school forever" and can be a great source of support for students looking to enter postcollege life. The school has a wealth of resources for students and over 950 student organizations for students to participate in. Those who attend Texas A&M tend to enjoy the experience. A full 91 percent of freshmen return for sophomore year.

STUDENT LIFE

These Aggies proudly declare that "there is rarely a dull moment" at Texas A&M. First off, sports fans should rejoice since we're told that "football is central to [student's] live[s] in the fall, with [the] stadium routinely seeing 80,000 in attendance." And, in general, Texas A&M students are pretty active. Many undergrads "spend their free time in the state-of-the-art rec center equipped with a climbing wall, a boulder wall, numerous [pieces of] exercise equipment, an indoor track, and countless exercise classes such as Zumba, Pilates, yoga, and many more." Additionally, "two-stepping and dancing is popular on the weekends." There are also plenty of "frat parties or house parties" to attend. And just off-campus students will find "four dollar movies, many dance halls, endless restaurants to eat at . . . a large mall . . . an ice skating rink, bowling alley, and miniature golf place." What more could a college student desire?

CAREERS

The Career Center at Texas A&M does a tremendous job of assisting undergraduates in their career search. Students can connect with over 3,000 potential employers, including more than eighty percent of the Fortune 500 companies. Clearly, these undergrads are in demand. Many students happily share that "the Aggie Network is [another] good [avenue] for getting jobs after graduation." Of course, prior to seeking

Texas A&M University—College Station

FINANCIAL AID: 979-845-3236 • E-MAIL: ADMISSIONS@TAMU.EDU • WEBSITE: WWW.TAMU.EDU

out interviews, undergrads can arrange one-on-one meetings to review resumes, cover letters, etc. Lastly, prospective (and current) students will be delighted to discover that the average starting salary, according to PayScale.com, for recent A&M grads is $54,300.

GENERAL INFO

Activities: Choral groups, concert band, dance, drama/theater, jazz band, literary magazine, marching band, music ensembles, musical theater, radio station, student government, student newspaper, student-run film society, symphony orchestra, television station, yearbook. **Organizations:** Campus Ministries, International Student Organization 1,000 registered organizations, 34 honor societies, 77 religious organizations. 20 fraternities, 36 sororities. **Athletics (Intercollegiate):** *Men:* baseball, basketball, cross-country, diving, football, golf, riflery, swimming, tennis, track/field (outdoor), track/field (indoor). *Women:* basketball, cross-country, diving, equestrian sports, golf, riflery, soccer, softball, swimming, tennis, track/field (outdoor), track/field (indoor), volleyball. **On-Campus Highlights:** Student Recreation Center, Kyle Field, Corps of Cadets, George Bush Presidential Library/Museum, Memorial Student Center. **Environmental Initiatives:** Aggie Green Fund, sustainable land use, green building practices, smart energy, optimization of energy clusters, waste management through recycling and composting.

FINANCIAL AID

Students should submit: FAFSA. Priority filing deadline is 3/15. The Princeton Review suggests that all financial aid forms be submitted as soon as possible after October 1. *Need-based scholarships/grants offered:* Federal Pell, FSEOG, State scholarships/grants, Private scholarships, College/university scholarship or grant aid from institutional funds. *Loan aid offered:* Direct Subsidized Stafford Loans, Direct Unsubsidized Stafford Loans, Direct PLUS loans, Federal Perkins Loans, State Loans, College/university loans from institutional funds. Applicants will be notified of awards on a rolling basis beginning 4/1. Federal Work-Study Program available. Institutional employment available.

BOTTOM LINE

Texas A&M's price tag depends on whether you are from the great state of Texas or not. In-state students pay only $6,149 in tuition, while out-of-state students will pay $24,742. In addition, student should expect to spend another $13,977 on housing, fees, books, and supplies. Three-quarters of the freshmen student body receive some aid, while almost half will take out loans. The average student will accrue $25,005 in debt during their Texas A&M career. The bottom line is that Texas A&M is a big school with big resources and big pride.

CAREER INFORMATION FROM PAYSCALE.COM

ROI rating	89
Bachelor's and No Higher	
Median starting salary	$55,200
Median mid-career salary	$98,300
At Least Bachelor's	
Median starting salary	$56,100
Median mid-career salary	$99,500
% alumni with high job meaning	52%
% STEM	29%

SELECTIVITY

Admissions Rating	89
# of applicants	33,970
% of applicants accepted	66
% of acceptees attending	46
# offered a place on the wait list	0

FRESHMAN PROFILE

Range SAT Critical Reading	520–640
Range SAT Math	550–670
Range SAT Writing	490–610
Range ACT Composite	25–30
Minimum paper TOEFL	550
Minimum internet-based TOEFL	80
% graduated top 10% of class	66
% graduated top 25% of class	91
% graduated top 50% of class	99

DEADLINES

Regular	
Deadline	12/1
Nonfall registration?	Yes

FINANCIAL FACTS

Financial Aid Rating	81
Annual in-state tuition	$6,679
Annual out-of-state tuition	$26,857
Room and board	$10,368
Required fees	$3,351
Average need-based scholarship	$9,818
% needy frosh rec. need-based scholarship or grant aid	94
% needy UG rec. need-based scholarship or grant aid	86
% needy frosh rec. non-need-based scholarship or grant aid	13
% needy UG rec. non-need-based scholarship or grant aid	8
% needy frosh rec. need-based self-help aid	48
% needy UG rec. need-based self-help aid	59
% frosh rec. any financial aid	75
% UG rec. any financial aid	70
% UG borrow to pay for school	43
Average cumulative indebtedness	$24,276
% frosh need fully met	37
% ugrads need fully met	28
Average % of frosh need met	73
Average % of ugrad need met	66

Trinity College (CT)

300 Summit Street, Hartford, CT 06016 • Admissions: 860-297-2180 • Fax: 860-297-2287

ABOUT THE SCHOOL

Trinity College is an "elite liberal arts school with a reputation matched by few other schools." Serious students flock here for the "gorgeous campus, outstanding teacher accessibility, good athletics, and an overall great academic environment." Replete with traditional New England architecture and set on a green campus which encompasses over 100 acres in downtown Hartford, Connecticut, students' number one reason for attending Trinity is "the strong sense of community and its unique identity as a college located on a beautiful green campus that is also in the heart of a city." From its "strong Division III athletics," to its "close faculty-student interaction," to "amazing study abroad opportunities," and a "great political science department" that benefits from being "two blocks away from the state capitol, which is great for internships," at Trinity "you get a chance to figure out what you are truly passionate about." Trinity's unique Guided Studies program, in which students undertake a fixed curriculum of interdisciplinary study to survey the entirety of Western civilization from the classical age to the present, forms the backbone of the school's academics for some and "really gives the student body an opportunity to try new fields of study." Says one happy Trinity undergraduate, "Even the president of the school . . . is accessible. He goes on the quest orientation hiking trip for first-year students and regularly attends various student events on campus."

BANG FOR YOUR BUCK

Trinity offers the prestige and individual attention of a small liberal arts school with the benefits its urban backdrop provides. Though the school's price tag is in line with other serious private colleges of its rank, students at Trinity are offered two main advantages: real personalized attention and truly distinct curricular options, which allow students to craft an individualized academic course of study. From its "interdisciplinary neuroscience major and a professionally accredited engineering degree program," to its "unique Human Rights Program, a Health Fellows Program, and interdisciplinary programs such as the Cities Program, Interdisciplinary Science Program, and InterArts," active learning with a host of flexibility forms the backbone of academic experience at Trinity.

STUDENT LIFE

Many students here hail from the tri-state area and the word "preppy" gets tossed about a lot in this "great community" where "you can walk across campus at any point in the day and run into ten of your friends." "Trinity's campus is beautiful and students here like to stick pretty close to home," says one of this "definitely not a suitcase school." Off campus, there are "concerts, plays, and all kinds of ways to entertain yourself"; Hartford has "amazing restaurants," movie theaters, and bowling alleys, and the campus movie theater (the Cinestudio) is a big haunt. Events thrown by the arts and cultural houses are popular weekend pastimes, and Greek life and school sponsored concerts/events are very well-attended. Mostly because of Trinity's small size, "the social scene is so unique and is one of the aspects that students past and present value the most."

CAREER

Trinity students are "very engaged and involved outside of class, often expanding their maturity and job experiences in internships [and] leadership opportunities." Career Services helps students out a lot with these jobs and internship searches through TrinityRecruiting (the online job listing service) with more than 200 internships for credit, and "alums are eager to help out the student body as well." Each student can take part in the two-day intensive Bantam Sophomore Success program, and alumni mentoring is available to everyone. Networking opportunities are especially fruitful if you want to go into finance or investment banking.

Trinity College

FINANCIAL AID: 860-297-2047 • E-MAIL: ADMISSIONS.OFFICE@TRINCOLL.EDU • WEBSITE: WWW.TRINCOLL.EDU

The starting salary for Trinity College graduates who visited PayScale.com was $47,800, and 54 percent said they felt their job had a meaningful impact on the world.

GENERAL INFO

Activities: Choral groups, dance, drama/theater, jazz band, literary magazine, music ensembles, musical theater, radio station, student government, student newspaper, student-run film society, yearbook. **Organizations:** Campus Ministries, International Student Organization, Model UN, 105 registered organizations, 5 honor societies, 5 religious organizations. 7 fraternities, 3 sororities. **Athletics (Intercollegiate):** *Men:* baseball, basketball, crew/rowing, cross-country, diving, football, golf, ice hockey, lacrosse, soccer, squash, swimming, tennis, track/field (outdoor), track/field (indoor), wrestling. *Women:* basketball, crew/rowing, cross-country, diving, field hockey, ice hockey, lacrosse, soccer, softball, squash, swimming, tennis, track/field (outdoor), track/field (indoor), volleyball.

FINANCIAL AID

Students should submit: FAFSA, CSS/Financial Aid PROFILE, Noncustodial PROFILE, Business/Farm Supplement. Regular filing deadline is 3/1. The Princeton Review suggests that all financial aid forms be submitted as soon as possible after October 1. *Need-based scholarships/grants offered:* Federal Pell, FSEOG, State scholarships/grants, Private scholarships, College/university scholarship or grant aid from institutional funds. *Loan aid offered:* Direct Subsidized Stafford Loans, Direct Unsubsidized Stafford Loans, Direct PLUS loans, Federal Perkins Loans, College/university loans from institutional funds. Applicants will be notified of awards on or about 4/1. Federal Work-Study Program available. Institutional employment available.

BOTTOM LINE

Whether they're drawn to this liberal arts hamlet for its "school spirit, amazing alumni, and career placement," or the feeling that they are attending a truly competitive college with "a city at your fingertips," undergraduates at Trinity have access to all the luxuries and opportunities that Trinity's reputation as a "little Ivy" affords. However, what sets the college apart is its small student-to-faculty ratio and commitment to individualized attention, which promises the added assurance that talented students won't fall between the cracks. The school earns high marks when it comes to financial aid despite its significant tuition of $50,350, with another $13,680 in room and board. Recent statistics signify that the school meets 100 percent of freshman financial need and remains committed to that percentage across all four years.

CAREER INFORMATION FROM PAYSCALE.COM

ROI rating	**88**
Bachelor's and No Higher	
Median starting salary	$49,900
Median mid-career salary	$86,500
At Least Bachelor's	
Median starting salary	$50,600
Median mid-career salary	$85,800
% alumni with high job meaning	54%
% STEM	9%

SELECTIVITY

Admissions Rating	**93**
# of applicants	7,570
% of applicants accepted	33
% of acceptees attending	22
# offered a place on the wait list	1,796
% accepting a place on wait list	32
% admitted from wait list	1
# of early decision applicants	506
% accepted early decision	59

FRESHMAN PROFILE

Range SAT Critical Reading	540–670
Range SAT Math	570–700
Range SAT Writing	550–680
Range ACT Composite	26–31
Minimum paper TOEFL	550
Minimum internet-based TOEFL	95
% graduated top 10% of class	64
% graduated top 25% of class	84
% graduated top 50% of class	98

DEADLINES

Early decision	
Deadline	11/15
Notification	12/15
Regular	
Deadline	1/1
Notification	4/1
Nonfall registration?	No

FINANCIAL FACTS

Financial Aid Rating	**97**
Annual tuition	$50,350
Room and board	$13,680
Required fees	$2,410
Average need-based scholarship	$41,684
% needy frosh rec. need-based scholarship or grant aid	95
% needy UG rec. need-based scholarship or grant aid	96
% needy frosh rec. non-need-based scholarship or grant aid	3
% needy UG rec. non-need-based scholarship or grant aid	6
% needy frosh rec. need-based self-help aid	74
% needy UG rec. need-based self-help aid	74
% frosh rec. any financial aid	48
% UG rec. any financial aid	45
% frosh need fully met	100
% ugrads need fully met	100
Average % of frosh need met	98
Average % of ugrad need met	100

Trinity University

ONE TRINITY PLACE, SAN ANTONIO, TX 78212-7200 • ADMISSIONS: 210-999-7207 • FAX: 210-999-8164

CAMPUS LIFE

Quality of Life Rating	94
Fire Safety Rating	94
Green Rating	60*
Type of school	Private
Affiliation	Presbyterian
Environment	Metropolis

STUDENTS

Total undergrad enrollment	2,273
% male/female	48/52
% from out of state	24
% frosh from public high school	73
% frosh live on campus	100
% ugrads live on campus	77
# of fraternities (% ugrad men join)	6 (17)
# of sororities (% ugrad women join)	7 (29)
% African American	4
% Asian	6
% Caucasian	55
% Hispanic	20
% Native American	<1
% Pacific Islander	0
% Two or more races	5
% Race and/or ethnicity unknown	2
% international	7
# of countries represented	66

ACADEMICS

Academic Rating	90
% students returning for sophomore year	90
% students graduating within 4 years	72
% students graduating within 6 years	83
Calendar	Semester
Student/faculty ratio	9:1
Profs interesting rating	93
Profs accessible rating	94

Most classes have 10–19 students.
Most lab/discussion sessions have
20–29 students.

MOST POPULAR MAJORS
Communication; Engineering Science;
Accounting

ABOUT THE SCHOOL

This private school in San Antonio, Texas, gives students a "great environment, great people, [and a] great education." The small student body—roughly 2,270—and the requirement that undergraduates must live on campus for three years gives the school a small-town feel in a big state. Trinity is a "small, liberal arts college . . . that has the comfort of a small secluded area [with the added] wonders of a big city." One Communication major says, Trinity is "a close-knit university with high standards of excellence and competency that challenge students, while creating a comfortable environment." The student to teacher ratio of roughly 9:1 helps foster this sense of community and the professors "know all of their students by name and are extremely accessible outside of class." With 47 majors offered, Trinity has something for everyone: "Some of the best aspects of Trinity are its emphasis on academic goals, assistance in preparing students for life after college, and, most importantly, the sense of community it provides between students, faculty, and alumni."

BANG FOR YOUR BUCK

Trinity meets an average of 94 percent of its students' financial needs and scholarship options draw in many prospective students, including international ones, who are eligible for financial assistance. One French and art history double major notes that Trinity is "warm and supportive but challenging—kind of like San Antonio's weather. The plentiful scholarship money didn't hurt either." Ninety-eight percent of freshmen get some form of financial aid, with 93 percent of other undergraduates receive financial assistance. Of those students receiving financial aid, 99 percent of them receiving need-based assistance. A Political Science major says that Trinity's "financial aid packages are great so there are many middle-class students and with such a smorgasbord of ethnicities, economic statuses, and cultures," the students "all learn from one another." According to the school's website, "All Trinity scholarships are renewable on an annual basis for up to eight semesters of undergraduate study, as long as the recipient meets each award's specified criteria." Most of these scholarships are merit-based but there are some that combine merit with financial need.

STUDENT LIFE

While "it's not uncommon to hear students worrying about tests," they are also "often looking forward to some big event over the weekend" such as themed parties or fundraisers for local charities. The school's location in San Antonio—"we are about five minutes from downtown"—also affords students access to clubs and restaurants. On campus, Greek life plays a significant role: the school has seven sororities and seven fraternities, with roughly 29 percent of women joining a sorority and 17 percent of men joining a fraternity. Though "Greek life is a popular way of getting involved," students can find "almost any type of . . . group on campus," where there are more than 115 registered student organizations. Even though students like to kick back and have fun, "when it's time to study, people study hard" and it's "not considered anti-social to not hang out with your friends a couple of nights before a big test. Overall, Trinity's students are an accepting fun-loving lot."

CAREER

According to PayScale.com, 55 percent of Trinity graduates consider their careers to be instrumental in making the world a better place. The average starting salary for a Trinity graduate is roughly $42,300, and popular jobs include marketing manager, financial analyst, and executive director. Popular majors at Trinity include Communication, Business Administration, and Computer Science. One Communication major singled out a grant the school received from AT&T that

Trinity University

allowed Trinity to "renovate the . . . communications lab [so] that is has [state-of-the-art] equipment," which helps to "further [the] interests and careers of students going into a media field." According to the school's website, Career Services "fosters career advancement and contributes to the growth and success of Trinity graduates." The office's website offers students access to TigerJobs, the school's online recruitment system. The school's websites emphasizes that "Career Services at Trinity is a comprehensive and centralized service that works with both students (from first-years to seniors) and alumni." Trinity's small size makes it so "everyone really knows everyone, even alumni, which is really great because it makes networking so much easier."

GENERAL INFO

Activities: Choral groups, concert band, dance, drama/theater, jazz band, literary magazine, music ensembles, musical theater, opera, pep band, radio station, student government, student newspaper, student-run film society, symphony orchestra, television station, yearbook, Campus Ministries, International Student Organization, Model UN. **Organizations:** 115 registered organizations, 24 honor societies, 7 religious organizations. 7 fraternities, 7 sororities. **Athletics (Intercollegiate):** *Men:* baseball, basketball, cross-country, diving, football, golf, soccer, swimming, tennis, track/field (outdoor). *Women:* basketball, cross-country, diving, golf, soccer, softball, swimming, tennis, track/field (outdoor), volleyball. **On-Campus Highlights:** Stieren Theatre, Laurie Auditorium, Coates Library, Bell Athletic Center, Coates University Center, Northrup Hall, and the Center for the Sciences and Innovation.

FINANCIAL AID

Students should submit: FAFSA, CSS/Financial Aid PROFILE. Priority filing deadline is 2/15. The Princeton Review suggests that all financial aid forms be submitted as soon as possible after October 1. *Need-based scholarships/grants offered:* Federal Pell, FSEOG, State scholarships/grants, Private scholarships, College/university scholarship or grant aid from institutional funds. *Loan aid offered:* Direct Subsidized Stafford Loans, Direct Unsubsidized Stafford Loans, Direct PLUS loans, Federal Perkins Loans, State Loans, College/university loans from institutional funds. Applicants will be notified of awards on or about 3/15. Federal Work-Study Program available. Institutional employment available.

BOTTOM LINE

A year at Trinity costs roughly $52,314, including tuition, room and board. With the average need-based gift aid for undergraduates being approximately $27,899, the average Trinity student graduates with $36,626 in loan debt, but 49 percent of graduates graduate with no debt.

CAREER INFORMATION FROM PAYSCALE.COM

ROI rating	89
Bachelor's and No Higher	
Median starting salary	$42,300
Median mid-career salary	$90,000
At Least Bachelor's	
Median starting salary	$43,900
Median mid-career salary	$93,400
% alumni with high job meaning	55%
% STEM	16%

SELECTIVITY

Admissions Rating	90
# of applicants	5,563
% of applicants accepted	48
% of acceptees attending	23
# offered a place on the wait list	257
% accepting a place on wait list	43
% admitted from wait list	34
# of early decision applicants	71
% accepted early decision	70

FRESHMAN PROFILE

Range SAT Critical Reading	580–690
Range SAT Math	580–680
Range SAT Writing	560–660
Range ACT Composite	27–32
Average HS GPA	3.5
% graduated top 10% of class	47
% graduated top 25% of class	75
% graduated top 50% of class	96

DEADLINES

Early decision	
Deadline	11/1
Notification	12/15
Early action	
Deadline	11/1
Notification	12/15
Regular	
Deadline	2/1
Notification	4/1
Nonfall registration?	Yes

FINANCIAL FACTS

Financial Aid Rating	90
Annual tuition	$39,560
Room and board	$12,754
Average need-based scholarship	$27,899
% needy frosh rec. need-based scholarship or grant aid	100
% needy UG rec. need-based scholarship or grant aid	99
% needy frosh rec. non-need-based scholarship or grant aid	36
% needy UG rec. non-need-based scholarship or grant aid	23
% needy frosh rec. need-based self-help aid	63
% needy UG rec. need-based self-help aid	67
% frosh rec. any financial aid	98
% UG rec. any financial aid	93
% UG borrow to pay for school	51
Average cumulative indebtedness	$36,626
% frosh need fully met	83
% ugrads need fully met	58
Average % of frosh need met	98
Average % of ugrad need met	94

Truman State University

100 East Normal Avenue, Kirksville, MO 63501 • Admissions: 660-785-4114 • Fax: 660-785-7456

CAMPUS LIFE

Quality of Life Rating	89
Fire Safety Rating	98
Green Rating	60*
Type of school	Public
Affiliation	No Affiliation
Environment	Village

STUDENTS

Total undergrad enrollment	5,853
% male/female	41/59
% from out of state	17
% frosh from public high school	88
% frosh live on campus	98
% ugrads live on campus	48
# of fraternities (% ugrad men join)	13 (8)
# of sororities (% ugrad women join)	6 (10)
% African American	4
% Asian	2
% Caucasian	80
% Hispanic	3
% Native American	<1
% Pacific Islander	<1
% Two or more races	3
% Race and/or ethnicity unknown	2
% international	7
# of countries represented	50

ACADEMICS

Academic Rating	80
% students returning for sophomore year	89
% students graduating within 4 years	55
% students graduating within 6 years	73
Calendar	Semester
Student/faculty ratio	16:1
Profs interesting rating	79
Profs accessible rating	83

Most classes have 20–29 students.
Most lab/discussion sessions have fewer than 10 students.

MOST POPULAR MAJORS

Business Administration and Management; Biology; Psychology

ABOUT THE SCHOOL

Truman students aren't shy about discussing their school's "extremely well-deserved academic reputation," nor should they be: the school is Missouri's only highly selective public university, and students are here due to hard work, in order to work hard. The "grade-conscious" students here at the "Harvard of the Midwest" receive an education grounded in the liberal arts and sciences, and the school keeps a constant eye on its applicability to their futures, incorporating critical thinking, writing, and leadership-skill-building opportunities along the way to a degree. Many experiential-learning opportunities exist all across campus, in which students can gain practical knowledge that will be relevant to future schooling and careers; the Career Center sets up a yearly Career Expo and Non-Profit Fair in order to expose students to employers and give them the chance to hone their interviewing, résumé, and professional skills. The classes are difficult, but "serve to develop the students into well-prepared graduates ready to face postcollege life"; many include a service learning component. Students are also able to diversify their studies across multiple subjects and throughout multiple countries by taking advantage of the numerous study abroad options, many of which can be covered by financial aid.

BANG FOR YOUR BUCK

Truman offers a private school education at a public price; students and their families can even set up a flexible payment plan through the Business Office. The school offers four separate types of loans for students, covering everything from tuition to a new computer to study abroad, and there are numerous federal and state aid options also available. Automatic scholarships are offered to incoming freshmen based on academic merit, and additional opportunities to apply for endowed foundation scholarships occur each spring. The school understands that everything costs money (except the application—it's free!), and their comprehensive financial aid programs can be used to make sure that students are able to focus on their studies. One out-of-stater says, "Between Truman scholarships and private scholarships, I'm basically being paid to go here." Basically, if a student wants to attend Truman, then numbers can be crunched.

While the deal Truman offers may seem too good to be true, the quality of the education on offer here remains high. Students report their professors "really push you to work hard," and "are available beyond their scheduled office hours and do their best to make sure we understand the material." Classes are "small and engaging," enabling a "fantastic one-on-one experience between professors and students."

STUDENT LIFE

Students coined the "term T.T.S. (Typical Truman Student) [...] to describe academically focused, very studious students." Here, "college life is hectic and amazing all at the same time." Truman brings "tons of really great activities, shows, bands, etc., to campus to keep us entertained," and though homework consumes much of a student's day, "there is always time to [... see] a comedian or performance." Kirksville, Missouri may not be a buzzing metropolis, but "part of the fun of Truman is to find unorthodox things to do"—"you can be a huge political advocate, involved in protests on the quad; you can become involved in community service locally and nationwide; or you can work in a lab to make discoveries." Students are pleased with the facilities, including "newly renovated" dorms, and the "excellent" library and say the campus is "beautiful, and the atmosphere is very welcoming."

Truman State University

FINANCIAL AID: 660-785-4130 • E-MAIL: ADMISSIONS@TRUMAN.EDU • WEBSITE: WWW.TRUMAN.EDU

CAREER

The fall semester gets a jumpstart at Truman with Career Week, hosted by the Career Center, complete with speakers, employer information sessions, and a career expo that has included Boeing, the Federal Bureau of Investigation, IBM, and Target. Other career calendar highlights are a spring Non-Profit conference, Alumni Mock Interview Day, and a host of grad school prep events like "How to Attend Graduate School for Free." Alumni who visited PayScale.com report an average starting salary of $39,900, and 56 percent believe their works hold a high level of meaning.

GENERAL INFO

Activities: Choral groups, concert band, dance, drama/theater, jazz band, literary magazine, marching band, music ensembles, musical theater, opera, pep band, radio station, student government, student newspaper, student-run film society, symphony orchestra, television station, campus ministries, international student organization. **Organizations:** 227 registered organizations, 18 honor societies, 16 religious organizations. 12 fraternities, 6 sororities. **Athletics (Intercollegiate):** *Men:* Baseball,basketball, cross-country, football, golf, soccer, swimming, tennis, track/field (outdoor), track/field (indoor), wrestling. *Women:* Basketball, cross-country, golf, soccer, softball, swimming, tennis, track/field (outdoor), track/field (indoor), volleyball.

FINANCIAL AID

Students should submit: FAFSA. Priority filing deadline is 4/1. The Princeton Review suggests that all financial aid forms be submitted as soon as possible after October 1. *Need-based scholarships/grants offered:* Federal Pell, FSEOG, State scholarships/grants, Private scholarships, College/university scholarship or grant aid from institutional funds. *Loan aid offered:* Direct Subsidized Stafford Loans, Direct Unsubsidized Stafford Loans, Direct PLUS loans, Federal Perkins Loans, Federal Nursing Loans, College/university loans from institutional funds. Applicants will be notified of awards on a rolling basis beginning 3/1. Federal Work-Study Program available. Institutional employment available.

BOTTOM LINE

Residents of Missouri pay $7,152 in tuition; nonresidents pay just $13,636, which is still a bargain. There is one full-ride award offered to incoming freshmen: the General John J. Pershing Scholarship, which includes an additional stipend for a future study abroad experience. The Harry S. Truman Leadership scholarship (for Missouri residents only) offers a limited number of $10,000 awards and a four-year leadership development program. Financial aid programs to help fund undergraduate research and study abroad experiences are also available.

CAREER INFORMATION FROM PAYSCALE.COM

ROI rating	87
Bachelor's and No Higher	
Median starting salary	$40,300
Median mid-career salary	$72,000
At Least Bachelor's	
Median starting salary	$42,200
Median mid-career salary	$72,600
% alumni with high job meaning	42%
% STEM	17%

SELECTIVITY

Admissions Rating	88
# of applicants	3,900
% of applicants accepted	79
% of acceptees attending	41

FRESHMAN PROFILE

Range SAT Critical Reading	580–730
Range SAT Math	560–680
Range ACT Composite	25–30
Minimum paper TOEFL	550
Minimum internet-based TOEFL	79
Average HS GPA	3.8
% graduated top 10% of class	47
% graduated top 25% of class	79
% graduated top 50% of class	97

DEADLINES

Regular	
Priority	12/1
Nonfall registration?	Yes

FINANCIAL FACTS

Financial Aid Rating	87
Annual in-state tuition	$7,152
Annual out-of-state tuition	$13,636
Room and board	$8,558
Required fees	$304
Average need-based scholarship	$7,171
% needy frosh rec. need-based scholarship or grant aid	99
% needy UG rec. need-based scholarship or grant aid	94
% needy frosh rec. non-need-based scholarship or grant aid	96
% needy UG rec. non-need-based scholarship or grant aid	79
% needy frosh rec. need-based self-help aid	70
% needy UG rec. need-based self-help aid	78
% frosh rec. any financial aid	99
% UG rec. any financial aid	86
% UG borrow to pay for school	56
Average cumulative indebtedness	$24,220
% frosh need fully met	43
% ugrads need fully met	36
Average % of frosh need met	88
Average % of ugrad need met	83

Tufts University

BENDETSON HALL, MEDFORD, MA 02155 • ADMISSIONS: 617-627-3170 • FAX: 617-627-3860

CAMPUS LIFE

Quality of Life Rating	93
Fire Safety Rating	98
Green Rating	94
Type of school	Private
Affiliation	No Affiliation
Environment	Town

STUDENTS

Total undergrad enrollment	5,290
% male/female	50/50
% from out of state	76
% frosh from public high school	56
% frosh live on campus	100
% ugrads live on campus	65
# of fraternities (% ugrad men join)	10 (18)
# of sororities (% ugrad women join)	4 (18)
% African American	4
% Asian	11
% Caucasian	58
% Hispanic	6
% Native American	<1
% Pacific Islander	<1
% Two or more races	4
% Race and/or ethnicity unknown	7
% international	9
# of countries represented	74

ACADEMICS

Academic Rating	93
% students returning for sophomore year	97
% students graduating within 4 years	88
% students graduating within 6 years	93
Calendar	Semester
Student/faculty ratio	9:1
Profs interesting rating	88
Profs accessible rating	84

Most classes have 10–19 students.
Most lab/discussion sessions have
10–19 students.

MOST POPULAR MAJORS
International Relations and Affairs; Biology;
Computer Science

#31 COLLEGE THAT PAYS YOU BACK

ABOUT THE SCHOOL
Some of the reasons Tufts students love their school are the "beautiful campus," "international focus," "diverse community," "proximity to Boston," and the "really chill vibe." This is a university that wants students to be "exploring passions and relating them to the world today." The size of the school is "not too big, not too small," but just right for many students. "Tufts is well known for being very liberal, focused on internationalism and global citizenship," a Religion major states. This is a place where "people aren't afraid to study and be intellectual." Often regarded as a "Little Ivy," Tufts offers a world-class academic education. Tufts professors are "highly accessible," "engaging and knowledgeable." "Professors have the students best interest at heart, so they do all they can to make sure we succeed," one student reports. A Political Science major says that "at Tufts, you're surrounded by so many intelligent, engaged, and interesting people in a supportive, collaborative learning environment."

BANG FOR YOUR BUCK
Although Tufts tuition is not insignificant, there are many opportunities for aid, loans, and scholarships. "There are a lot of work study programs offered at Tufts and a lot of people on complete financial aid," an International Relations student confirms. The Student Employment Office helps students get jobs on-campus or off and regularly posts jobs to the JobX and TuftsLife websites. The school has forty-four Tufts-specific scholarships and awards for everything from Fine Arts and Social Justice to various STEM majors. Prospective applicants can view the entire list online. Prospective applicants can also use the school's online Net Price Calculator to get an idea what kind of aid they can expect if accepted.

STUDENT LIFE
"The campus culture is thriving and alive," one student says, "and as such it really encourages students to merge their academic and social interests and pursue both in a passionate way." Your average student at Tufts is "fun, passionate," "geeky" and likely an "activist." "The variety of clubs and activities available is amazing" and most students get "involved in many clubs and activities, campaigns, grassroots organizing, athletic teams, volunteer organizations, jobs, etc." "The Tufts Dance Collective and Quidditch clubs are some of the most popular and fun," one student helpfully suggests. Unlike many universities, there are "not too many 'cliques'" here and students tend to get along with each other. "The best way to fit in at Tufts is to be yourself, even if that sounds cheesy." If there is a Tufts uniform, it's "skinny jeans, a vintage sweater, worn-in shoes, and framed glasses" along with a "MacBook Pro" softly playing indie music. On campus, there are "extensive" student-run events and many students show up "for theater, dance and musical performances." When students need to get off campus, Boston is "less than an hour" away.

Tufts University

FINANCIAL AID: 617-627-2000 • E-MAIL: ADMISSIONS.INQUIRY@ASE.TUFTS.EDU • WEBSITE: WWW.TUFTS.EDU

CAREER

"The school's strong reputation has helped me get summer jobs and internships," one student reports. This is a common sentiment among Tufts students. The university's reputation and proximity to Boston provide students with many opportunities to get a head start on their post-college careers. The "great alumni network" also helps students find "jobs or internships after college." The school frequently holds events like the Career Carnival and Tufts Career Fair along with consulting sessions. Fully 91 percent of the Class of 2013 had found full-time employment or were in graduate school by 2014. The website PayScale.com reports an average starting salary of $51,900 for Tufts grads and an average mid-career salary of $123,600.

GENERAL INFO

Activities: Choral groups, concert band, dance, drama/theater, jazz band, literary magazine, marching band, music ensembles, musical theater, opera, pep band, radio station, student government, student newspaper, student-run film society, symphony orchestra, television station, yearbook, Campus Ministries, International Student Organization, Model UN. **Organizations:** 160 registered organizations, 4 honor societies, 6 religious organizations. 10 fraternities, 5 sororities. **Athletics (Intercollegiate):** *Men:* baseball, basketball, crew/rowing, cross-country, diving, football, golf, ice hockey, lacrosse, sailing, soccer, squash, swimming, tennis, track/field (outdoor), track/field (indoor). *Women:* basketball, cheerleading, crew/rowing, cross-country, diving, fencing, field hockey, golf, lacrosse, sailing, soccer, softball, squash, swimming, tennis, track/field (outdoor), track/field (indoor), volleyball. **On-Campus Highlights:** The Aidekman Arts Center, Tisch Library, Edwin Ginn Library, Tisch Sports and Fitness Center, Ellis Oval, Meyer Campus Center.

FINANCIAL AID

Students should submit: FAFSA, CSS/Financial Aid PROFILE, Noncustodial PROFILE. Regular filing deadline is 2/15. The Princeton Review suggests that all financial aid forms be submitted as soon as possible after October 1. *Need-based scholarships/grants offered:* Federal Pell, FSEOG, State scholarships/grants, Private scholarships, College/university scholarship or grant aid from institutional funds. *Loan aid offered:* Direct Subsidized Stafford Loans, Direct Unsubsidized Stafford Loans, Direct PLUS loans, Federal Perkins Loans, College/university loans from institutional funds. Applicants will be notified of awards on or about 4/1. Federal Work-Study Program available. Institutional employment available.

BOTTOM LINE

The baseline tuition at Tufts is $49,520 for the 2014-15 academic year. Room and board are an additional $13,904. Adding the various fees, a student can expect a bill of $61,277 before any aid or scholarships. Students who are already on a health insurance plan can have $2,224 of that total waived.

CAREER INFORMATION FROM PAYSCALE.COM

ROI rating	92
Bachelor's and No Higher	
Median starting salary	$54,200
Median mid-career salary	$115,000
At Least Bachelor's	
Median starting salary	$55,400
Median mid-career salary	$115,000
% alumni with high job meaning	60%
% STEM	23%

SELECTIVITY

Admissions Rating	97
# of applicants	19,063
% of applicants accepted	16
% of acceptees attending	44
# of early decision applicants	1,839
% accepted early decision	39

FRESHMAN PROFILE

Range SAT Critical Reading	680–750
Range SAT Math	690–770
Range SAT Writing	680–750
Range ACT Composite	30–33
Minimum paper TOEFL	600
Minimum internet-based TOEFL	100

DEADLINES

Early decision	
Deadline	11/1
Notification	12/15
Regular	
Deadline	1/1
Notification	4/1
Nonfall registration?	No

FINANCIAL FACTS

Financial Aid Rating	95
Annual tuition	$51,304
Room and board	$13,566
Required fees	$1,126
Average need-based scholarship	$39,908
% needy frosh rec. need-based scholarship or grant aid	92
% needy UG rec. need-based scholarship or grant aid	93
% needy frosh rec. non-need-based scholarship or grant aid	6
% needy UG rec. non-need-based scholarship or grant aid	4
% needy frosh rec. need-based self-help aid	83
% needy UG rec. need-based self-help aid	89
% frosh rec. any financial aid	37
% UG rec. any financial aid	38
% UG borrow to pay for school	38
Average cumulative indebtedness	$26,185
% frosh need fully met	100
% ugrads need fully met	100
Average % of frosh need met	100
Average % of ugrad need met	100

Tulane University

6823 St. Charles Avenue, New Orleans, LA 70118 • Admissions: 504-865-5731 • Fax: 504-862-8715

CAMPUS LIFE

Quality of Life Rating	**97**
Fire Safety Rating	**95**
Green Rating	**89**
Type of school	Private
Affiliation	No Affiliation
Environment	City

STUDENTS

Total undergrad enrollment	6,662
% male/female	41/59
% from out of state	76
% frosh from public high school	58
% frosh live on campus	99
% ugrads live on campus	45
# of fraternities (% ugrad men join)	12 (31)
# of sororities (% ugrad women join)	12 (51)
% African American	4
% Asian	4
% Caucasian	77
% Hispanic	6
% Native American	<1
% Pacific Islander	<1
% Two or more races	4
% Race and/or ethnicity unknown	4
% international	3
# of countries represented	37

ACADEMICS

Academic Rating	**88**
% students returning for sophomore year	92
% students graduating within 4 years	72
% students graduating within 6 years	83
Calendar	Semester
Student/faculty ratio	9:1
Profs interesting rating	79
Profs accessible rating	85

Most classes have 10–19 students.
Most lab/discussion sessions have 10–19 students.

ABOUT THE SCHOOL

Tulane "is a place where learning is put center-stage." "The academic opportunities are unending" and are all about "preparing students for the 'real-world.'" "The campus is beautiful, the atmosphere is vibrant and professors are very friendly and helpful," one student says. Perhaps the biggest draw is the "location, location, location!" Students cannot stop raving about "the culturally diverse classroom of the city of New Orleans." "The people, the food, the vibe, the city, the weather, the festivals, the irreplaceable and second to none culture!" gushes one student. Perhaps this is why "the smart 'cool' kids go to Tulane." Tulane instituted a core curriculum as part of their post-Katrina Renewal Plan. This includes seminars for freshmen, public services classes, and a capstone program that gives students experience in their field. Tulane has "small classes taught by real professors." The "extremely personable and engaging" professors are "easy to talk to" and "very interested in their subject." As one student explains, "just like New Orleans, Tulane is quirky, classy (with underlying chaos), optimistic, and not without a sense of humor."

BANG FOR YOUR BUCK

Tulane is an especially attractive school to Louisiana residents. The school awards millions in both need-based aid and merit-based scholarships to applicants living in Louisiana. Tulane even offers guaranteed admission to Louisiana students who meet their academic requirements through the Focus Louisiana program. Students from other states have plenty of opportunity for aid and scholarships too. Tulane offers "no-loan assistance" to students whose families gross income is less than $75,000 a year. Everyone who applies is considered for Tulane's partial tuition merit scholarships, which range from $10,000 to $32,000. In addition, the school awards full-tuition scholarships that students can apply for as well as alternative financing options like a monthly payment plan to help families spread out expenses. Students who stay on as 5th Year masters students get discounted tuition during their additional year of graduate study.

STUDENT LIFE

The student body at Tulane reflects "the vivacious and colorful culture of New Orleans." The "super diverse student body" is hard to generalize, but most students are "smart, quirky, and unique." "The typical student is very friendly, academically motivated, and usually has some hidden talent," one student explains. "We're mainly Ivy-league rejects who all wanted to get out of our hometowns and have a new experience," a Philosophy student says. Greek life is big and "MARDI GRAS IS HUGE." "There's frequently live music," and students are always busy. "If you ask a Tulane student what they do in their free time be prepared for a laundry list of clubs and activities," one student warns. "Campus is a wonderful setting with just enough trees, quads, and bikes around to let you forget that you're in a major city." However, most students "love to explore the city" of New Orleans, which "is absolutely the best city to go to college in."

Tulane University

FINANCIAL AID: 504-865-5723 • E-MAIL: UNDERGRAD.ADMISSION@TULANE.EDU • WEBSITE: WWW.TULANE.EDU

CAREER

One of the biggest benefits of Tulane is the dedicated professors, many of whom make the extra effort to help students on their career paths. "I've had professors email me links to internships," one student reports. Another tells us, "My neuroscience advisor, Dr. Wee, is always working to network us with professionals so we can have a leg up after we graduate." As a core requirement of the undergrad curriculum, public service allows students to apply knowledge and skills from classroom study to real-world projects. Students also have good things to say about the jobs and opportunities that Tulane's Career Center provides. The Hire Tulane Grads website makes it easy for employers to post jobs and find qualified students, and Career Wave, an all day event, brings speakers from companies like Saks, Gil Group, and the NBA to campus. Payscale reports an average starting salary of $45,100.

GENERAL INFO

Activities: Choral groups, concert band, dance, drama/theater, jazz band, literary magazine, marching band, music ensembles, musical theater, pep band, radio station, student government, student newspaper, student-run film society, television station, yearbook. **Organizations:** 250+ registered organizations, 43 honor societies, 11 religious organizations. 12 fraternities, 12 sororities. **Athletics (Intercollegiate):** *Men:* baseball, basketball, cross-country, football, tennis, track/field (outdoor). *Women:* basketball, cross-country, diving, golf, swimming, tennis, track/field (outdoor), track/field (indoor), volleyball. **On-Campus Highlights:** Amistad Research Center, Newcomb Art Gallery, Reily Recreation Center, Howard Tilton Memorial Library, PJ's Coffee Shop.

FINANCIAL AID

Students should submit: FAFSA, CSS/Financial Aid PROFILE, Noncustodial PROFILE, Business/Farm Supplement. Priority filing deadline is 2/15. The Princeton Review suggests that all financial aid forms be submitted as soon as possible after October 1. *Need-based scholarships/grants offered:* Federal Pell, FSEOG, State scholarships/grants, Private scholarships, College/university scholarship or grant aid from institutional funds. *Loan aid offered:* Direct Subsidized Loans, Direct Unsubsidized Loans, Direct PLUS loans, Federal Perkins Loans. Applicants will be notified of awards on a rolling basis beginning 3/15. Federal Work-Study Program available. Institutional employment available.

BOTTOM LINE

The cost of tuition and fees at Tulane is $47,130 for the 2016-17 academic year. Room and board add another $13,758. Adding that together with the estimated costs of books and other miscellaneous fees, Tulane expects a total of $63,110 for resident students. Their estimated total for commuter students is $54,268. As noted above, Tulane has several programs aimed at providing aid to in-state applicants.

CAREER INFORMATION FROM PAYSCALE.COM

ROI rating	85
Bachelor's and No Higher	
Median starting salary	$44,700
Median mid-career salary	$80,100
At Least Bachelor's	
Median starting salary	$47,900
Median mid-career salary	$84,000
% alumni with high job meaning	48%
% STEM	11%

SELECTIVITY

Admissions Rating	94
# of applicants	26,257
% of applicants accepted	30
% of acceptees attending	21
# offered a place on the wait list	3,413
% accepting a place on wait list	27
% admitted from wait list	0

FRESHMAN PROFILE

Range SAT Critical Reading	620–710
Range SAT Math	620–700
Range SAT Writing	640–720
Range ACT Composite	29–33
Minimum paper TOEFL	600
Average HS GPA	3.5
% graduated top 10% of class	55
% graduated top 25% of class	85
% graduated top 50% of class	96

DEADLINES

Early action	
Deadline	11/15
Notification	12/15
Regular	
Deadline	1/15
Notification	3/15
Nonfall registration?	Yes

FINANCIAL FACTS

Financial Aid Rating	89
Annual tuition	$47,130
Room and board	$13,758
Required fees	$3,880
Average need-based scholarship	$31,397
% needy frosh rec. need-based scholarship or grant aid	99
% needy UG rec. need-based scholarship or grant aid	97
% needy frosh rec. non-need-based scholarship or grant aid	37
% needy UG rec. non-need-based scholarship or grant aid	26
% needy frosh rec. need-based self-help aid	71
% needy UG rec. need-based self-help aid	79
% UG borrow to pay for school	42
Average cumulative indebtedness	$32,040
% frosh need fully met	60
% ugrads need fully met 58	
Average % of frosh need met	97
Average % of ugrad need met	95

Union College (NY)

GRANT HALL, SCHENECTADY, NY 12308 • ADMISSIONS: 518-388-6112 • FAX: 518-388-6986

CAMPUS LIFE

Quality of Life Rating	87
Fire Safety Rating	95
Green Rating	94
Type of school	Private
Affiliation	No Affiliation
Environment	Town

STUDENTS

Total undergrad enrollment	2,269
% male/female	54/46
% from out of state	66
% frosh from public high school	65
% frosh live on campus	99
% ugrads live on campus	89
# of fraternities (% ugrad men join)	11 (37)
# of sororities (% ugrad women join)	6 (42)
% African American	4
% Asian	6
% Caucasian	73
% Hispanic	7
% Native American	<1
% Pacific Islander	0
% Two or more races	2
% Race and/or ethnicity unknown	0
% international	7
# of countries represented	33

ACADEMICS

Academic Rating	93
% students returning for sophomore year	93
% students graduating within 4 years	82
% students graduating within 6 years	88
Calendar	Trimester
Student/faculty ratio	10:1
Profs interesting rating	96
Profs accessible rating	95

Most classes have 10–19 students.
Most lab/discussion sessions have
10–19 students.

MOST POPULAR MAJORS
Economics; Psychology; Political Science
and Government

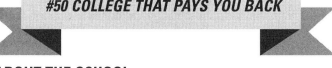

#50 COLLEGE THAT PAYS YOU BACK

ABOUT THE SCHOOL

Union College is a small, private institution located in upstate New York that operates on the trimester schedule. It offers more than forty majors, the most prominent of which are Biology, Economics, and Psychology, and a thriving study abroad program in which roughly 60 percent of students take part. Additionally, Union boasts a ten to one student-to-faculty ratio, with the most frequent class size coming in at between ten and nineteen students. Fifty-four percent of the student body is male, 46 percent is female, and 74 percent is white. A neuroscience major reports that "they give amazing scholarships, they have a great program for what I want to pursue, the atmosphere suited me extremely well, and I've never met friendlier people." Most students feel that "Union College is the perfect balance of the interdisciplinary liberal arts and engineering, where your extracurricular activities are just as important as academics," and also that there are "strong faculty-student interaction both in and out of the classroom," with one student noting "it is nice that the President of the school is willing to stop and talk with you, and knows your name." All students and faculty are assigned to one of seven Minerva Houses, community spaces which offer further opportunities for leadership, service, and faculty interaction. Overall, "Union is a work hard, play hard school with an active student body and accessible professors who are always willing to help."

BANG FOR YOUR BUCK

Tuition at Union College comes to $47,913, with the average aid package coming to around $39,479. Union meets the full demonstrated need of admitted students, and roughly 70 percent of students receive some form of aid. Students feel that "Union College is very generous with its financial aid and scholarship money," which is the sort of thing that practically anyone would want to hear. Multiple students report receiving full rides, and many others report receiving at least a partial merit scholarship. Union College also participates in academic opportunity programs like POSSE Scholars and Yellow Ribbon.

STUDENT LIFE

Every student on campus belongs to a Minerva House, and 39 percent of students of either gender are involved in Greek Life. The average Union student "comes from a upper middle class background in the northeast," and many find it remarkable that "students are able to have so much fun and do so well in their classes." It is noted that though there are students who are not from upper middle-class northeastern backgrounds, these students tend to fit in rather well. However, "while the rich New Englander is the 'typical' student, it is not saying that he isn't playing Dungeons and Dragons with the gaming kids." Drinking is a popular weekend activity, and yet there are atypical students in this aspect as well. Students feel that Union is making an effort to diversify the "typical" student body.

CAREER

Union College graduates report their average starting salary at around $50,800, and 68 percent report that their job has a great deal of meaning. Past that, students feel that "Union has an awesome career center that is always reaching out to students to help them with life after college with jobs, internships, resumes, etc. . . ."

Union College (NY)

FINANCIAL AID: 518-388-6123 • E-MAIL: ADMISSIONS@UNION.EDU • WEBSITE: WWW.UNION.EDU

Others add that "there are so many resources available in terms of funding, internships, and leadership opportunities." Students report being thrilled about the "undergraduate research opportunities" like the Sophomore Research Seminar or those through National Science Foundation awards, and the annual Steinmetz Symposium allows them to present their work to the entire campus community. A distinctive Union institution, the Minerva House program has produced sixty-two fellows selected to spend a year after graduation working on a global service project.

GENERAL INFO

Activities: Choral groups, concert band, dance, drama/theater, jazz band, literary magazine, music ensembles, radio station, student government, student newspaper, student-run film society, symphony orchestra, television station, yearbook, Campus Ministries, International Student Organization, Model UN. **Organizations:** 100 registered organizations, 13 honor societies, 7 religious organizations. 13 fraternities, 5 sororities. **Athletics (Intercollegiate):** *Men:* baseball, basketball, crew/rowing, cross-country, diving, football, ice hockey, lacrosse, soccer, swimming, tennis, track/field (outdoor), track/field (indoor). *Women:* basketball, crew/rowing, cross-country, diving, field hockey, ice hockey, lacrosse, soccer, softball, swimming, tennis, track/field (outdoor), track/field (indoor), volleyball. **On-Campus Highlights:** The Nott Memorial, Schaffer Library, Reamer Campus Center, Jackson's Garden, Memorial Chapel.

FINANCIAL AID

Students should submit: FAFSA, CSS/Financial Aid PROFILE, State aid form, Noncustodial PROFILE. Regular filing deadline is 2/1. The Princeton Review suggests that all financial aid forms be submitted as soon as possible after October 1. *Need-based scholarships/grants offered:* Federal Pell, FSEOG, State scholarships/grants, Private scholarships, College/university scholarship or grant aid from institutional funds. *Loan aid offered:* Direct Subsidized Stafford Loans, Direct Unsubsidized Stafford Loans, Direct PLUS loans, Federal Perkins Loans, College/university loans from institutional funds. Applicants will be notified of awards on or about 3/25. Federal Work-Study Program available. Institutional employment available.

BOTTOM LINE

The tuition at Union College comes to about $49,542. The average aid package comes to $35,500, with 80 percent of students receiving some aid. On average 100 percent of student demonstrated need is met. Union isn't cheap, but offers a great deal of financial aid to those who need it.

CAREER INFORMATION FROM PAYSCALE.COM

ROI rating	90
Bachelor's and No Higher	
Median starting salary	$51,700
Median mid-career salary	$99,200
At Least Bachelor's	
Median starting salary	$52,700
Median mid-career salary	$105,000
% alumni with high job meaning	38%
% STEM	27%

SELECTIVITY

Admissions Rating	94
# of applicants	5,996
% of applicants accepted	38
% of acceptees attending	25
# offered a place on the wait list	1,167
% accepting a place on wait list	54
% admitted from wait list	10
# of early decision applicants	399
% accepted early decision	60

FRESHMAN PROFILE

Range SAT Critical Reading	610–680
Range SAT Math	630–720
Range SAT Writing	600–680
Range ACT Composite	29–32
Minimum paper TOEFL	600
Minimum internet-based TOEFL	90
Average HS GPA	3.4
% graduated top 10% of class	71
% graduated top 25% of class	87
% graduated top 50% of class	97

DEADLINES

Early decision	
Deadline	11/15
Notification	12/15
Regular	
Deadline	1/15
Notification	4/1
Nonfall registration?	Yes

FINANCIAL FACTS

Financial Aid Rating	96
Annual tuition	$49,542
Room and board	$12,261
Required fees	$471
Average need-based scholarship	$35,500
% needy frosh rec. need-based scholarship or grant aid	98
% needy UG rec. need-based scholarship or grant aid	98
% needy frosh rec. non-need-based scholarship or grant aid	23
% needy UG rec. non-need-based scholarship or grant aid	9
% needy frosh rec. need-based self-help aid	93
% needy UG rec. need-based self-help aid	95
% frosh rec. any financial aid	84
% UG rec. any financial aid	80
% UG borrow to pay for school	67
Average cumulative indebtedness	$31,820
% frosh need fully met	100
% ugrads need fully met	100
Average % of frosh need met	100

University of Arizona

PO Box 210073, Tucson, AZ 85721-0073 • Admissions: 520-621-3237 • Fax: 520-621-9799

CAMPUS LIFE

Quality of Life Rating	92
Fire Safety Rating	91
Green Rating	93
Type of school	Public
Affiliation	No Affiliation
Environment	Metropolis

STUDENTS

Total undergrad enrollment	33,732
% male/female	49/51
% from out of state	31
% frosh from public high school	90
% frosh live on campus	71
% ugrads live on campus	20
# of fraternities	24
# of sororities	24
% African American	4
% Asian	6
% Caucasian	52
% Hispanic	25
% Native American	1
% Pacific Islander	<1
% Two or more races	4
% Race and/or ethnicity unknown	1
% international	6
# of countries represented	112

ACADEMICS

Academic Rating	72
% students returning for sophomore year	80
% students graduating within 4 years	43
% students graduating within 6 years	61
Calendar	Semester
Profs interesting rating	72
Profs accessible rating	73

Most classes have 20–29 students.
Most lab/discussion sessions have 20–29 students.

MOST POPULAR MAJORS

Psychology; Political Science and Government; Cell/Cellular and Molecular Biology

ABOUT THE SCHOOL

You can't fault undergrads at the University of Arizona for being mesmerized by a "beautiful" campus that's "full of history and traditions." Of course, we're also confident the fact that the UA "is a highly regarded research institution that promotes academic excellence" frequently proves to be equally enticing. After all, students who enroll here have access to a breadth of academic departments that's truly staggering. In fact, Arizona is one of only a few institutions to offer optical science and engineering as a major. These Wildcats also value the UA's "strong commitment to undergraduate involvement in research"—the 100% Engagement initiative aims to provide all students with the opportunity to participate in an immersive learning experience that uses collaboration, mentoring and reflection to help them launch successful, rewarding careers. The classroom experience here is typically characterized by "enthusiastic" professors who seem to "genuinely care about [the] students" and who often serve as Faculty Fellows (mentors and counselors) outside of class. Additionally, many are often adept at "applying [their lectures] to real world situations." And the vast majority are "willing to meet with students anytime." Lastly, as if all this wasn't enough, the "weather is amazing" to boot.

BANG FOR YOUR BUCK

The University of Arizona prides itself on offering "a good education at a good price." And it's not just Arizona residents who benefit. Indeed, the "UA also helps make the cost of education manageable by offering many scholarships to [qualified] out-of-state students." A thankful systems engineering major concurs sharing, "I am able to attend UA debt free [due to] . . . generous scholarship and financial aid packages." Some of those scholarships include the Arizona Excellence Tuition Award, which doles out scholarships ranging from $5,000 to $17,500 per academic year. Even better, this award is good for four consecutive years. In addition, the Achievement Award provides $4,000 per academic year to non-Arizona residents. This scholarship is need-based. Naturally, there are awards for Arizona residents as well. For example, in-state students may be eligible for the Wildcat Excellence Award. This provides scholarships ranging from $1,500 to $11,000 per academic year and is based upon academic merit. Scholarship Universe, the UA's award-winning scholarship management system, connects all students to potential external, institutional, and departmental funding.

STUDENT LIFE

Undergrads at the University of Arizona are seemingly always on the go. Of course, with more than 600 student clubs and organizations offered on campus, that's completely understandable. Students can participate in anything from "swing dance to intramural volleyball." These students also love supporting Wildcat athletics and "tailgates are common the weekends." In addition, Greek life is incredibly popular at the UA. A pleased senior shares, "On the weekends frats have huge party themes including ZBTahiti, AEPirates, Heaven and Hell, Swampwater, Pajama Jam, and many more." The UA's hometown of Tucson also offers "great live music, art and cinema." And outdoorsy types can take advantage of nearby natural wonders including Mount Lemmon, Gates Pass, Saguaro National Park, and the Catalina State Park.

CAREER

University of Arizona students feel assured of professional success. In fact, according to PayScale.com, the average UA grad receives a starting salary of $50,100. The website also highlights IBM Corporation, Honeywell Aerospace, Raytheon Missile Systems and the University of Arizona itself among the companies most commonly hiring UA

University of Arizona

FINANCIAL AID: 520-621-1858 • E-MAIL: ADMISSIONS@ARIZONA.EDU • WEBSITE: WWW.ARIZONA.EDU

grads. From webinars and podcasts to one-on-one career counseling, Career Services guarantees students enter the job market prepared. Perhaps most importantly, it hosts several job fairs throughout the year where students may have the opportunity to meet with companies such as Amazon, Bloomberg, ExxonMobil, American Express and Gap Inc., among many others. Since participation in the UA's 100% Engagement initiative allows students to earn an official notation on their academic transcripts, employers and graduate schools get a clear picture of students' skills and levels of engagement on campus.

GENERAL INFO

Activities: Choral groups, concert band, dance, drama/theater, jazz band, literary magazine, marching band, music ensembles, musical theater, opera, pep band, radio station, student government, student newspaper, symphony orchestra, television station, yearbook, Campus Ministries, International Student Organization, Model UN. **Organizations:** 504 registered organizations, 13 honor societies, 13 religious organizations. 24 fraternities, 24 sororities. **Athletics (Intercollegiate):** *Men:* baseball, basketball, cross-country, diving, football, golf, swimming, tennis, track/field (outdoor). *Women:* basketball, cross-country, diving, golf, gymnastics, soccer, softball, swimming, tennis, track/field (outdoor), track/field (indoor), volleyball. **On-Campus Highlights:** Flandrau Science Center, Center for Creative Photography, UA Museum of Art, Athletics Events, Arizona State Museum.

FINANCIAL AID

Students should submit: FAFSA. The Princeton Review suggests that all financial aid forms be submitted as soon as possible after October 1. *Need-based scholarships/grants offered:* Federal Pell, FSEOG, State scholarships/grants, Private scholarships, College/university scholarship or grant aid from institutional funds, Federal Nursing Scholarships. *Loan aid offered:* Direct Subsidized Stafford Loans, Direct Unsubsidized Stafford Loans, Direct PLUS loans, Federal Perkins Loans, Federal Nursing Loans, College/university loans from institutional funds. Federal Work-Study Program available. Institutional employment available.

THE BOTTOM LINE

Arizona residents attending the UA will receive a tuition bill of $9,864. Undergraduates hailing from out-of-state will be required to pay $29,017 in tuition. All students, regardless of residency status, can expect to pay $9,840 for room and board. Undergrads should also expect another $1,013 in required fees. Books and other academic supplies typically run students an additional $1,200. And those students who choose to commute will likely $1,500 in transportation costs.

CAREER INFORMATION FROM PAYSCALE.COM

ROI rating	84
Bachelor's and No Higher	
Median starting salary	$50,100
Median mid-career salary	$85,500
At Least Bachelor's	
Median starting salary	$50,400
Median mid-career salary	$87,000
% alumni with high job meaning	55%
% STEM	21%

SELECTIVITY

Admissions Rating	80
# of applicants	35,408
% of applicants accepted	76
% of acceptees attending	30

FRESHMAN PROFILE

Range SAT Critical Reading	480–600
Range SAT Math	480–620
Range SAT Writing	470–590
Range ACT Composite	21–27
Minimum internet-based TOEFL	70
Average HS GPA	3.4
% graduated top 10% of class	28
% graduated top 25% of class	54
% graduated top 50% of class	84

DEADLINES

Regular	
Priority	5/1
Deadline	5/1
Nonfall registration?	Yes

FINANCIAL FACTS

Financial Aid Rating	81
Annual in-state tuition	$9,864
Annual out-of-state tuition	$29,017
Room and board	$9,840
Required fees	$1,013
Average need-based scholarship	$10,726
% needy frosh rec. need-based scholarship or grant aid	94
% needy UG rec. need-based scholarship or grant aid	90
% needy frosh rec. non-need-based scholarship or grant aid	11
% needy UG rec. non-need-based scholarship or grant aid	7
% needy frosh rec. need-based self-help aid	56
% needy UG rec. need-based self-help aid	63
% frosh need fully met	12
% ugrads need fully met	9
Average % of frosh need met	62
Average % of ugrad need met	60

University of Arkansas—Fayetteville

232 Silas Hunt Hall, Fayetteville, AR 72701 • Admissions: 479-575-5346 • Fax: 479-575-7515

CAMPUS LIFE

Quality of Life Rating	**90**
Fire Safety Rating	**91**
Green Rating	**88**
Type of school	Public
Affiliation	No Affiliation
Environment	City

STUDENTS

Total undergrad enrollment	22,159
% male/female	48/52
% from out of state	40
% frosh from public high school	83
% frosh live on campus	89
% ugrads live on campus	26
# of fraternities (% ugrad men join)	19 (22)
# of sororities (% ugrad women join)	14 (37)
% African American	5
% Asian	2
% Caucasian	77
% Hispanic	8
% Native American	1
% Pacific Islander	<1
% Two or more races	3
% Race and/or ethnicity unknown	<1
% international	3
# of countries represented	85

ACADEMICS

Academic Rating	**73**
% students returning for sophomore year	82
% students graduating within 4 years	39
% students graduating within 6 years	62
Calendar	Semester
Student/faculty ratio	19:1
Profs interesting rating	71
Profs accessible rating	71
Most classes have 10–19 students.	
Most lab/discussion sessions have 20–29 students.	

MOST POPULAR MAJORS

Finance; Registered Nursing/Registered Nurse; Biology

ABOUT THE SCHOOL

The University of Arkansas—Fayetteville offers students a "great atmosphere" with "a lot of activities to get involved" with many spaces to help students "to relax and focus on your studies in an open and welcoming environment." The university offers eighty-one different majors, "the business college is excellent," the architecture program is likewise well-regarded, and the "honors college has a great reputation for getting people into medical school." Students agree that "the academics, though difficult, are great." Students say they are confident that their UA educations have made them "prepared for grad school," in part because the "quality professors with real world experience" "are willing to do anything it takes for the success of their students." Students appreciate the access they get to professors and administrators. One student explains, "I even have had a class taught by the Dean of the Honors College and have often seen the Chancellor strolling around campus. They are all happy to help in any way they can if the student is willing to put forth effort."

BANG FOR YOUR BUCK

The University of Arkansas-Fayetteville offers academic and college or departmental scholarships, as well as alumni sponsored scholarships and state scholarship programs. In addition, the New Arkansan Non-Resident Tuition award covers 70–90 percent of the difference between in-state and out-of-state tuition based on factors like grades, test scores, and state of residence. For all other states, the award covers either 50 or 80 percent of the out-of-state portion of tuition, again based on academic qualifications. The university also has a number of grant programs designed for students with demonstrated financial need, including the GO! Opportunities Grant Fund for students who graduated from Arkansas high schools or obtained a GED in Arkansas and the state sponsored Workforce Improvement Grant for students who are independent and already in the workforce. One student described their decision to attend, explaining, "I got a great scholarship package that not only paid for everything but I receive a little cash on the side and a book stipend."

STUDENT LIFE

Razorbacks are know to be "friendly and willing to help out," and competition on campus "is non-existent," unless it is on the football field. "When it is football season, everything stops and [everyone] goes to cheer on the [hogs]," one student tells us. While sports are hugely popular, students also praise campus initiatives that help engage in interdisciplinary collaborations, like the Campus Greens, which hosts speakers and helps finance and organize student led environmental initiatives.

CAREER

The UA Career Development Center maintains an active presence on campus, hosting multiple events every week during the school year. The Razorback Careerlink portal allows students and alumni to search through a database of full- and part-time jobs, internships, and co-op positions among companies and organizations that are specifically looking for UA students and graduates. The Career Development Center also lists the career paths of recent graduates so that students

University of Arkansas—Fayetteville

FINANCIAL AID: 479-575-3806 • E-MAIL: UOFA@UARK.EDU • WEBSITE: WWW.UARK.EDU

can see where other Razorbacks have ended up and get a real picture of the kinds of opportunities available to them. Graduates earn on average $47,200 in their early career and take in an average of 80,700 during their mid-career. Forty-nine percent of graduates report that they feel like the work they do makes the world a better place.

GENERAL INFO

Activities: Choral groups, concert band, dance, drama/theater, jazz band, literary magazine, marching band, music ensembles, musical theater, opera, pep band, radio station, student government, student newspaper, student run film society, symphony orchestra, television station, yearbook, Campus Ministries, International Student Organization 340 registered organizations, 39 honor societies, 32 religious organizations. 16 fraternities, 11 sororities. **Athletics (Intercollegiate):** *Men:* baseball, basketball, cross-country, football, golf, tennis, track/field (outdoor), track/field (indoor). *Women:* basketball, cross-country, diving, golf, gymnastics, soccer, softball, swimming, tennis, track/field (outdoor), track/field (indoor), volleyball. **On-Campus Highlights:** Bud Walton Arena, Old Main, Reynolds Razorback Stadium, Greek AmphiTheater, Senior Walk (every graduate's name engraved).

FINANCIAL AID

Students should submit: FAFSA. The Princeton Review suggests that all financial aid forms be submitted as soon as possible after October 1. *Need-based scholarships/grants offered:* Federal Pell, FSEOG, State scholarships/grants, Private scholarships, College/university scholarship or grant aid from institutional funds. *Loan aid offered:* Direct Subsidized Stafford Loans, Direct Unsubsidized Stafford Loans, Direct PLUS loans, Federal Perkins Loans. Federal Nursing Loans, State Loans, College/university loans from institutional funds. Applicants will be notified of awards on or about 4/1. Federal Work-Study Program available. Institutional employment available.

BOTTOM LINE

In-state tuition is $7,204 while out of state tuition is $21,522. On campus room and board is $10,332 and students are required to pay $1,616 in fees. The average incoming student gets $6,522 in need-based gift aid and the average need-based loan is 4,174. In total, 48 percent of students take out a student loan at some time during their educations a UA and on average students leave with a student debt load of $24,768.

CAREER INFORMATION FROM PAYSCALE.COM

ROI rating	85
Bachelor's and No Higher	
Median starting salary	$47,200
Median mid-career salary	$80,700
At Least Bachelor's	
Median starting salary	$48,400
Median mid-career salary	$81,900
% alumni with high job meaning	49%
% STEM	20%

SELECTIVITY

Admissions Rating	87
# of applicants	20,542
% of applicants accepted	60
% of acceptees attending	40
# offered a place on the wait list	160
% accepting a place on wait list	92
% admitted from wait list	85

FRESHMAN PROFILE

Range SAT Critical Reading	500–600
Range SAT Math	510–620
Range ACT Composite	23–28
Minimum paper TOEFL	550
Minimum internet-based TOEFL	79
Average HS GPA	3.6
% graduated top 10% of class	26
% graduated top 25% of class	54
% graduated top 50% of class	85

DEADLINES

Early action	
Deadline	11/1
Notification	12/15
Regular	
Priority	11/1
Deadline	8/1
Nonfall registration?	Yes

FINANCIAL FACTS

Financial Aid Rating	81
Annual in-state tuition	$7,204
Annual out-of-state tuition	$21,552
Room and board	$10,332
Required fees	$1,616
Average need-based scholarship	$6,868
% needy frosh rec. need-based scholarship or grant aid	81
% needy UG rec. need-based scholarship or grant aid	78
% needy frosh rec. non-need-based scholarship or grant aid	11
% needy UG rec. non-need-based scholarship or grant aid	8
% needy frosh rec. need-based self-help aid	67
% needy UG rec. need-based self-help aid	70
% frosh rec. any financial aid	79
% UG rec. any financial aid	72
% frosh need fully met	13
% ugrads need fully met	11
Average % of frosh need met	55
Average % of ugrad need met	56

University of California—Berkeley

110 SPROUL HALL, #5800, BERKELEY, CA 94720-5800 • ADMISSIONS: 510-642-3175 • FAX: 510-642-7333

CAMPUS LIFE

Quality of Life Rating	83
Fire Safety Rating	91
Green Rating	98
Type of school	Public
Affiliation	No Affiliation

STUDENTS

Total undergrad enrollment	27,496
% male/female	48/52
% from out of state	15
% frosh live on campus	95
% ugrads live on campus	26
# of fraternities (% ugrad men join)	(10)
# of sororities (% ugrad women join)	(10)
% African American	2
% Asian	35
% Caucasian	27
% Hispanic	14
% Native American	<1
% Pacific Islander	<1
% Two or more races	5
% Race and/or ethnicity unknown	3
% international	14

ACADEMICS

Academic Rating	81
% students returning for sophomore year	97
% students graduating within 4 years	73
% students graduating within 6 years	91
Calendar	Semester
Student/faculty ratio	17:1
Profs interesting rating	74
Profs accessible rating	66

Most classes have 10–19 students.
Most lab/discussion sessions have
20–29 students.

MOST POPULAR MAJORS

Electrical Engineering & Computer Sciences;
Economics; Computer Science

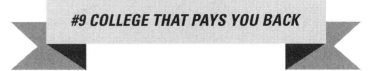

#9 COLLEGE THAT PAYS YOU BACK

ABOUT THE SCHOOL

University of California—Berkeley enjoys a reputation for quality and value that few other colleges can match. Large, diverse, and highly regarded, Berkeley is often ranked among the top public institutions in the world. Berkeley offers around 350 undergraduate and graduate degree programs in a wide range of disciplines. Best known for research, the school counts Nobel laureates, MacArthur Fellowship recipients, and Pulitzer Prize and Academy Award winners among its faculty. With an "all-star faculty and resources," professors here are "intelligent [and] accessible," with many departments boasting "the best [academics] in their field." Needless to say, undergraduate education is first-rate. The school maintains a low student-to-teacher ratio, and opportunities to get in on cutting-edge research at Berkeley abound. In fact, approximately half of the school's undergraduates assist faculty in creative or research projects during their time here. As some students note, "you don't get the coddling that the private universities show. You don't have a billion counselors catering to your every need." Though students note that survey classes here can sometimes be "enormous," professors "make themselves very accessible via e-mail and office hours." Berkeley maintains an incredibly high number of nationally ranked programs; however, engineering, computer science, molecular and cell biology, and political science are the most popular majors for undergraduates.

BANG FOR YOUR BUCK

Berkeley's Undergraduate Scholarships, Prizes and Honors unit of the Financial Aid Office administers three different scholarship programs. Twenty-five Berkeley Undergraduate Scholarships are awarded each year. The Regent's and Chancellor's Scholarship is Berkeley's most prestigious scholarship, and is awarded annually to approximately 200 incoming undergraduates. The by-invitation-only Cal Opportunity Scholarship is designed to attract high-achieving students who have overcome challenging socioeconomic circumstances. Award amounts vary for each of these scholarship programs, and are often based on financial need. All applicants to Berkeley are automatically considered for these scholarship programs. As a public institution, UC Berkeley's low in-state tuition makes this school very affordable. With a low cost and an active financial aid program, Berkeley is an ideal choice for high-achieving students from low-income families. According to its website, Berkeley serves more economically disadvantaged students than all the Ivy League universities combined. More than 30 percent of Berkeley undergraduates are eligible for Pell Grants. The Middle Class Access Plan helps middle-class families keep debt down by capping the parents' contribution.

STUDENT LIFE

At Berkeley "you are free to express yourself." "Conversations vary from the wicked party last night" to "debates about the roles of women in Hindu mythology." To simply label this school as "diverse" seems like an oversimplification. Here, people "think about everything." Students regard fellow students as "passionate" and "intelligent." Full of their signature optimism, they believe that "life at Berkeley has no limits"; they "study and hear obscure languages, meet famous scientists, engage with brilliant students, eat delicious food, and just relax with friends daily." Student life includes taking advantage of everything San Francisco has to offer across the bay, but

University of California—Berkeley

FINANCIAL AID: 510-642-6642 • WEBSITE: WWW.BERKELEY.EDU

even when remaining on campus, "there are clubs and classes that cater to everybody's needs and such a diverse group of people that it would be hard to not fit in."

CAREER

"Berkeley's greatest strengths are the amount of resources and opportunities it provides to students not only to allow them to explore numerous academic fields but to engage them in the community, in the country, and in the world." "There are internship opportunities for students from all disciplines, both on campus and in the surrounding cities of Berkeley, Oakland, and San Francisco." "Research opportunities are abundant" and "the career center is amazing." There are "endless options for student involvement" and employers like the school's "prestigious" reputation. According to the website PayScale.com, the average starting salary for graduates is $59,500 and more than 50 percent of alumni find their jobs to be highly meaningful.

GENERAL INFO

Activities: Choral groups, concert band, dance, drama/theater, jazz band, literary magazine, marching band, music ensembles, musical theater, pep band, radio station, student government, student newspaper, student-run film society, symphony orchestra, television station, yearbook, international student organization. **Organizations:** 300 registered organizations, 6 honor societies, 28 religious organizations. 38 fraternities, 19 sororities. **Athletics (Intercollegiate):** *Men:* Baseball, basketball, crew/rowing, cross-country, diving, football, golf, gymnastics, rugby, sailing, soccer, swimming, tennis, track/field (outdoor), water polo. *Women:* Basketball, crew/rowing, cross-country, diving, field hockey, golf, gymnastics, lacrosse, sailing, soccer, softball, swimming, tennis, track/field (outdoor), volleyball, water polo.

FINANCIAL AID

Students should submit: FAFSA, State aid form. Regular filing deadline is 3/2. The Princeton Review suggests that all financial aid forms be submitted as soon as possible after October 1. *Need-based scholarships/grants offered:* Federal Pell, FSEOG, State scholarships/grants, Private scholarships, College/university scholarship or grant aid from institutional funds. *Loan aid offered:* Direct Subsidized Stafford Loans, Direct Unsubsidized Stafford Loans, Direct PLUS loans, Federal Perkins Loans. Applicants will be notified of awards on or about 3/31. Federal Work-Study Program available. Institutional employment available.

BOTTOM LINE

For California residents, Berkeley is a great deal, ringing in at $11,220 annually for tuition and fees. In addition to tuition, the school estimates expenditures of $1,240 for books and supplies, though these costs vary by major. Nonresident tuition alone is $35,928 annually.

CAREER INFORMATION FROM PAYSCALE.COM

ROI rating	**94**
Bachelor's and No Higher	
Median starting salary	$59,500
Median mid-career salary	$114,000
At Least Bachelor's	
Median starting salary	$60,400
Median mid-career salary	$120,000
% alumni with high job meaning	50%
% STEM	31%

SELECTIVITY

Admissions Rating	98
# of applicants	78,924
% of applicants accepted	15
% of acceptees attending	46
# offered a place on the wait list	3,760
% accepting a place on wait list	65
% admitted from wait list	36

FRESHMAN PROFILE

Range SAT Critical Reading	610–730
Range SAT Math	640–770
Range SAT Writing	620–750
Range ACT Composite	29–34
Minimum paper TOEFL	550
Minimum internet-based TOEFL	80
Average HS GPA	3.87
% graduated top 10% of class	98
% graduated top 25% of class	100
% graduated top 50% of class	100

DEADLINES

Regular	
Deadline	11/30
Notification	3/31
Nonfall registration?	Yes

FINANCIAL FACTS

Financial Aid Rating	90
Annual in-state tuition	$11,220
Annual out-of-state tuition	$37,902
Room and board	$16,042
Required fees	$2,289
Average need-based scholarship	$19,087
% needy frosh rec. need-based scholarship or grant aid	97
% needy UG rec. need-based scholarship or grant aid	98
% needy frosh rec. non-need-based scholarship or grant aid	5
% needy UG rec. non-need-based scholarship or grant aid	3
% needy frosh rec. need-based self-help aid	50
% needy UG rec. need-based self-help aid	55
% frosh need fully met	19
% ugrads need fully met	23
Average % of frosh need met	78
Average % of ugrad need met	81

University of California—Davis

550 Alumni Lane, One Shields Ave, Davis, CA 95616 • Admissions: 530-752-2971 • Fax: 530-752-1280

CAMPUS LIFE

Quality of Life Rating	91
Fire Safety Rating	95
Green Rating	98
Type of school	Public
Affiliation	No Affiliation
Environment	Town

STUDENTS

Total undergrad enrollment	28,384
% male/female	41/59
% from out of state	3
% frosh from public high school	84
% frosh live on campus	92
% ugrads live on campus	25
# of fraternities (% ugrad men join)	40 (7)
# of sororities (% ugrad women join)	28 (10)
% African American	2
% Asian	32
% Caucasian	28
% Hispanic	19
% Native American	<1
% Pacific Islander	<1
% Two or more races	5
% Race and/or ethnicity unknown	2
% international	11
# of countries represented	121

ACADEMICS

Academic Rating	75
% students returning for sophomore year	92
% students graduating within 4 years	58
% students graduating within 6 years	85
Calendar	Quarter
Student/faculty ratio	18:1
Profs interesting rating	74
Profs accessible rating	70

Most classes have 20–29 students.
Most lab/discussion sessions have 20–29 students.

MOST POPULAR MAJORS
Biology; Psychology; Economics

ABOUT THE SCHOOL

The University of California, Davis is a large, public university that has come a long way from its agrarian roots. Today, its rigorous academics, vibrant campus community, and location near the state capital draw students from all over the world. UC Davis is known as a world-class research university, offering more than 100 interdisciplinary majors, as well as ninety graduate programs and advanced degrees from six professional schools. More than 70 percent of UC Davis students conduct research with a faculty member in a class, at a research center or in a laboratory. About 80 percent of students report participating in internships during their undergraduate career, including the school's eleven-week internship in Washington, D.C., open to students in any discipline. Davis's life sciences division receives top marks—in fact, the school claims to have more biology majors than any other campus in America. Science students also have access to Davis's multitude of world-class facilities, such as the Bodega Bay Laboratory and the Lake Tahoe Environmental Research Center. The school boasts top programs in engineering, enology and viticulture, and animal science, as well as the first Native American studies program in the country. UC Davis's quarter system affords "no time to fool around." "It is not really a school for a slacker."

BANG FOR YOUR BUCK

Davis offers many excellent scholarship opportunities. Besides awarding over $6 million in campus-based merit scholarship aid, the Undergraduate and Prestigious Scholarship Office also assists students in preparing for and applying to national and international competitive awards, such as the Rhodes, Marshall, Truman, and Goldwater Scholarships. The University of California's financial aid programs are designed to make a UC education accessible to students at every income level. In addition, UC has established the Blue and Gold Opportunity Plan to help low- and middle-income families. The program ensures that California undergraduates who are in their first four years of attendance at Davis (or two years for transfer students) will receive enough scholarship and grant assistance to at least fully cover their system-wide UC fees. For 2015–16, Davis students qualify if they have incomes below $80,000 and meet other basic eligibility requirements for need-based financial aid. In addition, UC Davis implemented the Aggie Grant Plan, which provides middle-income families with additional support. Many students receive grants to help cover costs in addition to tuition and fees, and many students with parent incomes above $80,000 will qualify for financial aid.

STUDENT LIFE

"It is fairly difficult to define 'typical' at UC Davis." "Students come from every background imaginable," yet "everyone can find their niche." "The student body is mostly made up of white and Asian students," but "Davis is a melting pot." "Many different cultures, ethnicities, and religions are present," and "everybody is really accepting." Students here are "goal-oriented," "down-to-earth, well-rounded, balanced, amiable, and intelligent." Most are "environmentally conscious" and strike a "good balance between academics and personal life." They love the Davis farmer's market and also mention an "indie theater... art galleries, and Davis sights like the arboretum." At Davis, "the green spaces are delightful." One student "particularly enjoys the wide open grassy fields." The school also hosts popular events such as concerts, Picnic Day, rallies, and rock climbing.

CAREER

"UCD offers a wide variety of internship, research, and career opportunities." "The internship and Career Center places more than 5,000 students in internships yearly." "We also have a plethora of abroad programs (including the Washington Program) at our

University of California—Davis

FINANCIAL AID: 530-752-2396 • E-MAIL: UNDERGRADUATEADMISSIONS@UCDAVIS.EDU • WEBSITE: WWW.UCDAVIS.EDU

disposal to ensure we come out well-rounded from experiences, not just book smart." Students seem confident that most "graduates from this school end up with successful jobs." Perhaps this is because "professors at UC Davis are very passionate about their careers . . . which in turn motivates students to be passionate in their studies and work." It seems as though this motivation translates positively into careers for most graduates. More than fifty percent of alumni visiting PayScale.com find their jobs to be meaningful. On the same site, the average salary for recent grads is close to $50,800.

GENERAL INFO

Activities: Choral groups, concert band, dance, drama/theater, jazz band, literary magazine, marching band, music ensembles, musical theater, radio station, student government, student newspaper, student-run film society, symphony orchestra, video production studio, campus ministries, international student organizations. **Organizations:** 700+ registered student organizations, 1 honor society, 67 religious/philosophical organizations. 32 fraternities, 34 sororities. **Athletics (Intercollegiate):** *Men:* Baseball, basketball, cross-country, football, golf, soccer, swimming, track/field, track/field, water polo. *Women:* Basketball, cross-country, field hockey, golf, gymnastics, lacrosse, soccer, softball, swimming & diving, tennis, track/field, volleyball, water polo.

FINANCIAL AID

Students should submit: FAFSA, State aid form. Priority filing deadline is 3/2. The Princeton Review suggests that all financial aid forms be submitted as soon as possible after October 1. *Need-based scholarships/ grants offered:* Federal Pell, FSEOG, State scholarships/grants, Private scholarships, College/university scholarship or grant aid from institutional funds. *Loan aid offered:* Direct Subsidized Stafford Loans, Direct Unsubsidized Stafford Loans, Direct PLUS loans, Federal Perkins Loans, College/university loans from institutional funds. Applicants will be notified of awards beginning 3/16.

BOTTOM LINE

In-state tuition for California residents is about $11,220 annually, while nonresidents are responsible for a total of $35,928 in tuition each year. All students need to add an additional $14,517 for room and board if they intend to live on campus. Once you factor in books and supplies and required fees, California residents and nonresidents can expect to pay about $32,208 and $56,916, respectively. The school's comprehensive aid packages can drastically offset the price for California students. For nonresident students, the additional $24,708 in supplemental tuition is a significant consideration, although scholarships as well as alternative and most federal loan funds can help offset these costs.

CAREER INFORMATION FROM PAYSCALE.COM

ROI rating	88
Bachelor's and No Higher	
Median starting salary	$51,000
Median mid-career salary	$94,600
At Least Bachelor's	
Median starting salary	$52,100
Median mid-career salary	$97,400
% alumni with high job meaning	57%
% STEM	34%

SELECTIVITY

Admissions Rating	90
# of applicants	64,510
% of applicants accepted	38
% of acceptees attending	22
# offered a place on the wait list	9,033
% accepting a place on wait list	30
% admitted from wait list	74

FRESHMAN PROFILE

Range SAT Critical Reading	510–630
Range SAT Math	560–710
Range SAT Writing	530–660
Range ACT Composite	24–30
Minimum paper TOEFL	550
Minimum internet-based TOEFL	60
Average HS GPA	4.0

DEADLINES

Regular	
Deadline	11/30
Notification	3/31
Nonfall registration?	No

FINANCIAL FACTS

Financial Aid Rating	80
Annual in-state tuition	$11,220
Annual out-of-state tuition	$35,928
Room and board	$14,517
Required fees	$2,731
Average need-based scholarship	$16,993
% needy frosh rec. need-based scholarship or grant aid	96
% needy UG rec. need-based scholarship or grant aid	96
% needy frosh rec. non-need-based scholarship or grant aid	2
% needy UG rec. non-need-based scholarship or grant aid	1
% needy frosh rec. need-based self-help aid	60
% needy UG rec. need-based self-help aid	56
% UG rec. any financial aid	61
% frosh need fully met	16
% ugrads need fully met	15
Average % of frosh need met	80
Average % of ugrad need met	78

University of California—Irvine

OFFICE OF ADMISSIONS & RELATIONS WITH SCHOOLS, 204 ALDRICH HALL, IRVINE, CA 92697-1075 • ADMISSIONS: 949-824-6703

CAMPUS LIFE

Quality of Life Rating	**70**
Fire Safety Rating	**88**
Green Rating	**99**
Type of school	Public
Affiliation	No affiliation
Environment	City

STUDENTS

@stats:Total undergrad enrollment	25,256
% male/female	46/54
% from out of state	3
% frosh from public high school	69
% frosh live on campus	79
% ugrads live on campus	41
# of fraternities (% ugrad men join)	23 (10)
# of sororities (% ugrad women join)	25 (10)
% African American	2
% Asian	37
% Caucasian	12
% Hispanic	25
% Native American	0
% Pacific Islander	0
% Two or more races	4
% Race and/or ethnicity unknown	4
% international	16
# of countries represented	70

ACADEMICS

Academic Rating	**79**
% students graduating within 4 years	72
% students graduating within 6 years	88
Student/faculty ratio	19:1
Profs interesting rating	69
Profs accessible rating	66
Most classes have 10–19 students.	
Most lab/discussion sessions have fewer than 10 students.	

MOST POPULAR MAJORS

Biology/Biological Sciences; Social Psychology; Business/Managerial Economics

ABOUT THE SCHOOL

There are more than 25,000 undergrads at the University of California—Irvine. The campus is situated in the warm, suburban town of Irvine, California. Many concur that on-campus life "revolves around academics" at UC Irvine. Students tell us that the school is an ideal place to study, as "it's quiet, almost pastoral, with Aldrich Park in the middle of the campus." Students here are able to choose from a slew of academic programs—many of them nationally renowned—and a vast number of courses. UCI is consistently ranked among the nation's best universities, with more than forty top-ranked academic programs. As you would expect from a large, well-funded, public research institution, cutting-edge research is the norm here. Three of UCI's researchers have won Nobel Prizes, and in 2010, one faculty member won the prestigious Templeton Prize. Big lecture courses are part of the deal, too, especially in your first year or two. Fortunately, many professors are at the top of their fields, and the faculty generally gets high praise from students. Upper-level classes get smaller. One of the campus's unique strengths lies in the way it combines the advantages of a large, dynamic research university with the friendly feel of a small college. The undergraduate experience extends beyond the classroom to participation in campus organizations, multicultural campus and community events, volunteer service projects, internships, study abroad, entrepreneurial ventures, and much more. One hub for community engagement, the Cross-Cultural Center, is home to fifty affiliated student groups and hundreds of programs each year. UCI's quiet, sprawling, suburban campus is located in sunny Southern California. The suburban environment often means lights-out relatively early for most undergrads. Even so, Irvine's location in dreamy Southern California leaves open the possibility for stimulating alternatives.

BANG FOR YOUR BUCK

UCI tends to attract the third-largest applicant pool in the University of California system (behind UC Berkeley and UCLA). With all the stellar resources available here and the plethora of nationally recognized programs, admission to UCI is an achievement that rivals the path set by its older and larger brethren. If you can get admitted, UCI offers generous financial aid assistance in the form of scholarships, loans, and grants. In addition to federal and state aid programs, UC Irvine offers a robust grant program for needy students. The Blue and Gold Opportunity Plan covers educational and student-services fees for California residents whose families earn less than $80,000 a year and qualify for financial aid. Blue and Gold students often qualify for additional grant aid to further help reduce the cost of attendance.

STUDENT LIFE

Since Irvine is a relatively quiet city, life at the school can be mellow. However, those who make the effort to get involved will be rewarded. "If you want to enjoy this school, you have to be involved in something," says a student. "The school is quiet, and they really don't promote student pride." However, "if you are adventurous and outgoing, there is plenty to do," and another student reports that "joining clubs has opened up a whole group of friends/ acquaintances." In terms of recreation, students "can typically enjoy time in libraries, nearby restaurants, the park, or pretty much anywhere nearby. It's not difficult to find things to do, since the campus is within walking distance to a great shopping center, and the mall is only a bus ride away." For those with access to a car who are willing to venture a bit further, there are a number of beautiful nearby beaches and "you are right near the hotbed

University of California—Irvine

FINANCIAL AID: 949-824-8262 • E-MAIL: ADMISSIONS@UCI.EDU • WEBSITE: HTTP://UCI.EDU/

of L.A. entertainment." So while UC Irvine might have a bit of a sleepy reputation, there's no shortage of things to do if you go out and look for them.

CAREER

The UC Irvine Career Center offers a number of resources for students exploring their options for life after graduation. One-on-one academic advising and career counseling are available; the school hosts many on-campus recruiting events and career fairs; and the Center's online database, known as Zotlink, lists jobs and internship opportunities and provides abundant information about professional development workshops and other career events happening on campus. It's easy to gain leadership experience through programs like Passport to Leadership, the Leadership Train, or the newly launched Student Leadership Portfolio, which helps students consider how their roles will relate to their futures (and resumes). Students widely report that a UC Irvine education does a great job of preparing them for what's to come.

GENERAL INFO

Activities: Choral groups, concert band, dance, drama/theater, jazz band, literary magazine, music ensembles, musical theater, opera, pep band, radio station, student government, student newspaper, student-run film society, symphony orchestra, yearbook, International Student Organization, Model UN. **Organizations:** 484 registered organizations, 18 honor societies, 51 religious organizations. 23 fraternities, 25 sororities. **Athletics (Intercollegiate):** *Men:* baseball, basketball, cross-country, golf, sailing, soccer, tennis, track/field (outdoor), volleyball, water polo. *Women:* basketball, cross-country, golf, sailing, soccer, tennis, track/field (outdoor), volleyball, water polo.

FINANCIAL AID

Students should submit: FAFSA, State aid form. Applicants will be notified of awards on a rolling basis beginning 4/1. The Princeton Review suggests that all financial aid forms be submitted as soon as possible after October 1. *Need-based scholarships/grants offered:* Federal Pell, SEOG, State scholarships/grants, Private scholarships, College/university scholarship or grant aid from institutional funds. *Loan aid offered:* Direct Subsidized Stafford Loans, Direct Unsubsidized Stafford Loans, Direct PLUS loans, Federal Perkins Loans, College/university loans from institutional funds. Applicants will be notified of awards on a rolling basis beginning 4/1. Federal Work-Study Program available. Institutional employment available.

BOTTOM LINE

Tuition, room and board, and everything else costs about $27,400 a year at UCI. (It's considerably less if you commute.) With all the sources of need-based and merit-based aid available here, most students don't pay anywhere near that amount. UCI is a truly a bargain if you can meet California's residency standards. On the other hand, if you are branded as a nonresident, the costs here approach those of a private school.

CAREER INFORMATION FROM PAYSCALE.COM

ROI rating	89
Bachelor's and No Higher	
Median starting salary	$49,900
Median mid-career salary	$97,700
At Least Bachelor's	
Median starting salary	$51,000
Median mid-career salary	$99,400
% alumni with high job meaning	50%
% STEM	30%

SELECTIVITY

Admissions Rating	95
# of applicants	71,768
% of applicants accepted	39
% of acceptees attending	21
# offered a place on the wait list	7,361
% accepting a place on wait list	55
% admitted from wait list	3

FRESHMAN PROFILE

@stats:Range SAT Critical Reading	490–620
Range SAT Math	550–690
Range SAT Writing	510–620
Minimum paper TOEFL	550
Minimum internet-based TOEFL	80
Average HS GPA	3.94
% graduated top 10% of class	96
% graduated top 25% of class	100
% graduated top 50% of class	100

DEADLINES

Deadline	11/30
Notification	3/31
Nonfall registration?	No

FINANCIAL FACTS

Financial Aid Rating	91
Annual in-state tuition	$11,220
Annual out-of-state tuition	$37,902
Room and board	$13,661
Required fees	$3,806
Average need-based scholarship	$18,593
% needy frosh rec. need-based scholarship or grant aid	97
% needy UG rec. need-based scholarship or grant aid	97
% needy frosh rec. non-need-based scholarship or grant aid	1
% needy UG rec. non-need-based scholarship or grant aid	1
% needy frosh rec. need-based self-help aid	75
% needy UG rec. need-based self-help aid	66
% frosh need fully met	25
% ugrads need fully met	21
Average % of frosh need met	85
Average % of ugrad need met	81

University of California—Los Angeles

1147 Murphy Hall, Los Angeles, CA 90095-1436 • Admissions: 310-825-3101 • Fax: 310-206-1206

CAMPUS LIFE

Quality of Life Rating	89
Fire Safety Rating	92
Green Rating	96
Type of school	Public
Affiliation	No Affiliation
Environment	Metropolis

STUDENTS

Total undergrad enrollment	29,585
% male/female	44/56
% from out of state	11
% frosh from public high school	74
# of fraternities (% ugrad men join)	35 (15)
# of sororities (% ugrad women join)	35 (15)
% African American	3
% Asian	29
% Caucasian	27
% Hispanic	21
% Native American	<1
% Pacific Islander	<1
% Two or more races	5
% Race and/or ethnicity unknown	2
% international	13
# of countries represented	110

ACADEMICS

Academic Rating	81
% students returning for sophomore year	96
% students graduating within 4 years	74
% students graduating within 6 years	91
Calendar	Quarter
Student/faculty ratio	17:1
Profs interesting rating	68
Profs accessible rating	66

Most classes have 10–19 students.
Most lab/discussion sessions have 20–29 students.

MOST POPULAR MAJORS

Biology; Business/Economics; Psychology

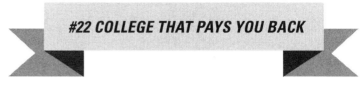

#22 COLLEGE THAT PAYS YOU BACK

ABOUT THE SCHOOL

In a word, the University of California, Los Angeles is about diversity—in what you can study, in what you can do with your free time, in ethnicity, in gender and sexuality, in everything. With more than 200 undergraduate and graduate degree programs on offer for its 40,000 students, there truly is something for everyone. The technology and research resources here are dreamy. There is comprehensive quality across the broad range of disciplines. There are more than 7,000 undergraduate and graduate courses. You can take classes here in pretty much any academic endeavor, and you will likely run across some of the best and brightest professors in the world. Brushes with fame are common here—with a location near Hollywood and a world-famous film and television school, the UCLA campus has attracted film productions for decades. That being said, you should be aware that bigness and breadth have their limitations (lots of teaching assistants, big classes, anonymity). But if you don't mind being a small fish in a big pond, chances are you'll have a great experience here. And with just a little bit of initiative, you might even make a splash. Perhaps more notable, "UCLA is the kind of school that pushes you to work hard academically but reminds you that interaction with people outside of the classroom is just as important."

BANG FOR YOUR BUCK

Even in a time of rising fees, UCLA remains far below most of the other top research universities in total costs for undergraduate study. A little more than half of the student population here receives need-based financial aid. This school prizes its diversity, and that definitely includes economic diversity. UCLA ranks at the top among major research universities in the percentage of its students that receive Pell Grants (which is free government money for low-income students). The university also offers the prestigious Regents Scholarship, intended to reward extraordinary academic excellence and exemplary leadership and community service accomplishments. Also, the career-planning operation here is first-rate, and there are extensive opportunities for internships with local employers. UCLA Financial Aid and Scholarships has both advisors and counselors available to help students complete financial aid applications, and to provide guidance throughout the process. In-person appointments can be scheduled, but the office also has walk-in hours. The UCLA website also provides access to certain scholarship opportunities, but the school also has a resource center on campus. The Scholarship Resource Center opened in 1996 to provide scholarship information, resources, and support services to all UCLA students, regardless of financial aid eligibility.

STUDENT LIFE

"UCLA is the mold that fits to you," says a happy student. "There is no 'typical student,' and everyone can easily find a group of students to fit in with. The benefits of 29,000 students and over 1,000 student groups!" The school has an extremely large campus and a very diverse student body, but it fosters an environment where everyone can find a place in the community: "Whether it be in Greek life, a club or organization, everybody has somewhere they can go to relax and have some fun. The apartments are close to campus, so nearly everybody lives in a small area with close proximity." And the benefits of going to school in a big, busy city are manifold: "LA is a vibrant and multicultural city. You have the beach to the west and the deserts/mountains to the east. EVERYTHING is accessible here in this city. If you want to go

University of California—Los Angeles

FINANCIAL AID: 310-206-0400 • E-MAIL: UGADM@SAONET.UCLA.EDU • WEBSITE: WWW.UCLA.EDU

surf during the week it's ten minutes away. The food here is amazing and brings out the inner foodie in everyone!" One student puts the student experience at UCLA very succinctly: "I, like most people here, love [my] life."

CAREER

"UCLA is about getting a top notch education at a (currently) affordable price that will start your career off on an excellent path," is a popular sentiment regarding how the school equips students for their future. The Career Center offers standard services like advising and counseling; job fairs; on-campus recruiting; job and internship search tools; resources for those applying to grad school or looking for international opportunities; and "JumpStart" workshops covering professional development topics in a wide variety of fields. Students seem very satisfied with what the school affords them: "Networking and marketing, you're always told of a ton of activities, internships, resource opportunities—there are constant career fairs and activities. Also, location-wise, L.A. is a huge cosmopolitan city, you've got the opportunity to work in anything." Out of UCLA alumni visiting PayScale.com, 49 percent report that they derive a high level of meaning from their job.

GENERAL INFO

Activities: Choral groups, concert band, dance, drama/theater, jazz band, literary magazine, marching band, music ensembles, musical theater, opera, pep band, radio station, student government, student newspaper, student-run film society, symphony orchestra, television station, yearbook, campus ministries, international student organization.

FINANCIAL AID

Students should submit: FAFSA. Priority filing deadline is 3/2. The Princeton Review suggests that all financial aid forms be submitted as soon as possible after October 1. *Need-based scholarships/grants offered:* Federal Pell, FSEOG, State scholarships/grants, Private scholarships, College/university scholarship or grant aid from institutional funds, United Negro College Fund. *Loan aid offered:* Direct Subsidized Stafford Loans, Direct Unsubsidized Stafford Loans, Direct PLUS loans, Federal Perkins Loans, Federal Nursing Loans, College/university loans from institutional funds. Applicants will be notified of awards on a rolling basis beginning 3/15. Federal Work-Study Program available. Institutional employment available.

BOTTOM LINE

For Californians, the cumulative price tag to attend UCLA for a year—when you add up fees, room and board, and basic expenses—is somewhere around $26,415. Your living arrangements can make a noticeable difference. If you can't claim residency in the Golden State, the cost totals $51,123. Almost all students who demonstrate need receive some form of aid, and the average cumulative indebtedness, at just $21,590, is relatively reasonable.

CAREER INFORMATION FROM PAYSCALE.COM

ROI rating	92
Bachelor's and No Higher	
Median starting salary	$51,800
Median mid-career salary	$96,900
At Least Bachelor's	
Median starting salary	$52,800
Median mid-career salary	$101,000
% alumni with high job meaning	47%
% STEM	21%

SELECTIVITY

Admissions Rating	97
# of applicants	92,728
% of applicants accepted	17
% of acceptees attending	21

FRESHMAN PROFILE

Range SAT Critical Reading	570–700
Range SAT Math	600–750
Range SAT Writing	580–720
Range ACT Composite	25–33
Minimum paper TOEFL	550
Minimum internet-based TOEFL	83
Average HS GPA	4.3
% graduated top 10% of class	97
% graduated top 25% of class	100
% graduated top 50% of class	100

DEADLINES

Regular	
Deadline	11/30
Nonfall registration?	No

FINANCIAL FACTS

Financial Aid Rating	84
Annual in-state tuition	$11,220
Annual out-of-state tuition	$35,928
Room and board	$13,452
Required fees	$1,743
Average need-based scholarship	$18,966
% needy frosh rec. need-based scholarship or grant aid	97
% needy UG rec. need-based scholarship or grant aid	97
% needy frosh rec. non-need-based scholarship or grant aid	2
% needy UG rec. non-need-based scholarship or grant aid	1
% needy frosh rec. need-based self-help aid	59
% needy UG rec. need-based self-help aid	62
% frosh rec. any financial aid	53
% UG rec. any financial aid	55
% frosh need fully met	25
% ugrads need fully met	25
Average % of frosh need met	83
Average % of ugrad need met	83

University of California—Riverside

3106 Student Services Building, Riverside, CA 92521 • Admissions: 951-827-3411 • Fax: 951-827-6344

CAMPUS LIFE

Quality of Life Rating	83
Fire Safety Rating	94
Green Rating	88
Type of school	Public
Affiliation	No Affiliation
Environment	City

STUDENTS

Total undergrad enrollment	18,608
% male/female	48/52
% from out of state	1
% frosh from public high school	90
% frosh live on campus	73
% ugrads live on campus	35
# of fraternities (% ugrad men join)	20 (6)
# of sororities (% ugrad women join)	20 (10)
% African American	4
% Asian	36
% Caucasian	13
% Hispanic	38
% Native American	<1
% Pacific Islander	<1
% Two or more races	5
% Race and/or ethnicity unknown	1
% international	3
# of countries represented	100

ACADEMICS

Academic Rating	75
% students returning for sophomore year	91
% students graduating within 4 years	48
% students graduating within 6 years	73
Calendar	Quarter
Student/faculty ratio	22:1
Profs interesting rating	70
Profs accessible rating	71

Most classes have 20–29 students.
Most lab/discussion sessions have
20–29 students.

MOST POPULAR MAJORS

Psychology; Business Administration and
Management; Biological and Biomedical
Sciences

ABOUT THE SCHOOL

Although perhaps not as famous as some of the other schools in the UC system, the University of California—Riverside (UCR) has much to boast about. For starters, this research university offers state-of-the-art facilities in genomics and nanotechnology. Its top-ranked entomology department draws insect-loving students like the proverbial moths to a flame. For those not inclined towards the sciences, UCR provides the largest undergraduate business program in the UC system, as well as the only undergraduate creative writing program among the UC schools. The school's "fantastic" honors program is another highly praised asset. With an emphasis on ethnic diversity and social consciousness, the school attracts a student population that stands out among other campuses across the country. As primarily a commuter school, UCR faces the challenge of keeping the social scene on campus lively and interesting despite having many of its students gone on the weekends. With more than 400 student organizations, the school strives to have a steady stream of events on and off campus, including concerts and movie screenings.

BANG FOR YOUR BUCK

More than 70 percent of undergrads at UCR receive some form of financial aid, and the school also offers a Blue and Gold Program for California applicants with a family income of up to $80,000 which covers the full cost of tuition through a combination of grants and scholarships. Merit-based Regents, Chancellor's and Highlander scholarships are also offered to freshmen with excellent academic qualifications, regardless of financial need. In addition to various forms of financial aid, UCR also provides additional services through its Internship Program, which places many students in paid positions with Fortune 100 companies as well as through its Student On-Campus Employment Program (SOCEP).

STUDENT LIFE

While students cite studying as a constant activity at Riverside, "the overall atmosphere is laid-back. People think about parties, such as most college students do. But a good majority of the students are very serious about their futures and do well in balancing their social lives with their academics." On the social side, UCR offers many on-campus activities, "such as athletic games, plays, and musical shows." Riverside may not be an exceptionally busy city, but students "go out often. Students can walk, take the bus, or drive their own car to any certain place such as the University Village or the mall." "During the weekdays it [is] normal to go out for happy hour at the local bars," says a student, and "there are a good amount of coffee shops for late night studying." Both Los Angeles and San Diego are nearby, so students with access to cars often venture a little further on the weekend to hang out or visit friends and family. "There is always something happening either on-campus or around the area," says a student. "All you need to do is choose to do one or the other; the whole college experience is what you make of it."

CAREER

Students at UCR study hard and are a very career-focused bunch. Most of them feel that the school has done an excellent job of preparing them for whatever the future may hold. The UCR Career Center offers academic counseling and one-on-one career planning; on-campus recruiting; online job and internship listings; advice for resume building and interview strategies; and many other services. The school also holds a variety of career fairs catering to students in different fields, from engineering to education to finance. Notable programming includes ORBITS, for first generation college students,

University of California—Riverside

FINANCIAL AID: 951-827-3878 • E-MAIL: ADMIN@UCR.EDU • WEBSITE: WWW.UCR.EDU

and the Job Discovery Series, with 135 career-representing panelists. Outside of the Center, one student reports that "my professors care about my success and guide me into the best career path by proposing internships," which seems to be indicative of most students' experience. Out of UCR alumni visiting PayScale.com, 44 percent report feeling as though they derive a high level of meaning from their jobs.

GENERAL INFO

Activities: Choral groups, concert band, dance, drama/theater, jazz band, literary magazine, music ensembles, musical theater, pep band, radio station, student government, student newspaper, student-run film society, international student organization. **Organizations:** 439 registered organizations, 9 honor societies, 27 religious organizations. 20 fraternities, 20 sororities. **Athletics (Intercollegiate):** *Men:* Baseball, basketball, cross-country, golf, soccer, tennis, track/field (outdoor), track/field (indoor). *Women:* Basketball, cross-country, golf, soccer, softball, tennis, track/field (outdoor), track/field (indoor), volleyball. **On-Campus Highlights:** Music festival-style concerts, new Lattitude 55, basketball games, Student Recreation Center and intramural sports, The Barn (music and comedy acts), Coffee Bean and Tea Leaf. The Highlander Union Building (HUB).

FINANCIAL AID

Students should submit: FAFSA, State aid form. Regular filing deadline is 6/15. The Princeton Review suggests that all financial aid forms be submitted as soon as possible after October 1. *Need-based scholarships/ grants offered:* Federal Pell, FSEOG, State scholarships/grants, Private scholarships, College/university scholarship or grant aid from institutional funds. *Loan aid offered:* Direct Subsidized Stafford Loans, Direct Unsubsidized Stafford Loans, Direct PLUS loans, Federal Perkins Loans, College/university loans from institutional funds. Applicants will be notified of awards on a rolling basis beginning 3/1. Federal Work-Study Program available. Institutional employment available.

BOTTOM LINE

For students who are California residents, the cost of tuition is about $11,200, which makes the school a good value for the price. For any out-of-state students, it is a different story. The tuition reaches up to around $37,900 plus another $16,400 for room and board. Whether you're an in-state or out-of-state student, do not forget to factor in the additional required fees and cost of books and supplies, which add up to a little bit over $4,600.

CAREER INFORMATION FROM PAYSCALE.COM

ROI rating	88
Bachelor's and No Higher	
Median starting salary	$46,300
Median mid-career salary	$92,100
At Least Bachelor's	
Median starting salary	$47,300
Median mid-career salary	$91,300
% alumni with high job meaning	46%
% STEM	22%

SELECTIVITY

Admissions Rating	92
# of applicants	38,505
% of applicants accepted	56
% of acceptees attending	19
# offered a place on the wait list	6,231
% accepting a place on wait list	60
% admitted from wait list	74

FRESHMAN PROFILE

Range SAT Critical Reading	500–600
Range SAT Math	520–650
Range SAT Writing	500–610
Range ACT Composite	22–28
Minimum paper TOEFL	550
Minimum internet-based TOEFL	80
Average HS GPA	3.7
% graduated top 10% of class	94
% graduated top 25% of class	100
% graduated top 50% of class	100

DEADLINES

Regular	
Deadline	11/30
Notification	3/31
Nonfall registration?	No

FINANCIAL FACTS

Financial Aid Rating	83
Annual in-state tuition	$11,220
Annual out-of-state tuition	$37,902
Room and board	$16,400
Required fees	$2,901
Average need-based scholarship	$17,712
% needy frosh rec. need-based scholarship or grant aid	97
% needy UG rec. need-based scholarship or grant aid	96
% needy frosh rec. non-need-based scholarship or grant aid	1
% needy UG rec. non-need-based scholarship or grant aid	2
% needy frosh rec. need-based self-help aid	78
% needy UG rec. need-based self-help aid	69
% frosh rec. any financial aid	89
% UG rec. any financial aid	85
% UG borrow to pay for school	69
Average cumulative indebtedness	$21,464
% frosh need fully met	24
% ugrads need fully met	20
Average % of frosh need met	85
Average % of ugrad need met	81

University of California—San Diego

9500 GILMAN DRIVE, 0021, LA JOLLA, CA 92093-0021 • ADMISSIONS: 858-534-4831 • FAX: 858-534-5723

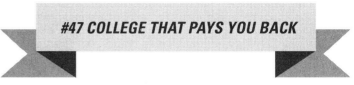

#47 COLLEGE THAT PAYS YOU BACK

ABOUT THE SCHOOL

Mathematics and the sciences reign supreme at the University of California—San Diego, and the school has an excellent reputation, huge research budgets, and an idyllic climate that have helped it attract eight Nobel laureates to its faculty. While research and graduate study garner most of the attention, undergraduates still receive a solid education that results in an impressive degree. The division of the undergraduate program into six smaller colleges helps take some of the edge off UC San Diego's big-school vibe (roughly 23,000 undergraduates) and allows students easier access to administrators. A quarterly academic calendar also keeps things moving. Campus life is generally pretty quiet. Students are divided on whether this school in scenic but sleepy La Jolla has a boring social scene or whether one simply has to look hard to find recreation. "There is always something to do on campus, and it is always changing! I never get bored!" But one thing is certain: some students work way too hard to afford the luxury of a social life. Students are often too busy with schoolwork to spend a lot of time partying, and when they have free time, they find hometown La Jolla a little too tiny for most college students. The town won't sanction a frat row, so Greek life doesn't include raucous parties, but the new 1,000-bed Village at Torrey Pines, built especially for transfer students, is one of the most environmentally sustainable student housing structures in the nation. Students also spend a lot of time at the beach or enjoying the school's intramural sports programs. One student summed up the dichotomy perfectly: "My school is all about science and the beach." Trying to study the hard sciences despite the distraction of the Pacific only a few blocks away is a mammoth task. And a fine public transit system makes downtown San Diego very accessible.

BANG FOR YOUR BUCK

More than half of UC San Diego's undergraduate students receive need-based support. The University of California's Blue and Gold Opportunity Plan (B&G) will cover students' UC fees if they are California residents and their families earn $80,000 or less and the student also qualifies for UC financial aid. For needy middle-class families earning up to $120,000, UC offers additional grant money that offsets half of any UC fee increase. In response to California's current economic climate, UC San Diego launched the $50 million Invent the Future student-support fundraising campaign, which will help fund scholarships and fellowships for all who need them.

STUDENT LIFE

A handful of undergrads seem to continually gripe that UC San Diego is "socially dead." However, plenty of students counter that there are definitely good times to be had, you simply have to "take control of your own college experience" and not just "go to class and [then retreat] to your room." For starters, San Diego offers "beautiful scenery and the perfect weather to go outside and play sports, chill at the beach or just hang out." Indeed, many undergrads tell us that there's a "huge surfing community." Additionally, students can typically find "small concerts or raves going on every week." The residence counsels also host lots of "fun programs such as Jell-o Fight, drive-in movies, casino nights, and much more." And there are a number of "spectacular" dance and play performances "that happen on campus."

University of California—San Diego

FINANCIAL AID: 858-534-4480 • E-MAIL: ADMISSIONSINFO@UCSD.EDU • WEBSITE: WWW.UCSD.EDU

CAREER

Professional success is practically synonymous with UCSD. Indeed, according to PayScale.com, the average starting salary for San Diego grads is $50,600. Students looking to jumpstart their search can easily turn to the Career Services Center. Here undergrads have the opportunity to meet with advisors to explore the breadth of career options, conduct assessments and research various industries. Most importantly, the Center hosts job fairs and networking events every quarter. These present great opportunities for undergrads to learn about internships, part-time gigs and full-time positions. Companies that have recently attended include Amazon, Boeing, Apple, Chevron Corporation, California State Auditor, Hulu, Groupon, Intel Corporation, and the Peace Corps.

GENERAL INFO

Activities: Choral groups, concert band, dance, drama/theater, jazz band, literary magazine, marching band, music ensembles, musical theater, opera, pep band, radio station, student government, student newspaper, student-run film society, symphony orchestra, television station, yearbook, campus ministries, international student organization. **Organizations:** 406 registered organizations, 5 honor societies, 46 religious organizations. 26 fraternities, 22 sororities. **Athletics (Intercollegiate):** *Men:* Baseball, basketball, crew/rowing, cross-country, diving, fencing, golf, soccer, swimming, tennis, track/field (outdoor), volleyball, water polo. *Women:* Basketball, crew/rowing, cross-country, diving, fencing, soccer, softball, swimming, tennis, track/field (outdoor), volleyball, water polo.

FINANCIAL AID

Students should submit: FAFSA, State aid form. Priority filing deadline is 3/2. The Princeton Review suggests that all financial aid forms be submitted as soon as possible after October 1. *Need-based scholarships/ grants offered:* Federal Pell, FSEOG, State scholarships/grants, Private scholarships, College/university scholarship or grant aid from institutional funds. *Loan aid offered:* Direct Subsidized Stafford Loans, Direct Unsubsidized Stafford Loans, Direct PLUS loans, Federal Perkins Loans, College/university loans from institutional funds. Applicants will be notified of awards on a rolling basis beginning 3/15. Federal Work-Study Program available. Institutional employment available.

BOTTOM LINE

California residents attending UC San Diego full-time pay roughly $15,050 in tuition and fees. Room and board costs come to about $12,477, not to mention additional costs for transportation, books, and personal expenses. Nonresidents pay more than $40,300 in tuition alone.

CAREER INFORMATION FROM PAYSCALE.COM

ROI rating	90
Bachelor's and No Higher	
Median starting salary	$52,400
Median mid-career salary	$103,000
At Least Bachelor's	
Median starting salary	$54,200
Median mid-career salary	$107,000
% alumni with high job meaning	58%
% STEM	38%

SELECTIVITY

Admissions Rating	97
# of applicants	84,198
% of applicants accepted	34

FRESHMAN PROFILE

Range SAT Critical Reading	560–670
Range SAT Math	620–750
Range SAT Writing	580–690
Range ACT Composite	27–32
Minimum paper TOEFL	550
Average HS GPA	4.14
% graduated top 10% of class	100
% graduated top 25% of class	100
% graduated top 50% of class	100

DEADLINES

Regular	
Deadline	11/30
Notification	3/31
Nonfall registration?	Yes

FINANCIAL FACTS

Financial Aid Rating	85
Annual in-state tuition	$13,672
Annual out-of-state tuition	$40,354
Room and board	$12,477
Required fees	$1,378
Average need-based scholarship	$18,147
% needy frosh rec. need-based scholarship or grant aid	92
% needy UG rec. need-based scholarship or grant aid	94
% needy frosh rec. non-need-based scholarship or grant aid	1
% needy UG rec. non-need-based scholarship or grant aid	1
% needy frosh rec. need-based self-help aid	82
% needy UG rec. need-based self-help aid	83
% frosh rec. any financial aid	77
% UG rec. any financial aid	63
% frosh need fully met	39
% ugrads need fully met	35
Average % of frosh need met	87
Average % of ugrad need met	87

University of California—Santa Barbara

OFFICE OF ADMISSIONS, 1210 CHEADLE HALL, SANTA BARBARA, CA 93106-2014 • ADMISSIONS: 805-893-2881 • FAX: 805-893-2676

CAMPUS LIFE

Quality of Life Rating	93
Fire Safety Rating	95
Green Rating	98
Type of school	Public
Affiliation	No Affiliation
Environment	City

STUDENTS

Total undergrad enrollment	20,607
% male/female	47/53
% from out of state	5
% frosh from public high school	84
% frosh live on campus	95
% ugrads live on campus	39
# of fraternities (% ugrad men join)	17 (8)
# of sororities (% ugrad women join)	18 (13)
% African American	2
% Asian	19
% Caucasian	35
% Hispanic	26
% Native American	<1
% Pacific Islander	<1
% Two or more races	8
% Race and/or ethnicity unknown	1
% international	7
# of countries represented	82

ACADEMICS

Academic Rating	82
% students returning for sophomore year	93
% students graduating within 4 years	68
% students graduating within 6 years	81
Calendar	Quarter
Student/faculty ratio	18:1
Profs interesting rating	81
Profs accessible rating	81

Most classes have fewer than 10 students.
Most lab/discussion sessions have
  20–29 students.

MOST POPULAR MAJORS

Biology; Economics; Psychology

#45 COLLEGE THAT PAYS YOU BACK

ABOUT THE SCHOOL

UCSB's beautiful campus is located 100 miles north of Los Angeles, with views of the ocean and the mountains, and typically benevolent Southern California weather. Perched above the Pacific coast, the University of California—Santa Barbara is a top-ranked public university with a multitude of world-class academic, extracurricular, and social opportunities. University of California–Santa Barbara is "a beautiful, laid-back learning institute on the beach," yet students say it's much more than a great place to get a tan. This prestigious public school is "one of the best research universities in the country," which "attracts many excellent professors" as well as a cadre of dedicated students. Maybe it's the sunny weather, but "professors here are more accessible than [at] other universities," and they are "genuinely interested in helping the students learn." This large university offers more than 200 major programs, of which business, economics, biology, communications, psychology, and engineering are among the most popular. Students agree that the competent and enthusiastic faculty is one of the school's greatest assets. Teaching assistants are also noted for being dedicated and helpful, especially in leading small discussion sessions to accompany large lecture courses. There are six Nobel laureates on the UCSB faculty, and the school offers many opportunities for undergraduates to participate in research.

BANG FOR YOUR BUCK

As a part of the prestigious University of California system, UCSB fuses good value and strong academics. It is a state school with over 20,000 students enrolled, so many classes are large. But with all the resources of a major research school at your fingertips, it's a definite bargain. The University of California operates the Blue and Gold Opportunity Plan. For in-state students with household incomes of less than the state median of $80,000, the Blue and Gold Opportunity plan will fully cover the mandatory UC fees for four years. California residents are also eligible for Cal Grants, a grant program administered by the state and open to college students that meet certain minimum GPA requirements. In addition to state and federal aid, there are a number of scholarships available to UCSB undergraduates. New freshmen with outstanding academic and personal achievement may be awarded the prestigious Regents Scholarship. There are additional merit awards offered through each of the university's four colleges, as well as through the alumni association.

STUDENT LIFE

University of California—Santa Barbara is "a place for strong academics, excellent research opportunities, all with a laid-back and vibrant student life." With its large student body—there are over 20,000 undergraduates—there's something for everyone. Students note that outdoor activities are popular, from surfing to hiking, and underscore that UCSB has "a beach on campus." There are about 500 registered student organizations on campus and students participate in activities as varied as "a Shakespeare flash mob group" and "aerial dancing class." The Greek system is also a mainstay of campus life, with the school housing eighteen sororities and seventeen fraternities. Roughly 12 percent of women join a sorority, with 8 percent of men joining a fraternity. The school strikes a balance, though, according to one Literature major, who describes the population at UCSB as "lots of Greeks [and] lots of geeks." For another student, the number of "clubs, internships, research opportunities, and avenues to create . . . your own extracurricular activities is almost intimidating."

University of California—Santa Barbara

FINANCIAL AID: 805-893-2118 • E-MAIL: ADMISSIONS@SA.UCSB.EDU • WEBSITE: WWW.UCSB.EDU

CAREER

According to PayScale.com, the average starting salary for a UCSB graduate is roughly $47,000 and popular careers include software engineer, mechanical engineer, and marketing manager. The most popular majors for UCSB students are Communication, Economics, and Sociology. While one Biochemistry major laments there are "basically too many students, and not enough open positions," other students praise the range of internship and post-graduation career opportunities, with one describing UCSB as "a springboard for the greatest young minds to launch into highly successful research and careers." The Career Services department at UCSB encourages students to take advantage of "GauchoLink," a frequently updated database of job and internship opportunities that also lists upcoming career-oriented events hosted by the school or by potential employers. Students are also able to store letters of recommendation with the Career Services department so as to streamline the process of applying for internships or jobs during their school tenure or after graduation.

GENERAL INFO

Activities: Choral groups, concert band, dance, drama/theater, jazz band, literary magazine, music ensembles, musical theater, opera, pep band, radio station, student government, student newspaper, student run film society, symphony orchestra, television station, yearbook, campus ministries, international student organization. **Organizations:** 508 registered organizations, 5 honor societies, 19 religious organizations. 17 fraternities, 18 sororities. **Athletics (Intercollegiate):** *Men:* Baseball, basketball, cross-country, diving, golf, gymnastics, soccer, swimming, tennis, track/field (outdoor), volleyball, water polo. *Women:* Basketball, cross-country, diving, gymnastics, soccer, softball, swimming, tennis, track/field (outdoor), volleyball, water polo.

FINANCIAL AID

Students should submit: FAFSA. Regular filing deadline is 3/2. The Princeton Review suggests that all financial aid forms be submitted as soon as possible after October 1. *Need-based scholarships/grants offered:* Federal Pell, FSEOG, State scholarships/grants, College/university scholarship or grant aid from institutional funds. *Loan aid offered:* Direct Subsidized Stafford Loans, Direct Unsubsidized Stafford Loans, Direct PLUS loans, Federal Perkins Loans. Federal Work-Study Program available. Institutional employment available.

BOTTOM LINE

Depending on where you live and what you study, the cost of attending UC Santa Barbara fluctuates. For California residents, the school estimates that total expenses come to about $35,289 annually. For out-of-state residents, the estimated annual cost comes to $61,917.

CAREER INFORMATION FROM PAYSCALE.COM

ROI rating	90
Bachelor's and No Higher	
Median starting salary	$49,400
Median mid-career salary	$96,300
At Least Bachelor's	
Median starting salary	$50,400
Median mid-career salary	$100,000
% alumni with high job meaning	49%
% STEM	16%

SELECTIVITY

Admissions Rating	96
# of applicants	70,444
% of applicants accepted	33
% of acceptees attending	19
# offered a place on the wait list	5,006
% accepting a place on wait list	58
% admitted from wait list	10

FRESHMAN PROFILE

Range SAT Critical Reading	550–670
Range SAT Math	580–700
Range SAT Writing	560–680
Range ACT Composite	24–30
Minimum paper TOEFL	550
Minimum internet-based TOEFL	80
Average HS GPA	4.0
% graduated top 10% of class	100
% graduated top 25% of class	100
% graduated top 50% of class	100

DEADLINES

Regular	
Deadline	11/30
Notification	3/5
Nonfall registration?	No

FINANCIAL FACTS

Financial Aid Rating	83
Annual in-state tuition	$12,240
Annual out-of-state tuition	$36,948
Room and board	$14,192
Required fees	$1,716
Average need-based scholarship	$17,948
% needy frosh rec. need-based scholarship or grant aid	95
% needy UG rec. need-based scholarship or grant aid	96
% needy frosh rec. non-need-based scholarship or grant aid	1
% needy UG rec. non-need-based scholarship or grant aid	1
% needy frosh rec. need-based self-help aid	80
% needy UG rec. need-based self-help aid	79
% UG rec. any financial aid	60
% frosh need fully met	28
% ugrads need fully met	25
Average % of frosh need met	83
Average % of ugrad need met	82

University of California—Santa Cruz

OFFICE OF ADMISSIONS, COOK HOUSE, 1156 HIGH STREET, SANTA CRUZ, CA 95064 • ADMISSIONS: 831-459-4008

CAMPUS LIFE

Quality of Life Rating	74
Fire Safety Rating	80
Green Rating	99
Type of school	Public
Affiliation	No Affiliation
Environment	City

STUDENTS

Total undergrad enrollment	16,231
% male/female	47/53
% from out of state	3
% frosh from public high school	87
% frosh live on campus	98
% ugrads live on campus	53
# of fraternities (% ugrad men join)	6 (5)
# of sororities (% ugrad women join)	11 (7)
% African American	2
% Asian	21
% Caucasian	33
% Hispanic	31
% Native American	<1
% Pacific Islander	<1
% Two or more races	7
% Race and/or ethnicity unknown	2
% international	4
# of countries represented	50

ACADEMICS

Academic Rating	75
% students returning for sophomore year	88
% students graduating within 4 years	56
% students graduating within 6 years	78
Calendar	Quarter
Student/faculty ratio	19:1
Profs interesting rating	67
Profs accessible rating	65

Most classes have 20–29 students.
Most lab/discussion sessions have 20–29 students.

MOST POPULAR MAJORS
Psychology; Business/Managerial Economics; Biology

ABOUT THE SCHOOL

UC Santa Cruz is a world-class research and teaching university, featuring interdisciplinary learning and a distinctive residential college system that provides a small-college environment within the larger research institution. Tucked within "a friendly and diverse community full of lovely scenery," a student observes how easy it is to "focus on scholastic endeavors in a beautiful forest setting." The university combines a multicultural, open community with a high-quality education, and the campus is very politically aware. Students enjoy the "medium-size school, where it is possible to get a university experience but the professors also want to learn your name." Undergraduates are provided with significant access to faculty and have a valuable opportunity to incorporate creative activities into their studies; they conduct and publish research and work closely with faculty on leading-edge projects. What sets instructors apart from those at a typical research-driven university is that "they are very passionate about their subject even when teaching undergrads," according to a surprised student.

BANG FOR YOUR BUCK

Along with quality instruction, internships and public service are common elements of the educational experience at UC Santa Cruz, which seeks to extend the classroom into the real world. Alternative Spring Break, for example, is an opportunity for students to immerse themselves in a service project such as building homes in Mexico and assisting with the rebuilding efforts in New Orleans. A unique human biology major requires an internship in the health field in a Spanish-speaking community, where students can volunteer in a hospital, spend time shadowing a physician, or assist in providing health services to underserved populations. Student Organization Advising and Resources (SOAR) sponsors internships which help students gain skills in leadership, networking, program planning, and outreach. To support students financially, UC's Blue and Gold Opportunity Plan covers UC tuition for students who qualify. In addition, a range of grants and scholarships can help cover student costs, including a scholarship sponsored by the UCSC Alumni Association, honoring high-achieving students who have compelling financial need.

STUDENT LIFE

"The 'stereotypical' Santa Cruz student is a hippie," and the school certainly has its fair share of those: "The typical student is very hardworking until about 9:00 P.M., when hikes to the forest are common practice and returning to your room smelling like reefer is acceptable," one undergrad explains—but "there are many different types who attend UCSC." "It seems that almost every student here has a personal passion, whether it be an activism or cause of some sort, etc.," one student writes. "Everyone is so . . . alive." "Most are liberal," and there's a definite propensity for earnestness; it's the sort of place where students declare without irony that they "not only possess a great respect for one another but the world and life in general. The world to an average UCSC student is a sacred and beautiful place to be shared and enjoyed by all its inhabitants."

University of California—Santa Cruz

FINANCIAL AID: 831-459-2963 • E-MAIL: ADMISSIONS@UCSC.EDU • FAX: 831-459-4452 • WEBSITE: WWW.UCSC.EDU

CAREER

UC Santa Cruz's Career Services creates hundreds of opportunities each semester for students looking to hone their skills and explore their options. On-campus internships through the Chancellor's Undergraduate Internship Program come with mentorship, a leadership seminar for credit, and a scholarship of $8,200 toward school registration fees. Students may also apply to spend a quarter in Sacramento, interning with students from other University of California campuses. It's easy to find federal, regional, and on-campus research gigs through an online database where students can search by major. Plus, Career Fairs, informational sessions, and Meet & Greets throughout the year ensure that students have plenty of chances to network and research potential fields.

GENERAL INFO

Activities: Choral groups, dance, drama/theater, jazz band, literary magazine, music ensembles, musical theater, opera, radio station, student government, student newspaper, student-run film society, symphony orchestra, television station, campus ministries, international student organization. **Organizations:** 138 registered organizations, 3 honor societies, 19 religious organizations. 6 fraternities, 11 sororities. **Athletics (Intercollegiate):** *Men:* Basketball, diving, soccer, swimming, tennis, volleyball. *Women:* Basketball, cross-country, diving, golf, soccer, swimming, tennis, volleyball. **On-Campus Highlights:** Arboretum, Farm and Garden, East Field House, Bay Tree Bookstore/Grad Student Commons, Pogonip Open Area Reserve.

FINANCIAL AID

Students should submit: FAFSA, State aid form. Regular filing deadline is 3/2. The Princeton Review suggests that all financial aid forms be submitted as soon as possible after October 1. *Need-based scholarships/grants offered:* Federal Pell, FSEOG, State scholarships/ grants, Private scholarships, College/university scholarship or grant aid from institutional funds. *Loan aid offered:* Direct Subsidized Stafford Loans, Direct Unsubsidized Stafford Loans, Direct PLUS loans, Federal Perkins Loans. Applicants will be notified of awards on a rolling basis beginning 4/1. Federal Work-Study Program available. Institutional employment available.

BOTTOM LINE

Over 16,000 students are enrolled at the university, with almost everyone originally from California, and the student population is split evenly between residents and commuters. Total cost of attendance, including tuition, room and board, fees, and books, for in-state students is $30,044 and $54,752 for out-of-state residents.

CAREER INFORMATION FROM PAYSCALE.COM

ROI rating	88
Bachelor's and No Higher	
Median starting salary	$48,400
Median mid-career salary	$89,300
At Least Bachelor's	
Median starting salary	$49,400
Median mid-career salary	$91,500
% alumni with high job meaning	45%
% STEM	20%

SELECTIVITY

Admissions Rating	94
# of applicants	44,871
% of applicants accepted	51
% of acceptees attending	16
# offered a place on the wait list	0

FRESHMAN PROFILE

Range SAT Critical Reading	520–640
Range SAT Math	550–670
Range SAT Writing	520–640
Range ACT Composite	23–29
Minimum paper TOEFL	550
Minimum internet-based TOEFL	83
Average HS GPA	3.8
% graduated top 10% of class	96
% graduated top 25% of class	100
% graduated top 50% of class	100

DEADLINES

Regular	
Deadline	11/30
Notification	3/31
Nonfall registration?	No

FINANCIAL FACTS

Financial Aid Rating	81
Annual in-state tuition	$11,220
Annual out-of-state tuition	$37,902
Room and board	$15,216
Required fees	$2,295
Average need-based scholarship	$19,335
% needy frosh rec. need-based scholarship or grant aid	93
% needy UG rec. need-based scholarship or grant aid	95
% needy frosh rec. non-need-based scholarship or grant aid	1
% needy UG rec. non-need-based scholarship or grant aid	1
% needy frosh rec. need-based self-help aid	75
% needy UG rec. need-based self-help aid	73
% frosh rec. any financial aid	61
% UG rec. any financial aid	66
% frosh need fully met	20
% ugrads need fully met	23
Average % of frosh need met	83
Average % of ugrad need met	83

The University of Chicago

1101 E 58TH STREET, ROSENWALD HALL SUITE 105, CHICAGO, IL 60637 • ADMISSIONS: 773-702-8650 • FAX: 773-702-4199

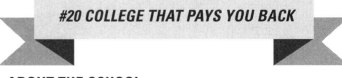

#20 COLLEGE THAT PAYS YOU BACK

ABOUT THE SCHOOL
The University of Chicago has a reputation as a favorite destination of the true intellectual: students here are interested in learning for learning's sake, and they aren't afraid to express their opinions. A rigorous, intellectually challenging, and world-renowned research university, the University of Chicago continues to offer a community where students thrive and ideas matter. Here, an attitude of sharp questioning seems to be the focus, rather than the more relaxed inquiry and rumination approach at some schools of equal intellectual repute. Many find welcome challenges in the debates and discussions that define the campus atmosphere; the typical Chicago student is task-oriented, intellectually driven, sharp, vocal, and curious. As one student surveyed said, "There is nothing more exciting, challenging, and rewarding than the pursuit of knowledge in all of its forms." The undergraduate program at Chicago emphasizes critical thinking through a broad-based liberal arts curriculum. At the heart of the experience is the Common Core, a series of distribution requirements in the humanities, science, and mathematics. No lecture courses here— Core courses are discussion-based, and enrollment is limited to twenty. Chicago's numerous major programs range from religious studies to linguistics, history, economics, and molecular engineering.

BANG FOR YOUR BUCK
The University of Chicago operates a need-blind admissions process, admitting qualified students regardless of their financial situation. Once admitted, the school guarantees to meet 100 percent of a student's demonstrated financial need. Under a program called "No Barriers," grants replace student loans for every student's need-based financial aid package. Highly qualified freshman candidates may also be considered for competitive merit scholarships. Scholarships are awarded to about 100 students annually; these scholarships. Scholarships are awarded to applicants on the basis of outstanding academic and extracurricular achievement, demonstrated leadership, and commitment to their communities. Notable merit scholarships include: the Odyssey Scholarship, a renewable scholarship and guaranteed summer internship for students from low- and moderate-income families; and University Scholarships, which are guaranteed for four years of study.

STUDENT LIFE
Students rejoice! The "social scene at UChicago is truly vibrant and encompasses a very wide spectrum." Indeed, it "allows you to dabble in a variety of groups; one weekend you can hang out at a frat playing flip cup or pong, while another weekend you can go out in downtown Chicago, drink wine with your sorority sisters, discuss Marx and Smith at an apartment party, or just simply watch a movie with your roommates." There are also "tons of [clubs to join], from numerous different martial arts to gymnastics to multiple magazines including a soft porn magazine to event planning for the school to tutoring kids and community service to cultural groups to a vegan society." And, of course, the city of Chicago also helps to guarantee boredom will be kept at bay. There is "always something to do like going to festivals, trying new restaurants, shopping, seeing a performance, listening to a concert, visiting museums, or experiencing a different culture."

The University of Chicago

FINANCIAL AID: 773-702-8655 • E-MAIL: COLLEGEADMISSIONS@UCHICAGO.EDU • WEBSITE: WWW.UCHICAGO.EDU

CAREER

Without a doubt, a University of Chicago education means that students will "enter a competitive job market prepared." This sentiment is supported by the fact that 95 percent of students have jobs or post-grad plans soon after leaving school. In fact, the average starting salary (according to PayScale.com) for recent UChicago grads is $50,600. The school's Career Advancement office maintains some unique programs to help ensure this success. For example, students can participate in the Jeff Metcalf Internship Program, which provides more than 2,000 paid internships each year throughout the country and abroad, or the Alumni Board of Governors Externship Program where they can shadow an accomplished professional.

GENERAL INFO

Activities: Choral groups, concert band, dance, drama/theater, jazz band, literary magazine, music ensembles, musical theater, pep band, radio station, student government, student newspaper, student-run film society, symphony orchestra, yearbook, campus ministries, international student organization. **Organizations:** 400 registered organizations, 5 honor societies, 36 religious organizations. 13 fraternities, 8 sororities.

FINANCIAL AID

Students should submit: FAFSA, Institution's own financial aid form or CSS/Financial Aid PROFILE. Priority filing deadline is 2/15. The Princeton Review suggests that all financial aid forms be submitted as soon as possible after October 1. *Need-based scholarships/grants offered:* Federal Pell, FSEOG, State scholarships/grants, Private scholarships, College/university scholarship or grant aid from institutional funds. *Loan aid offered:* Direct Subsidized Stafford Loans, Direct Unsubsidized Stafford Loans, Direct PLUS loans, Federal Perkins Loans. Applicants will be notified of awards on or about 4/1. Federal Work-Study Program available. Institutional employment available.

BOTTOM LINE

Yearly tuition to University of Chicago is a little more than $50,997, plus an additional $1,494 in mandatory fees. For campus residents, room and board is about $15,093 per year. Once you factor in personal expenses, transportation, books, and supplies, an education at University of Chicago costs about $71,550 per year. At University of Chicago, all demonstrated financial need is met through financial aid packages.

CAREER INFORMATION FROM PAYSCALE.COM

ROI rating	92
Bachelor's and No Higher	
Median starting salary	$50,600
Median mid-career salary	$107,000
At Least Bachelor's	
Median starting salary	$53,100
Median mid-career salary	$109,000
% alumni with high job meaning	56%
% STEM	22%

SELECTIVITY

Admissions Rating	99
# of applicants	30,069
% of applicants accepted	8
% of acceptees attending	61

FRESHMAN PROFILE

Range SAT Critical Reading	720–800
Range SAT Math	720–800
Range SAT Writing	700–780
Range ACT Composite	32–35
Minimum paper TOEFL	600
Minimum internet-based TOEFL	104
Average HS GPA	4.3
% graduated top 10% of class	98
% graduated top 25% of class	99
% graduated top 50% of class	100

DEADLINES

Early action	
Deadline	11/1
Notification	12/17
Early Decision	
Deadline	11/1
Notification	12/17
Deadline	1/17
Notification	2/20
Regular	
Deadline	1/1
Notification	4/1
Nonfall registration?	No

FINANCIAL FACTS

Financial Aid Rating	96
Annual tuition	$50,997
Room and board	$15,093
Required fees	$1,494
Average need-based scholarship	$42,467
% needy frosh rec. need-based scholarship or grant aid	98
% needy UG rec. need-based scholarship or grant aid	100
% needy frosh rec. non-need-based scholarship or grant aid	0
% needy UG rec. non-need-based scholarship or grant aid	0
% needy frosh rec. need-based self-help aid	13
% needy UG rec. need-based self-help aid	47
% frosh rec. any financial aid	64
% UG rec. any financial aid	62
% UG borrow to pay for school	34
Average cumulative indebtedness	$21,291
% frosh need fully met	100
% ugrads need fully met	100
Average % of frosh need met	100
Average % of ugrad need met	100

University of Colorado Boulder

552 UCB, BOULDER, CO 80309-0552 • ADMISSIONS: 303-492-6301 • FAX: 303-492-7115

CAMPUS LIFE

Quality of Life Rating	93
Fire Safety Rating	91
Green Rating	96
Type of school	Public
Affiliation	No Affiliation
Environment	City

STUDENTS

Total undergrad enrollment	27,010
% male/female	55/45
% from out of state	40
% frosh live on campus	95
% ugrads live on campus	29
# of fraternities (% ugrad men join)	18 (10)
# of sororities (% ugrad women join)	14 (19)
% African American	2
% Asian	5
% Caucasian	71
% Hispanic	11
% Native American	<1
% Pacific Islander	<1
% Two or more races	5
% Race and/or ethnicity unknown	1
% international	6
# of countries represented	113

ACADEMICS

Academic Rating	76
% students returning for sophomore year	86
% students graduating within 4 years	47
% students graduating within 6 years	71
Calendar	Semester
Student/faculty ratio	18:1
Profs interesting rating	78
Profs accessible rating	78

Most classes have 10–19 students.
Most lab/discussion sessions have
   20–29 students.

MOST POPULAR MAJORS
Physiology; Psychology; Communication

ABOUT THE SCHOOL

A large research institution of more than 25,000 undergraduates, the University of Colorado Boulder offers more than 150 fields of study. The school operates particularly strong programs in engineering and the sciences; students also hold the architecture, journalism, mass communications, and aerospace programs in high esteem. (The university is consistently among the top universities to receive NASA funding.) Since the school is large, there are many available academic choices and the diverse faculty reflects that, among them five Nobel Prize winners, nineteen Rhodes Scholars, and eight MacArthur Genius Grant Fellowships. "Being in a class taught by a Nobel laureate is not something everyone gets to experience." It is not uncommon for students to be on a five- or six-year plan as a result of the extensive amount of academic choices. When they do finish, CU graduates are likely to find themselves well prepared for the real world. The career services office offers counseling, job and internship listings, and on-campus recruiting to the general student population; in addition, the university has numerous online tools to help students prepare for the job market.

BANG FOR YOUR BUCK

For Colorado residents, scholarship opportunities include the Esteemed Scholars Program for freshmen, the CU Promise Program for freshmen and transfers, and the First Generation Scholarship, for students whose parents do not have college degrees. For both in-state and out-of-state students, CU offers this enticing guarantee: there will be no tuition increases during your four years of study. In addition, the top 25 percent of out-of-state admissions are eligible to receive the Chancellor's Achievement Scholarship. With well over 5,000 new freshman "Buffaloes" on campus each year, the school nonetheless provides an incredible array of resources. "CU is an amazing place because you can find an array of challenges and opportunities whether your drive is research, the arts, sports, a job, or tough classwork." "I am able to research in one of my professor's labs while receiving a great education." In select programs, students may earn a bachelors and a masters degree concurrently in five years.

STUDENT LIFE

University of Colorado Boulder tends to attract "very social" students. Therefore, that pretty much guarantees that undergrads can almost "always [find] something going on." For example, "during the weekends, there is always a party or two to attend, and once you are twenty-one the bar scene is quite popular." Moreover, CU Boulder is "a very politically aware campus and the students tend to have an opinion about different issues going on in the world." They also love simply chilling in their dorm. As one civil engineering major shares, "We have a ping pong table constantly in use, and it seems like there's always somebody playing music or playing a game or just hanging out and talking." Additionally, "most people usually watch the Broncos games together in the common room." Finally, seeing as though "Boulder is a beautiful place" many undergrads love participating in outdoor activities. Yes, this student population counts a number of "rock climbers, skiers, and backpackers" among their ranks.

CAREER

Students at University of Colorado Boulder are flush with career opportunities. Clearly, the fantastic Career Services office ensures that these undergrads know how to compete in competitive job markets. Freshman start with the StrengthsQuest program, to learn how to better maximize their skillsets on campus and beyond. Then the Buffs Professional Program leads them through professional development activities to help them stand out to future employers. Throughout the academic year, the office sets up a number of information sessions. This allows students to both network and explore a variety of career

University of Colorado Boulder

FINANCIAL AID: 303-492-5091 • WEBSITE: WWW.COLORADO.EDU

paths. Aside from the usual internship and job searches, the office helps undergrads find research opportunities that align with their interests and passions. In fact, many students are involved with cutting edge research. Of course, undergrads who have their sights set on finding a job will be happy to discover that CU hosts numerous career fairs. Even better—they are organized by industry. Therefore, students can attend events based around creative jobs, green jobs, finance jobs, and more.

GENERAL INFO

Activities: Choral groups, concert band, dance, drama/theater, jazz band, literary magazine, marching band, music ensembles, musical theater, opera, pep band, radio station, student government, student newspaper, student-run film society, symphony orchestra, campus ministries, international student organization. **Organizations:** 400 registered organizations, 28 honor societies, 30 religious organizations. 18 fraternities, 14 sororities. **Athletics (Intercollegiate):** *Men:* Basketball, cross-country, football, golf, skiing (downhill/alpine), skiing (nordic/cross-country), track/field (outdoor), track/field (indoor). *Women:* Basketball, cross-country, golf, lacrosse, skiing (downhill/alpine), skiing (nordic/cross-country), soccer, tennis, track/field (outdoor), track/field (indoor), volleyball. **On-Campus Highlights:** University Memorial Center (UMC), Student Recreation Center, Norlin Library, ATLAS Building, Farrand Field, CU Boulder's Outdoor Program at the Recreation Center.

FINANCIAL AID

Students should submit: FAFSA. Priority filing deadline is 3/1. The Princeton Review suggests that all financial aid forms be submitted as soon as possible after October 1. *Need-based scholarships/grants offered:* Federal Pell, FSEOG, State scholarships/grants, Private scholarships, College/university scholarship or grant aid from institutional funds. *Loan aid offered:* Direct Subsidized Stafford Loans, Direct Unsubsidized Stafford Loans, Direct PLUS loans, Federal Perkins Loans, College/university loans from institutional funds. Applicants will be notified of awards on a rolling basis beginning 3/15. Federal Work-Study Program available. Institutional employment available.

THE BOTTOM LINE

CU-Boulder's reasonable tuition is one of the school's major selling points. Tuition (including mandatory fees) for Colorado residents averages just about $11,500 annually. For nonresidents, tuition and fees average about $35,000. Room and board is an additional $13,590 annually. Books average $1,800 per year. Each year, more than 60 percent of CU-Boulder's undergraduates apply for and receive financial aid through a combination of loans, work-study programs, and scholarships. The average total need-based aid package amounts to over $16,000. The need-based gift aid to freshmen is approximately $10,000.

CAREER INFORMATION FROM PAYSCALE.COM

ROI rating	86
Bachelor's and No Higher	
Median starting salary	$50,000
Median mid-career salary	$89,900
At Least Bachelor's	
Median starting salary	$50,900
Median mid-career salary	$94,500
% alumni with high job meaning	49%
% STEM	21%

SELECTIVITY

Admissions Rating	82
# of applicants	31,326
% of applicants accepted	80
% of acceptees attending	25
# offered a place on the wait list	2,110
% accepting a place on wait list	17
% admitted from wait list	0

FRESHMAN PROFILE

Range SAT Critical Reading	530–640
Range SAT Math	540–660
Range ACT Composite	24–30
Average HS GPA	3.6
% graduated top 10% of class	28
% graduated top 25% of class	57
% graduated top 50% of class	89

DEADLINES

Early action	
Deadline	11/15
Notification	2/1
Regular	
Priority	11/15
Deadline	1/15
Notification	4/1
Nonfall registration?	Yes

FINANCIAL FACTS

Financial Aid Rating	85
Annual in-state tuition	$9,768
Annual out-of-state tuition	$33,316
Room and board	$13,590
Required fees	$1,763
Average need-based scholarship	$10,248
% needy frosh rec. need-based scholarship or grant aid	76
% needy UG rec. need-based scholarship or grant aid	77
% needy frosh rec. non-need-based scholarship or grant aid	5
% needy UG rec. non-need-based scholarship or grant aid	3
% needy frosh rec. need-based self-help aid	83
% needy UG rec. need-based self-help aid	85
% UG borrow to pay for school	44
Average cumulative indebtedness	$25,605
% frosh need fully met	42
% ugrads need fully met	36
Average % of frosh need met	81
Average % of ugrad need met	79

University of Connecticut

2131 HILLSIDE ROAD, STORRS, CT 06268-3088 • ADMISSIONS: 860-486-3137 • FAX: 860-486-1476

CAMPUS LIFE

Quality of Life Rating	85
Fire Safety Rating	91
Green Rating	98
Type of school	Public
Affiliation	No Affiliation
Environment	Town

STUDENTS

Total undergrad enrollment	18,395
% male/female	50/50
% from out of state	22
% frosh from public high school	88
% frosh live on campus	97
% ugrads live on campus	71
# of fraternities (% ugrad men join)	18 (8)
# of sororities (% ugrad women join)	15 (12)
% African American	5
% Asian	10
% Caucasian	62
% Hispanic	8
% Native American	<1
% Pacific Islander	<1
% Two or more races	3
% Race and/or ethnicity unknown	8
% international	4
# of countries represented	113

ACADEMICS

Academic Rating	75
% students returning for sophomore year	93
% students graduating within 4 years	67
% students graduating within 6 years	81
Calendar	Semester
Student/faculty ratio	16:1
Profs interesting rating	68
Profs accessible rating	67

Most classes have 10–19 students.
Most lab/discussion sessions have
10–19 students.

MOST POPULAR MAJORS
Psychology; Biology; Economics

ABOUT THE SCHOOL

With its "strong focus on academics" and "outstanding school spirit," it's easy to understand why students fall in love University of Connecticut. As a "highly ranked public university," UConn offers "a diverse learning environment" that really allows "students to achieve their goals." Undergrads are also quick to note that opportunities to conduct research abound. And they rush to share that the university has exceptionally strong programs in "agriculture, engineering and education." Importantly, UConn students find their time in the classroom "rewarding." Though professors "can be hit or miss," the vast majority are "engaging" and "passionate about their subject." As an actuarial student brags, "My professors are some of the best educators in their fields." Moreover, they are "very helpful and show that they care and are interested in their students." Perhaps this marketing undergrad sums it up best, "They really push you to do your best and are rooting you on the whole time."

BANG FOR YOUR BUCK

The financial aid office at the University of Connecticut works diligently to meet the needs of the student body. In fact, it supplies assistance to over 80% its undergraduates. One of the ways the university does this is by sponsoring a number of renewable merit scholarships. These include the highly competitive Nutmeg Scholarship which provides a full ride to exceptionally accomplished high school seniors from Connecticut and the STEM Scholarship which is given to students at the top of their class who have chosen to pursue a STEM discipline. Thankfully, incoming freshmen are automatically considered for these and more. Aside from scholarships, UConn also maintains a healthy work-study program. Students can find positions within any number of departments. Finally, it's important to note that undergrads who hail from New England may be eligible for a reduction in their tuition thanks to the New England Regional Student Program.

STUDENT LIFE

Life at the University of Connecticut is "nice because it offers a bit of everything." For starters, UConn is the place to be if you're a sports enthusiast. As an excited sociology major shares, "We have outstanding athletic programs from our D1 basketball to our intramural sports." The school also sponsors "hundreds of clubs" from the UConn Scouting Association and UConn Ballroom Dance Team to the Allied Health Science Club as well as many fraternities and sororities. Undergrads here are also good at making their own entertainment. For example, we're told that when it snows, "you'll catch tons of students tubing down HorseBarn Hill." And there's plenty of fun to be had when the weekend finally arrives. That's because "the Student Union holds late-night with karaoke, games, crafts, and other activities and the Jorgenson Theater holds everything from comedies to classical plays, concerts to award ceremonies, and everything in between."

CAREER

University of Connecticut students graduate ready to tackle the world. And that's exactly what they do. After all, according to payscale. com, the average starting salary for UConn alums is $52,600 and the

University of Connecticut

Financial Aid: 860-486-2819 • E-mail: beahusky@uconn.edu • Website: www.uconn.edu

average mid-career salary is an impressive $91,800. Of course, this isn't too surprising given that the Center for Career Development primes them for success. To begin with, undergrads can receive one-on-one counseling from a career consultant. This helps them create targeted goals and strategies. Students can also participate in the UConn Internship and Coop Programs which provide real-world work experience and plenty of opportunities for networking. In addition, the Center does a phenomenal job attracting companies for both career fairs and on-campus recruiting. Corporations that have been known to recruit UConn students include United Airlines, Half Full Brewery and Mass Mutual.

GENERAL INFO
Activities: Choral groups, concert band, dance, drama/theater, jazz band, literary magazine, marching band, music ensembles, musical theater, opera, pep band, radio station, student government, student newspaper, student-run film society, symphony orchestra, television station, yearbook, Campus Ministries, International Student Organization, Model UN 303 registered organizations, 29 honor societies, 17 religious organizations. 14 fraternities, 12 sororities. **Athletics (Intercollegiate):** *Men:* baseball, basketball, cross-country, diving, football, golf, ice hockey, soccer, swimming, tennis, track/field (outdoor), track/field (indoor). *Women:* basketball, crew/rowing, cross-country, diving, field hockey, ice hockey, lacrosse, soccer, softball, swimming, tennis, track/field (outdoor), track/field (indoor), volleyball. **On-Campus Highlights:** William Benton Museum of Art, Dairy Product Salesroom, Puppetry Museum, Green Houses, Jorgensen Auditorium and Connecticut Repertory Theater.

FINANCIAL AID
Students should submit: FAFSA. Priority filing deadline is 3/1. The Princeton Review suggests that all financial aid forms be submitted as soon as possible after October 1. *Need-based scholarships/grants offered:* Federal Pell, FSEOG, State scholarships/grants, Private scholarships, College/university scholarship or grant aid from institutional funds. *Loan aid offered:* Direct Subsidized Stafford Loans, Direct Unsubsidized Stafford Loans, Direct PLUS loans, Federal Perkins Loans, Federal Nursing Loans. Applicants will be notified of awards on a rolling basis beginning 3/1. Federal Work-Study Program available. Institutional employment available.

BOTTOM LINE
Connecticut residents will receive a tuition bill of $11,224. Unfortunately, undergrads hailing from out-of-state will pay significantly more—to the tune of $33,016. All students, regardless of where they grew up, will also have to pay $2,842 in university and student fees. Additionally, individuals planning to live on-campus can expect to pay $6,660 for their residence hall. Moreover, a seven-day meal plan runs another $5,776 a year. Finally, students should anticipate setting aside an additional $850 for books and supplies.

CAREER INFORMATION FROM PAYSCALE.COM

ROI rating	87
Bachelor's and No Higher	
Median starting salary	$51,900
Median mid-career salary	$89,100
At Least Bachelor's	
Median starting salary	$52,600
Median mid-career salary	$91,800
% alumni with high job meaning	49%
% STEM	18%

SELECTIVITY

Admissions Rating	89
# of applicants	31,280
% of applicants accepted	50
% of acceptees attending	23
# offered a place on the wait list	4,259
% accepting a place on wait list	45
% admitted from wait list	81

FRESHMAN PROFILE

Range SAT Critical Reading	560–660
Range SAT Math	590–690
Range SAT Writing	550–660
Range ACT Composite	26–30
Minimum paper TOEFL	550
Minimum internet-based TOEFL	79
% graduated top 10% of class	50
% graduated top 25% of class	85
% graduated top 50% of class	98

DEADLINES

Regular	
Deadline	1/15
Nonfall registration?	Yes

FINANCIAL FACTS

Financial Aid Rating	79
Annual in-state tuition	$11,224
Annual out-of-state tuition	$33,016
Room and board	$12,436
Required fees	$2,842
Average need-based scholarship	$10,102
% needy frosh rec. need-based scholarship or grant aid	68
% needy UG rec. need-based scholarship or grant aid	72
% needy frosh rec. non-need-based scholarship or grant aid	51
% needy UG rec. non-need-based scholarship or grant aid	36
% needy frosh rec. need-based self-help aid	72
% needy UG rec. need-based self-help aid	73
% frosh rec. any financial aid	49
% UG rec. any financial aid	48
% frosh need fully met	14
% ugrads need fully met	13
Average % of frosh need met	60
Average % of ugrad need met	61

University of Dayton

300 College Park, Dayton, OH 45469-1669 • Admissions: 800-837-7433 • Fax: 937-229-4729

CAMPUS LIFE

Quality of Life Rating	**97**
Fire Safety Rating	**81**
Green Rating	**83**
Type of school	Private
Affiliation	Roman Catholic
Environment	City

STUDENTS

Total undergrad enrollment	8,665
% male/female	52/48
% from out of state	49
% frosh from public high school	43
% frosh live on campus	93
% ugrads live on campus	71
# of fraternities (% ugrad men join)	11 (13)
# of sororities (% ugrad women join)	9 (20)
% African American	3
% Asian	1
% Caucasian	78
% Hispanic	3
% Native American	<1
% Pacific Islander	<1
% Two or more races	2
% Race and/or ethnicity unknown	2
% international	11
# of countries represented	70

ACADEMICS

Academic Rating	**79**
% students returning for sophomore year	91
% students graduating within 4 years	59
% students graduating within 6 years	76
Calendar	Semester
Student/faculty ratio	16:1
Profs interesting rating	86
Profs accessible rating	86
Most classes have 20–29 students.	
Most lab/discussion sessions have 10–19 students.	

MOST POPULAR MAJORS
Speech Communication and Rhetoric;
Marketing/Marketing Management;
Psychology

ABOUT THE SCHOOL

This Catholic, midsize national research university is "large enough to have all of the necessary resources and opportunities, but it is small enough to have a feeling of intimacy." The school adheres to a Common Academic Program (CAP) for its core curriculum and stresses service learning through community partnerships and civic engagement. One student notes, "University of Dayton takes community overboard (in a good way)." Professors always "relate experiences to the real world" and are "completely committed to seeing their students succeed." There is great connectivity between all levels of the university, and "students have the opportunity to meet with the President and administration and bring ideas up to them." All here agree that there is "a promising vision for the future of the school," with a great emphasis on making it easy for students to give back.

BANG FOR YOUR BUCK

The University of Dayton values transparency in its costs, and "what you pay as a first-year student is what you will pay as a senior"; scholarships and grants increase each year to offset tuition increases, and there are also no fees for classes, labs, or orientation. This allows families to better plan for the four years that a student is at school. Numerous university scholarships are available based on academics, merit, athletic ability, or legacy status (including those who are relatives of a Deacon in the Roman Catholic or Orthodox Church). There are also grants for students who demonstrate high financial need.

STUDENT LIFE

Almost the entire student body lives on this "beautiful, friendly, open-minded campus" in housing owned by the university (most of which has porches), which "helps keep a very strong community." Cook-outs, kiddie-pools, and porch parties are classic scenes in the UD student neighborhood. Students say that the greatest strength of the school is the atmosphere: "Everyone here is so relaxed and still gets what they [need] to do done." The Campus Activities Board hosts fun activities on the weekends such as movie nights, comedians, and trips to professional baseball games, and with all of the University of Dayton's clubs "you can always find a craft, dinner, social, 5k, service event, etc. to go to." Additionally, Flyer basketball is one thing all students gather around; the men's team appeared in the Elite Eight in the 2014 NCAA tournament. "It's great to see all the red on game days and going to the games is a blast," says a student.

CAREER

The University of Dayton Research Institute is a massive hub of engineering and science research, and there are numerous other centers and institutes that help promote leadership and internship opportunities, co-ops, and non-scientific research—common elements of a University of Dayton education. "We are not just sitting in a classroom for four years, we actually go out and see our learning in action," says a student. To prepare students for landing an internship, co-op or full-time job after graduation, Career Services offers career advising, mock interviews, and résumé critiques. Career Fairs are held each fall and spring, and the Hire a Flyer network gives students access to job openings and potential employers. Of the graduates who visited PayScale.com, the average starting salary was $50,600 and 46 percent reported feeling their job had a high level of meaning in the world. According to the school, 95 percent of UD graduates find employment, enroll in grad school, or join a volunteer program within six months of graduation.

University of Dayton

FINANCIAL AID: 800-837-7433 • E-MAIL: ADMISSION@UDAYTON.EDU • WEBSITE: WWW.UDAYTON.EDU

GENERAL INFO

Activities: Choral groups, concert band, dance, drama/theater, jazz band, literary magazine, marching band, music ensembles, musical theater, opera, pep band, radio station, student government, student newspaper, sustainability club, symphony orchestra, television station, yearbook, Campus Ministry, Model UN. **Organizations:** 240 registered organizations, 15 honor societies, 35 service groups. 11 fraternities, 9 sororities. **Athletics (Intercollegiate):** *Men:* baseball, basketball, cheerleading, cross-country, football, golf, soccer, tennis. *Women:* basketball, cheerleading, crew/rowing, cross-country, golf, soccer, softball, tennis, track/field (outdoor), track/field (indoor), volleyball. **On-Campus Highlights:** John F. Kennedy Memorial Union, Ryan C. Harris Learning-Teaching Center, University of Dayton Arena, Science Center, Kettering Laboratories, UDRI, ArtStreet, Marianst Hall, Chapel of the Immaculate Conception, RecPlex.

FINANCIAL AID

Students should submit: FAFSA. Priority filing deadline is 2/1. The Princeton Review suggests that all financial aid forms be submitted as soon as possible after October 1. *Need-based scholarships/grants offered:* Federal Pell, FSEOG, State scholarships/grants, Private scholarships, College/university scholarship or grant aid from institutional funds. *Loan aid offered:* Direct Subsidized Stafford Loans, Direct Unsubsidized Stafford Loans, Direct PLUS loans, Federal Perkins Loans. Applicants will be notified of awards on a rolling basis beginning 2/15. Federal Work-Study Program available. Institutional employment available.

BOTTOM LINE

Tuition at the University of Dayton is $40,940, but the school is all about "the real cost of tuition" and so has no additional fees or surcharges. Students who attend an official campus visit and file the FAFSA by March 1 also have their textbooks paid for by the school (up to $4,000 over four years). Ninety-four percent of students receive some manner of financial aid. Ninety-nine percent of needy students receive need-based aid, with the average freshman gift package being $22,645, and 62 percent of graduates borrow through a loan program, accruing an average of $35,740 in debt.

CAREER INFORMATION FROM PAYSCALE.COM	
ROI rating	86
Bachelor's and No Higher	
Median starting salary	$52,100
Median mid-career salary	$88,700
At Least Bachelor's	
Median starting salary	$53,800
Median mid-career salary	$91,100
% alumni with high job meaning	44%
% STEM	20%

SELECTIVITY	
Admissions Rating	86
# of applicants	16,968
% of applicants accepted	58
% of acceptees attending	22

FRESHMAN PROFILE	
Range SAT Critical Reading	510–620
Range SAT Math	520–630
Range SAT Writing	520–610
Range ACT Composite	24–29
Minimum paper TOEFL	550
Minimum internet-based TOEFL	80
Average HS GPA	3.6
% graduated top 10% of class	25
% graduated top 25% of class	58
% graduated top 50% of class	88

DEADLINES	
Early action	
Deadline	11/1
Notification	12/15
Regular	
Priority	11/1
Deadline	2/1
Notification	2/15
Nonfall registration?	Yes

FINANCIAL FACTS	
Financial Aid Rating	86
Annual tuition	$40,940
Room and board	$12,680
Average need-based scholarship	$22,645
% needy frosh rec. need-based scholarship or grant aid	100
% needy UG rec. need-based scholarship or grant aid	99
% needy frosh rec. non-need-based scholarship or grant aid	19
% needy UG rec. non-need-based scholarship or grant aid	20
% needy frosh rec. need-based self-help aid	85
% needy UG rec. need-based self-help aid	83
% frosh rec. any financial aid	98
% UG rec. any financial aid	94
% frosh need fully met	31
% ugrads need fully met	35
Average % of frosh need met	86
Average % of ugrad need met	84

University of Delaware

210 South College Ave, Newark, DE 19716-6210 • Admissions: 302-831-8123 • Fax: 302-831-6905

ABOUT THE SCHOOL

The University of Delaware is the largest university in the state. Delaware students benefit from a series of signature academic programs, where students rave about the "challenging classes and friendly professors." Other programs include service-learning, study abroad, and undergraduate research opportunities. Every freshman participates in First Year Experience, a program that allows them to meet other students in their major, learn about the school's resources, and generally feel more at home on campus. The school has renowned engineering, science, business, education, and environmental programs, and a new Health Services Complex houses clinics and core facilities for research. It is also one of only handful of schools in North America with a major in art conservation; the animal science program is esteemed as well, with a farm that's campus-adjacent for hands-on experience. Service learning at UD allows students to heighten their academic experience, and destinations run the gamut from Newark to Vietnam, New York to Costa Rica. The University Honors Program is the intellectual pearl of the university.

BANG FOR YOUR BUCK

Part of the billion-dollar endowment club, the University of Delaware can afford to award more than $100 million annually in federal, state, and institutional aid. All students who apply for Freshman admission by January 15 are automatically considered for scholarships. Every manner of scholarship is available merit, art, athletics and music. Some require additional documentation. Visit www.udel.edu/admissions for more information. The school's Commitment to Delawareans provides grants to cover the full demonstrated need of all first-time, in-state freshman. The most competitive candidates are in the running to be Distinguished Scholars and may receive full scholarships. According to the university, its commitment to affordability for all students "is seen through our reasonable tuition" and "a variety of scholarships, financial aid programs, and financing plans."

STUDENT LIFE

This is an "academically intense university," but everyone maintains "a balance between keeping up with your academics as well as having a good time on the weekends." For fun, UD students (who hail mainly from the East Coast) like "to tailgate at football games, go out to eat or see a movie on Main Street, attend parties off-campus, or just hang out with their friends." There is a coffeehouse series with local or on-campus musicians every week, along with many different fund-raising activities and clubs, which helps keep the general level of school spirit high. "If you look for them, there are a lot of great guest speakers, bands, and cultural events on campus at any time," says a student. With proximity to major cities (Philly, D.C., Baltimore, and New York), students are able to travel often and on the cheap.

CAREER

The "very helpful" Career Services Center is well-connected with outside organizations for lining up internship opportunities, and research opportunities within the university are equally as plentiful. In fact, according to the school, 85 percent of students complete some form of research, internship, or other experiential learning opportunity prior to graduation. Many specialized and general career fairs are held throughout the year, as well as on-campus informational sessions and interviews with UD employer partners. The Center helps students make career action plans, called CareerMAPs, and maintains a database of jobs, tips, and sample resumes; students applying to graduate school have access to a similarly robust pool of resources.

University of Delaware

FINANCIAL AID: 302-831-8761 • E-MAIL: ADMISSIONS@UDEL.EDU • WEBSITE: WWW.UDEL.EDU

UD graduates who visited PayScale.com reported an average starting salary of $50,300, and 46 percent said they felt their job had a high level of impact on the world.

GENERAL INFO

Activities: Choral groups, concert band, dance, drama/theater, jazz band, literary magazine, marching band, music ensembles, musical theater, opera, pep band, radio station, student government, student newspaper, student-run film society, symphony orchestra, television station, campus ministries, international student organization. **Organizations:** 400 registered organizations, 23 honor societies, 24 religious organizations. 24 fraternities, 19 sororities. **Athletics (Intercollegiate):** *Men:* Baseball, basketball, diving, football, golf, lacrosse, soccer, swimming, tennis. *Women:* Basketball, crew/rowing, cross-country, diving, field hockey, golf, lacrosse, soccer, softball, swimming, tennis, track/field (outdoor), track/field (indoor), volleyball.

FINANCIAL AID

Students should submit: FAFSA. Regular filing deadline is 3/15. The Princeton Review suggests that all financial aid forms be submitted as soon as possible after October 1. *Need-based scholarships/grants offered:* Federal Pell, FSEOG, State scholarships/grants, Private scholarships, College/university scholarship or grant aid from institutional funds. *Loan aid offered:* Direct Subsidized Stafford Loans, Direct Unsubsidized Stafford Loans, Direct PLUS loans, Federal Perkins Loans, Federal Nursing Loans. Applicants will be notified of awards on a rolling basis beginning 3/15. Federal Work-Study Program available. Institutional employment available.

THE BOTTOM LINE

The cost of attending the University of Delaware is comparatively cheap, especially if you're from Delaware. Annual tuition and fees hover around $12,830, while campus room and board will run you another $12,068. Out-of-state undergraduates pay $19,420 more in tuition. As part of its UD Commitment, the university works to make a UD education affordable to all qualified state residents and has pledged to meet their full demonstrated financial need (up to the cost of in-state tuition and fees). Over half of freshmen are recipients of financial aid packages averaging a little over $9,000 per enrollee.

CAREER INFORMATION FROM PAYSCALE.COM

ROI rating	87
Bachelor's and No Higher	
Median starting salary	$50,400
Median mid-career salary	$86,100
At Least Bachelor's	
Median starting salary	$51,100
Median mid-career salary	$90,100
% alumni with high job meaning	48%
% STEM	15%

SELECTIVITY

Admissions Rating	88
# of applicants	24,881
% of applicants accepted	63
% of acceptees attending	26
# offered a place on the wait list	2,138
% accepting a place on wait list	40
% admitted from wait list	0

FRESHMAN PROFILE

Range SAT Critical Reading	550–650
Range SAT Math	560–660
Range SAT Writing	550–650
Range ACT Composite	25–29
Minimum paper TOEFL	570
Minimum internet-based TOEFL	90
Average HS GPA	3.7
% graduated top 10% of class	33
% graduated top 25% of class	68
% graduated top 50% of class	94

DEADLINES

Regular	
Deadline	1/15
Nonfall registration?	Yes

FINANCIAL FACTS

Financial Aid Rating	88
Annual in-state tuition	$11,540
Annual out-of-state tuition	$30,960
Room and board	$12,068
Required fees	$1,290
Average need-based scholarship	$9,058
% needy frosh rec. need-based scholarship or grant aid	92
% needy UG rec. need-based scholarship or grant aid	82
% needy frosh rec. non-need-based scholarship or grant aid	62
% needy UG rec. non-need-based scholarship or grant aid	55
% needy frosh rec. need-based self-help aid	73
% needy UG rec. need-based self-help aid	79
% frosh rec. any financial aid	54
% UG rec. any financial aid	49
% frosh need fully met	51
% ugrads need fully met	47
Average % of frosh need met	76
Average % of ugrad need met	75

University of Denver

Undergraduate Admission, Denver, CO 80208 • Admissions: 303-871-2036 • Fax: 303-871-3301

CAMPUS LIFE

Quality of Life Rating	92
Fire Safety Rating	65
Green Rating	86
Type of school	Private
Affiliation	No Affiliation
Environment	Metropolis

STUDENTS

Total undergrad enrollment	5,758
% male/female	46/54
% from out of state	59
% frosh live on campus	93
% ugrads live on campus	44
# of fraternities (% ugrad men join)	9 (27)
# of sororities (% ugrad women join)	13 (29)
% African American	2
% Asian	4
% Caucasian	68
% Hispanic	10
% Native American	<1
% Pacific Islander	<1
% Two or more races	4
% Race and/or ethnicity unknown	3
% international	9
# of countries represented	43

ACADEMICS

Academic Rating	84
% students returning for sophomore year	86
% students graduating within 4 years	67
% students graduating within 6 years	77
Calendar	Quarter
Student/faculty ratio	11:1
Profs interesting rating	86
Profs accessible rating	85
Most classes have 10–19 students.	
Most lab/discussion sessions have 10–19 students.	

MOST POPULAR MAJORS
International Relations and Affairs; Finance; Psychology

ABOUT THE SCHOOL

There's no denying that University of Denver's profile is on the rise. And with its "small classroom settings," "focus on innovation [and] sustainability" and "excellent study abroad program[s]" it's easy to understand why. Of course, "being able to see the sun set over the mountains out [your] dorm window" doesn't hurt either. Academically, students have the opportunity to pursue a wide variety of disciplines. For starters, the university is "well-known for its hospitality and business programs." We'd also be remiss if we didn't highlight Denver's Josef Korbel School of International Studies, "regarded as one of the best schools for international relations in the world." Fortunately, no matter what they study, undergrads typically encounter "passionate" professors who are "experts in their field." And while their "expectations are high," they are also "actively engaged" and "willing to do [whatever it takes] to help students be successful."

BANG FOR YOUR BUCK

A number of undergrads are drawn to the University of Denver for the "great financial aid." And it's easy to understand why. The school truly strives to make sure its programs are affordable for all students, no matter their background. For example, Denver offers a variety of generous scholarships including the Chancellor award which provides $24,000 annually and the Provost award which offers $22,000 annually. Thankfully, DU's scholarships aren't limited to a select few. Indeed, roughly 70 percent of Denver's first-year students receive some type of merit-based aid. And these rewards are typically renewable assuming the student remains in good academic standing.

STUDENT LIFE

Overall, DU's student body tends to skew "preppy," though we've been assured that everyone, "no matter their race, ethnicity, religion [or] sexual preference [is] accepted and fit[s] in." Perhaps some of this openness can be attributed to the fact that the university is overflowing with extracurricular and social opportunities. To begin with, "Greek life is big." Additionally, "students love to cheer on their own sports teams as well as the professional teams in Denver." Of course, there's no need to fret if fraternities or athletics aren't your scene. A sophomore tells us that DU "has different activities like parades and fairs that students and their friends can enjoy, so it is really easy to be entertained." Lastly, given the school's proximity to the Rockies, it's no surprise that undergrads are "constantly driving up to the mountains to go skiing, snowboarding, hiking, etc."

CAREER

By and large, undergrads at University of Denver are confident in their post-graduation job prospects (The school reports that 97 percent of alumni have jobs and/or are enrolled in graduate school six months following graduation). And many students happily report that there are "countless opportunities for internships." This sunny outlook can certainly be attributed to the tireless efforts of DU's career services office. For starters, the office hosts multiple fairs throughout the academic year, including an innovative reverse career fair where students set up tables and employers circulate the room to share their job opportunities. Moreover, the office recently launched AlumniFire, which helps current students connect with Denver alums. And many students love to take advantage of the Career Center's drop-in program which allows them to swing by the office and quickly meet with a career advisor.

University of Denver

Financial Aid: 303-871-4020 • E-mail: admission@du.edu • Website: www.du.edu

GENERAL INFO

Activities: Choral groups, concert band, dance, drama/theater, jazz band, literary magazine, music ensembles, musical theater, opera, pep band, radio station, student government, student newspaper, student-run film society, symphony orchestra, Campus Ministries, International Student Organization, Model UN. **Organizations:** 160 registered organizations, 19 honor societies, 14 religious organizations. 9 fraternities, 13 sororities. **Athletics (Intercollegiate):** *Men:* basketball, diving, golf, ice hockey, lacrosse, skiing (downhill/alpine), skiing (nordic/cross-country), soccer, swimming, tennis. *Women:* basketball, diving, golf, gymnastics, lacrosse, skiing (downhill/alpine), skiing (nordic/cross-country), soccer, swimming, tennis, volleyball. **On-Campus Highlights:** Daniel Felix Ritchie School of Engineering and Computer Science, Ritchie Center (athletic facility), Newman Center (performing arts), Daniels College of Business building, Anderson Academic Commons (library).

FINANCIAL AID

Students should submit: FAFSA, CSS/Financial Aid PROFILE, Noncustodial PROFILE (if applicable). Priority filing deadline is 11/1. Regular filing deadline is 1/15. The Princeton Review suggests that all financial aid forms be submitted as soon as possible after October 1. *Need-based scholarships/grants offered:* Federal Pell, FSEOG, State scholarships/grants, Private scholarships, College/university scholarship or grant aid from institutional funds. *Loan aid offered:* Direct Subsidized Stafford Loans, Direct Unsubsidized Stafford Loans, Direct PLUS loans. Applicants will be notified of awards soon after admissions decisions. Federal Work-Study Program available. Institutional employment available.

BOTTOM LINE

Traditional, full-time undergraduates at University of Denver will face a tuition bill of $45,228 for the 2016-2017 academic year. Additionally, there are miscellaneous fees totaling $1,134. Students can also expect room and board to cost roughly $11,702. And they'll need to set aside another $1,200 for books (and various school supplies) as well as $1,275 for transportation. Lastly, it's estimated that undergrads will need $1,359 for personal expenses.

CAREER INFORMATION FROM PAYSCALE.COM

ROI rating	85
Bachelor's and No Higher	
Median starting salary	$47,800
Median mid-career salary	$82,100
At Least Bachelor's	
Median starting salary	$49,800
Median mid-career salary	$84,700
% alumni with high job meaning	55%
% STEM	9%

SELECTIVITY

Admissions Rating	87
# of applicants	15,036
% of applicants accepted	73
% of acceptees attending	13
# offered a place on the wait list	2,442
% accepting a place on wait list	19
% admitted from wait list	8

FRESHMAN PROFILE

Range SAT Critical Reading	550–660
Range SAT Math	560–660
Range SAT Writing	530–630
Range ACT Composite	23–30
Minimum paper TOEFL	550
Minimum internet-based TOEFL	80
Average HS GPA	3.7
% graduated top 10% of class	45
% graduated top 25% of class	80
% graduated top 50% of class	97

DEADLINES

Early action	
Deadline	11/1
Notification	12/31
Regular	
Deadline	1/15
Notification	3/15
Nonfall registration?	Yes

FINANCIAL FACTS

Financial Aid Rating	87
Annual tuition	$45,288
Room and board	$12,021
Required fees	$1,134
Average need-based scholarship	$29,644
% needy frosh rec. need-based scholarship or grant aid	46
% needy UG rec. need-based scholarship or grant aid	42
% needy frosh rec. non-need-based scholarship or grant aid	46
% needy UG rec. non-need-based scholarship or grant aid	41
% needy frosh rec. need-based self-help aid	46
% needy UG rec. need-based self-help aid	42
% frosh rec. any financial aid	85
% UG rec. any financial aid	83
% frosh need fully met	30
% ugrads need fully met	28
Average % of frosh need met	82
Average % of ugrad need met	83

University of Florida

201 CRISER HALL, GAINESVILLE, FL 32611-4000 • ADMISSIONS: 352-392-1365 • FAX: 352-392-3987

CAMPUS LIFE

Quality of Life Rating	87
Fire Safety Rating	60*
Green Rating	93
Type of school	Public
Affiliation	No Affiliation
Environment	City

STUDENTS

Total undergrad enrollment	35,043
% male/female	45/55
% from out of state	5
% frosh from public high school	70
% frosh live on campus	80
% ugrads live on campus	24
# of fraternities (% ugrad men join)	35 (20)
# of sororities (% ugrad women join)	28 (24)
% African American	6
% Asian	8
% Caucasian	57
% Hispanic	21
% Native American	<1
% Pacific Islander	<1
% Two or more races	3
% Race and/or ethnicity unknown	3
% international	1
# of countries represented	157

ACADEMICS

Academic Rating	74
% students returning for sophomore year	96
% students graduating within 4 years	67
% students graduating within 6 years	87
Calendar	Semester
Student/faculty ratio	21:1
Profs interesting rating	70
Profs accessible rating	71

Most classes have 10–19 students.
Most lab/discussion sessions have 10–19 students.

MOST POPULAR MAJORS
Psychology; Finance; Biology

ABOUT THE SCHOOL

The University of Florida is the prototypical large, state school that "provides its students with a well-rounded experience: an excellent education coated in incomparable school camaraderie." With a total enrollment of just over 50,000, this school is among the five largest universities in the nation, proffering "first class amenities, athletics, academics, campus, and students." Those students hail from all fifty states and more than 150 countries, all of whom are looking for more than your standard academic fare. UF certainly doesn't disappoint, as the school has "a great reputation and…great academic programs for the tuition price." The campus is home to more than 100 undergraduate degree programs, and undergraduates interested in conducting research with faculty can participate in UF's University Scholars Program. One unique learning community, Innovation Academy, pulls together students from thirty majors who share a common minor in innovation. The Career Resource Center (CRC) is a major centralized service that helps students prepare for their post-graduation experiences— UF "seeks to graduate academically ahead and 'real-world-prepared' alumni"—and organized career fairs are conducted regularly and the university is very successful in attracting top employers nationally to recruit on campus.

BANG FOR YOUR BUCK

The cost of attending University of Florida is well below the national average for four-year public universities. Annual tuition and fees hover around $6,381 (based on a typical schedule of thirty credit hours per year), while campus room and board will run you another $9,000-plus. Overall, Florida residents are the main benefactors of this great value. Out-of-state undergraduates pay a little over $28,000 more in tuition and fees and must also factor in higher transportation costs. The school prides itself on providing prospective students with financial aid packages that will help lower educational costs through a variety of "Gator Aid" options. Their website offers a net price calculator to help students and their families get a better idea of exactly how much it would cost to attend the school. In-state students should be sure to check out the Florida Bright Futures Scholarship Program, which offers scholarships based on high school academic achievement. The program has different award levels, each with its own eligibility criteria and award amounts.

STUDENT LIFE

Though students at UF study hard and things can get very serious during finals and midterms, fun abounds at school. "A lot of UF culture is based around sports. We are always going to or watching something," is a sentiment expressed by many students. "The sporting events are top notch and everyone [can] find a sport to cheer for because we are great at them all! Our intramural program and gym are also amazing." With sports tend to come parties, but while "many activities revolve around drinking and partying (especially during football season)," there are lots of other ways to enjoy yourself at school. "GatorNights are always fun," says a student. "Every Friday, there are different events from wax hands to comedians to sand candy and a lot more. Also, the clubs are great here. They have so many clubs, from Software Development to Aerial Dance and everything in between." There are opportunities to get away as well: "Occasionally

University of Florida

FINANCIAL AID: 352-392-6684 • WEBSITE: WWW.UFL.EDU

when looking for a change of scenery we embrace the nature around us and float down . . . Ginnie Springs or go to the school's lake." So no matter how you like to spend your time, UF should have something to offer.

CAREER

Students widely feel that UF does a great job at preparing them for life after school, from the first-rate academics to the "excellent" career services. The Career Resource Center offers an abundance of services, including academic advising and career planning, job fairs and recruiting events, resume critique and mock interviews, and resources for job and internship searches. Gator Shadow Day allows student to learn about careers by shadowing a professional at work. The Center also offers a program called Gator Launch to provide "underrepresented" students in the science and technology fields with special mentoring opportunities. All in all, students seem to leave happy. Of University of Florida alumni visiting PayScale.com, 53 percent report that they derive a high level of meaning from their jobs.

GENERAL INFO

Organizations: 961 registered organizations. **Athletics (Intercollegiate):** *Men:* Baseball, basketball, cross-country, diving, football, golf, swimming, tennis, track/field (outdoor), track/field (indoor). *Women:* Basketball, cross-country, diving, golf, gymnastics, lacrosse, soccer, softball, swimming, tennis, track/field (outdoor), track/field (indoor), volleyball.

FINANCIAL AID

Students should submit: FAFSA. Priority filing deadline is 3/15. The Princeton Review suggests that all financial aid forms be submitted as soon as possible after October 1. *Need-based scholarships/grants offered:* Federal Pell, FSEOG, State scholarships/grants, Private scholarships, College/university scholarship or grant aid from institutional funds. *Loan aid offered:* Direct Subsidized Stafford Loans, Direct Unsubsidized Stafford Loans, Direct PLUS loans, Federal Perkins Loans, College/university loans from institutional funds. Applicants will be notified of awards on a rolling basis beginning 4/15. Federal Work-Study Program available. Institutional employment available.

THE BOTTOM LINE

With relatively low tuition and a strong scholarship program for in-state students, UF is an especially good value for Florida residents. The Machen Florida Opportunity Scholars (MFOS) is a scholarship program for first-generation college freshmen from economically disadvantaged backgrounds. The scholarship provides a full grant scholarship aid package for up to four years of undergraduate education.

SELECTIVITY

Admissions Rating	94
# of applicants	29,837
% of applicants accepted	48
% of acceptees attending	51

FRESHMAN PROFILE

Range SAT Critical Reading	580–670
Range SAT Math	590–680
Range SAT Writing	570–670
Range ACT Composite	27–31
% graduated top 10% of class	72
% graduated top 25% of class	96
% graduated top 50% of class	100

DEADLINES

Regular	
Deadline	11/1
Nonfall registration?	Yes

FINANCIAL FACTS

Financial Aid Rating	85
Annual in-state tuition	$6,381
Annual out-of-state tuition	$28,658
Room and board	$9,910
Required fees	
Average need-based scholarship	$6,975
% needy frosh rec. need-based scholarship or grant aid	62
% needy UG rec. need-based scholarship or grant aid	66
% needy frosh rec. non-need-based scholarship or grant aid	87
% needy UG rec. non-need-based scholarship or grant aid	76
% needy frosh rec. need-based self-help aid	41
% needy UG rec. need-based self-help aid	50
% frosh rec. any financial aid	99
% UG rec. any financial aid	98
% frosh need fully met	27
% ugrads need fully met	25
Average % of frosh need met	99
Average % of ugrad need met	94

CAREER INFORMATION FROM PAYSCALE.COM

ROI rating	89
Bachelor's and No Higher	
Median starting salary	$49,500
Median mid-career salary	$86,300
At Least Bachelor's	
Median starting salary	$51,000
Median mid-career salary	$88,100
% alumni with high job meaning	52%
% STEM	20%

University of Georgia

TERRELL HALL, ATHENS, GA 30602 • ADMISSIONS: 706-542-8776 • FAX: 706-542-1466

CAMPUS LIFE

Quality of Life Rating	93
Fire Safety Rating	85
Green Rating	94
Type of school	Public
Affiliation	No Affiliation
Environment	City

STUDENTS

Total undergrad enrollment	27,547
% male/female	43/57
% from out of state	8
% frosh from public high school	71
% frosh live on campus	98
% ugrads live on campus	36
# of fraternities (% ugrad men join)	35 (22)
# of sororities (% ugrad women join)	27 (29)
% African American	7
% Asian	10
% Caucasian	71
% Hispanic	5
% Native American	<1
% Pacific Islander	<1
% Two or more races	4
% Race and/or ethnicity unknown	1
% international	2
# of countries represented	125

ACADEMICS

Academic Rating	78
% students returning for sophomore year	95
% students graduating within 4 years	62
% students graduating within 6 years	84
Calendar	Semester
Profs interesting rating	77
Profs accessible rating	72

MOST POPULAR MAJORS
Biology; Psychology; Finance

ABOUT THE SCHOOL

Programs in journalism, science, agriculture, and literature, among others, are the backbone of UGA's increasingly attractive profile as a world-class research institution that draws top faculty and students. "Everyone in Georgia strives to go to UGA," says a student. Students make note of the stellar, "experienced professors and research participation" opportunities, pointing out many of the classes—especially in the first two years—are large, and that it is to a student's advantage to go beyond just showing up. Smaller student-faculty ratios are available in honors program classes. UGA students are educated on a beautiful, 759-acre main campus located in Athens, Georgia, a quintessential college town known for its vibrant music and arts scene. "When classes are over and your studying is done, there is fun to be had all around Athens," including a full slate of on-campus and out-of-class activities on offer. Students can choose from more than 600 extracurricular organizations ranging from sororities and fraternities to pre- professional ("a great way to meet people"), environmental, and civic groups. There's an "incomparable" music scene, a hippie scene, and a jock scene—to name just a few—and all 34,000 students on campus have an easy time finding a group where they feel welcome. "I never tire of meeting new people, and UGA has so many people to offer. It's incredible," says a student. Students often gather around that other constant of UGA, the Georgia Bulldogs. "There are so many choices here, it's difficult to manage your time between studying and getting involved in all UGA has to offer," says a student. The University of Georgia Career Center provides centralized career services for students and is among the first in the nation to develop iPhone apps that connect students with potential employers. The university also offers an innovative Career Boot Camp, a day-long, intensive program that brings representatives of Fortune 100 companies to the campus to conduct exercises such as mock interviews.

BANG FOR YOUR BUCK

Georgia's merit-based HOPE Scholarship provides high school graduates who have a minimum 3.0 grade point average with a scholarship to cover the cost of tuition and a percentage of student fees and books. Ninety-seven percent of Georgia-resident freshmen at UGA receive the scholarship. UGA also offers the prestigious Foundation Fellowship, which provides an annual stipend of approximately $9,000 for in-state students (in addition to the HOPE Scholarship) and $15,700 for out-of-state students (plus an out-of-state tuition waiver). The fellowship provides numerous opportunities for national and international travel-study, faculty-directed academic research, and participation in academic conferences.

STUDENT LIFE

"Students are generally white, upper-middle-class, smart, [and] involved, and [they] have a good time," "seem to be predominantly conservative," and "are usually involved in at least one organization, whether it be Greek, a club, or sports." "The typical student at UGA is one who knows how and when to study but allows himself or herself to have a very active social life." The majority are Southerners, with many students from within Georgia. "The stereotype is Southern, Republican, football-loving, and beer- drinking. While many, many of UGA's students do not fit this description, there is no lack of the above," and "there is a social scene for everyone in Athens." "There are a great number of atypical students in the liberal arts," which "creates a unique and exciting student body with greatly contrasting opinions."

University of Georgia

FINANCIAL AID: 706-542-6147 • E-MAIL: ADMPROC@UGA.EDU • WEBSITE: WWW.UGA.EDU

CAREER

The UGA Career Center is a one-stop resource for major and career exploration, graduate school information, interviewing and resume prep, and, of course, the job search. On that front, DAWGLink has postings for full-time, part-time work, or internships, and the Intern For A Day program lets students get a taste of a particular field or career while shadowing a professional. The Center for Leadership and Service can connect students who want to volunteer (the Volunteer UGA Calendar is loaded with relevant panels and service opportunities) and even offers grants for student groups on campus to engage with the Athens community at large. Graduates generally earn average starting salaries of $45,900 (according to PayScale.com), and 47 percent derive a high level of meaning from their work.

GENERAL INFO

Activities: Choral groups, concert band, dance, drama/theater, jazz band, literary magazine, marching band, music ensembles, musical theater, opera, pep band, radio station, student government, student newspaper, student-run film society, symphony orchestra, television station, yearbook, campus ministries, international student organization. **Organizations:** 597 registered organizations, 22 honor societies, 35 religious organizations, 36 fraternities, 27 sororities. **Athletics (Intercollegiate):** *Men:* Baseball, basketball, cross-country, diving, football, golf, swimming, tennis, track/field (outdoor), track/field (indoor). *Women:* Basketball, cross-country, diving, equestrian sports, golf, gymnastics, soccer, softball, swimming, tennis, track/field (outdoor), track/field (indoor), volleyball. **On-Campus Highlights:** Zell B. Miller Learning Center, Sanford Stadium, Ramsey Student Center for Physical Activity, Performing and Visual Arts Complex, Tate Student Center.

FINANCIAL AID

Students should submit: FAFSA. Priority filing deadline is 3/1. The Princeton Review suggests that all financial aid forms be submitted as soon as possible after October 1. *Need-based scholarships/grants offered:* Federal Pell, FSEOG, State scholarships/grants, Private scholarships, College/university scholarship or grant aid from institutional funds. *Loan aid offered:* Direct Subsidized Stafford Loans, Direct Unsubsidized Stafford Loans, Direct PLUS loans, Federal Perkins Loans, State Loans, College/university loans from institutional funds. Applicants will be notified of awards on a rolling basis beginning 5/1. Federal Work-Study Program available. Institutional employment available.

THE BOTTOM LINE

The average in-state Georgia freshman pays $9,364 in tuition, while those from out of state cough up more than $27,574 a year. On-campus room and board costs just over $9,450. Recent graduates left UGA with approximately $22,087 in cumulative debt, on average.

CAREER INFORMATION FROM PAYSCALE.COM

ROI rating	89
Bachelor's and No Higher	
Median starting salary	$46,600
Median mid-career salary	$83,600
At Least Bachelor's	
Median starting salary	$47,600
Median mid-career salary	$84,100
% alumni with high job meaning	52%
% STEM	11%

SELECTIVITY

Admissions Rating	91
# of applicants	21,945
% of applicants accepted	53
% of acceptees attending	45
# offered a place on the wait list	954
% accepting a place on wait list	61
% admitted from wait list	6

FRESHMAN PROFILE

Range SAT Critical Reading	570–660
Range SAT Math	580–670
Range SAT Writing	560–660
Range ACT Composite	26–30
Minimum paper TOEFL	550
Minimum internet-based TOEFL	80
Average HS GPA	3.9
% graduated top 10% of class	53
% graduated top 25% of class	88
% graduated top 50% of class	99

DEADLINES

Early action	
Deadline	10/15
Notification	12/1
Regular	
Priority	10/15
Deadline	1/15
Nonfall registration?	Yes

FINANCIAL FACTS

Financial Aid Rating	83
Annual in-state tuition	$9,364
Annual out-of-state tuition	$27,574
Room and board	$9,450
Required fees	$2,258
Average need-based scholarship	$8,923
% needy frosh rec. need-based scholarship or grant aid	98
% needy UG rec. need-based scholarship or grant aid	92
% needy frosh rec. non-need-based scholarship or grant aid	24
% needy UG rec. non-need-based scholarship or grant aid	16
% needy frosh rec. need-based self-help aid	47
% needy UG rec. need-based self-help aid	54
% frosh rec. any financial aid	47
% UG rec. any financial aid	48
% UG borrow to pay for school	48
Average cumulative indebtedness	$22,087
% frosh need fully met	29
% ugrads need fully met	22
Average % of frosh need met	78
Average % of ugrad need met	72

University of Houston

4400 UNIVERSITY, HOUSTON, TX 77204-2023 • ADMISSIONS: 713-743-1010 • FINANCIAL AID: 713-743-9051

CAMPUS LIFE

Quality of Life Rating	85
Fire Safety Rating	94
Green Rating	78
Type of school	Public
Affiliation	No Affiliation
Environment	Metropolis

STUDENTS

Total undergrad enrollment	34,716
% male/female	51/49
% from out of state	2
% frosh from public high school	93
% frosh live on campus	50
% ugrads live on campus	19
# of fraternities (% ugrad men join)	25 (4)
# of sororities (% ugrad women join)	21 (4)
% African American	10
% Asian	22
% Caucasian	26
% Hispanic	32
% Native American	<1
% Pacific Islander	<1
% Two or more races	3
% Race and/or ethnicity unknown	1
% international	5
# of countries represented	117

ACADEMICS

Academic Rating	73
% students returning for sophomore year	86
students graduating within 4 years	20
students graduating within 6 years	51
Calendar	Semester
Student/faculty ratio	21:1
Profs interesting rating	73
Profs accessible rating	72
Most classes have 20–29 students.	
Most lab/discussion sessions have 20–29 students.	

MOST POPULAR MAJORS
Business Administration and Management;
Biology; Psychology

ABOUT THE SCHOOL

Situated in the heart of the fourth largest city in the United States, the University of Houston is a growing, up-and-coming research university located in an urban setting. The school is one of the most ethnically diverse colleges in the country, having "a thriving multicultural mix" within one of the nation's most international cities, also known as "the energy capital of the world." One undergraduate here loves the fact that "you meet people from different social/economic backgrounds every day and it's humbling and amazing!" Students communicate, share ideas, and build relationships with people from all over the world, enabling "political discussion and religious awareness to flow freely throughout the university." Despite the metropolitan environment, there is still a close-knit feel to the campus. With a great balance of residents and commuters, Houston is also nontraditional, "so you'll meet lots of people who are coming back to school after serving our country, having kids, or trying a few classes at a community college first." The location also makes it convenient for students who wish to work while attending, and Houston tries hard to accommodate them by providing evening, distance-learning, online, and Saturday classes. Enthused one satisfied beneficiary of these services, "commuters can still have school spirit!"

BANG FOR YOUR BUCK

Students tell us that the school's financial aid packages are "considerably higher than other institutions," and are instrumental in "helping bright kids from low-middle-income households build an optimistic future." Also, "tuition rates are quite low compared to its competitors." These and other accolades from students (and parents!) are quite common. "Such a great value." "Amazingly affordable." "A quality education that will be long-lasting and nationally recognized." Described as "amazing," "generous," and "substantial" by students, there are an abundance of scholarships available at Houston. "I got an all-expenses paid scholarship for being a National Merit Scholar!" The Tier One Scholarship program offers a distinguished, high-profile award intended to attract highly qualified students. Awarded to first-time-in-college freshmen, it covers tuition and mandatory fees for up to five years of undergraduate study. Selection is based on merit and consideration of a students need for financial assistance. Tier One Scholars also receive stipends for undergraduate research and for study abroad programs.

STUDENT LIFE

Students at UH are outgoing, friendly, and ambitious." "You will see every ethnicity and nationality you can think of" because "minorities are the majorities here!" Even though most students are commuters, many with full-time jobs and families, those that do live on campus seem quite happy to do so. "The spirit on campus is intoxicating!" remarks one resident. Others cite "the famous cougar paw hand signal" as a familiar gesture. Since students here are "like snowflakes," UH "has a club for everyone, for whatever you're into." There is also a bowling alley on campus, "rock climbing at the rec," and "a hangout spot, always bursting with life." Another UH tradition is "humans vs. zombies where we wear bandanas and chase each other with nerf guns in between classes!"

University of Houston

E-MAIL: VC@UH.EDU • FAX: 713-743-7542 • WEBSITE: HTTP://WWW.UH.EDU/

CAREER

"Opportunities are bountiful at UH." In the "nationally recognized" College of Business, students feel ready for the job market. They believe that UH prepares them "for a long term successful life in the career of their choosing." Professors at UH have an "amazing" amount of experience and "push their students to do their absolute best." "Not ONLY do they teach you about your subject, they show you how it applies to your career and how to make yourself a better person." "There are a number of student organizations that people participate in to show their enthusiasm for their chosen profession which also helps them find gainful employment doing what they love." Students take advantage of internships in Houston as well as opportunities with the major corporations that have "close ties to the University." According to the website PayScale.com, the average salary for recent graduates is $51,600.

GENERAL INFO

Activities: Choral groups, concert band, dance, drama/theater, jazz band, literary magazine, marching band, music ensembles, musical theater, opera, pep band, radio station, student government, student newspaper, student-run film society, symphony orchestra, television station, yearbook, campus ministries, international student organization. **Organizations:** 489 registered organizations, 32 honor societies, 39 religious organizations. 25 social fraternities, 21 social sororities. **Athletics (Intercollegiate):** *Men:* Baseball, basketball, cross-country, football, golf, track/field (outdoor), track/field (indoor). *Women:* Basketball, cross-country, diving, soccer, softball, swimming, tennis, track/field (outdoor), track/field (indoor), volleyball. **On Campus Highlights:** Student Center, Campus Recreation and Wellness Center, Student Center Satellite, Blaffer Gallery, TDECU Stadium.

FINANCIAL AID

Students should submit: FAFSA. Priority filing deadline is 4/1. The Princeton Review suggests that all financial aid forms be submitted as soon as possible after October 1. *Need-based scholarships/grants offered:* Federal Pell, FSEOG, State scholarships/grants, Private scholarships, College/university scholarship or grant aid from institutional funds. *Loan aid offered:* Direct Subsidized Stafford Loans, Direct Unsubsidized Stafford Loans, Direct PLUS loans, Federal Perkins Loans, State Loans. Applicants will be notified of awards on a rolling basis beginning 4/1. Federal Work-Study Program available. Institutional employment available.

BOTTOM LINE

In-state tuition is around $9,756 per year; for out-of-state students, the cost is $24,456. Room and board will come to $9,849; required fees, $954; books and supplies, $1,200. Nearly 50 percent of students borrow in some way to pay for school, and those that do can envision a cumulative indebtedness of $18,244.

CAREER INFORMATION FROM PAYSCALE.COM

ROI rating	**86**
Bachelor's and No Higher	
Median starting salary	$51,200
Median mid-career salary	$84,000
At Least Bachelor's	
Median starting salary	$51,600
Median mid-career salary	$85,700
% alumni with high job meaning	54%
% STEM	17%

SELECTIVITY

Admissions Rating	86
# of applicants	17,971
% of applicants accepted	60
% of acceptees attending	39

FRESHMAN PROFILE

Range SAT Critical Reading	510–610
Range SAT Math	540–640
Range ACT Composite	23–28
Minimum paper TOEFL	550
Minimum internet-based TOEFL	79
% graduated top 10% of class	30
% graduated top 25% of class	64
% graduated top 50% of class	89

DEADLINES

Regular	
Priority	12/1
Deadline	7/1
Notification	4/15
Nonfall registration?	Yes

FINANCIAL FACTS

Financial Aid Rating	80
Annual in-state tuition	$9,756
Annual out-of-state tuition	$24,456
Room and board	$9,849
Required fees	$954
Average need-based scholarship	$8,127
% needy frosh rec. need-based scholarship or grant aid	90
% needy UG rec. need-based scholarship or grant aid	82
% needy frosh rec. non-need-based scholarship or grant aid	9
% needy UG rec. non-need-based scholarship or grant aid	5
% needy frosh rec. need-based self-help aid	50
% needy UG rec. need-based self-help aid	63
% frosh rec. any financial aid	87
% UG rec. any financial aid	77
% UG borrow to pay for school	53
Average cumulative indebtedness	$22,763
% frosh need fully met	18
% ugrads need fully met	16
Average % of frosh need met	66
Average % of ugrad need met	63

University of Idaho

UI ADMISSIONS OFFICE, MOSCOW, ID 83844-4264 • ADMISSIONS: 208-885-6326 • FAX: 208-885-9119

CAMPUS LIFE

Quality of Life Rating	85
Fire Safety Rating	89
Green Rating	73
Type of school	Public
Affiliation	No Affiliation
Environment	Town

STUDENTS

Total undergrad enrollment	9,388
% male/female	52/48
% from out of state	23
% frosh from public high school	90
% frosh live on campus	86
% ugrads live on campus	23
# of fraternities (% ugrad men join)	17 (14)
# of sororities (% ugrad women join)	15 (14)
% African American	1
% Asian	1
% Caucasian	77
% Hispanic	9
% Native American	1
% Pacific Islander	<1
% Two or more races	4
% Race and/or ethnicity unknown	2
% international	4
# of countries represented	77

ACADEMICS

Academic Rating	74
% students returning for sophomore year	77
% students graduating within 4 years	28
Calendar	Semester
Student/faculty ratio	17:1
Profs interesting rating	72
Profs accessible rating	72

Most classes have 10–19 students.
Most lab/discussion sessions have
10–19 students.

MOST POPULAR MAJORS
Mechanical Engineering; Psychology;
Marketing/Marketing Management

ABOUT THE SCHOOL

Simply put, the University of Idaho is about "community, involvement and research." Of course, many students are drawn to the school because it has "one of the best agricultural programs in the northwest" as well as a "strong engineering program." Moreover, Idaho excels at turning its students into "problem solvers" who will ultimately "make a difference through knowledge, creativity, and...integrity." The university also delivers on its promise of "small classes" and "hands-on learning." Importantly, Idaho undergrads find that their professors are "more than accommodating to their students' needs." As one grateful senior shares, "They leave the floor open for students to ask questions if they do not understand the subject matter, and they also make themselves available often outside of classes so that if students need a little extra help, they can get it very easily." Even better, Idaho profs make it crystal clear that they're "excited to be here and share their knowledge with a new generation."

BANG FOR YOUR BUCK

Undergrads at Idaho are certainly thankful that they can receive a "quality education for a low cost." Of course, the price tag is still steep for many families. Fortunately, UI is able to offer some great financial aid packages. The school doles out more than $25 million in scholarship awards annually—some based upon need, some based upon merit and some due to outstanding achievement in a particular field. For example, the Go Idaho! Scholars Program automatically provides Idaho residents who meet specific GPA requirements with funding. These scholarships range from $1,000 to $4,000 and are guaranteed for four years. Idaho also operates a large work-study program, easily allowing students to make an active contribution to their education.

STUDENT LIFE

By and large, University of Idaho seems to net a "friendly" student body that "loves the outdoors and the simpler things in life." We've also been told that "Greek life is very common" and the "typical student is most likely in a fraternity or sorority." However, regardless of affiliation, most undergrads find their peers to be "very approachable." Students also happily report that there "are lots of clubs and activities and plenty of ways to reach out and find people with similar interests as you." For example, intramural sports "are very popular" as is "rock climbing [and] work[ing] out at the gym." Additionally, the "student government provides weekly entertainment in the form of movies, concerts, speakers, and comedians." Lastly, if undergrads are anxious to get off-campus, "downtown Moscow is [only] five minutes away and...has delicious, cheap restaurants, theaters, art galleries, and coffee shops."

CAREER

A University of Idaho degree definitely connotes success. After all, according to PayScale.com, the average starting salary for recent graduates is $46,700. Even better, the average mid-career salary is $84,400. And, most importantly, 56 percent of Vandals report being in a job that holds meaning. These stats can partially be attributed to a fantastic career center that works diligently to foster relationships with a variety of companies and organizations. The office is able to attract companies such as Boeing, E & J Gallo Winery, Hecla Mining Company, Hewlett Packard, Paragon Films, Inc., Peace Corps and

University of Idaho

FINANCIAL AID: 208-885-6312 • E-MAIL: ADMISSIONS@UIDAHO.EDU • WEBSITE: WWW.UIDAHO.EDU

Seattle City Light to its annual career fairs. And, thanks to the center's numerous resume and interview workshops, students are fully prepared whenever a potential opportunity arises.

GENERAL INFO

Activities: Choral groups, concert band, dance, drama/theater, jazz band, marching band, music ensembles, musical theater, opera, pep band, radio station, student government, student newspaper, student-run film society, symphony orchestra, television station, Campus Ministries, International Student Organization. **Organizations:** 190 registered organizations, 13 honor societies, 20 religious organizations. 17 fraternities, 15 sororities. **Athletics (Intercollegiate):** *Men:* basketball, cross-country, football, golf, track/field (outdoor), track/field (indoor). *Women:* basketball, cross-country, golf, soccer, swimming, track/field (outdoor), track/field (indoor), volleyball. **On-Campus Highlights:** Idaho Commons - food and meeting rooms, 18 hole golf course, Kibbie Dome - athletics, Student Recreation Center, Borah Theater, Rec Center/Outdoors Program, Frisbee Golf Course, Religious Centers. See our campus live with web cams at http://www.uidaho.edu/webcams.

FINANCIAL AID

Students should submit: FAFSA. Priority filing deadline is 2/15. The Princeton Review suggests that all financial aid forms be submitted as soon as possible after October 1. *Need-based scholarships/grants offered:* Federal Pell, FSEOG, State scholarships/grants, Private scholarships, College/university scholarship or grant aid from institutional funds. *Loan aid offered:* Direct Subsidized Stafford Loans, Direct Unsubsidized Stafford Loans, Direct PLUS loans, Federal Perkins Loans, College/university loans from institutional funds. Applicants will be notified of awards on a rolling basis beginning 3/30. Federal Work-Study Program available. Institutional employment available.

BOTTOM LINE

As you might have deduced, UI's price tag differs depending on whether or not you're a resident. Undergrads hailing from Idaho face a tuition bill of $5,162 whereas out-of-state students pay $19,970. Regardless of where a person grew up, room and board will cost $8,354. Students can expect to pay another $1,214 for books and supplies. And they'll need $2,622 for personal expenses and miscellaneous fees. Lastly, undergrads should set aside around $1,218 for transportation.

CAREER INFORMATION FROM PAYSCALE.COM

ROI rating	85
Bachelor's and No Higher	
Median starting salary	$45,800
Median mid-career salary	$84,800
At Least Bachelor's	
Median starting salary	$47,000
Median mid-career salary	$84,800
% alumni with high job meaning	58%
% STEM	19%

SELECTIVITY

Admissions Rating	81
# of applicants	8,515
% of applicants accepted	67
% of acceptees attending	28

FRESHMAN PROFILE

Range SAT Critical Reading	450–580
Range SAT Math	460–590
Range SAT Writing	450–580
Range ACT Composite	20–27
Minimum paper TOEFL	525
Minimum internet-based TOEFL	70
Average HS GPA	3.4
% graduated top 10% of class	20
% graduated top 25% of class	45
% graduated top 50% of class	73

DEADLINES

Regular	
Priority	2/15
Deadline	8/1
Nonfall registration?	Yes

FINANCIAL FACTS

Financial Aid Rating	84
Annual in-state tuition	$5,162
Annual out-of-state tuition	$19,970
Room and board	$8,354
Required fees	$2,070
Average need-based scholarship	$4,761
% needy frosh rec. need-based scholarship or grant aid	73
% needy UG rec. need-based scholarship or grant aid	76
% needy frosh rec. non-need-based scholarship or grant aid	90
% needy UG rec. non-need-based scholarship or grant aid	60
% needy frosh rec. need-based self-help aid	72
% needy UG rec. need-based self-help aid	77
% frosh rec. any financial aid	90
% UG rec. any financial aid	80
% frosh need fully met	39
% ugrads need fully met	30
Average % of frosh need met	80
Average % of ugrad need met	75

University of Illinois at Urbana-Champaign

901 WEST ILLINOIS STREET, URBANA, IL 61801 • ADMISSIONS: 217-333-0302 • FAX: 217-244-0903

ABOUT THE SCHOOL

In many ways, the flagship campus of the University of Illinois at Urbana-Champaign is the prototypical large, state-funded research university. It's hard to get admitted, but not too hard; however, it does stand apart. The admissions office reviews every candidate individually, which is rare. The library is stellar, and the amazing research resources are practically endless. With seventeen colleges and about 150 undergraduate programs to offer, students have a wide range of options, but even the best professors aren't going to hold your hand, and lower-level class sizes are mostly lectures filled with students. Despite this, many students agree that the professors are incredibly passionate and intelligent. Incredibly, nearly all faculty have PhDs. The engineering and business schools are the most prestigious and, therefore, offer the most competition. Agriculture, architecture, and psychology are also quite well respected.

University of Illinois is a magnet for engineering and sciences research. "The research resources are amazing," one pleased undergrad enthuses. Another student relates that "the library has almost any resource an undergraduate or even an advanced researcher would ever need." The university has been a leader in computer-based education and hosted the PLATO project, which was a precursor to the Internet and resulted in the development of the plasma display. That legacy of leading computer-based education and research continues today— Microsoft hires more graduates from the University of Illinois than from any other university in the world. The University of Illinois media organization (the Illini Media Co.) is also quite extensive, featuring a student newspaper that isn't censored by the administration since it receives no direct funding from it.

BANG FOR YOUR BUCK

The University of Illinois provides an incredibly wide array of undergraduate programs at a great price. A large percentage of the student population receives some form of financial assistance. The usual set of work-study, loans, and need-based grants is available, of course, along with a bounty of private and institutional scholarships. The school confers more than 1,500 individual merit-based scholarships each year. These awards vary considerably in value, and they are available to students who excel in academics, art, athletics, drama, leadership, music, and pretty much anything else. Alumni scholarships are available, too, if someone in your family is a graduate of U of I. There's an online scholarship database at Illinois's website that is definitely worth perusing. Application procedures vary, and so do the deadline dates.

STUDENT LIFE

The University of Illinois at Urbana-Champaign has a decidedly Midwestern feel. "Kids from out-of-state and small-town farm students" definitely have a presence, but, sometimes, it seems like "practically everyone is from the northwest suburbs of Chicago." There's a lot of ethnic diversity "visible on campus." On the whole, the majority of students are "very smart kids who like to party." "They really study fairly hard, and when you ask, it turns out that they're majoring in something like rocket science." One student notes that "students fit in through about 1,000 different ways. They find work friends, classmates, group members in an organization, you name it." A media studies student notes that "the townie culture here is what gets me. The bars in downtown Champaign are great and super relaxed, plus there is an awesome music scene that most people don't expect from a college town."

University of Illinois at Urbana-Champaign

FINANCIAL AID: 217-333-0100 • E-MAIL: UGRADADMISSIONS@UIUC.EDU • WEBSITE: WWW.ILLINOIS.EDU

CAREER

The typical University of Illinois at Urbana-Champaign graduate has a starting salary of around $55,000, and 48 percent report that their job has a great deal of meaning. Students feel that "you can't get any better alumni networking and leadership opportunities than you do at UIUC." Many students feel that "there are a lot of UIUC alumni in agencies" that they want to work for. Students applaud "the availability of highly regarded finance internships and full-time opportunities." The Career Center at Illinois offers multiple job fairs for several different sorts of careers and majors as well as other excellent resources like the job board I-Link and drop-in career counseling.

GENERAL INFO

Activities: Choral groups, concert band, dance, drama/theater, jazz band, literary magazine, marching band, music ensembles, musical theater, opera, pep band, radio station, student government, student newspaper, student-run film society, symphony orchestra, television station, yearbook, campus ministries, international student organization. **Organizations:** 1,000 registered organizations, 30 honor societies, 95 religious organizations. 60 fraternities, 36 sororities. **Athletics (Intercollegiate):** *Men:* Baseball, basketball, cheerleading, cross-country, football, golf, gymnastics, tennis, track/field (outdoor), wrestling. *Women:* Basketball, cheerleading, cross-country, diving, golf, gymnastics, soccer, softball, swimming, tennis, track/field (outdoor), volleyball. **On-Campus Highlights:** Campus Town restaurants and shops, Krannert Center for Performing Arts, Assembly Hall, Multiple Campus Recreation Centers, Illini Student Union, on-campus Arboretum; The Japan House; extensive athletic facilities; historic round barns; Siebel Computer Science Center; spacious green space at the Central and Bardeen Quads; Papa Dels Pizza and Za's Italian Cafe.

FINANCIAL AID

Students should submit: FAFSA. Priority filing deadline is 3/15. The Princeton Review suggests that all financial aid forms be submitted as soon as possible after October 1. *Need-based scholarships/grants offered:* Federal Pell, FSEOG, State scholarships/grants, Private scholarships, College/university scholarship or grant aid from institutional funds, United Negro College Fund. *Loan aid offered:* Direct Subsidized Stafford Loans, Direct Unsubsidized Stafford Loans, Direct PLUS loans, Federal Perkins Loans, College/university loans from institutional funds. Applicants will be notified of awards on a rolling basis beginning 3/15. Federal Work-Study Program available. Institutional employment available.

THE BOTTOM LINE

The University of Illinois requires all first-year undergraduate students (who do not commute) to live on campus. The cost for a year of tuition, fees, room and board, and basic expenses averages $26,708 for Illinois residents. For nonresidents, the average is about $41,868. The average student indebtedness upon graduation is $25,448. Around three-quarters of students are recipients of financial aid; the average need-based gift aid comes to nearly $13,700.

CAREER INFORMATION FROM PAYSCALE.COM

ROI rating	90
Bachelor's and No Higher	
Median starting salary	$56,400
Median mid-career salary	$97,700
At Least Bachelor's	
Median starting salary	$57,700
Median mid-career salary	$102,000
% alumni with high job meaning	49%
% STEM	26%

SELECTIVITY

Admissions Rating	90
# of applicants	35,819
% of applicants accepted	59
% of acceptees attending	33
# offered a place on the wait list	3,008
% accepting a place on wait list	62
% admitted from wait list	54

FRESHMAN PROFILE

Range SAT Critical Reading	590–690
Range SAT Math	700–790
Range SAT Writing	600–690
Range ACT Composite	26–32
Minimum internet-based TOEFL	80
% graduated top 10% of class	59
% graduated top 25% of class	90
% graduated top 50% of class	99

DEADLINES

Regular	
Priority	11/1
Deadline	12/1
Notification	2/13
Nonfall registration?	No

FINANCIAL FACTS

Financial Aid Rating	78
Annual in-state tuition	$12,036
Annual out-of-state tuition	$27,196
Room and board	$11,010
Required fees	$3,662
Average need-based scholarship	$13,702
% needy frosh rec. need-based scholarship or grant aid	80
% needy UG rec. need-based scholarship or grant aid	79
% needy frosh rec. non-need-based scholarship or grant aid	20
% needy UG rec. non-need-based scholarship or grant aid	11
% needy frosh rec. need-based self-help aid	78
% needy UG rec. need-based self-help aid	81
% frosh need fully met	14
% ugrads need fully met	11
Average % of frosh need met	69
Average % of ugrad need met	64

University of Maryland—Baltimore County

1000 Hilltop Circle, Baltimore, MD 21250 • Admissions: 410-455-2291 • Fax: 410-455-1094

CAMPUS LIFE

Quality of Life Rating	88
Fire Safety Rating	98
Green Rating	74
Type of school	Public
Affiliation	No Affiliation
Environment	Metropolis

STUDENTS

Total undergrad enrollment	11,243
% male/female	55/45
% from out of state	6
% frosh live on campus	75
% ugrads live on campus	34
# of fraternities (% ugrad men join)	11 (4)
# of sororities (% ugrad women join)	12 (5)
% African American	14
% Asian	24
% Caucasian	45
% Hispanic	7
% Native American	<1
% Pacific Islander	<1
% Two or more races	4
% Race and/or ethnicity unknown	4
% international	4
# of countries represented	96

ACADEMICS

Academic Rating	75
% students returning for sophomore year	86
% students graduating within 4 years	39
Calendar	Semester
Student/faculty ratio	20:1
Profs interesting rating	78
Profs accessible rating	73

Most classes have 20–29 students.
Most lab/discussion sessions have
20–29 students.

MOST POPULAR MAJORS
Computer and Information Sciences;
Biology; Psychology

ABOUT THE SCHOOL

Arguably the "best public college in Maryland," UMBC is an "extremely diverse school" that manages to maintain a "small community feel." And from the moment you set foot on campus, it's evident that the university is focused on "providing exceptional educational and research opportunities for students." Technically, UMBC is "geared towards science and technology majors." Indeed, undergrads are quick to highlight the "strong" engineering, biology and chemistry departments. However, don't despair humanities students. We're told that the "education and ancient studies programs are excellent" and that the interdisciplinary studies program is "amazing" as well. Inside the classroom, students are greeted by "very knowledgeable professors" who typically devote "most of the class time to real world discussion[s]." And, perhaps most importantly, professors at UMBC push students to "learn as much as [they] can, work as hard as [they] can and really think outside the box."

BANG FOR YOUR BUCK

Across the board, undergrads here brag that their school provides a "quality education at an affordable cost." Of course, it certainly helps that the university generally offers ample financial aid packages. Students (both in-state and out-of-state) benefit from a range of merit scholarships, which award anywhere from $1,000 to a whopping $22,000 annually. UMBC also runs the robust Scholars Program. Open to incoming freshmen applicants and based around seven different disciplines (cyber scholars, artist scholars, humanities scholars, public affairs scholars, women in technology scholars, STEM teacher education scholars and the Meyerhoff scholars), this competitive program combines financial aid with opportunities for advanced research, studying abroad, special seminars and directed internships.

STUDENT LIFE

Undergrads are thrilled to report that "UMBC is a place where it is cool to be smart, and everything about the campus, including the students, exudes 'nerd-chic'." Indeed, the "typical student…is interested in doing well academically and not just here to party until graduation." That being said, these students do kick back from time to time. And when they do, there's plenty in which to participate. For example, there's "a weekly movie, open mic nights, concerts, and game nights on campus." The school also offers "bus trips… to places like Larriland Pick-Your-Own Farm, New York City, Ocean City, Wisp (Snow tubing), etc. that are extremely affordable for the average poor college student." And, when all else fails, hometown Baltimore provides a number of entertainment and dining options.

CAREER

Thanks to UMBC's amazing Career Center, undergrads here are able to enter the job market with confidence. Starting from freshman year, the office works to empower students and help them plot their career goals. Undergrads can take advantage of a plethora of recruiting and networking events held on campus each year. More specifically, students have the opportunity to meet with representatives from companies/organizations like the Central Intelligence Agency, The Hershey Company, Lockheed Martin and the Nielsen Company (among others). And they can help ensure those meetings go well by attending one of the Career Center's many interviewing workshops or resume (and cover letter) writing seminars.

University of Maryland—Baltimore County

FINANCIAL AID: 410-455-2387 • E-MAIL: ADMISSIONS@UMBC.EDU • WEBSITE: WWW.UMBC.EDU

GENERAL INFO

Activities: Choral groups, dance, drama/theater, jazz band, literary magazine, music ensembles, musical theater, pep band, radio station, student government, student newspaper, student-run film society, symphony orchestra, Campus Ministries, International Student Organization, Model UN. **Organizations:** 250 registered organizations, 8 honor societies, 20 religious organizations. 11 fraternities, 12 sororities. **Athletics (Intercollegiate):** *Men:* baseball, basketball, cheerleading, cross-country, diving, lacrosse, soccer, swimming, track/field (outdoor), track/field (indoor). *Women:* basketball, cheerleading, cross-country, diving, lacrosse, soccer, softball, swimming, track/field (outdoor), track/field (indoor), volleyball. **On-Campus Highlights:** Students attend, and take part in, a world of excellent theatre, music and dance performances on campus. They go to art openings and lectures, start clubs and exchange ideas through the campus paper and literary magazines. Albin O. Kuhn Library and Gallery, The Commons (Student Center), Center for Art , Design and Visual Culture, Retriever Activities Center.

FINANCIAL AID

Students should submit: FAFSA. Priority filing deadline is 2/14. The Princeton Review suggests that all financial aid forms be submitted as soon as possible after October 1. *Need-based scholarships/grants offered:* Federal Pell, FSEOG, State scholarships/grants, Private scholarships, College/university scholarship or grant aid from institutional funds, United Negro College Fund. *Loan aid offered:* Direct Subsidized Stafford Loans, Direct Unsubsidized Stafford Loans, Direct PLUS loans, Federal Perkins Loans. Applicants will be notified of awards on a rolling basis beginning 3/25. Federal Work-Study Program available. Institutional employment available.

BOTTOM LINE

Maryland residents attending UMBC will face a tuition bill of $11,492. Out-of-state students will be expected to pay $24,492. Additionally, room and board (for those students planning to live on-campus) costs $11,568. Undergrads should set aside another $1,200 for books and school supplies and $1,292 for transportation needs. Students on financial aid are charged a loan fee of $74. Lastly, undergrads will likely want another $1,554 for personal and/or miscellaneous needs.

CAREER INFORMATION FROM PAYSCALE.COM

ROI rating	86
Bachelor's and No Higher	
Median starting salary	$49,700
Median mid-career salary	$84,800
At Least Bachelor's	
Median starting salary	$50,600
Median mid-career salary	$86,100
% alumni with high job meaning	54%
% STEM	36%

SELECTIVITY

Admissions Rating	89
# of applicants	10,629
% of applicants accepted	59
% of acceptees attending	25
# offered a place on the wait list	404
% accepting a place on wait list	100
% admitted from wait list	69

FRESHMAN PROFILE

Range SAT Critical Reading	540–640
Range SAT Math	570–670
Range SAT Writing	530–640
Range ACT Composite	24–30
Minimum paper TOEFL	460
Minimum internet-based TOEFL	48
Average HS GPA	3.8
% graduated top 10% of class	25
% graduated top 25% of class	54
% graduated top 50% of class	84

DEADLINES

Early action	
Deadline	11/1
Notification	12/15
Regular	
Priority	11/1
Deadline	2/1
Nonfall registration?	Yes

FINANCIAL FACTS

Financial Aid Rating	80
Annual in-state tuition	$11,264
Annual out-of-state tuition	$24,492
Room and board	$11,568
Required fees	$1,530
Average need-based scholarship	$8,172
% needy frosh rec. need-based scholarship or grant aid	76
% needy UG rec. need-based scholarship or grant aid	77
% needy frosh rec. non-need-based scholarship or grant aid	32
% needy UG rec. non-need-based scholarship or grant aid	12
% needy frosh rec. need-based self-help aid	53
% needy UG rec. need-based self-help aid	67
% frosh rec. any financial aid	74
% UG rec. any financial aid	70
% UG borrow to pay for school	51
Average cumulative indebtedness	$26,391
% frosh need fully met	20
% ugrads need fully met	12
Average % of frosh need met	63
Average % of ugrad need met	54

University of Maryland—College Park

MITCHELL BUILDING, COLLEGE PARK, MD 20742-5235 • ADMISSIONS: 301-314-8385 • FAX: 301-314-9693

CAMPUS LIFE

Quality of Life Rating	**72**
Fire Safety Rating	**89**
Green Rating	**99**
Type of school	Public
Affiliation	No Affiliation
Environment	Metropolis

STUDENTS

Total undergrad enrollment	27,443
% male/female	53/47
% from out of state	21
% frosh live on campus	93
% ugrads live on campus	42
# of fraternities (% ugrad men join)	36 (15)
# of sororities (% ugrad women join)	28 (19)
% African American	13
% Asian	16
% Caucasian	52
% Hispanic	9
% Native American	<1
% Pacific Islander	<1
% Two or more races	4
% Race and/or ethnicity unknown	2
% international	4
# of countries represented	65

ACADEMICS

Academic Rating	**73**
% students returning for sophomore year	95
% students graduating within 4 years	69
% students graduating within 6 years	86
Calendar	Semester
Student/faculty ratio	16:1
Profs interesting rating	70
Profs accessible rating	66

Most classes have 10–19 students.
Most lab/discussion sessions have 20–29 students.

MOST POPULAR MAJORS
Biology; Criminology; Economics

ABOUT THE SCHOOL

The University of Maryland—College Park is a big school. There are many different people from various backgrounds, as well as numerous student organizations on campus. Some incoming freshmen might find this intimidating, but thanks to the university's system of living-and-learning communities, which allows students with similar academic interests to live in the same residential community, take specialized courses, and perform research; this campus of almost 27,000 can feel a lot smaller and more intimate than it actually is. UMD offers a "top-notch honors program" for academically talented students, which offers special access and opportunities with a community of intellectually gifted peers. More than 100 undergraduate degrees are on offer here, and the university's location near Washington, D.C. means that top-notch research and internship opportunities are literally in your backyard. The university recently received funding from the Department of Homeland Security to create a new research center to study the behavioral and social foundations of terrorism. It's no surprise then that UMD's political science program is strong. A well-respected business program, top-ranked criminology program, and solid engineering school are also available. The school is also extremely invested in promoting sustainability across the university curriculum, and developing a sustainability ethic in campus culture.

BANG FOR YOUR BUCK

University of Maryland—College Park offers a comprehensive aid program for students who demonstrate financial need. But it's the university's full suite of merit-based scholarships that make a UMD degree an exceptional value. Highlights include the Banneker/Key Scholarship, the university's most prestigious merit scholarship, which may cover up to the full the cost of tuition, mandatory fees, room and board, and a book allowance each year for four years. The President's Scholarship provides four-year awards of up to $12,000 per year to exceptional entering freshmen. Maryland Pathways is a new financial assistance program set up by the university to assist low-income families by reducing the debt component and increasing grants to those who receive it. National Merit, creative and performing arts, and departmental scholarships are also available. To be considered for most merit scholarships, entering freshmen applying for the fall semester must submit their complete application for undergraduate admission by the priority deadline of November 1. The eligibility requirements for each scholarship vary. Award notifications begin in early March.

STUDENT LIFE

"The University of Maryland is a very large school," so "there is no 'typical' student here. Everyone will find that they can fit in somewhere." UMD is "an especially diverse school," and this makes people "more tolerant and accepting of people from different backgrounds and cultures." A student from New Jersey explains it this way: "Coming from a very diverse area, I thought it was going to be hard to find a school that had that same representation of minority and atypical students until I found Maryland. I don't think I have ever learned so much about different religions, cultures, orientations, or lifestyles. All of them are accepted and even celebrated" at UMD.

University of Maryland—College Park

FINANCIAL AID: 301-314-9000 • E-MAIL: UM-ADMIT@UGA.UMD.EDU • WEBSITE: WWW.MARYLAND.EDU

CAREER

The President's Promise initiative is the cornerstone of UMD's career philosophy, which focuses on helping students to articulate classroom learning in real-world settings. In cooperation with the comprehensive University Career Center, President's Promise connects students with career exposure and experiential learning opportunities (internships, job shadowing, service learning, study abroad, and research) in ways that complement the academic curriculum. One program, the Bright Futures Fund, supports unpaid interns with awards that range from $250 to $1,250. Opportunities to work with nearby federal agencies and labs, such as NASA's Goddard Space Flight Center and the National Institute of Standards and Technology, abound. More than 1,200 employers participate in UMD's career fairs annually or visit for on-campus interviews and networking events. Alumni who visited PayScale.com report a median starting salary of $52,700, and 54 percent derive a high level of meaning from their work.

GENERAL INFO

Activities: Choral groups, concert band, dance, drama/theater, jazz band, literary magazine, marching band, music ensembles, musical theater, opera, pep band, radio station, student government. **Organizations:** 724 registered organizations, 49 honor societies, 55 religious organizations. 32 fraternities, 24 sororities. **Athletics (Intercollegiate):** *Men:* Baseball, basketball, football, golf, lacrosse, soccer, track/field (outdoor), track/field (indoor), wrestling. *Women:* Basketball, cross-country, field hockey, golf, gymnastics, lacrosse, soccer, softball, swimming, tennis, track/field (outdoor), track/field (indoor), volleyball.

FINANCIAL AID

Students should submit: FAFSA. Priority filing deadline is 2/15. The Princeton Review suggests that all financial aid forms be submitted as soon as possible after October 1. *Need-based scholarships/grants offered:* Federal Pell, FSEOG, State scholarships/grants, Private scholarships, College/university scholarship or grant aid from institutional funds. *Loan aid offered:* Direct Subsidized Stafford Loans, Direct Unsubsidized Stafford Loans, Direct PLUS loans, Federal Perkins Loans. Applicants will be notified of awards on a rolling basis beginning 4/1. Federal Work-Study Program available. Institutional employment available.

THE BOTTOM LINE

College costs may be on the upswing, but the cost of an education at the University of Maryland—College Park is still a very good deal. Tuition and fees for Maryland residents comes to just $10,181 drawing in many from around the area; though nonresidents can expect to pay three times as much. All students who decide to live on campus can expect to pay an additional $11,758 in room and board. When you factor in the cost of books and supplies, the total cost of a UMD degree is $23,139 for all those who hail from the state, and $45,003 for those who don't.

CAREER INFORMATION FROM PAYSCALE.COM

ROI rating	86
Bachelor's and No Higher	
Median starting salary	$53,900
Median mid-career salary	$91,700
At Least Bachelor's	
Median starting salary	$54,800
Median mid-career salary	$94,400
% alumni with high job meaning	53%
% STEM	22%

SELECTIVITY

Admissions Rating	91
# of applicants	28,301
% of applicants accepted	45
% of acceptees attending	31

FRESHMAN PROFILE

Range SAT Critical Reading	590–690
Range SAT Math	620–730
Minimum internet-based TOEFL	100
Average HS GPA	4.2

DEADLINES

Early action	
Deadline	11/1
Notification	1/31
Regular	
Priority	11/1
Deadline	1/20
Nonfall registration?	Yes

FINANCIAL FACTS

Financial Aid Rating	81
Annual in-state tuition	$8,315
Annual out-of-state tuition	$30,179
Room and board	$11,758
Required fees	$1,866
Average need-based scholarship	$9,288
% needy frosh rec. need-based scholarship or grant aid	85
% needy UG rec. need-based scholarship or grant aid	80
% needy frosh rec. non-need-based scholarship or grant aid	12
% needy UG rec. non-need-based scholarship or grant aid	6
% needy frosh rec. need-based self-help aid	83
% needy UG rec. need-based self-help aid	91
% frosh rec. any financial aid	86
% UG rec. any financial aid	72
% UG borrow to pay for school	43
Average cumulative indebtedness	$26,818
% frosh need fully met	37
% ugrads need fully met	29
Average % of frosh need met	78
Average % of ugrad need met	75

University of Massachusetts Amherst

UNIVERSITY ADMISSIONS CENTER, AMHERST, MA 01003-9291 • ADMISSIONS: 413-545-0222 • FAX: 413-545-4312

CAMPUS LIFE

Quality of Life Rating	**91**
Fire Safety Rating	**92**
Green Rating	**98**
Type of school	Public
Affiliation	No Affiliation
Environment	Town

STUDENTS

Total undergrad enrollment	22,748
% male/female	51/49
% from out of state	20
% frosh live on campus	99
% ugrads live on campus	58
# of fraternities (% ugrad men join)	19 (8)
# of sororities (% ugrad women join)	12 (6)
% African American	4
% Asian	9
% Caucasian	67
% Hispanic	5
% Native American	<1
% Pacific Islander	<1
% Two or more races	3
% Race and/or ethnicity unknown	8
% international	4
# of countries represented	69

ACADEMICS

Academic Rating	**77**
% students returning for sophomore year	91
% students graduating within 4 years	66
% students graduating within 6 years	78
Calendar	Semester
Student/faculty ratio	17:1
Profs interesting rating	72
Profs accessible rating	66
Most classes have 10–19 students.	
Most lab/discussion sessions have 20–29 students.	

MOST POPULAR MAJORS
Psychology; Biology; Communication

ABOUT THE SCHOOL

The University of Massachusetts Amherst, comprised of over 1,400 scenic acres in the Pioneer Valley of Western Massachusetts and just ninety miles from Boston and 175 miles from New York, is the flagship of the five-campus University of Massachusetts system. UMass remains a powerhouse of education and research in the Northeast. "University of Massachusetts Amherst is a large research institution that has much more to offer than any small institution." Students' reasons for attending UMass Amherst are as diverse as they are, ranging from "the research opportunities" and its Commonwealth Honors College to the school's "newly built science buildings." However, "scholarship money, size, wide range of majors/programs, [and] location," consistently rank among admitted students' deciding factors. The College of Engineering, College of Information and Computer Sciences, and the Isenberg School of Management all have strong programs. The Commonwealth Honors Residential Community, a state-of-the-art living and learning complex opened its doors in the Fall of 2013. As one student outlines, the University of Massachusetts Amherst "is a multicultural school open to all beliefs and catered to enrich the lives of students in preparing them for the real world." This large research university is all about "giving students a great education while allowing them to find themselves and become an adult."

BANG FOR YOUR BUCK

UMass Amherst "offers the academic experience of a world-class research university in one of the best college towns in North America." The campus is "a top producer of internships, Fulbright Scholars, and Teach for America corp members." Student involvement "has placed the campus multiple times on the President's Higher Education Community Service Honor Role." Diversity is not only an attribute of the student community itself. Here students choose from over 90 academic majors and have the option to design their own through the school's BIDC program. As UMass Amherst is part of the Five College Consortium, undergraduates at this public university have the opportunity to extend their studies at nearby private colleges including Amherst, Hampshire, Mount Holyoke and Smith Colleges. Newly opened campus facilities include "state-of-the-art classrooms, studios, labs, and recreation center." "The campus is ranked in the top ten nationally for its sustainability work," and "cocurricular opportunities include [over 300] student-run clubs and organizations." The food is also consistently ranked among the best in the country and is a real value for the quality.

STUDENT LIFE

"There is no such thing as a typical student at UMass Amherst." An undergraduate population of more than 20,000 makes that impossible; most students here learn to balance fun and work. Students also "tend to fit the mold of their residence," undergrads tell us. One student writes, "Southwest houses students of mainstream culture. Students there can be seen wearing everything from UMass Amherst sweats to couture. Students in Central (especially Upper Central) tend to be the 'hippie' or scene type kids. Northeast houses . . . the more reserved types. Orchard Hill typically houses the more quiet types as well." On the whole, students "take our grades and the reputation of our school seriously. We take pride in being from UMass Amherst."

CAREER

At UMass Amherst, the Career Services database CareerConnect is a student's first (online) stop when searching for job postings, internships, and co-op opportunities. Of course, Career Services can also help you with major exploration, skill building, and networking. Another way to gain experience is to work for or co-manage one of the fourteen student-run, non-profit businesses on campus (like People's Market or the Bike Coop, to name a few). Finally, the Office of Civic Engagement and

University of Massachusetts Amherst

FINANCIAL AID: 413-545-0801 • E-MAIL: MAIL@ADMISSIONS.UMASS.EDU • WEBSITE: WWW.UMASS.EDU

Service-Learning offers several programs for community engagement that complement academic coursework. Alumni who visited PayScale.com reported median starting salaries of $49,400, and 48 percent derive a high level of meaning from their work.

GENERAL INFO

Activities: Choral groups, concert band, dance, drama/theater, jazz band, literary magazine, marching band, music ensembles, musical theater, opera, pep band, radio station, student government, student newspaper, student-run film society, symphony orchestra, television station. **Organizations:** Campus Ministries, International Student Organization, Model UN. 307 registered organizations, 39 honor societies, 19 religious organizations. 20 fraternities, 17 sororities. **Athletics (Intercollegiate):** *Men:* baseball, basketball, cross-country, diving, football, ice hockey, lacrosse, soccer, swimming, track/field (outdoor), track/field (indoor). *Women:* basketball, crew/rowing, cross-country, diving, field hockey, lacrosse, soccer, softball, swimming, tennis, track/field (outdoor), track/field (indoor). **On-Campus Highlights:** The Campus Center / Student Union, The Learning Commons, Recreation Center, The Mullins Center, The Fine Arts Center. **Environmental Initiatives:** Student-led effort resulted in first major public university to divest from direct fossil fuel holdings; new School of Earth and Sustainability; nationally recognized leader for using local food sources, recycling efforts, and clean and efficient energy infrastructure.

FINANCIAL AID

Students should submit: FAFSA. Priority filing deadline is 3/1. The Princeton Review suggests that all financial aid forms be submitted as soon as possible after October 1. *Need-based scholarships/grants offered:* Federal Pell, FSEOG, State scholarships/grants, Private scholarships, College/university scholarship or grant aid from institutional funds. *Loan aid offered:* Direct Subsidized Stafford Loans, Direct Unsubsidized Stafford Loans, Direct PLUS loans, Federal Perkins Loans, Federal Nursing Loans. Applicants will be notified of awards on a rolling basis beginning 4/1. Federal Work-Study Program available. Institutional employment available.

BOTTOM LINE

With a focus on framing learning within a professional dialogue, "opportunities to develop a résumé well before graduation are a hallmark of UMass Amherst." Students universally cite "financial affordability" as a popular factor when considering attendance. Annual in-state tuition and fees tally to $14,971 with an additional $11,897 for room and board. Out-of-state tuition is significantly more expensive at $32,204 annually. That said, UMass Amherst still offers major savings over private college tuition, and 85 percent of undergraduates receive some form of financial aid.

CAREER INFORMATION FROM PAYSCALE.COM

ROI rating	86
Bachelor's and No Higher	
Median starting salary	$48,600
Median mid-career salary	$84,200
At Least Bachelor's	
Median starting salary	$49,600
Median mid-career salary	$86,800
% alumni with high job meaning	47%
% STEM	16%

SELECTIVITY

Admissions Rating	88
# of applicants	40,010
% of applicants accepted	58
% of acceptees attending	20
# offered a place on the wait list	5,450
% accepting a place on wait list	23
% admitted from wait list	2

FRESHMAN PROFILE

Range SAT Critical Reading	550–640
Range SAT Math	580–670
Range ACT Composite	25–30
Minimum internet-based TOEFL	80
Average HS GPA	3.8
% graduated top 10% of class	32
% graduated top 25% of class	73
% graduated top 50% of class	97

DEADLINES

Early action	
Deadline	11/1
Regular	
Priority	1/15
Nonfall registration?	Yes

FINANCIAL FACTS

Financial Aid Rating	81
Annual in-state tuition	$14,971
Annual out-of-state tuition	$32,204
Room and board	$11,897
Average need-based scholarship	$9,905
% needy frosh rec. need-based scholarship or grant aid	91
% needy UG rec. need-based scholarship or grant aid	85
% needy frosh rec. non-need-based scholarship or grant aid	7
% needy UG rec. non-need-based scholarship or grant aid	54
% needy frosh rec. need-based self-help aid	76
% needy UG rec. need-based self-help aid	80
% frosh rec. any financial aid	90
% UG rec. any financial aid	85
% UG borrow to pay for school	70
Average cumulative indebtedness	$31,958
% frosh need fully met	14
% ugrads need fully met	13
Average % of frosh need met	81
Average % of ugrad need met	81

University of Michigan—Ann Arbor

1220 STUDENT ACTIVITIES BUILDING, ANN ARBOR, MI 48109-1316 • ADMISSIONS: 734-764-7433 • FAX: 734-936-0740

CAMPUS LIFE

Quality of Life Rating	93
Fire Safety Rating	88
Green Rating	94
Type of school	Public
Affiliation	No Affiliation
Environment	City

STUDENTS

Total undergrad enrollment	28,312
% male/female	51/49
% from out of state	38
% frosh live on campus	98
% ugrads live on campus	34
# of fraternities (% ugrad men join)	36 (17)
# of sororities (% ugrad women join)	28 (24)
% African American	4
% Asian	13
% Caucasian	62
% Hispanic	5
% Native American	<1
% Pacific Islander	<1
% Two or more races	3
% Race and/or ethnicity unknown	6
% international	7
# of countries represented	89

ACADEMICS

Academic Rating	89
% students returning for sophomore year	97
% students graduating within 4 years	75
% students graduating within 6 years	90
Calendar	Trimsester
Student/faculty ratio	15:1
Profs interesting rating	72
Profs accessible rating	76

Most classes have 10–19 students.
Most lab/discussion sessions have
20–29 students.

MOST POPULAR MAJORS

Experimental Psychology; Economics;
Business Administration and Management

#23 COLLEGE THAT PAYS YOU BACK

ABOUT THE SCHOOL

The University of Michigan—Ann Arbor is a big school with big opportunities, and we do mean big. The university has a multibillion-dollar endowment and one of the largest research expenditures of any American university, also in the billions. Its physical campus includes more than 34 million square feet of building space, and its football stadium is the largest college football stadium in the country. With more than 28,000 undergraduates, the scale of the University of Michigan's stellar offerings truly is overwhelming. But for those students who can handle the "first-class education in a friendly, competitive atmosphere," there are a lot of advantages to attending a university of this size and stature, and they will find "a great environment both academically and socially." You get an amazing breadth of classes, excellent professors, a "wide range of travel abroad opportunities," unparalleled research opportunities, and inroads into an alumni network that can offer you entry into any number of postgraduate opportunities. The school "provides every kind of opportunity at all times to all people," and students here get "the opportunity to go far within their respective concentrations."

BANG FOR YOUR BUCK

UM spent $341 million in 2012–13 on total undergraduate need-based and merit-aid. That is truly staggering and reflects an amount more than the total endowment of many schools. Students who are Pell-grant eligible may benefit from UM's debt-elimination programs. All in-state students can expect to have 100 percent of their demonstrated need met. The university's schools, colleges, and departments administer their own scholarship programs, so you should feel free to check with them directly. UM's Office of Financial Aid also administers a variety of scholarship programs that recognize superior academic achievement, leadership qualities, and potential contribution to the scholarly community. The majority of these scholarships are awarded automatically to eligible students. A full list of UM scholarships is available on the university's website. In addition to the scholarship programs offered by the school, there are also private scholarships available to prospective students. These are offered by a variety of corporate, professional, trade, governmental, civic, religious, social and fraternal organizations. While these applications can be time consuming, they can be worth it. Some are worth thousands of dollars. The University of Michigan has a full list of these scholarships—and their deadlines—on their website. The school is dedicated to helping prospective students gain a better understanding of how to pay for their education by providing access to financial aid counselors. Their website also features an application called M-Calc, a net price calculator, which allows students and their families to access an early estimate of the full-time cost of attendance the University of Michigan.

STUDENT LIFE

The Michigan student body is "hugely diverse," which "is one of the things Michigan prides itself on." There is a place for everyone here, because "there are hundreds of mini-communities within the campus, made of everything from service fraternities to political organizations to dance groups." As one undergrad puts it, "That's part of the benefit of 40,000-plus students!" Students also rave about "great programs like UMix . . . phenomenal cultural opportunities in Ann Arbor especially music and movies," and "the hugely popular football Saturdays. The sense of school spirit here is impressive." With over 1,200 registered student organizations on campus, "if you have an interest, you can find a group of people who enjoy the same thing."

University of Michigan—Ann Arbor

FINANCIAL AID: 734-763-6600 • WEBSITE: WWW.UMICH.EDU

CAREER

The Career Center offers a wealth of resources to students learning to be advocates for themselves post-graduation. The massive fall Career Fair jumpstarts the process for job-seekers (the Career Center even offers a smartphone App for navigating the floor plan), and the semester schedule is packed with programs and workshops like Career Crawls, which focus on themes such as choosing a major, or Immersions, a program which hosts half-day visits to an organization's workplace. Career Center Connector lists tons of job and internship opportunities while Alumni Profiles provide glimpses into grad's career choices and job search strategies. Other structured programs, like the Public Service Intern Program, link students with internship openings in the U.S. and abroad. Graduates who visited PayScale.com report an average starting salary of $56,800, and 48 percent believe that their jobs make the world a better place.

GENERAL INFO

Activities: Choral groups, concert band, dance, drama/theater, ethnic/environmental/gender groups, intramural sports, jazz band, literary magazine, marching band, music ensembles, musical theater, opera, pep band, radio station, social activism, student government. **Organizations:** >1,200 registered organizations, 31 honor societies, 98 religious organizations. 40 fraternities, 25 sororities. **Athletics (Intercollegiate):** *Men:* Baseball, basketball, cross-country, diving, football, golf, gymnastics, ice hockey, lacrosse, soccer, swimming, tennis, track/field (outdoor), track/field (indoor), wrestling. *Women:* Basketball, crew/rowing, cross-country, diving, field hockey, golf, gymnastics, lacrosse, soccer, softball, swimming, tennis, track/field (outdoor), track/field (indoor), volleyball, water polo.

FINANCIAL AID

Students should submit: FAFSA, CSS/Financial Aid PROFILE. Regular filing deadline is 4/30. The Princeton Review suggests that all financial aid forms be submitted as soon as possible after October 1. *Need-based scholarships/grants offered:* Federal Pell, FSEOG, State scholarships/grants, Private scholarships, College/university scholarship or grant aid from institutional funds. *Loan aid offered:* Direct Subsidized Stafford Loans, Direct Unsubsidized Stafford Loans, Direct PLUS loans, Federal Perkins Loans, Federal Nursing Loans, College/university loans from institutional funds. Applicants will be notified of awards on a rolling basis beginning 3/15. Federal Work-Study Program available. Institutional employment available.

BOTTOM LINE

UM's top-of-the-line education and comparatively low tuition make this school the definition of a best value. For Michigan residents, the estimated total cost of attendance for one year is about $26,331, including tuition, fees, room and board, books and supplies. For nonresidents, the price is almost exactly double the in-state rate at $56,604.

CAREER INFORMATION FROM PAYSCALE.COM

ROI rating	92
Bachelor's and No Higher	
Median starting salary	$58,000
Median mid-career salary	$96,000
At Least Bachelor's	
Median starting salary	$59,400
Median mid-career salary	$100,000
% alumni with high job meaning	51%
% STEM	28%

SELECTIVITY

Admissions Rating	96
# of applicants	51,761
% of applicants accepted	26
% of acceptees attending	45
# offered a place on the wait list	4,512
% admitted from wait list	2

FRESHMAN PROFILE

Range SAT Critical Reading	630–730
Range SAT Math	660–770
Range SAT Writing	640–730
Range ACT Composite	29–33
Minimum paper TOEFL	600
Minimum internet-based TOEFL	100
Average HS GPA	3.8

DEADLINES

Early action	
Deadline	11/1
Notification	12/24
Regular	
Priority	11/1
Deadline	2/1
Nonfall registration?	Yes

FINANCIAL FACTS

Financial Aid Rating	88
Annual in-state tuition	$14,401
Annual out-of-state tuition	$44,674
Room and board	$10,554
Required fees	$328
Average need-based scholarship	$15,400
% needy frosh rec. need-based scholarship or grant aid	83
% needy UG rec. need-based scholarship or grant aid	85
% needy frosh rec. non-need-based scholarship or grant aid	73
% needy UG rec. non-need-based scholarship or grant aid	65
% needy frosh rec. need-based self-help aid	75
% needy UG rec. need-based self-help aid	83
% frosh rec. any financial aid	68
% UG rec. any financial aid	61
% UG borrow to pay for school	44
Average cumulative indebtedness	$26,034
% frosh need fully met	77
% ugrads need fully met	81
Average % of frosh need met	86
Average % of ugrad need met	86

University of Minnesota, Twin Cities

240 WILLIAMSON HALL, 231 PILLSBURY DRIVE SE, MINNEAPOLIS, MN 55455-0213 • ADMISSIONS: 612-625-2008

ABOUT THE COLLEGE

The University of Minnesota, Twin Cities, offers more than 140 degree programs to its undergraduate student body of over 30,000. That equals a whole lot of opportunity. The university's top-ranked College of Pharmacy is complemented by exceptional programs in business and engineering. Off-the-beaten track majors are also available, as U of M has enough academic offerings to cover almost every esoteric interest you can imagine. This is a big research university, which means "there are incredible opportunities [for undergraduates] to work in ANY field of research." Instructors "enjoy teaching the material and getting to know the students personally." Qualified undergraduates may take graduate-level classes, too. It's a large school, so lower-level courses can get crowded—though freshman seminars, freshman composition, and foreign language classes are usually capped at twenty-five students or less. Study abroad opportunities here are expansive, and a good proportion of students take advantage.

BANG FOR YOUR BUCK

University of Minnesota offers a comprehensive program of need-based and merit-based aid. Each year, the incoming freshmen class receives over $25 million in academic scholarships to be used over the course of their college careers. Awards last four years, and range from $1,000–$12,000 each year. U of M offers a national scholarship program for nonresident freshmen that covers the difference between in-state and nonresident tuition. There are nine conventional residence halls, plus three new apartment-style facilities.

STUDENT LIFE

As is often the case at large schools, U of M offers a diversity of options depending on where your interests lie. "There is a lot of partying, but it can be avoided if you are not interested in it," is a sentiment echoed by many students, and both the University itself and the surrounding urban area offer many ways for students to have fun outside of class. "There are endless intramural sports, and sporting events, concerts, and different student groups and clubs that plan activities and have regular meetings," says one student, and another affirms that "there are so many events and activities on campus, it's hard to be bored." For those looking to explore, "uptown [Minneapolis] features some fantastic ethnic restaurants and kitschy shops as well as frequent art fairs and comedy clubs. Downtown features several theaters where student rates give us access to the best local performances." Students of all varieties seem to find the environment welcoming, and one raves that "we are also the most gay friendly, hipster, and bike friendly city in the nation (not to mention we're really proud of these three things)." So whatever it is you're into, at U of M you should be able to find exactly what you're looking for.

CAREER

U of M Career Services is somewhat unique in that each college has its own career center catering to the specific needs of its students. While these centers are linked through a main Career Services office, the majority of the services available at U of M, such as advising, career fairs, and job search tools, are offered through the individual colleges. As such, "academic advising and career services differ from college to college," but most students seem to be pleased with the quality of what is offered. One student reports that "my advisor and the career center are excellent guides," and another states that, "I'm always getting emails [from] the career center, all on-campus jobs offer training for finding jobs after graduation, and the information on post grad options are extremely easy to find." There are also resources available specifically for women, LGBT students, international students, and other demographic groups. According to the school, U

University of Minnesota, Twin Cities

FAX: 612-626-1693 • FINANCIAL AID: 612-624-1111 • WEBSITE: WWW.UMN.EDU

of M alumni have founded over 19,000 companies. Out of graduates visiting PayScale.com, 55 percent report feeling as though they derive a high level of meaning from their careers.

GENERAL INFO

Activities: Choral groups, concert band, dance, drama/theater, jazz band, literary magazine, marching band, music ensembles, musical theater, opera, pep band, radio station, student government, student newspaper, student-run film society, symphony orchestra, television station, international student organization. **Organizations:** 800 registered organizations, 76 religious organizations, 22 fraternities, 12 sororities, 7 multicultural fraternities, 5 multicultural sororities. **Athletics (Intercollegiate):** *Men:* Baseball, basketball, cross-country, diving, football, golf, gymnastics, ice hockey, swimming, tennis, track/field (outdoor), track/field (indoor), wrestling. *Women:* Basketball, cheerleading, cross-country, diving, golf, gymnastics, ice hockey, soccer, softball, swimming, tennis, track/field (outdoor), track/field (indoor), volleyball. **On-Campus Highlights:** Weisman Art Museum, McNamara Alumni Center, TCF Bank Stadium, Goldstein Gallery, Northrup Memorial Auditorium, Coffman Memorial Union, Mariucci Arena, University Theater, Rarig Center.

FINANCIAL AID

Students should submit: FAFSA. Priority filing deadline is 2/1. The Princeton Review suggests that all financial aid forms be submitted as soon as possible after October 1. *Need-based scholarships/grants offered:* Federal Pell, FSEOG, State scholarships/grants, Private scholarships, College/university scholarship or grant aid from institutional funds, Federal Nursing Scholarships. *Loan aid offered:* Direct Subsidized Stafford Loans, Direct Unsubsidized Stafford Loans, Direct PLUS loans, Federal Perkins Loans, Federal Nursing Loans, State Loans, College/university loans from institutional funds. Applicants will be notified of awards on a rolling basis beginning in February. Federal Work-Study Program available. Institutional employment available.

THE BOTTOM LINE

Tuition and fees at the University of Minnesota—Twin Cities runs about $12,546 per year for Minnesota, North Dakota, South Dakota, and Manitoba, Wisconsin residents. Nonresidents get a pretty good deal also: they can expect to pay in the range of $22,210 a year. Room and board is an additional $9,377, bringing the total cost of attendance to $23,519 for residents and $33,183 for nonresidents. University of Minnesota also fosters both learning and frugality with its unique thirteenth-credit tuition incentive in which every credit after thirteen is free of charge, keeping costs down for families and helping students achieve graduation in four years. Students typically take fifteen to sixteen credits each semester or 120 credits over four years.

CAREER INFORMATION FROM PAYSCALE.COM

ROI rating	87
Bachelor's and No Higher	
Median starting salary	$50,000
Median mid-career salary	$87,200
At Least Bachelor's	
Median starting salary	$50,500
Median mid-career salary	$88,900
% alumni with high job meaning	54%
% STEM	23%

SELECTIVITY

Admissions Rating	90
# of applicants	46,165
% of applicants accepted	45
% of acceptees attending	28

FRESHMAN PROFILE

Range SAT Critical Reading	560–700
Range SAT Math	620–740
Range SAT Writing	570–690
Range ACT Composite	26–31
Minimum paper TOEFL	550
% graduated top 10% of class	49
% graduated top 25% of class	85
% graduated top 50% of class	99

DEADLINES

Regular	
Priority	11/1
Deadline	12/15
Notification	3/31
Nonfall registration?	Yes

FINANCIAL FACTS

Financial Aid Rating	81
Annual in-state tuition	$12,546
Annual out-of-state tuition	$22,210
Room and board	$9,377
Required fees	$1,596
Average need-based scholarship	$9,919
% needy frosh rec. need-based scholarship or grant aid	84
% needy UG rec. need-based scholarship or grant aid	83
% needy frosh rec. non-need-based scholarship or grant aid	10
% needy UG rec. non-need-based scholarship or grant aid	7
% needy frosh rec. need-based self-help aid	80
% needy UG rec. need-based self-help aid	81
% UG borrow to pay for school	59
Average cumulative indebtedness	$26,006
% frosh need fully met	29
% ugrads need fully met	24
Average % of frosh need met	78
Average % of ugrad need met	73

The University of North Carolina at Chapel Hill

Campus Box #2200, Chapel Hill, NC 27599-2200 • Admissions: 919-966-3621 • Fax: 919-962-3045

CAMPUS LIFE

Quality of Life Rating	**90**
Fire Safety Rating	**96**
Green Rating	**94**
Type of school	Public
Affiliation	No Affiliation
Environment	Town

STUDENTS

Total undergrad enrollment	18,415
% male/female	42/58
% from out of state	17
% frosh from public high school	82
% frosh live on campus	100
% ugrads live on campus	52
# of fraternities (% ugrad men join)	34 (18)
# of sororities (% ugrad women join)	24 (18)
% African American	8
% Asian	10
% Caucasian	63
% Hispanic	8
% Native American	1
% Pacific Islander	<1
% Two or more races	4
% Race and/or ethnicity unknown	3
% international	3
# of countries represented	94

ACADEMICS

Academic Rating	**80**
% students returning for sophomore year	97
% students graduating within 4 years	82
% students graduating within 6 years	90
Calendar	Semester
Student/faculty ratio	14:1
Profs interesting rating	71
Profs accessible rating	68

Most classes have 10–19 students.
Most lab/discussion sessions have 10–19 students.

MOST POPULAR MAJORS

Biology; Psychology; Economics

ABOUT THE SCHOOL

The University of North Carolina at Chapel Hill has a reputation for top academics, top athletics, and great overall value. Chartered in 1789 as the first public university in America, UNC Chapel Hill has a long legacy of excellence. Although its relative low cost makes Carolina a great bargain in higher education, the school is all about "top-notch academics while having the ultimate college experience." Professors are at the top of their fields and "will work with you above and beyond the normal scope of their position to help you with any concerns or interests you could possibly have." The chancellor even "holds meetings for students to meet with her to discuss school issues." The journalism, business, and nursing programs are ranked among the best in the country, and students of any major may minor in entrepreneurship and compete for start-up funding in the Carolina Challenge. Study abroad programs are available in more than seventy countries. The student body is composed of students from every state and nearly 100 countries, and the university has produced more Rhodes Scholars over the past twenty-five years than any other public research university. There are "many opportunities to gain experience for a future career," and just by applying to Carolina, students are considered for opportunities such as the school's Honors Program, Carolina Research Scholars Program, Global Gap Year Fellowship, and assured enrollment in the university's business and journalism programs. The university's extensive career center counsels students throughout every stage of their education, and students are "at ease knowing that their hard work pays off."

BANG FOR YOUR BUCK

Carolina meets 100 percent of students' need, regardless of whether they are North Carolinians or out-of-state residents (entering students with need even receive laptop computers). Aid packages generally contain at least 60 percent in grant and scholarship assistance, with the remaining 40 percent in work-study and loans. Low-income students who are 200 percent below the federal poverty standard do not have to borrow at all to pay for their education—these students are designated Carolina Covenant Scholars and receive packages of grants, scholarships, and student employment. The university awards about 250 merit scholarships each year to students in the first-year class. These scholarships range in value from $2,500 to a full ride. Best of all, there is no separate application for merit scholarships; students are awarded scholarships, some of which are on a need-blind basis, based on information provided in the regular admissions application.

STUDENT LIFE

A feeling of generosity pervades UNC—"the epitome of Southern hospitality"—and extends beyond mere school spirit and the wearing of Tar Heels colors on game days. "Carolina is family," one student says. "Many of us here are crazy about sports," (even the fire trucks here are Carolina blue), "but most will do anything at all to help a fellow UNC student." Still, "there are few experiences that can top being in the risers at a UNC basketball game or rushing Franklin Street when UNC beats Duke," says a student. No matter what you're into, "life at UNC is full throttle," and "there are hundreds of active clubs and student organizations in which you can meet people with the same interests, or different interests." Students can participate in anything "from ballroom dancing to skydiving to paintball to religious groups" plus downtown Chapel Hill is just out the door.

CAREER

UNC's comprehensive Career Services assists students throughout their entire undergraduate education. First, volunteer Career Peers can

The University of North Carolina at Chapel Hill

FINANCIAL AID: 919-962-8396 • E-MAIL: UNCHELP@ADMISSIONS.UNC.EDU • WEBSITE: WWW.UNC.EDU

help prep undergrads for the job hunt by facilitating anything from mock interviews to marathon résumé-writing sessions. Careerolina is a one-stop shop for job and internship postings but also for information about on-campus recruiting, career fairs (recent guests include IBM, The Hershey Company, and NBC/Universal), and an assortment of workshops on topics like LinkedIn profiles or graduate school applications. Recent grads report average starting salaries of $46,100, and 53 percent believe their job holds a great deal of meaning.

GENERAL INFO

Activities: Choral groups, concert band, dance, drama/theater, jazz band, literary magazine, marching band, music ensembles, musical theater, opera, pep band, radio station, student government, student newspaper, student-run film society, symphony orchestra, television station, yearbook, campus ministries, international student organization. **Organizations:** 753 registered organizations, 30 honor societies, 55 religious organizations. 34 fraternities, 24 sororities. **Athletics (Intercollegiate):** *Men:* Baseball, basketball, cross-country, diving, fencing, football, golf, lacrosse, soccer, swimming, tennis, track/field (outdoor), track/field (indoor), wrestling. *Women:* Basketball, crew/rowing, cross-country, diving, fencing, field hockey, golf, gymnastics, lacrosse, soccer, softball, swimming, tennis, track/field (outdoor), track/field (indoor), volleyball. **On-Campus Highlights:** The Pit, McCorkle Place, Polk Place, Dean Smith Center, Student Union, Old Well, Coker Arboretum, Morehead Planetarium, Ackland Art Museum, Kenan Stadium.

FINANCIAL AID

Students should submit: FAFSA, CSS/Financial Aid PROFILE. Priority filing deadline is 3/1. The Princeton Review suggests that all financial aid forms be submitted as soon as possible after October 1. *Need-based scholarships/grants offered:* Federal Pell, FSEOG, State scholarships/grants, Private scholarships, College/university scholarship or grant aid from institutional funds. *Loan aid offered:* Direct Subsidized Stafford Loans, Direct Unsubsidized Stafford Loans, Direct PLUS loans, Federal Perkins Loans, State Loans, College/university loans from institutional funds. Applicants will be notified of awards on a rolling basis beginning 3/15. Federal Work-Study Program available. Institutional employment available.

THE BOTTOM LINE

The cost of attending Carolina is a real bargain—especially if your home state is North Carolina. In-state students can expect to pay about $8,834 in tuition and fees. Out-of-state students have it pretty good too; they can expect to cough up about $33,916 for the cost of tuition and fees for one year. Cost of living in Chapel Hill is pretty cheap too—you can expect room and board to run you just $11,218 per year.

CAREER INFORMATION FROM PAYSCALE.COM

ROI rating	**89**
Bachelor's and No Higher	
Median starting salary	$46,200
Median mid-career salary	$79,400
At Least Bachelor's	
Median starting salary	$47,100
Median mid-career salary	$81,500
% alumni with high job meaning	48%
% STEM	15%

SELECTIVITY

Admissions Rating	**96**
# of applicants	31,953
% of applicants accepted	30
% of acceptees attending	43
# offered a place on the wait list	3,144
% accepting a place on wait list	48
% admitted from wait list	5

FRESHMAN PROFILE

Range SAT Critical Reading	590–690
Range SAT Math	610–700
Range SAT Writing	590–700
Range ACT Composite	27–32
Minimum paper TOEFL	600
Minimum internet-based TOEFL	100
Average HS GPA	4.6
% graduated top 10% of class	77
% graduated top 25% of class	96
% graduated top 50% of class	99

DEADLINES

Early action	
Deadline	10/15
Notification	1/31
Regular	
Priority	10/15
Deadline	1/15
Nonfall registration?	No

FINANCIAL FACTS

Financial Aid Rating	**92**
Annual in-state tuition	$6,881
Annual out-of-state tuition	$31,963
Room and board	$11,218
Required fees	$1,953
Average need-based scholarship	$17,244
% needy frosh rec. need-based scholarship or grant aid	93
% needy UG rec. need-based scholarship or grant aid	91
% needy frosh rec. non-need-based scholarship or grant aid	6
% needy UG rec. non-need-based scholarship or grant aid	4
% needy frosh rec. need-based self-help aid	66
% needy UG rec. need-based self-help aid	73
% frosh rec. any financial aid	67
% UG rec. any financial aid	63
% UG borrow to pay for school	41
Average cumulative indebtedness	$20,127
% frosh need fully met	87
% ugrads need fully met	82
Average % of frosh need met	100
Average % of ugrad need met	100

University of Notre Dame

220 Main Building, Notre Dame, IN 46556 • Admissions: 574-631-7505 • Fax: 574-631-8865

ABOUT THE SCHOOL

As a private school with traditions of excellence in academics, athletics, and service, and with a vast, faithful alumni base that provides ample resources, the University of Notre Dame draws on its Catholic values to provide a well-rounded, world-class education. One student is thrilled to attend, noting that "as an Irish Catholic, Notre Dame is basically the equivalent of Harvard. I've always viewed the school as an institution with rigorous academics as well as rich tradition and history—and a symbol of pride for my heritage." Not all are Catholic here, although it seems that most undergrads "have some sort of spirituality present in their daily lives" and have a "vibrant social and religious life." Total undergraduate enrollment is just more than 8,000 students. ND is reportedly improving in diversity concerning economic backgrounds, according to members of the student body here. An incredible 90 percent are from out-of-state, and ninety countries are now represented throughout the campus. Undergrads say they enjoy "a college experience that is truly unique," "combining athletics and academics in an environment of faith." "It's necessary to study hard and often, [but] there's also time to do other things." Academics are widely praised, and one new student is excited that even "large lectures are broken down into smaller discussion groups once a week to help with class material and . . . give the class a personal touch."

BANG FOR YOUR BUCK

Notre Dame is one of the most selective colleges in the country. Almost everyone who enrolls is in the top 10 percent of their graduating class and possesses test scores in the highest percentiles. But, as the student respondents suggest, strong academic ability isn't enough to get you in here. The school looks for students with other talents and seems to have a predilection for athletic achievement. Each residence hall is home to students from all classes; most will live in the same hall for all their years on campus. An average of 93 percent of entering students will graduate within five years. Students report that "the administration tries its best to stay on top of the students' wants and needs." The school is also extremely community-oriented, and Notre Dame has some of the strongest alumni support nationwide.

STUDENT LIFE

Undergrads at Notre Dame report "the vast majority" of their peers are "very smart" "white kids from upper to middle-class backgrounds from all over the country, especially the Midwest and Northeast." The typical student "is a type A personality that studies a lot, yet is athletic and involved in the community. They are usually the outstanding seniors in their high schools," the "sort of people who can talk about the BCS rankings and Derrida in the same breath." Additionally, something like "85 percent of Notre Dame students earned a varsity letter in high school." "ND is slowly improving in diversity concerning economic backgrounds, with the university's policy to meet all demonstrated financial need." As things stand now, those who "don't tend to fit in with everyone else hang out in their own groups made up by others like them (based on ethnicity, sexual orientation, etc.)."

CAREER

At Notre Dame, The Career Center's mantra to students is "YOU must take ownership of your future." But, of course, career counselors and staff are there to support and assist students every step of the way. To that end, experiential career opportunities abound for freshmen

University of Notre Dame

FINANCIAL AID: 574-631-6436 • E-MAIL: ADMISSIONS@ND.EDU • WEBSITE: WWW.ND.EDU

and seniors alike: students can complete a Wall Street externship, shadow an alum at work, or be matched to a mentor in the industry of their choice. The Career Center funding program will even support students who need financial assistance to participate in a full-time summer internship. The university hosts several career and internship fairs each semester, along with networking programs like a Civil Engineering Luncheon or Consulting Night. Finally, Students visit Go IRISH, the center's primary recruiting database, for information about interviewing opportunities, employer information sessions, or opportunities that specifically seek a ND student or alum.

GENERAL INFO

Activities: Choral groups, concert band, dance, drama/theater, jazz band, literary magazine, marching band, music ensembles, musical theater, opera, pep band, radio station, student government, student newspaper, student-run film society, symphony orchestra, yearbook, campus ministries, international student organization. **Organizations:** 299 registered organizations, 10 honor societies, 11 religious organizations. **Athletics (Intercollegiate):** *Men:* Baseball, basketball, cross-country, diving, fencing, football, golf, ice hockey, lacrosse, soccer, swimming, tennis, track/field (outdoor). *Women:* Basketball, crew/rowing, cross-country, diving, fencing, golf, lacrosse, soccer, softball, swimming, tennis, track/field (outdoor), volleyball.

FINANCIAL AID

Students should submit: FAFSA, CSS/Financial Aid PROFILE, Noncustodial PROFILE, Business/Farm Supplement. Priority filing deadline is 2/15. The Princeton Review suggests that all financial aid forms be submitted as soon as possible after October 1. *Need-based scholarships/grants offered:* Federal Pell, FSEOG, State scholarships/grants, Private scholarships, College/university scholarship or grant aid from institutional funds. *Loan aid offered:* Direct Subsidized Stafford Loans, Direct Unsubsidized Stafford Loans, Direct PLUS loans, Federal Perkins Loans. Applicants will be notified of awards on a rolling basis beginning 3/28. Federal Work-Study Program available. Institutional employment available.

BOTTOM LINE

Notre Dame, while certainly providing a wonderful academic environment and superb education, does reflect this in the cost of attending the college. Annual tuition is $49,178. With room, board, and books, students are looking at close to $64,000 a year. Fortunately, over half of incoming needy freshmen are provided with need-based scholarship or grant aid. Over 75 percent of undergrads receive some form of financial aid.

CAREER INFORMATION FROM PAYSCALE.COM

ROI rating	90
Bachelor's and No Higher	
Median starting salary	$57,400
Median mid-career salary	$106,000
At Least Bachelor's	
Median starting salary	$59,000
Median mid-career salary	$111,000
% alumni with high job meaning	51%
% STEM	22%

SELECTIVITY

Admissions Rating	98
# of applicants	18,157
% of applicants accepted	20
% of acceptees attending	56
# offered a place on the wait list	1,602
% accepting a place on wait list	54
% admitted from wait list	0

FRESHMAN PROFILE

Range SAT Critical Reading	670–760
Range SAT Math	680–770
Range SAT Writing	650–750
Range ACT Composite	32–34
Minimum paper TOEFL	560
Minimum internet-based TOEFL	100
% graduated top 10% of class	91
% graduated top 25% of class	98
% graduated top 50% of class	100

DEADLINES

Early action	
Deadline	11/1
Notification	12/21
Regular	
Deadline	1/1
Notification	4/10
Nonfall registration?	Yes

FINANCIAL FACTS

Financial Aid Rating	94
Annual tuition	$49,178
Room and board	$14,358
Required fees	$507
Average need-based scholarship	$35,807
% needy frosh rec. need-based scholarship or grant aid	93
% needy UG rec. need-based scholarship or grant aid	94
% needy frosh rec. non-need-based scholarship or grant aid	56
% needy UG rec. non-need-based scholarship or grant aid	55
% needy frosh rec. need-based self-help aid	70
% needy UG rec. need-based self-help aid	76
% frosh rec. any financial aid	66
% UG rec. any financial aid	77
% UG borrow to pay for school	50
Average cumulative indebtedness	$27,237
% frosh need fully met	100
% ugrads need fully met	100
Average % of frosh need met	100
Average % of ugrad need met	100

University of Oklahoma

1000 Asp Avenue, Norman, OK 73019-4076 • Admissions: 405-325-2252 • Fax: 405-325-7124

CAMPUS LIFE

Quality of Life Rating	**92**
Fire Safety Rating	**90**
Green Rating	**77**
Type of school	Public
Affiliation	No Affiliation
Environment	City

STUDENTS

Total undergrad enrollment	22,132
% male/female	49/51
% from out of state	32
% frosh live on campus	87
% ugrads live on campus	30
# of fraternities (% ugrad men join)	28 (22)
# of sororities (% ugrad women join)	18 (29)
% African American	5
% Asian	6
% Caucasian	61
% Hispanic	9
% Native American	4
% Pacific Islander	<1
% Two or more races	7
% Race and/or ethnicity unknown	3
% international	5
# of countries represented	111

ACADEMICS

Academic Rating	**75**
% students returning for sophomore year	86
% students graduating within 4 years	38
% students graduating within 6 years	66
Calendar	Semester
Student/faculty ratio	17:1
Profs interesting rating	75
Profs accessible rating	76

Most classes have 10–19 students.
Most lab/discussion sessions have 20–29 students.

MOST POPULAR MAJORS

Registered Nursing/Registered Nurse; Psychology; Accounting

ABOUT THE SCHOOL

The University of Oklahoma combines a unique mixture of academic excellence, varied social cultures, and a variety of campus activities to make your educational experience complete. At OU, comprehensive learning is the goal for your life. OU students receive a valuable classroom learning experience, but OU is considered by many students to be one of the finest research institutions in the United States. Students appreciate the opportunity to be a part of technology in progress. With 459 student organizations on campus, "there's no way you could possibly be bored." "From the Indonesian Student Association to the Bocce Ball League of Excellence, there's a group for" everyone. "The programming board here brings in a lot of great acts and keeps us very entertained in the middle of Oklahoma," adds one student. "School spirit is rampant," and intercollegiate athletics are extremely popular—particularly football. "Not everyone likes Sooner football," but it sure seems that way. Students at OU "live and breathe football" in the fall when "the campus goes into a frenzy." Fraternities and sororities are also "a large part of social life." Some students insist that the Greek system isn't a dominant feature of the OU landscape. "You hardly notice their presence" if you're not involved, they say, and "the majority of students aren't involved." The "friendly and cute little town" of Norman is reportedly an ideal place to spend a day when not in class. Right next to campus is an area "full of" boutique shops and "a fine selection of bars and restaurants." "Norman is such a great town," gushes one student. "It's not too little to be boring but not too big to be impersonal."

BANG FOR YOUR BUCK

The University of Oklahoma's tuition and fees remain perennially low when compared to its peer institutions in the Big Twelve athletic conference, and OU is mighty proud of its dedication to providing financial assistance to students who want to attend. Alumni are loyal, and the fundraising machine is epic. In fact, OU's Campaign for Scholarships has raised over $247 million since its launch in 2005. As far as scholarships go, OU offers several merit- and need-based aid programs to students including those based on such criteria as academics, leadership, and extracurricular interests. Funds cover up to the full cost of tuition, and are available to Oklahoma residents and nonresidents.

STUDENT LIFE

"Greek life tends to dominate the social scene" at OU with sororities and fraternities making up a significant portion of the population. "Almost all students are in one or more student organizations." Most are "from Oklahoma or Texas, white, Christian, self-motivated, family oriented." Still OU is home to "a wide variety of students with different political, religious, and economic backgrounds." "Everybody is able to find other kindred spirits among the school community." And, more importantly, "there's a niche (and bar)" for everyone. It seems most students are involved in athletics in some capacity, even if it's just as a fan. "During football season, the campus is electric." The school also offers "amazing opportunities to see incredible art through theatre, dance, orchestra, and art exhibits." OU students attend free movies at the Union on the weekends, and Norman itself is "friendly and cute," a true "college town to the core."

University of Oklahoma

FINANCIAL AID: 405-325-5505 • E-MAIL: ADMREC@OU.EDU • WEBSITE: WWW.OU.EDU

CAREER

At OU, the "career services are impeccable," so naturally students feel "ready for the future." There are "creative programs that provide real-world experience" and "opportunities to really develop oneself outside the classroom." A student-run advertising and public relations agency or the National Weather Center are just a few places where students may hone their skills on campus. OU emphasizes community service through "million dollar help programs like the Writing Center, Free Action Tutoring, Project Threshold, etc." Students also receive career advice and counseling from professors who "leave their office doors open" and are happy to discuss "not only class but life after OU." Students feel a sense of global awareness at OU and a desire to better the world. Nearly sixty percent of alumni who visited the website PayScale.com regard their jobs as meaningful. And, according to the same site, the average salary for recent grads is $47,700.

GENERAL INFO

Environment: City. **Activities:** Choral groups, concert band, dance, drama/theater, literary magazine, marching band, music ensembles, musical theater, opera, pep band, model UN, radio station, student government, student newspaper, student-run film society, symphony orchestra, television station, yearbook, campus ministries, international student organization. **Organizations:** 459 registered organizations, 17 honor societies, 34 religious organizations. 28 fraternities, 18 sororities. **Athletics (Intercollegiate):** *Men:* Baseball, basketball, cheerleading, cross-country, football, golf, gymnastics, tennis, track/field (outdoor), track/field (indoor), wrestling. *Women:* Basketball, cheerleading, crew/rowing, cross-country, golf, gymnastics, soccer, softball, tennis, track/field (outdoor), track/field (in door), volleyball.

FINANCIAL AID

Students should submit: FAFSA. Priority filing deadline is 3/1. The Princeton Review suggests that all financial aid forms be submitted as soon as possible after October 1. *Need-based scholarships/grants offered:* Federal Pell, FSEOG, State scholarships/grants, Private scholarships, College/university scholarship or grant aid from institutional funds, United Negro College Fund. *Loan aid offered:* Direct Subsidized Stafford Loans, Direct Unsubsidized Stafford Loans, Direct PLUS loans, Federal Perkins Loans, College/university loans from institutional funds. Applicants will be notified of awards on a rolling basis beginning 3/15. Federal Work-Study Program available. Institutional employment available.

BOTTOM LINE

Total cost of attendance at OU runs about $21,112 per year for Oklahoma residents. Nonresidents can expect to pay about $35,483 a year. About 88 percent of undergrads here receive some type of financial assistance in the form of scholarships, grants, loans, work-study, and tuition waivers.

CAREER INFORMATION FROM PAYSCALE.COM

ROI rating	87
Bachelor's and No Higher	
Median starting salary	$49,000
Median mid-career salary	$87,200
At Least Bachelor's	
Median starting salary	$49,900
Median mid-career salary	$87,800
% alumni with high job meaning	56%
% STEM	20%

SELECTIVITY

Admissions Rating	86
# of applicants	12,002
% of applicants accepted	78
% of acceptees attending	45
# offered a place on the wait list	1,322
% accepting a place on wait list	100
% admitted from wait list	16

FRESHMAN PROFILE

Range SAT Critical Reading	520–670
Range SAT Math	540–670
Range ACT Composite	24–29
Minimum paper TOEFL	550
Minimum internet-based TOEFL	79
Average HS GPA	3.6
% graduated top 10% of class	37
% graduated top 25% of class	68
% graduated top 50% of class	93

DEADLINES

Regular	
Deadline	2/1
Nonfall registration?	Yes

FINANCIAL FACTS

Financial Aid Rating	90
Annual in-state tuition	$4,575
Annual out-of-state tuition	$18,897
Room and board	$10,280
Required fees	$6,306
Average need-based scholarship	$5,713
% needy frosh rec. need-based scholarship or grant aid	48
% needy UG rec. need-based scholarship or grant aid	58
% needy frosh rec. non-need-based scholarship or grant aid	65
% needy UG rec. non-need-based scholarship or grant aid	52
% needy frosh rec. need-based self-help aid	61
% needy UG rec. need-based self-help aid	69
% frosh rec. any financial aid	88
% UG rec. any financial aid	86
% UG borrow to pay for school	44
Average cumulative indebtedness	$27,255
% frosh need fully met	74
% ugrads need fully met	76
Average % of frosh need met	76
Average % of ugrad need met	79

University of Pennsylvania

1 COLLEGE HALL, PHILADELPHIA, PA 19104 • ADMISSIONS: 215-898-7507 • FAX: 215-898-9670

#30 COLLEGE THAT PAYS YOU BACK

ABOUT THE SCHOOL

The University of Pennsylvania (commonly referred to as Penn), as one of the eight members of the Ivy League, gives you all of the advantages of an internationally recognized degree with none of the attitude. Founded by Benjamin Franklin, Penn is the fourth-oldest institution of higher learning in the United States. The university is composed of four undergraduate schools, including The Wharton School, home to Penn's well-known and intense undergraduate business program. This, along with other career-focused offerings, contributes to a preprofessional atmosphere on campus. That comes with an element of competition, especially when grades are on the line. Penn students love the opportunity to take classes with professors who are setting the bar for research in his or her field. Professors are praised for being "enthusiastic and incredibly well-versed in their subject," a group who is "passionate about teaching" and who will "go out of their way to help you understand the material." Penn students don't mind getting into intellectual conversations during dinner, but "partying is a much higher priority here than it is at other Ivy League schools." Students here can have intellectual conversations during dinner, and hit the frat houses later that night. Trips to New York City and Center City Philadelphia are common, and students have plenty of access to restaurants, shopping, concerts, and sports games around campus.

BANG FOR YOUR BUCK

Transparency is embedded in Penn's financial aid process. The Student Financial Services website provides a chart of the percent of applicants offered aid and median award amounts for family income levels ranging from $0–$220,000 and higher. For 2015–2016, Penn committed more than $206 million of its resources for grant aid to undergraduate students. Over 78 percent of freshman who applied for aid received an award, and Penn's financial aid packages meet 100 percent of students' demonstrated need through an all grant, all grant aid program. According to the school, the average financial aid package for incoming awarded furst years in 2015 was $48,605. University Named Scholarships are provided through direct gifts to the university and privately endowed funds and enable Penn to continue to admit students solely on the basis of academic merit. The scholarship amount varies according to determined financial need. Staff at Penn provide strong support for applicants, with one student noting, "It was the only school to call me during the admissions process instead of just e-mailing me extra information."

STUDENT LIFE

This "determined" bunch "is either focused on one specific interest, or very well-rounded." Pretty much everyone "was an overachiever ('that kid') in high school," and some students "are off-the-charts brilliant," making everyone here "sort of fascinated by everyone else." Everyone has "a strong sense of personal style and his or her own credo," but no group deviates too far from the more mainstream stereotypes. There's a definite lack of "emos" and hippies. There's "the career-driven Wharton kid who will stab you in the back to get your interview slot" and "the nursing kid who's practically nonexistent," but on the whole, there's tremendous school diversity, with "people from all over the world of all kinds of experiences of all perspectives."

University of Pennsylvania

FINANCIAL AID: 215-898-1988 • E-MAIL: INFO@ADMISSIONS.UPENN.EDU • WEBSITE: WWW.UPENN.EDU

CAREER

Penn's Career Services is an amazing resource for students who wish to discover opportunities on- and off-campus. A bursting job board (with over 13,000 individual position postings), trips to New York City and Washington D.C. to learn about organizations and industries, as well as hundreds of employer information sessions give students tons of chances to network and research fields. One neat perk: along with other offices like Civic House, Kelly Writers House, and Penn Global, Career Services provides funding to finance research and unpaid (or lowly paid) summer internships. Career days a year bring over 600 employers to campus (Amazon, IBM, and Bloomberg, to name a few), and PennApps, a weekend-long "hackathon" for student developers, draws prospective employers like Intel and Microsoft for sponsorship and presentations. Alumni mentoring is also available to help students find their path. Penn grads who visited PayScale.com report median starting salaries of $59,300.

GENERAL INFO

Activities: Choral groups, concert band, dance, drama/theater, jazz band, literary magazine, marching band, music ensembles, student government, student newspaper, symphony orchestra. **Organizations:** 500+ registered organizations, 9 honor societies, 29 religious organizations. 36 fraternities, 13 sororities.

FINANCIAL AID

Students should submit: FAFSA, Institution's own financial aid form, CSS/Financial Aid PROFILE, Noncustodial PROFILE, Business/Farm Supplement. Priority filing deadline is 2/15. The Princeton Review suggests that all financial aid forms be submitted as soon as possible after October 1. *Need-based scholarships/grants offered:* Federal Pell, FSEOG, State scholarships/grants, Private scholarships, College/university scholarship or grant aid from institutional funds. *Loan aid offered:* Direct Subsidized Stafford Loans, Direct Unsubsidized Stafford Loans, Direct PLUS loans, Federal Perkins Loans, Federal Nursing Loans, College/university loans from institutional funds. Applicants will be notified of awards on or about 4/1. Federal Work-Study Program available. Institutional employment available.

BOTTOM LINE

A year's tuition is $45,556. You'll pay another $14,536 in room and board. Don't be alarmed: Penn offers loan-free packages to all dependent students who are eligible for financial aid, regardless of the family's income level. The average student debt, for the students who choose to borrow, is approximately $26,157. Students have noted the school's "generous aid program" as being "phenomenal."

CAREER INFORMATION FROM PAYSCALE.COM

ROI rating	92
Bachelor's and No Higher	
Median starting salary	$60,300
Median mid-career salary	$120,000
At Least Bachelor's	
Median starting salary	$62,000
Median mid-career salary	$124,000
% alumni with high job meaning	55%
% STEM	19%

SELECTIVITY

Admissions Rating	99
# of applicants	35,866
% of applicants accepted	10
% of acceptees attending	65
# offered a place on the wait list	2,651
% accepting a place on wait list	60
% admitted from wait list	9
# of early decision applicants	5,141
% accepted early decision	25

FRESHMAN PROFILE

Range SAT Critical Reading	670–770
Range SAT Math	690–780
Range SAT Writing	690–780
Range ACT Composite	31–34
Average HS GPA	3.9
% graduated top 10% of class	93
% graduated top 25% of class	98
% graduated top 50% of class	100

DEADLINES

Early decision	
Deadline	11/1
Notification	12/15
Regular	
Deadline	1/1
Notification	4/1
Nonfall registration?	No

FINANCIAL FACTS

Financial Aid Rating	94
Annual tuition	$45,556
Room and board	$14,536
Required fees	$5,698
Average need-based scholarship	$40,044
% needy frosh rec. need-based scholarship or grant aid	99
% needy UG rec. need-based scholarship or grant aid	99
% needy frosh rec. non-need-based scholarship or grant aid	0
% needy UG rec. non-need-based scholarship or grant aid	0
% needy frosh rec. need-based self-help aid	100
% needy UG rec. need-based self-help aid	100
% frosh rec. any financial aid	45
% UG rec. any financial aid	47
% frosh need fully met	100
% ugrads need fully met	100
Average % of frosh need met	100
Average % of ugrad need met	100

University of Pittsburgh

4227 Fifth Avenue, First Floor Alumni Hall, Pittsburgh, PA 15260 • Admissions: 412-624-7488 • Fax: 412-648-8815

CAMPUS LIFE

Quality of Life Rating	91
Fire Safety Rating	91
Green Rating	92
Type of school	Public
Affiliation	No Affiliation
Environment	Metropolis

STUDENTS

Total undergrad enrollment	18,908
% male/female	49/51
% from out of state	27
% frosh live on campus	97
% ugrads live on campus	44
# of fraternities (% ugrad men join)	22 (10)
# of sororities (% ugrad women join)	17 (10)
% African American	5
% Asian	9
% Caucasian	74
% Hispanic	3
% Native American	<1
% Pacific Islander	<1
% Two or more races	3
% Race and/or ethnicity unknown	1
% international	4
# of countries represented	48

ACADEMICS

Academic Rating	79
% students returning for sophomore year	92
% students graduating within 4 years	64
% students graduating within 6 years	82
Calendar	Semester
Student/faculty ratio	14:1
Profs interesting rating	70
Profs accessible rating	73

Most classes have 10–19 students.
Most lab/discussion sessions have
20–29 students.

MOST POPULAR MAJORS

Psychology; Biology; Registered Nursing/
Registered Nurse

ABOUT THE SCHOOL

An academic powerhouse, University of Pittsburgh is one of Pennsylvania's premier institutions. With 109 degree programs spread throughout eight undergraduate schools, students can study virtually any topic they desire. Impressively, strong prospective freshmen can be considered for guaranteed admission to fourteen graduate/professional schools, including dentistry, medicine and law. Additionally, Pitt has established a number of fantastic programs that enhance (and encourage) learning beyond the classroom. For example, the Outside the Classroom Curriculum (OCC) assists undergrads in finding internship, research, and volunteer opportunities where students gain practical experience (and a résumé boost). The Engineering Co-Op Program also helps students pair their education with a professional setting. And the stellar Honors College (offering a unique BPhil degree) maintains several prestigious programs, including the Brackenridge Summer Research Fellowships and the Yellowstone Field Program. Finally, hometown Pittsburgh provides students with a number of educational and cultural opportunities. Recently voted one of the most livable cities in the country, students frequently take advantage of the city's myriad bars, restaurants, museums and theaters (even getting a discount through PITTARTS).

BANG FOR YOUR BUCK

Pitt endeavors to help all students with financial need and limited resources. To begin with, all prospective freshmen who present an outstanding academic record (and complete an application by January 15) will automatically be considered for merit scholarships. These awards range from $2,000 to full coverage for tuition and room and board. Importantly, these scholarships are renewable up to three years, provided recipients meet predetermined GPA and progress requirements.

STUDENT LIFE

"The best part about Pitt is that there is no cookie cutter student." Although most do come from the northeast, "there are many atypical students when considering backgrounds, ethnicity, and beliefs." Students are "motivated," "studious," "hard working and friendly," "career minded, but not obsessive." They "balance school work and free time," and there are a "variety of ways to have fun" at Pitt "from museums, concerts, theatre, ballet, lectures, movie theaters, shopping, dining, and of course parties." Pitt is "a big school with all the perks of a small school" and most students "are involved in at least one activity." Students use their "free bus passes" to explore the city, dine at restaurants in Squirrel Hill and Southside, and attend Steelers and Pirates' games.

CAREER

"Pitt is excellent at helping students find jobs, internships, job shadowing opportunities, and other activities to help solidify a career path." There is an internship "guarantee" for all students after their first semester and "an entire department devoted to internships and job placement." "Pitt is one of the best schools to help students with experiential learning, whether it be through an internship, research experience, or even service learning experience." Students describe the career office as "very helpful and . . . always willing to point you in the right direction." There are career consultants available to help students along the way as well. Many also extol Pittsburgh itself as a hotbed of "career opportunities." According to alumni who've visited the website PayScale.com, the average starting salary for recent graduates is $50,300.

University of Pittsburgh

FINANCIAL AID: 412-624-7488 • E-MAIL: OAFA@PITT.EDU • WEBSITE: WWW.PITT.EDU

GENERAL INFO

Activities: Choral groups, concert band, dance, drama/theater, jazz band, literary magazine, marching band, music ensembles, pep band, radio station, student government, student newspaper, student-run film society, television station, campus ministries, international student organization. **Organizations:** 490 registered organizations, 20 honor societies, 24 fraternities, 18 sororities. **Athletics (Intercollegiate):** *Men:* Baseball, basketball, cross-country, diving, football, soccer, swimming, track/field (outdoor), wrestling. *Women:* Basketball, cross-country, diving, gymnastics, soccer, softball, swimming, tennis, track/field (outdoor), volleyball. **On-Campus Highlights:** Cathedral of Learning, William Pitt Union, Heinz Chapel, Petersen Event Center, Sennott Square. **Environmental Initiatives:** Steam plant which houses six 100,000 pound per hour national gas fired boilers; the Carillo Street Steam Plant provides partial steam service for both the University and the University of Pittsburgh Medical Center. Comprehensive building automation/energy management system that provides automatic control of building temperatures, lighting upgrades, occupancy sensors, and the expansion of the university's central steam and chilled water infrastructure to eliminate stand-alone chillers and boilers. The University pursues LEED certification for many large projects.

FINANCIAL AID

Students should submit: FAFSA. Priority filing deadline is 3/1. The Princeton Review suggests that all financial aid forms be submitted as soon as possible after October 1. *Need-based scholarships/grants offered:* Federal Pell, FSEOG, State scholarships/grants, Private scholarships, College/university scholarship or grant aid from institutional funds, Federal Nursing Scholarships. *Loan aid offered:* Direct Subsidized Stafford Loans, Direct Unsubsidized Stafford Loans, Direct PLUS loans, Federal Perkins Loans, Federal Nursing Loans, State Loans, College/university loans from institutional funds. Applicants will be notified of awards on a rolling basis beginning 3/1. Federal Work-Study Program available. Institutional employment available.

BOTTOM LINE

Pennsylvania residents should expect to pay $17,688 per academic year. Out-of-state undergraduates will need to shell out $28,828 annually. There are also additional, required fees totaling $930. Of course, the university offers a variety of grants, loans, and work-study opportunities.

CAREER INFORMATION FROM PAYSCALE.COM

ROI rating	87
Bachelor's and No Higher	
Median starting salary	$50,300
Median mid-career salary	$85,900
At Least Bachelor's	
Median starting salary	$51,400
Median mid-career salary	$87,100
% alumni with high job meaning	58%
% STEM	21%

SELECTIVITY

Admissions Rating	**90**
# of applicants	30,626
% of applicants accepted	54
% of acceptees attending	24
# offered a place on the wait list	2,382
% accepting a place on wait list	23
% admitted from wait list	30

FRESHMAN PROFILE

Range SAT Critical Reading	580–660
Range SAT Math	600–690
Range SAT Writing	570–670
Range ACT Composite	26–31
Minimum paper TOEFL	600
Minimum internet-based TOEFL	100
Average HS GPA	4.0
% graduated top 10% of class	50
% graduated top 25% of class	83
% graduated top 50% of class	99

DEADLINES

Nonfall registration?	Yes

FINANCIAL FACTS

Financial Aid Rating	**79**
Annual in-state tuition	$17,688
Annual out-of-state tuition	$28,828
Room and board	$10,950
Required fees	$930
Average need-based scholarship	$8,334
% needy frosh rec. need-based scholarship or grant aid	80
% needy UG rec. need-based scholarship or grant aid	70
% needy frosh rec. non-need-based scholarship or grant aid	8
% needy UG rec. non-need-based scholarship or grant aid	5
% needy frosh rec. need-based self-help aid	81
% needy UG rec. need-based self-help aid	86
% frosh rec. any financial aid	63
% UG rec. any financial aid	58
% UG borrow to pay for school	63
Average cumulative indebtedness	$38,045
% frosh need fully met	15
% ugrads need fully met	12
Average % of frosh need met	61
Average % of ugrad need met	55

University of Portland

5000 North Willamette Blvd., Portland, OR 97203-7147 • Admissions: 503-943-7147 • Fax: 503-943-7315

CAMPUS LIFE

Quality of Life Rating	**92**
Fire Safety Rating	**92**
Green Rating	**60***
Type of school	Private
Affiliation	Roman Catholic
Environment	Metropolis

STUDENTS

Total undergrad enrollment	3,770
% male/female	41/59
% from out of state	60
% frosh from public high school	60
% frosh live on campus	94
% ugrads live on campus	57
% African American	1
% Asian	12
% Caucasian	61
% Hispanic	11
% Native American	0
% Pacific Islander	2
% Two or more races	8
% Race and/or ethnicity unknown	2
% international	3
# of countries represented	38

ACADEMICS

Academic Rating	**86**
% students graduating within 4 years	71
% students graduating within 6 years	78
Student/faculty ratio	14:1
Profs interesting rating	88
Profs accessible rating	92

Most classes have 20–29 students.
Most lab/discussion sessions have 10–19 students.

MOST POPULAR MAJORS

Registered Nursing, Nursing Administration, Nursing Research and Clinical Nursing; Biology/Biological Sciences; Mechanical Engineering

ABOUT THE SCHOOL

The University of Portland is a Roman Catholic liberal arts school that offers "small classes" and a "tight-knit community" which emphasizes the importance of a "holistic education" that charges students "to constantly seek new and challenging ways to better the world and themselves." The university offers forty majors and thirty-three minors, as well as several academic research centers of interest, like the Dundon-Berchtold Institute, which sponsors student-faculty research in the area of applied ethics through fellowships and scholarships. The institute is open to students in any discipline and recent research topics range from political science to accountancy and mathematics education. Students say they have "great, hands-on professors" who are "highly knowledgeable, friendly, accommodating, and easily accessible." Students are just as impressed by the faculty's professional accomplishments; they say their professors "are amazing people who frequently go beyond the call of duty to ensure students are successful."

BANG FOR YOUR BUCK

In addition to federal and state grants, UP offers many institutional grants in scholarships for incoming students including academic merit-based scholarships, departmental scholarships, and over 400 endowed scholarships for students who meet various criteria. The school has a number of other fellowships and scholarships that are designed to encourage student research or activity. One unique example, Brian Doyle Scholarships in Gentle and Sidelong Humor, sponsors a creative, humorous project that students produce for the public. Students are automatically considered for institutional grants when they file the FAFSA, as part of the university's effort to meet demonstrated financial need. Many students count "a great scholarship" among the top reasons for choosing the University of Portland.

STUDENT LIFE

Students at UP are " dedicated to their studies, but still love to have fun." Many students come from Catholic high schools in the region and share a concern for environmental issues and global welfare. Students find pleasure in "on-campus activities like the coffee house they hold every week, the luau that occurs once a year, [and] the plays held throughout the year." There are over eighty-five groups and clubs for students to get involved with, many of which "are looking to address environmental concerns especially through upcoming events like Focus the Nation." The university also hosts "great ways for students to have fun on campus with improv shows, karaoke nights, and movies on the weekends."

CAREER

The University of Portland Career Center gives students a number of different resources to help them cut a career path. The center's Pilot MAP: 4 Year Career Plan provides students with a customizable timeline with themes for each year of their education. The program helps students explore how their interests may intersect with different majors and career paths, puts them in touch with campus resources

University of Portland

FINANCIAL AID: 503-943-7311 • E-MAIL: ADMISSIONS@UP.EDU • WEBSITE: WWW.UP.EDU

and experiential learning opportunities, and helps them enhance their interviewing and networking skills. Students are impressed by the wide selection of "academic internships and jobs available to students," and they say that professors are supportive of students "in activities outside of the classroom—such as volunteering, field experience, internships, clubs, etc." Graduates report an average early career salary of $52,500 and a mid-career average of $92,700. Forty percent of graduates say that their job makes the world a better place.

GENERAL INFO

Activities: Choral groups, concert band, dance, drama/theater, jazz band, literary magazine, music ensembles, musical theater, pep band, radio station, student government, student newspaper, student-run film society, symphony orchestra, yearbook, Campus Ministries, International Student Organization 40 registered organizations, 15 honor societies, 9 religious organizations. **Athletics (Intercollegiate):** *Men:* baseball, basketball, cross-country, golf, soccer, tennis, track/field (outdoor). *Women:* basketball, cross-country, golf, soccer, tennis, track/field (outdoor), volleyball. **On-Campus Highlights:** The Cove, St. Mary's Lounge, Howard Recreation Hall.

FINANCIAL AID

Students should submit: FAFSA. Applicants will be notified of awards on a rolling basis beginning 3/1. The Princeton Review suggests that all financial aid forms be submitted as soon as possible after October 1. *Need-based scholarships/grants offered:* Federal Pell, SEOG, State scholarships/grants, Private scholarships, College/university scholarship or grant aid from institutional funds, United Negro College Fund, Federal Nursing Scholarships. *Loan aid offered:* Direct Subsidized Stafford Loans, Direct Unsubsidized Stafford Loans, Direct PLUS loans, Federal Perkins Loans, Federal Nursing Loans, College/university loans from institutional funds. Applicants will be notified of awards on a rolling basis beginning 3/1. Federal Work-Study Program available.

BOTTOM LINE

Tuition at the University of Portland is $40,080, room and board is $11,902, and students pay $170 in fees—making the annual price tag $52,152 The average first-year student receives $23,025 in need-based gift aid and $5,198 in need based loans. On average graduates leave with $28,953 in student loan debt, and 61 percent of students take out college loans.

CAREER INFORMATION FROM PAYSCALE.COM

ROI rating	88
Bachelor's and No Higher	
Median starting salary	$50,200
Median mid-career salary	$90,500
At Least Bachelor's	
Median starting salary	$50,500
Median mid-career salary	$92,000
% alumni with high job meaning	52%
% STEM	18%

SELECTIVITY

Admissions Rating	89
# of applicants	11,202
% of applicants accepted	62
% of acceptees attending	14
# offered a place on the wait list	2,862
% accepting a place on wait list	25
% admitted from wait list	5

FRESHMAN PROFILE

@stats:Range SAT Critical Reading	540–660
Range SAT Math	550–640
Minimum paper TOEFL	525
Minimum internet-based TOEFL	71
Average HS GPA	3.65
% graduated top 10% of class	45
% graduated top 25% of class	77
% graduated top 50% of class	96

DEADLINES

Regular	
Deadline	2/1
Notification	10/1
Nonfall registration?	Yes

FINANCIAL FACTS

Financial Aid Rating	75
AAnnual tuition	$40,080
Room and board	$11,902
Required fees	$170
Average need-based scholarship	$22,689
% needy frosh rec. need-based scholarship or grant aid	76
% needy UG rec. need-based scholarship or grant aid	79
% needy frosh rec. non-need-based scholarship or grant aid	96
% needy UG rec. non-need-based scholarship or grant aid	92
% needy frosh rec. need-based self-help aid	68
% needy UG rec. need-based self-help aid	74
% frosh rec. any financial aid	98
% UG rec. any financial aid	95
% UG borrow to pay for school	61
Average cumulative indebtedness	$28,953
% frosh need fully met	10
% ugrads need fully met	6
Average % of frosh need met	69
Average % of ugrad need met	72

University of Richmond

28 WESTHAMPTON WAY, UNIVERSITY OF RICHMOND, VA 23173 • ADMISSIONS: 804-289-8640

CAMPUS LIFE

Quality of Life Rating	96
Fire Safety Rating	93
Green Rating	93
Type of school	Private
Affiliation	No Affiliation
Environment	City

STUDENTS

Total undergrad enrollment	2,889
% male/female	48/52
% from out of state	81
% frosh from public high school	56
% frosh live on campus	99
% ugrads live on campus	90
# of fraternities (% ugrad men join)	6 (17)
# of sororities (% ugrad women join)	8 (29)
% African American	6
% Asian	7
% Caucasian	59
% Hispanic	8
% Native American	<1
% Pacific Islander	<1
% Two or more races	4
% Race and/or ethnicity unknown	6
% international	9
# of countries represented	61

ACADEMICS

Academic Rating	97
% students returning for sophomore year	93
% students graduating within 4 years	83
% students graduating within 6 years	88
Calendar	Semester
Student/faculty ratio	8:1
Profs interesting rating	96
Profs accessible rating	96

Most classes have 10–19 students.
Most lab/discussion sessions have 10–19 students.

MOST POPULAR MAJORS
Business Administration; Leadership Studies; Biology

#48 COLLEGE THAT PAYS YOU BACK

ABOUT THE SCHOOL

While the University of Richmond offers the academic opportunities of a larger research university, it maintains the advantages of a small liberal arts college. The average class size is sixteen; 98 percent of classes have fewer than thirty students. No classes are taught by teaching assistants. A top-ranked undergraduate business program and the nation's first school of leadership studies are among the highlights here. Richmond's first-year seminar program includes courses taught by professors from all five of its schools. Every traditional undergraduate student is eligible to receive up to $4,000 for one summer research or internship experience before graduation. Some 600 undergraduates received $2 million in grants in 2016.

BANG FOR YOUR BUCK

The University of Richmond prides itself on its practice of need-blind admission, and this school invests a tremendous amount of time and money in making it possible for lower- and middle-income students to come here. Nearly half of students receive need-based financial aid, with an average award of more than $44,000. Virginians who qualify for financial aid and have a parental income of $60,000 or less receive an aid package equal to full tuition and room and board (without loans). The university also offers generous merit-based scholarships. Full-tuition scholarships are awarded to Richmond Scholars. Presidential scholarships are available for one-third tuition, and National Merit Scholarships, and National Hispanic Scholarships are awarded. Qualified students may be eligible for full-tuition Army ROTC scholarships and scholarships through the Yellow Ribbon Program. Through the Bonner Scholars Program, students make a four-year commitment to sustained community engagement and social justice education and receive a scholarship and funding for summer internships.

STUDENT LIFE

This mid-size private university in Richmond, Virginia, is "a place where you can truly make your education what you want it to be." One Global Health major says "I can't begin to fathom how differently not just my career but my entire life would be without the University of Richmond." There are 190 registered student organizations on campus, where 90 percent of undergraduates live (the university does provide help looking for non-dorm housing) and a Division I athletics program. "If partying isn't your scene," says one student, "there are plenty of other things to do, like watch movie[s] . . . or go into the city." Greek life does play a role on campus, where there are eight sororities and six fraternities. "Richmond is a small school with a [close-knit] community of students who know how to work hard academically but have fun at the same time," even if Greek life isn't for you.

CAREER

The average starting salary for a University of Richmond graduate is roughly $49,400, according to PayScale.com, and 48 percent of Richmond graduates say that their careers are helping to make the world a better place. Popular jobs after graduation include executive director, attorney, and senior financial analyst and the most popular Richmond majors are business administration, leadership studies, and biology. "The Office of Alumni and Career Services provides invaluable

University of Richmond

E-MAIL: ADMISSION@RICHMOND.EDU • FAX: 804-287-6003 • WEBSITE: WWW.RICHMOND.EDU

connections for arranging internship and employment opportunities for all students [year round]," says one student. The UR Summer Fellowships Program funds students' unpaid internships or their research projects alongside a faculty member. In addition to putting on a Fall Career Expo, Richmond's Career Services website offers students the chance to take advantage of SpiderConnect, an online database of potential jobs, internships, and networking opportunities with alumni. Despite its "small student body," one Political Science major praises Richmond's "large and active alumni network." Students can also take advantage of Richmond's Center for Civic Engagement, "an office solely dedicated to connecting students with volunteer opportunities."

GENERAL INFO

Activities: Choral groups, concert band, dance, drama/theater, jazz band, literary magazine, music ensembles, musical theater, pep band, radio station, student government, student newspaper, student-run film society, symphony orchestra, campus ministries, international student organization, Model UN. **Organizations:** 190 registered organizations, 6 honor societies, 14 religious organizations. 6 fraternities, 8 sororities. **Athletics (Intercollegiate):** *Men:* Baseball, basketball, cross-country, football, golf, lacrosse, tennis. *Women:* Basketball, cross country, diving, field hockey, golf, lacrosse, soccer, swimming, tennis, track/field (outdoor), track/field (indoor). **On-Campus Highlights:** Tyler Haynes Commons, Weinstein Center for Recreation and Wellness (Fitness Center), Robins Center (Athletic Center), Boatwright Memorial Library and Coffee Shop, Carole Weinstein International Center, Westhampton Green (Modlin Center for the Arts). **Environmental Initiatives:** Signing the ACUPCC and subsequent creation of the Climate Action Plan; waste diversion initiatives; energy conservation and efficiency projects.

FINANCIAL AID

Students should submit: FAFSA, CSS/Financial Aid PROFILE, Noncustodial PROFILE, copies of federal tax returns. Regular filing deadline is 2/1. The Princeton Review suggests that all financial aid forms be submitted as soon as possible after October 1. *Need-based scholarships/grants offered:* Federal Pell, FSEOG, State scholarships/grants, Private scholarships, College/university scholarship or grant aid from institutional funds. *Loan aid offered:* Direct Subsidized Stafford Loans, Direct Unsubsidized Stafford Loans, Direct PLUS loans, Federal Perkins Loans. Applicants will be notified of awards on or about 4/1. Federal Work-Study Program available. Institutional employment available.

BOTTOM LINE

The total cost for tuition, room and board, and everything else exceeds $63,000 per year at the University of Richmond. You'll get help though: A family's finances are never considered in the admission decision, and 100 percent of demonstrated financial need is met for U.S. students. Need-based financial aid and large scholarships are substantial.

CAREER INFORMATION FROM PAYSCALE.COM

ROI rating	**90**
Bachelor's and No Higher	
Median starting salary	$48,200
Median mid-career salary	$86,400
At Least Bachelor's	
Median starting salary	$48,600
Median mid-career salary	$93,200
% alumni with high job meaning	54%
% STEM	12%

SELECTIVITY

Admissions Rating	**94**
# of applicants	9,977
% of applicants accepted	31
% of acceptees attending	26
# offered a place on the wait list	4,070
% accepting a place on wait list	38
% admitted from wait list	10
# of early decision applicants	791
% accepted early decision	42

FRESHMAN PROFILE

Range SAT Critical Reading	600–700
Range SAT Math	620–720
Range SAT Writing	610–700
Range ACT Composite	29–32
Minimum paper TOEFL	550
Minimum internet-based TOEFL	80
% graduated top 10% of class	61
% graduated top 25% of class	89
% graduated top 50% of class	97

DEADLINES

Early decision	
Deadline	11/15
Notification	12/15
Regular	
Deadline	1/15
Notification	4/1
Nonfall registration?	No

FINANCIAL FACTS

Financial Aid Rating	**96**
Annual tuition	$49,420
Room and board	$11,460
Average need-based scholarship	$38,985
% needy frosh rec. need-based scholarship or grant aid	99
% needy UG rec. need-based scholarship or grant aid	98
% needy frosh rec. non-need-based scholarship or grant aid	23
% needy UG rec. non-need-based scholarship or grant aid	18
% needy frosh rec. need-based self-help aid	75
% needy UG rec. need-based self-help aid	80
% frosh rec. any financial aid	59
% UG rec. any financial aid	67
% UG borrow to pay for school	43
Average cumulative indebtedness	$26,250
% frosh need fully met	86
% ugrads need fully met	83
Average % of frosh need met	100
Average % of ugrad need met	100

University of Rochester

300 Wilson Boulevard, Rochester, NY 14627 • Admissions: 585-275-3221 • Fax: 585-461-4595

CAMPUS LIFE

Quality of Life Rating	**89**
Fire Safety Rating	**93**
Green Rating	**78**
Type of school	Private
Affiliation	No Affiliation
Environment	Metropolis

STUDENTS

Total undergrad enrollment	6,304
% male/female	50/50
% from out of state	59
% frosh from public high school	74
% frosh live on campus	100
% ugrads live on campus	90
# of fraternities (% ugrad men join)	18 (20)
# of sororities (% ugrad women join)	15 (26)
% African American	5
% Asian	11
% Caucasian	48
% Hispanic	7
% Native American	<1
% Pacific Islander	<1
% Two or more races	3
% Race and/or ethnicity unknown	7
% international	18
# of countries represented	114

ACADEMICS

Academic Rating	**86**
% students returning for sophomore year	96
% students graduating within 4 years	74
% students graduating within 6 years	88
Calendar	Semester
Student/faculty ratio	10:1
Profs interesting rating	75
Profs accessible rating	72
Most classes have 10–19 students.	

MOST POPULAR MAJORS
Economics; Biology; Psychology

ABOUT THE SCHOOL

Tucked away in lovely upstate New York, the University of Rochester offers students a "unique" collegiate experience. Undergrads rave about UR's "innovative curriculum," which "essentially [dictates that there are] no required classes." Alternatively, "students . . . chart out their own academic paths." In turn, this "encourages personal exploration rather than conventional general education." And with so many renowned disciplines, from its outstanding music conservatory to phenomenal programs in the applied sciences, it's understandable why students relish the opportunity to explore. Inside the classroom, undergrads delight in their "amazing" professors who "are at the top of their [respective] fields." Just as essential, they are "very approachable [in] a one-on-one situation." Finally, Rochester students cheerfully report that their peers "seem genuinely engaged and happy, and possess a quirky sense of humor." And they greatly appreciate that "while everyone here strives to do better it is in no way a cut-throat environment."

BANG FOR YOUR BUCK

Though a private university, Rochester strives to ensure that it's still affordable for qualified and capable students. These efforts are definitely appreciated and many an undergrad remarked that they chose UR because they received a "great financial aid [package]." In fact, 82 percent of the students here are receiving some form of need-based aid. And the average package is roughly $38,021. That includes a combination of loans, grants, scholarships and work-study. For undergrads wary about going into debt, be assured that Rochester does provide a variety of merit-based scholarships ranging anywhere from $2,000 per year to covering the full cost of tuition.

STUDENT LIFE

If you attend Rochester, you can virtually guarantee that you'll never be at a loss for something to do. As one senior explains, "Almost every weekend there are movies shown, dance performances, athletic events and other special programs held by one of our 250+ students organizations." A fellow senior rushes to add, "The a cappella shows here are immensely popular and easily sell out our biggest auditorium (we have four different a cappella groups)." Certainly, numerous undergrads can also be found at one of the many "parties hosted by the various frats." Fortunately, students assure us that everyone is welcome and no one is pressured to drink. Further, the "school has its own bus lines" which makes venturing into Rochester pretty easy. And we're told these undergrads love to head "off campus to bowl, ice skate, or go to the mall."

CAREER

University of Rochester students do pretty well for themselves. Indeed, according to PayScale.com, the average starting salary for these grads is $49,400. And how do these undergrads land such lucrative jobs? Why, through an excellent career services office! Rochester's Career & Internship Center sponsors weekly seminars that cover everything from finding internships to discussions of networking techniques and tips. The office also offers specialized boot camps for targeted career areas. For example, students may attend boot camps based around non-profit jobs or ones centered upon engineering and applied sciences. And, of course, we'd be remiss if we neglected to mention that the center also hosts several career fairs throughout the year. Students can connect with companies such as Apple, the Rochester Museum and Science Center, the Federal Bureau of Investigations (FBI), Wegmans Food Markets and Teach for America.

University of Rochester

FINANCIAL AID: 585-275-3226 • E-MAIL: ADMIT@ADMISSIONS.ROCHESTER.EDU • WEBSITE: WWW.ROCHESTER.EDU

GENERAL INFO

Activities: Choral groups, concert band, dance, drama/theater, jazz band, literary magazine, music ensembles, musical theater, opera, pep band, radio station, student government, student newspaper, student-run film society, symphony orchestra, television station, International Student Organization, Model UN. **Organizations:** 224 registered organizations, 6 honor societies, 14 religious organizations. 19 fraternities, 15 sororities. **Athletics (Intercollegiate):** *Men:* baseball, basketball, cross-country, diving, football, golf, soccer, squash, swimming, tennis, track/field (outdoor), track/field (indoor). *Women:* basketball, crew/rowing, cross-country, diving, field hockey, golf, lacrosse, soccer, softball, swimming, tennis, track/field (outdoor), track/field (indoor), volleyball. **On-Campus Highlights:** Eastman Theater, Memorial Art Gallery, Rush Rhees Library, Interfaith Chapel, Robert B. Goergen Athletic Center, Robert B. Goergen Hall for Biomedical Engineering, The Gleason Library.

FINANCIAL AID

Students should submit: FAFSA, CSS/Financial Aid PROFILE, State aid form, Noncustodial PROFILE. Priority filing deadline is 2/15. The Princeton Review suggests that all financial aid forms be submitted as soon as possible after October 1. *Need-based scholarships/ grants offered:* Federal Pell, FSEOG, State scholarships/grants, Private scholarships, College/university scholarship or grant aid from institutional funds. *Loan aid offered:* Direct Subsidized Stafford Loans, Direct Unsubsidized Stafford Loans, Direct PLUS loans, Federal Perkins Loans. Applicants will be notified of awards on or about 4/1. Federal Work-Study Program available. Institutional employment available.

THE BOTTOM LINE

Tuition at this private university will cost undergraduates $49,260. On top of that, on-campus room and board runs approximately $14,890. Students will face an additional $882 in required fees. And the university advises setting aside another $1,310 for books and miscellaneous supplies. Finally, undergrads commuting from off-campus should expect to spend roughly $300 for transportation.

CAREER INFORMATION FROM PAYSCALE.COM

ROI rating	**90**
Bachelor's and No Higher	
Median starting salary	$51,400
Median mid-career salary	$101,000
At Least Bachelor's	
Median starting salary	$55,700
Median mid-career salary	$111,000
% alumni with high job meaning	48%
% STEM	33%

SELECTIVITY

Admissions Rating	94
# of applicants	17,932
% of applicants accepted	34
% of acceptees attending	23
# offered a place on the wait list	2,507
% accepting a place on wait list	48
% admitted from wait list	0
# of early decision applicants	801
% accepted early decision	41

FRESHMAN PROFILE

Range SAT Critical Reading	600–710
Range SAT Math	640–760
Range SAT Writing	610–710
Range ACT Composite	29–33
Minimum paper TOEFL	600
Minimum internet-based TOEFL	100
Average HS GPA	3.8
% graduated top 10% of class	66
% graduated top 25% of class	92
% graduated top 50% of class	100

DEADLINES

Early decision	
Deadline	11/1
Notification	12/15
Regular	
Deadline	1/5
Notification	4/1
Nonfall registration?	Yes

FINANCIAL FACTS

Financial Aid Rating	93
Annual tuition	$49,260
Room and board	$14,890
Required fees	$882
Average need-based scholarship	$37,467
% needy frosh rec. need-based scholarship or grant aid	100
% needy UG rec. need-based scholarship or grant aid	99
% needy frosh rec. non-need-based scholarship or grant aid	15
% needy UG rec. non-need-based scholarship or grant aid	14
% needy frosh rec. need-based self-help aid	81
% needy UG rec. need-based self-help aid	83
% frosh rec. any financial aid	85
% UG borrow to pay for school	58
Average cumulative indebtedness	$30,873
% frosh need fully met	91
% ugrads need fully met	90
Average % of frosh need met	97
Average % of ugrad need met	95

University of Southern California

OFFICE OF ADMISSION/JOHN HUBBARD HALL, LOS ANGELES, CA 90089-0911 • ADMISSIONS: 213-740-1111 • FAX: 213-821-0200

CAMPUS LIFE

Quality of Life Rating	84
Fire Safety Rating	97
Green Rating	83
Type of school	Private
Affiliation	No Affiliation
Environment	Metropolis

STUDENTS

Total undergrad enrollment	18,810
% male/female	49/51
% from out of state	32
% frosh from public high school	54
% frosh live on campus	98
% ugrads live on campus	30
# of fraternities (% ugrad men join)	32 (26)
# of sororities (% ugrad women join)	26 (27)
% African American	4
% Asian	22
% Caucasian	40
% Hispanic	14
% Native American	<1
% Pacific Islander	<1
% Two or more races	5
% Race and/or ethnicity unknown	1
% international	13
# of countries represented	114

ACADEMICS

Academic Rating	81
% students returning for sophomore year	96
% students graduating within 4 years	77
% students graduating within 6 years	92
Calendar	Semester
Student/faculty ratio	9:1
Profs interesting rating	70
Profs accessible rating	67

Most classes have 10–19 students.
Most lab/discussion sessions have 20–29 students.

MOST POPULAR MAJORS

Social Sciences; Visual and Performing Arts; Business Administration and Management

ABOUT THE SCHOOL

Based in Los Angeles and known world round, the University of Southern California is a premier research institution and academic/athletic haven. USC "wants its students to do what they love without any restraint"; the school "is all about tailoring an education to the individual, and not vice-versa." Despite the size of the school, most classes are "very intimate and comfortable in setting" and students say that "even though it's a big school, it definitely has a small school feel." Professors are very passionate about their field of study and "always incorporate their personal experiences," but remain friendly and accessible. "Most of my professors insist that we call them by their first names," says a student. Make no mistake about the breezy SoCal life: the academics at USC are taken very seriously, and happily so. "It's clear that people do actually enjoy their classes," says one student.

BANG FOR YOUR BUCK

Though the sticker price may be high, USC administers one of the largest financial aid programs in the country and the majority of USC students receive financial aid to offset the cost. In addition to need-based aid, USC has more than a dozen robust scholarship programs, including departmental awards. USC Merit Scholarships (ranging in value from a few thousand dollars up to full tuition) include ten Mork Family Scholarships for full tuition plus a stipend; Stamps Leadership Scholarships for exceptional students whose test scores are in the top 1 to 2 percent nationwide; one hundred Trustee Scholarships for full tuition; and two hundred Presidential Scholarships offering half tuition.

STUDENT LIFE

The USC campus is "extremely diverse": the school enrolls more international students than any other U.S. university. The "great weather" of southern California goes without saying (the majority of students here are from in-state), and the sports scene here is huge. USC "is all about school spirit, great academics, Greek life, and football." There is plenty to keep students occupied outside of the classroom, including clubs, organizations, theatre, and music groups, and "the school does a really good job of bringing speakers and other events to campus." "There really is always something to do... Even walking to class everyday is awesome because you can definitely feel the vibe of an active campus." Many academic aspects and social aspects "combine for an ideal college experience" at USC, and "everyone can find their niche."

CAREER

The USC Career Center runs continuous workshops, counseling, information sessions, and events to help students discover and progress on their careers. An Internship Week and CareerFest (including career panels, networking mixers, and Employer Resume Review) are held every fall and spring, as are Explore@4 Career Panels where students can interact with alumni and industry professionals. The school also offers extensive internship and study abroad opportunities. USC graduates who visited PayScale.com reported an average starting salary of $51,700, and 52 percent felt they had a job with a meaningful impact on the world.

University of Southern California

FINANCIAL AID: 213-740-1111 • E-MAIL: ADMITUSC@USC.EDU • WEBSITE: WWW.USC.EDU

GENERAL INFO

Activities: Choral groups, concert band, dance, drama/theater, jazz band, literary magazine, marching band, music ensembles, musical theater, opera, pep band, radio station, student government, student newspaper, student-run film society, symphony orchestra, television station, yearbook, Campus Ministries, International Student Organization, Model UN. **Organizations:** 676 registered organizations, 49 honor societies, 74 religious organizations. 32 fraternities, 26 sororities. **Athletics (Intercollegiate):** *Men:* baseball, basketball, diving, football, golf, swimming, tennis, track/field (outdoor), volleyball, water polo. *Women:* basketball, crew/rowing, cross-country, diving, golf, soccer, swimming, tennis, track/field (outdoor), volleyball, water polo. **On-Campus Highlights:** USC Fisher Museum of Art, Galen Center (event & training pavilion), Leavey Library (open twenty-four hours), Heritage Hall, Tutor Campus Center.

FINANCIAL AID

Students should submit: FAFSA, CSS/Financial Aid PROFILE, Noncustodial PROFILE, Business/Farm Supplement. Priority filing deadline is 2/16. The Princeton Review suggests that all financial aid forms be submitted as soon as possible after October 1. *Need-based scholarships/grants offered:* Federal Pell, FSEOG, State scholarships/grants, Private scholarships, College/university scholarship or grant aid from institutional funds. *Loan aid offered:* Direct Subsidized Stafford Loans, Direct Unsubsidized Stafford Loans, Direct PLUS loans, Federal Perkins Loans, College/university loans from institutional funds. Applicants will be notified of awards on or about 4/1. Federal Work-Study Program available. Institutional employment available.

BOTTOM LINE

Though tuition runs around $49,464, 65 percent of USC undergrads (including international students) receive financial aid, with an average need-based package of $32,291. A whopping one hundred percent of average need was met. Of the 44 percent of students who took out a loan of some kind, the average debt upon graduation was $27,925.

CAREER INFORMATION FROM PAYSCALE.COM

ROI rating	88
Bachelor's and No Higher	
Median starting salary	$53,000
Median mid-career salary	$99,500
At Least Bachelor's	
Median starting salary	$54,300
Median mid-career salary	$102,000
% alumni with high job meaning	52%
% STEM	13%

SELECTIVITY

Admissions Rating	98
# of applicants	51,924
% of applicants accepted	18
% of acceptees attending	32

FRESHMAN PROFILE

Range SAT Critical Reading	620–730
Range SAT Math	650–770
Range SAT Writing	650–750
Range ACT Composite	30–33
Average HS GPA	3.7
% graduated top 10% of class	88
% graduated top 25% of class	97
% graduated top 50% of class	100

DEADLINES

Regular	
Priority	12/1
Deadline	1/15
Notification	4/1
Nonfall registration?	Yes

FINANCIAL FACTS

Financial Aid Rating	93
Annual tuition	$49,464
Room and board	$13,855
Required fees	$746
Average need-based scholarship	$32,291
% needy frosh rec. need-based scholarship or grant aid	86
% needy UG rec. need-based scholarship or grant aid	91
% needy frosh rec. non-need-based scholarship or grant aid	62
% needy UG rec. non-need-based scholarship or grant aid	46
% needy frosh rec. need-based self-help aid	89
% needy UG rec. need-based self-help aid	94
% frosh rec. any financial aid	68
% UG rec. any financial aid	65
% UG borrow to pay for school	44
Average cumulative indebtedness	$27,925
% frosh need fully met	98
% ugrads need fully met	93
Average % of frosh need met	100
Average % of ugrad need met	100

The University of Tennessee at Knoxville

320 Student Service Building, Circle Park Drive, Knoxville, TN 37996-0230 • Admissions: 865-974-2184

CAMPUS LIFE

Quality of Life Rating	88
Fire Safety Rating	95
Green Rating	92
Type of school	Public
Affiliation	No Affiliation
Environment	City

STUDENTS

Total undergrad enrollment	21,863
% male/female	51/49
% from out of state	11
% frosh live on campus	90
% ugrads live on campus	33
# of fraternities (% ugrad men join)	23 (16)
# of sororities (% ugrad women join)	18 (24)
% African American	7
% Asian	3
% Caucasian	79
% Hispanic	3
% Native American	<1
% Pacific Islander	0
% Two or more races	3
% Race and/or ethnicity unknown	3
% international	2
# of countries represented	63

ACADEMICS

Academic Rating	74
% students returning for sophomore year	85
% students graduating within 4 years	43
% students graduating within 6 years	70
Calendar	Semester
Student/faculty ratio	17:1
Profs interesting rating	69
Profs accessible rating	71
Most classes have 20–29 students.	

MOST POPULAR MAJORS

Biology; Psychology; Kinesiology and Exercise Science

ABOUT THE SCHOOL

The University of Tennessee at Knoxville offers students the great program diversity of a major university, opportunities for research or original creative work in every degree program, and a welcoming campus environment. UT blends more than 200 years of history, tradition, and 'Volunteer Spirit' with the latest technology and innovation. Life at UT is all "about education, community, and becoming a true Tennessee volunteer." "There's a great sense of unity." The faculty "tries extremely hard to encourage acceptance of several kinds of diversity." An "LGBTQ Resource Center" is available to students on campus. There is also a large 'Stop Bias' program that is promoted." In general, there are "tons of clubs and organizations to get involved with if you are passionate about something." Nine colleges offer more than 170 undergraduate majors and concentrations to students from all fifty states and 100 foreign countries, and UT students can make the world their campus through study abroad programs. More than 400 clubs and organizations on campus allow students to further individualize their college experience in service, recreation, academics, and professional development. The typical UT student "loves all aspects of the university's life, from its sports to its long-standing traditions." Students flock here for "family history, athletics, and to sing 'Rocky Top.'" "We love football just about as much as academics." However, academics here are just as intense as athletics. "Being a larger university, I have had many more opportunities than people I know at smaller schools in education as well as extracurriculars." "The University of Tennessee combines the best of all worlds: great education for a great price, sports, social life, and a ton of extracurriculars to choose from."

BANG FOR YOUR BUCK

UTK offers students the standard docket of work-study and state and federal grants and loans. Scholarships are plentiful. More than $46 million in scholarship funds are awarded annually, with four-year, one-year, and renewable scholarships available. A few highlights include: Bonham Scholarships, which are four-year awards based on academic merit. They provide six new recipients with $5,000 per year for four years. The Manning Scholarship honors Peyton Manning, a 1998 alumnus, who was the protoypical scholar-athlete. The scholarship awards recipients $6,000 per year for four years.

STUDENT LIFE

Students seem to relish life at Tennessee. A fairly sporty crowd, lots of undergrads flock to "the recreational facility called the T-RECS where you can work out, play basketball, swim, or play [just about] any other sport." And, of course, "[come] the fall, football dominates the social schedule of 90 percent of the students." Outside of athletics, "most dorms host socials at some point during the month with food included." Additionally, "Greek life is…huge…at UT." In fact, we're told that "fraternity row is the place to be on the weekends." Hometown Knoxville also provides plenty of fun. "The Smokey Mountains and outdoor activities are fewer than thirty minutes away, there are always concerts or events downtown on Market Square or in Old City, and there's always time to lounge in Worlds Fair Park or trek out on the wonderful Greenway system."

CAREER

Tennessee's Career Services does an amazing job helping these undergraduates kick-start their professional lives. No matter where they are in their education or their search, students can turn to this office for guidance and support. Indeed, many undergrads flock to receive help in perfecting their resumes and cover letters. They also learn how to research prospective employers and review

The University of Tennessee at Knoxville

FINANCIAL AID: 865-974-3131 • E-MAIL: ADMISSIONS@UTK.EDU • WEBSITE: WWW.UTK.EDU

proper interview etiquette. Impressively, the office offers classes like "Engineering Career Planning and Placement" to help students understand how to navigate certain industries. In addition, Career Services also hosts numerous job fairs throughout the academic year. Similar to their classes, many of the job fairs are centered around specific disciplines and professions. Undergrads can education fairs, social impact fairs, agricultural fairs and communications fairs (among others).

GENERAL INFO

Environment. City. **Activities:** Choral groups, concert band, dance, drama/theater, jazz band, literary magazine, marching band, music ensembles, musical theater, opera, pep band, radio station, student government, student newspaper, student-run film society, symphony orchestra, television station, yearbook, campus ministries, international student organization, Model UN. **Organizations:** 412 registered organizations, 27 honor societies, 39 religious organizations. 23 fraternities, 17 sororities. **Athletics (Intercollegiate):** *Men:* Baseball, basketball, cheerleading, cross-country, diving, football, golf, swimming, tennis, track/field (outdoor), track/field (indoor). *Women:* Basketball, cheerleading, crew/rowing, cross-country, diving, golf, soccer, softball, swimming, tennis, track/field (outdoor), track/field (indoor), volleyball.

FINANCIAL AID

Students should submit: FAFSA. Priority filing deadline is 2/15. The Princeton Review suggests that all financial aid forms be submitted as soon as possible after October 1. *Need-based scholarships/grants offered:* Federal Pell, FSEOG, State scholarships/grants, Private scholarships, College/university scholarship or grant aid from institutional funds. *Loan aid offered:* Direct Subsidized Stafford Loans, Direct Unsubsidized Stafford Loans, Direct PLUS loans, Federal Perkins Loans, State Loans, College/university loans from institutional funds. Applicants will be notified of awards on a rolling basis beginning 3/15. Federal Work-Study Program available.

BOTTOM LINE

Total cost of attendance for state residents at The University of Tennessee at Knoxville runs about $24,504 (including tuition, room and board, fees, and books). If you are from another state, you'll pay about $42,694.

CAREER INFORMATION FROM PAYSCALE.COM

ROI rating	**86**
Bachelor's and No Higher	
Median starting salary	$45,300
Median mid-career salary	$79,600
At Least Bachelor's	
Median starting salary	$45,900
Median mid-career salary	$81,500
% alumni with high job meaning	58%
% STEM	15%

SELECTIVITY

Admissions Rating	**88**
# of applicants	17,081
% of applicants accepted	76
% of acceptees attending	36

FRESHMAN PROFILE

Range SAT Critical Reading	520–630
Range SAT Math	530–630
Range ACT Composite	24–30
Minimum paper TOEFL	523
Minimum internet-based TOEFL	70
Average HS GPA	3.9
% graduated top 10% of class	54
% graduated top 25% of class	90
% graduated top 50% of class	100

DEADLINES

Regular	
Priority	11/1
Deadline	12/1
Nonfall registration?	Yes

FINANCIAL FACTS

Financial Aid Rating	**81**
Annual in-state tuition	$10,858
Annual out-of-state tuition	$29,048
Room and board	$10,238
Required fees	$1,810
Average need-based scholarship	$9,318
% needy frosh rec. need-based scholarship or grant aid	95
% needy UG rec. need-based scholarship or grant aid	89
% needy frosh rec. non-need-based scholarship or grant aid	0
% needy UG rec. non-need-based scholarship or grant aid	0
% needy frosh rec. need-based self-help aid	99
% needy UG rec. need-based self-help aid	99
% frosh rec. any financial aid	89
% UG rec. any financial aid	93
% UG borrow to pay for school	52
Average cumulative indebtedness	$24,272
% frosh need fully met	25
% ugrads need fully met	22
Average % of frosh need met	62
Average % of ugrad need met	57

The University of Texas at Austin

PO Box 8058, Austin, TX 78713-8058 • Admissions: 512-475-7339 • Fax: 512-475-7478

CAMPUS LIFE

Quality of Life Rating	**91**
Fire Safety Rating	**84**
Green Rating	**86**
Type of school	Public
Affiliation	No Affiliation
Environment	Metropolis

STUDENTS

Total undergrad enrollment	39,619
% male/female	48/52
% from out of state	5
% frosh live on campus	66
% ugrads live on campus	19
# of fraternities (% ugrad men join)	42 (15)
# of sororities (% ugrad women join)	30 (18)
% African American	4
% Asian	20
% Caucasian	44
% Hispanic	22
% Native American	<1
% Pacific Islander	<1
% Two or more races	4
% Race and/or ethnicity unknown	1
% international	5
# of countries represented	95

ACADEMICS

Academic Rating	**78**
% students returning for sophomore year	96
% students graduating within 4 years	52
% students graduating within 6 years	80
Calendar	Semester
Student/faculty ratio	18:1
Profs interesting rating	76
Profs accessible rating	68

Most classes have 10–19 students.
Most lab/discussion sessions have
10–19 students.

MOST POPULAR MAJORS
Biology; Economics; Psychology

ABOUT THE SCHOOL

Some students at the University of Texas at Austin (UT Austin) boldly make the claim that their school is considered the "Harvard of the South," and they would probably be able to make a strong case for it. Considered one of the best public schools in Texas, the massive UT Austin campus offers a world-class education through its wide array of programs in the sciences and humanities as well as state-of-the-art laboratories. Despite the large size of some of the classes, the students find their professors to be supportive. According to one student, "They are always willing to meet you outside of class, and they try their best to encourage students to speak up during class." Students flock to this research university not only for its robust academics but also for its famed athletic offerings. One student raves, "I think the greatest strengths are the level of education we receive and the athletics program. The classes here are very difficult and will prepare students very well for graduate schools or careers. The athletics program here is awesome." The football team (Go Longhorns!) certainly helps inspire the school's contagious school spirit. The school's 431-acre campus serves as home to a student body of over 51,000 (including graduate students) and offers boundless opportunities for students to get a rich and diverse social education. With over 1,000 student organizations, the campus is bustling with activities such as sports games, festivals, movie screenings, concerts, and cultural events. For those who need the rush of city life, the campus is just a few blocks away from downtown Austin, where students often frequent the numerous restaurants, bars, clubs, and live music venues, especially those on 6th Street, a major hot spot. Competitive academic programs, legendary athletics, a huge sprawling campus, the eclectic allure of Austin, a strong sense of Texas pride, and an unabashed love of a good party are the hallmarks of an education at the University of Texas at Austin.

BANG FOR YOUR BUCK

UT Austin works hard to make college affordable for the families of students who wish to attend. One effort, Texas Advance, provides scholarships to the university's brightest, most hard-working incoming freshmen with financial need. Many of these top-performing students will also be invited to participate in one of the university's selective academic-enrichment communities. 360 Connections set the tone once new students arrive on campus—these small groups help first-years make the most of all the opportunities for mentorship, research, internships and experiential learning that UT Austin has to offer. Meanwhile, the Office of Financial Aid offers money management information and programming needed to help all students and their families reduce the burden of unnecessary debt.

STUDENT LIFE

"Because of the huge Greek life at UT, a 'typical student' would be a sorority girl or fraternity boy," but—and it's a big but—such students "are hardly the majority, since UT is actually made of more 'atypical' people than most other schools. Everyone here has his own niche, and I could not think of any type of individual who would not be able to find one of his own." Indeed, "everyone at Texas is different! When you walk across campus, you see every type of ethnicity. There are a lot of minorities at Texas. Also, I see many disabled people, whom the school accommodates well. Everyone seems to get along. The different types of students just blend in together." Especially by Texas standards, "Austin is known for being 'weird.' If you see someone dressed in a way you've never seen before, you just shrug it off and say 'That's Austin!'"

The University of Texas at Austin

FINANCIAL AID: 512-475-6203 • WEBSITE: WWW.UTEXAS.EDU

CAREER

There is a huge career services presence at UT Austin, where each college has its own dedicated office. This way while all students have access to HireUTexas, the university's campus wide job board, they also have resources tailored to their particular schools and interests. For instance, students in the College of Liberal Arts may take courses (for credit!) that complement and make the most of their internship experiences. And ScienceWorks is the online hub for College of Natural Sciences students looking for jobs, internships, mentors and professional development events. Job and Internship Fairs are usually organized by school as well with multiple chances to network and meet potential employers each year. UT Austin graduates who visited PayScale.com report a median starting salary of $52,200, and 52 percent derive a high level of meaning from their work.

GENERAL INFO

Environment: Metropolis. **Activities:** Choral groups, concert band, dance, drama/theater, jazz band, literary magazine, marching band, music ensembles, musical theater, opera, pep band, radio station, student government, student newspaper, student-run film society, symphony orchestra, television station, yearbook, campus ministries, international student organization. **Organizations:** 1,000 registered organizations, 12 honor societies, 110 religious organizations. 40 fraternities, 32 sororities. **Athletics (Intercollegiate):** *Men:* Baseball, basketball, cross-country, diving, football, golf, swimming, tennis, track/field (outdoor). *Women:* Basketball, crew/rowing, cross-country, diving, golf, soccer, softball, swimming, tennis, track/field (outdoor), volleyball. **On-Campus Highlights:** Student Activities Center, Frank Erwin Special Events Center, Performing Arts Center, Harry Ransom Humanities Research Center, Blanton Museum of Art.

FINANCIAL AID

Students should submit: FAFSA, Institution's own financial aid form. Priority filing deadline is 3/15. The Princeton Review suggests that all financial aid forms be submitted as soon as possible after October 1. *Need-based scholarships/grants offered:* Federal Pell, FSEOG, State scholarships/grants, Private scholarships, College/university scholarship or grant aid from institutional funds. *Loan aid offered:* Direct Subsidized Stafford Loans, Direct Unsubsidized Stafford Loans, Direct PLUS loans, Federal Perkins Loans, State Loans. Applicants will be notified of awards on a rolling basis in the fall. Federal Work-Study Program available. Institutional employment available.

THE BOTTOM LINE

For students who are Texas residents, the cost of tuition is a little over $9,800 which makes the school very affordable for many. For any out-of-state students, the price tag jumps to $34,836 plus another $11,456 for room and board. Whether you're an in-state or out-of-state student, do not forget to factor in the additional cost of books and supplies, which add up to $750.

CAREER INFORMATION FROM PAYSCALE.COM

ROI rating	89
Bachelor's and No Higher	
Median starting salary	$52,200
Median mid-career salary	$97,200
At Least Bachelor's	
Median starting salary	$53,400
Median mid-career salary	$98,100
% alumni with high job meaning	48%
% STEM	24%

SELECTIVITY

Admissions Rating	92
# of applicants	43,592
% of applicants accepted	39
% of acceptees attending	46
# offered a place on the wait list	1,634
% accepting a place on wait list	71
% admitted from wait list	31

FRESHMAN PROFILE

Range SAT Critical Reading	570–680
Range SAT Math	600–710
Range SAT Writing	560–680
Range ACT Composite	26–31
Minimum paper TOEFL	550
Minimum internet-based TOEFL	79
% graduated top 10% of class	72
% graduated top 25% of class	92
% graduated top 50% of class	98

DEADLINES

Regular	
Deadline	12/1
Nonfall registration?	Yes

FINANCIAL FACTS

Financial Aid Rating	79
Annual in-state tuition	$10,144
Annual out-of-state tuition	$35,796
Room and board	$10,070
Required fees	
Average need-based scholarship	$9,048
% needy frosh rec. need-based scholarship or grant aid	75
% needy UG rec. need-based scholarship or grant aid	78
% needy frosh rec. non-need-based scholarship or grant aid	51
% needy UG rec. non-need-based scholarship or grant aid	29
% needy frosh rec. need-based self-help aid	67
% needy UG rec. need-based self-help aid	69
% UG rec. any financial aid	42
% UG borrow to pay for school	46
Average cumulative indebtedness	$25,349
% frosh need fully met	23
% ugrads need fully met	21
Average % of frosh need met	68
Average % of ugrad need met	69

The University of Texas at Dallas

800 West Campbell Road, Richardson, TX 75080 • Admissions: 972-883-2270 • Fax: 972-883-2599

CAMPUS LIFE

Quality of Life Rating	87
Fire Safety Rating	95
Green Rating	81
Type of school	Public
Affiliation	No Affiliation
Environment	Metropolis

STUDENTS

Total undergrad enrollment	15,575
% male/female	57/43
% from out of state	3
% frosh from public high school	90
% frosh live on campus	60
% ugrads live on campus	27
# of fraternities (% ugrad men join)	11 (2)
# of sororities (% ugrad women join)	11 (3)
% African American	6
% Asian	29
% Caucasian	37
% Hispanic	18
% Native American	<1
% Pacific Islander	<1
% Two or more races	4
% Race and/or ethnicity unknown	2
% international	3
# of countries represented	70

ACADEMICS

Academic Rating	72
% students returning for sophomore year	84
% students graduating within 4 years	48
% students graduating within 6 years	67
Calendar	Semester
Student/faculty ratio	21:1
Profs interesting rating	71
Profs accessible rating	71

Most classes have 10–19 students.
Most lab/discussion sessions have
20–29 students.

MOST POPULAR MAJORS

Biology; Computer and Information
Sciences; Game and Interactive Media
Design

ABOUT THE SCHOOL

A member of the UT system—it was founded as a graduate-level research center in 1969—the University of Texas at Dallas is working toward attaining the national prestige associated with its sister school, UT Austin. It is now home to more than forty centers, labs, and institutes. UTD administrators call its Academic Excellence Scholarship Program "the flagship program" of the university, and admitted students are automatically reviewed on the basis of SAT/ACT scores, class rank, GPA, National Merit status, National Achievement Scholarship Program recognition, and National Hispanic Honor Awards Program recognition, and other factors for merit-based scholarships. UTD is also competitive in its admissions process: its 61 percent acceptance rate is much lower than many state universities.

UTD focuses on producing employable graduates. The university offers a growing number of courses of study in science, engineering, arts, technology, and the social sciences, and boasts one of the top business schools in the state. In addition, the school's location just north of Dallas, in the heart of the Telecom Corridor, poises graduates for employment at one of the Dallas-Fort Worth area's over 3,000 tech companies. UTD students enjoy the free CareerWorks online job-recruiting system, which administrators call its "signature program."

BANG FOR YOUR BUCK

For high-performing students, UTD can provide the ultimate value: a free education. As a result of the Academic Excellence Scholarship Program and others, UTD attracts many of Texas's best and brightest with competitive scholarship offers: a striking number of students name scholarship funds as one of their top reasons for attending UTD, and the Eugene McDermott Scholars Program, which covers all expenses of a UTD education, stands out as a hallmark value opportunity. Academic Excellence scholarships are awarded each year to first-year students. Like the university itself, its ability to offer financial subsidies to its students is growing rapidly: "An ever-expanding breadth of degree programs and capital improvements," one administrator explains, "promise to push the university to the fore of education excellence" in the future. And on the employability point, UTD's Career Center "sponsors on-campus career expos, externships/job-shadowing programs, internships, and co-ops and industrial-practice programs in conjunction with the Jonsson School of Engineering and Computer Science and the Naveen Jindal School of Managements in-house career services."

STUDENT LIFE

Life on campus at UT Dallas is very focused on academics, with the consensus being that "people are here to work" and, as one student succinctly put it, "Study, study, study. Homework, homework, homework." "UT Dallas is not a party school," says a student, and others echo that sentiment, so "if you are into the party scene, you might have to look for it a little." A fair number of students report that "life at UTD consists of making your own fun, [so] don't rely on too many actual activities." However some students report a different experience: "There are a lot of clubs, even if some people may not know about them, meaning that there's something for everyone. Recently there's been a lot of campus improvement and it went from being ok looking to really nice, with a lot more areas for people to congregate. As a result campus has become a lot more lively." Additionally, students love to take advantage of the school's urban location in order to find things to do: "A lot of people go downtown for concerts/shows, museum visits, and general entertainment. There's plenty of delicious restaurants all over the place and people go out for bowling, laser tag, or the movies a lot because there's a lot of choices."

The University of Texas at Dallas

FINANCIAL AID: 972-883-2941 • E-MAIL: INTEREST@UTDALLAS.EDU • WEBSITE: WWW.UTDALLAS.EDU

CAREER

The UT Dallas Career Center offers many services for students looking ahead towards their futures. Advising is available to help students focus on their interests and develop professional goals; jobs and internship listings can be accessed via an online platform called CometCareers; and seminars are offered on résumé and cover letter writing and interview strategies. In addition to career fairs and on-campus recruiting, UTD offers an externship and job-shadowing program that pairs students with professionals from a variety of fields. Overall, students at UT Dallas report finding the Career Center "very helpful." Out of UT Dallas alumni visiting PayScale.com, 45 percent say that they derive a high level of meaning from their careers.

GENERAL INFO

Activities: Choral groups, concert band, dance, drama/theater, jazz band, literary magazine, music ensembles, musical theater, pep band, radio station, student government, student newspaper, student-run film society, symphony orchestra, television station. **Organizations:** 300+ registered organizations, 11 honor societies, 24 fraternities and sororities. **Athletics (Intercollegiate):** *Men:* baseball, basketball, cross-country, golf, soccer, tennis. *Women:* basketball, cross-country, golf, soccer, softball, tennis, volleyball. **On-Campus Highlights:** The Pub (coffeehouse), Comet Cafe, Student Union, Activity Center, University Village clubhouses, University Commons, Dining Hall, Food Court.

FINANCIAL AID

Students should submit: FAFSA. Priority filing deadline is 3/31. The Princeton Review suggests that all financial aid forms be submitted as soon as possible after October 1. *Need-based scholarships/grants offered:* Federal Pell, FSEOG, State scholarships/grants, Private scholarships, College/university scholarship or grant aid from institutional funds. *Loan aid offered:* Direct Subsidized Stafford Loans, Direct Unsubsidized Stafford Loans, Direct PLUS loans, Federal Perkins Loans, State Loans, College/university loans from institutional funds. Applicants will be notified of awards on a rolling basis beginning 3/1. Federal Work-Study Program available. Institutional employment available.

BOTTOM LINE

UTD undergraduates give their alma mater high marks on its dedication to rewarding academic performance with financial support. While at $12,162, the annual tuition price at UTD is higher than some state universities, the school exudes willingness to subsidize all or part of its students' education: 71 percent of UTD students receive some form of aid, only 36 percent of students incur debt to pay for tuition, and the average cumulative indebtedness is $21,174. Students see overall value in their UTD experience even beyond scholarships; one notes that he enjoyed "excellent and extremely affordable/convenient," living facilities, "especially in comparison to other college housing options offering the same services or lower-quality ones for double the price."

CAREER INFORMATION FROM PAYSCALE.COM

ROI rating	87
Bachelor's and No Higher	
Median starting salary	$50,300
Median mid-career salary	$83,800
At Least Bachelor's	
Median starting salary	$51,300
Median mid-career salary	$87,200
% alumni with high job meaning	45%
% STEM	20%

SELECTIVITY

Admissions Rating	88
# of applicants	11,237
% of applicants accepted	61
% of acceptees attending	40

FRESHMAN PROFILE

Range SAT Critical Reading	560–670
Range SAT Math	600–700
Range SAT Writing	520–650
Range ACT Composite	25–31
Minimum paper TOEFL	550
Minimum internet-based TOEFL	80
% graduated top 10% of class	33
% graduated top 25% of class	64
% graduated top 50% of class	88

DEADLINES

Regular	
Deadline	7/1
Nonfall registration?	Yes

FINANCIAL FACTS

Financial Aid Rating	83
Annual in-state tuition	$12,162
Annual out-of-state tuition	$33,654
Room and board	$10,668
Required fees	
Average need-based scholarship	$8,726
% needy frosh rec. need-based scholarship or grant aid	91
% needy UG rec. need-based scholarship or grant aid	87
% needy frosh rec. non-need-based scholarship or grant aid	17
% needy UG rec. non-need-based scholarship or grant aid	8
% needy frosh rec. need-based self-help aid	78
% needy UG rec. need-based self-help aid	86
% frosh rec. any financial aid	78
% UG rec. any financial aid	71
% UG borrow to pay for school	36
Average cumulative indebtedness	$21,174
% frosh need fully met	30
% ugrads need fully met	17
Average % of frosh need met	76
Average % of ugrad need met	65

The University of Tulsa

800 South Tucker Drive, Tulsa, OK 74104 • Admissions: 918-631-2307 • Fax: 918-631-5003

CAMPUS LIFE

Quality of Life Rating	**90**
Fire Safety Rating	**95**
Green Rating	**77**
Type of school	Private
Affiliation	Presbyterian
Environment	Metropolis

STUDENTS

Total undergrad enrollment	3,478
% male/female	58/42
% from out of state	43
% frosh from public high school	71
% frosh live on campus	83
% ugrads live on campus	71
# of fraternities (% ugrad men join)	7 (20)
# of sororities (% ugrad women join)	9 (22)
% African American	5
% Asian	4
% Caucasian	56
% Hispanic	5
% Native American	3
% Pacific Islander	<1
% Two or more races	1
% Race and/or ethnicity unknown	1
% international	26
# of countries represented	59

ACADEMICS

Academic Rating	**86**
% students returning for sophomore year	88
% students graduating within 4 years	52
% students graduating within 6 years	69
Calendar	Semester
Student/faculty ratio	11:1
Profs interesting rating	80
Profs accessible rating	80
Most classes have 10–19 students.	
Most lab/discussion sessions have 20–29 students.	

MOST POPULAR MAJORS
Petroleum Engineering; Psychology; Finance

ABOUT THE SCHOOL

This mid-size private research university in Tulsa, Oklahoma, combines "great academics with [Division I] athletics." With roughly 3,500 undergraduates, the school offers both the benefits of a large university with a "tight-knit community where everyone has a place to belong." The four undergraduate colleges within the university are the Henry Kendall College of Arts and Sciences, the Collins College of Business, the College of Engineering and Natural Sciences, and the Oxley College of Health Sciences. In addition to the Honors Program, the school also offers the Tulsa Undergraduate Research Challenge (TURC) program, which "combines advanced research in most disciplines, scholarship, and community service." Combined degree programs allow students in a number of majors to begin earning credits toward their masters degrees. One English major describes Tulsa students as "serious about school [and] academically minded." The academic environment is "definitely a studious one," according to an Engineering major. "Students push each other to excel through their demonstrated work ethic. We succeed together, and once our work is done, we know how to celebrate."

BANG FOR YOUR BUCK

The University of Tulsa meets roughly 81 percent of its students' financial needs, with approximately 87 percent of the undergraduates receiving some form of need-based aid. Eighty-nine percent of freshmen and 87 percent of all other undergraduates receive financial aid. One Marketing major notes that a key factor in choosing the school was that Tulsa was "willing to match financial aid offers made by other schools." The university's website emphasizes that "while each family differs in its resources, its priorities and its attitudes toward money, TU follows policies and practices to treat families equitably in the process." In terms of scholarships, the university provides multiple in-house opportunities, from the Presidential Scholarship for incoming students with exceptional academic promise to scholarships available for students demonstrating academic merit and leadership, and offers web links and information about outside scholarship opportunities for students depending on their interests, background, or academic path. Tulsa "has great academics and recruits really intelligent students," including a high number of National Merit Scholars, says one Biology student. The school also helps "students a lot financially with their wide variety of scholarships."

STUDENT LIFE

With 178 chartered student organizations, there "are many opportunities to get involved in events and community service on campus." In addition to on-campus offerings, there are also "vast opportunities to enjoy art in Tulsa. The Philbrook Museum offers free admission with a valid TU student ID and the Gilcrease Museum is managed by the university." Greek life plays a social role on campus, which houses nine sororities and seven fraternities. Twenty-three percent of women join a sorority and 21 percent of men join a fraternity. One Economics major notes that "I have lots of Greek friends who are perfectly happy to make friends both inside and outside their sororities and fraternities. The Greek organizations seem to want to include the rest of the school in a lot of their events." Tulsa students also enjoy "Hurricane Thursday events," which are "events the school puts on every [week]. It is something fun to go to and hang out with everyone." The right mix is important to Tulsa students: "TU is the only school that hit the right balance of the all the things I was looking for—great professors, challenging classes, not-too challenging classes, [and] a campus full of events and things to do."

University of Tulsa

FINANCIAL AID: 918-631-2526 • E-MAIL: ADMISSION@UTULSA.EDU • WEBSITE: WWW.UTULSA.EDU

CAREER

According to PayScale.com, the average starting salary for a Tulsa graduate is roughly $56,800, and popular careers include petroleum engineer, reservoir engineer, and attorney. While some students note that the school's career services could cater to a wider base than just engineering students, others praise Tulsa's availability of "internship and [post-college] opportunities" along with "chances to meet possible employers." The university's website provides access to a feature called "Golden OpporTUnities," where current and past students can peruse over 500 potential jobs or internships. In addition to hosting four job fairs a year on campus, the Office of Career Services also offers resume assistance and interview preparation for students, as well as facilitates job presentations for interested student-led organizations and clubs on campus. Faculty support student success, as well, through academic mentoring or by incorporating real-world projects into their coursework so that undergrads can hone their teamwork and professional presentation skills before graduation.

GENERAL INFO

Activities: Choral groups, concert band, dance, drama/theater, jazz band, literary magazine, marching/pep band, music ensembles, musical theater, opera, preprofessional groups, radio station, student government, student newspaper, orchestra, television station, Campus Ministries, multicultural organizations, recreational clubs. **Organizations:** 178 chartered organizations, 37 honor societies, 19 religious organizations, 7 fraternities, 9 sororities. **Athletics (Intercollegiate):** *Men:* basketball, cheerleading, cross-country, football, golf, soccer, tennis, track/field (outdoor), track/field (indoor). *Women:* basketball, cheerleading, crew/rowing, cross-country, golf, soccer, softball, tennis, track/field (outdoor), track/field (indoor), volleyball.

FINANCIAL AID

Students should submit: FAFSA. Priority filing deadline is 3/1. The Princeton Review suggests that all financial aid forms be submitted as soon as possible after October 1. *Need-based scholarships/grants offered:* Federal Pell, FSEOG, State scholarships/grants, Private scholarships, College/university scholarship or grant aid from institutional funds. *Loan aid offered:* Direct Subsidized Stafford Loans, Direct Unsubsidized Stafford Loans, Direct PLUS loans, Federal Perkins Loans. Applicants will be notified of awards on a rolling basis beginning 3/15. Federal Work-Study Program available. Institutional employment available.

BOTTOM LINE

Tuition at Tulsa runs roughly $35,790 annually, with an additional $11,996 approximately for room and board, books, and fees. Forty-two percent of Tulsa students have borrowed through one of the various loan programs, while the average need-based gift award for freshmen is roughly $8,400 (and $6,900 for other undergraduates). The average financial aid package offered to Tulsa students is approximately $24,900, and on average, Tulsa graduates leave school with around $29,161 of debt.

CAREER INFORMATION FROM PAYSCALE.COM

ROI rating	88
Bachelor's and No Higher	
Median starting salary	$56,400
Median mid-career salary	$88,900
At Least Bachelor's	
Median starting salary	$59,200
Median mid-career salary	$91,700
% alumni with high job meaning	51%
% STEM	31%

SELECTIVITY

Admissions Rating	94
# of applicants	6,762
% of applicants accepted	44
% of acceptees attending	24

FRESHMAN PROFILE

Range SAT Critical Reading	560–700
Range SAT Math	570–700
Range ACT Composite	26–32
Minimum paper TOEFL	550
Minimum internet-based TOEFL	80
Average HS GPA	3.9
% graduated top 10% of class	73
% graduated top 25% of class	91
% graduated top 50% of class	99

DEADLINES

Early action	
Deadline	11/1
Notification	12/15
Regular	
Priority	2/1
Nonfall registration?	Yes

FINANCIAL FACTS

Financial Aid Rating	88
Annual tuition	$37,580
Room and board	$11,116
Required fees	$540
Average need-based scholarship	$5,648
% needy frosh rec. need-based scholarship or grant aid	33
% needy UG rec. need-based scholarship or grant aid	36
% needy frosh rec. non-need-based scholarship or grant aid	96
% needy UG rec. non-need-based scholarship or grant aid	93
% needy frosh rec. need-based self-help aid	50
% needy UG rec. need-based self-help aid	55
% frosh rec. any financial aid	91
% UG rec. any financial aid	86
% UG borrow to pay for school	49
Average cumulative indebtedness	$37,008
% frosh need fully met	55
% ugrads need fully met	48
Average % of frosh need met	86
Average % of ugrad need met	82

University of Utah

201 South 1460 East, Room 250 S, Salt Lake City, UT 84112 • Admissions: 801-581-7281 • Fax: 801-585-7864

CAMPUS LIFE

Quality of Life Rating	**91**
Fire Safety Rating	**89**
Green Rating	**92**
Type of school	Public
Affiliation	No Affiliation
Environment	Metropolis

STUDENTS

Total undergrad enrollment	23,794
% male/female	56/44
% from out of state	20
% frosh from public high school	92
% frosh live on campus	45
% ugrads live on campus	13
# of fraternities (% ugrad men join)	10 (5)
# of sororities (% ugrad women join)	7 (8)
% African American	1
% Asian	6
% Caucasian	70
% Hispanic	11
% Native American	<1
% Pacific Islander	1
% Two or more races	4
% Race and/or ethnicity unknown	1
% international	6
# of countries represented	93

ACADEMICS

Academic Rating	**74**
% students returning for sophomore year	89
% students graduating within 4 years	28
% students graduating within 6 years	64
Calendar	Semester
Student/faculty ratio	16:1
Profs interesting rating	76
Profs accessible rating	71
Most classes have 10–19 students.	
Most lab/discussion sessions have 10–19 students.	

MOST POPULAR MAJORS

Psychology; Economics; Communication

ABOUT THE SCHOOL

Salt Lake City's University of Utah, affectionately called "the U," is a large public school that offers extensive "academics and research [in] a student-oriented institution" with a "fun atmosphere." Over 100 majors and minors are offered in 19 colleges and schools, including a university studies major that allows students to create an "individualized major in an area not otherwise available" at the university. The university awards BA, BS, BFA and BMus degrees, and its well-respected Hinckley Institute of Politics hosts "one of the best internship programs in the country." Additionally, the U boasts "one of the best music programs in the state" and "the Middle East department is second-to-none." Student can also customize their degree by adding an emphasis to their major or by pursuing one of the school's two-dozen undergraduate certificates. The U has "incredible" professors who bring "a challenging curriculum and a wide variety of perspectives" to their classrooms, and many have "won awards and recognition in the academic world."

BANG FOR YOUR BUCK

The U has a wide array of scholarships for incoming, first-year students, including academic scholarships, diversity scholarships, and need-based awards. There are also grants to help students with financial need, which the university describes as the cornerstone of its aid program for students with demonstrated need. The University of Utah says that it places a high-priority on providing need-based aid "to ensure that an economically diverse student population can enroll at the university." Many students cite "good scholarship" opportunities as a major factor when deciding to attend the University of Utah.

STUDENT LIFE

According to one student, anyone who is willing to put in the effort will find plenty of opportunities to take advantage of at the U: "The opportunities are not limited to the brightest students; rather, they are available to any proactive student." Campus events through "student government, clubs, and other extracurricular activities" abound at the U, where involved students become "very close-knit." Students praise the ample research opportunities available on campus and say that many students get "involved in the local community." Students say that the free "lecturers and discussion panels hosted by the school are intriguing and insightful." Campus activities include seasonal sports and "some of the best outdoors in the nation. Killer snow, amazing hills, mountains, lakes and streams." While "the typical student is probably married and working on completing a degree to support themselves, their spouses, and possibly their children," everyone can "fit in great because there are hundreds of different student groups and opportunities to get involved. It's easy to find a niche."

CAREER

The University of Utah's Career Services office offers students a number of ways to prepare themselves for the job market. Career coaches help students understand how to leverage their talents and interests into fulfilling careers by planning research opportunities and experiential learning. Career services also hosts three on-campus volunteer, internship and job fairs throughout the year, including a science and engineering focused career fair. The renowned Hinckley

University of Utah

FINANCIAL AID: 801-581-6211 • E-MAIL: ADMISSIONS@SA.UTAH.EDU • WEBSITE: WWW.UTAH.EDU

Institute for Politics places student from all disciples into internships every year. Students say they are able participate "in several meaningful extracurricular activities," and have access to top-notch "lab equipment, job opportunities, internships, or study abroad programs." University of Utah graduates who visited PayScale.com report an average early career salary of $49,400 and mid-career salaries average at $89,200. Sixty percent of graduates say their job helps to make the world a better place.

GENERAL INFO

Activities: Choral groups, concert band, dance, drama/theater, jazz band, literary magazine, marching band, music ensembles, musical theater, opera, pep band, radio station, student government, student newspaper, student-run film society, symphony orchestra, television station, Campus Ministries, International Student Organization, Model UN 238 registered organizations, 41 honor societies, 9 religious organizations. 7 fraternities, 6 sororities. **Athletics (Intercollegiate):** *Men:* baseball, basketball, cheerleading, diving, football, golf, skiing (downhill/alpine), skiingnordiccross-country, swimming, tennis. *Women:* basketball, cheerleading, cross-country, diving, gymnastics, skiing (downhill/alpine), skiingnordiccross-country, soccer, softball, swimming, tennis, track/field (outdoor), track/field (indoor), volleyball. **On-Campus Highlights:** Rice Eccles Stadium, Jon M. Huntsman Center, Huntsman Cancer Institute, Utah Museum of Fine Arts, Utah Museum of Natural History, Marriott Library Red Butte Gardens Olympic Cauldron Park Fort Douglas Museum and Cemetery Kingsbury Hall/Gardner Hall.

FINANCIAL AID

Students should submit: FAFSA. Priority filing deadline is 3/15. The Princeton Review suggests that all financial aid forms be submitted as soon as possible after October 1. *Need-based scholarships/grants offered:* Federal Pell, FSEOG, State scholarships/grants, Private scholarships, College/university scholarship or grant aid from institutional funds, Federal Nursing Scholarships. *Loan aid offered:* Direct Subsidized Stafford Loans, Direct Unsubsidized Stafford Loans, Direct PLUS loans, Federal Perkins Loans, Federal Nursing Loans, State Loans, College/university loans from institutional funds. Applicants will be notified of awards on a rolling basis beginning 4/1. Federal Work-Study Program available. Institutional employment available.

BOTTOM LINE

In-state tuition at the University of Utah is $7,408 and out-of-state tuition runs $25,929 per academic year. On campus room and board is $9,425 and students pay $1,110 in fees. The average first-year student receives $7,988 in need-based gift aid, $4,195 in need-based loans, and on average students leave with $19,056 in student loan debt. Only 39 percent of students take out some form of loan during their U of U undergraduate education.

CAREER INFORMATION FROM PAYSCALE.COM

ROI rating	86
Bachelor's and No Higher	
Median starting salary	$48,100
Median mid-career salary	$86,100
At Least Bachelor's	
Median starting salary	$49,600
Median mid-career salary	$88,500
% alumni with high job meaning	60%
% STEM	16%

SELECTIVITY

Admissions Rating	79
# of applicants	12,174
% of applicants accepted	81
% of acceptees attending	34
# offered a place on the wait list	0

FRESHMAN PROFILE

Range SAT Critical Reading	500–640
Range SAT Math	510–660
Range SAT Writing	490–620
Range ACT Composite	21–28
Minimum paper TOEFL	550
Minimum internet-based TOEFL	80
Average HS GPA	3.6
% graduated top 10% of class	25
% graduated top 25% of class	53
% graduated top 50% of class	86

DEADLINES

Early action	
Deadline	12/1
Notification	1/15
Regular	
Priority	12/1
Deadline	4/1
Nonfall registration?	Yes

FINANCIAL FACTS

Financial Aid Rating	80
Annual in-state tuition	$7,408
Annual out-of-state tuition	$25,929
Room and board	$9,425
Required fees	$1,110
Average need-based scholarship	$6,910
% needy frosh rec. need-based scholarship or grant aid	88
% needy UG rec. need-based scholarship or grant aid	82
% needy frosh rec. non-need-based scholarship or grant aid	13
% needy UG rec. non-need-based scholarship or grant aid	6
% needy frosh rec. need-based self-help aid	82
% needy UG rec. need-based self-help aid	90
% frosh rec. any financial aid	75
% UG rec. any financial aid	64
% UG borrow to pay for school	39
Average cumulative indebtedness	$19,056
% frosh need fully met	15
% ugrads need fully met	12
Average % of frosh need met	67
Average % of ugrad need met	63

University of Virginia

OFFICE OF ADMISSION, CHARLOTTESVILLE, VA 22906 • ADMISSIONS: 434-982-3200 • FAX: 434-924-3587

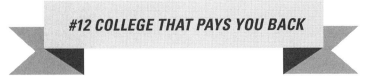

#12 COLLEGE THAT PAYS YOU BACK

CAMPUS LIFE

Quality of Life Rating	89
Fire Safety Rating	88
Green Rating	94
Type of school	Public
Affiliation	No Affiliation
Environment	City

STUDENTS

Total undergrad enrollment	16,736
% male/female	44/56
% from out of state	28
% frosh from public high school	71
% frosh live on campus	100
% ugrads live on campus	40
# of fraternities (% ugrad men join)	31 (23)
# of sororities (% ugrad women join)	15 (25)
% African American	6
% Asian	13
% Caucasian	60
% Hispanic	6
% Native American	<1
% Pacific Islander	<1
% Two or more races	5
% Race and/or ethnicity unknown	6
% international	5
# of countries represented	118

ACADEMICS

Academic Rating	85
% students returning for sophomore year	97
% students graduating within 4 years	87
% students graduating within 6 years	93
Calendar	Semester
Student/faculty ratio	15:1
Profs interesting rating	77
Profs accessible rating	77

Most classes have 10–19 students.
Most lab/discussion sessions have
20–29 students.

MOST POPULAR MAJORS
Business/Commerce; Biology; Economics

ABOUT THE SCHOOL

The University of Virginia's offerings live up to Thomas Jefferson's presidential legacy. UVA seamlessly blends the academic advantages of the Ivy League with the social life and the price tag of a large state school. The wealth of academic and extracurricular activities available here is paralleled at just a handful of schools around the country, and the school "values academia while fostering an enjoyable atmosphere for students." While class sizes can be large, and getting into the courses you want can be difficult, students rave about their engaging and inspiring professors, "who care and keep students from being 'numbers.'" Graduation rates are among the highest in the country, and the university has one of the highest graduation rates for African-American students. UVA also takes its history and traditions very seriously. The student-administered honor code is a case in point; sanctions can be harsh, but only for those who disrespect it. "Students claim full responsibility for their grades and actions, while being engaged and challenged in all aspects of life," says a student.

BANG FOR YOUR BUCK

UVA has one of the largest per-capita endowments of any public school in the country and exerts a tremendous effort to ensure that its undergraduates have access to an affordable education regardless of economic circumstances. Around half of undergraduates receive some form of financial aid, and the university aims to meet 100 percent of every student's demonstrated need. There are loan-free financial aid packages for low-income students and new Blue Ridge Scholarships for high achieving students with high financial need. There are caps on need-based loans for middle-income families. By limiting debt—or eliminating it altogether, in the case of students with the most need— UVA ensures that you can afford to attend the university as long as you can get admitted and maintain decent grades. Scholarships abound for Virginia residents, including the Virginia Commonwealth Award, which gives recipients up to $3,000 per academic year. There are plenty of other scholarships, too, available based upon need, academic achievement, and specific donor criteria. UVA's signature program, Jefferson Scholars, covers the tuition, fees, room and board of extraordinary students.

STUDENT LIFE

Students here "often get typecast as homogeneous and preppy." Overall "life at UVA is pretty chill, but when exams roll around life can be very hectic." Due to the top-notch academics, one student says, "during the week I typically spend most of my time studying." It's not all work and no play, however, as "people are committed to academics but play hard on the weekends. Parties off-grounds, going to bars, hanging out with friends, seeing shows and performances, going to dinner, etc." are all popular. "While the UVA party scene is definitely predominant, both the University and the city of Charlottesville provide plenty of alternative opportunities for entertainment." "It seems that almost every day of the week there is something university-sponsored to attend," says a student, and physical activity is big too: "[Students] like playing sports, going running, going hiking in the areas around Charlottesville, playing Frisbee on the lawn, etc. Everyone always seems to be outdoors during nice weather." The

University of Virginia

Financial Aid: 434-982-6000 • E-mail: undergradadmission@virginia.edu • Website: www.virginia.edu

wealth of things to keep busy pays off for students. "Life at school is usually buzzing," says a student, and another raves that "I can't imagine being happier anywhere else."

CAREER

University Career Services offers all of the standard resources for undergrads, including advising and one-on-one career planning; job fairs and on-campus recruitment; internship and job search services; and professional development services like résumé building and interview coaching. It also offers specialized career events in a variety of fields, such as commerce, engineering, nursing, education, and government and non-profits. The new Internship Center is a hub for all things internship related, like the University Internship Program that provides field placement based on what students are learning in the classroom. One student raves that "UVA really excels in career training and placement." Career Exploration Workshops and other self-assessments ensure that undergrads are attuned to their personal styles and interests. "The students [at UVA] are very ambitious and career-focused," and out of alumni visiting PayScale.com, 48 percent report that they derive a high level of meaning from their jobs.

GENERAL INFO

Activities: Choral groups, concert band, dance, drama/theater, jazz band, literary magazine, marching band, music ensembles, musical theater, opera, pep band, radio station, student government, student newspaper, student-run film society, symphony orchestra, television station, campus ministries, international student organization.

FINANCIAL AID

Students should submit: FAFSA, CSS/Financial Aid PROFILE. Priority filing deadline is 3/1. The Princeton Review suggests that all financial aid forms be submitted as soon as possible after October 1. *Need-based scholarships/grants offered:* Federal Pell, FSEOG, State scholarships/grants, Private scholarships, College/university scholarship or grant aid from institutional funds, Federal Nursing Scholarships. *Loan aid offered:* Direct Subsidized Stafford Loans, Direct Unsubsidized Stafford Loans, Direct PLUS loans, Federal Perkins Loans, Federal Nursing Loans, College/university loans from institutional funds. Applicants will be notified of awards on or about 4/5. Federal Work-Study Program available. Institutional employment available.

BOTTOM LINE

There is a large disparity here between tuition and fees for in-state versus out-of-state students. That's not unusual, just something to note. It's also important to keep in mind that 100 percent of applicants with financial need have their needs met. The sticker price for tuition, fees, room and board, and personal expenses for Virginia residents is somewhere in the neighborhood of $24,440 per year. For residents of other states, it's more than twice as much at $55,102. Financial aid packages for freshmen include an $19,312 grant on average.

CAREER INFORMATION FROM PAYSCALE.COM

ROI rating	93
Bachelor's and No Higher	
Median starting salary	$54,700
Median mid-career salary	$97,600
At Least Bachelor's	
Median starting salary	$56,400
Median mid-career salary	$102,000
% alumni with high job meaning	52%
% STEM	24%

SELECTIVITY

Admissions Rating	97
# of applicants	30,840
% of applicants accepted	30
% of acceptees attending	40
# offered a place on the wait list	3,547
% accepting a place on wait list	59
% admitted from wait list	19

FRESHMAN PROFILE

Range SAT Critical Reading	620–720
Range SAT Math	630–740
Range SAT Writing	620–720
Range ACT Composite	29–33
Average HS GPA	4.2
% graduated top 10% of class	89
% graduated top 25% of class	97
% graduated top 50% of class	99

DEADLINES

Early action	
Deadline	11/1
Notification	1/31
Regular	
Deadline	1/1
Notification	4/1
Nonfall registration?	No

FINANCIAL FACTS

Financial Aid Rating	93
Annual in-state tuition	$11,060
Annual out-of-state tuition	$41,722
Room and board	$10,726
Required fees	$2,654
Average need-based scholarship	$20,035
% needy frosh rec. need-based scholarship or grant aid	85
% needy UG rec. need-based scholarship or grant aid	84
% needy frosh rec. non-need-based scholarship or grant aid	9
% needy UG rec. non-need-based scholarship or grant aid	8
% needy frosh rec. need-based self-help aid	62
% needy UG rec. need-based self-help aid	64
% frosh rec. any financial aid	55
% UG rec. any financial aid	50
% UG borrow to pay for school	35
Average cumulative indebtedness	$24,905
% frosh need fully met	100
% ugrads need fully met	100
Average % of frosh need met	100
Average % of ugrad need met	100

University of Washington

1410 Northeast Campus Parkway, Seattle, WA 98195-5852 • Admissions: 206-543-9686 • Fax: 206-685-3655

CAMPUS LIFE

Quality of Life Rating	**85**
Fire Safety Rating	**95**
Green Rating	**99**
Type of school	Public
Affiliation	No Affiliation
Environment	Metropolis

STUDENTS

Total undergrad enrollment	31,063
% male/female	48/52
% from out of state	17
% frosh live on campus	65
% ugrads live on campus	25
# of fraternities	32
# of sororities	16
% African American	3
% Asian	24
% Caucasian	42
% Hispanic	7
% Native American	<1
% Pacific Islander	<1
% Two or more races	7
% Race and/or ethnicity unknown	1
% international	15
# of countries represented	83

ACADEMICS

Academic Rating	**80**
% students returning for sophomore year	94
% students graduating within 4 years	63
% students graduating within 6 years	84
Calendar	Quarter
Student/faculty ratio	21:1
Profs interesting rating	74
Profs accessible rating	72

Most classes have 20–29 students.
Most lab/discussion sessions have 20–29 students.

MOST POPULAR MAJORS

Business Administration and Management;
Computer Science; Engineering

ABOUT THE SCHOOL

Known as "U-Dub," the University of Washington's flagship campus in Seattle is the largest university on the West Coast, providing excellent "course options, location, and a good price range." Its resources are truly astonishing, creating a "diverse student body with an aim to learn about diverse subjects." The school's "great libraries and huge online databases . . . make researching for papers (almost) a snap!" The Career Center at UW ensures that students have access to a myriad of internship and other experiential-learning opportunities. UW International Programs and Exchanges (IPE) provides hundreds of study abroad and internship options to UW students, and the school "boasts a great level of awareness of international issues." UW offers more than seventy student exchanges with universities around the world that are available to undergraduates from most fields. Students pay their regular UW tuition and fees and are able to attend classes at the partner university for a semester or an academic year. Husky athletics always draw huge crowds, and the school "has an electric campus" even on nongame days. More than 770 student clubs and organizations are on offer. The Greek community is big without being overwhelming.

BANG FOR YOUR BUCK

The University of Washington is committed to making students' education affordable by providing financial assistance in a number of areas—from grants and loans to scholarships and work-study opportunities. The University of Washington offers a full range of grant opportunities for students who qualify. More than $152 million in grants were received by UW undergraduates in 2010–11. The average freshman grant was $11,800. Both merit- and need-based scholarship awards are also available, and the university provided $28.5 million in scholarships. UW's Husky Promise program guarantees full tuition and standard fees will be covered via grant or scholarship support for eligible Washington residents. The cutoff income level that UW has set for eligibility is the highest in the nation for comparable programs.

STUDENT LIFE

"At such a large university, there is no 'typical' student," undergrads tell us, observing that "one can find just about any demographic here and there is a huge variety in personalities." There "are quite a lot of yuppies, but then again, it's Seattle," and by and large "the campus is ultraliberal. Most students care about the environment, are not religious, and are generally accepting of other diverse individuals." Otherwise, "you've got your stereotypes: the Greeks, the street fashion pioneers, the various ethnic communities, the Oxford-looking grad students, etc." In terms of demographics, "the typical student at UW is white, middle-class, and is from the Seattle area," but "there are a lot of African American students and a very large number of Asian students." All groups "seem to socialize with each other."

CAREER

Internship, leadership, and service learning experiences are all on the menu at the University of Washington, where offices like The Career Center and the Center for Experiential Learning and Diversity are dedicated to connecting students with opportunity. For example, students and faculty work side-by-side on projects through the Undergraduate Research Program, or undergrads may join in the Community for Social Progress, which links academics with service learning in the community. HuskyJobs

University of Washington

FINANCIAL AID: 206-543-6101 • WEBSITE: WWW.WASHINGTON.EDU

consolidates job postings, internships, and volunteer opportunities, as well as information about employers who are interviewing on campus, all in one handy place. Even better, career workshops aren't just for enrolled students—the two-day Dependable Strengths Seminars are geared toward alumni or community members "in any stage of career transition."

GENERAL INFO

Activities: Choral groups, concert band, dance, drama/theater, jazz band, literary magazine, marching band, music ensembles, musical theater, opera, pep band, radio station, student government, student newspaper, student-run film society, symphony orchestra, television station, campus ministries, international student organization. **Organizations:** 711 registered organizations, 13 honor societies, 52 religious organizations. 32 fraternities, 16 sororities. **Athletics (Intercollegiate):** *Men:* Baseball, basketball, crew/rowing, cross-country, football, golf, soccer, tennis, track/field (outdoor). *Women:* Basketball, crew/rowing, cross-country, golf, gymnastics, soccer, softball, tennis, track/field (outdoor), volleyball. **On-Campus Highlights:** Henry Art Gallery, Burke Museum, Meany Hall for Performing Arts, football games at Husky Stadium, Waterfront Activities Center (WAC). **Environmental Initiatives:** College of the Environment. Environmental Stewardship and Sustainability Office; Strategy Management Finance and Facilities. This office supports the Environmental Stewardship Advisory Committee (ESAC). Charter signatory of the American College & University Presidents Climate Commitment (ACUPCC); development and submission of a Climate Action Plan.

FINANCIAL AID

Students should submit: FAFSA. Priority filing deadline is 2/28. The Princeton Review suggests that all financial aid forms be submitted as soon as possible after October 1. *Need-based scholarships/grants offered:* Federal Pell, FSEOG, State scholarships/grants, Private scholarships, College/university scholarship or grant aid from institutional funds. *Loan aid offered:* Direct Subsidized Stafford Loans, Direct Unsubsidized Stafford Loans, Direct PLUS loans, Federal Perkins Loans, Federal Nursing Loans. Applicants will be notified of awards on or about 4/1. Federal Work-Study Program available. Institutional employment available.

BOTTOM LINE

In-state tuition at the University of Washington is about $9,694 annually, and out-of-state tuition is in the ballpark of $33,732. Room and board can be as much as an additional $11,691. Students graduate with about $21,180 in debt on average.

CAREER INFORMATION FROM PAYSCALE.COM

ROI rating	89
Bachelor's and No Higher	
Median starting salary	$53,500
Median mid-career salary	$92,600
At Least Bachelor's	
Median starting salary	$55,000
Median mid-career salary	$94,400
% alumni with high job meaning	59%
% STEM	25%

SELECTIVITY

Admissions Rating	89
# of applicants	36,840
% of applicants accepted	53
% of acceptees attending	35

FRESHMAN PROFILE

Range SAT Critical Reading	540–660
Range SAT Math	580–710
Range SAT Writing	530–650
Range ACT Composite	26–31
Minimum paper TOEFL	540
Minimum internet-based TOEFL	76
Average HS GPA	3.8

DEADLINES

Nonfall registration?	Yes

FINANCIAL FACTS

Financial Aid Rating	81
Annual in-state tuition	$9,694
Annual out-of-state tuition	$33,732
Room and board	$11,691
Required fees	$1,059
Average need-based scholarship	$15,500
% needy frosh rec. need-based scholarship or grant aid	74
% needy UG rec. need-based scholarship or grant aid	84
% needy frosh rec. non-need-based scholarship or grant aid	11
% needy UG rec. non-need-based scholarship or grant aid	6
% needy frosh rec. need-based self-help aid	71
% needy UG rec. need-based self-help aid	82
% frosh rec. any financial aid	60
% UG rec. any financial aid	60
% UG borrow to pay for school	40
Average cumulative indebtedness	$21,180
% frosh need fully met	40
% ugrads need fully met	23
Average % of frosh need met	82
Average % of ugrad need met	82

University of Wisconsin—Madison

702 West Johnson Street, Suite 101, Madison, WI 53715-1007 • Admissions: 608-262-3961 • Fax: 608-262-7706

CAMPUS LIFE

Quality of Life Rating	**94**
Fire Safety Rating	**82**
Green Rating	**60***
Type of school	Public
Affiliation	No Affiliation
Environment	City

STUDENTS

Total undergrad enrollment	31,662
% male/female	49/51
% from out of state	33
% frosh live on campus	92
% ugrads live on campus	26
# of fraternities (% ugrad men join)	26 (9)
# of sororities (% ugrad women join)	11 (8)
% African American	2
% Asian	6
% Caucasian	76
% Hispanic	5
% Native American	<1
% Pacific Islander	<1
% Two or more races	3
% Race and/or ethnicity unknown	<1
% international	8
# of countries represented	108

ACADEMICS

Academic Rating	**82**
% students returning for sophomore year	96
% students graduating within 4 years	57
% students graduating within 6 years	85
Calendar	Semester
Student/faculty ratio	17:1
Profs interesting rating	79
Profs accessible rating	76

Most classes have 10–19 students.
Most lab/discussion sessions have
20–29 students.

MOST POPULAR MAJORS

Political Science and Government; Biology;
Economics

ABOUT THE SCHOOL

Mostly known as "an amazing research institution," the University of Wisconsin—Madison offers 157 majors and abundant opportunities in study abroad, internships, research, and service learning, all of which operate under the Wisconsin Idea: the principle that education should influence and improve people's lives beyond the university classroom. "If you are proactive, you basically have the means and resources to pursue any academic or creative feat," promises a student. The "challenging" academic atmosphere "definitely makes you earn your grades," but academic advising is readily available, and students know when to hunker down and hit the books. "At UW, the students who are out partying Saturday night are the same ones you will see in the library Sunday morning," says a student.

Even within the large school, there are plenty of chances for a student to create a smaller world. The university residence halls feature seven learning communities that give students the chance to live and learn with other students who share their interests, and provide a more seamless experience that blends residential and academic life on campus. There are also First-Year Interest Groups, which are groups of students who enroll in a cluster of three classes together. "No one's going to hold your hand and point you to what it is you want," but whoever you are, "there is a group for you and a ton of activities for you." Madison has "such a beautiful campus with so many different scenes." You "can spend part of your day walking downtown and enjoying the city, followed by a relaxing afternoon by the lake and trails," and then by night, "just being at a football, basketball, or hockey game makes your adrenaline pump and the heart race!"

BANG FOR YOUR BUCK

No matter whether you're paying in-state or out-of-state tuition, think of the (reasonable) cost as granting access to a complete jackpot of resources. From intangibles (such as access to some of the state's brightest minds) to more easily defined benefits (research opportunities and internships galore), students can take their time here and make anything they want of it. Also, a UW grad is a Badger for life, and the alumni connection will serve you well for the rest of yours.

STUDENT LIFE

At Madison, "studies come first." However, "there is always something fun for free going on on campus, as well as in Madison itself." There are movies at the union, concerts, ballroom dancing, and "gorgeous Lake Mendota" just to name a few of the "countless options." "People are always thinking progressively, both politically and socially." Students like to ponder the "big existential as well as moral questions," but that doesn't stop them from "grabbing a beer" or "just being weird." There are also "amazing opportunities to network and meet people through student organizations." "There is a niche for everyone from the outdoors lovers (Hoofers) to the organized sports lovers (intramurals) to clubs focused on the most obscure subjects."

CAREER

"Madison provides large amounts of FREE resources for their students to use from Resume Writing Services to the Career Fair to the thousands of clubs available for students to join." Also, there are "various internships and organizations to get involved in." Madison "focuses you on the future," and the professors are "not only

University of Wisconsin—Madison

FINANCIAL AID: 608-262-3060 • E-MAIL: ONWISCONSIN@ADMISSIONS.WISC.EDU • WEBSITE: WWW.WISC.EDU

professors, but active participants in their field." Career Services hosts meet-ups, informal gatherings where students can learn everything from resume and cover letter writing to how to interview well and navigate the job search. There are also "countless opportunities for undergraduate research and internship opportunities" where students can "apply their learning to real life." So it's no wonder that according to PayScale.com, more than fifty percent of alumni find their jobs meaningful. According to the same site, the average starting salary for graduates is $48,500.

GENERAL INFO

Activities: Choral groups, concert band, dance, drama/theater, jazz band, literary magazine, marching band, music ensembles, musical theater, opera, pep band, radio station, student government, student newspaper, student-run film society, symphony orchestra, television station, yearbook, international student organization. **Organizations:** 985 registered organizations, 27 honor societies, 26 fraternities, 11 sororities. **Athletics (Intercollegiate):** *Men:* Basketball, cheerleading, crew/rowing, cross-country, football, golf, ice hockey, soccer, swimming, tennis, track/field (outdoor), wrestling. *Women:* Basketball, cheerleading, crew/rowing, cross-country, golf, ice hockey, soccer, softball, swimming, tennis, track/field (outdoor), volleyball. **On-Campus Highlights:** Allen Centennial Gardens, Kohl Center, Memorial Union Terrace, Chazen Museum of Art, Babcock Hall Dairy Plant and Store.

FINANCIAL AID

Students should submit: FAFSA. The Princeton Review suggests that all financial aid forms be submitted as soon as possible after October 1. *Need-based scholarships/grants offered:* Federal Pell, FSEOG, State scholarships/grants, Private scholarships, College/university scholarship or grant aid from institutional funds. *Loan aid offered:* Direct Subsidized Stafford Loans, Direct Unsubsidized Stafford Loans, Direct PLUS loans, Federal Perkins Loans, Federal Nursing Loans. Applicants will be notified of awards on a rolling basis beginning 4/1. Federal Work-Study Program available. Institutional employment available.

BOTTOM LINE

Tuition and room and board varies depending on which state you're from. Wisconsin residents can expect to pay around $20,580 for a year (including room and board and required fees), and nonresidents are looking at about $42,830. A tuition reciprocity agreement exists between Wisconsin and Minnesota. About 94 percent of needy freshman students receive need-based scholarships or grant aid that do not have to be repaid, and additional scholarships, work-study, and federal and campus loans are available.

SELECTIVITY

Admissions Rating	92
# of applicants	32,780
% of applicants accepted	49
% of acceptees attending	39

FRESHMAN PROFILE

Range SAT Critical Reading	560–660
Range SAT Math	630–760
Range SAT Writing	600–690
Range ACT Composite	27–31
Average HS GPA	3.9
% graduated top 10% of class	54
% graduated top 25% of class	91
% graduated top 50% of class	100

DEADLINES

Regular	
Deadline	2/1
Nonfall registration?	Yes

FINANCIAL FACTS

Financial Aid Rating	88
Annual in-state tuition	$9,273
Annual out-of-state tuition	$31,523
Room and board	$10,092
Required fees	$1,215
Average need-based scholarship	$10,169
% needy frosh rec. need-based scholarship or grant aid	94
% needy UG rec. need-based scholarship or grant aid	96
% needy frosh rec. non-need-based scholarship or grant aid	9
% needy UG rec. non-need-based scholarship or grant aid	8
% needy frosh rec. need-based self-help aid	74
% needy UG rec. need-based self-help aid	79
% UG borrow to pay for school	49
Average cumulative indebtedness	$26,994
% frosh need fully met	35
% ugrads need fully met	37
Average % of frosh need met	76
Average % of ugrad need met	78

CAREER INFORMATION FROM PAYSCALE.COM

ROI rating	**90**
Bachelor's and No Higher	
Median starting salary	$49,600
Median mid-career salary	$88,800
At Least Bachelor's	
Median starting salary	$50,700
Median mid-career salary	$91,400
% alumni with high job meaning	57%
% STEM	26%

Vanderbilt University

2305 WEST END AVENUE, NASHVILLE, TN 37203 • ADMISSIONS: 615-322-2561 • FAX: 615-343-7765

CAMPUS LIFE

Quality of Life Rating	97
Fire Safety Rating	91
Green Rating	92
Type of school	Private
Affiliation	No Affiliation
Environment	Metropolis

STUDENTS

Total undergrad enrollment	6,871
% male/female	49/51
% from out of state	66
% frosh from public high school	66
% frosh live on campus	100
% ugrads live on campus	92
# of fraternities (% ugrad men join)	17 (35)
# of sororities (% ugrad women join)	16 (53)
% African American	9
% Asian	13
% Caucasian	51
% Hispanic	8
% Native American	<1
% Pacific Islander	<1
% Two or more races	5
% Race and/or ethnicity unknown	5
% international	7
# of countries represented	48

ACADEMICS

Academic Rating	93
% students returning for sophomore year	97
% students graduating within 4 years	87
% students graduating within 6 years	92
Calendar	Semester
Student/faculty ratio	8:1
Profs interesting rating	91
Profs accessible rating	89

Most classes have 10–19 students.
Most lab/discussion sessions have
10–19 students.

MOST POPULAR MAJORS

Engineering Science; Social Sciences;
Multi-/Interdisciplinary Studies

#16 COLLEGE THAT PAYS YOU BACK

ABOUT THE SCHOOL

Vanderbilt offers its 6,900 undergraduate students a heady blend of superior academic offerings, an exceptional urban environment, and a community at once steeped in tradition and enmeshed in state-of-the-art research. Students are engaged in learning at all times, whether as part of the interdisciplinary curriculum, during The Commons first-year living and learning residential community, engaging in research and creative endeavors, exploring global cultures through study abroad, or participating in one of more than 420 student-led organizations. A campus-wide honor system ensures that Vanderbilt students navigate the university's tough academics with integrity. Students from the sixty-nine degree programs in Vanderbilt's four undergraduate schools participate in research aside world-renowned professors in fields ranging from neuroscience to child psychology, from music education to nanotechnology. During their four years as undergraduates, approximately three-quarters of Vanderbilt students take advantage of internships, research positions, service projects, and/or study abroad programs, which enhance their academic experiences, building valuable skills important to future careers. Vanderbilt's ethos of service permeates campus, and students routinely engage in projects designed to make a difference in their communities.

BANG FOR YOUR BUCK

Vanderbilt goes above and beyond to ensure that promising students can have access to a Vanderbilt education no matter what their financial situation may be. To meet this goal, Vanderbilt makes three commitments: the admissions process is need-blind for U.S. citizens and eligible non-citizens; Vanderbilt meets 100 percent of demonstrated need for all admitted students; and Vanderbilt's financial aid packages do not include loans. The financial aid program does not use income bands or cutoffs; there is no specific income level that automatically disqualifies a family from receiving need-based financial aid, benefiting middle-class as well as low-income families. In addition to need-based financial assistance, Vanderbilt offers merit scholarships to a highly selective group of the most talented applicants. Applicants for these merit scholarships must demonstrate exceptional academic records and leadership in their communities. The majority of merit scholarships are awarded as part of three signature scholarship programs: the Ingram Scholarship Program, the Cornelius Vanderbilt Scholarship Program, and the Chancellor's Scholarship Program. All three signature awards include full tuition for four years, plus summer stipends.

STUDENT LIFE

Vanderbilt students inform us that they are "VERY busy" yet also continually manage to "have sooooo much fun." As one American Studies major boasts, "Every day, I get half a dozen Facebook event invites to this performance or that party or this benefit or that campus speaker." Moreover, "athletic events are . . . a great time [and] everyone tailgates for the football games." Additionally, "the men's basketball team is very popular as well." Greek life is also fairly prevalent. Fortunately, students insist that "fraternity parties are mostly open events, so anyone, Greek or non-Greek, can enjoy the social scene." Lastly, "the music, art, shopping, food, nightlife, coffee

Vanderbilt University

FINANCIAL AID: 800-288-0204 • E-MAIL: ADMISSIONS@VANDERBILT.EDU • WEBSITE: WWW.VANDERBILT.EDU

shops, outdoors, etc. in Nashville serve as a playground for infinite fun for Vandy students."

CAREER

Vanderbilt's superb reputation definitely provides students with a leg up. As one mechanical engineering student brags, "Going to a Top 20 has been great for the job hunt." Undergrads happily report that they can always turn to professors during their search. For example, if "you need help finding a job . . . [professors] are very willing to write you a letter of recommendation." They also constantly dole out "great advice on how to create a career that we will love when we graduate." Of course, Vandy's career services office is a fantastic resource as well. It sponsors numerous events to help undergrads narrow their focus and discover opportunities. For example, students can attend a "What is Consulting?" workshop with representatives from Deloitte. They can just as easily swing by a law school fair or an engineering and information technology industry day. All of these events, plus a healthy emphasis on internship placement, help ensure Vanderbilt undergrads will end up on a career path that suits them well.

GENERAL INFO

Activities: Choral groups, concert band, dance, drama/theater, jazz band, literary magazine, marching band, music ensembles, musical theater, opera, pep band, radio station, student government. **Organizations:** 420 registered organizations, 17 honor societies, 22 religious organizations. 17 fraternities, 16 sororities. **Athletics (Intercollegiate):** *Men:* Baseball, basketball, cross-country, football, golf, tennis. *Women:* Basketball, bowling, cross-country, golf, lacrosse, soccer, swimming, tennis, track/field.

FINANCIAL AID

Students should submit: FAFSA, CSS/Financial Aid PROFILE. Deadline for submitting is 2/1. The Princeton Review suggests that all financial aid forms be submitted as soon as possible after October 1. *Need-based scholarships/grants offered:* Federal Pell, FSEOG, State scholarships/grants, Private scholarships, College/university scholarship or grant aid from institutional funds. *Loan aid offered:* Direct Subsidized Stafford Loans, Direct Unsubsidized Stafford Loans, Direct PLUS loans, Federal Perkins Loans, Federal Nursing Loans, College/university loans from institutional funds. Applicants will be notified of awards on or about 4/1. Federal Work-Study Program available. Institutional employment available.

BOTTOM LINE

In addition to being need-blind in the admissions process, Vanderbilt meets 100 percent of a family's demonstrated financial need through Opportunity Vanderbilt. Best of all, need-based financial aid packages for eligible students have been loan-free since 2009.

CAREER INFORMATION FROM PAYSCALE.COM

ROI rating	93
Bachelor's and No Higher	
Median starting salary	$57,300
Median mid-career salary	$102,000
At Least Bachelor's	
Median starting salary	$58,200
Median mid-career salary	$104,000
% alumni with high job meaning	58%
% STEM	25%

SELECTIVITY

Admissions Rating	99
# of applicants	32,442
% of applicants accepted	11
% of acceptees attending	46
# of early decision applicants	3,702
% accepted early decision	24

FRESHMAN PROFILE

Range SAT Critical Reading	700–790
Range SAT Math	720–800
Range SAT Writing	690–770
Range ACT Composite	32–35
Minimum internet-based TOEFL	100
Average HS GPA	3.8
% graduated top 10% of class	87
% graduated top 25% of class	97
% graduated top 50% of class	99

DEADLINES

Early decision	
Deadline	11/1
Notification	12/15
Regular	
Priority	1/1
Deadline	1/1
Notification	4/1
Nonfall registration?	No

FINANCIAL FACTS

Financial Aid Rating	99
Annual tuition	$44,496
Room and board	$14,962
Required fees	$1,114
Average need-based scholarship	$40,267
% needy frosh rec. need-based scholarship or grant aid	89
% needy UG rec. need-based scholarship or grant aid	92
% needy frosh rec. non-need-based scholarship or grant aid	56
% needy UG rec. non-need-based scholarship or grant aid	42
% needy frosh rec. need-based self-help aid	39
% needy UG rec. need-based self-help aid	49
% frosh rec. any financial aid	69
% UG rec. any financial aid	65
% UG borrow to pay for school	22
Average cumulative indebtedness	$21,506
% frosh need fully met	98
% ugrads need fully met	99
Average % of frosh need met	100
Average % of ugrad need met	100

Vassar College

124 RAYMOND AVENUE, POUGHKEEPSIE, NY 12604 • ADMISSIONS: 845-437-7300 • FAX: 845-437-7063

CAMPUS LIFE

Quality of Life Rating	**81**
Fire Safety Rating	**87**
Green Rating	**84**
Type of school	Private
Affiliation	No Affiliation
Environment	Town

STUDENTS

Total undergrad enrollment	2,435
% male/female	44/56
% from out of state	74
% frosh live on campus	99
% ugrads live on campus	96
% African American	5
% Asian	11
% Caucasian	59
% Hispanic	11
% Native American	<1
% Pacific Islander	0
% Two or more races	6
% Race and/or ethnicity unknown	<1
% international	7
# of countries represented	48

ACADEMICS

Academic Rating	**93**
% students returning for sophomore year	94
% students graduating within 4 years	86
% students graduating within 6 years	91
Calendar	Semester
Student/faculty ratio	8:1
Profs interesting rating	93
Profs accessible rating	84

Most classes have 10–19 students.
Most lab/discussion sessions have
10–19 students.

MOST POPULAR MAJORS
Psychology; Political Science and
Government; Economics

ABOUT THE SCHOOL

A coed institution since 1969, Vassar was founded in 1861 as the first of the Seven Sister colleges. Located in Poughkeepsie, New York, this private liberal arts school where there is very little in the way of a core curriculum allows students the freedom to design their own courses of study. This approach, students agree, "really encourages students to think creatively and pursue whatever they're passionate about, whether medieval tapestries, neuroscience, or unicycles. Not having a core curriculum is great because it gives students the opportunity to delve into many different interests."

Student life is campus-centered, in large part because hometown Poughkeepsie does not offer much in the way of entertainment. It's a very self-contained social scene; virtually everyone lives on Vassar's beautiful campus. A vibrant oasis in the middle of nowhere, it's easy for students here to get caught in the "Vassar Bubble." There are clubs and organizations aplenty, and the school provides interesting lectures, theatre productions, and a wide array of activities pretty much every weeknight. Weekends, on the other hand, are more about small parties and gatherings. More adventurous students make the relatively easy trek to New York to shake up the routine.

The lack of core requirements is valued by students as "a great opportunity… to explore anything they want before settling into a major." The faculty is "super accessible" and "fully engaged in the total Vassar community." "My professors are…spectacular at illuminating difficult material," says a junior psychology major. Classes are small and "most are very discussion-based"; while academics are rigorous and challenging here, students describe themselves as self-motivated rather than competitive, contributing to a relaxed and collaborative atmosphere.

BANG FOR YOUR BUCK

Vassar has a need-blind admissions policy and is able to meet 100 percent of the demonstrated need of everyone who is admitted for all four years. Vassar awards more than $57 million dollars in scholarships. Funds come from Vassar's endowment, money raised by Vassar clubs, and gifts from friends of the college and all are need-based. In addition to a close-knit community, beautiful campus, engaged professors, and rigorous academics, study abroad opportunities abound.

STUDENT LIFE

The students at Vassar are an eclectic group who "will do things in any way but the traditional way" and who revel in their individuality. Think "smart and passionate hipsters" out to prove they have something to offer the world. Students say "the vibe of the whole school is so chill," but does not hamper a "vibrant extracurricular scene." In fact, Vassar is "bursting at the seams" with over 120 student organizations. There are "a ton of intramural sports teams," several very popular a cappella groups, plenty of political organizations, a large performing arts contingent, and "basically anything else you can think of." New York isn't far, but there are always a decent amount of weekend activities right on this close-knit campus such as "concerts, comedy shows, plays, dances, etc."

Vassar College

FINANCIAL AID: 845-437-5230 • E-MAIL: ADMISSIONS@VASSAR.EDU • WEBSITE: WWW.VASSAR.EDU

CAREER

The Career Development Office at Vassar "helps students and almumnae/i envision and realize a meaningful life" after graduation. To that end, the CDO provides career and major exploration, sets up information interviews, and will even help students put together a four-year plan to maximize their college experience. Both VCLink and The Vassar Alumnifire network provide job and internship listings for summer and post-college. PayScale.com reports that the starting salary for recent grads averages $44,800 and that 47 percent of grads visiting their website believe their work makes the world a better place.

GENERAL INFO

Activities: Choral groups, concert band, dance, drama/theater, jazz band, literary magazine, marching band, music ensembles. **Organizations:** 105 registered organizations, 11 religious organizations. **Athletics (Intercollegiate):** *Men:* Baseball, basketball, crew/rowing, cross-country, diving, fencing, lacrosse, rugby soccer, squash, swimming, tennis, track/field (outdoor), volleyball. *Women:* Basketball, crew/rowing, cross-country, diving, fencing, field hockey, golf, lacrosse, rugby, soccer, squash, swimming, tennis, track/field (outdoor), volleyball. **On-Campus Highlights:** Library, Shakespeare Garden, Class of 1951 Observatory, Frances Lehman Loeb Art Center, Center for Drama and Film. **Environmental Initiatives:** composting nearly 100 percent of food waste on site purchasing local food.

FINANCIAL AID

Students should submit: FAFSA, CSS/Financial Aid PROFILE, Noncustodial PROFILE. Regular filing deadline is 2/15. The Princeton Review suggests that all financial aid forms be submitted as soon as possible after October 1. *Need-based scholarships/grants offered:* Federal Pell, FSEOG, State scholarships/grants, Private scholarships, College/university scholarship or grant aid from institutional funds. *Loan aid offered:* Direct Subsidized Stafford Loans, Direct Unsubsidized Stafford Loans, Direct PLUS loans, Federal Perkins Loans, College/university loans from institutional funds. Applicants will be notified of awards on or about 3/30. Federal Work-Study Program available. Institutional employment available.

BOTTOM LINE

The sticker price at Vassar for tuition, fees, and room and board runs about $63,280 for a year. That said, Vassar has a need-blind admission policy, and financial aid is extremely generous. It's probably harder to get admitted here than it is to afford going here. Meeting financial standards is less important than exceeding high academic standards and intellectual pursuits that venture far outside the classroom.

CAREER INFORMATION FROM PAYSCALE.COM

ROI rating	90
Bachelor's and No Higher	
Median starting salary	$44,800
Median mid-career salary	$85,500
At Least Bachelor's	
Median starting salary	$44,800
Median mid-career salary	$85,500

SELECTIVITY

Admissions Rating	96
# of applicants	7,556
% of applicants accepted	26
% of acceptees attending	34
# offered a place on the wait list	1,017
% accepting a place on wait list	48
% admitted from wait list	2
# of early decision applicants	692
% accepted early decision	39

FRESHMAN PROFILE

Range SAT Critical Reading	670–750
Range SAT Math	660–740
Range SAT Writing	660–750
Range ACT Composite	30–33
Minimum paper TOEFL	600
Minimum internet-based TOEFL	100
% graduated top 10% of class	72
% graduated top 25% of class	96
% graduated top 50% of class	99

DEADLINES

Early decision	
Deadline	11/15
Notification	12/15
Regular	
Deadline	1/1
Notification	4/1
Nonfall registration?	No

FINANCIAL FACTS

Financial Aid Rating	99
Annual tuition	$50,550
Room and board	$11,980
Required fees	$750
Average need-based scholarship	$45,109
% needy frosh rec. need-based scholarship or grant aid	98
% needy UG rec. need-based scholarship or grant aid	100
% needy frosh rec. non-need-based scholarship or grant aid	0
% needy UG rec. non-need-based scholarship or grant aid	0
% needy frosh rec. need-based self-help aid	100
% needy UG rec. need-based self-help aid	100
% frosh rec. any financial aid	61
% UG rec. any financial aid	58
% UG borrow to pay for school	47
Average cumulative indebtedness	$17,847
% frosh need fully met	100
% ugrads need fully met	100
Average % of frosh need met	100
Average % of ugrad need met	100

Villanova University

AUSTIN HALL, 800 LANCASTER AVENUE, VILLANOVA, PA 19085 • ADMISSIONS: 610-519-4000 • FAX: 610-519-6450

CAMPUS LIFE

Quality of Life Rating	96
Fire Safety Rating	96
Green Rating	91
Type of school	Private
Affiliation	Roman Catholic
Environment	Village

STUDENTS

Total undergrad enrollment	6,994
% male/female	49/51
% from out of state	78
% frosh from public high school	52
% frosh live on campus	99
% ugrads live on campus	69
# of fraternities (% ugrad men join)	14 (17)
# of sororities (% ugrad women join)	14 (42)
% African American	5
% Asian	7
% Caucasian	74
% Hispanic	8
% Native American	<1
% Pacific Islander	<1
% Two or more races	2
% Race and/or ethnicity unknown	2
% international	2
# of countries represented	49

ACADEMICS

Academic Rating	88
% students returning for sophomore year	96
% students graduating within 4 years	85
% students graduating within 6 years	90
Calendar	Semester
Student/faculty ratio	12:1
Profs interesting rating	90
Profs accessible rating	98
Most classes have 10–19 students.	
Most lab/discussion sessions have 10–19 students.	

MOST POPULAR MAJORS

Finance; Registered Nursing/Registered Nurse; Mass Communication/Media Studies

ABOUT THE SCHOOL

The rich Augustinian Catholic tradition creates a real sense of community at Villanova University, stemming from rigorous academics, service, spirit, and a perennially good basketball team. "Everyone actively [pursues] their own area of academic interest," and "if you want to succeed, the community will do everything in its power to make sure you can do so." There is a great support system set up to help students achieve academically (professors, advisors, tutors, writing/math/ language learning centers) and there are "a lot of projects across majors that have real-world applications and are designed to help students in the long run." All degree programs—from science to engineering, business to nursing—are rooted in the liberal arts. The writing-intensive curriculum begins freshman year with two-semester Augustine and Culture Seminar Program, in which students are divided into small discussion- and dialogue-driven classes; students are also housed near their classmates in "Learning Communities" to further foster relationships and create "a healthy, competitive environment that helps students grow together."

BANG FOR YOUR BUCK

Though the sticker price is high, the vast majority of Villanova students receive need- or merit-based scholarships and grants to offset the cost. Many scholarships are available. The merit-based Presidential Scholarship covers all tuition, room and board, books, and fees; twenty-eight are awarded each year, six of which go to historically underrepresented groups. Villanova Scholarships begin at $2,000 a year for academic achievers; students commuting from their families' homes can receive partial tuition Commuter Scholarships; and the Villanova/Coca-Cola First Generation Scholarship Program awards five partial scholarships per year to academically outstanding undergraduates who are the first in their families to attend college and have financial need.

STUDENT LIFE

Students here are active. Most of campus has a focused atmosphere during the week ("This isn't a school where people wear sweat pants or pajamas to class."), with extracurriculars (community service is big here) and intramurals taking up swaths of time. However, weekends are more relaxed. The school is "close enough to Philadelphia that you take advantage of all the city has to offer" and there are shuttles to the nearby King of Prussia mall. Performances (musicians, hypnotists, cultural shows) are well attended, and students "get creative when staying on campus." The orientation program means "each new student makes twenty new friends off the bat" and "it seems like everyone falls into a niche here very easily and everyone is happy." To top it off, nothing is quite like a basketball game at the Pavilion, the stands "packed with students proudly wearing their navy blue Nova Nation t-shirts."

Villanova University

FINANCIAL AID: 610-519-4010 • E-MAIL: GOTOVU@VILLANOVA.EDU • WEBSITE: WWW.VILLANOVA.EDU

CAREER

The Villanova Career Center hosts career fairs in the spring and fall to help hook students up with internships and jobs, and there are smaller, industry-based fairs held for students interested in nursing and teaching throughout the year. There is a "great presence of recruiters on campus," and potential employers collect student résumés and conduct on-campus interviews through the Career Center. Hundreds of alumni also take part in the Career Connections Advisor Program, and Villanova "does an impeccable job coordinating volunteer opportunities for students." Villanova reports that the average starting salary for recent graduates was $57,300 and the university had a 97% success placement rate (employed, continuing education or other planned activities).

GENERAL INFO

Activities: Choral groups, concert band, dance, drama/theater, jazz band, literary magazine, marching band, music ensembles, musical theater, pep band, radio station, student government, student newspaper, student-run film society, symphony orchestra, television station, yearbook, Campus Ministries, International Student Organization, Model UN. **Organizations:** 250 registered organizations, 34 honor societies, 15 religious organizations. 13 fraternities, 14 sororities. **Athletics (Intercollegiate):** *Men:* baseball, basketball, cheerleading, cross-country, diving, football, golf, lacrosse, soccer, swimming, tennis, track/field (outdoor), track/field (indoor). *Women:* basketball, cheerleading, crew/rowing, cross-country, diving, field hockey, lacrosse, soccer, softball, swimming, tennis, track/field (outdoor), track/field (indoor), volleyball, water polo. **On-Campus Highlights:** St. Thomas of Villanova Church, Davis Center for Athletics and Fitness, Villanova University Shop, Connelly Center and Cinema, Bartley Hall Exchange.

FINANCIAL AID

Students should submit: FAFSA, CSS/Financial Aid PROFILE, Noncustodial PROFILE. Priority filing deadline is 2/7. The Princeton Review suggests that all financial aid forms be submitted as soon as possible after October 1. *Need-based scholarships/grants offered:* Federal Pell, FSEOG, State scholarships/grants, Private scholarships, College/university scholarship or grant aid from institutional funds. *Loan aid offered:* Direct Subsidized Stafford Loans, Direct Unsubsidized Stafford Loans, Direct PLUS loans, Federal Perkins Loans, Federal Nursing Loans. Applicants will be notified of awards on or about 4/1. Federal Work-Study Program available. Institutional employment available.

BOTTOM LINE

It costs $46,966 in tuition to attend Villanova, and an additional $12,720 for room and board. Fifty-four percent of undergraduates receive some sort of financial aid, with an average of 79 percent of need being met and the average need-based financial aid package running $30,020.

CAREER INFORMATION FROM PAYSCALE.COM

ROI rating	88
Bachelor's and No Higher	
Median starting salary	$55,300
Median mid-career salary	$101,000
At Least Bachelor's	
Median starting salary	$56,700
Median mid-career salary	$103,000
% alumni with high job meaning	46%
% STEM	21%

SELECTIVITY

Admissions Rating	93
# of applicants	16,206
% of applicants accepted	48
% of acceptees attending	22
# offered a place on the wait list	4,807
% accepting a place on wait list	47
% admitted from wait list	2

FRESHMAN PROFILE

Range SAT Critical Reading	590–690
Range SAT Math	610–710
Range SAT Writing	590–690
Range ACT Composite	29–32
Minimum paper TOEFL	550
Average HS GPA	4.0
% graduated top 10% of class	55
% graduated top 25% of class	87
% graduated top 50% of class	98

DEADLINES

Early action	
Deadline	11/1
Notification	12/20
Regular	
Priority	12/15
Deadline	1/15
Notification	4/1
Nonfall registration?	No

FINANCIAL FACTS

Financial Aid Rating	82
Annual tuition	$46,966
Room and board	$12,720
Required fees	$650
Average need-based scholarship	$30,020
% needy frosh rec. need-based scholarship or grant aid	91
% needy UG rec. need-based scholarship or grant aid	91
% needy frosh rec. non-need-based scholarship or grant aid	24
% needy UG rec. non-need-based scholarship or grant aid	27
% needy frosh rec. need-based self-help aid	84
% needy UG rec. need-based self-help aid	86
% frosh rec. any financial aid	55
% UG rec. any financial aid	54
% UG borrow to pay for school	55
Average cumulative indebtedness	$33,588
% frosh need fully met	20
% ugrads need fully met	17
Average % of frosh need met	80
Average % of ugrad need met	79

Virginia Polytechnic Institute and State University

UNDERGRADUATE ADMISSIONS, 201 BURRUSS HALL, BLACKSBURG, VA 24061 • ADMISSIONS: 540-231-6267

CAMPUS LIFE

Quality of Life Rating	**99**
Fire Safety Rating	**86**
Green Rating	**97**
Type of school	Public
Affiliation	No Affiliation
Environment	Town

STUDENTS

Total undergrad enrollment	25,384
% male/female	57/43
% from out of state	24
% frosh live on campus	98
% ugrads live on campus	37
# of fraternities (% ugrad men join)	29 (14)
# of sororities (% ugrad women join)	12 (19)
% African American	4
% Asian	9
% Caucasian	70
% Hispanic	5
% Native American	<1
% Pacific Islander	<1
% Two or more races	4
% Race and/or ethnicity unknown	3
% international	5
# of countries represented	116

ACADEMICS

Academic Rating	**77**
% students returning for sophomore year	94
% students graduating within 4 years	0
% students graduating within 6 years	83
Calendar	Semester
Student/faculty ratio	16:1
Profs interesting rating	77
Profs accessible rating	83
Most classes have 20–29 students.	
Most lab/discussion sessions have 20–29 students.	

MOST POPULAR MAJORS
Engineering; Biology; Business Administration and Management

ABOUT THE SCHOOL

Virginia Polytechnic University (Virginia Tech) is one of only two senior military colleges within a larger state university. (Texas A&M is the other.) This affords students a unique learning experience while benefiting from opportunities in a university with 174 undergraduate degree options. Unlike at your typical tech school, students at Virginia Tech happily discover that they don't have to forfeit a variety of exciting extracurricular activities in order to achieve an excellent education. VT's programs in engineering, architecture, agricultural science, and forestry are all national leaders, while the outstanding business program offers top-notch access to occupations in the field. Significant research is being conducted in each of the school's nine colleges. Nonetheless, undergrads are continually surprised by the genuine interest the school's first-rate faculty takes in students and their educations. At Virginia Tech, professors are dedicated to their students, a fact that is continually demonstrated by their open office doors, frequent e-mail communication, and willingness to accept undergraduates as researchers.

BANG FOR YOUR BUCK

Sixty percent of Virginia Tech students receive some form of financial aid. Students can receive funds from federal, state, private, and university scholarships, as well as Stafford and Perkins loans, work-study, and federal Pell Grants. Some scholarships consider a student's financial need, while others are awarded independently, based on a student's academic or athletic achievement. Students can browse the numerous scholarship opportunities online through the school's scholarship database.

Membership in the Virginia Tech Corps of Cadets offers excellent opportunities for supplemental scholarships. About 650 cadets receive $1.5 million in Emerging Leaders Scholarships. In addition, 429 cadets garnered $7.8 million in Army, Navy, and Air Force ROTC scholarships. The cadets, of course, have access to other scholarships and financial aid. But the Emerging Leaders and ROTC scholarships provide more than $9 million in total aid to members of the 857-student corps.

STUDENT LIFE

Virginia Tech is "the perfect mix of studies and fun." People here are generally intellectual and "will have discussions on almost anything, including political issues and global issues." Off the clock, most students love Hokie Sports, and a typical student is "someone who has a love for all things Virginia Tech. You will find them at every...football game." "There is nothing like a home game during football season," agrees another student. Blacksburg is "in the middle of nowhere" but there is a nearby mall, grocery stores, and lots of local restaurants, and "school-related and Greek life functions are the main sources of weekend activities." There are hundreds of student organizations to get involved with, and "there are 30,000 people around you that are the same age as you. You find stuff to do."

CAREER

Virginia Tech "does excellent with job placement after graduation." There are many opportunities for internships and full-time positions through the "amazing Career Services" as well as career fairs for

Virginia Polytechnic Institute and State University

FINANCIAL AID: 540-231-5179 • E-MAIL: VTADMISS@VT.EDU FAX: 540-231-3242 • WEBSITE: WWW.VT.EDU

every major. Though Virginia Tech isn't necessarily known for liberal arts, the College of Liberal Arts and Human Science has been gaining serious momentum over the years, and "there are also a lot of connections to D.C. for jobs in these fields." The department maintains a host of online and in-person resources, such as Resumania! résumé review services, on-campus interviewing programs, and an online database of jobs and internships. Fifty percent of Virginia Tech graduates who visited PayScale.com said they thought their job had a meaningful impact on the world, and reported an average starting salary of $53,800.

GENERAL INFO

Environment: Town. **Activities:** Choral groups, concert band, dance, drama/theater, jazz band, literary magazine, marching band, music ensembles, musical theater, pep band, radio station, student government, student newspaper, year book. **Organizations:** 600 registered organizations, 32 honor societies, 53 religious organizations. 29 fraternities, 12 sororities. **Athletics (Intercollegiate):** *Men:* Baseball, basketball, cheerleading, cross-country, diving, football, golf, soccer, swimming, tennis, track/field (outdoor), track/field (indoor), ultimate Frisbee, water polo. *Women:* Basketball, cheerleading, cross-country, diving, lacrosse, soccer, softball, swimming, tennis, track/field (outdoor), track/field (indoor), ultimate Frisbee, volleyball, water polo. **Environmental Initiatives:** The Virginia Tech Climate Action Commitment Resolution and Sustainability Plan.

FINANCIAL AID

Students should submit: FAFSA. Priority filing deadline is 3/1. The Princeton Review suggests that all financial aid forms be submitted as soon as possible after October 1. *Need-based scholarships/grants offered:* Federal Pell, FSEOG, State scholarships/grants, Private scholarships, College/university scholarship or grant aid from institutional funds. *Loan aid offered:* Direct Subsidized Stafford Loans, Direct Unsubsidized Stafford Loans, Direct PLUS loans, Federal Perkins Loans, College/university loans from institutional funds. Applicants will be notified of awards on a rolling basis beginning 4/1. Federal Work-Study Program available. Institutional employment available.

BOTTOM LINE

Virginia Tech's high-quality education and low tuition make this school an excellent investment. For Virginia residents, the estimated total cost of attendance for one year is $20,750, including tuition, fees, and room and board. For nonresidents, the price is around $36,791. In the popular school of engineering, the cost per credit hour is a bit higher than other major fields.

CAREER INFORMATION FROM PAYSCALE.COM

ROI rating	89
Bachelor's and No Higher	
Median starting salary	$54,500
Median mid-career salary	$96,700
At Least Bachelor's	
Median starting salary	$55,400
Median mid-career salary	$100,000
% alumni with high job meaning	47%
% STEM	32%

SELECTIVITY

Admissions Rating	88
# of applicants	22,280
% of applicants accepted	73
% of acceptees attending	39
# offered a place on the wait list	2,118
% accepting a place on wait list	73
% admitted from wait list	0
# of early decision applicants	2,023
% accepted early decision	52

FRESHMAN PROFILE

Range SAT Critical Reading	540–640
Range SAT Math	570–680
Range SAT Writing	530–640
Minimum paper TOEFL	550
% graduated top 10% of class	41
% graduated top 25% of class	82
% graduated top 50% of class	99

DEADLINES

Early decision	
Deadline	11/1
Notification	12/15
Regular	
Deadline	1/15
Notification	4/1
Nonfall registration?	Yes

FINANCIAL FACTS

Financial Aid Rating	81
Annual in-state tuition	$10,496
Annual out-of-state tuition	$26,536
Room and board	$8,266
Required fees	$1,989
Average need-based scholarship	$6,809
% needy frosh rec. need-based scholarship or grant aid	65
% needy UG rec. need-based scholarship or grant aid	70
% needy frosh rec. non-need-based scholarship or grant aid	47
% needy UG rec. non-need-based scholarship or grant aid	35
% needy frosh rec. need-based self-help aid	66
% needy UG rec. need-based self-help aid	73
% UG rec. any financial aid	75
% UG borrow to pay for school	53
Average cumulative indebtedness	$28,873
% frosh need fully met	15
% ugrads need fully met	17
Average % of frosh need met	62
Average % of ugrad need met	64

Wabash College

PO Box 352, 301 W. Wabash Av, Crawfordsville, IN 47933 • Admissions: 765-361-6225

CAMPUS LIFE

Quality of Life Rating	89
Fire Safety Rating	92
Green Rating	71
Type of school	Private
Affiliation	No Affiliation
Environment	Village

STUDENTS

Total undergrad enrollment	868
% male/female	100/0
% from out of state	23
% frosh from public high school	92
% frosh live on campus	100
% ugrads live on campus	91
# of fraternities (% ugrad men join)	9 (54)
% African American	6
% Asian	1
% Caucasian	74
% Hispanic	7
% Native American	<1
% Pacific Islander	0
% Two or more races	3
% Race and/or ethnicity unknown	2
% international	7
# of countries represented	14

ACADEMICS

Academic Rating	94
% students returning for sophomore year	85
% students graduating within 4 years	70
% students graduating within 6 years	73
Calendar	Semester
Student/faculty ratio	10:1
Profs interesting rating	98
Profs accessible rating	98

Most classes have 10–19 students.
Most lab/discussion sessions have
10–19 students.

MOST POPULAR MAJORS

History; Political Science and Government;
Economics

#38 COLLEGE THAT PAYS YOU BACK

ABOUT THE SCHOOL

There are still all-male liberal arts colleges out there, and Wabash College is among the last and the best of them. Wabash College is one of just three remaining men's liberal arts colleges in the nation. Even so, Wabash's solid reputation and even more solid endowment ensure that the tradition of quality, single-sex education will continue into the foreseeable future. Academically, a flexible curriculum and rigorous academic programs define the Wabash experience. With a student body of fewer than 1,000 students, the school boasts an excellent student-to-teacher ratio of ten to one. First-rate professors and a hands-on administration enhance the Wabash experience, along with special programs designed to complement classroom learning with real-world experience. For example, the school's Immersion Learning Courses allow students to link their classroom work to a seven- to ten-day trip within the United States or overseas, at no additional cost to the student.

Wabash students adhere to the elegant Gentleman's Rule, which simply requires them to behave as responsible students both on and off campus. Though the student body has grown more diverse in recent years, Wabash men are typically very bright, very ambitious, and very conservative. Not all are religious, but those who are take their faith very seriously. Weeknights at Wabash are all about academics, while weekends are filled with parties. Life at Wabash is very Greek-oriented—half of students belong to a fraternity. Purdue, Ball State, Butler, and Indiana University are all nearby, should students crave the occasional getaway, and women from neighboring schools often travel to the Wabash campus on the weekends. Hometown Crawfordsville is small—home to only 15,000 permanent residents—but Indianapolis is fewer than fifty miles to the southeast.

BANG FOR YOUR BUCK

The school can afford to distribute aid generously. Admissions are based on academic ability, not ability to pay. At Wabash, nearly 100 percent of student financial need is met. Merit-based aid is also plentiful. Wabash's scholarship program includes Honor Scholarships, which are renewable up to $160,000 over four years. Wabash also offers President's Scholarships (renewable; minimum of $92,000 over four years), Dean's Scholarships (renewable; minimum of $72,000 over four years) and Fine Arts and Alumni Awards (renewable; up to $60,000 over four years). There are also merit-based scholarships for students who demonstrate exceptional character and excellence in leadership, such as the Lilly Award, which covers the full cost of tuition and room and board.

STUDENT LIFE

The men of Wabash are "politically, athletically, and socially aware," and "conversations prove to be intellectual and fun with neither category outweighing the other." School work is a priority during weekdays, but weekends give way to letting off steam through visits to other schools (often to visit girlfriends), athletics, or parties. The Student Senate pays for a variety of social activities to keep students occupied (such as lazer tag and ski trips), and there's always good old discussions with friends, watching movies, and playing video games. Students are strongly organized by living units and the majority of the school is involved in a Greek organization; extracurriculars likes clubs and sporting events are where a lot of people will get together. One of

Wabash College

E-MAIL: ADMISSIONS@WABASH.EDU • FAX: 765-361-6437 • WEBSITE: WWW.WABASH.EDU

the biggest uniting factors is Wabash sports: "We live and die by our sports teams," says a student.

CAREER

The alumni support from Wabash "is amazing"; many "have high ranking and prestigious positions and love reaching out to the students offering different internship and job opportunities." The Schroeder Center for Career Development help students to take full advantage of the "boundless career opportunities" that a Wabash education offers, bringing in recruiters, offering professional development workshops, and connecting students with peer advisors. There are a number of unique services through the office: the Career Test Drives program allows students to try out different careers via first-hand experience (typically shadowing alumni); the Bash Bunks program helps students to find short-term housing with alumni; and the Suit Yourself Program lets students borrow all of the dress clothes they need for interviews and events free of charge.

GENERAL INFO

Activities: Choral groups, concert band, drama/theater, jazz band, literary magazine, music ensembles, pep band, radio station, student government, student newspaper, student-run film society. **Organizations:** 65 registered organizations, 7 honor societies, 5 religious organizations. 9 fraternities. **Athletics (Intercollegiate):** *Men:* Baseball, basketball, cross-country, diving, football, golf, soccer, swimming, tennis, track/field (outdoor), track/field (indoor), wrestling. **On-Campus Highlights:** Allen Athletics and Recreation Center, Wabash Chapel, Hays Hall, Trippet Hall, Lilly Library, Malcolm X Institute of Black Studies. **Environmental Initiatives:** Campus-wide recycling. Environmental Concerns Committee driving LEED Certification. Green bikes.

FINANCIAL AID

Students should submit: FAFSA. Regular filing deadline is 2/15. The Princeton Review suggests that all financial aid forms be submitted as soon as possible after October 1. *Need-based scholarships/grants offered:* Federal Pell, FSEOG, State scholarships/grants, Private scholarships, College/university scholarship or grant aid from institutional funds. *Loan aid offered:* Direct Subsidized Stafford Loans, Direct Unsubsidized Stafford Loans, Direct PLUS loans, College/university loans from institutional funds. Applicants will be notified of awards on or about 3/31. Federal Work-Study Program available. Institutional employment available.

BOTTOM LINE

Few students pay the full cost of attendance at Wabash. Most students receive generous aid packages in the form of loans and scholarships, drastically offsetting the price. Therefore, most undergraduates pay just a fraction of the estimated $50,340 cost to attend (which includes tuition, room and board, plus other expenses).

CAREER INFORMATION FROM PAYSCALE.COM

ROI rating	91
Bachelor's and No Higher	
Median starting salary	$44,700
Median mid-career salary	$94,800
At Least Bachelor's	
Median starting salary	$59,300
Median mid-career salary	$108,000
% alumni with high job meaning	56%
% STEM	18%

SELECTIVITY

Admissions Rating	87
# of applicants	1,247
% of applicants accepted	61
% of acceptees attending	31
# offered a place on the wait list	32
% accepting a place on wait list	97
% admitted from wait list	16
# of early decision applicants	48
% accepted early decision	88

FRESHMAN PROFILE

Range SAT Critical Reading	510–610
Range SAT Math	530–640
Range SAT Writing	470–600
Range ACT Composite	22–28
Minimum paper TOEFL	550
Minimum internet-based TOEFL	80
Average HS GPA	3.7
% graduated top 10% of class	35
% graduated top 25% of class	71
% graduated top 50% of class	95

DEADLINES

Early decision	
Deadline	10/15
Notification	11/16
Early action	
Deadline	11/1
Notification	12/7
Regular	
Priority	12/1
Deadline	1/15
Nonfall registration?	Yes

FINANCIAL FACTS

Financial Aid Rating	91
Annual tuition	$40,400
Room and board	$9,600
Required fees	$650
Average need-based scholarship	$25,192
% needy frosh rec. need-based scholarship or grant aid	99
% needy UG rec. need-based scholarship or grant aid	98
% needy frosh rec. non-need-based scholarship or grant aid	20
% needy UG rec. non-need-based scholarship or grant aid	15
% needy frosh rec. need-based self-help aid	78
% needy UG rec. need-based self-help aid	82
% frosh rec. any financial aid	99
% UG rec. any financial aid	95
% UG borrow to pay for school	91
Average cumulative indebtedness	$32,916
% frosh need fully met	72

Wake Forest University

P.O. Box 7305, Reynolda Station, Winston Salem, NC 27109 • Admissions: 336-758-5201 • Fax: 336-758-4324

CAMPUS LIFE

Quality of Life Rating	**91**
Fire Safety Rating	**95**
Green Rating	**87**
Type of school	Private
Affiliation	No Affiliation
Environment	City

STUDENTS

Total undergrad enrollment	4,871
% male/female	47/53
% from out of state	79
% frosh from public high school	65
% frosh live on campus	100
% ugrads live on campus	77
# of fraternities (% ugrad men join)	14 (39)
# of sororities (% ugrad women join)	9 (58)
% African American	6
% Asian	5
% Caucasian	74
% Hispanic	6
% Native American	<1
% Pacific Islander	<1
% Two or more races	3
% Race and/or ethnicity unknown	<1
% international	6
# of countries represented	27

ACADEMICS

Academic Rating	**95**
% students returning for sophomore year	93
% students graduating within 4 years	83
Calendar	Semester
Student/faculty ratio	11:1
Profs interesting rating	96
Profs accessible rating	98
Most classes have 10–19 students.	
Most lab/discussion sessions have 10–19 students.	

MOST POPULAR MAJORS
Political Science and Government; Business/Commerce; Psychology

ABOUT THE SCHOOL

Wake Forest combines the best tradition of a small liberal arts college with the resources of a national research university. Founded in 1834, the university believes deeply in its responsibility to educate the whole person, mind, body, and spirit. One student says, "I was very impressed with the quality of the facilities and professors." They certainly need all the help they can get, as Wake Forest academics are rigorous. Wake has a nurturing environment, with professors and faculty that care about the well-being and personal growth of their students. "Small classes with a lot of discussion are common." Small class sizes create opportunities for intense discussion, and though the workload may be heavy at times, professors are extremely accessible outside of class for additional help or questions. Professors, not graduate assistants, are the primary instructors. Students have access to top-flight scholars from the very first day of their college career. Wake Forest also offers extraordinary opportunities for undergraduate students to get involved in faculty research projects.

BANG FOR YOUR BUCK

"Wake Forest's generous financial aid program allows deserving students to enroll regardless of their financial circumstances." Wake Forest is one of a small group of private institutions that agrees to meet 100 percent of each regularly admitted student's demonstrated financial need. Nearly two-thirds of the students here receive some form of financial aid. In addition, each year Wake Forest awards merit-based scholarships to less than 3 percent of its first-year applicants. These scholarships are renewable through four years, subject to satisfactory academic, extracurricular, and civic performance. Though criteria differ slightly, the programs all recognize extraordinary achievement, leadership, and talent. Most scholarships do not require a separate merit-based scholarship application. The competition is steep, with recipients generally standing at least in the top 10 percent of the class. "Wake Forest's Reynolds and Carswell merit-based scholarships cover tuition, room, board, and summer grants for individually-designed study projects. Gordon Scholarships are awarded to up to seven students each year to students among constituencies historically underrepresented at Wake Forest."

STUDENT LIFE

There are a ton of traditions peppered throughout the school year, and a good percentage of students are involved in the Greek system. "Most people go out on Fridays and Saturdays, and some go out for 'Wake Wednesdays' as well," says a student. Movies and shopping are common ways to relax, and it is "very accessible to get to downtown Winston-Salem to spend the night in a more upscale part of town." A lot of students are strongly involved in community service, and also love going and supporting the Wake football and basketball teams "in southern attire." On warm days you will find students out on the quad "throwing [the] football ... or just sitting around talking," or hiking and rock climbing at nearby Pilot Mountain. Shorty's (an on-campus restaurant) is "a great place to hang out with friends any night of the week," and there is also "an impressive variety of on-campus dining options."

Wake Forest University

FINANCIAL AID: 336-758-5154 • E-MAIL: ADMISSIONS@WFU.EDU • WEBSITE: WWW.WFU.EDU

CAREER

The Office of Career and Professional Development is known to be one of the best in the nation, and "for a school this size, that's incredible." The resources that are available there "almost guarantee you the best internships and jobs" and whether it's résumé reviews, career counseling, intern searches, or job application help, the OPCD provides all students with unprecedented career support. Numerous career fairs and an annual three-day Career Trek to different major cities lets students personally immerse themselves in a variety of each city's industries. Wake Forest graduates who visited PayScale.com reported an average starting salary of $53,300, and forty-eight percent said they felt their job had a meaningful impact on the world.

GENERAL INFO

Activities: Choral groups, concert band, dance, drama/theater, jazz band, literary magazine, marching band, music ensembles, pep band, radio station, student government, student newspaper, student-run film society, symphony orchestra, television station, yearbook, campus ministries, international student organization. **Organizations:** 168 registered organizations, 16 honor societies, 16 religious organizations. 14 fraternities, 9 sororities. **Athletics (Intercollegiate):** *Men:* Baseball, basketball, cheerleading, cross-country, football, golf, soccer, tennis, track/field (outdoor), track/field (indoor). *Women:* Basketball, cheerleading, cross-country, field hockey, golf, soccer, tennis, track/field (outdoor), track/field (indoor), volleyball. **On-Campus Highlights:** Charlotte and Philip Hanes Art Gallery, Museum of Anthropology, The Z. Smith Reynolds Library, Wait Chapel, Benson University Center.

FINANCIAL AID

Students should submit: FAFSA, CSS/Financial Aid PROFILE, State aid form, Noncustodial PROFILE. Regular filing deadline is 1/1. The Princeton Review suggests that all financial aid forms be submitted as soon as possible after October 1. *Need-based scholarships/grants offered:* Federal Pell, FSEOG, State scholarships/grants, Private scholarships, College/university scholarship or grant aid from institutional funds. *Loan aid offered:* Direct Subsidized Stafford Loans, Direct Unsubsidized Stafford Loans, Direct PLUS loans, Federal Perkins Loans, State Loans, College/university loans from institutional funds. Applicants will be notified of awards on a rolling basis beginning 4/1. Federal Work-Study Program available. Institutional employment available.

BOTTOM LINE

At Wake Forest University, the total cost for tuition and fees, room and board, books, and supplies comes to about $60,000. Fortunately, the average financial aid package for freshman includes a grant totaling $40,000. Additional aid is available in the form of scholarships, work-study, and loans.

CAREER INFORMATION FROM PAYSCALE.COM

ROI rating	89
Bachelor's and No Higher	
Median starting salary	$49,100
Median mid-career salary	$92,100
At Least Bachelor's	
Median starting salary	$51,400
Median mid-career salary	$94,600
% alumni with high job meaning	46%
% STEM	12%

SELECTIVITY

Admissions Rating	95
# of applicants	13,281
% of applicants accepted	29
% of acceptees attending	33
# of early decision applicants	1,050
% accepted early decision	48

FRESHMAN PROFILE

Range SAT Critical Reading	590–690
Range SAT Math	620–730
Range SAT Writing	610–710
Range ACT Composite	28–32
Minimum paper TOEFL	600
% graduated top 10% of class	77
% graduated top 25% of class	93
% graduated top 50% of class	99

DEADLINES

Early decision	
Deadline	11/15
Regular	
Deadline	1/1
Nonfall registration?	No

FINANCIAL FACTS

Financial Aid Rating	92
Annual tuition	$48,746
Room and board	$14,748
Required fees	$562
Average need-based scholarship	$40,740
% needy frosh rec. need-based scholarship or grant aid	93
% needy UG rec. need-based scholarship or grant aid	93
% needy frosh rec. non-need-based scholarship or grant aid	55
% needy UG rec. non-need-based scholarship or grant aid	50
% needy frosh rec. need-based self-help aid	93
% needy UG rec. need-based self-help aid	95
% frosh rec. any financial aid	39
% UG rec. any financial aid	34
% UG borrow to pay for school	39
Average cumulative indebtedness	$36,546
% frosh need fully met	80
% ugrads need fully met	77
Average % of frosh need met	99
Average % of ugrad need met	99

Washington University in St. Louis

CAMPUS BOX 1089, ST. LOUIS, MO 63130-4899 • ADMISSIONS: 314-935-6000 • FAX: 314-935-4290

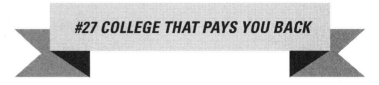

#27 COLLEGE THAT PAYS YOU BACK

ABOUT THE SCHOOL

Washington University in St. Louis provides its students with a total educational experience designed not only to prepare each student to find success in whatever career path he or she chooses, but also to make a contribution to society. The school is "rich with great people, amazing extracurricular opportunities, an underrated city just down the street, and an education that will challenge you." Academic flexibility allows students to study across academic disciplines in the university's five undergraduate schools, and these programs "are flexible enough to allow students to pursue academic interests in business, arts and sciences, art and architecture, and engineering all at once." Students at Washington University have the benefit of working alongside some of the brightest students in the world as they learn from world-renowned faculty who love to work with undergraduates. The Skandalaris Center for Entrepreneurial Studies is one of many community-building hubs that create innovative opportunities on campus. Professors "are engaged and lively," and faculty interactions can include research and mentoring, not only in the natural sciences, but in all fields, including through freshman programs. "You can tell everyone just loves to be here," says a student.

BANG FOR YOUR BUCK

WUSTL offers a personalized approach to financial assistance. The university's financial aid office takes the time to understand each family's individual financial circumstances and award financial assistance that is tailored to a particular family's unique situation. (This works out particularly well for middle-income families with mitigating factors affecting their ability to pay.) In addition, WUSTL is committed to ensuring that no student is forced to leave school due to a change in his or her family's financial circumstances. A short online form makes applying for financial assistance simple, and awards range up to the full cost of attendance. In addition to generous academic scholarships and need-based aid, WUSTL strives to reduce the amount of student loans being borrowed by students. One hundred percent of need is met for all admitted students. Many students qualify for financial assistance awards which meet their demonstrated need without the use of student loans. Merit-based scholarships are also offered. The John B. Ervin Scholars Program and Annika Rodriguez Scholars Program cover up to the full cost of tuition plus a stipend, and focus on leadership, service, and commitment to diversity and are open to applications in all academic areas.

STUDENT LIFE

Every student at WUSTL "seems to be quirky in their own way and people generally embrace that about each other." "Everyone's involved in something awesome. It inspires you to do more with your time here," says a student. This intelligent, happy group say that "most weeknights are spent working all night or going to meetings and then working," ("There is a lot of studying going on, so we take a lot of 'study breaks' as a floor") but weekends are for kicking back. Dinner at the Loop (a strip with a variety of stores, restaurants, and entertainment venues) is a fun routine, and "going out into the city, shopping at the mall, going to the frats, or even staying in to play nerdy games are very common here." Potlucks are also a frequent occurrence, and you can also find "movie nights, poetry slams, performances, and other things to do."

Washington University in St. Louis

FINANCIAL AID: 888-547-6670 • E-MAIL: ADMISSIONS@WUSTL.EDU • WEBSITE: WUSTL.EDU

CAREER

Washington University "does an excellent job of preparing students" for their future careers, setting students on a Four Year Plan for the career process from the first days that they set foot on campus. The Career Center helps hook students up with "great internship opportunities" based upon their major, maintains an online recruiting platform (CAREERlink) to further facilitate student proactivity, and offers one-on-one advising for students at all stages of their job search. Road shows each year take students to Chicago, Los Angeles, and New York where they can network with alumni and with industry professionals. Forty-eight percent of WUSTL graduates who visited PayScale.com said they felt their job had a meaningful impact on the world, and alumni have an average starting salary of $55,000.

GENERAL INFO

Activities: Choral groups, concert band, dance, drama/theater, jazz band, literary magazine, music ensembles, musical theater, opera, pep band, radio station, student government, student newspaper, student-run film society, symphony orchestra, television station, campus ministries, international student organization. **Organizations:** 350 registered organizations, 19 honor societies, 17 religious organizations. 10 fraternities, 8 sororities. **Athletics (Intercollegiate):** *Men:* Baseball, basketball, cross-country, diving, football, soccer, swimming, tennis, track/field (outdoor), track/field (indoor). *Women:* Basketball, cross-country, diving, golf, soccer, softball, swimming, tennis, track/field (outdoor), track/field (indoor), volleyball.

FINANCIAL AID

Students should submit: FAFSA, Institution's own financial aid form, CSS/Financial Aid PROFILE, Noncustodial PROFILE. Regular filing deadline is 2/1. The Princeton Review suggests that all financial aid forms be submitted as soon as possible after October 1. *Need-based scholarships/grants offered:* Federal Pell, FSEOG, State scholarships/grants, Private scholarships, College/university scholarship or grant aid from institutional funds. *Loan aid offered:* Direct Subsidized Stafford Loans, Direct Unsubsidized Stafford Loans, Direct PLUS loans, Federal Perkins Loans, State Loans, College/university loans from institutional funds. Applicants will be notified of awards on or about 4/1. Federal Work-Study Program available. Institutional employment available.

BOTTOM LINE

Undergraduate tuition and fees ring in at about $49,770 annually. Add another $15,596 for room and board, and you're looking at a $65,366 baseline price tag, not including books, supplies, personal expenses, or transportation. Don't fret: Financial aid is generous and merit-based aid is available as well.

CAREER INFORMATION FROM PAYSCALE.COM

ROI rating	92
Bachelor's and No Higher	
Median starting salary	$55,500
Median mid-career salary	$105,000
At Least Bachelor's	
Median starting salary	$58,300
Median mid-career salary	$113,000
% alumni with high job meaning	51%
% STEM	25%

SELECTIVITY

Admissions Rating	98
# of applicants	29,259
% of applicants accepted	17
% of acceptees attending	35
# of early decision applicants	1,652
% accepted early decision	37

FRESHMAN PROFILE

Range SAT Critical Reading	690–760
Range SAT Math	710–790
Range SAT Writing	690–770
Range ACT Composite	32–34
% graduated top 10% of class	89
% graduated top 25% of class	100
% graduated top 50% of class	100

DEADLINES

Early decision	
Deadline	11/15
Notification	12/15
Regular	
Deadline	1/15
Notification	4/1
Nonfall registration?	No

FINANCIAL FACTS

Financial Aid Rating	96
Annual tuition	$48,950
Room and board	$15,596
Required fees	$820
Average need-based scholarship	$37,617
% needy frosh rec. need-based scholarship or grant aid	95
% needy UG rec. need-based scholarship or grant aid	97
% needy frosh rec. non-need-based scholarship or grant aid	10
% needy UG rec. non-need-based scholarship or grant aid	6
% needy frosh rec. need-based self-help aid	73
% needy UG rec. need-based self-help aid	63
% frosh rec. any financial aid	50
% UG rec. any financial aid	53
% UG borrow to pay for school	29
Average cumulative indebtedness	$24,243
% frosh need fully met	99
% ugrads need fully met	99
Average % of frosh need met	100
Average % of ugrad need met	100

ellesley College

ADMISSION, 106 CENTRAL STREET, WELLESLEY, MA 02481-8203 • PHONE: 781-283-2270

ABOUT THE SCHOOL

Students spend a tremendous amount of time reading and writing papers at Wellesley. Spending part of junior year abroad is a staple of a Wellesley education. The Wellesley College Center for Work and Service (CWS) offers grants and stipends, which allow students to pursue what would otherwise be unpaid research and internship opportunities. When they get their diplomas, Wellesley graduates are able to take advantage of a tenaciously loyal network of more than 30,000 alums who are ready to help students with everything from arranging an interview to finding a place to live. Wellesley's close-knit student population collectively spends large segments of its weekdays in stressed-out study mode. Students don't spend all of their weekdays this way, though, because there are a ton of extracurricular activities available on this beautiful, state-of-the-art campus. Wellesley is home to more than 150 student organizations. Lectures, performances, and cultural events are endless. Wellesley is twelve miles west of Boston, and access to cultural, academic, social, business, and medical institutions is a powerful draw. On the weekends, many students head to Boston to hit the bars or to parties on nearby campuses. While enrolling just 2,474 undergraduates, Wellesley offers a remarkable array of more than 1,000 courses and fifty-four major programs; plus, "you can cross-register at MIT (and to a limited extent at Brandeis, Babson, and Olin.)" From research to internships to overseas studies, Wellesley "provides great resources and opportunities to all its students."

BANG FOR YOUR BUCK

With an endowment worth more than $1.5 billion, Wellesley is rolling in the riches. Admission is completely need-blind for U.S. citizens and permanent residents. If you get admitted (no easy task), Wellesley will meet 100 percent of your demonstrated financial need. Most financial aid comes in the form of a scholarship; it's free money, and you'll never have to pay it back. Packaged student loan amounts are correlated to family income. No student will graduate with more than $15,200 in packaged student loans. Students from families with a calculated income between $60,000-$100,000 will graduate with no more than $10,100 in packaged student loans. And students from families with the greatest need, with a calculated income of $60,000 or less, will graduate with $0 in packaged student loans.

STUDENT LIFE

Because Wellesley is an academically rigorous school full of driven women, "most of the weekday is spent in class or studying." But when students want to take a break from the books, "there are always seminars and panel discussions and cultural events to attend. The diverse community and the multitudes of campus groups means there's always something to do." Once the weekend hits, "there's a large split. There are girls that don't party, or hardly party. And then there are girls who party every weekend." "On campus parties are hard to find and are normally broken up because of a noise complaint from a studying neighbor." As such, "the girls who are interested in men frequently spend their weekends venturing off campus to MIT or Harvard for parties," or head into Boston for "a girl's night out—go to a movie, maybe see a play, go karaoke, or just have dinner in the city." But no matter how you want to spend your free time, Wellesley has you covered: "It's nice to know that whatever you feel like doing on a Friday night, you'll always have company—whether you want to stay in and watch a movie or go into Boston to party."

Wellesley College

FINANCIAL AID PHONE: 781-283-2360 • E-MAIL: ADMISSION@WELLESLEY.EDU • FAX: 781-283-3678 • WEBSITE: WWW.WELLESLEY.EDU

CAREER

The typical Wellesley woman is often described as "career oriented" by her peers, and fortunately "Wellesley has an amazing alumni network and a career service center that helps students gain access to all sorts of job, internship, and community service opportunities." The Center for Work and Service offers ample resources, including career advising, help with finding jobs and internships, and tools for students seeking to continue their education in graduate school. True to its name, the center also offers guidance for women looking for service opportunities within existing organizations on and off-campus, and even offers funding for students looking to start their own initiatives. The support doesn't end after students graduate: "Wellesley's alumnae network is one of the strongest I found in my college research, and Wellesley's career placement services will assist alumnae no matter how much time has passed since they graduated."

GENERAL INFO

Activities: Choral groups, dance, debate society, drama/theater, jazz band, literary magazine, music ensembles, neuroscience club, quidditch team, radio station, Shakespeare society, student government, student newspaper, student-run film society, symphony orchestra, ultimate frisbee team, yearbook, campus ministries, international student organizations. **Organizations:** 160 registered organizations, 6 honor societies, 30 religious organizations. **Athletics (Intercollegiate):** *Women:* Basketball, crew/rowing, cross-country, diving, fencing, field hockey, golf, lacrosse, soccer, softball, squash, swimming, tennis, track/field, volleyball.

FINANCIAL AID

Students should submit: FAFSA, CSS/Financial Aid PROFILE, Noncustodial PROFILE. Priority filing deadline is 3/1. The Princeton Review suggests that all financial aid forms be submitted as soon as possible after October 1. *Need-based scholarships/grants offered:* Federal Pell, FSEOG, State scholarships/grants, Private scholarships, College/university scholarship or grant aid from institutional funds. *Loan aid offered:* Direct Subsidized Stafford Loans, Direct Unsubsidized Stafford Loans, Direct PLUS loans, Federal Perkins Loans, State Loans, College/university loans from institutional funds. Applicants will be notified of awards on or about 4/1. Federal Work-Study Program available. Institutional employment available.

BOTTOM LINE

The total cost for a year of tuition, fees, and room and board at Wellesley is over $63,900. However, this school has the financial resources to provide a tremendous amount of financial aid. Your aid package is likely to be quite extensive, and students leave with just $12,455 in loan debt on average. That's chump change for an education worth more than $250,000.

CAREER INFORMATION FROM PAYSCALE.COM

ROI rating	90
Bachelor's and No Higher	
Median starting salary	$49,000
Median mid-career salary	$78,400
At Least Bachelor's	
Median starting salary	$49,900
Median mid-career salary	$83,700
% alumni with high job meaning	59%
% STEM	15%

SELECTIVITY

Admissions Rating	96
# of applicants	4,667
% of applicants accepted	30
% of acceptees attending	42
# offered a place on the wait list	1,182
% accepting a place on wait list	58
% admitted from wait list	12
# of early decision applicants	354
% accepted early decision	42

FRESHMAN PROFILE

Range SAT Critical Reading	650–740
Range SAT Math	640–740
Range SAT Writing	670–750
Range ACT Composite	30–33
% graduated top 10% of class	78
% graduated top 25% of class	97
% graduated top 50% of class	100

DEADLINES

Early decision	
Deadline	11/1
Notification	12/15
Regular	
Deadline	1/15
Notification	4/1
Nonfall registration?	No

FINANCIAL FACTS

Financial Aid Rating	97
Annual tuition	$48,510
Room and board	$15,114
Required fees	$292
Average need-based scholarship	$46,012
% needy frosh rec. need-based scholarship or grant aid	96
% needy UG rec. need-based scholarship or grant aid	97
% needy frosh rec. non-need-based scholarship or grant aid	0
% needy UG rec. non-need-based scholarship or grant aid	0
% needy frosh rec. need-based self-help aid	91
% needy UG rec. need-based self-help aid	90
% frosh rec. any financial aid	61
% UG rec. any financial aid	61
% frosh need fully met	100
Average % of frosh need met	100
Average % of ugrad need met	100

₂esleyan University

ᵥYLLYS AVENUE, MIDDLETOWN, CT 06459-0265 • ADMISSIONS: 860-685-3000 • FAX: 860-685-3001

CAMPUS LIFE

Quality of Life Rating	**91**
Fire Safety Rating	**93**
Green Rating	**95**
Type of school	Private
Affiliation	No Affiliation
Environment	Town

STUDENTS

Total undergrad enrollment	2,897
% male/female	47/53
% from out of state	92
% frosh from public high school	50
% frosh live on campus	100
% ugrads live on campus	99
# of fraternities (% ugrad men join)	4 (10)
# of sororities (% ugrad women join)	1 (3)
% African American	8
% Asian	8
% Caucasian	53
% Hispanic	11
% Native American	<1
% Pacific Islander	<1
% Two or more races	6
% Race and/or ethnicity unknown	6
% international	9
# of countries represented	55

ACADEMICS

Academic Rating	**95**
% students returning for sophomore year	95
% students graduating within 4 years	92
% students graduating within 6 years	94
Calendar	Semester
Student/faculty ratio	8:1
Profs interesting rating	92
Profs accessible rating	89

Most classes have 10–19 students.
Most lab/discussion sessions have
 10–19 students.

MOST POPULAR MAJORS
Psychology; Economics

ABOUT THE COLLEGE
Wesleyan University is a member of the historic Little Three colleges along with Amherst and Williams Colleges, and has long been known as one of the "Little Ivies." Just like an Ivy League school, Wesleyan is home to exceptional academics, fantastic resources, and brilliant students. "Wesleyan was a clear fit for me based on the artistic and diverse environment and the academic possibilities offered," says one junior. There are no required core courses at Wesleyan, giving each student the opportunity to chart their own intellectual path. "Academically, the university is in ranks with the most elite American universities, but it has a special social quirkiness that really sets it apart." As a result, the university attracts students with a high level of intellectual interest and curiosity. "I knew it would allow me to grow," says one student, "[and] become someone that I would look up to. At other schools, I just would have been comfortable and would have stayed the same." Professors are passionate about their work and are always available to meet with students outside of class. Breaking bread at a professor's home is not uncommon for students. "Whether in a class of seven, or a class of 100, my professors have always gone out of their way to help me in whatever I was struggling with; or sometimes just to get to know me," tells one senior. Wesleyan's rigorous academics produce the goods: the university produces more history doctorates per undergraduate history major than nearly any other college or university in the United States, and medical, dental, and veterinary school acceptances have ranged from 65 to 75 percent in recent years.

BANG FOR YOUR BUCK
There's a Wesleyan alum wherever you go, and a Wesleyan degree will open doors for you for the rest of your life. The university eliminates loans in the financial aid package for most families with incomes under $60,000 and reduces packaged loans for other low income families so that many financial aid students can graduate with no loans or much reduced loan indebtedness. A student reveals that she "received a very good financial aid packet." The average freshman grant is $42,797.

STUDENT LIFE
Wesleyan is a top-notch school and as such, it's not surprising that students spend a lot of time on their studies. However "most Wes students get all their work done and still have time to go out and have fun. This is not easy, but well worth it." Many students site the incredible diversity of activities and interests on campus as one of their favorite things about the school. "People go to performances, sporting events, lectures, protests, restaurants, open mics, parties, campus events...etc.," raves one happy student. "Anything from an Indian dance festival to an open forum on the economic recession to a frat party that is also a charity event for a school in Kenya." More broadly, a nearly universal sentiment among students at Wesleyan is that the "incredible" students themselves are the greatest assets the campus has to offer. "Everyone is passionate about something: maybe it is their coursework, video games, theater, but there is always SOMETHING." "I chose Wesleyan because of the engaging and open-minded students I met when I visited there," says a senior, "four years later, the student body is still my favorite part of Wes."

Wesleyan University

FINANCIAL AID: 860-685-2800 • E-MAIL: ADMISSIONS@WESLEYAN.EDU • WEBSITE: WWW.WESLEYAN.EDU

CAREER

The Career Center at Wesleyan offers a number of services and resources for students looking to explore their interests and plan for their futures. One-on-one academic and career counseling is available; the Center sponsors career fairs and offers resources to help students network with alumni and prospective employers; it schedules workshops to help student build their professional and job-seeing skills; and it also provides a variety of resources for students looking for opportunities overseas. Students seem happy with the opportunities the school affords them, and report that "there's not a single class I've taken here that I won't carry with me after college." Out of Wesleyan alumni visiting PayScale.com, an unusually high 62 percent report feeling as though they derive meaning from their jobs.

GENERAL INFO

Activities: Choral groups, concert band, dance, drama/theater, jazz band, literary magazine, music ensembles, musical theater, pep band, radio station, student government, student newspaper, student-run film society, symphony orchestra, yearbook, campus ministries. **Organizations:** 220 registered organizations, 2 honor societies, 10 religious organizations. 4 fraternities, 1 sorority. **Athletics (Intercollegiate):** *Men:* Baseball, basketball, crew/rowing, cross-country, diving, football, golf, ice hockey, lacrosse, soccer, squash, swimming, tennis, track/field (outdoor), track/field (indoor), wrestling. *Women:* Basketball, crew/rowing, cross-country, diving, field hockey, ice hockey, lacrosse, soccer, softball, squash, swimming, tennis, track/field (outdoor), track/field (indoor), volleyball.

FINANCIAL AID

Students should submit: FAFSA, CSS/Financial Aid PROFILE, Noncustodial PROFILE. Regular filing deadline is 2/15. The Princeton Review suggests that all financial aid forms be submitted as soon as possible after October 1. *Need-based scholarships/grants offered:* Federal Pell, FSEOG, State scholarships/grants, Private scholarships, College/university scholarship or grant aid from institutional funds. *Loan aid offered:* Direct Subsidized Stafford Loans, Direct Unsubsidized Stafford Loans, Direct PLUS loans, Federal Perkins Loans, College/university loans from institutional funds. Applicants will be notified of awards on or about 4/1. Federal Work-Study Program available. Institutional employment available.

BOTTOM LINE

The total retail price here for tuition, room and board, and everything else comes to about $65,500 per year. Financial aid here is beyond generous, though, and the full financial need of all undergraduate students is met with a combination of loans, part-time employment, and grants.

CAREER INFORMATION FROM PAYSCALE.COM

ROI rating	**90**
Bachelor's and No Higher	
Median starting salary	$46,400
Median mid-career salary	$97,600
At Least Bachelor's	
Median starting salary	$48,500
Median mid-career salary	$103,000
% alumni with high job meaning	53%
% STEM	16%

SELECTIVITY

Admissions Rating	96
# of applicants	9,822
% of applicants accepted	22
% of acceptees attending	35
# offered a place on the wait list	1,877
% accepting a place on wait list	47
% admitted from wait list	1
# of early decision applicants	960
% accepted early decision	39

FRESHMAN PROFILE

Range SAT Critical Reading	620–730
Range SAT Math	630–740
Range SAT Writing	630–750
Range ACT Composite	29–33
Minimum paper TOEFL	600
Minimum internet-based TOEFL	100
% graduated top 10% of class	72
% graduated top 50% of class	100

DEADLINES

Early decision	
Deadline	11/15
Notification	12/15
Regular	
Deadline	1/1
Notification	4/1
Nonfall registration?	No

FINANCIAL FACTS

Financial Aid Rating	96
Annual tuition	$50,312
Room and board	$14,904
Required fees	$300
Average need-based scholarship	$41,244
% needy frosh rec. need-based scholarship or grant aid	92
% needy UG rec. need-based scholarship or grant aid	95
% needy frosh rec. non-need-based scholarship or grant aid	1
% needy UG rec. non-need-based scholarship or grant aid	1
% needy frosh rec. need-based self-help aid	92
% needy UG rec. need-based self-help aid	95
% frosh rec. any financial aid	53
% UG rec. any financial aid	48
% UG borrow to pay for school	45
Average cumulative indebtedness	$24,860
% frosh need fully met	100
% ugrads need fully met	100
Average % of frosh need met	100
Average % of ugrad need met	100

Wheaton College (IL)

501 COLLEGE AVENUE, WHEATON, IL 60187 • ADMISSIONS: 800-222-2419 • FAX: 630-752-5285

ABOUT THE SCHOOL

A Christian liberal arts college located just outside of Chicago, Wheaton College combines nationally recognized academic excellence with a mission that emphasizes Christian faith. The school's motto, "For Christ and His Kingdom," reflects Wheaton's ethos that education empowers students to build a stronger church and work for the betterment of society as a whole. The school offers over forty majors including six in the highly regarded Conservatory of Music, and "prepares [students] for working and serving in the real world" through numerous study abroad programs, academic exchanges, and outreach initiatives. Given the school's top-notch reputation and low student-to-teacher ratio, it's not surprising students rave about their professors. Students are "continually astounded at the quality of the professors" who "express a level of enthusiasm for their respective subjects that their students cannot help but catch." Students universally praise faculty members who "make a huge effort to get to know [us] personally" and "genuinely want to help us grow in both our academics and our faith as Christians." For students, Wheaton offers "a place where [their] values will be represented while being challenged in an environment that is respected well outside of [their] sphere."

BANG FOR YOUR BUCK

Wheaton College offers both need-based and merit-based financial assistance in the form of grants, scholarships (including three new Presidential Leadership Awards for 2016-17), loans, and work-study. In addition to participating in a number of Federal and State assistance programs, the school offers need-based Wheaton Grants of up to $25,000 as well as many opportunities for other scholarships. Department-specific merit scholarships are available in many subjects, such as Physics, Engineering, and Education, and to students in the Conservatory of Music. Wheaton also expresses a commitment to "Christ-Centered Diversity" and multiculturalism, and offers scholarships to students of color, international students, and students from underserved communities. A debt forgiveness program is also available for students and alums who become missionaries. In 2014 Wheaton introduces several new programs, such as the merit-based Arthur Holmes Faith and Learning scholarship of $20,000 payable over four years, and a Yellow Ribbon Program that works with the VA to make additional funds available to veterans. Overall, 79 percent of Wheaton undergraduates are receiving financial aid, making it a solid choice for students who may require some assistance in paying for college.

STUDENT LIFE

Though rigorous academics often mean that "you can't expect to have a ton of free time at Wheaton," students still "love to hang out and do fun things together in addition to working hard in their classes." Spiritual life and worship is a huge part of the Wheaton experience, and in keeping with Wheaton's Christian values "alcohol is not allowed in any of the dorms and even off-campus students may not drink during the semester." So while a few students party and drink, most "do the fun part without alcohol or drugs." Instead, students "are tasked with creating their own fun" by "watching films, attending special lectures, and participating in school-sponsored events such as swing dances, winter formals, and the Christian concert series." Additionally, many students cite intense conversations with friends about "our relationships with Christ, our hopes and dreams, what we find interesting in the world," as one of their favorite aspects of student life, saying that "lengthy discussions that drag on into the wee hours are fairly common." Additionally, Wheaton students frequently travel into Chicago on weekends to eat, shop, or just hang out, made possible by a train system that is easily accessible from campus.

Wheaton College (IL)

FINANCIAL AID: 630-752-5021 • E-MAIL: ADMISSIONS@WHEATON.EDU • WEBSITE: WHEATON.EDU

CAREER

Wheaton's Center for Vocation and Career offers a number of services including one-on-one career counseling, job fairs and networking opportunities, and professional development activities such as resume critique and mock interviews. "Students look constantly toward the future," have "high goals," and are "career-minded," and the school largely satisfies their needs. Students feel that "a Wheaton education reaches beyond the classroom to developing all aspects of the student in preparation for future life and vocation." Similarly, "Wheaton has changed me for the best and has brought me to a point where I feel ready to enter the professional world." Many majors require internships for which students can turn to alumni in the WiN network for networking and leads. Of Wheaton alumni visiting PayScale.com, 62 percent report feeling as though their job has a high level of meaning.

GENERAL INFO

Activities: Choral groups, concert band, dance, drama/theater, jazz band, literary magazine, music ensembles, musical theater, opera, pep band, student government, student newspaper, student-run film society, symphony orchestra, Campus Ministries, International Student Organization, Model UN. **Organizations:** 85 registered organizations, 13 honor societies, 12 religious organizations. **Athletics (Intercollegiate):** *Men:* baseball, basketball, cross-country, football, golf, soccer, swimming, tennis, track/field (outdoor), track/field (indoor), wrestling. *Women:* basketball, cross-country, golf, soccer, softball, swimming, tennis, track/field (outdoor), track/field (indoor), volleyball. **On-Campus Highlights:** Billy Graham Center - archive, museum, Wade Center - English authors collections, Meyer Science Center, Todd M. Beamer Student Center, Wheaton College Center for Faith, Politics and Economics.

FINANCIAL AID

Students should submit: FAFSA, Institution's own financial aid form. Priority filing deadline is 12/1. The Princeton Review suggests that all financial aid forms be submitted as soon as possible after October 1. *Need-based scholarships/grants offered:* Federal Pell, FSEOG, State scholarships/grants, Private scholarships, College/university scholarship or grant aid from institutional funds. *Loan aid offered:* Direct Subsidized Stafford Loans, Direct Unsubsidized Stafford Loans, Direct PLUS loans, Federal Perkins Loans. Applicants will be notified of awards on a rolling basis beginning 3/1. Federal Work-Study Program available. Institutional employment available.

THE BOTTOM LINE

Tuition for a year at Wheaton College is listed as $34,050, with room and board totaling an additional $9,560. Combined with books and supplies, students can expect to spend approximately $44,410 per year to attend Wheaton. This is somewhat less than many private schools, and the college offers a number of financial aid programs, with 100 percent of need-qualifying freshman students receiving need-based financial aid at an average award of around $22,035 in total gift aid. So for students looking for a top-tier education in a Christian environment, Wheaton College offers an exciting and accessible opportunity.

CAREER INFORMATION FROM PAYSCALE.COM

ROI rating	88
Bachelor's and No Higher	
Median starting salary	$43,500
Median mid-career salary	$90,200
At Least Bachelor's	
Median starting salary	$44,500
Median mid-career salary	$89,400
% alumni with high job meaning	73%
% STEM	10%

SELECTIVITY

Admissions Rating	90
# of applicants	1,971
% of applicants accepted	70
% of acceptees attending	44
# offered a place on the wait list	409
% accepting a place on wait list	29
% admitted from wait list	27

FRESHMAN PROFILE

Range SAT Critical Reading	600–710
Range SAT Math	600–700
Range SAT Writing	590–700
Range ACT Composite	27–32
Minimum paper TOEFL	587
Minimum internet-based TOEFL	95
Average HS GPA	3.7
% graduated top 10% of class	54
% graduated top 25% of class	81
% graduated top 50% of class	96

DEADLINES

Early action	
Deadline	11/1
Notification	12/31
Regular	
Deadline	1/10
Notification	4/1
Nonfall registration?	Yes

FINANCIAL FACTS

Financial Aid Rating	84
Annual tuition	$34,050
Room and board	$9,560
Average need-based scholarship	$21,380
% needy frosh rec. need-based scholarship or grant aid	100
% needy UG rec. need-based scholarship or grant aid	99
% needy frosh rec. non-need-based scholarship or grant aid	35
% needy UG rec. non-need-based scholarship or grant aid	32
% needy frosh rec. need-based self-help aid	75
% needy UG rec. need-based self-help aid	77
% frosh rec. any financial aid	86
% UG rec. any financial aid	79
% UG borrow to pay for school	58
Average cumulative indebtedness	$26,593
% frosh need fully met	26
% ugrads need fully met	26
Average % of frosh need met	88
Average % of ugrad need met	87

Whitman College

345 Boyer Ave, Walla Walla, WA 99362 • Admissions: 509-527-5176 • Fax: 509-527-4967

CAMPUS LIFE

Quality of Life Rating	**96**
Fire Safety Rating	**81**
Green Rating	**76**
Type of school	Private
Affiliation	No Affiliation
Environment	Town

STUDENTS

Total undergrad enrollment	1,470
% male/female	42/58
% from out of state	64
% frosh live on campus	100
% ugrads live on campus	64
# of fraternities (% ugrad men join)	4 (44)
# of sororities (% ugrad women join)	4 (44)
% African American	1
% Asian	5
% Caucasian	73
% Hispanic	7
% Native American	<1
% Pacific Islander	0
% Two or more races	7
% Race and/or ethnicity unknown	2
% international	5
# of countries represented	27

ACADEMICS

Academic Rating	**97**
% students returning for sophomore year	93
% students graduating within 4 years	79
% students graduating within 6 years	87
Calendar	Semester
Student/faculty ratio	8:1
Profs interesting rating	97
Profs accessible rating	98

Most classes have 10–19 students.
Most lab/discussion sessions have 10–19 students.

MOST POPULAR MAJORS
Biology; Psychology; Economics

ABOUT THE SCHOOL

Whitman College attracts students who represent the Whitman mosaic: down-to-earth high achievers with diverse interests. One student says, "I wanted to attend a college where I would be intellectually challenged and stimulated. Now that I'm a second-semester senior, I can say that what I've learned in my classes at Whitman will benefit me for the rest of my life." The college is known for combining academic excellence with a down-to-earth, collaborative culture, which includes "professors who take the time to chat with students, invite them to dinner in their homes, organize field trips, [and] enlist students to help them in their research projects." For a real-life example, look no further than Whitman's tradition of awarding summer, annual, and per-semester grants for student-faculty research collaboration, aimed at turning each student into a "whole, intelligent, [and] interesting person." "Internships, study abroad, work, research opportunities (in and out of the sciences) are abundant at Whitman. Grants are easily accessible for those who have valid reason to seek them." The recently established Whitman Internship Grant program provides a stipend of approximately $2,500 to students completing unpaid summer internships that are relevant to their educational goals and career interests. It allows them to get creative with internships and to take part in opportunities that best match their academic or career interests. "Whitman has so many strengths, but I think the most important is that the students and faculty at Whitman promote and maintain a great, collaborative, and intellectually active atmosphere for academics," says one student.

BANG FOR YOUR BUCK

A full suite of scholarships are on offer here, covering up to the full cost of tuition and fees for four years. Highlights include the Whitman awards, which are renewable, four-year merit-based scholarships, ranging from $9,000 to $14,000 to entering students who have excelled academically. Whitman's Paul Garrett and Claire Sherwood Memorial Scholarships range from $2,500 to $50,000 depending on demonstrated financial need. The scholarship includes a trip to NYC to visit corporate headquarters and graduate schools on the East Coast. The Eells Scholarship covers the full cost of tuition for four years and includes a research grant. Talent awards are available in art, music, and theater. Whitman's outside scholarship policy allows students to add scholarships they receive from non-Whitman sources on top of the college's awarded scholarship up to the total budget.

STUDENT LIFE

Whitman students widely report that the school is a "work hard, play hard" kind of place. While students "do not let partying or other non-academic endeavors get in the way of their studies," they find many ways to unwind and have fun. They cite games and sports, from organized intramural events to pick-up Frisbee on the lawn, as a constant activity, especially in nice weather. On the weekends there are plentiful parties thrown by fraternities, clubs, or informal groups of friends, but "there is also absolutely no pressure to drink or do drugs." There are also "many school-sponsored dances and events that are well-attended," and Whitman often brings in guest lecturers, "cool indie bands," and other acts to entertain students. The school also sponsors "numerous outdoor program trips and activities, like hiking, cliff jumping, kayaking, climbing, etc." And no matter where their interests lie students love to spend time with their peers, who provide "the perfect combination of silliness and actually being able to have an intelligent and enlightening conversation."

Whitman College

FINANCIAL AID: 509-527-5178 • E-MAIL: ADMISSION@WHITMAN.EDU • WEBSITE: WWW.WHITMAN.EDU

CAREER

Whitman's Student Engagement Center provides a number of services to help students prepare for life after college. It offers traditional resources like job and internship search tools, career counseling, help with resumes and cover letters, and career fairs. The school also organizes "Whitman Hubs" in several cities to provide students and alumni with professional networking opportunities. The SEC sponsors special events and programs geared towards students interested in entrepreneurship and community service. Many students praise the career resources that the school offers, and of Whitman alumni visiting PayScale.com, 49 percent report that they derive meaning from their jobs.

GENERAL INFO

Activities: Choral groups, concert band, dance, drama/theater, jazz band, literary magazines, music ensembles, musical theater, radio station, student government, student newspaper, student-run film series, symphony orchestra, campus ministries, international student organization. **Organizations:** 80 registered organizations, 3 honor societies, 7 religious organizations. 4 fraternities, 4 sororities. **Athletics (Intercollegiate):** *Men:* Baseball, basketball, cross-country, golf, soccer, swimming, tennis. *Women:* Basketball, cross-country, golf, lacrosse, soccer, swimming, tennis, volleyball. **On-Campus Highlights:** Reid Campus Center, Penrose Library.

FINANCIAL AID

Students should submit: FAFSA, CSS/Financial Aid PROFILE, Noncustodial PROFILE. Regular filing deadline is 2/1. The Princeton Review suggests that all financial aid forms be submitted as soon as possible after October 1. *Need-based scholarships/grants offered:* Federal Pell, FSEOG, State scholarships/grants, Private scholarships, College/university scholarship or grant aid from institutional funds. *Loan aid offered:* Direct Subsidized Stafford Loans, Direct Unsubsidized Stafford Loans, Direct PLUS loans, Federal Perkins Loans. Applicants will be notified of awards on or about 4/1. Federal Work-Study Program available. Institutional employment available.

BOTTOM LINE

Whitman College is one of the nation's top liberal arts colleges. The total cost of tuition, room and board, and everything else adds up to around $57,700 per year. Both need-based and merit aid is available to help offset costs. Every spring, Whitman offers a financial-planning night that addresses not only loans but also financial issues for graduating students. Whitman offers internships during the summer that allow the students to work in the same area as their degree and hopefully help with employment when they graduate.

CAREER INFORMATION FROM PAYSCALE.COM

ROI rating	90
Bachelor's and No Higher	
Median starting salary	$42,400
Median mid-career salary	$101,000
At Least Bachelor's	
Median starting salary	$44,800
Median mid-career salary	$104,000
% alumni with high job meaning	55%
% STEM	25%

SELECTIVITY

Admissions Rating	93
# of applicants	3,790
% of applicants accepted	43
% of acceptees attending	22
# offered a place on the wait list	872
% accepting a place on wait list	42
% admitted from wait list	18
# of early decision applicants	166
% accepted early decision	76

FRESHMAN PROFILE

Range SAT Critical Reading	600–720
Range SAT Math	600–700
Range SAT Writing	600–700
Range ACT Composite	27–32
Minimum paper TOEFL	560
Minimum internet-based TOEFL	85
Average HS GPA	3.7
% graduated top 10% of class	54
% graduated top 25% of class	88
% graduated top 50% of class	98

DEADLINES

Early decision	
Deadline	11/15
Notification	12/20
Regular	
Priority	11/15
Deadline	1/15
Notification	4/1
Nonfall registration?	Yes

FINANCIAL FACTS

Financial Aid Rating	87
Annual tuition	$45,770
Room and board	$11,564
Required fees	$368
Average need-based scholarship	$30,721
% needy frosh rec. need-based scholarship or grant aid	100
% needy UG rec. need-based scholarship or grant aid	100
% needy frosh rec. non-need-based scholarship or grant aid	37
% needy UG rec. non-need-based scholarship or grant aid	42
% needy frosh rec. need-based self-help aid	78
% needy UG rec. need-based self-help aid	81
% frosh rec. any financial aid	80
% UG rec. any financial aid	77
% UG borrow to pay for school	47
Average cumulative indebtedness	$21,192
% frosh need fully met	49
% ugrads need fully met	42

Willamette University

900 State Street, Salem, OR 97301 • Admissions: 844-232-7228 • Fax: 503-375-5363

CAMPUS LIFE

Quality of Life Rating	**91**
Fire Safety Rating	**98**
Green Rating	**98**
Type of school	Private
Affiliation	Methodist
Environment	City

STUDENTS

Total undergrad enrollment	1,905
% male/female	44/56
% from out of state	78
% frosh from public high school	75
% frosh live on campus	99
% ugrads live on campus	68
# of fraternities (% ugrad men join)	4 (28)
# of sororities (% ugrad women join)	4 (25)
% African American	2
% Asian	9
% Caucasian	62
% Hispanic	12
% Native American	1
% Pacific Islander	<1
% Two or more races	10
% Race and/or ethnicity unknown	2
% international	1
# of countries represented	14

ACADEMICS

Academic Rating	**92**
% students returning for sophomore year	87
% students graduating within 4 years	71
% students graduating within 6 years	79
Calendar	Semester
Student/faculty ratio	10:1
Profs interesting rating	94
Profs accessible rating	91
Most classes have 10–19 students.	
Most lab/discussion sessions have 10–19 students.	

MOST POPULAR MAJORS
Biology; Economics; Psychology

ABOUT THE SCHOOL

As soon as you set foot on Willamette University's campus, you instantly feel the "great [sense of] community" that surrounds you. And with its "great reputation" and countless "study abroad and internship opportunities" enrolling here is a no-brainer for many students. Importantly, Willamette's "small size fosters a support system that allows students to branch out and be involved with a wide range of academic and extracurricular activities." Students also appreciate the school's liberal arts curriculum, quickly highlighting the "strong" biology and psychology programs along with an "amazing" politics department. Just as essential, undergrads generally feel "respected" by both professors and the administration and mention that all parties "are very receptive to new ideas." And, of course, accessibility is paramount. As one senior boasts, "It's not unusual to be asked to dinner at a professor's house . . . and there is no one—not even our president—who doesn't have open office hours, or isn't willing to make an appointment to meet with a student."

BANG FOR YOUR BUCK

Undergrads at Willamette really value the diversity found on their campus. And many chalk that up to a stellar financial aid office. An art history major explains, "The student body is more than just rich white kids. People come from everywhere and it's the financial aid packages that make it possible." Still skeptical? Well, the average aid package doled out to undergrads is $33,652. Though, we should mention that the average need-based loan is $5,335. Fortunately, there are also plenty of merit scholarships to be had. And the beauty is that all applicants are automatically considered, so there's no additional paperwork.

STUDENT LIFE

Don't let their laid back demeanor fool you; Willamette undergrads are a busy and active lot. As one student shares, "There is a huge population that is involved in clubs on campus, anything from soccer club to juggling club or knitting club." These Bearcats are also full of school spirit. Hence they "love to support varsity sports teams, attend theatre productions [and] listen to our a cappella groups perform." We're also told that "parties happen" but "they're low-key compared to larger schools." Finally, there's plenty to take advantage of when students are itching to get off-campus. Undergrads frequently "take trips to Portland and the ocean, and also head out to the mountains for skiing as well as hiking along paths decorated with waterfalls."

Willamette University

FINANCIAL AID: 877-744-3736 • E-MAIL: BEARCAT@WILLAMETTE.EDU • WEBSITE: WWW.WILLAMETTE.EDU

CAREER

Willamette students are surrounded by professional opportunity. Though hometown Salem might not be a bustling metropolis, undergrads insist that plenty of job possibilities exist, especially given that "the capitol [building is] across the street to one side, and the [Salem] hospital to the other." Moreover, students don't have to go the search alone. Indeed, "professors are very willing to help students find internships, jobs and research opportunities." And undergrads can surely turn to Career Services as well. The office provides everything from job postings to résumé advice. Additionally, students who are unsure of the professional path they want to pursue can receive career counseling and testing. And all undergrads may use the office to connect with successful alumni. Lastly, PayScale.com reports that the average starting salary for Willamette alums is $41,300.

GENERAL INFO

Activities: Choral groups, concert band, dance, drama/theater, jazz band, literary magazine, music ensembles, musical theater, opera, student government, student newspaper, student-run film society, symphony orchestra, Campus Ministries, International Student Organization, Model UN. **Organizations:** 107 registered organizations, 7 honor societies, 4 religious organizations. 4 fraternities, 4 sororities. **Athletics (Intercollegiate):** *Men:* baseball, basketball, cross-country, football, golf, soccer, swimming, tennis, track/field (outdoor), track/field (indoor). *Women:* basketball, cross-country, golf, soccer, softball, swimming, tennis, track/field (outdoor), track/field (indoor), volleyball. **On-Campus Highlights:** Hallie Ford Museum of Art, Montag Student Center, Sparks Athletic Center, Willamette Bistro, Mill Stream and Star Trees on campus.

FINANCIAL AID

Students should submit: FAFSA. Priority filing deadline is 2/1. The Princeton Review suggests that all financial aid forms be submitted as soon as possible after October 1. *Need-based scholarships/grants offered:* Federal Pell, FSEOG, State scholarships/grants, Private scholarships, College/university scholarship or grant aid from institutional funds. *Loan aid offered:* Direct Subsidized Stafford Loans, Direct Unsubsidized Stafford Loans, Direct PLUS loans, Federal Perkins Loans. Applicants will be notified of awards on a rolling basis beginning 4/1. Federal Work-Study Program available. Institutional employment available.

THE BOTTOM LINE

Tuition at Willamette generally runs undergrads (and their families) $46,900. In addition, those students opting to live on-campus will likely pay another $11,600 for room and board. Beyond that, the university also charges $317 in required fees. Lastly, undergrads should anticipate spending approximately $950 on books and other academic supplies.

CAREER INFORMATION FROM PAYSCALE.COM

ROI rating	**86**
Bachelor's and No Higher	
Median starting salary	$42,000
Median mid-career salary	$85,200
At Least Bachelor's	
Median starting salary	$43,600
Median mid-career salary	$87,500
% alumni with high job meaning	62%
% STEM	17%

SELECTIVITY

Admissions Rating	**87**
# of applicants	6,332
% of applicants accepted	78
% of acceptees attending	11
# offered a place on the wait list	433
% accepting a place on wait list	39
% admitted from wait list	32

FRESHMAN PROFILE

Range SAT Critical Reading	550–670
Range SAT Math	550–660
Range SAT Writing	550–650
Range ACT Composite	25–30
Minimum paper TOEFL	560
Minimum internet-based TOEFL	85
Average HS GPA	3.8
% graduated top 10% of class	40
% graduated top 25% of class	73
% graduated top 50% of class	97

DEADLINES

Early decision	
Deadline	11/15
Notification	12/31
Early action	
Deadline	11/15
Notification	12/31
Regular	
Priority	1/15
Notification	3/1
Nonfall registration?	Yes

FINANCIAL FACTS

Financial Aid Rating	**86**
Annual tuition	$46,900
Room and board	$11,600
Required fees	$317
Average need-based scholarship	$27,843
% needy frosh rec. need-based scholarship or grant aid	99
% needy UG rec. need-based scholarship or grant aid	99
% needy frosh rec. non-need-based scholarship or grant aid	26
% needy UG rec. non-need-based scholarship or grant aid	16
% needy frosh rec. need-based self-help aid	80
% needy UG rec. need-based self-help aid	79
% frosh rec. any financial aid	95
% UG rec. any financial aid	92
Average cumulative indebtedness	$26,643
% frosh need fully met	22
% ugrads need fully met	15
Average % of frosh need met	84

William Jewell College

500 COLLEGE HILL, LIBERTY, MO 64068 • ADMISSIONS: 816-781-7700 • FAX: 816-415-5040

CAMPUS LIFE

Quality of Life Rating	**90**
Fire Safety Rating	**88**
Green Rating	**60***
Type of school	Private
Environment	Town

STUDENTS

Total undergrad enrollment	1,053
% male/female	42/58
% from out of state	40
% frosh from public high school	90
% frosh live on campus	98
% ugrads live on campus	84
# of fraternities (% ugrad men join)	3 (34)
# of sororities (% ugrad women join)	4 (40)
% African American	4
% Asian	1
% Caucasian	78
% Hispanic	4
% Native American	<1
% Pacific Islander	<1
% Two or more races	6
% Race and/or ethnicity unknown	2
% international	5
# of countries represented	22

ACADEMICS

Academic Rating	**85**
% students returning for sophomore year	82
% students graduating within 4 years	56
% students graduating within 6 years	62
Calendar	Semester
Student/faculty ratio	10:1
Profs interesting rating	93
Profs accessible rating	92

Most classes have 10–19 students.
Most lab/discussion sessions have
 10–19 students.

MOST POPULAR MAJORS
Biology; Business Administration and
Management; Registered Nursing/
Registered Nurse

ABOUT THE SCHOOL

This small liberal arts college—enrollment is roughly 1,060 students—in rural Missouri "is all about being personal—both in classes and student life." One Political Science major sums up Jewell as "a serious school with serious students, wonderful professors, and a satisfying student life." Even though Liberty, Missouri, might not be on everyone's radar, Kansas City is within driving distance and students will frequent its restaurants and other attractions. "A typical student at Jewell," says a Business Administration major, "is . . . committed to academics but knows how to balance a social life as well. Students at Jewell fit in right away due to the [welcoming] upperclassmen." The small class sizes—the average student to professor ratio is 10:1—are important and students emphasize that they feel like individuals "not like a number." Students praise the "great" and "intelligent" professors and emphasize that "Jewell has strong academics and great athletics"—it's a Division II school—and "gives everyone the chance to feel . . . involved" due to the size of the student body.

BANG FOR YOUR BUCK

Though some students note the economic equality imbalance, others praise the school for its "substantial" financial aid and scholarships. The school meets an average of 67 percent of its students' demonstrated need and 99 percent of freshmen (and 96 percent of other undergraduates) receive some form of financial assistance; in 2014–2015, the school awarded $18.5 million in aid. Every student who applies to Jewell is automatically considered for academic, merit-based scholarships, says the school's website. Sports scholarships are common among the large number of student-athletes at Jewell and several students cite the generous sports-related financial aid offers as key motivators in choosing the school. The school's website also provides, in an easily searchable list separated by major, outside scholarships for current and prospective Jewell students.

STUDENT LIFE

"Jewell offers incredible opportunities to become involved," says one Political Science major. "My first year, I averaged sixteen meetings per week." It's "easy to become involved" on campus, where there are seventy registered student organizations. The school sponsors events like "free bowling, ice skating, [and] movies" and students often travel to Kansas City. Greek life plays a significant role on campus—there are four sororities and three fraternities. Roughly 36 percent of women join a sorority and 42 percent of men join a fraternity. A Nonprofit Leadership major notes that even as an "independent," it's easy to become "very close to numerous Greeks and also participate in many Greek events." Jewell is "like a big family" and you "cannot go anywhere on campus without running into a friendly face." As of fall of 2014, Jewell introduced "Jewellverse," a program that promises to provide an iPad Pro to all students and faculty—and to be replaced at the beginning of the junior year—to facilitate "mobile learning" and the move towards a "paperless campus."

William Jewell College

FINANCIAL AID: 816-415-5975 • E-MAIL: ADMISSION@WILLIAM.JEWELL.EDU • WEBSITE: WWW.JEWELL.EDU

CAREER

According to PayScale.com, the average starting salary for a Jewell graduate is roughly $45,700. Fifty-nine percent of Jewell graduates state that their careers are beneficial to making the world a better place. According to the school's website, 99 percent of Jewell graduates are employed or in graduate school within six months of graduation. On the school's Outcomes and Career Services pages, students are able to search a database of alumni in order to facilitate networking connections for potential jobs and internships. The school's proximity to Kansas City allows students to gain career experience in a variety of internship settings. One Psychology major notes that "if you're not in class, you're at an internship." Jewell offers seven-week, one-credit sessions for career planning multiple times throughout the year, as well as giving students the opportunity to apply to the Career Mentor Program, which matches them up with a professional in their chosen field.

GENERAL INFO

Activities: Choral groups, concert band, dance, drama/theater, jazz band, literary magazine, music ensembles, pep band, student government, student newspaper, symphony orchestra, Campus Ministries. **Organizations:** 70 registered organizations, 13 honor societies, 7 religious organizations. 3 fraternities, 4 sororities. **Athletics (Intercollegiate):** *Men:* baseball, basketball, cheerleading, cross-country, football, golf, soccer, swimming, tennis, track/field (outdoor), track/field (indoor). *Women:* basketball, cheerleading, cross-country, golf, soccer, softball, swimming, tennis, track/field (outdoor), track/field (indoor), volleyball. **On-Campus Highlights:** The Perch—campus coffee shop, Mabee Center— athletic facility, The Quad—central campus quadrangle, Yates-Gill College Union— student union building, Ely Triangle—first-year residence hall, Fitness Center.

FINANCIAL AID

Students should submit: FAFSA. Priority filing deadline is 3/1. The Princeton Review suggests that all financial aid forms be submitted as soon as possible after October 1. *Need-based scholarships/grants offered:* Federal Pell, FSEOG, State scholarships/grants, College/ university scholarship or grant aid from institutional funds. *Loan aid offered:* Federal Perkins Loans, Federal Nursing Loans. Applicants will be notified of awards on a rolling basis beginning 11/1. Federal Work-Study Program available. Institutional employment available.

BOTTOM LINE

A year at Jewell costs roughly $43,230: $32,210 for tuition, $9,280 for room and board, and $1,200 for books and supplies. The average need-based financial aid package for undergraduates is $23,550, while the average freshman receives roughly $21,698 in need-based gift aid. Sixty-eight percent of undergraduates have borrowed from one of the various loan programs; financial assistance is not available to international students. The typical Jewell student graduates with roughly $29,885 of debt.

SELECTIVITY

Admissions Rating	89
# of applicants	1,456
% of applicants accepted	49
% of acceptees attending	34

FRESHMAN PROFILE

Range SAT Critical Reading	500–640
Range SAT Math	490–620
Range ACT Composite	23–28
Minimum paper TOEFL	550
Minimum internet-based TOEFL	80
Average HS GPA	3.8
% graduated top 10% of class	30
% graduated top 25% of class	59
% graduated top 50% of class	90

DEADLINES

Priority	12/1
Nonfall registration?	Yes

FINANCIAL FACTS

Financial Aid Rating	85
Annual tuition	$32,210
Room and board	$9,280
Required fees	$720
Average need-based scholarship	$23,559
% needy frosh rec. need-based scholarship or grant aid	100
% needy UG rec. need-based scholarship or grant aid	94
% needy frosh rec. non-need-based scholarship or grant aid	100
% needy UG rec. non-need-based scholarship or grant aid	93
% needy frosh rec. need-based self-help aid	72
% needy UG rec. need-based self-help aid	75
% frosh rec. any financial aid	100
% UG rec. any financial aid	99
% UG borrow to pay for school	72
Average cumulative indebtedness	$31,581
% frosh need fully met	56
% ugrads need fully met	27
Average % of frosh need met	80
Average % of ugrad need met	78

CAREER INFORMATION FROM PAYSCALE.COM

ROI rating	86
Bachelor's and No Higher	
Median starting salary	$41,400
Median mid-career salary	$74,200
At Least Bachelor's	
Median starting salary	$41,200
Median mid-career salary	$75,500
% alumni with high job meaning	61%
% STEM	10%

Williams College

Box 487, WILLIAMSTOWN, MA 01267 • ADMISSIONS: 413-597-2211 • FAX: 413-597-4052

CAMPUS LIFE

Quality of Life Rating	68
Fire Safety Rating	60*
Green Rating	92
Type of school	Private
Affiliation	No Affiliation
Environment	Village

STUDENTS

Total undergrad enrollment	2,099
% male/female	49/51
% from out of state	87
% frosh live on campus	100
% ugrads live on campus	93
% African American	8
% Asian	12
% Caucasian	54
% Hispanic	13
% Native American	<1
% Pacific Islander	0
% Two or more races	6
% Race and/or ethnicity unknown	0
% international	8
# of countries represented	54

ACADEMICS

Academic Rating	94
% students returning for sophomore year	97
% students graduating within 4 years	88
% students graduating within 6 years	96
Calendar	4/1/4
Student/faculty ratio	7:1
Profs interesting rating	81
Profs accessible rating	85

Most classes have fewer than 10 students.
Most lab/discussion sessions have 10–19 students.

MOST POPULAR MAJORS
Economics; English; History

#25 COLLEGE THAT PAYS YOU BACK

ABOUT THE SCHOOL

Founded in 1793, Williams College emphasizes the learning that takes place in the creation of a functioning community: life in the residence halls, expression through the arts, debates on political issues, leadership in campus governance, exploration of personal identity, pursuit of spiritual and religious impulses, the challenge of athletics, and direct engagement with human needs. The school is an "amalgamation of the most thoughtful, quirky, and smart people that you will ever meet as an undergraduate." The rigorous academic experience "is truly excellent," and a typical student says, "I feel like I am learning thoroughly." Professors are accessible and dedicated. Distinctive academic programs include Oxford-style tutorials between two students and a faculty member that call for intense research and weekly debates. These tutorial programs offer students an opportunity to take a heightened form of responsibility for their own intellectual development. In January, a four-week Winter Study term allows students to take unique, hands-on pass/fail classes.

BANG FOR YOUR BUCK

The endowment at Williams approaches $2 billion. That's substantially more than the annual gross domestic product of most countries. This colossal stash bountifully subsidizes costs for all students, including the cost of books and course materials for any student receiving financial aid and the costs to study all over the world. The fact that Williams is simply awash in money also enables the school to maintain a need-blind admission program for domestic students—including those who are undocumented or have DACA status—and meets 100% of the demonstrated need of all students. More than half of the college's international students—60% to be exact—receive financial aid and their average grant exceeds $60,000 annually. Merit-based scholarships are a historical artifact here. All financial aid is based purely on need. Williams also offers a generous financial aid program for international students. Convincing this school that you belong here is the difficult part. If you can just get admitted, Williams guarantees that it will meet 100 percent of your financial need for four years. You will walk away with a degree from one of the best schools in the country with little to no debt.

STUDENT LIFE

The typical Williams student is "quirky, passionate, zany, and fun." As one junior reports, "Williams is a place where normal social labels tend not to apply . . . So that football player in your theater class has amazing insight on Checkhov and that outspoken environmental activist also specializes in improv comedy." Nestled in the picturesque Berkshires of Massachusetts, campus is "stunning" and secluded, which means there is a real sense of community and caring here. Entertainment options include "lots of" performances, art exhibits, plays, and lectures. Some students have a healthy "obsession" with a cappella groups, and intramurals are popular, especially Ultimate Frisbee and broomball ("a sacred tradition involving a hockey rink, sneakers, a rubber ball, and paddles"). On Mountain Day, a unique fall tradition, bells ring announcing the cancellation of classes for the day, and students hike Stony Ledge to celebrate with donuts, cider, and, of course, a cappella performances. Opportunities for outdoor activities abound.

Williams College

FINANCIAL AID: 413-597-4181 • E-MAIL: ADMISSION@WILLIAMS.EDU • WEBSITE: WWW.WILLIAMS.EDU

CAREER

The Career Center at Williams empowers students to forge their own career path and gives them all the tools they need to get started. Each semester's calendar is packed with informational sessions, and cover letter writing or job fair success workshops. The aptly named "Who Am I & Where Am I Going" workshops helps students explore potential fields, and many students complete "real world" internship or work experience before graduation. The Williams Network connects students with opportunities and the "extensive alumni network," help graduates get plum jobs all over. Graduates who visited PayScale.com report an average starting salary of $50,200 and 55 percent find a great deal of meaning in their work.

GENERAL INFO

Activities: Choral groups, dance, drama/theater, literary magazine, music ensembles, radio station, student government, student newspaper, student-run film society, symphony orchestra, yearbook, international student organization. **Organizations:** 110 registered organizations, 3 honor societies, 8 religious organizations. **Athletics (Intercollegiate):** *Men:* Baseball, basketball, crew/rowing, cross-country, diving, football, golf, ice hockey, lacrosse, skiing (downhill/alpine), skiing (nordic/cross-country), soccer, squash, swimming, tennis, track/field (outdoor), track/field (indoor), wrestling. *Women:* Basketball, crew/rowing, cross-country, diving, field hockey, golf, ice hockey, lacrosse, skiing (downhill/alpine), skiing (nordic/cross-country), soccer, softball, squash, swimming, tennis, track/field (outdoor), track/field (indoor), volleyball. **On-Campus Highlights:** Paresky Student Center, Schow Science Library, Williams College Museum of Art, Center for Theatre and Dance, Chandler Gymnasium, Sawyer Library.

FINANCIAL AID

Students should submit: FAFSA, CSS/Financial Aid PROFILE, Noncustodial PROFILE. Priority filing deadline is 2/1. The Princeton Review suggests that all financial aid forms be submitted as soon as possible after October 1. *Need-based scholarships/grants offered:* Federal Pell, FSEOG, State scholarships/grants, Private scholarships, College/university scholarship or grant aid from institutional funds. *Loan aid offered:* Direct Subsidized Stafford Loans, Direct Unsubsidized Stafford Loans, Direct PLUS loans, Federal Perkins Loans, College/university loans from institutional funds. Applicants will be notified of awards on or about 4/1. Federal Work-Study Program available. Institutional employment available.

THE BOTTOM LINE

Williams College is very similar to an Ivy League school. It has boundless, state-of-the-art resources in everything; a diploma with the Williams brand name on it will kick down doors for the rest of your life; and it's absurdly expensive. The total retail price here for tuition, room and board, and everything else comes to about $65,480 per year. Financial aid here is beyond generous, though, and you'd be insane to choose a lesser school instead because of the sticker price.

CAREER INFORMATION FROM PAYSCALE.COM

ROI rating	92
Bachelor's and No Higher	
Median starting salary	$50,200
Median mid-career salary	$110,700
At Least Bachelor's	
Median starting salary	$54,000
Median mid-career salary	$112,000
% alumni with high job meaning	46%
% STEM	26%

SELECTIVITY

Admissions Rating	98
# of applicants	6,883
% of applicants accepted	18
% of acceptees attending	45
# offered a place on the wait list	1,603
% accepting a place on wait list	36
% admitted from wait list	9
# of early decision applicants	593
% accepted early decision	41

FRESHMAN PROFILE

Range SAT Critical Reading	670–780
Range SAT Math	660–770
Range SAT Writing	670–780
Range ACT Composite	31–34
% graduated top 10% of class	93
% graduated top 25% of class	98
% graduated top 50% of class	100

DEADLINES

Early decision	
Deadline	11/15
Notification	12/15
Regular	
Deadline	1/1
Notification	4/1
Nonfall registration?	No

FINANCIAL FACTS

Financial Aid Rating	96
Annual tuition	$51,490
Room and board	$13,690
Required fees	$300
Average need-based scholarship	$46,007
% needy frosh rec. need-based scholarship or grant aid	99
% needy UG rec. need-based scholarship or grant aid	100
% needy frosh rec. non-need-based scholarship or grant aid	0
% needy UG rec. non-need-based scholarship or grant aid	0
% needy frosh rec. need-based self-help aid	100
% needy UG rec. need-based self-help aid	100
% frosh rec. any financial aid	50
% UG rec. any financial aid	49
% UG borrow to pay for school	43
Average cumulative indebtedness	$16,593
% frosh need fully met	100
% ugrads need fully met	100
Average % of frosh need met	100
Average % of ugrad need met	100

Wofford College

429 North Church Street, Spartanburg, SC 29303-3663 • Admissions: 864-597-4130 • Fax: 864-597-4147

CAMPUS LIFE

Quality of Life Rating	**89**
Fire Safety Rating	**90**
Green Rating	**60***
Type of school	Private
Affiliation	Methodist
Environment	City

STUDENTS

Total undergrad enrollment	1,613
% male/female	50/50
% from out of state	45
% frosh from public high school	62
% frosh live on campus	96
% ugrads live on campus	92
# of fraternities (% ugrad men join)	6 (45)
# of sororities (% ugrad women join)	4 (54)
% African American	8
% Asian	3
% Caucasian	81
% Hispanic	3
% Native American	<1
% Pacific Islander	<1
% Two or more races	3
% Race and/or ethnicity unknown	1
% international	1
# of countries represented	15

ACADEMICS

Academic Rating	**91**
% students returning for sophomore year	88
% students graduating within 4 years	77
% students graduating within 6 years	82
Calendar	4/1/4
Student/faculty ratio	11:1
Profs interesting rating	92
Profs accessible rating	88

Most classes have 20–29 students.
Most lab/discussion sessions have
  20–29 students.

MOST POPULAR MAJORS
Biology; Finance; Business/Managerial
Economics

ABOUT THE SCHOOL

Without a doubt, the minute you arrive at Wofford you feel a "family vibe" permeating the campus. Indeed, above all, this is an institution where everyone "look[s] out for each other and help[s] one another succeed." Certainly, the college's size fosters a "close-knit community" and virtually guarantees "individualized attention." And the "amazing [study] abroad program" definitely attracts many students. Academically, undergrads find their classes to be "challenging" and "rigorous." And while professors undoubtedly "expect a lot," they "are [also] willing to assist in any way they can." Undergrads here boast that instructors "have an open door policy, and they encourage students to stop by even if they do not need help[;] many even give home or cell phone numbers." Finally, as one elated Spanish major sums up his experiences, "[Wofford is] an exceptional liberal arts school that provides each student with a well-rounded education that prepares them for a successful future."

BANG FOR YOUR BUCK

Wofford has a well-earned reputation for awarding "generous" financial aid packages. This sentiment is immediately supported by a fortunate computer science major who shares, "They gave me enough financial aid to go for free." Though not all undergraduates will receive aid packages quite that substantial, there's still plenty of money to be had. In fact, 94 percent of students receive some form of need-based aid, with the average package topping out around $28,377. And in recent years, Wofford has distributed $45.5 million in aid among its students. This money comes from a variety of scholarships. The college has been commended for helping low- and middle-income students.

STUDENT LIFE

Wofford is generally "a hub of activity and students can participate in school sponsored events [on a daily basis]." Undergrads will find everything "from painting on the lawn to an oyster roast." Opportunities also abound for getting "involved with the Spartanburg community through service organizations such as tutoring elementary school students, working with Habitat for Humanity and the Humane Society." Additionally, Greek life is pretty big at Wofford. The college just completed a new Greek Village for sorority and fraternity activities. One student adds, "Football games are also fun and really popular with the student body." Lastly, Spartanburg has "a beautiful downtown area [where undergrads] like to walk around and shop."

CAREER

Perhaps one of Wofford's "greatest strength[s] is preparing . . . students for the business world." The college "stress[es] the importance of internships and will do everything they can to help students in the job and graduate school application process." Naturally, a lot of this assistance comes from the career services office. For starters, the school runs a robust internship program. Wofford students have interned at a range of companies, everywhere from NASA to The Aspen Institute and ABC News. Undergrads also have the opportunity to meet with career coaches who help with everything from resume review to developing a career strategy. Wofford also offers programs in entrepreneurship. All of this diligence certainly pays off. After all, the average starting salary for recent Wofford graduates is $44,300, according to PayScale.com.

Wofford College

FINANCIAL AID: 864-597-4160 • E-MAIL: ADMISSION@WOFFORD.EDU • WEBSITE: WWW.WOFFORD.EDU

GENERAL INFO

Activities: Choral groups, concert band, dance, drama/theater, literary magazine, music ensembles, pep band, student government, student newspaper, yearbook, campus ministries. **Organizations:** 105 registered organizations, 10 honor societies, 8 religious organizations. 7 fraternities, 4 sororities. **Athletics (Intercollegiate):** *Men:* baseball, basketball, cross-country, football, golf, riflery, soccer, tennis, track/field (outdoor), track/field (indoor). *Women:* basketball, cross-country, golf, lacrosse, riflery, soccer, tennis, track/field (outdoor), track/field (indoor), volleyball. **On-Campus Highlights:** The Roger Milliken Arboretum, Roger Milliken Science Center/Great Oaks Hall, Main Building/Leonard Auditorium, Franklin W. Olin Building, Village Student Housing, Gibbs Stadium, Richardson Physical Activities Building, Russell C. King Field and Switzer Stadium, Stewart H. Johnson Greek Village, Joe E. Taylor Athletic Center. Under construction are the Rosalind Sallenger Richardson Center for the Arts (open, spring 2017) and the Jerry Richardson Indoor Stadium (open, fall 2017).

FINANCIAL AID

Students should submit: FAFSA. Priority filing deadline is 3/1. The Princeton Review suggests that all financial aid forms be submitted as soon as possible after October 1. *Need-based scholarships/grants offered:* Federal Pell, FSEOG, State scholarships/grants, Private scholarships, College/university scholarship or grant aid from institutional funds. *Loan aid offered:* Direct Subsidized Stafford Loans, Direct Unsubsidized Stafford Loans, Direct PLUS loans, Federal Perkins Loans. Applicants will be notified of awards on or about 3/15. Federal Work-Study Program available. Institutional employment available.

THE BOTTOM LINE

Students who set their sights on attending Wofford should anticipate a tuition bill of $40,245. Aside from tuition, undergraduates can expect to pay $11,635 to cover the cost of room and board. They'll also need an additional $1,200 for books and other miscellaneous academic supplies.

CAREER INFORMATION FROM PAYSCALE.COM

ROI rating	88
Bachelor's and No Higher	
Median starting salary	$46,200
Median mid-career salary	$89,000
At Least Bachelor's	
Median starting salary	$47,400
Median mid-career salary	$87,300
% alumni with high job meaning	64%
% STEM	26%

SELECTIVITY

Admissions Rating	88
# of applicants	2,795
% of applicants accepted	72
% of acceptees attending	22
# offered a place on the wait list	174
% accepting a place on wait list	39
% admitted from wait list	24
# of early decision applicants	86
% accepted early decision	85

FRESHMAN PROFILE

Range SAT Critical Reading	520–630
Range SAT Math	530–630
Range SAT Writing	520–620
Range ACT Composite	23–29
Minimum paper TOEFL	550
Minimum internet-based TOEFL	80
Average HS GPA	3.57
% graduated top 10% of class	42
% graduated top 25% of class	72
% graduated top 50% of class	94

DEADLINES

Early decision	
Deadline	11/1
Notification	12/1
Early action	
Deadline	11/15
Notification	2/1
Regular	
Deadline	2/1
Notification	3/15
Nonfall registration?	Yes

FINANCIAL FACTS

Financial Aid Rating	86
Annual tuition	$40,245
Room and board	$11,635
Average need-based scholarship	$30,032
% needy frosh rec. need-based scholarship or grant aid	100
% needy UG rec. need-based scholarship or grant aid	99
% needy frosh rec. non-need-based scholarship or grant aid	38
% needy UG rec. non-need-based scholarship or grant aid	30
% needy frosh rec. need-based self-help aid	50
% needy UG rec. need-based self-help aid	54
% frosh rec. any financial aid	96
% UG rec. any financial aid	94
% frosh need fully met	44
% ugrads need fully met	39
Average % of frosh need met	90
Average % of ugrad need met	91

Worcester Polytechnic Institute

ADMISSIONS OFFICE, BARTLETT CENTER, WORCESTER, MA 01609 • ADMISSIONS: 508-831-5286 • FAX: 508-831-5875

CAMPUS LIFE

Quality of Life Rating	93
Fire Safety Rating	91
Green Rating	96
Type of school	Private
Affiliation	No Affiliation
Environment	City

STUDENTS

Total undergrad enrollment	4,299
% male/female	67/33
% from out of state	57
% frosh from public high school	66
% frosh live on campus	96
% ugrads live on campus	49
# of fraternities (% ugrad men join)	13 (31)
# of sororities (% ugrad women join)	6 (49)
% African American	2
% Asian	5
% Caucasian	63
% Hispanic	8
% Native American	<1
% Pacific Islander	0
% Two or more races	3
% Race and/or ethnicity unknown	6
% international	12
# of countries represented	74

ACADEMICS

Academic Rating	90
% students returning for sophomore year	96
% students graduating within 4 years	76
% students graduating within 6 years	85
Calendar	Quarter
Student/faculty ratio	13:1
Profs interesting rating	85
Profs accessible rating	87
Most classes have fewer than 10 students.	

MOST POPULAR MAJORS
Computer Science; Electrical and Biomedical Engineering; Mechanical Engineering

#36 COLLEGE THAT PAYS YOU BACK

ABOUT THE SCHOOL

Worcester Polytechnic Institute is a small university in Massachusetts with a primary focus on technology and the applied sciences. Undergraduates can choose from more than fifty majors and minors across fourteen academic departments, and though the school is world-renowned for engineering WPI prides itself on offering an extremely flexible curriculum that emphasizes the importance of a well-rounded education. In addition to abundant research opportunities the school offers several "projects programs" in the sciences and humanities. These include an Interactive Qualifying Project that challenges students to apply technology to solve a societal problem, often by working and studying abroad. Students say that these programs "give [them] a chance to learn real world skills and work together rather than against each other." "I love the fact that WPI develops technical professionals' soft skills and doesn't only focus on the numbers," students say, and while there are some unpopular professors most "genuinely want all of their students to not just succeed academically but to understand the material." Furthermore, the majority are "interested in helping students, and don't prioritize their own research above being a good professor."

BANG FOR YOUR BUCK

WPI offers several financial aid options in the form of scholarships and grants, loans, and work-study. Need-based aid comes from a variety of State and Federal programs, such as the Pell Grant, as well as institutional scholarships. The school also offers an extremely high number of merit-based scholarships for which students are automatically considered upon application, with several awards that average $12,500 to $25,000. There are special merit scholarships available to students of color, and to students studying in specific disciplines such as chemistry or pre-med. Ninety-five percent of students are receiving need-based aid, and many students cite financial assistance as a determining factor in their decision to attend WPI.

STUDENT LIFE

Though "the work in classes requires you to spend significant time studying," WPI is "a place for more than just rigorous academics." Thirty to 40 percent of students are involved in Greek life and there are abundant clubs and activities on campus. "Students are very involved in campus organizations" and in addition to structured groups there are dances, a winter carnival, Saturday gaming nights, a comedy festival, a play festival, and weekend movie nights, among many other offerings. Off campus in Worcester, "there are constantly shows and concerts, there is an ice rink, a climbing gym, and movie theaters." Many students also travel to Boston on weekends. "At WPI you are always on the go with work, academics, and extra curricular activities, but we are the best time managers I know."

CAREER

Due to WPI's emphasis on real-world experience and applied science and technology, it's not surprising that the students are a career-focused bunch. All students participate in two projects, with external sponsors, before graduation. The Career Development Center is generally well regarded, offering career fairs and company presentations, services like résumé building and interview prep, and advice for students on how to

Worcester Polytechnic Institute

FINANCIAL AID: 508-831-5469 • E-MAIL: ADMISSIONS@WPI.EDU • WEBSITE: WWW.WPI.EDU

use networking and social media to their advantage. A WPI education is "about preparing students for successful careers in their respective fields upon graduation through practical applications of the knowledge and skills that are taught," and "a large percentage of the student body will leave WPI with a fairly good job when they graduate." Evidence seems to bear out that observation, as WPI has been frequently cited for graduating their students into high-paying careers. Beyond the finances, 43 percent WPI alumni visiting PayScale.com report feeling as though their job has a high level of meaning.

GENERAL INFO

Activities: Choral groups, concert band, dance, drama/theater, jazz band, literary magazine, marching band, music ensembles, musical theater, pep band, radio station, student government, student newspaper, student-run film society, symphony orchestra, yearbook, International Student Organization. **Organizations:** 200 registered organizations, 14 honor societies, 7 religious organizations. 13 fraternities, 6 sororities. **Athletics (Intercollegiate):** *Men:* baseball, basketball, crew/rowing, cross-country, diving, football, soccer, swimming, track/field (outdoor), track/field (indoor), wrestling. *Women:* basketball, crew/rowing, cross-country, diving, field hockey, soccer, softball, swimming, track/field (outdoor), track/field (indoor), volleyball. **On-Campus Highlights:** Student invented fountain, Campus Center, Robotics Lab, Fire Protection Engineering Lab, biomedical and life sciences research center at Gateway Park, Sports & Recreation Center..

FINANCIAL AID

Students should submit: FAFSA, CSS/Financial Aid PROFILE, Noncustodial PROFILE. Regular filing deadline is 2/1. The Princeton Review suggests that all financial aid forms be submitted as soon as possible after October 1. *Need-based scholarships/grants offered:* Federal Pell, FSEOG, State scholarships/grants, Private scholarships, College/university scholarship or grant aid from institutional funds. *Loan aid offered:* Direct Subsidized Stafford Loans, Direct Unsubsidized Stafford Loans, Direct PLUS loans, Federal Perkins Loans, State Loans, College/university loans from institutional funds. Applicants will be notified of awards on or about 4/1. Federal Work-Study Program available. Institutional employment available.

THE BOTTOM LINE

Tuition and fees for a year at WPI are listed as just over $47,194, with room and board totaling an additional $13,000. Combined with books, supplies, and fees, students can expect to spend approximately $56,860 per year to attend Worcester Polytechnic Institute. In addition to many merit-based scholarships WPI offers a numerous need-based programs, with 99 percent of freshmen receiving some form of financial aid. Between robust aid packages and lucrative career prospects for graduating students, Worcester Polytechnic Institute could be a great investment for those interested in the science, technology, and engineering fields.

CAREER INFORMATION FROM PAYSCALE.COM

ROI rating	91
Bachelor's and No Higher	
Median starting salary	$63,700
Median mid-career salary	$112,000
At Least Bachelor's	
Median starting salary	$64,300
Median mid-career salary	$114,000
% alumni with high job meaning	52%
% STEM	87%

SELECTIVITY

Admissions Rating	94
# of applicants	10,172
% of applicants accepted	49
% of acceptees attending	22
# offered a place on the wait list	2,472
% accepting a place on wait list	56
% admitted from wait list	3

FRESHMAN PROFILE

Range SAT Critical Reading	570–680
Range SAT Math	640–740
Range SAT Writing	560–670
Range ACT Composite	27–32
Minimum paper TOEFL	550
Minimum internet-based TOEFL	79
Average HS GPA	3.8
% graduated top 10% of class	65
% graduated top 25% of class	91
% graduated top 50% of class	98

DEADLINES

Early action	
Deadline	11/1
Notification	12/20
Regular	
Deadline	2/1
Notification	4/1
Nonfall registration?	Yes

FINANCIAL FACTS

Financial Aid Rating	87
Annual tuition	$46,364
Room and board	$13,736
Required fees	$630
Average need-based scholarship	$22,103
% needy frosh rec. need-based scholarship or grant aid	100
% needy UG rec. need-based scholarship or grant aid	96
% needy frosh rec. non-need-based scholarship or grant aid	32
% needy UG rec. non-need-based scholarship or grant aid	34
% needy frosh rec. need-based self-help aid	53
% needy UG rec. need-based self-help aid	53
% frosh rec. any financial aid	98
% UG rec. any financial aid	95
% frosh need fully met	55
% ugrads need fully met	45
Average % of frosh need met	79
Average % of ugrad need met	77

Yale University

PO Box 208234, New Haven, CT 06520-8234 • Admissions: 203-432-9300 • Fax: 203-432-9392

CAMPUS LIFE

Quality of Life Rating	94
Fire Safety Rating	62
Green Rating	95
Type of school	Private
Affiliation	No Affiliation
Environment	City

STUDENTS

Total undergrad enrollment	5,537
% male/female	51/49
% from out of state	93
% frosh from public high school	57
% frosh live on campus	100
% ugrads live on campus	84
% African American	7
% Asian	17
% Caucasian	47
% Hispanic	11
% Native American	1
% Pacific Islander	0
% Two or more races	6
% Race and/or ethnicity unknown	1
% international	11
# of countries represented	89

ACADEMICS

Academic Rating	96
% students returning for sophomore year	99
students graduating within 4 years	87
students graduating within 6 years	96
Calendar	Semester
Student/faculty ratio	6:1
Profs interesting rating	90
Profs accessible rating	86
Most classes have 10–19 students.	

MOST POPULAR MAJORS
Economics; Political Science; History

#7 COLLEGE THAT PAYS YOU BACK

ABOUT THE SCHOOL

As one of the triple towers of the Ivy League, when you say you attend "Yale, you don't really have to say much else—those four letters say it all." Beyond the gothic spires ("It reminds me of Hogwarts," says a student) and ivy-clad residence halls, Yale University truly lives up to its reputation as one of the preeminent undergraduate schools in the nation. At this world-class research institution, 5,000-plus undergraduates (who are "are passionate about everything") benefit not only from "amazing academics and extensive resources" that provide "phenomenal in- and out-of-class education," but also from participation in "a student body that is committed to learning and to each other." Cutting-edge research is commonplace and great teaching the norm, and three quarters of courses enroll fewer than twenty students. A popular test-the-waters registration system allows students to sample classes for up to two weeks before they commit to their schedule, and the school "encourages its students to take a range of courses." "The wealth of opportunities in and out of the classroom made the choice very clear to me," says a student. The education they're getting prepares them for leadership on a massive scale. Case in point: Yale alumni were represented on the Democratic or Republican ticket in every U.S. presidential election between 1972 and 2004. Still, no matter the end result, it's clear that "the people at Yale are genuinely interested in learning for learning's sake, not so that they can get a job on Wall Street."

BANG FOR YOUR BUCK

Here's a shocker: you don't have to be wealthy to have access to a Yale education. Thanks to a multibillion-dollar endowment, Yale operates a need-blind admissions policy and guarantees to meet 100 percent of each applicant's demonstrated need. In fact, Yale's annual expected financial aid budget is larger than many schools' endowments. Yale spends more than $100 million dollars on student financial aid annually. The average scholarship award is around $35,000, and it's entirely need-based—no athletic or merit scholarships are available. Seven hundred and fifty Yale undergraduates will have a $0 expected parent contribution next year—that's more than 10 percent of its student body. Yale even provides undergraduates on financial aid with grant support for summer study and unpaid internships abroad.

STUDENT LIFE

A typical Yalie is "tough to define because so much of what makes Yale special is the unique convergence of different students to form one cohesive entity. Nonetheless, the one common characteristic of Yale students is passion—each Yalie is driven and dedicated to what he or she loves most" which "creates a palpable atmosphere of enthusiasm on campus." Yale is, of course, extremely challenging academically, but work doesn't keep undergrads from participating in a "a huge variety of activities for fun." "Instead of figuring out what to do with my free time, I have to figure out what not do during my free time," says a student. There are more than 300 student groups on campus including the Yale Daily News, the oldest collegiate daily newspaper still in existence, as well as "singing, dancing, juggling fire, theater . . . the list goes on." Many students are politically active and "either volunteer or try to get involved in some sort of organization to make a difference in the world."

Yale University

FINANCIAL AID: 203-432-2700 • E-MAIL: STUDENT.QUESTIONS@YALE.EDU • WEBSITE: WWW.YALE.EDU

CAREER

As its name would suggest, the Yale Office of Career Strategy (OCS) offers a host of resources to students before they even embark on the job hunt. A comprehensive collection of online career profiles helps students gain an overview of potential fields, and walk-in appointments with career advisers ensure that all of their questions get answered. OCS sponsors numerous internship programs, often drawing upon Yale's extensive alumni network for leads on opportunities. The Yale Career Network is another great way to network with keen alumni. Yalies report average starting salaries of about $58,500, and 59 percent of those grads who visited PayScale.com say they find a high level of meaning in their work.

GENERAL INFO

Activities: Choral groups, concert band, dance, drama/theater, jazz band, literary magazine, marching band, music ensembles, musical theater, opera, pep band, radio station, student government, student newspaper, student-run film society, symphony orchestra, television station, yearbook, campus ministries, international student organization. **Organizations:** 350 registered organizations.

FINANCIAL AID

Students should submit: FAFSA, CSS/Financial Aid PROFILE, Noncustodial PROFILE. Regular filing deadline is 3/1. The Princeton Review suggests that all financial aid forms be submitted as soon as possible after October 1. *Need-based scholarships/grants offered:* Federal Pell, FSEOG, State scholarships/grants, Private scholarships, College/university scholarship or grant aid from institutional funds, United Negro College Fund. *Loan aid offered:* Direct Subsidized Stafford Loans, Direct Unsubsidized Stafford Loans, Direct PLUS loans, Federal Perkins Loans, State Loans. Applicants will be notified of awards on or about 4/1. Federal Work-Study Program available. Institutional employment available.

THE BOTTOM LINE

Annual tuition to Yale is $49,480. Room and board in one of Yale's residential colleges is $15,170 per year, bringing the total cost to about $62,200 annually, not to mention costs of books, supplies, health insurance, and personal expenses. Yale guarantees to meet 100 percent of all students' demonstrated financial need; as a result, the cost of Yale education is often considerably lower than the sticker price.

CAREER INFORMATION FROM PAYSCALE.COM

ROI rating	96
Bachelor's and No Higher	
Median starting salary	$60,300
Median mid-career salary	$104,000
At Least Bachelor's	
Median starting salary	$61,400
Median mid-career salary	$120,000
% alumni with high job meaning	68%
% STEM	21%

SELECTIVITY

Admissions Rating	99
# of applicants	30,236
% of applicants accepted	6
% of acceptees attending	69
# offered a place on the wait list	1,098
% accepting a place on wait list	65
% admitted from wait list	73

FRESHMAN PROFILE

Range SAT Critical Reading	720–800
Range SAT Math	710–800
Range SAT Writing	710–790
Range ACT Composite	31–35
Minimum paper TOEFL	600
Minimum internet-based TOEFL	100
% graduated top 10% of class	96
% graduated top 25% of class	99
% graduated top 50% of class	100

DEADLINES

Early action	
Deadline	11/1
Notification	12/15
Regular	
Deadline	1/1
Notification	4/1
Nonfall registration?	No

FINANCIAL FACTS

Financial Aid Rating	97
Annual tuition	$49,480
Room and board	$15,170
Average need-based scholarship	$47,960
% needy frosh rec. need-based scholarship or grant aid	100
% needy UG rec. need-based scholarship or grant aid	100
% needy frosh rec. non-need-based scholarship or grant aid	0
% needy UG rec. non-need-based scholarship or grant aid	0
% needy frosh rec. need-based self-help aid	73
% needy UG rec. need-based self-help aid	85
% frosh rec. any financial aid	51
% UG rec. any financial aid	50
% frosh need fully met	100
% ugrads need fully met	97
Average % of frosh need met	100
Average % of ugrad need met	100

INDEX OF SCHOOLS BY NAME

NOTES

NOTES

NOTES

NOTES

NOTES

NOTES

NOTES

NOTES